Tom Peters

TWO COMPLETE BOOKS

Tom Peters

TWO COMPLETE BOOKS

Thriving on Chaos

A Passion for Excellence

with Nancy Austin

GRAMERCY PRESS
NEW YORK

This 1995 edition is published by Gramercy Press,
distributed by Random House Value Publishing, Inc.,
40 Engelhard Avenue, Avenel, New Jersey 07001,
by arrangement with Random House, Inc., New York.

Random House
New York • Toronto • London • Sydney • Auckland

Printed and bound in the United States of America

8   7   6   5   4   3   2   1

Contents

Foreword

By Jeffrey Kagan
President, Kagan Telecom Associates, Atlanta Telecommunications
industry analyst, consultant, columnist, speaker

Unless you've been taking a Rip Van Winkle-length nap for the last few years, you've no doubt noticed a change that is altering the way America does business: The once well-ordered and definable telecommunications industry segments that separate the telephone (local, long distance, cellular), computer, television, cable, entertainment, shopping and information industries have been converging in a thick, technological fog. But as the fog lifts, we are given a glimpse of the emerging information superhighway and with it, all the amazing technologies which will change our lives forever. While this techno-road remains under construction, it is currently open to businesses wishing to gain a competitive edge.

Revolutionary business guru Tom Peters has spent the last decade sounding the alarm regarding today's information revolution. Thanks in no small part to his forward-thinking, businesses that have followed his prescriptions are flourishing—even during this chaotic period of change.

MCI is one of those flourishing companies. By combining its customer-centered focus with an ability to adapt quickly to a changing business environment, it has developed an uncanny genius for listening to the market and giving customers exactly what they want—even before they know they want it.

We can learn much from both Peters and MCI. Peters had made a lifelong commitment to investigating successful companies to learn what makes them successful. He then shares his findings with the rest of the corporate community in an effort to improve the way America does business. And MCI—a long-time leader in the telecommunications industry—has displayed the foresight to evolve past its boundaries as a mere phone company into one of the premier architects of the information superhighway.

I've been following the ideas of both Peters and MCI for more than a dozen years and it is clear to me that they are both reading from the same script: Both are sources of powerful ideas which are at once revolutionary, yet as vital as oxygen to breath for companies wanting to make the successful transition to the information age.

We cannot pick up a newspaper without reading about the communications revolution, information technology, or the internet. But some journalists write about the info highway as something far in the distant future, a thing yet to be built. Others write about it as being here today and talk about the tools currently available to us. No wonder we are confused.

Let's put the confusion to rest once and for all: The information superhighway is not only real, it is available today for the average business person or consumer to use. I use it everyday; most people do to one extent or another. In fact, it's not new at all, but has been around for over 150 years. Back in 1844, Samuel Morse transmitted the first message, "what hath God wrought," over the telegraph. Of course, this particular advance wasn't referred to as the information superhighway. If anything, it was more like an information dirt road, but it was the foundation of our nation's information and communication infrastructure. From there, it has continued to evolve from simple Morse code to the telegram, telephone, radio transmissions, television, cable TV, information services, audio and video conferencing, the internet and beyond.

Sure, ten years from now technology will be far beyond where it is today— as today's telephone is beyond yesterday's telegraph—but that doesn't mean there isn't a wealth of business-building tools at our disposal right now. In fact, a technology paradox is underway, pushing the price of technology into a virtual free-fall and making it affordable for even the smallest of businesses. This affordability is quickly transforming technology from an extra tool used to gain a competitive advantage, to, in many cases, the actual price of admission into the corporate arena. Unfortunately, many companies aren't implementing these affordable solutions, positioning themselves in competitive quicksand.

Though plenty of amazing interactive, multimedia magic is still on the way, many of us don't realize that there are plenty of new tools—CD ROM, the internet, E-mail, video phone calls—for us to use today to build our business. These new tools can help us better solve today's problems, and prepare to address tomorrow's challenges, which, believe it or not, are knocking at our door right now. We don't understand the sheer power we literally have at our fingertips today, so we end up rehashing solutions to yesterday's problems, using the same old tools—such as computers, fax machines and modems— and coming up with the same old solutions.

There is a revolution occurring in the communications and information industries. Yet, in these times of intense change, our core beliefs regarding how business—and even the world around us—operates are being shaken at their roots. As we make the bumpy transition to an information society in the larger context of a global marketplace, we are not only privileged, but overwhelmed to be *the* generation ushering in this incredibly exciting time filled with historic challenges and opportunities.

The winds of change are definitely blowing in Washington. Over the past few years when I've met with current House Speaker, Congressman Newt Gingrich, his enthusiasm in welcoming the new information age has shone brightly. Ditto for Vice President Al Gore, who has also shown strong leadership and a clear desire to do the same thing. In fact, it was Gore who coined the term "Information Superhighway" a decade ago. This is one issue where both Republicans and Democrats see eye-to-eye and will do everything in their power to ease our transition to an information-driven age. Clearly, both sides of our government want this information society to become a reality as soon as possible. They aren't standing in its way. Instead, they are diligently clearing a path so the movement's larger players don't trip. They want open, fair competition to take over.

So, that means the rest is up to us. We have to stop thinking in old terms and open our minds to new solutions. We must think outside the lines and beyond comfort zones. Technology is going to be the force that will allow companies to compete in the global information economy—with the new tools we have at our disposal we can solve old problems and face new ones. As all these technologies and industries continue to converge, additional tools will continue to become available for us to use in our everyday businesses. Furthermore, modern technology has made many such tools available and affordable today for even the smallest of businesses!

While our children are much more comfortable with new technology than we are, we, in turn, are more comfortable with it than our parents and grandparents were. We are one generation away from purging this technology paranoia which is hindering our competitiveness. This is important, because we've reached a time when even the slightest delay in embracing future technologies can spell certain disaster. Truly the biggest mistake we can make is assuming our competition, both domestic and global, is as intimidated by new technology as we are, and thus is not moving to quickly integrate these new advances into its businesses.

A real revolution, the kind of technological revolution Peters has been shouting about for more than a decade, is now fully underway and the wake-up call is being sounded from the highest of peaks. This is a crucial generation of historic change. For all the Mr. Flintstones busily toiling in the rock quarries who don't embrace these modern business tools, well, let's just say they'll learn their lessons when the dust clears and they find they are running the best darn buggy whip businesses of the 1990s.

I've met many executives who swear they will never get E-mail or implement video-conferencing. They said the same thing back in the mid-80s about fax machines and computers. I've got news for them: If their customers and competitors use this stuff, they will too. When it comes to losing business to the technology-superior competition, it's funny how suddenly we can't do without the same advances they have.

Predictably, businesses will be the first to take advantage of the emerging technologies. Like the explosion of computers and fax machines, each new service will first get entrenched in the office before making its way into our homes. Although with 40 million Americans working at least part-time from home in a growing trend called Telecommuting, the transition may be quicker than ever. For instance, although the power of E-mail and video conferencing is just beginning to be realized, they will be the preferred communication methods of the next few years. As prices continue to drop and quality continues to rise, they'll become as ubiquitous as the fax machine—in the office and at home. It's no longer a question of if, only when.

We'll also be doing business on-line. Virtually every business will be able to place a storefront on the internet, enabling it to sell products and services to millions of people worldwide. Indeed, these potential customers make up a dream demographic: young, educated and affluent. Opening a storefront in cyberspace is affordable for most businesses today and many companies are already making a fortune from it. Others are simply positioning themselves for what will surely be the biggest business opportunity of this generation. Again, it's not a question of if, only when.

Because the truth is, customer expectations are rising. The public's desire for service at any time and at any price is driving much of this communications revolution. Customers are no longer satisfied waiting hours for a return call or days for information to arrive in the mail. People want information now! And if you cannot give them that level of responsiveness, they'll turn to one of your competitors who does. Incidentally, these are things Peters has been telling us for years. The watermark is clearly rising and it is the new technologies that will help today's businesses meet that customer-focused challenge.

But to fulfill customers' increased demands, you must possess the necessary technology. There's no doubt that telecommunications is changing forever. Your old-fashioned phone company, for example, is quickly fading into oblivion. In order for today's telecommunications companies to flourish in coming years, they must be more than just a pipeline for content, they must provide the new technologies and even the actual content in many cases.

There has been a lot of lip service to meeting the challenge, but very few phone companies have actually developed real, tangible products and services that allow their customers to utilize the business-building power of these technologies. Fortunately, MCI is doing just that. For years it has been first to market innovative long distance products, and now it is the first company to introduce an incredibly powerful interactive software package, called networkMCI Business, which gives business its first solid opportunity to use the info highway.

Moreover, at a time when we are all on information overload, MCI is developing tools to help business manage and efficiently use information, rather than just pumping out more and more unneeded data. As usual, not only is MCI responding to a market need with real solutions, it is the first phone company to do so. In fact, most people don't know MCI has been behind the scenes, leading the way in building and running the information highway for many years. It has supplied the high-speed lines that make up the backbone of the internet, allowing volumes of information to travel from point A to point B in the blink of an eye. Adding further width to the company's position as a world class leader in the information revolution, Vinton Cerf, the father of the internet, is once again occupying the Captain's chair at the MCI internet operation.

MCI is no longer just a phone company, it is a full-service communications and information provider. And this is what other phone companies will have to be in order to flourish in the new information society. Either that or be relegated to a mere commodity of telephone services—which it looks like many of today's phone companies are destined to become. As Lee Iacocca used to say, "You can either lead, follow or get out of the way." On the information highway, if you don't lead or follow, forget about getting out of the way. You'll quickly become roadkill.

As one leader to another, it's natural that MCI (through Gramercy Press) is publishing some of the best work of Tom Peters, who is perhaps the nation's most valuable leader in revolutionary business ideas. Companies of all sizes can learn valuable lessons from both Peters and MCI. I have the utmost respect for both. Any business person who wants to make a smooth transition to the information society—and take advantage of the innovative technologies that will change the way we live and do business forever—will do well to absorb the powerful ideas contained in these pages. Consider this book your wake-up call.

Introduction

I made my mark in 1982 with *In Search of Excellence,* co-authored with Bob Waterman. Just five years later, I began *Thriving on Chaos* with "There are no excellent companies."

Yikes!

We (Bob and I) meant what we said about excellence in 1982. I meant what I said in 1987.

What happened during those five years? And what's happened since then?

Bob Waterman and I came from a stodgy environment, that of the high-powered, high-priced consultancy McKinsey & Co. We were big company oriented to a fault. Our breakthrough in *In Search of Excellence* was to look for things that were working . . . in big companies.

Truth is, I'm still proud of the "eight basics" in *In Search of Excellence*: a bias for action, close to the customer, productivity through people, etc. Nonetheless, many (perhaps one-third) of our "stars for the ages" in 1982 were experiencing difficulties by 1987 and full-fledged trauma three or four years later—e.g., IBM. It's not, I think, that the eight principles were wrong. More to the point, the global village arrived with a vengeance, new technology shortened the trip around the world to a few nanoseconds, a global entrepreneurial revolution spawned thousands of flexible, innovative companies—and any number of 1982's bellwethers were just too inflexible to react.

In fact the new upstarts are to the point. Though Bob Waterman and I had written *about*—and, we thought, *for*—big companies, many/most of the people who showed up at my seminars came from high-growth, medium-sized companies. Good as they were, they were perpetually paranoid—and ready to take next steps.

These energetic enterprises became the motherlode for my research. And the basis for *A Passion for Excellence,* co-authored with Nancy Austin. I think the framework of *A Passion for Excellence* (see page 553) makes sense; but the framework, to be honest, is not the story. The story *is* the little stories from hither and thither.

The practical nuggets are what most idea-hungry readers loved about the book. While I like some of my other books better because of their "more logical structure," *A Passion for Excellence*'s followers told me, by the thousands, this was/is their favorite—because they can open it, read ten pages, and find an idea to work on today.

Thriving on Chaos was an extension of *A Passion for Excellence . . . and* a big step forward. An extension in that it was a continuation of my effort to cater (in the best sense) to busy readers; hence the 45 items that constitute a full-fledged guide to organizing. The huge (for me, at any rate) step forward was to emphasize (obsess on) flexibility, adaptation and experimentation.

When I said "no excellent companies" I meant that there are no "principles for the ages." Even the most thrilling ideas can atrophy and/or become burdens (e.g., "close to the customer" at IBM became "close to the *wrong* customer"). Therefore we—leaders at all levels—should be perpetually prepared to toss out baby parts along with the bathwater, and constantly reinvent.

In the years since *Thriving on Chaos* these ideas have taken slightly different shapes, as global integration and competition has superheated. Still, I'm willing (mostly) to stake my reputation on the words and ideas of *A Passion for Excellence* and *Thriving on Chaos.*

True, some of the companies profiled herein have taken a licking. But I am comfortable with that. I do *not* believe in pat formulas, do *not* believe in principles for all time.

I *do* believe in taking steps, *now,* to try new things. In fact, I think *In Search of Excellence*'s principle No. 1, "A Bias for Action" is the most important lesson for any individual, organizational unit or business.

Test it. Try it. Get on with it. ("Just do it" in Nike speak.) The passion for constant experimentation (and the willingness to suffer repeated black eyes from experiments that fail) is measure No. 1 for today's managers.

The pages that follow contain no right answers. They do contain a host of ideas put into action by real people. I'd be surprised if you can't find a few (or, hopefully, a few dozen) that make sense for you.

Good luck. And, oh yes, Just Do It!

Thriving on Chaos

A HANDBOOK FOR
A MANAGEMENT REVOLUTION

To
ROGER MILLIKEN
and
WILLIAM DONALD SCHAEFER

two whose flexibility of mind and raging
impatience with inaction have inspired
the most dramatic and fruitful
organizational revolutions
I've witnessed

Three outstanding attitudes—obliviousness to the growing disaffection of constituents, primacy of self-aggrandizement, [and the] illusion of invulnerable status—are
persistent aspects of folly.

Barbara Tuchman
The March of Folly

Contents

Preface

RX: REVOLUTION!

Few would take exception to the conclusion that our sales forces are not sufficiently cherished. But how many are ready to consider doubling the sales force—in the next 36 months? And all would nod when urged to get marketers out with customers more. But would you sign up for putting marketers in the field 50 percent of the time? Improving quality—we all salute that, too. But will you accept a challenge to cut defects by 90 percent in 36 months? I'd guess that most would agree when the idea of tying pay to performance (for everyone) comes up. But are you ready to institute a bonus that amounts to 50 percent of base pay (a third of total pay)?

Revolution: It's a word business people have trouble with, and justifiably so. But our competitive situation is dire. The time for 10 percent staff cuts and 20 percent quality improvements is past. Such changes are not good enough.

Many of the ideas in this book will be new to readers of *In Search of Excellence* and *A Passion for Excellence;* others will be familiar. But *the rate of change demanded by the prescriptions in this book and the boldness of the goals suggested will be unfailingly new—and frightening.*

So this book *is* about a revolution—a necessary revolution. It challenges everything we thought we knew about managing, and often challenges over a hundred years of American tradition. Most fundamentally, the times demand that flexibility and love of change replace our longstanding penchant for mass production and mass markets, based as it is upon a relatively predictable environment now vanished.

Titling a book is never easy—the "selling proposition" must be presented in no more than a half-dozen words. Finding the right title here was especially tough. After much discussion I decided to be adamant about "revolution," palatable or not. But the most vigorous debate involved the choice of a preposition: "amidst" versus "on." The competitive situation was (and will be) chaotic—so "chaos" was easy. And it's not hard to sign up for "thriving." But was it to be "Thriving *amidst* Chaos" or "Thriving *on* Chaos"?

To thrive "amidst" chaos means to cope or come to grips with it, to succeed in spite of it. But that is too reactive an approach, and misses the point. The true objective is to take the chaos as given and learn to thrive *on* it. The winners of tomorrow will deal *proactively* with chaos, will look at the chaos per se as the source of market advantage, not as a problem to be got around. Chaos and uncertainty are (will be) market opportunities for the wise; capitalizing on fleeting market anomalies will be the successful business's greatest accomplishment. It is with that in mind that we must proceed.

West Tinmouth, Vermont   TOM PETERS
June 1987

I

PRESCRIPTIONS FOR A WORLD TURNED UPSIDE DOWN

Facing Up to the Need for Revolution

Can America make it? A huge trade imbalance, a sliding currency, falling real wages and a dismal productivity record. A decade ago, these were the hallmarks of a struggling British economy. Today they characterize an American economy which is struggling . . . against fierce competition from the Far East.

> *Financial Times* (of London)
> May 9, 1987

EXCELLENCE ISN'T

There are no excellent companies. The old saw "If it ain't broke, don't fix it" needs revision. I propose: "If it ain't broke, you just haven't looked hard enough." Fix it anyway.

No company is safe. IBM is declared dead in 1979, the best of the best in 1982, and dead again in 1986. People Express is the model "new look" firm, then flops twenty-four months later.

In 1987, and for the foreseeable future, there is no such thing as a "solid," or even substantial, lead over one's competitors. Too much is changing for anyone to be complacent. Moreover, the "champ to chump" cycles are growing ever shorter—a "commanding" advantage, such as Digital Equipment's current edge in networks that allow vast numbers of computers to interact with one another, is probably good for about eighteen months, at best.

There are two ways to respond to the end of the era of sustainable excellence. One is frenzy: buy and sell businesses in the brave hope of staying out in front of the growth industry curve. This is the General Electric idea: in the last six years, it has acquired over 325 businesses at a cost of over $12 billion, and dumped more than 225, getting $8 billion in return.

The second strategy is paradoxical—meeting uncertainty by emphasizing a set of new basics: world-class quality and service, enhanced responsiveness

13

through greatly increased flexibility, and continuous, short-cycle innovation and improvement aimed at creating new markets for both new and apparently mature products and services.

The latter is Ford's approach to transformation. Quality really has become Job One at Ford. The once all-powerful finance function has assumed a less dominant role, and manufacturing, the prime source of quality, is no longer low in the organizational pecking order. And product development techniques have been set on their ear with the unconventional, but wildly successful, Team Taurus approach; it combined supplier, worker, dealer, and customer input from the start.

If the word "excellence" is to be applicable in the future, it requires wholesale redefinition. Perhaps: "Excellent firms don't believe in excellence—only in constant improvement and constant change." That is, excellent firms of tomorrow will cherish impermanence—and thrive on chaos.

THE ACCELERATING AMERICAN DECLINE

You need not look far to find cause for alarm:

1. Our average business productivity grew at 3 percent a year from 1950 to 1965. From 1965 to 1973, the rate was 2 percent; and since 1973, it's barely crept along at 1 percent. Manufacturing productivity looks worse. It grew at 2.5 percent a year from 1950 to 1985; that contrasts with Japan at 8.4 percent, Germany and Italy at 5.5 percent, France at 5.3 percent, Canada at 3.5 percent—and much-maligned Britain at 3.1 percent.

2. U.S. per capita GNP, called by some the truest measure of a nation's international economic standing, slipped below Japan's in 1986; it also trails the per capita GNP of such European nations as West Germany, Switzerland, Sweden, and Denmark.

3. The average wage for a 25–34-year-old white male declined 26 percent from 1973 to 1983 in constant dollars; the comparable figure for 35–44-year-olds was little better, a decline of 14 percent. This figure is more useful to look at than others. Given the increase in work force participation by women, overall family income has slowly risen. But the economic fate of the individual white male remains the bellwether indicator of progress (or lack of it).

4. The national savings rate, long the lowest in the industrial world, continues to decline. Despite supply-side economic stimulants such as the 1981 tax cut, savings as a share of disposable personal income plummeted from 7.5 percent to 3.9 percent from 1981 to 1986. At year's end 1986, it stood at 2.8 percent. Only our dramatic shift as a nation from premier net lender to premier net borrower has kept investment afloat.

5. In 1986, 138 banks failed, the largest number in one year since the Great Depression; the pace in 1987 is ahead of 1986's. By contrast, 10 banks toppled in 1981.

6. Economists estimate that as many as 30 million people have been dislocated by the "restructuring" in manufacturing during the last decade. Since 1980, the Fortune 500 have shed a staggering 2.8 million jobs.

7. The plain truth is that every major manufacturing or service firm—from the Bank of America and Citicorp, to Du Pont and General Motors, to IBM and Intel and the Hospital Corporation of America—is undergoing trauma.

Alarming as these indicators are—and a host of similar ones—it is the chaos in trade that is most revealing of our poor performance. It alone provides the harsh, industry-by-industry evidence of our decline.

The fact that the trade deficit is currently (April 1987) running at $152 billion, despite the dollar's plunge against the yen and mark since September 1985, is a powerful indication that, while the problem may have been exacerbated by the dollar's strength of a few years back, we are getting clobbered primarily because of the generally poor quality of what we produce and a failure, as a result of questionable service and slow responsiveness, to make use of our onshore, close-to-the-world's-biggest-market advantage.

Textile-makers all but gave up decades ago, and begged for protective relief; while foreign wages were and are often still low, the industry's repeated failure to modernize and adapt to new market needs was the root cause. Then, one by one, steel, autos, and machine tools also begged for—and got—access to the protectionist trough. Finally, 1986 brought the spectacle of Silicon Valley's once proud barons spending more time in Washington than at the factory; their pleas for protection against Japan's alleged "dumping" (selling below cost to gain market share) culminated in the imposition of tariffs of 100 percent on certain Japanese electronics products. But though Japanese hands are not entirely clean, it was long-term disinterest in the factory (the nuts and bolts of producing top-quality products) and arrogance toward even large customers that most severely damaged our semiconductor industry—not Japanese "dumping" or protectionist barriers within Japan.

In 1986, despite continuing bright spots such as computers and aircraft, even the trade balance in high-technology goods went into the red. That was also a first-time losing year for construction equipment and agriculture. In the latter case, despite billions in subsidies, we have simply not awakened to the fact that most of the rest of the world, including India and China, is now self-sufficient in grain. Commodity prices in general remain in a trough, and any upticks are likely to be temporary. That is, the United States can no longer depend on its natural resources to be a source of enduring trade surplus.

A Decline in Service Too

The various service industries are faring little better than manufacturing and agriculture. A formidable $41 billion positive trade balance in services in 1981 has all but disappeared. In a recent *Harvard Business Review* article, "Will Service Follow Manufacturing into Decline?," James Brian Quinn and Christopher Gagnon were glum:

It will take hard and dedicated work not to dissipate our broad-based lead in services, as we did in manufacturing. Many of the same causes of lost position are beginning to appear. Daily we encounter the same inattention to quality, [over]emphasis on scale economies rather than customers' concerns and short-term financial orientation that earlier injured manufacturing. Too many service companies have . . . concentrated on cost-cutting efficiencies they can quantify, rather than on adding to their product's value by listening carefully and . . . providing the services their customers genuinely want. Haven't we heard this once before? The cost of losing this battle is unacceptably high. . . . If [services] are disdained or mismanaged, the same forces that led to the decline of U.S. manufacturing stand ready to cut them to pieces.

That's bad news indeed, since the service sector now employs 75 percent of us.

Some Rays of Light, but on Net, Trouble

To be sure, the picture isn't entirely grim. And many of these indicators have their flip sides. For instance, although Japanese productivity growth has been several times ours in recent years, we still hold an absolute productivity advantage over the Japanese. In absolute terms they are far ahead of us in targeted industries (steel, autos, semiconductors), but far behind in others (agriculture, the service sector as a whole).

And while the Fortune 500 continue their job-shedding binge, our vital capital markets, among other things, have spurred a small-business-led surge in job creation, in high-tech as well as hamburgers.

Yet, while the bag is mixed, almost all leading indicators—e.g., productivity growth, competitive assessments of leading industries such as financial services and semiconductors, the trade balances with almost any other industrialized nation—clearly show that our postwar economic hegemony is at an end. Though we still harbor fond memories of days when the rules of the game governed everyone but us, we are now, at best, "one of the big players"; decisions of the Japanese and German ministries of finance are at least as important as those of the U.S. Federal Reserve Board or Department of the Treasury.

All of this is, of course, exacerbated by our failure to come to grips with our awesome budget deficit. One simply can't (1) run a constant deficit of $100 to $200 billion a year, (2) blithely devalue the dollar by over 50 percent vis-à-vis Japan, and (3) shift from chief creditor to chief debtor nation overnight—while expecting the economic waters to remain calm. The U.S. standard of living has declined, by definition, as the dollar has plummeted. More inflation surely looms if the dollar is not stabilized. And a recession may well lie ahead.

Thus, it is essential to address the macroeconomic folly of continued deficits, among other matters. But it is equally important not to be lulled by the glib talk of macroeconomic wizards. Sound macroeconomic policy will help, but the underlying source of our problematic economic performance is a cataclysmic change in competitive conditions, which has in surprisingly short order turned almost every traditional U.S. strength, at the level of the individual firm, into weakness.

AN ERA OF UNPRECEDENTED UNCERTAINTY

Merging and Demerging: Shuffle for Shuffle's Sake

Madness *is* afoot. On the same day in early March 1987, Chrysler buys AMC and USAir swallows Piedmont.

The Chrysler move comes amidst predictions of overcapacity in U.S. auto production—and not long after a decision at General Motors to shut down eleven plants. In the airline industry, prior to late 1986, only USAir, Piedmont, Delta, and American had eschewed major mergers; they also happened to be the four most profitable airlines, with number one American making twenty-four times as much as United, which was the largest airline in 1986 and fraught with problems after trying to swallow much of Pan Am. In 1987, Texas Air will be biggest, after swallowing Continental, Eastern, and People Express. Its digestion problems are all too well documented. So why have the four best so quickly succumbed to major mergers?

Don't look to GE for an answer. On the one hand, its former top strategic planner (now a line executive vice-president) is quoted by *Business Week* in early 1987 as saying that nine out of ten acquisitions "are a waste of time and a destruction of shareholders' value." Then the same article goes on to report that GE is thinking of acquiring United Technologies—a conglomerate with revenues of $16 billion.

Certainly most studies suggest that, in general, mergers don't pan out. For instance, business strategist Michael Porter, of the Harvard Business School, recently concluded a study of merger behavior among thirty-three big U.S. firms from 1950 through 1980. As a group, they subsequently unloaded 53 percent of all their acquisitions during this period and sold off a whopping 74 percent of their acquisitions in unrelated new fields (those purchases that were to have made them safe by positioning them in "guaranteed" growth sectors, according to the press releases). Likewise, when consultants McKinsey & Co. made an extensive study in 1986 of mergers between 1972 and 1983 that involved the two hundred largest public corporations, they determined that a mere 23 percent were successful (as measured by an increase in value to shareholders). The highest success rate (33 percent) was found with small acquisitions made in related fields, the lowest (8 percent) resulted from the merger of large firms whose operations were in unrelated areas.

Structural economist Frederic Scherer has observed, after years of meticulous study: "On average, mergers decrease efficiency." An economist at the Securities and Exchange Commission was more blunt: Asked to comment on a proposal to further relax antitrust restrictions, he replied, "Most industries in which we

have competitive difficulties are not exactly filled with pigmy companies. . . .
You don't put two turkeys together and make an eagle."

The mergers do grab headlines. But Ray Miles, dean of the business school
of the University of California at Berkeley, is not alone when he points out,
"Current 'merger mania' notwithstanding, it seems likely that the 1980s and
1990s will be known as decades of large-scale disaggregation." New terms such
as "breakup value" and "de-integration" are heard daily in the halls of the
Fortune 500. A 1987 *Forbes* analysis of Litton Industries, caustically titled "But
the Grass Looked Greener Over There," speaks eloquently to the overall issue
of frenzied buying and selling:

> Restructuring. The magic word of the mid-1980s. Just say the syllables:
> re-struc-tur-ing. They cure all ills, excuse all past mistakes and justify huge
> writedowns in assets. But does restructuring always accomplish what it
> originally sets out to accomplish? The trouble with much of what goes on
> in the name of restructuring is that it is a policy for tomorrow based on
> today's known circumstances. Take the case of Litton Industries, Inc. That
> $4.5 billion (revenues) conglomerate has been repeatedly restructured in its
> 33-year history. The latest restructuring, completed in 1985, refocused the
> company into three main lines of business, each of which looked extremely
> promising when the restructuring began four years earlier. Alas. Soon after
> the reorganization was essentially complete, each of the three chosen busi-
> nesses ran into problems. . . . The Litton of the future is essentially in place,
> says [its chief executive officer]. "Now our job for the next several years
> is to make what we have perform." But one wonders: Will Litton have to
> restructure again in a few years? Or will management finally settle down
> to making what it has work?

Mergers and de-mergers are just one part of the madness. Strategies change
daily, and the names of firms, a clear indicator of strategic intent, change with
them. In rapid succession, U.S. Steel became USX, American Can became
Primerica, and United Airlines became Allegis for a while. General Electric has
been a bit more coy than the rest; it has not made the official change to GE,
but "encourages" the use of the initials rather than the words. The new names
share a common trait—they're all more vague than their predecessors.

So U.S. Steel is almost out of steel, as the change in its name suggests. And
why not? The year of the change, 1986, brought LTV, the second-largest U.S.
steelmaker after swallowing Republic Steel in 1984, to bankruptcy. The company, with $8.2 billion in revenues, became the biggest industrial firm ever to
go belly up. (Texaco, at $32 billion, eclipsed the record in early 1987. Most
record-breaking feats these days seem to be bad-news stories.)

Internationalism: Yes and No

Despite protectionist movements in the United States and other nations,
transactions that cross international borders are sharply on the rise. Seldom

does a week pass without major joint ventures among partners from more than one country. Nomura buys into Salomon Brothers. Boeing and the Japanese make a deal. McDonnell-Douglas then attempts to join up with Airbus Industries in an effort to match Boeing's newest partnership.

Global financing is also changing the landscape. On the one hand, financial markets are opening up rapidly, and everyone is increasingly connected to everyone else. High-speed computers and communications technology make possible the arrangement of the most exotic financing in a dozen currencies in a matter of days—which facilitates such developments in manufacturing as "global sourcing," wherein firms shop freely among several nations, usually for the lowest-cost source of numerous components. This in turn brings increasing de-integration or "hollowing" of firms; tasks routinely done inside most firms, from watering the plants in the lobby to manufacturing subcomponents, are now subcontracted to outsiders small and large, domestic and foreign.

But strong as the trend toward transcending national boundaries is, the countertrend is also strong. Protection is one element. Debt is another. The United States has lent a trillion dollars to developing countries, and about two-thirds of that debt is held by private banks. Huge debt restructurings are common, and more major defaults, such as Brazil's in early 1987, are anticipated. The quandary is inescapable. The only way the debt-strapped nations can pay back their loans is by exporting what they produce, whether manufactured goods or commodities. This drives them to aggressive selling tactics, which trigger a further protectionist response. Talk about Catch-22.

Predictability Is a Thing of the Past

Nothing is predictable. Currency-exchange transactions now total $80 trillion a year, only $4 trillion of which is required to finance trade in goods and services. The rest is essentially currency speculation, one reason that the overall financial situation has been labeled the "Casino Society." The prices of the major currencies, once stable within 1 percent over decades, now swing 5 percent a week, and 50 percent a year. The prices of energy, agricultural products, and metals are also volatile.

So we don't know from day to day the price of energy or money. We don't know whether protection and default will close borders, making a mess of global sourcing and trade alike, or whether global financing will open things up further.

We don't know whether merging or de-merging makes more sense, and we have no idea who will be partners with whom tomorrow or next week, let alone next month.

We don't know who our competitors will be, or where they will come from. New foreign competition appears each day—not only in new services and end products (1986 was the year of the Hyundai and the Yugo, and 1987 brings Daihatsu, the ninth Japanese auto company to export to the United States), but also in the form of the invisible subcomponents of purportedly American products (at one point most of the innards of the IBM personal computer were made abroad).

New competitors financed by venture capital and a sustained market for Initial Public Offerings (IPOs) spring up like mushrooms in banking and health care and pizza delivery and temporary business services, and in semiconductors, supercomputers, and biotechnology, too. Other "new" competitors are units spun off from big firms (often following a hostile takeover or a leveraged buy-out, two of a vast number of new financing schemes speeding the pace of corporate overhaul) or downsized, newly autonomous units within big firms.

Technology's Unsettling Impact—On Everything

Technology is yet another wild card affecting every aspect of doing business. As mentioned, it has revolutionized financing. It has also forever changed:

1. Manufacturing: The technology of miniaturization is (a) reducing optimal factory size dramatically and (b) allowing factories of all sizes to turn out a huge variety of products, with greatly reduced setup times.

2. Design: Such innovations as computer-aided engineering are slashing the length of design-to-manufacture cycles.

3. Distribution: Electronics, computer, and telecommunications technologies are making it possible to (a) shorten substantially the time required between order and delivery, (b) poll customers instantly, (c) engage in almost numberless permutations and combinations of globe-spanning partnerships. They are also (d) breathing new life into the independent user, such as the corner grocer, whose optical scanner and computer give him newfound power in dealing with big producers. Likewise, (e) distribution companies, such as Ingram in books and McKesson in drugs, make it possible for smaller user firms to achieve almost all the purchase-price economies that big buyers can achieve.

4. Product definition: There is a blurring of service/product distinctions, given the enhancement of almost every product, from tractors to bank cards, by "software" services and the "intelligence-added" features provided courtesy of the microprocessor.

Consumers Are on the Move Too

On the consuming end of things, more uncertainty is added. Tastes are changing: (1) Thanks to the Japanese, Germans, and others, there is a vastly increased awareness of quality. (2) The rapid rise in the number of women in the work force and of two-wage-earner families leads to new needs (e.g., convenience goods and services). (3) Changes in the kinds of jobs available and, hence, in the distribution of incomes may create something like a two-class society—with an increased number of "haves" demanding greater variety and quality, and an increased number of "have-nots" demanding more durable basic goods, in the face of increasingly poor prospects. And (4) with a TV or two in every home, and a car or two in most driveways, the demand for these products is shifting from a desire for the product per se, almost regardless of quality, to a demand for customized alternatives with special features tailored for ever narrower market segments.

The Interaction of Forces: All Bets Are Off

Of course, more important than any one of these sets of uncertainties—financial, international, technological, or markets/tastes—is the interaction among them. For instance, the drive for more product variety is abetted by the technology which can meet such needs, the explosion of international competitors (producers of both end products and subcomponents) with a piece of the action, and the similar, finance-driven explosion of start-up domestic firms vying for a piece of the more specialized action too.

Sum up all these forces and trends, or, more accurately, multiply them, then add in the fact that most are in their infancy, and you end up with a forecaster's nightmare. But the point is much larger, of course, than forecasting. The fact is that *no firm can take anything in its market for granted.*

Suppose you are considering next year's strategy for a maturing product. Here's what you might well find:

▶ a new Korean competitor
▶ an old Japanese competitor continuing to reduce costs and improve quality
▶ a dozen domestic start-ups, each headed by talented people claiming a technology breakthrough
▶ one old-line domestic competitor that has slashed overhead costs by 60 percent and is de-integrating via global sourcing as fast as it can
▶ another old-line domestic competitor that has just fended off a hostile takeover; in doing so, it may have (odds 50 percent) sold off the division that competes with you to another strong competitor with a great distribution system
▶ a competitor that has just introduced an electronics-based distribution system that wires it to each of its 2,500 principal distributors, slashing the time required to fill orders by 75 percent
▶ yet another competitor that is tailor-making its products to suit the requirements or tastes of tiny groups of customers, thanks to a new, flexible Computer Integrated Manufacturing (CIM) system
▶ consumers demanding consistently high quality in every component of the product, from inner workings to fits and finishes
▶ a wildly gyrating currency market that confounds your own global sourcing decisions
▶ the probable interruption of supply from two offshore manufacturing plants where governments have defaulted on loan interest and principle payments

It is because this scenario is now *average*—for every banker, health care administrator, public utility executive, and soup maker, let alone computer maker—that our organizations *all* require major surgery. Violent and accelerating change, now commonplace, will become the grist of the opportunistic winner's mill. The losers will view such confusion as a "problem" to be "dealt" with.

OLD ASSUMPTIONS ASKEW

Today, only a small motivated firm with . . . highly qualified labor and good vertical mobility instead of oppressive hierarchy can hold up in a world whose principal characteristic is instability.

> Andrea Saba
> *Submerged Industry,*
> on the dominant role of
> the gray economy in spearheading
> Italy's economic revival

Henry Ford made great contributions, but his Model T was not a quality car.

> W. Edwards Deming
> father of statistical
> process control and the
> Japanese quality revolution

U.S. industry, run as it was by our forefathers in the tradition of our ancestors, grew big and powerful and restless. We built the biggest steel mills, the biggest oil refineries, the biggest chemical plants, the largest automobile assembly lines, the largest smelters in the world. Boy, could we make product! We didn't always make the best, but we made the most at the lowest price and U.S. industry became a model for the rest of the world. We were the model for size, productivity, for efficiency— but not necessarily for quality. You've heard the expressions, "It ran like a Swiss watch," or "It had the precision of a German machine." We in the U.S. really didn't care. We left the specialized, high quality niche in the marketplace to others, while we concentrated on huge scale, high volume, mass production economics. . . . But then in the '60s and '70s we began to get some hint . . . that some of our assumptions were askew. For one thing, we started to experience some competition from foreign producers—not just because they could make their products cheaper and faster, but because they were, for God's sake, better. The car didn't fall apart at 30,000 miles, and when you bought their television set, it didn't mean taking the repairman into the family.

> Dr. Irving G. Snyder, Jr.
> Vice President and Director
> of Research & Development
> Dow Chemical USA
> from a speech: "The
> Quality Revolution—It
> Just Ain't in Our Genes"

Two assumptions at the very core of our economic system are now causing untold harm: (1) bigger is better, and biggest is best; (2) labor (human beings at work) is to be ever more narrowly specialized, or eliminated if possible.

THE AMERICAN PENCHANT FOR GIANTISM

Big, not best, has always been the American calling card. In fact, I bet you can't drive more than seventy-five miles in any direction, from anywhere in the United States, without running into a "biggest in the world" of some sort. Wide-open spaces and an apparently limitless frontier set it all in motion. U.S. farmers, starting with the Pilgrims, would cultivate land, wear it out, and blithely move west five miles. Today almost every farm you see is a history lesson told by hulks of rusted cars and agricultural equipment, and homes and yards are filled with broken Christmas toys and power lawn mowers.

Have you ever seen a rusted auto or tractor body in Germany, Switzerland, or Japan? The Europeans and the Japanese have lived within limits for centuries, and have had to be more careful with resources—that is, quality-conscious.

When we began to manufacture, we adopted agriculture's early habits—mass, not quality. Big railroads spurred us on by making vast markets for cheap goods accessible to industry. Railroad tycoons then used naked power to create and control huge business combinations; independents who wouldn't go along faced outrageous rail rates and were often forced out of business. The rise of big combines coincided with the War Department's perfection of mass-production techniques starting in the Civil War and culminating little more than a half-century later, during World War I. Britain may have invented most tools of mass production, but Americans copied and perfected them, and applied them to commercial use. (It's ironic that we are now the premier inventors, and Japan the "copycat" perfecters.)

This all-American system—long production runs, mass operations—paid off with victory in World Wars I and II, and cemented subsequent U.S. economic dominance. But we won World War II with *more* tanks and planes, not, in general, *better* ones. And then overseas economies revived and started looking to our enticing markets. Their only entryways were through niche markets and by offering superb quality to overcome our skepticism, such as that engendered by the inferior image of Japanese products in 1955.

The emphasis on quality fit nicely with European and Japanese skills, in particular their bent for craft (non-specialized) labor and their use of the worker as the primary means of adding value to a product. As well, their historic lack of excessive vertical integration (as in the Ford Motor Company, which once owned the iron mines from which came the iron for the steel forged in the River Rouge mills that in turn went into the cars) provided unique flexibility and was the basis for the short production runs needed to conquer small niche markets. We stuck to our penchant for big, becoming enamored of large-scale automation after World War II. The Japanese took our unused designs for smaller, more

23

flexible machine tools, cornered that market, and also raised rapid product changeover to a high art.

And so today, we are in trouble. Quality and flexibility will be the hallmarks of the successful economy for the foreseeable future. A recent poll of Korean businessmen, *Fortune* reports, revealed that "they preferred Japanese suppliers to American by a margin of two to one. The Koreans complained about mediocre product quality, slow delivery times, and poor service, and added that U.S. companies were reluctant to accept small orders." (This is all the more dramatic, given the longstanding enmity between the Japanese and the Koreans.)

The Koreans are right, but it is gut-wrenching to turn our backs on bigness. GE chairman Jack Welch tells security analysts he wants his company to be number one in "market value"—to be worth the most on the stock market. Does he want to be remembered for superb products? for creating jobs? Who knows? He seldom talks about products; and as for jobs, GE has slashed over 100,000 jobs from its payroll, not counting acquisitions, since he came aboard. And as one *Forbes* writer puts it, GE's Fairfield headquarters "has the look and feel of a colossal investment banking house on the prowl for takeover targets"—with nary a product in sight.

Size drives even entrepreneurs, who all too quickly drift from a desire to be special to a desire to be big, and, they anticipate, safe. People Express founder Don Burr's ill-fated acquisition of Frontier Airlines is all too typical.

Listen to the chatter when the Fortune 500 comes out. Few chiefs comment on their profit or return on assets. The question is: "What's your rank?" "Making the Fortune 500"—an attribute based on size alone—is the Holy Grail for most nonmembers; moving up is the Holy Grail for most members.

The Japanese Passion Whose Time Has Come

There are two principal schools of thought about the Japanese miracle. Economists would have us believe their success is due to consistent, conservative macro-economic policy—the confluence of interest between companies and their bankers, and between the bankers and the government. For instance, the conservative alliance represented by the all-powerful Ministry of Finance and the more visible Ministry of International Trade and Industry (MITI) directs low-cost loans to targeted industries and protects youthful (or recovering) industries. The sociologists and management theorists sing a different tune, explaining the same phenomenon in terms of group cohesion, lifetime employment, and other management and family (e.g., child-rearing) practices.

The plain fact is, of course, that both have a point. Both factors have contributed to Japan's success.

But there are other, more novel explanations that make sense too. One such focuses on the unique, age-old Japanese passion for smallness, in a world where the advantages of smallness seem to be fast eclipsing the once generally perceived value of giantism. For instance, in *Smaller Is Better: Japan's Mastery of the Miniature,* Korean writer O-Young Lee suggests that "Japan, with its tradition of smaller is better . . . its sensitivity to information, is perfectly positioned to take the lead in the coming age of reductionism."

Lee does a thorough job of tracing the roots of Japan's attachment to smallness. Japanese fairy tales, for example, feature "little giants" who turn needles into swords, bowls into boats, in contrast to such characters of Western folk legend as Paul Bunyan. But the language may provide the most important clue. For instance, the Japanese word for "craftsmanship" is literally "delicate workmanship," and that for feminine beauty is "detailed woman." On the other hand, "large" is literally "not delicately crafted" and "worthless" is "not packed in." There are many more prefixes, more frequently used, that mean "small" than "big." And so on.

The folding fan, miniature gardening, the tea ceremony, and other ritual staples of Japanese life all stem, according to Lee, from a passion for reductionism. For meditation, the Japanese naturally gravitate to small spaces—small inner courts, say, within already small houses—while Americans (and Koreans and Chinese, for that matter) head for the wide-open spaces when they need to reflect. In fact, the Japanese are contemptuous of almost everything large, says Lee, adding that "Nothing comes harder to the Japanese than living with objects of no use. They cannot bear the unnecessary, the excess."

This deep-seated Japanese trait has major economic consequences in these, the early days of the electronic (miniaturization) age. Sony, for instance, has pioneered in miniaturization—of tape recorders and radios (the Walkman), of VCRs (see also page 197), and of the disk audio, and now video, player.

Though it was a U.S. firm that invented the transistor, and initially supplied transistors to Sony, it was Sony which first mastered the consumer application of the technology. Many other examples, of course, could be added, such as the development of the first electronic calculator by Sharp in 1963. Lee concludes: "That reduction is a hallmark of Japanese electronics should come with little surprise if we recall our discussion of the [Japanese] rock garden. . . . the essence of rock gardening aesthetic was summed up in the words of the garden designer Tessen Soki: 'A thousand miles is shrunk down to one foot.' " (Japan's total dominance of the market in miniaturized consumer goods is illustrated by its astonishing $9 billion positive trade balance in consumer electronics alone,* which is nearly half the size of its more ballyhooed automotive surplus.)

In summary, says Lee, "It has been a thousand years since Sei Shonagon wrote, 'All things small, no matter what they are, all things small are beautiful.' How ironic that we should now be hearing the same refrain from the other side of the Pacific!"

One need look no further than a 1987 Mazda ad in a Lufthansa in-flight magazine for evidence supporting Lee's thesis. The ad simply could not have been conceived in America. Its beautiful artwork features a photograph of

---

*The overall annual U.S. electronic trade deficit with Japan runs over $20 billion.

eleven ancient, delicately crafted Japanese wooden combs. The ad's lead was "Combing Through the Details." The copy proceeds:

A comb looks like a very simple item. But it is deceptively simple. We tend to forget that in the past combs were all hand made. That every tooth, and the space between each tooth, was filed to the same width. This uniformity is all the more astonishing when we remember it was achieved by eye. One mistake and the comb would be ruined. This made combs valuable possessions. And the fact that they were personal items engendered the belief in ancient Japan that one's comb was the repository of one's soul. No wonder the making of it was approached with an almost religious devotion. The comb, an example of how devotion to the basics can lead to simply stunning results. Mazda. Where a devotion to the basics of automotive engineering leads to simply stunning results.

The ad, then, (1) uses the small and delicate as exemplar (a comb in this instance), (2) underscores the tie to ancient Japan and craftsmanship, and (3) "sells" the emphasis on details as Mazda's principal competitive strength.

Now GM has tried a similar tack, using the lead line "No one sweats the details like GM." The similarity is superficial, to say the least. "Sweat" and the image of delicate and ancient combs are, figuratively and literally, worlds apart!

Re-interpreting History I: Has Big Ever Been More Efficient?

The new market realities demand flexibility and speed. The new technologies permit their achievement—but only if we turn our backs decisively on our love affair with size and its handmaidens, stability and predictability. And a useful step in weaning ourselves from the obsession with size might be to recognize that it has never yielded the promised results.

"Bigness has not delivered the goods, and this fact is no longer a secret." With these words, economists Walter Adams (a former president of Michigan State University) and James Brock launch their 1986 book *The Bigness Complex.* After a review of hundreds of studies, they conclude: "Scientific evidence has not been kind to the apostles of bigness and to their mythology."

Adams and Brock don't even require us to deal with the many forces—the instability, the technology of miniaturization, the explosion in products, services, and competitors, and the changing markets just described—that are all currently pushing toward the predominance of smaller enterprises or business units. They argue, and my own observations coincide with theirs, that the highly touted economies of scale have never been all they were cracked up to be.

In fact, astute observers of the industrial landscape have been questioning the efficiency of bigness for decades. A report on U.S. Steel done by a management consultant in the 1930s concluded even then that the firm was "a big, sprawling, inert giant, whose production operations were improperly coordinated; with an inadequate knowledge of the costs or the relative profitability of the many thousands of items it sold; with production and cost standards generally below those considered everyday practice in other industries; with inadequate knowledge of its domestic markets and no clear appreciation of its opportunity in foreign markets; with less efficient production facilities than its rivals had."

Also in the 1930s, the legendary General Motors chairman Alfred Sloan turned self-critical, observing that "in practically all our activities we seem to suffer from the inertia resulting from our great size. . . . There are so many people involved and it requires such a tremendous effort to put something new into effect that a new idea is likely to be considered insignificant in comparison with the effort that it takes to put it across. . . . Sometimes I am almost forced to the conclusion that General Motors is so large and its inertia so great that it is impossible for us to be leaders."

In a classic 1956 study, economist Joe Bain examined the cost advantages flowing to multi-plant, as opposed to single-plant, firms in twenty industries. In no case was owning more than one plant a major advantage! More recently, Frederic Scherer studied the fate of fifteen former subsidiaries of conglomerates that had been sold to their former managers. All but one showed substantial improvements in profit—despite the heavy burden of debt incurred in the buy-outs. Among the reasons for the dramatic improvement, Scherer notes these: "Cost-cutting opportunities that had previously gone unexploited were seized. Austere offices were substituted for lavish ones. Staffs were cut back sharply. . . . Inexpensive computer services were found to substitute for expensive in-house operations. Make vs. buy decisions were reevaluated and lower-cost alternatives were embraced. Efforts were made to improve labor-management relations by removing bureaucratic constraints that had been imposed by the previous conglomerate's headquarters. Tight inventory controls were implemented, cutting holding costs by as much as one-half."

The movement toward efficiency through smallness is accelerating in virtually every industry today. Language itself provides the first clue:

▶ In steel, there is an unsung U.S. success story—the one-third of the market now held by profitable, fast-growing firms such as Nucor Corporation and Chaparral Steel. These two have excelled in "mini-mills." Now, the *mini-mill* is about to be eclipsed by the *micro-mill:* further miniaturization, thanks to new technologies, will make it economical to dot little mills every 25 miles or so along the road, in support of local markets.

▶ A recent *Industry Week* analysis of Allen-Bradley observes that "the Milwaukee-based firm found that its motor starters were losing market share to imports. . . . The design was obsolescent. . . . the company designed and built a . . . *minifactory* [my emphasis] to make them in Milwaukee. Allen-Bradley has cashed in on the flexibility of its *'factory within a factory'* [my emphasis]. It has boosted the variety of starters from 125 originally to 600—without adding floorspace or hardware. . . . Its flexibility gives the company a quick-response capability that translates into a marketplace edge. . . . Now it exports motor starters again and is recouping its domestic share as well."

▶ In photo-finishing, the *mini-lab* is allowing corner shops with a $250,000 line of credit to do what only Kodak could do ten years ago. The same is true in optometry, where the same word is in vogue.

▶ The evidence even cascades from the shelves of the corner grocery store, where, for example, the products of a host of *micro-brewers* are pushing the venerable Budweiser to the rear.

More sweeping evidence comes from *U.S. News & World Report*'s year-end analysis for 1986. It attributes much of the productive vitality of the Los Angeles basin—population about 13 million—to the astonishing fact that "some 90 percent of those employed in the . . . area work in small firms with fewer than 50 people that can change course fast to stay competitive."

Once upon a not-so-ancient time, as noted above, Ford owned the mines that provided the iron that went into the steel from which its cars were made. Today, too much of such vertical integration is hurting many of the old industrial giants. For instance, most of Chrysler's $500-per-car cost advantage over GM accrues from the fact that it purchases 70 percent of its components outside the firm; the comparable GM proportion is 30 percent. Not surprisingly, de-integration is now a strategic priority at GM. As Gordon Forward, founder of Chaparral, puts it, "The big is coming out of manufacturing in this country." The *Economist* confirms the trend:

> Disbursement of production towards ever-smaller manufacturing units is progressing remorselessly. . . . Industrial boutiques [those new terms again], run by small, independent operators with all the latest computer-aided . . . techniques are emerging as contractors to mainstream corporations, many of which might eventually be forced to offload their own manufacturing units and buy in tailor-made products. . . . [That is], Henry Ford's soul-destroying, wealth-creating assembly lines are out of date. Most of the things factories make now—be they cars, cameras or candlesticks—come in small batches designed to gratify fleeting market whims. The successful manufacturing countries in the 21st century will be those whose factories change their products fastest.

Reinterpreting History II: Has Big Ever Been More Innovative?

After efficiency, the second advantage of bigness touted by its advocates has been innovativeness. On this point, the authors of *The Bigness Complex* begin by presenting the advocates' conventional wisdom—

> Ostensibly, giant firms might be presumed for a variety of reasons to be superior inventors and innovators: They can afford to hire armies of the best brains and to outfit them in elaborate, extensive and sophisticated laboratories. Their massive size should permit them to bear the potential losses of risky research into fundamentally new products and production processes. They can further reduce risks by operating a large portfolio of

individual projects, so that the success of any one project can compensate for the failures and losses of other projects. They have established channels of distribution and that should enable them to quickly bring new products to market.

—and then proceed to slash away:

Reality and the available evidence show that despite all these theoretical advantages, small firms . . . are far more efficient innovators than industrial giants . . . small firms are more prolific inventors than giant companies; small firms exert significantly greater research and development effort than large ones; small firms devise and develop inventions at substantially lower costs than large firms; and the giant organizations seem to suffer a number of debilitating and apparently endemic disadvantages as regards invention and innovation.

Adams and Brock review numerous studies, such as one by the National Science Board (part of the National Science Foundation) which reveals that only 34 percent of major technical innovations come from giant firms (over 10,000 employees)—far less than those firms' share of industrial output. Moreover, "the smallest firms produced about four times as many innovations per R&D dollar as the middle-size firms and 24 times as many as the largest firms."

They continue with this *coup de grâce:* "Nor do giant firms display any appetite for undertaking more fundamental and risky research projects. That is, contrary to the image that bigness is conducive to risk-taking, there is no statistically significant tendency for corporate behemoths to conduct a disproportionately large share of the relatively risky R&D or of the R&D aimed at entirely new products and processes. On the contrary, they generally seem to carry out a disproportionately small share of the R&D aimed at entirely new products and processes." Yet another study reveals that large firms spend three to ten times more than small ones to develop similar new products. Even firms venerated for research, such as Du Pont, are challenged by these authors: "A study . . . found the bulk of the firm's commercially important products to have been invented *outside* the firm."

Brock and Adams do a much-needed job in conveying the macro-economists' view of the shortcomings of size. Eli Ginzberg of Columbia University and George Vojta, formerly Citicorp's top strategic planner, examine the phenomenon from the managerial perspective in *Beyond Human Scale: The Large Corporation at Risk:*

The large corporation at risk moves along a familiar path. Growth in earnings and return on capital tend to moderate. Often the deceleration of the rate of profits conceals an accumulation of potential corporate deficits, which are permitted to remain hidden, at least for a time, by accounting conventions and/or regulatory procedures. . . . [A] slow secular decline in a major arena is often misread as a cyclical phenomenon that time will cure. This misreading allows top management to procrastinate before taking corrective action. . . .

Burdened by the high costs of internal coordination and ineffective utilization of its human resources, the large enterprise is increasingly vulnerable to the entry of small and medium firms into its markets. Its vulnerability is usually in the specialized segments of these markets, where the small firm can be more attentive and responsive to selected customer groups. These new competitors, unburdened by massive prior investments and free of the heavy costs of internal coordination, are frequently able to offer superior products and thereby capture the small end of the market. The large-scale competitor must therefore focus increasingly on the upper end, where transaction size and gross profitability are still large enough to cover its costs. Over time, many large corporations must yield large segments of what had earlier been highly profitable markets to the new competition. . . . At this stage the firm is on the brink of major trauma. It confronts large write-offs, is vulnerable to takeover bids, and may even have to file for bankruptcy.

While these two studies contain damning evidence, neither emphasizes the degree to which current trends are underscoring the inadequacies of bigness. The best contemporary analysis has been done by Michael Piore and Charles Sabel of MIT in *The Second Industrial Divide.* They catalogue "the break-up of mass markets," "the decomposition of large markets," "the disintegration of mass markets," "particularized demand," and, the ultimate, "fragmented markets becoming pulverized." Surprisingly, they are not talking about new arenas such as biotechnology and semiconductors, but about chemicals, steel, textiles, autos, and computers. And they propose a survivor's strategy, "flexible specialization," by which they mean smaller economic units or firms providing a wider variety of products for narrower markets. I will discuss such a strategy below. The point here is simply this: What has been the most venerated tradition in American economics, or, indeed, the American psyche—that big is good; bigger is better; biggest is best—isn't so. It wasn't so. And it surely won't be so in the future.

THE OTHER AMERICAN TRADITION:
MINIMIZATION OF LABOR'S ROLE

If bigness is now problematic (and never really was very good), what about that other sacred cow of the American economic belief system, the minimization of the role of labor? It began with a unique American device—the specializing of jobs into narrow skills. The Japanese and Europeans have a centuries-old craft-guild tradition (based on broad-based skills). Extreme specialization never took root in either setting. But neither the craft tradition nor the craftsmen came to America with the great waves of immigrants; instead, there were masses of illiterate peasants to labor in our giant factories. And when labor finally did organize, the result was to lock in place the narrow job jurisdictions that the moguls of mass production had so painstakingly invented.

The central idea behind narrow job classifications is the conception of labor as a mechanical tool; cost minimization (low wages) and the widespread application of labor-replacing automation are natural concomitants. So is the fact that old American firms and, more frighteningly, new ones thoughtlessly ship work offshore to find cheaper labor. No one speaks more eloquently of the stark choices we face than Robert Reich in *Tales of a New America:*

> . . . high wage economies can no longer depend on standardized mass production. Big Ideas . . . can be shipped in blueprints or electronic symbols anywhere on the globe. Workers in South Korea, Taiwan, or Mexico can churn out turbo-charged automatic vacuums just as well as American workers can, and for far lower wages. Indeed, today [an inventor] is as likely to license a South Korean or Taiwanese company to manufacture the [Big Idea] as he is to sell out to Westinghouse. If Westinghouse does get hold of [the] Big Idea, it is apt to build its own factory overseas.
>
> In a world where routine production is footloose and billions of potential workers are ready to underbid American labor, competitive advantage lies not in one-time breakthroughs but in continual improvements. Stable technologies get away. Keeping a technology requires elaborating upon it continuously, developing variations and small improvements in it that better meet particular needs. . . .
>
> Where innovation is continuous, and products are ever more tailored to customers' particular needs, the distinction between goods and services begins to blur. Thus when robots and computerized machine tools are linked through software that allows them to perform unique tasks, customer service becomes a part of production. When a new alloy is molded to be a specified weight and tolerance, service accounts for a significant part of the value added. . . . Reports that American workers can no longer compete in manufacturing and must shift to services are only half-right. More precisely, they can keep high wages only by producing goods with a large component of specialized services, or to state the same thing differently, providing services integral to the production and use of specific goods.
>
> The point is this: In the new global economy, nearly everyone has access to Big Ideas and the machines and money to turn them into standardized products, at about the same time, and on roughly the same terms. *The older industrial economies have two options: They can try to match the wages for which workers elsewhere are willing to labor. Or they can compete on the basis of how quickly and well they can transform ideas into incrementally better products* [my emphasis].
>
> The first path—toward stable mass production—relies on cutting labor costs and leaping into wholly new product lines as old ones are played out.

For managers this path has meant undertaking (or threatening) massive layoffs, moving (or threatening to move) to lower-wage states and countries, parceling out work to lower-cost suppliers, automating to cut total employment, and diversifying into radically different goods and services. For workers this path has meant defending existing jobs and pay scales, grudgingly conceding lower wages and benefits, shifting burdens by accepting lower pay scales for newly-hired workers, seeking protection from foreign competition, and occasionally striking.

The second path . . . involves increasing labor value. For managers this path means continuously retraining employees for more complex tasks, automating in ways that cut routine tasks and enhance worker flexibility and creativity, diffusing responsibility for innovation, taking seriously labor's concern for job security and giving workers a stake in improved productivity via profit-linked bonuses and stock plans. For workers this second path means accepting flexible job classifications and work rules, agreeing to wage rates linked to profits and productivity improvements, and generally taking greater responsibility for the soundness and efficiency of the enterprise. The second path also involves a closer and more permanent relationship with other parties that have a stake in the firm—suppliers, dealers, creditors, even the towns and cities in which the firm resides.

On this second path, all those associated with the firm become partners in its future. . . . Each member of the enterprise participates in its evolution. All have a commitment to the firm's continued success. Both paths can boost profits and improve competitiveness in the short run. But only the second can maintain and improve America's standard of living over time.

A Grim Prognosis

Today's and tomorrow's winning hand is becoming increasingly clear—quality and flexibility. Essential to them both are (1) smaller units and (2) highly skilled workers serving as the chief source of incremental improvements in products and services.

Is it a simple case of what "goes around, comes around"? Long-standing Japanese and European traditions—less dependence on big scale, more dependence on broadly skilled labor—are now conducive to economic success. Our denigration of these two factors may prove disastrous.

Worse yet, we have no tradition to fall back on as we seek new models. This is not, as some have labeled it, a "back to basics" movement. Quality and flexibility through skilled labor have never been an American custom.

THE SHAPE OF THE NEW
AMERICAN COMPETITOR

Uniformity has given way to broader choices. . . . Mass markets have splintered. Size has lost its significance as it becomes increasingly clear that a company's rank in the *Fortune 500* is of limited importance.

Martin Davis
Chairman, Gulf+Western
Fortune, December 1985

In the face of the uncertainties catalogued above, there are those who *are* thriving, in every economic sector. Interestingly, the winners increasingly share common traits. Most pronounced is the emergence of the specialist producer of high value-added goods or services,* or niche creator, which is either a stand-alone firm or a downsized, more entrepreneurial unit of a big firm.

Specialists in Steel, Autos, and Chemicals . . .

A quick *tour d'horizon* admits no exception to this trend. Begin with the toughest of industries, steel. While USX, LTV, Bethlehem, and the rest of the integrated firms totter, mini-mill/micro-mill leaders such as Nucor Corporation and Chaparral, and specialists like Worthington Industries, thrive. Productivity in each of these large firms is several times the industry average. Worker involvement is uniformly high, and quality and responsiveness to customers are phenomenal. In many markets, business is being won back from overseas.

The auto market is flying apart. Hyundais dot the highway. Chrysler's president says we will soon have "the Big Thirty, not the Big Three," and industry analyst Maryann Keller comments that "The U.S. market [has become] a collection of niche markets." Chrysler was following a niche strategy when it acquired AMC primarily for its Jeep Division. And Ford has won by adding value to its product through design distinction and high quality. GM, on the other hand, has been losing out: aiming for the "mass market" that no longer exists, it produced look-alike models, and did not deign to enter small niches, such as that for four-wheel drive and turbos, until very late in the game. The huge firm, says Keller, was "nibbled to death rather than chewed" by smaller, more highly focused competitors.

In chemicals, big firms are writing off billions of dollars in assets in basic

---

*The term "high value-added" will be routinely used throughout the book. By it I simply mean products or services which emphasize innovative design tailored for narrow markets and resulting from more intense listening to customers; superior quality; exceptional service and responsiveness to customers. This is in contrast to the Model T strategy—"any color as long as it's black"— followed by so many firms to this day.

commodity chemicals aimed at undifferentiated markets; they are racing, instead, into what the industry calls "downstream" (closer to the river's mouth, or customers) products—numerous specialty, high value-added chemicals to address the narrow needs of smaller markets. Monsanto had a rosy profit picture in 1986; in just five years it has reduced its dependence on bulk chemicals from 26 percent to 3 percent of assets. Du Pont is creating numerous swift-moving business units, closer to the market.

. . . and Computers and Semiconductors

In September 1986, *Financial World* reviewed the computer industry, observing: "Despite analysts' predictions of an industry shakeout, that only a handful of huge companies would survive, the computer industry is actually *more* fragmented than ever." The *Economist,* in January 1987, concurred: "The way in which market forces have humbled IBM is a lesson to trustbusters everywhere. Only a few years ago the American Justice Department and the EEC Commission threatened to break it up or maim it, so as to end its near-monopoly of the computer market. Today it is struggling to remain a blue-chip. In 1986 it suffered a 27 percent fall in net profits . . . while increasing its sales by a tiny 2.5 percent to $51 billion. Can IBM now mount as successful a counter-attack against its competitors as it did against too-hasty trustbusters?"

In fact, IBM is under attack from the world of the future (Hypres is succeeding, where a quarter-billion-dollar IBM development project failed, in introducing the first products using exotic Josephson Junction technology)—and in supercomputers (Cray et al.), superminicomputers (Convex et al.), engineering work stations (Apollo et al.), minicomputers and networks (Digital Equipment et al.), and personal computers (Apple et al.). A February 1987 issue of *High Technology* assesses the state of the vital "parallel/multiprocessor computers" market. It lists nineteen products, from Elxisi's 6400 to Sequent's Balance 2100 to BBN's Butterfly to NCube. Elxisi? BBN? Who?

In semiconductors, the commodity, or so-called merchant chip, market, once dominated by Fairchild, National Semiconductor, et al., has all but been lost to Japan. We were victimized even in this new arena by our century-old addiction to mass production and our aversion to labor. With a few exceptions such as IBM, which produces chips only for internal consumption, the big U.S. producers emphasized invention over polishing manufacturing skills. Mass production facilities were built willy-nilly as product demand soared. The best engineers did not go into production. Silicon Valley's labor practices, except for engineers, often make Detroit's look humanistic. Since demand exceeded supply in the days in which these firms' philosophies were taking shape, rudeness, not responsiveness, was the approach to customer affairs.

Now the worm has turned, as it did on Detroit. Computer companies and other purchasers not only found the Japanese chip to be of higher quality, they found the Japanese firm to be more responsive to their needs—from 6,000 miles away—than their next-door neighbors.

The way out of the box, if there is one, appears to be customer-centered specialization. Thus Intel is betting much of its future on an entrepreneurial Application Specific Integrated Circuit (ASIC) unit—a group whose operations are entirely separated from those of the rest of the firm. The greater good-news story in U.S. semiconductors, however, may be the 113 specialist start-ups between 1977 and 1986 that constitute the so-called Third Wave; only six have failed, and the new bunch will do over $2 billion in sales in 1987. Some, such as LSI Logic, which was just founded in 1981 but is projecting sales of $300 million in 1987, have become powerhouses. They give us a wide lead in what may well turn out to be the most important part of the industry.

Forget Bigness in Packaged Goods Too

The story is repeated in packaged goods and foods. Take Kitchen Privileges of Alexandria, Virginia, a specialist firm that serves specialists. It is a commercial kitchen (seventeen ovens, walk-in freezer, etc.) specifically designed to be rented. And it is, by giants such as Campbell Soup, to help test-market new products, and by start-ups like Ultimate Brownies. Consumers, especially in the burgeoning two-worker-family sector, are demanding more and more fresh specialized products. Big producers such as Campbell and entrepreneurs by the thousand are satisfying them by deluging a market increasingly fragmented into niches with goods designed to fit.

Campbell has in fact had two sweeping reorganizations in the last five years. The first created over fifty fleet-of-foot business units, the second decentralized marketing into regional offices in an effort to get closer to the distribution channel. Flexible manufacturing systems the firm is introducing add yet another dimension of responsiveness.

Procter & Gamble is following a similar path, attempting to streamline its very hierarchical, functionally centered organization. The firm's past successes cannot be denied, but its old approach is far too cumbersome for today's fast-changing markets.

Ditto the Service Sector

The situation in the service sector is no different. The business section of the January 3, 1987, issue of the Kansas City *Times* proclaims: "Niche stores again outdo retail giants in holiday sales." The new household names and profit stars in retailing are firms such as The Limited, The Gap, and Nordstrom. Even the specialists are specializing—The Limited's Victoria's Secret, Limited Express, and Henri Bendel; The Gap's Banana Republic. Meanwhile, the giants, from Safeway to Carter Hawley-Hale, sputter, fight takeover threats, and attempt to transform their cavernous retail spaces into collections of Limited-like boutiques. (Counter-trends can be found, to be sure, such as warehouse stores in retailing. However, these stores will likely end up with a very limited share of the market. In fact, sales per store in warehouse operations have been declining since 1983.)

In financial services, the "financial supermarket," with its one-stop shopping for all financial services, died stillborn: for example, Merrill Lynch, formulator of the idea, sold off its commercial real estate unit in 1986. And the giant banks, with rare exceptions, look much less "solid" than only a few years ago; the Bank of America is the premier acute-care case—while superregionals such as Banc One of Columbus, Ohio, are surging ahead and smaller specialists such as the University National Bank & Trust of Palo Alto, California, are growing fast and yielding eye-popping returns to assets. Indeed, a look at *Business Week*'s 1986 list of the top 200 banks reveals that the further down the list you go, the better the returns get. Only one of the twenty-three biggest banks (The Morgan) returned more than 1 percent on assets, while fully twenty of the smallest fifty topped that magic mark.

In health care, too, the mega-firms like American Medical International and Hospital Corporation of America were seen as the wave of the future just a few years ago. They roamed the countryside gobbling up small hospitals, and some experts were predicting that most health care in the United States would be delivered by a half-dozen firms by the mid-nineties. Now the giants are struggling. On May 31, 1987, for instance, HCA announced that it was selling off 104 hospitals, for $1.8 billion; it is left with 75, some 50 psychiatric centers, and a number of management contracts. On the other hand, regional hospitals that have specialized are doing well. So are ambulatory-care centers and superspecialists such as ServiceMaster, a Chicago-area firm whose principal business is contracting to clean hospitals. It's over a billion dollars in size, with a five-year return to equity that was tops among the *Business Week 1000* in 1986. (Incidentally, ServiceMaster is going great guns with its mundane but specialized service in Japan, too.)

More evidence of the specialist advance in services is the burgeoning of temporary services and franchising. Only a few years ago the word "temp" brought to mind stenographers and receptionists. The industry, which grew at a compound annual rate of almost 20 percent from 1970 to 1984, now provides temporary semiconductor workers, trial lawyers, and even executives. Call Kelly today for that secretary substitute, and they'll ask you if you want a WordStar or a MacWrite person.

Typical of the specialist winner in franchising is Minit-Lube, or "McOil Change," as *Forbes* dubbed the several-hundred-unit chain:

> Stand in the spotless driveway of Minit-Lube, a fast-growing auto lubrication franchise, where cars are streaming into Minit-Lube's bays, three abreast. Why is this chain so successful? Perhaps it is because, aside from the drive-through car bays, Minit-Lube looks nothing like a greasy automotive business. It's clean, painted white and surrounded by neatly trimmed, lush landscaping. . . . The place should have been named McOil Change. The customer pulls up, is greeted by a smiling employee trained to make

eye contact. The customer then places the standard order—a check or fill of brake and power-steering fluids, motor oil, battery water and filters for air and oil. Thereafter, a uniformed service team springs into action. One pops the hood to check and fill fluids. Another vacuums the interior and cleans windows. A third, from a pit below, works his way along the drive shaft, grease gun and wrench in hand, lubricating joints, draining the oil and replacing the filter. Within ten minutes the driver is on his way. The bill: $20. Sears charges the same just for an oil change and lubrication, and it can take up to an hour.

The Winning Look Is Clear

This tour is hardly complete, but it does give the flavor of the sorts of firms that are turning up winners. And even were most of the recent mergers to reverse history's trend and work, the movement toward specialization and more moderately sized business units would in no way be blocked. A GE swallows an RCA, but its first move is to put each acquired business unit, such as NBC, through a starvation diet, similar to the one GE's homegrown corporate and business unit staffs have been subjected to. The truly close-to-the-market units within GE and its acquisitions, and within Du Pont, IBM, and P&G, are being reshaped to look and act more like The Limited, Minit-Lube, or Worthington Industries.

Take all the evidence together, and a clear picture of the successful firm in the 1990s and beyond emerges. It will be:

▶ flatter (have fewer layers of organization structure)
▶ populated by more autonomous units (have fewer central-staff second-guessers, more local authority to introduce and price products)
▶ oriented toward differentiation, producing high value-added goods and services, creating niche markets
▶ quality-conscious
▶ service-conscious
▶ more responsive
▶ much faster at innovation
▶ a user of highly trained, flexible people as the principal means of adding value

Figure 1 summarizes the case I've made so far. A series of forces, arrayed on the left side of the chart, are interacting with one another to create a completely new context for doing business, labeled "outcome." The outcome can only be dealt with, I believe, by firms which share a common set of traits, labeled "shape of a winner."

It is that shape, and the attainment of it in short order, which this book addresses.

Generic Uncertainty

- Oil @ $5 or $35 a barrel
- 1 trillion Eurodollars
- $80 trillion in annual currency = trading/gyrating exchange rates
- Casino society (junk bonds, availability of venture capital, strong market for initial public offerings, leveraged buyouts)
- $1 trillion in developing-country debt
- Mergers, divestitures, de-integration, joint ventures
- Record business and bank failures (and record start-ups)

Technology Revolution

- Design (fast collection of customer data, reduced design-to-manufacture time)
- Manufacturing (smaller, more flexible factories)
- Distribution (electronic linkages, power to customers)

New Competitors

FOREIGN
- Developed (e.g. Japan, Germany)
- Newly industrialized (e.g. Korea)
- Rapidly industrializing (e.g. Brazil)

DOMESTIC
- Smaller firms resulting from the entrepreneurial explosion
- Downsized and de-integrated units within big firms, spun-off elements from big firms

Changing Tastes

- More options
- Two-wage-earner families
- More affluence (top third)
- Less affluence (bottom third)
- Saturation of markets for the "commodities" of yesteryear
- Demand for superior quality

Figure 1: **Forces at Work and Their Apparent Resolution**

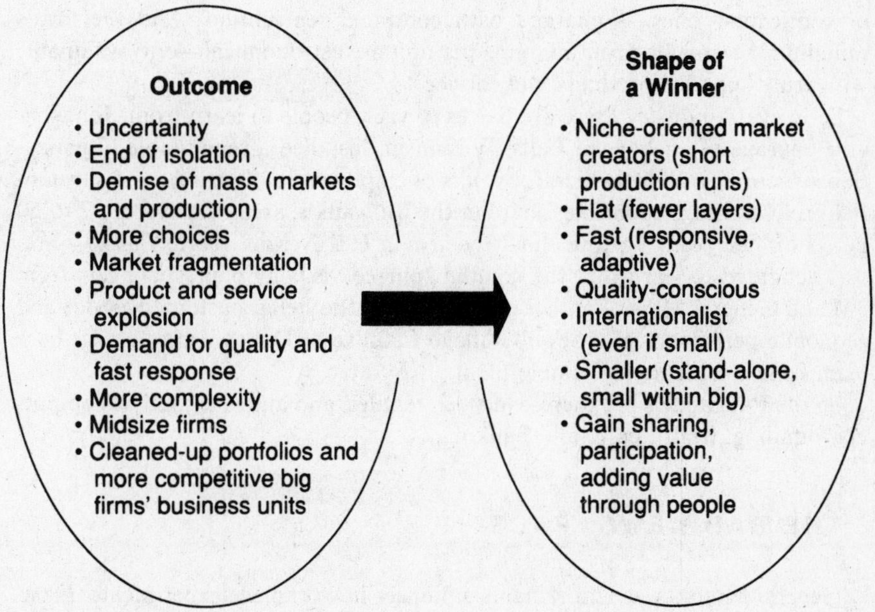

Outcome

- Uncertainty
- End of isolation
- Demise of mass (markets and production)
- More choices
- Market fragmentation
- Product and service explosion
- Demand for quality and fast response
- More complexity
- Midsize firms
- Cleaned-up portfolios and more competitive big firms' business units

Shape of a Winner

- Niche-oriented market creators (short production runs)
- Flat (fewer layers)
- Fast (responsive, adaptive)
- Quality-conscious
- Internationalist (even if small)
- Smaller (stand-alone, small within big)
- Gain sharing, participation, adding value through people

THE GOOD NEWS: THERE IS GOOD NEWS

You want evidence of transformation not led by major mergers? How about Ford at $60 billion, Chrysler at $23 billion, Dana at $4 billion, Brunswick at $3 billion, Milliken at $2 billion, Campbell Soup at $4 billion, McKesson at $6 billion? You want examples of those squarely in the middle of it? Try Du Pont or Procter & Gamble. How about winners who have hiccuped but so far not made a major misstep in tumultuous markets? Consider Cray, Apple, Digital Equipment, Nucor, Worthington, Chaparral, ServiceMaster, American Airlines, Banc One, Federal Express, The Limited, Nordstrom.

But is there anyone big who seems to have known the formula all along? I began this discussion by declaring that there were no excellent companies. Were I to admit an exception, it would be 3M. If ever there was a perpetual-motion machine, it is this $9 billion firm. Its trick has been to understand value-added differentiation and perpetual market creation long before such tactics became necessary. Every unit of the corporation, whether it serves "mature" markets or exotic new ones, is charged with continual reinvention. And the firm's minimum acceptable profit margins per unit are astronomical—only attainable with truly superior products and service.

So in every industry there are places to visit, people to learn from. Johnsonville Sausage of Sheboygan Falls, Wisconsin, installed a remarkable organization structure, with little hierarchy, lots of employee involvement, and substantial profit-sharing; its market share in the Milwaukee area soared from 7 to 50 percent in ten years. I wrote about the firm in *U.S. News & World Report*—and was delighted to learn that the column spurred visits by plant managers from 3M and General Mills. Another column, about the stellar customer service and economic performance of Sewell Village Cadillac of Dallas, led to a visit by a team from a Procter & Gamble plant.

So the role models are there—in steel, textiles, and autos, as well as computers, retailing, health care, and banking.

THE BAD NEWS: PACE

General Motors was and remains a pioneer in workplace experiments. From its joint venture with Toyota called the New United Motor Manufacturing, Inc. (NUMMI), to its assembly plant in Lakewood, Georgia, a lot has been going on.

But not enough. The firm's relative cost position has deteriorated. Its management ranks, despite radical (by past standards) surgery, remain hopelessly bloated. Its committee-driven designs still lag and its product development cycles are still two to three times longer than those of its best competitors. And it still can't figure out how to take on small markets. Top that off with a bad case of merger indigestion from Hughes and EDS alike. Moreover, technology, rather than people, is still its theme. (All of this was, almost certainly, what led to GM's precipitous 20 percent loss of market share in just one year, as of May 1987. Never mind whether or not GM will recover, as it may well do—the simple fact that the world's largest industrial firm could tumble that fast, despite extraordinary incentives to car buyers aimed at stemming the tide, is stunning evidence of the changing times.)

No one is complacent. Ford, though topping GM in profits in 1986 for the first time in sixty-two years, knows it has barely scratched the surface in its attempt to achieve superior quality and shorter product development cycles. It looks to Toyota as the premier firm in its industry. IBM is scurrying, too; one long-time observer of the firm estimates that its payroll has 50,000 more people than it needs to accomplish its current mission.

But is even Ford moving fast enough? It's not at all clear. Radical changes in organizational structure and procedures are called for. Layers of management must be reduced in most big firms by 75 percent. Product development time and order lead time must be slashed by 90 percent. Electronic/telecommunication linkups to customers and suppliers must be developed posthaste. Just listening to customers and dealers needs to become the norm—and as yet it's not.

All this adds up to a requirement, not for structural or procedural tinkering, but for a revolution in organization: more autonomous units—guided by a coherent vision rather than by memorandums and managers-as-cops, and manned by involved workers with a big stake in the action and hell-bent upon constant improvement. And this in turn means that new attitudes are also required—especially commitment on the part of managers to the idea that suppliers, workers, unions, distributors, and customers are all partners in the common endeavor.

But the wholesale changes in attitude have not yet occurred, and without them we are doing immeasurably dumb things. We are, for example, letting work drift offshore in pursuit of the lowest-cost production. But, as I'll argue below, to lose control of the plant is to lose control of the future—of quality, responsiveness, and the source of most innovation, which in manufacturing industries occurs in the palpable, on-premises interaction among plant team, designer, marketer, and customer.

We are misusing automation. Americans still see it as a tool to reduce the need for labor, not as a tool to aid labor in adding value to the product. In consequence, efforts to staff our plants with robots are not working.

We are still churning businesses, via merger and divestiture, in hopes of obtaining some ideal portfolio, fit for the future. There is none. No industry is safe. There is no such thing as a safe, fast-growth haven. The new attitudes toward people and adding value are required as much in financial services and entertainment as in autos and steel. Look at the revolution wrought by The Limited or Federal Express, linking people power and computer network power; most service firms are light-years behind.

This book is dedicated to Roger Milliken of Milliken & Co. His genius in 1980 was to see that the answer to competition in the "mature" textile market was unparalleled quality attained largely through people. He revolutionized the company then. But he's almost unique because he saw in 1984 that the first revolution was wholly inadequate to meet the worldwide competitive challenge. So he made another revolution, reordering every relationship in the firm in pursuit of unparalleled customer responsiveness. Two revolutions in six years.

It is Roger Milliken's brand of urgency—and taste for radical reform—that must become the norm. For Milliken's two revolutions (and the firm was a star to begin with) are still only barely meeting the competitive challenge.

IMPLICATIONS FOR PUBLIC POLICY

This book is meant to serve as a handbook for management. Management, I believe, holds the key to a competitive resurgence in the United States. Nonetheless, certain policy prods could help immeasurably in speeding the necessary transformation.

As a conclusion to this introductory analysis, I will offer only the barest of outlines—suggestions for several steps that policymakers can take:

1. Promote more, not less, competition. That is, turn up the heat. First, pass no protectionist legislation. Protect an industry, ancient and recent history alike suggest, and it gets sloppier, or at least fails to improve at an acceptable rate. Playing fields are not, and never have been, level. We should utilize existing trade management legislation, which is fully adequate, and not add more. The objective is to get better and different, not to try to hide from a newly energized world economy. (In this regard, the trade bill which will likely pass in 1987—the most restrictive since Smoot-Hawley in 1930—is a giant step backwards.)

Second, don't tie the corporate raiders' hands. Raiders are no altruists, and their acts cause much unnecessary pain. And, to be sure, some of the moves corporations make to forestall raiders are dysfunctional—for example, making inappropriate mergers so as to create a balance sheet that scares a raider off, or shuttling jobs offshore in a crash, but ultimately misguided, effort to slash costs. But on balance, the raiders are, along with the Japanese, the most effective force now terrorizing inert corporate managements into making at least some of the moves, such as downsizing, that should have been made years ago.

Third, get rid of the entire capital-gains tax after a certain holding period passes. The start-up firms are the breath of fresh air in the economy—we encouraged them with the 1981 capital-gains tax break, and have now discouraged them with the omnibus tax act of 1986. In general, support financial incentives that favor start-ups and spin-offs/divestitures such as leveraged buyouts.

2. Retool and involve the work force. The work force must become the prime source of value added. We need to give employers the incentive to hire people and constantly upgrade skills. First, provide a special tax incentive for all funds, including employee wage costs, spent on training and pay-for-knowledge programs. Provide a further tax incentive for wage increases that result directly from skill upgrading. Provide general tax deductibility for employee off-the-job skill upgrading, whether or not it's related to the current job. I also support, to aid displaced workers, some form of Individual Training Account, as proponents have labeled it. Sizable tax-deductible contributions by employees, similar to IRAs, might be made over an extended period. The money would revert to the employee at retirement or some such time, but upon displacement would be issued, in voucher form, for use in certified training programs.

A second, sweeping plank is aimed at giving employers an even higher incentive to hire and involve employees. Inspired, in particular, by the ideas discussed by Martin Weitzman in *The Share Economy,* I propose, for employers, that a major, old-fashioned investment tax credit plan be allowed on wages distributed as bonuses via profit-distributing bonus plans and quality- and productivity-based gain-sharing plans. For employees, I suggest a big tax exemption, possibly with limits, for all income from profit-distribution and productivity-based gain-sharing plans. (Such a bold incentive would be required to compensate for greater uncertainty—the real possibility of lower pay in bad times.)

Third, greater employee assurance is required as foreign competition heats up even further, and smaller firms become increasingly dominant. Extended and increased trade adjustment assistance is desirable to combat the former (though it should be highly skewed to force rapid enrollment in retraining programs, for instance). Portable pensions and other dislocation-ameliorating housing and health-care programs will be required as well.

3. Stop the mindless offshore job drift. The loss of jobs per se may be less significant than the loss of control of our destiny, as certain manufacturing activities migrate offshore. I propose a new form of domestic content legislation. The term is usually applied to the percentage of domestic content in imports. My alternative is to provide some tax credit for domestic products, based upon the percentage of domestic content, up to, say, 50 percent. A particularly thorny subset of this issue is start-ups—for instance, high-tech firms—that never do establish their own manufacturing operations. The capital-gains tax formula for start-ups could be a sliding one, depending on the percent of value added by onshore manufacture.

4. Push internationalism. We need to shed our lingering isolationism. Concepts I support include (a) a value-added tax (VAT) to pay for the programs I have proposed here, but excluding goods sold for export, (b) tax benefits favorable to Americans working abroad, (c) provision of more readily available financing sources for smaller or mid-sized firms seeking export markets, and (d) educational incentives to induce much more foreign-language education.

5. Support expanded research and development. The R&D tax credit and the basic-research credit which supports business and university linkages will both be phased out by the end of 1988, thanks to the 1986 tax act. At the least, they should be restored. Support for high levels of basic research, especially in non-defense areas, is a must. Additionally, we might provide special tax breaks

43

to firms that bring university researchers on board, or that support cooperative education programs, especially in engineering and science.

This brief sketch is not meant to be exhaustive. It does not include any mention of major policy levers that influence the overall business climate (arenas where others are more expert than I), and it includes only some of the types of policies that would hasten the transformation of our firms.*

I find myself turning more frequently to public policy considerations because of my growing frustration. The changes are being made—by management. The changes can be made—by management. But they are not being made fast enough by management. The issue is not the unions. Nor is it "unfair" Japanese practices, unless learning our language or paying attention to details that commercial and individual consumers care about is unfair.

We must look at what's working, and move fast to adapt and emulate the best. The speed of the transition is the most pressing issue.

---

*It also flies in the face of the basic intention of tax reform—less use of the tax code to manipulate firms' outcome. While I acknowledge the adverse consequences of thousands of special interest loopholes, I think this is precisely the wrong time to turn our back on the most effective weapon to aid rapid industrial transformation—tax policy.

2

Using the Prescriptions: The Essentials of Proactive Management

"NICE TO DO" BECOMES "MUST DO"

The history of the forty-five prescriptions that are the essence of this book is the history of *In Search of Excellence*. In short, a "nice-to-do" in 1979 (when the excellence research began) has become a "must-do" in the late 1980s.

It soon became apparent that the "excellence phenomenon," and the associated explosion of concern with management's performance, was not leading to rapid enough transformation by most firms. The modest effort of my colleagues and myself to focus on application of the principles for success we had described was spearheaded by a five-day executive seminar. It is officially called Implementing In Search of Excellence.

The spirit of implementation of the new, especially in sizable organizations, is best embodied by Kelly Johnson's original Lockheed "Skunk Works" (discussed extensively in *A Passion for Excellence*). A modest-sized band toiled under Johnson's guidance for forty-four years. In the process it delivered working prototypes, and often production models, of some forty-one new aircraft or other complex systems. Included were the F-104 Starfighter, the durable C-130, the renowned U-2, and the exotic SR-71 "blackbird" spy plane.

Again and again Johnson would deliver the goods in a tenth the expected time at a tenth the expected cost—and with a product both advanced and reliable. This sort of "corpocracy" beater was the symbol we were looking for. So the seminar became Skunk Camp, and the participants, naturally enough, became Skunks. Though the words are amusing, the objective, as with Johnson's original band, was deadly serious.

The people who came surprised us. After a first session attended mostly by our heroes (chicken magnate Frank Perdue, Dana turnaround boss Ren McPherson, et al.), the regular meetings were dominated by: (1) people who headed midsized companies and (2) action takers, such as plant or division managers, from giant firms.

Plant managers from Ford and Crown Zellerbach attended, as did division general managers from 3M. But more typical was the response of Buckman Labs. The firm is a privately held, $110 million maker of specialty chemicals based in Memphis, Tennessee; already well run, it has sent some twenty-four executives, from both U.S. and foreign operations, to our seminars.

The sessions, then, were filled with activists, not theorists. They bought the message of *Search* and *Passion,* and were hell-bent and determined to get on with it. So we were increasingly pressed by our customers to move beyond the case studies and examples in the two books to hard-edged answers to the question: "What in the heck are we supposed to *do*?" Thus "the promises" were born, drafted early one morning, seven in number. They have evolved into these prescriptions. I'll address their structure presently.

A different kind of evolution was more important. The original tone of presentation was: "Here's some nifty stuff you might do first, folks. Take it or leave it." But the evidence kept pouring in: America wasn't cutting it in any industry, either service or manufacturing. Banks, hospitals, and semiconductor firms alike were shutting their doors. GM, IBM, and Du Pont were quaking.

So a nice-to-do "reduce product development cycle time" became a hard-edged "reduce product development cycle time by 75 percent," and then became "reduce product development cycle time by 75 percent in the next two to three years." An innocuous "reduce the layers" became a sharp "no more than five layers in an organization of any size"—and "get rid of all first-line supervisors." "Get people involved" became "get everyone involved in almost everything, train like the dickens, and introduce major pay-for-knowledge and profit-distribution plans—NOW."

Thus the hastily sketched, "nice to do" promises have become a manifesto for radical organizational reform, a handbook for a management revolution. And the objective is not to be excellent, because "to be" implies stasis and there is no place to stand anymore; the only excellent firms are those that are rapidly evolving.

PRESCRIPTIONS FOR A WORLD TURNED UPSIDE DOWN

Five areas of management constitute the essence of proactive performance in our chaotic world: (1) an obsession with responsiveness to customers, (2) constant innovation in all areas of the firm, (3) partnership—the wholesale participation of and gain sharing with all people connected with the organization, (4) leadership that loves change (instead of fighting it) and instills and shares an inspiring vision, and (5) control by means of simple support systems aimed at measuring the "right stuff" for today's environment.

In each area except the last I will present ten prescriptions. Each of the total of forty-five, with no exceptions, is an urgent call for radical reform. Following the logic developed in the preceding chapter, for instance, the first "customer" prescription demands a radical shift of the firm's entire portfolio toward highly differentiated products, delivered via a strategy aimed at creating niche markets. It is my advice for bankers, retailers, hospital administrators, computer makers, and city managers alike.

The next prescription uses another "hot" word, urging a quality revolution. Why revolution? Simple. I've looked at dozens of "quality programs" closely, hundreds casually, and read and talked with the gurus. Everybody has a quality program—but only the tiniest handful, such as Ford, Milliken, and the Paul Revere Life Insurance Company, are really making a difference. Thus I spell out twelve steps, each bold, which represent the minimum basis for a quality revolution.

And on the challenges go, all the way to the last of the forty-five, which stresses integrity. Of course, integrity has always been important. But even its meaning has changed. If we are to depend increasingly on people's wholesale involvement, then integrity is more of an issue than ever—integrity, as I've come to see it, means that if there are no employee bonuses, there are no executive bonuses. It means trusting first-line employees to do all the quality control, after providing them with the tools and training required to execute.

The endpapers of this book list the forty-five prescriptions in abbreviated form. Two obvious questions pop out at once: What do you do first? How do you pace the introduction of the ideas?

There is a happy and an unhappy answer. The happy answer is that many of the prescriptions support each other. Doing one aids implementation of another. For instance, the twenty-five people, leadership, and systems prescriptions all exist solely to speed the customer and innovation goals established in the customer and innovation sections.

The bad news: *You can't do it all at once, but you must.* Fail to get on with almost all of this agenda at a brisk pace and you're in for trouble. Part of the reason is that explosion of domestic and foreign competitors: Some competitor is already beating you to the punch on most of these bold ideas in some segments of your market right now. But you can't do everything at once, and I do provide some guidelines for getting started. Still, your own sense of your competitive situation must be the guide to picking a starting point. And, of course, various parts of the organization can work with different intensity on different ideas.

Hard Evidence Supports Each Bold Goal

It's essential to note that there is no speculation involved in any of these prescriptions. First, they are born of the radically altered business environment in which we find ourselves. They are need-driven, pure and simple.

Second, each idea has already been anticipated by a few leaders in virtually every industry. There's not a hint of "it would really be nice to wire ourselves up to our customers." PPG (once Pittsburgh Plate Glass), Milliken, Federal Express, McKesson, et al. have done it. More are doing it every day.

The Prescriptions and the Public Sector

Maryland governor William Donald Schaefer led the dramatic transformation of Baltimore during his fifteen years as mayor. A compulsion for action, unmatchable energy, and an astonishing ability to be in touch with the city's people marked his tenure. That is why he joins Roger Milliken in my dedication.

In a late-1986 letter to me, Schaefer stated that "the same principles of success prevail" in the public as in the private sector. Many would debate Schaefer on that point. I'm not one of them. My own career includes over four years in two managerial assignments in Washington, one as a young Navy lieutenant at the Pentagon, one as a White House coordinator of drug treatment and law enforcement programs. Both jobs were humble ones, especially the first. So I have observed failure and success as an insider, and from watching the likes of Schaefer and General Bill Creech, former commander of the giant Air Force Tactical Air Command, whose dramatic organization turnaround was chronicled at length in *A Passion for Excellence*.

It *is* the same. Even the language is the same among the best in the public sector—that is, the customer is identified and made central to all affairs in the top schools, cities, state agencies. Such is the talk even in a newly invigorated IRS. Procedures have been radically simplified by the best public sector leaders. First-line-employee involvement and improvement programs in pursuit of responsive service are the essential concern of the top public sector bosses.

To address the similarities while attempting to deal with linguistic differences, I have included a brief section called "Public Parallels" at the end of those prescriptions whose translation to the public sector, in my experience, has been most difficult.

The Prescriptions as Management Theory

The prescriptions constitute a first draft, if you will, of a theory of management. I add this point because it is increasingly clear that we need a new theory of management, or at least some new generally accepted principles. It is audacious to proclaim these prescriptions as a first draft of generally accepted principles, yet I do.

They draw from the most thoughtful theorists of both macro- and microeconomics. They join the firm to worldwide financial flows and expected international conditions (and uncertainties). They are also consistent with the more sound of the various sociological and psychological theories on the internal states of organizations. Consideration is given to information theory, especially to so-called internal transaction costs (better called communication and coordination costs) that affect scale economies, flexibility, and responsiveness so greatly. Finally, the diverse impacts of changing technology on every aspect of the internal and external dealings of the organization are considered. Thus while all of the prescriptions are grounded in empirical evidence, all have been passed through a number of purely theoretical frameworks as well.

Why is this important to the practitioner, who is, after all, the book's customer? For at least two reasons, as it turns out. First, it is an essential test of soundness that extreme empirical observations—and, by conventional standards, the prescriptions are extreme—be consistent with some larger set of theoretical ideas. Otherwise, the extreme observations could be suspect as anomalies from which it is dangerous to generalize.

Second, each manager, from newly promoted supervisor to the chief executive of a big firm, has, and indeed needs, a pocket theory of management. It is seldom formal, to be sure, but more likely an implicit list of "ten things I really believe" that can be wheedled out of anyone with some effort. So each reader-practitioner has a theory. I want to challenge it, or reinforce it, as the case may be.

That said, what is the theory, beyond the specifics of each of the forty-five prescriptions? In summary:

1. The customer responsiveness prescriptions add up to a view of a "porous" organization listening intently to its customers and adjusting rapidly. The porosity induces the flexibility and responsiveness necessary to satisfy minute differences in demand—thence, an ever-changing portfolio of highly differentiated, high-value-added products/services. If we are to sustain our relatively high-wage economy, we must learn to add value across the board.

2. The prescriptions for fast-paced innovation suggest that more starts on new things, in every function, by every person, must be made in order to adapt as fast as the ever-faster-changing environment requires. Given that premise, the need arises for tolerance of well-intended failures and persistent champions of innovation if the state of excitation necessary to deal with the exploding competitive picture is to be maintained.

3. The flexibility-through-empowered-people prescriptions, which deal with high involvement, minimal hierarchy, and increased rewards based upon new performance parameters (quality, responsiveness), are wholly consistent with the more freewheeling, fast-reacting organization pictured in the customer and innovation sections. Highly trained and thus more flexible workers, with a big stake in the action, are a must for constant adaptation to customer needs and constant innovation.

4. The leadership prescriptions essentially address only two questions: First, "how do you induce people to love change as much as they've hated it in the past?" And then, "how do you lead/guide/control what looks like anarchy by normal standards?" That is, how do you deal with very short production runs *and* higher quality *and* treating every customer as a "market segment," and also get line workers involved in everything from budgets to quality control, while paring middle management to the bone? New notions of "control," such as creating an inspiring vision and being out and about, replace traditional controls by means of written policy directives filtering down from a remote headquarters.

5. The systems prescriptions add up to revolution, too: They redefine the

traditional—and ever-important—process of measurement and control. Measure the "right stuff" (quality, flexibility, innovation) is the plea. Share information, heretofore considered confidential, with everyone in order to engender fast action on the line. That is, systems must *abet* our revolutionary agenda rather than impede it, as they most often do today.

These are the general themes you can expect. I can't overstate the extreme nature of the challenge I unashamedly lay down. Some months ago, after a marketing conference, I did some scribbling on a napkin while flying home. I listed the major activities of a business. Then I listed the way it "was/is" and the way it "must become" as column headings. To my dismay, in all ten basic areas, almost a 180 degree flip-flop was required. I called my sketch "a world turned upside down." This list, summarized as Figure 2 (see pages 42–43), provided a major spur to the writing of this book.

The themes are already familiar: a flow of power to the field, the need to act fast, adapt fast, and destroy traditional functional barriers—all in the service of rapid, value-added market creation. But as you subsequently read and reflect on these prescriptions, pay special attention to the time "denominator"—for example, in the fourth customer prescription you'll find the outrageous *demand* that you link up electronically with 75 percent of your biggest customers within the next 24 months. I have become a fanatic about quantifying—but a new sort of quantifying. I insist upon quantifying the "soft stuff"—quality, service, customer linkups, innovation, organizational structure, people involvement, and even how much time you spend breaking down inappropriate inter-functional barriers. We must move from lip service to the ideas of *In Search of Excellence, A Passion for Excellence,* and 1,000 other books just as good or better, to setting challenging goals for implementation. It's an unalterable fact: others in your industry, from Korea to Kalamazoo, are meeting and exceeding my most "outrageous demands" as you read this.

USING THIS BOOK

Many strategies are available for organizing a book. I have chosen a handbook format. In the course of hundreds of seminars, numerous important ideas have surfaced. In each of the five major business areas, there were hundreds of candidates for the final list of five or ten prescriptions.

As a result, though we have forty-five specific "suggestions" (prescriptions), each one, even at this level of dis-aggregation, is complex. Each prescription includes some supporting data (case examples, summaries of others' research), but is principally organized into specific suggestions for action. Finally, based upon my experience, a short list of possible near-term "first steps" is presented.

I propose that you skim any of the five sections and pick the areas that appear most relevant to your current competitive situation. Size up yourself (and your competition) vis-à-vis the sweeping proposals that a given prescription lays out. Then (1) move to corroborate the validity of the idea in your own setting and (2) select some pragmatic steps to be taken in two weeks to sixty days that will allow you to both (a) collect data and (b) seek pilot sites for first tests of the proposals.

The Tension

I hope to induce tension. On the one hand, it is imperative—in each and every one of the forty-five areas—that you consider bold goals, really bold goals, in fact. On the other hand, it is at least as important that you pick some "next 72 hours" steps—i.e., get going!

In May 1987, I was part of a seminar with an established building products firm. The discussion quickly turned to responsiveness to customers (distributors). The group worked on some challenging goals, and developed one for an order turnaround process that amounted to a 100 percent improvement on their current performance. Some gasped and more than a few snickered at the possibility of such a "promise."

Yet I stood up and threw cold water on the idea, suggesting that, given the competitive scene, the group consider an improvement of 400 to 600 percent—and described several other groups, from similar old-line firms, that had done at least that much.

I think I was right—and so, later, did the firm's president (he acknowledged, for instance, that some small competitors were already beating my "bold goal" suggestion). Such non-incremental goals, which will require you to "zero base" the business and seek completely new ways of organizing everything—from accounting systems to organizational structure to training to equipment layout and distribution network relations—are a commonplace necessity today.

Rather than accepting or rejecting the call for boldness, we (the group and a colleague and I) decided to accept the 400 to 600 percent improvement as given for the next 36 hours of the seminar, acting as if it could be done. So we plunged headlong into the process of looking for dramatic and mundane first steps, to be taken in the next two days to sixty days, that would facilitate implementation of the goal.

I can't conclude with a hearty "They did it." I can tell you that they accepted the challenge, did come up with very practical—and bold and mundane—first steps, and mounted several pilots, which produced promising results in the thirty days immediately following the end of the seminar (at which point this book went to press).

I commend them—and such an approach.

Figure 2: **A World Turned Upside Down**

	Was/Is	Must Become
1. Marketing	Mass markets, mass advertising, violent battles to shift a share point, functional integrity of marketing pros	Market creation, niche focus, innovation from being closer to markets, thriving on market fragmentation, ceaseless differentiation of any product (no matter how mature)
2. International	"Global" brands which are managed from the U.S., international as an adjunct activity, for big firms only	Focus on new market creation, development done offshore from the start, essential strategy for firms of all sizes
3. Manufacturing	Emphasis on volume, cost, hardware, functional integrity	Primary marketing tool (source of quality, responsiveness, innovation), part of product design team from the start, short runs, flexibility, people *supported by* automation
4. Sales and Service	Second-class citizens, "move the product" predominates	Heroes, relationship managers (with every customer, even in retail), major source of value added, prime source of new product ideas
5. Innovation	Driven by central R&D, big projects the norm, science- rather than customer-driven, cleverness of design more important than fits and finishes, limited to new products	Small starts in autonomous and decentralized units the key, everyone's business, driven by desire to make small and customer-noticeable improvements

	Was/Is	Must Become
6. People	Need tight control, try to specialize and diminish role	People as prime source of value added, can never train or involve too much, big financial stake in the outcome
7. Structure	Hierarchical, functional integrity maintained	Flat, functional barriers broken, first-line supervisors give way to self-managed teams, middle managers as facilitators rather than turf guardians
8. Leadership	Detached, analytic, centralized strategy planning, driven by corporate staffs	Leader as lover of change and preacher of vision and shared values, strategy development radically bottom-up, all staff functions support the line rather than vice versa
9. Management Information Systems (MIS)	Centralized for the sake of consistency, internally aimed	Information use and direct customer/supplier linkups as a strategic weapon managed by the line, decentralization of MIS a must
10. Financial Management and Control	Centralized, finance staff as cop	Decentralized, most finance people to the field as "business team members," high spending authority down the line

Caveats

I have proposed a piecemeal reading of the book, in an effort to deal with real-world implementation. There are two major problems with such an approach—issues of attitude and issues of connectedness.

Attitude. The book—each part, each prescription—is about attitude: for instance, turning the organization inside out (making it porous to customer and distributors and suppliers) and turning it upside down (encouraging participation, information-sharing, and wholly new roles for supervisors/managers at all levels).

There is, then, a feel to the prescriptions taken as a whole—what they add up to in terms of the way we think about people, customers, relationships (adversarial versus cooperative)—that requires a more or less front-to-back reading. Unless you address the deep-seated attitude issues (see the prior discussion of scale economies and labor's historic role), you miss the point.

Connectedness. There are two issues here. First, each of the five or ten prescriptions in each section is closely interrelated with the others in that section. Each section's introduction, as well as some of the commentary in each prescription, underscores this point. For instance, most participation programs fail. The reasons are many, including failure to train, failure to simplify structure, and failure to reward (pay for) good performance. Thus, the ten prescriptions for achieving flexibility through people are close to meaningless if taken separately; they must be considered together, as a unit. (That doesn't mean that you don't "start somewhere." Rather, you must keep all ten in mind at all times—and work on all ten, albeit at different rates in different places.)

The second issue here is the relation of each set of five or ten prescriptions to the other four sets. Each of the five sets is designed to support the other four, and vice versa. You cannot achieve, say, the customer responsiveness goals unless you buy into all the rest. Furthermore, everything in the book follows from the first set of prescriptions, and especially the first six. This book is market-driven! The first six customer responsiveness strategies are essential for survival. The rest of the book, in many respects, is about implementing these strategies.

Format

Handbooks, by definition, are meant for ready—and repeated—reference. That is why we've chosen a format that breaks the book not into chapters, but into 45 parts, each containing one of the prescriptions. Moreover, each prescription begins with a summary which covers its main points and specifies the most important subsidiary goals. Additionally, most prescriptions contain detailed lists of suggested actions, based upon the best practice of firms that are most successfully preparing for the future.

I strongly urge you to use the central elements of each prescription as a basis for competitor comparison. How are you doing on *each* dimension of the prescription? How is your best (new, small, old and refurbished, international) competitor doing? Do my goals sound outrageous? If so, think again, please—that is, look again at the very best unit in your firm, or your very best small competitor. Careful reflection, I suspect, will reveal that in fact someone in your industry has already surpassed each of the apparently ever-so-bold goals prescribed herein.

This handbook is intended to push you to the limit, time and again. Get to work on a practical improvement project, assess the early results—and then look at the bold goals (and evidence for their necessity); then redouble your efforts, and your pace.

Learning to Love Change

There is no prescription which says it outright. Yet it lurks on every page. It is the true revolution to which the title refers. The world has not just "turned upside down." It is turning in every which way at an accelerating pace.

To meet the demands of the fast-changing competitive scene, we must simply learn to love change as much as we have hated it in the past. Our organizations are designed, down to the tiniest nuts and bolts and forms and procedures, for a world where tomorrow is today, plus or minus one-one-thousandth of one percent.

Our factories are not built to compete with micro-brewers (beer) and micro-mills (steel) or "boutique factories" (very specialized shops with very specialized and advanced machine tools). Our accounting systems are not designed to deal with machines that can produce hundreds of different parts an hour. And our strategic planning systems are not designed to deal with the appearance of a host of new and largely unexpected competitors in a given year.

Every variable is up for grabs, and we are meeting (not meeting, in general) the challenge with inflexible factories, inflexible systems, inflexible front-line people—and, worst of all, inflexible managers who still yearn for a bygone era where presiding over the opening of new wings of hospitals and new plants was about the most strenuous chore to be performed.

Today, loving change, tumult, even chaos is a prerequisite for survival, let alone success. It is to that end—exploring what it means to succeed by loving change—that this book is devoted.

II

CREATING TOTAL *C*USTOMER RESPONSIVENESS

SECTION SUMMARY

Only those who become attached to their customers, figuratively and literally, and who move most aggressively to create new markets—for fast-growing and mature products alike—will survive.

Figure 3 describes the relationships among the ten customer responsiveness prescriptions. C-1, the Guiding Premise, follows from the case developed in Part I. Success—in health care, food, or computers—will go to those who add value by developing customized products or services that create new market niches.

Prescriptions C-2 through C-6 are the Five Basic Value-Adding Strategies for attaining the superordinate objective specified in C-1. These are: C-2, the provision of exceptional quality, as perceived by the customer; C-3, the provision of exceptional service, emphasizing the intangible attributes of any product or service; C-4, the achievement of extraordinary responsiveness by creating electronic or other tight linkages to the customer; C-5, exploiting international market opportunities, regardless of firm size or market maturity; and C-6, positioning the business unit or organization in a way that creates a clear sense of its uniqueness in everyone's mind—customer, distributor, supplier, employee.

The Five Basic Value-Adding Strategies are in turn supported by the Four Capability Building Blocks. The first, C-7, is a pervasive obsession—including every person and every function in the organization—with listening to customers. The next two delineate revised—and heroic—roles for neglected functions: C-8 demands the transformation of manufacturing from "cost center to be optimized" to a prime marketing tool; C-9 proposes the elevation of the sales and service functions to positions of commanding importance and the lionizing of their people. The fourth basic capability building block—achieving fast-paced innovation—is the subject of the next set of prescriptions, I-1 through I-10.

The customer responsiveness prescriptions add up to a revolution in corporate life—the wholesale external orientation of everyone in the firm, the achievement of extraordinary flexibility in response to what in the past would have been called customer whims. C-10 summarizes the "feel" of that revolution.

Figure 3: **Creating Total Customer Responsiveness**

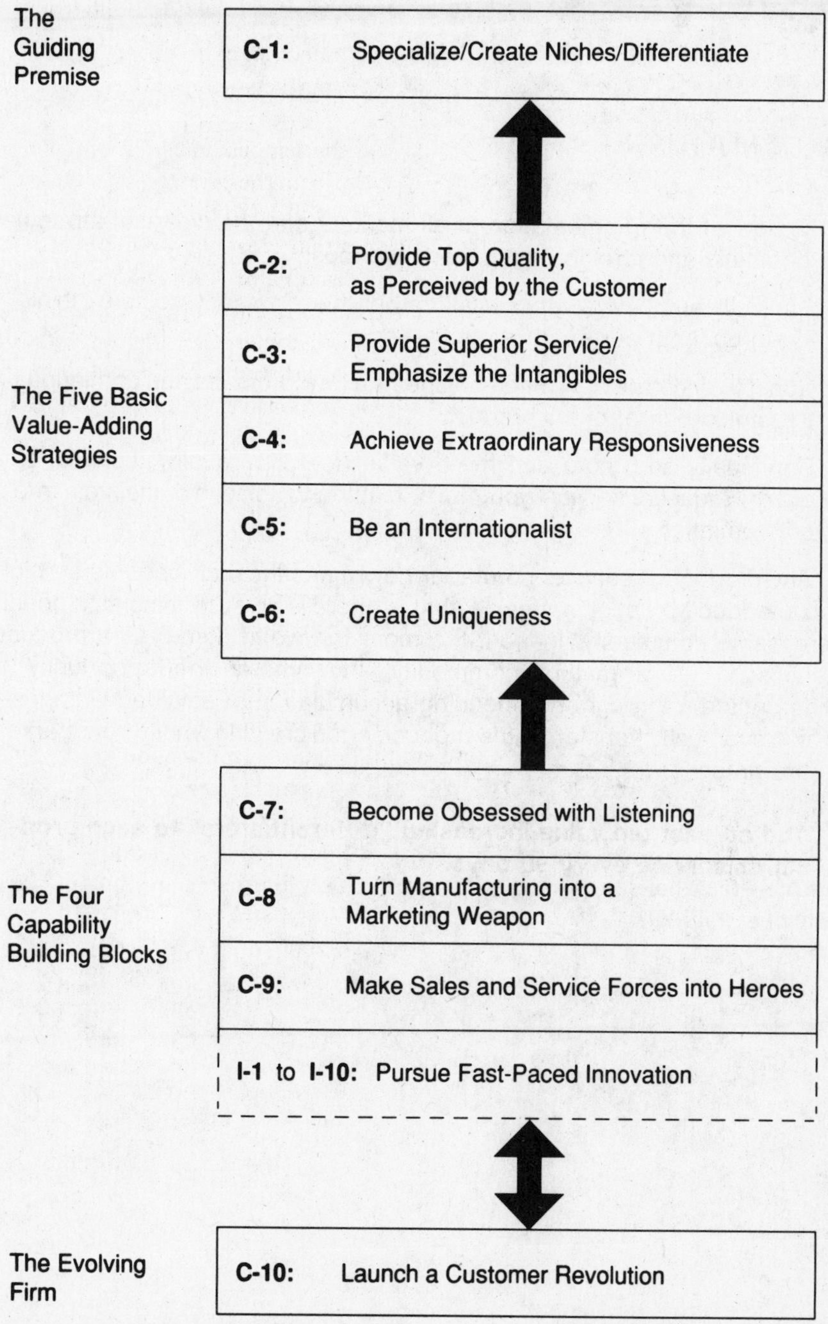

The
Guiding
Premise

| C-1: | Specialize/Create Niches/Differentiate |

The Five Basic
Value-Adding
Strategies

C-2:	Provide Top Quality, as Perceived by the Customer
C-3:	Provide Superior Service/ Emphasize the Intangibles
C-4:	Achieve Extraordinary Responsiveness
C-5:	Be an Internationalist
C-6:	Create Uniqueness

The Four
Capability
Building Blocks

C-7:	Become Obsessed with Listening
C-8	Turn Manufacturing into a Marketing Weapon
C-9:	Make Sales and Service Forces into Heroes

I-1 to I-10: Pursue Fast-Paced Innovation

The Evolving
Firm

| C-10: | Launch a Customer Revolution |

59

C-1

SUMMARY

In view of the fragmentation of all markets and the clear-cut strategies of domestic and foreign competitors, we must:

► Radically emphasize "specialist" rather than "mass"/"volume" thinking throughout our entire portfolio—now.

► Constantly create new market niches via new products and continuous transformation of every product.

► Continually add more and more value (features, quality, service) to every product or service, youthful or mature, to achieve or maintain true differentiation.

Any product or service, no matter how mundane, can become a "high-value-added" product or service; that is, there is no such thing as a nondifferentiable commodity. Indeed, the more the world perceives a product/service to be a mature commodity, the greater the opportunity to differentiate it through the unending accumulation of small advantages—which eventually transforms the product, often creating wholly new markets in the process.

Add at least ten value-increasing "differentiators" to each product or service every 90 days.

Specialize/Create Niches/Differentiate

. . . the Japanese pulled the rug out from under U.S. manufacturing. They figured they could break America's stronghold in many markets only by offering customers a broader choice of goods. That would attack the key weakness of mass manufacturing: It depends on long, stable production runs. By totally revamping the factory and finding methods that could rapidly inject a stream of new products into the market, [they ensured that] the U.S. would be unable to keep pace. It was a stunning strategic coup that marked the end of an era. The Japanese created a manufacturing infrastructure that can respond with blazing speed to market demands and changing opportunities. . . . few U.S. companies have the manufacturing talent necessary to mount an effective response. The experts can tick off only 30 or so.

Business Week, April 1987

The fastest growing companies on the fringe of this year's *Fortune 500* hold strong positions in specialized markets.

"The Riches in Market Niches"
Fortune, April 1987

The car market has become increasingly fragmented. . . . General Motors will have to become Specific Motors, offering . . . a wider variety of cars for narrower markets . . . in the new world of low-volume production runs.

"The Economy of the 1990s"
Fortune, February 1987

More than anything else, today's [successful] hospitals specialize, specialize, specialize.

Training, April 1987

There has been an explosion in the last four or five years in specialty foods.

Louie Gonzalez, Safeway Stores
May 1987

On an Eastern Airlines flight early in 1987, I noticed something odd in the little pocket at the front of the cabin where schedules are usually placed. It turned out to be a MasterCard credit application—or, rather, an application for an Eastern Airlines MasterCard. Each time you use the card, at a restaurant or photo shop, you get bonus miles.

Two days later, in Rutland, Vermont, I saw another newly printed credit card application while purchasing some pots and pans. The Vermont National Bank, with the Contemporary Downtown Business Association as co-sponsor, was offering a Downtown Rutland Shopping Card—"no annual fee, low annual interest rate of 16.5%, 25 day grace period, free 'Downtown Dollars.'" (Free "Downtown Dollars" means a rebate of 1 percent on all purchases, issued twice a year, and usable at any participating merchant's establishment.)

These two examples are typical of the blizzard of new financial service products that are being launched daily—from both traditional and nontraditional sources, and encompassing partnerships of all sorts.* Similar blizzards mark any industry you can name. For instance, there's the Oklahoma City hospital beset with cost problems, whose cinnamon rolls happened to win a citywide bake-off; it now has a separate catering division providing bakery products for Marriott, among others.

MARKET CREATORS

A banker friend offers this advice: "Niche or be niched." In Part I of this book I made the case which underpins this prescription. For a series of reasons, including (1) an explosion of new and relatively small competitors, as well as foreign competitors looking for toeholds in every U.S. market, (2) growing instability in the marketplace, and (3) the technology revolution, we are fast entering the era of the flexible specialist. The observation is as valid for the service sector as for manufacturing. And it is as valid for large firms, which must reshape themselves to keep up, as for small or midsized ones.

The language is a dead giveaway: "micro-brewers" (beer), "mini-mills" and "micro-mills" (steel), "minilabs" (photo finishing, optometry), "minifactory," "industrial boutique," "boutique farming," "designer tomatoes," "custom semi-conductor," "gourmet semiconductor," "de-integrate," "de-organize," "de-massify," "collection of niche markets," "flexible manufacturing systems," "de-merge," "hollow [corporation/hospital]," "store within a store," "factory within a factory," "particularized demand," "de-layering," "subcontracting," "temporary services," "de-conglomerate," "sell off," "spin off," "breakup value," "flattened [organizational] pyramid," "[market] fractured into subseg-

---

*In fact, there has recently arisen a whole new segment of the credit card business, called "affinity cards." For instance, Ducks Unlimited of Reno, Nevada, offers a Visa card with a picture of a duck landing on a marsh; some of the interest paid in by cardholders goes to preserve marshland for ducks.

ments." None of these terms was in use in 1975. Yet I ran across each, some several times, in the space of a month in late 1986.

A recent analysis by the highly respected Strategic Planning Institute (SPI), using their extensive PIMS (Profit Impact of Market Strategy) data base,* shows that return on investment in market segments of less than $100 million averages 27 percent, while the return in large ($1 billion and over), less differentiated markets averages 11 percent—quite a difference. And in their landmark study of midsized firms, *The Winning Performance: How America's High Growth Mid-Size Companies Succeed,* Don Clifford and Dick Cavanagh observed that niche-creating, high-value-adding strategies marked over 95 percent of their winners in every sector of the economy.

I made a brief tour of the landscape in Part I, suggesting the sorts of changes that are occurring. Figure 4 summarizes that tour and includes a few other examples as well: name the industry and you'll find (1) the emergence of specialist small and midsized firms and (2) large firms trying to reconfigure to better enable themselves to compete in the specialist world.

Thus, this first prescription reflects the fast-changing macro- and microeconomic environment. If you are not reconfiguring your organization to become a fast-changing, high-value-adding creator of niche markets, you are simply out of step.

The attitudes that mark the niche market creators, as opposed to traditional market sharers, are aptly described by Silicon Valley marketing expert Regis McKenna:

> *Marketing should focus on market creation, not market sharing* [my emphasis]. Most people in marketing have what I call a "market-share mentality." They identify established markets, then try to figure a way to get a piece of the market. . . . All these strategies are aimed at winning market share from other companies in the industry.
>
> In fast-changing industries, however, marketers need a new approach. Rather than thinking about *sharing* markets, they need to think about *creating* markets. Rather than taking a bigger slice of the pie, they must try to create a bigger pie. Or better yet, they should bake a new pie.
>
> Market-sharing and market-creating strategies require very different sorts of thinking. Market-share strategies [emphasize] advertising, promotion, pricing, and distribution. Customers are interested primarily in price and availability. The supplier with the best financial resources is likely to win.
>
> Market-creating strategies are much . different. In these strategies, managers think like entrepreneurs. They are challenged to create new ideas.

---

*The PIMS data base contains detailed, confidential data on product lines from over 3,000 business units representing all sectors of the economy. The data base was formed within General Electric in 1972. SPI is now an independent entity in Cambridge, Massachusetts. *The PIMS Principles,* by Drs. Robert Buzzell and Bradley Gale, published in 1987, summarizes the SPI research.

The emphasis is on applying technology, educating the market, developing the industry infrastructure, and creating new standards. The company with the greatest innovation and creativity is likely to win.

. . . If companies think only about sharing the markets, they will never get involved in emerging businesses. They'll take a look at the business, decide that the "pie" is too small, and move on to other possibilities.

That is exactly what happened in the personal-computer business. Dozens of major companies investigated the market for inexpensive computers in the mid-1970s. At the time, these computers were used primarily by hobbyists—that is, enthusiasts who enjoyed tinkering with the machines. . . .

But a few companies, companies such as Apple and Tandy, looked at the business with a market-creation mentality. They looked beyond the hobbyists and saw that small businessmen and professionals might eventually use the machines—if only the machines were designed and marketed a bit differently. Rather than focusing on what *was* they focused on what *might be.*

Figure 4: **The Trend Toward Niche Market Creation in America**

Sector	Typical Thriving Niche Creators	Major Firms Reorganizing/Becoming Niche Creators
Manufacturing/ Agriculture		
Steel and Metals	Worthington, Nucor, Chaparral, Alleghany Ludlum, Fansteel, Stahl Specialty, Philips	Inland
Autos		Chrysler, Ford
Chemicals	Liquid Air, Sealed Air, Safety-Kleen, Hexcel Chemical Products, Buckman Labs	Du Pont, Monsanto
Textiles	Nantucket Industries, Russell Corp., Golden Needles Knitting and Glove	Milliken
Forest Products	Elgin Corrugated Box, Trus Joist	

Figure 4 *(Continued)*

Sector	*Typical Thriving Niche Creators*	*Major Firms Reorganizing/Becoming Niche Creators*
Semiconductors	LSI Logic, Siliconix, Cypress Semiconductor	Intel, Advanced MicroDevices, Texas Instruments
Computers	Cray Research, Sun Microsystems, Convex, Compaq, Apple	IBM, NCR
Packaged Goods	Salad Singles, Orval Kent, Dreyer's Grand, Anchor Steam	Campbell Soup, Procter & Gamble
Farming	Perdue Farms, Chianina Lite Beef, Inc., Denair	

Service

Retailing	The Limited, Nordstrom, The Gap, 7-Eleven	Sears, Safeway, Kroger
Distribution	McKesson, Williams-Sonoma, Ingram	Spiegel
Financial Services	Banc One, Stillwater National, Citytrust, University National Bank & Trust, Barnett Banks	Continental Illinois
Health Care	ServiceMaster, Emergency Management Services, Nuclear Medical Associates, Health Management Professionals, Caremark, El Camino Hospital, the Mayo Clinic	Hospital Corporation of America
Temporary Services	Editorial Experts, The Mortgage Professionals	
Trucking/Busing	Ryder System, Peter Pan	

Midsize firms and fast-growth industries are not the only arenas in which specialization and market creation can occur. Other PIMS analyses point out that differentiation works as well in declining as in growing markets. Economist William Hall goes further, concluding after extensive research that the top differentiators in "mature" industries (e.g., tires, cigarettes) actually outperform the best differentiators in growth industries. Thus, any firm's strategy can—and should—be shifted radically toward niche creation.

DIFFERENTIATING "COMMODITIES"

Anything—a first draft said "almost anything," but I scrapped the "almost"—can be turned into a value-added product or service for a well-defined or newly created market. Consider:

The Milliken shop towels. "Shop towel" is a euphemism for "rag." Textile-maker Milliken & Co. has a vital rag/shop towel business (towels, dust mops, and the like for factories, hospitals, and similar establishments), growing like the blazes with returns on investment of more than 50 percent. How can a domestic textile producer do that?

Simple: A rag is not a rag. The shop towels are sold to industrial launderers who in turn rent them to the ultimate user. Milliken trains the salespeople of its customers (the industrial launderers), develops promotional material for them, and held a whopping thirty-three days of executive-level "user conferences" for customers in 1985. A few other services in 1986 included: Shop Towel Product Workshop I–IV; telecommunications seminars; seminars on selling skills; audiovisual sales aids for their customers; production seminars; customer tours of Milliken plants; on-line, computer based order entry and freight optimization systems to maximize responsiveness and minimize shipping costs; market research assistance; use of the Milliken Data Access System, which gives the customer, via computer link-up, access to various Milliken marketing aids; sales leads generated by participation in conventions; participatory management seminars; Customer Action Teams (see below, C-4); and Partners for Profit seminars on quality improvement. In other words, the works. And the list expands each month. Beyond even all this, though, customers most commend Milliken for its extraordinarily rapid response to special needs.

Learning to sell mops and rags is no picnic at Milliken. Classroom training for a neophyte rag salesperson amounts to twenty-two grueling weeks, followed by a year's on-the-job trial with small accounts. Most computer firms don't prepare their salespeople that well!

Milliken has turned the humble shop towel into a high-value-added, greatly differentiated product. In fact, it has created a new product and a new market through its value/service/responsiveness-added approach. Milliken essentially runs its customers' businesses for them, using the rags sold as an excuse to provide value-adding services. This "for certain" commodity is not a commodity at all. Moreover, doing business this way has become typical for Milliken. It launches hundreds of Customer Action Teams and Partners for Profit programs each year; every one is an unabashed attempt to de-commoditize a product and create a new market, by constantly improving quality, adding features, and increasing service and responsiveness—in order to improve its customers' profitability.

Elgin's boxes. During the last fifteen years, most big paper companies have been hemorrhaging badly, with frighteningly low utilization rates in their giant plants. Their main defensive tactic has been vicious price-cutting. Yet since 1970 independent producers of corrugated boxes have increased their share of the market, in that $16 billion industry, from 12 to 30 percent. Elgin Corrugated Box Company of Elgin, Illinois, provides a fine example of one of these smaller winners. Business is so good that the $13 million firm will add a new plant in 1987 to serve its low-growth market around Chicago. Why?

Elgin's logo gives away one-third of the secret: "Our job is to make QUALITY product at the best [production line] speeds we can. Not to run FAST with the best quality we can." Quality is Elgin's hallmark—in a host of big and small ways. It spends on better ink for the printing on the box. It uses a more expensive A-flute corrugation (the flute is the inner fold of paper between the two outer layers), requiring more material, rather than the more common C-flute; the former is much stronger. Jury-rigged machines (old, but adapted many times) make sharper corners—and so on, ad infinitum.

The other two components of Elgin's competitive edge are service and responsiveness to its customers' needs. Elgin has not been late in shipping an order (it fills roughly 280 per week) for over six years! Moreover, it gleefully takes on small, difficult orders that larger firms won't touch. Its relatively small, flexible plant makes such custom work both possible and profitable. And the small custom orders often lead to big ones. "If they'll do the tough stuff for us," says one customer, "then we'll give them the bread-and-butter orders too."

In sum, Elgin does not consider its boxes a "commodity"; to the contrary, it adds value to its product every step of the way—and gains a decisive advantage in a business that many have written off as "dying" in our high-wage economy.

(Elgin, Illinois, is home to another specialist in another competitive industry. Community hospitals are struggling, with hospital occupancy rates at 65 percent and declining despite the loss of thousands of beds nationwide each year since 1965. Yet the 300-bed community hospital in Elgin is thriving, having specialized by creating "radiation therapy facilities that rival those of the Mayo Clinic," according to *Healthcare Forum.*)

"Gold Seal" laser parts—and more. A Silicon Valley laser products firm got all its employees engaged in product improvement, focusing on such "mundane" areas as packaging. Packaging for even a tiny $500 laser part was upgraded: Instead of a nondescript plastic bag, there was a gold seal label, an ebony-colored mounting for the part, and a vacuum seal (increasing shelf life).

The company successfully offered the "new" product—to highly sophisticated customers—at a 20 percent premium.

In another part of the business, the president and his senior colleagues gave customers—doctors who often have trouble with laser calibration—their home phone numbers. Sales increased by 30 percent. The phone didn't ring much; the president got only one call in the first 120 days. But the gesture alone doubled customer confidence in and comfort with the product.

The list could be added to endlessly. One division of American Standard, the world's premier supplier of quality toilets, bathtubs, etc., is confronted with all the problems of a mature business. The billion-dollar division has recently added a $25,000, top-of-the-line, combined bathtub and home entertainment center. It includes a device that gives you a video picture, from the tub, of whoever is knocking at the door. The division's overall objective is nothing less than re-conceiving the role of the bathroom.

Or take American Express Travelers Cheques—97 years old in 1987 and going strong. Over $20 billion worth will be sold this year, and revenues are growing at 20 percent a year, despite a declining dollar that has made foreign travel much more expensive. The key? Amex keeps developing new features. Refund approval, after losing your checks, now takes less than six minutes; replacement checks will be delivered almost anywhere in three hours or less.

And young Federal Express does much more than just meet the promise of guaranteed overnight delivery which launched the company; it is constantly expanding its service offerings. For instance, a huge distribution center in Memphis stocks such urgently needed items as medical supplies and computer parts. They are stockpiled by Federal Express customers, such as IBM; one quick call and Federal Express will have the critical item on its way to an IBM customer in dire need.

Differentiation makes a difference! Furthermore, anything, from rags to laser parts, can be differentiated—and differentiated decisively over time.

Constant Differentiation: Japan's Edge

A deeply ingrained habit of constant differentiation is the essence of Japan's economic success. It's called kaizen, which management consultant Masaaki Imai describes as "ongoing improvement involving everyone." It is, he says, "the most important difference between Japanese and Western management." Economist Masanori Moritani, in his book *Japanese Technology,* elaborates: "One of the characteristics of competition in Japan is the establishment of small distinctions between one's own product and similar products made by other manufacturers. These tend to be minor improvements in convenience, function, miniaturization and the like. . . . Five, six or even as many as ten companies may be producing virtually identical products, but upon close examination, you will find a number of small innovations in each. Since each firm is rapidly making such improvements in its goods, the cumulative effect is immense. In two or three years, the product can be completely transformed."

A Word or Two of Caution

Though there is no limit to the ability to differentiate profitably, there can be misguided differentiation:

1. Don't offer wildly exaggerated differentiation that the market doesn't want. Take Regent Air, former provider of luxury cross-country flights—at $3,240 per round trip. The firm found a severely limited market at that price. It shut down in 1986.

2. Don't negate useful—and expensive—differentiation by underattending to other parts of the product-service package. The fruits of differentiation may also be denied as a result of weakness in a neglected part of an operation. For instance, how many "new look" $175-a-night hotels have sprung up, with stunning architectural opulence—but where service is more reminiscent of a $20-a-night fleabag? Customers' memories of the poor service tend to far outweigh the impressive decor. Many of these hotels have found occupancy far below expected levels, and as overbuilding in this segment continues, I'd predict some outright failures.

A similar pitfall is illustrated by the marketing classic from the pet food industry. A renowned manufacturer broke the bank on market research—for instance, testing numerous packaging variables to make the new product uniquely attractive to the purchaser. It paid off, at first. But soon low repeat purchases scuttled the product. Everyone loved it—except the dogs.

3. Don't let premature implementation of exotic technology trip you up. Some producers of highly differentiated products fail as a result of being too far ahead of their time. The first automated teller machines and the first picture phones in the United States were fiascoes. A decade or more passed before automated tellers caught on—and the jury is *still* out on picture phones.

4. Don't forget that it's not differentiated until the customer understands the difference. Sometimes a new idea is on target, but still is not "sold"—i.e., communicated—effectively. Scandinavian Air System's chief, Jan Carlzon, tells of a fare-reduction campaign launched years ago at the Swedish domestic airline, Linjeflyg. The program was called "F50," to indicate fares at an attractive 50 percent off. But F50 flopped. When Carlzon took over the airline, he retained the idea, but renamed it the "Twenty Dollar Plan," signifying the actual fare. The switch from technical argot to plain talk caused the program to catch fire. Carlzon explains: "What people don't understand doesn't exist."

While differentiation is a winning strategy, it obviously requires thoughtfulness. That said, however, the plain fact is that nine out of ten executives underestimate their ability to differentiate. Who would have ever thought that Milliken could charge a premium price for rags, or that Federal Express, by guaranteeing overnight delivery, could charge a premium amounting to several hundred percent on mail?

Quantify Your Differentiators

I offer one last demanding piece of advice: Quantify. I am attempting to quantify almost everything. It can be done, no matter how apparently qualitative the attribute. Therefore I urge you to set a tough, quantitative target for adding "differentiators," as I call them, to every product and every service you provide. Specifically, I suggest ten every 90 days—and frankly, that's far too low.

The point is that though the differentiators are individually mundane, they can be collectively awesome in impact, redefining an entire segment of an industry, as Milliken's "shop towels" do. No one is stuck with a commodity. To the contrary, I repeatedly observe that the more the world perceives the product to be a commodity, the greater the opportunity to differentiate and create new and unexpected niches through the unending accumulation of small advantages.

A FINAL WORD ON ADDING VALUE:
THE HAPPY-SAD STORY OF PEOPLE EXPRESS
AND THE MODEL T

No person changed the industrial landscape in this century more profoundly than Henry Ford. The $360 Model T automobile provided previously unimaginable opportunities to the American public, and monuments to Ford are deservedly large. Yet Ford held on far too long to the narrow vision that his Model T represented, and almost lost the company as a result. He yielded market share to General Motors, which eventually nearly closed the price gap and then beat Ford hands down by providing a diverse product line and by offering financing for all GM customers.

Today Ford is having its greatest relative resurgence in over sixty years—which is how long it took to recover from the Model T mentality. And today—oh, irony!—GM is suffering from a strategy reminiscent of the Ford of old, emphasizing volume and cloning all its models to look alike, while it is Ford that has regained its touch through distinctive styling (e.g., the Taurus) and features (e.g., turbos), and generally superior quality (with special attention to fits and finishes).

The recent swallowing of People Express Airlines by Texas Air recalls Ford's nearly catastrophic decline earlier in this century—and despite the unhappy ending, founder Don Burr nonetheless deserves monuments almost as great as those to Ford. For, like Ford, Burr significantly expanded the horizons and possibilities for millions of Americans by making air transportation affordable. Thanks to him, it's now hard to remember that less than a decade ago flying was almost the exclusive province of businesspersons and the well-to-do.

Rushing to take advantage of the federal deregulation of airlines, Burr and People Express forced overwhelming and lasting changes on other, more established air systems—such as the across-the-board use of efficient hub-and-spoke networks. Perhaps the changes would have come without Burr or People Express (would there have been some other version of the Model T without Ford?). Still, Burr's boldness surely shortened the process by years.

So what happened? Over a four-year period, competitors, by reducing their overhead drastically, closed much of the once imposing difference between People's cost per seat per mile and their own, while at the same time continuing to provide the amenities that People did not. The result: Burr was left with a customer-perception problem similar to that which the Model T eventually acquired—available in "any color as long as it's black." Despite the belated investment of hundreds of millions of dollars in a new terminal and a new reservation system, People was burdened by ineradicable memories of the dingy and congested North Terminal at Newark, of ridiculous overbooking incidents and a primitive reservation system that turned the entire community of travel agents against the airline.

At the same time, while matching People on price, other airlines poured more and more money into reservation systems and other notable value-adding differentiation strategies. American Airlines, in particular, under aggressive chief Bob Crandall, did almost step for step to People what GM, under Alfred Sloan, did to the first Mr. Ford. And now, with People gone, fares are on the rise, though they will never again reach heights that will exclude most of the public from flying. (Frank Lorenzo of Texas Air, which acquired People, continues to play the "discounter's roulette," but the plain fact is that the days of no-frills flying—air travel as a commodity—are probably gone, and the deepest discounts have an increasing number of strings attached.)

An almost exact parallel seems to be unfolding in the telecommunications industry. MCI was the all-time giant-slayer, destroying AT&T's monopoly. Even more proactively than People, in the early 1980s MCI took advantage of the drift toward less regulation, providing a no-frills alternative long-distance service to AT&T's at a discount of up to 50 percent. In doing so it started a major and permanent revolution from which many customers have benefited immeasurably.

Again, however, the price gap is closing, and MCI's no-frills image is fast becoming an almost intractable millstone, as AT&T's genuinely high level of service and superior transmission quality are now proving to be a decisive value-added advantage.

The strategic implications of these three cases, and a host of other, less prominent ones that could have been discussed, are profound. A no-frills provider takes advantage of or creates a true discontinuity by providing a widespread, low price/low cost, undifferentiated product or service. In the marketplace, both older and newer players respond as basic economic theory proclaims they must—by narrowing the price/cost gap. Once the gap is somewhat narrowed and a new, substantially lower-than-the-start plateau is reached, the winning strategy for the long haul becomes differentiation—via service, quality, and variety.

The first Henry Ford at Ford, People Express's Don Burr, and MCI's Bill McGowan deserve the accolades that have been heaped upon them. But the pioneer no-frills provider almost inevitably sows the seeds of its own destruction. Its position is ultimately fragile and vulnerable to the clever differentiator, which will likely win both the customers and the profits over the medium to long term. (It is important to note, in the context of this book's emphasis on the speed of market transformation, that Ford had a run of 19 years with the Model T, from 1908 to 1927; People and MCI were in trouble within a couple of years of their great triumphs.)

PUBLIC PARALLELS

Public sector manager: Send off to the governor's office in Michigan for the state's latest annual report. Michigan is back! Unemployment is surprisingly low; vitality on numerous fronts is high. The annual report details a vast array of innovative, "value-added" programs that have spurred development, despite the auto industry's continued disarray and domestic manufacturing's downsizing. A small business explosion has been encouraged; retraining has been supported. State pension funds have been tapped to provide venture capital for start-up firms. Unique partnerships have been formed by the bushel.

In *The High-Flex Society,* economist Pat Choate offers another example of a state's value-adding, differentiation strategy:

Franklin [Electric Company], an electric motor manufacturer, decided to open a plant in Wilburton, Oklahoma, in 1981. Since the company needed a hundred workers to wind, assemble, test, and package submersible electric motors, it asked the Oklahoma State Department of Vocational and Technical Education to prepare a training program for the workers who would be hired. The company and the department formed a team composed of company representatives and state training specialists and engineers. Together, they identified specific training needs and devised a pre-employment orientation for trainees, manuals for the various jobs, and a schedule for all activities. . . . The state provided equipment for worker orientation. The company provided the training equipment the workers would use once [its] facility was in operation, making the curriculum realistic and job-specific. Faculty was drawn from both state personnel and company supervisors. . . . The Franklin experience is by no means unique. By 1985, seventeen years after Oklahoma began providing such customized training assistance, the service had been used by more than 500 firms. Some have been large international companies such as General Motors and Weyerhaeuser, while many have been smaller companies such as Franklin.

Start-up training is only part of the training service Oklahoma provides.

To ensure that those who require remedial assistance can also participate in these programs, Oklahoma offers individual pre-entry-level training. . . . The program is popular with Oklahoma political leaders because it produces visible results at a low cost—the average sum per trainee has been $141. Most important, graduates have a very good chance of getting a job. Nearly three-quarters of the more than fifty thousand persons who enrolled in this program between 1968 and 1985 finished the training and were employed. . . .

In 1980, the state initiated an extension program to help firms increase their productivity. Much as county agents assist farmers in applying improved agricultural techniques, these industrial specialists counsel firms on how to improve production processes, time management, work scheduling, and employee involvement. This program has been particularly popular with small and medium-sized firms, which typically have had little opportunity to consult with productivity experts.

The relentless pursuit of jobs has become a city and state obsession. Some follow the same low-cost strategy that so many "commodity" manufacturers use; they offer a vast array of tax-reducing holidays and gimmicks. The danger is that they get trapped, as do their industrial counterparts, in a downward spiral: price is their only weapon, and as the amenities (education, infrastructure) deteriorate, no price is low enough to induce employers to come. The smart boosters, therefore, while surely price-conscious, principally use a value-adding, differentiating strategy—stressing amenities and creative, growth-oriented partnership programs.

FIRST STEPS

1. Read on. Prescriptions C-2 through C-6 develop the five basic value-adding, differentiation-oriented, market-creating strategies: (a) top quality, (b) service that emphasizes the intangibles, (c) responsiveness, (d) becoming an internationalist, and (e) creating true uniqueness in the customer's mind.
2. Take one slumbering product or service, or one in each product or service family. In the next 60 days, meet intensively with (a) end-user customers, (b) members of the distribution channel, (c) suppliers, (d) people at all levels from all functions in your organization. Devise a low-investment strategy for *radical* differentiation of the product or service via value-adding steps; relaunch the product or service in the next six months.
3. Finally, add such a "differentiation assessment" to your normal strategic-planning program. But beware—grand plans are not the answer; start adding differentiators now.

C-2

SUMMARY

With high-quality products and services being provided by new, especially foreign, competitors; and with quality being increasingly demanded by industrial and individual customers, every firm must:

▶ Mount a quality improvement revolution.

▶ Ensure that quality is always defined in terms of customer perceptions.

A quality revolution means eating, sleeping, and breathing quality. Management obsession and persistence at all levels are essential. But the passion must be matched with a detailed process. And, always, the customer must be present—as the chief definer of what's important.

Cut supplier, company, and distribution system product/service failure rates by 90 percent in the next three years. Get everyone involved, starting in the next 90 days, in a radical program of continuous quality improvement.

Provide Top Quality, as Perceived by the Customer

The best of ours are [now] about as good as the worst of theirs, and that is a tremendous achievement.

> Robert E. Cole
> University of Michigan,
> commenting on the improvement
> in U.S. auto quality vis-à-vis Japan
> *Fortune,* February 1987

Percentage of West Germans who say "Made in America" is a mark of quality: 6.

> Roper survey, reported
> in *Harper's,* March 1987

Tennant Company was known for producing top-quality floor maintenance equipment. But during my visits with our Japanese joint-venture partner in the late 1970s, I had been hearing complaints—sometimes bitter—about hydraulic leaks in our most successful machines. Back home, I began asking questions: Why were the hydraulic leaks happening only in the machines we sent to Japan, and not in those we were selling in the U.S., where, in fact, we were selling many *more* of the same machine?

As it turned out, the leaks weren't just happening in Japan. The machines we sold here at home were leaking too. The difference was that U.S. customers accepted the leaks. If a drop of oil appeared on a freshly polished floor, they simply wiped it up. In Japan, the leak was cause for complaint. Japanese customers expected better quality. . . .

At about the same time, we faced our first serious competition in Japan from the lift-truck division of Toyota when it announced its entry into the sweeper business. The news spread in our company, and suddenly everything we'd been hearing about Japanese cars, Japanese stereos, and Japanese television sets versus U.S. cars, stereos, and television sets began to take on new meaning.

Those events, all happening in 1979, motivated us to begin our journey toward quality. We have found that like all important ideas, quality is very simple. So simple, in fact, that it is difficult for people to understand.

Roger Hale
chief executive officer
Tennant Company
in *Quest for Quality*

It has always been remarkable to me the extent to which people can hold certain assumptions inviolate even in the face of compelling evidence to the contrary. Nowhere has my amazement been greater than when I've watched healthcare professionals confront the issue of quality. There is a common assertion, of course, that "quality is a given"—that the quality of care provided by physicians and hospitals is "roughly equivalent." . . . Unfortunately, it is a ridiculous contention. . . . The power of owning a "high quality" position can be overwhelming. In Baltimore and in the surrounding area extending in a 100-mile radius, for instance, consumer preference for Johns Hopkins consistently runs above 50 percent. Similar patterns can be discerned for Massachusetts General and the Cleveland Clinic. In an era when most hospitals are hard put to define how they differ from their neighbors, no point of differentiation is likely to prove more powerful than quality.

J. Daniel Beckham
Healthcare Forum
March–April 1987

THE CRUSHING QUALITY PROBLEM

Every day's news brings new, painful evidence. A poll shows that Koreans prefer Japanese over American suppliers by a wide margin (see Part I)—chief reason: problematic American quality. An analyst reviews Japan's closed markets; a principal reason for them—Japan's low opinion, across the board, of the quality of American products. The Limited, fearful of a trade war and in response to the declining dollar, is trying to line up American suppliers to replace part of its vast overseas network. The chief roadblock—the unreliability of American suppliers on quality.

The United States is getting clobbered in steel, autos, semiconductors, construction, and financial services alike. The causes, the voices of protectionism would have us believe, are closed markets, aggressive marketing (dumping), and differences in cost, particularly of labor. But the plaintive voices of customers and the cold, hard data tell a different story: For the most part, the quality of made-in-America goods and services is questionable; perhaps "stinks" is often a more accurate word. Yet, fifteen years after the battering began, quality is still not often truly at the top of the American corporate agenda.

THE LONG IGNORED EVIDENCE:
QUALITY EQUALS PROFIT

The evidence of the value customers place on quality surrounds us—from Federal Express, The Morgan Bank, Nordstrom, American Airlines, and Disney in the service sector to Maytag, Ford, and Digital Equipment in manufacturing. And the anecdotal evidence is matched by systematic evidence. For example, every survey of auto quality shows that U.S.-made cars, except, recently, for Ford's, still bring up the rear by a long shot—and the loss of market share to foreign producers continues even in the face of the increasing prices of many foreign cars as the dollar declined.

The remarkable PIMS data base, also cited in C-1, is decisive. For a decade after establishing the data base, PIMS researchers argued that market share was the primary begetter of profits. But a re-analysis of the data led to a startling and more robust conclusion: High market share does indeed bring profit; however, sustainable market share comes primarily through leadership in what the PIMS researchers call "relative perceived product or service quality"—"relative" meaning vis-à-vis competitors, and "perceived" meaning as seen through the customer's rather than the provider's eyes. PIMS researchers now call relative quality "the most important single factor affecting a business unit's [long-term] performance," and a recent PIMS newsletter to members concluded: "When we examine the options for maintaining the lead in value, we find that changes in relative quality have a far more potent effect on market share than do changes in price."

PIMS assesses both technical and "soft" factors (judgments about a firm's responsiveness, for example) in customers' views of competing product offerings, holding price constant. On average, those firms whose products score in the top third on relative perceived product quality outearn those in the bottom third by a two-to-one margin. Moreover, this conclusion does not vary substantially by sector (service sector vs. manufacturing sector, consumer products vs. industrial-user goods), geography (North America vs. Europe), or market trajectory (low growth vs. high growth, low inflation vs. high inflation).

TRW provides a useful test, since it is a microcosm of the U.S. economy, with products ranging from one-megabit semiconductors to auto parts and financial and information services. In 1985, Dr. John Groocock, recently retired vice-president for quality at TRW, applied the PIMS ideas to his $6 billion firm; using customers' evaluations of quality as his measure, he assessed 148 product lines in forty-seven TRW business units, and compared them with 560 product lines of the company's competition.

The results? The top third of TRW's business units (with a quality score, as perceived by customers, of 4.6 out of a possible 5) out-earned the bottom third (with a score of 1.9—which amounts to "average quality" vis-à-vis competitors) by a three-to-one margin. The top third had a 26.6 percent return on assets employed, versus 8.9 percent for the bottom third. The top third's 7.7 percent return on sales more than doubled the bottom third's 2.9 percent. Groocock concluded: "The PIMS results for quality are so impressive that it is surprising that they have had so little effect on American management."

A 1985 Gallup survey for the American Society for Quality Control assessed the extent to which customers are willing to pay more for quality; the results startled even those who commissioned the survey: "It would appear that most consumers are willing to pay to get the quality in a product they desire. . . . On average consumers report that they would pay about a third more for a better quality car ($13,581 versus $10,000). Consumers would be willing to pay about 50 percent more for a better quality dishwasher ($464 rather than $300) and proportionately more for a television or sofa they thought was of better quality ($497 rather than $300 for a TV, $868 rather than $500 for a sofa). Finally, consumers claim they would, on average, pay twice as much for a better quality pair of shoes ($47.00) than for an average quality pair ($20.00)." The proportion who would pay nothing extra for the higher quality was 10 percent for automobiles, 4 percent for dishwashers, 3 percent for shoes, 6 percent for TVs, and 4 percent for sofas. Frighteningly, the survey also found that people with higher incomes and Westerners, two consumer categories considered "leading indicators," were by far the most dissatisfied with the quality of American products.

For ten years I have pored over studies and observed grocers, retailers, express mail companies, and hardware distributors; manufacturers of textiles and steel (from structural grade construction steel to precision parts for transmissions) and washing machines and autos. I have studied furniture makers and makers of two-by-fours and high-tech wood joists and producers of cardboard boxes and tents. I have examined the methods and results of theme park operators, baseball franchise owners, chicken and beef and vegetable and pig farmers, cookie makers, ice-cream makers, soup makers, computer makers, and semiconductor makers. My unequivocal findings: (1) customers—individual or industrial, high tech or low, science-trained or untrained—will pay a lot for better, and especially *best,* quality; moreover, (2) firms that provide that quality will thrive; (3) workers in all parts of the organization will become energized by the opportunity to provide a top-quality product or service; and (4) no product has a safe quality lead, since new entrants are constantly redefining, for the customer, what's possible.

So why does all this remain the best-kept secret in North America?

QUALITY IN THE U.S.A.:
SOME QUANTITATIVE ASSESSMENTS

The U.S. auto industry remains central to the American economy, affecting semiconductor makers and health care providers as well as its own workers and communities. Protection from imports in the form of quotas was laid on in 1981, to provide a "breathing space"—now in its sixth year—during which the United States would "catch up."

The results? While there has been some improvement, the yawning gap in quality between the domestic product and the foreign (especially Japanese) has not closed. The Rogers Survey, done only for industry insider use, but leaked and published in *Fortune,* measures "TGWs," or Things Gone Wrong, in the first eight months of new-car ownership per 100 cars produced. Chrysler is worst with an average score of 285 and GM is next to last at 256. Ford, which was last among domestic producers in 1980 with a score of 392, has leapt to best by far, with a score of 214. The average for Japanese models, however, is still miles ahead, with a score of 132 TGWs. Indeed, the worst Japanese performer is about equal to the best of GM and Chrysler, confirming Bob Cole's comment.

Pollster and industry consultant J. D. Power of Los Angeles is best known for its influential automobile CSI—Customer Satisfaction Index. On the quality component of the index, the Japanese are decisively in the lead, with an average score of 134 (on this index, higher is better). The Americans have passed the Europeans, but manage only a 90 (average is 100). Ford again leads comfortably with an above-average 107, and Chrysler and GM bring up the rear. In this poll, GM at 83 edged out Chrysler at 85 for most awful.

Another important Power survey assesses dealers' opinions on vehicle reliability and dependability. By this measure, 63 percent of cars manufactured in Asia were considered "very acceptable" and 9 percent were considered "unacceptable." Only 23 percent of cars made in the United States were very acceptable, while 26 percent were unacceptable.

Finally, *Consumer Reports* conducts a major "frequency of repair" survey each year. The most recent results, from 450,000 respondents, are not comforting. Just 1 percent of GM's cars were ranked "above average," while 69 percent scored "below average." Japan, by contrast, had 88 percent above average and *none* below average. Chrysler scored better than GM on this poll, with 13 percent above and "only" 70 percent below average. But hold on. That includes Chrysler's Japanese-made cars; remove them and the 13 percent drops to 4 percent, and the 70 percent jumps to 83 percent.

The purpose of printing these numbers is to underscore the chasm that exists between us and our competitors in the area of quality. The problem is not, as former UAW president Doug Fraser once said to me, that "we did take our eye off the ball a bit." We are behind by orders of magnitude—and not only in autos. We must squarely confront this fact, in order to realize the urgency with which we must attack the quality issue.

More important than the numbers is the generic impression—America doesn't make quality goods, and is worse on service/responsiveness than on quality. Such a perception gap would take a decade or more to reverse, even if we were hard at work today. I belabor this point, because I still encounter such skepticism among U.S. executives (much more than from any line worker). "Where's your evidence?" they commonly ask. I'm inclined to be smart-alecky and say, "Where's your counterevidence?" But I usually don't say that. Instead,

I produce the evidence. And yet, as often as not, though I cite the source and produce the originals of the studies I still get blank stares; and not infrequently, in the face of the hard evidence, the skepticism is not only not removed, but turns to raw belligerence of the "it's just not so" variety. Then, I usually get very quiet—because I am scared.

TWELVE ATTRIBUTES OF A QUALITY REVOLUTION

If you accept the above—the bad-news evidence and the indications that quality pays—what do you do about it? The answer is a systematic program. Glib words. Tough to execute. Many have started. Most have foundered. In the last few years, I have read all I could find on the subject and observed close up uniquely successful quality improvement programs at IBM, Tennant Company, Milliken & Co.,* Ford, the Paul Revere Life Insurance Company, First Chicago (the bank), Worthington Industries, the Air Force's Tactical Air Command, Federal Express, and several other organizations. The top programs share a dozen traits:

1. Management obsessed with quality. First comes top management's attention—or obsession, as I prefer to call it. What does that mean? It's visceral—the anguish and anger of Roger Milliken at a tiny defect in a tiny order. I've watched him call his whole great ship to general quarters over a "small" problem that others wouldn't even have seen or heard about, let alone acted upon.

One of the best descriptions of the emotional component of mounting a quality revolution appeared in *The Big Time,* a study of the Harvard Business School's class of 1949. Conrad Jones, a top executive at the consultants Booz, Allen & Hamilton, painted this picture:

> . . . Let me tell you about two meetings I sat in on. Both were with companies that were having some problems with quality control. One company was professionally managed. Their approach to the problem was to analyze everything. How many doors, say, were falling off? What *percentage* of doors were falling off? How much would it cost to stick 'em back on? What were the chances of getting sued? How much advertising would it take to counteract the bad publicity? Not once did they actually talk about the doors, the hinges, or why the hell they were falling off. They weren't interested in solving the problem, they just wanted to manage the mess. The other meeting was at Coleman Stove. . . . They were having a problem with some boilers that were cracking. So picture it—the Executive Committee assembles, there's the usual small talk. . . . Then the service department comes in with the reports, the clipboards, the yellow pencils,

---

*Quality expert Phil Crosby says that these first three firms have the best quality improvement programs in America.

and everybody hunkers down for a serious discussion. Well, you know how long that meeting lasted? About thirty seconds: Old Man Coleman sits bolt upright in his chair and bellows out: "You mean we've got goods out there that aren't working? Get 'em back. Replace 'em, and find out why, goddammit." And that was the end of the meeting. There was no financial analysis. There was no legal analysis. There was no customer-relations analysis. There was *no* goddam analysis. The issue was the integrity of the product—which meant there was no issue at all. We stand by it, and that's that.

I will soon turn to talk of systems and measurements, but it is essential to begin with emotion. In a recent New York *Times* article, Gulf + Western chairman Martin Davis, ruminating on today's uniquely tumultuous environment, asserts, "You can't become emotionally attached to any particular asset." An "asset" presumably means a business, its products and its people. What bunk! I can't conceive of one of the Nordstrom brothers saying that, or Leon Gorman, L. L. Bean's chairman, or Federal Express founder Fred Smith, or Roger Milliken, or "Old Man Coleman." Quality begins precisely with emotional attachment, no ifs, ands, or buts. As Apple's former top manufacturing executive (now chief financial officer) Debi Coleman puts it: "I don't think you should ever manage anything that you don't care passionately about."

Top management commitment means lots of big and little things. For instance, is quality at the top of the agenda—every agenda? (See also prescription L-3.) At Milliken, President Tom Malone reports that the first four hours of every monthly President's Meeting (an operating review) are devoted exclusively to quality. "And it would be that way," he adds, "if the office were burning down as we met."

A Texas Instruments executive describes a variation on this theme: "In years past, we traditionally held quarterly reviews with top corporate executives. For the past three years or so, these financial reviews have been discontinued. In their place, we hold a review four times per year with top management that is devoted solely to quality and productivity."

Jim Harrington, senior IBM quality manager and 1986 chairman of the American Society for Quality Control, makes the more general point: "Now step back and take a look at your calendar. Are you spending as much time controlling the quality of your department's output as you are investing in cost and schedules? . . . If you don't have time for quality and don't value it enough to be interested in it, how can you expect your employees to? . . . Plant managers hold production status meetings in which quality, schedules, and costs are reviewed. Normally, schedules are addressed first, then costs, then quality—if there is time. . . . [But] if quality is really the most important factor, then it should be first on every agenda."

Another key to top management commitment is the potent use of symbols. (Again, see also prescription L-3.) A few years ago a new Ford Thunderbird was a sure bet for *Motor Trend*'s "car of the year," an assessment that not only strokes egos but means big dollars too. As in the world of Hollywood's Oscars, however, a car must be released for production by a certain date to qualify. In what one Ford executive described as "the shot heard round the world," the company held up the release, forgoing the almost certain prize, because the car's quality was not yet up to snuff for a production model. In the most powerful way, Ford had demonstrated its new commitment to quality—the commitment that played such a vital role in the company's extraordinary performance in 1986.

Likewise, Tennant executives brought the company to full alert with a single symbolic stroke as they launched their quality program in 1980. As a first step, before their ameliorative quality improvement program was in place, they cut the number of rework mechanics, the firm's highest-paid assemblers, in half—from twenty to ten (there are only two today). The message: There will be no more rework—we will do it right the first time.

A third element of top management commitment is perhaps the most challenging—persisting through program doldrums. A serious quality commitment is forever. Some have called Toyota the most quality-oriented big company in quality-conscious Japan. One key to its success has been the mundane suggestion system, made not so mundane at Toyota. We often act as if Japan's giants sprang to life as world-class organizations. Not so. In 1960, Toyota's suggestion system snared just 5,001 submissions (about six-tenths of one suggestion per worker), only 33 percent of which were implemented. Twenty-two persistent years later, in 1982, that number had increased 381-fold, to 1,905,682 suggestions, or 32.7 per worker. Moreover, 95 percent were implemented.

With no exception, quality program leaders report that programs stall around the 12–18-month mark, no matter how much energy and organization have gone into them. Award programs become stale. Team leaders are worn out. The first full round of training is complete. The easy-to-find problems have been solved. Moreover, there are doldrums every couple of years thereafter—forever. At these points, which appear unavoidable, most lose heart. Commitment means gritting your teeth and dreaming up as many new wrinkles as you can to pump life back into the program.

There is a final element of commitment. As my seminars, at which a mass of ideas has been presented, wind down, obviously frustrated participants frequently shout out, "So what, exactly, do I do first?" Here's the answer I give: "Starting this afternoon, don't walk past a shoddy product or service without comment and action—ever again!"

A brochure is going out to customers. You've already missed your deadline. Five thousand have been printed, inserted into envelopes, addressed and sealed, and are packed and ready to be taken to the post office. Your small unit's cash flow is pinkish to red in hue. And then you discover a single typo on page two, in the small print. Should you walk past it or act? Easy. Act—throw it out!

It doesn't matter whether the firm has 15 or 150,000 employees. Whether you are section head or chairman of the board. If you knowingly ignore a tiny act of lousy service or poor quality, you have destroyed your credibility and any possibility of moral leadership on this issue. Period.

I have dwelled on management commitment for the very reason that most experts ignore it. Yes, they put it at the top of their list, in a knee-jerk fashion; but they devote about two paragraphs in a 500-page book to it, and then move on to the nuts and bolts, the "real stuff." They never define precisely what this seemingly soft and squishy item means. Yes, it is about attitudes; but the attitude of abiding and emotional commitment must also be translated into practical actions, which show up on the calendar each day.

Pounding Away

Recall Roger Hale's comment about the floor cleaner's hydraulic leak, noticed only by his Japanese customers. He launched the Tennant quality revolution in 1979. Hale did many things right, and made a number of errors, too. But above all, he and his firm have persisted. Miracles have occurred, but they are unfailingly miracles of pounding away. Let's return to the hydraulic leak, and look at Tennant's progress, as reported in *Quest for Quality:*

First Year (1981): Team learned about hydraulics, including the best assembly methods. Team set own goals. Average performance: 1 leak per *216* joints. Note: Average machine has about 150 joints; therefore, almost every machine leaked.

Second Year: Developed extensive training programs. Developed and printed training manuals. Trained managers, supervisors, assemblers, and engineers. Purchasing department set supplier goals. Replumbed test machines [using] new methods; reduced number of joints and overall fitting and hose costs by 10 percent per machine. Average performance: 1 leak per *509* joints.

Third Year: Reduced number of hydraulic hose and fitting suppliers from 16 to 2. Average performance: 1 leak per *611* joints.

Fourth Year: Introduced newly plumbed products at year end.

Fifth Year: Gave training update to all assembly people. Reduced number of suppliers from 2 to 1. Note: Reduced hose and fitting costs by 10 percent by single-sourcing. Average performance: 1 leak in *1,286* joints. Not one customer reported a leak from any machine shipped this year. Received National Fluid Power Association's PRO Award for our work in this area.

Sixth Year: Average performance: 1 leak per *2,800* joints. Zero field-reported leaks.

Now, that's hanging in!

---

2. There is a guiding system, or ideology. Most quality programs fail for one of two reasons: They have system without passion, or passion without system. You must have both.

This is not the place, nor am I the expert, to make a recommendation other than "Have a system." There's a lot of controversy here: Should you follow Deming (W. Edwards Deming, father of the Japanese quality revolution via statistical process control)? Or Phil Crosby, author of *Quality Is Free,* and so prominent that GM bought a 10 percent stake in his firm? Or Armand Feigenbaum's "Total Quality Control"? Or Joseph Juran? Or invent a system of your own?

Eventually you will develop your own scheme if you are successful. But I strongly recommend that you not begin with a Chinese menu. Pick one system and implement it religiously. Frankly, it makes little difference which system you choose, among the top half-dozen or so, as long as it is thorough and followed rigorously.

3. Quality is measured. "What gets measured gets done" is a wonderful old saw. "Measurement is the heart of any improvement process. If something cannot be measured, it cannot be improved," says IBM's Harrington. You must start by measuring the "poor-quality cost," precisely and in detail. Poor-quality cost includes such items as manufacturing (or any other function's) rework, warranty costs, cost of repair or return of poor goods from suppliers, and inspection costs. IBM, Milliken, et al., after substantial initial resistance, have decisively demonstrated that the cost of poor quality can be measured in every function—from the executive secretarial pool to engineering to the sales force to the plant.

The measurement must begin at the outset of the program. Among other things, if done right, it will inject energy into the program as the size of the problem—and the opportunity—comes into view. Though the experts agree on little else, they do concur on the poor-quality cost: it absorbs about 25 percent of all your people and all your assets in manufacturing firms to do the rework and other tasks caused by poor quality; the costs of poor quality in service firms absorb a staggering 40 percent of people and assets. IBM says the costs of poor quality run from 15 to 40 percent of gross revenues, depending on the maturity of the product.

Measurement should be visible. Electronic scoreboards glow in many Milliken plants, tracking quality progress by the hour; big charts and readable graphs are on public display in accounting, personnel, and data processing too. Huge TICs (team improvement charts) dot IBM.

It can also be straightforward, as Richard Schonberger describes it in *World*

Class Manufacturing: "Data recording comes first. The tools are cheap and simple: pencils and chalk. Give those simple tools for recording data to each operator. Then make it a natural part of the operator's job to record disturbances and measurements on charts and blackboards. The person who records data is inclined to analyze, and the analyzer is inclined to think of solutions." Schonberger goes on to illustrate with, for instance, the system of Display Boards that marks Hewlett-Packard's Greeley, Colorado, operation.

Caution: Though I am a "measurement freak," as one colleague put it, I acknowledge a downside. Measurement must be done by the participants; that is, by the natural work group, team, or department itself. It must not be done "to" such groups by an accounting department or by an "audit" or "inspector" brigade. If it is, there is a high risk (1) that the process will become bureaucratic and (2) that turf fights and squabbles over interpretation of data will break out, setting true involvement back considerably. Ford is so finance- and numbers-driven that it avoided measurement for a long time, fearing that the powerful finance bureaucracy would usurp the quality program, as it had so many others.

4. Quality is rewarded. In the people prescriptions, I will discuss forms of rewards in general (see P-7). At this juncture, I simply want to urge you to reward contributions to quality improvement.

Quality targets are part of Ford's executive compensation plan. For Ford managers in general in 1986, 40 to 65 percent of their bonus was based on contributions to quality, just 20 percent on contributions to profit. Quality targets are the primary incentive variable in Perdue Farms' executive pay scheme. They are part of everyone's performance evaluation at IBM. Adding a big component of quality-based incentive compensation caused an early breakthrough in top management's attitude at Tennant.

Rewards based on quality are part of IBM's program with suppliers too. For instance, with one division's cable suppliers, the premium price is paid for 0.0 to 0.2 percent defects; for a 0.21 to 0.3 percent defect level, $2.00 per cable is knocked off the price; for 0.31 percent and over, there is a $4.00 reduction. With this system in place, a defect rate that had averaged 0.11 percent for years rapidly dropped to .04 in 60 days—and stayed there.

5. Everyone is trained in technologies for assessing quality. Instruct everyone in problem cause-and-effect analysis, rudimentary statistical process control, and group-problem-solving and interaction techniques. Some train only first-line supervisors. This is a serious mistake. The chairman of the board should take the course—Roger Milliken went to Crosby's Quality College; IBM's chairman took its basic course. More important, every person in the company should be extensively trained.

"Training is the key," says a Tennant executive; every Tennant manager had taken at least five courses in quality control by 1985. Richard Schonberger's *World Class Manufacturing* includes a chapter titled "Training: The Catalyst." He warns: "Western industry must put substantially more resources into training to match the prodigious sums the World Class Manufacturing companies in Japan and Germany invest in it." Japanese consultant Masaaki Imai concurs:

"There is a Japanese axiom: 'Quality control starts with training and ends in training.' "

6. Teams involving multiple functions/systems are used. Once more, ideological firestorms await you. Paul Revere's quality program quarterback, Pat Townsend, champions *non*voluntary quality circles—and makes a vigorous and well-documented case, replete with success. The Japanese, on the other hand, use only voluntary quality circles. Tennant sides with the Japanese. Crosby rejects quality circles as such, but embraces teams: Error Cause Removal Teams or Corrective Action Teams formed as needed, with members drawn from various sites as necessary, to take on a specific problem. The team disbands when the problem is solved, and thus doesn't deteriorate into a weekly sewing circle—that is, another bureaucratic exercise.

In any case—and many would place this point at the top of their lists—it is vital to engage in multi-function problem-solving and to target business systems that cross several functional boundaries (order entry, engineering changes, etc.). Ford and IBM both say they wasted years before realizing that most quality improvement opportunities lie outside the natural work group (for instance, a section of fifteen within accounts receivable). Tennant and Milliken launched multi-function teams from the start. In fact, Tennant's first team was a multi-function group working on an automatic floor scrubber; it reduced defects per machine from 1.3 to 0.4 in its year of existence. Tennant tries to be sure that every team has members who can run interference in each major function.

Masaaki Imai contends that the "natural" work group is *not* the key to Japanese success. Instead, he says, "Cross-functional management is the major organizational tool in realizing [Total Quality Control] improvement goals." IBM's quality improvement process emphasizes the systems that hold the functions (and firm) together. An "owner" has been assigned to each business system—for example, one that deals with implementing engineering changes, which may start in the field, involve a lab or two, several plants, and eventually field service. Typically, IBM and others found that such processes, which bridge functions and units, fall through the cracks and are not relentlessly updated. IBM has now raised business system quality improvement to a near-science. Every system is painstakingly and quantitatively scored as to effectiveness. Special Process Improvement Teams grind away, and a sophisticated, thirteen-step Process Analysis Technique has been developed and honed.

IBM's reasons for the move are clear, as explained by corporate quality director Edward Kane:

The billing process consists of 14 major cross-functional activities which are logically related but physically dispersed among 255 marketing branches and 25 regional offices, a similar number of field service locations, and several headquarters operations and manufacturing sites. The work is cross-functional and nonsequential within any function. It is tied together by a complex information system. Overall, 96 percent of the invoices are accurate, but because of the high cost of adjusting those that are incorrect, *54 percent of the total resource was devoted to cost of quality* [my emphasis].

A deeper issue emerges here for the first time that is addressed more fully in the people prescriptions (especially P-9). We must fundamentally shift our managerial philosophy from adversarial to cooperative. Protecting functional fiefdoms and hoarding information is the American middle management norm. The seemingly straightforward plea in this prescription for cross-functional quality teams peels off but one layer of a big onion.

7. **Small is very beautiful.** There is no such thing as an insignificant improvement. Paul Revere's Townsend expounds:

Many teams received credit for things as simple and as small as moving a file cabinet ten feet closer to the one person who has frequent use of it. A quality idea? Technically, perhaps not—but the inconvenient location of that cabinet had most likely been a matter of irritation fifteen times a day for the person who had to walk the extra dozen or so steps. Could it have been moved prior to the Quality Has Value process? Perhaps in theory it could have been, but the person being inconvenienced did not believe it, or did not want to go through the hassle of asking permission through however many layers of management that it would have taken.

Milliken leaders declare that the plaudits now go to those who admit to/revel in having lots of problems—that is, lots of quality improvement opportunities. It's no longer okay to give the traditional, macho "everything's on schedule" response—amidst the rubble of an obviously noncompetitive factory or distribution operation.

8. **There is constant stimulation.** Create endless "Hawthorne Effects."* I referred to the 12–18-month doldrums before. The antidote is new goals, new themes, new rewards, new team champions, new team configurations, new celebratory events. Change everything, in fact, except the structure of the basic system (see point #2 above).

No item in the improvement process is too small to use in generating and sustaining momentum—or too insignificant for concern. In a program Revere's Townsend launched in his second year, as part of an effort to keep things lively, names were randomly drawn out of a pot each week; if the person picked happened to be wearing his or her Quality Has Value pin, he or she was awarded a free lunch. Townsend discovered that women were not well represented among the winners. The reason, it turned out, was the pin. Designed by a man, it had a tie tack fastener, which made holes in women's dresses or blouses. When an optional charm design was offered, the participation of the women shot up. On such details are wars—and quality revolutions—won or lost.

*After the 1930s Western Electric experiments which inadvertently demonstrated that productivity increased when a work situation was constantly attended to and stimulated, regardless of the precise type of intervention—lights up, productivity up; lights down, productivity up again.

9. There is a parallel organization structure devoted to quality improvement.
Create a "shadow quality organization." Tennant's includes a Steering Committee, a Recognition Committee, a Zero Defect Day Celebration Committee. Unexpected stars have been born in the process; Tennant executives note: "Champions can . . . come from the ranks of the hourly workers. A welder who became involved in one of the first quality small groups in his department became its informal leader. Then he volunteered for the second company-wide Quality Team. From there he went to the Zero Defect Day planning committee. As he learned more and did more, he became an articulate spokesman for quality within the company. In 1983, he and his co-workers were asked to make a presentation at the Tennant Company-sponsored Japanese Management Association Meeting. Now, this former welder is a supervisor—and a champion for quality company-wide." At Revere, too, the parallel structure has become a new source of promotion and an unofficial alternate career advancement channel.

Caution: Many correctly warn that if such "parallel" structures are not carefully controlled, they can deteriorate into a new, inertia-inducing layer of bureaucracy.

10. Everyone plays: Suppliers especially, but distributors and customers too, must be a part of the organization's quality process. The task, once more, is a challenging one. Milliken trains its suppliers. Milliken and Tennant form joint improvement teams with suppliers (Milliken's are called Partners for Profit—see C-1). Symbols help: IBM calls all suppliers Business Associates. Ford takes out full-page ads in papers such as *The Wall Street Journal* and *USA Today* to praise suppliers with top quality records. More fundamentally, what's required is mutually dependent, lasting relationships (see also I-2, on team product development, particularly the discussion of Ford's Taurus project). Almost all agree, for instance, that the number of suppliers must be drastically reduced— recall Tennant's hydraulic leaks, which were also much reduced when the number of suppliers was reduced, in two steps, from sixteen to one.

Tennant's Doug Hoelscher, vice-president for engineering/manufacturing/ purchasing, reports on an early approach to a supplier:

> . . . I got the phone number of our largest supplier—not surprisingly, the one with which we were having the largest number of quality-related problems. I was apprehensive about calling the president to tell him that there "might be" some quality-related problems with his product that he "might not" know about.
>
> His response: "Why the hell are you calling me? I have people to handle these kinds of things."
>
> I took a deep breath and explained that at Tennant Company we were trying a new approach. Our CEO and I wanted to become more involved with our counterparts in key supplier companies, and we had set a goal of reducing our supplier base by 10 percent per year over the next five years. I seemed to have his attention. I told him I hoped he was interested in keeping our business and invited him to a meeting. He reluctantly agreed.

At the meeting, we showed him documentation outlining the percentage of parts received from his company that we had to reject because of poor workmanship. It became obvious to him that the product he was selling was not of the quality his people had led him to believe. His shoulders drooped. "What do you want me to do?" he asked.

"Ship us the product as promised," we said. We then explained that we didn't expect zero-defect products immediately, and that we could work with him to meet our expectations. We had three requirements:

1. Set annual improvement goals.
2. Meet with us annually to review progress against those goals.
3. Become a fully-qualified supplier by meeting those goals.

In turn, we said, we would send him semi-annual reports showing his company's performance. As long as he continued to show improvement and eventually became qualified, we would continue to purchase from him.

The result has been a much more satisfying relationship with a key supplier. His company did set and meet goals. We continue to purchase parts from them, and they are a part of our group of major suppliers. We now provide quarterly updates to each member of that group, and many participate in our ZD [Zero Defects] Day programs. Meeting our quality goals has become a joint effort. When a company depends as we do on · outsiders for so many components of its product, cooperation for quality not only makes sense, it is absolutely essential.

Analogously, all parts of the company must be part of the program—MIS, personnel, accounting and treasury, sales, order entry, shipping. Quality programs limited to the factory or operations center will fizzle. Milliken and Revere are especially proud, and rightly so, of the intensive involvement of their field sales/service forces in quality control. These independent-minded domains are usually very skeptical about participating, but can become the source of phenomenal improvements.

11. When quality goes up, costs go down. Quality improvement is the primary source of cost reduction. I continue to hear all too much chatter about the "quality/cost trade-off." For one kind of quality—i.e., extra features—there is, of course, a trade-off. The hand-stitched leather seats in an Aston-Martin cost a bundle. But overall, perfecting quality saves money. As noted, poor quality has a huge, documentable cost.

In *Augustine's Laws,* Norman Augustine, president of Martin Marietta, has recast data from a study of the room air conditioner industry, conducted by Harvard's David Garvin. The result is depicted in Figure 5. Augustine concludes: "As greater quality is built into a product, the cost of achieving quality does not increase but rather decreases."

The elementary force at work is simplification. Almost all quality improvement comes via simplification of design, manufacturing, layout, processes and procedures. For example, the redesign of the second generation of Hewlett-Packard's HP-150 touch screen personal computer reduced the number of parts

Figure 5: **Room Air Conditioner Industry**

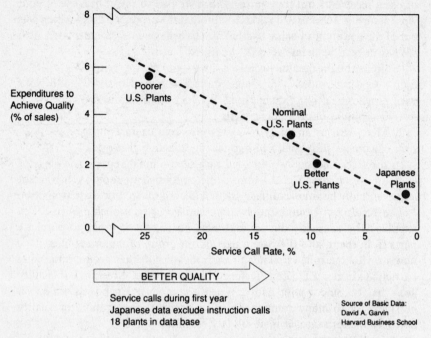

Expenditures to Achieve Quality (% of sales)

Service Call Rate, %

BETTER QUALITY

Service calls during first year
Japanese data exclude instruction calls
18 plants in data base

Source of Basic Data:
David A. Garvin
Harvard Business School

from 270 to 130 and the number of suppliers from 120 to 50. Quality soared and costs plummeted.

In fact, there is an interesting asymmetry which has profound consequences. Cost reduction campaigns do not often lead to improved quality; and, except for those that involve large reductions in personnel, they don't usually result in long-term lower costs either. On the other hand, effective quality programs yield not only improved quality but lasting cost reductions as well. And all this doesn't even touch upon increased revenues from more sales resulting from improved quality.

12. Quality improvement is a never-ending journey. There is no such thing as a top-quality product or service. All quality is relative. Each day, each product or service is getting relatively better or relatively worse, but it never stands still. Ford is doing well now, but Toyota, which Ford sees as its principal competition, is implementing 5,000 new suggestions a day.

These dozen factors, as imposing as they may collectively be, still don't begin to do justice to the best quality improvement programs. There is something almost mystical about them: "This program is what we're all about." "It's who we are." "This program *is* Tennant." Such is the stem-to-stern feel of the programs that deserve to be called quality revolutions. Sadly, anything less than an all-out, "This *is* us" approach will fall into disuse within 18 months, becoming one more "program of the year" skeleton that haunts management's effort to be taken seriously about anything.

The goals must—and can—be bold. I recommend a target of 90 percent reduction in defects in three years, with a 25 percent reduction in the first 12 to 18 months. Between 1978 and 1984, Tennant reduced the cost of poor quality from 17 to 8 percent of sales, cut manufacturing rework hours from 33,900 to 6,800 a year (while sales were growing), and introduced state-of-the-industry warranties to boot. To aim for less is to be less than serious.

Some Startling Results from a Quality Program in Action

A few examples, from *Excellence: The IBM Way,* by H. James (Jim) Harrington, underscore the huge potential that IBM found as its quality program got into full swing:

▶ Error-free installation of new products. When a major new system is launched, though computing power is significantly increased from the start, it usually takes years to iron out bugs that result in downtime. After starting its quality program, IBM audaciously decreed that this post-launch learning curve would, ipso facto, no longer exist. A new machine was to have better "availability" than the machine it replaced and the competition's best—from the start. Harrington reports: "For years we had believed that a defect-free installation of our large computers was impossible because of their complexity. . . . But once we focused on error-free installation, the process immediately began to improve. Today the 308X series is seven times better than its predecessor product in terms of defect-free installation . . . [and] installation time has been cut by a factor of three."

▶ Enormous improvement opportunities in mature products. IBM uses about 2,000,000 flat ribbon cables a year to connect electronic circuits. Harrington says, "This is a well-known technology moved out to vendors years ago. . . . Massive amounts of rework had been built into the product estimate and treated as normal expected yield. A young industrial engineer . . . mustered up enough interest from management so that a team was assigned to attack the high defect rates." Scrap per cable dropped from 94 cents to 28 cents, and rework dropped from 25 to 4 percent. Problems in final tests fell from 12 to 1.2 percent. "Our annual savings," Harrington notes, "are $5,000,000."

▶ Software coding yields to the improvement process. Process improvement technologies were applied to software, where quality is in part measured in terms of defects per 1,000 lines of code. An institute was even set up to abet the process. A threefold improvement ensued over a six-year period.

▶ Stunning results from improving mundane accounting practices. Accounting data entry was 98 percent accurate at the outset. But that means 20,000 to 30,000 miscodes per day! In two years, the number dropped to 0.4 percent, a fivefold improvement.

▶ Supplier partnerships hit paydirt. "In the 1970s we made the mistake of talking to our suppliers in terms of AQLs [Acceptable Quality Levels] when we should have been talking parts per million," says Harrington. "I am convinced that if in the 1970s we had been talking parts per million, today we would be talking parts per billion." Typical improvements, from 1980 to 1983, measured as defects per million: transistors, from 2,800 to 200, a 14-fold improvement; transformers, 4,200 to 100, a 42-fold rise in quality; and capacitors, from 9,300 to 80, a 116-fold rise.

Such are the opportunities, from the complex to the less complex, from the new to the old, from hardware to software to accounting.

QUALITY MUST BE JUDGED AS THE CUSTOMER PERCEIVES IT

The advice this prescription has proffered so far is vital. But it still misses the boat. After four wildly successful years of pounding away at "quality," Milliken found that a second revolution was required—to become more responsive to customers. Tennant and Ford, and even IBM, have likewise moved beyond early definitions of quality improvement and are paying more attention to the customer.

Crosby will assert that his process is oriented toward the customer. I am his fan, but he is not. Getting better, within specifications (which are at least, in theory, partially determined by the customer), is not enough. Dow's Irving Snyder is on target:

Quality is not just an inspector. It's not just in the product. . . . But what is it? How do we define it so that we can get a handle on it and cope with it? . . . I asked about 50 methods editors to help me define quality in terms of the key element they work with—specifications. Here are some of the answers I received: "A specification is a minimum requirement to which we produce a product." "A specification tells the manufacturing plant what to produce." "A specification tells the salesperson what he'll be selling." "A specification spells out the limits within which we can produce a satisfactory product." These were all very interesting, I told them. But nobody picked up on the fundamental reason we have specs in the first place, and that is: "Specifications should define what it takes to satisfy the customer." Period. This is what quality is all about: the customer's perception of excellence. And quality is our response to that perception.

Let me give you an example. One of our customers in Europe came to us several years ago with his own testing spec for carpet foam backing. We were a bit put out that someone thought they could test it better than we could. We told him not to worry. Dow measures for foam stability, molecular weight distribution, particle size conformity, percent of unreacted monomer, adhesion strength—all the vital things. We told him, "You're going to get the best there is, real quality!" Well, three times we tried to ship him the order, and three times he sent it back. Now, that gets annoying. So we asked him, "What's the deal?" And he told us, "Your product can't pass my roll-stool test!"

"Roll-stool test? What's that?" Well, what he did was take the bottom half of an office chair, that is, the undercarriage and casters, put a weight on it, and spin it around on a piece of test carpet 30,000 times. He even had a little counter to keep track, day and night. If the carpet sample didn't delaminate from the foam, you passed the test and got the order. Ours didn't pass, so back we went to the laboratory. Eventually, we gave him a product that would withstand 80,000 revolutions before delaminating. The lesson was painfully clear: Quality is what the customer says he needs, not what our tests indicate is satisfactory.

Caution: The Customer's Perception of Quality Can Be Perverse

I have owned a GMC truck for over a year. Nothing major has gone wrong with it—no dropped transmission or oil leaks. It's worse than that: About eight little things have gone wrong, such as the failure of a light which indicates whether or not the truck is in four-wheel drive and a loose, rattling latch on the glove box.

The problem is that even collectively these irritating problems aren't enough to warrant the inconvenience of a visit to the dealer. Therefore, and here's the rub, each time I get in the truck, it's as if a brightly lit map of GM's failure to attend to detail flashes before my eyes.

Frankly, in terms of my perceptions, GM would have been better off if the transmission had failed. I would have gotten it fixed immediately, it would have been done with, and my memory of it would have dimmed.

The Moral Dimension of Quality

In the winter of 1987, a new magazine appeared, *Quality: America's Guide to Excellence.* One of the lead articles began with this statement: "We have to grant quality its moral dimension. . . . It should be recognized as a virtue—something to be sought for its own sake—not just a profitable strategy. To the Swiss, with their passion for grace and precision in everything from pocket knives to highway bridges, quality is second nature. Can we import not just Swiss products but the attitudes behind them?"

Quality is practical, and factories and airlines and hospital labs must be practical. But it is also moral and aesthetic. And it is perceptual and subjective. It is delivering above expectation. It is a startling little touch that makes you smile at the designer's or production shop's care for you, the customer. Marketing expert Phil Kotler, of Northwestern, calls this the "delight factor"—it's at the opposite end of the perception scale from the "perverseness" phenomenon noted above.

Ford is coming to understand this. Its Taurus and Sable are filled with such features, including my favorite, a coffee cup holder. Many are following in

Ford's footsteps. Some declare that a packaging and industrial design renaissance is sweeping from Europe and Japan to the United States.

On the other hand, we have a long way to go. As I was changing a tire recently, I was struck by the rough surface of the $8.95 lug wrench I was using. It could be a work of art, like the $8.00 mallet I bought in Hammerfest, Norway, in the summer of 1986—it's so attractive that when I'm not using it, I display it on a shelf in my den!

The Japanese aesthetic sense is centuries old. Within the Toyota or Sony Walkman lie the modern outcroppings of the tea ceremony. After all, the Shinto religion, according to Joseph Campbell in *The Masks of God: Oriental Mythology,* is marked by "seamstresses [who] hold requiem services for lost and broken needles." *Inc.* provides corroboration:

> Although Japanese lumbermen and construction firms had long been customers for whole logs shipped from the Pacific Northwest, they had rarely bought finished lumber from the region's mills. Quality had been a big part of it: as with so many other products from consumer appliances to food, the Japanese tended to be finicky customers. And in the case of lumber, they liked it cut to exacting traditional Japanese specifications. How the wood looked—not merely how strong it was or how much it weighed—was a primary concern.
>
> . . . [F]orester Adolph Hertrich followed the path traveled so many times by the Japanese themselves during the 1960s as they began their industrial conquest of the United States. He traveled extensively throughout Japan, meeting with potential customers and inspecting the facilities of their Japanese lumber suppliers, taking careful notes wherever he went. . . . By the mid-1970s, he had begun to redesign his mill from head saw to edger to trim saw. . . . And most important, foremen were instructed by Japanese specialists on the complex lumber-grading systems that are based on such aesthetic factors as color and graining—categories that change depending on the region of Japan in which a customer is located. It took Hertrich and his people two years before they were finally confident and able to impress prospective Japanese customers. And to press the point still further, they even built a traditional Japanese guest house from their own lumber and invited overseas guests to spend the night there. To the Japanese businessman, who has always suffered from some cultural discomfort when dealing with Westerners, this willingness to accommodate was a powerful and persuasive marketing strategy.
>
> And it has paid off handsomely. Today, while many local mills lie idle, Vanport's 170 nonunion workers labor at double shifts. Sales last year reached $27 million, 90% of which are destined for Japan. The company has been consistently profitable.

From the Taurus gas cap to the roll-stool test, from guest houses in Oregon to ceremonies for broken needles, quality is a complex subject. The twelve-trait program to revolution is a big part of it, but not all of it by a long shot.

PATTERNS AND PRIORITIES
IN QUALITY PROGRAMS

Each of the quality improvement programs I have observed most closely, at Milliken, Tennant, IBM, Ford, and the Paul Revere Life Insurance Company, has followed a tortuous path to success. The similarities are instructive.

Milliken began in 1981 with a pure quality improvement thrust, helped by Phil Crosby. It focused from the start on quality teams within the natural work area, cross-functional teams, and suppliers. About two years into the process Milliken added the reluctant sales group to its quality program. At the three-year mark, it shifted attention to customer issues, mounting a series of multi-functional teams to work on them. The final phase of the Milliken program took the customer emphasis a giant step further, aiming for order-of-magnitude improvements in overall customer responsiveness.

Tennant's program, also spurred by Crosby, has followed a similar path, beginning with the emphasis on quality and including suppliers and cross-functional teams from the outset. About seven years into their program, Tennant, too, came to the conclusion that a new emphasis on the customer was needed, that customers had not been central enough to the program during its early years.

IBM worked on quality within the natural work group at first. About three years into the program, the abiding importance of cross-functional systems to the quality of almost everything became evident. Systems improvement emerged as the all-out obsession of the quality process. Now, in 1986 and 1987, IBM has learned that it, too, was not listening adequately to its customers. Customers have become the focus of renewed concern.

The early Ford emphasis was on employee involvement, working with the unions; it focused on the natural work group. Then, as mentioned, Ford, like IBM a couple of years before it, moved radically in the direction of quality improvement via an emphasis on cross-functional systems improvement. Six or seven years into the process, Ford is now focusing attention on the customer.

Paul Revere began with an emphasis on the individual work group at headquarters, but moved quickly to include field selling and servicing operations. Step three for Revere was the inclusion of cross-functional activities.

Two points emerge. First is the not immediately obvious need to emphasize improvement in the subtle but controlling cross-functional systems; as noted, Ford and IBM believe they lost years by not realizing the importance of these systems. Second, even in the best programs the quality improvement activities, though they certainly had a dramatic impact on customers' acceptance of the product, were not sufficiently focused on the customer. Groocock of TRW and Crosby worked together at ITT for years and, technically, they define quality quite similarly. Yet Groocock's clear emphasis, developed in his work at TRW, is on the customer; Crosby, by contrast, gives lip service to the customer, but is primarily concerned with meeting technical specifications.

It is noteworthy that Crosby's favorite exemplars, Milliken, Tennant, and IBM, have reached similar conclusions, several years into the process. Their improvements in quality had not automatically taken them close enough to the customer, especially according to the customers' *perceptions* of quality.

So the natural progression goes something like this: (1) quality within the natural work group; (2) quality jointly with suppliers; (3) quality in field sales and service and marketing operations; (4) quality improvement through cross-functional teams and systems improvement; and finally (5) a shift of emphasis to the customer. Figure 6 surveys the experiences of the five firms.

Though these prescriptions are written to suggest that one should "do it all," it is clear that the agenda is overfull. One could argue that Milliken or Tennant or Ford or IBM or Revere could have changed its tune earlier, from the natural work group to the field to cross-functional systems to the customer, but I'm not sure of that. In all cases, there was much to learn. "Do it all at once" is tempting, but not very practical, advice.

Figure 6 : **Patterns of Progression**

STEP	MILLIKEN	IBM	TENNANT	FORD	PAUL REVERE
1. Quality within natural work group	1*	1	1	1	1
2. Quality with suppliers	1	1	1	2	
3. Quality with field sales/service	2	1	2		2
4. Cross-functional teams	1	1	1	2	3
5. Quality via systems improvement	4	2	2	3	1
6. Quality as close to the customer	3	3	3	4	
7. Quality as total customer responsiveness (see C-4)	4				

* 1 means did at the outset; 2 means next wave of emphasis, etc.

PUBLIC PARALLELS

Reread #3 and #11 in the description above of a quality revolution. Poor-quality cost is as sound a notion in the public sector as in the private. With increasing budget pressure, a quality revolution will allow you to have your cake and eat it too: improve service delivery and cut its cost simultaneously.

Incidentally, the same caution holds in the public as in the private sector. Quality is defined by the customer's perception of service delivery, not the legislative parameters of a particular program. Callousness or indifference in the delivery of an inherently helpful service destroys much of its benefit.

FIRST STEPS

1. What do you feel about quality and its role—in your gut? Is it a consuming passion, or one more competitive weapon? Think about this question for a long time.
2. Starting today, if you are serious, never again knowingly walk past poor quality—in any form—delivered by your firm without taking dramatic and decisive action, almost regardless of the cost.
3. Collect reams of data on quality—internally and from customers. Go off-site for three days of intense debate. Are you up to mounting a true quality revolution? Will anything short of such a revolution do?
4. From the start, ensure that the customer is a major part of the program, and that the customer's perceptions drive the program. Embarrassing or not, invite customers to every quality analysis/program meeting—from the outset.

C-3

SUMMARY

Increasingly, competitive advantage in a crowded market will stem from "service added":

▶ Become a service fanatic, emphasizing service in the customer's terms.

▶ Consider every customer to be a potential lifelong customer, generating word-of-mouth referrals; therefore, emphasize the relationship with the customer over time.

▶ Attend especially to the intangible attributes of the product or service.

Service pays! Customers for hamburgers, aircraft engines, fashion goods, bank loans, health care, and semiconductors buy far more than an interest rate or technical specifications. Over the long haul, relationships, based upon perceptions formed over time, are more important than so-called tangible traits. Every product and service can be completely redefined on the basis of "service/intangibles added." Service, on average, is so bad that a barrage of tiny positives can overwhelm the customer and the competition. Remember, the average customer is neither a crook nor an idiot. Caution: Service is more than smiles—at the very best it's attitude and supporting systems.

Measure customer satisfaction, in customers' terms and emphasizing the intangibles. Measure it regularly for all members of the distribution channel. Tie measurement directly to compensation and performance evaluation. Design support systems, training programs, etc., based upon the "lifetime value" of the customer. Append at least three tangible and three intangible "service added" features to every product/service offering, every 90 days.

Provide Superior Service/Emphasize the Intangibles

The United States has been terrible as it applies to customer service. When the history of American business is written, I think that's going to be the most incredible part of the historian's view of what we did during the sixties and seventies. I mean, we killed the goose that laid the golden egg. . . . Somehow, management let employees believe the customers weren't important.

> Fred Smith
> founder, Federal Express
> March 1987

WHERE SUPERLATIVE SERVICE IS THE NORM

So you want to buy a suit? Well, one of our seminar participants did. He is an executive for a large national retailer, headquartered in Portland, Oregon. His two daughters and his wife are Nordstrom fans. They constantly bubble about it and pester him to shop there. He was frankly fed up with all the talk. Moreover, despite their comments to the contrary, he secretly suspected that Nordstrom charged an arm and a leg. (Nordstrom's policy is to match anyone's price for a garment, if asked to do so.)

But he did need a suit badly. And a major sale was going on. At worst, he figured, he didn't have too much to lose, especially with the sale. Reluctantly, he went to Nordstrom.

The service in the store was good, he had to admit. And he did find a fine suit on sale, although he also picked up a second suit—at full price. Nordstrom promises same-day alterations. He noted, however, that there was a little asterisk next to the promise—next-day alteration was promised during sales. He chortled at this small chink in the armor.

He came back at 5:45 P.M. the next day to pick up his suits. It was fifteen minutes before closing. He needed the suits for a trip that night.

To his surprise, though he'd only been there once, his salesperson greeted him by name! The fellow then trotted upstairs to pick up the suits. Five minutes passed. The salesperson reappeared—without the goods. They hadn't been finished.

Though he needed the suits, our friend admits to secret glee. Without the suits, he took off for a Monday appointment in Seattle, after which he proceeded to Dallas for the big meeting of the trip.

He checked into his hotel and went up to his room. A message light informed him that a package had arrived for him. A bellhop fetched it—Federal Express, mailing fee $98. Yes, it was from Nordstrom. In it were his two suits. On top of them were three $25 silk ties (which he hadn't ordered) thrown in gratis! There was also a note of apology from the salesperson, who had called his home and learned his travel arrangements from one of his daughters. With a smile of resignation, he admits that he's now a believer.

Specialty retailer Nordstrom has grown sevenfold since 1978, from $225 million to $1.9 billion. Its ad budget is a small fraction of the industry's average, yet sales per square foot, tops among department stores, are three times higher than the industry norm. Moreover, Nordstrom has generated growth internally (no acquisitions) and made most of its gains in the viciously competitive Southern California market.

Its secret? A matchless level of service. If you live in the West, you can't talk about Nordstrom service, because practically everyone has a bizarre Nordstrom story, and you will be inundated with "But I can top that." And that's the point. Though the Portland executive's story is a bit extreme, only slightly less remarkable tales are truly commonplace. ("The store was officially closed. They kept it open for 15 minutes while I looked for a present for my friend. I was already late to the party. And they wrapped it, too, with no sense of being rushed. It was the most beautiful package at the party"—ho hum.)

The sparkling dressing rooms have fresh flowers. No dressing-room matron impedes your entry, demanding to know how many pieces you're carrying in, then giving you an appropriately coded tag to certify the number. No thief-proof wires on the coats (I call them "Macy lines") prevent you from trying them on.

Your salesperson can cash checks, take returns, and do gift wrapping on the spot, instead of shuttling you off to a long line in an out-of-the-way and dingy corner. And those returns? Nordstrom takes anything. Employees even declare that Jim Nordstrom once said, "I don't care if they roll a Goodyear tire into the store, if they say they paid $200 for it, give them the $200." And, yes, the salesperson will routinely know your name after one trip, as was the case with our Oregon friend. He or she will be collecting numerous other facts as well in precious "personal books."

Sophisticated bankers from Morgan, IBM marketing executives, and Harvard marketing professor Ted Levitt are variously given credit for developing the term "relationship management." It is usually applied to sales of mainframe computers, huge corporate loans, and similar sizable transactions. Nordstrom applies the term to retailing with unparalleled skill and zest. Even if you haven't had a problem, as a regular customer you can expect a flood of gifts (flowers on your birthday, etc.) and personal notes from your Nordstrom salesperson.

But Nordstrom won't talk to outsiders like me. Why? Fear of giving away secrets? No, sincere humility. Vice-president Betsy Sanders proclaims, "If we were as good as people say, then there wouldn't need to be shopping malls, only Nordstrom!"

SERVICE PAYS HANDSOMELY

Nordstrom, Federal Express, IBM, The Morgan Bank, Frito-Lay, American Express, McDonald's, Disney, and all too few others seem to understand that service pays. The PIMS data base once more provides decisive support. It split a sample of firms into those rated as better and those rated as worse than average on service—by their customers. The better performers on service charged about 9 percent more for their goods. They grew twice as fast as well, and picked up market share at 6 percent a year, while the also-rans lost share at 2 percent a year. The bottom line: a 12 percent return on sales for the top half in service as seen by the customer, versus a paltry 1 percent for the rest. Some difference!

Beneath such gross indicators are more finely tuned ones. A study by Technical Assistance Research Programs revealed these facts: Twenty-six of every twenty-seven customers who have a bad experience with you fail to report it. The principal reason is not surprising: They expect no satisfaction if they do bug you. The scary part comes next—some 91 percent of those who complain won't come back. Scarier yet, the statistic on dropouts holds as true for $1,000 purchases as for $1.79 ones. And perhaps worst of all, the average person who has been burned tells nine to ten colleagues; 13 percent of the malcontents will spread the bad news to twenty or more people.

There is some hope. The data show that, depending on the industry, you can get 82 to 95 percent of these customers back, if you resolve the complaint in a timely and thoughtful fashion. Other studies are even more optimistic. A well-handled problem usually breeds more loyalty than you had before the negative incident.

Finally, the study yields a clincher: It costs five times more to go out and get a new customer than it does to maintain a customer you already have. Anyone who's been a salesperson for even a day agrees that there's no lousier way to live than depending on cold calls. Developing expanded business with today's customers and thriving via the "word" on your reputation that they broadcast is a less stressful—and more profitable—way to live. Yet all too often our market development budgets, in allocations of both time and money, are skewed toward snazzy activities aimed at attracting first-time users, with today's customer taken for granted.

FOCUS ON THE "OUTER RINGS":
THE TOTAL PRODUCT CONCEPT

The Total Product Concept of Harvard's Ted Levitt provides a device to aid systematic analysis of this prescription:

Figure 7

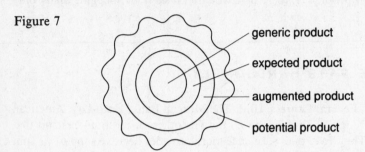

generic product

expected product

augmented product

potential product

Consider Nordstrom: At the *generic* level, the store provides four walls and the categories of goods traditional to an upscale specialty clothing retailer. At the *expected* level, hours are standard and fashions are timely. At the *augmented* level, Nordstrom spends heavily to "overstaff" the sales floor by traditional standards—with "overpaid" people by traditional standards. It likewise "overspends" to ensure the availability of more sizes and colors than usual. And it "overspends" again to maintain numerous, close-to-the-market buying offices which cater to specialized, local tastes.

It is at the *potential* level, however, that Nordstrom really lives its "No Problem at Nordstrom" logo: the flowers in the dressing rooms; a grand piano, with pianist, in each store; the losses from the few who doubtless do take advantage of the "return anything" policy; the empowerment of salespeople to deal with almost all problems on the spot; the routine performance of exceptional acts of service, such as the ones described above.

As you, the customer, traverse Levitt's rings, from generic to potential, you realize that Nordstrom is not "a specialty clothing retailer." It is, and many have so labeled it, "an experience," "a phenomenon," or, as one of my computer company friends calls it, "a provider of a lifetime, user-friendly relationship, only marginally associated with clothing per se!"

In the same vein, Federal Express has redefined "mail service." And Ray Smith of the Louisville Redbirds has transformed minor-league baseball: spotless washrooms, cleaned several times per game; seats steam-cleaned and hand-wiped before each game; freshly squeezed orange juice and the best nachos around; players available to sign balls; kids encouraged to run on the field after the game; and an endless array of special events make his game the choice for summer family entertainment in Louisville—with attendance that, even with a poor field record, tops that of some major-league clubs.

The bottom line—and please stop and reflect on this if you don't at first agree—is this: Nordstrom, Federal Express, et al. have created fundamentally new products and new markets by skewing their attention to the outer two rings in the Levitt scheme. Moreover, they have invariably done so through a thousand tiny differentiating actions, none of which is earth-shaking by itself.

This is so important because the converse attitude is all too prevalent. Spend time around engineering firms, and most of the chatter is about their products' technical performance—the generic circle. Hang out with bankers, and again the generic—the price of money—dominates conversation. While I acknowledge the importance of the generic, I am urging a flip-flop: <u>most of the organization's attention should center on repositioning the product and creating whole new markets by emphasizing the two outer Levitt rings.</u>

Figure 8

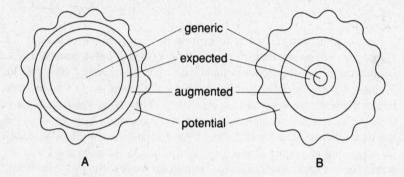

The value of this advice is rising from "useful" to "essential"—"service added" is increasingly becoming the competitive battleground in every market. That is, traditional strategic thinking, in retailing and manufacturing, can be depicted as Figure 8A, in which the "generic" dominates. The effective organization of tomorrow—auto company, custom semiconductor maker, insurance firm—will pay attention as shown in Figure 8B, that is, will emphasize service added via the "augmented" and "potential" rings.

ATTEND TO THE INTANGIBLES

Little Things Mean a Lot

Computer retailer ValCom launched a program called CARE, for Customers Are Really Everything. The centerpiece has been working at an expanding list labeled "A Little Thing Means a Lot." Small touches, such as the following, are constantly added to the firm's selling package: "Send monthly newsletter to customers with spotlight on key customers. Spot management visits to key accounts. Send small gifts to customers. Send thank-you notes with store logos.

Salespeople saying thank you with sales invoice. Call back customers 30 days after sale is delivered—see how they are doing. Provide support service index for customer's Rolodex of names and addresses. Return phone calls the same day. Put label on computer with phone number of store. Take a picture of the customers and their computer system and post it in your store; mail them a copy. Have framed customer satisfaction letters on store walls. Provide bag with store logo on it for customer to carry diskettes, ribbons, etc. 'Keep-in-touch' program: mail thank you once every three months to current customers acknowledging their continued support. Circle/highlight phone number to call for questions on invoice." It adds up.

Little things mean a lot even in what appears to be the most clear-cut commodity arena. Here's a letter addressed to the Granite Rock Company of Watsonville, California:

March 24, 1987

Dear Sirs:

I am sending you this letter to express my gratitude with your service. I was very impressed with the human manner (as opposed to a machine-like manner) that my situation was handled. . . . I had ordered 7.25 yards for a simple 10 × 40 slab, broom finish. When the driver showed up on time, to say the least, we were off to a great start. The driver was friendly, and cooperative which I would say is not a common trait. After pouring out the truck [he] noticed I was having a hard time . . . as my laborer didn't show up, and he helped to speed things up. . . . As it turned out I was one wheel-barrow short and had no way to make it work without it. After using the truck's radio to communicate with the batch plant and drivers, he found a truck very near by with less than a yard on its way back to the plant. The second driver was able to find the job quickly, save my ass and do it all politely. To top it off I was only charged for the extra one-quarter yard I used, as opposed to a one-yard minimum. . . . If my service was a fluke then oh-well, but I tend to think that it was all a reflection of the attitude in which Granite Rock is run. Also there is no way to say clearly enough how nice it is to have pleasant drivers who are able to be a service instead of just another randy ass concrete truck driver. You can be sure I will call upon this company again when we have work in your area.

Sincerely,
Contractor

The Power of Call-Backs

At a recent seminar, we devoted a half-day to the perception of service. The talk among insurance company executives, hospital administrators, and auto-component manufacturers at one point gravitated to "call-backs." It seemed that each succeeding participant had a more astounding tale to tell about the potency of a call from an executive or manager following a purchase or a repair. Even, said one, a call to see if a bid had arrived was received with wonderment— no one had ever bothered to do that before, according to a crusty auto company purchasing executive.

This small, human touch in an increasingly impersonal world can go a long way toward cementing a customer relationship. Domino Pizza's top franchisee (based on repeat business), Phil Bressler, attributes much of his success to calling 100 customers per week. He insists that call-backs be given priority over the shop's nightly accounting closeout. His explanation: "Nobody's ever bought a pie from us because we had a great closeout."

High-tech Intangibles

So the transformational possibilities of Levitt's outer rings hold for pizzas and concrete. They hold as well for manufacturing firms, as Caterpillar, Boeing, and IBM demonstrate daily. They hold for health-care service: a group of hospital administrators at one of our seminars came up with about 250 service intangibles beyond the generic procedure for which the patient is admitted. Indeed, even (or especially) in the arena of the highest technology, the intangibles are paramount, as Regis McKenna points out in *The Regis Touch:*

[I]t is common for a company to boast that its product . . . is 25 percent more powerful than any competing product. Indeed, an incredible number of positioning strategies center on price and "specsmanship." (That is, promoting a product by its superior technical specifications, or "specs.") . . . Companies are much better off if they establish positions based on what I call "intangible" factors, qualities such as reliability and service. Unlike price and technical specs, intangibles don't fit neatly onto a product-comparison chart. . . . But intangibles are much more powerful as positioning levers. . . .

The power of intangible positioning became clear to me a few years ago when I was doing a market survey for Intel. As part of the survey, I talked to a number of engineers about a certain memory chip. I remember asking one engineer why he selected the Intel chip. This chip was a fairly technical product, and you might have expected the engineer to answer in technical argot: "The memory had an access time of so many nanoseconds," or "Its power dissipation is only such-and-such." That didn't happen. Instead, the engineer told me his company buys almost all its chips from Intel, so it was natural to buy the new chip from Intel too. Had he evaluated the new product? Not really. "We just tend to buy from Intel because we have a business relationship there," he explained. "We know where they are going and we trust the company. . . ." Most buying decisions are made the same way. Product managers spend days, if not weeks, drawing up charts and graphs that compare products on the basis of specifications and price. But buying decisions are rarely based on these objective standards. The important product comparisons come from the minds of those in the marketplace. And in people's minds, it is intangible factors that count.

Under-promise, Over-deliver

With competition heating up in every market, firms are forced to promise the moon to get an order, especially that first order. Right?

Wrong. With an explosion of competitors, many of them new and without track records, reliability, rather than overly aggressive promises, is the most valuable strategic edge, especially for the mid- to long haul. While getting faster at responding to customers is imperative (see C-4), living up to commitments has never been worth more.

A survey of banks, summarized by Citytrust marketing vice-president Skip Morse, supports this point. Banks with lower customer ratings tend to respond, for instance, to an early-morning customer query with, "We'll be back to you by noon," or "We'll be back to you." Then they get back to the customer at, say, 3 P.M. The top-rated banks, such as The Morgan, reply, "We'll be back to you by close of business today"—and they are—at 4 P.M., for example.

The paradox: Those banks which, objectively speaking, perform better—that is, which actually get the job done first—are frequently rated lower by customers than those they have apparently outperformed. Customers turn thumbs down on banks that fail to keep promises (3 P.M. instead of noon) or that are vague ("We'll get back to you"), and unfailingly prefer slightly less aggressive promises if these are honored.

I experienced the same phenomenon in quick succession at a hotel and a service station. Although the hotel's menu promised that room service would start at 6:15 A.M., when I called at 6:20 A.M., I was subjected to a tinny tape-recorded message saying, "Room service will be open at six-thirty." Though I'm a morning coffee devotee, the 15 minutes is no big deal, in absolute terms. But the delay was infuriating in light of the promise made; my perception was that I was getting rotten service—a perception compounded by the hotel's high rates.

Similarly, when I ordered an unusual-sized tire from a local service station, I was surprised and delighted to be assured (twice) that I could pick it up just four hours later. I was busy then, so I said I'd return the next morning and left that station feeling much better about its unusually high gas prices, which appeared to be offset by its service responsiveness.

I rearranged the next morning's schedule, and popped in at 9 A.M. To my dismay, the tire hadn't even been ordered—and my morning was shot. One more shattered expectation. And once again the issue was the perception, not the absolute: I had originally expected getting the tire to take a couple of days, at least, and had been more than willing to wait.

I realized how important all this was when I had an ever so tiny reverse experience of "over-delivery," and from an airline no less. Airlines just don't tell the truth very often. We all know that "ten minute delay" is a code phrase for either (1) "hour delay" or (2) "I don't have the foggiest notion when, or if, the darn thing will ever take off."

But once I felt the power of the truth. A downpour swept La Guardia, and all takeoffs were halted. When we moved onto the taxiway after the storm had passed, and with the underventilated plane already approaching Black Hole of Calcutta status, the pilot said, "We're fifteenth in line, and we'll be off in forty-five minutes." There were lots of groans, but we settled in. About 30 minutes later we were off—and I felt as though I'd been given a great gift. The fact is that it's memorable over a year later. Now had that pilot followed the routine—"There are a buncha planes ahead of us. It'll be 'bout fifteen minutes"—the same 30-minute wait would have been just one more "over-promise, under-deliver" episode.

Some intriguing evidence from the health-care field bears on this issue. Surgical patients who are told, in detail, of the nature of post-operative agony recover as much as one-third faster than those left in the dark.

Suppose a patient is told that she or he will suffer severe shortness of breath for four or five days following surgery. Even if the symptoms persist a bit longer than average, the patient is prepared to deal with it. The uninformed patient panics, believing that the operation was a failure. No amount of post-operative explanation helps ("They're lying—I'm dying"). Even if the uninformed patient's shortness of breath lasts less than the norm, his or her emotional distress frequently sets back overall recovery.

We all seek predictability. In fact, the more uncertain, frightening, and complex the situation (such as today's competitive scene), the more we grasp for predictability. That's why I'm not at all surprised at the bank study or health-care findings.

And yet, as much as we may relate to such stories of frustrating, unkept promises when we are on the receiving end (patient, individual consumer, commercial purchaser), we tend to underrate this concern when we plan our own firm's strategy.

Take, for instance, groups I have worked with from two fine companies (building products, packaging materials), both renowned for top-flight product quality. Both have been meeting with customers to learn how they are perceived in the marketplace. Both have been surprised that their renowned quality has been less the focus of attention than their good, or occasionally bad, record for responsiveness. That is, despite quality that is demonstrably superior to their chief competitors', more than 80 percent of the customer feedback harps on responsiveness and reliability. Quite frequently, "second-rate firms" (as their competitors—my clients—see them, based upon relative quality) have received high overall marks from customers because they have unfailingly met their commitments.

"I can't get over it," one executive pondered. "I expected them to talk about various quality enhancements, including some problems we've had with a new product. Instead, they went on and on about a small, late order here or an especially responsive act there."

Quality is important, to be sure. So is absolute response time. And price. But at least as important as any of these is keeping your word. In fact, I've boiled it down to a simple formula:

$$CP = \frac{D}{E}.$$

Customer perception (CP) equals delivery (D) divided by expectation (E). Maximizing CP is essential in the squishy, real world, where perception of the intangibles is really everything.

Treat the Customer as an Appreciating Asset

When the Federal Express courier enters my office, she should see "$180,000" stamped on the forehead of our receptionist. My little twenty-five-person firm runs about a $1,500-a-month Fed Ex bill. Over ten years, that will add up to $180,000. I suggest that this simple device, calculating the ten-year (or, alternatively, lifetime) value of a customer can be very powerful—and has sweeping implications.

Grocer Stew Leonard got me started on this. He says, "When I see a frown on a customer's face, I see $50,000 about to walk out the door." His good customers buy about $100 worth of groceries a week. Over ten years, that adds up to roughly $50,000. We all agree that repeat trade is the key to business success. This simple quantifying device provides a way to add potency to the idea.

Here are two other examples. Average lifetime auto purchases will total about $150,000, not including repair work. Given the remarkably low dealer loyalty of car buyers these days, might it not make a difference if dealers and their employees focused on this big number? Or suppose you frequent a good restaurant twice a month for a six-person business dinner. You're worth about $75,000 every ten years to that establishment.

Imposing as they are, these figures are just the tip of the iceberg. The repeat customer is also any firm's principal vehicle for powerful word-of-mouth advertising. Conservatively, suppose a lifelong, happy customer sells just one colleague on becoming a lifelong customer of your fine restaurant, grocery store, or Federal Express, as the case may be. Suddenly, the regular customer's value to the restaurant doubles from $75,000 to $150,000, including that likely word-of-mouth referral. And that sign on my receptionist's forehead should now be read by the Fed Ex person as $360,000 rather than $180,000.

There's a third step in the progression. If the restaurant's waiter handles five tables a night, he or she is catering to 5 × $150,000, or $750,000, worth of potential business. The numbers are stunning for Fed Ex. If our courier has forty regular stops at businesses my size (which would be normal), she is managing each day a "portfolio" of customers worth 40 $\times$ $360,000, or $14 million, to Federal Express!

So the three-step formula is: First, estimate the ten-year or lifelong value of a customer, based upon the size and frequency of a good customer's average transaction. Then multiply that number by two, to take into account the word-of-mouth factor. Finally, multiply the new total by the average number of customers served per day by the sales, service, dispatch, or other front-line person or group. The result is the lifelong value of the "customer portfolio" that that individual or group deals with each day.

The implication is clear: If you look at customers in this or a related way, you are likely to take a new view of hiring, training, compensating, and spending on tools to aid the customer-serving process. Take that waiter, managing $750,000 of your future each night. Are you still sure you want to brag about the low average wages you pay? Are you certain that skimping on uniform quality makes sense? Does the investment in a small computer system to support order taking still look as expensive as it did? Suddenly, Stew Leonard's insistence that everyone in the store go through the lengthy Dale Carnegie public-speaking and attitude courses is seen in a different light. So is the high pay at Federal Express, and its seemingly lavish spending on support tools, such as the Cosmos computer system that soon will include a terminal in each delivery truck. (On the reverse side, it makes the failure of People Express to invest in service support tools incomprehensible.)

Consider another element of the pay scheme. Most firms don't discriminate between sales commissions that come from new business and those that come from repeat and add-on business. A few go so far as to pay higher commissions for new business and cut back on commissions for repeat orders, which presumably require less work. The contrary should be standard. In fact, sales commissions and/or salaries ought to be skewed substantially toward incentives for repeat and add-on business. We want our salespeople not to take today's customers for granted. Repeat and add-on business usually results from a host of small but, in total, time-consuming touches—such as acting as a go-between with the engineering or service department; our incentives should say unequivocally, "Spend that time!"

This advice is now more important than ever. With "service added" an increasingly important strategy, all sales are fast becoming "system sales." All transactions must be looked at as relationship-building opportunities.

It boils down to this: When you build a plant, it starts depreciating the day it opens. The well-served customer, on the other hand, is an appreciating asset. Every small act on her or his behalf ups the odds for repeat business, add-on business, and priceless word-of-mouth referral.

Try this calculation yourself. One hospital administrator did at a seminar of ours. Upon finding that the average nurse "managed" $2 million in business each day, he mounted an aggressive program to enhance the status of the nursing department. A European software executive did the same thing at a seminar I attended with several of his big customers present. He looked around the table, did a hasty mental calculation, and whistled: "We have 720 million guilders [\$360 million] in 'lifetime' business in this room." Turning to his associates, he added, "You'd better listen to what they have to say."

Not "Gee Whiz," but a Way of Life

Thus I urge, in this prescription, that you emphasize service and, in even broader terms, the intangibles—that is, augmented and potential product traits. The overall profitability numbers and the specific cases, from high tech to low, in service and manufacturing, support me. The challenge is to view *every* element of *every* operation through the customer's lens; to constantly attempt to—literally—*redefine* each element of the business in terms of the customer's perceptions of the intangibles.

There *is* a catch. I've now been to dozens of seminars where lists of ideas for enhancing customer perceptions, often with hundreds of items, are readily made. Most of the ideas are inexpensive, so few fiscal barriers to implementation exist. Yet one of two outcomes usually ensues—only a small share of the ideas is implemented or, even if the whole list is implemented, that's the end of it.

Nordstrom's edge is that "the list," if you will, represents an attitude, a way of life. There is no end. It is always expanding. It is everyone's business. For while the attributes of service can be dissected into small and delightfully doable bits, the mind-set required to hack away, year after year, at a "service added" strategy is far from common. Preoccupation with the outer two rings in the Levitt scheme must become a lifetime affair for tomorrow's successful firms.

MEASURE CUSTOMER SATISFACTION

Measure! And reward on the basis of the measures. Quality—the poor-quality cost, customer evaluation of quality—can be measured; I emphasized that in prescription C-2. Service can be measured too. Yet few do it. And most of those who do (1) do so too infrequently, (2) don't emphasize the intangibles, and (3) haven't the confidence to pay for performance in this area.

After years of observation, I have arrived at ten considerations that are key to effective measurement of customer satisfaction:

1. Frequency. Formal surveys every 60 to 90 days are a must. Do informal surveys monthly at least. A major annual image survey should be the program's cornerstone. Perdue Farms and Citytrust survey daily; Domino's Pizza does so weekly—yet all too many pat themselves on the back for doing a semiannual survey. Such a low frequency doesn't cut the mustard.

2. Format. A third party must do the systematic annual image survey and probably should do the 60–90-day surveys. And they should be expensive—so you'll take them seriously. The results, even if embarrassing, must be widely shared. Informal "focus groups" of a few customers ought to be called in to every operation—manufacturing, distribution, accounting, not just marketing—

on a biweekly or monthly basis. Debriefings with key accounts (annually or semiannually) must include formal survey questions and open-ended discussions with all levels and functions in key account operations. Mount informal (or formal) "call three customers each week" programs for senior managers in all functions, including specified rituals for sharing and discussing the data generated by the calls. Summaries of all customer complaint correspondence (statistical plus some actual letters and call transcripts) should be made available to all. Systematic "lost sale" follow-up programs are also a must.

3. **Content.** Ask some standard quantifiable questions—e.g., "How many complaints did you get in the first 90 days after the product went on sale?" "How many hours do you take to respond to customer queries of various sorts?" Put energy into devising ways to quantify the qualitative questions—e.g., "How were we to do business with?"—on a scale of one to ten. And be sure, in all such measuring, to test "us" against your "best competitor" (best overall, best in the area, newest, etc.).

4. **Design of content.** Do continual, systematic "naïve" listening from as many angles as possible (see also prescription C-7). No single measure or survey instrument is best, or even good. Coordination and cross-checking among many is essential. The chief roadblock to program success is moving beyond obvious measures to the difficult-to-articulate, controversial (especially to engineers, accountants, manufacturers, marketers, and kindred spirits) perceptual variables that ultimately determine long-term customer relations/repeat business/account growth. Take the example of the bank survey: Would your questions get at the value of "underpromising" on delivery?

5. **Involve everyone.** Informal focus groups must include all functions, all levels of seniority. Hold in-plant key-account reviews with all hands in attendance. Visits to customer sites should include, over time, *all* functions, *all* levels from line workers to top management. Suppliers, wholesalers, and other members of the distribution channel should also take part, formally and informally.

6. **Measure everyone's satisfaction.** Measure the satisfaction of all direct and indirect customers: the ultimate user and every member of the distribution channel—dealer, retailer, wholesaler, franchisee, rep, etc.

7. **Combinations of measures.** Reduce measures to a composite quantitative score for (a) some individuals (e.g., salespersons, service persons), (b) groups (a dispatch or reservation center team), (c) facilities (factory or operations office or store), and (d) divisions.

8. **Relation to compensation and other rewards.** Once measures, developed in partnership with the people being measured (ideally, everyone), are fully agreed upon and checked out for reliability over time, move to include them in compensation plans (e.g., incentive compensation for salespersons, gainsharing programs for others). Consider making this the prime variable in sales incentive compensation (instead of volume of sales); or at least use it as a "go–no go" switch (e.g., if a person is not in the top half on the continued customer satisfaction measure, he or she is not eligible for any awards based on the volume of sales).

9. Symbolic use of measures. Key customer satisfaction measures should be publicly posted in every part of the organization.

10. Other forms of measurement. Every job description (if you have them—see S-2) should include a qualitative description of the person's "connection to the customer," and every performance evaluation should include an assessment of the person's degree of "customer orientation."

Do Something, Anything, Now!

If you're not doing anything about measurement right now (and most aren't), then consider this fallback advice. After a speech in Atlanta, a young man pulled me aside: "So what am I supposed to do?" I'd just covered the list above, and I replied: "Do those ten things." "No," he insisted, "what am I supposed to DO?" Frustrated, I thought for a moment, then blurted out: "Look, just drag fifteen customers in from somewhere, buy 'em lunch or dinner, and ask them what the heck is on their minds." "Thanks, that's great," he said, obviously satisfied, and took off.

I hope he got as much out of the exchange as I did. The measurement list is a product of a lot of work. But if it puts you off, just drag fifteen . . .

Cautionary Tales about Measurement: Tripping over Words

Seemingly innocuous terms can lead us way off course with the measurement of customer satisfaction. Here are five loaded phrases:

1. "Not symptomatic": A bank executive was discussing customer satisfaction measurement. He said that when a problem only showed up once—a particular error on a statement, for instance—then there was little or no follow-up beyond a cursory apology, because it was "not symptomatic of a larger problem."

At some of my seminars, I get detailed feedback from hundreds of people. There is invariably some criticism. Sadly, I have found every criticism symptomatic of larger issues—some continuing form of inattention or inflexibility on my part. I readily find all too sensible reasons why a particular critic reacted the way she or he did. *Every* customer complaint *is* symptomatic of a shortcoming—moreover, it usually represents a lurking improvement opportunity. Treat every snafu (a) as symptomatic of impending doom and (b) as a budding opportunity for market creation and product redefinition—and act accordingly.

2. "Objective" versus "subjective": One manager insists: "Cleanliness is subjective. By definition, it can't be measured." So what's objective? The same manager responds: "What percent of orders went out on or before the date due."

First, cleanliness can be measured. Just add a question to your next survey: "How clean was the store, on a scale of one to ten, where ten is 'like an operating room'?" Or: "Relative to fast-food places where you've eaten recently, how clean was our operation?" Choices might include "awful," "below average," "average," etc.

Second, this particular manager's example of objectivity is anything but. A high-tech firm boasted it was beating order-due dates 98 percent of the time. But customers were not knocking down the doors with repeat business. It turned out that the "due date" was actually a tortuously negotiated date: if the custom asked for the order by January 17, a harried plant manager might insist th February 25 was the best he could do. So what's the big deal in beating that kin of "due date" by even a week? When the firm switched to the "customer reques date" (reasonable or not) as its measurement base, meeting or beating it slumped to a tawdry 32 percent. After a year of hard work it has climbed back to 68 percent—and repeat business has grown.*

So anything can be measured and made "objective." But measurement per se does not ensure objectivity.

3. "Ninety-seven percent satisfied": An IBM executive says, "We make 300,000 components. Don't say to me, '97 percent are okay.' Say instead, '9,000 were defective.' Sounds a little bit different, doesn't it?" He adds: "You don't really want 9,000 angry customers, do you?" A hospital administrator concurs: "Remember, 95 percent 'happy' patients in a 600-bed hospital means that 30 are thinking about suing you for malpractice at any given point!"

4. "On average": The use of averages is downright dangerous. For instance, "On average, we ship parts within 37 hours of order entry," or "The average customer requires 0.84 service visit per year." But more study reveals that the 37-hour "average" also means 89 hours for the "worst-off 10 percent"; and the 0.84 service visit translates into two or more visits for 26 percent of your customers. Gear your measures to focus attention on the worst-off 1, 5, 10, or 25 percent of customers.

5. "Unsystematic": I'm all for systematic surveys of 700 randomly selected customers or noncustomers. But I also applaud very unsystematic rituals, despite the disdain they draw from MBA analysts. Once a month, George Gendron, editor-in-chief of *Inc.* magazine, calls a half-dozen people who have not renewed their subscriptions. When I saw him last, he was flying off from the East Coast to Denver just to talk to one of those unhappy subscribers. "Her notion of what was wrong and what could be improved was positively brilliant," he said. The MBA's conception of "systematic" didn't apply in this case, but the business was well served.

Watch your language!

THE HUMAN TOUCH IS NOT ENOUGH: TECHNOLOGY'S ROLE

It is important to conclude with a word of caution. While courtesy is powerful medicine, it is only half the story. Federal Express thrives because of its great

*Go back and re-read the section on customer perception, expectation, and delivery. Make sure that the denominator on the righthand side of the equation ("expectation") is the *true* customer expectation, not one that you've finagled.

"people orientation" (involvement, incentive compensation, empowerment to take the initiative to solve problems, etc.). But that's matched by equally great support systems. The Limited's success has resulted from the same blend of people and technology/systems. Likewise, Nordstrom matches its people emphasis with hard-dollar expenditures on inventory, salary and commissions, numerous local buying offices, and in-store amenities. American Express, McDonald's, and Frito-Lay match a people orientation with a systems emphasis too. Even grocer Stew Leonard fits this mold. His customer orientation, through people, is matchless—but he was also one of the first grocers, small or large, to do daily computer analysis of the profitability of every item he sold; Leonard was a decade ahead of Safeway on systems that are just now becoming commonplace in the industry.

On the other hand, that other express, People, is out of business. The smiles were tops. But they couldn't compensate for an awful reservation system which infuriated passengers and travel agents alike.

PUBLIC PARALLELS

With respect to those two outer rings of Levitt's, there are no limits for the imaginative public sector manager. Ron Hartman, general manager of Baltimore's Mass Transit Administration, offers up a fine example: "Two years ago we received a series of complaints on one of our premium park-and-ride express bus lines from a suburb to downtown Baltimore. Several buses were continually late. We fixed the problem, but felt we owed the riders more for the inconvenience. One day after the service got back to normal, we took advantage of the fact that it was the Christmas season. On a cold December morning, instead of the usual bus showing up, we decorated a bus with lots of crepe paper and tinsel, stuck a Christmas tree in the fare box to offer the service free, hooked up a tape recorder playing carols, and dressed the driver like Santa Claus. We offered cookies, coffee, and candy canes as commuters boarded. We still get letters from those customers and most continue to ride with us."

Sad to say, though, I can point to few public sector operations that emphasize the "outer rings," or even measure customer (constituent) satisfaction. But then all too few private firms measure it, to their detriment. On the other hand, extensive, systematic measurement is plausible and would surely be useful for any public entity—a school, a transportation or sanitation district, etc.

Many public sector managers are reluctant to seek such feedback, because they are afraid it will be too expensive to deal with, will open up a can of worms, and will result in suggestions that will be beyond their bailiwick—"Keep the library open seven days a week, twenty-four hours a day," etc. But the reality is that the lion's share of consumers of private and public services are sane and thoughtful. IBM's average customer does not respond to a survey with "Redesign the whole top of the line." The majority of suggestions will be in the line of "You always run out of soup spoons," "The towel dispenser is too high for kids to reach." If you sample regularly, and respond quickly, you will be inundated with small, practical, generally inexpensive—and implementable— ideas. Then both you and the customer/citizen win.

FIRST STEPS

1. Take one product or service that you offer. Bring in customers, informally. Spend a day working on the "two outer rings"—the augmented and the potential product. What do you offer? What do competitors offer? How do customers perceive the offering?
2. Calculate the ten-year or lifetime value of a customer. Then review, with representatives from all functions, what you do proactively to encourage relationship building. Focus especially on key front-line jobs that affect the *perception* of responsiveness to the customers. Check biases in sales and service compensation systems vis-à-vis repeat business. Perhaps start your own "Little Things Mean a Lot" program for recent purchasers and lifelong customers.

C-4

SUMMARY

Given changing technology, the opportunity granted by being close to the U.S. market, and the moves of competitors, we must:

▶ Achieve total customer responsiveness (TCR) via bold, new partnerships with suppliers/distributors/customers.

▶ Seek out and create new markets *with* our partners.

▶ Introduce "hustle" as a key strategic concept—fast moves, fast adaption, and tight linkages will become a way of life.

Adversarial relations with suppliers, distributors (and all members of the distribution channel), and ultimate end users must be quickly replaced with partnership relations. Major electronic/telecommunication linkages and other tactics to enhance speed/responsiveness must be quickly achieved. They represent the ultimate offensive strategic opportunity, but must also be done quickly for defensive reasons—others will get there first and lock in customers for years to come.

In the next 24 months, mount major partnership projects with 75 percent of your major suppliers/distributors/customers. Slash jointly held inventories and the lead time required for order fulfillment (including delivery times on new models and styles) by 90 percent. Continually add value-enhancing, ever-tighter links to every member of the distribution channel.

C-4

Achieve Extraordinary Responsiveness

Strategy, its high-church theologians insist, is about outflanking competitors with big plays that yield . . . a sustainable advantage. It is questionable whether this proposition is itself sustainable. . . . The competitive scriptures almost systematically ignore the importance of hustle and energy. While they preach strategic planning, competitive strategy, and competitive advantage, they overlook the record of a surprisingly large number of very successful companies that vigorously practice a different religion. These companies don't have long-term strategic plans with an obsessive preoccupation on rivalry. They concentrate on operating details and doing things well. Hustle is their style and their strategy. They move fast, and they get it right.

[H]igh profits [at top financial service institutions] stem largely from superior execution or forceful opportunism, not structural competitive barriers. Different execution styles lead to considerable variations in bottom-line results. Many wholesale banks have the same cost of funds, offer similar products and services, and use the same kinds of sales forces to reach the same customers. Yet some are more profitable than others. They "get it right." . . . They get a higher share of corporate cash balances because the account officers get and stay close to their clients. They know the clients so well that they make suggestions before the clients know they need them. . . . "Lost" wire transfers are found promptly. They're informed, fast, and available.

Amar Bhide,
"Hustle as Strategy"
Harvard Business Review,
September/October 1986

Creating well-defined market niches is not enough. Neither is TQC, total quality control. Nor is superior service with an emphasis on the intangibles. Add TCR, total customer responsiveness, to prescriptions C-1 through C-3.

LINK UP OR ELSE!

This prescription covers, for instance, extensive electronic linkups among supplier, factory, delivery truck, distributor (agent, etc.), and customer. Citicorp, Federal Express, drug distributors McKesson and Bergen Brunswig, American Airlines, American Hospital Supply, Merrill Lynch, truckers Ryder and P-I-E Nationwide, Milliken, and The Limited are typical of the pioneers here. It also means getting physically closer to your customer, with programs and resources—Campbell Soup, Frito-Lay, and PPG are among those showing the way in this. And it concerns computer-integrated manufacturing and flexible manufacturing systems in general. But it is at least as much about forming partnerships among functions within the firm and with suppliers, distributors, sales reps, and ultimate customers. Adversarial relations in these arenas, characteristic of most firms historically, spell competitive discomfort today and doom tomorrow. TCR most generally means "hustle," as Amar Bhide defined it, or "sustaining a constant sense of urgency," as Elgin Corrugated Box Company president Bob Wilson calls it.

The stakes are high—survival. The goal is breathtaking. This prescription, in a host of major areas, demands 75 to 90 percent improvements in the next 24 to 48 months. As you read this, others, possibly including your competitors, are taking on—and achieving—such goals. Winners will do it; losers won't. And once more there's a cautionary note: Though the goals must necessarily be bold, they will not be achieved by a leapfrog, big bang, or one-shot application of new technology. Change in the structure of the organization and in decades-old attitudes must precede, or at least parallel, technology's application. In the quality prescription C-2, I repeatedly warned that passion without systems was a lousy formula; so were systems without passion. The same, with minor variations, holds true of TCR.

An Alarming Contrast

It was a coincidence. My *Business Week* arrived at home on a Friday in April 1986. I came across a story about Custom Vêtement Associates, the U.S. subsidiary of French garment maker Vestra. A custom-tailored suit has always meant a ten-week wait to me. No more. U.S. retailers such as Saks have been given "terminals made for the French national Videotex system," *Business Week* reported. "These link retailers with the main manufacturing operation in Strasbourg. Tailors take key measurements from customers and plug them into a terminal. Every night the data are sent to a central computer in New York and beamed via satellite to France. In the morning, after nine inspectors look at different pieces of data, a computer-controlled laser cutter selects the appropriate material and cuts the garment. A staff of tailors does the finishing touches, and the suit is shipped within four days."

By chance, I purchased a truck for my Vermont farm the next day, Saturday.

I bought American—GMC. Not until I got it home did I realize that the spare tire gobbled up almost all the truck's effective storage space. The solution was clear: buy a simple A-frame bracket to mount the tire on the rear of the vehicle. Of course, this was impossible on Saturday, when I discovered the problem, or Sunday. Very few dealers in the United States keep their parts or service operations open on weekends—that is, when customers are around. On Monday, I stayed home and went to the dealership. In place of the Custom Vêtement computer terminal was the usual parts book, several feet long and made of flimsy (and by now ragged) paper. Nonetheless, I managed to place the order. I was informed, however, that there was no way of knowing when the part might be in; I should call in "three or four days," just to find out when it might arrive. It depended on whether the regional distributor had it, and so on. To make a long story short, it took over three weeks to get the simple part (a GM part) and another week to get and complete an appointment for installation. Five weeks later and over $400 poorer, I had a $20,000 truck that would now carry a second bag of groceries!

WAYS TO CONNECT WITH THE CUSTOMER

Going Local

High Technology editor Bob Haavind said the obvious in a recent editorial: "So where can U.S. manufacturing industry hope to gain an edge? In fact, domestic manufacturers have a tremendous potential advantage relative to off-shore competitors simply by being close to the market. Amazingly, few American firms make much use of this obvious advantage."

Some, of course, do. Frito-Lay has long maintained a big lead in the snack-food business by "overspending" to get close to the customer. The $3 billion subsidiary of PepsiCo, which contributes about $350 million in pre-tax profits to its parent, sends out 10,000 route salespersons each day. And now, despite its commanding lead in market share, Frito-Lay has taken additional steps to tighten its linkages to its customers. For example, the company is moving significant marketing muscle to the field. Marketing staff members, once located in the Dallas headquarters, will now be installed in eight regional offices in an effort to make brand strategy more "bottom up than top down," according to the firm's marketing vice-president. The share of the marketing budget devoted to local needs will rise dramatically. Frito-Lay's director of field marketing declares, "Basically, there's no such thing as a national program for promotions coming out of Frito-Lay anymore. We will tailor our marketing to our prime trading areas." Frito-Lay's president, Mike Jordan, adds, "We are tailoring our program to meet the needs of individual chains. . . . That was not one of our strengths in prior years."

Frito-Lay's new approach is also being used by stablemate Pepsi-Cola. Both programs are carbon copies of an even more aggressive effort by Campbell Soup,

119

mentioned briefly in Part I. In 1982, once stodgy and hierarchical Campbell reorganized into fifty-two business units to speed product development and niche-market creation. A fourfold increase in the pace of product development ensued. Typical of the outcome is the success of the unleashed Canadian unit. Allowed to break with the conventional wisdom of packaged-goods marketers (dominated by a mass-market, economy-of-scale mind-set), the $300 million subsidiary recently introduced, for instance, a new brand of V-8 juice for French-speaking Canadians, whose taste in tomatoes is different from that of their English-speaking counterparts. It's been a smashing success.

The second bold move at Campbell came in April 1986, when, in a break with the monolithic Procter & Gamble marketing model, it created twenty-two powerful regional marketing offices. Field brand managers, sales, and big budgets are being applied to local needs on an unprecedented scale. (Incidentally, P&G is now following suit, though at a slower pace.)

Get "Wired": Installing Electronic Linkages

Once again, Frito-Lay shows the way. Soon every one of its delivery trucks will have an onboard computer terminal, linked to the rest of the distribution system. Federal Express, with its Cosmos system (see C-3), has gained a great advantage in the same fashion.

Drug distributor McKesson's electronic linkages to its customers—independent pharmacies—*are* the successful firm's strategy. In the 1970s, Foremost-McKesson was a diversified elephant, limping along with dairies, pasta makers, and drug distributors in its portfolio. Near the end of the decade the company undertook radical surgery. It sold off virtually all nondistribution activities and invested about $125 million in a state-of-the-art computer-telecommunications system. The system not only made the renamed McKesson Corporation more profitable, but it also saved and made profitable McKesson Drug's more than 12,000 then struggling independent pharmacist customers, who can now compete with chains on price—and often beat them on availability. Orders can be placed at any time via a hand-held programmable computer that hooks up to a common phone line. Deliveries are made daily, and the rarest drugs can be readily obtained. McKesson's once imperiled independent customers have increased their business significantly in the last half dozen years and McKesson's drug distribution business has grown fourfold, from $1 billion in 1978 to almost $5 billion today, with a spiffy 20 percent return on assets to boot.

Beyond price and availability, McKesson has added numerous other features to assist—*and lock in*—its customers. Software packages, such as ECONOPRICE, ECONOCHARGE, ECONOCLAIM, ECONOPLAN, and ECONOFICHE, print continuously updated labels based on the retailer's own formula, aid in the management of accounts receivable, speed third-party (insurer) claim processing for prescription drugs, optimize the utilization of shelf space, and provide microfiche information on such things as drug interaction and Medicaid numbers. McKesson does get displaced from time to time, but all these linkages make it no mean feat to do so.

Reviewing the McKesson systems, researchers Louis Stern and Patrick Kaufmann noted these benefits from so-called Electronic Data Interchange (EDI): "(1) Reduced order lead times; (2) higher service level; (3) fewer out-of-stock situations; (4) improved communication about deals, promotions, price changes, and product availability; (5) lower inventory costs; (6) better accuracy in ordering, shipping, and receiving; and (7) a reduction in labor costs." Not bad.

Among others choosing similar strategies are McKesson's fierce rival, Bergen Brunswig, which has followed McKesson's lead; also in health care, pioneer American Hospital Supply (now owned by Baxter Travenol), which has installed supply order terminals in over 5,000 hospitals and health care establishments, sewing up this business (for now); American Airlines, which pioneered years ago with its Sabre system—now in over 10,000 travel agents' offices, and thus creating "total [customer] dependence," says *Business Week;* P-I-E Nationwide, a Jacksonville, Florida, trucking firm, which developed Shipmaster software for an IBM compatible PC and a modem linking it to carriers; and several pioneer financial service firms, such as Aetna, which have established electronic links with brokers.

Retailing has perhaps witnessed the biggest shift in this direction. In *Managing in the Service Economy,* Harvard's James Heskett comments on Italian knitwear maker Benetton, which "has pioneered a retailing approach throughout Europe that promises to influence a number of other retailers worldwide: It substitutes information for assets. Because its first retail outlet offering knitted outerwear in colorful fashions was very small, the Benetton family developed an approach to retailing that makes effective use of small spaces. Unlike its more traditional competitors with stores of perhaps 4,000 square feet, a typical Benetton outlet is not more than 600 square feet. Little space is wasted in floor selling or 'back room' storage. An electronic communications system supported by a manufacturing process allows for dyeing to order and for rapid replenishment of the items in greatest demand during a fashion season. The result is a higher rate of inventory turnover in the store and a level of sales-per-square-foot that is often several times that of Benetton's competitors. Benetton's assets support many more sales because it has injected both communications and [flexible] production technology into its service."

In fact, Benetton can make changes in inventory in ten days that take most retailers months. The only more masterful retailer may be The Limited. Its system includes the world's largest and most automated distribution center (in Columbus, Ohio), dedicated Boeing 747s bringing daily orders from over 300 factories around the world, and instantaneous data linkages among the retail outlets, the distribution centers, and the far-flung factories. All of this, for example, allowed the chain to bring a 500,000-unit order of its popular Outback Red line of sportswear to market in just ten weeks. It found the fabric, cut it, stitched it, and shipped it at a pace probably ten times faster than its competitors

121

could have done. Sadly, The Limited stands as testimony to Bob Haavind's indictment of U.S. manufacturers. Domestic producers generally can't meet The Limited's requirements for responsiveness—which is now (spring 1987) causing special pain, since protectionist trade policies and the falling dollar are forcing the company to seek domestic suppliers as a safety valve.

TOTAL CUSTOMER RESPONSIVENESS

Manufacturing firms in general, and heavy manufacturers in particular, have been remarkably slow, as in so many other areas, to jump on this bandwagon. It surprised me to see a report in a February 1987 issue of *High Technology* commenting on a Chrysler plant which "transmits [by computer] its production schedule to the [supplier] TRW plant." This should not be news. It should be the norm.

Milliken Mounts Another Revolution

It is becoming the norm at textile manufacturer Milliken. "It's a 'bet the company' move," an executive explains. That's a startling statement. The firm has long been its industry's leader in R&D and manufacturing technology. Finding that its traditional strengths were not adequate to meet the stepped-up challenges it faces from overseas, in 1981 Milliken mounted the all-out and successful quality improvement program discussed in C-2.

Even so, the foreign onslaught continued unabated, with most of the industry reeling from it. So Milliken mounted yet another revolution in 1985. Executives are now demanding, across the entire estimated $2.25 billion firm, nothing less than cuts of 90 percent in the time it takes to develop products and deliver them.

The first phase of Milliken's total customer responsiveness program consisted of mounting over 1,000 Customer Action Teams (CATs). Each was a self-contained effort to unearth new market opportunities in partnership with an existing customer. To launch a team, the customer had to agree to supply team members and join with Milliken representatives from manufacturing, sales, finance, and marketing in seeking creative solutions to better serving current markets or creating new ones. Each year hundreds of such projects are completed and hundreds of new ones are launched.

The details of a typical project make clear the sweeping nature of the firm's program. A two-year Partners for Profit program with apparel maker Levi Strauss has revolutionized the way the two firms do business together. First, Milliken capitalized on its unparalleled quality program. Given Milliken's flawless track record—statistically demonstrated—in the delivery of top quality, Levi agreed to omit its own inspection of inbound Milliken-supplied goods. Moreover, close cooperation between the two firms enabled Milliken to produce fabric to Levi's exacting color standards and in roll sizes that maximize Levi's ability to utilize the material.

Since the first inspection can be skipped, Milliken can ship directly to Levi's factories, eliminating the need for Levi to warehouse the material. Next, the two firms, abetted by state-of-the-art data and telecommunication linkups among numerous plants, were able to eliminate even Levi's in-plant sorting and storage. The Milliken delivery truck is now a meticulously stocked "warehouse on wheels." With exact, time-coded order information, the truck brings precisely what Levi needs to the plant entrance, and the fabric is off-loaded, in appropriate reverse order, then carried directly to the specific in-plant machine where the garments will be cut and sewn. To accomplish this ultimate reduction in work in progress, an especially complex cooperative maneuver was required. At a remote facility, Levi makes electronic tags that guide its in-plant utilization for each roll of fabric. Via yet another sophisticated, on-line hookup, the appropriate tags arrive at the Levi finishing plant just as the Milliken truck pulls up, and are attached as the truck is unloaded.

The net of all this is a monumental cost saving and reduction in delivery time for Levi Strauss. Milliken, of course, shares the dollars-and-cents benefit, but, more important, keeps an order onshore that might otherwise have been lost to overseas competition. In addition to the cost savings that come from the elimination of inspection, inventory, and warehousing, Levi achieves previously unheard-of flexibility, which, in turn, helps it respond more aggressively to today's lightning-fast changes in fashion and taste. With demonstrations of responsiveness such as this under its belt, Milliken was even able to grab some Limited Stores business that had long been filled by that firm's affiliated offshore plants.

The Milliken program is just gearing up, but cycle-shortening results are already astonishing. In a major carpet business, a six-week sample and product delivery cycle previously thought irreducible was cut to just five days. Another business's historic eighty-day cycle was reduced to three days—and twenty-four-hour response 100 percent of the time is now seen as an achievable goal.

The Basic Interactive Elements of TCR, as Demonstrated at Milliken

Several elements, working in tandem, marked this latest Milliken revolution:

► First, reminiscent of the quality revolution, was top management commitment. TCR was Revolution II. Letters from Roger Milliken never cease referring to the sense of urgency associated with this new operation.
► Second, the unparalleled success of the earlier quality program was the necessary foundation: Without it, various partners such as Levi would have had no sound basis to move forward.
► Third, the CATs and the projects with suppliers in the quality program paved the way for a wholesale shift from adversarial to partnership relations within and outside the firm. In 1980 Milliken epitomized the hierarchical, authoritarian, highly functionalized corporate organization. The CATs pulled sales, marketing, and the two strongest baronies, accounting and manufacturing,

together, and this made possible the cooperation and the lowest-level, no-delay decision-making that, much more than technology (as so many are finding out to their dismay), are the keys to TCR.

▶ The fourth step was another breakthrough—a complete shake-up, accomplished in 90 days across sixty plants, of the manufacturing organization structure. In one move in 1985, the span of control in the plants went from one supervisor for every six nonsupervisors to a ratio of one to thirty-six. The freed-up supervisors, mostly called process engineers, are now first-class expediters. They ensure that new product samples are shepherded through the highly programmed system with alacrity and that phone calls from the various functions (customers, suppliers, etc.) are returned fast, with action taken. The increased number of in-plant process engineers is consistent with Japanese factory organization; in fact, Milliken president Tom Malone launched the reorganization after carefully collecting data on Japanese factory organization in the course of over a dozen visits to that country.

Previously undreamed-of feats of multi-plant, multi-functional cooperation are now the daily norm with no letup in quality standards, which are constantly being tightened. This last point is vital. Since they were to be required to be so much more flexible, the company's plant managers at first pleaded for relief from quality standards. And indeed, the achievement of better quality and more flexibility simultaneously is a tall order. Perfection in product would seem to be at odds with satisfying small orders on a moment's notice. But once again, Milliken took chapters from Japan's book. Robert Hall, of Indiana University, elaborates in *Attaining Manufacturing Excellence:* "All Japanese motorcycle companies introduce several new models per month into plants already producing a large mix. Each day, after production is complete, some of the time remaining is used for trying the new tooling and arrangements for upcoming models. When it appears that production can go without a hitch, the new model is inserted into the production lineup for the succeeding schedule month. Any necessary finishing changes are incorporated at the end of the first or second month of production." This requisite increased flexibility is possible only because of much tighter linkages among design, engineering, and manufacturing in Japan than in the United States. (This trait, also taught to the Japanese by American W. Edwards Deming, will be the subject of prescription C-8 and several others.)

Responsiveness as Competitive Edge: GE Plastics

Milliken is not alone among manufacturers in using TCR as an offensive competitive weapon. The grinding wheel (for metal finishes) division of the old-line Norton Company of Worcester, Massachusetts, has given terminals to all its distributors, which makes it "easier to do business with us and harder to leave," according to division general manager Richard Kennedy.

Or consider GE's multi-billion-dollar engineering plastics operation, built from scratch in just a couple of decades. This science-based operation was predicated on technological advantage—GE Chairman Jack Welch, who holds a Ph.D. in chemical engineering, got his start there. Today, the business sees its future strategic advantage coming from "service/responsiveness added." The new strategy's instant success brings together all of our familiar themes: (1) attitude/commitment, (2) service through people, and (3) support systems (training, computer systems, electronic linkages).

Paul Jones manages the Plastics Business Group's Sales Service Center in Albany, New York. He describes the origins of the strategy of emphasizing, then centralizing, customer service:

> We were spread out—customer service was located within our marketing organizations, within the product businesses, within manufacturing, traffic, credit, collections, finance. The people in the plants were stuck in trailers. They were back in the bowels of the organization where nobody could really find them except by a telephone call. They had a 20-year-old system that we were working with; the time-sharing system badly needed upgrading. Cost is not the important thing. Customer service can be an offensive thrust for us. . . . Nobody else had done it in the industry. Somebody's gonna do it, and I want to be the first to do it. At first, [only] a very small minority of people really could understand that this is the best way to go. But as time went on, it [became] nearly unanimous. We have a showcase customer service center. We bring customers through. We show it off as much as we can. It's a mindset throughout the whole organization to get people to see that this can be an offense. These [customer service] people can get pounds [the selling unit for plastics] for us. They can go after top line [revenue enhancement] rather than just acting as mechanics, just going through the bureaucratic procedures and telling the customer, "Well, you'll get it when we run it."

The system was centralized, and exceptional energy went into recruiting and training eighteen Customer Service Coordinators, selected from over 1,000 applicants. Jones explains the organization's approach to hiring and development: "We wanted aggressive people, we wanted ambitious people who would fight for their customer. . . . We looked for people who were very quick on their feet, very articulate. We looked for nice people. We put them through all sorts of telephone training, presentation skills, how to order wine at a restaurant, everything. We got them so involved. These people aren't just plugged into a phone; they go see their customers, they travel with the salespeople. Their jobs are to spend ten percent of the time traveling with the customers. We did all those things before we ever sat them down in front of our new computer system."

The objective—largely achieved—was to turn the new heroes, in the business's mainstream and under the close and watchful eye of top management, into true "advocates for the customer," people who, says Jones, "won't take 'no' [from some other part of the Plastics Group] for an answer."*

It's working in sales—and in attitude. The customers understand—and so does GE: "The surveys . . . will come back and say, 'Patty does an outstanding job for me, but,' and it's the 'but' that we have to focus on, the people downstream, the package that was ripped when it came in, the bag that had a tear in it, the pallet that had broken, it was the wrong color or what have you. It may have been Patty that had put the thing in with the wrong color number. The customers never believe that. Their customer service coordinator is beyond reproach. They never make a mistake as far as the customer's concerned. They are super people, and we've got to maintain them."

Next came the systems: "We got away from people located all the way across the country, taking orders, using this [holding up a paper tablet] as their order entry method and writing things down. Maybe it got into the system, maybe it didn't. We literally burned every bridge. We threw away the old computer system, even threw away the old computer. We went to a completely brand-new system with centralized people, brand-new people, trained, oriented solely towards servicing the customer."

Next came electronic linkages—still in an embryonic stage, but of the highest urgency, as Jones explains: "We've had to do it. We had customers . . . requesting electronic data interchange. They want to enter their orders electronically. . . . If we didn't do that, we were going to walk away from hundreds of millions of dollars a year. . . . So a very high-priority item for us right now is to go to the electronic hook-ups. We are finding that customers really want their computer to talk to ours. They don't want us to put in a little terminal, a personal computer, that they can dial up. They don't want to have a GE Order Entry Center. They just want to put their demands in—MRP [Material Requirements Planning] system, whatever you want to call it—so they can have access to us via their system, electronically. . . . They want acknowledgement electronically, they want us to tell them when we're going to ship electronically, they want us to send them shipping information electronically, invoice them electronically; they want to pay us electronically."

Taken together, these elements are starting to add up to a first-order competitive advantage. Moreover, a host of additional, unexpected advantages are popping up at every turn: "[Our average Customer Service Coordinator] will have 60 to 70 customer contacts a day apiece. They can ask all sorts of questions. They do surveys with customers on advertising. We do surveys on what other competitors are doing—'Joe, old buddy, you and I talk to each other every day. What's happening to your market? Are distributors more of a threat, are people selling direct?' It's a fantastic tool. Our customer service organization, properly trained, can gather information for us to feed back into the management of the business, and they do it in a way that leaves the customer flattered that they're

*Domino's Pizza Distribution (Domino's $540 million [in revenues] dough, topping, and equipment supplier) is training a similar elite group of "store advocates" who will act as the franchisees' ombudsmen with the firm.

asking. We're not on an intelligence-gathering mission. The customer is glad we're asking. It shows concern."

Such strategies, though far from the norm right now, will fast become the norm—or else!

Responsiveness: Training Your Customer's People

Recall, in C-1, the discussion of Milliken's shop towel business. Milliken has almost made the towel the least important part of the transaction—the company essentially provides consulting services (sales aids, advice on quality-improvement programs) which enhance its customers' overall capability.

No one understands such a strategy better than ServiceMaster, based in Downers Grove, Illinois. ServiceMaster (mentioned in Part I) manages its customers' housekeeping, food service, and maintenance operations. The heart of the firm's strategy is to train and develop the customers' workers—in jobs that are generally lightly regarded.

ServiceMaster, like McKesson et al., has numerous, highly technical support systems. But these merely complement the core program which helps the customers' people upgrade their skills, contribute ideas—and achieve extraordinary productivity and low turnover in job categories that traditionally have sky-high turnover rates.

Thus, training your customers' employees becomes yet one more opportunity to redefine responsiveness and make it an offensive marketing strategy.

Make Just-in-Time (JIT) an Offensive Strategy

Just-in-time inventory management is usually conceived of as something manufacturers do *to* their suppliers, achieving linkups "backward" toward the vendor. The Milliken idea essentially turns this on its head. Milliken proactively seeks out opportunities to assist customers, using some variant of voluntary just-in-time inventory management as a marketing strategy, linked "forward," toward the customer. Robert Hall provides another example, illustrating the attitude change that must accompany such a strategy: "A corrugated box company began thinking about providing quality JIT service to a variety of customers. A few of them were beginning to ask for it. The company's operating people could foresee considerable improvement in quality, setup times, lot sizes, and deliveries, but it immediately became obvious that the traditional sales strategy would no longer be valid. It had specialized in large, low-price orders wangled by methods occasionally employing football tickets and Christmas booze. *The sales force could no longer be box sales people but rather service representatives in the true sense—analysts of each customer's operations* [my emphasis]. How did the customers schedule? At what rate did they use boxes? What did quality mean to them? Should the company target small, short lead time orders as well as large ones?"

The ultimate expression of this TCR/JIT strategy is being applied by PPG.

Without being asked, and with no assurance of a contract in perpetuity, the Coatings and Resins Division at PPG has built six satellite plants (with another four under construction) within three miles of auto assembly plants to which it is the sole supplier. Radical inventory reduction for the customer is ensured, though at least as important is the general level of responsiveness, enhanced by tight computer linkages and workers dedicated to a single customer. Though PPG has no guarantees, it's not difficult to conclude that it would be tough to displace.

The sweeping revision of the traditional new relationships is captured by Hall in *Zero Inventories:* "The development of [the] system of direct hand-off of material throughout an industry suggests many aspects of supplier relationships which do not now prevail in much of industry. Supplier-customer relationships need to extend over a period of time, and both parties need to trust each other with more details of their operations than is often true. This [also] means more faith that each will not try to invade the other's business ([a fear] usually expressed by customer companies who decide to 'pull business in-house')." In fact, most just-in-time experiments have failed to reach their potential, not because of inadequate computerization, but because of a fundamental failure on the part of participants to understand the new attitude of trust, cooperation, and mutual investment for the long haul required to make the system hum.

SUMMARY: THE NINE (AT LEAST) FACTORS NECESSARY TO ACHIEVING TCR

The sweeping nature of the change this strategy entails cannot be over-estimated:

1. A wholesale change of attitude. First, the firm must replace adversarial dealings with partnership thinking, "backward" toward suppliers and "forward" toward the distribution channel and the ultimate end user, as well as among the various functions within the firm. Second, hustle and flexibility must become the norm. What has traditionally been seen as disruptive must now be seen as the chief source of opportunity—if the factory is not a hotbed of short-lead-time, customized orders, trouble is brewing.

2. Reorganization of the Milliken sort is almost imperative. Basically, reducing layers of management (flattening the organization), breaking down the barriers between functions, and upping the percentage of expediters are prerequisites to TCR.

3. The closer linkages demand a superb level of basic product quality, as at Milliken.

4. The continual interchange of electronic data, à la The Limited and McKesson, is essential.

5. People involved in managing customer contact through the new system must become company heroes and receive superb training, as at GE.

6. Forward (distribution channel, customer) and backward (supplier) integration is necessary. Though traditional economies of scale are fast disappearing and vertical de-integration (shifting operations to subcontractors) is becoming commonplace, a potent new form of vertical re-integration, via data exchange and other partnership programs (rather than ownership of assets), is partially or wholly supplanting it.

7. Co-location, electronic and physical, is important. Whether it's a terminal in the truck as at Frito-Lay, or a computer in the druggist's back room as at McKesson, or a plant two miles away as at PPG, or a regionalized marketing effort like Campbell Soup's, the smart service provider will achieve direct or indirect physical presence in the customer's operation.

8. The system must be constantly enhanced, via software packages, à la McKesson, and training of customer personnel in the use of the system.

9. TCR becomes a prime marketing tool. First, it is a defensive necessity; if you don't get your hooks into the distribution channel/customer, someone else will—and probably is doing it as you read this. Second, the strategy is ultimately offensive. An infinite stream of add-on features, like the McKesson ECONOPRICE program, can add more and more value to the provider-user relationship over time, making separation increasingly difficult. The economists have a term for this strategy—"first mover advantage." It is derived from such activities as oil or gas pipeline-building, and embodies a very simple—and powerful—idea: Whoever builds the first pipeline (or supplies the first terminal with readily usable software) will likely ship the oil for a long time to come.

New attitudes, reorganization, some form of co-location, electronic telecommunications links, and value-added software hooks add up, then, to TCR—and a monumental change in basic business relationships. In fact, there are no manufacturing or service firms anymore. Already, 70 percent of manufacturing's value-added is coming from service activities, such as research and distribution. And progressive service firms, such as McKesson or Federal Express, are more capital-intensive than manufacturers on average. This prescription, then, is really about the transformation of every product or service firm into a service-added firm. Linkages—personal, physical, and electronic—are altering the way the game of competitive business is played. Even General Motors now acknowledges this; tight customer-dealer-firm-supplier linkages are the heart of the Saturn project strategy. (GM, in fact, acquired Ross Perot's Electronic Data Systems in 1984 for the precise purpose of pursuing a link-up strategy.) And traditionally arrogant semiconductor manufacturers are turning in the same direction, providing custom chips designed in tandem with customers—and beginning by permitting customers access to what till then had been closely guarded design and production secrets.

Indeed, there are no limits to this idea. A Michigan hospital voluntarily provided all its doctors with computer terminals—to aid admissions, for example. Doctors were not compelled to use the hospital; no strings were attached. Yet once the system was in place and the doctors' staff learned to use it, admissions soared. More software hooks were then sunk into the docs—

for example, the provision of overall office management accounting programs.

Use Your Imagination: Have Congress Assist with TCR!

In 1986, Deluxe Check of Minneapolis earned a whopping $121 million after-tax on $867 million in sales of, that's right, checks. Service is its hallmark (see also S-1), and it will do anything to speed an order to its customers. In fact, it went so far as to lobby Congress successfully for special legislation. Deluxe received permission to install U.S. Postal Service substations in each of its 62 plants. With such a station on the premises, the process of shipping is shortened—one more tiny step toward achieving one of the highest after-tax return on sales in the Fortune 500. Thus, there is no limit to the imagination that can be applied to the pursuit of matchless responsiveness.

FIRST STEPS

1. Take one or two major customers (end users or members of the distribution channel) and form an immediate joint task force to assess opportunities for closer linkages.
2. Mount pilots within the next 90 *days* in two or three locations at least— that is, get going! Make a plan for the achievement of such linkages a major part of your next round of strategic planning in every business unit. Consider incremental programs, to be sure, but also be careful to ensure that revolutionary thinking is a part of the process.
3. Throughout the effort, be constantly cognizant of the all-important, deep-seated attitudinal issues that underlie the "techniques." If you fail to see customers, suppliers, and members of the distribution channel as partners instead of adversaries, the rest of the program, including perhaps large dollar investments, will be more than wasted—it may well boomerang.

C-5

SUMMARY

In view of the true globalization of the economy, smaller firms as well as large ones, in service as well as manufacturing, must:

► Become true internationalists, at least selling to and designing in, and probably manufacturing in, Europe and Japan/Asia.

► Follow the unfailing international success principles: persisting, building relationships/learning the culture, choosing partners carefully/ mastering the distribution system, decentralizing, and tailoring the product or service to local needs and tastes.

► Examine joint venture and other alliance opportunities of all sorts, though not with an expectation that such partnerships will substitute for patient market development.

Internationalism is not just for the Boeings. Smaller firms not only can succeed overseas, but must consider international opportunities in their early years. International operations must always be built upon patient market and relationship development, not an American strong suit.

Every firm over $2 million in revenues should take first steps to examine international-market-creation opportunities in the next 12 months. Every firm over $25 million should be alarmed if it is not doing 25 percent of its business overseas, including some in Japan.

C-5

Be an Internationalist

Japan Winning the [Export] Race in China: Persistence, Patience Key
      Headline, lead article "Business Day"
      The New York Times
      April 29, 1987

American management in the past has been singularly blind to the needs of human beings. Management wants to eliminate the human equation from business. . . . That puts businessmen at a disadvantage overseas because so many businesses are based on human relations and friendship. They say, "How the hell could you do business by making a friend? What's that got to do with the bottom line?" As it turns out, it has everything to do with it. . . . We're impatient. But all over the world, if you have friends, you can do anything. That's how the system works.

> Edward T. Hall
> Author of *The Silent Language*
> and, most recently, co-author of *Hidden Differences: Doing Business with the Japanese;*
> from an article in the July issue of *Science 85*

Ready or not, Americans, the global village has arrived. London's financial market restructuring in late 1986, called "Big Bang," is only one of the latest bits of evidence. Then, in early 1987, the value of stocks listed on the Tokyo exchange surpassed the value of those listed on the New York exchange. The former head of Citicorp, Walter Wriston, describes today's reality in *Risk and Other Four-Letter Words:*

> Natural gas owned by Indonesia's oil agency, Pertamina, flows out of a well discovered by Royal Dutch Shell into a liquification plant designed by French engineers and built by a Korean construction company. The liquified gas is loaded onto U.S.-flag tankers, built in U.S. yards after a Norwegian design. The ships shuttle to Japan and deliver the liquid gas to a Japanese public utility, which uses it to provide electricity that powers an electronics factory making television sets that are shipped aboard a Hong Kong–owned container ship to California for sale to American farm-

133

ers in Louisiana who grow rice that is sold to Indonesia and shipped there aboard Greek bulk carriers. All of the various facilities, ships, products, and services involved in the complex series of events are financed by U.S., European, and Japanese commercial banks, working in some cases with international and local government agencies. These facilities, ships, products, and services are insured and reinsured by U.S., European, and Japanese insurance companies. Investors in these facilities, ships, products, and services are located throughout the world. This illustration is not only factual, it is typical of transactions that take place over and over again daily throughout the globe.

There is a startling paradox here: On the one hand, we are all, like it or not, participants in a single global market. Service and manufacturing firms, large and small, are exporting to the United States. Sometimes we see it: Honda, Mercedes, Heineken. And sometimes we don't: Korean construction firms are building our buildings, and there is almost no product that doesn't have some foreign subcomponents. Likewise, our smaller as well as larger firms, in service or manufacturing, are finding unique market opportunities abroad.

On the other hand, the explosion of products and the technology revolution, described in Part I, are making all international markets more local; catering to local tastes, not so-called global branding (one kind of tomato soup for 125 countries), is essential.

Yet for a host of deep-seated reasons, such as a continuing isolationist mentality and "Yankee impatience," too many of our firms are (1) either failing to consider overseas opportunities, especially in their formative years, or (2) failing at early attempts to do business offshore, then withdrawing with tail between legs.

This prescription, though broadly concerned with internationalism, emphasizes the Japanese market for three reasons. First, Japan is our bellwether competition. Second, the Japanese market is tough to crack, but (1) it has been conquered by a surprising number of American firms (though all too many give up on it) and (2) the keys to success in Japan are the keys to success in any international market. And third, I strongly believe that America must develop a "westward focus"; the Pacific Rim *is* the market of tomorrow.

A Case in Point: The United States and Japan in China

There is no love lost between Chinese and Japanese. Despite the hiatus in relations between 1949 and 1972, there is true affection between Chinese and Americans. In 1986, Japan's exports to China were valued at $12.4 billion, amounting to a 29 percent share of Chinese imports. Hong Kong came next ($5.6 billion) and the U.S. was third, with $4.7 billion—38 percent of the Japanese total.

The reasons for the sparkling Japanese success, cited in a *New York Times* (April 29, 1987) analysis, and confirmed by my own conversations with U.S.

executives residing in China, go far beyond propinquity, and include the following: (1) a commitment to the market (300 Japanese firms are established there, versus 170 U.S. firms); (2) a presence, marked by offices in many cities and the initially unprofitable establishment of a strong infrastructure (e.g., spare-parts depots in numerous locations); (3) a willingness to learn the difficult Chinese language (the *Times* reports, for instance, that the big, but relatively smaller, Sanwa Bank has five offices in China, with a total of twelve Japanese employees, of whom nine speak Chinese, while huge Citicorp has three offices, with only one Chinese-speaking American); (4) a willingness in the early years to forgo profit in order to gain market share; (5) the willingness of Japanese employees to accept longer assignments (three to five years versus a U.S. average of two to four) with less lavish, closer-to-the-people living accommodations than their American counterparts; and (6) the insistence of most American firms on reams of paperwork and on the involvement of lawyers where the Japanese operate like the Chinese—more informally, creating personal bonds.

Recall that earlier, in C-4, we talked of hustle as strategy. A Western diplomat said to the *Times* of the Japanese, "[They] do better because they are better. They have a long-term perspective, they're persistent, and they're out knocking on doors." An American businessman echoes the sentiment: "They are incredibly good. If they see a possible opportunity, they go all out. They rush people in from Tokyo or Hong Kong. . . . They fight for it. The Americans are more likely to throw up their hands and walk away from it. The Americans are like fish out of water."

CRACKING THE TOUGHEST INTERNATIONAL MARKET: JAPAN

Some American firms, from some surprising quarters, are thriving overseas—and in Japan:

▶ Memphis is many people's definition of an insular town. Buckman Labs, the specialty chemical firm, is headquartered there. Though not a giant by Du Pont/Dow standards, it has been doing business offshore since 1946, when an unplanned layover in Puerto Rico started the senior Mr. Buckman down that path. The midsized firm conducts business in no fewer than sixty-seven countries, including Japan, and several of its plants are overseas. Market penetration in several countries is higher than in the United States.

▶ American Family Life Assurance of Columbus, Georgia, is not one of the insurance giants. But in 1985, selling a specialized cancer policy, the firm did $350 million in business in Japan—more than it did in the United States. And then there's Materials Research Corporation of Orangeburg, New York. It just built its second plant. This one is outside the United States, in Oita, Japan. The company sells machines that coat and etch silicon chips to Japanese firms. Or take ServiceMaster (the cleaning contractor has fifteen major hospital contracts in Japan), Loctite (adhesives maker), and Molex (electrical connector manufacturer)—all of them setting the standards *in Japan.*

Consider more broadly the supposedly toughest market for Americans, laden with pernicious systemic as well as natural barriers—Japan. In the high-tech arena, IBM makes and sells computers worth more than $3 billion in Japan. The sales in Japan of Hewlett-Packard's Japanese subsidiary top $400 million, and grew at the rate of 27 percent per year from 1980 through 1984. Xerox, NCR, and Texas Instruments are also American high-tech giants winning on Japanese soil; the latter's semiconductor operations in Japan are equal in quality to the best Japanese producers.

But, you say, computers and such are international by nature—what about the most American of American firms? Well, how about 7-Eleven's 2,000 stores in Japan, doing more than $250 million in sales? How about McDonald's, which sells fast food worth $400 million in Japan, enough to worry the Japanese that its next generation might lose their skill with chopsticks?

Tupperware, Kentucky Fried Chicken, Coca-Cola, Schick, 3M, S. C. Johnson (Johnson Wax), Shaklee, Bristol-Myers, Polaroid, Otis Elevator, Franklin Mint, Baskin-Robbins, Medtronic, Quaker Oats, and Johnson & Johnson also star on the Japanese scene. Estimates vary about the totals. The Japanese Ministry of International Trade and Industry (MITI) estimated that 1,000 solely or substantially owned U.S. subsidiaries in Japan had revenues there of $55 billion in 1981. A more recent estimate pegs 1984 sales from the top 200 U.S. subsidiaries on Japanese soil alone at $44 billion. That is, it can be done. (Incidentally, none of these revenues from subsidiaries producing in Japan count in the trade balance. Those who carp about closed markets conveniently ignore the success stories I've just reviewed.)

Persist!

IBM, a strong believer in internationalism from its earliest days, began doing business in Japan in the 1920s, and put a manufacturing plant there in 1939, when the firm had less than $25 million in total revenues. T. J. Watson, modern IBM's founder, lived by the creed "World Peace Through World Trade." At times he may have overdone it; he was bitterly criticized, for instance, for sticking with his German trading partners almost until the United States entered World War II.

IBM has invested heavily and, more important, become a part of Japan's and Europe's insider network through the only magic that exists in international affairs of all sorts—persistence and patience. It has continuously modified products for offshore markets and done significant basic and applied research and engineering offshore. The most recent step-up of its commitment to Japan and Asia was moving its entire Pacific Basin headquarters from Mt. Pleasant, New York, to Tokyo in 1984.

The rest of the success stories bear the same stamp. Edmund Fitzgerald, chairman of Northern Telecom, commented in 1986 on the supposedly uncrackable Japanese telecommunications market: "[This is] the first time in history that American-made digital central office switches will be moving into the core network of NTT [Nippon Telephone & Telegraph]. One of our initial advisors on that told us, 'You can do business with Nippon Telephone, but you must be patient and persistent.' That was the best advice we ever got. It took a lot of patience and a lot of persistence, but it was worth it." ROLM, as a small firm (before being acquired by IBM and gaining access to its deep pockets), succeeded in Japan—but only after senior officers made twenty-odd visits, just to conclude the first, tiny sale. Similarly, American Hospital Supply worked for five years to land its first, small order. Disney spent five years negotiating the licensing agreement for its Tokyo theme park. Coca-Cola, which today has a 60 percent share of the Japanese soft-drink market, also suffered a full decade of red ink.

A small forest products company from the Northwest, without the resources of Coke et al., is now spurting ahead in Japan. But it took four years of regular visitation on the part of senior managers to get a first, small, foot-in-the-door order. The opportunity finally came when another supplier, this one Japanese, couldn't react fast enough to meet its Japanese customer's need. The American firm was given insufficient time to do the impossible—but it did it, and soon a trickle of orders became a torrent.

Build Relationships/Learn the Culture

Relationship-building among senior executives is important to international business of all sorts, but uniquely so in Japan. American impatience militates against such a major investment of time. It's no coincidence that America's top international firms—e.g., IBM, Boeing, The Morgan—are also the masters of relationship-building in our domestic markets too.

Learning the culture is essential. This starts, by definition, with language skills, another arena of unique American ineptitude and arrogance, especially when it comes to Asia. Even today, only about 10,000 Americans are studying Japanese. Worse yet, that number is only 2,000 more than in 1973. In *Second to None: American Companies in Japan,* a study of over a thousand successful subsidiaries of United States firms operating in Japan, journalist Bob Christopher recalls a highly placed Japanese official remarking that he has never met a U.S. salesperson who speaks fluent Japanese. Nearly ninety percent of U.S. executives in Japan don't even bother to try to learn the language, according to one poll. And while you might get away with doing business in English in the office during the day, real business—after-hours relationship-building—is conducted almost exclusively in Japanese; furthermore, fewer than 1 percent of Japanese wholesalers, so essential to success, speak English. Christopher also attacks the short tenure, typically two to four years, of most U.S. executives who come to Japan. Such a brief sojourn aborts any chance of becoming an "insider." More generally, Americans' insensitivity to other cultures is demonstrated by

United Nations polls which report that among citizens of developing countries, Americans place last in empathy for foreign cultures.

Choose Partners Carefully/Master the Distribution System

Dealing with local customs and institutions on local terms is vital. Take Japan's distribution system. In America, 1.5 middlemen handle the average product between producer and ultimate consumer; in Japan, that number is 4.3. The labyrinth of Japanese distributors drives Americans and Europeans crazy. An illustration of the system's complexity: Mitsubishi's consumer electronics products are distributed in Japan through 26,000 separate franchisees, three and a half times the number of outlets McDonald's has in the United States, despite a Japanese population that is just half the size of ours. Christopher calls the system "bloated," "byzantine," and "nightmarish." Nevertheless, it is there; no amount of American haranguing about market openness will change it one whit. Schick's success (70 percent of the Japanese market for stainless-steel razor blades) resulted from a consistent distribution strategy focused on one powerful partner. Gillette, which dominates the U.S. market, designed a losing strategy in the same market: It involved more than 150 distributors; the fragmentation prevented Gillette from achieving a coherent image with retailers. Apple Computer committed a cardinal sin by making a deal with a powerful distributor, then going behind its back through other channels. Apple's penalty for violating the rules where relationships are so important was a 1 percent share of the 1.2-million-unit personal computer market in 1984, despite its head start.

Many accuse the Japanese of "not letting us into the system." While this is true in some cases, there is a difference between not being allowed in and not having the patience to learn even the distribution system, though it does seem a lifetime's occupation.

For small firm or large, choosing and working with partners is a necessity almost anywhere overseas, but especially in Japan. The form of the partnership can vary. Xerox teamed up with Fuji, and Kentucky Fried Chicken in Japan is 50 percent owned by Mitsubishi. Each gained instant credibility through the partnership. IBM, though, has always gone it alone in Japan, and there are lots of possible hybrid alternatives in between. In any case, deep study and thoughtfulness are required—and once more, characteristic American impatience is completely unacceptable. Numerous hastily formed partnerships, yielding short-term financial returns, have bombed in the long run, because time-consuming relationship-building was ignored. Partnership relations are no substitute for continuous attention.

Decentralize

A decentralized organizational structure is required. Harvard's Raymond Vernon spoke frankly about our problems in a 1980 *Harvard Business Review* article. After large U.S. firms met with early success overseas, many rescinded the initial decentralization which had contributed in unseen ways to that success:

Several factors explain the American propensity for one-way transmission [U.S. to overseas] multinational networks. Most important, [the bulk of] subsidiaries were created during a period in which U.S.-based companies characteristically had a technological lead over their competitors, generating and selling products that would represent the market of the future. As long as U.S. companies were secure in their innovative leads, there was no great need to use foreign subsidiaries as listening posts.

A second factor has been the premature obliteration of international divisions in many U.S. companies. As the foreign interests of American companies grew and flourished in the postwar period, the international divisions were often the star performers. But their success was eventually their undoing. By the middle 1960s, one American company after another reorganized itself to acknowledge the increased importance of its foreign business. According to one study undertaken in the early 1970s, the typical pattern consisted of abolishing the international division and setting up a series of so-called global product divisions to do the worrying about foreign products.

In a recent study covering a group of 57 large U.S.-based multinationals a colleague and I ran into some disturbing indications suggesting that some of these reorganizations may have been wildly counterproductive. A subset of our sample, organized along global product lines, exhibited rather striking characteristics. This group of companies seemed to show decidedly less interest in its foreign operations than those with an international division. Ten years after they had introduced their new products into the United States, the global product companies were only producing about 50 percent of their products in overseas locations. By contrast, the other companies in the sample were manufacturing more than 80 percent of their new products in foreign plants. . . .

Some companies have recognized the danger in the newer organizational form and are returning to the old way of doing things. A prime example is Westinghouse, which went from an international to a global product division and back to an international division again.

Tailor the Product or Service to Local Tastes

Finally, there's the issue of the product itself—it must be of high quality and suit local tastes and requirements. In general, given the worldwide economic recovery of the last thirty years and true globalization of the sort described by Walter Wriston, our ability to dominate through technology alone has all but disappeared. No one can succeed now except via value-added differentiation, especially on the basis of quality and service, and these have not been strong suits of the United States in the past. They must become so, but nowhere more than in Europe and Japan, the world's most finicky customers when it comes to quality.

Closely related is the issue of tailoring products or services to suit customers' needs (or whims). In the easy post–World War II days, we pushed products overseas when they started to decline at home, milking them for all they were worth. Today, there usually must be substantial customizing—or even new products designed for foreign markets. Coca-Cola took the lime taste out of Sprite to cater to Japanese tastes. Kodak changed its film to adapt to Japanese notions of attractive skin tones, and also altered its graphic arts products, because most space-starved Japanese professionals don't have darkrooms.

Of course, nothing is cut-and-dried. Tupperware was told that Japanese women don't throw home parties, but it persisted and found that the party formula was uniquely suited to the norms of Japanese social intercourse. Analogously, Disney was successful even though it insisted upon maintaining its squeaky-clean image and thus ignored the Japanese convention of selling sake at recreation parks. Coca-Cola also bucked convention at least once with advertisements that featured drinking out of the bottle U.S.-style, inadvertently starting a craze labeled "drinking bugle style" (from the billboard picture of people drinking from an inverted Coke bottle). Thus, you can overdo "Japanizing" or tailoring to any nation's habits, thereby throwing away the product uniqueness that may be your primary advantage. On balance, though, I and most experts strongly come down on the side of modifying the product to suit the market.

There is a raging debate over the issue of global brands. Global-brand advocates, not the least of whom are the new monster ad agencies resulting from the recent wave of mergers, tout the power of a global image. I acknowledge their viewpoint, but my evidence weighs in strongly on the side of decentralized operations and at least some nation-by-nation product tailoring in nine cases out of ten.

Pizza Hut, for example, is known around the world—in large measure because of its flexibility, catering to the tastes of different countries. In Japan, that means squid toppings. In Mexico, jalapeños are a favorite. In Korea, it means no salt.

The stories of foul-ups—due to faulty tailoring—are numerous, and often amusing (if you're not involved). When Coca-Cola moved into China, it chose Chinese characters for its signs that sounded like "Coca-Cola." Unfortunately, after thousands of signs went up the company discovered that the characters meant "Bites the Wax Cowboy." Coke went back to the drawing board, sorted through hundreds of additional characters, and came up with a set that had an appropriate sound, and when translated became "Makes the Mouth Rejoice." It was an important improvement—as sales increases subsequently confirmed.

"MADE IN THE U.S.A." FOR EXPORT

One Who Got It Right

Eighty miles north of Indianapolis you exit I-69 and head into Van Buren, Indiana, population 1500. Headquartered there is Weaver Popcorn, holder of sixty percent of the Japanese popcorn market.

Weaver's 59-year-old tradition is quality. Nobody does it better in the United States. Their prowess in plant genetics is well known, and they've unquestionably set the standard for excellence in this specialized industry.

With a towering reputation, and a rare American exhibition of patience (a lot of visits that others would have called fruitless), Weaver earned a few small orders in Japan.

They sallied forth with their very best, America's finest, and were rebuffed. The reason—a blow to the corporate ego: the quality wasn't right. Rather than take a few random teacup-size samples, the Japanese had hand-inspected hundreds of pounds of the popcorn—and found impurities.

Aha, you say—yet another example of Japan's closed minds and markets. But Weaver was challenged, not insulted, by the rejection. This modest-size company recalled the entire order, shelling out a substantial $65,000 without flinching. Employees were chagrined—and the Japanese were impressed. "You reacted to that problem the way a Japanese company would have," said one to Weaver's man in Japan.

Weaver did not stop there. Uniquely advanced optical inspection equipment, which cost over a half-million dollars was ordered and installed to meet Japan's standards. It was not required for the U.S. or European market that constituted the vast majority of Weaver's sales. But the smallish Weaver did it anyway—and quickly grabbed the lion's share of the Japanese market.

Many Others Who Get It Wrong

The pathetic tales of our attempts to foist nonmetric measurement, left-hand-drive cars and refrigerators as big as houses on the Japanese are too horrid to recount in greater detail. Sadly, such fiascos are anything but behind us, in products high-tech and low-, in countries from Japan to Ireland.

In *Trade War,* Steven Schlossstein, who spent six years in Japan with The Morgan, recalls a conversation with Kakimizu Koichi, executive director of Japan's Overseas Economic Cooperation Fund:

> "The Americans still talk about market access," he said, warming up. "As if Japan is still closed to the outside world, like it was over a century ago under the Tokugawas. But they forget, or do not understand, the problems that are unique to Japan. May I give you one example?"
>
> "Please," I said.
>
> He shifted his erect posture slightly and closed his eyes as he called the

details into memory. "As you know, our islands sit on a deep geologic fault, and we are susceptible to severe earthquakes. Everyone remembers how Tokyo was destroyed in 1923, but we get tremors in Japan almost every day. What does that suggest to you?"

"Safety in building design?" I said.

"And safety in product design," he added. "The Japanese government specifies very strict standards in product design because of that fact. Like space heaters. Japanese homes and apartments do not have central heating, so we use small kerosene heaters. If they topple over during an earthquake, the fire hazard is great."

He gestured dramatically with his hands, throwing them up in the air, simulating an explosion.

"So when foreigners want to sell space heaters in Japan, they must conform to our standards," he said. "The Swedes make very good kerosene heaters, engineered even more stringently than we require. In all simulated tremor tests, they never tip over. They are superbly designed. The Americans, on the other hand, simply package their domestic space heaters and ship them to Japan. Now, which do you think we will approve for sale in our market?"

I shook my head. "No contest," I replied. That was easy.

"So attention to precision and detail is essential if a foreign manufacturer wants to be successful in this market. Let me show you something." He reached into a drawer and withdrew a plastic picture album. Instead of vacation snapshots, it was filled with banknotes. "I used to collect foreign money when I was at the Ministry," he said. "Look at this yen note."

He handed me a standard 500-yen bill. There was Prince Itoh Hirobumi, a Meiji oligarch, with that familiar two-dollar look. I tried to make the leap from the earthquake-induced kerosene heater fires to pocket money. That was not so easy.

"Look at the white borders," he said, "how even and exact they are, on all four sides. Notice the *precision.*"

I noticed. For the first time. Who ever pays attention to the borders on greenbacks? He pulled out a handful of various yen notes. They all had identical borders and were, indeed, precise. Then he laid down some American bills. George Washington and Ben Franklin were not surrounded by a force field of identical white borders. The borders were uneven, crude by comparison.

The implication was obvious.

If our federal government was so sloppy when it made its own national currency, how could the Japanese expect American companies to be any better when they produced manufactured goods for export?

Sad to say, my partner Ian Thomson, an accountant, and I replicated Koichi's experiment. After I told Ian the story we both pulled out five-dollar bills. Sure enough, the borders varied on each bill, and between the two.

Many U.S. firms had great initial success exporting their products after World War II, when other countries' industries were flattened and few alternatives to American imports existed. We didn't have to work very hard, be very patient, or emphasize relationships—others were begging for our goods, regardless of design flaws, questionable quality, or our indifference to their culture. Not so today. Today "learn and listen" and "earn your way in" will be the only keys to lasting success. But thanks to such factors as opening financial markets, those American companies of any size and in any industry that will make the patient investment required will find boundless opportunities.

A Last, and Revealing, Case from Boeing

Perhaps a single, almost inadvertent statement captured the sense of the challenge—and the opportunity—for me. My luncheon partner was the head of helicopter operations at that masterful internationalist, Boeing. We were talking about selling capital goods overseas. "Well," he said casually, "as a rule of thumb, I expect one of my people to put in about sixty hours of specific homework to prepare for an average twenty-minute meeting with a middle-level government or industry official." That's preparation! And it is in addition to the wide experience Boeing requires of its overseas people. It is exactly such standard operating procedures which are the "secrets" of overseas commercial success, from Bahrain to Seoul—precisely the "secrets" that appear to elude so many U.S. pretenders (honorable but impatient) in the world of international markets.

Reprise

The customer responsiveness prescriptions feature the Five Value-Adding Strategies, of which this is one. That is, becoming an internationalist, regardless of firm size or product maturity, ranks on my list with the provision of superior quality and service.

This prescription is among a large set of ideas that have moved from the "nice to do" to the "must do" category. I cannot overemphasize the need for the average firm to "think (and do) international." Isolation is dead, like it or not, and regardless of any vagaries of Washington's trade policies over the next few years.

At the very least, every firm will be dealing with foreigners as suppliers (of subcomponents, for instance). Being oriented toward the markets and habits of others is a necessary defensive tactic (competitors will be doing so) as well as an extraordinary opportunity for the producer of top-quality products and services.

FIRST STEPS

1. Every $2 million firm, in service or manufacturing, has international potential. Start thinking about it early. The big-firm equivalent: If you're $25 million or larger, and not doing 25 percent of your business overseas, and at least a little bit in Japan, you are avoiding today's realities and opportunities, and you risk being out of touch in general.
2. How to start: Spend time. Listen. Visit, only half purposefully at first. Make friends. Keep cool. Be patient. If you're not prepared to spend six weeks a year overseas, don't bother to start. Caution: If your first proposed product or service offering is not substantially tailored to meet the foreign market's needs—packaging, colors, instruction manual, vagaries of distribution, let alone basic function—odds are you're headed for a discouraging setback.

C-6

SUMMARY

As market fragmentation accelerates, we must:

▶ Strive more valiantly than ever to achieve uniqueness, as an organization, in the customer's mind.

▶ Get to the point where everyone in the organization can understand and state its uniqueness (strategic distinction in the marketplace).

Being unique—standing out from the growing crowd of competitors, products, and services—is an essential for survival. Such uniqueness, to be implemented, must be understood and lived by everyone in the organization. While niche-market-oriented, higher-value-added strategies are increasingly the winning hand, low-cost producers can be successful. On the other hand, an "in between" or "stuck in the middle"—i.e., not unique— strategy is unfailingly disastrous.

Can you state your "uniqueness" in twenty-five words or less? Test the level of agreement, randomly and regularly, with new and long-term employees—and with suppliers, distributors, and customers. Is your uniqueness, as practiced day to day, clear to all of these participants in your business?

Create Uniqueness

Sorting things out, for consumers of personal or industrial goods, is increasingly difficult. Markets are fragmenting. Customer choices are exploding. The strategy for success, spelled out in C-1, is differentiation and niche-market creation. But that is a product or service strategy. There is a larger question: How is the firm (or a division) positioned in the customer's mind? Sure, the ABC Company makes a terrific widget for the narrow XYZ market. But what do consumers most generally think about when they consider buying any of ABC's products? The answer to that question will determine more of your long-term success in a chaotic marketplace than any specific choice about positioning a specific service or product for a specific niche.

DON'T GET STUCK IN THE MIDDLE

I found myself nodding continuously as Mike Kami, a respected consultant on corporate strategy, stormed back and forth on the stage in front of an audience of 2,000 people from Hardee's, the restaurant chain. In a one-hour presentation, he probably used the word "uniqueness" at least thirty times. He'd shout, "What's so special about your company?" "How are you *different* from your competitors?" "Ex-act-ly how?" "What is your *uniqueness in the marketplace?*"

A 1985 *Forbes* article criticized the strategy of Federated Stores, suggesting that their approach lacked clarity. By contrast, *Forbes* applauded Federated's rival Dayton-Hudson, which is deemphasizing investment in its traditional department stores (and other off-the-main-line activities) and directing most of its energy at the relatively narrow retail segment represented by its Mervyn's and Target divisions. "The point about Dayton-Hudson's strategy," said *Forbes*, ". . . is not which segment of retailing they chose, but that they chose one." In other words, don't just stand there, be something.

Sometimes a firm loses its uniqueness. Sears lived by the slogan "Quality at a good price" for decades. In the seventies its retailing strategy became confused. Customers wondered, was it the old Sears? Or, as some of the company's activities suggested, was it becoming an upscale outfit? The customers gave Sears an unequivocal answer. As one retail executive put it: "Those who saw

Sears as K Mart shopped at K Mart. Those who thought it was Macy's shopped at Macy's." Spotty retailing results, except for white goods, continue to plague the giant firm.

Substantial analytic evidence supports the importance of uniqueness in the marketplace. Strategy expert Michael Porter of Harvard contends that there are only three successful generic strategies: (1) "overall cost leadership," (2) "differentiation" (by which he means leadership in quality or service or innovation across a broadly defined market), and (3) "focus" (a niche strategy). Porter concludes:

> The three generic strategies are alternative, viable approaches to dealing with . . . competitive forces. . . . Sometimes the firm can successfully pursue more than one approach as its primary target, though this is rarely possible. . . . *Effectively implementing any of these generic strategies usually requires total commitment, and organizational arrangements are diluted if there's more than one primary target* [my emphasis]. . . . The firm failing to develop its strategy in at least one of the three directions—a firm that is "stuck in the middle"—is in an extremely poor strategic situation. The firm lacks the market share, capital investment, and resolve to play the low-cost game, the industry-wide differentiation necessary to obviate the need for a low-cost position, or the focus to create differentiation or low cost in a more limited sphere. The firm stuck in the middle is almost guaranteed low profitability. It either loses the high-volume customers who demand low prices or must bid away its profits to get this business away from low-cost firms. Yet it also loses high-margin businesses—the cream—to the firms who are focused on high-margin targets or have achieved differentiation overall. The firm stuck in the middle also probably suffers from a blurred corporate culture and a conflicting set of organizational arrangements and motivation system.

That doesn't leave much. Figure 9, adapted from Porter's *Competitive Strategy,* summarizes this point.

Empirical tests of Porter's thesis have confirmed its validity. A 1985 study, reported in the *Journal of Business Venturing,* produced dramatic results. Not surprisingly, firms classified as having "high relative quality, low relative price" led the pack with a 36 percent return on investment. However, those that rated "high on relative quality, [but also] high in relative price" fared almost as well—a 34 percent return on investment. Acceptable profitability also marked the opposite, or low-cost, outcome: Firms with "low relative quality, low relative price" had a return of 15 percent. The poorest performers by far were those stuck in the middle: The firms categorized as "middle relative quality, middle relative price" managed only a 2 percent return on investment.

This supports Porter's view—with an important modification, consistent with prescriptions C-1 through C-4. While Porter doesn't distinguish between the payoffs of low-cost and high-differentiation strategies (look at the end points of the curve in Figure 9), the study (see the details in Figure 10) decisively demonstrates that the high-differentiation strategy is more profitable. The study does strongly support the U shape of Porter's curve. However, the high-quality/high-price "end" of the curve tops the low-quality/low-price "end" by more than a two-to-one margin, 34 percent versus 15 percent.

Figure 9

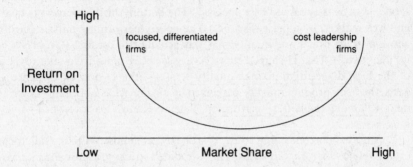

But this analysis still fails to deal with my greatest concern: Even if the low-price/cost, low-quality strategy is somewhat profitable, it does not appear to be sustainable. Recall the discussion in C-2 about the revision of the PIMS findings, from an emphasis on the positive relationship between market share and profit to an emphasis on sustainable market share, which is driven by high relative quality. Also see *A Passion for Excellence* for an extensive discussion of this point.

Further strong corroboration of the risk of the "in-between" or "stuck-in-the-middle" strategy comes from Dr. John Groocock's analysis of TRW, using the PIMS methodology and referred to in prescription C-2. Recall that the top third of TRW's divisions, rated on the basis of customers' perception of quality, outperformed the bottom third by three to one. In C-2 I did not report on the

Figure 10: **Return on Investment as a Function of Quality and Price**

Relative Price	*Relative Quality*			
	Low	*Medium*	*High*	*Average*
High	17	18	34	23
Medium	9	2	16	9
Low	15	11	36	21
Average	14	10	29	17

149

middle third of TRW's divisions; it turns out that these fifteen of TRW's forty-seven divisions fared far worse financially than those rated lowest. The middle third on relative quality had a 1.4 percent return on sales (compared with 2.9 percent for the bottom third and 7.7 percent for the top third) and a 5.1 percent return on assets employed (compared with 8.9 percent for the bottom third and 26.6 percent for the top third).

The study has grave implications when one looks beneath the surface. The top third in Groocock's study charged premium prices, and the product or service was usually rated "best in class." The bottom third had average quality, and was marked by a price discount. The poorly performing middle third had above-average prices and quality that was usually tied for first (Groocock calls it "joint best"). That U-shaped curve is very sensitive indeed. To take advantage of the high-differentiation/high-quality strategy, the Groocock evidence suggests, the firm/product must be perceived by customers as noticeably better, not merely "among the better" performers. Thence Kami's favorite word—uniqueness.

Yet another corroborating study, this one by economist William Hall, focused exclusively on mature industries. The "straddle" strategy, as he called it, proved deadly once again. Only those achieving "lowest delivered cost relative to competition coupled with an acceptable delivered quality" and those achieving "the highest product/service/quality differentials position" thrived.

The implications we can draw from these empirical tests actually square with common sense. As one seminar participant put it: "It's simple, when you think about it. The average consumer doesn't go to the yellow pages and say, 'Where can I find a product with an average number of defects at an average price?' You either want something great, and you'll pay for it. Or if you don't care excessively about the quality [or can't afford it], you want it as cheap as possible."

True as that statement has doubtless always been, it is more true than ever today. With an explosion of products and competitors, the consumer, individual or commercial, is overwhelmed by choices. Your distinction had best stand out—unequivocally.

I'm reminded of a first-rate radio ad from the stellar computer dealer, BusinessLand. A clock ticked loudly. After a few seconds an announcer came on with a message like this: "Seven seconds have passed. Somewhere, yet another software program has been introduced. BusinessLand is the expert at sorting through this jungle and giving you the most professional advice concerning the bewildering and exploding array of options out there." And, indeed, BusinessLand's profitable uniqueness is that (1) it does just that and, more important, (2) it is widely seen by customers as doing it better than anyone else.

UNIQUENESS REQUIRES CONSENSUS, NOT PERFECTION

The uniqueness idea, then, has sound analytic, anecdotal, and common-sense underpinnings. But what does it mean on a day-to-day basis? "How unique?" and "Whose definition?" are among the important questions.

Years ago, my friend Allan Kennedy, co-author of *Corporate Cultures,* and I had a lively discussion about how precise a corporate strategy has to be. Our conclusion: It must be "not wrong" and be widely "bought into" by everyone in the organization. That is, the "perfect" strategy, designed by corporate planners and altered annually in accord with minute shifts in market conditions (low cost this year, high quality the next), is worth little or nothing if it is not widely understood, accepted, and the basis for daily action throughout the firm. The fact that the team at the top supports the strategy is far less important than that the people on the loading dock support it—at 2 A.M., when no supervisor, let alone a vice-president, is around. In *Leaders,* by Warren Bennis and Burt Nanus, an exemplary chief executive makes the same point: "Leadership is heading into the wind with such knowledge of oneself and collaborative energy as to move others to wish to follow. *The angle into the wind is less important than choosing one and sticking reasonably to it.*"

So what is your organization's "uniqueness" as perceived by the marketplace? Can you state it in twenty-five words or less? Is the strategy statement printed on wallet-size cards that are given to everyone? Is it immortalized in granite—as grocer Stew Leonard's is? Leonard used to have his philosophy displayed on the store's wall—"Rule #1: The customer is always right. Rule #2: If the customer is wrong, see Rule #1." In late 1985, he went a step further, obtaining a three-ton chunk of granite and embedding it in concrete at the store's front entrance. The two rules were chiseled into the stone. Much of Leonard's reason for planting this heavy reminder is to discipline himself and the organization: "Every time a customer walks by it, they are reminded that that's how they should judge us. We'd better live up to it. There's no place to hide."

Make Uniqueness Everyone's Business

More important, would *everyone* in the organization choose roughly the same twenty-five words you chose to describe your uniqueness? The dirtiest of several tricks we sometimes play at our seminars is this: We ask each participant, "Sometime before you leave here, please call a person, at entry level, who has been on your payroll for no more than ten working days. Ask her or him to define your 'uniqueness' in twenty-five words or less. [When we're really feeling snippy, we sometimes ask for fifteen or even ten words.] If that person doesn't use virtually the same words you use, then, we contend, you have no strategy!" By that time you can hear a pin drop.

But our challenge is precisely the point. If the new receptionist doesn't understand, within hours of signing on, that you aim to be nothing less than "the most responsive temporary service agency for paralegal and paramedical needs in the Greater Milwaukee Area," you are in trouble, or at least in grave danger of not living up to your grand design.

There is much more to be said, and I will do so in the sections on people and leadership (principally L-2). But it cannot be said often enough that the deeper issue is not an ability to repeat the words (though it's a start, and most fall short even at this level), but psychological "buy-in" and commitment.

In a *Sporting News* article on the top coaches in the National Basketball Association, Coach Doug Moe of the Denver Nuggets commented, "You have to make your players believe that you believe in whatever you're doing. It doesn't matter what the style is, as long as you believe in it." While I've suggested here that the dimensions of uniqueness do matter (e.g., don't get stuck in the middle), Moe's point remains valid. Many of the people and leadership prescriptions will deal with the attributes of leadership, followership, values, and commitment which turn the stated uniqueness into a powerful driving force. That is, in summary, your statement of "what we are" has to be (1) roughly right, (2) enduring, (3) succinct, (4) memorable, (5) believable, and (6) energizing to all.

THE PRACTICAL VALUE OF UNIQUENESS

Suppliers, distributors, and customers must be in tune with your twenty-five-word statement of distinction if you are to realize the full power of your uniqueness. The one- or two-word idea or image customers have of Maytag ("Old Lonely"), Federal Express ("Absolutely, Positively, Overnight"), or Nordstrom ("No Problem at Nordstrom") is worth billions to each firm. The new three-person temporary service agency thrives or not exactly in proportion to the spread of a consistent word-of-mouth image about its uniqueness.

Suppliers have a book on your uniqueness too. No supplier tries to pull a fast one on Milliken when it comes to quality of material. If you want Milliken's business, you know in advance that outrageous quality standards, raised each year, await you; but you also know that if you can meet those stringent standards, a lifelong relationship, perhaps as Milliken's sole source, is yours. The value to Milliken is contained in the fact that the best suppliers, knowing Milliken's uniqueness, seek it out, and are honored to have its business.

The power of this idea cannot be overstated. Mike Kami is right to rant and rave about uniqueness. From a market perspective, there are better and worse generic strategies; but above all, the numbers decisively demonstrate that mixed strategies are disastrous. And the internal value of uniqueness as a source of empowerment is the basis for that market value. If we've all learned one thing in the last decade, it's that brilliant execution is more important than a brilliant strategy. And the *sine qua non* of brilliant execution is that (1) everyone knows which way the boat is heading, (2) the course is being consistently steered, and (3) the route is an exciting one, worthy of enlistment.

PUBLIC PARALLELS

Cities are competing for employers, and are often trying to revitalize the urban core. The idea of "what's special" about Colorado Springs, or Columbus, Ohio, is decisive in determining the city's future. Likewise, the value of the empowerment of every employee—in the police department, or at P.S. 29—also derives from a feeling of uniqueness.

FIRST STEPS

Informally poll your customers (citizens, patients, commercial consumers), suppliers, and distributors. Then poll your manager colleagues, in the city planning department, the distribution center, the executive suite. Is there strong or weak agreement as to your organization's uniqueness? If it's weak (or an "in-between" strategy), put this issue at the top of your agenda, far ahead of budget preparation or strategy formulation; these latter two activities are, after all, no more than reflections of your effort to achieve uniqueness.

C-7

SUMMARY

To execute strategies C-1 through C-6, several Capability Building Blocks are essential. First, we must:

▶ Become "transparent" to (that is, listen to) customers—end users, reps, distributors, franchisees, retailers, suppliers. Listen frequently. Listen systematically—and unsystematically. Listen for facts—and for perceptions. Listen "naïvely." Use as many listening techniques as we can conjure up.

▶ Make sure that field input from those closest to the customer (e.g., sales/service/stores) gets a thorough hearing with engineers/designers/buyers—without distortion, and with immediate follow-up. (Most new product ideas are "out there," in customers' minds and practical needs, waiting for *someone* to listen—and act.)

▶ Ensure that our CIS (customer information system) is as rich and substantial—and as much discussed—as our typically inward-oriented MIS (management information system).

Listening to customers *must* become everyone's business. With most competitors moving ever faster, the race will go to those who listen (and respond) most intently.

Marketers should be in the field at least 25 percent and preferably 50 percent of the time. *Everyone* should make several customer visits per year. Add at least one new, "naïve" customer listening device to your department's repertoire (regardless of the department) each 60 days.

C-7

Become Obsessed with Listening

You can see a lot by observing.

Yogi Berra

Re "Why the Bounce at Rubbermaid?": I plan to wrap copies of your article around bricks and throw them through the office windows of selected MBA brand managers I've met. These are the guys and gals who don't believe any research results unless they're based on a sample of 10,000 questionnaires.

Now here's Mr. Gault [Rubbermaid's CEO] actually *talking* to his customers to find out how to improve his products. . . . What will American business think of next? This kind of interactive market research is said to be common practice in Japan, but many of our managers simply assume that they know—and know better than—their customers. The message on my brick will read, "Get out of your office and *meet* your buyers!"

Allyn Thompson
Letter to the Editor
Fortune, May 1987

Prescriptions C-1 through C-6 constitute the basic value-adding strategies necessary to deal with today's chaotic environment. The remainder of the prescriptions in this book deal with "how to get there from here," beginning, in this customer responsiveness section, with the first of the Capability Building Blocks.

First among equals is listening to customers, with an ear to their practical, application-oriented needs. "Listening," like so many of these apparently simple ideas, turns out to be anything but simple. Since it must be practiced if we are to survive, it will become a mindset and a way of life for everyone—or else.

Yes, even listening has changed; or, rather, must change. To be sure, traditional modalities of market research remain important. If you are launching a new line of widgets, at some stage sizable numbers of people must be brought into a room and hooked up to galvanic skin response (GSR) detectors—that is, electrodes—to get their reactions to tastes or bag colors.

But, first, even this traditional mode of market research is being drastically altered. New computer simulation models allow you to do much more with much less data, much faster. Additionally, given the widespread availability of data bases together with a host of supporting software to allow clever interpretation of what's in them, data analysis that just a few years ago only a P&G could do and pay for is now possible for small firms as well.

Even that, however, is not the real point. More important is that with product life cycles shrinking, you've got to get whiffs of new trends earlier. Moreover, everyone needs to get in on the act. The organization prepared to move fast is the listening-intense organization—not only in sales and marketing, but in engineering and manufacturing and even (see C-4) management information systems (MIS).

Most are not ready, especially the big firms. The P&Gs of the world are victims of listening that is too methodical; by the time it's done, someone else may well have stolen the market. A few of the giants (P&G itself, Campbell, Frito-Lay) are moving to address such problems through reorganizations to get closer to the market (see C-4) and through team-based product development (see I-2).

The science and engineering-driven firms are beset by worse woes: (1) an arrogance born of success in a less competitive world, and (2) an American penchant for separating the "science types" from the translators—both the sales and marketing groups and the manufacturers (see C-8, I-3). Allied-Signal's chief planner, Lee Rivers, laments, "The U.S. does more basic research than anyone else. But other people have found more effective ways to turn [U.S.-born] scientific knowledge into products, goods, and services." Those other ways, practiced especially well by the Japanese, are led by listening, always with an ear toward application. *Industry Week,* in May 1987, reported on the U.S. problem: "Take ceramics, for example, which many see as a key material for the future. While U.S. firms have set a research target of reducing the grain size of the ceramic powder, the Japanese approach has been to start at the applications stage, says advanced-materials expert Michael Eckstut at Booz, Allen & Hamilton Inc. Japanese ceramic companies work with automakers to develop useful products, he notes. 'The Japanese know that what is important to the end customer is not grain size or [process] characteristics, but a product that can withstand so many degrees for 50 hours, or something you can bang on 50 times a day. That is the technology leverage, not the grain size.' So while the U.S. outspends Japan in ceramics research, the Japanese are spending where they're more likely to get results. That's one reason Japan is faster at getting ideas to the market."

An ear for application—at Campbell Soup or Allied-Signal or Ben & Jerry's Ice Cream of Waterbury, Vermont—is an ear constantly close to the market. It's as simple, and as fundamental, as that.

WHAT IT MEANS TO REALLY LISTEN:
THREE CASES

David-Edward Limited

June 13, 1985

Dear Mr. Peters,

As a manufacturer of a high-quality upholstered furniture line for the contract market, we are dependent upon design specifications generated by interior designers that we define as our customers. Like most manufacturers in our field, we have usually designed our product, our policies and our procedures and then promoted them to those people. . . .

I decided to bring together a group of 12 prominent designers in our area and ask their opinions, not of our company specifically, but of our industry in general. I . . . encourag[ed] them to talk to me about their requirements, both practical and psychological. The first pilot meeting was extremely successful. . . .

With the success of the first meeting, we organized what I called the David-Edward Listening Tour. Between December 15th and April 15th, I visited 27 cities in the U.S. In each case, we invited a dozen or so prestigious designers to meet with me for two hours over breakfast. . . .

We recorded all of the sessions and I sent abstracts of these recordings to all participants. The information we received has been invaluable. We have modified products, programs, policies, and procedures to provide what our customers say they really need. . . .

Our representatives are predicting a 25 to 45 percent [sales] increase over the next six months. In addition, we were also able to reach a different audience than the one we call on in true sales calls. We got the really hard-to-see people to see us. Interesting that they wouldn't give me 15 minutes to listen to me in their offices, but would allow me two hours in my hotel if I would listen to them.

Finally, we are now perceived as an industry leader, as a firm which cares, and then does something about what we hear. A story will be written about us in an up-coming issue of our most prestigious trade magazine and our competitors are wondering how to compete with a nonrepeatable psychological coup.

Sincerely,
Philip C. Cooper, President
David-Edward Limited
Baltimore, Maryland

Pacific Presbyterian Medical Center

Robin Orr administers the thirteen-bed Planetree Model Hospital Project at San Francisco's Pacific Presbyterian Medical Center. The typical counter between the nurses and patients was the first thing to go at Planetree. The formal medical records are always open to the patient; moreover, he or she and the family are vigorously encouraged to write comments on the record. Patients are also urged to question a doctor's decision to prescribe any drug.

Interaction is further facilitated by medical library privileges and the suggestion that patients should read up on such things as their ailment, drugs, and drug side effects. The nursing arrangement provides another listening (and involvement) post. One nurse has overall responsibility for coordinating the patient's care throughout the hospital stay and afterwards. Working with the coordinating nurse, he or she makes joint decisions about every aspect of the stay and treatment. And there's a patient advocate nurse who irons out any miscommunications between doctors, nurses, and the patient—interceding long before a minor irritant festers into a full-blown problem.

Dr. Philip Lee, president of the San Francisco Health Commission (not associated with Pacific Presbyterian), says, "When patients understand the nature of their treatment, and understand how to best work with their health-care team, there is clear evidence that shows hospital stays shorten [some studies indicate a major reduction], and returns to the hospital are far less frequent."

Patients and their families rave about the program. Initially skeptical doctors are signing up in droves to take part. Orr is invited to speak about the program at meetings in cities from Dallas to Helsinki. Others are undertaking pilot projects similar to Pacific Presbyterian's. And cost per day (over and above the benefits of shorter stays and fewer repeat visits) runs no more than standard care.

The Lutheran Parish at Bendersville

Dan Biles calls the pulpit a lousy listening post. He's minister of the Lutheran parish in Bendersville, Pennsylvania (population 500). When he arrived in 1985, he astonished the local people with what he calls Ministry by Wandering Around, by being the first minister in over *twenty years* to stop by the corner coffee shop to sit down and have coffee with the local farmers in what he describes as a "one-intersection town." He concludes: "Nobody had ever thought to do something that simple—at least not for a long time. By stopping at the coffee shop, I build relationships. . . . It makes the church more visible also. It's the kiss of death for a minister to stay in his office. . . . A lot of pastors and synod staff people ought to be spending 80 percent of their time out of their office doing MBWA." Dan Biles also visits every parishioner's home at least once a year—he observes that people speak more freely on their home turf. Incidentally, attendance at Sunday services quickly shot up by 25 percent.

CHARACTERISTICS OF GOOD
CUSTOMER LISTENING

After years of dealing with managers beset by turbulent conditions, my correspondence from police chiefs, mayors, school principals, hospital administrators and businesspersons occupies many a file cabinet. The most moving letters by far are the hundreds about "simple listening." In fact, if I had a file labeled "religious conversion"—that is, correspondence from those whose management practices have truly been transformed—I suspect that 50 percent of its contents would deal with just one, narrow topic: going out anew, with a "naïve" mind-set, and listening to customers. (Another 25 or so percent would be from managers who had done the same thing with their people—another version of "naïve" listening—see P-3 and L-5.)

Let's return to Philip Cooper, Robin Orr, and Dan Biles. To begin with, good listeners get out from behind the desk to where the customers are. In Cooper's case, the president of a $6 million firm visited twenty-seven cities in six months to engage in face-to-face customer contact. In Orr's situation, it was not just getting out from behind the desk, but getting rid of the desk—or clinic counter, to be precise. With Biles, the corner coffee shop was an important adjunct to the elevated pulpit.

Further, good listeners construct settings so as to maximize "naïve" listening, the undistorted sort. Cooper went one-on-twelve: one of him and a dozen of "them." He begged them to talk; he came with no slick presentation. Orr has a coordinator who is specifically charged to listen as well as a passive listening device (the chart that is to be written on), and she also provides education so that the patient will be prepared to ask wisely. Biles's frequent, leisurely, low-pressure visits to the coffee shop and parishioners' homes are a clear sign of his intent to listen, not preach—in his case, literally.

Finally, good listeners provide quick feedback and act on what they hear. Cooper sent abstracts of the talks (proof of listening, if you will) to the participants. And his company acted in short order to change a host of things on the basis of what was heard. At Planetree, the feedback is the nurses' and doctors' willingness to consider patient input in all decision making.

Don't you just wonder why no other minister bothered to hang out at the coffee shop in twenty years? I would, if that file I mentioned weren't so thick. Now I just shake my head when another letter comes in: "Dear Tom: I visited our four far west offices for the first time in five years. You wouldn't believe . . ." "Dear Tom: My ready mix [concrete] plant manager used to tell me he couldn't fit this or that into his schedule. Whenever he'd do so, I'd plop him in my truck and take him out to the customer, so he could explain face to face why he couldn't help the guy. You'd be amazed . . ." "Dear Tom: Whenever there's a customer problem, of any magnitude, we now take along an operations center person on the customer call. Their eyes really open when they hear the customer describe the consequences of what looked like a little thing to them."

So listening means: (1) hanging out (on their turf), (2) listening naïvely (comments on the patient's chart) and with intensity, and (3) providing fast feedback and taking action.

Listening with Intensity

Consider giving out home phone numbers. One division of Trus Joist, a $200 million high-technology forest products firm, has several thousand customers. A year or so ago, it sent each one a "Customer Service Card." It looks and feels like a credit card and the graphics are attractive. It prominently displays the division's toll-free customer-hot-line number. An equally well-done plastic insert for the customer's Rolodex accompanied it. Good enough, but there's more. On the back of the card and the Rolodex insert are ten home phone numbers—the division general manager, the national marketing manager, the product applications engineer, the division controller, the three plant managers in Oregon and Louisiana, and the customer service manager from each of those plants. (The general manager reports heavy use of the toll-free number—but no home phone calls.)

How about a "high roller" contest? That is, turn the tables and instead of honoring cost-cutting, honor spending—money and time in support of customer listening. Why not give an award to the factory manager who has logged the most miles and the biggest phone bill on customer calls and visits. Do the same thing among staff vice-presidents, distributors, center managers, and marketers. Present spot bonuses and/or certificates for acts of meritorious listening to customers. Make this a spirited campaign.

Spending Time and More Time "Hanging Out" in the Marketplace

Silicon Valley's Regis McKenna takes a tough-minded stance on intensity. Every marketer should be "on the road *half the time* [my emphasis]. . . . You get that . . . sixth sense only by spending time in the marketplace. You need to live and breathe the market. You need to talk to market participants on a continuing basis." McKenna concludes: "It is ironic, but true, that in this [era] of electronic communications, personal interaction is becoming more important than ever."

Japanese management expert Kenichi Ohmae sounds very much like McKenna's double:

Despite the increased ease of collecting and analyzing market data, the answer does not lie in better information systems or more corporate planners. . . . The most successful Japanese consumer-electronics companies send their product design engineers around the world for about *six months each year* [my emphasis] to study the latest customer needs and survey the competitive scene. They visit customers and dealers. They attend trade shows. They hold regional product conferences with dealers and salesmen to get direct feedback on what improvements they can make in the design and marketing of their products—a technique they regard as far superior to sending out questionnaires from corporate headquarters. In short, these people are sensitive to the *use* of the product. . . . For instance, by observing California's youngsters on roller skates, a Sony engineer came up with the concept of the Walkman, a portable cassette player. . . . The traditional approach to product development is to study the market and then have design engineers convert the marketing experts' concept into a product design. That division of labor has disappeared in many Japanese firms in recent years. . . . The engineers do the marketing in a less quantified and less sophisticated way, but move right into product design. It's more of an entrepreneurial approach where the people close to the market and product create the business. . . . Speed has become an important element of strategy.

So Ohmae and McKenna preach the six-months-in-the-field standard. This prescription is more modest: I demand "at least 25 percent" of time on the road for marketers—though I quickly add "preferably 50 percent."

Taking What You Hear Seriously—and Acting Fast

Ohmae sounds another important note, about getting information collected in the field into the design loop quickly. An emphasis on destroying functional barriers runs through many of these prescriptions (see especially C-8, P-9). In the case of this one, fewer functional barriers means that the raw listening can be translated more rapidly into new product and service ideas—essential in today's speeded-up world.

In "The New Product Learning Cycle," published in *Research Policy,* innovation experts Modesto Maidique and Billie Jo Zirger report a study of 158 products in the electronics industry, half failures and half successes. Many of the "unsuccessful products were often technological marvels that received technical excellence awards and were written up in prestigious journals." Too much exotic technology at far too high a price, they add, "is the story of virtually every one of our product failures." The successes, on the other hand, came first and foremost from intense involvement with customers. For instance: "In some cases the attempt to get customer reaction went to an extreme. . . . A test equipment manufacturer conducted design reviews for the new product at their lead customer's plants." Second, as Ohmae also observed, the successful firms had better—and faster—interaction among their "create, make, and market functions." Feedback was quick, undistorted—and taken seriously.

Taking feedback seriously remains a prime difficulty. Engineers and research scientists have long assumed that salespeople offering up customers' ideas are simply providing dream lists that would make their (the salespeople's) life easier. Senior management must intervene directly to ensure that ideas from the field are given a thorough hearing. A division of Toshiba America has turned this notion into a first-order strategic advantage. The general manager, looking for a competitive edge, realized that he was sitting on a gold mine of customer listening—the 4,000 calls a month that come into his service center. He reversed the traditional attitude of "handle this quickly and close the file," deciding instead to treat the calls as 4,000 golden opportunities to get customer ideas. To signal his seriousness, he had the service phone bank team report to top management each month on what they heard. He now considers this input—and the actions taken based upon it—to be the cornerstone of a remarkable success against larger and better-funded rivals. The story of GE's industrial plastics group, recounted in C-4, is a carbon copy—including exceptional results obtained in short order.

Involve Everyone in Customer Listening

If intensity and rapid feedback are the most important aspects of real listening, the involvement of everyone in the process follows closely. Customer listening is not just a marketing, sales, and service job. At one end of the spectrum, every clerk and machine operator should be involved. At the other end, the ivory tower researcher should also be thrown into the fray. A very high-tech firm finally cajoled its top R&D person, who epitomized the "what can I learn from these jerks" mentality, into visiting customers. He got very excited, and the president took advantage of his reaction by pushing him in front of a video camera to extol the virtues of getting out and about with customers. The tape is played in every training session.

Use Every Listening Post You Can Find

One important point, then, is not to leave listening and market research to the experts. Another deals with what constitutes "good listening." The answer is clear: any angle you can dream up. One highly successful banker is an avid reader of local banking newsletters from around the country. He's an avowed thief (see I-4). In his fast-paced world, new products are being introduced daily. He reads voraciously to get the first scent of anything that he might copy. And while he has a talented marketing department, by setting an example through his ceaseless circulation of little tidbits about this and that, he encourages everyone to get attuned to doing his or her own listening/"market research."

In *The Intuitive Manager,* Roy Rowan reports the following from a conversation with an executive of a data service firm: "I've never been surprised by research. Research is more of a confirmation tool than a discovery tool." That is, it has its place, but is no substitute for everyone's listening. Apple CEO John Sculley, who learned his craft at PepsiCo, is blunter still: "No great marketing decisions have ever been made on quantitative data."

You Must Persist

I mentioned that most of my "religious conversion" mail deals with listening. But even a genuine conversion is not enough.

A Canadian bank executive recalled a listening program that one of his regions instituted in 1986. For about two weeks, all managers spent some time each day calling customers, asking "How are we doing?" and "How can I help?" The results, he reports, were phenomenal. The customer feedback was terrific ("How magnificent that you thought to call"), morale skyrocketed, and a bushelful of new business ensued.

Yet this executive came to me in frustration. The program had been started a year earlier, and he'd just finished a review visit to the region. "The first thing I asked," he said, "was 'How's the [listening] program going?' 'Really great,' I was told. What that meant, it turned out, was that the regional manager agreed that last year's efforts had been a smashing success. But he hadn't replicated it. For the life of me, I can't figure out why he hadn't kept it up. He's not kidding me. He's a tough manager. I know it worked, and I know he genuinely thought it was a stunner. So my question is, how do we keep up the momentum?"

I had no answer, except to urge that he persist in asking "How's the listening program going?" question at every opportunity, and that he force-feed the process until it caught on. Clearly, even an earth-shaking positive experience is not in and of itself enough to insure self-perpetuation.

Words: "Educate" versus "Listen"

Nothing gets my dander up faster than the numerous conversations that go something like this:

"We've really got to get in closer touch with our customers, communicate with them better."

"Yes, we have a big problem there."

"They don't understand the new features. It's all there. We just need to spend time with them."

"Yes, you're right, we've got to educate them."

Observe the quick deterioration, from (1) get in touch to (2) communicate to (3) *they* don't understand to (4) educate *them*. How quickly listening has become talking and telling.

To "educate" is to transmit our ideas to an unschooled student or neophyte. Educating presumes we know whereof we speak. Few of us do, at least when it comes to customers in today's turbulent world. Surely we know why we think our product or service or new feature is great; how we think it will help our potential customer. But can we be sure that our favorite features match the customer's perception of what he or she needs? They seldom do. The customer's perception of our product is based on a compound of history, word-of-mouth information, a bad experience five years ago (long and conveniently forgotten by us), and perhaps a competitor's recent small act of courtesy, or a "trivial"

163

new competitor feature ("not technologically significant," sniff our engineers) that is just what the doctor ordered for this *particular* customer.

The Right Mindset: Treat the Customer as Foreigner

In fact, we'd be much better off if we could pretend that our customers are foreigners who do not speak our language. They don't. Take a person who comes from the world of commercial banking. One of his customers might come from the world of contractors; the next from the world of women's wear boutiques. The language and customs are dramatically different for each. Few of the banker's customers will speak "Banker."

Sadly, most of us don't really listen to our "foreigners." Worse still, we act as we all too frequently do when we're around a foreign person who doesn't speak our language and tries to ask us directions. As soon as it becomes clear that we aren't getting through, we shout even louder in our own tongue. He or she speaks just enough of our language (for example, the customer knows where the accelerator pedal is in the car) to convince us that if only we could yell a little louder, the advantages of the new overhead cam design would get through his or her obviously thick skull.

Each of us carries around a crippling disadvantage—we know and probably cherish our product. After all, we live with it day in and day out. But that blinds us to why the customer may hate it—or love it. Our customers see the product through an entirely different set of lenses. Education is not the answer; listening and adapting is.

Make Listening Fun

Listening can even be fun! That's the point of the VPI, or Very Promotable Item. Wal-Mart Stores' growth has been phenomenal, from $50 million per year in sales to over $15 billion in just fifteen years; from 15 to 1,000 stores in that same period. Now, in 99 out of 100 cases of such growth, executive detachment from the market follows—detachment in which lie the seeds of eventual decline. Wal-Mart, however, led by the indomitable Sam Walton, has battled the negative side effects of growth as successfully as any company I know. Executives, including Sam himself, are regularly out and about with their customers. The terrible "Taj Mahal phenomenon" has not set in: Wal-Mart's "headquarters" in Bentonville, Arkansas, are every bit as spartan as they were a decade ago.

Of all Wal-Mart's defenses against hardening of the corporate arteries, though, the VPI is my favorite. Each of the top executives (and, as of 1985, their spouses) picks out an item of store merchandise that he or she will directly sponsor throughout the year. For instance, Sam (who chooses three items instead of one in deference to his position) selected a five-gallon plastic fisherman's bait bucket in 1985. He was responsible for tracking its progress throughout the year, for pushing store managers to merchandise it aggressively, for giving those managers ideas about how to display and price the item, and for keeping tabs on it whenever he's in a store.

The most beneficial effect of the program is simply that it keeps senior management's hand in the business in a very direct way. In a word, each Wal-Mart executive remains an engaged merchant. And the hoopla that has arisen around VPIs contributes to that effect. The executives must publicly announce their choices. Moreover, they must religiously track sales and margins and—for good or ill—report on them, regularly and in full public view. The program is fun and engaging. It is humanizing—and often humbling. Some items bomb. One of Sam's did recently. The program thus effectively reminds the now-greats of a huge operation of the vagaries of the real world in which their field forces live.

YOU NEED A CUSTOMER INFORMATION SYSTEM (CIS)

A new acronym—CIS—provides a summary of this prescription. We all know about MIS, or management information system. But how's your CIS, or customer information system?

The CIS consists of formal market research and customer surveys (see C-3). It also consists of calling a couple of customers a week, of the VPIs at Wal-Mart and Listening Tours like the one at David-Edward, of giving out home phone numbers to thousands of customers, of encouraging patients to comment on their medical records, of passing articles around the office.

You see, we are what we eat. As I said, our seminars are peppered with dirty tricks; I'll share another of the nastiest. "When you get back to work," I urge, "check your in-box. Measure it, quantitatively. How many papers, or pages, deal with internal affairs such as the minutes of committee meetings or personnel actions. And how many deal directly with customers—survey results, complaints (or kudos), correspondence?" I add: "Of your 'closely watched' numbers (the half-dozen litmus test indicators that almost all effective managers seem able to recall from memory), how many are customer-centered?"

My challenge is usually met with teeth-grinding and reluctant agreement when I suggest that, for most of us, 90 percent or more of our "information flow" is internal in emphasis, not external. If that's so for you—go check your in-box—then quite simply and unequivocally you are not listening to your customers or markets. We are all victims of our in-box. We process what's there, and that's about that. If what you're processing is internally focused, then so are you.

Reprise

Listening, in sum, has three main objectives: (1) to develop, fast, an applications-oriented (practical) source of new product ideas; (2) to keep in "naïve" touch with the host of things, involving every department, that (a) bug customers and (b) simultaneously present improvement opportunities (this is the essence of C-2 through C-4); and (3) to motivate everyone in the organization through unfiltered involvement with the person who really signs the paycheck—the customer.

Furthermore, it calls for turning the organization inside out. The image in my mind's eye is a bit grotesque. I see the organization purposefully becoming a burn victim. It peels away everyone's outer, protective layers of skin and opens up more nerve cells to the painful sting of the exploding customer/competitor world. Right now our protective layers are making us noncompetitive. Too few people, at too few levels, in too few functions, listen too little and too late—and ignore what they hear too often, and act too late.

PUBLIC PARALLELS

From my colleague Jayne Pearl I gathered this gem:

How do you deliver good service when your customers are crooks and crime victims? Lieutenant Greg Stock of the Santa Barbara, California, Police Department sent his officers and himself on a "managing by wandering around" mission. Stock explains: "After my Dirty Harry stage, after I'd been an undercover cop, I was promoted and put in charge of twenty-five young officers. I realized that most of us only see crooks and jerks all day and night, or their victims. Like me, most start out with lots of vim and vigor, but we get skeptical and hardened. A lot of people out there are paying our salaries. This is a way to let them know what a good job we're doing, get a wider basis of support and experience for the officer." Not surprisingly, his idea was not eagerly embraced at first. Stock says he presented the idea as a challenge, to play up to their macho instincts. "I told them, 'Not all you guys will be able to do this, to deal with getting some doors slammed in your face.' And the general response was 'Hey, I'm not afraid of anything.' " The response was unanimously positive. The officers just ring a few doorbells every day, introduce themselves, give out a "business card" with emergency phone numbers and encourage the citizens to call for any reason. Stock says, "Our product—providing public peace and safety—will never go out of demand, and we don't have the incentive of having to be profitable. It's easy to get complacent and give rotten service—unless we keep challenging ourselves."

The device, once more, is simple—yet compelling. Beneath its simplicity, however, is the pervasive mindset that this prescription has emphasized: "I'm here to listen—and help." Not: "Let me tell you . . ."

FIRST STEPS

1. Perform the in-box test right now. How much of the content is "external"? Unless the percentage is greater than 50, go on to step 2.
2. Invent one personal listening ritual and start on it today—call three customers, follow up on one complaint, follow up one lost sale.
3. Gather a group of salespeople and bring up (or get them to bring up), and then analyze, a half dozen cases of failure to successfully transmit information collected in the field to marketers, merchants, or designers. Develop a process to shorten and upgrade that feedback loop, such as the presence of top executives at a monthly meeting where such ideas are discussed and commitments to action made.

C-8

SUMMARY

To remain competitive, the long-neglected factory must cease to be viewed as a cost center. Instead, we must:

▶ Make manufacturing or operations a—or the—prime marketing tool.

▶ Give manufacturing/operations people respect and a lead role at the firm's top decision-making table.

▶ Realize that manufacturing/operations is the prime source of: (1) superior quality, (2) day-to-day product/service innovation, and (3) responsiveness/lead-time shortening.

▶ Through new technology, increase factory flexibility; but beware that changes in organizational structure and attitudes must precede the new technology's widespread application—this means destroying traditional functional barriers and inducing a radically increased level of day-to-day, nonhierarchical interaction among factory team members, designers, engineers, marketers, and field forces—and customers and suppliers.

▶ Get customers into the factory; get factory people out to the customers.

The factory, though radically changed in shape (smaller, fewer people), is more important than ever. Though de-integration often makes sense, beware of the numerous hidden costs of subcontracting, especially overseas sourcing in pursuit of lower cost (or even higher quality). Vital day-to-day innovation, flexibility, and responsiveness come from palpable, casual, close proximity, as well as from formal interactions among internal functions (design, manufacturing, marketing, sales, service), suppliers, customers, distributors, etc.

Reassess every decision to let all or a bit of manufacturing go, especially offshore, in light of this prescription. Get all manufacturing managers into the field at least 15 percent of the time. Every production worker should make at least three customer visits per year. Get droves of customers into the factory on a regular basis. Get most engineers onto the factory floor—living there.

C-8

Turn Manufacturing into a Marketing Weapon

We have seen a growing number of clients in the electronics, toys, fashion, and consumer goods businesses "coming home" from abroad in 1986. The quality, supply, labor and communications issues that drove these companies offshore initially have become greatly influenced by the real need to "hang on to your valued clients." Companies that sought long-term survival with expected cost reductions and manufacturing efficiencies through foreign operations have learned the hard way that it is easier to control your own destiny through better management techniques, local manufacturing effectiveness programs, "Just-in-Time" materials scheduling efforts, subcontracting arrangements and the related training programs. The "higher-quality producer" may again be your U.S. competitor that uses these techniques.

> David M. Richardson
> Boyden International
> letter to *The Wall Street Journal*,
> November 7, 1986

Manufacturing must become a, if not the, primary marketing tool in the firm's arsenal. Quality, maintainability, responsiveness (length of lead times for delivery), flexibility, and the length of the innovation cycle (for both incremental improvement of current products and major new product development) are all controlled by the factory.

Marvin Runyon left Ford in 1980 after a distinguished career to head Nissan's new operation in Smyrna, Tennessee. His reason was the lack of respect, at the time, for the manufacturing function at Ford, as evidenced by lower salaries for factory managers and manufacturing executives than for marketing and finance people at comparable levels. Though Ford has made major progress since then, the outright disrespect for manufacturing, especially manufacturing's awesome potential marketing and market-creation power, is still typical of most old—and, more frightening, young—firms. Decisions by start-ups and old firms alike

169

to move manufacturing offshore, or even to subcontract onshore, in the single-minded pursuit of lower labor costs are often ill conceived.

MANUFACTURING STRATEGY: AMERICAN QUICK FIX VS. JAPANESE INCREMENTALISM

In *Tales of a New America,* Robert Reich sees the current pattern as the prime threat to our future well being: "Americans have made money from transferring our Big Ideas to [the Japanese]. They have made money by selling them back to us as terrific products and parts. What is left out of this calculation is the value of experience. They learn how to organize themselves for production—integrating design, fabrication, and manufacturing; using computers to enhance their skills; developing new flexibility; creating new blends of advanced goods and services. They learn how to make the kind of small, incremental improvements in production processes and products that can make all the difference in price, quality and marketability. In short, they develop the collective capacity to transform raw ideas quickly into world-class products."

Harvard's Bob Hayes spotlights the danger of letting manufacturing slip mindlessly offshore: "When the [offshore manufacturer eventually] enters the market, he's worked with the process on a daily basis, has a sense of the wider potential of the technology, of possible applications that you wouldn't have been thinking about. . . . He who can do nothing but sell is at a great disadvantage."

So what is the problem? Reich and Hayes among others believe that it is our neglect of incremental improvements which can transform a product over time. We wait for the breakthrough idea, counting on the distant lab rather than the factory working in daily contact with the product—and customers—to save us.

That's looking at the problem from the outside in, from the market's perspective. But look at it from the inside out, from the firm's view, and exactly the same picture emerges. We denigrate labor's role, overspend on big-bang automation, remove the engineers (process and research) from the shop floor, and continue to flail away at mass production. We lose responsiveness and under-emphasize quality. And, ironically, even the cost savings that mass production and automation are supposed to abet seldom materialize. As Ross Perot puts it: "We resort too often to the unhelpful practice of trying to solve a problem with larger doses of capital. Automation can become a narcotic." In a January 1987 speech to the Detroit Economic Club, he lamented that "despite spending $40 billion for robotics-equipped plants and other capital improvements, GM lost market share and went from being the low-cost producer to the high-cost producer among the Big Three."

We Must Stop Rejecting the Simple

In his fine history of automation, *Forces of Production,* David Noble traces our passion for the complex to automation's earliest days: "The technical commùnity [had] a preference for formal, abstract approaches . . . an obsession with control . . . an enthusiasm for computers . . . a delight in remote control, an enchantment with the notion of machines without men . . . a fetish for novelty and complexity . . . coupled with an arrogant disdain for proven, yet simpler, methods."

Indeed, there were numerous, and more basic, approaches available. However, they involved substantial machinist input. That was anathema in the anti-labor environment in America following World War II. And, of course, these rudimentary models flew in the face of inertia, bureaucracy, and the untold millions spent by big contractors to support the complex systems and military procurement specifications that effectively blocked other ways of doing things. Producers of the simpler—and proven—systems were shut out; so were smaller potential users—the independent machine shops.

All these forces were reversed in Japan. Labor organizations favored machinist input. The extensive subcontracting system and the big firms jointly encouraged small-shop use of advanced, flexible machining technology. And Japan had no military or academic bias for complex systems. Thus Noble reports that "by 1982, 90 percent of Japanese machines were of the simpler design." Moreover, two-thirds of the advanced systems in Japan itself are in small shops.

The combination of America's love of mass and complex, abstract solutions shows up in the premier customer battleground of the future—flexible manufacturing systems. Our performance has been appalling. Barnaby Feder of the *New York Times* reports on a 1986 study:

[Harvard's Ramchandran Jaikumar] studied 35 flexible manufacturing systems in the United States and 60 in Japan in 1984—a sample, he says, of more than half the installed systems in both countries. The United States came out of the comparison looking to him like "a desert of mediocrity." Rather than narrowing the competitive gap with Japan, the technology of automation is widening it further. . . . American manufacturers make and export the flexible systems. The computer-controlled machine can handle a wide variety of parts and tasks. . . . But the American manufacturers usually program the flexible systems to produce larger runs of a few products, just as if they were only current versions of the conventional machinery that has dominated assembly lines since the days of Henry Ford. . . . As a result, the average number of parts made by an American flexible manufacturing system in Jaikumar's study was 10, in contrast to the Japanese average of 93. And the Japanese used their system to handle 22 new parts for every 1 introduced by the Americans, allowing them to offer a wider variety of products more suited to the demands of individual customers. . . . The Japanese [assigned] small groups of engineers to develop flexible systems and then posted them on the factory floor where they could operate them, sometimes for years. Not surprisingly, the Japanese systems are frequently reprogrammed. . . . American manufacturers, by contrast, have tended to use fairly large engineering teams with many specialists to design and install systems. The engineers often end up building systems that are far more flexible then their intended use requires. When the engineering group is then disbanded or moved to a new project, the poorly trained and underskilled workforce that is often left behind is loath to tamper with the unnecessarily complicated systems.

This bodes poorly. It is the single most frightening instance of our strengths of yesterday becoming the burdens of today. We still rely on mass, complexity, and abstraction—in pursuit of low-cost, long-run production. Not only do we fail to achieve the low cost, but our prior rejection of simple solutions (marked by high labor involvement) and current inability to adopt such systems are crippling us in the market, where flexibility is the chief basis for future manufacturing competitiveness.

Hands Off: The Losing Marketing Strategy

In the late 1940s, General Electric led the charge in developing complex, all-encompassing automation systems, overtly aimed at eliminating as much labor as possible. Ironically, GE's chief scientist, Roland Schmitt, is now arguing in effect for amending the ivory-tower-driven approach his own company pioneered. In a 1987 editorial in *High Technology,* titled "Wanted: Hands-on Engineers," he concludes:

There's . . . the issue of effective execution—of strong performance all the way to the finish line. Here research is *not* the answer. Although we certainly need cadres of highly skilled engineering researchers, the vast majority of today's engineers need to be trained less like researchers and more like the practicing, dirt-under-the-fingernails engineers of yesteryear.

By treating everything as a research problem, we tend to devise elegant, inventive solutions without adequate attention to cost, manufacturability, and quality. Meanwhile, the Japanese exercise their skills on features that have significant customer value, while observing stringent guidelines for cost and quality.

The reason for emphasizing theory, at the expense of design and hands-on practice, has been to give the engineering graduate a command of the fundamentals rather than mere exposure to obsolete machines and superficial shop techniques. That objective is laudable, but its implementation has been carried too far. Students who will work in an economically competitive culture are being trained instead in a culture of research and analysis— the culture of their professors. Thus our educational system imparts mostly academic values, which emphasize optimum solutions, while putting little emphasis on such considerations as speed, cost, and customer satisfaction—the values of the marketplace.

Following the marketing and manufacturing principle of kaizen, or constant improvement, the Japanese tinker, invent, and add customer-friendly features incrementally. In *Restoring Our Competitive Edge,* Bob Hayes of Harvard and Steve Wheelwright of Stanford observe that to Americans capital investment primarily means the construction of new plants, while the Japanese principally see it as the constant improvement of machinery that they already have. Just a quarter of U.S. capital investment typically goes to improving the performance of existing machinery, while 60 percent of Japanese capital investment is devoted to that end. Likewise, a recent McKinsey & Co. study calculated that the Japanese spend just one-sixth to one-third as much as we do on big-bang automation: "The bulk of their [efficiencies] come from the home-grown approaches to design and manufacturing of production equipment."

In *World Class Manufacturing,* Richard Schonberger reports on Toyota No. 9 Kamigo engine plant, which *Automotive Industry* magazine considers ". . . the most efficient engine plant in the world." Schonberger points out that it is equipped with twenty-year-old machines from America, "retrofitted so they don't miss a beat. . . . Quality problems are nipped in the bud, so there is little rework to do, and little need to keep buffer stock. . . . Most machines can be set up in one or two minutes, so there is no reason to run large batches." The result is enhanced flexibility—and responsiveness.

In *Attaining Manufacturing Excellence,* Robert Hall observes that experts who have seen both Japanese and American plants conclude: "(1) New American plants often have excellent technology that is at least equal to Japanese and usually better. That is, any technology gap still slightly favors Americans. (2) American computer systems and software are almost always superior to Japanese. They are larger, more complex, and more powerful, but this can be a weakness as well as strength if the systems mask wasteful practices that should not exist. (3) Japanese are almost always superior in their ability to improve existing plant and equipment: tooling improvement, defect elimination, layout improvement and so forth. The conclusion is that Americans have trouble putting the pieces together and making the most of what they have." In a chapter appropriately titled "Attaining the Effect of Automation Without the Expense," he adds: "Spending big money quickly on automation is not wise. In the end, its effectiveness depends as much on organizational preparation as on money and technical prowess. Plus, equally skilled competitors cannot be beaten just by outspending them. Major automation cannot be effectively 'installed'; it must be accompanied by a way of organizational life."

Unfortunately, the phenomenon described above is not proprietary to the Japanese. The German success story is similar: Engineers live on the shop floor, and are brought up in a dirty-fingernails tradition. Investment in increasing the skills of labor is monumental. (Steelmaker Krupp spent $51 million training 4,200 would-be workers in 1986.) High quality and short production runs are the norm—success with flexible manufacturing systems has been stunning.

PHENOMENAL RESULTS FROM INCREMENTALISM IN THE UNITED STATES

What, then, is the answer for the United States? Adopt incrementalism our-selves, says Hall: "Manufacturing excellence results from a dedication to daily progress. Making something a little bit better every day, [using] every em-ployee's skill. . . . Manufacturing excellence tries to improve activities that contribute to customer well-being in ways often unseen and frequently unap-preciated."

Richard Schonberger reveals the power of these ideas when practiced in the United States. *World Class Manufacturing* ends with an Appendix titled "Honor Roll: The 5-10-20s"; that is, 84 plants he's discovered on North Ameri-can soil which have been following the constant-improvement strategy and have achieved a *fivefold, tenfold, or twentifold* improvement in manufacturing lead time. Here are some representative examples:

3M, Weatherford, Oklahoma (floppy discs): WIP [work in progress inventory] cut from six hundred to six hours, space per unit cut sixfold, productivity tripled.

Omark, Guelph, Ontario (saw chain): Lead time cut from twenty-one days to one, flow distance cut from 2,620 to 173 feet.

Omark, Onalaska, Wisconsin (gun cleaning kits): Lead time cut from two weeks to one day, inventory cut 94 percent.

Omark, Woodburn, Oregon (circular saw blades): Order turnaround time cut from ten to fourteen days with 75 percent fill rate to one or two days with 97 percent fill rate, WIP cut 85 percent, flow distance cut 58 percent, cost cut 35 percent.

Hewlett-Packard, Greeley, Colorado (flexible disc drives, tape storage units): WIP cut from twenty-two days to one day, whole plant on JIT [just-in-time].

THE LOOK OF CUSTOMER-RESPONSIVE MANUFACTURING

I've come across no better American exemplars of a customer-responsive approach to manufacturing than at Worthington Industries and Elgin Corru-gated Box Company. Here's what I found:

1. Process engineers live on the shop floor, working with line operators to extend the use of material and machines.

2. Every machine had been modified scores of times, usually by several generations of operators. Time and again, at Elgin, I'd hear: "This cost $1,500. Joe here did it while he was recovering from a strained back. The machine now does something that no one else [in the industry] can do. If he'd gone out to get this manufactured, it would have cost $70,000—if the big-equipment guys would even have done it." At Worthington, a spare-time project led to a component calibration task being moved in-house; what used to take up to ten days and cost $500 now takes a few hours and costs less than $10. (At Golden Needles Knitting and Glove, a jury-rigged—by people on the floor—Japanese machine does a complex, open-finger knitting job that the machine's Japanese producers still don't believe is possible. One result: Golden Needles is the just-in-time sole source for NUMMI's work gloves.)

3. The old and new reside comfortably next to each other. An advanced Worthington machine is powered by three U.S. Navy submarine engines, vintage 1943; it is controlled, however, by the latest computer technology—reprogrammed by a Worthington electrician, not a computer programmer. (Similarly, Luciano Benetton brags of his old $5,000 machines, retooled and reprogrammed many times "and now valued at half a million dollars apiece.")

4. Functional barriers are virtually nonexistent. (See I-2, P-9, L-8.) All quality control at Worthington is done by the operators, who have the latest measurement equipment to aid them. They also do all except major maintenance, having wholesale access to unlocked parts and tool rooms. All salespeople train extensively on the machines. Sales reviews are held on the shop floor regularly. Order information is available to all.

Many have called the absence of functional barriers and the staff's role as support for the line keys to Japanese manufacturing success. Masanori Moritani comments in *Japanese Technology:*

> A [major] strength of Japanese [manufacturing] technology is the close connection between development, design, and the production line. In Japan this is considered simple common sense, but that is not always the case in the United States and Europe. . . .
>
> Outstanding college-educated engineers are assigned in large numbers to the production line, and many are given an important say in business operations. Many manufacturing-industry executives are engineers by training, and a majority have had extensive firsthand experience on the shop floor. In Japanese firms, the production department has a strong voice in development and design. In addition, engineers involved in development and design always visit the production line and talk things over with their counterparts on the floor. . . .
>
> In certain respects, French television manufacturers outshine their Japanese competitors in the development of top-of-the-line models. Soft-touch and remote control were introduced by the French well before the Japanese began using them. But while France may spend a great deal on producing splendid designs for their deluxe models, the quality of the actual product is inferior to Japanese sets. This is because French designers do not fully understand the problems encountered on the shop floor, and because the design work is not done from the perspective of the person who actually has to put the machine together. In short, there is a serious gap between

development and production, a product of gaps between various strata in the company hierarchy itself.

5. Process and product innovation goes on constantly. Machine operators at Elgin and Worthington routinely work with customers, in the plant, to solve problems.

6. Customers are in the plant all the time, and plant workers are out with customers all the time. I've never visited a Worthington (or Milliken) facility when customers weren't present—not just touring, but working. (Milliken sees its sparkling plants as its best sales offices. One executive flatly asserts, "We've never lost an order if we've gotten the customer to visit.") Managers in Worthington factories are routinely expected to spend about 15 percent of their time on the road with customers. The average machine operator will make two or three customer visits a year, often overnight stays. (Gene DeFouw of ALOFS, a Grand Rapids company that manufactures assemblies and stampings, describes the results of factory/customer connections: "We sent all of our people involved to see the product at work, to meet their counterparts [at GM]. Now, when a problem arises [the customer's] response is to call 'a friend,' not buck it up through the system and 'memo-ize' it. . . . And that 'friend,' I can assure you, comes running." DeFouw then half-ruefully cited several recent experiences with his own Japanese equipment suppliers. Modifying a machine for one small customer is normal behavior on their part. So is chartering a plane to bring an inexpensive spare part several thousand miles following a breakdown. "When I asked why," he recalls, "they said, 'We want you to grow so we can grow with you.' It was that simple.")

7. The plant managers have worked on the floor, modified machinery—and done a stint or two in sales. One Worthington Steel plant manager is typical. He hired on in the summer while he was an undergraduate in business at Ohio State. Turning down an offer from IBM, he went to Worthington full-time after graduation. He's been inside every machine in the plant, and once worked with Austrian equipment producers for months modifying a new machine. He talks like a Ph.D. metallurgist and/or mechanical engineer, but has no formal training in either discipline. He had a tour in sales, and was successful.

It nets out this way: (1) Elgin and Worthington are constantly innovating, with customers, in product and process; (2) their flexibility and responsiveness are unparalleled in their giant industries; (3) they produce top quality (Worthington, for instance, scores four times better than the industry average); (4) they have generally oldish machines that have been modified to achieve state-of-the-art in performance; and (5) both are low-cost producers to boot. Not a bad set of specs. Both, in sum, are brilliant market creators who use the factory as their prime marketing arm.

Market Creation Through Manufacturing at Chaparral

Chaparral Steel of Midlothian, Texas, is a pioneer in mini-mill technology. It has the lowest costs in the U.S. steel industry, and lower costs even than its Asian competitors—for instance, it can produce steel at one-half what it costs a typical Japanese mill. Founder Gordon Forward is a technologist, yet surprisingly he has no research department. He explained to the *Harvard Business Review:*

Our largest challenge is to cut the time it takes to get technology out of the lab and into operations [my emphasis]. . . . Let's go back to what I think happened at some of the bigger companies in the industry. Well, nothing happened. Sure, there was research. But I often thought that those companies had research departments just so CEOs could say something nice about technology in their annual reports. The companies all put in vice presidents of research. The companies all built important-looking research centers, places with 2,000 people in a spanking new facility out in Connecticut or somewhere, with fountains and lawns and little parks. Those places were lovely, really nice. But the first time I went into one of them I thought I was entering Forest Lawn. After you spend some time there, you realize you *are* in Forest Lawn. Not because there are no good ideas there, but because the good ideas are dying there all the time. . . . Many of the ideas weren't all that hot. . . . You know, someone would come up with a harebrained scheme that would burn out the refractory lining of a furnace. Now, if this fellow had only had some production experience, he would know perfectly well that iron oxide, pure iron oxide, is a solvent for refractories. But chances are, he doesn't even talk to anybody in production. . . . I'm not arguing that pure research has no place in our industry. But what we had was a lot of technical work that never got linked to real production needs. It was partly the fault of all those folks in the research centers, but it was also the fault of production people who were suspicious of any new ideas. They saw change as a challenge to their positions. . . . They also treated the research people as safety valves. You can guess the way they thought. "If all those smart Ph.D.'s are responsible for new ideas, we don't have to worry about them. Besides, most of the ideas are nonsense anyway. Just get out of our way and let us make the stuff we're supposed to make." It's what happens when you treat research as a staff operation.

So we've tried to bring research right into the factory and make it a line function. We make the people who are producing the steel responsible for keeping their process on the leading edge of technology worldwide. If they have to travel, they travel. If they have to figure out what the next step is, they go out and find the places where people are doing interesting things. They visit other companies. They work with universities. Working with the universities is particularly important . . . the attraction for the university

177

people is that they get to work with Chaparral people who can go back and really make something happen. They know they're not working with someone who's just going to return to the office and write a report. . . . *The lab is the plant* [my emphasis]. Sometimes I bite my lip because it tries things that scare the daylights out of me. Of course, we don't give the whole plant over to laboratory work, but the whole plant really is a laboratory—even though it is one of the most productive steel mills in the world. We don't stop operations to try crazy things, but we do try to do our research and development right on the factory floor. You know, if you put a production fellow and a maintenance fellow and an engineer together, you're gonna find out pretty quickly whether something has a chance of getting off the ground. And if it does, having them there means that you have a pretty good chance of getting it up and working—and fast. . . .

[The manufacturing people] have to be darn good at production but also talented technologists. There are no folks in the lab somewhere backing them up. . . . We've had to create some of [these people]. . . . [For instance, there is] our sabbatical plan . . . for our people at the front line, [at] supervisor level. Some time ago, when we sat down and asked ourselves what kind of company we wanted to be, we knew we were going to have to be aggressive. We knew we had to stay on top of new technology. And we knew that the best way to get technology into the workplace is through people. Now, that may sound great, but how do we do it? We all felt that most factories stifle young people, cripple them with bureaucracy. We wanted Chaparral to give people freedom to perform, to really tap a person's ego. . . . Many of us had noticed how young people in our industry were scared stiff on the first day that they became foremen. For a year or two they would find the job exciting. They might take a management course, seek out new responsibilities, try to learn new things. But after about three years, it all became rote. . . . They could stop thinking and go get their excitement somewhere else—off the job. So we thought, let's get them out of their regular jobs and put them on a kind of sabbatical. Let's give them some special projects. . . . Sometimes we have these people travel. Or we have them visit other steel mills. . . . Or we have them look into a new kind of furnace we're considering or a new program we're working on for our computer. Sometimes they just spend time [out visiting] with customers.

Forward, too, readily sends his factory troops to the customers when the need arises:

If we have bent bars coming off our production line and they're causing problems for our customers, we might send a superintendent over with the salesperson or the person who did the bundling or somebody from production or metallurgy. It's everyone's job. We mix crews. We send off maintenance people along with some people from the melt shop and from the rolling mill. We want them to see Chaparral the way our customers do, and we also want them to be able to talk to each other. We want them to exchange information and come back with new ideas about how to make improvements or new ways to understand the problem. . . . [It's] where the issue of staff versus line comes in again. It's all a line responsibility—or should be. Everyone can help and share product quality and customer satisfaction and be held directly responsible. . . .

About four years ago, we made everyone in the company a member of the sales department. That means people in security, secretaries, everyone. When you think about who talks to customers, you realize that a lot of people do—on the phone, when customers visit on a tour, whatever.

BUILD CUSTOMER-RESPONSIVE MANUFACTURING

At Chaparral we find the same key principles described at Elgin and Worthington, and found among Japan's (and Germany's) winners: (1) destruction of functional barriers; (2) engineers on the mill floor, not detached; (3) research treated as ongoing, incremental experimenting in conjunction with manufacturing and customers; (4) an attitude of scrounge/test/modify/hustle/act; and (5) everyone's involvement with customers.

Sales, marketing, service, quality, innovation, flexibility, and responsiveness all emanate from manufacturing at Elgin, Worthington, Milliken, Chaparral, et al. It's obvious, then, why Hayes, Reich, and others dread the mindless abandonment of manufacturing in pursuit of lower costs alone. It's not only the loss of manufacturing jobs that hurts, but the loss of the ability to be market-oriented that occurs when manufacturing is either dismantled or treated as little more than a cost center.

The same factors should inject a note of caution into American manufacturing's current love affair with vertical de-integration. It is often wise, and frequently because it brings in innovation useful to customers from a host of in-tune offshore or onshore suppliers. But de-integration in the narrow-minded pursuit of low cost ignores all of the marketing attributes that the factory could and should possess.

"Feel" is a word that businesspersons find troublesome. It is too mushy. And yet "feel" is in many ways the essence of this argument. It is from hands-on interaction—among suppliers, customers, foremen, line machine operators, researchers, heads of distribution centers—that day-by-day advances in innovation and responsiveness flow. If one does de-integrate, onshore or off, the feel must be kept intact. Many have learned of late that this is easier said than done, especially with offshore producers, and even if you encourage frequent travel. The problem is that, often as not, it is chance meetings and conversations—over time—that lead to the tests of new ideas with merit. If the raw number of interactions plummets, then it becomes frighteningly unlikely that the thousands of minor, incremental innovations in product and process necessary to stay competitive will occur.

Develop a New "Model" of the Role of Manufacturing

In summary, we must shake a series of misconceptions about manufacturing, and adopt new ways of doing things:

Conventional Wisdom

New Wisdom

The cost advantages of our competitors force us to go offshore.

Huge productivity improvements—via people more than capital—are readily available in every industry. Models from every industry surround us, if only we will take the trouble to look. Take steel—Nucor, Worthington, and Chaparral are each three or four *times* more productive than the industry as a whole.

As long as we retain design/engineering and marketing, we keep control.

Most innovation comes from the interchange, on a daily and often unplanned basis, between those functions *and* manufacturing. Moreover, the chief American selling point should be unparalleled flexibility—this is lost when manufacturing withers.

Good people don't want to go into manufacturing.

True, given the way we have treated manufacturing over the last three decades. As some are demonstrating, though, this can be reversed in fairly short order. The factory can become the leading edge, the launching point for a brillant career, rather than a dead end.

"Comparative advantage" arguments lead us away from manufacturing and toward service activities.

It is true that not as many people will work in factories in the future, but that is not an anti-manufacturing argument. In the firm of the future, comparative advantage will come from the value added via quality, service, flexibility, responsiveness, and constant innovation. The factory, no matter how many work there, drives *all* of these attributes. This holds true for the

Conventional Wisdom　　　　　　*New Wisdom*

emerging "factory" in the service businesses—trading rooms, Automatic Teller Machines, etc., in the bank; reservation systems among airlines; total systems at McKesson, The Limited, and Federal Express—see C-4. Studies now reveal that service businesses are on average *more* capital-intensive (have more "factory," if you will) than manufacturing.

FIRST STEPS

Are you working through decisions to de-integrate, to ship manufacturing offshore? These may turn out to be sound moves, but reassess them in light of the tenets presented here. Are you sure you can retain (or achieve) world-class responsiveness? constant innovation?

If you are not considering such moves, begin a thorough review of manufacturing/operations with an eye toward revenue generation rather than cost minimization. Each manufacturing activity's operating or strategic plan should be written and reviewed from a marketing perspective.

C-9

SUMMARY

To achieve the radically customer-centered strategies laid out in prescriptions C-1 through C-6, we must:

▶ "Overinvest"—total dollars, numbers of people and per capita—in front-line sales, service, distribution, and sales/service/distributor support people and support systems.

▶ Make these people the company heroes—by paying them well; training them "excessively," in class and on the job; providing them with outstanding tools; giving them the opportunity to participate in the structuring of their jobs and support systems; and listening to them.

▶ "Overinvest" in support for and time spent with the wholesalers, retailers, reps, franchisees, and other members of your distribution channel—select them carefully, but then regularly weed out the poorest performers.

Ironically, the most lightly regarded people in most organizations, public or private, are those who are closest to the customer (patient, citizen) and most directly responsible for the quality and responsiveness of service delivered. This tradition must be reversed with a vengeance, if total customer responsiveness is to become reality.

Consider doubling: (1) the number of salespersons, direct or in support of reps/franchisees; (2) the sales training budget; and (3) the sales support system budget.

C-9

Make Sales and Service Forces into Heroes

This prescription and the preceding one deal with the two most neglected elements of the typical American corporation: (1) manufacturing (2) sales and service. These two must simply achieve preeminence if we are to become competitive once again. They are the basic capability building blocks that permit a firm to execute the new—and necessary—strategies laid out in C-1 through C-6.

THE PAYOFF FROM PUTTING SALES AND SERVICE FIRST

The customer game is ultimately won or lost on the front lines—where the customer comes in contact with *any* member of the firm. The front-line team *is* the firm in the customer's eyes. Therefore, the front-line team must be treated as the heroes they genuinely are—and supported with tools (training, systems) that allow them to regularly serve the customer heroically. Surprisingly, all too few firms understand this:

▶ Could it be so simple? Buckman Labs thrives, despite new competitors and a relatively flat worldwide market demand for its products. Since 1980, it has more than trebled its sales force from 90 to 275; sales have increased at exactly the same rate, with a lag of about a year—which is the time it takes one of its technical salespersons to get up to speed. The chief executive officer harbors no doubts: "Sales increase at the rate of adding salespersons."

▶ The personal/home computer business—producers and distributors alike— sagged in 1985, yet retailer BusinessLand had a sales surge of almost 200 percent; today, it nears the half-billion-dollar mark in revenues. In addition to in-store personnel, it fields a 750-person sales force that has cracked the business market for personal computers wide open. That's a feat that even Apple hasn't yet accomplished. Some rate BusinessLand's sales force as one of the top three or four in the computer industry. Though recruiting top talent to begin with, the firm lavishes $600 or more a month in new training on each salesperson.

▶ Attention is showered on the mechanics at $100 million Sewell Village Cadillac. The best make upwards of $100,000 a year. The training is tops, and the computerized support systems are exceptional.

To this list add such companies as ServiceMaster, Marriott, Disney, IBM, Federal Express, Nordstrom, Stew Leonard, Safety Kleen, Snap-On Tools, and Trus Joist. These firms live for their sales, service, and customer support people. Some have unions (e.g., Frito-Lay, Disney), and some don't—it's the care, feeding, attitude, pay, and support systems that count. Regional vice-president Betsy Sanders of Nordstrom captured the spirit in a talk to a group of technology executives:

"How many of you know Nordstrom?"

All hands go up.

"How many of you have a positive image of Nordstrom?"

Once more, all hands go up.

"How many of you know me?"

No hands go up.

"How many of you know Jim or Bruce Nordstrom?"

No hands.

"How many of you know our store manager in Palo Alto, or wherever you might have visited us?"

Still no hands.

"How many of you know us via security analysts' reports?"

No hands again.

"You see, Nordstrom *is* the salesperson to you. It's not me, not Bruce Nordstrom, not a security analyst's recommendation. It is that *one* person you are in contact with when you are in the department you want."

As I've noted, Nordstrom's salespersons are paid well. There are plenty around, and management is also always on the floor to help. Moreover, the salespersons are supported by Nordstrom's high inventories, and by the phenomenal one-day turnaround time for alterations. Further, they are allowed to do almost anything—cash checks, take returns, gift-wrap.

In light of all this support, Sanders says, "We demand a lot from them!" Nordstrom, then, simultaneously dotes on and asks a lot from their front-line people. Frito-Lay does the same. In *The Marketing Edge: Making Strategies Work,* Harvard's Tom Bonoma explains that it's pay and support—and something else:

> Despite the rigidity of the [Frito] system and, indeed, some potential Mickey Mouse requirements of the system, the salesperson does things other companies can't get their salespeople to do. [Salesman Jess] Pagluica routinely took the time to "flex" each bag of Fritos or whatever he was putting on the shelf, smoothing out the wrinkles so that the display would look better. . . . He religiously counted every package of goods coming into

the store, was scrupulous in crediting the customer for damaged goods, and in general was almost frighteningly zealous about what he was doing. A visitor from another planet might have thought that the display was an altar, and [Frito] his religion. Most puzzling of all, Pagluica was a union man!

When [people] examine the system in detail, they come up with a number of reasons why the system works so well. Of course the commissions Jess Pagluica is paid have a lot to do with his willingness to "flex" the bags, and the training he has received allows him to understand that the neater display is likely to get more sales from the shopper than a sloppy one. There are good opportunities for advancement in the [Frito] system; the company is paying Jess's way through night school, and he has high aspirations to become a [Frito] regional manager in time. The system of multiplication tables on the backs of invoices, the optical scan invoices themselves, and account call patterns make good sense, and Jess understands how using these can help him make more money and [Frito] move more goods.

But none of this . . . really explains why Jess runs. Jess runs, one comes to learn from listening to him, because he believes in Frito-Lay as a company, as a vendor of high-quality snack products, and as a good place to work. He knows, accepts, and, best, believes the marketing theme of the firm that "we have two seconds to reach the customer with our fine line of high quality snack foods," and he wants customers, both trade and end user, to want Frito-Lay products. He understands in his belly that he is the link that makes or destroys the company's interaction with the customers.

Bonoma adds that it's top management's abiding belief in the sales forces, a belief passed on not only to the field but also to all those who support the field, which ultimately makes the difference. Former Frito-Lay president Wayne Calloway (now chairman of Frito's parent, PepsiCo) put it bluntly: " 'Service to sales' is stamped on everyone's underdrawers around here."

An emphasis on the sales and service force has served firms such as Frito-Lay well for a long time. But the Frito/Nordstrom "secret" has been oddly shielded from others, who look principally to creative buying/designing and/or low-cost production/operations for their strategic advantage. Today (and tomorrow even more so), "service added," as described in C-1, C-3, and C-4 may well be the best strategy for survival, let alone winning. The care and feeding of the sales and service force—and more, turning them into innovators—is of monumental importance. Sadly few have a tradition of such attention to fall back on.

Tom Bonoma provides another example of the compulsions of field-driven firms:

Consider Dan Siewert, President of Cole National Corporation's Optical Division (CNCOD). CNCOD runs more than five hundred optical departments leased from Sears and other retail chains. . . . Siewert's performance since coming to the Optical Division can only be considered stunning. . . .

Just one visit to Siewert's office makes the . . . culture of the division clear. . . . The district sales managers are the "heroes" of the division; it is about them that people talk and about sales increases and "small wins" in the field. The story is told repeatedly, for example, about the regional manager who did not have enough advertising money for both production costs and talent costs to make a local "spot" commercial, so dressed herself up as a television set and handled the talent problem herself. She reported a 37 percent sales gain!

As to rituals, the president (not an assistant or subordinate) reviews sales numbers with the district managers monthly; weekly reviews are held with direct supervisors, and daily sales statistics are collected.

Exceptional feats performed by sales and service people are the daily fare of hallway chatter at CNCOD, Frito-Lay, et al. But these superhuman feats have not in fact been performed by bionic men and women; they have been performed by ordinary people who have been told, in a host of ways, that the firm exists to support them.

The converse attitude, however, is the norm. Retailers skimp hopelessly on clerks. Nordstrom's Sanders concurs: "I never blame another store's salespeople for lousy service. There aren't enough of them. They get no support. They're paid miserably. They're lowest on the totem pole. What else would you expect?"

In high-technology firms, I observe a similar pattern. Salespeople, even if well paid, are psychologically neglected. Top sales management often doesn't sit on decision-making committees; top field service management almost never does. Sales is not on the fast track for hotshots, and a sales tour is not even a requisite way-stop for aspirants to general management.

Acknowledge the Role of Service and Support People in Achieving Customer Responsiveness

I am a fan of salespeople—lots of them, well paid, superbly trained, and supported by the most advanced systems, such as the intricate question-answering system, all out of the customer's view, at Disney parks. However, I want to emphasize even more strongly the potential role of service people. They suffer greater relative neglect, yet can provide even more payoff.

Service means in-the-field service personnel, but it also means others such as the people who answer the phone in the reservation or order-entry center and the personnel in the distribution center. I can only stutter my dismay at the shabby facilities, low pay, and lack of respect these people usually receive.

At Disney, the sweepers are heroes. At Marriott, the bellhops and the people in the reservation center have attention showered upon them. Toshiba America made its service support phone operators into heroes—and made a strategic leap as a result.

These, however, are bright spots in a generally gloomy picture—as witness the experience of the founder of a field-service trade association representing the electronics industry. Wishing to assess the state of thinking in field-service management, he searched through the Library of Congress for texts on the subject. To his dismay, even using a liberal definition of what would qualify, he could find only two books.

We can no longer afford to neglect this increasingly crucial strategic area. While formal study is hardly the answer, we need urgently to get more organized—and especially more imaginative—about field service, service support, and service support systems management, and to develop a specific strategy for these functions (see also C-3 and C-4).

The centerpiece of such a strategy must, in turn, be a plan for upgrading the role and prestige of service and service support people in general (recall GE's newly ennobled Customer Service Coordinators—also in C-4); service management must be singled out from top to bottom. Top service management must be a part of all the firm's policy-making bodies. The service management career path must become a feeder to general management positions. And service managers must routinely become a prominent part of design teams and multi-function teams dealing with the paramount issue of enhancing overall company responsiveness.

A Strategy for Inducing Sales and Service Force Heroics

There are at least nine critical factors for enhancing attention to sales, service, and support people (see also prescriptions P-1 through P-10):

1. Spend time with them. If you're not visiting stores and distribution centers at 2 A.M., and dispatch offices *very* regularly, you don't care about these functions. It's that simple.

2. Pay them well. Are your distribution center people paid well above the norm, with gain-sharing incentives to boot? If not, fix it now.

3. Recognize them. The boss's time counts. So do little things. A high-technology firm held a two-day offsite meeting for distribution people, looking for new opportunities. The firm was careful to make sure that the setting and trappings were as lavish as those it provides for top management affairs.

4. Listen to them. Like Toshiba (see also C-7), provide regular senior management forums in which sales and service and support people can be heard.

5. Make sales and service a feeder route to general management and/or a necessary way-stop on the path to general management.

6. Empower them. Like Nordstrom or Federal Express, give the sales and service people wide latitude to act as "the company" when they are in the field or on the phone, and especially when they are confronting a problem.

7. Train them. No firm I know has ever overtrained sales, service, and support people. And make sure it's the right kind of training. One study of retail sales training revealed that twelve times as many hours were devoted to "cash register technique" and the policy manual as to selling skills and dealing with the problems of customers.

8. Support them technically. Make sure that the systems are in place which

187

allow them to do their job to the fullest extent possible. Federal Express people have time to spend on the customers and their needs/problems precisely because they are not burdened with a cumbersome set of forms to fill out. The system does the rote work, and provides, for example, instant information in response to any query via the truck's on-line computer system and the courier's hand-held computer.

9. Hire enough of them! Think hard about the example of Buckman Labs, about Frito-Lay, BusinessLand, and Nordstrom. All four have far too many salespeople, by industry standards. Seriously consider doubling or tripling your sales force (assuming minimal annual market growth) over the next three to five years.

As to the last point, I sadly observe that most firms' sales and service managements don't know how to dream. They are bewildered by the "what if you doubled the sales force" question. When there is a general 10 percent cutback, they automatically take a 10 percent cut too. Cost containment, not revenue enhancement, drives most firms.

When Japanese firms are faced with hard times, on the other hand, their instincts are the opposite. Assembly-line workers at automobile companies are sent out to sell. (Toyota recently sent 25,000 to the field.) Operations people in banks are sent out to seek new deposits. IBM, among U.S. firms, has followed this path, most recently in late 1986, when it moved 5,000 operations people into marketing (sales). To turn Seattle First National Bank around, chairman Richard Cooley used this Japanese tactic with great success. In fact, his temporarily unleashed "back room" people matched the firm's regular salespeople at signing up new accounts.

Then there is the "productivity increase" trap. We know that salespeople—or anyone else—can always be 10 percent more productive. If we are projecting flat or 5 percent market growth, we focus on making the salesperson 5 to 10 percent more productive, rather than adding to the force. I'm all for prudence and making sales and service people more productive. But return once again to our opening example: "We add a salesperson, and a year or so later, we've got $400,000 more revenue," says the chemical company president. No, it's not that simple. But surely it's a point well worth considering.

CATER TO DISTRIBUTORS, FRANCHISEES, WHOLESALERS, AND MANUFACTURERS' REPS

Now extend the discussion of sales and service persons to include members of the distribution channel not on the firm's payroll. The story is a carbon copy. Steelcase, a top-flight office-furniture maker, works only through dealers. McDonald's continues to soar. The dealer or franchisee is a cherished member of the family at both firms; it's almost as simple as that. Yet again, few seem to get it. Three salespeople "cover" 200 dealers or reps, or support 200 franchisees. Harvard's Bonoma has coined the revealing term "global mediocrity":

... Management attempts to make up for poor-quality distribution relationships with more distributors. Instead of fixing its distribution management structures and learning new ... habits about the "partnering" aspects of distributor relationships, management often just keeps adding distributors in an attempt to get the "right" ones that will have high vendor commitment despite few signs of reciprocity on the vendor's part.

Consider ... ten years' distribution history for a large recreational product supplier. ... Management seems to go in "great cycles" on the distribution problem, first overrecruiting marginal distributors, then in subsequent years winnowing out marginal ones. As the list gets winnowed, however, management appears to be dissatisfied still that it has the "right" partners, and rerecruits more distributors to begin the winnowing process again. Each time this happens, distributor sales, on average, go down. . . .

Indeed, management at this company spent little to no money and gave less attention to building the dealer "commitment" it claimed it so sorely wanted. Instead, it had a total of seven salespeople to manage the entire dealer net, did little training, and gave the salespeople wide latitude in both signing up new dealers and terminating old ones. In essence management ducked the marketing "homework" of making its current distributor relations work over the years by continual distributor replacement; when it recognized this and concentrated on building the commitment it spent so much time talking about, sales per dealer went up remarkably.

Bonoma reinforces these points, describing major differences in dealing with franchisees:

Two [real] donut chains, let's call them A and B, incorporate about the same time, using similar strategies of franchising for distribution breadth. Chain A's managers, wishing to retain as much control as possible over the delivered product, implement their strategy by charging high initial and ongoing royalties from franchisees, and putting in place a rigorous system for spot-checking restaurants by corporate staff. Management in Chain A knows it is "trading off" some greater number of potential franchisees for the higher royalties and tight controls, but it does so gladly. The corporate coffers, fattened by royalties, are used for an intensive franchisee support program to aid the franchised store owners. . . .

Things go well for both chains for some period, until headquarters management at both companies becomes dissatisfied with the "share of stomach" that donuts have in the overall menu of fast foods. Looking at consumers' behavior, both managements reason that if there were a broader menu ... customers might be more likely to stop at their outlets ... when donut demand is low. Expanding the menu requires the addition of stoves and griddles in the franchisee outlets. . . . The question is: Which chain will have an easier time getting its franchisees to part with the incremental investment necessary to make the strategic switch?

Clearly Chain A, with its fewer but better managed and perhaps more profitable franchisees, will be more likely to be able to make the strategic move toward a full-line fast food restaurant. Chain B, with its cadre of poorly controlled, independent, and too numerous outlets, which have received little from corporate except a product recipe and a sheaf of forms, may be expected to have a much more difficult time with the strategic switch.

A Strategy for Enhancing the Role of the Members of the Distribution Channel

My observations of the good news and the bad square precisely with Bonoma's, suggesting the following strategy:

1. Once more—time and attention. For instance, are the people in the distribution channel partners and members of the family invited in to every crucial setting (and not just on a token basis), listened to long before a proposal becomes a policy, seen as the prime source of new service and product ideas?

2. Give a lot, expect a lot, and if you don't get it, prune. Recall Bonoma's Chain A/Chain B example. Chain A gave a lot and demanded a lot; Chain B gave little and got little. Be a "Chain A" type. And if the dealer/rep/franchisee doesn't eventually come through, let him go.

U.S. automakers suffer from poor service delivery by their dealers, as well as from questionable quality. Yet they steadfastly refuse to do much about the former, trapped by the "global mediocrity" syndrome. As Cadillac dealer Carl Sewell says, "If GM would just drop a couple of dealers for giving lousy service, and broadcast it on the front page of *Automotive News,* we could turn the thing around."

Similarly, I've talked with many executives of fast-food and hotel chains who haven't dropped a franchisee in years. I acknowledge that it's tough; among other things, it means forgoing immediate revenue. Moreover, if you haven't enforced your rules (or never had any), tedious, even legal, disputes can ensue.

Reps scream the loudest when I suggest that they drop suppliers who are unreliable on quality or delivery, especially well-known suppliers. Yet even a few lousy suppliers cripple the rep.

My advice: If you're not setting high standards—with reps, dealers, wholesalers, and franchisees—and then pruning the bottom 2 or so percent each year, you are in for trouble in the customer responsiveness department.

3. Provide bold—extensive, expensive—support. This suggestion exactly parallels my closing point in connection with field sales, service, and support people. Think about doubling or trebling the support force that services your dealers and reps. Don't skimp on systems support either. Be bold! When I look at Frito-Lay or Disney, for example, I simply cannot conceive of anyone, in the public or private sector, overdoing it.

The American businessperson's holy grail is cost containment. Yet the surest way to cut unit costs is to spread them over greater revenue. This entire set of customer prescriptions, but none more than this one, suggests a new premier objective: revenue enhancement. (See also C-10.) Execution of the winning strategies laid out in prescriptions C-1 through C-6 begins by turning our neglected field troops and their supporters—those closest to the customer—into the company's heroes, rather than one more "cost element" to be optimized or minimized.

PUBLIC PARALLELS

Sadly, the public sector analogue is exact regarding this prescription. The nurse in the public hospital and the elementary and secondary school classroom teacher should be the nation's heroes. They are not.

In Vermont, the people who drive the snow-clearing vehicles in the winter stand tall with their fellow citizens. Business—indeed life itself—would grind to a halt were they to give less than their all, and we know it. Likewise, the utility lineman after a storm, or the firefighter, is at least a hero during his or her short interludes of dramatic action.

But what about the garbage collectors and bus drivers? And the clerks in the planning and zoning office? And the crews that patch potholes? They are the front-line deliverers of a city's most visible day-by-day services. The public, including numerous elected officials, has a nasty habit of lumping all these people together and calling them "public dole bureaucrats."

To be sure, the public sector has its share of obfuscating, narrow-minded bureaucrats. And I'm on their case as much as I'm on the case of obfuscating, mischief-making private sector bureaucrats. But Betsy Sanders's analysis holds for the public sector too—when you see a front-line employee with a lousy attitude, and an "I just enforce the rules" mentality, it's not the clerk's fault at Podunk's City Hall any more than it's the clerk's fault at Macy's in Palo Alto.

Baltimore's transit boss, Ron Hartman, came up with an innovative answer to this. He wanted to reward good performance from bus drivers. Not fazed by the public sector's inability to give tangible rewards, he figured that downtown merchants benefited from good transit service. So he solicited gifts from them to give to top drivers (such as free meals and movie tickets) in return for free advertising space on the buses.

Every time a driver gets a positive letter from a customer, she or he gets an award. And roving supervisors carry movie tickets and restaurant chits with them. If they notice a driver performing a meritorious act, they give out an award on the spot.

FIRST STEPS

Can you answer the question: "Do my sales and service and indirect support people feel like heroes?" If not, get out and get that answer— among other things, ask customers (end users and all members of the distribution channel). Commit now to three visible activities per month with (1) field sales and service people and (2) their indirect counterparts at such places as reservation and distribution centers.

C-10

SUMMARY

With everything up for grabs in every market, we must:

▶ Become customer-obsessed.

Opportunity now lies, not with perfecting routines, but with taking advantage of instability—that is, creating opportunities from the daily discontinuities of the turbulent marketplace. To do this, the customer, in spirit and in flesh, must pervade the organization—every system in every department, every procedure, every measure, every meeting, every decision.

Make a customer-obsessed revolution. Routinely look at the smallest nuance of the tiniest program through the customer's eyes—that is, as the customer perceives it, not you. Make champions of change in support of the customer, not guardians of internal stability, the new corporate heroes in every function.

C-10

Launch a Customer Revolution

When he was mayor of Baltimore, Don Schaefer, the present governor of Maryland, had a sheet of drawing paper taped to the wall of his office, handwritten with a black felt-tipped pen. It read:

#1. PEOPLE
#2. Do It Now.
#3. Do It Right The First Time
#4. Do It Within Budget
#5. Would You Like To Live There?

If you pass the first four hurdles, but can't leap the fifth, you've missed the whole point.

That's a true customer orientation. Every action, no matter how small, and no matter how far from the firing line a department may be, must be processed through the customer's eyes. "Will this make it easier for the customer?" "Faster?" "Better?" "Less expensive?" "Will the customer be more profitable because of it?"

No department, including legal and accounting, should exist to "protect the firm." If you want to avoid badly aged receivables, there's a simple solution: Make every customer pay 100 percent of the purchase price in cash at the time of ordering. The problem, of course, is that you'll have no customers.

EMPHASIZE REVENUE ENHANCEMENT

The business equation is simple: Profit equals revenue minus cost. Or maybe it's slightly more complicated: <u>Long-term profit equals revenue from continuously happy customer relationships minus cost.</u>

Many firms' cost structures are out of whack, to be sure. Nonetheless, our obsession for the past few decades has been with cost containment rather than revenue enhancement. The ten prescriptions for achieving total customer responsiveness suggest shifting the focus to revenue enhancement—e.g., when

195

times are tough, add salespersons, don't cut the sales department's travel budget.

Domino's Phil Bressler, addressing fellow franchisees, states the case for revenue enhancement in plain language:

A couple of my managers just went out and bought some nonprofitable stores. The first thing they wanted to know is how to get 'em profitable. And the first thing I said was "Forget it." When you forget profitability, it comes to you. When you worry about it, the customer invariably gets hurt. We've got one guy who took over a $6,500 [per week in revenue] store and he's got it up to $12,500 in four months. He's running horrible costs, and he's barely making money. I just keep telling him, "Forget about it," because he's going to have a $20,000-a-week store in about three months. Sales building is the way to profitability. You can only cut your costs so low before they hurt the customer. You can never raise your sales too high. Just to emphasize, we do a house-by-house analysis in our store in Towson [Maryland], which has the best market penetration of any Domino's Pizza store in the country. It does $35,000 a week, $2.00 per address, $6.49 average ticket price. So we've got a lot of customers, but we found that among the 17,000 addresses, we only have 1,700 customers. Ten percent! I felt like just going crazy. We should be doing $70,000 a week. But that's our best market penetration [among 3,800 stores] in Domino's Pizza. So look at the potential you have. You only have 10 percent of your area, at most. The sky's the limit.

Even when our theories have focused on revenue enhancement, the approach has often been flawed. We have overemphasized: (1) buying market share through low price, (2) increasing sales through marketing devices, and (3) buying and selling businesses until some on-paper Nirvana of "cash cows" and growth stars has been collected in one optimal portfolio.

The advice here is contrarian. I suggest: (1) any product can be wildly differentiated and made into a value-added winner, even—perhaps especially—in the oldest, dullest, and most ordinary commodity-like arenas; (2) not only does quality pay—everywhere—with new business, but it is better than free, actually leading to huge cost reductions as it goes up; (3) "service-added" and an emphasis on the intangibles may be an even better basis for differentiation than quality, though it does cost money; (4) radical increases in responsiveness are possible, and they, too, may save money (because they are impossible without flatter organizations with less management, they require less inventory, etc.); and (5) market creation (creating new niches) and relationship building with customers and members of the distribution channel should replace marketing gimmicks and devices as the mainstay of achieving a thoroughly customer-obsessed firm.

The above turns marketing on its ear, in big ways and small. TRW's Groocock comments on how hard it is to get a market research department to do quality-oriented market research; that is, to focus on the relative quality of your and your competitors' offerings. Silicon Valley's McKenna observes the wrenching difficulty in moving firms from a market-sharing mentality to a market-creating mind-set, from an emphasis on glitzy advertising and promotional gimmicks to an emphasis on word-of-mouth-reputation development, and from an emphasis on the tangible traits of a product or service to an emphasis on intangible traits.

All of the changes rest on the base of people's attitudes. Above all, the customer prescriptions deal with new skills, not new devices. We emphasize, in C-2 through C-4, that the passion for quality, service, and responsiveness has to be matched with world-class systems—the techniques of Crosby or Deming, the support systems that mark The Limited or Federal Express. That element is vital. Nonetheless, an overall emphasis on customer-oriented skill building is primary: (1) problem-solving skills for all to achieve consistent quality improvement; (2) naïve listening skills to understand the intangible attributes of a product in the customer's eyes; (3) a shift from adversarial to cooperative relations within the firm aimed at smashing age-old structural barriers and hierarchies in order to achieve lightning-fast responsiveness; (4) learning to work as partners with suppliers and distributors, rather than as contractually driven adversaries; (5) empowering front-line sales and service people to solve (and want to solve) most problems on the spot, rather than buck them up or blame them on "the system"; and (6) treating every customer, for groceries or a supercomputer, as (a) a "market segment" with special needs and (b) as someone with whom we wish to develop a lasting relationship.

REVOLUTION IS MANDATORY

To turn virtually all our basic assumptions upside down is a daunting task. But it is the easier of the two challenges which these prescriptions lay down. The second half of achieving a customer obsession reminds you that we are looking toward epic increases, not incremental ones:

1. In C-1, I did not ask you to "think about a value-added orientation." I asked you to shift your entire portfolio toward value-added products and services—fast. And I then insisted that every product or service can be wildly differentiated; and, further, no matter how wildly differentiated it is, you should set monthly quantitative targets for differentiating it more.

2. In C-2, I didn't ask for quality improvement, I asked for a *revolution,* carefully choosing that word. Remember Toyota's march from 5,000 to almost two million suggestions, IBM's hundredfold improvement in quality in old technologies. And remember "Old Man" Coleman's passion for perfect stoves, boilers, etc. Moreover, I offered compelling evidence that (a) the payoff in revenue enhancement from quality improvement is enormous, *and* (b) as a side benefit you can save money (remember, poor-quality costs run from 25 to 40 percent of people and assets) if you really do it right the first time.

3. In C-3, recall the Nordstrom vignettes: They, too, constitute a revolution—that is, a revolutionary attitude about the limitless possibilities for serving the customer and adding intangible benefits to your products—and reaping profits.

4. In C-4, once again revolution was the rallying cry. Slash lead times by 90 percent—and many are doing just that. Link up electronically with 75 percent of your customers in the next 24 months—or be prepared to go broke when a competitor does so first. Smash functional factory barriers and get all functions working together to do everything several times faster than it's now being done.

> Note: All of these apparently squishy traits (C-1 through C-4) can be—indeed, must be—measured: differentiators added, quality as perceived by customers and the cost of quality, the customer's perception of service and the intangibles, and response times. There is nothing "soft" about these matters.

5. Small firm as well as large: Go international. Go even to Japan, and prosper. That's what C-5 demanded. The emphasis was once again on skill building and hard work: Learn the language. Visit numerous times, only semi-purposefully, to begin to build relationships. Tailor everything to local requirements from the start. And expect years with modest returns.

6. C-6 boils down the challenges of C-1 through C-5. Develop a twenty-five-word statement of uniqueness that captures the essence of your approach to distinction in the marketplace. Make sure that the most recently hired mailroom denizen understands it, within twenty-four hours of his or her coming on board. Strategy statements which include all the "right stuff" are great, but they are useless until understood, believed, and cared about on the loading dock at 2 A.M.

7. With C-7, concerning listening skills, I began the examination of what is necessary to achieve the market survival strategies represented by C-1 through C-6. Developing a true listening orientation poses radical challenges, too: every marketer in the field 50 percent of the time; every production worker out with customers several times a year. Top it off with an attitude that says, "Treat customers as though they speak a foreign language"—they do.

8. In C-8—revolution once more. Turn manufacturing (or operations) from a "cost center" to the chief marketing weapon. Every aspect of the factory or operations center must be aligned with the customer obsession—including all hands' direct involvement with customers.

9. The idea of C-9—turning sales, service, and support people into the firm's heroes—also bespeaks revolution. And once more it's essential to quantify. Think about Nordstrom's "overstaffing" (and its sevenfold growth since 1978, in tough markets, without acquisitions), about Frito-Lay's well-equipped 10,000-person sales force (and $330 million in annual profit), and the chemical firm that can't help itself—add a salesperson, and a year or so later a half million in revenues accrues. I asked you to consider doubling the sales force. And I

asked you to take the top service and distribution people to the Breakers in West Palm Beach for their annual meeting, as you may have been doing with your top salespeople for years.

This last customer prescription attempts to capture the flavor of the nine *other* revolutions I've asked for so far. The sum of the nine revolutions represented by C-1 through C-9 is the customer-obsessed organization.

GET STARTED—NOW

The good news is: You have no choice. No organization, from the newest boutique on Union Street in San Francisco to Dayton, Ohio's public utility, from IBM and Du Pont to GM, is secure. Each of these prescriptions, then, is a "must-do." And no city or state is safe. Like it or not, the competition for jobs is now brutal. Employers are asking for the impossible: bigger tax breaks and better schools and highways and employee training. Moreover, cities and states are competitively selling their services to others, from energy to data systems management, in an effort to increase their revenue and spread their costs further. In health care, it's the same story: more market-driven, value-added distinctions—and simultaneously lowered costs.

To say that you have no choice is not to say, "Take on all ten at once." Recall the brief note on "patterns" at the end of C-2. I traced the evolution of five successful quality/responsiveness programs and suggested that Ford et al. had been wise not to try everything at once.

I still think that is sound advice. But the spirit of C-10 says something more. While you must wrestle with the timing of specific programs for quality and listening, you should and can get to work on shaping the organization toward a wholesale customer orientation, across the board, this afternoon.

Detailed programs, such as new training and supporting systems, are necessary parts of this revolution (see also I-1 through I-10, P-1 through P-10). But instilling a "we live for customers" attitude can become your overriding action agenda today. Tack your own version of Governor Schaefer's chart on your real or mental wall this afternoon, and pass every action through Schaefer's sieve #5: "Would you like to live there?"—i.e., how does it feel to the customer?

FIRST STEPS

The last word is reserved for Domino's Bressler: "At the crew meetings, I get the crew together and ask each one of them, 'What have you done for the customer today?' We put up all the stories, what they've done, and then we vote. I give the manager who's done the best deed for the customer an award. And then I tell him to go give one to one of his people. So they hold the same contest at their store. That gets your people to think about what the customer is." In a way, it is that simple; this final vignette speaks a thousand words about the underlying mind-set of the customer-obsessed organization—and leader.

What ten small, measured steps will you take this week to begin to instill a "customer obsession" throughout your unit or firm?

III

PURSUING FAST-PACED *I*NNOVATION

SECTION SUMMARY

If responding with almost unimaginable alacrity to customer whims (creating new, value-added markets) is the superordinate objective, fast-paced innovation is the chief enabling device—and the subject of prescriptions I-1 through I-10 (see Figure 11).

Strip away the nonessentials, and innovation—in personnel and accounting as well as in product development, in schools and police departments as well as in industry—is a numbers game. Thus, the Guiding Premise here, I-1, is: Invest in application-oriented small starts.

What turns a low-odds start into a successful innovation? There are Four Strategies: I-2, team-based product development, which involves all key functions (and key outsiders including suppliers, distributors, and customers); I-3, encouraging rapid and practical tests (pilots) in the field, instead of getting bogged down writing long proposals unsupported by hard data; I-4, the practice of "creative swiping" (and adaptation) of ideas from *anyone, anywhere,* including competitors; and I-5, selling the new product or service via systematic word-of-mouth marketing "campaigns."

Four principal Management Tactics to Encourage Innovation are next: I-6, support for persistent and passionate champions, necessary to sustain innovators in general in the face of low odds and corporate rebuffs; I-7, "managing" your daily affairs to purposefully stand up for innovation efforts (which I call "modeling innovation"); I-8, supporting thoughtful failures (from which something is learned) and defying silly rules which impede fast action-taking; and I-9, "demanding" innovation through measurement and reward systems which apply "hard"-number targets to what has been traditionally conceived as a "soft" variable.

Finally, I-10 describes the newly adaptive firm, in which the general capacity to innovate is maximized.

It is essential to note that while these prescriptions are separable, the true impact comes from all ten working to reinforce one another.

Figure 11: **Pursuing Fast-Paced Innovation**

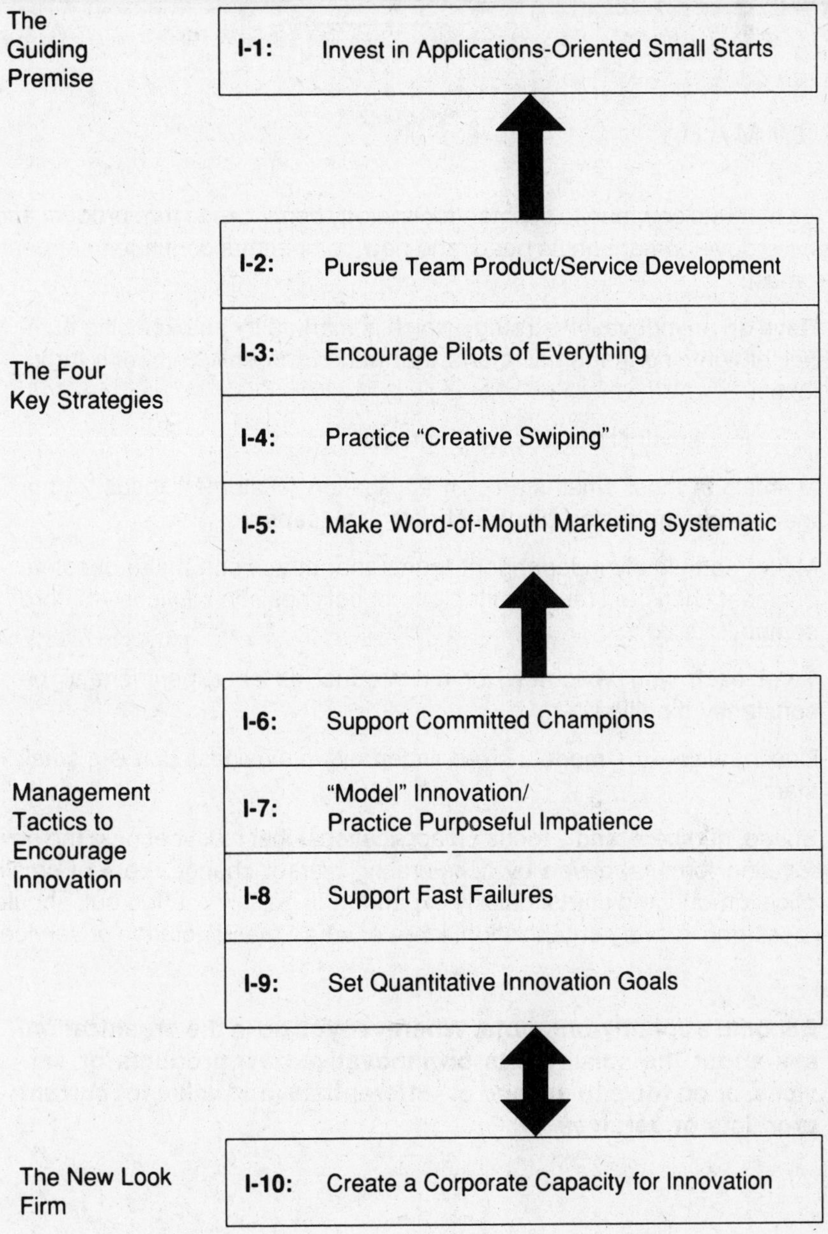

The
Guiding
Premise

| I-1: | Invest in Applications-Oriented Small Starts |

The Four
Key Strategies

I-2:	Pursue Team Product/Service Development
I-3:	Encourage Pilots of Everything
I-4:	Practice "Creative Swiping"
I-5:	Make Word-of-Mouth Marketing Systematic

Management
Tactics to
Encourage
Innovation

I-6:	Support Committed Champions
I-7:	"Model" Innovation/ Practice Purposeful Impatience
I-8	Support Fast Failures
I-9:	Set Quantitative Innovation Goals

The New Look
Firm

| I-10: | Create a Corporate Capacity for Innovation |

203

I-1

SUMMARY

As markets continue to splinter, technology continues to turn product and service development on its head, and new competitors continue to appear, we must:

► Develop an innovation strategy which is marked by an explosive number of lightning-fast small starts that match the environment's turbulence.

► Aim most small starts at small markets.

► Maintain in most small starts an application (customer) focus, rather than overemphasizing giant technological leaps.

► Mount completely independent teams that attack and make obsolete our most cherished (and profitable) product lines and services—before competitors do.

► Treat each would-be, new, or old product as an experiment to be constantly modified.

► Decentralize—the modest-sized, independent business unit *is* a small start.

Speed, numbers, and a focus on application—that must become the new innovation formula, driven by accelerating market change. Lots of small, application-oriented starts, quickly expanded or quickly snuffed out, should be occurring in every organization, large or small, manufacturing or service.

Become a Johnny-one-note: Wherever you go in the organization, ask about the small starts on innovative new products or services, or on tools to expand or differentiate (add value to) current products or services.

Invest in Applications-Oriented Small Starts

U.S. firms have a tendency to shoot for the best technology or massive markets while ignoring other, less glamorous products for which there is a market demand.

> *Industry Week*
> on Japan's success in R&D
> May 1987

You can't get the CEO of a $5 billion company excited about a $100,000 market like ceramic scissor blades or razor blades. We shoot right from the start for the ceramic [auto] engine. We don't want to go through the learning process in smaller markets.

> Dr. Lee Rivers
> Director of Corporate Planning
> Allied-Signal

Where is all this great stuff coming from? It's not really coming out of IBM. . . . It's coming out of little two- and three-man companies, because they're finding out that forty guys can't do something that three people can do. It's just the law of human nature.

> Roger Smith
> Chairman, General Motors
> on the source of innovative systems
> for the Saturn Project
> *Detroit Free Press,* March 1985

[Breakthrough] projects the entrepreneurs initiated and carried through had one essential quality. All had been thoroughly contemplated by the regnant experts and dominant companies, with their large research staffs and financial resources, and had been judged too difficult, untimely, risky, expensive and unprofitable.

> George Gilder
> *The Spirit of Enterprise*

THE UNPREDICTABILITY OF INNOVATION
DEFEATS EXCESSIVE PLANNING

The essence of successful innovation is, and always has been, constant experimentation. Plans and basic research are important, but frequent tests in small markets are more important.

▶ The Sharper Image catalog is advertising Porta Copy. It's a hand-held copier from Japan, measuring 6¼″ × 3¼″ × 1¾″ and weighing less than two pounds. It is not from Xerox, or even Fuji Xerox, and it represents a typical Japanese market foray: it is (1) customer/application-oriented; it is (2) a small product for (3) a small market (at first, anyway); and (4) the technology is not yet perfected.

▶ Japan first entered the European auto market via Finland. No one worried about a Japanese "incursion" there; it was out of sight—almost literally. In the small, "invisible" Finnish market, the Japanese experimented with new features for European consumers. Only later, with trial—and error—largely out of the way, did they launch their full-blown European "invasion."

In Part I, I discussed the systematic evidence of the dismal record of giant firms with regard to innovation: it costs them three to ten times more to develop comparable products; they are late in development or adoption of most new technologies; and they are not, as conventional wisdom has long had it, more prone to take on risky projects (in fact, they are much less prone to do so). This may have been tolerable in the past—U.S. Steel (now USX) survived for decades in our oligopolistic market despite its late adoption of every major new technology. But this will no longer do.

As McKinsey director Dick Foster argues in *Innovation: The Attacker's Advantage,* most big firms are trapped by inertia. The few that do maintain their innovative edge learn to be "close to ruthless in cannibalizing their current products and processes *just when they are most lucrative* [my emphasis] and begin the search again, over and over." The best, he adds, "abandon the skills and products that have brought them success."

This is strong language. What are the root causes of the almost inevitable loss of innovativeness in bigger firms? The list is topped by (1) slowness to move to test new ideas, (2) a bias toward conceptual research rather than application, and a concomitant overdependence on (3) ponderous planning systems and (4) Big Projects. Planning and thoughtful resource allocation surely make sense, but innovation is an inherently messy and unpredictable business, growing more so every day. And the unpredictability cannot be removed, or perhaps even substantially reduced, by excessive planning.

Patterns of Innovation: The (Typical) Case of the VCR

What do RCA, CBS, Bell & Howell, Polaroid, Magnavox, Kodak, Sears, MITI, David Sarnoff, and Bing Crosby have in common? What do Masaru Ibuka, Alexander Poniatoff, Cartridge Television Inc., Andre Blay, George Atkinson, and Stuart Karl have in common? The first set is a partial list of famous names that tried to invent or sell video recorders—and failed. The second list consists of the unknown producers and distributors who succeeded in making the VCR revolution (some subsequently also failed).

The making and marketing of the VCR in the 1970s and 1980s, as recounted in *Fast Forward* by James Lardner, is a garden-variety story of a major innovation. The mega-projects in mega-firms yielded nothing. Gut instincts prevailed. The wrong people bought the product—and then misapplied it. The wrong people sold it. A (then) young company with a small reputation (Sony) was pitted against MITI—and won. Little (then) Ampex of Redwood City, California, called "Hobby Lobby" by RCA, did in RCA, David Sarnoff, and the gigantic David Sarnoff Research Center. Then Ampex, with desks sporting signs that said "Help stamp out transistors," was done in by Sony. Tiny start-up Cartridge Television Inc. of Palo Alto, California, did it even faster than Sony—but made the mistake of selling through Sears, and is now defunct. Sears et al. were usurped by Blay, Atkinson, and company, who created a whole new distribution industry—video stores. (In the end, the Beta-max-format machine of now-big Sony lost out to the longer-playing VHS format of Matsushita et al.)

Listed below are four attributes of the VCR story, each of which has implications for innovation generally.

1. The "big guys" build big, non-adaptive, complex projects—and fail. RCA and CBS had head starts on video recording. Their projects were marked by (1) old ideas (RCA et al. unimaginatively saw the video recorder as just a "souped-up audio recorder"), (2) engineers in vast numbers in isolated labs, and (3) executive ego. They failed, as did Kodak, Magnavox, Bell & Howell, Zenith, et al. The big guys, with big (internal) political stakes, don't proceed by trial and error. They bet on one big project and can't afford to have it turn out poorly. Lardner reports, "[The American projects] were conceived on such an expensive scale as to leave no room for trial and error, . . . no opportunity to bring a flawed product to market (as Sony had done . . .), learn from it, and persist."

2. The "little guys" fight adversity, move fast, and often fail too—but create the revolution. Ampex, Cartridge Television Inc., and Sony did what RCA et al. could not do. Physically far from the center of things and underfunded, they thought new thoughts and moved fast. All three eventually failed.

All fought long odds. Sony, for instance, was stalled for years trying to buy, for only $25,000, the rights to use Bell Labs' transistor. MITI, carefully controlling Japan's export of then scarce funds, saw the matter as an untried company dealing with an untried technology; and besides, Toshiba, Hitachi, et al. were working with RCA on the transistor. (Sony eventually won approval and, despite the delays, beat the big guys in Japan as well as the United States by years in starting production.)

3. The winners were customer- (consumer-) oriented, though the path to the consumer was tortuous and required remarkable persistence. Ampex was engineering-driven. Sony was consumer-driven. Ampex engineers saw a market for only thirty machines; they stuck with vacuum tubes and added bells and whistles to meet every single customer's need.

Sony founder Masaru Ibuka (less well known than his partner Akio Morita) said that the U.S. players were misled by defense and space work, where money and complexity were no issue: ". . . They have no idea how to apply high technology to [the] consumer field. But I changed [the] idea. 'First for consumer' is my idea." This bias persists in Sony to this day. The firm beat Matsushita and Philips (the original inventor) with a CD player that was one-twentieth the size and one-third the cost of earlier models. Lardner reports that Sony executive Kozo Ohsone carved out a block of wood about an inch-and-a-half thick and five inches square, barely bigger than the disc itself. The idea was "to persuade the engineers. I told them we would not accept the question 'Why this size?' That was our size and that was it." (The origins of the Sony Walkman are similar—based upon consumer use; the designer observed Californians on roller skates—see C-7.)

In all these cases, Sony proudly turned its back on market research and produced simple, "user-friendly" designs by gut instinct.* Even so, the course of the revolution was not foreseen. For instance, early VCR sales were to schools, where the complex Ampex machine was intended for use by the audio-visual professional; Sony designed for the teacher or student, not the expert (Steven Jobs did something similar at Apple). Nevertheless, the early machines were still far too complex and inflexible, and Sony's breakthrough with its landmark U-matic was not a consumer sale, but a sale to CBS News, which bought a U-matic and a lightweight Japanese video camera produced by Ikegami to cover Nixon's 1974 visit to Moscow. Lardner concludes: "Decisively rejected by the [school] market for which it had been intended, the U-matic became a stunning success just the same."

4. History repeated itself in every phase of the process. The distribution drama was a replay of the saga of invention itself. While Sears et al. stumbled in normal channels, Andre Blay succeeded: outsider Blay founded the Video Club of America. Soon George Atkinson, equally unknown, made the next leap, renting to Howard Johnson, Holiday Inn, Shakey's Pizza, et al. Lardner comments: "The studios . . . found themselves dealing with the 'video software dealer,' a species of small businessperson whose existence they had never contemplated." The trend of hits by the "wrong" players knew no bounds in this standard story of innovation. As the initial home movie rental trend peaked, the VCR boom spawned the "how to" video boom, but, as Lardner explains, "it was

---

*This went too far, however, when Sony persisted with the Betamax format in the face of the even more customer-friendly design of the VHS.

not every Hollywood executive who could make the necessary mental leap." Thus, it was young Stuart Karl who turned from waterbeds to home video and created *Jane Fonda's Workout,* starting another revolution.

As usual, the big guys fought change every inch of the way. Much of Lardner's book is devoted to the studios' litigation with Sony over copying tapes. The studios also fought movie rentals, assuming it would destroy movie-going; instead, it turned out that video rental regulars were inclined to go to movies more often.

Face It, We All Guess Wrong About the Future

"For God's sake, go down to reception and get rid of a lunatic who's down there. He says he's got a machine for seeing by wireless! Watch him—he may have a razor on him."—Editor of the *Daily Express* of London, refusing to see John Baird, the inventor of television, in 1925.

"Who in the hell wants to hear actors talk?"—Harry Warner, founder of Warner Bros. Studio, in 1927.

"I think there is a world market for about five computers."—Thomas J. Watson, chairman of IBM, in 1943.

"There is no reason for any individual to have a computer in their home."—Ken Olsen, president of Digital Equipment, in 1977.

For the story of the VCR, I could have substituted the saga of upstart McDonald's and the launching of the fast-food revolution; American Express and the credit card; or Genentech (versus the big pharmaceutical houses) and the commercial application of biotechnology. The established experts and the big companies and their planners are wrong time and again. Even if they were once pioneers, they seem rapidly to become overly conservative about the future (e.g., the video recorder as just a "souped-up audio recorder") and overly optimistic once a product comes along (not foreseeing the decade or more of trial and error—twenty-five years in the case of the VCR—between the first, halting prototype and widespread use).

ACT SMALL/START SMALL/BREAK INTO SMALL UNITS OR TEAMS: A SOLUTION FOR BIG FIRMS

Big firms must act like a collection of smaller ones when it comes to innovation:

▶ Numerous small starts—experiments, really—must constantly be made.
▶ The small starts must usually be aimed at small markets.
▶ The small starts for small markets should have an applications orientation.
▶ Multiple, major, unbridled efforts must regularly be launched to knock your best products and services off their profitable perches before some new competitor does so.

▶ Radical, continual decentralization must be pursued—"horizontal" growth via the addition of new business units, rather than "vertical" growth by development of bigger, functionally organized units.

In short, while innovation requires thoughtfulness (I am a staunch fan of high R&D spending), it nonetheless boils down by and large to a speed and numbers game—in the marketplace, not the boardroom.

Break the "Think Big" Mind-set

Big firms have a tough time thinking small. In *The Next Economy,* economist and businessman Paul Hawken offers an insightful look at the flawed reasoning of large American enterprises, concluding with a half dozen "letters" to business chieftains in which he proposes strategies to deal with the changing nature of business. In one to Clifton Garvin, Jr., then Exxon's chairman, he observes: "Because you are a big business, you are trapped by doing things in large ways. But it is one thing to start a business that becomes large and entirely another to start things on a large scale. You should imitate nature, where meaningful beginnings are almost always unnoticeable. I suspect no one could have predicted that the commodity firm of Clark & Rockefeller [the eventual Esso/Exxon] would [become] the world's largest company."

3M does better at making small starts than any other giant firm I've come across. No project is too small for its consideration, despite its $9 billion size. Team product development (see I-2) at Procter & Gamble, Du Pont, and other firms also marks a major effort to downsize and speed up development efforts. A major reorganization at Campbell Soup in 1982 to create small business units (see Part I and C-4), IBM's formation of Independent Business Units, Milliken's launching of thousands of Customer Action Teams (see C-4), and even GM's decision to start up Saturn as a separate corporation (its first such move in over fifty years) are all part of the same effort.

Surround "Big" (if Necessary) by "Small"

The small-starts idea has endless variations. Big, hyperorganized projects must be surrounded by small-start projects and partial projects. For instance, a senior GM manager describes several innovations developed by informal groups outside the main "planning process" that paved the way for major project successes in his firm. From just one maverick band came (1) the soft bumper system for the 1973 Corvette, (2) the "friendly fender" for the Fiero, (3) fiberglass wheels for 1986 models, (4) a fiberglass spring (the invention involved "commandeering a computer"), and (5) fiberglass bumper beams for the 1980 Corvette. He concludes: "The paperless skunkwork operation gets things done in one-tenth of the time with very little money." At Pacific Bell, a system was required for automating a million transactions. Two estimates were received, one from a big, outside firm (three years, $10 million) and one from a major Pacific Bell unit (two years, $5 million). Meanwhile, three South California employees took a crack at the task—and did it in sixty days for $40,000.

Act Small/Buy Small: Another Big-Firm Solution

Still another uncharacteristic, small-start route can be followed by big firms—tiny acquisitions. For example, a few years ago, The Limited, with over 2,800 shops, bought a four-store chain, Victoria's Secret. Today they've expanded that "small start" to 160 stores—and are starting again, with the purchase of a single Manhattan store, Henri Bendel, in 1986.

The Small Start: Genuine Autonomy Required

Despite the success stories, acting small, if you are big, is much easier said than done. A new-product team in a big company has a tough time achieving true independence. *Innovation: The Attacker's Advantage* traces, for instance, Du Pont's loss of leadership to Celanese when tire cord shifted from a nylon to a polyester base. To its credit, Du Pont, with a 75 percent market share in nylon-based cord, hedged its bet by mounting experimental efforts in polyester once it learned that others were doing so. Unfortunately, however, Du Pont's start-up polyester team was forced to test its experimental product at the tire cord development center—run by the dominant (and very profitable) nylon department. Not surprisingly, the kindly advice and worldly cautions offered by the experts in that setting brought Du Pont's polyester project to a standstill. Meanwhile, Celanese, with no entrenched and profitable position in nylon to defend, entered the market for polyester tire cord with alacrity and quickly captured a 75 percent share. Thus, the small start alone is not enough. The small start unit must be truly independent of the current dominant business.

Keep the Funding Lean and the Apparatus Simple

Another big-company, big-project factor that impedes innovation bears particular mention here—too much money. In my experience, the well-funded big team seldom produces much of anything. Likewise, the small acquisition inundated with the new parent's money usually veers off course. The pressure is off. The project becomes too elaborate. Failures are met with more spending and more elaboration. Every nut, bolt, or piece of software is designed afresh, even if the project is presented as an "urgent, bet the company" move. One study cited in *The Bigness Complex* underscores this, observing that most successful innovation is the product of relatively primitive machinery—and that includes the most exotic of high-tech wizardry. Here's a description of the primitive scrounging associated with one of the most sophisticated high-energy-physics experiments ever undertaken:

At Saclay, outside Paris, the French learned that they had promised that the scintillator in their gondolas would turn out five times more light than was physically possible. They spent the next two years rethinking scintillator technology, and searching for a plastic that would give them enough light without costing more than the whole UA1 detector put together. When they found one that would do the trick, it turned out to have been purified by a German chemist in his spare time at home. So they talked the chemist's firm into developing the plastic as a research project, which meant that they could get the 12 tons they required. Then they found a shower-stall manufacturer in Belgium that would turn the German plastic into high-tech physics apparatus. They moved their computers and their sophisticated testing equipment into the shower factory to check the plastic as it rolled off the assembly lines.

The account is from *Nobel Dreams,* which describes Carlo Rubbia's winning of the 1984 Nobel Prize in physics. Rubbia's win ended years of European frustration at the hands of Americans: "Until Rubbia came along, the United States had owned high-energy physics. From 1950 through the end of the last decade, Americans had made virtually every major discovery and won nearly every Nobel Prize. . . . No matter how tough the European competition was in physics, the Americans always beat them. In the seventies, European physicists seemed to be regrouping. Yet even though CERN [the European Organization for Nuclear Research] had the most powerful accelerator in the world by a factor of ten, and a budget as great as all of the U.S. labs put together, the American physicists still somehow came up with the three most notable and clearcut discoveries of the decade, and all the Nobel prizes." Author Gary Taubes concludes that the long-frustrated Europeans "had a problem with money. Unlike the Americans, they had too much of it."

Small Starts/Small Stops: Cut It Quick if Necessary

Small starts (in small markets) can be (1) cut off quickly and (2) modified quickly. "Big" projects involve big political stakes (recall RCA and the VCR); when failure is imminent, it is (1) hidden or (2) "fixed" by further elaboration (which usually leads to bigger failures). Furthermore, "big project" failures usually lead to such a souring of attitudes toward an idea that it cannot be readily resurrected, even in an entirely new form.

Small Starts/Application Bias: Invent for the User

The small start by the small, independent team is usually application/market/customer oriented—by definition. The emphasis on a small market means that the project is already aimed at a narrow, practical application.

"Big" projects, on the other hand, are usually driven by the science or "the big idea." Customer involvement and customer-derived content are minimal.

Small Starts: Beyond New Products

"Small starts" as an approach to innovation applies to every activity, not just new product or service development (see also I-3). *The Economist* reported on the innovation pattern of the few American firms that have been successful at adopting flexible manufacturing approaches:

> [These firms] are neither "visionaries" nor "ostriches." People in the trade call them "evolutionists." All of them have been nibbling away at computer-integrated manufacturing *without committing themselves to overly ambitious projects* [my emphasis]. As a rule, they have tended first to computerise their machine tools, creating "islands of automation." Next, they have streamlined their scheduling departments, slimming down the wadges of bumph [masses of paper] they produce. Only then have they linked the two departments together, so the machines receive their instructions and materials precisely when, and only when, they are needed.

Topping *The Economist*'s list (and my own) among those who have followed this "small starts" strategy are Hewlett-Packard, Allen-Bradley, and Chrysler. An executive of a European systems software house concurs. Successful European firms have followed what he calls a "prototype" strategy, starting small and learning one's way forward. Less successful firms have spent years and tons of money developing a rigid master plan. They have been locked in from the start, as a result of attitude and of capital expenditure, to a grand design that seldom holds up, but which they are unwilling to scuttle as implementation begins.

ACT SMALL/START SMALL: A GOOD IDEA FOR SMALL FIRMS, TOO

The small-start advice applies equally to small firms. I've observed that most initially successful small firms fail because a good *second* product or service isn't developed in a timely fashion. That's usually because a dominant founder attempts to replicate the process that brought about his or her first success. Since so many fortuitous events are involved in a success, including a raging fire in the belly, the odds of replication are slight. Seeding multiple small starts is as much a must for the three-year-old $1.5 million firm as for AT&T, though the scale of a "small start" will differ in the two cases.

NO EXCEPTIONS TO THE SMALL-START STRATEGY

What About the Japanese?

Many react to the discussion of small starts with some variation of "But aren't the hyper-organized Japanese the epitome of 'big start'/'big project' thinking?" The answer is a resounding "no." Jim Abegglen and George Stalk, Jr., in *Kaisha: The Japanese Corporation,* argue that instead, incremental improvements and rapid response to competitors, achieved through factory- and customer-driven actions, are the key to Japan's success:

Kaisha respond and rarely leave an initiative by competitors unmet. The response is often very fast and, in the case of manufactured products, is offered with a flurry of new product introductions. . . . Western management generally prefers a more carefully considered process of responding to competitors' initiatives. Some initiatives are met and others are rationalized away. Typical rationalizations include the arguments that the new [Japanese] products are not significant improvements or that the market does not really want the product.

The effects of these very different responses to competitive initiatives are beginning to show. For example, Japanese automobile manufacturers are selling cars with four-valve engines, electronically controlled suspensions, ceramic engine components, turbochargers with intercoolers, lightweight nonmetallic body panels, synthesized-voice hazard and diagnostic warnings and more. Most of these innovations are unavailable in Western automobiles except, occasionally, in the highest premium optional offerings. Similar product innovation gaps are observable in Japanese air conditioning equipment, machine tools, robotics, vending machines, and parking meters, to name just a few.

The common Western response to emerging innovation gaps appears dangerously naïve. The line of reasoning goes something like this: "The Japanese competitors are not using any technology or innovation we are not already aware of. We could do the same if we wanted to. Anyway, it does not do us much good to copy them—our challenge is to 'leap frog' them." While the Western competitors consider the virtues of an appropriate response to Japanese innovation, the gap that has to be leaped continues to widen, and the probability of a successful leap continues to fall.

Thus, in the first place, the Japanese treat every product as an ongoing experiment and are constantly engaged in improving it. Second, the typical Japanese firm's close integration of design, engineering, and manufacturing induces constant experimentation. Third, Japan's big firms are less vertically integrated than ours (about half as much), and smaller subcontractors are counted on for innovation. Fourth, the Japanese have begun in almost all new markets with penetration of small, applications-oriented niches. Fifth, Japan has a small-business sector that was more vital than ours from the end of World War II until 1975. From robotics to autos, new Japanese firms have played a vital, if largely unnoticed, role in that nation's dramatic resurgence.

What About Boeing (or the U.S. Navy)?

"But you can't develop the 757 by the 'small starts' approach" is another rejoinder to the small-starts idea. "Yes and no" is my answer.

First, recall that the original Kelly Johnson Skunk Works was devoted to aircraft design. That is, moderate-sized, off-line activities can produce complex, systems-oriented projects. Second, Boeing is a perfect example of "small starts *within* big projects." Boeing's product development is driven by the close, intense, continuous involvement of its customers (e.g., airlines, national governments). Aircraft are literally designed using customers' input: prototypes of every bit and piece are presented by either side, and merits are debated constantly. Furthermore, the key to speedy aircraft design is trial and error. Parts of new aircraft are tried out as redundant systems on current aircraft. Finally, subcontractor involvement is another hallmark of aircraft development. Thus, Boeing will work with engine-makers GE, Pratt & Whitney, and Rolls Royce and with thousands of others who will design and tinker with aspects of the craft.

Thus, the effective giant project in fact epitomizes the "small starts" approach. It is blooming, buzzing confusion which eventually gets molded into a complex system. Those most open to customer/supplier involvement and innovation are most likely to succeed (see also the discussion of the Ford Taurus team development effort in I-2).

On an even larger scale, the writer and defense expert Tom Clancy contemplates treating the fleet of the U.S. Navy as a "portfolio" of experiments. Clancy (writing in *U.S. News & World Report* of June 15, 1987) contrasts the Soviet and American approaches to designing new classes of submarines:

> We shouldn't be afraid to do what the Russians do—build a few submarines with combat capacity but that are really experimental platforms. Congress won't let the Navy do that. That's stupid because that's the only way you learn. We should today have three or four boats in the fleet that are just to test out new ideas—instead of taking every new idea we come up with and putting them all in one platform at once. What the Russians do better than we do is they're willing to experiment. They are willing to make a failure once in a while just to learn. The American military is regarded by everybody in the media as the "welfare queen": They can't risk a failure, because even if they learn something from the failure, everybody's going to say they were fools for trying it. It enforces a kind of conservatism that is fundamentally unhealthy.

In other words, the small-start idea has universal application.

215

JUST WHAT IS A "SMALL START"?

Small-start possibilities are many. Consider:

▶ The 3M rule: Tradition demands that each scientist devote 15 percent of his or her time to projects of his or her own selection.
▶ Another longstanding 3M tradition, which ordains that each division sponsor venture-like projects by people from *other* divisions who have come to them for support.
▶ The Hewlett-Packard routine whereby most divisions have an informal list of things to work on; as teams disassemble, the next project is picked up.
▶ The Japanese strategy of entering industries via small, applications-oriented niches.
▶ That willingness of a Limited to look to tiny acquisitions as a way to test important waters.
▶ The IBM habit of funding multiple, independent, fully staffed teams to work—in parallel, with rigid separation enforced—on any big project.
▶ The slightly less formal Cray Research approach of forming duplicate entrepreneurial teams to attack big pieces of projects.
▶ The Boeing approach of inventing together with customers and suppliers who innovate in parallel on small bits and pieces.
▶ Regular "sabbaticals" for supervisors at Chaparral Steel (see C-8), during which they work on special innovation projects with universities, customers, and suppliers; researchers and production hands, too, are constantly tinkering, together, on the plant floor, which is seen as a lab.
▶ Milliken's propensity to form—at the drop of a hat and without formal charter—a dozen-person team including a customer and a supplier to ferret out or create a small new market opportunity.
▶ A less formal version of the first 3M rule—that is, managers regularly and informally supporting groups to work on alternative approaches to bits and pieces of major projects.

"Small starts," then, is principally an attitude of hustling, testing, and scrounging, aimed at shortening the development cycle by hook or by crook. It's an attitude that results in a seven-person team being pulled together and provided work space in twenty-four hours—or less—once a problem or opportunity or new competing product surfaces. And it means never betting all the chips on the Big Project or the central R&D lab—Gordon Forward of Chaparral is dead serious when he describes Big Steel's research centers as "Forest Lawns" (C-8).

The Ten Preconditions of a "Small-Starts" Approach

Achieving a small-starts approach is like making a quality revolution (see C-2). It requires a thoroughgoing revision of attitude in every element of the corporation. A small-starts approach demands:

1. Letting everyone get out with customers, listening (see C-7, C-8, I-4, P-1).
2. Getting customers into the organization, involved in the plant and lab in particular (see C-8).
3. Establishing a "do a pilot" rather than "write a proposal" mentality (see I-3, I-8).
4. Using small teams in general for almost any task (see P-2).
5. Viewing suppliers as partners—co-innovators—instead of as adversaries (see I-2).
6. Removing bureaucracy to allow teams to get on with it (see I-8, P-10, L-8).
7. Flattening the structure and working fast across functional boundaries (see P-8, P-9, L-8).
8. Developing an instinctive "market creation" rather than "market sharing" orientation (see C-1).
9. Treating the product as an experiment, to be constantly improved (see C-1, I-8, I-10).
10. Management's *living* the message of rapid tests (see I-3, I-7, L-9).

PUBLIC PARALLELS

The small-starts approach is at least as important in the public sector as in the private, because it removes the public sector's favorite excuse for inaction—the inability to gain political and fiscal support for major new programs. Here I argue that small tests and partial tests turn out to be the most efficient way to innovate, regardless of the budget climate. Every school district (and school), every police force and transit district, should be a hotbed of little trials. Moreover, every public-sector senior manager should be, like his private-sector counterpart, on the lookout for small starts. "How many experimental classes does the principal have? Is the public works chief trying out different scheduling routines to achieve maintenance objectives with minimal service disruption?"

A specific manifestation of "small starts" has been the dramatic success in several states, such as Massachusetts, Michigan, and Pennsylvania, with new business incubator plans. Rather than putting all their eggs (their economic well-being) in the big firm/big plant basket, they are seeking to create a climate favorable to start-ups. Those choosing the big plant have often fallen victim to the vicissitudes of the quarter-to-quarter changes in capital spending plans of big firms, and the grotesque market demand fluctuations (with attendant grotesque employment fluctuations) that occur after the monster facility opens.

FIRST STEPS

1. Review your formal and informal product development budget. What share of it constitutes "big bets" and what share is aimed at small starts? Ensure that every unit's strategic plan is strongly weighted toward the latter, or at least that there is evidence of numerous small starts.
2. Beginning today, constantly talk up small starts, yours and others'. To aid this process, conduct a formal review of the almost certain explosion of new product and service offerings in your markets (odds are high that most will have come from the "wrong" place—via a small start by an unexpected player).
3. Talk these ideas up in every department; *every* activity should be engaged in small starts that will enhance and further differentiate *every* product and service offering, whether in development or mature.

I-2

SUMMARY

To speed new-product/service development to a pace approaching that dictated by new market needs, we must:

▶ Use multi-function teams for *all* development activities.

▶ Staff such new-product/service development teams almost from the outset with full-time people from all primary functions—e.g., design/engineering, marketing, manufacturing/operations, finance, and perhaps field sales/service and purchasing.

▶ Involve outsiders—suppliers, distributors, and customers—in new-product/service development from an early date as well.

▶ Be especially aware of the trap of "shared resources"—that is, partially committed people or facilities.

The use of multi-function teams is the chief tool for speeding up product development.

Use multi-function teams for all new-product/service development activities. The objective: to introduce (multiple) novel sources of innovation and reduce new-product/service development cycle times by at least 75 percent in the next two to three years.

Pursue Team Product/Service Development

It takes five years to develop a new car in this country. Heck, we won World War II in four years.

> H. Ross Perot,
> founder, Electronic Data System;
> former board member, GM

Lots more tries than ever are required to keep pace with changing times (I-1). But how do we ensure that the development cycle for new projects/products/services gets shortened enough to help us keep pace with new, ingenious competitors?

Recall the assertion of Chaparral Steel boss Gordon Forward that his largest challenge is to cut the time it takes to move technology from the lab into commercial use. His answer is to put the engineers and researchers on the shop floor with operators and purchasing people. The mill becomes a hotbed of experimentation, with all the principal players in minute-to-minute contact. Forward's approach is still unusual in the United States, and that's unfortunate, because <u>the single most important reason for delays in development activities is the absence of multi-function (and outsider) representation on development projects from the start.</u>

Rip apart a badly developed project and you will unfailingly find 75 percent of the slippage attributable to (1) "siloing," or sending memos and minutes up and down vertical organizational "silos" or "stovepipes" for decisions, and (2) sequential problem solving: design hands off to engineering, which translates the idea into detailed specifications; when engineering is finished, it passes the task on to manufacturing, which only then begins to worry about how the product is to be made; when manufacturing is finished, it passes the project to purchasing; from purchasing it goes to marketing; and from marketing to field service and sales. One group essentially finishes its "higher order" task before passing the job "down" to the next-level executor. Interaction among functions is minimal; what's done is always within the context of the hierarchy of functions—design, then engineering, at the top; manufacturing and sales at the bottom.

The answer is to commingle members of all key functions, co-opt each function's traditional feudal authority, and use teams (see also P-2, P-8). 3M has always done it; so has Hewlett-Packard. Frito-Lay slashed product development time when it adopted the team approach in the mid-seventies, a course made easier by the firm's already well-entrenched disrespect for bureaucracy and hierarchy. Today, even the most functionally oriented, hierarchical firms, such as Du Pont and Procter & Gamble, are scurrying to break down old organizational barriers and do innovation "all at once."

A CASE STUDY: FORD'S TEAM TAURUS

Among the traditional firms, none is working harder—or more effectively—at team product development than Ford. Team product development customarily features the removal of barriers between design/engineering and production and, to some extent, marketing and sales and purchasing. It can go much further. Team Taurus did, creating in the process a car that won kudos for design and quality—and coming in under the proposed product development budget by almost one-half *billion* dollars to boot.

Traditionally product development at Ford was sequential. Mary Walton describes it in *The Deming Management Method:*

> [D]esigners designed a car on paper, then gave it to the engineers, who figured out how to make it. Their plans were passed along to the manufacturing and purchasing people, who respectively set up the lines and selected the suppliers on competitive bids. The next step in the process was the production plant. Then came marketing, the legal and dealer service departments, and then finally the customers. In each stage, if a major glitch developed, the car was bumped back to the design phase for changes. The farther along in the sequence, however, the more difficult it was to make changes. In manufacturing, for example, "We wouldn't see the plans until maybe a year before production started," [Taurus project leader Lew] Veraldi said. "We would go back to engineering and say can you do it this way. They'd say, 'Go peddle your papers. It's already tooled. I can't afford it.' "

That's all changed, Walton reports, again quoting project leader Veraldi:

> "With Taurus . . . we brought all disciplines together, and did the whole process simultaneously as well as sequentially. The manufacturing people worked right with the design people, engineering people, sales and purchasing, legal, service, and marketing.
>
> "In sales and marketing we had dealers come in and tell us what they

wanted in a car to make it more user-friendly, to make it adapt to a customer, based on problems they saw on the floor in selling.

"We had insurance companies—Allstate, State Farm, American Road . . . [tell us] how to design a car so when accidents occur it would minimize the customer's expense in fixing it after a collision." One of the problems mentioned by insurance companies was the difficulty in realigning a car that had suffered front-end damage. As a result, Taurus and Sable have cross marks engraved on a suspension tower under the hood to define the center of gravity as an aid in front-end alignment. Team Taurus included Ford's legal and safety advisers, who advised on forthcoming trends in the laws so "we could design for them rather than patching later on."

Manufacturing was brought into the act early. Veraldi observes: "We went to all the stamping plants, assembly plants, and put layouts on the walls. We asked them how to make it easier to build. We talked to hourly people." Team Taurus collected thousands of suggestions and incorporated most of them. "It's amazing," he said, "the dedication and commitment you can get from people. . . . We will never go back to the old ways because we know so much [about] what they can bring to the party."

The Power of Supplier Involvement

Mary Walton reports that perhaps the most profound difference was in relationships with suppliers:

The common way of doing business is to choose the lowest bidder on advertised specifications. For Taurus, the company identified its highest quality suppliers and sought their advice in the beginning stages. In return for their contributions, Ford pledged to make them, as far as possible, the sole supplier.

One of those companies was A. O. Smith in Milwaukee, a family-owned corporation whose major division made automotive subframes, the steel structures on which were mounted the engine, the transmission, and the control arms for the wheels. The company was the world's largest manufacturer of car and truck frames. In 1980, Ford sought Smith's advice. . . . [For instance,] Ford had done the drafting in the past. But Smith offered to have its own drafting department, which was staffed by experts on that particular part of the car, do the drafts and give them to Ford for approval. "There was a willingness to accept each other's experts that had not existed before," [Ford executive vice president Paul] Smaglick said.

A. O. Smith did have to submit a bid, even after the cooperative effort, but the contract was awarded three years before production and was for five years, rather than the traditional one, another significant sign of movement toward partnership. And A. O. Smith's response was matched by others. Walton reports: "One lighting firm developed louvered interior lights that cut down on reflection on the driver's side when [they were] on elsewhere in the car. Another firm produced a carpet in which all the fibers lay in the same direction for uniform appearance. A plastics company came up with an optional fold-out tray for tailgate parties for the station wagon. Said Veraldi, 'Those are the little attention-to-detail items that we've never done before.' "

As production time neared, Walton reports, customers were given extensive sneak previews, and their ideas resulted in modifications: "In another departure, prototypes were built nine months before the first cars would come off the line. . . . [They were] tested by potential new car buyers, resulting in more changes for the better. The traditional way of making changes was to produce the car and wait for customer complaints. 'That's stupid, isn't it?' Veraldi observed, 'because the first three months, customers get something that is less than good.' "

Wholesale Involvement Yields Wholesale Success: Even Ford Was Surprised

So, from beginning to end, Walton notes, unprecedented involvement was the theme: "The prototypes were also taken to suppliers so that their workers could see the car. In the past, said Veraldi, 'The supplier would make the part, fit it to a gauge, and ship it to a plant. . . . The workers had never seen the final product they make in a car. All they do is they see a molding, or an engine, or a door. They would never see the result of their efforts in a car. . . .' When the car came to A. O. Smith, the employees got the day off to look it over. Two hundred workers at a plant that supplied exterior moldings signed a poster pledging their commitment to quality as a thank-you. . . . Framed, the poster hangs on Veraldi's office wall."

Thus the "team" in Team Taurus included, among others: (1) designers, (2) engineers, (3) manufacturing people, including hourly workers, (4) lawyers, (5) marketers, (6) dealers, (7) suppliers, including hourly workers, (8) representatives of insurance companies, and (9) customers.

Systematic studies as well as such case studies support the efficacy—actually order-of-magnitude superiority—of the team approach. For instance, Modesto Maidique and Billie Jo Zirger's study of new product launchings in high technology firms, cited earlier (C-7), determined that a critical distinguishing factor between success and failure was the "simultaneous involvement of the create, make and market functions" from the outset of the project. Similarly, analyses of Japanese successes emphasize their attention to manufacturability from the start of development efforts, the location in one place of engineers, designers, and manufacturers, and a conception of management unconstrained by traditional American functionalism (see also C-8).

TEAM DEVELOPMENT: THE SUCCESS FACTORS

The vital success factors, then, include these:

1. Multi-functional involvement. Multiple-function representation means, at best, the Ford approach: customers, dealers, suppliers, marketers, lawyers, manufacturing personnel, engineers, designers—and nonmanagers as well as managers; and all of these from the start.

Short of that, following the lead of Hewlett-Packard and 3M as well as lessons learned from Milliken's Customer Action Teams (see C-4), I suggest that development teams at a minimum consist of (a) a designer/engineer, (b) a representative of manufacturing, (c) a purchaser, (d) an accountant, (e) a marketer, and (f) a field sales or service representative.

2. Simultaneous full-time involvement. Key team members—at least design, manufacturing, and marketing—must be represented full-time from the start. The involvement of others, even of lawyers, should be full-time for the duration of the most intense activity. The idea here is simple co-optation. There is no such thing as a part-time passion. The part-time team member is not really a team member. The part-timer knows where his or her bread is buttered, and is first and foremost a "functional representative," more interested in discovering reasons why things won't work than driven by the champion/entrepreneur's passion to smash down barriers and make things work. The part-timer is evaluated and paid by the "home" function; a win is seeing to it that no "surprises" occur when she or he goes back home, and the product comes their way for manufacturing, field service, etc.

Rewards should go to teams as a whole. Evaluation, even for members who are only full-time for a while, should be based principally upon team performance. This is simple to state, but tough to execute. It's a piece of a larger issue—the actual shifting of the entire focus of evaluation, including pay and promotion, from functional performance (evaluated by the next three layers of management up) to team performance, where a team leader, regardless of which function she or he comes from, dominates the evaluation process.

But what about the member of the purchasing department who may be full-time for only a few months in a multi-year process? The ideal answer is an approach like Chaparral's, where functional barriers essentially don't exist (see C-8, P-1). Short of that, it is vital that the purchasing team member be rewarded, in the short or the long run, by his contribution to the team's success, rather than the purchasing department's success. If a purchasing person was on two teams, for two months each during the year, most of his or her annual evaluation should be based upon the team leaders' appraisals, not that of the nominal boss in purchasing.

A related element is rewards for cooperation. A few pioneering firms give large and numerous awards to honor acts of cooperation. For instance, if you, the manager, give out ten dinners or $100 checks or send fifty thank-you notes this month—why not make a rule, formal or informal, that at least half of these acts of recognition must go to people in other functions who have helped you and your teams? (See also P-9, L-8.) The chief issue is attitude, but such awards can help change attitudes, over time.

3. Co-location. Walls of concrete and plaster are very important—and inimical to team work. Numerous studies chronicle the astonishing exponential decrease in communication that ensues when even thin walls or a few dozen feet of segregation are introduced. Hence <u>all team members must "live" together.</u> It's as simple as that. Want factory people and engineers to talk? Put them in the same room, with no dividers. Space management is yet another tough nut to crack, but I can state unequivocally that regardless of expense, you can't overdo it when it comes to putting people close together.

4. Communication. Communication is everyone's panacea for everything—but nowhere more than here. In *A Passion for Excellence,* the original Skunk Works at Lockheed was described. This renegade band regularly completed complex projects in a tenth or less of average development time, at a tiny fraction of expected cost. Tom West's Data General skunkwork (the subject of *Soul of a New Machine*) and Gerhard Neumann's exceptional General Electric aircraft engine development operation were also analyzed. Many things were special about these three leaders, but nothing more than their insistence on constant communication across typically troublesome functional boundaries. Daily meetings and brief, written status reports, circulated to everyone, were the norm in all three cases. There is no substitute.

Effective decision-making forums are a special communications consideration. It is essential that regular decision-making sessions be held, with all functions represented. More important is instituting what I call the "no substitutes" rule. That is, whoever attends the meeting representing purchasing, even if it's a junior clerk who's the only one around that day, must be authorized to sign off for purchasing as a whole for whatever is on the day's agenda. Decisions subsequently undone, because a junior rep attended a meeting for his or her boss, are another leading source of project delays—and then sore feelings about wasted time, which cause further delays.

New technologies that allow machine-to-machine communication are essential; this is the essence of computer-integrated manufacturing (CIM), for instance. Yet this software, especially if developed by a central and detached engineering group, can do more harm than good. Most CIM failures (which means most CIM projects at this point) result from not taking into sufficient account issues of organization/people/attitude, and in particular from designing systems too complex to allow constant adjusting and tweaking on the factory floor.

5. The "shared resource" trap. Recall, in I-1, the discussion of Du Pont's loss of the tire cord market to Celanese. The problem was shared resources—a tire cord development center that reported to the established nylon department; it slowed the powerless polyester team's test efforts. I can hardly in good faith urge duplication of every resource for every development project. On the other hand, the Du Pont story is the norm, not the exception. In fact, recent research reported in the *Journal of Business Venturing* concludes that the sharing of resources between new-product/service teams and main-line activities—including manufacturing, marketing, and sales—is a leading cause of sandbagged product development and introduction efforts.

My best advice is to urge that you at least try to wholly dedicate bits of labs or factories, or parts of marketing or field service operations, to the new-product efforts when you feel you can't afford full duplication. That is, approximate duplication as best you can, even if the costs seem high. They usually aren't when measured in retrospect.

6. Outside Involvement. Suppliers, dealers (or other distribution channel members), and ultimate customers must become partners in the development process from the start. Much, if not most, innovation will come from these constituents, if you trust them (i.e., show them all information from the start) and they trust you. This is one of the most important instances of the urgent need for a shift from adversarial to cooperative relationships.

THE INNOVATIVE MIND-SET: BEWARE OF INCREMENTALIST THINKING

New car model development cycles used to be six or seven years. Now they're down to about four to five years in the United States, and three to four in Japan. Not good enough, say the Japanese, who are shooting for one to two years.

Their approach? They determine not what "can be" but what "must be": The cycle *will* be one to two years. The question then becomes: How do we organize to accomplish it?

The difference between the formulations "can be" and "must be" turns out to be profound. In May 1987 I had discussions with a highly successful Swedish firm on this subject. They have reduced new product development cycle times by about 50 percent, using many of the tools Ford used, including Computer Aided Engineering (CAE) systems, simultaneous rather than sequential product development, and partnership relations with suppliers. But now Japanese corporations, large and small, are showering their market with new products. Can the Swedes make another cut of 50 to 75 percent?

The first answer was tentatively "no." They went through each element that influenced the cycle—new tooling, design, etc. They could foresee a 25 percent reduction here, maybe 50 percent there, and very little in a few places—nothing approaching 75 percent overall (or even 50).

Then we shifted the fundamental premise of the discussion: "Given: You *must* cut product development cycle time by 75 percent. How do you organize to do so?"

Recall the determination of Milliken & Company to cut its lead time by 90 percent, discussed in C-4: The key was an earth-shaking reorganization. This, I proposed, was the way the Swedish firm must think. This is the way their Japanese competitors are thinking.

The solution thus begins with a whole new mind-set, and involves radical new ways of organizing (e.g., *much* flatter organizations, with a total transformation of middle management's role—see P-8, P-9). With a revolutionary mind-set, the firm is now more confident of success—any number of radical organizational ideas were indeed brought to the surface.

FIRST STEPS

1. Immediately re-assess one critical development project that's in its early phases—are suppliers, distributors, customers, purchasing, manufacturing, field sales and service, and marketing deeply involved, along with design/engineering? If not, experiment with involvement of each of these groups. Launch a radical experiment in team/simultaneous development with a forthcoming new product venture.
2. Consider radical organizational/relationship options needed to slash product cycle time drastically (75 percent at least) in the next couple of years.
3. Bite the bullet, if you are a functional manager. Start proactively lending your people, full-time at critical junctures, to project teams—whether you are an accountant or a purchasing manager. When you form your next team, isolate it physically, and attempt to get full-time help, at least for short periods of time, from the two or three most important contributing functions.

   Shift the basis of evaluating your people to focus on their contribution to others' teams. Reward those who did well in team settings, even or especially if it caused some pain to your function. Likewise, go out of your way to honor those who aided your teams, and especially their bosses, who allowed them to do so.

I-3

SUMMARY

With ever more confusion in the market, it becomes increasingly important to replace talk with tests; we must:

▶ Substitute pilots and prototypes for proposals.

▶ Find trial sites and field champions for new programs/projects/products as far from headquarters as possible.

"Piloting," rather than the constant rehashing of abstract proposals, must become a way of life. We need to dramatically speed up the first test or partial test of the first prototype, subassembly, store within a store, training module, software subsystem, pre-test market.

Cut your average "time to first tangible test" of everything by 75 percent, in every arena, in the next 24 months.

Encourage Pilots of Everything

[D]on't get too prepared. . . . A lot of people who want to go into business want to know everything. They never do anything. My idea . . . is get out on the damn field and start kicking that ball. . . . All I had was the inspiration. I didn't know that much about soccer. I didn't know there were even two sizes of soccer balls. . . . So the next thing with the inspiration is "get out and start doing something." The doing part of it is picking up a phone, calling a few friends, and saying, "Why don't you meet me over on Mercer Island and I've got an idea here. I really feel it." So when they come over, I pull out a soccer ball. They already have their crutches, and we start kicking it. . . . Then things start happening.

> Don Bennett, businessman
> and first amputee to climb
> Mount Rainier, on the founding
> of the Amputee Soccer League;
> from *The Leadership Challenge*

The first EDSer to see a snake kills it. At GM, the first thing you do is organize a committee on snakes. Then you bring in a consultant who knows a lot about snakes. Third thing you do is talk about it for a year.

> H. Ross Perot,
> founder, Electronic Data Systems;
> former board member, GM

The formula implied by the above—test it now, at least some piece of it, in the real world—has always been a key to success. Now it's much more. It's become a key to survival.

PILOTING YOUR WAY TO (RAPID) SUCCESS

Take an innovation in a staff department. You are the head of training in a $150 million firm, which urgently needs a spanking-new, high-visibility international management program. The president has been after you to get going for six months. What is the fastest and most effective way to move toward development and large-scale implementation?

You've been chatting about the subject around the office. Now a vigorous young woman comes to you with her strongly held idea for such a program. What do you do? One course is to ask her to write a proposal to float with the executive committee. Another is to bring it up casually at a meeting with your peers or seniors to see how it flies. The second approach is better than the first, but it's still dumb. There's a much better answer.

First, forget the international headquarters staff three doors down. They've fought this idea for years on the pretext that "if it ain't entirely broke, why try to fix it"—in other words, hands off! Instead, sit down with your young would-be champion and go through a list of the international line managers whom you know best, or better yet, whom she knows. Pick out a couple. The persons you've identified should not be skeptical about trying something new. They probably should not even be very senior. They should be people who you or your champion know will be excited about this topic. They must be line managers.

Find some pretext to send the young champion off on a brief field trip to visit with the foreign managers you've identified—to gather live, raw, far-away-from-headquarters input from them at the outset. And then the proposal? Not yet. When your eager champion gets back, have her write up three or four pages of rough notes. Fewer and rougher is better; high polish puts people off. Then, the next time you're meeting with international managers (perhaps you could stop in for lunch or coffee during a training session), pull out those unimposing notes. Chat about a couple of the key points with several of the managers—once again, those most likely to be friends instead of foes. Have your champion do the same sort of thing as opportunities present themselves. Then gather a little more data. Perhaps send your champion off to a couple of companies you've heard about that have interesting new international training programs. Circulate notes from those visits to the people you've both talked with.

And so on. The objective is to strike some sparks—to get several committed champions to own the idea. Not you or even your senior international counterparts, but your young champion and a few enthusiastic mid-level line persons in the field.

Test Bits and Pieces Unobtrusively

Can you segment, or "chunk," the project? That is, can you find a little piece of it that can be 75 percent developed in the field by one of your new field champions? If so, get on with it posthaste, and test it casually. That is, stuff some of the partially developed new material into an ongoing training program, perhaps as an extra half-day or a substitute half-day. Have the field champions run through the program with a few of their people. As the opportunity arises, expand the network of champions. By now, pilots of chunks should be popping up in various places, and word should be leaking out. After some months of this, it is finally time to float the proposal more formally.

Piloting Shortens the Process

Some of you are by now saying that this takes longer than making proposals to senior management. That's a typical rejoinder. I beg to differ.

The process is best represented by an exponential curve. There is a slow, low-level, virtually invisible start, followed by a wildly efficient takeoff as word of mouth, led by the *field* rather than by headquarters, starts to do the selling for you. Most pieces of the program have been tested (piloted) by the *field*, refined by the *field*—and are working and getting better and more *field*-oriented daily. Other managers have begun to insist that their operation be the next pilot site for this exciting, new, *field*-designed course.

Mastering the Quick Pilot Mentality

I've chosen an innocent training program as my example. The process is precisely the same with a new product or service, a new accounting procedure, a new distribution procedure, a new factory layout, a new partnership program with a supplier, a new approach to a union.

Traits of pilot-driven innovation include: (1) test sites in the field; (2) a committed champion or two at home; (3) some carefully nurtured line champions far from home; (4) network building via word-of-mouth reports of experience with pilots; (5) chunking the project into small parts for the most rapid testing; (6) casual introduction of chunks into ongoing routines, so as not to prematurely upset the status quo; (7) rapid sharing of the precious bits of real, test-generated data as they accumulate; (8) field design and ownership of the chunks; and (9) protection of the champions by you, the senior manager.

The beginning of the process—the time when commitment can be killed—is most crucial. Most significantly, no valid market data exist at first—none can exist about something untried. So it is precisely at the outset that proposals get shot down or become the topic of endless, hypothetical debate. Any new idea is, by definition, disruptive. It also automatically challenges the wisdom of seniors who have been in place a long time and who didn't think of it in the first place. Building a ground swell, through pilot projects in the field, with line operators as champions, simply turns out to be the most effective—and efficient—way to implement anything.

I acknowledge the dogmatic nature of the previous statement. "Most effective" and "efficient" are strong words in a complex world. I generally avoid them like the plague. But not this time. The stakes are too high. We must learn to innovate fast. "Try," "test," "adjust," "try again," "fail," "modify," "scrap," "start over"—this must become the normal pattern. Regis McKenna calls all products continuous experiments. The Japanese view manufacturing (indeed, life) as a battle to achieve constant improvement. I see life in business analogously, as a series of pilots—committed people, on the nearby shop floor or 6,000 miles away, constantly performing real-world tests on small chunks of the new.

If you walk through a store or distribution center and you can't find a dozen tests of systems or partial systems going on, you should worry.

If you find a senior engineer or buyer or MIS manager wasting most of his or her time "working up the chain" with proposals, rather than "working down"—that is, seeking pilot sites and champions far away from headquarters—you should worry even more.

We don't need proposals. Or, rather, we need a new form of proposal. The most useful proposal aimed at an executive committee is one that has been thoroughly presold to everyone on the basis of hard evidence in support of the new, evidence gained in numerous pilot projects designed by and contributed to by each key executive's own field people.

The piloting mentality is best fostered by chatting it up. When any idea surfaces, instinctively ask these questions: (1) Where are you going to test it? (2) Who is the field-test sponsor? (3) Who "owns" it, you or the field sponsor? (4) Are you sure? (5) When are you going to test it? (6) Can't you test a piece of it sooner? (7) Can't you do the first test in less time? (8) Can't you chunk it more? Later, the questioning shifts: (1) What did you learn from this pilot or that? (2) What have you done with that learning? (3) How's your network growing? (4) Is someone from X or Y function part of it? (5) Does the field still own it?

"Soft" Analysis versus "Hard" Pilots

Is this approach "soft"? No! It is hard—the very hardest. It is rational, and it is "scientific." In fact, it amounts to the organization's embracing the essence of the scientific method—empiricism and the experimental method. Piloting is the data-based approach. By contrast, decision making by proposal churning is whistling in the wind; it is the truly soft and ultimately less rational route.

Piloting Is Dirt-Cheap!

The best news of all is that this piloting/chunking/testing mind-set, far from creating expensive and time-consuming chaos, actually creates inexpensive order and powers the way to rapid success. That is, the whole firm becomes engaged in collecting real-world data from real-world tests as fast as possible. People are not wasting time speculating and posturing and politicizing and proposal writing. When they talk in the halls, they talk of data and evidence.

Further, those who are making tests and learning on the firing line, instead of speculating at staff meetings, are the new, honored elite. In fact, staff people generally are no longer around headquarters all that much in the fast-learning organization—their role is now to be out and about, seeking field champions and sponsors and test sites and spreading information about pilot successes throughout the network, in hopes of starting a bandwagon in the *field* for an idea.

The simple historical point is this: In every arena, from Citicorp and PepsiCo and GE at their best, to Lockheed's Skunk Works over a forty-four-year period, we find some organizations, big and small, that do things, not "a little faster," but five or ten or twenty or fifty times faster. Their secret is encompassed by this prescription: Move forward on the basis of hard facts and quick testing, not speculation.

But that's history. The difference between yesterday and today is dramatic: Now, there is no choice. A host of new or downsized competitors are working to undermine your defenses. Many are small and unencumbered by bureaucracy. The small players are also no longer handicapped by traditional diseconomies of scale, thanks to the technology revolution. You are vulnerable. The smaller firms are, in a sense, pilots. You will either answer their challenge—and the challenge mounted by the faster-moving teams at Campbell Soup and Du Pont and Milliken and Procter & Gamble—or lose much of your business in short order.

A CASE STUDY: HOW TO FOSTER A QUICK-TEST ENVIRONMENT

Most ad industry experts are in agreement: the "noise" (volume of competing advertising messages) is so high today that to be a success, one's message must increasingly be startling, outrageous, or "intrusive," to use the insiders' term.

Such a proposition didn't sit well at conservative Young & Rubicam ($4.2 billion in billings), long known for its methodical research. But Y&R is shedding its stodgy image (witness its stellar new campaign for Colgate's low-tartar toothpaste). Much of the credit goes to a systematic program to induce risk-taking via quick tests, launched in 1984 by the creative director of the New York office, John Ferrell. Here are several of the steps Ferrell took:

(1) He began with a pep talk to all 300 employees in the creative department. The new message: Take risks. Such an exhortation, of course, would have had little effect without numerous reinforcements.

(2) A key to the transformation was creation of The Risk Lab. Its objective is to provide a chance for creative people to test far-out ideas early in the ad development process, rather than late, when much is at stake with bosses, account executives (ad agencies' senior sales people), and client officials. (a) Ferrell gave the director of creative research, Stephanie Kugelman, a new title, Dr. Risk. (b) Kugelman moved out of the 18th-floor research department offices,

and camped out, a week at a time, on various floors in the creative department; when she was in residence, the floor's reception area even sported a sign, "The Doctor Is In." (c) Kugelman would give an instant reaction, on behalf of the research community, to wild and woolly ideas; moreover, in a major departure from conventional practice, she would hastily pull together a panel of consumers to provide a "quick and dirty" test for a new idea (again, without risking supervisor or client opprobrium). (d) Kugelman's role is now being institutionalized; she and five researchers are moving permanently out of the research department and into offices in the creative area.

(3) Procedures were modified, too. Before, all research pro and con (and confusing and equivocal), would be packaged in an imposing document. Now, research information is boiled down to one summary page. None of this denigrates the role of research, but it does mute its overpowering influence on the decision-making process. As Ferrell remarked to *The New York Times,* "So many research methods are designed to say don't take any risks at all."

Thus, between exhortation, some fun, co-location of warring functions, de-bureaucratizing, purposeful reduction of a dominant function's influence, and devices to aid fast tests before an idea gets politically "locked in," Y&R is waking up.

TEST IT FAST: A QUANTITATIVE TARGET

Time is short. Aim for a 75 percent reduction in "time to first tangible test" for the average project, achieved over the next 24 months. Smaller and midsized firms are doing it as a matter of course. Team product development and the nurturing of champions (prescriptions I-2 and I-6) are powerful aids in this effort. But both of those tools lose most of their potency if you fail to pilot in accordance with the guidelines established here.

PUBLIC PARALLELS

This prescription is even more applicable to the public than to the private sector. I remember chiding a city's middle managers. Most were spending the majority of their time floating proposals for this or that, trying to stretch an already badly stretched budget.

"But why," I said, "should anyone support this or that new program? You have no evidence that it works." "Precisely" was the reply. "We need demonstration money to try it." In one case, demonstration money meant $250,000 for a nine-month test, with a formal evaluation due six months later. After some heated debate, we came to agree that a "quick and dirty" test could be performed in 90 days in the field (out of sight of top management) for $5,000 to $20,000; moreover, there was a champion already out there, a person who'd wanted to have a go at it for years.

In fact, there is always someone "out there" ready to take a whack at it, whether we're talking about a school district or a complex military technology project. Furthermore, almost anything can be subjected to a partial test in 90 days for $25,000 or less. (This is not speculation. I've repeatedly seen it done in supercomputers and financial services alike.)

"Devote 100 percent of your time (or 50 percent, to be realistic) to getting that one, real, first piece of test-generated evidence," I counsel public managers. "Then float the $250,000 proposal." Even better, try several partial pilots before going to the trough to try to pry loose the scarce resources.

Another part of the conversation goes like this: "But what if the little one blows up? The whole deal will be scotched before we've even tried to get the money." You can probably guess my answer: "Better to know now, and get a little egg on your face, than to find out later, at great expense, and get the frying pan thrown at you too."

FIRST STEPS

1. Ensure, through every form of recognition you can dream up, that the organization's heroes are those who are piloting, not merely speculating.
2. Formally (and informally) ask at each staff meeting, on each visit, in each performance appraisal: What are you testing? Where are the pilots?
3. Always be on the lookout for pilots and tests, as you walk through the hotel or purchasing office, review major account sales programs, visit customers and suppliers. Commend them on the spot, including any interesting failures (see prescription I-8).

I-4

SUMMARY

In today's ever-accelerating business environment, you must:

▶ Put NIH (Not Invented Here) behind you—and learn to copy (with unique adaptation/enhancement) from the best! Do so by aggressively seeking out the knowledge of competitors (small and overseas, not just tired old foes) and interesting noncompetitors.

Become a "learning organization." Shuck your arrogance—"if it isn't our idea, it can't be that good"—and become a determined copycat/adapter/ enhancer.

What *ten* ideas have you swiped—and implemented with appropriate enhancement—from competitors and noncompetitors in the last 60 days? If you've adopted/adapted fewer than ten, beef up your "creative swiping" program immediately.

Practice "Creative Swiping"

Kobayashi: When we want to do something, we just try to learn and absorb all the possible answers, alternatives and developments not only in Japan, but in Europe, in developing countries and in the U.S. Then, by combining and by evaluating the best of all this, we try to come up with the optimum combinations which are available. For instance, we are very sophisticated copycats. I have accompanied many executives, many union people going abroad to study—groups, of course. All top executives of chain stores, for instance, make two or three trips a year to Europe or to the U.S. . . .

Interviewer: To do what?

K: To learn something. To get something new.

I: Are you saying, then, that one of the secrets of Japanese success has to do with their desire, their urge to get the best . . .

K: . . . to collect information from all parts of the world. If any Japanese manager wants to develop a new product, he likes to find out all the possible seeds—instead of the needs, here.

I: Seeds?

K: Seeds-oriented. Try to find a good seed rather than try to identify the needs here. For instance, the transistor—when the former chairman of Sony saw the article in *Fortune* magazine about the transistor, he imported it. I have been speaking over and over again of the obsession; the urge to absorb is quite high and intensified here.

> Interview with Professor
> Kaoru Kobayashi, from
> *Japan: The Most Misunderstood
> Country*

The Presidio Theaters in Austin, Texas, have been a spectacular success. Presidio's flagship Arbor Cinema Four, though in the ninety-eighth-largest market in the country, regularly places among the ten top-drawing theaters in America for any given movie. From theater seats found in France to a sound system developed by Lucasfilm, Presidio prides itself on having stolen the seeds of virtually every idea it's implemented. But the chain is careful to steal only from the best! Charlie Chick, Presidio's president, calls it "creative swiping."

Only the best steal from the best. When Honda launched the upscale Acura project, it picked BMW as its principal competitor—Best in Class. The Acura design team was given just one year to beat BMW. Early signs suggest that they either succeeded or came remarkably close.

BECOMING OBSESSED WITH COMPETITORS

Americans, in semiconductors and retailing alike, are generally terrible at analyzing their competitors, especially in comparison with our competitor-obsessed Japanese rivals. We don't do enough of it, and if we do do it, we usually relegate it to an egghead "competitive analysis" unit, stuck on a hilltop light-years from our centers of operations. Directly related is our cherished go-it-alone, pioneer spirit which leads us to look down our noses at *any* copying. It's the NIH [Not Invented Here] syndrome and it can be deadly.

Challenge Number One: Determining Who the Competition Is

The first question is: *Who*, exactly, is the competition? Too often, firms have focused on old rivalries. Sears worried about Penney, Ford worried about GM, and Xerox studied Kodak—and vice versa. Sears's real problem is K Mart and Wal-Mart at the low end, Mervyn's in the middle, Nordstrom at the high end, and cataloguers from Spiegel to Banana Republic.

A California department-store merchandising executive stunned me. When talking about competitors, she restricted her remarks to other department stores. "But what about The Limited, Victoria's Secret, The Limited Express, The Gap?" said I, no expert. "Aren't they the real source of your woes?" The executive's information on any competitor was weak; it was especially superficial concerning these newer and more venomous ones.

Xerox's obsession in the mid-seventies with crosstown rival Kodak's new (and good) high-price copiers effectively led it to ignore the little stings from Savin, Canon, et al. in pipsqueak market segments. Then, suddenly (or so it seemed), these mice moved out of their corners and became lions; Xerox lost more than half its market share before it stemmed the tide.

On the other hand, a Ford executive delighted me recently when he said, "Our competitor is Toyota." For too long, Detroit's leaders ignored the hard data and continued to focus on the current enactment of the old rivalry between Barney Olds and Henry Ford, Sr. In fact, some Detroit sources say that GM really began to panic only when Ford's Taurus and Sable took America by storm—that is, when a fellow denizen of Detroit had clearly captured the buying public's imagination.

So determining the "who" is no trivial task. You must check out: (1) foreign firms, with special emphasis on the first, unobtrusive entry into small niches (this has been a favored Japanese tactic, in everything from small engines to machine tools to copiers); (2) small domestic firms, especially their entries into tiny, premium (and profitable) niches; (3) new, big domestic rivals trying to shed their troubles by intruding on your patch; (4) the very best competition, region by region (even stellar firms such as Frito-Lay have a relatively small share of the market in large parts of the United States); and (5) oddball forays through distribution channels and from competitors you wouldn't expect (e.g., TV home shopping, and the explosion of cataloguers in retailing).

Analyzing the Competition: The Obvious and Beyond

Even gross indicators, such as market share by segment, relative revenue, and relative earnings, can give you a good start on competitive analysis. These are crude measures, yet I am surprised at how few (1) collect the data, (2) update them regularly, and (3) share them widely within the firm. Every person in the company should have ready, visible access to the numbers on market share—yours and your competitors'—updated weekly; it is a good first step toward getting the competitors "in the air." (Once again, beware of new incursions. Gross share data is less important than share by segment. A loss of one-quarter share point overall might be mainly attributable to a 20 percent share loss in an unobtrusive but important niche.)

But even the best numeric analysis is not without pitfalls, as one expert on competitive analysis ruefully acknowledges. *Fortune* profiled Wall Street analyst Maryann Keller, the most respected follower of the auto industry. Despite a high batting average, "Keller's record has not been flawless. As a stockbroker, she missed a great opportunity Chrysler offered in 1982, arguing for GM instead. 'Chrysler was a disaster financially, and I believed that GM, with all its financial power, would prevail,' she says. 'After all, how could a company that has everything going for it blow it? It's the one time in my life where I let the numbers rule my judgment. I will never make that mistake again.' "

The next level of analysis focuses on the technical traits of your competitors' products, as gleaned from "reverse engineering" (ripping apart their products) and studies of comparative cost structures. This is a big step beyond market-share analysis, but there is a trap in overemphasizing a comparison of generic product traits too (see C-3). Such analysis can obscure factors that may be more important in predicting the outcome of future marketplace skirmishes. Frankly, Coca-Cola can learn more about the course of its future wars with PepsiCo by thoroughly studying Pepsi's nonbureaucratic, no-nonsense, "test it, try it . . . now" environment than by chemical analysis of any soft drink.

Thus, at yet a third level, it is essential to focus on common-sense business queries: How do the competitors organize for R&D? How high in the pecking order are the service managers and sales managers? How much and what kind of training is given to the people who answer the phones? How high is the division manager's spending authority? The answers to such questions are terrific indicators of a potential competitor's responsiveness. For instance, if a competitor has an organizational structure with only three layers and gives great spending authority to general managers, it is likely to be quick to respond to change.

MAKE COMPETITIVE ANALYSIS EVERYONE'S BUSINESS

After the "who" and the various levels of "what" comes the "how." I support having expert technicians doing "reverse engineering," and I do think there's a place for small economics units churning out worldwide competitive analysis statistics. But there is a more basic dimension.

Competitive analysis should be everyone's business. The objective is to turn everyone on to it—service people, check-processing people, MIS people. There are two reasons to do so. First, they can be exceptionally good sources. At conventions, or in chats with friends and neighbors, they can pick up a great deal of information, if they are tuned in to the general process—and then listened to. That is, the MIS professional will be the first to hear that a competitor is developing a sweeping new electronic linkup with hundreds of major customers. He or she will hear it (1) from their computer service/salesperson, (2) from a customer, (3) from an MIS person in a bank who heard about it from a friend, (4) from a former employee now at a software house who heard it from a friend, or, most likely, (5) from a braggart who's doing the software in the competitor's MIS department! The pressing question is: Will he or she merely "be fascinated" by the tidbit? Or are there ready channels, formal and informal, for swapping the information fast, getting it to the right division, or marketer, or whomever? Most such intelligence goes nowhere because of conventional barriers to communication or, worse yet, because of an attitude of nonurgency, which means no alarm bell is tripped in the back of the MIS person's head.

Take the simplest case. Does the average retail salesperson look at other retailers' ads or arrangements in the mall on the way to work? Why not start a monthly contest, with $100 (or $50 or $500, or dinner for two at the best restaurant in town) going to whoever picks up the best "I walked by Saks and saw" idea? You could design a full-fledged suggestion system devoted exclusively to ideas from competitors.

So the average person can be of great service, if he or she is given a mission, a sense of urgency, and a forum in which to be heard.

Competitive Analysis as Motivation

The second, and perhaps more important, benefit of getting every employee to think about the competition is the effect upon general readiness to accept change. I've heard GM executives flatly deny the extent of the erosion of GM's market share within hours of my talking to a leading analyst. Their retort is some dubious, oddball interpretation that makes "awful" look merely "bad."

If GM's executives are trying to confuse me, think what they must do to their employees. If you want to induce a sense of urgency, share the gory details of any loss of market share (especially big losses in tiny segments), of polls that show the extent to which customers prefer the vehicles or traveler's checks of others. Almost all employees are smart. If they are inundated with the unvarnished news, the odds that even onerous change will look acceptable go way up.

FIGHTING NIH ("NOT INVENTED HERE")

As a manager, trade in "Not Invented Here" for "Not Invented Here, But Swiped from the Best with Pride."

The best leaders (see L-5) are the best note-takers, the best "askers," the best learners. They are shameless thieves. Grocer Stew Leonard heard a great little idea from an executive in the Department of Defense at a meeting I attended in late 1986; he implemented it within the week. There was no NIH. No "Gee, if it's DOD, it must be bad." The only operative question was: "Will it work [with a twist or two] for us?"

For Leonard this is second nature; in fact, *A Passion for Excellence* highlighted his One Idea Club and One Idea Club van—a device for transporting a dozen people to a competitor's (or interesting noncompetitor's) operation, nearby or far away, to look for small, good, immediately implementable ideas.

Citytrust prospered under former president Jon Topham, who had the same passion. His attitude is: "Somebody, somewhere, big or small, near or far, has introduced a service we could copy with enhancements—today."

Above all, keep it simple. Competitive analysis buffs have made a mess of competitive analysis. They brought the term to our vocabulary, which was a fine service. But then they did what most experts do with good ideas, turning the process into an arcane discipline and quasi-science which can be understood and conducted only by a mandarin class—namely, them, and for a high fee.

There is, as noted, a place for ultrasophisticated competitive analysis. But the prime objective of this prescription is to turn *everyone* into a vacuum cleaner, trying to understand—and often copy—the best of what our new and most thirsty competitors are up to.

NIH is marked by an endless number of denials: (1) We can't copy old rivals because "if they did it, (a) it must be dumb or (b) we wouldn't want to look like them." (2) We can't copy new rivals, especially foreign ones, because "we're not Japanese, you know." (3) We can't copy small rivals if we're big, because "you can't do that sort of thing if there are more than 500 people on the payroll." (4) Or big ones if we're small—"Hey, we don't have AT&T's deep pockets." (5) And we can't copy from nonrivals because "that stuff will only work in (a) groceries, (b) semiconductors [or any other industry except ours]."

As usual, the problem is attitude, and the solution lies in changing it to: (1) being positive rather than negative about competitors' products, especially tiny features (after all, you couldn't have invented everything first); (2) being positive

243

about other industries' products and services from which you can learn; and (3) opening up the organization, at all levels and in all functions, to the buzz of "what's going on out there that's interesting."

In the successful Taurus/Sable program, Ford bought cars from around the globe. They assessed over 400 features, from major performance parameters to the ease with which the gas cap could be removed. The objective was to become Best in Class (BIC) on most of these features; with a creative mix of copying *and* marginal improvement, Ford feels it reached BIC status on 80 percent of the 400.

COPYING AND UNIQUENESS

Prescription C-6 was unequivocal: Success depends on uniqueness. How do you square that with being a copycat?

The answer is threefold. First, every idea you "steal" should be adapted and enhanced to fit your special circumstances. Second, though your goal should remain the achievement of uniqueness, uniqueness most often comes not from a breakthrough idea, but from the accumulation of thousands of tiny enhancements (the Milliken shop towel—see C-1) that utterly transform the product and create new markets in the process. Most of these enhancements will have been done first by somebody else in some other market—e.g., those who are linking up electronically with customers are, at one level, "swiping" from American Airlines' Sabre system. In particular, tiny companies are, de facto, experiments worth watching.

Third, copying does not interfere with breakthrough thinking; to the contrary, it improves the chances of achieving a breakthrough. For instance, the most creative scientists are synthesizers. They pull together disparate ideas and reshape them to solve a current conundrum. Thus, Charles Darwin's "breakthrough" formulation about evolution came after reading Thomas Malthus, whose 60-year-old ideas on overpopulation meshed in Darwin's mind with his original data from the Galápagos Islands. *The Origin of Species* is at once "unique" and a first-rate example of creative swiping.

In business, this process generally means the ability, for example, of drug distributor McKesson to learn about electronic linkages from American Airlines—and to uniquely apply the concept to achieve commanding strategic advantages in a different industry.

Note, however, that such creative swiping is by no means plain copying, which in a fast-moving world is increasingly useless. Simply copying a competitor today precludes creating your own unique basis for advantage. Creative swiping, which amounts to adapting ideas from unconventional sources, aims solely at creating uniqueness.

In sum, I continue to counsel an urgent quest for uniqueness. The overall vision/positioning of a firm in the marketplace should not be copied from anyone. But the enhancement of each tiny element of the vision can greatly benefit from the hard work that others, in almost any organization, are doing to improve quality, service, responsiveness, etc.

REMINDER: CUSTOMERS' PERCEPTIONS ARE WHAT COUNT

I conclude with a reminder about a critical word from the prescription dealing with listening to customers (C-7)—naïve. Customers like our competitor's products for whatever reason *they* choose. On *our* tests, we might seem better than the competitor on eight out of eleven traits; but if our market share is 15 percent, we're obviously missing something. As a friend at Ford put it: "I remind [my colleagues] that despite our improved quality, design, and profitability, each and every minute, over four out of five car buyers worldwide decide that they don't like Fords, vis-à-vis *some* competitor. Why?"

Why? What can we learn? What can we copy and enhance? These are critical questions.

PUBLIC PARALLELS

The Venture Project was a model study in competitive analysis in the public sector. A Participative Management Project was launched in Walnut Creek, California. One result was an awareness that the city could learn from others.

In 1986 four California cities—Walnut Creek, Irvine, Palo Alto, and Palm Springs—joined in a learning (competitive analysis) venture. Venture Teams from each city spent an intense week visiting the other three cities. The observations were written up and widely shared, resulting in the implementation of a raft of practical ideas. While acknowledging that some programs are unique to a particular city, one participant quickly added: "In most cases there is a product that can be used either socially, organizationally, or economically to benefit others."

Most significant was the underlying spur to action described in the project's summary report: "City managers can no longer act as caretakers of their cities' resources, but must act as entrepreneurs to guide their cities to be more efficient and productive." (The project's first round was so successful that it was continued, with participants visiting private-sector organizations in search of new ideas.)

Some private operation, some entrepreneur somewhere, is doing just about everything any city is doing. What does the best private firm picking up garbage charge and what is the quality of its service? Precisely this sort of comparison, of course, has been a major impetus to the growing "privatization" of public services.

You can also consider every neighboring city a competitor. How is it that

XYZ makes a profit on its airport while you must subsidize yours to the tune of tens of millions? Maybe the reason is different labor conditions beyond your control (watch out for the old enemy, NIH)—but then again, maybe it's not. Maybe it's an accumulation of a thousand factors, the majority of which are under your control.

Most important, any public sector operation can mount its version of the One Idea Club and turn the organization into a hotbed of learning and swiping. What city, county, state is doing what about X or Y? What are schools in East Oshkosh doing about ABC? The public sector consists of thousands of schools, sanitation departments, and fire and police operations. Some are lousy, as some firms in the private sector are lousy. But surely the best 10 percent have something (lots, I'd judge) to teach each and every one of us.

FIRST STEPS

In the next 90 days, mount a contest in each department, including accounting and personnel. Which one can come up with the most implementable ideas? Awards might be for (1) best idea overall, (2) most ideas from outside the organization, (3) highest percentage of participation, (4) best idea from a small competitor, (5) best idea from a big competitor, (6) best idea from a foreign competitor, (7) best idea from a noncompetitor. The emphasis should be on quantity, not the magnitude of any idea, since the aim is to get everyone looking for tiny differences.

Consider institutionalizing such a program through a "swiped-idea fair" (once or twice a year) or a special Not-Invented-Here-But-Swiped-with-Pride suggestion system.

I-5

SUMMARY

Since the exploding array of new products and services is causing more and more confusion in the marketplace, and in the minds of early buyers of industrial or consumer goods, we should:

▶ Organize new-product/service marketing efforts around explicit, systematic, extensive word-of-mouth campaigns.

Purchasers buy the new based principally upon the perceptions of respected peers who have already purchased or tried the product. The twist this prescription adds is the idea that word-of-mouth campaigns for the new and untried can be as systematically pursued as can the use of traditional marketing tools, such as advertising. Such programs are increasingly important, as the number of competitors and their offerings increase exponentially, and their products' life cycles decrease dramatically. Influencing the early sorting-out process must be managed with great skill.

Use *systematic* word-of-mouth campaigns as the keystone for launching all new products and services. The campaign should include specific and detailed strategies to land a half-dozen progressive (probably not big) customers prior to full-bore roll-out.

Make Word-of-Mouth Marketing Systematic

Buying a new personal computer? Trying to figure your way through the jungle of new personal financial services? Where are you likely to go for counsel? Certainly you don't sit in front of the TV waiting for an ad to appear. And you're not likely to "let your fingers do the walking." You probably ask a respected friend, neighbor, or colleague who's been down the same route recently.

Now switch sides. If you were the would-be seller of a new service or product, how could you tie into that network of friends and experts who advise potential buyers? Most sales of services, complex products, and especially new products and services, come via word of mouth. As a seller, you need not passively sit by. You can be just as organized, thoughtful, and systematic about "word-of-mouth advertising" as about media buys.

However, marketers tend to over-rely on mass media advertising and under-rely on the careful development of reputational campaigns, according to Regis McKenna. He goes on:

> Word-of-mouth communication can take on many different forms. Industry participants form "old-boy networks" to keep each other informed about new developments. One recent market-research report showed that such a network plays a key role in the telecommunications industry. Gaining access to the network is critical to success. . . .
>
> Word of mouth is so obvious a communications medium that most people do not take time to analyze or understand its structure. To many people, it is like the weather. Sure, it is important. But you can't do much about it. You never see a "word-of-mouth communications" section in marketing plans. . . .
>
> Of course, much of the word-of-mouth communication about a company and its products is beyond the company's control. But a company can take steps to put word of mouth to its advantage. It can even organize a "word-of-mouth campaign."
>
> . . . [T]he company must decide who should receive the message—and who from within the company should deliver it. By the nature of word-of-

mouth communications, it is not possible to spread the message too widely. Luckily, there is no need to. Word of mouth is governed by the 90-10 rule: "90 percent of the world is influenced by the other 10 percent." . . . A word-of-mouth campaign should be based on targeted communication. Word of mouth is not an efficient means for distributing information widely. . . .

The targets for a word-of-mouth campaign fall into several categories:

The financial community. Who backs a company is often more important than how much money is behind it. . . . A company's initial backers can use word of mouth to spread the company's message.

Industry-watchers. Rapid-growth industries are filled with consultants, interpreters, futurists, and soothsayers who sort out and publish information through word-of-mouth. . . .

Customers. Companies can use word of mouth to reach customers at trade shows, technical conferences, training programs, and customer organizations. [New-product test] sites and early customers become especially important.

The press. More than 90 percent of the major news stories in the business and technical press come from direct conversations. All journalists have networks of sources they use for background, opinions, and verifications. It is valuable to become part of this word-of-mouth network.

The selling chain. The selling network includes sales representatives, distributors, and retailers. . . . word of mouth is needed to generate enthusiasm and commitment toward the product.

The community. Every person who is interviewed, or delivers a package, or visits a company walks away with an impression. If company employees communicate properly, every person who comes in contact with the company becomes a salesperson for the company, a carrier of good will about the company.

Ev Rogers of the University of Southern California is the leading expert on "diffusion of innovation." He has examined how new ideas and new products spread. His dozens of studies have analyzed new commercial products, the adoption of birth control techniques, and agricultural technology to determine the reasons behind the typical thirty-year and forty-year delays in the widespread dissemination of innovations—delays which mark even products and services which demonstrate crystal-clear, decisive advantages from the start.

Rogers, like McKenna, emphasizes the overriding power of networks: "Most individuals do not evaluate an innovation on the basis of scientific study of its consequences. Most depend mainly upon a subjective evaluation of an innovation that is conveyed to them from other individuals like themselves who have previously adopted the innovation. This dependence on the communicated experience of near-peers suggests that the heart of the diffusion process is the imitation by potential adopters of their network partners who have adopted previously." Study after study that Rogers reviews reveals that: (1) an innovation takes off only after "interpersonal networks have become activated in spreading subjective evaluations" and (2) "success is related to the extent that the change agent or marketer worked through opinion leaders."

I write, I must admit, with the zeal of a true believer. My first book, *In Search of Excellence,* was launched by an unsystematic (but, in retrospect, thorough) word-of-mouth campaign. A 125-page presentation of what became the book's principal findings was first bound in 1980, fully two years before the book was published, and circulated surreptitiously among business executives. My co-author, Bob Waterman, and I eventually printed 15,000 presentation copies to meet the underground demand, much to the misguided consternation of our publisher, who was certain we were giving away most of our future sales. We also assiduously courted opinion leaders in the media over a period of several years. Thus, within days of the book's launching, supportive reviews appeared, and the network of 15,000 (plus at least an equal number of photocopied knockoffs) hurried to buy the real thing, often in bulk for their subordinates. We could not have more effectively marketed the book if we had planned the process meticulously.

GETTING WORD OF MOUTH ORGANIZED

The important point, to which McKenna speaks so passionately, is that the process can be systematized. For instance:

▶ Careful charting of official and unofficial opinion leaders can be conducted.
▶ Disproportionate selling time can and should be aimed at highly reputable, would-be early adopters.
▶ Sales incentives should encourage working with early adopters.
▶ Events that pair happy new customers with a wider audience can be staged on both a one-shot and an ongoing basis.
▶ User newsletters can be established, then circulated to targeted nonusers.
▶ Testimonials can be systematically gathered and circulated.
▶ All of these programs and others can be put together in a detailed, written, step-by-step "word-of-mouth" campaign plan.

THE SEARCH FOR SMALL, PROGRESSIVE BUYERS

The most critical word-of-mouth activity is, of course, targeting early adopters. Above all, look for the innovative adopters, not necessarily the big ones. Sure, you'd like to launch your new workstation by signing up GM. Yes, you'd like the chairman of the town's biggest firm to be the first to buy your new personal financial planning service. But such giants, though certainly helpful to word-of-mouth diffusion, are usually laggards when it comes to adopting new products and services. Therefore, you'd be wise to look to smaller firms or individuals with a reputation for progressiveness; they're much more likely to become early adopters. Pouring almost all of your energy into getting a couple of these leaders on board is usually a worthwhile strategy.

FIRST STEPS

Take one new product and ask these questions: (1) Am I devoting 75 percent of my marketing effort—dollars and energy—to activating a word-of-mouth network? (2) Are all of my salespersons devoting a specific—and sizable—share of time (and money) to user network development and expansion? Are they compensated for doing so? (3) Is *every* employee a conscientious network developer among his or her colleagues? Based upon the answers, develop a sixty-day word-of-mouth blitz (targeted very precisely on a few key progressive customers) to re-launch or enhance product/service acceptance.

I-6

SUMMARY

To match the accelerating rate of change in the environment, numerous innovation projects must be mounted, which requires us to:

▶ Encourage as many "determined beyond reason" (though pragmatic if you look more closely) champions to come forth.

▶ Accept some level of champion-induced disruption, far beyond the traditional norm.

▶ Draw out champions in personnel as well as engineering, around the edges of big and well-planned projects as well as in independent ventures.

Any one innovation project, whether in accounting or in new-product development, has low odds of success. We must learn to cherish those with a passionate enough attachment to a new idea to push for it, though most such people will be rough around the edges and most of the projects will fail.

Each *day,* find one or two specific opportunities to publicly applaud/guard/clear the way for champions. Let no visit to any unit, especially support functions, go by without taking the opportunity to cheer at least one new-project champion and one audacious, but hitherto unnoticed, supporter of that champion.

Support Committed Champions

I used to think that anyone doing anything weird was weird. I suddenly realized that anyone doing anything weird wasn't weird at all and that it was the people saying they were weird that were weird.

> Paul McCartney
> original Beatle

The reasonable man adapts himself to the world; the unreasonable one persists in trying to adapt the world to himself. Therefore, all progress depends on the unreasonable man.

> George Bernard Shaw
> *Man and Superman*

CHAMPIONS ARE REQUIRED

What are the management tactics that allow us to achieve the thoroughgoing innovative attitude described in I-1 through I-5? The need for spirited champions inside the firm heads the list.

▶ In *The Spirit of Enterprise,* George Gilder pays tribute to the entrepreneur: "[T]he entrepreneurs sustain the world. In their careers, there is little of optimizing calculation, nothing of delicate balance of markets. They overthrow establishments rather than establish equilibria. They are the heroes of economic life." He viciously attacks conventional economic theory, which, he insists, denies their role: "The prevailing theory of capitalism suffers from one central and disabling flaw: a profound distrust and incomprehension of capitalists. With its circular flows of purchasing power, its invisible-handed markets, its intricate interplays of goods and moneys, all modern economics, in fact, resembles a vast mathematical drama, on an elaborate stage of theory, without a protagonist to animate the play."

▶ America's premier expert on small business, David Birch of MIT, notes in the same vein that small businesses are uniquely successful at innovating and meeting market needs, in part because of "their [leaders'] unfettered and somewhat undisciplined efforts."

▶ In *Star Warriors,* science reporter William Broad quotes a Lawrence Livermore Labs manager concerning the development of a supercomputer by a tiny team there: "Curt and Tom were considered off-the-wall crazy because it was well known that the big computer companies would have done it if it had been possible. The fact that it hadn't been done meant that it was foredoomed—they were absolutely wasting their time. They got an enormous amount of ridicule. Just because people say you're crazy doesn't mean you're going to win, but sometimes it sure looks like a necessary condition for success."

All of the above support this prescription: Learn to acknowledge—and love—those protagonists.

Inside the firm or outside it, the product/project champion *is* special. He or she is a dreamer, and also a scrounging pragmatist. The champion takes on activities that have low odds for success but are high-odds matters to him or her precisely because of the passionate attachment.

By any rational analysis, the odds of any project's success are low. The barriers are monumental: As if low odds based on technology, manufacturability, and the explosive market where everyone is trying everything weren't enough, everyone inside the firm is out to get the champion of a new product—or a new accounting technique. Machiavelli spoke of the champion's plight in *The Prince:* "It ought to be remembered that there is nothing more difficult to take in hand, more perilous to conduct, or more uncertain in its success, than to take the lead in the introduction of a new order of things. Because the innovator has for enemies all those who have done well under the old conditions, and lukewarm defenders among those who may do well under the new."

Those who attack the innovator, moreover, have a seemingly valid point. Why, they ask, should we disrupt a production line to test a device which has little likelihood of succeeding? Why divert precious equipment in the R&D lab to a flaky project? Why work overtime in the purchasing office to procure a new epoxy resin for some oddball with a wacko idea, using up credibility with a supplier in the process? Why burden a marketer, on a stretched three-man marketing staff, with a two-week assignment to check out a woolly notion?

So this is the *logical* response to the champion in pursuit of a low-odds venture. It thereupon induces a self-fulfilling prophecy: Only the sort of person who is passionately committed to stand up to all this static and ridicule is likely to succeed. Such a person is almost a sure bet to be egotistical, impatient, and disruptive. And those traits in turn further enhance the odds of stiff rebuffs from any establishment's managers.

Only the "Unreasonable" Champion Can Succeed

Richard Pascale, co-author of *The Art of Japanese Management,* describes a unique Japanese entrepreneur: "Any account of Honda's successes must grasp at the outset the unusual character of its founder, Soichiro Honda. . . . Honda was an inventive genius with a large ego and mercurial temperament, given to bouts of 'philandering' (to use his expression). In the formative stages of his company, Honda is variously reported to have tossed a geisha out a second-story window, climbed inside a septic tank to retrieve a visiting supplier's false teeth (and subsequently placed the teeth in his mouth), appeared inebriated and in costume before a formal presentation to Honda's bankers requesting financing vital to the firm's survival (the loan was denied), hit a worker on the head with a wrench, and stripped naked before his engineers to assemble a motorcycle engine."

Gary Taubes reports in *Nobel Dreams* on Carlo Rubbia:

> On December 10, 1984, Carlo Rubbia finally got his Nobel Prize. . . . Rubbia is arguably the most powerful man in high-energy physics. . . . His is a discipline in which political savvy, physical endurance, money, and maybe guts, can be as important as scientific insight. . . . [H]e is renowned for his frenetic energy and his inability to sit still—or even to stay in one city or one country for more than a week—as much as for his physics and his political acumen.
>
> Rubbia had an incurable passion for physics. If his proposals were rejected by the management, he would do experiments under the table. He would set up his equipment on test beams and, if questioned, explain that he had only been checking his apparatus. . . .
>
> He was considered one of the three toughest men to work for at CERN, and as far as I can tell, few physicists who worked for him liked him. . . . He was unsteadfast. Frequently he failed to finish what he had started. He tended to create extravagant experiments, then leave them for other extravagant experiments as soon as they showed signs of coming up with unextravagant results. He had a reputation for impetuosity, for lacking the patience to do the kind of excruciatingly careful analysis high-energy physics demands. And physicists who knew Rubbia at the time suggested that, as a result, his numbers were inaccurate as often as not. "I would feel badly if I did something wrong," explained one senior physicist who worked with Rubbia in the sixties. "For Carlo, that's not what counts. Clearly, he has a different kind of thing that drives him." Bernard Sadoulet, who first met Rubbia in 1969, put it more bluntly: "His numbers are what they are. They are usually wrong—but if they suit his purpose, nothing is wrong."

Rubbia's career faced ruin several times in the 1970s because of questionable data. Yet he fought back. Because of his reputation, he was at times pushed to the back of the line, but that just created another barrier to batter down: "Rubbia went through contortions to get precedence. He tried to have detecting equipment built quickly in the machine shops at CERN, but was informed that his competitors had priority there, too. He then borrowed some equipment from a Harvard colleague, flew it from Boston to Geneva checked as luggage, and rolled it into the path of the colliding beams while the technicians were taking a half-hour tea break. He took the first pictures of protons in collision and showed them a few weeks later at the American Physical Society meeting in New York. It was called a tour de force."

When he got support for his vital experiment, which eventually led to the prize, he and a partner went out in search of a team: "One physicist described [the recruiting process] as the Rubbia roadshow: polished transparencies, lots of hyperbole, plenty of striding back and forth and gesticulating, and remarkable amounts of enthusiasm." And once the team was assembled, Rubbia pushed. "[H]e would control the detector to the best of his paranoid abilities. 'Paranoid' is the word Rubbia himself uses. He would push his physicists to work on a timescale that they considered impossible. He would tell them he wanted some device in a weekend that they thought would need three months, and they would eventually get it to him in two weeks. They would never know quite how they were able to do it so fast. But Rubbia expected it, and it wasn't worthwhile giving him another reason to scream, since he found so many without their help."

In Rubbia we see all the successful champion's characteristics writ large: (1) energy, (2) passion, (3) idealism, (4) pragmatism, (5) cunning, (6) towering impatience, (7) an unrealistic unwillingness to allow any barrier to set him back, and (8) love-hate relationships among his subordinates.

Would you hire Soichiro Honda? Would you hire Carlo Rubbia? If you had hired them, would you have kept them on when even their integrity was under attack? Be honest with yourself.

The role of the absurdly committed champion is an established fact, from the battlefield to the fast-food industry. Yet historically, the pace of change was such that you could survive, at least, without many champions.

Not so today. Today we are confronted by a brutal conundrum. Because of all the interacting sources of uncertainty described in Part I, the odds for the success of any one project are going down fast—after all, twenty-seven firms in your market are trying the same thing you are, with new ones added every day. Increasingly, then, we need to innovate faster just to survive; put another way, we need many *more* people to sign up for projects with much *lower* odds for success just to stay even. In short, we need impassioned champions by the thousands. Yet the impassioned champion is anathema to everything that traditional, civil, organized corporate endeavor stands for. But we must hire him, even though he will alienate some good people, irritate almost everyone, and in the end fail anyway more often than not. The picture is not meant to be pretty. Rubbia hardly comes across as a "nice guy." Neither did Honda in his inventive days. But in saying that, I steadfastly refuse to sugarcoat the truth: Most successful innovators, in training departments, factories, and labs, have a bit of the Rubbia in them. If they didn't, they'd never have had the gumption to start—and never, never have had the will to stay the course.

THE MISSING LINK: MANAGERS MUST
ACT AS EXECUTIVE CHAMPIONS

So what's the manager to do? You must become what I call an executive champion—a nurturer, protector, facilitator, and interference runner for as many energetic champions as you can induce to sally forth. Moreover, if you are a senior executive, you must encourage other managers also to view their role, in large measure, as that of executive champion.

You must individually and collectively dance a tightrope: (1) hire your Rubbias, (2) provide them with pillows rather than accountants to punch when things are at a low ebb, (3) protect others from them and them from others, often for long periods of time, and (4) occasionally fire them if they do stray too far off the reservation.

EVERYBODY CAN (MUST) BE A CHAMPION

So far, I have dealt only with the gloomy half of the story, with the oddballs who must be kept from self-destructing before the job is done. The deeper issue is how to elicit something only a little short of Rubbia's energy from larger numbers of people already on the payroll—in the operations center even!

Take this story from Ford, reported by William Allan of Scripps Howard in 1986:

> A few months ago, Ford Motor Co. gave up on the EXP, its two-seat sports car. Two seaters—MR2, Fiero, Civic, 300ZX—are so popular even Cadillac is planning one, but EXP sales were sluggish. Its styling was stale, and for a sports car it was plain lazy. . . .
>
> But when the news of EXP's planned demise reached Ford's Wayne, Michigan, assembly plant, there was a revolution of sorts. . . . Losing an entire model line sent visions of layoffs through the plant. "We hated to lose a whole model. Building another car line gives the plant security," said John Latini, plant manager.
>
> The employees, with a bit of assistance from Latini, went down to the body shop and pirated parts from the other models and put together what they thought was a much better-looking EXP. "Ford had actually canceled the EXP, but we took the front end and both bumpers off a prototype of the current Escort GT. We had to smooth some sheet metal back along the body, but it looked real good," Latini said. . . . The employee pumpkin wasn't ready for the big dance just yet. Detroit doesn't work that way. But the plant's version was good enough to be shipped to Ford's Design Center, where the pros smoothed out some rough edges.
>
> The result is the 1986 Escort EXP. During its first three months it posted steadily increasing sales. . . .

259

I contend, then, that many average people have a lot of the Rubbia in them, and we must find ways to unleash it. Several prescriptions in this book will focus on how to do so—to engender commitment and passion in everyone for constant improvement of everything. The trick is not mere exhortation to "become an impassioned champion." We must do many things right, in tandem, to up the odds of champions coming forth to take on risky projects—and even moving a filing cabinet ten feet is a risky act in many places (see C-2).

Among them, we must: encourage rapid testing of everything in small pilot projects (I-3); model innovation ourselves (I-7); proactively support failure and defiance of the rules, as long as core values are not violated (I-8); train the daylights out of people (P-4); rid the organization of senseless bureaucracy (P-10) and excess layers of management (P-8); reconceive every manager's role as one of facilitator rather than cop (P-9); and give people a stake in the action when their taking the initiative works out (P-6).

PUBLIC PARALLELS

It should go without saying that the passionate champion is the engine of innovation in the public sector as well, from the army in battle to the neighborhood school. Moreover, he or she shows all the "difficult" traits exhibited by champions in the private sector. Thus, the role of executive champion in the public sector requires even more deftness because of public scrutiny. The executive champion must provide succor for both the champion and the aldermen the champion offends.

FIRST STEPS

1. Whenever a project team is about to be formed, do you instinctively think first of the passion of the champion or would-be champion when you are searching for a project leader, or do you focus on other skills? I suggest the former. Regardless of your level in management, do you think of yourself as facilitator (or nurturer, protector) of champions? Or do you think of yourself as master project administrator, managing other plan-driven project administrators? Keep the distinctions at the front of your mind when it's time to appoint the next team or project leader.

2. Each day, give yourself a grade on how well, as evidenced by specific actions, you have defended, guarded, and made things easier for champions. If you can't point to specific actions taken each day, you are simply not engendering innovative activity at the pace required for survival.

I-7

SUMMARY

To get the constant innovation necessary for survival, managers must:

▶ Personally symbolize innovativeness in their daily affairs.

▶ Seek out opportunities to stand foursquare with innovators.

Seeing is believing! Would-be champions will be encouraged to come forth when senior managers demonstrate, by their actions, that they support constant innovation, even when it's a bit disruptive. It is essential that managers make a constant effort to recognize innovators (and applaud the details of their victories over organizational inertia), at all levels and in all functions.

Each *day,* seek out at least one opportunity to stand on the side of innovation and innovators. Practice "purposeful impatience" daily: applaud the new, rough-cut or not, and yawn at even good performance that involves no bold moves and no fast-paced experiments. Create an Innovators Hall of Fame, and include members from support functions in at least equal numbers to those from the engineering, design, or merchandising function.

"Model" Innovation/Practice Purposeful Impatience

A wonderful story is told about Lee Iacocca when he wanted to add a convertible to Chrysler's line. Following standard operating procedures, he asked his chief engineer to craft a model. The engineer, consistent with (actually better than) industry standards, replied, "Certainly. We can put together a prototype in nine months." Several bystanders report Iacocca's furious response: "You just don't understand. Go find a car and saw the top off the damn thing!" Iacocca got his prototype—and in short order. He then proceeded, so the story goes, to engage in some "systematic" market research. He drove around Detroit with the top down on the new prototype, and when the number of people waving at him reached a level he thought satisfactory, he ordered the car built—and it's a fact that a big success ensued.

Is the tale apocryphal? Parts of it surely aren't, as I've heard the story confirmed again and again. In any event, it has given rise to the two key terms in this prescription: "purposeful impatience" and "model innovation in your daily affairs."

A MANAGER'S DAY-TO-DAY ACTIVITIES: SYMBOLS OF SUPPORT FOR (OR REJECTION OF) INNOVATION

1. Be careful of your mundane actions. Do your office routines, whether you are in the executive suite or the supervisor of the seven-person accounts receivable department, exhibit the "saw the top off the damn thing" attitude that you are asking of others? Or are you inconsistent? Do you encourage people to by-pass functional barriers and deal directly with their counterparts in other functions, but then get bent out of shape when someone does this and gets you in hot water with a fellow vice-president? Do you encourage cutting the paperwork to speed the pace of action, but continue to spew out twenty-three memos per day?

Do you applaud when someone scrounges computer time, breaking a little

263

china, and succeeds in speeding up a project? And do you continue to applaud—or at least shrug it off—if the effort fails and it turns out that the scrounged computer time means a delay in receiving a 275-page report you've anxiously been awaiting because the president wants it?

You want committees sharply reduced. But have you appointed any new ones lately? You want product development teams to have a full-time operations person on them from the start. But do you then scream when an operations snafu arises, attributable (it is said) to the fact that Ms. Jones was detailed to one of those teams?

The new rules for innovation that these prescriptions propose controvert most conventional wisdom. You, the boss, must live up to them—especially the small, but symbolically significant, ones.

2. Behave with purposeful impatience. I believe in civility—most of the time. But not when it comes to an exercise like this: "We need three more days to get the computer run on the cost buildup from the division controller's office; they're tied up with the corporate monthly operating review." Don't put up with it. Ever again.

That is, you must make it clear that people are paid to beat down functional barriers—preferably by building solid relationships in every function. They are not being paid to guard turf and process "cover your tail" memos up and down the organization (see also P-8, P-9).

So the answer to the plea for "three more days" is: "Uh-huh. Well, you've got forty-five minutes to get the numbers; that's when the presentation starts." Or: "You've been involved with this project for eleven months. You should know the numbers we need from memory." Or: "Fine. We'll sit here in the boardroom and wait. Anybody know a good carry-out restaurant?"

It is essential—today more than ever—not to put up with traditional excuses that come from the victory of boardroom-brand civility and functional primacy over taking action.

3. You want innovation? Just ask for it. A bank president called a two-day meeting at a remote location to work with his top forty officers on some strategic issues. The group trundled off at one point for a "breakout session," where teams traditionally get together to noodle over some key issue, coming back with a vague report about "the important parameters." This time the president's guidance was unconventional: "You've got two hours to come up with big savings, without layoffs. . . . See you in 120 minutes." They did return—and with the savings. A significant share of the ideas were implementable. One group brought $700,000 back to the table, and exceeded that brash target in practice.

At Milliken's four-day annual retreat for top managers, I've seen groups of twenty from disparate functions and businesses wrestle with a thorny issue for two hours, knowing they had to come up with a lengthy action list, to be implemented—and reported on—in 30 days. They unfailingly do it. No one says, "But my boss is not here, I can't commit our group to that." It's your job as a senior manager, says Milliken, to know what you can and can't commit to—and you'd better be able to offer a lot, or you and your boss are both going to be in hot water. Little time is spent on nuances, less on bureaucratic bickering. The issue is: "We're going to crack this nut," and that's that. They quickly go around the table; each participant has a minute or two to discuss her or his idea—*and* to propose a 30-day action plan, such as "Meet with X at plant Y and shorten this step in the paper processing. Due date 3/18/87." The meeting chairman nods quickly, the item is duly recorded, and on they go: "Fine. . . . Okay, Dave, what does the New York sales office have to say about the new product sample preparation process?" Bang. Bang.

It may sound impossible. I couldn't believe my own eyes at first. But I've seen it at Milliken four years running, and at a number of other firms as well. It can be done.

4. Seek out and celebrate the innovators. There are mavericks who do the impossible in support departments such as MIS—for instance, a software code writer who finishes what's typically a month-long debugging task in a weekend. It turns out that although he's in North Dakota, he has scrounged computer time from a little-used mainframe in Barcelona, then cajoled a couple of vendor people into helping out, too.

Somehow, you must develop routines that aid you, as boss, in hearing about him. It's not easy, since he generally works from midnight until 10 a.m. in a hidden corner of a faraway building (most computer installations are in low-rent neighborhoods or rural states). Once he surfaces, call immediately (or fly in) and make a fuss over his herculean effort. (One California bank executive gives awards to persons who tell her about innovators that are almost equal to those she gives the innovator per se. It's a great strategy for unearthing unsung stars in faraway places.)

5. Establish a Hall of Fame in every unit—and insist that it be full. And though big annual innovation awards are desirable, a month is probably the longest you should go without some sort of award. Even on-the-spot awards should be more or less formalized. Give all managers an informal quota. I don't favor a rigid target like "four per month." But I do recommend that you carefully track the results and cajole those who seem to be reluctant to give out such awards: "No innovations in purchasing again this month, I see. Could that be right, John?" Or include in the monthly operations review a brief "Innovation Report" that lists the innovations, innovators, and innovators' bosses; the repeated absence of any executive's name adds to the pressure on him/her to produce.

6. Reward small innovations as well as large ones. Wholesale participation in innovating is essential. This will be spurred by vigorously celebrating small innovations, not just breakthroughs. (Interestingly, American financial awards for suggestions average ten percent of the savings that the suggestions subsequently generate. Japan's far more numerous awards average only one percent of savings. The Japanese reason—correctly—that lots of small awards induce more tries.)

7. Support the supporting cast. Be sure that those in the support functions who help the innovators get about as much credit, in both fanfare and dollars, as the hotshot software engineer or children's wear merchant. We need to replace buck-passing with rapid action. One vital aid is ensuring that the Hall of Fame trophy for the beat-the-competition introduction of the 2938R test machine, the Fangouli line of women's wear, or the new salad-bar format includes the names of the people who helped out from purchasing, accounting, training, and the like—and includes them prominently, not in a footnote.

The reasoning is straightforward. Most improvements and time reductions in the product/service development process will come from turning the largely unseen supporting cast into committed champions. Therefore, treat them that way. Consider, for example, George, the accountant who voluntarily goes all out doing a complex cost analysis in three days that usually takes two weeks. He turns a touted designer into a hero, but misses his son's first Little League game in the process, and gets his immediate boss's nose bent out of shape to boot, because the boss's pet project slipped a bit. George deserves a medal, and more than a bronze one. But—and here I repeat, but this is vital—you must first work like the devil to find him! The chief engineer never fails to bring around "Jane the genius circuit designer," but George never gets to tag along. If you are really wired in, you'll personally send Joey, George's boy, two box-seat tickets—for Joey and George—for a game during the Padres' next home stand. The plaque in the Hall of Fame gallery should prominently feature George too.

I've seen all of these management spurs to innovation in action. They are individually powerful, and collectively dynamite. However, they require a thoroughgoing penchant for innovation and close attention to its outcroppings—on a day-to-day basis.

FIRST STEPS

1. Get a close associate to act as your conscience. He or she should let you know, bluntly, each time you start acting like the problem rather than the solution—that is, fostering inertia and barrier-building rather than action-taking and barrier destruction.
2. Simply demand action without muss and fuss. Raise a big rumpus—that is, walk out—the next time you hear "X couldn't get the data because . . ."
3. Seek at least one opportunity each day to say in effect, "Saw the top off the damn thing"—that is, do a quick modification, don't reinvent the wheel.
4. Go out of your way to publicly pat an innovator on the back. Recognize at least one innovator a week, even if only with a simple note.
5. Be relentless in systematically seeking out and celebrating the invisible supporters of the successful project team, especially those from off-line functions who helped out at some peril to themselves. Make sure that you reward at least two supporters for every front-line innovator; do some personal digging to get at these supporters.

I-8

SUMMARY

To speed action-taking—and reduce innovation cycle time—as necessary to be competitive requires us to make *more* mistakes, *faster;* we must:

► Support *failure* by actively and publicly rewarding mistakes—failed efforts that were well thought out, executed with alacrity, quickly adjusted, and thoroughly learned from.

► Actively and publicly reward defiance of our own often inhibiting regulations.

► Personally seek out and directly batter down irritating obstacles—often as not small ones—that cumulatively cause debilitating delays and which champions cannot readily clear from their own paths.

Inaction is the chief enemy of speedy innovation. These prescriptions, as a whole, are designed to induce faster action-taking. This necessarily translates into making *more* mistakes and defying silly bureaucratic rules and traditions.

Revel in thoughtful failures that result from fast action-taking. If you haven't yet cheered at least one interesting failure today, applauded an act of defiance, and removed one tiny hurdle from a champion's path, you are not foursquare behind fast innovation.

I-8

Support Fast Failures

You've got to have an atmosphere where people can make mistakes. If we're not making mistakes, we're not going anywhere. The scientific method is designed for mistakes.

> Gordon Forward
> President, Chaparral Steel

Many people dream of success. To me success can only be achieved through repeated failure and introspection. In fact, success represents the 1 percent of your work which results only from the 99 percent that is called failure.

> Soichiro Honda
> founder, Honda Motor

[Limited founder Les Wexner] actually likes mistakes; buyers are graded not only on their successes, but also on their failures. Too many hits means the buyer isn't taking enough chances. . . .

This is not a company that lingers over its mistakes. Wexner's divisions dump tons of [unsalable] clothing into the off-price and bargain-basement market each year. "When you eat like an elephant, you s—— like an elephant," Wexner has said.

> *Forbes,* April 1987

Gordon Forward worships at the altar of science—and cherishes mistakes. Honda says he mucks up 99 percent of the time. Wexner goes further and rewards failures, and is wary of too much success. What is the meaning of so much passion for failure by well-known superachievers?

COMPLEXITY + NEED FOR SPEED = MAKE MORE MISTAKES (OR ELSE)

There's little that is more important to tomorrow's managers than failure. We need lots more of it. We need faster failure. It is fair to say that if we can't increase the gross national failure rate, we're in for a very rough ride indeed.

269

(Actually, the economy's brightest star is the increase in failures. That is, our accelerated rate of business start-ups has brought record levels of job creation—and an accompanying record rate of failures.)

After a speech I gave in April 1987, a bank executive from Colorado urged me to "title your next book *How to Learn to Love Failure.*" Nothing, he avowed, is more vital in financial services, where new products are introduced daily, new competitors emerge weekly (recall Eastern Airlines' MasterCard in C-1), and product life cycles are shrinking dramatically.

The logic is simple: (1) We must innovate, in every department, faster. (2) Innovation obviously means dealing with the new—i.e., the untested. (3) Uncertainty is rising. (4) Complexity is rising. (5) Uncertainty is only removed and complexity dealt with by action. (6) To act on the new in the face of increasing complexity yields failure. (7) To act speedily yields speedy failure. (8) Rx for speedy innovation: More failure, faster. (9) Rx for dramatically speeded-up innovation: Dramatically increased rates and amounts of failure.

Plans can only go so far, and not very far at that. Literally thousands of variables—people (you, your boss, your champion, your accountant, etc.), technology, competitors (and their people, technology . . .), timing, macro-economic forces, random external events—are at play in successfully introducing the most basic training course, let alone a new computer, a memory chip, a fashion line, a menu change at a 100-restaurant chain, or a consulting service. Those variables, beyond the few that any formal plan covers, can only be addressed (and then tinkered with) when the project sees at least the partial light of day (this was the main message of I-3).

Perhaps a 750-page plan can anticipate 10 percent of the possible snafus. But it takes nine months to prepare. Those nine months are an eternally lost opportunity to do real-world testing, failing, and adjusting. A 25-page plan anticipates 8 percent of the problems, and can be completed in a tenth of the time. The point is this: There is an almost irreducible number of failures associated with launching anything new. For heaven's sake, hurry up and get them over with!

Get Over the "F-Word" Hurdle

When I talk with businesspersons I find they certainly understand, and sign up for the obvious logic of, the discussion above. Yet they have a terrible time coming to grips with the word "failure." In fact, several people, when asked in a seminar to discuss the role of fast failure in speeding up innovation, could not bring themselves to do so directly. The closest they could get was "the hated 'F' word" and "outcomes of the other variety."

To increase the speed of innovation and dramatically accelerate product development cycles as required by competitive conditions, we must quickly come to grips with the word "failure" and the issue of failure. The timely achievement of anything new entails vigorous public support of failure—not just support for "good tries," but public support for failures themselves.

Talk Up Failure

The goal is to be more than tolerant of slip-ups. You must be like Wexner and actively encourage failure. Talk it up. Laugh about it. Go around the table at a project group meeting or morning staff meeting: Start with your own most interesting foul-up. Then have everyone follow suit. What mistakes did you make this week? What were the most interesting ones? How can we help you make more mistakes, faster?

Literally give awards, perhaps fun ones—a bent golf putter, an old tennis shoe (bronzed), or a model of two cars crashing into one another—for the most interesting/creative/useful/fastest failure. Ask everyone to repeat this exercise with his or her people, weekly or monthly. Have an annual "Hall of Shame" banquet where you give awards for the fastest/most useful—and the dumbest and most embarrassing—foul-ups. Also include "interesting fast failures" as a regular category in your newsletter.

On the informal side, add a leaf to the one-minute manager's ritual: instead of looking to "catch someone doing something right," look to catch someone doing something wrong! Make it a habit to send thank-you notes to people who make innovative, fast failures; send such a note around the office when an interesting, fast failure comes to your attention.

"Fail Forward"

To be sure, pay attention to Mr. Honda's formulation—"failure and introspection." To support speedy failure is not to support (or tolerate) sloppiness. It is imperative to demand (1) that something be learned from each failure, and (2) that it be quickly followed with a new modification.

Dave Boyer is president of Teleflex, a profitable maker of high-tech control systems, based in Limerick, Pennsylvania. The firm's automotive division has rapidly grown from $10 million to $60 million, attributable to a rate of new-product introduction which has resulted in 50 percent of sales coming from products launched in the last year. The key to that success rate is what Boyer calls "failing forward." That is, failing fast—and learning from it so as to make the next and smarter step quickly. The Teleflex team talks openly about "failing forward," and sees this openness as a prime ingredient in their success.

You Can't Wait to Dot All the "i's"

There is an important caveat to the above. I said that supporting fast and useful failure does not imply supporting sloppiness. That's true only to a point. Sloppiness could be interpreted to mean not tying up every loose end, not waiting until all the data are in. But the fact is that we can't afford to wait until all the data are in because by then the market will be lost. We must trust instinct, and we must launch tests with only some of the data in. So be careful to tolerate fast-paced moves (and subsequent failures) when only some of the answers are

271

available, and when the fastest way to get more of the answers is to test, not talk (it usually is the fastest way).

"Fast Failure" and "Do It Right the First Time": No Conflict

How do you reconcile the inevitability of failure and the quality gurus' plea that you "do it right the first time"? Aren't the two ideas at odds?

To begin with, so far I've been dealing with the introduction of a new product or service or training program or accounting software package; the emphasis has been on addressing the vagaries of the market (including the internal-to-the-firm market for, say, a new training program). Introducing the new, which by definition goes beyond the routine and accepted, will be accompanied by failure—period.

More generally, though, the "do it right the first time" philosophy rests squarely on the acknowledgment of failure and the need for constant tinkering. That is, we are presumably not now doing it up to maximum potential (not doing it right the first time) because we haven't: (1) worked with suppliers on problems, (2) trained and encouraged our people to analyze existing problems, and (3) assessed and updated systems which cause bottlenecks.

So implementing "do it right the first time" means acknowledging that each job, routine, and system is a hotbed of endless opportunities for improvement. The simple definition of an "opportunity" is that something is now broken, regularly failing, or at least not working as it might. Furthermore, new and improvement-conscious competitors are constantly making their product better; if we are not constantly improving (which means testing and adjusting—and failing, since each test deals with the novel), we are by definition falling behind, relatively—and relatively is what counts.

So "do it right the first time" and the quest for constant improvement depend on (1) acknowledging current failures, and (2) making lots of fast failures as we constantly experiment with new ways of doing things.

Seek Out "Little" Failures: Become a "Failure Fanatic"

Today's essential quest for constant improvement of everything only comes from constant adjustment of routines, both trivial and great. To adjust any process means dealing with new conditions—which means (once again) failing ("if you're not falling down, you're not learning" is the skier's dictum). It is impossible to overstate the degree to which tiny failures (minuscule errors resulting from trying new things—e.g., changing the way an order entry form is handled) feel like big ones on the front line in most companies.

To induce constant improvement, *everyone* must be failing faster, including the newest mail clerk, trying to improve his or her method of sorting the mail. The idea of supporting—seeking out and vigorously applauding—numerous little failures is essential. For the littlest novel effort feels like a huge risk to most, and it traditionally has been ("we don't pay people to screw things up, Ms.

Jones"). We must, then, especially on the front line, become "failure fanatics," constantly in search of a little mistake to applaud, even a dumb one made in an effort to improve something.

THE DIRE RESULTS OF FAILING
TO SUPPORT FAILURE

It is so frightening to observe, as I repeatedly do, organizations where the fear of revealing the tiniest of errors is sky-high. Here's what ensues: (1) Small failures are individually hidden and fester until they accumulate, causing big failures much further down the line; (2) small failures, since they are unacceptable, do not quickly lead to adjustments, but are followed by a huge effort to fit a square peg into a round hole; (3) data are faked (or very liberally or partially interpreted) so that failures can be seen as successes; (4) data are hidden from those in other functions who could help, because the lead function's boss doesn't want to lose face with his or her peers; (5) those at the top are kept in the dark and partially misled (at least by omission), and then commit themselves further and further on the basis of incorrect knowledge—which makes subsequent exposure of failure even harder; (6) no learning takes place, especially among politicized seniors, because no failures ever come to the surface, and normal human give-and-take, chiding and crowing, is replaced by stilted posturing; (7) real tests are delayed and delayed as more and more simulations are done, in a panicky, time-consuming effort to make sure that no failure occurs on the first test—now highly visible and expensive; and, finally, (8) truth, fun, and speed all go down the drain.

SUPPORT DEFIANCE OF REGULATIONS
THAT SLOW THINGS DOWN

The innovation prescriptions boil down to tactics for speeding up the pace of action-taking. And there is an even more audacious requirement than the last one (support for fast failure): Actively and publicly hail defiance of the rules, many of which you doubtless labored mightily to construct in the first place.

To be sure, this does not mean condoning lawbreaking, abusing a fellow employee (or customer or supplier), or allowing shoddy products to go out the door, even to a test market. These few core values should not be defied.

Here I refer to lauding the breaking of bureaucratic rules, regulations, and conventions which, even when written out, unnecessarily slow down action-taking. But how can you teach respect for the law and individuals, promote perfection in quality and service, and then race around cheering out-and-out defiance?

In a perfect world, there'd be no Mickey Mouse rules, written or otherwise (see P-10, L-8 for my suggestions on getting rid of such nuisances). Furthermore, you'd have no functional jealousies and turf-guarding to clog up the works. But the world of sizable organizations is not perfect and won't be, no matter how hard we work at eliminating bureaucracy. So it is not inconsistent to urge an obsession with quality and at the same time to cheer on someone who ignores petty rules and traditions in order to scrounge some parts or commandeer a computer or 250 square feet of factory space to quickly knock out a prototype. The process of seeking constant quality improvement or enhanced flexibility requires us to break silly rules that impede communication and fast action.

Telling Stories About "Constructive Defiance"

The leader's chief tool here is storytelling (see also L-3). Storytelling allows you to make your point with precision—to distinguish precisely, through example, between "good defiance" and the unacceptable violation of core values. So I suggest that you use storytelling (in person at all-hands meetings, in newsletters, on videotape) to laud innovators' appropriate defiance and, at the same time, their adherence to shared values. Thus, you can publicly laugh at the details of their scrounging of this and that, and at the same time applaud the quality of their work and their respect for their teammates. More specifically, I propose that you go out of your way to recount at least one vignette which illustrates constructive defiance, as I call it, in pursuit of speedy innovation each time you give a little talk; include at least one story of constructive defiance in each newsletter.

Few Rules Should Be Inviolable: "Place Your Waterline Low"

The late Bill Gore (founder of W. L. Gore & Associates, makers of Gore-Tex and medical products) had a superb metaphor for managing risk-taking. "You can try anything, as long as it's above the 'waterline,' " he'd say. "Above the waterline" meant anything that didn't affect the basic integrity of the organization. "If you want to drill holes below the waterline," he'd add, "you need to check with your sponsor [the W. L. Gore equivalent of boss]."

I've found that metaphor useful—to a point. That is, the practical issue becomes where management places the waterline. Bill Gore placed it as shown in Figure 12A; very little was below it. You were encouraged to try almost anything. In fact, the last time I saw him, in 1986, he bragged that a European associate had bought a plant (albeit for a song) without telling him!

I find that the conventional listener is enamored with the waterline metaphor. However, in his or her mind, it's placed as shown in Figure 12B. Virtually nothing is above it. The message: Experiment (and risk failure) as long as the issue is trivial. While I can't provide exact advice on waterline placement, I can urge you to edge toward Bill Gore's version. Constant risk-taking and experimentation are required today simply to survive.

Figure 12

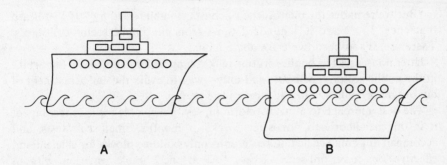

A   B

CLEAR AWAY THE HURDLES THAT IMPEDE INNOVATORS' PROGRESS

The final element of this prescription is a suggestion that you adopt a "running the copier" mentality. Innovation project teams get bogged down for numerous reasons, and most of them turn out to be trivial: The team is unable to cadge an extra 100 square feet of office space, even though the project has a high priority. They have to go through a lengthy capital appropriations ritual to get a personal computer. As boss, often the biggest boost you can give your innovation teams comes from seeking out opportunities to knock down these small hurdles, the ones that people are not likely to talk to you about because they are so mundane they don't merit "bothering you." Take heed of the words of Fred Brooks, legendary chief designer of IBM's pathbreaking System 360: "How does a project get to be a year behind schedule? One day at a time." The accumulation of little items, each too "trivial" to trouble the boss with, is a prime cause of miss-the-market delays. As boss, you must consciously seek out opportunities to help in little ways. You must view yourself as basher-in-chief of small barriers and facilitator-in-chief of trivial aids to action rather than "the great planner."

Performing this barrier-bashing activity also presents one more opportunity to symbolize innovation (see I-7). When you, as chief, directly intervene to clear the "little stuff" out of the way, you are not just being helpful to the team. You are also sending a powerful message to all involved that you don't want such barriers to interfere with innovation-minded project teams in the first place. Flailing away at the little hurdles—and publicly clucking at the hurdle-makers—is all part of the process of upping the pace of activity.

275

PUBLIC PARALLELS

"But we're under the microscope of constant public scrutiny." If I've heard that once, I've heard it a hundred times from my public sector colleagues. Therefore, it's implied, we can't abide failure.

Utter nonsense! The public scrutiny makes support for failing *more* important in the public sector. The best—and only—way to avoid the embarrassment of big program failures is to encourage little ones.

The best approach to a major reform in, say, police practice is to test bits of it in one neighborhood, for a few weeks or months. Small-scale tests, and accompanying small-scale failures, are the only building blocks for efficient and effective long-term, full-scale success. "All at once" implementation, without such tests and failures, is a recipe for disaster—and true public embarrassment.

FIRST STEPS

I suggest that you (1) publicly applaud at least one fast failure, (2) reward at least one act of constructive defiance, (3) knock down at least one seemingly trivial barrier in a team's way, and (4) perform at least one small facilitating act this week. Insist that each of your subordinate managers do the same.

I-9

SUMMARY

Since a stepped-up rate of innovation has become essential, we must:

▶ Measure innovation.

What gets measured gets done. While there are difficult issues of specification and definition, innovation can be measured. Even imperfect measures provide an accurate strategic indication of progress, or lack thereof.

For every profit center, fast-growing or stagnant, establish a uniform and tough quantitative target for the percentage of revenues stemming from new products and services introduced in the previous 24 months; be liberal in your definition of what constitutes "new." As a starting point, consider a target of 50 percent; this is far too low for some industries, and perhaps too high for others.

Set Quantitative Innovation Goals

Business Week proclaimed in mid-1986 that Digital Equipment's resurgence could be measured by the 85 percent of sales coming from products introduced in the last 18 months—and contrasted it with IBM's 40 percent over a comparable period. The magazine added that the Digital figure has become an obsession in IBM's executive suite. There's doubtless more to the current state of the ongoing contest between IBM and Digital, but this simple analysis does get directly to the heart of the matter: Innovation can be measured, and thought about—quantitatively.

As usual in these prescriptions, attitude is the root issue—in this instance, getting innovation "in the air." But also as usual, I've discovered no better way to get at these "soft" concerns than by measuring what most consider impossible-to-quantify phenomena. Precise measurement involves sticky matters of definition, as we shall see. However, even crude measures focus the debate. *Business Week*'s crude 85 percent versus 40 percent turns out to be a pretty good indication of IBM's nagging sluggishness in an ever accelerating marketplace.

MEASURING INNOVATION: FIVE KEY FACTORS

You must consider five key factors when measuring innovation:

1. Definition: What constitutes an innovation. It *is* difficult to define innovation. I acknowledge that, and suggest that you worry about it. But then I also suggest that you reach a quick compromise and move to action—in this case, measurement.

Just what is a new product? Surely it's Apple's new Macintosh SE computer. But what about a new cable for that computer? It's the addition of a breakfast menu at a fast-food chain. But is it the addition of a new jelly for morning muffins at the same chain? It's a new photo-finishing kiosk in a retail store, but is it the availability of a new extra-large or extra-small size in one line of shoes?

My strong bias is toward a broadly inclusive definition of what constitutes a new product, for at least three reasons. First, small can turn out to be big. In the early seventies Frito-Lay went after big wins, focusing new-product development energy on whole new categories. Its batting average was low. A new emphasis on "line extensions" marked the late seventies. Line extension connotes small changes in general. But Frito-Lay found out that small was often big. A new bag size opened the market to new customers with new needs. The addition of a new flavor in an old product created a new market.

The story is repeated in other arenas. A building material is repackaged to make it easier for construction workers to handle it on the job. The small change creates new and growing demand for the product. Even in very high technology, a small, user-friendly twist creates unexpected new uses and new customers, and thence new markets.

The second reason for a broad definition of innovation is that the accumulation of small innovations is the premier source of big innovations. The objective is to create history fast—the rapid transformation of every product and service. This was the essence of C-1 through C-4. And recall, from prescription I-1, Regis McKenna's concept of a product as a continuous experiment. Apple has changed the bellwether Apple II dozens of times in a few short years. Each change creates new uses, and over time total transformation has occurred. So, too, has any given department in Nieman-Marcus been modified time and again until it bears only superficial resemblance to its original form.

In fact, research concludes that most landmark products (called "technological guideposts" in engineering- and science-based firms) do not involve breakthroughs. Instead, they are the culmination of many changes, each small, which eventually lead to wholesale user adoption of the product.

The final reason to emphasize small innovations is psychological. "Have innovation on the mind" and "act fast everywhere" are the underlying imperatives of all ten of these prescriptions. Focusing on small innovations improves the odds of generating lots of wins and greater involvement in and enthusiasm for innovation in general.

But isn't there a danger in ignoring the breakthroughs and working far too long on buggy whips and vacuum tubes? Of course there is. But in general, overemphasizing the search for the miracle solution is more dangerous than overemphasizing day-to-day, user-friendly improvements.

2. Rewards: Linked to the innovation goal. Tie compensation and evaluation to the quantitative innovation goal. Measurement stirs up discussion, but the clincher is tying evaluation to it. That was the message on quality (prescription C-2) and service (C-3); the same tune is being hummed here.

3M has pioneered. Compensation, especially at senior levels, has been linked to the percentage of sales that come from new products introduced in the previous couple of years. We urge that you move in the same direction, once you put the issue of definition behind you.

I don't want to make this seem easy. It's not. The aim of measuring innovation is to foster more action, faster, and there is a danger—and this applies to quality measurement schemes as well. The main objective might be derailed if measuring ends up creating bureaucratic pettifogging—for example, if it leads people to revise catalogues weekly to make more colors available on a particular product in order to satisfy the innovation measurement system's appetite. That's obviously not the point.

To beat back the chances of such a bureaucratic drift, arrive at a broadly agreed-upon definition of what constitutes innovation. Then rate executives and others on the basis of the definition, sorting them into three or four broad categories; reward on that basis. And if the definition you chose leads to nitpicks and dysfunctional behavior, change it.

3. Uniform innovation targets. The most important nuance again comes courtesy of 3M: Consider making every business unit's innovation target exactly the same. The theory is simple. Every division, old and mature or new and exotic, should be responsible for regular regeneration. The sandpaper gang should not be let off the hook, or treated as a "cash cow," to use that unfortunate term from the 1970s.

I can't overemphasize the importance of this. In C-1, I presented decisive evidence that (1) all markets, including mature ones, are fragmenting and becoming increasingly dominated by value-adding specialists; (2) highly differentiated mature products are the biggest moneymakers; and (3) any product can be fundamentally differentiated/transformed—a store is no longer "a store," but becomes an "experience," etc. Were I not for target uniformity, I would be led to suggest tougher innovation targets for older and more sluggish divisions or units. The divisions involved in new markets will be forced automatically by competition to act fast. The units with older, established markets can easily (1) become complacent if they are doing well or (2) fall into the "it's a commodity, so only price/cost counts" mind-set.

4. Widespread use of the innovation target. Once more, an atmosphere with chatter about innovation is the central objective. Track and measure innovation, quantitatively and qualitatively. Put innovation goals in every manager's set of objectives. Have quarterly or monthly innovation review meetings in every function, including training and accounting. Start each weekly or monthly staff or operations review meeting with five minutes on innovation programs. Get innovation measures into the formal accounting system. Share information on innovation with everyone. Post measurements of progress conspicuously.

Talk it up!

5. The involvement of all hands. Finally, this measurement process should include everyone. You should emphasize a single, big measurement (e.g., IBM's 40 percent versus Digital's 85 percent and 3M's single target). But at a secondary level, performance evaluation criteria should have "innovation requirements" (note that there's an analogy here to the "customer connection" proposed in C-3). And this should be as true for cash register clerks as for bench scientists and division general managers (see also I-10, L-9).

FIRST STEPS

1. Do immediate, rough-cut measurement of innovation. Define it loosely and tightly and compare the numbers. Let each department or division do it themselves; *don't let central accounting run the show!* Try some rough comparisons with competitors. Get customers into the act, for they usually give more weight than insiders to minor innovation—and customer-oriented—advances.

2. After observing the stability and usefulness of the measure, move to include it in evaluation and compensation within 18 months from now.

I-10

SUMMARY

The turbulent marketplace demands that we:

▶ Make innovation a way of life for everyone.

We must learn—individually and as organizations—to welcome change and innovation as vigorously as we have fought it in the past, in accounting as well as in new-product development. The corporate capacity for continuous change must be dramatically increased.

Assess each and every action in light of its contribution to an increased corporate capacity for change.

Create a Corporate Capacity for Innovation

BUILDING INNOVATION SKILLS IS A LONG-TERM COMMITMENT

I concur with strategy expert Mike Porter's condemnation of mergers, either to diversify or to acquire market share. They are "a drug," he says, "which makes managers feel good in the short term, but ultimately saps the energy and creativity of the firm." Most so-called strategic alliances, so popular these days, don't work either. Porter goes so far as to say they "are never the solution to a company's strategic dilemma." The alliance is usually aimed at papering over a severe weakness rather than working to correct it; the flaw usually becomes more pronounced, not less, when the teammates attempt to work together. Restructuring, in its conventional guise, comes in for severe criticism, too. Porter agrees that it may be necessary and useful as far as it goes. "But restructuring," he observes, "is not a strategy." It atones for past sins (e.g., excessive layers of management); it does not build for the future (i.e., create new and necessary skills). He faults imitation, too. Imitators, unlike innovators, "lack the conviction to set themselves apart."

All of these commonplace approaches to dealing with today's business environment have one thing in common: they are attempted short cuts. All share a fatal flaw. They sidestep the painstaking effort required to create the core capabilities necessary to achieve sustainable competitive advantage in a turbulent setting. No skill is more important than the corporate capacity to change per se. The company's most urgent task, then, is to learn to welcome—beg for, demand—innovation from everyone. This is the prerequisite for basic capability-building of any sort, and for subsequent continuous improvement.

Elicit Innovation from Everyone

Creating a basic innovative capacity means inducing a steady, high-volume flow of new projects, products, and services (I-1, I-9). It requires nurturing and ensuring an adequate number of passionate and at times disruptive champions (I-6). It means measuring managers on how much innovation they've induced (I-9). But the challenge ends up being much more broad-based. Everyone, in every function, must constantly pursue innovation; the average firm's overall capacity for innovation must increase dramatically.

It is ironic that we usually argue that Americans are innovators while the Japanese are copycats. There is a good case for the opposite conclusion. To be sure, we Americans love our cowboy entrepreneur heroes, our touted buyers in retailing, our engineers and deal-makers, and our matchless stream of Nobel Prize winners. But we are the ones who treat our workers as rote executors. And our first-line supervisors too. We even treat our middle managers as administrators—not creators of a new (or constantly improving) order. The Japanese, on the other hand, have created a corporate capacity for innovation. They are the ones who insist that every person be constantly involved in improvement projects—every boss, every nonboss, every salesperson and researcher and supplier and subcontractor. Consultant Masaaki Imai even quantifies the trait for managers: "Japanese management generally believes that a manager should spend at least 50 percent of his time on improvement."

The best American firms and leaders, without reference to Japan (to them it's neither Eastern nor Western, but a simple matter of common sense), live the same doctrine. At W. L. Gore & Associates, for instance, the principal success measure for every job—from the mail room to the lab—is innovation, the degree to which the worker (or manager) has changed/improved things. The operative question is: "How is your twenty square feet of the accounts receivable department different (and better) from the way it was ninety days ago?"

The Constant Search for New Ideas

In a related vein, I have long observed that one of the primary distinguishing characteristics of the best leaders is their personal thirst for and continued quest for new/small/practical ideas. The two people to whom this book is dedicated, Governor Don Schaefer of Maryland and Roger Milliken, are voracious note-takers (see L-5). Certainly neither one, nor their kindred spirits, ever turned his back on a so-called breakthrough idea. It's just that they long ago gave up believing in miracles; instead, they depend on a mass of small innovations—from everyone—to raise every element of their operations to stratospheric levels of performance.

The idea of being in touch (C-7), swapping and swiping ideas (I-4), and testing them without muss and fuss (I-3) is central. As we saw in prescription C-8, the Japanese and Germans and the best American manufacturers insist that engineers live on the factory floor, getting a feel for the action and being immediately available to assist workers in improvement projects. Being in touch also means breaking down functional barriers. I have emphasized this in relation to new products in prescription I-2, which urges multi-function staffing for new-product teams.

And being in touch and swapping ideas also mean customers, suppliers, and distributors wandering the company's hallways and plants; and everyone from the company wandering the customers' operations. All of this is more important than ever, because the world-class manufacturing or service firm will be more highly integrated than before, albeit in new ways. Just-in-time inventoi y management will apply "backward" to vendors and "forward" to distributors and end users. Computerized design tools will link buyers and engineers to plants and operations centers—and to the customer, too. That is, everyone in every function will be a full-scale partner in the value-adding team. Therefore constant innovation by everyone will be requisite.

OWN UP TO THE MAGNITUDE OF THE TASK

"Improvement" is an innocuous term. Even "innovation" is fairly innocuous. "Change" is not. Change means disruption, by definition. Whether it's holding a welding torch at a slightly different angle, moving a file cabinet ten feet, or installing just-in-time inventory management across ten plants, change *is* disruptive. Constant change by everyone requires a dramatic increase in the capacity to accept disruption. Consider our daily affairs: When a road on the way to work is under repair for sixty days, it's a pain in the neck to search out a new route, especially if you were used to stopping at a particular deli on the old route for the world's best cappuccino and buttermilk doughnuts.

I use this trivial example because we should not downplay what a tall order this prescription, I-10, amounts to. This is especially so given the traditional American mechanical model of management derived from mass production, in which disruption of any sort has been a very dirty word. In fact, in seminars the most common rejoinder that I get to the idea of constant innovation is: "But isn't there a high cost to this chaos and anarchy that you're proposing? Surely we don't want that mail-room clerk you talk about being inventive! We want the damned mail on our desks by 9:30 A.M. For heaven's sake, when do you get any work done with all this 'innovation' going on about you?"

The question is fair only in the context of the old model, in which the worker is seen as a pair of hands, with the head a necessary evil. The reality is that millions—*literally* an unlimited number—of innovation/improvement opportunities lie within any factory, distribution center, store, or operations center. And you can multiply that by more millions when you can involve the factory and distribution center and store working together as a team. And multiply again when you add in involvement in innovation by suppliers and customers.

Only when we come to understand that the ideas are principally on the front line (or in the supplier's operation), not in R&D or "higher up," will the fear of disruption recede. For when the new understanding is stamped in, we will begin to search for ways to give workers more time to work at innovation, rather than threatening them at every turn.

Learning to See Disruptions as Opportunities

At Milliken, slipping in an urgently needed new-product sample used to be the ultimate disruption to the very orderly—"rigid" is not an unfair term—factory production environment. Top management became painfully aware that a much higher rate of such "disruptions" (that is, more new products) was its sole path to survival. The firm's major reorganization described in prescription C-4 was aimed at turning former disruptions into a normal way of life, with no loss of efficiency or diminution in quality.

Turning Adversaries into Partners

Most innovation in the future will demand that historically adversarial relations—(1) between many functions in the firm, (2) between labor and management, (3) between suppliers and the firm, (4) between the firm and its distributors/customers—be replaced by cooperative relations. (See, for instance, C-2 on working with suppliers and on the use of cross-functional teams in quality improvement efforts, and I-2 on speedy team product development.)

Establishing new relationships requires listening, creating a climate of respect and trust (P-1 through P-10, S-4, S-5), and coming to understand the mutual benefits that will ensue if partnership relationships are firmly established.

Creating Innovation Capacity

Creating a corporate capacity for constant innovation is a staggering task, the antithesis of the short-cut approach discussed at the beginning of this prescription. It requires all of the skills covered in the nine innovation prescriptions immediately preceding. Further, I-10 provides an ideal introduction to the next twenty prescriptions. Constant innovation, from everyone in every function, can only occur if each person is uniquely valued for—and trained to make and paid for—her or his potentially awesome contribution (P-1 through P-10). The capacity for change (a shift from love of stability to love of change) is also the implicit topic of all ten leadership prescriptions (L-1 through L-10).

FIRST STEPS

1. I-10 is different from the other innovation prescriptions, and therefore the first step is different—it calls for reflection. Think beyond the practical steps, such as inducing pilots of everything (I-3). Focus on the overall capacity (willingness) of your organization to embrace innovation. Subject every personal action, especially small ones, to this acid test: Does the action increase or decrease the corporate capacity for change? That is, is it on the side of increasing risk-taking and piloting, of encouraging champions to come out of the woodwork? Does it help

reduce the fear of the unknown (through kidding about useful failure, for instance)? Or is it on the side of encouraging over-analysis and inaction? If you can't fill in the blank in the following sentence, "This specifically fosters a greater willingness to innovate (especially on the usually fearful front line) because _____," then modify the action you were about to take. Encourage each person working for you to pass every minute daily action through the same filter.

2. Begin to emphasize the shift from adversary to partner by watching your language: How do you describe people in other functions, union leadership (if applicable), suppliers, franchisees? Begin by ensuring that your language toward the traditionally adversarial group is the language of a partner. And, as in Step #1 above, pass each small act through a filtering operation: Does this impede or accelerate the shift from adversary to partner?

IV

ACHIEVING FLEXIBILITY BY EMPOWERING *P*EOPLE

SECTION SUMMARY

The first twenty prescriptions depict a newly flexible, responsive, and adaptive organization. The implicit, and at times explicit, theme has been "through people"—people *must* become the primary source of value added, not a "factor of production" to be optimized, minimized, and/or eliminated.

The first two of the ten prescriptions here (see Figure 13) constitute the Basic Premise: P-1 boldly asserts that there is no limit to what the average person can accomplish if thoroughly involved; P-2 adds that this power can most effectively be tapped when people are gathered in human-scale groupings—that is, teams, or, more precisely, self-managing teams.

The next prescriptions, the Five Supports, are the tools required to achieve wholesale involvement by everyone: P-3, an atmosphere marked by constant opportunities (both formal and informal) for everyone to be listened to—and then recognized for their smallest accomplishments; P-4, substantial line effort devoted to recruiting that focuses explicitly on desired values and qualities (ability to work on teams, for instance); P-5, a radical emphasis on training and retraining—that is, constant upgrading of skills; P-6, incentive pay, based upon contribution and performance, for everyone; and P-7, provision of some form of employment guarantee for a major part of the work force, assuming acceptable individual performance.

These supports can assist in achieving P-1 and P-2 only if the Three Inhibitors are removed: P-8, simplifying structure by reducing layers and eliminating all front-line supervision as we know it; P-9, changing the role of middle managers from cop and guardian of functional fiefdoms to basher of barriers between functions in order to induce true autonomy and speed action-taking at the front line; and P-10, eliminating silly bureaucratic procedures and, worse still, demeaning regulations and dispiriting work conditions.

A 1985 study by consultants at A. T. Kearney discovered that some 80 percent of Fortune 500 firms had started some type of quality circle program since 1980; unfortunately, 83 percent had dropped the effort within 18 months of its inception. Why?

The principal reason is a tendency simply to form "teams" and in effect tell their members to "get interested and participate." The remedy is to work on all ten of these prescriptions at once. I admit that doing it "all at once" is a tall order. Yet accomplishing the objectives of this set of prescriptions—upon which all else (e.g., C-1 through C-10) depends—is uniquely resistant to piecemeal implementation. Obviously, progress and breadth of implementation will vary from prescription to prescription. But you must at least get started on all ten more or less simultaneously. That is, involvement means nothing without training; involvement and training mean nothing unless overly complex, bureaucratic procedures are eliminated; and so on.

When General Motors and Toyota joined together in the NUMMI venture described in prescription P-1 and referred to elsewhere in these pages, a formal, guiding philosophy was developed. It included these elements: (1) "Kaizen, the never-ending quest for perfection"; (2) "the development of full human potential"; (3) "Jidoka, the pursuit of superior quality"; (4) "build mutual trust"; (5) "develop team performance"; (6) "every employee as manager"; and (7) "provide a stable livelihood for all employees." These seven features, supported by simple systems, extensive training, and a host of other devices, have resulted in startling performance improvement in short order. One *can* break NUMMI's success into a series of discrete factors—but although each *is* essential, it is the interaction among all of them, at work simultaneously, which has proved to be NUMMI's secret.

Figure 13: **Achieving Flexibility by Empowering People**

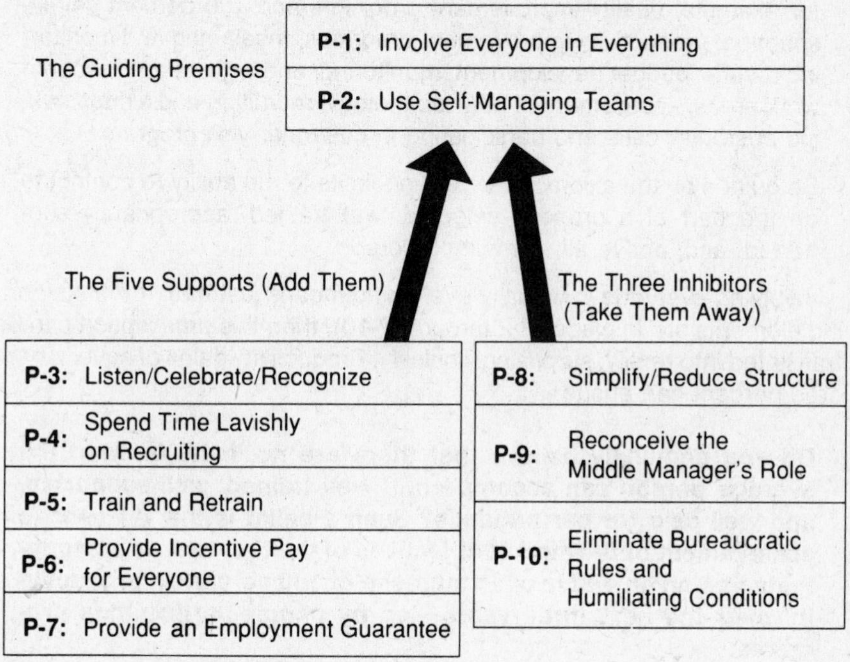

The Guiding Premises

| **P-1:** Involve Everyone in Everything |
| **P-2:** Use Self-Managing Teams |

The Five Supports (Add Them)

The Three Inhibitors (Take Them Away)

P-3: Listen/Celebrate/Recognize	**P-8:** Simplify/Reduce Structure
P-4: Spend Time Lavishly on Recruiting	**P-9:** Reconceive the Middle Manager's Role
P-5: Train and Retrain	
P-6: Provide Incentive Pay for Everyone	**P-10:** Eliminate Bureaucratic Rules and Humiliating Conditions
P-7: Provide an Employment Guarantee	

P-1

SUMMARY

Executing the business strategies laid out in the first two sets of prescriptions (C-1 through C-10, I-1 through I-10) requires the unstinting involvement of everyone in the firm. Therefore, we must:

▶ Involve all personnel at all levels in all functions in virtually everything: for example, quality improvement programs and 100 percent self-inspection; productivity improvement programs; measuring and monitoring results; budget development, monitoring, and adjustment; layout of work areas; assessment of new technology; recruiting and hiring; making customer calls and participating in customer visit programs.

▶ Be guided by the axiom: There are no limits to the ability to contribute on the part of a properly selected, well-trained, appropriately supported, and, above all, committed person.

Involving everyone in virtually everything means just that. If the supporting elements are in place (P-2 through P-10), then this prescription can be translated into reality, surprisingly quickly. Productivity gains of several hundred percent can ensue.

Do you genuinely believe that there are no limits to what the average person can accomplish, if well trained, well supported, and well paid for performance? Such a belief is the #1 spur to achievement of the market objectives of the first twenty prescriptions. Set an objective of an increase of 100 percent in productivity over the next three years—led by people-participation programs.

Involve Everyone
in Everything

Powerlessness corrupts. Absolute powerlessness corrupts absolutely.
> Rosabeth Moss Kanter
> Harvard Business School

Something happened that must not happen again. Somewhere, somehow, the employees got the idea that they were in the driver's seat. That they had control in their hands. This is an attitude, gentlemen, that must be reversed. This is the fantasy that must be eradicated.
> Lemuel Boulware
> GE industrial relations executive
> commenting to top management
> after a 1946 strike

I'm not going to have the monkeys running the zoo.
> Frank Borman
> former chairman, Eastern Airlines,
> discussing worker participation,
> *The Washington Monthly,* June 1986

The customer prescriptions emphasized quality, service, quick response, and heretofore unheard-of flexibility. The innovation prescriptions demanded numerous champion-powered small starts, team product development, and making innovation everyone's responsibility.

Execution of these two sets of prescriptions is impossible without the wholesale involvement mandated by P-1. In fact, despite the accelerating technology/automation revolution, our organizations must become more dependent on people (line workers). To be sure, fewer people will work on the line in a given factory or operations center, but those who do will be more important to and responsible for the company's success than ever before. Prescription C-8 noted the problems American firms have had in implementing flexible systems. All too often we throw money at the wall in the form of overly complex automation schemes designed in some ivory tower and hope it sticks. More important, the successful manufacturing firm is turning to a "service-added"/"responsiveness-added" strategy that is people-intensive.

Thus, we turn to the people prescriptions as a practical matter, in order to execute the strategies laid out in C-1 through C-10 and I-1 through I-10. And once again, this set of prescriptions is "must-do," not a "nice-to-do." Surviving depends upon quality, flexibility, and constant innovation, which in turn depend upon people.

ACKNOWLEDGING THE ROOT OF THE PROBLEM: ATTITUDES OF MANAGEMENT

It's absurd! We don't want for evidence that the average worker is capable of moving mountains—if only we'll ask him or her to do so, and construct a supportive environment. So why don't we do it?

Why do we mindlessly ship jobs offshore, when evidence surrounds us—even from the toughest industries—that we can compete on quality and cost, despite our high wages, if only we take advantage of the work force's potential?

Harvard economist Robert Reich, as noted in Part I, puts the blame on our 150-year love affair with mass production. We, alone, have consistently tried to make labor ever more narrowly specialized and, in the end, to eliminate it. When automation was introduced by U.S. firms such as General Electric, the ad copy made it clear that the objective was (1) to get tighter control over labor and then (2) to eliminate as many people as possible as fast as possible through all-encompassing "big bang" systems.

In my view this mind-set has proved disastrous, especially of late. Indeed, the chief reason for our failure in world-class competition is our failure to tap our work force's potential. By contrast, as discussed in Part I, Japan and Germany, among others: (1) have always had a craft labor tradition and thus have not ceaselessly pursued the narrowing and specialization of job content; (2) have on the contrary looked to automation to enhance labor's value, utilizing labor's input to program simpler and more flexible machines (designed in the United States, but rejected by Americans in favor of complex systems—see C-8); and (3) have sought competitive advantage through constant, rapid refinement of products via a philosophy of constant improvement.

I am frustrated to the point of rage—my files bulge with letters about the power of involvement. Sometimes it's planned, and I'll talk about that. Sometimes it's inadvertent. But the result is always the same: Truly involved people can do anything!

Consider this statement from Nucor Corporation's president, Ken Iverson: "I've heard people say that Nucor is proof that unions per se have a negative impact on worker productivity. That's nonsense! That conveniently ignores vital questions like: What's the quality of direction being given the workers? Where are the resources the workers need to get the job done efficiently? Where's the opportunity for workers to contribute ideas about how to do the job better? The real impediment to producing a higher-quality product more efficiently isn't the workers, union or nonunion; it's management." W. Edwards Deming is a little kinder, insisting that management is merely 90 percent of the problem.

Ralph Stayer is president of Johnsonville Sausage of Sheboygan Falls, Wisconsin. Recall that the firm, mentioned in Part I, has increased its share of the greater Milwaukee market from 7 to over 50 percent since 1978. How? Stayer explains: "Workers felt here's where I get my money and I have fun elsewhere. In the final analysis, a person's work determines what they are in life. I can tolerate being a mediocre golfer, but not a mediocre human being. I didn't really change stuff to get a better product [though that's what ensued]. What I decided to do, if I take my business and turn it this way and that, I can bring out the greatness in people. . . . I listened to people more, asked them how they do things. . . . I didn't find much resistance, but I did find inertia. Their lifelong learning was to take directions and orders, not to be asked questions. I wanted to help people become the instrument of their own destiny."

Tennant executives (see C-2) were proud of their long-standing tradition of being "people-focused." Yet in looking back at the start of their exceptional quality improvement program in 1979, they realized that even their assumptions had been askew: "We frowned on any activity *except* the job. We didn't ask production employees to help design new products or improve procedures. But the quality emphasis gave us an opportunity to tap the knowledge and skill of the people who do the production work."

And yet, a poll of post–World War II graduates of leading business schools done in late 1986 produced these results: 98 percent of the MBAs felt that "Japan's blue-collar workers work harder than their American counterparts." Do they see management as at all responsible for this "fact"? Apparently not. In answer to the next question, 69 percent of the MBAs swore allegiance to themselves, signing up for this statement: "The United States has more capable managers in business and industry than the Japanese."

THE POWER OF INVOLVEMENT—EVEN IF INADVERTENT

Let me begin again, more systematically, with three cases illustrating the astonishing effects of worker participation. None of the three involves training, structural change, pay incentives, or any of the other supports that I'll recommend in this section on people. They simply offer a glimpse of what I believe is the compelling, natural human thirst to be engaged:

▶ Pieter Martin, manufacturing manager of Buckman Labs' plant in Ghent, Belgium, wanted to improve communication between departments. When he installed what he thought would be a perfect communications system, he noticed an unintended result. Martin had invested $5,000 in walkie-talkies for eighteen employees that would allow the warehouse workers to contact the shipping department, for instance, or the lab supervisor to call the production line without bothering the maintenance crew. But the walkie-talkies of two of the workers didn't work right—they picked up all the interdepartmental chatter. Martin says, "They didn't tell us. And eventually I noticed that at meetings those two were so involved, asking lots of questions and offering solutions to problems in other departments." When he discovered the reason was the "flawed" walkie-talkies, he didn't try to get them fixed. Instead, he traded them in for a downgraded system to allow everyone to listen in on everyone else.

▶ The $25 million video products firm was growing, but its operations department was fast slipping out of control. The groups involved in purchasing, scheduling, order entry, packaging/labeling, and shipping were always at odds. Foul-ups were costing millions. The operations vice president tried everything. He had an outside systems expert look at the difficulties. He dove in himself. He called in each of the dozen key people for individual counseling. Defeated, he decided that hiring a full-time "coordinator" would be the only lasting solution.

But, in a Catch-22 twist, the problem was so advanced that there were no funds for hiring the coordinator. So, on an interim basis, he pulled the dozen together, unloaded his continuing frustrations, and simply begged them to meet once a week and talk about the problems. It couldn't hurt. He informed them that he would be available to give advice, as needed. He then effectively washed his hands of the discouraging mess, even turning over to the leaderless "group" the authority to sign off on items worth tens of thousands of dollars.

It didn't take a genius to see that things started to improve within just a couple of weeks. And the nagging problems didn't just get better, they began to disappear. Another few weeks went by; he was surprised that no one had called to ask his advice.

Some time later he received the long-awaited tap and was asked to show up at a meeting the following week to provide some expert counsel on a technical issue. Upon arrival, he found a formal, professional agenda at his assigned seat, and discovered that he—the nominal boss—was on call for item number six. The pace was brisk and the handling of items was efficient. A couple of other outside experts appeared before he did, including the local UPS manager, who had been asked by the committee to solve a nagging distribution coordination problem.

The VP's turn routinely came and went. As the meeting moved along, his only irritation was somewhat minor. The youngest and only female participant was taking notes. "Just one more example of delegating the crummy task to the junior woman," he grumbled to himself. Then, as the meeting ended, she raised her head from her note-taking and commented: "Well, that will do it for this week. I pass along my role as chairman. Whose turn is it to run the show next week?"

► The AMAX coal mine was about to run out of material at its main operating face. Three expert studies, one by an outside consultant, demonstrated decisively that extension of the current operation was uneconomic. A $24 million project was required to extend the mine's life.

A new engineer, who didn't know any better, broke tradition by going underground and wandering the face, chatting with miners. One old-timer, a member of the United Mine Workers, was perplexed at the impending shutdown of the current face. He laid out a relatively inexpensive approach to keeping it open. The green engineer allowed as how the scheme sounded plausible to him.

The engineer quickly put together a proposal triggered by the miner's idea. It costed out at $4.8 million, and management was grudgingly convinced it was worth a try, if the engineer could get volunteers. He asked, and thirty UMW members came forward, along with a handful of supervisors and engineers.

The project immediately ran into trouble; a roof caved in as the group began a tricky attempt to drill through a fault. The mine boss, a skeptic to begin with, gave the young engineer a weekend to fix the problem or "pack up your gear and get out." On Saturday, the engineer met with the entire team all day, laying out the situation and soliciting ideas. A revised scheme was quickly concocted. It worked superbly.

The project became a model of participation in any number of ways. For example, after the first emergency session, the entire team adopted the habit of meeting every Saturday to discuss progress and problems. Team involvement included equipment reclamation too. Given top management's skepticism, the group was allotted the two worst machines for the job—machines ticketed for the scrapheap at project's end. The miners—UMW stalwarts all—entirely reconfigured the old equipment in the course of the project. The two worst machines emerged as the best pieces of equipment in the mine's inventory, far superior to much newer models.

At one level, then, the message of this prescription is involvement by hook or by crook. That is, do it! Of course, the more systematic questions are: How much? At what pace? With what tools?

MANAGING THE WORKPLACE TO MAXIMIZE INVOLVEMENT

Worthington Industries and Chaparral Steel produce steel of superb quality—but have *no* quality inspectors. "Our people in the plants are responsible for their own product and its quality," says Chaparral's Gordon Forward. "We expect them to act like owners." Forward goes on:

It's really amazing what people can do when you let them. Take our security guards, for example. Normally, when you think of security guards at four o'clock in the morning, they're doing everything they can just to stay awake. Well, ours also enter data into our computer—order entry, things like that. They put the day's quality results into the computer system each night. We upgraded the job and made a very clear decision not to hire some sleepy old guy to sit and stare at the factory gate all night. Our guards are paramedics; they run the ambulance; they fill up the fire extinguishers; they do the checks on the plant; now we're even considering some accounting functions.

In the plant, our supervisors do their own hiring. The two people we have in personnel [for a 1,000-person operation] do some initial screening and look after group health insurance and a few other things. But the supervisors run their own shows. They're responsible for training their people and for their safety. They have room to grow. Every time a new piece of equipment comes into the plant, the foremen and their crews decide how we are going to operate it. Or if we upgrade some equipment and find a new, better way to operate it, those people make those decisions too.

It should be evident that the removal of barriers between functions and the abolition of nitpicking job specialization are essential to such involvement. Certainly it has been near the heart of the success at NUMMI. The landmark UAW-NUMMI agreement reduced job categories from eighty to four. A parallel plan encourages workers to learn upwards of a dozen jobs. The practical consequences are, of course, considerable. But the psychological ones are even more important. One worker, who was employed at GM's operation in Fremont, California, before it shut down and reopened as NUMMI, explains his liberation: "For six years, all I did was ashtrays. Now I don't know which of the nineteen things I'm trained for so far I'll be doing." That sounds rather innocuous. But think about your day. It may go well or poorly, but it's not likely to be boring or mind-numbing. Problems will arise that will keep you engaged. Engagement is the point.

And what have been the results? The same UAW workers who were disaffected GM employees in 1981 are now producing what some statistics confirm is the top-quality car made in the United States.* Productivity quickly became tops among GM's plants, despite a below-average level of automation. An absenteeism record and a grievance rate that were among the worst in GM in 1981 are now among the best—with those same people.

GM has taken its lumps in this book. But its vast operation also includes models of the best of what can be; the firm's problem has been a failure to implement widely the lessons learned from its best operations. One bellwether is its successful Delco-Remy plant in Fitzgerald, Georgia, which provides a good laundry list of just how far involvement can go. The *average* workers there:

---

*NUMMI alternates production of the Toyota FX and Chevrolet Nova. The former is selling. The latter, still burdened with lackluster design and a lingering perception of shoddy GM quality, has not done well. (No layoffs are in the works, however.)

▶ handle all quality control (experts are on tap only if needed in specific cases)
▶ do all maintenance and make minor repairs on machines
▶ keep track of their own time; there are no time cards (no clock)
▶ handle the "housekeeping" (no janitors)
▶ participate in a pay-for-knowledge program (for learning almost every job in the plant)
▶ are organized in teams which engage in regular problem-solving activities
▶ are responsible for safety
▶ have full-time access to the lock-free tool room
▶ do budget preparation and review (capital and operating)
▶ help determine staffing levels
▶ advise management on equipment layout and generate requirements for new equipment
▶ are in charge of all recruiting and run the assessment center for new recruits
▶ decide on layoff patterns (whether to lay people off or have everybody work shorter hours, for example)
▶ rotate as leaders of work teams

Sadly, NUMMI and Fitzgerald, with their extraordinary records for low absenteeism, high quality, and high productivity, are still far from the norm, at GM and elsewhere.

CREATING A CLIMATE THAT ENCOURAGES SPONTANEOUS INITIATIVE-TAKING

The ultimate stage of involvement is the regular, spontaneous taking of initiative. For instance, Tennant Company executives brag about their welders in *Quest for Quality:* "Traditionally, the welding department's procedure was to weld several individual machine parts . . . then send them to the stockroom, where they were stored until the department had an order to produce a particular machine. The company's engineers wanted to streamline the operation by welding more and storing fewer units. They devised a system with a $100,000 price tag that was rejected by management as too expensive. Even a scaled-down, $25,000 version was deemed too costly. A small group of welders tackled the problem. They designed an overhead monorail that could carry welded parts from one station to another so a frame could be welded together from start to finish without leaving the department. The welders weren't deterred by cost. They discovered a supply of I-beams in a local junkyard and bought them for less than $2,000. In *two days* [my emphasis] they installed the monorail. In the first year of its use, the new system saved . . . more than $29,000 in time and storage space."

Service firms have the same opportunities as do manufacturers. Consider the case of a janitor, the sole person on duty at a commissary of Domino's Pizza Distribution Company. He took an off-hours call from a franchisee about to run out of pepperoni. (Having a franchisee run out of anything is the cardinal sin at Domino's Distribution.) On his own initiative, he located keys to a truck, loaded the vehicle with one small box of pepperoni, and drove hundreds of miles to keep the franchisee from closing down. It never occurred to him that Distribution, as the subsidiary is called, would want him to do anything else—and he was right.

And how about the relatively junior telecommunications expert at Federal Express who, following a blizzard in the California Sierras, was faced with the prospect of having no phone service for several days? With no coaching—and no need to seek approval from above—he rented a helicopter (using his personal American Express card), was dropped onto a snowbound mountaintop, trudged three-quarters of a mile in chest-deep snow, and fixed the line to get Fed Ex back in business. This occurrence, though spontaneous, was hardly accidental. Federal Express, like Domino's, constantly emphasizes (through management example, the absence of stifling bureaucracy and structure, exhortation, recognition, and formal training) that all workers are routinely expected to take whatever initiative is required to fix problems and/or extend first-rate service to a customer. In fact, not to act this "outrageously" (by the standards of others) is cause for a poor evaluation.

The question confronting us in the remainder of this section is how to induce such involvement and initiative-taking as a matter of course.

Sometimes some seem to be learning. I'll stumble across an article, such as one in a late 1986 issue of the San Jose *Mercury News,* titled, "McDonnell Looks to Rank and File to Help Set Management Strategy." It reports: "In a departure from its traditional top-down management style, the St. Louis aerospace giant is trying a new tactic: It's asking some of the company's lowest-paid workers how to run the business better."

But then a few days later I hear two different sorts of tales. A family friend works in a New Jersey construction products plant. To cut costs, they removed *all* the pay phones. She had a father who was desperately ill, and was infuriated. Another friend does duty on the swing shift in a midwestern chemical plant. "They out and out told us," he says, " 'You're not here to use your heads.' " The plant's products are used in medical procedures, and when he went into the hospital last year, my friend asked a nurse if a particular procedure involved his company's product. "She said it didn't," he reports. "If it had been our stuff, I wouldn't have let them do the procedure. I'd have demanded [a competitor's product]." Is that damning?

I conclude with a simple and heartfelt request: Spend some time by a lake and just think about all of this. Recall the extraordinary feats of Domino's janitor and the junior telecommunications expert at Federal Express. Recall the effects of the inadvertent involvement of the two people tied into the walkie-talkie system at Buckman Labs, and what happens routinely at Worthington, Johnsonville, and Nordstrom. Recall the welders at Tennant, the AMAX miners, the Chaparral night watchman, the turnaround at NUMMI—with the union involved—and the long list of normal worker activities in Fitzgerald, Georgia.

Do you really think the average worker can become so engaged? Can earn his or her salary several times over? Let me remind you that the increases in productivity associated with my examples, not to mention the improved quality, often amount to a hundred percent or more (the national average, remember, is less than 2 percent a year). That is why I demand, in this prescription, that over the next 36 months you shoot for an increase of 100 percent in productivity via participation-led programs.

Yes, we are fighting 150 years of converse assumptions about specialization, jurisdiction, participation, skill enhancement, and initiative taking—and the will of the worker. But the eleventh hour is upon us. Just what do I, and Chaparral's Gordon Forward, and Buckman's Pieter Martin, and Johnsonville's Ralph Stayer, Worthington's John McConnell, and Fred Smith of Federal Express, have to do to convince you?

DO SOMETHING!

Involvement can start with anything. Maybe even a party. The point is to find *some* window into the process. GM's pioneering efforts at Buick City provide a good example of seeking an opening, any opening:

> The QWL [Quality of Work Life] process began in Buick in 1975. The general manager provided the initial impetus based upon his participation in a union-management QWL seminar sponsored by the GM-UAW National Quality of Work Life Committee. This meeting so impressed him that he encouraged his staff to participate in a similar seminar with the leadership of UAW Local 599, which represents the 16,000 production and maintenance workers at Buick in Flint, Michigan.
>
> The first meeting was held in October 1975. Among other accomplishments, a joint committee was established to oversee the QWL process. After about a half dozen off-site meetings, the third of which was held at the UAW Family Education Center as guests of the union, a decision was made to provide an opportunity for the workers to become involved in some form or fashion. Since neither party was quite sure of how the process might work and how people might react to the joint invitation, they agreed upon the safe step of an open house. The voluntary participation of employees was sought in the planning, organization, and administration of a division-wide open house for Buick families and friends. The open house was so successful that it was followed over the next two years by a bond drive, a blood donor campaign, a hospital fund-raising, and a United Way of Michigan campaign.
>
> Because the people so impressed management with their talents, their eagerness, and their desire to become more involved, the manufacturing manager began to look for a way to institutionalize the high level of involvement.

303

And, indeed, much has happened since. Yet the opening was critical. Having a party is surely not the only way to begin. But it's a pretty good one, it turns out.

PUBLIC PARALLELS

The public parallels are exact, with one possible catch: union-management tension. Sadly, most management-union agreements to do such things as reduce job specialization categories have been made with a gun to the heads of both parties—the threat of going bust. Perhaps a stringent budgetary environment in the public sector will lead to the same sorts of useful pressure—on both unions *and* management.

Despite this, it remains a fact that W. Edwards Deming's assessment of management as 90 percent to blame for lack of enthusiastic participation among front-line employees applies to the public as well as the private sector. Any manager, low-level or high-, in a union or nonunion environment, can accomplish 75 percent of what's advocated here, regardless of the setting. As usual with our prescriptions, attitudes are fundamental.

FIRST STEPS

1. Spend a week or two working a regular shift in a factory or operations center. Make a list of the tasks that the first two levels of supervision are now doing. Talk with colleagues. Think about inadvertent or planned acts of front-line initiative-taking in your past experience. How many of the tasks that supervisors perform could be done by first-line people?
2. Experiment with some enhanced, new skill training for first-line people, starting in the next 60 to 120 days. Bring informal groups together to talk about job redefinition. If you can do it in the context of competitive necessity, so much the better. Involve first- and second-line supervisors in your frightening (to them—see P-2) deliberations from the start.
3. In the course of the next six months, form a study group of fifteen (principally line managers at all levels). Visit at least ten American factories or operations centers which are undertaking dramatic participation-led programs. At the end of that study, consider committing to the quantitative productivity improvement goal established above.

P-2

SUMMARY

To achieve the level of involvement described in P-1, which is necessary to become appropriately flexible, quality-conscious, and thence competitive, we must:

▶ Organize as much as possible around teams, to achieve enhanced focus, task orientation, innovativeness, and individual commitment.

The modest-sized, task-oriented, semi-autonomous, mainly self-managing team should be the basic organization building block. Be aware that the wholesale use of a self-managing team structure probably calls for elimination of the traditional first-line supervisor's job.

Regardless of whether or not the fit is perfect, organize *every function* into ten- to thirty-person, largely self-managing teams. Eliminate all first-line supervision as we know it (see also P-8).

P-2

Use Self-Managing Teams

P-1 set the stage. Wholesale worker involvement must become a national priority if we are to create the competitive strengths necessary just to maintain, let alone improve, our national economic well-being. The next nine prescriptions address how to achieve this goal. At the top of the list is the use of teams, variously called quality circles, semi-autonomous work groups, and self-managing teams.

Use them. That's the first piece of advice. The self-managing team should become the basic organizational building block. Train them; recruit on the basis of teamwork potential; pay them for performance; and clean up the bureaucracy around them, dramatically changing the roles of middle managers and staff experts (these are topics of subsequent prescriptions).

Team-based organization, though not widespread in American business, is hardly a new idea. And it is certainly not Japanese-inspired or some product of a mysterious Asian group mentality. True, the twelve-person section is the basic Japanese organizational unit, but teams, in the form of eight-person squads, have been the bedrock of Western military organization, for instance, for hundreds of years.

EXAMPLES TO LEARN FROM

The good news is that numerous examples are available for observation and analysis. General Motors, for instance, has been experimenting for a dozen years now, at a host of union and nonunion sites. One early experiment, at the Delco-Remy plant in Fitzgerald, Georgia, was described in P-1, where the subject was the exceptional involvement of individual workers. The Fitzgerald plant is entirely team-based. Figure 14 shows the interlocking nature of operating and support teams, all the way to the top of the organization chart.

But, you say, what can I learn about team-based organizations from a new, nonunion plant like Fitzgerald? Consider, then, GM's Cadillac engine plant in Livonia, Michigan, which was reorganized in the early 1980s. Fundamental to the transformation were these elements: (1) A planning team, consisting of (2) management and union leaders, as well as (3) several hourly employees, worked

Figure 14: **The Fitzgerald Plant Organization**

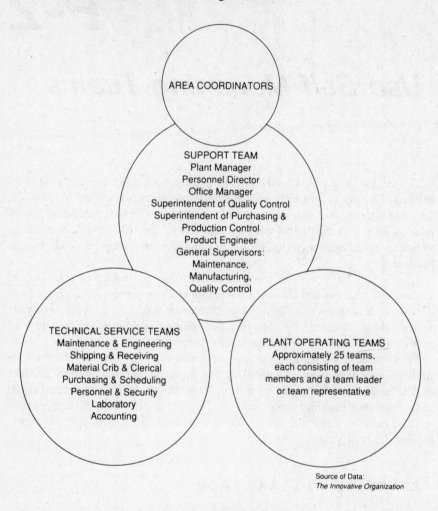

AREA COORDINATORS

SUPPORT TEAM
Plant Manager
Personnel Director
Office Manager
Superintendent of Quality Control
Superintendent of Purchasing &
Production Control
Product Engineer
General Supervisors:
Maintenance,
Manufacturing,
Quality Control

TECHNICAL SERVICE TEAMS
Maintenance & Engineering
Shipping & Receiving
Material Crib & Clerical
Purchasing & Scheduling
Personnel & Security
Laboratory
Accounting

PLANT OPERATING TEAMS
Approximately 25 teams,
each consisting of team
members and a team leader
or team representative

Source of Data:
The Innovative Organization

(4) full-time for (5) almost a year on plant organization and operation. (6) Visits to other sites were made. (7) The previously secret account books were opened up. (8) An operating philosophy was hammered out, called the Livonia Engine Plant Operating Philosophy. (9) A team structure was arrived at. Former plant manager Bob Stramy and two colleagues report the planning team's principal finding in *Transforming the Workplace:* "The most powerful and influential conclusion concerns the Livonia Planning Team's unqualified support and promotion of the team concept as a central and unifying force throughout the new organization. So urgent and prominent was this ideal, moreover, that it immediately became the recurrent main theme of the evolving operating plan and its orchestration over the months of planned implementation."

The team focus at Livonia meant that (10) every person in the organization became part of a group of eight to fifteen people. (11) Importantly—and appropriately—the groups came to be called, not work groups, but business teams.* (12) The "business team" is a highly autonomous group (especially by prior standards), responsible for scheduling, training, problem solving, and many other activities. The teams, for instance, (13) developed their own quantitative performance indicators. (14) They meet at least once a week as a group. (15) Pay-for-knowledge, as at Fitzgerald, encourages everyone (16) to learn virtually every job in the plant. (17) Most awards for suggestions are team-based (this is yet another commonplace Japanese practice), and (18) individual performance appraisals emphasize support for the business team. As at NUMMI (which is also team-based), (19) job specialization has been virtually eliminated. Only a single job category remains at Livonia: "quality operator."

Early productivity and quality results were exciting.

MAKING SELF-MANAGING TEAMS WORK: ALTER THE CONTEXT

First-Line Supervisors Must Change (and Mainly Disappear)

The most difficult issue in most shifts from a traditional structure to self-managing teams is not the worker. It's figuring out what to do with the first-line supervisor. At Livonia, the second level of supervision, that of general foreman, was entirely eliminated, and the number of first-level supervisors (the foremen) was reduced by 40 percent; the foreman's role was retitled team coordinator. An outside observer of GM's numerous team-based experiments concluded:

The most difficult role change in a team-based plant is from traditional production supervisor to an area advisor for a group of shop floor work teams. Advisors are usually chosen through a process of self-selection and careful screening. They are then trained in participative management, group facilitation, and problem-solving skills, often together with the union committeemen. Advisors are responsible for quality, cost, schedule, and people development goals, as well as boundary management for their groups. Their style should become more participative and less directive as work teams gain skills. The dramatic increase in the scope of the advisor's role and in the skills needed to do it well often lead to feelings of ambiguity and confusion. In this area, as in so many others, top plant management must provide a flexible support system for advisors which is designed to help them grow into their roles.

*Goodyear's most successful plant, in Lawton, Oklahoma, has chosen a similar designation. Each of 164 teams of five to twenty-seven people is a "Business Center," responsible for quality control and productivity measurement and enhancement.

Ford's extensive Employee Involvement (EI) programs have been headed in the same direction. For instance, at Sharonville, Ohio, "a decision [was reached in 1981] by the plant manager, supported by the division, to reorganize the plant hierarchy. *The general supervisor level was completely eliminated* [my emphasis]. In its place, each zone superintendent was assigned an assistant known as a manufacturing planning specialist who, as the name implies, was to provide planning and coordinating assistance to each superintendent. The individual was not to be in a position of line authority. His position description called for another responsibility which was to have a profound effect on the future 'management' and growth of the EI process. He was to act as the departmental coordinator for all present and future EI problem-solving groups, working closely with his own superintendent and the plant co-coordinators."

By 1987, several of the most advanced Ford and GM experiments had removed all formal supervisor designations, except for plant manager, in operations of up to 1,000 people. At Johnsonville Sausage, mentioned in prescription P-1, all formal supervision has been eliminated from its four plants; even the plant manager position has been eliminated. Teams (called Pride Teams) manage almost everything.

Where the first-line supervisor's job is not being de facto eliminated, it is being changed. Training expert Jack Zenger reports that his phone has been ringing off the hook. Hundreds of firms have consulted him about increasing spans of control from, say, one supervisor to ten non-supervisors to one supervisor to 50 to 75 workers (see P-8).

With such a shift in span of control, the job goes through an automatic and radical adjustment. An over-the-shoulder style of management is not even physically possible under the new circumstances—see Figure 15. However, the casualty rate among efforts to retrain and transform the supervisor from detail person/cop to facilitator is very high, especially in traditional firms.

In conclusion, if you do not drastically widen the span of control, and shift the supervisor's job content, the self-managing team concept will not work— period. •

Pitfalls on the Road to Self-Managing Teams

One way to sidle toward team organization is to install quality circles, which were also discussed in prescription C-2. The route is not easy, however, for a well-functioning circle program requires changes in traditional supervisorial attitudes and practices almost as radical as those demanded by total team-based management. And the pitfalls are similar. One recent assessment based upon extensive experience throughout Martin-Marietta listed these problems:

▶ misunderstanding of the concept and process by upper and middle management, creating false expectations
▶ resistance to the concept and process by middle managers and supervisors, often verging on outright sabotage

▶ empire-building by the quality circle office, substituting the illusion of immediate success for the long-term goal of institutionalizing the quality circle process

▶ poor and "one-shot" training for circle members, supervisor-leaders, and managers

▶ failure to prepare the organization to provide incentives for participation in quality circles

▶ failure to prepare the organization to provide the information and support necessary for members to solve problems

▶ failure of the organization to implement circle proposals

▶ failure of the organization to measure the impact of quality circle participation—on defect rates, productivity rates, attrition rates, accident rates, scrap rates, grievance rates, lost-time rates, and so on

▶ failure to develop and codify a set of process rules prior to forming the first circles

▶ moving too fast—forming more circles than the quality circle office or the organization can deal with adequately

Figure 15: **The Changing Nature of First-Level Supervision**

Old	*New*
• 10 people reporting to him or her	• 50 to 75 "direct reports"
• scheduler of work	• coach and sounding board for self-managing team leaders/coordinators, working on training to emphasize skill development
• rule enforcer ("manager" of the union contract on management's behalf, if applicable)	• facilitator, getting experts to help the teams as needed
• lots of planning	• lots of wandering
• focused "down" (or "up") the structure	• focused "horizontally," working with other functions to speed action-taking
• transmitting middle/top management's needs "down"	• selling teams' ideas/needs "up"
• providing new ideas for workers	• helping workers/teams develop their own ideas; providing ideas for cross-functional systems improvement

THE MARKET WILL DEMAND A SELF-MANAGING TEAM STRUCTURE

New flexible manufacturing systems and the decentralized availability of the information needed for fast product changeover are leading to the wholesale adoption of cellular manufacturing, which essentially concentrates all the physical assets needed for making a product in a self-contained configuration which is tailor-made for team organization.

Participants in these increasingly fast-paced settings have no choice but to depend upon each other. Moreover, because of just-in-time inventory management and other techniques, it is essential that the teams/work groups be in constant, nonabrasive contact with all the operation's other functions. Thus the transformation of the traditional, internally directed first-line supervisor/cop into the externally directed coordinator/facilitator is a must, not a "nice-to-do."

The power of self-managing teams has been demonstrated in numerous settings. Why do they work? Quite simply, people of groups of ten to thirty can get to know one another well, can learn virtually every one else's tasks, can be gotten together with little fuss, and under enlightened leadership can readily achieve unit cohesion and esprit.

Team-Based Structures Work Everywhere

At the highest level of abstraction, this prescription constitutes one more attack on vertical, functional organizational structures, and on big scale in general. The evidence from watching well-trained teams perform is that extreme specialization was always dumb. Maintenance, budgeting, inventory management, and even customer contact can all be done by the twenty-five-person group. More generally, I urge you to emphasize mainly self-sufficient units, or what I call the small-within-big principle, throughout the organization. Even traditionally centralized activities, such as MIS, purchasing, and accounting, can be radically decentralized; I will say more about this in prescription P-8, which deals exclusively with structure.

Are there any limits to the use of teams? Can we find places or circumstances where a team structure doesn't make sense? Answer: No, as far as I can determine.

That's unequivocal, and meant to be. Some situations may seem to lend themselves more to team-based management than others. Nonetheless, I observe that the power of the team is so great that it is often wise to violate apparent common sense and force a team structure on almost anything. Even if a store or factory or distribution activity doesn't neatly break down into bands of ten to thirty, shift layouts around, "inefficiently" if necessary, to gain the potential power of a self-managing team structure. There is ample evidence that American economic performance will increasingly depend on quality, service, constant innovation/improvement, and enhanced flexibility/responsiveness. Committed, flexible, multi-skilled, constantly retrained people, joined together in self-managing teams, are the only possible implementers of this strategy.

FIRST STEPS

1. Start a test with a team structure in one facility within the next 180 days. The steps should be a small-scale version of the Livonia experience described above.
2. If you are already a user of teams (in the factory, say), develop an action plan for expanding the idea to all operations. Pick one department (MIS, for instance) and get going in the next 90 days.
3. Home in immediately on the crucial role of the first two levels of supervision. Can the supervisors be retrained or shifted to purely support jobs if you adopt some form of self-managing team structure? At the very least, the supervisor will undergo a traumatic shift of role (assuming you keep the role); don't let this surprise you—or dissuade you from proceeding. Above all, don't evade the issue. The failure to dramatically change the roles and numbers of supervisors has torpedoed the lion's share of self-managing team experiments.

P-3

SUMMARY

Wholesale involvement is necessary to engender the level of quality, service, and flexibility required by today's markets (P-1). Intense communication is required to foster that involvement; we must:

▶ Listen constantly, congregate, or share ideas/information, and recognize achievement.

▶ Celebrate—informally and formally—the "small wins" that are indicative of the solid day-to-day performance turned in by more than 90 percent of your work force.

Unprecedented information-sharing, interaction, and recognition are required to induce the attitude change and horizontal communication necessary to foster widespread involvement and commitment.

Develop formal and informal devices aimed at spurring intense, proactive listening—these should range from "chats with the chairman" to extensive formal surveys. Invest lavishly in regular get-togethers—at least bimonthly, for all hands, in each facility. Support this with ancillary devices—such as weekly (or more frequent) newsletters, videos, or audios. Hold a minimum of five celebratory "events," small or large, each month; top this off with a minimum of ten thank-you notes per week for jobs—particularly small ones—well done.

Listen/Celebrate/Recognize

The first two prescriptions in this section stressed the involvement of everyone in virtually everything. End specialization. Use self-managing work groups as the basic structural unit in the organization. All this, however, requires new attitudes. How do we foster them?

CREATE A LISTENING ENVIRONMENT

Create an environment where listening is cherished—and opportunities for structured *and* unstructured listening are rife. Listening means managers listening to their people, of course. And it means teammates listening to each other—recall in the previous prescription that in several cases a major portion of each worker's evaluation rested upon his or her contribution to the team as a whole. Listening also means people paying attention to those in other functions, battering down the time-honored, action-slowing functional boundaries at every opportunity.

Informal Listening

Listening can be informal; for instance, the daily "kaffeeklatsch" tradition in each work area at giant Hewlett-Packard. It is the weekly breakfast of the president and twenty randomly selected employees which was used to stimulate a transformation at Rockwell's Semiconductor Division.

The top managers of a Canadian forest products company felt they were top-flight communicators until a survey revealed that employees felt they stank—at listening. Solution? The two owners undertook a series of thirty dinners in the course of the next year. Ten employees and their spouses, eventually including everyone at the mill, went to dinner with the bosses. After the meal, there was a sociable and often long and intense question-and-answer session. "We all want to be listened to," says the president. "By the end of the evening I'd often see a remarkable change in attitude on the part of even the crustiest of the union guys."

315

Formal Listening

Casual get-togethers, then, are an essential part of listening—coffee klatches, breakfasts, dinners. So are more formal affairs. The president of Rockwell Semiconductor also devotes one day each month to tours of his major facilities, making sophisticated, no-holds-barred, no-information-withheld presentations to all hands. Our friends in the forest products company topped off their dinner routine with an informative weekly newsletter. It, too, holds back nothing, covering last week's affairs and next week's; delivery comes punctually at the end of the day shift on Fridays.

More? Tandem Computer's Friday Beer Busts, described in *A Passion for Excellence.* They sound like fun, and are, often involving a theme or a special food. But the activity, held religiously at each Tandem facility around the world at four o'clock each Friday, is also a deadly serious opportunity to break down barriers in what is already a remarkably informal, communication-intense environment.

More extreme? Federal Express brings all 3,000 managers together about once every eighteen months for several days to meet, talk, clear the air.

How about such listening "devices" as surveys? Some—such as IBM, for example—use them as a primary feedback (listening) device. The key is the feedback. IBM spends lavishly on the questionnaires, but so do many others. IBM departs from the norm in using the surveys as a basis for the evaluation of managers. Furthermore, when surveys indicate a major problem, a SWAT team from division headquarters is often on the site almost instantaneously. The whole process feeds on itself: Since employees know that action will result, they take the survey very seriously.

The Essentials of a Listening Environment

Here are some key factors in the creation of a listening environment.

1. The bare-bones essential, not to be underrated, is provision of a forum per se in which eventually you can talk and listen in a nonthreatening environment. I add the word "eventually," because putting listening programs in place does not ensure instant "straight talk." There must also be a sincere desire to listen—and hear—and the patience to persevere until the floodgates open. But without a "listening opportunity structure," probably including several of the informal and formal devices described above, little or no progress toward participation and enhanced commitment will ensue.

2. Next is a physical location—a place to listen. The most successful experiments with self-managing teams almost always include the provision of well-equipped rooms where teams can meet for problem-solving. At Chaparral Steel, each operation has a problem-solving room—with an added fillip: it is equipped exactly like the corporate boardroom. As the president says, the decisions being made in the plants are at least as important as those being made in the board-room—shouldn't the setting and amenities reflect that?

3. Feedback and action reinforce the intent. Remember that these are forums for listening, not preaching. The breakfast meetings at Rockwell were stilted at first, until attendees realized that (a) they weren't going to get in trouble with their bosses by talking and (b) the president was acting on what they were saying. At that point, the dam broke and ideas poured in not only at the meetings but in general. Likewise, as noted, the power of IBM's surveys lies in the fact that they elicit active responses.

4. Training is essential. I spoke of "listening training" for everyone at Tennant (see C-2). One suggestion program has a "writer" assigned to it who helps sometimes inarticulate people translate their ideas onto a form; another uses audiotapes similarly as a vehicle for making suggestions. Training in group problem-solving and in the identification of problem causes and effects (see C-2) is also essential. Supervisors are especially in need of help; in traditional settings, the supervisor plays a talking role, not a listening role.

5. Opportunities must be frequent. Here are several possibilities: (a) set aside work hours for team meetings (a ten- or fifteen-minute meeting each day at the start of the shift, an hour at the end of the shift once a week) for problem-solving, and also encourage employees to call after-hours meetings with pay as needed; (b) as at Tandem, hold informal weekly sessions that involve others beyond the immediate work group; (c) issue a weekly, or at least biweekly, rough-and-tumble, no-holds-barred newsletter; (d) hold a monthly or bimonthly, no-holds-barred, state-of-the-plant/operations center/division/company (as appropriate, but the more inclusive, the better) session, during working hours, with at least 50 percent of the time devoted to questions and answers; (e) make formal annual surveys involving a quick-action feedback routine; and (f) establish some set of systematic rituals, such as the boss hanging out in the cafeteria two mornings a week.

6. Attitude is vital. The last point, of course, deserves to be first. Recall prescription P-1. If you don't believe there's much worth listening to, you'll make a mess of this. Remember, this prescription is a *tool* in service to a much larger idea.

How much time does it take? Lots. Does it cost a lot? Quite often the answer is yes, in terms of hard dollars for shipping thousands of people to the site of the annual get-together and soft, "opportunity cost" dollars associated with having people meet with each other regularly during working hours.

CREATE PUBLIC FORUMS FOR RECOGNITION (TEACHING)

The construction of public forums for the recognition of achievement is closely entwined with listening. Among other things, well-constructed recognition settings provide the single most important opportunity to parade and reinforce the specific kinds of new behavior one hopes others will emulate.

Thus, recognition activities become a key listening and communication device, beyond their straightforward motivational influence on those being recognized.

Begin with an elementary question. Exactly how much recognition is desirable? To survive a day in the average check-processing or factory operation, or in the dispatch office, is tough. A machine breaks down. A customer unexpectedly demands a rescheduling. The colleague next to you has two kids sick with German measles and is distracted all day. That is to say, survival—for the average person on the average day—is not easy. Making it through five such days in a row is heroic. That's why my least favorite phrase is "a fair day's work for a fair day's pay." An informal poll of friends unearthed not one who had done merely a fair day's work for a fair day's pay. Our own, albeit self-centered, view of our performance is that we always do more than required, surmounting those numerous—but very real—daily and daunting hurdles with élan and dispatch. This seemingly high self-assessment is shared by almost 100 percent of the working population. And it is, by and large, a correct assessment.

I therefore believe that substantial recognition for fairly mundane actions—which are never really mundane—as well as for truly exceptional performance is called for, and is usually markedly absent.

Recognition: "Little Things" with High Impact

Consider this. A new owner of Fletcher Granite Company in Westford, Massachusetts, observed a record-breaking productivity effort by one of his employees. On impulse, he grabbed a two-way radio and publicly lauded this prodigious feat, with everyone listening in. A colleague of the worker later reported to the president: "Lou is walking on cloud nine. He's been here thirty-five years, and it's the first time the boss has recognized his work." What a sad-happy story! Want to hear another 200 to 300 like it? I've got them in my files. Here's just one more.

Sam Preston recently retired as executive vice-president of S. C. Johnson (Johnson Wax, etc.). He had a habit of sending little notes, with a bold "DWD" scrawled across the top, after coming across a sparkling effort. The "DWD" stands for "Damned Well Done." At his retirement party, Preston was stunned. People came up and thanked him for DWDs sent fifteen years before. Recognition is that memorable and that infrequent—even at S. C. Johnson, which has been one of America's top people-oriented companies for decades.

A Menu of Recognition Devices

Start with informal recognition:

▶ Keep mental or calendar notes of informal, semi-spontaneous celebratory events. Plan to do a minimum of five each month. Begin by stopping at the bakery on the way to work and picking up two dozen doughnuts to "award" at coffee break to a project team that passed a minor milestone—on schedule—the day before yesterday.

▶ Have a special meal at the distribution center cafeteria to celebrate ninety days of meeting the promise of "95 percent fulfillment within 24 hours of receiving the order." Have hamburgers made of top sirloin—and have management do the cooking and serving and cleaning up. "Ninety days at 95 percent" hats or T-shirts wouldn't hurt either. P.S.: Recalling one of the other major themes in this book—be sure to invite people from outside the center who helped you reach the goal, such as the three people in MIS who worked three straight weekends to help you simplify a critical, bottleneck-creating system.

▶ Consider a ritual like that of the top property manager of Marriott's in Albuquerque, New Mexico. He makes it a rigorous habit to send out at least 100 thank-you notes a month to his staff for jobs well done. You don't think you can find a hundred things worth saying thank you for? That's a prime indicator that you are out of touch.

▶ Trinkets. Simple observation suggests that most of us are trinket freaks—if they represent a genuine thanks for a genuine assist. A very successful Skunk Works manager sends skunk-adorned mugs, belt buckles, etc., to those in *other* functions who have stuck their necks out and helped his woefully undermanned operation.

Recognition on a grand scale: The Domino's Pizza Distribution Olympics are a fine example. The second annual Olympics were held in Dearborn, Michigan, on May 13, 1986. As usual, the games did not begin until the tripod (its bowl in the shape of a pizza) was ignited. But the torchbearers were no ordinary athletes. They were Domino's Pizza president, Tom Monaghan, a rags-to-riches entrepreneur, and Anthony Scales, a double amputee, who is "fast, does his job as a tray scraper and dough maker extremely well," according to his boss.

Distribution's compound annual growth over the last eight years has been 75 percent. Employment has soared to well over 1,700 people at 35 commissaries across the United States, Canada, and West Germany. How does Domino's manage such extraordinary growth, especially with its unusually young work force (the average age is 28)? The Olympics, brainchild of Distribution president Don Vlcek, is part of the answer.

The Olympics provide a showcase for the skills that underpin Distribution's success. Management obsessively measures and regularly rewards good job performance and customer satisfaction (customers in this case are Domino's franchisees), but the games may be even more memorable than Distribution's monthly bonuses. Moreover, they help maintain the company's focus and cohesiveness in the face of extremely rapid growth.

Competition for the May 1986 Olympics started in September 1985. The first round took place in each of the commissaries. At the beginning of the next year, about 650 local winners proceeded to the three regional rounds, which spawned 78 regional winners. Finally, the regional winners and their spouses moved on to Dearborn for the "national games," covering fourteen areas of competition. The "veggie slicing" contest emphasizes quantity and quality of vegetables, individual appearance, and sanitation. "Traffic management" measures skills at routing and coordinating team members and their delivery vehicles. Other categories include "dough making and catching," "store delivery," "driving," "loading," and "maintenance."

Less predictable contests involve the accountants, testing not only their speed and accuracy in bookkeeping and reporting but their interpersonal skills as well. For instance, in one contest, the accountant must handle a simulated phone call from a franchisee who is very late in paying his bill. Phone skills are also tested in contests among customer service reps and receptionists. Other contests rate team leadership.

One particularly nice touch is the involvement of Distribution's franchisee-customers, who comprise the majority of the judging panels. But most significant is the fact that the lead-up to the event has become a year-long process, not just a one-shot deal that is quickly forgotten. The first year's pizza "athletes," especially the runners-up, went home to their commissaries determined to "go for the gold" next year.

The stakes in Dearborn in 1986 were high. Sixteen winners in the fourteen main categories received top prizes of either $4,000 each or a lavish vacation for two.

The Olympics thus represent a serious commitment by management. Counting the prizes, Distribution spends $800,000 on the regional and final games, and that excludes the unrecorded costs of local competitions. But the investment has an invaluable return—honed skills plus a powerful sense of camaraderie and overall excitement that propels mostly young, inexperienced people through a system in which there is great potential for stress.

The Essentials of Successful Recognition Programs

Factors that make the difference between success and failure in granting recognition include these:

1. All recognition for acts of special merit must be heartfelt. Though, as noted, I define "special merit" more broadly than most, promiscuous recognition is self-defeating. I observe that great managers, like great teachers, are themselves most highly rewarded by the accomplishments of their employees. The best teachers say, "Look at what Andrea or Cliff did. Isn't that incredible?" The not-so-good ones talk about how they are being innovative in their lesson plans. In other words, if the accomplishments of your team are not really a source of excitement to you, don't engage in what will come across as patently phony acts of recognition, whether as simple as "DWD" or as grand as Distribution's Olympics.

2. Big awards for herculean efforts are a must, perhaps limited to 2 to 5 percent of the work force. But numerous awards for small acts of heroism are at least as important.

3. You can think systematically about all this. Domino's carefully designed Distribution Olympics is a case in point. Moreover, Distribution's management sits down after each year's programs and carefully assesses details and major themes, making numerous modifications for the next year. Here's another: The president of a forest products company instituted annual recognition dinners at each of his facilities last year. He sent me a copy of the detailed twenty-page "critique" he distributed to each operations manager after the entire round was complete (he attended every one). The document assessed everything from treatment of spouses, to table settings, to length of speeches, to procedures for picking people to be recognized, and the observations were carefully considered in planning the next year's event.

4. Celebrate what you want to see more of. Obvious as this dictum is, we ignore it too often. If you want more cross-functional barrier-breaking, make sure that every celebration includes hitherto unsung helpmates from other functions. Or, to the same end, do what one insurance company did—at least 50 percent of each manager's awards for good performance went to those in *other* functions who helped his or her team. Likewise, if you want to build team spirit, make sure that the gala for the gang at the distribution center is equal in lavishness to that for the top sales people; and make sure that most of the awards go to teams of people, not individuals.

Celebrate. Recognize. Communicate. Teach.

Inc. magazine called "Stew's News," the Stew Leonard's dairy store newsletter, "the ultimate company newsletter." I'd have to agree. I'll let the content do the talking. The November–December 1986 issue had 42 overflowing pages and over 300 pictures:

Cover: "This year's Hall of Fame winners!"—large photo.

Page 2: An editorial by Stew, Sr., on recognition given by outsiders to the dairy, ending with a strongly worded admonition: "Guard against being lulled to sleep."

Page 4: Story about employee Art Rosenblatt's idea that increased clam chowder sales by 30 percent; he designed a container so "it looked more homemade."

Page 5: A peppy article, "Come on, Stew, is the customer ever wrong?" Answer: No (with numerous specific supporting examples).

Page 8: Poem by an employee: "Ode to my Stew Leonard's fellow employees."

Page 9: 44 customer comments from the thousands per month that are popped into the store's suggestion box. About one-third were suggestions, one-third criticisms ("Your veal chops are cut too thin"), and one-third praise ("My therapist suggested I come here to cure my depression. It worked!! I love Stew Leonard's").

Page 10:   Article on customers; headline: "Thanks, Dody Forrest [the writer, an employee], for the Great Article."

Page 11:   "What's new at Stew's," reviewing new features around the store.

Pages 15–16:   Awards being given out at the Christmas party, with photos.

Page 18:   Large star symbol at the top, feature on "Two Stars in Fresh Products," with big picture and description of what they did.

Page 20:   Article by an employee on teamwork.

Pages 21–22:   Dozens of birthday and work anniversary pictures.

Page 35:   "Dairy Personals"; e.g., "D.T. I love you. Signed your assistant carpenter."

Page 37:   "Let's welcome our new employees," with list of names.

Back Cover: "Super Star of the Month," featuring big photos and detailed write-up of accomplishments.

What's going on here? (1) Celebration and recognition galore; (2) detailed teaching/feedback via descriptions of specifics as to why people won awards quotes from customer suggestion slips; (3) precise communication of the spirit, cooperativeness, and all-hands participation that mark Stew Leonard's. The newsletter, produced by employees, is itself a model of participation. It also achieves a nice blend of formality and informality. The paper stock is of high quality and the printing is tops. But it is done in typescript, with lots of fairly rough sketches; you'd be proud to take it home and keep it, but it completely avoids any suggestion of PR department glitz.

PUBLIC PARALLELS

My public sector friends are quick to point out that their elected aldermen would scream bloody murder if they took the fifty top performers to Disney World for a four-day annual recognition event, or even downtown to Hardee's.

True—and irrelevant. Obviously, thank-you notes are possible. So are plaques, Halls of Fame, mugs, and T-shirts. Beyond that, let your imagination guide you. In 1986 I spoke at a dinner meeting honoring the teachers of Irving, Texas. An aggressive superintendent had worked with an aggressive school board chairman to raise private funds to celebrate the teachers' efforts.

As for petty cash, if the city won't let you buy doughnuts for the gang that worked overtime to get the budget presentation for the supervisors ready on time, dip into your own pocket. The spontaneous "I care"/"Thank you" act, at a cost of $17.95, is worth as much to the people recognized as many a stilted corporate affair costing $225,000.

FIRST STEPS

1. Mount at least a Rockwell-variety, informal breakfast program. Immediately. The first step is to get a firsthand feel as to whether or not people think they are being listened to.
2. Start observing your own meetings, and ask a colleague to observe you. How much listening and open exchange takes place within your organization?
3. Don't run out and launch a major recognition program! Chew the recognition idea over first, with great concern for genuineness. Also review prescription P-7, which deals with compensation: *I am pointedly not proposing coffee mugs with decals as a substitute for profit distribution or a decent wage.* After you've thought through these things, then consider a major affair—in the context of your overall people program.

P-4

SUMMARY

Prescriptions P-3 through P-10 are supports for P-1 and P-2, which in turn are necessary for survival in the current environment. The process of engendering commitment, the first step toward involvement, and organization featuring self-managing teams can be radically enhanced (or detracted from) by the recruiting process. To get off on the right foot, we must:

▶ Invest heavily—in line persons' time—in recruiting.

▶ Avoid psychological testing and interviewing by staff psychologists like the plague—hiring is a line responsibility, too important by far to delegate to "experts."

▶ Use selection criteria which emphasize appropriate "soft stuff" that will be directly important to the company in the future—teamwork potential, customer orientation—as much as or more than "hard stuff."

Per P-5, for instance, we must invest substantially more money in training people than ever before. Per P-1, we will ask people to give more of themselves. Per P-2, we will put people into arenas with modest numbers of formal supervisors compared to the past. For all these reasons and more, which add up to more autonomy and the need for mutual trust, the recruitment process takes on added significance.

Interviewees for all jobs who pass initial screening should spend a day or two in at least a half dozen lengthy interviews. Senior line people, peers, and even potential subordinates, starting with the receptionist, should be part of the formal evaluation system. The interview should unequivocally stress the attitudes and skills necessary to thrive, for cashier and bench scientist, in an ever more ambiguous and fast-changing world.

Spend Time Lavishly on Recruiting

It's a simple fact. The average person, in the bank operations center or factory, will be supported by much more capital equipment in the future. All of these prescriptions have had one underlying theme: The average person will be asked to contribute much more than in the past. It doesn't follow that we need all be bionic people, but it does mean that we'd better worry about issues such as commitment from the outset.

The task of transforming raw recruits into committed stars, able to cope with the pace of change that is becoming normal, begins with the recruiting process per se. The best follow three tenets, unfortunately ignored by most: (1) spend time, and lots of it; (2) insist that line people dominate the process; and (3) don't waffle about the qualities you are looking for in candidates. These practices join the long list of those that must move from the nice-to-do to the must-do category.

LOOK FOR WHAT YOU VALUE

The most effective recruiting processes are intense, and straightforward in their objectives:

► As an applicant for a job at Hewlett-Packard, if you pass an initial screening, you're in for at least a dozen long interviews. A division general manager of a $75 million operation will likely spend an hour or so with final candidates for a first-line purchasing job. Other interviewers include bosses at two or three levels and numerous peers and potential subordinates; each also spends an hour or more. They make the time. Daily committee meetings can wait.

Moreover, each of the interviewers zeroes in on the traits that most people would call mushy and unmeasurable. When I taught in Stanford University's MBA program, I observed students returning from a long day of interviewing at HP, baffled that the interviewer seemed to take little interest in their ability to manipulate a balance sheet or understand which direction electrons flow in. Instead, HP interviewers were determined to figure out whether or not they'd be good team players. A typical "question" might go like this: "Describe in detail an experience you had working in an intense, long-lasting small group." It makes sense, of course, given that so much of HP's work is carried out by small teams engaged in high-pressure projects.

▶ Grocer Stew Leonard considers retailing experience or skills at the cash register secondary. First, he seeks outgoing people who are likely to be genuinely friendly toward colleagues and customers. "We can teach cash register. We can't teach nice," says Stew. And as at HP, judgments about these traits start with the receptionist.

Similarly, at retailer Nordstrom, regional vice-president Betsy Sanders reports that the chief criterion is not prior retailing experience, but "friendliness." And retailer Luciano Benetton uses virtually the same guidelines for selecting Benetton franchisees; he doesn't demand any merchandising experience, but asks that the operators have what he calls "the right spirit" to run one of his thousands of shops. A chief bellman at Marriott—who is involved in recruiting—adds: "I don't want them if they've worked at other hotels. Too many bad habits. I want them to be friendly and outgoing. I'll teach them how to be a good bellhop."

Most people argue that it is impossible to judge such squishy "soft" traits accurately; hence, while acknowledging their importance, they fail to give them a decisive role in candidate evaluation.

However, the companies cited here have become just as adept at judging an applicant's potential courtesy or teamwork skills as they are at assessing mathematical, accounting, or other so-called hard competencies. It's simply a matter of painstakingly zeroing in on specific behaviors and asking detailed questions whose answers reveal the presence or absence of these vital attributes. Tom Melohn, co-owner of North American Tool & Die (NAT&D), an exceptionally profitable $10 million firm, recalling interviews with several candidates for one clerical job, explains: Most applicants began by asking about hours, money, and other mechanics. The one he picked, however, "asked all kinds of questions about our approaches and procedures. Clearly, she wanted to understand the business. She was also able to handle complex tasks and seemed genuinely excited at the end of the [trial] half day."

GREAT ON PAPER IS NO GUARANTEE

In the recruiting process, beware of credentials. Education is a source of much of the nation's productivity increase over the decades. I acknowledge that, and I am an advocate of more, not less. On the other hand, American firms tend to overemphasize not only the MBA (to a disgraceful degree) but technical diplomas as well.

In *Kaizen,* Maasaki Imai reports that innovative Honda Motor, responsible for a disproportionate share of automotive technical breakthroughs in its short history in that business, "has only three Ph.D.s on its engineering staff. . . . One is founder Soichiro Honda, whose Ph.D. is an honorary degree, and the other two are no longer active in the company. At Honda," Imai concludes, "technological input does not seem to require a Ph.D." That's some contrast to GM. Remember that the same philosophy of developing technical skills on the job is followed by steel's high-tech star, Chaparral; Worthington Industries, and many if not most of the other stellar manufacturers mentioned in prescription C-8, follow the same path.

By deemphasizing paper credentials, the Japanese and Chaparral et al. encounter much less static when they attempt to assign engineers to the plant. A much higher share of Japanese than American engineers work in the plant on projects that at first blush appear to be rather mundane, and far from the exotic design chores that highly trained engineers think should be their lot.

"Great People" Don't Equal "Great Teams"

Do wall-to-wall great people—on paper—make great teams? Not necessarily. In the first twelve years of their existence, the National Football League's Tampa Bay Buccaneers have had an unprecedented six first choices in the college draft. First choice in the draft is awarded to the team with the past season's worst record among the NFL's twenty-seven members; overall, Tampa's twelve-year record is worst by far.

WHY INTENSIVE RECRUITING WORKS

The recruiting process followed by HP, Nordstrom, et al. has such an impact for a series of reasons, some quite subtle:

▶ A lengthy set of interviews unmistakably demonstrates that the firm cares enough about the candidate and the working environment to get people at all levels deeply involved in recruitment. Those who are hired start with the key values of HP or Nordstrom instilled by the recruiting process itself. And since those firms live their values so openly, if the person is going to be uncomfortable, he or she will probably become so during the lengthy courtship—and drop out then. (Most of those who do so nonetheless become fast friends of the firm, as a result of the obvious care and concern lavished on them.)

▶ The heavy investment of time by line managers and peers has an even more significant outcome. It puts the monkey squarely on the backs of the bosses and colleagues of the new hire. It's up to them to look directly for what they want (e.g., "good with customers") and then to affirm their choice by making the new person into a partner and a success. Their judgment is on the line.

They can't blame any problems on "the jerk recruiters who only care about grade-point averages."

Tom Melohn of NAT&D, which has reduced turnover from 27 percent to 4 percent since 1978, sums it up nicely: "I strongly believe in the importance of having a work force that shares the same values. For that reason, I interview each candidate before other managers do. That takes time, obviously." And that's demonstrating commitment—from the top.

A corollary is the virtual noninvolvement of personnel or human resource departments. After an initial screening, recruiting should be considered far too important to delegate to any staff "experts." In this vein, I strongly oppose the use of a company psychologist to interview candidates, and the use of psychological testing in general. These devices impart precisely the wrong message about the company's value system. They suggest you are looking for flaws rather than strengths, and for pat "personality profiles" rather than interesting human beings. Further, it is an unequivocal indicator to the candidate that you value staff experts over line input. It also makes it darned tough for line managers, no matter how highly they esteem a candidate, to overrule a negative evaluation by the highly paid, jargon-spouting psychologist.

Finally, the use of such techniques suggests that there *are* pat answers, and evades the hard work of really figuring out what you (line person) want and how to discern whether it's present.* (That is, the judgments that Nordstrom is making are much more subtle—and thoughtful—than anything that could be provided by a given profile on the Minnesota Multiphasic Personality Inventory test.)

In the course of a year and a half, one professional service firm's managing partner reduced turnover from 30 percent a year to zero in a critical professional-skill area in which the local labor pool suffered a chronic shortage. He attributes the dramatic turnabout to the transfer of the entire recruiting process from the "pros" (human resource people, psychological testers, and the company psychologist) to the line. Similar results are occurring even in auto plants, where first-line people are being given wholesale responsibility for running in-plant assessment centers (see the story of GM's Delco-Remy plant in prescription P-1).

DO YOU KNOW YOUR VALUES?

The recruiting message is simple: line people looking for no-nonsense traits that will be of use in the world of tomorrow. There's an unspoken assumption behind this—that you know what your values are, or must be.

---

*I have no problem with using the personnel department to provide extensive training in the interview process, to help the line interviewers figure out how to get at indications of the traits they are looking for.

Most don't. Most recruiting practices, which mirror the firm's values, for better or for worse, are reflections of yesterday's needs; and bureaucratic (overly complex) reflections to boot.

"To get your recruiting straight, you'd best have your values straight," says Melohn of NAT&D. I talk so frequently in these prescriptions about the need to welcome change rather than fight it. Do you look for "flexible people"? Would you know how to screen or ask questions based on that criterion? (Without a doubt, in this area at least, the best predictor of the future is the past. "Flexible people" tomorrow will have been flexible yesterday—will have sparkled in ill-defined assignments, contributed to the creation of new ventures, such as a new college periodical. Substantial research, for instance, has been devoted to discerning who is likely to be "entrepreneurial." It turns out that tomorrow's entrepreneurs will have been entrepreneurial from the start—e.g., will have figured out a new technique for selling Girl Scout cookies at age 12.)

PUBLIC PARALLELS

Many of my public sector colleagues applaud these ideas, but inform me that the public's idea of fairness requires them to use extensive written tests and to depend heavily on credentials (a minimum of seven courses on the theory of elementary-grade lesson plans are required for a teaching certificate, etc.).

I certainly acknowledge the abuses of nepotism and politically inspired hiring that these rules were designed to prevent. However, I believe that even written tests, and especially written interview protocols, can at least be substantially tailored to allow you to look for the kinds of criteria that I've suggested drive Hewlett-Packard or Nordstrom.

In particular, look at your district's best teachers or your city's best police sergeants, and extract success criteria from that review in an objective manner. My bet is that the best will be light on credentials and heavy on other, so-called softer factors. Use these as a basis for your written selection process.

FIRST STEPS

1. Look at your stars: in engineering, in accounting, in the operations center—especially those best adapting to the environment's fast-paced needs. What makes them tick? What is their background? Have any group that's recruiting begin the process by working up a practical list of "what works with that job," based upon the traits of these top performers. Have the group work to turn that list into a series of practical, desirable traits; then create a set of interview questions around those traits. Above all, the traits and questions should pass the "common sense" test and be free of theoretical, "ought to need" attributes.

2. Do you specifically emphasize "soft" values (e.g., teamwork potential) in your recruitment process? Take one job designation you are about to start recruiting for and think through what the values are. Write them down, and write down a series of questions that would help you determine their presence or absence in an interview. Add these questions to your next round of recruitment interviews. Again, make sure they are in common-sense language, not boilerplate or psycho-babble.

3. Recall P-1: Consider turning the front-line recruiting process over to the front line! Begin by involving front-line employees in interviews, and gradually give them full responsibility. Further consider, as some have done, giving sizable bonuses for bringing in candidates who are hired and are subsequently successful. (Review I-5: Word of mouth is as powerful in recruiting, especially in tight labor markets, as it is in new product sales.)

4. Have you canceled any recruiting interviews in the last three months because you were unexpectedly harried? What does that say to the recruit—and everybody you work with—about your valuation of the hiring process and people in general?

P-5

SUMMARY

The need for involvement—and flexibility—has an obvious corollary: Train and retrain. We must:

▶ Invest in human capital as much as in hardware.

▶ Train entry-level people; retrain them as necessary.

▶ Train everyone in problem-solving techniques to contribute to quality improvement.

▶ Train extensively following promotion to the first managerial job; then train managers every time they advance.

▶ Use training as a vehicle for instilling a strategic thrust.

▶ Insist that all training be line-driven—radically so; all programs should consist primarily of input from the line, be piloted in several line locations, and be taught substantially by line people.

Work-force training and constant retraining—and the larger idea of the work force as an appreciating (or depreciating) package of appropriate (or inappropriate) skills—must climb to the top of the agenda of the individual firm and the nation. Value added will increasingly come through people, for the winners. Only highly skilled—that is, trained and continuously retrained—people will be able to add value.

Consider doubling or tripling your training and retraining budget in the course of the next 24 to 36 months. Less serious consideration means a failure to come to grips with both the nature of the problem—and the magnitude of the opportunity.

P-5

Train and Retrain

Above all, [IBM's Thomas] Watson trained, and trained, and trained.
                              Peter Drucker, *Management*

We've documented the savings from the statistical process control methods
and problem-solving methods we've trained our people in. We're running
a rate of return of about 30 times the dollars invested—which is why we've
gotten pretty good support from senior management.
                              Bill Wiggenhorn
                              Director of Training, Motorola
                              June 1987

BEATING THE COMPETITION THROUGH SKILL ENHANCEMENT

Recall from prescription C-2 that success requires increasing the relative
quality of a firm's product or service—relative, of course, to the competition.
When we think of our work force, we should emphasize the same word, "relative," also vis-à-vis the competition.

The work force is indisputably our principal asset. Each day its overall level
of useful skills (as well as its commitment and energy) is either increasing or
decreasing relative to that of the competition. The operative strategic question,
then, is obvious: What have you done today to enhance (or at least insure against
the decline of) the relative overall useful-skill level of your work force vis-à-vis
competitors?

Much of the answer lies in your response to a series of questions about
training: Who? How much? How relevant to tomorrow's needs? And how
would the competition answer these same questions?

Work-force training must become a corporate (and indeed national) obsession. It is not. And it is on this variable that the outcome of the overall
competitive struggle may most strongly depend.

A National Disgrace, An Epic Opportunity

Our investment in training is a national disgrace. That should come as no surprise. Despite lip service about people-as-our-most-important-asset, we value hardware assets over people, and have done so for the last century.

The ideas in the people prescriptions are not startling—or, at least, should not be. Involved and committed people can move mountains. Yet the fact that this set of prescriptions needs to be presented at all speaks to our long-time national deemphasis on human capital. Ross Perot once said that "brains and wits will beat capital spending ten times out of ten"; he was referring to the production line, not just the laboratory. TRW policy analyst Pat Choate estimated in 1986 that "The federal government contributes $3,200 to plants and technology for every dollar it chips in for employee training through tax incentives."

Even when we do train, we get it backwards. *Training* magazine's 1986 survey reports that while 69 percent of organizations with over 50 people on the payroll provide training for their middle managers and 70 percent train their execs, only 25 percent train production people, 30 percent train salespeople, and 34 percent train customer service people. Digging deeper, *Training* finds that for those who do provide training, much more (in terms of time spent per person) goes to managers than to nonmanagers.

Analyze the competition, and the story gets grimmer. The Japanese, Germans, and others outspend us wildly on training, especially in-company skill refurbishment and upgrading.

In short, our training track record is pathetic. Worse, it's getting worse. That is, as the pace of change picks up, the rate at which skills become obsolete—for scientist, machine operator, and actuary alike—is quickening. The customer prescriptions featured value added through quality, service, and responsiveness; factory/operations center hands and sales and service people are the necessary heroes. The innovation prescriptions were clear—*everyone* must innovate. Everyone *must* be prepared (1) to contribute ideas and (2) to work together with less supervision (see P-2). And only constant training will provide the basis for constant adaptation.

TRAIN EVERYONE—LAVISHLY

Some few American firms learned the training secret long ago:

▶ Training has been IBM's secret weapon for decades. At one point, the senior Watson had just a one-person staff—an education director. An ad last year featured an IBM worker at the company's Lexington, Kentucky, site who had undergone major retraining a half-dozen times in a twenty-five-year career to fend off technical obsolescence. IBM pioneered in training women for service jobs in the 1920s. Its sales training course is still arguably the best in the land.

And its training for entry-level managers is legendary—the firm is one of the rare ones that do not assume that supervising "comes naturally."

Training immediately follows each promotion at IBM. Everyone must spend at least 40 hours in the classroom each year. When IBM moved into alternate distribution channels a few years ago, all of its employees received a basic course in retailing. And when it launched its quality program (C-2), it formed Quality Institutes (special training schools) in the early 1980s as the spearhead of its remarkable quality improvement program; over 150,000 people were trained in quality control during the first five years of the program. Today IBM is facing major problems in many of its markets. It is doing many things to turn the tide, but none more important than massive retraining aimed at equipping the work force for the new challenge.

► Federal Express and Disney have thrived with similar training rigor. Unlike IBM, both firms have a large number of employees who are unlikely to spend their careers with the firm. Nonetheless, both treat everyone as a potential career employee. The training Federal Express gives its customer service people in Memphis and Disney's training of a 17-year-old would-be jungle boat driver far surpass the training many technical firms give their machinists.

Others have turned to training in a time of need, or to pursue new opportunities. Recall Milliken's 22 weeks of in-class training for its rag (shop towel) salespersons, and Tennant's training, used to push its top-drawer quality program along. As the second epigraph at the beginning of this prescription suggests, Motorola has turned to training to stay competitive in its high-tech markets. The firm's leadership in U.S. semiconductor products is supported by an allocation of over 2.5 percent of its payroll to training; in addition, it extensively trains suppliers, including Japanese firms.

Consider these additional examples as well:

► In four short years beginning in 1982, Pat Carrigan, the first woman to manage an assembly plant at GM, turned around a horrid situation at Lakewood, Georgia. Her strategy? A partnership with people. She cited three principal tactics: (1) a two-week pre-start-up training program for everyone, following a long shutdown during the depths of the 1981–83 recession; (2) an ongoing training program that gave 3,000 people some 360,000 hours of training in 24 months; (3) establishment of some 133 work groups, covering 90 percent of the work force—the only tactic that did not involve training. Overall success indicators at Lakewood include a drop in absenteeism at the troubled plant from 25 percent to 9 percent between 1981 and 1985. A moving, formal union tribute to Carrigan marked the end of her term at Lakewood.

► When Nissan moved to Smyrna, Tennessee, it started right—or average, by Japanese best-company practice. It spent $63 million ($7 million courtesy of the state of Tennessee) training about 2,000 workers, or over $30,000 per person, before the plant started operation. Not only does that ensure well-trained people; it also sends a "you're important to us" message to each and every individual. Sadly, the typical American manager's response to the Nissan story is some variation of "They're nuts. Give 'em that much training and they're sure to leave." People will hasten to leave if you treat them well? Some logic! Neither common sense nor the hard evidence supports this view.

▶ Computer maker Amdahl of Sunnyvale, California, took a chance with something akin to the Nissan approach. In 1981 line workers asked management how they could get a leg up in the company. The director of manufacturing and operations, Bernie Sussman, responded by offering employees who never went to college a chance at higher education. Amdahl's program, designed with local De Anza Junior College, offers courses such as quality assurance, materials in process, production and inventory control, management principles and accounting. Students who complete the two years earn 41 college credits, which can be applied to an Associate Arts (AA) degree. Bill Flanagan, vice-president of manufacturing, notes that classes are taught on site and employees can attend up to five hours of class a week on company time. Amdahl also picks up the tab for books. Total cost: $125,000 a year. In early 1987, 58 employees were enrolled. Of the 40 who have completed the program, 38 are still working at Amdahl; in fact, the turnover rate among participants (5 percent) is half the company's overall turnover rate. Furthermore, 30 of the "graduates" have been promoted. After completing the program, Flanagan's secretary went on to earn a business administration degree; another woman who worked on the wiring assembly line for more than two years is currently a staff assistant in the finance department.

▶ Grocer Stew Leonard swears by Dale Carnegie training. That's hardly surprising, since his customer-first philosophy stresses warmth and courtesy. His seriousness is demonstrated by the offer to send anyone—including a 20-hour-a-week high school part-timer—to a full 14-week, $600 Dale Carnegie course. One wall at Leonard's displays photos of the 800-plus graduates of the course; Leonard's overall training tab of $1,000 per employee per year is four times the grocery industry average. With this kind concern so evident, Leonard has a long waiting list for every job in the store. His turnover is tiny by industry standards, and his talent pool for promotion is unsurpassed.

Each of these examples illustrates an instinctive "training first" approach to (1) jumping off to a good start (IBM, Fed Ex, Disney, Leonard, Nissan) or (2) responding to crisis/opportunity (Motorola, GM/Lakewood, Tennant, Milliken). Sadly, such instincts are unusual in America.

ELEMENTS OF A GOOD TRAINING PROGRAM

The following attributes will mark successful training programs for the future:

1. Extensive entry-level training that focuses on exactly the skills in which you wish to be distinctive. Disney, IBM, Federal Express, Stew Leonard, and Nissan provide models: their training "overemphasizes" the skills that define their uniqueness. Leonard focuses on courtesy and communication skills; the shoddy training of most retail clerks focuses on how to run the cash register—and what a message that sends! Disney teaches Walt's vision directly, as well as acting and atmospherics; it sends another clear message through its extensive training—in customer servicing skills—for sweepers, parking-lot attendants, and ticket sellers. Federal Express has made a science of training its Memphis-based customer service force in how to deal with antsy customers.

2. All employees are treated as potential career employees. One might not ordinarily think of a cleaning contractor like ServiceMaster as a place for people to have careers. But ServiceMaster is different. Promotion from within is its invariable policy, and its training is offered in the context of career development. Retailer Nordstrom takes exactly the same view, in another industry that traditionally has low company loyalty. The Amdahl example above is illustrative of the payoff that can come from shifting to a "career" attitude toward employees, in that case with production people.

3. Regular retraining is required. IBM, as noted, and Milliken are among those who force everyone into the classroom each year. This is a must. Moreover, constant skill broadening should be everyone's goal. Pay-for-knowledge programs, discussed in P-1 and P-2 (see also P-6), are an important and too often overlooked ingredient.

4. Both time and money are generously expended. Regular time off from work, as in the Amdahl program (which, remember, was not directly related to the participants' current job), is a signal of serious interest in the worker's development. Generous tuition contributions are another vital sign of interest.

You can't overspend on training. At least, the odds are very low. Recall prescription C-9, where I encouraged you to consider doubling the sales force. Take the same approach to training: What could you accomplish if you doubled or tripled the training budget? Keep Nissan's $63-million-and-over-$30,000-per-person pre-start-up figure in mind—it's unlikely that you'll be pushing beyond that benchmark.

But a word of caution: Throwing money at a problem is unfailingly stupid, be it training, automation, or basic research. Most training is now ill conceived. Many training departments are not run by highly respected executives. So, take it a step at a time, with quality the goal—but think very boldly too.

5. On-the-job training counts too. Nordstrom provides what's possibly the best training program among retailers. Yet very little takes place in the classroom. The Nordstrom "trick" is "overstaffing"—salespersons *and* managers, on the sales floor. There is always a manager available to help. And since the firm's emphasis is on careers, each employee is encouraged to act as a coach from the start; success at doing so is a component of everyone's evaluation. Nordstrom is a living classroom, every day.

6. There are no limits to the skills that can profitably be taught to everyone. Johnsonville Sausage, in conjunction with a local community college, and Worthington Industries, courtesy of the finance department, teach basic, but complex and not sugarcoated, economics to everyone. Tennant, Motorola, and others, in their quest for quality improvement, have learned that over time almost everyone can absorb well-conceived courses in complex problem analysis and statistical process control.

7. Training is used to herald a commitment to a new strategic thrust. In the 1960s and 1970s, General Electric used training as the flagship for strategic change on several occasions. Inflation accounting, strategic planning, and technology management courses spearheaded major strategic programs in each area. Almost 100,000 managers and service professionals went through programs lasting several days in each case. Senior executives devoted enormous amounts of time to course development and teaching per se. Hewlett-Packard successfully followed a similar approach with manufacturing, marketing, and strategic planning in the early 1980s.

8. Training is emphasized at a time of crisis. Don't cut the training budget when crises come; increase it! That's what Carrigan did at Lakewood, Georgia (GM). It's also the logic of the path chosen by Motorola, Tennant, and IBM when mounting their respective quality revolutions. Massive and lengthy retraining to aid redeployment at times of technological change or wrenching competitive dislocation is another aspect; Digital Equipment, IBM, Ford, and GM are learning this skill (see P-7, on employment security, for more detail).

9. All training is line-driven. Even when the skill to be taught is a new one, the line must take the lead in developing program input, and then again in the teaching. Without these ingredients, the line has no personal stake in the program, and it is soon discovered that the would-be student is "too busy to spare three days" for training. Senior and junior line people must be temporarily assigned to training to work out the details of course content. The training department person is the pedagogy expert, but not the content leader. Some firms have gone the final step—to insist that the line pay for all training programs. That puts extraordinary pressure on the training department to listen. The objection is that more conservative programs will result, and this is doubtless true to a certain extent; but a conservative program "owned" by the line is far more useful than a radically innovative program written off as "the training department's fantasy after they consulted with academics."

10. Training is used to teach the organization's vision and values. "Control" and "management" in the future will flow through an empowering vision and shared values (see both the leadership and systems prescriptions). The best training programs, at all levels, from beginner to brush-up, must be seen as a prime opportunity to underscore these values. Top management must be involved in every training program as teachers, using the opportunity to discuss and transmit the vision that holds the firm together in turbulent times.

Training Supervisors: Now More than Ever

Supervising is a skill. Of course it is, you say, nodding. Yet most first-level managerial training courses are awful. There's no urgency in getting the new supervisor to attend: "We're stretched as it is; wait until the ABC project is beyond the critical stage"—but somehow it never quite is, or there's a DEF project that follows. Moreover, the content of these courses, like the courses for retail clerks that primarily teach how to use a cash register, typically emphasizes mechanics—the twenty-three official preliminaries to firing someone—and seldom stresses leadership or coaching. When the next promotion comes, the story is repeated; the far different task of managing managers is all but ignored. All of the above amounts to a frightening omission—and lost opportunity. There is no more difficult transition in a career than the one from nonboss to boss; the second-toughest is to boss of bosses. These passages should be marked by programs commensurate with their significance.

The historic de-emphasis of these transitions has been unfortunate. The future consequences of such neglect are unacceptable. The first-line supervisory and middle-management job must change dramatically (see P-2, P-9, especially). Timely training in the newly required skills is essential.

Consider Revolution

The ten elements of a good training program and the suggestions about management training add up to a tall order. Most firms are "working on" all of them to some extent. The prescription here, though, asks you to consider a revolution: (1) Review the training budget *before* the capital budget. (2) Do a thorough competitive assessment of your investment in skill development and career enhancement (for the work force as a whole) vis-à-vis domestic and foreign competitors. (3) Evaluate the content of every course relative to the opportunities suggested, especially in prescriptions C-1 through C-10. (4) Do a "zero base" assessment of your training department; you are probably not a fan of training, because you've mixed line rejects and detached "training professionals" together, creating courses that smart line operators avoid sending people to like the plague. (5) Consistent with the first four points, treat your training (skill level) assessment as the essence of strategic opportunity. If you don't spend as much time on this assessment as on the evaluation of the capital (hardware) budget, you have entirely missed the point of all ten of the prescriptions in this section.

The "revolutionary decision," following the sort of assessment just suggested, may well require the establishment of a rather grand "corporate university." Many are turning in this direction—especially to remedy deficiencies in the skills of high school graduates. Note, however, that there is a great opportunity to do this wrong: (1) to emphasize the glitz and glamour of a new facility, filled with computer-controlled audio/video monster machines; (2) to fail to tie the curriculum directly to the firm's key strategic needs; and (3) to emphasize executive training at the expense of total corporate skill enhancement. If you can avoid these pitfalls, the opportunity is both strategic and limitless.

FIRST STEPS

1. Go out and survey the five very best first-line training programs you can find. Do it in the next 60 days, and make sure the survey team has no controllers, and no more than one trainer, and is dominated by highly respected line people.
2. Next, insist that each top manager attend a large share (at least three or four days' worth) of one front-line training program as it is currently provided.
3. Presuming that steps one and two suggest vast opportunity, do not immediately retool the training department; instead, start by thoroughly revamping *one* entry-level course in the next four months. The project leader should be a respected line person, with a trainer as deputy.
4. Following step #3 above, move to include a "zero-base" assessment of the current training staff and the magnitude of the opportunity in next year's strategic plan. The strategic assessment task should be handled by division general managers (or the equivalent), with trainers as "staff" to the assessment group. A major part of the group's work should consist in overall measurement of your total corporate skill pool/skill level—make it quantitative, and in contrast to your competition's. (If such an assessment does not unearth dramatic opportunities, you've probably done it wrong, or else your overall vision is too limited—i.e., it does not sufficiently emphasize the value-adding, market-creation objectives that are discussed most fully in C-1 through C-6.)

P-6

SUMMARY

Involvement of skilled workers on a grand scale (see P-1, P-2, P-4 especially) is essential to achieving future competitiveness. To further enhance worker commitment to proactively seeking constant improvement, we must:

► Provide bold financial incentives for everyone. Incentive pay for everyone is the "clincher," the ultimate recognition for a contribution to improved company performance—and not widely used. But incentives programs must be accompanied by a genuine and clearly perceived opportunity to influence the results. Incentives should focus on the ten- to thirty-person work group.

Above-average pay yields above-average work—or at least the converse is true. Consider putting everyone on salary. Pay-for-knowledge incentives to learn several jobs are a must. Include everyone in a profit-distribution/gain-sharing incentive pay scheme. A variable target of at least 25 percent of base pay is reasonable. Feedback (performance pay) should be quick—monthly at least. Employee share ownership should be strongly encouraged, through an Employee Stock Ownership Plan (ESOP) or similar program.

Provide Incentive Pay for Everyone

A Yankelovich poll of Japanese and American workers is illuminating. On the statement "I have an inner need to be the best I can, regardless of pay," American workers, maligned by so many (especially American managers), surprisingly outscored the Japanese. On the much more practical question concerning "who would benefit most from an increase in [worker] productivity," the tables were turned. Some 93 percent of Japanese workers thought that they would benefit, while only 9 percent of American workers felt that way. Self-interest probably rules in both countries, but our workers keenly believe that increased productivity and self-interest don't go hand in glove. Japanese workers' traditional 25 to 50 percent bonus after a good year doubtless helps induce the feeling that there is a direct link between contribution and outcome.* In fact, in Japan the total sum distributed as bonuses usually exceeds a firm's after-bonus profit.

PROFIT DISTRIBUTION: AN OLD IDEA IN NEED OF DUSTING OFF

The idea of incentive pay for everyone is hardly new to Americans. A century ago, in 1887, Procter & Gamble installed a profit-sharing plan that divided profits between the company and its workers in the same proportion that labor costs bore to total costs (in an era, remember, when labor costs were a much bigger slice of the pie than today). That is, if wages were 50 percent of all costs, the workers' bonus would be one-half of profits. President Cooper Procter stated at the time: "The chief problem of big business today is to shape its policies so that each worker will feel that he is a vital part of his company with a personal responsibility for its success *and a chance to share in that success* [my emphasis]."

*From 1970 through 1980, the average bonus was 4.52 months' pay for people in firms of over 500 employees, 3.21 months' pay for those in firms of 30 to 100 employees.

Sadly, Procter's statement is equally apt today. A century later, it is still less than 20 percent of the U.S. work force that participates in a profit distribution plan or other productivity-based gain-sharing plan. Furthermore, just 10 percent own shares of stock in their company, despite the generous incentives granted by the historic Employee Share Ownership Plan (ESOP) legislation passed in 1974.

As prescription P-1 and several of its successors suggest, I observe that America's productivity and quality problems—for the individual firm and for the nation—are directly linked to a failure to involve people in their jobs, and a failure to seek their assistance in the achievement of consistent quality and productivity improvement.

Such involvement is the paramount step. But if managers ask people to give of their creative talents and commitment, and to take apparent risks by doing such things as proposing labor-saving ideas, those people should share handsomely in any profit that results. The widespread failure to reward people for higher involvement is a missed opportunity of the first order.

A FIVE-PART INCENTIVE PAY PROGRAM

Base Pay Above the Norm

It is commonly assumed that the high wages of unionized steelworkers doomed integrated steel manufacturing in this country. The high pay at Nucor, Chaparral, and Worthington Steel makes a mockery of this. All three firms are several times more productive than average, with superb quality and responsiveness to boot. Yet Worthington, for instance, sets its base wage within the top 25 percent of local wages, and then adds to that with a profit-distribution formula that usually averages 80 percent of the base wage each 90 days.

Retailing is notorious for low pay. But Nordstrom soars in an increasingly competitive market with superb service—and wages that are pegged about $2.00 per hour above retail's average in a given area; the premium wage is then further enhanced by an unusual 6.75 percent sales commission. Top salespersons can clear $70,000. Federal Express pays very well too. A part-time Courier-Pak sorter in the Memphis Hub started at $9.75 an hour in 1986 and received a profit-sharing bonus and a sizable tuition refund.

University National Bank & Trust of Palo Alto is a top-performing example of the new brand of relatively small specialist banks. In 1986 the fast-growing institution earned three times more (on assets of $180 million) than the average California bank (1.27 percent versus 0.43 percent). Chairman Carl Schmitt explains his approach to pay: "It's one thing to have a strategy, but you have to also make it work. To do that, you have to hire good people. Then you gotta pay them." UNB&T's average salary and benefits per employee rank seventy-sixth out of seventy-eight California banks (with total deposits between $100 million and $500 million). "That sounds terrible!" says Schmitt. "But the way they rank it, the lowest-paying banks are at the top [of the list]. Now that's an interesting window to the industry's attitude—that it's better to have lower salaries, to keep costs down. That's not how we think and that's not our practice."

In general, I recommend: (1) base pay somewhat above the geographic area average for comparable jobs—which means that total pay, with incentives added, will be substantially above average. I also urge (2) that everyone be put on salary.

Pay-for-Knowledge

Prescriptions P-1 and P-2 discussed pay-for-knowledge, including the specifics of several programs.

Since only the employee trained in a number of skills will provide the bedrock for the constant adaptation that will mark the new breed of winners, such programs are a must. Incentives might encourage learning the jobs of at least two teams in an average factory or operations center setting; that would amount to twenty to twenty-five jobs. Three to five significant pay incentive steps should be associated with the progression of skill acquisition.

Productivity and Profit-Based Incentive Pay

▶ Lincoln Electric is a Cleveland-based manufacturer of welding machines and induction motors. It suffered over a 40 percent decline in revenues during the 1981–83 recession, yet it laid no one off, and has not done so since the early 1940s (see also P-7).

Lincoln was an early adopter of the Scanlon Plan, named after Joe Scanlon, a USW worker who developed the incentive scheme in an effort to save La Pointe Steel during the Great Depression. The original Scanlon Plan splits profits and cost savings from suggestions with the work force. At Lincoln, each employee gets a semi-annual "Merit Rating," which results in the addition or subtraction of "points" from a starting score of 100, based on "ideas and cooperation, output, dependability, and quality." The points are then valued according to the firm's current profit level. From 40 to 55 percent of pre-tax profits go into the bonus pot. The bonus has averaged 95 percent of base wages each year, since 1940. With sales back up to pre-recession heights in 1984, some 2,405 workers split $42 million—about $15,000 per person. Employees also own 40 percent of the firm's stock.

The payoff for Lincoln is productivity that is 250 percent above industry average, making it possible for the firm to continue to be the world's low-cost producer in a tough industry.

▶ Nucor's team-based bonus system is key to its astounding productivity, which keeps it ahead of even foreign producers on costs. The firm's production people are grouped into units of fifteen to thirty-five people. The principal incentive program works like this: A standard for an activity is set at 90 percent of the average time historically required to do the task,* and the team bonus is determined by how much the team beats the standard. For instance, if the team does 60 percent better than the standard, its members get a 60 percent bonus, *paid the next week.* The resulting compensation is exceptional. For instance, the average pay in recessionary 1983 for an hourly worker at Nucor's 525-person mill in Darlington, South Carolina, ran over $30,000; more than 75 percent of the workers had been unskilled when hired just a few years before.

▶ Worthington Industries follows another, equally successful formula to keep its productivity, quality, and responsiveness tops. It distributes 17 percent of pre-tax profits each quarter on the basis of divisional performance (e.g., the steel operations). This translates into about 80 percent of the already high base wage, as noted. Attaining membership in the plan works this way: Each facility has an elected committee of nonmanagers. After a ninety-day probationary period, a worker is eligible to become "permanent" and join the profit-distribution plan. The committee of peers at the facility votes the person in or out, or calls for additional probationary time. Employees also own over 30 percent of Worthington's stock, and stock awards are granted for such things as superior attendance. Everyone at Worthington is on salary, and is therefore not docked for absenteeism, which runs only 1 percent. Productivity is about 200 percent better than the industry average.

▶ At Steelcase, tools for maintaining top market share in an increasingly competitive market include profit- and productivity-based bonuses averaging 60 percent of base pay. On top of that, the firm invariably contributes 15 percent of total compensation (the maximum allowable by the IRS) to a deferred profit-sharing plan. Bonuses are based in part on individual performance, and also include quarterly and annual profit distribution.

▶ At Publix, a Florida grocer, where employees own 100 percent of the stock: (1) each store pays a quarterly cash bonus equal to 20 percent of its profits; (2) there is a standard Christmas bonus equal to two weeks' pay; and (3) 10 percent of profits (in addition to the 20 percent for the quarterly bonuses) goes into a deferred profit-sharing plan, divided among all employees with over 1,000 hours per year.

▶ Andersen Corporation of Bayport, Minnesota, continues to be the nation's largest and most successful manufacturer of windows and patio doors. A mundane product? Don't tell that to the firm's work force of 3,500 or to its customers, for whom Andersen provides high-quality, customized products. In 1986, the workers divided up a profit-distribution bonus—a tradition since 1914—of $72 *million,* coming in *one* check and equivalent to eight months and three weeks' pay! (If they invest the bonus money, in a home for instance, they get the further assistance of a Thrift Bonus Program.)

---

*It is vital that the standard be based on past averages, and devised in cooperation with the workers. "Merit pay" plans in which the standard is some shifting "optimum" mandated by a stopwatch or the boss's whim foster suspicion, not commitment.

The employees, called "working partners," also own 30 percent of the firm's stock, and are eligible for a substantial personal productivity bonus. The Andersen approach is straightforward. The Minneapolis *Star and Tribune* summarizes: "[The three basic] principles are to make products that are different from, and better than, others in the marketplace; to hire the best people *and pay the top wages in the industry* [my emphasis], and to provide full employment year-round." The last-mentioned, in a notoriously cyclical business, is a bold objective indeed—but with rare exceptions, it has been faithfully followed by the firm, which has grown from $50 million in revenue in 1966 to $790 million in 1986. Productivity at Andersen runs at twice the industry average.

These few examples are typical of the most progressive profit-distribution plans. Each, moreover, comes from a tough industry, where keeping pace with the competition is difficult indeed. Drawing on them and many others, here's what I recommend:

1. Productivity-and-quality-based incentives that emphasize team performance and profit-distribution incentives based upon the performance of the facility, division, and, to some extent, the corporation as a whole. The team and the facility/division are the basic building blocks (see also P-2); identification with these groups should be maximized, and the lion's share of variable compensation should follow from team/facility/division performance. Individual incentives are fine as long as they are not too complicated. However, I urge that specifically suggestion-based individual incentives be handled outside the normal incentive compensation system, as a special case. Furthermore, suggestion-based incentives should emphasize numerous small awards, rather than big ones.

2. A variable incentive bonus level that works out to a minimum of 20 percent of the total paycheck.

3. Monthly distribution of bonus money, separate from the regular paycheck.

4. A simple and understandable bonus formula. Worthington's chief financial officer, Joe Stegmayer, shakes his head in dismay when he talks of the people who visit his company to learn about their plan: "They call back to tell us what they're doing. And if they're doing anything, it's usually '7.33 percent of pre-tax profits, above $100,000 per facility, if a target return on adjusted net assets of 12.6 percent is also reached.' No one can figure it out. That means people's motivation to increase profits will not improve." Worthington's formula, 17 percent of pre-tax profits, has stayed the same since the plan began in 1966. (One thing has changed at Worthington. Profit distribution used to be based on facility rather than divisional performance. The firm shifted to the latter so that fully booked plant managers would have an incentive to shift orders to other plants more able to meet them rather than hoard them at their own operation—adding unnecessary costs through overtime pay—in hopes of gaining higher profits for their own facility.)

A Time of Trouble: The Best Time for Incentive Pay

Business Week in late 1986 reported a save-the-business agreement reached by grocer A&P. The Philadelphia local of the United Food & Commercial Workers (UFCW) agreed to a 25 percent pay cut in exchange for participation in a major incentive scheme: "If a store's employees could keep labor costs at 10 percent of sales—by working more efficiently or by boosting store traffic—they'd get a cash bonus equal to one percent of the store's sales. They'd get an 0.5 percent bonus at 11 percent of sales or 1.5 percent at 9.5 percent of sales. It was a gamble in the low margin supermarket business, but it worked. . . . Philadelphia A&P workers now earn $10.40 an hour in base wages plus an average of eighty-five cents an hour in one-time bonuses. The average food store wage in Philadelphia is $10.60. . . . Overall labor costs have been cut from 13 percent to 11 percent, versus an industry average of 12 percent."

Business Week adds: "Just as important is the effect of the bonus incentive on per-store sales, which have jumped 24 percent since 1984, to $7 million a year. With a vested interest in improving the way their stores are run, workers have made useful suggestions in bi-monthly meetings with store managers and at the regional level. In Richmond, Virginia, employees suggested that the pathway between the checkout lanes and the store shelves be widened, because in peak times the checkout lines stretched into the aisles, and customers would leave rather than fight the crowd. In one black and Italian neighborhood in Philadelphia, employees suggested adding large sections of popular ethnic food. Previously all A&P stores had to carry the same items. 'You'd be amazed at the willingness of people to participate when they can say anything without fear of reprisal,' says Thomas R. McNutt, president of UFCW Local 400 in Landover, Maryland. . . . A&P's rivals said [it was] crazy to offer one percent bonuses in a business where profit margins aren't much larger. But the dividends from the Philadelphia experience have silenced them."

Employee Share Ownership

Lowe's Companies is the biggest U.S. lumber and hardware retailer, with 309 stores in 21 states. It has been a model of the power of ESOPs to add to a firm's strength in a fragmented, competitive market. Workers at Lowe's own 25 percent of the company. The firm contributes 12 to 15 percent of payroll to its plan each year. Ownership is taken seriously at Lowe's. Each store elects a representative to an advisory committee, which hears management reports and makes recommendations. Each store holds a monthly meeting, where employees discuss changes in such things as operating procedures and merchandising. Against this backdrop, Lowe's has achieved productivity 200 to 300 percent above industry average, while employee theft is less than one-sixth of normal.

In 1974, fewer than 500,000 American workers owned stock in their companies. Now, over 8,000 ESOPs involve 8 million workers. The great explosion was fueled by the 1974 legislation that allows employers tax deductions for up to 25 percent of payroll that they contribute to an ESOP. In *Employee Ownership in America,* Corey Rosen, Katherine Klein, and Karen Young make the first comprehensive analysis of ESOPs, assessing some thirty-seven plans in depth. They review prior studies that sometimes demonstrate productivity increases of 200 to 300 percent following installment of an ESOP.

Averages aren't really the point, though. After extensive analysis, the authors home in on several possible factors that could determine the success or failure of an ESOP. Three, in combination, determine effectiveness: (1) employer contribution has to be high (at least 8 to 10 percent of payroll); (2) a true philosophy of employee-as-partner has to exist (this is the topic of the ten prescriptions in their section, taken together); and (3) multiple mechanisms for worker participation must be in place and actively used.

Among the factors that, perhaps surprisingly, were *not* decisive contributors to success were: (1) percentage of the company stock owned by employees; (2) extent of voting rights (which can range from virtually none to normal shareholder rights); (3) the reason for installing the plan (altruism versus a leveraged buyout, for instance); and (4) stock price performance following the installation of the ESOP. I find the insignificance of that last factor of special importance. The immediate rebuttal I hear to the ESOP idea from executives is: "Sounds great when the stock price is soaring. But what about lousy years and bear markets?" As usual, this is a residue of our insulting view of workers' intelligence. Executives with stock options understand that markets go up and that markets come down. Why do the same executives suppose that the people who work for them can't understand such things? The study by Rosen et al. suggests decisively that they do.

In summary, I strongly urge consideration of an ESOP, with a contribution of at least 8 to 10 percent of payroll—as long as the factors that Rosen et al. found important are also in place.

Executive Incentives

The suggestions here are simple: (1) very low base pay compared to very high incentive pay and (2) rewards based upon what you want to happen.

I am mindful of the critics' continuing concern about American management's obsession with short-term profitability. Nonetheless, especially in big firms, I observe the opposite phenomenon: executives have huge salaries that don't tumble when performance tumbles.

In a bad year, Nucor's Ken Iverson bragged that he was the lowest-paid of the Fortune 500 chiefs. I heartily applaud such bragging. The partners in the Trammell Crow real estate company draw a minimal base salary of less than $20,000; the rest of their compensation depends upon performance in the course of the year.

Here's what can happen. A bank's subsidiary was struggling. The parent devised a clever incentive scheme to perk things up. It capitalized the unit with $2.5 million in preferred stock and $500,000 in common stock. Then 40 percent of the common was given outright to the unit's managers. They were allowed to pocket dividends and stock appreciation, after profit was used to pay dividends on all the preferred stock.

Suddenly, the newly enfranchised and recently voracious-for-more-capital managers decided they had too much money. They returned $1.5 million, or 60 percent, of the preferred immediately, reducing preferred equity to $1 million. They gave up cars and perks as well, and even tried to move the unit's office to a low-rent neighborhood (the corporate parent intervened). Profits in the previously somnolent unit quintupled in the first year.

I don't particularly recommend such a plan, and perhaps in time it could lead to an excessive focus on the short term. It is, however, a dramatic illustration of the power of a clear executive incentive.

I propose base salaries of $200,000 or less for all corporate chiefs (and $75,000 or less in firms of $25 million or less), with incentives based on a mix of short- and long-term performance. And when times are tough, managers, especially top executives, should take the first and hardest hits. In a bad year, the pay of Nucor's workers will plunge 20 percent on average; executive pay will drop 70 percent.

Second, base bonuses upon the strategic skills you want to improve or emphasize. Once again, if you want to underscore the importance of superior quality, base your incentives on some measurement of quality and the improvement thereof. Ford, Tennant, Perdue Farms, and others do. If you want to emphasize customer service, pay on the basis of customer service ratings; IBM does, all the way to the top. If increased innovation is your target, reward executives, as 3M does, on the basis of the share of revenues stemming from recently introduced new products. If you want inter-unit cooperation, award big bonuses for bold acts of inter-unit support.

A Gigantic Opportunity

This Five-Part Incentive-Pay Program could add up to a lot of bucks. And it does at Steelcase, Nucor, Worthington, Lincoln Electric, Publix, Nordstrom, et al. But then, and this has been the point of all of these prescriptions, there's an enormous gain to be had: Nordstrom—200 percent above the industry average in sales per square foot; Lowe's—productivity 200 to 300 percent above average, with little shrinkage; Lincoln Electric—productivity running 250 percent above average; Nucor—productivity 300 percent above average; Worthington—productivity 200 percent above the norm, quality 300 percent above average; Andersen—productivity that's 100 percent above standard. And all of these firms are in markets growing more competitive each day.

It is distressing to see jobs mindlessly shipped offshore, and then to learn that Lincoln, in a violently competitive market from which most Americans have withdrawn, is the world's low-cost producer, while paying its average employee in excess of $40,000 a year in a merely okay year. When will the rest of us learn to "get revolutionary" about the people involvement/pay issues?

WARNING: INCENTIVES WITHOUT INVOLVEMENT WILL BACKFIRE

There are several caveats to consider before mounting a radical performance incentive plan. The worst possible thing you can do is to accept some of these suggestions without opening the doors to involvement—that is, without giving the person who is part of an incentive scheme access to the financial numbers, to training, and to the opportunity to influence the now variable pay outcome. To do otherwise is maddening; it says, in effect, "Here you are, chum. Look at the carrot [big variable incentive]. But—ha! ha!—you have no tools to reach out for it." The way to increase productivity is to allow access to an unlocked tool room, so the modem can be obtained when needed; to train extensively in cause-and-effect problem analysis; to give access to a meeting room where the team can do analysis and implementation planning. If these tools (and a host of others) are absent, the effect of the incentive is to underscore the worker's impotence. It will backfire badly.

Moreover, let me make clear what this prescription is *not.* It is *not* a reversion to the old saw: "In the end, money is the only incentive that counts." No! Involvement and the opportunity to influence the outcome come first; the money is a fine form of recognition for the help rendered. In fact, John McConnell of Worthington Industries calls his firm's generous incentive programs "just one more form of recognition." So it is, then, the coupling that counts: Involvement is important. Control over the outcome (e.g., minimum bureaucracy and supervision) is essential. And incentive pay confirms that the worker has done well using the tools and freedom thus granted.

There is, I earnestly believe, no downside. There is no evidence that workers are incapable of comprehending or bearing the pain of a poor year if (1) they have a chance to do very well in a good year and (2) they were involved in the decisions and actions that led to the outcome.

PUBLIC PARALLELS

First, there are public parallels. All levels of government are now experimenting vigorously with pay-for-performance programs. A pilot project in the U.S. Navy at China Lake, California, for instance, has sharply reduced the number of pay bands, and has dramatically increased the share of wage increases awarded on the basis of merit.

None of these programs, that I know of, approaches the radical proportions of Lincoln Electric's. On the other hand, the public pay system has been so constrained for so long that even small changes have dramatic impact. Pay-for-performance programs should also be on every public manager's agenda.

FIRST STEPS

In the next 60 days, study ten radical incentive schemes, inside and outside your industry. After day 60, consider (1) a radical scheme and (2) a three-to-five-year process for phasing it in. (This is the only prescription where I don't recommend an incremental/pilot approach. Pay is too sensitive an issue, psychologically. Once you commit, you must follow through, or suffer a very great loss of credibility.)

P-7

SUMMARY

In order to demand constant risk-taking from everyone for the sake of continuous improvement; and in order to pave the way for flexible response and constant change/reorganization, we should:

▶ provide a guarantee of continuous employment for a large share of the work force (subject to acceptable individual performance)

▶ develop a wide range of tactics, from retraining (see P-5) to short-term redeployment to understaffing by 5 or 10 percent, to ensure that layoffs rarely if ever occur.

Instability of circumstance requires constant change in technology, work procedures, structures; the formation of joint ventures and alliances; the drastic shortening of product life cycles; the institution of such procedures as just-in-time inventory management. To deal with all this turmoil, the worker must embrace change and flexibility to a previously unimaginable degree. While training and changes in attitude will help, some form (sweeping, I believe) of employment guarantee is necessary to certify management's intent to place primary emphasis on its skilled work force.

After a probationary period of 6 to 18 months, provide a guarantee of continuous employment to your permanent work force (where "permanent" is defined as enough people to handle 90 percent of normal demand). Develop, ahead of time, a specific strategy for dealing with precipitous drops in demand, including major redeployment (to maintenance, sales). Develop an ongoing retraining program to precede/accompany the introduction of, say, new technology.

Provide an Employment Guarantee

If we have too many people, we consider it a management problem, not an employee problem.

> Lowell Mayone
> Vice-President,
> Hallmark
> May 1987

When a company has a layoff, it's most often the management's fault. . . . In a recession people want to test me, to see if I'm brave enough to have a layoff. I'm willing to take that ridicule because it's paid off to hold on to our people. I don't have layoffs to see how brave I am. . . . We have a big investment in the people. . . . It's also good business for our people to have confidence that we will not lay them off just to help our profit short-term. This faith in the company is important.

> Ken Olsen
> President, Digital Equipment,
> in a 1982 speech to Wall
> Street analysts,
> 1982

In May 1987, UAW vice-president Bill Casstevens announced ratification of an agreement with Case-IH (Tenneco's farm equipment subsidiary) that "marks the first time the UAW has negotiated full employment protection in a major contract."

Case-IH won numerous provisions for job flexibility (a two-thirds reduction in job classifications, the ability to require more overtime) and a 39-month wage freeze in return for guaranteed employment levels (GELs) that cover 3,500 employed and 1,600 laid-off Case-IH workers. The base of 3,500 will be maintained with a guarantee of 40 hours of pay per week, regardless of changes in technology or market conditions. Moreover, when normal attrition occurs, for every two "quits" (retirements, etc.) one worker will be brought back from layoff. If increasing demand leads to sustained higher employment, the prevalent GEL will automatically go up. The landmark agreement also includes such provisions as earmarking a substantial portion of any future increase in the employees' cost-of-living allowance (COLA) to a major retraining program (this will represent the employees' contribution to the program, which may be added to by the company if necessary).

The pact follows the UAW's historic 1984 agreement with GM that included a "no layoff" provision protecting all workers with more than a year's seniority from unemployment due to the introduction of new technology, outsourcing decisions, and negotiated productivity improvements.

Critics call such agreements no more than a flurry of defensive actions on the part of floundering manufacturing unions—last-ditch attempts to protect a few overpaid jobs at the expense of (1) competitiveness (competitive wage rates) and (2) future/new workers. The hue and cry about the latter reached epic proportions when the pilots' and flight attendants' unions accepted American Airlines' landmark two-tier wage structure (significantly lower pay for entering employees) in return for lifetime employment guarantees for current workers.

Doubtless there is some truth to such claims. The numbers alone suggest that union strength is waning in the U.S. as competition surges and many basic worker rights are assured by legislation and judicial decisions. But be that as it may, guaranteed employment (1) has non-union origins that are over 175 years old and (2) is an idea whose time has come—i.e., it's yet another of the "nice to do's" turned "must do."

Not a New Idea

Most trace the idea of employment security back to 1806 and the cotton mill owned by Robert Owen in New Lanark, Scotland. Faced with an abrupt reduction in the supply of raw materials (an American embargo), almost all millers shut down and fired their workers. Owen stopped the machinery, but kept paying full wages and turned people to maintenance tasks during the four-month crisis.

Owen reaped the reward that is, today, the heart of the matter. His workforce was subsequently much more amenable to managerial, organizational, and technological changes. Constant innovation, supported by workers, led to extraordinary long-term profitability relative to competitors.

The U.S. has a long tradition of enlightened firms offering employment security. Though no written provision (other than to do the utmost to avoid layoffs) has ever existed at non-union IBM, the company has followed a de facto no-layoff policy for over 60 years. It has used a series of tactics (to be discussed below) to avoid layoffs. Procter & Gamble (largely non-union) introduced a minimum 48-weeks-per-year "guarantee" for production people back in 1923.

Other venerable and new guarantors include S. C. Johnson (Johnson Wax), Hewlett-Packard, Hallmark, Digital Equipment, Federal Express, Worthington Industries, Nucor Corporation, and Lincoln Electric. The last-named, for instance, guarantees 30 hours of pay a week minimum for every employee who has been on the payroll for two years.

THE POWER OF EMPLOYMENT GUARANTEES

The Work in America Institute is the foremost proponent of guaranty programs, having studied hundreds of creative experiments throughout the country. Its list of advantages is consistent with my own observations, and includes increased employee willingness to:

1. Accept management-proposed changes that might otherwise threaten security.
2. Volunteer ideas for improving performance and productivity, even when labor-saving changes may result.
3. Maintain an optimal pace of work, without fear that the job may run out.
4. Give up restrictive practices (such as jurisdictional lines and obsolete work rules), which are designed to protect jobs.
5. Agree to perform tasks outside their normal job definition, when there is need to do so.
6. Accept inconveniences, such as mandatory overtime, when persuaded of the need.
7. Volunteer for, and profit from, training that expands the boundaries of their job.

Other benefits to employers that the Institute observes include:

1. Maintenance of productivity because of higher morale and preservation of employee skills.
2. Retention of skilled workers.
3. Reduction or elimination of the large costs associated with layoffs, particularly where "bumping" occurs—for example, distorted production scheduling, delayed start-ups when recession ends, retraining of bumped employees.
4. Greater flexibility in deploying human resources to keep operations going.
5. Savings in employer costs associated with severance pay, early-retirement incentives, and other layoff schemes requiring substantial financing.
6. Avoidance of post-recession costs of hiring and training new workers to replace those who find other jobs during layoff.
7. Reinforcement of group loyalties and strengthening of employee loyalty to the firm.

These substantial benefits have long been affirmed by pioneers such as IBM, P&G, and Lincoln. But that's not the point. The point is that the preceding list reads like a summary of the tactics necessary to implement the survival strategies laid out in this book (see especially C-1 through C-10, I-1, I-10, P-1), namely that firms must, above all, (1) become more flexible and (2) achieve the benefit of constant, employee-driven improvements in quality, service, and productivity.

It is almost a psychological truism to state that *only* some guarantee of security will enable firms to induce employees to (1) constantly take risks (improve things, add new skills), and (2) be flexible enough to deal with constant change. This is the principal paradox with which management must deal (see also L-1): the engendering of heretofore unheard-of flexibility requires an equally heightened level of underlying stability—but a stability born of trust and the shared understanding of a vision, not stability based on tedious contracts and lengthy procedure manuals. Trust comes from the heart, from attitude—and from a guarantee that the newly empowered risk-taker in the maintenance shop has a relatively safe nest to which he may return.

WHAT IS A GUARANTEE?

"Lifetime employment" as practiced in Japan is the image that usually springs to mind. But the Japanese guarantee is less of a model than it seems. For one thing, "lifetime employment" covers, according to most estimates, just 15 to 35 percent of the work force, and applies almost exclusively to males in big firms. Furthermore, it is maintained through a series of strong-arm tactics such as (1) pulling in subcontract work, on short notice, from small firms, (2) using women in temporary, unprotected roles to absorb peak demand, and (3) massive redeployment of people to sales, for instance, in troubled times.

"Guarantee" turns out to be an elastic term in general. Except for those in union contracts, few guarantees are given in writing. Most, including IBM's, are oral agreements to move heaven and earth to avoid layoffs, backed up by what really counts—a decades-long track record of having done precisely that. Even Lincoln Electric's "guarantee," sustained through the toughest of times for over 50 consecutive years (with the exception of layoffs required by the return to normal production at the end of World War II), is not hard and fast; it can be changed, with six months' advance notice, by a vote of the firm's board of directors.

Here are a few of the variables that are often used to define whose employment is guaranteed, and some of the tactics used to maintain the guarantee. First, the who. Once again, the Work in America Institute provides a useful laundry list of practices:

1. *Different classes of employees* may enjoy different degrees of employment security. For example, managers normally have greater security than blue-collar employees.

2. *Permanent* employees have more employment security than temporary employees.
3. *Length of service* may determine the degree of security.
4. *Certain changes,* but not others, may be covered. For example, employees may be secure against technological changes, but not against plant closures.
5. *Occupation and wages may be altered.* Employees may be assured of permanent employment, but not necessarily in the current position or occupation or at the current wage level, and not necessarily with the current employer.
6. *Employment may be offered in a different location.* For example, a displaced employee may be transferred to a different job in the same community by outplacement to a different employer.
7. *Certain aspects of employment* may be protected and not others, such as weekly earnings, an hourly rate, a minimum number of working hours per year, and so on. Thus, the job is protected, but the terms of employment are modified temporarily.
8. Security may be contingent on *acceptance of certain conditions,* such as mandatory overtime, internal transfer at management's discretion, and blurring of jurisdictional lines.
9. *Negotiated concessions* may be required, such as wage reductions, benefit modifications, and work-rule relaxations.
10. Security may apply for a *limited period of time* (such as for the duration of a collective agreement), or for the work life of the employee (as in the case of the newspaper typographers, longshoremen, and others).

In general, the more restrictive the definition of "guarantee," the less trust is engendered and the less the benefit to the firm. I strongly recommend a broad definition—accompanied by the adoption of certain tactics designed to make sure the firm can live up to its promise.

MAKING A GUARANTEE FEASIBLE

There are three primary tactics that enable a firm to offer a guarantee—and stick with it:

1. Careful hiring (understaffing) and extensive use of overtime/temporaries/subcontractors. Most "guarantee" firms purposefully understaff with permanent (guaranteed) employees—often by a considerable number.

This in turn requires very tight control over hiring. For example, at Lincoln Electric every new hire must be approved by four vice-presidents. A more common device is granting permanent employment to the numbers needed to handle less than normal market demand. Thus, IBM's giant typewriter operation in Lexington, Kentucky, is staffed to meet 85 percent of normal demand. Overtime is used to make up about 10 percent of the remainder (ten to twelve

Saturdays per year are expected as a condition of employment, and up to twenty-two Saturdays per year can be required as a matter of course in times of high demand). For the final 5 percent or so, subcontracting and temporary help are used.

Motorola, in its semiconductor operation, also staffs for 80 to 85 percent of normal demand, but rather than extensive overtime or subcontracting, the firm uses "contract workers" to meet shortfalls; they are hired on six-month contracts, at the same pay as permanent workers. Control Data (which targets for just 70 percent of normal demand), Hewlett-Packard (a major user of subcontractors), and Nucor are others who staff their facilities with fewer permanent employees than required to meet normal demand.

It is imperative to add that such "lean" permanent staffing can only be effective if work practices are nonrestrictive, with everyone trained to perform multiple tasks—the second primary tactic.

2. Redeployment and retraining. From Japan to Kansas City, redeployment and retraining is a conventional tactic for those who guarantee employment.

Hallmark, which is also a very cautious hirer, (a) switches assignments (in stark times, factory workers take on maintenance and housekeeping jobs), and (b) lends employees to the community (for instance, in the 1981–82 recession, several factory workers weatherproofed houses).

Shifting people to sales in tough times is a common Japanese practice, which IBM has followed, too. In 1981–82, Lincoln increased revenues by $10 million by shifting factory and office workers temporarily to sales. Kimberly Clark used the same tactic with seventy-five factory workers—and reports an added benefit: After returning to the factory, the seventy-five had a much greater appreciation of the importance of quality to customers.

During the same slump, semiconductor equipment-maker Materials Research Corporation had scientists and engineers call on customers. They also had factory and office crews perform housekeeping, security, and maintenance functions; groups, including supervisors, rotated through the tasks on ninety-day assignments. MRC's overall responsiveness to the slump proceeded in stages: (a) attrition, which was unsuccessful (it works notoriously poorly during general downturns), (b) redeployment, as noted above, and, finally, (c) generic education. That is, people, with full pay, were encouraged to go to school to upgrade skills that would be useful to them and the firm over the long haul.

Retraining has long been IBM's middle name (see P-5). Digital Equipment has undertaken massive retraining/redeployment of factory workers more recently, offering such options to 4,500 workers between 1984 and 1987; some 3,800 have accepted. For instance, about 100 supervisors have moved into sales. Because of automation, retraining and redeployment at Digital are expected to continue at the rate of 2,200 to 2,500 factory people per year for the foreseeable future—despite booming demand.

Buick is using retraining/redeployment as a major tool to deal with technological change. Its Employee Development Center in Flint, Michigan, guarantees a minimum one-year stay to each person displaced by technological development, regardless of seniority. While retaining full pay and fringe benefits, the worker is retrained for other Buick jobs.

Pacific Bell, faced with massive overstaffing following the breakup of the Bell System in 1984, has cut employment from about 100,000 to 70,000 with no layoffs. The reduction, induced by programs such as sweet early-retirement packages, has caused uneven staffing shortages. Redeployment and retraining have been potent tools to ease the adjustments. Overall, the program has been so effective that despite the cuts, grievances have fallen from nearly 5,000 per year to less than 100 in the six months through May 1987.

3. Work sharing and short work weeks. If cautious hiring, conscious under-staffing, cutting back on temps, pulling in subcontracting, working at discretionary tasks (e.g., performing deferred maintenance), shifting to revenue enhancement activities (sales calls by engineers, factory hands, et al.), and retraining fail, firms that guarantee employment use shortened workweeks and work-sharing. Nucor, Lincoln, and Hewlett-Packard have been among those who cut back substantially on hours. At Nucor in bad times, three- or four-day weeks are not uncommon (executives incur bigger penalties, via cuts in compensation); in good times, six-day weeks are common.

Job-sharing is still not legal in many states, but is increasingly being used where allowed.* The case of Motorola's semiconductor operation is typical. In the 1981–83 recession it took four successive steps: (1) a hiring freeze, (2) elimination of all overtime, (3) the pulling in of virtually all subcontracting, and, finally, (4) job-sharing.

THE COSTS OF RENEGING ON A GUARANTEE

Though few non-union guarantees are in writing, most have been effective by dint of long practice. But what if times change drastically, and layoffs become a must? That's happened at such venerable firms as Kodak.

The story is mixed, and depends on the firm's approach. Meatpacker Hormel's guaranteed-hours program was considered a landmark, especially in a highly seasonal industry. However, faced with very tough competitive conditions, management invoked a narrow interpretation of its contract with the union, demanding substantial wage cuts. The result was a rancorous, sometimes violent, nine-month strike, in which faith was shattered on both sides.

The other side of the coin is represented by Advanced Micro Devices (AMD), a semiconductor-maker forced to renege on a hard-and-fast no-layoff promise. Since the company (1) genuinely tried many alternatives, and (2) was so much more generous than its industry neighbors such as National Semiconductor, the breach of promise was not met with an outcry.

*In job- or work-sharing, an employer spreads unemployment, via reduced hours, over the whole work force. In some cases, state law allows compensation via unemployment insurance for the hours lost.

DEALING WITH MANAGERS

The organizational structures of U.S. corporations continue to feature bloated management ranks, with reductions of 50 to 80 percent still required at many firms (see P-8). How does an employment guarantee square with the need for continued management-pruning?

First, the thrust of this prescription is directed to the nonmanagerial work force. Our managerial population, in big firms at least, has been until recently, de facto, guaranteed employment. With rare exceptions, managers have stayed on even as downturns required huge nonmanagerial layoffs, often of long duration.

So management must be cut back. However, I applaud the efforts of Digital Equipment (et al.) to redeploy supervisors. Retraining, redeployment, and lavish early-retirement programs should be used to accomplish as much as possible of the management cutback without firings.

If these tactics don't work (and managers are generally more reluctant than workers to accept redeployment), make the necessary cuts in one step, rather than extending the process. The latter induces perpetual fear (and risk aversion) throughout the firm. After the cut, extend the guarantee to managers as well as nonmanagers.

THE LARGER CONTEXT

An employment guarantee involves three major issues: (1) providing security in return for flexibility/risk-taking on everyone's part, (2) treating the work force as a long-term "asset" worthy of constant re-investment (e.g., retraining), and (3) shifting from a mind-set that sees cost reduction as a primary goal (with labor a "factor of production") to a revenue enhancement strategy.

Pragmatically, the first issue governs. We must achieve more flexibility and a willingness not only to accept change, but to wholeheartedly participate in its speedy implementation.

The second issue, discussed in Part I, represents a monumental shift in attitude to perceiving the work force as the prime source of value added—via quality, service, responsiveness, and constant improvement of everything by everyone. This strategy is a must (see C-1 through C-10), and guaranteed employment—and attendant continual retraining (see P-5)—is a cornerstone of its execution.

Finally, I can only wish that American managers will come to consider job creation (or maintenance) as one of their chief obligations. As noted, this suggestion does not fly in the face of pleas to cut overstaffing. It does suggest that the firm's long-term goal and guiding premise should be to maintain current employment levels or increase them via revenue enhancement. Revenue maximization, not short-term cost minimization, should become the new lodestar (see C-10).

FIRST STEPS

Develop a plan for using temporaries, subcontractors, and overtime in conjunction with staffing at 85 to 90 percent of normal demand requirements. Consider what retraining and redeployment needs would have to accompany a no-layoff guarantee. After a thorough review, begin a program of attrition and the use of, say, temporaries (perhaps as Motorola does, with a six-month contract at wages equal to those of permanent employees) before committing to the guarantee. If you do commit to a guarantee, phase it in over a one-to-five year period, with new features predicated upon the achievement of various growth and productivity improvement goals.

P-8

SUMMARY

Excessive organizational structure is a principal cause of slow corporate response to changed circumstances. We must:

► Radically reduce layers of management.

► Assign most "support" staff—in accounting, personnel, purchasing, etc.—to the field, reporting to site (line) managers.

► Establish a radically increased ratio of non-supervisors to supervisors—a "wide span of control"—at the organization's front line.

Structure kills. Most are moving to reduce it. Few are moving fast enough. Excess middle management staff—often to the tune of several hundred percent—still exists in most big firms and even in many smaller and mid-sized firms.

No more than five layers of management are necessary, regardless of firm size; limit layers in any facility to three at most. Get staffs out in the field, and encourage them to be "business team members" rather than narrow functional specialists (see also P-9). Minimum spans of control at the front line should be one supervisor for every 25 to 75 nonsupervisors.

Simplify/Reduce Structure

The most important thing American industry needs to do is reduce the number of management layers. . . . [It's] one thing we're really fanatical about. We have four management layers. We have a foreman, and the foreman goes directly to a department head, and the department head goes directly to the general manager, and he goes directly to this office.

> F. Kenneth Iverson, chairman
> Nucor Corporation
> (1986 sales: $755 million)

We have the poorest productivity growth in any Western industrialized country. And managerial ineptitude has put us into this box. The way to get higher productivity is to train better managers and have fewer of them. Four years ago we had more than 1,200 people at corporate headquarters. We're coming down to 250.

> William Woodside, chairman
> Primerica
> (formerly American Can)
> February 1987

MANAGEMENT'S TIME BOMB: EXCESSIVE STRUCTURE

We are being strangled by bloated staffs, made up of carping experts and filling too many layers on the organization chart. Today's structures were designed for controlling turn-of-the-century mass-production operations under stable conditions, with primitive technologies. They have become perverse, action-destroying devices, completely at odds with current competitive needs.

The consultants McKinsey & Company recently examined thirty-eight advanced manufacturing technology systems; they concluded, according to *Boardroom Reports:* "The first step in accomplishing successful plant floor implementation of new manufacturing approaches is the clearing out of *all* [my emphasis] the middle managers and support service layers that clog the wheels of change.

These salaried people are often the real barriers to productivity improvement, not the hourly workers on the floor." Similarly, the Yankee Group (a Boston consulting firm) concluded, as I did in P-2, that there will be no need for foremen in future factories; information technology will provide all the data needed, and routines for digesting it, to the front-line worker.

James O'Toole, professor of corporate strategy at the University of Southern California, in a study of "span of control," has observed that it averages one supervisor to ten nonsupervisors in the United States. The Japanese ratio runs 1:100, often 1:200. Not surprisingly, O'Toole concludes: "In general, American workers appear to be oversupervised."

Review the discussion above: (1) Iverson says structure is the primary management issue, and makes do with four layers (and a headquarters complement of a little over a dozen) to run a firm with almost a billion dollars in assets—and to make a profit, in steel. (2) The chairman of Primerica, a manufacturing firm (American Can) turned service company with $5 billion in revenues at the end of 1986, finds he can cut central staff by 80 percent. (3) Normally conservative McKinsey & Company, reviewing the disastrous results of attempts to install new and flexible manufacturing systems in the United States, says get rid of all middle management; and the Yankee Group contends that we soon won't need foremen. (4) Researcher Jim O'Toole says the ratio of supervisors to workers on America's industrial front lines may be out of whack by a factor of ten.

Treat people well, involve them in everything (P-1). Put them on self-managing teams (P-2). Make a "customer-oriented revolution" (C-10). Nurture volatile champions in every function (I-6). Do all these things and more, and still you will be doomed to suffer the failure of or unmercifully slow implementation of your strategy if you are saddled with a ten-layer organizational structure.

My co-authors and I downplayed the importance of structure in *In Search of Excellence* and again in *A Passion for Excellence.* We were terribly mistaken. Good intentions and brilliant proposals will be dead-ended, delayed, sabotaged, massaged to death, or revised beyond recognition or usefulness by the over-layered structures at most large and all too many smaller firms.

THE ORIGINS OF STRUCTURAL BLOAT

Almost seventy-five years ago, Du Pont created what may have been the first modern divisionalized organization structure, with separate units containing all the functions necessary to do business (R&D, engineering, purchasing, manufacturing, distribution, sales). General Motors soon followed suit. It has been estimated that between the end of World War II and 1970, 90 percent of the Fortune 500 decentralized into divisional structures.

Decentralization was the right strategy—it still is. But the "clean," business-minded structures envisioned by the pioneers lost their zip over time, and success didn't help. Many decentralized units grew big, with some divisions encumbered by ten or more layers of management.

Decentralization Is Reversed

But worse was to come. The "operations research paradigm" appeared during World War II; optimization of everything (e.g., manufacturing, engineering) became the cry. The optimizer is by definition a centralizer, a hyper-organizer. Function after function—purchasing, for example—was de facto recentralized at such companies as GM, despite the nominal retention (on paper) of the decentralized divisional structure. Then came the new marketing theories, which required central coordination of ad budgets, for instance; then the dominance of finance people, with their complex centralized control systems. The enormous increases in transportation costs in the 1970s led the centralizers to take over distribution, too, in the name of "optimal efficiency." New requirements in personnel (resulting from equal opportunity and safety legislation) led to big, central personnel staffs. New sensitivities—the environmental and consumer movements, for example—led to centralized approaches to the outside world via massive public relations and lobbying operations that attempted to control the "decentralized" division's outside contacts, even with local press. Each development, sensible in itself, fostered the further growth of expert central staffs. Each central staff addition meant (1) more requests to the line for reports, and (2) more requests that this or that report be coordinated with numerous others; moreover, each staff was increasingly requested to coordinate almost everything with every other central staff. The mess (and resultant inertia) increased exponentially.

To deal with the mess, still more layers and "offices of" were added—the idea of the group executive, the office of the chairman; and each of these in turn developed private staffs (1) to consolidate their power and (2) to deal professionally with the queries of other staffs. Even Kafka would have been challenged to describe the situation adequately.

The Final Blow: Matrix's "Dotted Lines"

Meanwhile, the thrilling early successes of NASA's project organization structure brought us a new idea, the "matrix"—yet another form of de facto centralization. Every group was to be "wired" to every other group (organization charts show dense clouds of dotted lines going this way and that) to gain "synergies" that would come from coordinating everything and everyone with everything else and everyone else. In the mid-seventies, new marketing themes developed, wedded to the matrix concept. For instance, "global branding" became an excuse for gutting international divisions of the authority that had devolved to them in their glory years; recentralization left the illusion of local control intact, but in reality put New York–based, English-only-speaking, MBA-toting market modelers in charge of Thailand and Luxembourg and all stops in between.

Stir in the mainframe computer, central data banks, instant telecommunications, and exploding global financial networks calling for centralized cash management—and by 1975, anything approaching true decentralization was dead in most sizable firms. At about that time, the competitive crunch hit. And the first response was? You guessed it—*more* centralization, this time in the name of centralized control over costs ("rationalization") to achieve efficiency.

Structural Weaknesses Become Apparent—but Are Tough to Fix

Increasingly, the new competitors that most effectively started chipping away at the giant firms' profitable niches were smaller, less complicated, and more focused—Honda nibbled at GM, Nucor at U.S. Steel, Digital at IBM, Federal Express at the U.S. Postal Service, and so on (see Part I). It is now all too apparent that our overly centralized, over-layered organizations are dysfunctional. But saying that, even understanding it, and doing something about it are two different things. We are so hooked on the tools, logic, and false comfort of expert staffs and centralized systems that the task is an enormous one. Furthermore, we have developed a generation of big business managers (and continue to develop them in our MBA factories) who have become so dependent on these systems that they have lost all feel for the totality of a business operation. It is a travesty even to call them "businessmen," in any historic sense of that term.

Thus, we must change habits developed over several decades—at a time when certain tools such as telecommunications networks are becoming more powerful. Such tools *can* be used in the service of an autonomous unit (see C-4); whether or not they will be so used by more than a few is an altogether different matter. The danger is that they will be used, as so often in the past, to further centralize operations once more in the name of the great management deity, "synergy."

Logic Will Not Help

Suppose you agree with all this, and are ready to move forward. You may (probably will) be ensnared by a last irony. Each isolated element of the overdetermined structure looks necessary—on paper. Every job in the "charts and boxes" structures makes sense; you and your predecessors weren't fools. You didn't add staff jobs capriciously. Far from it; you were always reluctant to add to "headquarters headcount." And yet it's still two or three or five times too high. Bellwether firms are developing new products five times faster than you are. And your sluggishness, make no mistake, is chiefly attributable to all those layers.

CREATING THE STRUCTURE OF THE FUTURE

Limit Management Layers to Five

Peter Drucker in his classic book *The Practice of Management* recommends seven layers as the maximum necessary for any organization. But that was in 1954, a more placid era. I insist on five layers as the maximum. Incidentally, that's the number of layers with which the Catholic Church makes do to oversee 800 million members. As Eli Ginzberg and George Vojta observe in *Beyond Human Scale: The Large Corporation at Risk:* "Many writers on organization have termed the Catholic Church the most venerable large institution in the West, as it has achieved and maintained a position of leadership and power for over a millennium and a half. A key organizational characteristic of the Church is that despite its size it has avoided excessive layering."

In fact, even the five-layer limit should apply only to very complex organizations such as multi-division firms. Three layers—supervisor (with the job redefined to deal with a span of control no smaller than one supervisor for twenty-five to seventy-five people), department head, and unit boss—should be tops for any single facility, such as a plant or operations or distribution center. That's about the way Nucor does it: foreman (wide span of control), department head, general (facility) manager, president. Chaparral Steel makes do with a similar arrangement: foreman/general manager (who is highly empowered to make decisions and cross functional boundaries), superintendent, vice-president, president.

Put Staff in the Field

Much of the problem of sluggishness, it is true, comes from sheer excess of staff and layers of staff. On the other hand, where the staff is located and what they do are as important as how many there are. Colleagues from several firms, such as Mars, Inc., where a thirty-person headquarters guides a $7 billion company, say that they're not altogether sure they have fewer staff people per revenue dollar than other firms do. Their companies' effectiveness, they suggest, stems from the placement of virtually all staff people in factories, sales branches, and distribution centers. They do not populate corporate or other central headquarters. And indeed, I regularly observe that when you put an accountant (or someone from "personnel") in the field, as a member of a business unit of manageable size, she or he automatically and almost instantaneously changes. Ginzberg and Vojta invented the term "business-mindedness" to describe the shift in such managers' perspectives from "inward" to "outward":

> The overall aim is to create a climate of "business-mindedness" in the large corporation. In other words, the behavior of managers must be pri-

marily geared to success in the marketplace over the long pull, in contrast to their current preoccupation with fighting their way up the corporate hierarchy through alliances and maneuvering. . . .

In corporations in which power-related behavior patterns are well established, which means in almost all large corporations, managers spend a great deal of their time and energy trying to keep informed of developments that can affect the future of their groups. They attend many meetings for the sole purpose of insuring that the group's franchise or turf is not reduced. The extent to which they find it necessary to expend energy in such defensive tactics means that they can direct less effort to improving the group's business performance and, ultimately, the profitability of the corporation as a whole.

The moral of such behavior is not lost on junior and middle managers. They soon realize that the evaluation of their work by supervisors, peers, and subordinates depends as much upon how they are perceived as on how competently they perform, on politics rather than performance. Such a climate favors cautious organizational maneuvering rather than business risk-taking. . . .

The long-range impact of such risk-avoiding behavior can have devastating effects. If young managers are shielded from having to operate in an entrepreneurial environment in which they are held accountable for the resources under their command as well as for the consequences of their decisions, they will move up the hierarchy without ever having been forced to operate in an exposed business setting, in which the market calls the shots.

The Effect of Fewer Layers: Less Is More

The good news from those who are experimenting radically is that less is more:

▶ A meticulous 1985 study of forty-one large companies by management consultants A. T. Kearney contrasted winning and losing companies on the basis of long-term financial performance. Winners had 3.9 fewer layers of management than losers (7.2 versus 11.1) and 500 fewer central staff specialists per $1 billion in sales.

▶ In *World Class Manufacturing,* Richard Schonberger returns time and again to the topic of "better support with [fewer] people," based upon his extensive observations of hundreds of revolutions in structure at the factory level of organization. One chapter on staff roles, for instance, discusses "better maintenance with fewer people in the plant maintenance department" (operators do their own maintenance, faster—and cheaper, when prevention of failure is considered), "better quality with fewer people in the quality department" (self-inspection, with appropriate training, becomes the norm), "better accounting with fewer accountants" (for instance, direct costing replaces cumbersome overhead allocations when just-in-time inventory management and operator maintenance take place), "better production control with fewer production controllers" (self-contained, so-called cellular manufacturing units abet this), "better material management with fewer materials staff" (just-in-time leads to less complex processes in the factory), and "better information with less data processing" (again, simplification is the cause).

▶ The Brunswick Corporation cut its layers by 40 percent—and turned a losing situation around in short order. At first, the expectation was that expert staff in the divisions would have to be increased to take up the tasks previously performed by those now cut from corporate staffs. It didn't work out that way. What all frustrated businesspersons joke about turned out to be hard fact. The division staffs were immediately able to reduce their numbers, too. That is, it turned out that much of what the division staffs had been doing was not productive work, but simply generating responses to requests flowing down from the corporate center and group-lead staffs.

▶ *Industry Week* conducted a special study in late 1986 on the realigning of middle management in big firms:

> William Dowdell, a 45-year-old manager of printing-plate systems for Du Pont, . . . heads an experimental operating unit created 18 months ago. [He] is a perfect example of how companies are restructuring managerial responsibility. Before the new unit was formed, Mr. Dowdell managed the marketing arm of the photo products division. . . . That unit found it difficult to make money, because decisions on pricing . . . new products rarely kept up with the competition. *Indeed, major decisions required between 30 and 40 signatures for approval* [my emphasis]. "It was incredibly frustrating," Mr. Dowdell recalls. "That kind of bureaucracy just stifles creativity." In the old structure the photo products division consisted of three subunits, each of which reported to a vice president. Under the experimental arrangement, Mr. Dowdell was put in charge of the entire $45-million-a-year division and given responsibility for all marketing, manufacturing, and research and development work. And, since Mr. Dowdell no longer has to obtain all those approvals for a project, the bureaucratic paper shuffling has stopped. . . . "It's amazing to see the change in people—the enthusiasm they have—when we released them from the paper chase and made them part of the process," Mr. Dowdell says. Not only have the profits of the photo products division firmed up—since it now meets competition head on—but improvements in printing-plate technology have enabled the unit to produce a magazine for the industry. That project would never have got off the ground under the old structure, Mr. Dowdell says.

▶ A small example from Mountain Bell is also instructive at the micro-level. A new manager in a town of 20,000 was determined to emphasize customer service. The problem, as he quickly saw it, was that "there was no one person any customer could turn to. No one was really responsible for anything." The group closest to the action was hopelessly factionalized. Thirty nonmanagers were overseen by seven first-line supervisors, each of whom guarded his functional turf jealously. The new manager rapidly concluded that "there was no horizontal communication." Moreover, at the top of the already overorganized heap sat yet another two managers (second-line supervisors). The new boss acted swiftly, clearing out five of the seven first-line bosses and one of the two at the next level up. Even the two first-line supervisors no longer managed separate functions; the thirty nonmanagers were reorganized into one, undifferentiated team. Communication improved dramatically—and customer service along with it: complaints per hundred subscribers per month rapidly dropped by 75 percent.

These examples, and a host more like them, are staggering in their implications—not merely that "less is more," but that "a lot less is a lot more." Pruning central staff/layers by 50 to 90 percent leads to more responsiveness and better staff work. It all adds up to this: If you have more than a handful of people at headquarters, if you have more than a few layers, you are in trouble—or fast heading for it. It's as simple and stark as that.

CHANGING CORPORATE STRUCTURES: ISSUES AND (SOME) ANSWERS

Slash the central staff and layers. Then slash the decentralized staffs and layers. Assign the staff work to the line. And things get better. But there's more to it than that. Attacking the issue of structure requires us to take on a bewildering array of difficult issues:

1. **Powerful forces still apparently push toward centralization.** Many—such as transportation network optimization, telecommunications linkups, common data base management—are actually on the rise. Only an abiding contrary belief in the observed power of the smaller, niche-creating unit (see Part I, C-1, and I-1) will help you deal with these forces. Examine your company's problems vis-à-vis foreign competitors, and consider experimenting somewhere with a new structure (for instance, despite its current problems, GM deserves lots of credit for the radical nature—structurally—of the new Saturn operation).

2. **Most senior managers have developed a psychological dependence on the instant—if irrelevant—answers to everything that are provided by big central staff groups.** Examples such as Dowdell of Du Pont suggest that top management can go from thirty signatures to one, but it is painful, which is why most move so slowly. Perhaps only radical experiments such as Du Pont's will wean top management from its past. But a failure or two (which is guaranteed to occur), even a small one, can stall progress.

3. **What do we do, as a firm or nation, with the huge excess of middle managers?** There's no easy answer here either. Many can be devolved to the field, but many will not survive the transition. Extensive retraining is a mini-

mum (see P-5, P-6). But a whole generation who did their jobs well and a new generation of women and minorities finally making it into management's lower and middle ranks have been cast adrift—and we must continue the shift, faster still. (Part I hints at some of the adjustment assistance that is needed as a matter of policy; but most proposals, mine and others', still don't deal adequately with the immensity of this problem.)

4. What do we do with the first-line supervisor population, of whom 90 percent are redundant? Retraining for a new role may, again, help some (see P-5, P-6, P-7); but there are no easy answers. Demotions back to nonsupervisorial status seldom work out. The harsh truth, though, is that line jobs will not be salvageable unless the excess hierarchy at the crucial front line is moved out.

5. True decentralization will require such things as order-of-magnitude increases in the spending authority of unit managers. How can we quickly develop general managers whom we trust with such large sums? Once more, no easy solutions are on the horizon. As noted, most of today's functional experts are not "businessmen." For every Dowdell of Du Pont there are several who fail as managers of newly autonomous units. Training doesn't seem to help much, either, for those who have spent a lifetime climbing the ladder at headquarters. Sadly, the most practical solution is a kind of musical chairs—move 'em in and move 'em out, and hope that one out of several will rise to the challenge.

6. How can we develop alternative control schemes when the complement of intervening, inherently conservative staff layers virtually disappears? Here there are some answers, though once again not easy ones, since they come up against deep-seated attitudes. When I suggest that you slash the layers, I'm not asking you to slash away, lay off 75 percent of the staff, expand the span of control from 1:7 to 1:50—and then wash your hands of the whole mess. New controls must replace the old ones. What will they be? Customer contact, the subject of several of the first set of prescriptions, for one. True closeness to the market and constant commerce with customers and suppliers turns out to be an amazingly effective control device. The power of the market (i.e., angry customers constantly visiting) is more of a disciplining force than a passel of visiting staff managers with a 2,000-page analysis. Likewise, the people prescriptions are aimed at substituting a new form of control—self-control born of the involvement and ownership that follows from, among other things, training people on the line to take on many traditionally supervisory roles. Being fully responsible for results will concentrate the mind more effectively than any out-of-touch cop on the staff. Finally, the leadership prescriptions also spell out new roles and new forms of control. Getting out and about to listen, concentrating on shaping and clarifying your vision, and the like are alternatives to the feeling (usually an illusion today) of control that exists when you are in the boardroom surrounded by clever MBAs whose glowing lap-top computers can spew forth multicolored contingency answers to any question in seconds. None of this, however, will turn out to be easy. And making senior management comfortable with these arrangements—that's an especially tough nut to crack; only successful experience will crack it.

7. How can we deal with the apparent turmoil of some inevitable duplication that results from the creation of independent business units working in closely related markets—e.g., several (uncoordinated) sales calls on the same customer, products from different divisions that at least partially compete with one another, incompatible computer systems and data bases? Once more, we must experiment. Some duplication, in practice, will occur; but accumulating evidence suggests it will fall far short of our worst fears. (And even if it is fearsome, we must still move. The embarrassment of a few snafus with multiple sales calls is a lot less than the embarrassment of losing your market to five mid-sized competitors, each of whom is five to ten times faster than you.)

Fighting Your Instincts

This list of seven presents a nightmarish challenge—and an absence of comforting answers. Your firm's competitive position is probably declining. Every instinct, honed over decades, says crack down, grasp the reins more tightly, opt for the always impressive paper efficiencies of more centralization. But following your instincts here can be catastrophic. Just look who's killing you—a firm which is a tiny fraction of your size. (GM is five times bigger than Honda, for instance. IBM is 25 times bigger than Apple, and six times bigger than DEC.)

You must, sad to say, bite the bullet, and take drastic action (or at least experiment boldly)—without good answers to most of the basic questions posed above. But you can choose among an increasing number of places to visit— ongoing experiments of the most radical sort. Visit Nucor or Chaparral and see how to live with four layers of management. Visit Mars to observe how a thirty-person group runs a giant firm. Visit the new-look Ford or GM plants, to observe how union and management have dealt with the demise of job specialization and the elimination of supervisors. See how Brunswick makes do with half the layers it had. Find out how Johnsonville Sausage (see prescription P-2) gets on without even facility managers. Or how half-billion-dollar Lincoln Electric makes do with a span of control of 1:100—and yet achieves productivity that's several times the industry average.

Here, as elsewhere, you are asked to consider radical steps. But I am not speaking as a theorist, only urging in the strongest terms that you consider what others have done.

FIRST STEPS

1. Don't hire a consultant to help you with this!
2. Visit: Schedule at least 5–10 trips in the next 6–12 months to interesting companies experimenting with radically new structural configurations. On each trip, stay for several days. Do this by yourself, or put together a line-dominated team to study 5–15 interesting firms.
3. Consider taking radical action—fast. A policy of letting people go a few

at a time, day by day and year by year, is aborting the transformation of many companies, since every remaining person lives in terror of the other shoe dropping.

4. *Structure and the unit manager:* If you are in the middle of the pyramid, I'll spell out a new role in the next prescription, P-9. But let me make a few suggestions here. Get out of the office and into the field. Get every person in your unit out into the field. If this is a physical impossibility (you run central computing), get everyone in regular touch by phone with his or her "customers" before problems arise; induce your "customers" to visit you. Also, make sure that every person is working on at least one special project in the field, that everyone on your staff is assigned to a field operation for at least one specific project of 30 to 60 days' duration each year. You can do these things, and they will help.

P-9

SUMMARY

One of the most dramatic requirements associated with increasing responsiveness is to shift the organization's entire "way of being" from a "vertical" (hierarchical) to a "horizontal" (fast, cross-functional cooperation) orientation. To do that, we must:

▶ Reconceive the middle management job as one of facilitator and functional-boundary smasher, instead of expert and guardian of functional units.

▶ Use a "reverse pyramid" organization chart, with front-line people "on top" and supervisors and middle managers below them in a support-and-facilitation role.

The middle manager, apparently in the way of the required organizational revolution, *can* become the most important player in the newly conceived structure—but his or her role must be wholly changed from the traditional one.

Dramatically shift reward (formal and informal) and evaluation systems for middle managers in order to emphasize "making things happen" across formerly sacred functional boundaries.

Reconceive the Middle Manager's Role

Management excellence cannot come from fragmented contributions by various functional staffs; that is, if quality assurance has exclusive jurisdiction over a quality program, if production control has an inventory program, and so on. Each staff seeks to impose another set of techniques, each set demanding adjustments and attention from an already choked line organization. Only so much can be assimilated at a time, and it should be cohesive. . . . Japanese are good integrators. . . . Americans are accustomed to thinking that integration of a company is only in one place—at the top, where strategy is made.

Robert Hall
Attaining Manufacturing Excellence

Perhaps the biggest change of all for manufacturing engineering is getting used to the idea that the best way to make a contribution is found on the factory floor, not in the equipment manufacturers' catalogs. The [manufacturing engineer] must spend some time with equipment sales reps but should spend more with machine operators, setup crews, maintenance technicians, and supervisors. Most of the tangible wealth of industry is in old equipment that is falling apart fast. Most of it is worth rescuing.

Richard Schonberger
World Class Manufacturing

I, like many others, have repeatedly attacked middle managers. And we do indeed have too many layers, too much staff. Yet the leanest of sizable organizations does need *some* middle managers. What should their role be?

We must start by acknowledging the problem. Jan Carlzon dramatically reversed the fortunes of the Scandinavian Air System (SAS) in the early 1980s. It lost millions in 1979–80, but achieved high profitability and won "Airline of the Year" status just twenty-four months later, while the rest of the European airline industry lost billions.

Carlzon accomplished his miracle through an extraordinary improvement in service. The new company heroes were the first-line service providers. Carlzon explicitly ordered them to go around their managers, right to the top if necessary, to clear hurdles out of the way. He acknowledges that he "hot-wired the system" to achieve immediate results.

Now he sees the need for a second, more lasting and more profound revolution. In his first effort, which he now calls the First Wave, he was dismissive of middle managers—the "layer of insulation," as he described them. He admits he gave them "no viable alternative" to their old and traditional role as "rule interpreters." They were the scapegoats. Now, in the Second Wave, he believes, that must be changed. Middle managers are to be autonomous—but no longer as rule interpreters or as protectors of "functional integrity" in the traditional, vertical, "functional stovepipe," "functional silo" organizational structure. Instead, middle managers are to be responsible for seeking out and battering down the very functional barriers that they were formerly paid to protect. They are to be charged with making things happen, come hell or high water. In other words, as Carlzon concludes in his book *Riv Pyramiderna!* (Flatten the Pyramids),* "the distribution of roles is radically different."

MAKING THE MIDDLE MANAGER PART
OF THE SOLUTION

It would be impossible to overestimate what a profound shift this constitutes for Western management. British researcher Malcolm Trevor and his associates studied Japanese and European managers in European settings, and summarized their research in *The Japanese Management Development System.* Their conclusion about British managers applies to the United States as well: "As a country, the UK is cursed by [managerial job] specialisms. . . . [The] Japanese expected that managers would not stick to functional boundaries. . . . British managers were over-concerned with a formal chain of command but little concerned with horizontal communication. . . . British managers hoarded information that [the Japanese] managers [in Japanese-owned operations] intended them to share. . . . For British managers, sharing information can be seen as a danger to their own career prospects."

For the Japanese, the authors add, "jobs are ambiguous, are roughly defined. . . . Job contents change all the time. . . . [There are] no divisional fences." This connotes no lack of discipline on the part of the Japanese, to be sure, but a different interpretation of what the managerial job is all about. A typical Japanese manager, they continue, "follows company rules and procedures very strictly, but . . . his job area is very flexible." There is no sense of contradiction between rule-following and job flexibility. In the West, managements at firms such as Chaparral, Worthington, and Hewlett-Packard historically, and Ford,

---

*The title of the English translation is *Moments of Truth.*

Du Pont, Omark, P&G, and Milliken have been experimenting with lower-level integration of functions. The emphasis has been on team-level, multi-function coordination, not on the several (at least two or three) layers of management immediately above the team. None has gone as far as the Japanese; none except Carlzon has so precisely defined the revolutionary shift in the role of middle management that would be required to do so.

Back in the 1940s, Rensis Likert developed a "linking pin" idea of organization; Herman-Miller implemented it, and GM experimented with it in several places. The core idea is that each level of management is a member of a multi-functional team that includes the next level up.

But Likert's essential idea doesn't go far enough. For one thing, it focuses on coordination, and "coordination" *as it is practiced* emphasizes that horrid role of protecting one's function. While coordination does include "getting together," to "coordinate," often as not in practice, is to stall in the name of "checking this out three layers up" before acting. The objective here is to go one giant step further, as Carlzon suggests. Every middle manager should spring out of the gate each morning as a dedicated, proactive boundary basher. He or she is not just passively "coordinating" but is aggressively seeking ways to force activity that involves multiple functions to occur faster. In this new role, the middle manager must become: (1) expeditor/barrier destroyer/facilitator, (2) on-call expert, and (3) diffuser of good news. In short, the middle manager must practice fast-paced "horizontal management," not traditional, delaying, "vertical management."

Task #1: Turning the Organization Upside Down—and Sideways

The organization chart must be turned upside down. Carlzon did it; so does retailer Nordstrom (Figure 16, p. 370). First-line management's role is to support the front-line people. Middle management's role is to act largely as facilitator, greasing the skids and speeding up actions, especially those actions (most) requiring cross-functional, multi-unit cooperation. Middle management is no longer to be the umpire, in charge of constraining, preventing, or slowing action in the name of turf, rights, or integrity. As you can see, the Nordstrom organization chart even includes the idea of a "helping hand" aimed "upward."

What precisely does this mean? At Milliken, close on the heels of SAS in moving this idea forward, the new breed of middle manager is becoming an out-and-out expediter (see C-8 also). Days are spent on the phone, inducing faster interaction among functions, in an all-out attempt to shorten product development time, for instance. No longer does the manager conceive of his or her job as protecting the well-oiled factory mechanism from disruptions caused by the aggressive New York sales team, who in the past were generally seen as "playing lapdog to customers with unreasonable demands." The idea now is to welcome those demands, no matter how "unreasonable" at first blush.

It's essential to connect this idea to prescriptions P-1 and P-2. That is, the new breed of middle (or even first-level) managers, per our model, will have turned

Figure 16: **Nordstrom Organization Chart**

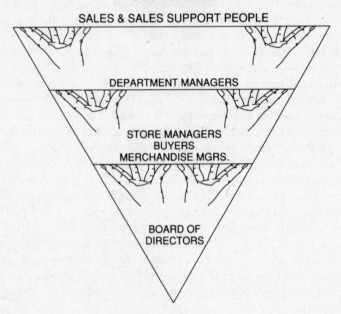

CUSTOMERS

SALES & SALES SUPPORT PEOPLE

DEPARTMENT MANAGERS

STORE MANAGERS
BUYERS
MERCHANDISE MGRS.

BOARD OF
DIRECTORS

over the lion's share of their traditional tasks as experts and referees—their responsibility for maintenance, inspection, scorekeeping, scheduling, hiring, etc.—to the self-managing team structure "below" them. Thus they are less concerned on a minute-to-minute basis with the quality of the widgets flowing past them. Instead they (1) make sure that their work teams are trained and equipped to do their own inspection, (2) then turn their attention to eliminating cross-functional bottlenecks that cause quality and scheduling—and cost—problems, and finally, (3) proactively seek ways for the operating unit as a whole to increase responsiveness. Evidence suggests that 75 percent of middle managers' time must be spent on horizontal rather than vertical (down or up) communication.

The SAS Example

In this role, the middle manager is given a new life—the power and incentive to say "yes," and make things happen, rather than merely the negative power to say "no," and delay/stop things. At SAS, for instance, the middle manager in maintenance at a geographic location is asked to proactively seek out his or her counterpart in baggage-handling to try to create projects that cross functional barriers and make things work better, rather than act as the simple guardian of maintenance's rule book. The manager's duty is to solve problems—

now, on the spot—rather than passing them up to the regional level and writing memos about why things did not happen.

In *Riv Pyramiderna!* Carlzon specifically explains the kind of thinking that is to be eliminated, and what it is to be replaced with:

Consider the following before-and-after scenario of how flattening the pyramids might make an airline staff better able to serve its passengers' needs.

Let's say that you've pre-ordered a special vegetarian meal for your SAS flight from Stockholm to New York. Nervously, you approach the check-in counter to find out whether your meal has been delivered to the plane.

"I don't know," the agent sighs. "I'm sorry, but I'm busy, and I'm not familiar with the food service."

"But what can I do?" you ask.

"You'll have to ask at the gate," she replies. "They'll certainly be able to help you there."

The agent quickly moves on to help the next person in line. Given no alternative, you go to the gate and ask again.

The gate attendant is friendly, but he doesn't know where your meal is either. "I wish I could help, but I don't have anything to do with food service. Just check with the stewardess when you get on board and things should certainly work out."

Reluctantly, you board the plane. When you ask the stewardess about your vegetarian meal, she is bewildered. She hasn't heard anything about special food orders, but the plane is about to take off and nothing can be done now. "You should have contacted us earlier," she reprimands. "There would have been no problem if only we had known in time."

In this situation, the hierarchical organizational structure has caused the airline to ruin three "moments of truth" [Carlzon's term for fleeting contacts with a customer]. No one the passenger encountered had the authority to handle the specific problem, and no one dared step out of his normal role to try to solve it.

Let's now suppose that the organization has changed its structure by flattening the pyramid and putting a team of people in charge of the Stockholm-New York flight from start to finish.

The team has 15 members, two of whom function as "coaches," one indoors and one out by the plane. The indoor coach sits in on the flight crew's briefing and consults with them about pre-flight information such as the appropriate time to begin boarding, whether any infants . . . are on the passenger list, and whether anyone has ordered a special meal.

In the morning, the indoor team assembles at the check-in counters to solve passengers' ticketing problems, assign seats, handle fragile baggage, and so forth. When a mother arrives with her baby, she is . . . told that a suspended cradle has already been put on board and that the seat beside hers will be kept free if at all possible.

When you arrive at check-in and ask about your vegetarian meal, you won't be hurriedly dismissed by the agent behind the counter. Thanks to the new team arrangement, your meal request becomes that agent's responsibility. She can confirm that it is already on board—or take steps to make sure it's loaded by the time you step into the plane.

As more and more passengers check in, the SAS team gradually moves to the departure gate, where they nod to their passengers in recognition. They are well acquainted with the flight to New York and can answer all the usual questions: how to transfer from JFK to La Guardia, why there is a stopover in Oslo, the actual flight time, and whether the captain will announce when they are flying over Greenland.

Problems are solved on the spot, as soon as they arise. No frontline employee has to wait for a supervisor's permission. No passenger boards the plane while still worried or dissatisfied.

In some few, critical areas, the new conception of the middle manager's role may even result in more middle management jobs, not fewer. Robert Hall, for instance, observes in *Attaining Manufacturing Excellence* that "the need for manufacturing engineers to unplug work flow may call for greater staffing in that area." When one starts thinking of managers as expediters, it is no longer so obvious that their numbers should always be minimized.

Task #2: To Be an Expert on Call

In *World Class Manufacturing,* Richard Schonberger identified staff experts on call to support the line—when requested—as a key attribute of the best manufacturing settings. He observed:

Having salaried people (engineers, schedulers, buyers, plant managers—everybody) on call is common in Japan and also seems to be ingrained in Japanese subsidiary plants outside of Japan. The concept was in place at Kawasaki in Nebraska *circa* 1981. . . . Doug Sutton, chief of scheduling, told me, "Boy, is it ever different at Kawasaki than when I worked at [U.S. firm]. I hardly spend any time in my office." Doug was out on the floor solving problems much of the time during the work day. Most were probably not scheduling problems. They were problems of all kinds. In the JIT [just-in-time] concept, job titles mean little and responsibilities blur. One American company, Hewlett-Packard, has a tradition of having salaried support people's desks on the factory floor, intermingled with work stations. That is part of the fabled "HP Way." In my judgment Hewlett-Packard is further along in implementing JIT than any other non-Japanese-owned company except, perhaps, Omark Industries. And why not? HP had a head start, since the problem-solvers were already located in the right place next to where the production problems occur.

There is no question that special expertise is needed, but now the provider plays the role of consultant to teams doing their own problem analysis, rather than holder of the stopwatch. The command to which our new managers must learn to respond is: "Don't call us. We'll call you." It suggests that if they wish to justify their existence, they'd better have something valuable—to the line—to offer.

Task #3: Passing on the Good News

The final new and revolutionary role of middle management is to spend more than half its time on the road, passing on news of the experiments in plant X or distribution center Y to others throughout the system. (Dana Corporation is typical of those who have done this with senior staff.) "Passing on" rather than "shoving down the throat of" is an essential distinction. The newly conceived middle manager/senior staff expert is a clearinghouse and walking/flying newsletter, not an arbiter of taste who *tells* operating people what's good and that "distribution center A and B *shall* implement the idea that was so successful at center C." The distinction is vital.

Getting Started

All the above is easy to say, exceedingly difficult to implement. In effect, we are calling for a reversal of a hundred years of tradition and a 180 degree shift of attitude among people who were originally "hired to make sure that instructions are followed," to use Carlzon's language. Hired and promoted, often several times, I'd add—because, by definition, these managers have been the very best at making sure that instructions are followed to the letter, and that their bosses farther up the functional stovepipe are never held to account for a foul-up. "Blame the other function first, before they blame you," has been the operative rule. Now we are asking these master corporate politicians and memo writers to seek out minute-to-minute opportunities to transcend the rules (that is, break them, at the margin) and make things happen. Wrenching change after wrenching change is required—to begin with, the visit and the phone call replace the "memorandum for the record" as the prime mode of communication. The requirements will include:

▶ Extensive training, (with heavy executive involvement) to underscore the firm's serious commitment to the new conception of the role and to teach practical skills, such as team-building.
▶ Performance evaluation and compensation systems that emphasize teamwork across functions and enhanced action and risk-taking, rather than the creation of tidy audit trails that show that the XYZ function was "within its rights to slow thus and such down."
▶ Physical relocation, to get middle managers out of their departmental centers and into operations centers and distribution centers (see also P-8).

Most important, the managers of staff managers and the firm's top executives must seek out daily opportunities to pat the newly reminted managers on the back for acting as facilitators rather than cops. This, too, will be difficult, because the managers of managers, former cops themselves, have long operated successfully in an environment of safe and orderly inaction, rather than proactive problem-solving, with its inherent (by past standards) untidiness.

FIRST STEPS

1. Begin the process with some subtlety. Focus, without fanfare, on rewarding (pat on the back, mention in the newsletter) facilitation of the most minor sorts between functions. Assiduously seek out examples of multi-plant, multi-function affairs that went smoothly and fast, under ordinarily trying circumstances; find out who provided the lubricant, and praise him or her to the skies—especially if the managers in question took proactive action to prevent a slowdown or to meet an impossible customer demand. Set quantitative goals for yourself—a pat a day for an act of skid-greasing.

    Also, practice the reverse of this: (a) Don't accept any more memos (or even oral reports at staff meetings) that are basically excuses for inaction, or that blame other functions for foul-ups. (b) Spot-check to see how many action items on a typical meeting's agenda are being solved on the spot, versus how many stay unresolved ("I'll have to check 'up the line' on that and get back to you"); raise hell about the latter.

2. Move to include proactive cross-functional facilitation as a *major* element in performance evaluation systems and objective-setting routines for managers at all levels (see also P-10).

3. I hate to be nasty, but ceremoniously fire or demote an upper middle manager who, after training and coaching, still flagrantly puts roadblocks in the way of critical tasks in the name of functional integrity, and then tries to cast the blame on others.

P-10

SUMMARY

Even the use of self-managing teams, training, and the radical shift in structures and management roles are not enough to ensure the level of involvement described in P-1. We must go further:

▶ De-bureaucratize: radically reduce and simplify paperwork and unnecessary procedures.

▶ "De-humiliate": eliminate policies and practices (almost always tiny) of the organization which demean and belittle human dignity.

▶ Become a housekeeping fanatic.

Directly attacking the "Mickey Mouse" of excessive paperwork and demeaning rules is required to take the lid off the organization—and genuinely invite wholesale participation and commitment necessary for survival.

Reduce all manuals by 50 to 75 percent this year (and then do the same thing next year). Stamp out memos! Send none. Respond to none. Send back all memos sent to you with a "received but not read" stamp. Rid yourself immediately of obvious and nauseous insults such as executive parking spaces. Eliminate ten "demeaners" every 60 days. Ask lots of questions such as: Do you really need an office? Do you really need a policy manual? Keep stores (including their back rooms), plants, distribution centers, sales branches, etc., spotless. Keep rest rooms shining and graffiti-free, and don't skimp on dollars for the enhancement of personal space on the line; plan to introduce five new "housekeeping" improvements every 90 days at every facility.

Eliminate Bureaucratic Rules and Humiliating Conditions

I find it mind-boggling. We do not shoot paper at the enemy.
> Admiral Joseph Metcalf
> on the 20 tons of paper and file cabinets
> aboard the Navy's newest frigates
> *Newsweek,* May 1987

Quick response to perpetual turmoil is now a competitive necessity. People's involvement, commitment, and empowerment, in turn, are the keys to speedy organizational action. Training, team configuration, reduced structure, and new roles for middle managers aid speedy action-taking. But if the bureaucratic rigmarole remains, all of the above add up to naught.

Moaning about bureaucracy is a time-honored management prerogative. Now, however, bureaucracy is beyond moaning about; it is a block to survival. The campaigns against bureaucracy must become strategic priorities of the first order.

SIGNS OF HOPE

There are people and firms which have beaten back bureaucracy's seemingly inevitable encroachment:

- ▶ *The New York Times* recently reported that anti-bureaucrat Ken Iverson of Nucor Corporation maintains an "executive dining room": "[He] has designated as the executive dining room the Chinese restaurant and the delicatessen—usually the deli—in the shopping center across the street from Nucor's headquarters in Charlotte, N.C."
- ▶ A division general manager in a large high-technology firm raised spending authority, without approvals, for his engineers—from $25 to $200. The accountants screamed. Following imposition of the new standard, spending

plummeted by 60 percent. He explains: "That wasn't the point, cutting costs. It was to quit treating them like kids. But you know what happened, of course. With the $25 limit, it's 'Let's see how many $24.99s we can tack together, without authorization.' It was a time-consuming game—'We can out-Mickey Mouse you, boss.' Now, with the $200, people say, in effect, 'Hey, that's a lot of money I'm responsible for.' They look at it as theirs."

▶ In *The Intuitive Manager,* journalist Roy Rowan reports: "[Ross] Perot claims he operated a memo-less company. Like Napoleon, who reputedly tossed out all written reports from his generals, figuring he'd already heard the important news, Perot prefers to conduct all of his business by personal contact. 'Written reports stifle creativity,' he says."

▶ *Fortune* reports on James Reid, running an exceptionally profitable auto-components firm, Standard Products: "He drives a compact Oldsmobile. His company, on the verge of the *Fortune 500* (sales in fiscal 1986: $433 million), is still run from a drab two-story brick building in Cleveland's warehouse district. Reid's 15-by-20 office will never adorn the pages of *Architectural Digest.* But, he says, 'I can do as much thinking here as in an office 50 times this size.'"

▶ $1.9 billion retailer Nordstrom gets by with a one-sentence policy manual: "Use your own best judgment at all times."

Bureaucracy—excessive rules, regulations, and paperwork—is not a must. Ross Perot ran a company worth several billion dollars without writing memos. By raising spending limits and thus cutting down on game playing, an executive cuts spending—and improves morale and speeds action-taking. A billion-dollar company finds that a corner deli makes a great executive dining room, and so on.

Everyone talks about cutting the red tape. A few do it. Why not the rest of us? How do you reduce the policy manual to just a single sentence? Or raise engineers' spending limits, in one step, by almost a factor of ten? Or stop sending *any* memos?

I cannot provide you with the will to do these things. I can simply tell you (1) that they can be done, (2) that they must be done if we are to (a) move faster and (b) liberate people—managers and nonmanagers alike—to perform up to their potential, and (3) that they have been done, with gusto, by others like you.

LIBERATION THROUGH THE ELIMINATION OF EXCESSIVE PROCEDURES

Start with the voluminous rules. Nordstrom V.P. Betsy Sanders acknowledges that the one-line "policy manual" drives Nordstrom's lawyers crazy. So be it, she adds.

The point is that it frees Nordstrom employees from an astonishing amount of Mickey Mouse. Sad to say, rule books are only referred to in order to slow action, defend turf, and assign blame. Have you ever heard of anyone going to a rule book to figure out how to speed things up?

University of Chicago philosopher Ted Cohen has commented that since sports are so rule-driven, most innovation revolves around how to be ingenious at cheating without getting caught: "How *much* of a head slap is legal for a defensive end trying to slow down a tight end?" How far can Reggie Jackson "stick his fanny in front of a ball [to deliberately get hit and be awarded first base] in the World Series?" Moreover, says Cohen, it's precisely because there are so many rules and rule enforcers (umpires and referees in sports, supervisors in business) that "the player feels he may abandon the responsibility for decent conduct because someone is around."

Less Is More (Again)

At Nordstrom, the absence of manuals is anything but an invitation to chaos. Nordstrom supervisors are always coaching and teaching. Indeed, says Sanders, their chief duty is to coach salespersons on *"exactly* what it means to 'use your own best judgment.' " The absence of childish rules shifts the employee's focus of innovation to precisely where the firm wishes it to be: in pursuit of serving the customer better, rather than in pursuit of evasion of the rules about toilet breaks. In fact, self-control is such a powerful control that entry-level turnover is high.

At a Mars, Inc., subsidiary, fewer rules means less fuss—and more emphasis on the business task at hand. A principal labor contract was up for renewal. A rookie management negotiator set an objective about which most of his peers were highly skeptical—to replace the inch-thick document with one of five pages or less. He was successful, and as a result of his efforts, among other things a grievance record that had been about average was cut to a trickle. There are simply no little nitpicking details—"subparagraph 7.13.b.2.ii"—left for either side to get hot and bothered about on a day-to-day basis. Dayton Power & Light followed a similar path. The firm opened negotiations early, and worked for six months with the union to define the nature of the changing, ever more competitive business environment for utilities. The upshot, another twelve months later, was a reduction in the length of the contract from 200 pages to 14, the first being their statement of shared philosophy. In short order a profound change in attitude has ensued, with people working together to confront problems. NUMMI and the UAW also forged a streamlined contract, starting with a statement of philosophy; similar positive results have followed (see the section summary preceding P-1, and P-2).

Or consider Worthington. No union has ever organized one of its field start-up operations, but it has acquired several unionized companies. Though top management strongly discourages applying pressure to decertify, five operations have done so. Worthington senior managers observe that front-line employees have little problem living without the protection of a union contract. But first-line supervisors have had the devil of a time adjusting. One executive notes: "You just took away their reason for being. They were there, as they saw it, to administer the contract on management's behalf. They were there to catch guys goofing off. Now, suddenly, no rule book, no time clocks, no scheduled breaks [you take a break when you conveniently can], no locks on the tool-room door, no forms to be signed to check out a tool or a spare part. What's left for them to do? Very little, by the old standards. Some don't make the transition."

A Practical Agenda

Here's an approach to getting on with the task of reducing bureaucracy:

1. As a manager, "model" nonbureaucratic behavior. (Also see L-3, L-8.) Demand that any report sent to you be reduced to, say, three pages or less. Starting today, do not send memos to anyone for any reason. Use the phone or personal contact. Also, prune the number of reports you receive by 50 to 80 percent in the next six to twelve months. Further, send back without comment—and repeatedly if necessary—all "information copies" of memos. (I studied this at one point. The conventional humorous wisdom turned out to be hard truth. Well over 90 percent of several hundred memos I analyzed were of the "cover your ass" variety—designed only to clear the writer of any hint of blame should anything subsequently go awry.) Finally, send back, without comment and repeatedly, any decision documents that should not be addressed to your level. One senior political appointee within the Department of Defense, in the Installation and Logistics secretariat, arrived on the job to find that tiny architectural changes were sent all the way to Washington for his approval. He put no comment on them whatsoever, but just started sending them back. People eventually caught on, and the flow stopped.

And if you're a lower-level manager? All of this can at least be done "downward"—that is, eliminate the rules you can control and refuse to be nitpicky about enforcing the ones you can't control. But a surprising amount of bureaucracy fighting can be done "upward." When you get a memo from your boss, pop into his or her office with an answer—don't call your staff to general quarters and retire to your office for three days to write a treatise in response.

2. Announce and implement your own "stamp out the silly [and action slowing] regulations" operation. One manager, for instance, designed an engaging ritual to involve all his group in eliminating irritating rules and regulations: "I bought a bright red mailbox and placed it in the division hallway. I commissioned a cartoon around the theme 'Send back to Mickey Mouse.' " He acts within a week on the suggestions about what regulations should be cut, and awards a porcelain Mickey Mouse statue each month to the person who identifies the biggest nuisance. A U.S. Army brigadier general who attended one of our seminars picked up on this idea and is implementing it vigorously and with great effect—and fun—in a large command.

3. Cut every procedure manual within your bailiwick in half over the next twelve months. Then do the same thing again in the following year. Sure, you're not chairman, chief executive officer, mayor, or general. But at least get your own house in order and stop being the principal cause of spreading havoc and wasting your people's time.

4. Urge the lawyers or contracts department—none too gently—to experiment with handshake agreements or contracts of no more than two pages. It can be done.

Roots of a Bureaucracy-Free Environment

I would be greatly remiss if I failed to note a caveat here. This business of eliminating rules and regulations is a big deal—a matter of replacing detailed, written "what if" strictures with trust (see S-4, S-5 also). Take the last suggestion. The way to eliminate lengthy supplier contracts is to join in long-term partnerships with a much smaller than normal number of quality suppliers. The same thing applies to all the others. You won't reduce the paperwork in a lasting fashion until you remove the underlying cause for it—mistrust and adversarial relations. This is why 9.9 out of 10 "paperwork reduction" committees fail to achieve any lasting change.

STOP TREATING PEOPLE WITH CONTEMPT

Knocking off humiliating practices is the second part of this prescription. A blast from Ross Perot, while at GM, captures the spirit: "In Pontiac [Michigan], GM executive parking garages are heated, while the poor guys who work in the plant freeze their tails off walking to work in the snow. It costs $140,000 a year to heat one parking garage. I'd shut that thing down. It has nothing to do with cars."

U.S. Steel ignominiously became USX in 1986; it has reduced its USW worker population from 94,000 in 1974 to less than 30,000 today. Yet *Business Week* reported acidly in 1985: "On the 61st floor [of the firm's headquarters] in Pittsburgh, uniformed stewards deliver coffee on silver trays to executive suites."

During a visit I made to Columbus in 1986, a Worthington employee and I struck up a conversation about the American steel industry. It was right after LTV had declared bankruptcy. The guy just couldn't fathom how the chairman of that company had the nerve to bring home a $700,000 salary, and pay himself a whopping bonus to boot, for driving a firm over the edge. Neither could I. In fact, the final break between Ross Perot and GM came when that firm's problematic performance in 1986 led it to decline to pay a profit-sharing bonuses of $1,000 to hourly workers—while giving executives all they were "entitled" to by traditional practice. "You can't look the troops in the eye and say, 'It's been a bad year; we can't do anything for you,' but then say, 'By the way, we're going to pay ourselves a $1 million bonus,'" Perot said.

I suspect that Perot would have been equally peeved at Lee Iacocca. Upon being questioned by the press as to how he reconciled his $20.6 million total compensation in 1986 with Chrysler's cuts in merit pay for other employees, he replied, "That's the American way. If little kids don't aspire to make money like I did, what the hell good is this country?"*

This is difficult material to talk about. How does one remain calm? Each of these examples is mind-numbing. So humiliating to the very work force whose renewed energy, talent, and flexible response to change we need for survival. So easy to avoid—in theory. So revealing of dysfunctional, age-old assumptions—in practice.

We insult employees with executive parking spots, heated, no less; with executive dining rooms; with bonuses and "strategy meetings" in lavish settings for the top 100 officers and their spouses even after lousy years. Roger Smith announces eleven plant closings and 27,000 more potential layoffs—then retreats behind double-locked—or triple-locked (depending on whose story you believe)—glass doors to contemplate the wasteland he's created (his $1.4 million in compensation in 1986 doubtless eased the pain a bit).

Stop! I want to scream. It's dumb. I don't say this for humanitarian reasons, much as I believe in such reasons. My point is pragmatic: How do you humiliate and demean someone and then expect him or her to care about product quality and constant improvement?

Nucor's Ken Iverson found multicolored hard hats when he arrived at the company: white for workers, blue for foremen, green for department heads. He replaced them with one color—green—for everyone.

At NUMMI the separate entrances for managers and workers were eliminated, as was the executive lunchroom. The brother of the president of Toyota was the first NUMMI chief; many remarked that they were stunned to see him eating regularly with line workers in the common cafeteria. Perhaps the importance of eliminating humiliating practices is underscored by the very fact that so many, from both inside and outside the industry, noted his presence in the cafeteria; it stood out among the many positive things NUMMI had done.

Other humiliations are more subtle. Psychological assessment tests (see prescription P-4) and, certainly, urinalysis are demeaning. A Boise Cascade worker was recently suspended for smashing a camera hidden in the ceiling of a locker room to detect theft from lockers; employees hadn't been consulted on its installation. Can you imagine what would have happened if the firm's security chief had secretly installed a hidden camera in the executive washroom?

The Mickey Mouse rules that smell of contempt and distrust are part of the negative signals we send. By a great deal of our entry-testing, we make it clear that we assume the candidate is a misfit or a thief or drug addict or all three. Then we confirm it daily after he or she comes aboard. For instance, do you want

---

*It might be the American way—and important to our entrepreneurial vitality. But as we consider the more important role of the work force in the future, we should at least acknowledge that it's not the only capitalist way. The compensation ratio between labor and top management runs 1 to 80 in the United States, versus 1 to 25 in West Germany and 1 to 7 in Japan.

a dollar's worth of stamps in a hurry to get a customer letter out in a timely fashion? It is presumed you are a cheat, and want them for personal use, so you have to fill out a fifteen-line form to get them. Need a spare part to fix a broken machine? Fill out a two-page form, get two supervisors to sign it (if the part costs more than $2.95), and then pass through the double-locked door to the supply room. And then we turn around and have the nerve to ask people to "do it right the first time," to take an interest in the machine. How absurd!

It goes from top to bottom. The "hourly" can't check out a screwdriver. The engineer is trusted with only $25 (though you're "betting the company" on his or her design skills). And the division general manager, overseeing 700 people and $25 million in assets, has a signature authority of $1,000. The message sent could not be more clear if it were printed on a banner dragged behind a plane flying over the Super Bowl.

Start Now—Do SOMETHING Fast

There are two answers to the above. One is removing the "humiliators." Start with the physical stuff, such as executive parking spots, executive dining rooms, separate entrances for managers and nonmanagers, the use of limos—right now. Next, scour every procedure book, looking—with the help of those being demeaned—for the small and large put-downs and irritants. Consider a team effort such as the Gnat Patrol from a BFG operation in Oklahoma that seeks out and swats petty annoyances. I propose that you go so far as to set quantitative goals: For instance, remove ten procedural "demeaners" every 60 days.

BECOME A HOUSEKEEPING FANATIC

Despite the best efforts of a professional photographer, the photo appearing in *Fortune* in mid-1986 of a Japanese-owned and -managed auto-component factory in the Midwest was somewhat washed out. Washing out occurs when there is too much reflected light. In this case, the reflected light came from the mirror-like, highly polished floors and the metal fittings. There go the Japanese, cheating again. This time it's unreasonably clean plants—on U.S. soil.

I shouldn't have to say this. There should be no more obvious point. If the workplace looks shabby, if the toilets are foul, with graffiti on the walls, how can you *dare* preach about commitment, participation, quality, and service? Worthington Industries founder John McConnell was considering buying a company a while ago. One of his acid, pre-acquisition tests is a tour of the facilities. In the employee cafeteria, he found netting temporarily rigged beneath the ceiling—to catch the crumbling plaster and keep it out of the food. It led him to question the whole deal. If management was that insensitive to its work force, could the company be salvageable?

In the spring of 1985, British coal miners went back to work after a year-long strike. *Newsweek* reported: "The miners filed into the pit baths to change for work. They found the floor sprinkled with paint chips from the peeling walls. There was no hot water, and the pipes, after a year's neglect, needed repair. 'To see this is an insult,' said . . . an official of the local. 'It's degrading.' " The strike had been rancorous, the worst of this century. When it ended, the objective for both sides should have been to get on with the job at hand, to seek both the efficiencies and the increased cooperation necessary if the coal industry is to survive. One way not to up the odds of the industry's survival is to insult the miners. Yet by allowing the miners to return to filthy conditions, British coal management, intentionally or not, did exactly that.

I wonder about these things a lot. How can you possibly preach service to your fast-food franchise employees and then not have an unlimited supply of clean uniforms ready, so that they can change whenever they spill something? It's so obvious: It is psychologically impossible to deliver good service in a dirty uniform. Don't you suppose, on a gray day, that the cleanliness of the Fed Ex truck peps the driver up? You bet it does.

And what's so very obvious for service employees, or any employees in contact with customers, goes double in the factory. How can you ask a quality circle to deliberate seriously in a cramped, noisy corner of a filthy cafeteria? How can you allow grime to collect on the floor of the auto dealership's service bay and then send directives to mechanics on the importance of customer service? How can you possibly chide a distribution center team for a high error rate on deliveries and ignore the fact that the toilets are foul, that the employees' locker room hasn't been painted for ages, that the saltshakers on the canteen tables don't work, that one vending machine (out of only three to serve 125 people) is chronically out of order, that the controller reduced the number of pay phones in the break area from four to two?

There is so much you can do. Perhaps fresh flowers on cafeteria tables. Will tough factory hands respond? Answer, without exception in my experience: yes. Don't expect thank-you notes. But do expect such small touches to pay off many times over. Spend money on this kind of improvement. Most of it doesn't cost much—flowers and paint, for example. Some amenities do cost more: brighter lights in the parking lots or better landscaping. But if you're smart, this part of the facilities budget will be the last to feel the cost cutter's ax. Delay purchasing a new piece of machinery if you must—but don't delay refurbishing the chairs and tables in the cafeteria—and start eating there yourself, regularly.

Heroes with Paint Buckets and Washrags

▶ Ron Kowal, director of manufacturing and purchasing at Tennant, talks about a very special painter:

Frank Smith is a good example of an employee who takes quality seriously. Frank is one of the people responsible for making sure the

Tennant Company factory has the reputation of being one of the cleanest in the country. A painter in the maintenance department, he has been painting interior and exterior walls and ceilings at Tennant Company for years. Frank has applied hundreds of gallons of white paint each year at the request of department managers, who remembered once in a while to thank him for the good job. Nevertheless, Frank knew he was doing an important job. And there is no doubt in our minds that a clean plant is one of the highest priority objectives in any quality process. When people take pride in work areas, they will also take pride in their work.

About six years ago, as part of the quality emphasis, Frank decided to put a little extra into his job. He began creating wall murals—pictures of fish, grouse, or deer, paintings of Tennant company products, slogans about quality, or whatever the people who work in the area requested. Every year, requests for his work increase, along with the positive comments on what a great job he is doing. Frank proves that quality can be achieved in more ways than assembling products. He achieves quality with a brush, a ladder, a bucket of paint, and a fertile imagination.

▶ The authors of *The 100 Best Companies to Work for in America* report on the billion-dollar maker of office furniture:

> The emphasis on quality and pride in workmanship extends to Steel-case's truck fleet, which comprises 97 tractors and 213 trailers. It's one of the largest truck fleets in the country—and it boasts the best safety record of any private fleet. Steelcase has such a rigorous maintenance program that some of its trucks last one million miles. Its vehicles are kept in spotless condition. New drivers are required to spend their first six months on the job doing nothing but washing trucks. Drivers have their names on door panels. In 1984, a new driver, 30-year-old Paul Rosendahl, was so impressed with the pride and the spit and polish that he recorded a song, "Blue and Chrome," to salute the Steelcase trucks.

PUBLIC PARALLELS

Reducing bureaucracy: Maryland governor Don Schaefer provides eloquent testimony: "It is strange to see sometimes how our elected officials change. When they run for the first time for a major office . . . for example, mayor of a large city—they are in shirtsleeves. They have some crudely made banners (prepared, of course, by your average citizen). They virtually demand of the people they meet while campaigning that they be called by their first name or nickname. They shout to the rooftops that if you have a problem—call me.

"Yet, what happens after they are elected? Dare you still call them Bob or Bill or Don? How do they respond to your problem (if you can ever get to them)? Do they simply just waltz past you now as you wait in a line at a restaurant? And do they wave to you through the tinted-glass back window of their chauffeur-driven limousine as they splash backed-up gutter water all over your clothes?"

The new Model Installation Program of the Department of Defense, brainchild of Deputy Assistant Secretary of Defense Bob Stone, is another effort making a difference. Its bulletin, the "Graduate Journal," subtitled "Turning Writers into Fighters," chronicles success at reducing bureaucracy. Here are some snippets from a recent issue collected by a staff dedicated to making visits to the MIP sites and spreading the good news (see P-9, Task #3):

▶ The 200-page construction manual will be replaced by a four-page guide that removes detailed restrictions, emphasizes quality, and gives installation commanders more influence over what gets built.
▶ Eighteen housing regulations will be replaced by one that gives lots more authority to commanders.
▶ Commanders will be able to buy locally when it's smart to do so; when [the Government Services Agency] has the best deal, we're making it easier for commanders to buy from them.
▶ DOD can now buy the cheapest airline ticket available rather than pay a more expensive government rate.

The task is daunting, but the philosophy is now taking hold. Thousands of accumulating success stories, spurred by the development of a word-of-mouth network, are increasing efficiency and responsiveness, and returning control to the field.

De-humiliating: Go back and reread this prescription. About nine-tenths of the suggestions concern things that are inexpensive or free, so there is no financial bar to implementation. And if you instill the attitude this prescription aims at, employees, public or private, will often chip in themselves. In several crippled firms, following a new boss's obvious determination to put workers first, I've seen the most incredible outpouring of plants from home, and after-hours repair projects sprout up overnight.

FIRST STEPS

I don't care if you've waited twenty-seven years for it, get rid of the damned reserved parking spot right this bloody minute. (*Then* you can consider asking "them" to "do it right the first time.")

Actually, dozens of inexpensive (in terms of money or time) First Step suggestions are contained in this prescription. What's holding you up?

V

LEARNING TO LOVE CHANGE: A NEW VIEW OF *L*EADERSHIP AT ALL LEVELS

SECTION SUMMARY

The dictionary defines "axiom" as "a statement universally accepted as true." Management, as it has been professionalized and systematized, has developed many axioms over the past century. But in the past twenty years, the stable conditions (large-scale mass production) that led to the slow emergence of these universals have blown apart. So now the chief job of the leader, at all levels, is to oversee the dismantling of dysfunctional old truths and to prepare people and organizations to deal with—to love, to develop affection for—change per se, as innovations are proposed, tested, rejected, modified and adopted.

This set of prescriptions (see Figure 17) begins with the Guiding Premise, L-1, that leaders must above all confront—and master—a series of paradoxes—that is, willingly embrace (test, learn about) across-the-board challenges to conventional wisdom.

Mastering the paradoxes and what they stand for (L-1) requires the Three Leadership Tools for Establishing Direction: L-2, developing and preaching a vision which clearly sets your direction, yet at the same time encourages initiatives from everyone to perfect and elaborate the challenge that vision lays out; L-3, channeling interest by living the vision via your calendar (what you do—and do not—spend time on), which is the single most effective tool for establishing faith in the vision amidst otherwise debilitating uncertainty; and L-4, practicing visible management, for the purpose of preaching the message and enhancing the leader's understanding of the context where it counts—on the front line, where true implementation takes place.

The principal challenge is to empower people (everyone) to take new initiatives—that is, risks (as they see it)—on a day-to-day basis, aimed at improving and eventually transforming every routine in the firm. Of course, prescriptions P-1 through P-10 addressed this. But there are four enabling leadership prescriptions (Leading by Empowering People) as well: L-5, on becoming a compulsive listener, since listening (especially to those at the front) remains the truest signal that "I take you seriously"; L-6, on cherishing the people at the front—demonstrated in a host of ways, from pay scales to invitations to staff meetings; L-7, on delegating "authority" in a way that truly empowers; and L-8, vigorous and visible pursuit of bureaucracy bashing.

The last two leadership prescriptions urge you to get directly on with the new "it": L-9 proposes that everyone be evaluated on the simple but revolutionary question: "What have you changed lately?" L-10 suggests that leaders must epitomize change in every action in order to create an overwhelming sense of urgency throughout the organization.

As in the prior sections, the leadership prescriptions, though separable, should be considered as a whole. While you can't do "everything at once," no one prescription makes much sense in a vacuum.

Figure 17: **Learning to Love Change: A New View of Leadership at All Levels**

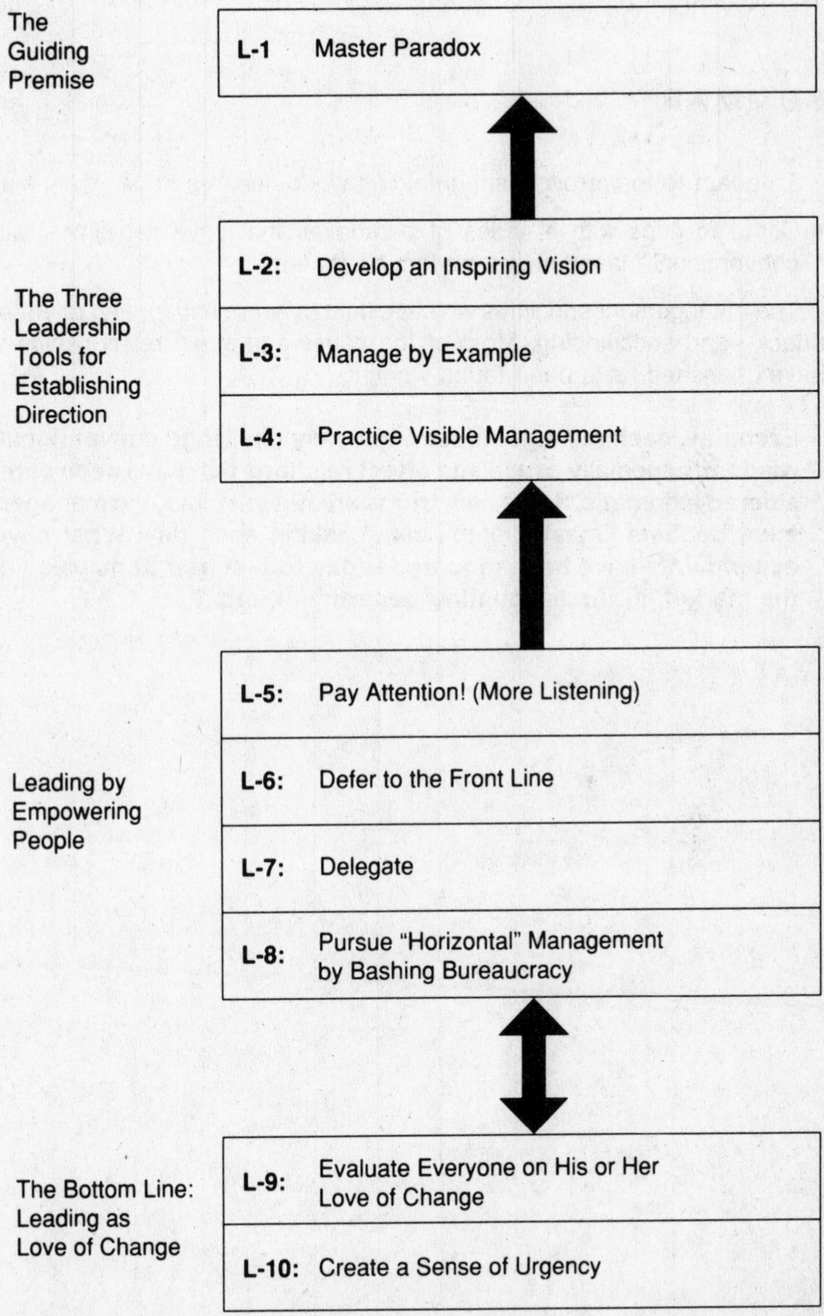

The Guiding Premise	**L-1**	Master Paradox

↑

The Three Leadership Tools for Establishing Direction	**L-2:**	Develop an Inspiring Vision
	L-3:	Manage by Example
	L-4:	Practice Visible Management

↑

Leading by Empowering People	**L-5:**	Pay Attention! (More Listening)
	L-6:	Defer to the Front Line
	L-7:	Delegate
	L-8:	Pursue "Horizontal" Management by Bashing Bureaucracy

↕

The Bottom Line: Leading as Love of Change	**L-9:**	Evaluate Everyone on His or Her Love of Change
	L-10:	Create a Sense of Urgency

L-1

SUMMARY

To adapt to tomorrow's fast-unfolding world, leaders at all levels must:

► Come to grips with a series of paradoxes that have set almost all conventional management wisdom on its ear.

The management principles we have held dear are undergoing relentless attack—and succumbing. Most of the cause-and-effect relationships we have cherished have been found wanting.

Each day, each manager must practically challenge conventional wisdom, especially cause and effect relations that have been considered axiomatic. Since new truths are not yet clear, the manager must become "master empiricist," asking each day: What new experiments have been mounted today to test new principles (in the market, in the accounting department, etc.)?

Master Paradox

Perhaps we would be well advised at this juncture, since formal knowledge can no longer help us to understand a world in which the pace of change and development is so great, to think of the jester's role in relation to the king. Since the jester did not speak on behalf of any respectable body, he was able with impunity to draw attention to abuses which the king should suppress, to raise uncertain matters in an admonishing tone, to be receptive to things which the established authorities were either unwilling or unable to see. The contrast is thus between the perception of the jester and the knowledge of the authorities. Is there a similar contrast between perception and scientific thought? . . . Science makes progress by distinguishing between what it regards as meaningful and what it considers to be merely static, i.e., a disruptive factor which can be ignored. Perceptiveness on the other hand deals with problems which as yet have no significance but which acquire significance in the future.

Isabelle Stengers*
"Order Through Chaos"
May 1987

Paradox: A statement that seems contradictory, unbelievable or absurd but that may actually be true in fact.

Webster's New World Dictionary

Today's successful business leaders will be those who are most flexible of mind. An ability to embrace new ideas, routinely challenge old ones, and live with paradox will be the effective leader's premier trait. Further, the challenge is for a lifetime. New truths will not emerge easily. Leaders will have to guide the ship while simultaneously putting everything up for grabs (see L-2), which is itself a fundamental paradox.

Here are eighteen paradoxes, large and small, which are indicative of the chaotic business environment now unfolding:

*Isabelle Stengers is co-author, along with Nobel Laureate (Chemistry) Ilya Prigogine, of *Order Out of Chaos*. The quotation here is from an essay in the 1987 Annual Report of Buro voor Systeemontwikkeling bv, the Netherlands' largest systems software house.

1. More stability of purpose/employment is necessary to deal with less stability in the environment. More flexibility and responsiveness are the survivors' watchwords. However, more flexibility will only be engendered when there is a clearer vision (see L-2), more trust, and fewer adversarial dealings. That is, you can't ask a fearful person to break all the conventional rules and regularly take what feel like (and are, by past standards) risky initiatives.

2. More competition requires more cooperation. More competitors and competitors' products require more flexibility/responsiveness and higher quality, for instance. This in turn means supporting partnerships between: (a) companies and their (often sole source) suppliers, (b) companies and other companies that can bring in critical new skills needed in a market area (especially overseas), (c) the performers of various functions, to speed action-taking where it counts, at the front line, (d) management and the work force (and the union, if applicable), and (e) the company and its distributors/franchisees/reps. If we are to compete effectively, we must learn to cooperate with all these sets of partners.

3. More productivity will come through more people—not fewer. Winners will learn to add value through the work force (its attention to quality, service, and responsiveness). Losers will continue to willy-nilly replace people with machines, in the vain hope of competing with Brazil or Indonesia on cost. More sales and service people and expediters in the factory will be needed to add more value—i.e., to enhance revenue. Better-trained people in the factory will provide massive productivity improvements over time. While I acknowledge corporate bloat (see P-8, for instance), sensible job creation in pursuit of revenue enhancement must nonetheless replace today's most frequent management boast: the number of people cut in the last eighteen months.

4. Success will stem from more love of the product—and less attachment to it. To get everyone enthusiastic about constantly improving the product requires commitment to it as well as to them (see C-2). On the other hand, products will be made obsolete more frequently by competitors' offerings or by our own, competing efforts (see I-1). Thus, a commitment to ceaseless improvement of the product must reside side by side with a willingness to scrap it when we develop a replacement (or someone else does).

5. We must be wary of the economics of scale—but create more complex alliances. Efficiencies of scale in the traditional sense are going—or already gone—for a host of reasons (see Part I). On the other hand, more joint ventures and partnership arrangements are required to thrive, especially overseas.

6. More de-integration goes hand-in-hand with more re-integration (on new dimensions). Vertical integration is fast being reduced; subcontracting of anything and everything is becoming routine. Yet closer linkages, via electronic/ telecommunication channels, for instance (see C-4), are a must. Thus while one (traditional) form of "big scale" (vertical integration) is being undone, another form (electronic linkages and new partnerships) is emerging.

7. "Big yields low cost" can and must rapidly give way to "small yields low cost." New, miniaturized technology and the adoption of techniques such as cellular manufacturing and just-in-time inventory management are leading to lower costs from smaller units that feature short production runs and great flexibility. Smaller units also may have much less overhead, and they are more likely to subcontract services such as accounting—yielding still more cost reduction.

8. More productivity ensues from having fewer suppliers. Conventional wisdom pits suppliers against one another to obtain low-bid contracts. Success now will stem from high quality (lifetime cost of product, not initial contract cost—see C-2) and supplier responsiveness to constantly shifting customer/market demands; this, in turn, will come only from partnership relations, based on trust, with a few suppliers.

9. The more a market seems "commodity-like," the more adding small increments of value pays off. Adding numerous small increments in service, quality, and responsiveness actually makes a bigger difference—is more valuable—in mature markets than in growth markets. Surprisingly, the low-price strategy is the weapon of last resort in all markets; adding value is the first choice—regardless of market circumstance.

10. More products (with shorter production runs) does not mean lower quality. The necessary reorganization of the plant into manufacturing cells, for instance, and much greater involvement of the work force—plus appropriate automation to support (not supplant) people—allow more complex production scheduling (short runs, fast responses) to coincide with higher quality. There need not be (and cannot be, given the competitive situation) any tradeoff between quality and flexibility.

11. High quality yields lower costs. Quality and cost, within a wide performance range, are not part of a "tradeoff" equation. Increasing quality, which generally results from simplification of design and manufacture, radically reduces costs.

12. Higher quality comes with fewer inspectors. Once again, people are the key. Virtually all inspection should be self-inspection—and this can be accomplished if the work force is involved, committed, trained, supported with appropriate tools, relieved of bureaucratic Mickey Mouse, and paid for performance.

13. Accelerating the success rate comes only from accelerating the failure rate. Revolutionary improvement in quality, service, and responsiveness will only occur when all are participating in the day-to-day enhancement of the product/service; that is, when all are taking risks to try new methods. Numerous failures always (according to the laws of science) precede any success. Therefore, speeding up the success rate requires speeding up the failure rate.

14. Tighter control can be achieved through more decentralization. The new, decentralized organization features (1) well trained and highly involved people (everyone) and (2) units "transparent to" (permeated by) the customer. Truly decentralized, externally (customer-) obsessed units, with a clear vision and high involvement, are more under control in today's volatile environment than traditional, centrally controlled units—which are inflexible and more out of touch by definition. The latter focus on slow, power-driven, "vertical" decision-making; the former emphasize market-driven decision-making and fast adaptation.

15. Tighter adherence to policy is accomplished when less time is spent in the office. Proactive adaptation to a volatile environment comes when people are both inspired by a useful vision and empowered to act. These two traits follow from visible management—not hierarchical, committee-driven, out-of-touch management. The old form of organization via rulebook and policy manual is not able to keep up today. Teaching flexibility (and modeling it) is an out-of-the-office task (see L-3, L-4); flexibility in turn engenders control— empowered people pursuing (and elaborating) a clearly transmitted vision.

16. Strategic planning exercises led by staffs are being supplanted by strategic capability building led by the line. The long-range strategic plan, of voluminous length, is less useful than before. But a strategic "mind-set," which focuses on skill/capability-building (e.g., adding value to the work force via training to prepare it to respond more flexibly and be more quality-conscious), is more important than ever.

17. More appropriate measurement is achieved with fewer measures. Anything can be measured. The winners' measures will emphasize the vital performance parameters—e.g., quality, service, flexibility, responsiveness, and employee skills/capabilities (see S-1). True control stems from a very few, simple measures of high integrity, understood by all (also covered in S-1). More flip charts measuring the important variables and fewer 800-page printouts dealing with arcane cost information are the success prescription.

18. Success will come to those who love chaos—constant change—not those who attempt to eliminate it. The fleet-of-foot, value-adding, niche-market creator (see C-1) thrives on the very uncertainty that drives others to distraction. Stability and predictability are gone for good—and therefore must not be the implicit or explicit goals of organizational design, the layout of factory or operations center, pay schemes, strategic planning, objective-setting exercises, accounting systems, or job evaluations. Victory will go to those who master instability by constantly working on responsiveness-enhancing capabilities.

THE LEADER AS EMPIRICIST

These eighteen paradoxes are but a small sample—yet they violate all the core organizing assumptions of the last hundred or more years. Consequently, the leader at any level will not convince his or her boss (traditional middle manager or outsider members of the board) of these still heretical ideas through argument. His or her role must therefore become that of "empiricist in chief" (see also I-3, on "piloting"). That is, the firm must become a hotbed of tests of the unconventional. It must become an experimenting (and learning), adaptive, change-seeking organization. It must ceaselessly send its people, at all levels and in all functions, out to visit other interesting firms, universities, customers, suppliers, distributors, competitors (see C-7, I-4). The unit manager willingly lends people to project teams full-time and other functions for lengthy assignments, so that they can learn more faster, and be part of useful tests aimed at dealing proactively with change. The organization learns from the best, swipes from the best, adapts, tests, risks, fails, and adjusts—over and over.

Recall that Chaparral Steel president Gordon Forward calls his mill a laboratory. That is the right image. Every person becomes an empiricist and every department becomes a laboratory. The experiments deal with procedures and rules and forms of supervision and communication patterns, as well as with new products and services.

Nothing can be "institutionalized." All products not being rapidly improved are, ipso facto, falling rapidly behind. This morning's new widget is being made obsolete by two early-afternoon start-ups. A fast failure—followed by a fast adjustment—becomes the organization's most cherished event, demanded from everyone, daily.

THE CORE PARADOX

The core paradox, then, that all leaders at all levels must contend with is fostering (creating) internal stability in order to encourage the pursuit of constant change. The vision must be clear enough (consistent, etc.—see L-2) to encourage continual risk-taking and failing, or else the continual testing and stretching and enhancing—changing—of everything will not occur, or not occur fast enough.

This dichotomous task has not been imposed upon leaders before. They must preach the vision with verve—over and over. And at the same time, they must insist upon and then revel in the constant tests that re-form (expand, contract, destroy) the very same vision. The ship will seem somewhat out of control by the old standards. That is, the madness of thousands of simultaneous experiments—including some by the newly hired reservations clerk—is the only plausible path to survival. What once amounted to being "in control" (i.e., being guided by a plodding hierarchy of bureaucrats, conservators of the past) is a design for disaster today. "In control" by the old standards is "out of control" (fast slipping behind) by the new standards.

TIPS FOR THE PARADOX-LOVING MANAGER

Here are a few tips to deal with the task of simultaneously nurturing stability and instability:

1. Be out and about (see L-4). Only by being "at the front" will you be able to "feel" the pace and progress—and the problems—where it counts, on the line.

2. Demand empiricism. Demand hard tests and fast tests and partial tests of everything, by everyone (see I-3).

3. Listen and provide listening forums. Everyone must be listening, sharing, recognizing small successes, laughing at small failures (see P-3, for instance), and urging even faster tries.

4. Learn to love and laud failures. As previously mentioned, one seminar participant proposed that *How to Learn to Love Failure* be this book's subtitle. It's a good idea: "test fast, fail fast, adjust fast" must become the organization's battlecry (see I-8).

5. Proclaim the virtues of speedy "horizontal" action-taking. Be vociferous in support of tests and fast failures that have resulted from eschewing excessive "vertical" decision-making and instead foster fast "horizontal" action-taking, i.e., involving multiple functions at the front line (see P-9, L-8).

6. Define and chat up the common denominators. I suspect that superb quality, flexibility, and everyone's wholesale participation will top most firms' menus. Define these constants through "preaching"—and especially through example (see L-3). Tie this idea to #2 above (empiricism); that is, preach principally by using examples of nifty, somewhat risky experiments that seem to be forwarding the new cause—especially experiments conducted on the front line, by front-line people and multi-function teams.

7. Let customers—and soaring goals—do the "teaching." The most effective control in the midst of madness is control which is externally inspired. Constant customer listening, coupled with a vision that proclaims the goal of being the very best in the customer's terms will act as an almost moral context for (and control over) the firm's ongoing revolution—that is, the firm that is engaged in continual experiments with everything, by everyone. If customers populate every cranny of the organization, literally (and symbolically), the sense of urgency and the basis for self-control will increase immeasurably, and fast—and never slip (see C-10 also).

8. Make it fun. Only fun—in the sense of taking pleasure in accomplishment and interesting foul-up alike—will allow you to thrive amidst the ravages of change in a world turned upside down. It's the basis for yet one more paradox: The economic stakes have never been higher; therefore, it's never been more important not to take yourself too seriously. "We are in the midst of a great and crazy adventure, creating our brave new rulebook by error and trial as we go along"—that must be the tone (see L-10).

9. Promote those who deal best with paradox. Perhaps this goes without saying: If the ability to deal with these paradoxes is the key to success, then we should promote, at all levels, those who show the greatest facility in doing so. A new breed of managers is required. Full-speed execution will not occur until the new breed is in place. It is imperative to dig into the ranks, or do whatever else is necessary, to get them in place as rapidly as possible.

FIRST STEPS

Openly address and discuss, in every forum, the practical implications of the paradoxes described above. Make sure that you find at least one excuse per day to raise issues surrounding at least one of these paradoxes. And then mount a quick test. And then talk about that test, whether successful or not.

L-2

SUMMARY

In a time of turbulence and uncertainty, we must be able to take instant action on the front line. But to support such action-taking at the front, everyone must have a clear understanding about what the organization is trying to achieve. We must:

▶ Develop and live an enabling and empowering vision. Effective leadership—at all levels—is marked by a core philosophy (values) and a vision of how the enterprise (or department) wishes to make its mark. Look inward, work with colleagues, work with customers, work with everyone to develop and instill such a philosophy and vision.

▶ Ensure that the vision is at once (1) specific enough to act as a "tie breaker" (e.g., quality is more important than volume) and (2) general enough to leave room for the taking of bold initiatives in today's ever-changing environment.

▶ Become the vision's foremost itinerant preacher: Do not let a single day pass without taking at least two or three opportunities to deliver your three-minute "stump speech" on the vision and to "showcase" events and people (small events and front-line people rather than big events and senior executives) that are illustrative of initiatives which support the vision. When it comes to vision and philosophy: (1) consistency is not the hobgoblin of small minds, and (2) God is in the details.

Quite simply, the vision must supplant the rule book and the policy manual. "Hustle" in service to the customer was the message of C-1 through C-10. "People's involvement is everything" was the rallying cry of P-1 through P-10. How does the leader direct this front-line energy and quick initiative-taking? A soaring purpose—a vision and corporate values responsive to today's and tomorrow's needs—is the answer. Day-to-day flexibility and innovation by everyone can only occur if the outline/charter/vision is unmistakable—and exciting.

Via soul-searching listening, assessment of the external situation, and solicitation of all points of view, develop a succinct vision that is clear and exciting, and at the same time leaves wide latitude for the pursuit of new opportunities.

L-2

Develop an Inspiring Vision

The very essence of leadership is [that] you have to have a vision. It's got to be a vision you articulate clearly and forcefully on every occasion. You can't blow an uncertain trumpet.

Father Theodore Hesburgh
former president, Notre Dame University
Time, May 1987

The corporation has shared information widely (S-3); you understand you are in a competitive pickle. You're part of a profit-distribution plan (P-6), you've been well trained (P-5), and the unnecessary structure has been removed (P-8); there are no supervisors around. But it's 2:35 A.M. The truck is almost loaded. The last order comes out on the dock, and the deliverer scoots off into the shadows. Something is amiss, you feel (but you're not sure), as you go over the packing label. What do you do?

The driver is chomping at the bit, and costing a fortune. The guy who passed the order on to you is senior to you by two years, supposed to know what he's doing. Odds are high you're all wet. Do you give in to your suspicion, and push the red button—or do you let it go?

To survive in today's quality-conscious environment, the answer had better be "push the panic button." But it will be only if the firm's vision and values are unmistakable; if they make what's of overarching importance clear, and at the same time leave vast latitude for initiative-taking—by everyone.

Some understand the role of vision in the brave, new, turbulent world:

▶ In *Leaders,* Warren Bennis and Burt Nanus conclude: "Leaders articulate and define what has previously remained implicit or unsaid; then they invent images, metaphors, and models that provide a focus for new attention. By so doing, they consolidate or challenge prevailing wisdom. In short, an *essential* factor in leadership is the capacity to influence and *organize meaning* for the members of the organization. . . . Managers are people who do things right and leaders are people who do the right thing. The difference may be summarized as activities of vision and judgment—*effectiveness* versus activities of mastering routine—*efficiency*. . . . [The subjects in our study] viewed themselves as leaders, not managers. This is to say that they concerned themselves with their organizations' basic purposes and general direction. Their perspective was 'vision-oriented.' . . . There were no 'incrementalists.' These were people creating new ideas, new policies, new methodologies. They changed the basic metabolism of their organizations. These leaders were, in Camus' phrase, 'creating dangerously,' not simply mastering basic routines. . . . Their visions or intentions were compelling, and pulled people toward them. Intensity coupled with commitment is magnetic. And these intense personalities do not have to coerce people to pay attention; they are so intent on what they are doing that, like a child completely absorbed with creating a sand castle in a sandbox, they draw others in."

► In *The Leadership Challenge,* Jim Kouzes and Barry Posner discuss Phil Turner, facilities manager for Raychem Corporation (he has since been promoted to plant manager for the company's Wire and Cable Division): "We had the chance to sit in with him one day when he was talking with his supervisors. Phil was describing the daily life of the people who work in facilities. A typical day-in-the-life might begin with this phone call: 'Phil, the toilet is overflowing in the men's room. Would you send somebody over to fix it?' Or, 'Phil, the air-conditioner is broken in our building. It feels like it's 110 degrees in this place. Would you send someone over to fix it?' . . .

"Phil related to his managers how one could get the impression that the people who work for Raychem were ungrateful. . . . 'But . . . I don't think that's what they are trying to tell us at all. I think what they are trying to tell us is that they care about their space. I have a vision for this department. I got the idea from [an executive vice-president]. The other day, [he] came by my office. The door was open and he walked in. He put his hand on my shoulder and said, "Phil, I want to thank you for planting those flowers outside my office window. They make me feel good." So I think our job is to make people feel good,' declared Phil."

Developing a vision and, more important, living it vigorously are essential elements of leadership. And they are not, as the case of Phil Turner shows, the exclusive province of mayors, governors, and chief executives. Vision occupies an equally important place of honor in the supervisor's or middle manager's world.

"CREATE DANGEROUSLY"—OR GO BELLY UP

The leaders Bennis and Nanus describe were "creating dangerously," "chang[ing] the basic metabolism of their organization." This radical definition of leadership must become the norm today. A supervisor or the chief executive of a big firm not bent upon "creating dangerously" is apt to lose his or her job and go out of business. It's as simple and as grim as that.

Following and administering rules might have been dandy in the placid environments of yesteryear. Not today. Managers must create new worlds. And then destroy them; and then create anew. Such brave acts of creation must begin with a vision that not only inspires, ennobles, empowers, and challenges, but at the same time provokes confidence enough, in the midst of a perpetual competitive hurricane, to encourage people to take the day-to-day risks involved in testing and adapting and extending the vision.

Don't Let It Become a Fad

Failure, today, is failure to change. The leader's vision is at once the license to dare to be better and the beacon and "control system" which keeps the process of mastering new worlds from deteriorating into directionless anarchy.

Sadly, "visioning" has become a fad in business circles. The idea of an effective enterprise being energized and guided by a succinct and uplifting philosophy that dares everyone to take risks to realize its challenge is a compelling one—especially as an alternative to guidance via necessarily static, 300-page strategic plans and 1,700-page policy manuals written for yesterday's placid conditions. And, indeed, this alternative form of control/motivation is essential in a setting where, for survival's sake, flexibility and constant change must replace rigidity. For this very reason, the idea of developing a vision is too important to be trivialized by the explosion of handbooks on "how to get vision" in twenty-seven easy steps. Thus, the line I tread here is a thin one. No leadership topic is more important. There are some things that can be said based on others' experience. But no precise path to "finding one" can—or should—be described. The process of discovery is personal, and the essence of the art of managing/leading in chaotic times.

Visions: A Broad Definition

Visions are aesthetic and moral—as well as strategically sound. Visions come from within—as well as from outside. They are personal—and group-centered. Developing a vision and values is a messy, artistic process. Living it convincingly is a passionate one, beyond any doubt. Posters and wallet-sized cards declaring the vision and corporate values may be helpful, but they may not be. In fact, they can hinder and make a mockery of the process if the vision and values are merely proclaimed, but not lived convincingly.

The "What" of Visions

1. **Effective visions are inspiring.** Steve Jobs, at Apple, wanted no less than to start a revolution in the way the average person processes information, thinks, and deals with his or her world. Fred Smith, founder of Federal Express, had a vision of truly reliable mail service. The Nordstrom family seeks to create "an experience" with their stores. And Raychem's Phil Turner, cited above, wants to create revolution, too, through an uplifting idea about what the maintenance of facilities can accomplish for all his fellow workers.

411

These leaders were not simply engaging in "market creation," as important as that is (see C-1). They were engaged in a crusade, and asked employees with nerve and verve, and customers and suppliers, to join them. To experience Apple or Fed Ex or Nordstrom, even as a customer, is to have your world changed permanently.

By contrast, inspiring visions rarely (I'm tempted to say never) include numbers. Earnings-per-share targets, however inspiring to the chief's pocketbook and the stockholders, are seldom uplifting to 10 or 10,000 people. While the numbers are important—especially in a world where corporate raiders await in every alleyway—they are a by-product of spirited performance, not its cause. Rather than numbers, the most effective visions ask for the best in one way or another—the highest-quality widgets, the best service ever in retailing history, the best customer relations in banking, the widest selection of clothing ever, a life-transforming experience for customers (of Apple or Outward Bound or Mrs. Field's Cookies); furthermore, they make it clear that "the best" will only be attained by the willing risk-taking of everyone on the payroll, starting with the just-hired teller or bellhop.

2. Effective visions are clear and challenging—and about excellence. One of Bennis and Nanus's leaders was Sergiu Comissionà, renowned conductor of the Houston Symphony: "When asked what he was like, his musicians answered, 'Terrific.' But when asked why, they wavered. Finally they said, 'Because he doesn't waste our time.' That simple declarative sentence at first seemed insignificant. But when we finally watched him conduct and teach his master classes we began to understand the full meaning of that phrase. . . . *It became clear that Comissioná transmits an unbridled clarity about what he wants from the players. He knows precisely and emphatically what he wants to hear at any given time. This fixation with and undeviating attention to outcome—some would call it an obsession—is only possible if one knows what he wants* [my emphasis]. And that can come only from vision, or as one member of Comissionà's orchestra referred to it, from 'the maestro's tapestry of intentions.' There is a high, intense filament, we noticed in our leaders—similar to Comissionà's passion about the 'right' tone—and in any person impassioned with an idea. . . . The visions these various leaders conveyed seemed to bring about a confidence on the part of the employees, a confidence that instilled in them a belief that they were capable of performing the necessary acts. *These leaders were challengers, not coddlers* [my emphasis]. Edwin H. Land, founder of Polaroid, said: 'The first thing you naturally do is teach the person to feel that the undertaking is manifestly important and nearly impossible. That draws out the kind of drives that make people strong.' "

3. Effective visions make sense in the marketplace, and, by stressing flexibility and execution, stand the test of time in a turbulent world. Prescription C-6 emphasized "uniqueness." How does the firm position itself—make itself distinctly different from all its competitors? Further, C-6 said that some forms of uniqueness were better than others, emphasizing a limited number of effective, generic strategies: Quality, service, responsiveness, and constant creation of new niche markets, even for seemingly mundane products, are the essence of a market-oriented strategy that has high odds of success over time. The vision that will be effective in the marketplace emphasizes the creation of enduring capabilities that will allow the organization to execute the strategy. The vision is thus paradoxical: It is relatively *stable*—focusing on superior quality and service, for instance. But it is *dynamic* in that it underscores the constant improvement (individual skill-building, for instance) and constant try-fail-adjust cycles that keep the skills/capabilities up to date. (See also L-1 and S-3, on strategic planning.)

4. Effective visions must be stable but constantly challenged—and changed at the margin. Johnson & Johnson's simple credo has served it well. Yet J&J has a periodic, highly articulated Credo Challenge. Key ideas seldom if ever change, but minor alterations add up to substantial adaptation over time. Kodak's smooth-running machine served it well for decades—while no effective competition was on the horizon. In the late 1970s, battered by newer film and camera makers, it had to renew its commitment to old tenets grown flabby, and make adjustments for tomorrow as well.

The vision must act as a compass in a wild and stormy sea and, like a compass, it loses its value if it's not adjusted to take account of its surroundings. People Express, for example, confused its early success as a "phenomenon" with the requirements of long-term customer satisfaction. When the firm was no longer a "phenomenon"—as others matched People's prices and then their costs—the bases for sustained attractiveness to customers, such as an adequate reservation system, were found to be sadly lacking. The very arrogance which led to the firm's bold start blinded it to a changed world.

5. Effective visions are beacons and controls when all else is up for grabs. Only fast-moving, structurally trim, action-oriented firms will survive. They will be populated by self-managing teams and marked by the total absence of first-line supervisors and fewer middle managers. So who's in charge? As a Tandem Computer executive puts it: "The controls are not a lot of reviews or meetings or reports, but rather the control is understanding the basic concept and philosophy of the company." The immense effort involved to achieve "buy-in" by everyone and the discipline required to live the vision with unswerving consistency are what transform this single sentence from Tandem into practical reality.

To turn the vision into a beacon, leaders at all levels must model behavior consistent with the vision at all times (see L-3 and L-4 especially). Bennis and Nanus are once again instructive: "Trust is the lubrication that makes it possible for organizations to work. Trust implies accountability, predictability, reliability. . . . The truth is that we trust people who are predictable, whose positions are known and who keep at it."

Jim Kouzes and Barry Posner heard a slightly different, somewhat broader statement of this same idea from Stanford University president Donald Kennedy, who says:

The leader's job is to energetically mirror back to the institution how it best thinks of itself. I just try to keep reminding students of certain things . . . about their opportunities, their obligations about public service and the like. And I try to pick what [the dean of students] calls "teachable moments." Like the recent honor code violations. This strikes me as a moment to use to try to get people to understand what we are doing. People say, "You've got a massive cheating incident, the honor code doesn't work." I say, "Wait a minute, what do you think the honor code is for?" "Well, the honor code is to prevent cheating." "Gee, are you sure about that? If the honor code is to prevent cheating, there are surely better ways. Give me a lot of police and I'll end it around here. And you think everyone will cheer about that?" "Well, no." And so you start talking about what the honor code is for. And about responsibility.

6. **Effective visions are aimed at empowering our own people first, customers second.** As mentioned, visions must be consistent with market realities—and to be sure, the vision of a Federal Express, for example, attracts customers. But the first task of the vision is to call forth the best from the company's own people.

7. **Effective visions prepare for the future, but honor the past.** A contemporary German philosopher has stated: "Whoever supplies memory, shapes concepts, and interprets the past will win the future." Oddly, visions are about the past as much as about the future. Ronald Reagan, whatever his faults, called upon us to create new opportunities for the future by recalling our entrepreneurial, high-spirited past. The most effective visions draw upon enduring themes to make us feel more confident about stepping out in new directions to deal with a brave new world. Thus, a call for renewed emphasis on quality may be rooted in the tradition of craftsmanship of the firm's honored founder. A call to shed slovenly ways and innovate rapidly can be tied to the organization's early and glorious entrepreneurial days, when it succeeded by catching then established firms napping. A call for greater work-force involvement and less bureaucracy may be related to the company's and the nation's pioneer days when self-reliance reigned.

The continuity is stressed for the very purpose of paving the way for change: "As you seek to change every procedure and job description to aid responsiveness, remember the bygone days when *we* whipped big competitors by being faster and fleeter of foot." That is: "You are safe in that you honor our most cherished traditions as you seek to break out of today's constraining bonds."

8. **Effective visions are lived in details, not broad strokes.** A vision is concise, encompassing, a picture of sustaining excellence in a major market. But, as in the example of Stanford president Donald Kennedy using honor code violations as a "teachable moment," or Phil Turner's planting a few flowers at Raychem, the vision lives mainly in the details of its execution. This is the theme of L-3 and L-4. Calendars, notes on memos, and who gets invited to meetings are the "stuff" of visions on a moment-to-moment basis. They form the basis for reliability and trust as nothing else can.

Getting a Vision

To describe the eight key traits of an effective vision is not to describe how to get one. You've just been promoted to your first supervisory job or to chairman of the board, or founded a small company, or become head of New York's Eastern Regional Boy Scout Commission—and you realize the unique opportunity such a moment presents to shape your part of the organization. You want to present a compelling vision. So what do you do? Do you go to the mountaintop? Can you hire a consultant to give you one? (If so, how much does it cost?) Do you form a team to hammer one out? Do you solicit "vision input" from the front line? From customers?

All of these and none is the confusing answer. Here are a few ideas about how you might proceed:

1. Look to your prior experiences. You don't come to the table cold. You've been part of the organization (or some organization) for years, starting with Sunday school or a Brownie troop. What have you learned? What really bugs you the most about such groups? What's been nifty? What's been memorable? What seems to have been going on at work when people were really soaring? When they were at each other's throats?

A vision and a set of values come first from these past experiences. Here's your chance—first-line supervisor or chairman. Fix what's been wrong in every place you've been before: Not enough communication? Set up daily, informal rap sessions. Too much politics? Stamp out incipient politics by pouncing on those who attempt to butter you up—begin this on hour one of day one in the new job. Too much bureaucracy gumming up the works? Cut out five reports right now, and stop all memo writing. Lousy attitudes toward customers? Insist that any customer call be put through to you instantly, even if you are in a closed-door meeting with your boss or your boss's boss.

2. Fiddle around, but make haste. Make lists. Doodle. Write ideas on index cards. Talk with others—from all walks of life—and seek their advice. Reflect on all such numerous inputs—but move fast. The organization is most malleable on day one; it becomes less so with each passing hour. The metaphor, from national politics, of a president's "honeymoon" is apt; term after term it's proved accurate. That is, you've got about a hundred days to get on with it.

Set down your ideas, loosely or precisely. Take some immediate steps of the sort described above. Begin in a fairly dramatic fashion, albeit using small events as your fodder.

3. Try some participation. After noodling a bit, you might schedule fifteen meetings in the next thirty days with disparate groups—first-line people from each function, first-line supervisors from each function, first-line supervisors from a mixture of all functions, suppliers, customers, wholesalers, community leaders. Chat about your ideas. Seek their list of top-ten irritants, their ten best experiences in the company or function; and keep on scratching away.

4. Clarify over time. Perhaps a two- or three-day session with those who report directly to you is in order. Again, swap stories, dreams, precise internal and market assessments, wallow in the data (mainly anecdotes). Ask them to come to the party with lots of data, gathered by doing their own smaller-scale version of what you've been up to. Maybe the result will be a formal declaration of values, maybe not. Maybe it will be two flip charts' worth of handwritten ideas that everybody sticks up in his or her own office. Perhaps it will eventually be turned over to a printer and circulated to everyone on wallet-sized cards and posters alike. But then again, maybe it never will.

5. Remember, listening is basic. Paradoxically, visions are seldom original. Bennis and Nanus observe: "The leader may have been the one who chose the image from those available at the moment, articulated it, gave it form and legitimacy, and focused attention on it, but the leader only rarely was the one who conceived of the vision in the first place. Therefore, the leader must be a superb listener, particularly to those advocating new or different images of the emerging reality. . . . Successful leaders, we have found, are *great askers,* and they do pay attention."

Living the Vision First

The printing of the cards and slogans is the least important part of all this. By then, if the process is to work, it's a done deal, bought into, already being lived. The most important part is wallowing in the ideas and then, as they become increasingly clear, living them.

1. "Live, then post." In fact, if you began with a formal declaration, you are probably doomed. You don't know what it really means, let alone anyone else. You are likely to be continually trapped by a thousand tiny inconsistencies as you wobble toward clarity. That is, some small personnel decision or some small customer decision requires you to do the thinking you should have done before turning on the printing press. Such inconsistencies, after a formal declaration, convict you of hypocrisy and set the process back, perhaps derailing it forever. Remember, honeymoons are not very long; you seldom get a second chance. So, in the end, act fast when it comes to living the emerging eternal values; go slow when it comes to sloganeering.

2. Preaching it: The Stump Speech. Part of living the vision is in the details that will mark prescriptions L-3 and L-4—paying attention via time spent and getting out to the front line, where true implementation occurs. But there is a "preaching" element too, which I call developing a "stump speech," a term whose origins are, of course, political. The boss with a vision—supervisor or chairman—is political, in the very best and purest sense of that word. He or she, running an accounting department or a police department, is constantly out "campaigning"—campaigning for the support, energy, and whole-hearted participation of everyone in the organization.

I suggest a three- to five-minute "stump speech," with many variations. Use it at least a couple of times a day, almost regardless of setting. No opportunity is, in fact, inappropriate for reiterating the vision, using a pertinent detail that happens to be at hand. If possible, end the speech with a couple of examples of people in the ranks living the vision in their daily affairs—not in a dramatic fashion, but in a small way that illustrates the way the vision affects daily operating routines; try harder still to have that example encompass a small risk (not small to him or her) that someone took to enact the vision.

3. Another part of living the vision is pure emotion. One crew member said of Dennis Conner, the winning skipper in the 1986 America's Cup race, "He gives confidence to the whole crew." Los Angeles Ram running back Eric Dickerson said of his coach, John Robinson, "He makes you think you're invincible." Football commentator John Madden reports a comment by a Chicago Bears lineman on the team's quarterback, Jim McMahon, "In the huddle, your eyes just glue into him. I'd jump out in front of a bus and block it for him."

This brings us back full circle to the paragraph from Bennis and Nanus's *Leaders* that prefaced this prescription. The vision lives in the intensity of the leader, an intensity that in itself draws in others. This is the final ingredient.

Caveat: Beware of Stasis

The very purpose of the vision is to provide the bedrock upon which constant evolutionary, opportunistic change can take place. However, it is all too easy for even the most compelling vision (initially) to become static, impeding the very change it is meant to induce.

IBM's main premise, to provide the best service of any firm in the world, has gotten a bit tattered in recent years. It often came to mean, as a by-product of IBM's success, the best service to the managers of central information systems. When information processing began to be radically decentralized, IBM's tough account managers often joined with the client MIS director in rearguard actions to fight change. The vision had come to be interpreted in a limited—and limiting—way.

The vision must provide stability—it inspires the confidence necessary to induce constant risk-taking in pursuit of its execution/perfection/expansion. But it must not become constrained by yesterday's success pattern, or by a narrow interpretation of market need. The vision must be infused with no-holds-barred customer/competitor listening (see C-7, I-4); it must be coupled with stringent innovation goals (see I-1, I-9); and it must be abetted by flat, non-bureaucratic, close-to-the-market organization (see P-8)—all of which in themselves encourage initiative-taking which will over time change the operational definition of the vision at the margin or, eventually, dramatically. It is true, nonetheless, that despite all these spurs, the vision still stands a good chance of getting rusty, and even enlightened exercises such as Johnson & Johnson's Credo Challenge are not likely to stave off some narrowing over time.

"Beware" is hardly practical advice, but it is a first step. The absence of bold new initiatives, in pursuit of objectives that may seem somewhat contrary to the vision, should be cause for alarm. Don't let the vision be shot through with holes, but be damned sure some of your best and brightest are shooting at it—with bazookas as well as snipers' rifles. Recall the advice of Richard Foster, from *Innovation: The Attacker's Advantage*—winners, he says, are those who have constantly attempted to make obsolete their most cherished skills and products. While always true to some degree (Foster reviews centuries of history), the implications of his analysis are stunning as we look to the breathtakingly more turbulent future.

FIRST STEPS

The process of developing a vision, though it represents the "highest level of abstraction," is quintessentially a trial-and-error process. Reread this prescription; take any angle on the process you can think of—but start today.

L-3

SUMMARY

In these uncertain times, when the need to accelerate the pace of change is paramount, we must:

▶ Lead, as never before, by personal example—in particular, calling attention to the new by means of our primary leadership tool: our calendars; that is, the way we spend our time.

▶ Reinforce attention to the new direction by the second most powerful day-to-day leadership tool—promotion decisions.

▶ Understand the power of our smallest actions: Amidst uncertainty, when people are grasping at straws in an effort to understand the topsy-turvy world about them, their symbolic significance is monumental.

People in organizations are all boss-watchers, especially when external conditions are ambiguous. For better or worse, what you spend your *time* on (not what you sermonize about) will become the organization's preoccupation. Likewise, the proactive use of symbols, such as the sorts of stories you tell and the people you invite to meetings, sends powerful signals to the organization about what's important. The final confirmation of "what really counts around here," when things are changing, is who gets promoted—risk-takers and harbingers of the new, or "the same old crowd."

Modify your calendar by 15 percent in the next six weeks to call attention *quantitatively* to your top priority. Eventually, spend no less than 50 percent of your time, visibly and directly, on your top priority. Dip down in the organization and intrude in *every* promotion decision; keep a *quantitative* scorecard on the degree to which promotions reflect the top strategic priority. Pause briefly and consider the symbolic significance of *every* act, given that others are especially thirsty today for clues about your organization's priorities.

Manage by Example

Example is leadership.
>   Albert Schweitzer

My moment of truth came toward the end of my first ten months. It was one of those nights in the office. The clock was moving toward four in the morning, and I was still not through with the incredible mass of paper stacked before me. I was bone weary and soul weary, and I found myself muttering, "Either I can't manage this place, or it's unmanageable." I reached for my calendar and ran my eyes down each hour, half-hour, quarter-hour to see where my time had gone that day, the day before, the month before. . . . My discovery was this: I had become the victim of a vast, amorphous, unwitting, unconscious conspiracy to prevent me from doing anything whatever to change the university's status quo.
>   Warren Bennis
>   while president of the
>   University of Cincinnati,
>   as reported in *The Leadership Challenge*

I did the thirty-day [calendar] review and a general review of the last six months. I became shocked and then saddened as the truth [about how I was spending my time] slowly sank in.
>   Hospitality industry executive
>   Skunk Camp participant, 1985

I started by delivering on my number one promise—I have cleared my calendar so that about 60 percent of my time is available for listening, walking around, etc. I have even set aside all airplane travel time for "innovative dreaming," in fact that's where I am now. I previously used this time for "in-basket clearing."
>   Senior civilian executive
>   U.S. Army Corps of Engineers
>   Skunk Camp participant, 1986

ATTENTION GETTER #1: A CHANGE
IN YOUR CALENDAR

I have studied leadership and strategy implementation for over twenty years, reviewing hundreds of books, thousands of studies, and observing a host of effective and ineffective leaders. Literature on management style is best measured by the ton, as is true for topics such as conflict resolution, consensus-building, "forging a team at the top," choosing an optimal structure, and goal-setting techniques. More recently "how to create the 'right' culture" seems almost to have become a boardroom obsession.

To be sure, many sound ideas have surfaced concerning each of these important topics. Yet I am willing to stick my neck out and state unequivocally that all of them, taken together, pale by comparison to the power of this one: changing your calendar.

Changing your calendar is not sufficient to bring about desired organizational change. But it is necessary. It is quite simply impossible to conceive of a change in any direction, minor or major, that is not preceded by—and then sustained by—major changes, noticeable to all, in the way you spend your time.

At one level, this prescription seems almost tautological. As managers, we don't do the business of the enterprise anymore—drive the municipal bus, patrol the beat, sell the shoes or computer. Therefore, *we are our calendar,* the signals we send about what's important and what isn't. That seems to be what Warren Bennis found out in the course of trying to institute changes at the University of Cincinnati.

At another level, the power of the calendar exists because virtually everyone is a boss-watcher. In ways both direct and convoluted, the agenda of others soon come to mirror that of the boss. And this is true—to the point of being a truism—on the shop floor, in the elementary school, on the garbage route, and in the executive suite.

Why, then, since the powers of example (that is, the calendar) are both ageless and indisputable, do we stress them here? Quite simply because their creative use is more essential today than ever before.

All organizations must now be jerked rapidly in new directions. Moreover, the requisite change in direction is taking place against a backdrop of ever more confusing messages from the environment—cut costs but achieve better quality; decentralize and recentralize. Even if conventional planning tools were once effective as direction setters (a questionable assertion), they are much too slow—and not blunt enough—for today's needs.

Telecommunications engineers have a precise term for all this: "signal-to-noise ratio." When you are transmitting through the air, or via a transatlantic cable, there is lots of interference or "noise," such as random electromagnetic signals. Your transmitted signal must be strong enough (i.e., of great enough amplitude, distinct from all others) to override the noise—in other words, the signal-to-noise ratio must be high enough—so that the signal arrives clear and unequivocal at the receiving location.

Turbulence in the environment is now causing unprecedented noise. If the organization is to be led clearly to implement its vision (see L-2), our "signal amplitude" had better be great indeed. Only when the front line receives crystal-clear signals that leaders, at all levels, are foursquare behind them will they be comfortable enough to take the risks necessary to make the far-reaching changes required. And the only for-certain confirmation of the commitment of leaders is the way they spend their time. In summary, to signal the need for dramatic change, the calendar must be altered dramatically—unmistakably enough and visibly enough to overwhelm the growing noise level.

So it boils down to this: Want to call attention to your new quality program, or your new people participation program, or your new innovation program? There's only one way that counts with the organization's members: Spend time on it—lots of it.

A Possible Scenario: Making Your Calendar Send Your Message

Is quality your necessary and consuming passion?

► Start *every* meeting—even if the topic is a new computer for the Düsseldorf office—with a quality review.

► Schedule a full-dress quality review once a month with those who report directly to you and an informal report on quality at the start of each week's routine staff meeting.

► Go outside the firm to a number of seminars on the topic—even if you're chairman of a $20 billion company—and let everybody know you went, and took notes.

► Meet once or twice a week with longtime customers or suppliers, on their turf, to discuss quality; then circulate detailed notes on the meeting.

► Make sure your desk is stacked high with books on quality—for all to see.

► Regularly call people at all levels of the organization to ask questions about quality.

► Circulate dozens of articles on the topic—to hundreds of people, with a simple note appended, such as "Can we make use of this? Let me know."

► Have a three-day "off-site session" with front-line quality managers from each facility.

► Start routinely poking around—in person—in the bowels of the organization, even in functions outside your own; chat up everyone who's willing to discuss the topic with you; mainly ask questions at first.

► Get anyone and everyone to send you reports on some aspect of quality in their operation.

And then, and here's the rub, add up all this activity to determine, exactly and quantitatively, just how much gross calendar time you are spending on the matter. You simply must have at least one daily activity that is clearly—i.e., visibly (stands out against the background "noise")—devoted to it. You should set a bold, quantitative weekly and monthly target as well, and then track your progress, and publicize your schedule (and schedule changes) for everyone to see.

The Message Is in the *Amount* of Time Spent

Though the issue might well be quality, you need not spend so-called "quality time" on it. That is, you don't need to get everything right at first; you simply need to get quality demonstrably on your agenda. No doubt you will be at sea in the beginning; implementing a new strategic thrust is not easy: "Just what the hell *is* quality anyway?" You won't know whom to meet with, whom to call, what to ask or talk about, whom to believe. The odd thing is that it really doesn't matter. What matters is that everyone who works for and with you observes you embracing the topic with both arms—and your calendar. What they need to observe is your obvious, visible and dramatic, determination to batter down all barriers to understanding, and then implementation.

Your energy and intensity—as shown chiefly by your time spent—will signal everyone who comes in contact with you, directly and indirectly, that you are in dead earnest, which is really the point. In surprisingly short order, even if the organization is a big one, their calendars will mysteriously start to match yours. The firm will slowly begin to come to life around the issue. Many efforts will be misdirected or useless. A few may even be harmful. No matter. Slowly the lumbering beast called the unit or organization (whether with 17 or 17,000 occupants, whether public sector or private) will shift its sights. And if you sustain your effort—as proved by that damnable calendar—attention to, and experimentation with, the new strategic thrust will be sustained as well. Over time, you and the obviously sensible people on your payroll will inexorably begin to do more things "right."

Creative Uses of the Calendar: (1) Turning Any Occasion into a Soapbox Opportunity and (2) Self-Cooptation

Is it as easy as just changing your calendar? Yes. And no. It is that easy—after the fact. But it's no easier than losing weight and then keeping it off. After all, your calendar, as it is now, is not the calendar of an idiot. It was "chosen" by you. Perhaps you feel it was foisted on you by superiors, or just grew topsy-turvy, like Bennis's, out of maliciousness or mindlessness. And it is true, you are in part a victim—but never, I contend, decisively so. You may well be forced to go to meeting X and declaim on topic Y. But even in that extreme case, you can always—yes, always—turn the presentation into a soapbox opportunity to preach the quality (or service, or participation, or innovation) gospel: "Let me begin my discussion of European computer selection with a review of its impact on quality as perceived by our customers." It would be darned tough to stop you from doing that!

Another example: Former Secretary of Health, Education, and Welfare John Gardner had a number of pet projects, but the "system" stymied him. He broke somewhat free when he started to schedule seemingly insignificant speeches, a year in advance, on one of those pet topics. Suppose he had a keen interest in cancer research. In February of one year, he might schedule a speech to an obscure cancer research consortium for March of the following year. Once on the master calendar, the event becomes "real" to the bureaucracy. About six to eight weeks before the speech, the system starts to cough up papers and speech drafts on the subject, and meetings automatically get scheduled to discuss the forthcoming event; in other words, Gardner would grab hold of the "mindless system," and use this subtle lever to make it attend to his desires.

In less august surroundings, we all have similar opportunities. Each year, for instance, I deliberately schedule about ten or fifteen speeches to groups that will force me to think about new topics I'm interested in. As the day approaches, I'm often mad as the dickens at myself for having scheduled such a "disruption." But I know I've got to show up, so I start working on the new topic; the result is that a small number of what I call "self-cooptation" events often set the tone for the rest of my work.

Measure (Quantify) Your Progress

Specifically, I propose that you begin by shifting at least 15 percent of your time toward your top priority in the next six weeks, and follow up with another 15 percent (for a total of 30 percent) in the six weeks after that. Indeed, it is certain that the first figure can be 25 percent, or even higher. I have seen any number of superb leaders almost totally clear the decks to get on with a new agenda. Remember the busy executive from the U.S. Army Corps of Engineers who quickly shifted 60 percent of his normal working time, and then his airplane time too.

In the face of most organizations' need for revolutionary change, this shift in the use of your time must soon add up to even more than I've suggested so far—to fully 50 percent of your time devoted to the new, revolutionary strategic priority. Nothing less will shake most organizations from their lethargy fast enough to restore competitiveness.

Bob Townsend, author of *Up the Organization* and *Further Up the Organization,* offers even more dramatic counsel, based upon the turnaround he engineered at Avis. He urges you to devote 100 percent of your time to the critical issue. For instance, at one point Townsend determined that Avis's financial reporting was a mess. He was unable to measure anything accurately, or even know how he stood at the end of the day. He relieved the controller, and then, over the furious objections of the board of directors, formally appointed himself full-time controller. He moved out of the president's office and into the controller's office for several months, until the problem was in hand and a replacement had been selected. As he says, the extreme demonstration of concern sent "a darned clear message." Talk about a high "signal-to-noise ratio"!

There Can Be No Surrogates

There is in fact no alternative to you acting as standard bearer for a dramatic strategic shift. You may, if you are chief executive, appoint a "representative"— a "quality czar," for example. But beware. He or she can be no more than your point person, and never a true surrogate. There can be no substitutes when it comes to the way the members of the organization assess your priorities and the seriousness of your intent. You are either "on" the topic—or you are not.

ATTENTION GETTER #2: PROMOTING CONVERTS TO THE NEW PROGRAM

For us boss watchers (all of us, that is) the way our bosses spend their time, not what they say, is the top attention director. Ultimate confirmation of the seriousness of the intent signaled by a change in the calendar is who gets promoted—attention getter #2.

For example: The firm must shift from an inward-looking to an outward-looking focus. The process started a year ago. The calendar of the unit chief, or the top executives, says, "This is for real." Now a general management job pops open in the second most important unit in the company. Who gets it?

The three most obvious candidates are all longtime toilers in the trenches, several times promoted, talented beyond doubt. But all three have been luke-warm about the new thrust. Their backgrounds are all oriented heavily toward finance (rather than sales or marketing).

Does one of the three get the job, or does the person at the top dip down and anoint a somewhat younger line marketer who has been out front, at no small personal risk, on the new strategy? Everyone in the firm, from junior distribution supervisor to the crusty old director of MIS and the corporate sales VP, is focused on this bellwether appointment. It is the acid test.

The picture need not be so stark. It need not be "marketers" versus "finance persons." Suppose one of the three finance people, by chance the most junior, had taken to the new program like a duck takes to water, long before even the chief had demonstrated he would stay the course. Or suppose it's an old tiger, the oldest of the three, with only eighteen months to go to retirement—but he got out in front while the relative youngsters lay back, testing the chief's mettle.

The latter two examples are taken from personal observation. A big firm undertook a shift to a quality-before-cost-and-volume orientation. The "old boys" were certain that when push came to shove the chairman would return to penny-pinching, "cost is what really counts around here" ways. Then, two years into the program, the chairman confounded the reluctant dragons by appointing someone fifteen years their junior as chief operating officer—and heir apparent. He came from a relatively small division—but he had been the most energetic by far in implementing the quality thrust. In the second case, a

63-year-old was named vice-chairman of a big firm for precisely the same reason. He, at age 61, had far surpassed those fifteen years his junior in his zeal for a new, customer-oriented strategy in an operation that had been primarily numbers-oriented—and he had previously been a card-carrying member of the inward-looking finance fraternity.

In both instances, those on the scene, from top to bottom, describe the surprising promotion as decisive proof that the new strategy was no flash in the pan.

I am not suggesting that you mindlessly scour the woods for some bootlicking youngster who has taken to the new approach for the purpose of self-aggrandizement. But zeal for the new will always vary among candidates for a key job. Make sure that you pick a convert; at least don't pick someone, regardless of past loyalty, whom everyone judges to have been dragging his or her heels.

Go one step further. Though I am an avowed fan of decentralized organizations and delegating authority, I strongly urge that any boss get personally involved in every promotion in his organization, even those three or four layers down. There aren't all that many promotions per year in firms of ordinary size, particularly in a division or in an operations center. Each one is a precious item, a signal of matchless amplitude. Autonomy be damned—you can't let those gems slip through your fingers. Scream about "quality over volume" as a division general manager, but then permit three of the next six first-line supervisor promotions to go to "ship the product" fanatics, and you can effectively kiss your strategically crucial program goodbye. Down on the line, where it counts, you are a dead duck—and a hypocrite.

And, as usual, quantify. Keep a running scorecard on promotions. What's your overall batting average? E.g.: "Six first-line promotions—four filled with converts or zealots; none filled with heel draggers."

MANAGING (LEADING) AS SYMBOLIC ACTION

Len Bias was not just another drug-overdose victim. Rock Hudson was not just another AIDS victim. The arrival of the planet's five-billionth human citizen is not just another birth.

On the other hand, we don't even know who that five-billionth person was, or, in fact, whether he or she was born in 1986 or 1987. And the deaths of Bias and Hudson rate only routine entries in the dusty record books of Maryland's Prince Georges County and Los Angeles County. Nonetheless, each of these occasions has a significance far beyond the simple statistical one, affecting the broader and graver issues of drug abuse, AIDS, and overpopulation.

Storytelling

People, including managers, do not live by pie charts alone—or by bar graphs or three-inch statistical appendices to 300-page reports. People live, reason, and are moved by symbols and stories.

We read ceaselessly about President Reagan's talent as a storyteller. Even his most stalwart fans regularly blush at the gap between statistical reality and his chosen story. But no one, friend or foe, snickers at the skill and power with which he has created compelling images that have moved the nation and defined controversial policies.

Researchers, somewhat ruefully to be sure, attest to the power of stories. One study involving MBAs—those persons more likely than almost any others to profess devotion to pie charts—is illuminating. Stanford researcher Joanne Martin attempted to convince a number of Stanford MBA students of the sincerity of a firm's policy of avoiding layoffs. Dividing them into separate groups, she presented one group with an illustrative story; another group received a wealth of statistical evidence indicating the firm had far less involuntary turnover than normal for the industry; a third group got both story and stats; a fourth group was given an executive's statement about the firm's policy. The most convinced group? The "story only" one—even more than the group that got both the story and the statistics.

Managing at any time, but more than ever today, is a symbolic activity. It involves energizing people, often large numbers of people, to do new things they previously had not thought important. Building a compelling case—to really deliver a quality product, to double investment in research and development, to step out and take risks each day (e.g., make suggestions about cost-cutting when you are already afraid of losing your job)—is an emotional process at least as much as it is a rational one.

It requires us, as managers, to persuade people quickly to share our sense of urgency about new priorities (see L-10); to develop a personal, soul-deep animus toward things as they are; to get up the nerve and energy to take on the forces of inertia that work against any significant program for change. The best leaders, especially in chaotic conditions (effective generals, leaders of revolutions), almost without exception and at every level, are master users of stories and symbols.

Furthermore, they are not ashamed of it. Martin Luther King talked openly about creating "a sense of drama" at crucial moments. Douglas MacArthur's first actions upon arriving in Japan at the end of World War II (such as landing unarmed) were masterpieces of the use of symbols. So was the carefully orchestrated arrival in France following the Allied landings on D-Day of the officially powerless Brigadier General Charles de Gaulle: within days he established dominance amidst total chaos through the skillful use of symbols representing the glory of France. And to jolt a quality program into gear, numerous managers I know have saved up defective products for a week and piled them on the factory floor in plain view of all involved; or even carried them by the bucketful into a board-of-directors meeting.

I am not suggesting that you quit collecting statistics. Numbers are important. Moreover, you should make sure that your "story of the week" bears a strong relation to overall developments, that it is a valid outcropping of an emerging trend.

Fortunately, or unfortunately, the average day or week serves up a set of good-news and bad-news stories that are plausible and that conform to systematically collected data. Resolve to collect three good-news and two bad-news stories concerning your top strategic priority within the next week. Talk about them, write about them. Ask others to collect—and use—good-news/bad-news stories in a similar fashion.

Everything Is Symbolic: Some Questions to Ask Yourself

A hundred forms of symbolic action add up to the clearest of pictures of the firm's (and leader's) true, rather than espoused, concerns:

1. What questions are asked first? You talk quality, but you always have the volume/cost report come first. Priorities are clear to one and all.

2. Where do you visit? You say partnerships with suppliers are the key to quality. Yet your calendar shows that of your sixty-five formal visits outside the firm this year (to attend outside board meetings, for example), only one has been to a supplier; moreover, three visits to suppliers were canceled at the last moment because of "pressing priorities."

3. Is there a pattern to the notes you pen on memos? Many reply to memos by penning notes in the margins. Are yours always merely topical, or do they have an overall theme? For instance, no matter what the topic, do you use your notes as reminders about innovation opportunities (if that's your theme)?

4. What does the "look" of the business reveal? You talk austerity and openness, yet hide behind your secretary and continue to allow officers to fly first-class "because of their burdensome schedules." What's on the menu in the executive dining room or corporate cafeteria? What's on the menu in the plant cafeteria?

The Manager as Pattern, Like It or Not

In the end, the manager's minute-to-minute actions provide a living model of his or her strategic vision. "Modeling," the behavioral scientists tell us with rare accord, is the chief way people learn. This is true in general, but now more than ever, when the search for themes by people beset with uncertainty and fear is at an unprecedented level.

Studies show that each day, like it or not, is marked by thousands of symbolic acts. Your personal note on a memo will be copied by hundreds and deciphered by thousands before nightfall. Your seemingly minor personnel decision will be debated in every outpost of the company, within minutes of your "secretly" making it. Your candid conversation with a salesperson during a customer call you made together flashes through the grapevine. Your inadvertent decision to park in a different slot this morning is causing reverberations of 5.9 on the Richter scale: "What's it mean?" You are spewing forth signals by the thousand, to thousands, each day. This is a plain fact. Whether or not you approach this inevitable set of signals opportunistically is up to you. But never doubt that you will send them—or that others will make a pattern from them, no matter what you do. What this pattern will suggest to those others, however, can be influenced dramatically. Grab hold of these opportunities. You *are* a rich, daily pattern to others. You *must* manage it in today's environment, when the conventional systems (such as policy proclamations and strategic planning) are overwhelmed by the pace of change and proving to be wholly inadequate. Only proactive management of the torrent of signaling activities can create the pace of implementation necessary for business survival.

There are those who object that a manager such as I describe is paying too much attention to style, not enough to substance. This is nonsense. Because the fact is, there is no perceived substance without symbols. Trust and credibility come through everyone's observation of the manager's symbolic integrity, not his or her "policy documents."

FIRST STEPS

1. Change that calendar—this afternoon. Change just one hour this week (surely you can do that). Change six days in the next six weeks to unmistakably reflect your top strategic priority.
2. Watch your symbols! Perhaps with the help of a friend, assess the degree to which your minute-to-minute behaviors closely reflect (or contradict) your strategic themes. Make this assessment daily, or at least weekly—starting right now.
3. Can you, without hesitation, point to one symbolic activity *each day* which not only showed you foursquare in support of your top priority, but also showed you making a tough choice that demonstrably placed yesteryear's top priority in second place?
4. Stop, right now, a mindless decision about a promotion, about to go to someone everyone assumes is the "best person for the job." Make sure the next promotion decision sends an unequivocal message throughout the unit or firm as a whole about your commitment to your top priority.

L-4

SUMMARY

To deal with a world turned upside down for everyone, a world in which clear guidance is hard to come by, and where rules and paper no longer reign supreme, we must:

▶ Practice visible management.

▶ Act to reduce information distortion.

▶ Get rid of our offices, or take several steps in that direction.

Visible management is a requisite today. All are confronted with change. Change is the only source of opportunity—and yet change has been anathema, especially to American organizations designed for stability and mass production of goods and services. To enable all organization members to get comfortable with change and constant risk-taking, management must be ever present, training, coaching, cajoling—and caring and comforting. A prime side-benefit of such a direct presence is a radical reduction in information distortion, which is now more dangerous than ever (delusion has a higher-than-ever price tag).

You are out of tune with the times if you are in the office more than one-third of the time.

Practice Visible Management

The most effective leaders, from Mohandas Gandhi to Sam Walton of Wal-Mart, have always led from the front line, where the action is. Today, any leader, at any level, who hopes for even limited success must likewise lead from the trenches. The changes are first discovered out where the customer is, where the small new competitor is, and where the disgruntled dealer is, not in the stillness of the meeting room on an overhead transparency.

When a trend, in today's world, is well enough known to put on paper, it's too late; the market is lost.

Furthermore, today's requisite flexibility will, as the people prescriptions argued, only come when every person is, and feels, empowered to take action at the front line. We, as leaders, will only know if they are so empowered (or still encumbered by silly, action-stifling rules) by being there.

So you be the judge:

Case One:

Dear Mr. Peters,

I have just completed perhaps the most educational month of my business career (including four years of business school).

I am responsible for the parts department of a large Caterpillar dealership. As part of a renewed emphasis on customer service, I spent a week working in the warehouse of one of our largest customers. What an eye opener! Being on the receiving end of one of our Caterpillar parts shipments rather than the shipping end was informative, to say the least. I learned firsthand why this customer was complaining about certain aspects of our parts service, because *I* was the one who had to open the boxes, sort through the parts, and process the paperwork. Now I believe this customer, and will act on his concerns, where before, I would tend to shrug off his complaints as "just part of doing business." Actually working *with* customers is the key to finding out what they *really* think of our company.

To follow that up, I have spent two days a week working as a warehouseman on our day and night shifts. Again, my eyes were opened. Not only did I find out how our warehouse really operated, I found out that our warehouse people are genuine *heroes!* They have a hard, monotonous job, but they show up day after day, year after year, with smiles on their faces and willing to do their best. I can't tell you how impressed I was with their professionalism, dedication, and willingness to work with me. Before, I viewed them as employees on the low end of the pay scale. Now I view them as friends, worthy of all the respect and support our company can provide.

[These activities have] opened my eyes to the obvious—that my job is to learn to think as our customers think, and to provide the kind of environment that will let the people I work with think, innovate, make mistakes, have fun, and do their very best.

> Sincerely,
> General Parts Manager
> (February 1987)

Case Two:

Although I will almost always be in my office not later than 7:30 in the morning, I do not want to see anyone until approximately eight o'clock, nor do I want people hanging around in the outer office. Again, because of the time demands on everyone, if you want to see me about a particular subject, call [my secretary] and leave a message as to the subject matter. It is my intention to see you as quickly as possible to resolve the problem or discuss the matter at hand. But I want no one just drifting around the office to visit or address a particular problem.

> Excerpt from a memo to all
> vice-presidents by a new chief
> executive officer of a
> multibillion-dollar service company

Between the two, who would you bet on?

Getting out and about is a dandy idea. But it is more than that. It is an attitude toward managing and leading. It is a way of life. It is virtually a theory of organization unto itself. That is, it deals with the fundamental way in which communication, including executive communication, takes place in and among collectivities called organizations—communication that deals with gathering the information necessary for decision-making, with making a vision concrete, with engendering commitment and risk-taking, with caring about people beset with an unprecedented disruption of normal routines.

Getting away with not getting out may have been possible yesterday. It is not today.

THE PERILS OF INFORMATION DISTORTION

I was appalled by a feature in the January 12, 1987, issue of the Detroit *News* titled "The Hazards of Business Fads." In it the president of the American Management Association, Tom Horton, took on "managing by wandering around" with a vengeance. Or, the paper reports, "by stumbling around, as Horton says. It's his nomination for most ridiculous recent management fad." The article quotes Horton's argument: " 'The theory is that the captain needs to get away from the bridge and roam the ship. But somebody's got to be steering the ship.' Good managers, he points out, don't wander aimlessly; their visits are planned and purposeful."

This is utter nonsense, for several reasons:

▶ Management enemy number one, perhaps at all times but today for certain, is information distortion, especially when the information comes professionally packaged, accompanied by computer-generated sixteen-color graphics. As a longtime consultant, I know almost every trick of the trade when it comes to distorting information behind crisp logic and clever schematics.

The world today is uniquely "messy," with a host of new variables surfacing at lightning speed. The manager had better be as "messy" as the world; that is, she or he must have an undistorted feel for the uncertainties out there on the line. Information-processing scientists even have a term to describe this need: requisite variety. That is, the variety of your sources must match the complexity of the real problem, or you will be led to erroneous conclusions.

In the office, whether you are chief of a big organization or a small one, you are shielded from the truth by a bewildering array of devices, prudent or malicious, all designed to "save" you from trivia and complexity so that your mind can be clear as you confront the "big picture" decisions. Instead, your mind is all too likely to be empty of all but prepackaged data, leading you to make uninformed decisions.

▶ The action and the information necessary for implementation are on the front line, as the parts manager from Caterpillar quoted above learned so swiftly. The team plugging away in the distribution center on the 11 P.M. to 7 A.M. "graveyard" shift knows more about the company's problems with quality and service and about new competitors than the bosses do, all nine levels of them, from center supervisor to CEO. But to get at that information, and to "feel" what is keeping people from acting on it, you must visit and chat with these knowledgeable people where and when the action is—at 3 A.M., on the loading dock.

▶ Ambling must be semi-aimless to ensure numerous sources and perspectives. Psychologists used to preach to guilty dads: "It doesn't matter how much time you spend with your kids, it's the quality of the time that counts." Common sense, as well as subsequent studies, says that's bunk. Most good experiences with kids (or anybody else) are inadvertent, a sideshow to the planned purpose of an activity. As philosopher Vilfredo Pareto put it: "Logic is useful for proof, but almost never for making discoveries." That meticulously planned state visit by the chief of the 16- or 16,000-person unit or firm will be fashioned by subordinates to ensure that the views they've espoused to the boss before won't be distorted by, say, an irate customer.

▶ The distortion of information is everyone's problem. It is worse in the White House than in the corner store. But not by as much as you'd think. Distortion in the ten-person outfit can be mind-boggling. Oddly enough, if you're a "good guy" or "good gal," it doesn't help either. That is, if you're well liked, easy to get along with, committed to service, you're still in trouble—because the gems whom you've hired don't want to disappoint you. They therefore unintentionally shade the truth. Three or four sequential, little shadings rout veracity. So no matter what your style, Simon Legree in pinstripes and vest or warm and tender in shirt sleeves, you've got a problem.

But let's return to Horton's bridge. I think he means "someone's got to be in charge." I half agree. Recall prescription L-2; the leader in turbulent times must articulate a vision that others (1) sign up for and (2) are empowered by. But stamping in the vision, the essence of the new leadership, is not best done from the bridge. It is best done on the front line, where exemplars who are taking "little" risks to implement the new way can be found and singled out for all to see. Moreover, it's out there where the leader finds answers to the more fundamental question: Does the vision make sense in its implementation?

Furthermore, the main reasons a captain gets stuck on the bridge add up to a frightening Catch-22: (1) his vision is muddy, (2) he doesn't dramatize examples of effective initiative-taking, (3) he fails to break down functional barriers to action-taking, and (4) he doesn't effect true delegation. Thus, even minor decisions flow up to the top—and the captain gets ever more firmly stuck on the bridge (1) deciding about trivial affairs (2) based upon distorted information (3) provided by equally out-of-touch staffs who (4) stay at home themselves to await the boss's call for more overhead transparencies.

Visible Management: A Return to the Old School?

Horton's objection about aimlessness is one of two principal gripes about "managing by wandering around." The second is the polar opposite—some see it as a repudiation of the delegation of responsibility through management by objectives. They contend that visible management can be a return to close, over-the-shoulder, KITA (kick them in the ass) supervision. While I'd admit that such an interpretation is plausible, the point of being out and about, as I conceive it and observe it at its best, is the antithesis of KITA—it is to listen and facilitate, not give commands and inspect. That's easy to say, but recall that a major thrust of the people prescriptions dealt with a revolution in the first-line supervisor's role. Extensive training and coaching are required to shift an old-timer from out-and-about-as-KITA to out-and-about-as-facilitator-and-listener.

The Special Case of Offices

Consider the all-too-characteristic course of a mom-and-pop enterprise. Years ago, when the company was founded, the owner sat in a chair at a little desk out on the shop floor. Then he moved into a cubicle with a three-foot partition around it. Later the walls were extended up to the ceiling. Then a door was added. More and more frequently it was observed to be closed. Next came a secretary's desk outside his office. Then she was given a cubicle, then high walls, then a door. An executive row began to form.

And now you check in with a security guard and get a plastic card. Then, escorted, you ride an elevator to the middle floor. Next, you shift to another elevator for the trip to the top floor. Then you check in a second time at a reception desk on the top floor. You wait, and a new escort appears. You are taken down a long, imposing hall with a fourteen-foot-high ceiling, punctuated by dark oak doors on either side—almost all of them closed. At the end of the hall, you enter *his* door and are passed off to his personal secretary, who seats you in the anteroom. Eventually, his door opens. . . .

And this man, I invariably find, wonders why he has gotten out of touch. He doubtless believes he stays close to his company's product by using it. But each nut and bolt in his edition of the product has, of course, been inspected ten times before it gets to him.

This sort of detachment plagues most of us, not only chairmen of Fortune 500 companies. It starts with that initial shift from the plain desk to the cubicle, and occurs one step at a time, mostly invisible, through a 100-step (or, more likely, 1,000-step) process. I observe the problem in corner stores, in restaurants, in twenty-five-person shops, in schools, in hospitals, in municipal offices.

One executive reversed the process. During a Skunk Camp, Ted Santo, a senior manager from Dayton Power & Light, called home to order a drastic step: he had his office dismantled. Several months later he wrote:

My office is indeed gone. I wanted to wait a while before describing the effects to you so I could be sure of my feelings and to be sure my feelings wouldn't change over time. It has been seven months now and I still don't miss it. I love the "freedom" it has given me to move about or wander. I find myself meeting people more often and on their turf.

As luck would have it, I have been promoted recently and have gained the responsibility for three new departments. Fortunately, without a "large stuffy office," I have the freedom to jump around all four work areas. My former office would have been even more of a hindrance to me now then it was before.

The reaction to the demolition of my office was profound. People genuinely thought I had gone off the deep end. Also, people thought I had worked years for my beautiful office and that I had earned it. Besides, they were looking forward (especially my staff) to their big office someday. Since then, they have accepted it, although I still catch a fair amount of ribbing over it.

I do maintain a small work area in two departments: a round table with three chairs and a file cabinet in an open area by the entrance door. This allows me to correspond with my secretarial support, correspond on the phone and handle my mail efficiently. However, I am in full view of everyone, and, therefore, I am more accessible to all. I love it!

Consider the two cases carefully. I strongly urge you to turn back the clock as far as you can. If you don't go so far as to dismantle your office, at least consider:

▶ dispensing with all executive secretaries, and sharing a secretary with three or four other executives. ("The world" will adjust—the flow of paperwork to you will actually go down to match the newly diminished secretarial capacity; I guarantee it.)

▶ dispensing with the secretary's office, and the door to your office.

▶ ensuring that your office is no bigger or better appointed (if you're chief) than the office of the manager of the factory/operations center.

▶ starting to answer your own phone, all the time when you're in (when you're out—which, remember, should be at least two-thirds of the time—let the overall office secretary take messages).

GETTING ON WITH VISIBLE MANAGEMENT

Ten Steps:

1. Put a note card in your pocket and write on it: "Remember, I'm out here to listen." I don't carry such a card, but I used to. I've now got the habit down to the point where I can merely say to myself before each meeting, "Shut up. Shut up. You are here to listen." In two-person sessions, I sometimes informally keep track of the time I talk versus the time I spend listening.

2. Take notes, promise feedback—and deliver. Fix small things on the spot, or within twenty-four hours. Send thank-you notes to individuals or small groups, perhaps summarizing what you thought you heard, within twenty-four hours of the meeting. Listening is abetted by note-taking; note-taking also lets the other persons know you are serious. But the clearest indicator is that something happens—either on the spot or soon after you get back to the dreaded office: A directive is issued wiping out a silly regulation you found was irritating everyone; or a faulty toilet is fixed up in three hours; or new lights are installed in the parking lot within the week. (Recall the discussion about the role of symbols in L-3. Make sure that two or three "little" things like this happen fast.)

3. Cycle your actions through the chain of command. Do it, yes—that is, take direct action on some small stuff (or maybe large, if you're sure you understand the issue). But tell the chain of command what you are up to; let them take—and take credit for—the bulk of your follow-up actions.

4. Protect informants. As you demonstrate your commitment by listening and fixing things, you will hear more and more unvarnished truth, often drifting in through side channels. Use it with care, and make sure, by using your own network, that no informant gets burned by an irate supervisor. And if a supervisor ever comes down on someone who was candid with you about a problem, remove him or her from managerial responsibility on the spot.

5. Be patient. When you start to wander, even in a ten-person purchasing operation, you will be treated cautiously and as if you were a bit mad. You are sometimes challenging a decades-long routine of comfortable, if nonproductive, noncommunication. Only repetition, and lots of it, will lead to opening up. Only repeated instances of swift follow-up and action by you will make it worthwhile for them to talk freely. Only evidence that you will protect informants will turn the tide. It takes time to demonstrate all these things.

6. Listen, yes; but preach a little too. Don't preach as in sermonize, but use tiny, concrete opportunities—dealing with housekeeping, or excessive paperwork—to preach, via example, your guiding theme. Don't scream at too much paperwork. Laugh at it, instead: "Why, surely this is a mistake—a two-page form requiring three signatures to requisition a $17.95 spare part for this machine, so you can repair it before it breaks and stops the line?" Then declare that form dead as of that moment—and check next week to make damn sure that it did, in fact, die.

7. Give some, but not much, advance notice, and travel alone. The limited advance notice is not meant to "catch" people; it is meant to head off the truth-inhibiting trappings of state visits that accrue to the hinterlands forays of even middle managers, especially from corporate "headquarters." And whatever your "management level," don't bring a staffer/note-taker with you. Take your own damn notes!

8. Work some night shifts, take a basic training course. Follow the path of the parts manager from Caterpillar. Of course you might be treated "oddly." But if your commitment is sincere, you will be responded to genuinely. You cared enough to try, awkwardly or not, and that trying sets you apart. Human beings respect human acts, and even respect the awkwardness, because we've all been odd man out ourselves on numerous occasions.

9. Watch out for the subtle demands that you put on others which cut down on their practice of visible management. You may preach getting out and about for all, but then you call for some data "right away, I've got a meeting with the investment bankers in two hours." You have just sent a bulletin, printed in six-inch-high red letters: "Getting out is great, but be in the office whenever I capriciously beckon." Bye-bye, visible management.

10. Use rituals to help force yourself and your colleagues to get out and about. Ask numerous, pointed questions that can only be answered through firsthand knowledge: "You know, we have an awful lot of errors in shipping. How does the system work? What do the people on the night shift think about the new computer? Let's go through a couple of individual orders in detail. How does the paper actually get transmitted from Joe to Jane? Does it come to Joe's desk? Who brings it? How long does it take?" Keep homing in until subordinates have no choice but to go out and find out for themselves. But watch out for gimmicks doomed to fail. I used to believe in "meeting-free days" that would allow people to get out and about. It never works, given the perceived crises that always arise (and seem to demand a meeting).

The primary tool for inducing visible management, recalling L-3, is the behavior you model. You planned a visit to a distribution center on the other side of the country, your first in eighteen months. A minor crisis arises. Cancel or not? Don't cancel. Let your able team handle the crisis. Go on with the visit. That sends an unmistakable message.

What If Your Boss Is an Ogre?

My file has more than one like this: "My boss is in the office 90 percent of the time. He expects me to be at the ready when a question arises, as it often does, before or during one of his endless meetings. So how am I supposed to be out and about with my seven-person economics forecasting group and our 'customers' throughout the firm?"

It won't be easy, I'd be the first to agree. But here are three possible strategies:

▶ Chronicle your three worst failures in the last year. Odds are, they occurred because you were out of touch. Admit your guilt to the boss, and propose a plan, including visits to your customers, as a way to avoid repeating the sin this year.
▶ Build customers' demand for your services. When a line executive vice-president comes to your boss, a staff vice-president, and asks for you to visit the Rubber Products Division in Sacramento, he'll have little choice but to acquiesce.
▶ At least you can get your gang of seven out of their offices. They, after all, are probably mimicking your behavior. Don't let them. Force them out, and their real-world contacts will doubtless enhance your work product—and maybe induce your boss to see the merit of your getting out.

Pay special attention to the last of the three strategies. Our bosses may be able to force us to do dumb things, but they can't force us to transmit the dumb things on down to our people. Manage down, not up—always begin by cleaning up your act in those areas where you clearly do have discretion.

The Power of Very Visible Management:
The Revolution at Valley Medical

The Association of Western Hospitals gave one of its prized Innovation Awards (sponsored jointly with 3M) for 1986 to Valley Medical Center, in the Seattle area. The association's magazine reports on the turnaround:

[CEO Richard Roodman explains:] "Valley Medical Center developed a very poor reputation in the Seattle community for the quality of care delivered. In fact, it was known as 'Death Valley.' . . . The night I was hired there were 150 protesters outside a room where a public session was going on and they were carrying pickets and banners that said 'It's cheaper to die.' The press had a field day."

Indecision, lethargy, demoralization, insecurity, feelings of betrayal—these were some of the conditions that the VMC medical staff and employees were experiencing when [Roodman] came on board. "The culture was one in which there was a total absence of pride," he said. "The employees basically felt left out. No one had seen the administrator in five or six years . . . they had *heard* there was a guy there. . . ."

To further complicate the situation, the community "hated" VMC. . . . *Within approximately two weeks* [*of being hired*], *Roodman visited nearly 700 employees* [my emphasis]. He wrote each of them a letter and mailed it to his or her home, and met with medical staff and formal and informal leaders. . . . "What we decided to do was develop a skeleton of what we wanted to accomplish and then we asked for *their* ideas," he said. "We got close to 600 people—union representatives, department managers, members of the community—and we went around the area and met with the chambers of commerce, the elected officials, the mayors. We tried to work the formal and informal structure of the medical staff into the process. We went to the volunteers, the auxiliary . . . we tapped the chaplains . . . we did all this in about three months."

The result of these and other innovative approaches to the web of problems at VMC was a long-range plan that involved *people* in a variety of ways. The plan focused on five different areas: patient and community responsiveness (quality issues), medical staff relations, human resources, marketing, and financial management.

The article concludes with an impressive array of statistics attesting to VMC's subsequent success. It all started with a powerful dose of getting out and about.

FIRST STEPS

1. Take ten small steps in the next ten days to get closer to raw information. Take one step before the sun sets today!
2. Starting today, have all customer calls put through to you directly. Is your theme quality? If so, put a red "quality" phone on your desk. Publish the phone number; anyone with a good-news or bad-news quality story is to call you directly (your secretary mustn't even have the number on his or her phone console).
3. The next time you pick up the phone to ask someone to stop by and see you, check yourself. Go visit the person instead—it is precisely by such (individually) "small" actions that you get your time in your office down to one-third—or less.

L-5

SUMMARY

While keeping in touch with the first winds of the new has always distinguished superior leaders, it is now a necessity. Today's effective leader must:

▶ Become a compulsive listener.

Today's successful leaders will work diligently to engage others in their cause. Oddly enough, the best way, by far, to engage others is by listening—seriously listening—to them. If talking and giving orders was the administrative model of the last fifty years, listening (to lots of people near the action), is the model of the 1980s and beyond.

Rip one front-line job apart: Listen to those who hold it. Learn their frustrations. Then act to clean up the mess and encourage them to do what must be done to react to today's volatile environment. Repeat with another job every 120 days.

Pay Attention! (More Listening)

Continuous improvement and flexibility—those are words that can't be repeated enough. What do they mean, practically? Turning over "control" and responsibility for action (test, modify, improve, repeat the cycle) to the front line, shifting the bulk of communication from "vertical" (up and down the hierarchy) to "horizontal" (people from multiple functions working together at the front line to do/create new, rapid responses to every customer need).

"Empowering" really boils down to "taking seriously." No one denies where the answers are: on the firing line. How do we get people to come forth and give the answers, to take risks by trying new things bound to fail at times? Near the top of the list is listening—that is, taking people seriously by the act of listening per se, and making it clear that you do take people seriously by what you do with what you hear.

The most effective leaders, political or corporate, empower others to act—and grow—in support of a course that both leaders and followers find worthy. The leader's job is at once to articulate the empowering vision (L-2), and to stay in touch with followers to ensure that she or he is in tune with the needs of the real world where the vision is implemented. Studies of effective leaders demonstrate that they do not induce narrow obedience to a precise objective among followers. To the contrary, powerful leaders make followers more powerful in pursuit of a commonly held dream, jointly defined. Furthermore, the listening leader inspires other leaders (managers at all levels) to be listeners too. The listening organization is in turn the one most likely to pick up quickly on changes in its environment.

Listening and Visible Management

Visible management (see L-4) involves listening, too, of course. What's the difference here? First, the prime "listening objective" put forth in L-4 was to reduce the distortion of information flowing to the boss, to enable him or her to make better decisions, for instance. Second, visible management is also about parading and symbolizing the vision—it has a "telling" component. Third, and most important, listening to the front line, in particular, is too important to be a subsidiary point. There are many who would say that unvarnished listening is the chief distinguisher between leadership success and failure, especially in times such as these when the empowerment of everyone is paramount. Oddly enough, to listen, per se, is the single best "tool" for empowering large numbers of others.

THE LISTENERS

There's a certain image of Roger Milliken that I keep in my mind's eye. It's from his firm's annual strategy meeting at Calloway Gardens, Georgia, in 1986. Four grueling, down-to-the-wee-hours-of-the-morning sessions, no recreation—this is a survival exercise, as Roger sees it. He's just come out of a meeting with his company presidents and a few handpicked outsiders, in this case from Dana, IBM, and Du Pont (and me). At the meeting, he probably asked sixty questions an hour. Each principal question was followed by five or ten more to get at the details, always the details—the real implementation story, not the gloss. In two-and-a-half hours he probably filled a quarter of a yellow legal pad with notes. (The next morning he'll turn the copious notes from this and other such sessions into his traditional meeting's-end speech—at which time he will announce a score of specific programs that will set the tone for the next twelve months.)

The participants of the meeting are exhausted from the intensity of this tireless 70-year-old, who's held the chief executive's job for over forty tumultuous years. We race back to our rooms for a fifteen-minute breather before the next grueling session commences—twenty-five action-packed small-group reports in ninety minutes. I happen to look up. There is Roger, pacing the corridor in front of his room, dictating at a staccato pace—yet more notes.

Listen. I don't know when it first occurred to me that I was observing a pattern. At our first Skunk Camp I watched Frank Perdue, the chicken king, and grocer *sans pareil* Stew Leonard engage in an Olympian struggle: Who would take the most notes?

Leonard won hands down, but even runner-up Perdue topped the rest of us put together, I'd bet. Both have been at their jobs, engaged, for decades. What was the subject? Milliken's president, Tom Malone, was describing the firm's quality program. Perdue, Mr. Quality to me already, rudely interrupted him dozens of times. He wanted clarification. Malone, a scientist, is as clear a speaker as I've heard, but he wasn't concrete enough for Frank. The reason quickly became clear. The next morning Perdue was up at 3 a.m. discussing with his people on the East Coast the implementation of the stuff he'd heard the day before. A major new executive compensation plan focused on quality and a landmark corporate training center were among the big ideas Perdue took from the seminar—and implemented in short order.

Stew Leonard didn't wait until 3 A.M. He was on the phone at lunch break.

"Are you sure you know what this means?" I asked. "It makes sense, doesn't it?" was Stew's reply. Well, yes, I agreed. "So why wait?" Leonard snapped back. I had no rebuttal to that one.

Another time, I gave a talk to a civic group in Baltimore. Mayor Don Schaefer attended. My speech lasted two and a half hours. I've had Fortune 500 CEOs and governors attend my sessions. Most come for the opening remarks and to be seen, then scoot out as soon as the lights are dimmed, or fidget endlessly and talk to a stream of aides rushing in and out half bent over so as not to disturb others in the front row—and doing so all the more because of their pronounced scurrying. Well, Schaefer sat there for two and a half hours, and he took as many notes as I used to take in a semester-length engineering course. I next saw him at a purely social occasion, a 1987 Toast honoring his over fifteen years as Baltimore's mayor. Several speakers appeared at the event—and true to form, Schaefer took copious notes, on napkins, on the menu, on various scraps of paper. The results of Schaefer's scribbling were legend in Baltimore—when the mayor took notes, action memos were sure to follow, including very pointed advice.

EFFECTIVE LISTENING IS ENGAGED LISTENING

There's an important emotional component to this. There's listening, and then there's engaged listening. The note-taking habit is a tip-off to the latter, but there's more to it than that. Engaged listening may be the principal mark of concern that one human being can evince for another, in any setting.

Once more, Roger Milliken provides a role model. Despite his decades in the business—to be sure, he's "seen it all"—he's like a kid when attending a session with dozens of team presentations from the front line. He'll turn to me with stunned amazement: "Can you believe that? Look at what they did." All news from the front is engaging to him, and especially if it comes from junior people who've caught fire and pushed Roger's vision further than anyone had a right to expect.

We've all been victims of the other side of the story. The vice-president goes on a field trip. He's been isolated for so many years that he really doesn't have, or feel he has, anything to talk to that truck driver about. After all, he's just reviewed twenty-three pages of "driver productivity indicators" with the boss of the driver's boss's boss. Why bother with the driver herself? Questions at best are brief and pro forma. The boss hasn't got the inclination, or nerve, to really dig in and ask about the forms and procedures. Trucks sure as heck don't interest him; he has a limousine. In fact, I'm not being fair. Down deep he's probably greatly embarrassed that he doesn't have anything to say or ask. He's scared to death of revealing his ignorance (especially to her), though to do so would doubtless break the logjam.

Prescription C-9, among others, made it clear: The drivers and the dispatchers will become the heroes of the newly responsive organization—or else. Leaders are only as good as they are: *They* have the answers to *your* problems. You must get passionately interested in the view, and the impediments, as seen from the dispatch center and rolling along I-80 with your products jostling in the back of the vehicle.

Engaged Listening Is Strategic!

When I deal with this issue of "engaged listening" in seminars, I'm at a loss to give prescriptive advice. It's not possible to prescribe "engagement" in any direct way. I can, however, give you a tip that will help. This "stuff" is strategic. If you can muster the nerve (that is what it takes) to get engaged with that truck driver (or reservations center person), I guarantee you that a lengthy discussion of the "little things" that rule their lives in your organization will collectively reveal the *strategic* stumbling blocks to higher quality, more responsiveness, etc. Wonder why your $80 million investment in a new reservations (or distribution) computer system is not reaping the benefits promised by senior staff experts? The people in the reservations center know. If you can stomach the repeated "You should've asked us about————" (to which you reply, stunned, "They didn't ask you?" . . . "No"), you'll end up with an earful.

Listen because they are your heroes; but if that's not your view, listen because the answer to strategic conundrums lies within the "little" roadblocks to their executing the vision.

You Must Have the Guts to Ask Dumb Questions

I was blessed early in my consulting career at McKinsey & Company. My first boss, Allen Puckett, is one of the smartest people I know. He was smart enough and comfortable enough with himself to ask really elementary (some would say dumb) questions.

He'd be with an oil executive from Getty who was paying us a bundle to be there. The fellow would, unself-consciously, be talking a private language: rigs, wildcatters, landsmen, scouts, stepouts, tertiary recovery. Whenever Allen would hear a word he didn't understand, he'd ask. "What's tertiary recovery?" he'd say. "Stepouts?" The rest of us were scared stiff; we assumed that since we were being paid an exorbitant fee, we shouldn't ask dumb questions. But the result was we'd lose 90 percent of the strategic value of the interview because we were afraid to display our ignorance by asking, "What's a barrel of oil?"

Mostly, it's the "dumb," elementary questions, followed up by a dozen even more elementary questions, that yield the pay dirt. "Why in the heck does this form go *there* next?" and "Who has to sign it?" are probably the two most vital questions when it comes to discussing the reason a firm is slow to act on something. "Experts" are those who don't need to bother with elementary questions anymore—thus, they fail to "bother" with the true sources of bottle-necks, buried deep in the habitual routines of the firm, labeled "we've always done it that way."

BREAKING DOWN FUNCTIONAL BARRIERS
BETWEEN WARRING FIEFDOMS: THE POWER
OF PATIENT LISTENING

Numerous scholarly monographs and case studies offer complex theories about ingrained stereotypical assumptions and resistance to change, the principal bases for the incessant battles that take place between major functions in any organization. But the most effective tactic I have observed for overcoming these stereotypes is the manager at the local level taking the initiative and offering, in a nonthreatening way, to sit down and chat with everyone involved; that is, from all functions. It takes a while—perhaps a long time—for any noticeable change to occur. But with lots of patience, the results can be startling. Here are two typical cases:

▶ During a seminar a debate about why doctors and administrators seem unable to cooperate bogged down. A woman who had crafted a brilliant turnaround of a troubled hospital in the Boston area proclaimed, "Look, we just assume that doctors don't want to cooperate and we treat them based on that assumption. I simply declared that I was going to be in my office on the same morning each week, with coffee and Danish, and I'd be pleased if any of the medical staff would drop by and join me toward no particular end. It was slow to catch on, I'd be the first to admit it. There were a lot of lonely breakfasts, but now it's the most important and real 'staff meeting' of the week."

A young man chimed in with another, equally pointed anecdote. He said he held an informal staff meeting every two weeks with a group in his hospital. They went to a local pub for burgers and shop talk. For no particular reason, a year or so into the process, he invited some doctors to attend. They did. He was surprised, and asked one why he'd showed up. "Why not?" came the reply. "You always have this lunch, and no one ever invites us. Why do you think we wouldn't want to attend whenever we can?" Decades of stereotyping was the clear reason.

In fact, over the course of several seminars with several hundred senior hospital managers, we collected a list of dozens of ways of breaking down the barriers. They almost all had the same theme: Find a setting that is not charged with tension and invite voluntary participation at some form of "let's chat" get-togethers. My favorite was the administrator who reported this strategy: "Eat your way through the medical staff." During a year's time, she had scheduled about seventy-five lunches, never with more than one doctor at a time; the cumulative outcome was a revolution in relations between the medical staff and the rest of the hospital.

▶ Les Wexner, founder of The Limited, provides corroboration. After acquiring the Lerner store chain in 1986, he cut off a host of hard-nosed suppliers in order to deal with bloated and outdated inventory. Naturally, the suppliers responded with a passel of lawsuits. The Limited's Bob Grayson, who is now chief executive of Lerner, was tossed into the wolf pack of New York garment makers. Grayson, whom Wexner calls "a good Iowa farm kid" and a hell of a merchant, discovered the power of the kaffeeklatsch. He said he'd show up at Lerner's midtown Manhattan headquarters at the crack of dawn each morning to read *Women's Wear Daily* and be available to discuss the business with anyone who cared to come. It started small—very, very small—but it's still growing to this day. Suppliers, with whom relations started so poorly, are there in droves. The Limited's once very strained relations with suppliers, in the toughest environment imaginable, were substantially reversed.

After careful consideration, I conclude that this is an especially good tactic for breaking the stereotypical images that keep warring functions apart, in all organizations. Some manager must take the lead to disarm, sit down, listen, and accept repeated rebuffs. After all, she is often facing decades of bruised feelings. More important, she must wait it out until it becomes clear to her "adversaries," not that she is in any way a "good gal," but that she has the conviction to sit quietly, to start a dialogue, in order to salvage or enhance the increasingly threatened organization on whose payroll all "sides" depend for bread, butter, and recognition.

The only danger, and it is a grim one, is a badly damaged ego. Sitting and sitting and waiting and waiting for the first coffee-and-Danish attendee is the ultimate in passivity if being out in front leading the charge is your style.

FIRST STEPS

1. Develop some personal listening ritual immediately. For instance, once every couple of weeks have an hour-long discussion with some first-line person. Think of yourself as a consultant called in on a nitty-gritty systems improvement assignment. Track down, in great detail, the nature of one or two critical tasks the person performs—precisely what's done, why it doesn't get done faster, and so on. (Use the outcome as you wish. This little listening device, repeated regularly, will unfailingly yield strategic insights.)
2. Start some form of "coffee and Danish" in the next 30 days.

L-6

SUMMARY

The flexible organization's leaders will put a disproportionate emphasis on the care and feeding of front-line people (see also C-8, C-9, P-1 through P-10). We must:

▶ Ensure that the front-line people—the implementers, the executors—know that they are the organization's heroes.

▶ Honor staff people to the extent that they support line people, not on the basis of the beauty or the elegance of their paper solutions to intractable problems.

▶ Promote managers (or promote to manager)—of line and staff functions alike—only those who create excitement among their people and colleagues from other functions; do not promote dull ducks, turf guardians, or those who do not take their greatest pleasure in the accomplishments of others, particularly their subordinates.

Success in today's environment will come when those on the front line are honored as heroes, and empowered to act—period. A prime leadership task is to ensure that honor goes to the line and those who support it most vigorously.

Review your actions at the end of each day. Have you made your "bias" for front-line operators—and for those on staffs who support them most vigorously—unmistakably clear?

L-6

Defer to the Front Line

Harvard Business Review: Everybody talks about ["Celtics Pride"]. It's at the heart of the Celtics' mystique. What is it?
Boston Celtics President Red Auerbach: It's the whole idea of caring.

From an interview in the
Harvard Business Review, March/April 1987

The "visible" half of execution—the marketing professionals—can perform only as well as the "invisible" operations area allows it to. Moreover, the quality of operations can also determine an institution's ability to innovate. . . . Executives can promote quality operations by giving that area an independent identity . . . [and] status along with identity. "Class" divisions between lending officers and backroom operators are crippling. Institutions that are serious about the quality of their operations give employees compensation, recognition and opportunities for advancement comparable to what they offer marketing professionals. Citibank made John Reed [now chairman] its youngest senior vice president [in 1969] largely due to his role in operations. At Goldman Sachs, the partner in charge of operations is widely regarded as the third most powerful person in the firm, and the firm actually recruits promising business school graduates for that function.

Amar Bhide
"Hustle as Strategy"
a *Harvard Business Review* article
on financial service institutions

I love 'em all. [The offensive linemen are] my guys. Anytime I felt bad about something, . . . I always went over to where they were warming up at practice. We would always warm up in groups—offensive linemen here, wide receivers there, running backs over here. . . . Somehow, just being with the offensive linemen always made me feel better. Maybe it was because they were such solid guys—solid as rocks.

John Madden
Football commentator
former NFL coach

John Sculley has masterminded a remarkable turnaround at Apple Computer. The nature of it is nicely captured in one comment: "Implementers aren't considered bozos anymore." That is, those who write the manuals, answer the phones, sell the product, spend time with dealers, build the product, and are engaged in constant improvement of the product are the new Apple heroes. There's nothing wrong with talented designers, to be sure. They are essential. But there is something very wrong with any company that is over-dependent upon talented designers to pull its bacon out of the fire.

Bacon will increasingly be pulled out of the fire at 2 A.M. on the loading dock and at the reservation center. That is, it is pulled out of the fire by the people who work on the firing line. The role of everyone else—from president to junior accountant—is to enhance the ability of the front line to do its job.

ARE YOU LINE-ORIENTED?

Here are a few of the indicators that reveal the status of line personnel:

1. Pay. There are two key indicators here—entry-level pay and managerial pay. Prescription P-6 and others described the high front-line pay at Andersen Corporation, Lincoln Electric, Federal Express, Worthington, Nucor, Nordstrom, and others. Pay was often "off the scale" by others' standards—and so was productivity—several *hundred* percent above average.

From my days at McKinsey & Co., I remember one study especially well. Over a fifteen-year period, senior staff executives at an old-line manufacturing firm came to be paid almost 60 percent more than senior line executives (with comparable titles). That is, an accounting boss, sitting on the corporate staff at Level 4, made half again as much as a manufacturing boss at the same level. What was important in this firm? It was clear as day—how close your office was to the chairman's, and the brilliance and beauty of your paper solutions. The staff ran the line. The bright young men and women on the way up wanted to get on that staff, and not get stuck in isolated factories, distribution centers, sales branches, or any other kind of operational function.

Managerial pay is a dead giveaway. To underscore the line's role, line managers (operations, sales, distribution) should be paid somewhat more than their staff (personnel, accounting) counterparts—or at least not paid less.

2. What's hot? What do the best and the brightest head for? Operations or the corporate controller's staff? The line-oriented firm's objective must be enhancement of the line jobs. Over the long haul, this can be best accomplished via the promotion pattern ("three of the last five general manager promotions went to people who spent most of their careers in the line functions"). The problem can be addressed immediately by: (1) insisting that entry-level college graduates or MBA recruits start on the line (those that don't buy in aren't hired), and (2) offering better pay and a clearer career track to those who start on the line, and (3) lavishing symbolic attention on line people.

3. Where the action is. Do people in your firm blanch at the prospect of a three-year tour as deputy director of the Spanish affiliate? Or distribution manager for the southwestern United States? Making "boondocks" operating jobs the plums (a chance to demonstrate independent initiative), rather than those closest to the throne, is essential to achieving a line orientation.

4. Who calls the shots. Does the operating review consist of a parade of lonely line people called in one by one for a ritual grilling by three top executives and twenty staffers—with another twenty staffers, with "backup data" by the pound, sitting in the anteroom? Or is the line "overrepresented," with a few key staff people in attendance? This indicator—attendance at decision-making forums— is a first-rate tip-off of a firm's orientation.

5. What the calendar says. Recall L-3 (leading by example) and L-4 (visible management). Quite simply, does senior management spend more time with customers, suppliers, and line operators—especially front-line people—than huddled in session with staffers?

This means both the chairman and the president. In some firms, the chairman is "Mr. Outside"—dealing with analysts, the board, etc.—and the president is "Mr. Operations." This is the GM pattern, for instance. It doesn't cut the mustard. The top gun must demonstrate commitment to the line—by time spent. This is especially so in this era of uncertainty, when the firm's top priority is often retooling line skills and reestablishing contact with long-neglected customers and distributors.

6. Who gets the recognition. Does the boss send notes congratulating young staffers on superb presentations, but fail to discover and praise similar accomplishments in the field—25, 250, or 2,500 miles away? The lion's share of recognition should go to line people; measure this *quantitatively*—track yourself by the week.

7. The language you use. Recall John Sculley's remark. Hang out at most corporate headquarters and you soon come to believe that in most firms everyone on the line is considered a "bozo." As one (line) friend put it to me: "They've never met a dumb marketing staffer or a smart sales manager in their lives." That's precisely the wrong feel. Linguistic disrespect leads to subtle—and not so subtle—denigration when decisions are being made and pay/honors are being apportioned.

8. What the "little things" reveal. Would a vice-president turn down an invitation to the chairman's dinner party at his Long Island estate in order to visit a new plant in County Cork, Ireland, because he wants to be with his newest troops on Christmas Eve? Would the chairman publicly applaud the decision? Or ignore it? Or would the hallway talk be about "naïve Joe"? "He'll learn. The rough edges wear off in time. He's spent too many years away from the pulsebeat [the halls of power]."

These and a host of other indicators provide clear evidence of the organization's concerns. The good news is that each of the eight can be managed. The first step is to take the list seriously, do an assessment of your own firm using a list like this—and then get meticulously to work reversing the polarity of the firm's interests, if it is not line-oriented.

LEADERSHIP THAT HONORS THE LINE

Pride in the Accomplishments of Others

A related trait is taking obvious pride in the work of others, especially people on the firing line. In *20 Teachers,* author Ken Macrorie talks about an extraordinary high school woodworking teacher, Sam Bush. Bush spent most of his time with Macrorie bragging about his charges: "Isn't this beautiful work?" "Do you see this mirror?" "Isn't that turning done beautifully?" "And the way that design is laid on there?" "That piece means something special to me because it was done by a boy who was falling apart in life and couldn't get it together in the shop either."

Bush takes genuine pride in his students' work. He describes his accomplishments, not in terms of techniques taught, but in terms of his genuine and transparent thrill at *their* accomplishments. Obvious as this may sound, it is at once unusual and a trait of exceptional leaders in all walks of life. (A psychologist's recent study of child-rearing practices employed by the parents of successful businesspersons concluded that constant, outright—and often public and obnoxious—bragging about the child's accomplishments topped the list of successful parenting traits.)

Bragging about the achievements of the front-line troops can rekindle long dormant spirits; it is also a matter of increasing importance, given the demand of the times for stellar contributions from every front-line person.

This idea can readily be turned into hard-boiled management advice: <u>Only promote people whose greatest pleasure is bragging about the accomplishments of their front-line troops.</u>

"Measuring" Managers' Attention to the Line

How do you "measure" it? Simple. Suppose you're a regional vice-president making a site visit to a hotel. Where does the property manager take you first? To her office to review "the numbers" or a "summary presentation"? Or is she bubbling with energy and determined to make you walk every inch of the property looking at tiny touches and meeting the people responsible for them?

Does she introduce you only to the four assistant managers, including one who finished the night shift three hours ago, whom she ordered to stay around? Or does she introduce you to everyone (and know them by name), beginning with the bellhops and housekeepers? Does she have them explain to you what they're doing, while she glows with pride? Or does she explain, while they hover in the background?

It's easy to make judgments, once you start focusing on these differences, which usually are this extreme. Be careful, though. You might have brought this on yourself. You, and perhaps several of your predecessors, may have clearly signaled that "I've seen a million hotels in my time"—and that you are interested in skipping the umpteenth tour of the scullery in favor of "getting into the numbers." That is, the first task is to get your own priorities straight and signal them unequivocally.

Incidentally, this same advice holds for the evaluation of staff managers. Do they bubble on about great analyses and paper coups? Or do they brag about Judy, who is on temporary assignment to Brazil for ninety days, to work on implementing a just-in-time inventory management system with the operations manager there? That is, do they brag about (1) their people and (2) their support for the line? Or do they emphasize their central watchdog-analyst's role?

Promotion Priority: Creating Excitement as a "Hard" Leadership Trait

Promote those people who create excitement, zest, and enthusiasm among their colleagues (before they become a boss), subordinates (after they become a boss), and even their peers in other functions (see also L-10). This applies to accounting or personnel supervisors as well as shift foreman in the factory and engineering section heads.

I clearly remember the advice my first boss gave me when I became a consultant at McKinsey & Company. The organization, on any given day, is divided into project teams. Selecting your next project makes or breaks your career—and your mental well-being. How do you select that next project? "It's simple," said my mentor. "Choose somebody you'd like to work with, whom you'd learn from, who would be fun to be around in a tense situation." He shocked me by adding: "Don't worry *at all* about the content of the project." He was so right. An uninspiring boss can turn the most exciting strategic project into a dispiriting exercise. The genuinely engaged and enthusiastic boss can turn a dull inventory management problem into the most exciting thing since NASA put Neil Armstrong on the moon.

The key is to trust your judgment, not psychobabble spewed forth by the Ph.D.s in the personnel department. Promote people who love people, who cherish their subordinates' accomplishments, and who create excitement. It's easy. People with these traits usually show their mettle about midway through their first week on the job. They're talented, fun to be around—and they bring the place to a high pitch of spirited performance, years before the mantle of manager is first placed upon them.

Promote Leaders Who Lead

This prescription epitomizes the common-sense underpinnings of the entire set. Great football franchises—Pittsburgh, Oakland/Los Angeles, Washington, Chicago, Miami, Dallas—are marked, over the course of decades, less by Hall of Fame quarterbacks and halfbacks than by top-flight nose tackles, free safeties, linebackers, centers, and special teams. It's not that marketers and engineers (quarterbacks and fullbacks) aren't important. They are. It's just that the emphasis must be placed—especially today, when all competition is as intense as NFL competition—on the people who more fully determine the outcome *over time*—those troops on the line. In fact, each of these teams has had great "marketers" (Roger Staubach of Dallas, Ken Stabler of Oakland) from time to time. But the basis for sustaining performance has been year-in-and-year-out front-line brilliance.

Basically, I'm asking that you take leadership seriously. Promote into leadership positions those who perform like leaders. That sounds silly—at first. But we too often give our support chiefly to the "squared away" young man or woman who gives brilliant presentations, who is terrific to be around at lunch or dinner with an important client. I'm not against analysis and good presentations and social graces in front of clients. But I am in favor of understanding that success ultimately comes from making the implementers into heroes.

The point, as always it seems, is a "must-do." Executing the winning customer strategies (C-1 through C-4 especially) requires line leadership—the willingness of front-line people to take the initiative, to listen to customers, to act fast. The desirability of great quarterbacks and marketers is not diminished. However, the presence of great linemen and nursing staff is decisive for future success.

FIRST STEPS

1. Go back to the eight questions that determine a line-versus-staff mindset. How do you stack up? Use your next visit as fodder: Change your routine in five ways that enhance the line, not at the expense of staff, but to make it first among equals.
2. Hold off and reflect upon a current promotion decision. Are you evaluating the candidate on the basis of (a) his or her attitudes toward subordinates' accomplishments and (b) his or her ability to create excitement? That is, are you really looking at *leadership?* Or are you using technical traits as the primary determinant?
3. I can give no advice on making yourself care and enhancing your desire to be around offensive linemen, except for one small thing: Spend time with them. They're the greatest. I think you'll soon see that. If you don't, I sincerely propose that you quit and become a management consultant.

L-7

SUMMARY

Delegation of responsibility has been a central topic in management texts through the ages. But today's marketplace, which demands heretofore unheard-of front-line freedom to initiate far-reaching actions, propels the subject toward the top of the list. To be responsive, we must:

▶ Examine each act of delegation through the lenses of (1) really letting go, (2) not inadvertently "taking back," and (3) carefully setting the context for delegation by (a) establishing high standards, (b) developing commitment to a jointly shared vision, and (c) encouraging mutual faith and respect.

Delegation is "hot"! We must learn to let go, or suffer the consequences of unacceptably slow action-taking. Other prescriptions, such as P-8, have urged the elimination of most traditional forms of control. So we must learn the subtle art of delegation anew—more delegation than ever with fewer than normal formal controls.

Increase true delegation—radically. But first institute a new and paperless form of control—a shared vision (L-2) and remarkably high standards. Review every act of delegation, assuming such alternate controls have been established, to see if you are "really letting go" to the extent required to inspire others to take true and vigorous responsibility. Carefully monitor your casual remarks to those to whom you've delegated, ensuring that you don't inadvertently rescind the grant of autonomy.

Delegate

The Tower Board Report issued early in 1987 on the Iran-Contra affair gave delegation in general a black eye. That's unfortunate. The thrust of virtually all of these prescriptions is freeing up the organization to work faster and with less traditional hierarchy and supervision. That is, much more delegation is required today than ever before.

DELEGATION: THE SINE QUA NON OF EMPOWERMENT

Even without considering today's stepped-up need for delegation, the plain fact is that nine of ten managers haven't delegated enough. Oh, yes, they think they have. They hand over tasks and pass out assignments routinely. But only rarely does the "delegate" really catch fire and become empowered with true ownership—and its concomitant, the true burden of responsibility.

What goes wrong? To begin with, there's the difference between letting go and Really Letting Go. But wait, you say, doesn't Really Letting Go mean anarchy, chaos, and confusion, i.e., of the Iran-Contra sort?

Effective delegation does mean Really Letting Go—for instance, high spending authority (outrageously high, by old standards), relatively infrequent formal reporting, geographic separation, and, above all, psychological distancing—in other words, the works. But . . .

There is a big, qualifying "but"—true delegation, of the Really Letting Go variety, will result in superb performance only if these four counterforces are simultaneously at play:

▶ The boss (that is, delegator) has ridiculously high standards, which she or he lives, transmits, and uniformly demands.
▶ The boss has a crystal-clear vision about where the ship's headed (see L-2) in which she or he and the delegate have faith (in fact, the delegate is made the living embodiment of the vision).
▶ The boss wholeheartedly believes in people, and will be deeply disappointed, as a mentor, if the delegate fails or at least fails to make a herculean effort—all

the more so since the boss has made it clear (albeit indirectly) how far out on a limb she or he has gone to let the delegate take on this task.

▶ The boss lets the delegate bite off a lot more than he can chew if he is insistent upon doing so, but stops just a touch short of letting him bite off an absurd amount.

Subtle Cues Add Up to Really Letting Go: Four Cases

Take this seemingly simple case. British mystery writer P. D. James is also a superb management analyst; here's an apparently innocuous passage from her 1986–87 best-seller, *A Taste for Death:*

Dalgliesh had accepted that the agreement must be kept; [Kate Miskin] would meet Carole Washburn alone. He had given her no instruction and offered no advice. Other senior officers would have been tempted to remind her of the importance of the meeting, but this wasn't his way. She respected him for it, but it increased her burden of responsibility. Everything might depend on how she handled the encounter. [Adam Dalgliesh is James's Sherlock Holmes, a respected senior detective. Kate Miskin is the only woman in Dalgliesh's new, elite unit. Carole Washburn is a murder suspect.]

That single paragraph, within the novel's context, reveals most of the attributes of successful delegation. Dalgliesh really does let go—on several levels. Most obviously, he lets the relatively junior Miskin go alone to a most crucial meeting. But there are several additional levels of letting go involved. To begin with, Dalgliesh's elite unit is new, and has been formed despite political objections. This is its first "visible" case. Moreover, the case is dragging, and Dalgliesh is being sniped at by the press and entrenched political enemies. Under these circumstances, to allow the youthful Miskin to go ahead, alone, takes on added significance. Dalgliesh is risking opprobrium from the press, from his own bosses, and from within his team as well—his seasoned colleagues are perturbed at his appointment of a relatively young woman. Finally, at the deepest, though seemingly most insignificant, level of letting go—that is, the Really Letting Go level—Dalgliesh pointedly has not reminded Miskin of the meeting's importance, a fact that she is well aware of (as you and I would be).

What does she doubtless feel? Terror, along with pride, at being on Dalgliesh's team. He is a stern taskmaster, seldom given to praise. His standards are widely known to be Olympian. But she also knows that he has faith in her. The meeting sequence is just the most recent indication. Dalgliesh is not sentimental, and certainly no radical feminist. She has been chosen early in her career because he thinks she's darned good.

In sum, we see the full-blown paradox of true delegation in this brief vignette. On the one hand, the boss lets go: (1) formal delegation, (2) a monumentally important task, (3) he is sticking his neck way out by delegating (both internal and external foes are sharpening their knives), and (4) he ups the ante by pointedly not reminding her of all of the above.

On the other hand, she has hardly been sent on an anarchist's mission. That is: (1) the boss is a commanding professional and has made it clear that she's in this position because she's talented and he trusts her skills, even though he knows it will force her to test the limit of her capabilities, and (2) his standards are extremely high. The autonomy granted is real and significant, but it is matched by the psychological pressure to perform up to one's limits and to the highest standards.

Consider three shorter cases. Two involve me, the third a close friend. I began to learn to "really" delegate only after being forced into it. Ten years ago I was heading a small unit that was doing quite well. I had a stellar supporting cast. Yet, when crucial presentations came, I made them. And why not, since I'd been on board since the beginning—and my superiors had made it clear to me that it was my show—and my neck.

As the unit was approaching its third anniversary, I was in a severe automobile accident—knocked completely out of action for two or three months. My major interest became soap operas and midday TV game shows. Then, as the reports began to come in, it became abundantly clear what a talented team I had. It was disconcerting, but one heck of a learning experience. Rather than behave decently (as I would have put it then) and cancel the numerous engagements that I had booked, every single activity had been taken on by a team member. And while, a decade later, I still harbor the suspicion that I might have done any one activity 2 percent better than they, the reality is that a dozen people caught fire—all at once.

In the fall of 1986, a similar event occurred. A colleague had made a promise years before to contribute to a significant project that I too was interested in. She never quite got around to it. I kept my hand in, often bailing out the project before an about-to-pass deadline with last-minute heroics, all the while wondering why my colleague's promise remained unfulfilled. Then a family tragedy caused me to be unavoidably out of touch as a critical project deadline approached. Without a word from me, my long-dormant associate grabbed the reins. Once more, I'd like to believe that I could have done the task 1 percent better—we all hold such rationalizations dear. What I do know is that out of the woodwork she came, and the task was brilliantly done. Now her superb contributions are routine. We've still never discussed any of this.

A close friend had a similar experience. He had been letting go of a big operation of his making for about two years. Rather, he had been "sorta letting go." Suddenly, he was gone—on a long-planned trip, 10,000 miles from home. His interests didn't change entirely, however, and just three weeks after departing he called to get an update—and discovered that once it had become clear that he had "really gone," a series of hitherto unthinkable things had occurred. One senior colleague, in particular, had suddenly become wholly engaged in the operation—and effectively so, to the point of patching up a very frayed relationship with another principal player.

Each of these three examples involves some subtle attributes of Really Letting Go. "Sorta letting go," it's clear, doesn't work. It took a life-threatening accident, an unequivocally about-to-be-missed deadline, and a several-month-long, 10,000-mile journey to do the trick. In every instance there was not a shred of doubt on the part of the newly inspired participants that the "boss" had let go.

Beware the Subtle Cues That Add Up to "Really Taking Back"

The process is extremely delicate, which explains why so few do really catch fire as we'd hoped at the time of the act of delegation. Bob Townsend relates a cautionary tale: "You tell a guy to get on with it. He's on his own. You make that clear. Two days later, on the way out at about seven in the evening, you poke your head into his office ever so briefly. You say, as a last, inadvertent aside, 'Have you checked with Bernie on your plans?' If you had stuck around another ten seconds to watch his reaction, you would have seen physical deflation, like a balloon when its air is let out. And his color fades, too. You just stole the whole damn thing back from him, and in about five seconds. And worst of all, you didn't mean it. Or even know it, for that matter. I mean, he would have checked with Bernie anyway!"

The first four "case studies" related above all suggested that moving to true delegation means crossing an imaginary line which transfers psychological ownership to the delegates: This is the real thing, there's no going back. Recall the example from *A Taste for Death:* The apparently trivial act of refraining from reminding Kate Miskin that an important meeting was, in fact, important (nothing, it would seem, could be more trivial) was the key to upping the ante and putting the monkey squarely on her back. Townsend's caveat is frightening—how easy it is to then grab the whole thing back.

Checklist: Are You Letting Go?

Whenever you are delegating, then, you must address a lengthy series of questions:

▶ Have you first transmitted the overarching vision with clarity? That is, does the delegate, through demonstrated behavior, clearly "buy in"?
▶ Have you set high standards in the past that make it clear what level of performance you demand?
▶ Have you demonstrated in the past, in small ways, that you trust the delegate's judgment?
▶ Do you have a track record for jumping in at the last moment (before a deadline) to pull the irons of others (to whom you've delegated) out of the fire?
▶ Do you consciously avoid attending meetings (i.e., avoid the seemingly innoc-

uous excuse for attending: "just to be informed; it's your show") when the delegate is meeting with (a) his or her team, (b) outsiders, such as customers or vendors, (c) more senior people (including your own boss)?

▶ Have you bitten your tongue and stayed out of the delegate's hair when "back channel" reports (i.e., gossip) inform you that "Joe's in over his head," "Joe didn't check with me on thus and such"?

▶ Have you staved off your boss (or staff experts) who want status reports ("He's awfully young, I assume you're on top of this")?

▶ Have you avoided excessive reporting (a paragraph a week is okay—preferably handwritten; 10 pages is not okay)?

▶ Have you given the manager formal authority (a high dollar sign-off level) to insure he doesn't need to come running every five minutes?

▶ Have you provided (in most cases) a separate physical location for his/her team (at least an enclosed, separate space; at best a grubby space in another building—even a block away helps)?

▶ When she or he calls (or stops by) for advice or to "touch bases," do you (a) avoid giving direct orders ("Hey, I'm rusty on that, you might go see Mary or Jean" is the best response) and (b) keep the "touch bases" conversation from being an approval-granting (by you) session (practice the art of the slightly disengaged "uh huh," rather than "sounds good" or "good work")?

▶ Have you made it clear, by your total (and visible) inaction as a critical deadline approaches that (a) you are not going to jump in and (b) you are not even going to raise the volume of questions ("uh, Joe, uh, three days to the presentation, huh?" He knows that!)?

ESTABLISHING THE CONTEXT FOR DELEGATION

I've pounded on the idea of letting go, and its subtlety and fragility. Let's take a closer look at the issues of faith, mutual respect, and high standards. Napoleon and Moshe Dayan had something in common. Napoleon made it clear, in word and in deed, that he would not leave wounded soldiers behind to be savaged by the enemy. A crucial part of the Dayan legend likewise involves the lengths to which he went to ensure that his wounded Israeli soldiers would not be picked up by their foes.

The same chord was struck by legendary Green Bay Packer coach Vince Lombardi. He said that you didn't have to like your football players but you must love them and respect them. The University of Alabama's equally legendary coach, Bear Bryant, was in the same mold. Former Oakland Raider quarterback Ken Stabler said that Bryant was indeed a tough son-of-a-gun; but he quickly added that you could abide it, because Bryant made it abundantly clear that he had total respect for you.

Napoleon, Dayan, Lombardi, and Bryant asked their soldiers and players, time and again, to do the impossible, to do more than they had ever dreamed they were capable of. And time and again, to the dismay of so many enemies and opponents, the people responded. The bosses were tough. But beneath it was abiding love and respect for the people who were asked to go out and meet a challenge greater than they had ever met before.

Management expert Karl Weick studied musicians. In one experiment, he gave a talented jazz ensemble a new piece of music that no member had ever seen. He told them it was a little-known piece by a famous composer. Then he gave them a second novel piece, which was in fact by the same composer; this time, however, he told them it was by Joe Doaks. The experiment was repeated numerous times with several groups to ensure the validity of the results.

When musicians played the new (to them) work of the unknown (Doaks) the first few times, they made numerous mistakes. However, their first attempt with the new (to them) piece by the "renowned composer" resulted in far fewer mistakes. That is, the confidence induced by the famous name alone led to substantially more competence on the part of the musicians from the outset.

Why include Napoleon, Dayan, Lombardi, Bryant, and a jazz ensemble in a discussion of delegation? Most treatments of delegation focus almost exclusively on the letting go, with a bit on formal controls needed to keep track. Few discussions of delegation emphasize the role of faith, belief, vision, caring, intensity, and the psychodynamics that the effective leader sets up with his followers. To discuss delegation without this misses the point.

Small things enhance delegation. Even smaller things destroy it. It happens in a context. Paradoxes abound, such as really letting go, but establishing an inspiring moral context for the importance of the task—including the leader's obvious confidence and caring.

The Mayor Believes in You

Laurie Schwartz had worked for Mayor Don Schaefer but had taken off to pursue a career in the private sector. After a chance get-together at a Christmas party, he once again tapped her. She had indicated that she might be available for one of his famous "special projects." Without another word, he invited her to a meeting. He didn't tell her what it was about, even after she joined a confab of senior business people from Charles Street.

With amenities quickly out of the way, the mayor got down to business. "I want you to meet Laurie Schwartz. She," he declared, "is now Ms. Charles Street. She's going to get us going here." (Baltimore's main business street was not being transformed at a pace that was up to Schaefer's soaring standards.) And that was that. Charles Street was Schwartz's. The mayor dragged her back down to City Hall, where the city's department heads were assembled. "Laurie's back," the mayor announced. "She's running Charles Street, and you're to do whatever she says."

The charge was about that simple, though the execution obviously was not. A couple of years later, Charles Street was fast becoming a gem, with over 100 million new dollars invested in it. Laurie Schwartz was the cheerleader, the quarterback, the de facto chairman of the board.

Did Schaefer really believe that she could pull off this miracle? One suspects he did. It is clear that he delegated the responsibility to her unequivocally. She was out on a limb. She had said she was somewhat interested in doing something for him; in return, he had lobbed a key part of the city her way.

Schaefer had done a frightening thing to her. She believed in him, believed in his compelling vision, believed in his track record of making the impossible seem almost routine. Moreover, she believed that he believed in her, and that he wouldn't have done this "to her" unless he thought she *could* pull it off. So she now had the monkey on her back for a piece of his—their—vision. It was her ball, in her court. Deliver or else, her psyche said; and that's precisely what His Honor had intended.

DELEGATE TO ACT "HORIZONTALLY"

Delegation has traditionally meant "pushing decision-making to the lowest level." That has been the thrust of this prescription, too. The implicit (or explicit) target is the individual and his or her work group (see P-2 on self-managing teams, for instance).

But there is another "half" of delegation, growing in importance. That is, delegation to the front line and self-managing group to act "horizontally," to seek out fast connections with other functions, without checking "up."

This "horizontal" delegation was a theme of P-8 and P-9. It is also the theme of the next prescription, L-8, which urges nothing less than a full-blown "horizontal style" of management.

FIRST STEPS

1. Make it a habit to examine and reexamine regularly every important act of delegation. Have you really snipped all the strings—physical, psychological, etc.—necessary to transfer psychological ownership? While I believe as a rule in spontaneity, also take care that your language in chance encounters doesn't make that monkey jump back your way.
2. But examine the context equally carefully. Is there real agreement about the vision? Are your standards known to be high?

L-8

SUMMARY

We must pursue fast-paced action at all costs, and therefore:

▶ Vigorously and gleefully, with all hands participating, take the lead in destroying the trappings of bureaucracy.

▶ Manage the organization "horizontally"—that is, insist that "vertical" obfuscating be replaced with proactive (no checking "up"), "horizontal," front-line cooperation in pursuit of fast action.

Test. Try. Modify. Test. Act. Or: Act, act, act. To do so means to become an avowed and public hater of bureaucracy, and to ceaselessly pursue more spontaneous communication among functions (at the front line).

Let no day pass without acting as a visible model by engaging in at least one feat of bureaucracy destruction. Ensure that most of these publicized feats of bureaucracy-bashing are in service to a "horizontal style" of management, which minimizes up and down (vertical) communication and replaces it with fast, front-line cooperation across functional boundaries.

Pursue "Horizontal" Management by Bashing Bureaucracy

In December 1986, I gave a speech to young graduates of the U.S. Navy's Civil Engineer Corps Officers School. The centerpiece was a list of ten suggestions. At the top: "I beg each and every one of you to develop a passionate and public hatred for bureaucracy." I meant it.

The central point of this prescription is its proactive nature. Don't appoint a paperwork reduction committee (see P-10). Such an approach might be dandy, but I mean something much more proactive. Become an emotional, vociferous, repetitive, public hater of bureaucracy. Become a nuisance!

ENERGETIC BUREAUCRACY-BASHING

Rant and rave. Tear up papers. Refuse to read them. Don't attend meetings. You may put your career in jeopardy in the short run, for having a lousy attendance record. But if you don't put it in jeopardy for that, it will likely be in jeopardy in the long run, when the business goes bust or the city can't pay its debts or the weapons system won't work.

Be outrageous. Get rid of all your file cabinets—think of it as the white-collar equivalent of installing a just-in-time inventory management system. Put big cardboard boxes around your desk, and throw all the junk you receive into them—unread. Put a big red label on the boxes: "This week's unread paperwork."

Whenever you get a report, read only the first two pages. Call the sender: "I didn't understand your report."

"I'll come down to your office and explain."

Your office, a short time later:

"Of course you didn't understand it, you only read the first two pages of my thirty-nine-page report."

"My eyes tire. I can't read anything longer than two pages. It's age, I'm sure. I'm thirty-eight [or twenty-six or fifty-two] now."

"I think I get the point. Shorten it up."

"No, you don't get it at all. Next time, just come down and explain—like you did just now. Don't write a damn report!"

Be colorful. Have a Friday afternoon ceremony, once a month at 4 P.M. Bring beer and invite your people out to the incinerator. Burn all the paper you received but did not read.

Invite them next month to a spot in the woods. Bring beer and shovels. Dig a hole. Tote out a small wooden casket. In it place all the forms and rules and discontinued reports that you and they have tagged for immediate elimination. If you've got real nerve, bury the office copier next to the casket. Wear mad garb. Lead a chant as the casket and copier are lowered into the ground: "No more paper, no more forms."

(Yes, I know you may be the highly respectable chairman of a staid $1.5 billion company. "Antic" is not exactly your middle name. But then what's so bloody honorable about your miserable earnings record and the 4,000 jobs you've shipped offshore in the last six years?)

You've got two choices: (1) find your own style of doing this or (2) go broke. I realize the danger of losing the reader here: "You can't do that around here." "It's not me." I urge you to reassess those oh-so-reasonable responses: (1) We all agree that urgency is essential to survival today. (2) We all agree that getting rid of "bureaucracy" induces urgency (no number of "motivational devices," including gobs of incentive money, will overcome our petrified forest of barriers). (3) And, sadly, we all agree (those of us who are honest, anyway) that we don't know what to do about the problem, other than rail at it. (4) Therefore, I am merely suggesting that we match the need to address these radically shifting times with a radical and proactive strategy: fun, energy, anger, participation, vigor—and time and attention—in urgent pursuit of demolishing the barriers, especially the excessive "vertical processing" of information that slows action down among functions at the front by orders of magnitude.

Involvement and Celebration: Part and Parcel of Bureaucracy-Bashing

Make bureaucracy-demolition fun—and participative. Get everyone to nominate forms and procedures for elimination. Have a committee, made up principally of junior line people, assess the suggestions and act on them within a week. Insist that they accept at least 50 percent.

Give an award to every individual who makes a nomination, a bigger award for every nomination accepted—then group and unit awards. Perhaps even put "anti-bureaucracy effectiveness" in your performance evaluation scheme.

Have a semiannual or annual luncheon or dinner, labeled: "Beating Back Bureaucracy: Luncheon of Irate Red-Tape Cutters." (Bronze shears of various sizes would make nice trophies.)

Formalize a separate, anti-bureaucracy suggestion system, individual- or group-based. There's no end to such ideas. Fun and participation are the keys. A more serious matter—survival—is the goal.

Is a project stuck at a fairly important milestone? A negotiation with a supplier bogging down? Spend lavishly on airfare (and long-distance phone calls). Get on the plane, visit with the supplier or customer or project team—and don't leave until the darn thing is fixed. Forget the committee meetings that you missed in the process—most of them were to worry about how to deal with other project teams around the company that were stuck or with other negotiations that were bogged down.

In fact, go a step further. Give awards to the persons who spent the most money (or logged the most miles) in pursuit of unblocking stalled projects or negotiations; give a concomitant award to the person who missed the most meetings while in pursuit of speeding up stalled affairs. (See L-10 for a broader discussion of inducing a sense of urgency.)

INSTALLING A "HORIZONTAL STYLE" OF MANAGEMENT

Consider your group to be a company. Every other function is, by definition, either a vendor or a customer. Treat them with the respect and care with which you'd deal with outsiders. Practice relationship management, customer listening, customer visiting, and, mainly, reward your "salespersons"—i.e., everyone—for getting and keeping your "customers" happy. Hold "vendor"/ "customer"-appreciation days and open houses.

Suppose you are in manufacturing. Invite the division controller's staff to your next beer bust. Send one of your shift foremen to the chief cost accountant's office on a sixty-day temporary assignment. Teach "customer-serving" habits—accounting in this case—to your supervisors. Send thank-you notes to an accountant who did a job swiftly for you, with a copy to his or her boss and boss's boss.

Devote 15 percent of your monthly operations presentation to specific examples of smooth cross-functional cooperation. Devote 20 percent of your discretionary bonus money to awards for those in other functions who have assisted you; devote another 20 percent to rewarding your own people for meritorious acts of proactive skid greasing.

Hold a surprise party for a team from MIS that took the trouble to spend a weekend getting bugs ironed out of a new program's software—to help your unit. Send one of your machine operators to a full-blown, twenty-week information systems department training program so that he or she can be a well-schooled prime contact when the next new manufacturing software package is on the drawing boards.

Keep daily or weekly score for yourself or your unit: For instance, perform a dozen "barrier bashers" each month.

Poke fun at the bureaucracy, bureaucrats, and barriers that interfere with "horizontal" management. Regardless of how deeply you buy and live this message, you will still act like a bureaucrat and turf guardian several times a day. That's wonderful news, because it means you can unfailingly preface an attack on others with an attack on yourself!

At each weekly staff meeting, consider including a "report card" on yourself. Cite your violations: paperwork excess, turf guardianship, and so on. Have a half-dozen such categories. Give yourself a grade on each one—a bureaucrat's grade on your dealings with each key "customer"/"vendor" functions you work with—and an overall grade. Then post the results. Give people hell, lightheartedly (present a duncecap) or in earnest, who have "checked in" with you on a horizontal-action issue instead of acting on their own.

Have a different person present a report card on your function as a whole each week. Anybody who has the temerity to give the function an A on anything buys lunch for everyone and makes coffee all the next week. The chosen report-card preparer should be encouraged to spend several hours collecting instructive stories and preparing the report card.

The logic is impeccable: Two towering hindrances to quality, service, responsiveness, fast innovation, and people involvement are functional barriers—"vertical" management—and bureaucracy. Therefore, it follows logically that two of the leader's top strategic priorities ought to be proactively attacking bureaucracy and working at that "horizontal style."

"Hot Buttons"

In *The Leadership Challenge,* Jim Kouzes and Barry Posner tell of a productive barrier-bashing device that was also great fun: "At Sequent Computer, company president Casey Powell at one critical point handed out buttons. Most of the company would wear green 'How Can I Help?' buttons, but people on the critical path would get red 'Priority' buttons. People with green buttons were to do anything to remove obstacles for those people with the red buttons. Powell wore a green button. . . ."

FIRST STEPS

Review the numerous practical, and participative, devices for establishing "horizontal" management included in this prescription. In the next thirty days, select two activities and begin to implement them.

L-9

SUMMARY

To up the odds of survival, leaders at all levels must become obsessive about change. They must:

▶ In the matter of formal and informal evaluations of leaders (managers at all levels), focus less on measures that deal with such things as budgets, and more on the explicit questions: "What, exactly, have you changed lately? What, exactly, have your subordinates changed lately?" Additionally, every meeting should commence with a rapid, explicit review of exactly what has been changed since the last session, even if it was yesterday; every newsletter should emphasize change; and so on.

Change must become the norm, not cause for alarm. The bottom line: If you can't point to something specific that's being done differently from the way it was done when you came to work this morning, you have not "lived," for all intents and purposes; you surely have not earned your paycheck by any stretch of the imagination. Furthermore, the incremental changes of today must almost unfailingly be in support of non-incremental change— that is, a bold goal to be achieved in record time.

Make "What, exactly, have you changed?" the most common question in the organization. Ask it a dozen times a day, at least.

L-9

Evaluate Everyone on His or Her Love of Change

Are sales consistent with your forecast? Did you exceed budget? These are reasonable and important questions. They are standard fare for performance appraisals or quarterly or monthly reviews. They deal, as the experts say they should, with results that presumably are more or less under the manager's control.

But I believe these are the wrong questions for the times. They are tangential to the main event. We should be asking something more fundamental: "What, precisely, exactly, unequivocally, have your changed—today?" And: "Are you sure?" And: "What's next?" And: "Exactly what bold goal does the change support?"

The questions are deceptively simple. Most often they go unasked. Yet I firmly believe they are far and away the most crucial questions for all today's managers, at all levels.

A vice-president from IBM said flatly that this question—What have you changed?—has become the most frequent query at all levels throughout his firm. Discussions with IBMers down the line confirm his assertion. And well they should. IBM's industry is in chaos—and will remain so for years—and there is mounting evidence that on some dimensions the giant company has not been keeping pace.

From computers to retailing to health care to government, managers of all functions and at all levels are confronted with an unprecedented amount of turmoil. Just over a dozen years ago, when I was working with McKinsey & Co., my colleagues and I didn't even bother to take inflation into account while making twenty-year cash-flow projections for quarter-billion-dollar petrochemical facilities. Moreover, we were confident in our ability to predict supply, demand, and commodity prices for wheat and corn (we were concerned with a fertilizer facility) with a fine degree of accuracy, over a twenty-year period. Feedstock (oil and gas) prices, we felt, were also predictable. As for the value of the dollar compared to other currencies—it never crossed our minds to consider wide fluctuations.

Today all of those variables—and a host of others—are just that: highly variable (see Part I). Nothing is "for sure" over a *three-month* time horizon, let alone one of *twenty years.*

NEW TIMES DEMAND NEW QUESTIONS

This radically new environment demands radically new forms of organization and radically new forms of evaluation of those who manage. To be sure, making budget remains a valid aim. But while it may be a necessary condition for survival, it is no longer even close to a sufficient one—for the shift supervisor, let alone the division general manager.

The IBM executive continues: "We must reexamine every relationship, every element of doing business, every process, every procedure. The only plausible criterion for success is: 'Are you changing enough, rapidly enough, to successfully confront the future?' "

To adapt to a radically altered environment, each procedure—in MIS, accounting, personnel, manufacturing, product development, distribution—that links up with other functions, each relationship with suppliers and distributors, must be "zero-based," that is, wholly reassessed and, in nine cases out of ten, changed in its essentials. We must, then, measure each manager directly on his or her ability to change things dramatically.

How Many? How Much? How Fast? How Bold?

Are you looking for new opportunities to exploit technology? Opportunities to, say, link your data base electronically with that of your key—and probably even smaller—suppliers and middlemen and customers? Have you launched a new training program to expose all hands to one or another aspect of an altered future? Are front-line people being empowered to change things and cross traditional functional boundaries at a moment's notice without checking "up" first? Are temporary organizations being created on twenty-four hours' notice, and then scrubbed fifteen or thirty days later when the task is done?

It's no longer adequate to ask: "How many people, up from whatever last year, did you process in basic sales training?" It's necessary to ask:

▶ "How, *exactly,* have you changed basic sales training to match possible future scenarios—within the last three months?"

▶ "How much material in the sales refresher course has been updated in the last six months?"

▶ "How many new case studies are you using?"

▶ "Why *these* new cases?"

▶ "Whom have you recently asked to advise you on course content whom you *never* asked before?"

▶ "Are you *sure* that your advisers—from inside and outside the firm—are diverse enough to mirror the changing conditions in the real world?"

▶ Is all of this change dramatic enough/fast enough to allow us to surge ahead of our competitors—or at least keep pace with the new ones entering the market each day?

CREATING NEW RITUALS

"What have you changed lately?," "How fast are you changing?," and "Are you pursuing bold enough change goals?" must become pressing questions asked of any manager, at any level, in any function, as a matter of course. For instance, during each staff meeting, go around the table posing the question to each colleague. Don't spend much time, perhaps no more than ten minutes for ten people. But do it, ritualistically. Make the simple question a prime element in your formal performance appraisal system, as well as in your informal monthly sit-down appraisal: "What have you changed? How much have you changed? What are you planning to change next? What are your direct-reports changing? What have they changed in the last two days, two weeks, two months? How bold are the goals of your change program?"

My assessment of the surprising continued vitality of 3M, PepsiCo, and Citicorp, arguably three of the fastest-moving giant firms in the United States, is that they are, above all, impatient. They'll reorganize on a dime, while others barely have the energy to do so every half-dozen years. In fact, my own measure is that if you aren't reorganizing, pretty substantially, once every six to twelve months, you're probably out of step with the times. These firms don't stand on ceremony. They never stop exploring ways to get it right—for now. And they don't fret much about getting it wrong—as long as it's fixed fast. They are brash experimenters, moving in tandem—through error and trial—with the pace of the dynamic markets in which they participate. And yet even they are showing signs of slippage; remember the opening sentence of this book: There are no excellent companies. No one big (almost no one at all), in my judgment, is changing fast enough.

DEALING WITH THE ARGUMENTS OF NAYSAYERS

There are three routine rebuttals to this idea. The first is: "Aren't you advocating wheel-spinning? You don't really want change for change's sake, now, do you?"

I'd be the first to acknowledge that I've seen many instances of very unproductive, frenzied behavior. I don't support that. The manager's job is to make sure that frenzy for frenzy's sake does not occur. On the other hand, I'm not a Pollyanna. I don't believe in pure win-win situations. There is something to be traded off. In today's environment, when you boil it all down, the principal enemy is inertia, in smaller firms as well as in large ones. Thus, on net, a fair dose of change for change's sake, even including some wheel spinning, is preferable to continued inertia.

The second argument is more fundamental: "You've gone on and on about work-force commitment and achieving the highest level of quality and service. Don't these things, which by their nature suggest stability (how can anything be better than best?), fly in the face of 'changing everything'?" Once more, the answer is not simple. Constant change programs surely do threaten many people, especially traditional supervisors and middle managers. But constant change is thoroughly consistent with pursuing perfection in quality and service. Indeed, it is a must, for no one among the increasing array of competitors is standing pat. In the time it takes to read this prescription, Toyota will have implemented another fifty suggestions—that is, will have gotten better (there is no best for long).

But the threat posed to stability by constant, incremental changes is the least of it. For I have just proposed radically changing the organization's structure annually or even more frequently—it's a must. Changing all the procedures and then changing them again—another must. Smashing the market into bits, and then smashing it into even finer bits—a must as well. Restlessly altering the structures and markets and procedures depends upon keeping the vision and value system constant, more constant and more prominent than ever before—replacing control by procedure with control by vision and trust. The vision and managers' consistent, daily actions in support of it is the sea anchor, the basis for keeping people from running aground as the waves of change toss them to and fro.

Yes, it is a paradox (see also L-1): In the face of more change, more stability (but not the paper-driven kind) is essential. Charts and boxes and stability based upon lengthy job descriptions and your place in the organizational structure must be replaced by vision, values, and stability based on trust.

The final argument: "You keep asking for pursuit of incremental change; now you're saying 'dramatic change,' 'bold goals.' Can you reconcile the two?" Yes, on two scores. First, there is no choice. The goals must be bold, even to stand still. Hence incrementalism must always be in pursuit of the dramatic minimum improvements set out in these prescriptions.

Moreover, the most efficient and effective route to bold change is the participation of everyone, every day, in incremental change (see I-1 on small starts and I-3 on pilots, especially). Most bold change is the result of a hundred thousand tiny changes that culminate in a bold product or procedure or structure. The dramatic success symbol is usually just that, a symbol. The road to it is paved with a million experiments, a million false steps—and the wholehearted participation of everyone.

THE ACID TEST: CHANGE IS THE MANAGER'S DAY-TO-DAY BOTTOM LINE

Lately I've been ending my speeches with a snide observation which directly concerns this prescription: "If you are interested in keeping your jobs, ask yourself at the end of the day, every day, 'What exactly and precisely and explicitly is being done in my work area differently from the way it was done when I came to work in the morning?' The average manager starts each and every day as an expense item ('wealth dissipator,' in the words of Brunswick's Jack Reichert), not a revenue enhancer. You must earn the right to draw your substantial managerial salaries. The only way to do so is by making things different and better. Different and better today can only mean—changed, acted upon. If you can't put your hands on something—a coaching session that's leading to demonstrably new behavior, a changed form or eliminated rule— that's being done differently in the afternoon from the way it was done in the morning, then you haven't been alive." Furthermore, that specific something changed today had better have been changed in pursuit of a very bold goal (i.e., a 90 percent decrease in defects in the next thirty-six months). That is, the moment's tangible change must be in pursuit of dramatic change.

It's tough medicine. The manager, in today's world, doesn't get paid to be a "steward of resources," a favored term not so many years ago. He or she gets paid for one and only one thing—to make things better (incrementally and dramatically), make things different (incrementally and dramatically), to change things, to act—today.

FIRST STEPS

What exactly, precisely, have you changed today? What precise bold goal is that change connected with? Ask yourself. Ask everyone, junior or senior, with whom you came in contact this very day. Repeat, daily, for the rest of your career!

L-10

SUMMARY

Since our foremost need is to change more, faster, we must:

► Induce a sense of urgency and hustle throughout the organization.

► Seek to minimize potentially paralyzing fears, despite the uncertainty which makes fearfulness legitimate.

To achieve the awesome but minimum acceptable agenda laid out in the thirty-nine previous prescriptions, the organization must be energetic, from stem to stern. A principal leadership challenge, then, is to go all out to create a sense of urgency.

Every managerial act must be seen as an unequivocal support for urgency in pursuit of constant testing, change, and improvement.

L-10

Create a Sense of Urgency

George Washington University business researcher Peter Vaill, the pioneer scholar of a field called "high performing systems," says that the stellar outfits— whether Brownie troops or factories—all have a certain feel, or "aesthetic motivation." A U.S. Air Force general I know insists that the best air squadrons "hum." Similar words or expressions include "electric," "electricity in the air," "in synch."

Most of us "learned" about this phenomenon in grade school. Some classrooms "hum," are "electric," are "in synch." Most lack any such spark. So, too, with training departments, retail buying offices, and software development groups.

The challenge this book lays down is all about "hustle" (see C-4 and Amar Bhide's superb description of "hustle as strategy"). We must challenge everything, change everything, improve everything. We must cut this cycle time and that by 75 to 90 percent (and do it fast), become orders-of-magnitude more responsive, implement thousands of individual and team suggestions each day just to keep up with the Joneses (the Hondas, Electroluxes, Limiteds).

The necessity of learning to love change permeates this book. Most of the prescriptions, sometimes indirectly, have taken aim at inducing flexibility and minute-to-minute risk-taking. Figure 18 is a partial listing, some forty key factors whose primary effect, working in tandem, is to create organizational fluidity— i.e., love of change (and the ability to make changes) by everyone. They range from the power of information provided to the front line (detailed knowledge of competitors, for instance, is an unsurpassed spur to action) and the removal of excessive "layers" of structure, to extensive worker training in how to solve problems and a straightforward call to evaluate everyone on the basis of how much he or she has, in fact, changed (I-9, I-10, L-9)—and lately, to boot.

But even if you do all these things (an imposing challenge), there will still be something missing—an intangible (that maligned "soft" word) "X-factor": electricity, hum, hustle, or whatever else you choose to call it. This prescription urges you to add the "X-factor" to your organization, whether it's a small team in the loan department or a large multinational institution.

Well, just what is it? After all, this is a book of practical suggestions. Allied-Signal, a then-sluggish firm embarking on a turnaround, ran advertisements a couple of years ago that featured otherwise stodgy-looking executives without suit jackets and with their shirt sleeves rolled up; the inscription read: "We mean business." I don't know what the ad's effect was (on customers or employees), but its flavor is to the point here. We must break out of the old molds, and fast. Rolled-up sleeves are hardly the whole answer, but they do provide a hint.

Figure 18: **40 Factors That, Reinforcing One Another, Induce Flexibility**

1. The visible presence of new, flexible competitors
2. Visible display of the exploding array of new products
3. Talking up sales lost to revolutionary new technologies
4. Spruced-up old competitors intruding into your market
5. Business failures and restructurings in your industry
6. Good competitor analysis available to all
7. A belief that new market creation is the premier business success strategy
8. A belief that any product can be constantly improved
9. Unvarnished customer listening programs of every description
10. Constant measurement of customer satisfaction
11. Unadulterated feedback from sales and service forces
12. Customer (and supplier and distributor) visits by everyone: us to them, them to us
13. An environment that encourages numerous "small starts" and instant pilot tests of everything
14. Vociferous support for fast, thoughtful failures
15. Encouragement to fight NIH (not invented here) and "swipe" ideas from anywhere
16. Support for somewhat eccentric champions at all levels who may break the rules (who exhibit "constructive defiance"); praise of risk-taking supporters of champions
17. The use of "fully staffed," self-sufficient product development teams
18. Skill training and constant retraining; training in jobs in other functions; training in problem-solving techniques (cause and effect analysis)
19. Involvement in a "pay for performance" plan
20. Membership on a self-managing team, responsible for most of its own support activities such as budgeting and capital planning
21. A chance to be a team leader
22. Removal of bureaucratic impediments
23. Removal of humiliating rules
24. Provision of an attractive (clean and peppy) work environment
25. Constant rewards and celebrations for small accomplishments
26. Guaranteed employment
27. Fewer (or no) first-line supervisors

28. Middle managers who encourage constant front-line contact among functions
29. Middle managers who act as "on call" experts, spending most of their time helping teams; likewise, middle managers (experts) living "on the floor" of the factory or operations center, or distribution center
30. No more than five layers of structure
31. The use of small units, "small within big" configurations, everywhere
32. Senior management in touch with the line; strong, demonstrated top management support for the front line
33. Encouragement to "be the best" and "be unique" on some important performance dimension
34. Supervisors (and others) who are promoted on the basis of their ability to create an exciting work environment
35. Suggestions systems, reward systems, and other devices that invite zestful bureaucracy-bashing and constant cross-functional contact
36. Everyone evaluated on what/how much they have changed/improved
37. Wholesale information availability to everyone
38. Basic business forecasting and evaluation systems that emphasize trust, fairness, and integrity
39. People evaluation systems that emphasize "degrees of winning"
40. Genuine "bottom-up" setting of objectives and appraisal of performance

CREATING A SENSE OF URGENCY

How do you create urgency, hustle, and electricity? Part of the answer, of course, lies in a review of Figure 18; are you making use of all of these factors—at once? The rest involves management (leadership) by example—but example that doesn't so much emphasize, for instance, the quantity of time spent on your top priority (see L-3) as it does the presence of that intangible "X-factor." That is, if you want hustle—well, hustle yourself:

1. Cut out excessive trappings of office. Begin at home. Answer your own phone. Damp down the regal splendor of the office (regal is relative; this applies equally to first-line supervisors and chairmen of $10 billion firms). Don't travel with executive assistants. Etc. (See P-10, L-8.)

2. Follow a spartan routine. Give up executive perks and increase your people's perks. I can't tell you to fly coach or drive a 1965 pickup; I can tell you that doing so helps others take your "lean, mean, and urgent" speech seriously.

3. Be enchanted by the product or service. Want others to be excited about the 2379B widget, or the new "home bakery" you've added to your 125 supermarkets? The answer is simple (to state): *you* must be—and act—excited. If it's not crystal-clear to all that you love "it" (and "it" may be a new training program), then it's hard to imagine that "they" will love it.

Love it? How? I can't say how, as in how to love; but I can say what, as in

483

what love means. The what is—being fascinated by it; asking questions about it; showing it off to everyone; displaying it everywhere; bragging about it (and its creators); examining it regularly; using it (if possible). It is, yes, intangible, but it boils down to engagement. If you're not engaged, others' sense of urgency will be damped immeasurably. (See C-2.)

4. "Go to the sound of the guns" (customers). The late Lieutenant General Melvin Zais (featured in *A Passion for Excellence*) advised would-be generals to do this—to seek the center of the maelstrom. Maryland's Governor Don Schaefer, a World War II Army veteran, puts this near the top of his list. When he was Baltimore's mayor, "go to the sound of the guns" meant go to the neighborhoods.

In business, the sound of the guns is wherever the customer is. Again, recall L-3 (Manage by Example). Want others to become obsessed with customers? You go first, Ms./Mr. Leader. A big (and longtime) customer calls from the other side of the country with a "little problem" with the first shipment of a new product. The board meeting is only forty-eight hours away. You've got very tough queries coming. So what do you do? Call the sales vice-president and order him to "get on it"? No. You go to the sound of the gun/customer. With some public fanfare, you toss your board presentation out, order up a charter jet (charters are okay when a big customer is involved), and *you* go there. Buy a clean shirt when you arrive; don't wait to pack a bag. It's almost that simple: Become a "hustling fool" (as a friend calls it) when the customer beckons; a whole lot of other such "hustling fools" will quickly be born in your organization.

This suggestion also applies, without modification, to lower-level managers and staff managers. Be observed (by your people) canceling an important meeting with the boss in order to rush to a customer's side (which, if you are in a staff job such as MIS, may mean a factory manager for whom you are installing a new CAM system). Yes, it is risky; but the risk you take as well as the nature of the act itself will go a long way toward instilling that "X-factor."

5. Redouble your commitment to "symbolic management." Much of L-3 (and L-4, L-6) was about symbols. All of this, the last leadership prescription, is about symbols. Creating a sense of urgency is, make no mistake, a symbolic exercise. It may come naturally. But it may not. If not, there is good news: You can learn to think symbolically—in fact, you must.

The most important step is heightened self-awareness: Put each small action through an "X-factor" filter. Does it foster or impede a sense of urgency? A perfectly reasonable decision, such as sending a proposal for a new product back for more staff work, when put through the "X-factor" sieve, should be reversed. Yes, you could learn more from another six weeks of study; but the presenter, a staff manager, said he was ready to charge ahead. Even though you're not sure, throw caution to the winds (at the margin) and tell him to proceed.

The more subtle trick is achieving a "bottom-up" perspective on urgency. What looks eminently reasonable to you often as not looks from below like waffling based upon power politics or mistrust of the line.

6. Laugh/cry/smile. "Hustle" and "electricity" are purely emotional. The era of the effective but detached manager, supervisor, or chief executive is gone. Necessary urgency throughout the organization and detachment at the top (or in any managerial post) cannot coexist.

This is not a "style tip." Former Oakland Raider football coach John Madden was a screamer, shouter, and arm-waver. Dallas Cowboy coach Tom Landry has a contained style. But talk to their players, as I have; both are paragons of emotionality. That is, both are transparently intense; their will to win and their passion for flawless execution are unmistakable.

I am not, then, urging you to be more extroverted or introverted. I am advising you that involvement, especially with the work of the front line (see also L-6), is a must for survival in a world where the front line's willingness to take spontaneous initiatives counts for more with each passing day.

One form of emotional involvement, laughter, deserves a special comment. Urgency and laughter go hand in glove. "Get going" and "try something" are among this book's central tenets. To speed action-taking, we simply must learn to laugh at our own (personal, organizational) bureaucratic, action-delaying foibles (L-8); and we must learn to laugh at interesting and useful mistakes (or "fast failures"—see I-8). In general, a spirited environment is marked by laughter—enthusiasm for being on a team and trying darn near anything to make the service or product better.

7. Be the first to get in to work. I have some qualms about this one because of the possibility of a "macho" misinterpretation. But I believe it is essential. Let me indulge once more in a sports analogy. My memory reaches back to the great Oakland Athletics team of 1972 (few now recall that Oakland is the only team in the last thirty years to win three consecutive world series, starting in 1972). Young Vida Blue pitched for the A's and was a whirlwind. Blue did a lot well, but I vividly recall one of his habits in particular. Pitchers are in general cerebral sorts by baseball standards and march to the tune of a different drummer; among other things, they walk, often with studied slowness, off the mound at the end of an inning. Not Blue. He trotted off. And that simple trot came to symbolize the hustling, scrounging, brilliantly successful A's.

I urge you, then, to come to work first, and trot off and onto the mound. Your personal display of spunk, of energy and zest for your task and life in general, especially if you are visible to the line, will be the single most important determinant of the organization's energy.

URGENCY AND FEAR

The fearful organization is not a hustling organization. Fear, of tiny failure or impending layoff (management or non-management), is the chief enemy of urgent action and flexibility. Unfortunately, in many of our biggest firms, the middle or first-level manager, on whom we must ultimately depend for survival, has lots to fear. Until that fear is erased or minimized, hustle—urgent testing of the untried—will not become common. Information hoarding rather than sharing (information is power, after all) and action-delaying tactics (not to act is not to risk failure) become the norm in fearful organizations. Political maneuvering (in an effort to make oneself apparently valuable to someone who looks like a survivor) goes up too.

Dealing with fearfulness requires any number of strategies, which either have already been discussed (see C-10 on establishing a revenue-enhancing attitude, I-8 on supporting failures, P-7 on tactics to accompany guaranteed employment, and P-4 on retraining managers and others) or will be discussed (see S-4 and S-5 on integrity and trust).

But beyond all these is yet another leadership "X-factor." Wartime military leadership provides the best and most obvious analogue. By definition, wartime command involves, day in and day out, the ultimate source of fear—sudden death for those in the prime of life. Military leadership offers two answers: confidence and accessibility.

Confidence means non-paralysis, a willingness to act, and act decisively; to start new things and cut failing ventures off. It does not mean false confidence about the future—complacency or unwarranted certainty about the correctness of the organization's strategy. Such false confidence, amidst obvious turmoil, is correctly read as foolishness, inducing more fearfulness—i.e., loss of confidence—rather than less. (The continued unwillingness of many corporate chieftains to face up to reality in the face of plummeting market share provides ample demonstration of complacency, and of its dire consequences—a continued lack of a sense of urgency on the part of the rest of the organization. GM in 1986 and Xerox and Kodak in the mid- and late seventies come to mind.)

So demonstrating confidence means demonstrating self-awareness of the competitive problems (which we all have) and then exhibiting a willingness to move fast to test strategies that will lead to fast adaptation. Move fast, above all, does not mean "get it right"—it does mean experiment fast, bravely, and continually. (And, I reiterate, it means having the guts to cut off the failed experiment before it becomes an elephantine disaster, then plunging ahead with a new one posthaste.)

I cannot, obviously, provide a formula for "getting confident." I can suggest that confidence only comes not when you are rolling the dice on a "big idea," but when you know you're working successfully at implanting the basic skills which will turn the organization into a hotbed of experiments aimed at improving everything dramatically and creating little new markets at a record clip.

The second tactic for fighting fear is accessibility, discussed in L-4 and L-6 as well. When times are chaotic, in war or in an increasingly crowded marketplace, just to *see* the leadership, to be around the leaders, to observe their humanity, is a tonic. (Even the leader who appears appropriately fearful helps instill confidence—if he or she is still willing to act boldly.) To "stand beside" at time of need is the best killer of fear. It doesn't necessarily lead to acts of extraordinary bravery (or risk-taking in the market), but it does induce a willingness to shed paralyzing fright and move forward, begin acting (testing). And to act, to have everyone taking those minuscule moment-to-moment risks (which are, of course, not cumulatively minuscule at all) is the essence of urgency and, ultimately, success.

FIRST STEPS

Pass every action, starting now, through the "scullery filter": That is, "Will the new worker in the scullery (or housekeeping or accounting department) view this as an example of our organization's new sense of urgency, will it be viewed neutrally, or will it look like delay and 'business as usual'?" If you cannot decisively answer "foster a sense of urgency, readily apparent to all," then the act is a step back, not even neutral. You have no time to waste; every tiny act must be an unmistakable demonstration to the scullery crew that a newfound sense of urgency has been unleashed.

VI

BUILDING *S*YSTEMS FOR A WORLD TURNED UPSIDE DOWN

SECTION SUMMARY

Systems are more important than ever, principally because today's systems cause real harm. For starters, if the market logic set forth in Part I and in prescriptions C-1 through C-10 is valid, we are measuring the wrong things. Second, our systems, as conventionally conceived, channel information narrowly and restrict the power to act. Thus the systems prescriptions (see Figure 19), like the leadership prescriptions, are aimed at both controlling (directing attention to appropriate strategic concerns) and decontrolling (empowering everyone to act).

The Guiding Premise, prescription S-1, is a paradox: Measure more by measuring less. That is, simplify systems (in some instances replace computer printouts with flip charts), but make sure that they measure "the right stuff"—e.g., quality, innovation, flexibility, and even such especially "soft" traits as effectiveness at bureaucracy-bashing.

Reconceiving the System Tools of Control and Empowerment is the topic of the next two, enabling prescriptions: S-2, revising performance appraisal, management by objectives, and job descriptions through simplification (or elimination in the case of job descriptions) and redirection toward what's important; S-3, sharing information (and power, since information is power) widely, increasing spending authority, and instituting simplified, relevant, nonbureaucratic, "bottom-up" strategic planning.

The "glue" that binds a company together in an uncertain world, and provides the stability necessary to encourage constant experimentation, is trust, which can be abetted by systems. The last two prescriptions address this central topic of Establishing Trust via Systems: S-4 makes the case for conservative financial and nonfinancial goal-setting; and S-5 focuses on maintaining total integrity.

The fifteen leadership and system prescriptions (1) revise the nature of control, (2) radically decentralize the power to take action, and (3) come to grips with the stability-instability paradox—the need to provide more stability in order to encourage the greatly increased day-to-day risk-taking necessary to deal with that instability in a world turned upside down.

Figure 19: **Building Systems for a World Turned Upside Down**

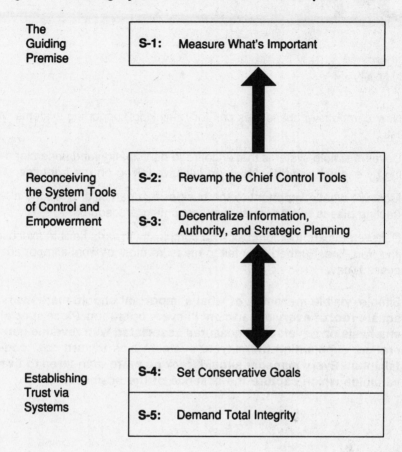

S-1

SUMMARY

New competitive challenges call for rethinking supporting systems. We must:

► Develop simple systems that encourage participation and understanding by everyone and that support initiative-taking on the front line.

► Measure what's important to the business; in particular shed the distracting biases of traditional cost-accounting procedures.

Our systems are too complex. The complexity thwarts flexible execution at the front line. Further, they fail to measure most of what's important to success today.

Simple, visible measures of what's important should mark every square foot of every department in every operation. Place special emphasis on developing measures associated with revenue generation, supplanting the current systems bias toward cost containment. Every manager should track no more than three to five variables which capture the essence of the business.

492

S-1

Measure What's Important

Measurement is too often equated with how many pounds of numerical indicators the senior manager receives weekly. There is little feel for the data at any level. Line—especially front-line—involvement in its use or formulation is limited. Ironically, the need for flexibility in an increasingly complex environment requires systems to be made less complex.

In addition, our systems invariably measure "the wrong stuff." We know how to measure costs—using models whose assumptions were created decades ago for a much different world. Sources of long-term revenue enhancement—such as quality, service, flexibility—are virtually absent from most measurement systems.

KEEP IT SIMPLE (AND VISIBLE)

Keep It Simple: Flip Charts and Line Involvement

Flip charts, two-variable management, back-of-the-envelope calculations—surely these were yesteryear's way of life, inappropriate to today's complex setting.

Not so. An accounting firm executive recalls his surprise at the "systems" used by NUMMI (the GM-Toyota venture). He had expected state-of-the-art—that is, complex—measurement techniques. "Instead," he says, laughing, "it was flip charts, red and green lights depicting a system's status . . . absurdly simple, but to the point."

A primary test of a sharp manufacturing operation, according to Richard Schonberger in *World Class Manufacturing,* is the presence of living, and simple, measures: charts on the wall assessing the causes of delay, updated hourly by crayon or marker pen; physical space for teams to meet near the line, equipped with blackboards that can be covered with simple, to-the-point analyses.

Schonberger makes no bones about the method: "Data recording comes first. The tools are cheap and simple: pencils and chalk. Give those simple tools for recording data to each operator. Then make it a natural part of the operator's job to record disturbances and measurements on charts and blackboards. The

493

person who records data is inclined to analyze, and the analyzer is inclined to think of solutions." He goes on to describe the feel of a pragmatic, measurement-happy environment:

> . . . One [plant] stands out for its attention to keeping the walls covered with measured data on the basics. It is the Hewlett-Packard plant making the HP-3000 series 500 minicomputer. . . . [Simple] charts are everywhere in the California plant where the 3000-500 is produced. The charts have been in use for several years with excellent results. . . .
>
> A main wall near the center of the manufacturing floor has three large charts posted on it. One shows the JIT [just-in-time] material flow. Another chart shows the total quality control process. The third, centered between the other two, contains a wealth of data plotted on graphs and charts, mostly on performance in printed circuit assembly (PCA). One graph plots PCA throughput time: down from fifteen days in 1982 to 1.5 days in 1984. Another shows WIP [work-in-progress] inventory: down from $676,000 in 1983 to $200,000 in 1984 to $20,000 in 1985. Three more graphs show scrap, floor space, and labor hours in PCA—all cut roughly in half. Several more graphs show declining defects. . . . Every day PCA people post detail sheets showing number of bent leads, missing parts, and other nonconformities, and they plot defect total on the graphs weekly. . . .
>
> In short, the plant is set up for *visual management* [my emphasis]. A manager, a quality engineer, a supplier, a customer, or a visiting class from a college campus can make a circle tour of the compact facility in an hour or two and know what is right and what is wrong. Compared with this, managing a plant by examining periodic reports seems like looking through binoculars the wrong way. . . .
>
> World-class manufacturing surely does require strategic leadership. I am convinced that the best strategy is doing things better and better in the trenches. The best leadership is that which insists on visible measures of what is going on in the trenches and on action there to achieve a high rate of improvement.

The essential variables are these: (1) simplicity of presentation, (2) visibility of measurements, (3) everyone's involvement, (4) undistorted collection of primary information throughout the operations area, (5) the straightforward measurement of what's important, and (6) achievement of an overall feel of urgency and perpetual improvement. Unfortunately, all six of these elements are missing in systems that govern the average operation I've observed.

Getting started on achieving this sort of environment involves all of the activities covered in the people prescriptions (P-1 through P-10). Once more, the outcomes are readily describable, but they hinge on attitude—a belief that people can accomplish their tasks and that they wish to accomplish them.

Of special importance, recalling previous discussions (especially P-8), is the idea of staff on call. The information-intense environment—with the information used by those who collect it—is based upon "bottom up" initiative. Decisions on what to collect, when to collect it, how to record it, and how to use it must remain the almost exclusive province of well-trained front-line people, aided only on an "as needed" basis by the experts.

Keep It Simple: One or Two Measures That Count

. . . the manager good at monitoring has at his fingertips [a few general measures] with which—he or she feels—the pulse of the business can be tracked. Whether or not the variables identified are causally related to the effects measured in a scientific sense is immaterial; the point is, the manager has driven his or her understanding of the business to such a fine point that he or she has isolated the two or three really useful measures about the products, company, and industry and religiously tracks these as a test of progress and a barometer of change.

Tom Bonoma
The Marketing Edge

For senior managers, the idea of simplicity, as captured in this comment by Tom Bonoma, means boiling what's important down to a couple of variables that capture the strategic essence of the unit or firm.

The uniqueness of wildly profitable Deluxe Check (see C-4) lies in remarkable customer responsiveness, going back to an "order" written by founder W. R. Hotchkiss on August 18, 1936. He declared that henceforth all orders would go out no later than the day after they were received, adding that "no money should be spared" to achieve this end.

This dictum still drives the firm, and the two simple service statistics measuring their success are prominently reported in the firm's annual report. In 1986, Deluxe shipped 97.1 percent of orders in accordance with its promise; 99.6 percent of those orders were error-free.

How is this achieved? While appropriate automation marks Deluxe's sixty-two plants, simple, visible systems are the essence of success. For instance, each day's order slip is a different color. Tuesday's is orange, and one plant manager comments: "At 4:30 Wednesday, I don't want to see any orange around here."

Detailed, computerized data collection systems are a must, but operating managers must also "know the [essential] numbers" from memory. "No orange by late Wednesday afternoon" is easy to remember. And the greater the complexity swirling around us, the more important it is to maintain this kind of grasp on reality. The operating manager must not slip into a morass of complexity, answering every question, as so many do, with: "I'll have accounting run the numbers, and we'll get an estimate in four or five days." Requisite lightning-fast responses demand keeping a feel for things at all times.

Thinking About Vision, Symbolic Action, and Recognition as a "Control System"

Recall the discussion of managing as symbolic action (see L-4). In particular, I stressed the role of stories in guiding an institution. Analogously, prescription L-2 emphasized the role of a succinct vision. In an ambiguous environment, people need something to provide day-to-day guidelines in handling an endless series of novel circumstances.

The old hierarchical organization provided a simple answer: Buck everything up the line for decision. We no longer can afford the luxury of such time-consuming deliberations. We must increasingly depend on front-line people to make the right choices. Further up the line, but far short of corporate staffs, we must depend on senior functional or general managers to make decisions on strategic affairs.

The best "systems" to ensure correct choices are (1) a clear vision, (2) sharing stories that illustrate how others, at all levels, have reacted to novel situations consistent with the vision, and (3) recognition for jobs well done, those that illustrate imaginative responses in the face of numbing uncertainty.

These devices—vision, symbolic action, recognition—are a *control system,* in the truest sense of that term. The manager's task is to conceive of them as such, and to consciously use them. There is nothing soft about a Federal Express, Domino's, Nordstrom, or Deluxe Check "story" or recognition affair. It purposefully defines what each firm means by "go the limit to serve the customer."

MEASURING WHAT'S IMPORTANT

Current Systems Mislead

Our traditional measurement systems are dangerously misleading. Take the standard cost-accounting system. It "allocates" overhead costs such as the accounting department, engineering, utilities, machinery, and management to direct labor. That is, direct labor "hours" are the most readily counted indicator; all of the other expenses are appended to this one, visible expense. In fact, each typical "direct labor hour" may carry an overhead "burden," as the accountants call it, of as much as 1,000 percent. That's why, when a manager is pushed by higher-ups to cut costs, there is but one sensible target under this accounting regimen: to cut direct labor, which, on the books, includes that huge "burden." Thus, for accounting purposes, when he cuts a direct labor hour, he will usually be credited with the reduction in the "burden" as well, whether it actually occurs or not.

Suppose the manager decides to subcontract production of a labor-intensive part. He saves 100 hours of direct labor a month at $20 per hour ($2,000 in all). But on the books, he saves not only the direct labor costs but the 1,000 percent burden (worth ten times the labor) as well—for credited monthly savings of

$22,000. The subcontract to a smaller, low-overhead, perhaps offshore operation costs, say, $5,000 a month. The net "booked" saving, then, is $17,000 a month. Much applause goes to the plant manager.

Unfortunately, the real story is different from the accounting story. In fact, actual factory overhead is not reduced much or at all by the act of subcontracting (you can't shut off the heat around one idle machine). Most likely, overhead is increased, because the plant manager (or someone, somewhere) has to negotiate and administer a contract with the new supplier and handle the incoming components. Not to mention the increased uncertainty of delivery and quality in the early days of dealing with any supplier—that also carries real costs. So the true net saving is the $2,000 saving in direct labor minus the $5,000 subcontract cost minus, say, $1,000 in real, added overhead—or a loss of $4,000. Nonetheless, thanks to the miracle of "modern" accounting, the plant manager still takes that bow.

Such perverse outcomes are standard, according to H. Thomas Johnson and Robert S. Kaplan in *Relevance Lost: The Rise and Fall of Management Accounting.* In fact, the authors report, some experts claim that "cost accounting is the number one enemy of productivity." Industrialists trained in engineering, such as Andrew Carnegie, used accounting to assist line managers in decision-making on the factory floor. But slowly, as professionally trained accountants began to take control of the system, accounting's emphasis shifted from being a management tool for the factory floor to financial reporting. And it's those oh so frequent financial reporting requirements laid on by agencies such as the SEC and the IRS that necessitate, for instance, allocating all overhead costs to direct labor and the cost of goods sold—which in time leads to the kind of flawed decision-making described above. That is, to determine profit for the fleeting "accounting period" across numerous products in a factory (a meaningless number from a proactive managerial standpoint), you must, by hook or by crook, assign every dollar of expense to something. Direct labor is the easiest "something," even though the result misdirects decision-makers.

The "expensing" of activities such as research, worker-skill upgrading, and process improvement is another prime example of a traditional cost-accounting device that can have a deleterious effect on performance. Since these investments in the future are treated, *for accounting purposes,* as "expenses of the period" (wholly written off each thirty days, for instance), they fall prey to the short-term cost cutter. That is, cutting R&D is a 100 percent cut—you get full credit; thus it's a fat target. Were it "capitalized" as a building is, when you cut it you'd only get a few percent credit in the short term—and the temptation would be reduced accordingly.

Another error of this sort involves hidden cross-subsidies among products that make it difficult, especially with today's conventions, to measure true product profitability—a particularly dangerous problem in these times, when short production runs for an ever wider variety of products are becoming the norm. You must know whether a product is making money or not; our present systems cloud the issue. A related sin is our fixation on short-term measures,

497

which makes it almost impossible, for instance, to assess the long-term costs of developing a product.

A last example involves purchasing: Most purchasing departments still are evaluated principally on the contract cost of procurement. Almost always, however, they fail to factor into these "contract costs" how the poor quality of purchased goods can diminish final product quality—tarnishing the ultimate producer's reputation and driving up other, hard-dollar costs (fixing defective supplier material, warranty work).

The Essential Variables Are Ignored—But Can Be Measured

Bad as these problems are, however, there are sins of outright omission in traditional accounting that are far worse. Our fixation with financial measures leads us to downplay or ignore less tangible nonfinancial measures, such as product quality, customer satisfaction, order lead time, factory flexibility, the time it takes to launch a new product, and the accumulation of skills by labor over time. Yet these are increasingly the real drivers of corporate success over the middle to long term, as emphasized in the first forty prescriptions in this book.

The good news is that nontraditional measures are popping up. Prescription C-2 offered several examples of the thoughtful measurement of poor-quality cost, for instance, at Tennant, IBM, and Milliken. Firms such as Ford, Tennant, and Perdue Farms use quality objectives as a basis for compensation. IBM continues to refine the measurement of quality, most recently devoting substantial effort to the quantitative measurement of business systems (see C-2); that firm also uses direct incentives (rewards and penalties for quality) in supplier contracts.

Quality is slowly becoming a basis for purchasing department evaluation. For instance, Schonberger reports on Uniroyal's Rubber Division, which adopted a scheme in which quality accounted for 40 percent of its Vendor Service Rating; price carried a 25 percent weight, on-time delivery 20 percent, and service 15 percent. But obvious as such schemes might seem, they are still very rare. A discussion with acquisition quality managers at the Department of Defense underscored the point. Quality is receiving lip service at DOD these days, but one frustrated senior civilian executive reported: "The files are filled with vendors who've delivered 20 to 30 percent defective parts for years; yet we still won't cut them off."

Getting quality into the routine measurement system is not easy. In *The Chain of Quality,* TRW's John Groocock (see also C-2) describes the effort he made when he took on his first quality assignment at ITT Europe. In Harold Geneen's ITT, nothing was taken seriously until it was measured and included in the intricate financial review process. If quality were to be a priority, Groocock reasoned, it would have to edge its way into that all-consuming system. So early on he sought an accountant as an ally:

He was responsible for accounting systems throughout the company, and reported to the controller. He showed me how to write a controller's procedure and together we did so. He suggested we should make quality costs a quarterly report instead of a monthly report. That seemed rational. Quality costs do not change all that rapidly, and he said it would save the divisional controllers, who were already greatly overworked, a substantial amount of effort. I had never asked a senior accountant for anything before in my life and was surprised that he was taking my request so seriously. However, I felt intuitively that, as most of the financial system was on a monthly reporting, a quarterly measure would always be a low-prestige bother (it would never become institutionalized). . . . So I kept my nerve, dug my heels in, and got away with monthly reporting. . . . We circulated the draft controller's procedure to the division quality managers and controllers and quickly incorporated their comments. Most of them felt it was not serious and that it would not really happen. Early in December the controller's procedure was signed off. People had been surprised to find that they could not think of any good reason for disapproving it. No one had stood up and shouted "Nonsense!" during my presentation at the conference. The division people had their chance to table rational objections, and these were taken into account. My colleague in accounting devoted so much personal effort that he was becoming a champion himself. Suddenly, it was no longer an academic exercise, and amazingly at the end of February, most of the required reports for January 1967 came in (January is a quiet month for accountants). The delinquents were a minority and were exposed to the pressure that minorities suffer, and soon came into line. I nursed the fledgling system for three years, and after I went to Brussels as Director of Quality ITT Europe (ITTE) in 1969, I championed the system throughout Europe for the next eleven years.

Other prescriptions supply other examples of companies that are measuring "the right stuff." McKesson (C-4) measures its responsiveness to its customers. Schonberger's *World Class Manufacturing* underscores the importance of measuring responsiveness, which he calls lead time: "The number of believers in zero lead time as a superordinate target is still small but growing fast. One by one, top companies are coming to the conclusion that reducing lead time is a simple and powerful measure of how well you are doing. The manufacturing people at both Motorola and Westinghouse have chosen lead time reduction as a dominant measure; various divisions of Hewlett-Packard and General Electric have too. Lead time is a sure and truthful measure, because a plant can reduce it only by solving problems that cause delays. Those cover the gamut: order-entry delays and errors, wrong blueprints or specifications, long setup times and large lots, high-defect counts, machines that break down, operators who are not well trained, supervisors who do not coordinate schedules, suppliers that are not dependable, long waits for inspectors or repair people, long transport distances, multiple handling steps, and stock record inaccuracies. Lead times drop when those problems are solved. Lead times drop fast when they are solved fast."

The innovation prescriptions also emphasize measurement. Prescription I-9, for instance, features 3M's measurement of innovation, and its linkage between executive pay and a precise, quantitative innovation target. The people prescriptions, especially P-6, advise rewarding everyone on the basis of measured quality and/or productivity improvement, and present many novel schemes for doing so. The people prescriptions also emphasize the need to foster cross-functional cooperation. We aren't used to measuring or rewarding on this basis, but a 1986 story in *Fortune* about American Express suggests it can be done:

> [Chairman Jim Robinson] started preaching the virtues of intramural cooperation. Amex, he said, is "one enterprise." . . . He then reinforced his pitch with steel rods, requiring senior executives to identify two or three promising One Enterprise synergy projects in their annual strategic plans and work on them during the year. He made it corporate policy to evaluate every manager and professional employee on their contributions to One Enterprise, and then he handed out extra bonuses to senior executives who did their bit for the cause.
>
> One of the two bonuses paid in 1985 went to [the] chairman of American Express Bank. He received $80,000 because the bank had worked on a dozen or so successful synergy projects, including introducing Shearson investment bankers to its overseas clients and selling $240 million of money orders and traveler's checks for the card division. . . .
>
> In addition to providing his senior executives with financial incentives to cooperate, Robinson relies on a watchdog to make sure the middle managers do so too. [The manager of corporate strategy] issues . . . a monthly report on the status of each One Enterprise project, which [is] circulated among the company's top 100 executives. The report gives managers collaborating with other managers unusual visibility; it also turns the high beams on task forces that get bogged down in internal politics. In those cases [the report indicates] "no progress" in the Project Status column: "After two or three months of that kind of attention . . . people start finding ways to resolve their differences."

I have, in fact, attempted to provide quantitative measures for most of these prescriptions. Figure 20 summarizes several of them. Unfortunately, the course is largely uncharted. There are a few, pioneering examples, such as those just mentioned. In most instances, however, you are on your own, with my sketchy outline as guidance. But the issue is of the utmost significance. "What gets measured gets done" has never been so powerful a truth.

Figure 20: **A Sample of Unconventional Measures Proposed in This Book**

Prescription	*Measure*
C-1: Niche Creation	Number of "differentiators" added to each product every 90 days.
C-2: Quality	Relative perceived product quality; poor-quality cost; rewards based on quality goals. Devise quality measures in every unit. Evaluate suppliers on the basis of quality.
C-3: Service	The ten attributes of customer satisfaction; customer evaluation of the intangibles; the lifetime value of a customer.
C-4: Responsiveness	Speed of response to customer needs; percentage of customers covered by tight (electronic or other) linkages; new links (electronic or other) added to each product each 90 days.
C-7: Listening	Informal listening ("call three customers per week").
C-8: Factory as Marketing Arm	Customer visits to factory; factory manager and nonmanager visits to customers.
C-9: Sales, Service, and Distribution	Time spent with sales and service people; rate at which additions are made to sales and service force; number of franchisees/distributors pruned.
I-1: Small Starts	Number of small starts; percentage of time/R&D budget devoted to small starts.
I-3: Pilots	Number of pilot tests of anything going on in each area.
I-4: Competitive Analysis	Number of ideas "swiped" from competitors per month.
I-5: Word of Mouth	Percentage of ad/marketing budget devoted to word of mouth.

(continued on next page)

Figure 20 *(continued)*

Prescription	Measure
I-6: Support Innovators	Number of awards to innovators; number/percentage of awards to unsung supporters of innovators per month.
I-8: Support Fast Failure	Number of awards for interesting failures, constructive defiance of rules.
I-9: Share of Revenue from New Products	Percentage of sales coming from new products introduced in the last 12, 24, 36 months.
P-2: Teams	Percentage of people in team configurations.
P-3: Recognition	Number of recognition acts/events per month.
P-5: Training	Hours/dollars devoted to skill upgrading.
P-6: Compensation	Percentage of total compensation from profit-distribution bonus plan/pay-for-knowledge program.
P-9: Middle Management Role	Number of acts of boundary-bashing; number of awards going to boundary-bashers.
P-10: De-bureaucratize	Number of demeaning and debilitating regulations renounced per month; number of amenities added to each facility per month; your "housekeeping," scored vis-à-vis competitors.
L-3: Manage by Example	Time spent per day/week on top priority.
L-4: Visible Management	Percentage of time out of the office; percentage of time with customers, front-line people.
L-6: Line Focus	Number of line versus number of staff at meetings; line versus staff salaries; time spent with line people.
L-9: "What Have You Changed?"	Amount of things changed; formally evaluate everyone accordingly.

FIRST STEPS

1. Assign each business unit and department the task of developing in 30 days five rough, unconventional, paper-and-pencil measures of what's going to be important to their unit's ability to support the firm's mission.
2. Use the measures, in rough form, in formal reviews. Insist that two-thirds of the new measures emphasize (a) customers (e.g., quality, service, listening), (b) flexibility/responsiveness, (c) innovativeness, and (d) the relative increase/decrease in the value of the workforce's skills, taken as a whole.

S-2

SUMMARY

In an effort to induce flexibility, we must turn our backs on, or radically redefine, the three staples of control over individuals—performance appraisals, the setting of objectives, and job descriptions. We must:

► Simplify these three primary control systems.

► Focus on what's important (e.g., flexibility rather than rigidity).

► Make the process of developing objectives, etc., truly "bottom up."

► Make the documents "living" ones, subject to constant discussion rather than infrequent, pro forma review.

These three control systems, like the measurement systems just discussed in S-1, are increasingly doing more harm than good. As typically constituted, they attempt to achieve a specificity of result inconsistent with today's fluid, competitive environment. If we can't fix them, we should scrap them.

Performance appraisals should be ongoing, based upon a simple, written "contract" between the person being appraised and his/her boss. Limit objectives to no more than three per period (quarter, year). Eliminate job descriptions.

Revamp the Chief Control Tools

W. Edwards Deming has contended that performance appraisal is the number one American management problem. He says it takes the average employee (manager or nonmanager) six months to recover from it.

I think Dr. Deming is about right, though I'd add the setting of objectives and job descriptions to the list of personnel control devices that are downright dangerous—as currently constituted.

Like the cost-accounting systems described in S-1, these are systems started for useful reasons which (1) have become increasingly bureaucratic, run by "experts" (often personnel departments in this case, rather than accountants as in S-1), and (2) are frighteningly out of touch with today's and tomorrow's needs. They are stability-inducing systems at odds with a world where flexibility is the chief survival requirement.

PERFORMANCE EVALUATION AND PAY SCHEMES THAT ARE SIMPLE AND TO THE POINT

Performance evaluation is essential—more than ever, in fact. It is a tool for directing attention, and attention today must be directed to new targets (see C-1 through C-4, for instance). Throughout the first forty prescriptions, I implicitly endorsed performance appraisal—at various times suggesting that it emphasize quality, constant innovation, and functional-barrier destruction.

The following attributes can turn performance appraisal from a minus to a plus:

1. **"Appraisal" must be constant,** not focused principally on the big annual (or semiannual) appraisal "event." (Dr. Deming points out that, in contrast to American dependence on the one or two big events, specific feedback to the average Japanese employee comes daily.) To ensure this, middle managers should evaluate first-level managers on the degree to which the first-level managers give their people constant feedback, both good and bad.

Above all, the annual (or quarterly or semiannual) appraisal review should never come as a surprise. The employee should be fully aware of his or her status and progress throughout the year.

2. Appraisal is—and should be—very time-consuming. We usually fail to give regular and direct feedback (painful negative feedback in particular) in the course of day-to-day affairs. Now it's time to fill out the semiannual appraisal form. We put it off until late on Sunday afternoon prior to "appraisal meeting week." Then we hurry through it, accompanied by a stiff scotch or two. Likewise, we rush through the scheduled meetings at the rate of seven or eight a day. (We hold them—as opposed to slipping the form under the door—only because the personnel department representative says we must.) Then the office is a shambles for the next few weeks. A few find their superb self-images confirmed; most are stunned, hurt, and disappointed. In no case has the meeting been a useful one for either the appraiser or the target.

Successful appraisal requires four different sorts of time: (a) day-to-day time spent giving constant feedback; (b) preparation time for the annual or semiannual evaluation; (c) execution time for the appraisal meetings, which should be spread out rather than bunched by the dozens in a single week; and (d) group time, during which fellow managers are consulted and appraisal criteria coordinated. (This last category not only provides the manager with input, but also engenders a sense of fairness and equity throughout the organization.)

3. There should be a small number of performance categories, and no forced ranking. I'm well aware of "category inflation," in which 90 percent of the people end up being graded as nine or ten on a one-to-ten scale. Nonetheless, there is simply nothing dumber (and more debilitating) than labeling one-third to one-half of your people losers, which is exactly what virtually all forced-ranking systems do. Surely, all the time you've spent recruiting and coaching has resulted in a work force more than half of which is doing an adequate job. Label an individual a loser and you will induce that person to behave like a loser. In particular, the person so labeled will work at keeping out of sight, and therefore cease to take even small risks, which is intolerable in today's environment.

This is not a plea to go easy on your "problem" people. They deserve counseling and a second and third chance, to be sure; given that nod to genuine due process, I am behind you when you make the necessary decision to demote or let go. But forced ranking doesn't help you go after those who need serious help, and its unintended fallout creates a large number of unnecessarily disaffected employees.

I suggest a system in which about 10 to 20 percent receive a "superior" evaluation; another 70 to 85 percent are satisfactory; and no more than 5 to 10 percent or so are in a questionable/unsatisfactory status. The lumping of 70 to 85 percent in one "grade" does not in any way limit your ability to pay tribute to jobs well done by individuals and groups. Recognition (see P-3, L-6) and group/team financial and other awards (see P-2, P-6) are the heart of the true evaluation—and motivation—system. Bob Townsend, in *Further Up the Organization,* urges just three categories, with attendant bonuses: "unsatisfactory (no bonus), satisfactory (bonus of X, on average), outstanding . . . equal to 2X or greater." Townsend adds ruefully: "Keeping it simple means fighting the experts. . . . [Yet] every change [of rules or percentages] means loss of understanding, loss of trust, loss of motivation."

4. Minimize the complexity of formal evaluation procedures and forms. I am against complexity. I am not against putting comments in writing. You, as manager, and each subordinate should jointly and literally sign off on a one-to-two-page written "contract," drafted initially by the subordinate, that includes the following: (a) one or two specific annual or semiannual objectives; (b) one or two personal/group/team growth or career-enhancement objectives; (c) one or two objectives for skill improvement in deficit areas; and (d) one objective that relates to the group's (or team's) overarching strategic theme—such as quality improvement. The format should be open-ended prose. Formal reviews of progress should be scheduled at least bimonthly, and informal reviews should be more frequent. You (the manager) should be able to recall—from memory—the content of each and every contract.

One executive, in a financial services firm, responded to this idea with: "Aren't you catering to your bias—after all, you're a writer, and prose seems natural. I'm a numbers guy."

I objected vigorously. First, I'm an engineer by training—and disposition. And a measurement fanatic, as this book demonstrates (see S-1). My point, I said, was that numbers too often focus on highly abstract outcomes. We need, instead, to emphasize capability building—developing the skills that will give us strategic advantage over the long haul. We need to talk about "building sales-force capability and support systems," "achieving flexibility," and "cutting product development time" more than about achieving "15 percent earnings-per-share growth." The latter target may be admirable, but is not much related to the skill enhancement necessary for adjusting to the changing world.

Of course, I have no objection to quantitative indicators of the enhancement of the skills of the sales force or the shortening of development cycles, for instance. But I'd also want to see an objective statement such as "be rated, by 1989, by third-party survey as having the premier sales force in the region."

5. Performance appraisal goals ought to be straightforward, emphasizing what you want to happen. You want quality improvement to rank as number one for your group? Rank it number one in the performance evaluation, and ask each manager to have one key objective—the first one—dealing with it directly (recall that Tennent did this—C-2). If barrier-dismemberment is the key for a middle manager, put it first in the jointly edited "contract."

Grocer Stew Leonard doesn't beat about the bush: Everyone's evaluation asks of them how they contributed to "STEW." The "S" stands for customer satisfaction, the "T" for teamwork, the "E" for excellence, and the "W" for Wow! The last is Leonard's favorite word, referring to the sense of excitement which he believes is the essence of the store's achievement. In other words, Leonard's evaluation is unequivocal about what he deems important to the business's continuing success.

6. Make the pay decisions public. Most bridle at this, but the benefits are several. In the absence of public disclosure, speculation is rife, and the picture it paints usually distorts or darkens the truth. More important, public disclosure causes embarrassment only if there truly is an inequity, about which, regardless of its convoluted historical basis, you should be embarrassed.

7. Make formal appraisal a small part of overall recognition. I have argued vociferously here for appropriate use of appraisal, especially to direct attention to new concerns. I even stated it was more important than ever before. That said, the thrust of the first forty prescriptions is clear—recognition (listening, celebration, pay, involvement) should/must come from a host of ongoing activities, of which performance evaluation is but one.

Together the seven attributes of performance appraisal outlined here add up to a common-sense approach. The rejoinder I most frequently get is: "But how can you not resort to complex categories—level 9 [of 23], pay step 7 [of 10]"—in a complex organization?"

The answer harks back to prescription P-8:

▶ First, keep the organization simple, with few layers. That is, there should be only a handful of managerial and nonmanagerial (professional, scientific) categories, or levels.

▶ Second, each should have a small number of wide, overlapping steps for pay purposes.

▶ Third, fight conventional wisdom in one last way—allow stellar professionals (salespersons, engineers) to outearn, sometimes by a wide margin, their bosses. I'll go a step further: 10 to 25 percent of each sales manager's salespersons and 10 to 25 percent of each R&D manager's engineers/scientists should be outearning their boss. "Let the top pros remain pros" (if they wish) is the guiding advice—don't force them to become frustrated managers.

▶ Fourth, "spend time." Managers develop a sense of what's equitable on the basis of hours and hours of discussion—at the time of formal reviews, when opportunities for promotions arise, etc.

OBJECTIVES THAT EMPHASIZE THE ACHIEVABLE

Put a 5-foot-10-inch person into 6 feet 3 inches of water, and odds are he'll learn to swim. He may sputter and spit a bit, but he can always hop up off the bottom and get air. Put that same person in 7 feet 4 inches of water, and you may have a dead body on your hands.

In any managerial forum, the topic turns at some point to goal-setting. Most American managers seem all too ready to toss the people who report to them into the 7-foot-4-inch-deep tank. This is what I hear: "You've got to push your people. Shoot for the moon. That's what motivates 'em. Give 'em half a chance and they'll sign up for a goal 10 percent less than last year's, even though the market is way up." And so on.

I have come to hate the term "stretch target," as it is commonly used. Yet I fervently believe in "stretch." I believe, however, in the 6-foot-3-inch variety for the 5-foot-10-inch participant. There is an attribute of goal-setting that stands out in creating a highly charged environment—teaching people that they are winners and that they can succeed, which in turn induces them to take on more, risk more. Thus, the prime objective of goal-setting should be to turn 90 percent of the people in your firm into confident winners who will take the new and always greater risks required by the chaotic times we live in.

That does leave room for "stretch"—it's a must. Without it, there is no sense of accomplishment. But the real art for the manager lies in creating challenging but achievable targets. That may mean, for example, creating just a two-inch hurdle to "teach" a previously demoralized individual (or group) that she or he (or it) is a winner.

This is not just theoretical speculation. I am an inveterate reader of biographies. Consider Field Marshal Bernard Montgomery and General George Patton; the two have something surprising in common. In North Africa, both (at different times) launched their careers in the limelight after inheriting winless and dispirited armies. And both rapidly reversed these armies' fortunes—using exactly the same technique to begin the turnaround. Both focused on the instantly "doable"—pushing their men to achieve *something,* and thereby leading them to realize they weren't born losers. In both cases, appearance and fitness were the chosen vehicles. A first "stretch target" (of the two-inch variety) was to demand spotless uniforms and to launch an intensive physical fitness program. A study titled "Excellence in the Surface Navy" describes a similar turnaround by a successful ship captain: "He began by 'planning victories for the ship.' By this he means that he was constantly on guard, looking for competition that the ship could enter into reasonably sure that it would emerge victorious. This could be something as trivial as challenging other ships in the task group to a sailing competition, knowing full well that their ship was the only one that had any sailboats, to seeking recognition as the top ship to complete refresher training in a given year. In either case, the crew's image of itself was enhanced by such actions."

The right attitude is one I call "degrees of winning," rather than "winners and losers." This is especially important today. We are required to teach so many fundamentally new things—how a manager can be a facilitator instead of a cop, how to stop emphasizing volume and enhance quality, how to manage a flexible organization instead of a stable one, how to make everyone rather than a handpicked few an agent for change and a risk taker responsible for constant improvement. Building new skills, when large numbers of people are involved, depends above all on generating momentum and commitment. Momentum and commitment come from learning that you can act as needed in—and succeed in—the brave new world. "Punishment," the behavioral scientists have long told us (with compelling documentation), is a futile strategy in general, but especially when new behaviors are required, as they are today. Punishment drives us to hide and be even more averse to risk.

A final word and pleasant surprise: If you work with your team to set achievable goals, you may find yourself managing goals downward—and "unstretching" them, if you will. Social psychology experiments reveal time and again that once people (singly or in groups) get on a roll, they set their objectives too high! They rapidly come to believe they can leap any building of any height in a single bound; by overreaching, they set themselves up for demotivating disappointments. The best route to long-term success, especially where new skills need to be learned, is therefore to meticulously set tailor-made targets that do indeed stretch, but which can be hurdled by almost everyone.

A Comment on Management by Objectives

Management by objectives (MBO) is one more great idea that has been neutered by bureaucrats in nine out of ten applications. That is, MBO (like performance appraisal) is a superb tool if the objectives are (1) simple, (2) focused on what's important, (3) genuinely created from the bottom up (the objectives are drafted by the person who must live up to them, with no constraining guides), and (4) a "living" contract, not a form-driven exercise.

Peter Drucker "invented" MBO in 1954, in *The Practice of Management.* Interestingly, Drucker never capitalized the words, nor did he use the three words by themselves. He spoke of (lowercase) "management by objectives *and self-control* [my emphasis]"—that is, nonbureaucratic self-management was the avowed purpose. The antithesis, an accountant-driven extra layer of bureaucracy, was what usually ensued, as the fine idea became encumbered over time by complex top-down techniques.

So by all means keep MBO—but get rid of the capital letters, restore Drucker's "and self-control," and follow the four rules proposed above. Once more, the point is underscored by the times—we can't afford systems that implicitly abet inflexibility, as most MBO routines do today.

SCRAP JOB DESCRIPTIONS

Who would fight "you gotta know what you're supposed to do"? No one, until the job description starts to constrict options—which is almost inevitable. Perhaps a case could be made for job descriptions in a stable, predictable, very vertically oriented (functional) organization. Today, in all cases the "j.d." is a loser.

Begin by answering this question: Have you—the average reader has been successful—ever read your job description? Most, if they're honest, will admit that they haven't. If you haven't read your job description, yet have had a successful career as a nonmanager and manager, what's the big deal about job descriptions? I have never read a job description in any of my incarnations. I've done stints as a U.S. Navy Seabee battalion operations officer and a detachment commander (overseas); a Pentagon junior assistant (in the Office of the Chief of Naval Operations); the President's senior drug abuse adviser; and a junior consultant, senior consultant, and partner at McKinsey & Co. My failure to read my job descriptions has never been a handicap. In fact, it doubtless helped me from time to time. By not reading my job descriptions, I've never been burdened by knowing exactly what I'm officially *not* allowed to do or with whom exactly I am required to "interface" on a project. (To be very honest, and this speaks volumes, I'm not sure whether any of my jobs, even in the Navy, had a job description.)

In the typical job description, with the stroke of a pen the boss sets all her or his managerial worries to rest. She or he conjures up the tasks that need completing (however impossible they may be), and then sets any nasty worries about coordination aside by endlessly listing all the groups that are to be "interfaced with" in the process of executing the "wish list."

This misleading comfort is, in my experience, unavoidable in written job descriptions. The only solution therefore is to scrap them.

While I am an archenemy of job descriptions, I am an unabashed supporter of great coaching as the alternative. That is, I wholeheartedly acknowledge the validity of "you gotta know what you're supposed to do." Especially today. I was blessed with uncommonly good coaches throughout the formative years of my career. I've found those who rely on job descriptions to be those who, in general, favor paper over people. In contrast, great coaches put in grueling hours teaching values—and, most important, they teach the "how-to's" of successful day-to-day risk-taking; that is, their coaching emphasizes flexibility under fire, not inflexibility. They do not try to replace that painstaking coaching effort with the typical job description, a four-page document which "covers all the bases."

The job description is a cop-out, pure and simple. But it is more (or less) than that. It is imperative today that managers and nonmanagers be induced to cross "uncrossable" boundaries as a matter of course, day after day. Standing on the formality of a written job description (as an excuse for inaction, or the reason you have to "check up—and up and up—the line") is a guaranteed strategy for disaster.

NEW SYSTEMS IN SUPPORT OF FLEXIBILITY

Performance evaluations, objective setting, and job descriptions are three staples of management "control." All, though sound of purpose, typically become bureaucratic. They stamp in distinctions and rigidity, rather than stamping them out. They impede fluidity.

To throw them out (job descriptions) or revamp them (performance evaluations, objective setting) is not to promote anarchy. Control, in service to the new business requirements, is brought about through a shared and inspiring vision (see L-2), by coaching—and by treating people as fully participating parties (P-1 through P-10). The contract for performance evaluation, for instance, must be as fluid as the fluid, highly competitive system in which it exists.

PUBLIC PARALLELS

The worst offenders on performance appraisals and job descriptions are in the public sector. The reasons, as usual, are sound. The turn-of-the-century reform movement, led by Teddy Roosevelt and others, struck at the caprice, favoritism, and corruption of the political machines. They replaced hooliganism with professionalism.

As with most movements, this one went too far. Today, there is an especially virulent form of corruption induced by overly rigid systems. This new corruption, in service to the "system's imperative," is nonresponsiveness to constituent needs. A second form of corruption is the shocking waste of time and talent poured into beating the system. In my public sector incarnations, I saw that the master job description writer was prized indeed; she or he could make almost anything come to pass, through painstaking construction of job requirements that would jump scores of regulated hurdles and end up with the desired placement of Ms. X in job Y.

I have no illusion about the elimination of job descriptions in the public sector. I do believe, on the basis of my observations, that such systems can be greatly simplified. Most regulations, written in response to legislation or executive orders, amount to killing gnats with a sledgehammers. The average public sector operation is choked on bureaucratic garbage of its own design, not that of misguided legislation. Goals of 75 to 95 percent reduction in system complexity (including all those described in this prescription) are within the domain of the *average* mid-level or senior public sector manager.

A promise to ask, at least five times each day, "Who says we have to do it this [complicated] way?" will launch the attack on systems gridlock—especially if you create an environment where everyone starts asking such questions.

FIRST STEPS

1. In one division or department, replace a complex system of performance appraisal with a contract written in plain prose. (Invest heavily in group discussion with those affected before doing so. It is essential that the "security" of the current, complex, objective-appearing system not be wholly compromised; the people to be evaluated must "buy in" and understand why the new system does not mean they will be prey to the whims of their managers.)
2. In conjunction with the establishment of a vision (L-2), eliminate job descriptions entirely or in one part of the organization this year. Again, substantial discussion, involving everyone, must accompany this move.

S-3

SUMMARY

To deal with the new strategic requirements for success, all the tools to induce and support action-taking must be available at the front line. Therefore, we must:

► Share virtually all information with everyone.

► Decentralize control systems, and decentralize the accountants/systems people who oversee them.

► Provide very high levels of expenditure authority for division general managers—and all other levels as well.

► Decentralize strategic planning.

The ability to take action close to the market—and fast—is the first requirement for competing. Therefore both information availability and the authority to move forward at the front line are musts.

Share, publicly and visibly, virtually all information about operating results—with everyone. Provide training to abet understanding this newly available information. Spending authority for business unit managers should be $20,000 to $50,000 (in a $25 million unit); spending authority for facility heads (and all others) should be proportionately as high. Make strategic planning an exclusively "bottom up" activity, with two-thirds of the content focusing on skill/capability-building rather than prediction of the future.

Decentralize Information, Authority, and Strategic Planning

An individual without information cannot take responsibility; an individual who is given information cannot help but take responsibility.

Jan Carlzon
from *Riv Pyramiderna!*

Promoting information exchange . . . was the original purpose of Quality Control circles in Japan, and it still is probably the most valuable use of circles.

Richard Schonberger
World Class Manufacturing

UNLEASH INFORMATION POWER

There are few greater liberating forces than the sharing of information. There is no such thing as "delegation" or "motivation" without extensive information.

Knowledge is power—it always has been; it always will be. Power—at the front line—is one more "must-do," not a "nice-to-do." Without power, there will be no (or, at least, no timely) action.

One stutters with amazement: The meeting is with executives of a food-processing company in the Midwest, over one billion dollars in size, privately held. The discussions turn to the distribution of profit-based bonuses, and the ins and outs of the facility (such as a factory) versus the division as the basis for distribution. A plant manager, who would be among those most affected by any scheme, has surprisingly little to say. I probe, and am stunned to learn that he has never been privy to data on the profitability of the facility he runs.

How can he manage? How can he be "motivated" to improve? How can he cope at all? A twenty-year veteran (and obviously successful), he acknowledges that there's "lots of conventional wisdom about individual product profitability" but no one really knows the score. In fact, a detailed corporate study had just revealed that an all-time favorite, a product thought to be a "cash cow," had in fact been losing money for years. This was clearly seen when costs were allocated more logically (see S-1).

This story is bad enough in any circumstance. It is terrifying in this case. New competitors are offering a bewildering array of new products. If the firm can't figure out what it takes in the plant to profit on a given product, it is doomed.

Information hoarding, especially by politically motivated, power-seeking staffs, has been commonplace throughout American industry, service and manufacturing alike. It will be an impossible millstone around the neck of tomorrow's organization. Sharing is a must.

Sharing means, apropos the preceding vignette, the availability of all data to facility managers. Equally important, it means availability of virtually all data to everyone, all the time.

"Everyone" includes the front-line team. Moreover, much of the most important information should be posted.

Yes, post the quality, scrap rate, and efficiency statistics. Let the whole factory team know—and visiting customers and vendors too. First Chicago, a bank with $40 billion in assets, worked with customers to develop some 700 performance measures (encompassing a large number of business units); these are the spearhead of its highly touted quality improvement program. Charts track progress on each of the indicators. Weekly performance reviews depict progress, or lack thereof, on each measure in terms of a stringent goal. The reviews, with dirty and clean linen alike aired, are always attended by customers and suppliers. The bank's executives believe that being publicly "on report" on what were previously the most confidential (or simply not tracked) measures is a great spur to performance. As they see it, there is no downside risk.

Leaks: The Phony Threat

The possibility that information will slip into the hands of competitors is the chief objection to widespread information sharing. It is a phony excuse on several scores.

First, there is no evidence that people on the line do leak the information. Firms such as Tandem Computer and Herman-Miller have long shared their corporate secrets—with everyone. More recently, firms such as GM have been sharing previously sacrosanct cost and operating performance data with front-line employees. There is just not a shred of evidence that such information gets leaked. (As one executive wryly observed: "If there's any evidence of leaking in general, it's usually vice-presidents who are the culprits.")

Second, determined competitors will have ferreted out, indirectly, what's important anyway—so you end up hiding the data only from those who could best use it on a day-to-day basis, the machine operators or first-line supervisors.

Finally, the specter of leaks is beside the point. Even if they were to occur, the value, for motivation and fast decision-making, of making information available to all is so high as to make any debate meaningless.

Is there any information that shouldn't be shared? Not much. Certainly patent information, confidential personnel records, and information about would-be acquisitions are off limits—for legal as well as common-sense reasons. But that's about all.

The evidence is unequivocal. People's thirst for understanding, especially amidst the new and permanent turbulence we now face, is unlimited; and with some training, their skill in interpretation is always extremely high, according to those who have been the most liberal sharers.

The Multiple Facets of the Power of Information

Information motivates in several ways:

1. It provides critical confirmation that the firm sees the worker as a partner and problem solver. The absence of such information confirms the worker's impotence.

2. The widespread availability of information is the only basis for effective day-to-day problem solving, which abets continuous improvement programs. Recall Jan Carlzon's comment at the beginning of this prescription: Without information, taking responsibility for improvement is highly unlikely.

3. Sharing information on the front line inhibits the upper-level power game playing that is the prime enemy of flexibility and moving fast. Basically, most power plays (and thence delays) are born of information hoarding. One group doesn't want to share a problem it may have caused. Another sees its unique data base as a way to control or delay action on a proposal it doesn't favor. Make information available to all, and most such behavior disappears—fast.

4. Visible posting of information radically speeds problem solving and action taking. There is an inherent human tendency to "butt in"—and it's great in this case. Post information on something, and a million experts bloom; most are helpful. Information—charts, graphs, operating data—is the organization's lubricant. When the plant or distribution center becomes one big billboard, a thousand chance interactions are triggered.

5. Information sharing stirs the competitive juices. Unit-versus-unit comparisons do this. But so do simple charts and graphs, even without such comparisons. Just about everyone would rather get better than get worse, especially when spurred by the increasingly intense competitive environment. Put a chart on the wall, and you've upped the odds that the suggestion box under it will be filled with ideas on how to make the performance curve go up.

6. (Useful) information begets more (useful) information. When information is "around"—a lot of it, publicly posted—people start asking all sorts of useful questions, and require more (and more relevant) information. Time and again, new measures are invented by groups close to a machine or process who have finally been let in on its secrets.

517

7. Information abets flattening the organizational pyramid (see P-8 and P-9). Information availability inherently shifts skill and responsibility to the front line and facilitates front-line communications across functional barriers ("horizontal management"). Information in and of itself is the chief substitute for first-line supervisors—and many staff experts too.

Training in the Use of Information

But information availability is not enough. It must be accompanied by extensive training in ways to develop the information, record it, analyze it, and act upon it. Successful firms such as Worthington Industries and Johnsonville Sausage go so far as to provide extensive training in economics and accounting for everyone (see P-4). All the best-quality programs involve training in problem analysis and data collection and interpretation, as well as in group problem-solving skills to promote the interchange of information and speed implementation (see also C-2, C-8).

HIGH SPENDING AUTHORITY

This prescription is really about the nuts and bolts of systems-induced autonomy. Information is a primary source of power, and a major stimulant of initiative- and risk-taking close to the action. Ranked right along with it is spending authority.

Again and again I find the most insultingly low spending authority granted to people—at all levels. It is especially self-defeating in a setting where everyone is being asked to act fast and take the initiative. All too commonplace is (1) the division general manager with $5,000 in "sign-off" authority (despite "control" over $40 million in assets), (2) the factory or operations center manager (600 employees) with $1,000 in authority, (3) the shift site manager or functional boss with $250 in authority, (4) the engineer or supervisor with $50 in authority, and (5) the first-line employee who must fill out a page-long form, with a supervisor's signature, to buy a $2.95 roll of tape needed in a practical problem-solving venture.

First, such low spending authority is demeaning and demotivating. We "trust" people to take the initiative and "make things happen," but give them no authority to do so. Second, it is self-defeating to that essential strategic need—hustle. Speed of execution depends not on big leaps, but on a million tiny actions taking a fraction of the time they used to. These in turn are driven by the ability to buy a roll of tape, a $100 tool off the shelf from Sears (rather than spending six weeks and $300 to "procure it" through channels), and take a $1,000 visit to a remote site, at a moment's notice, to speed up a project or move a new customer or supplier relation along another inch or two.

Here are the spending authorities I support:

▶ Front-line employee—$250
▶ First-line supervisor—$2,000
▶ Bench scientist or engineer—$2,000 to $10,000 (depending on seniority)
▶ Plant or operations center manager (two hundred people)—$5,000 to $25,000
▶ Division general manager ($25 million operation)—$20,000 to $50,000

The guidelines at Worthington are close to this, though much higher at the "lowest" level—$2,000 for a first-line employee (typical is the employee who went out and hired people and bought equipment to remove snow, making it easier for everyone to come to work). Chief Financial Officer Joe Stegmayer adds that "Nowhere is any of this written. . . . we want people to think, do it, and worry about it later. A person is never disciplined or chastised for spending money. In fact, we want people to make mistakes or they aren't being aggressive enough. If a person continues to make mistakes, however, then there's a problem."

More Control with Higher Spending Authority

Increasing spending authority does not entail a loss of control. To the contrary, it begets more control of the most powerful sort—self-control. Low spending authority leads to shenanigans—avoid a $1,000 limit by making an endless stream of $999.95 requisitions. High spending authority says to the worker, or unit boss, "I take you seriously." The monkey is on his or her back to live up to the trust.

And, to be sure, those who abuse the trust badly should be severely disciplined. Of course, it's not quite that easy; the leadership prescriptions come into play here. That is, the out-and-about leader (L-4), preaching the vision (L-2) and reinforcing it with stories about appropriate behavior (L-3), is essential to true delegation (L-7). Once more, I remind you that we are talking about substituting one form of control (vision, values, and visible management) for another (control by demeaning, voluminous rules).

The Leader's Job: Teaching About Limits

As a new consultant at McKinsey & Co. in 1974, I was immediately assigned to a team evaluating a huge addition to a southwestern petrochemical facility. An early task (second week) was to "check out supply and demand for [certain agricultural chemicals] in Canada over the next twenty years."

Arriving in Calgary, I soon decided that *I* needed a consultant. So I hired a Canadian energy specialist, for about $5,000, to do an analysis for me. No one told me to do it; nor did anyone approve my move. As a matter of fact, other than understanding that "you do whatever it takes to get an answer, fast," I don't know what led me to make such a bold (for a newcomer) move.

Sure enough, the answer helped the project along, but I also got a "coaching" lesson from my boss. He lavishly applauded my initiative as "good McKinsey tradition," but allowed as how I might have given him a jingle before doing the deal. He assured me he would have approved my effort, and I'm sure to this day that he would have.

The story is a fine example of how to teach initiative-taking—and limits. There was no spending limit imposed and in a similar crunch I would have done what I did again (I subsequently did many times), yet I also learned a lesson about touching bases first (which I subsequently also did). Thus my zest for reaching out—and the firm's support for such initiatives—was left intact, and, if anything, enhanced, while controls were maintained. This is all just common sense, not mysterious at all—and organizations can (and must) be run this way.

GENUINE "BOTTOM UP" STRATEGIC PLANNING

Sound strategic direction has never been more important—which is why the strategic planning process must be truly decentralized. Yet strategic planning, as we conventionally conceive of it, has become irrelevant, or worse, damaging.

What is a good strategic *plan*? There is none. But there is a good strategic planning process. A good strategic planning process (1) gets everyone involved, (2) is not constrained by overall corporate "assumptions" (e.g., about the general economics picture), (3) is perpetually fresh, forcing the asking of new questions, (4) is not to be left to planners, and (5) requires lots of noodling time and vigorous debate. As for the document per se, it (1) is succinct, (2) emphasizes the development of strategic skills, and (3) is burned the day before it is to go to the printer—that is, it is a living document, not an icon.

Flexibility is the necessary watchword. Sound thinking and debate about the future, marked by the asking of novel questions, foster flexibility of thought and action. Two-hundred-page plans do not. Moreover, flexibility is made possible by strategic capabilities and the habit of hustle (the ability to execute strategies quickly); strategic plans can address these topics, but seldom do.

Tomorrow's successful corporation will be a collection of skills and capabilities ever ready to pounce on brief market anomalies. Any useful strategic plan, or planning process, must focus upon the development and honing of these skills (which translates into readiness to seek and exploit opportunities), rather than emphasize static approaches to market development. That is, the strategy should focus primarily on such things as the time and energy to be devoted to creating revolutionary quality improvement (see C-2) or getting linked up fast with almost all of our customers (see C-4).

The "new" strategic plan, and planning process, must necessarily be "bottom-up." Assessing the ability (and necessary skills) to execute—to be responsive, flexible, attentive to customers—starts on the front line. Obviously, as the process moves forward, it will involve debate among senior officers, and compromise. But it should never lose touch with or sight of the front line, where execution takes place.

In fact, each facility, as well as each business unit and function, should have a strategic plan. The plan should not exceed a dozen pages, and perhaps two-thirds of it should be devoted to strategic skill/capability development in the context of the corporation/business unit's vision and the most significant external forces at work.

The plan, whose development involves everyone, should be shared with everyone after completion. At that point, there is a serious case to be made for destroying it—if not in practice, at least in spirit. Its value is as an assemblage of thoughts, not constraints. The process of developing it is close to 100 percent of its value—or perhaps more than 100 percent of its value. Slavishly following the plan despite changing conditions (now the norm), because of the time and political capital spent in assembling it, is counterproductive.

Finally, the content and format of the plan and the planning process should be modified substantially every year. Most plans and planning processes readily become bureaucratic (within two years), whereas the sole purpose is to be thought-provoking. Only changes in process which demand wholly new questions—from near the front line especially—will ensure vitality and usefulness.

FIRST STEPS

1. Do not hesitate or equivocate. Schedule an "all hands" meeting with your small or large group in the next 30 days. Share all operating information with them, leaving behind a printed version. Insist that every manager post key indicator charts, developed by front-line people, in every work area within the next 60 days.
2. Institute a thoroughgoing review of all spending authorities—this should not be an accountant-led review, but should be line-led, focusing on specific instances of delays in operations caused by limited spending authority.
3. Scrap your current strategic planning process—now. Burn your current strategic plan. Announce, in the next 30 days, that first-line input to the new process will be actively solicited—and demanded.

S-4

SUMMARY

Given the rising uncertainty that surrounds each project, and the firm as a whole, we must:

▶ Set conservative financial targets in all arenas—revenue, earnings, depreciation.

▶ Develop a true "appeal" system, which allows line managers ultimately to reject, if necessary, targets handed down to them.

▶ Set conservative growth targets, insisting in particular that infrastructure development—e.g., distribution networks, sales and service forces, the management talent bank—lead, not lag behind, projected revenue growth.

Above all, in an increasingly volatile environment, financial systems must have integrity and not be marred by unrealistic estimates. Likewise, if in a growth situation, we must be sure that the basic skills (e.g., distribution) are in place to support the exploitation of the opportunity.

Financial objectives should be small in number and conservative—only rarely should a manager fail to meet his or her objectives. Every growth plan must be backed up by the near-certainty of available supporting infrastructure.

Set Conservative Goals

This prescription is part of a paradox. The world is uncertain; so we must move at the snap of a finger to exploit any opportunity. To be ready and capable of this, however, we must be able to rely absolutely on our financial control systems and on the projections and promises we make. That is, the system must thrive on integrity and trust (see S-5). These two traits demand conservatism, not puffery, in our objective setting and budget promises.

Likewise, in order to grow through instant response to any opportunity, we must be certain that our execution skills—e.g., trained workers and managers, a well-oiled distribution system—are firmly established. To support aggressiveness in pursuit of new markets, then, we need conservatism of underlying systems.

There is an analogy in sports. A former all-pro defensive back, who once led the National Football League in interceptions, attributed his success to being the first to start and the last to finish the boring drills that make up everyday practice. "Any one interception," he said, "is just luck. But to increase the odds of 'getting lucky,' I needed to study and study the film and run and run with our guys who were running my [opponent's] patterns. I then stand a better chance of being in the right place any time the ball is a little bit off target."

Similarly, the most daring musicians are the ones who have mastered the basics so well that they can step out and try, at the margin, new variations. The boldest generals are invariably the truest masters of logistics; boldness under fire can only occur if the refueling operation runs like clockwork.

"SIGN UP"—AND DELIVER

In too many firms, budget drills, though nominally bottom-up, are in fact top-down. Targets are sent down, and you sign up—or else. So you do sign up, and some succeed. Many more fall short, and given the generally unrealistic nature of the estimates, you can't punish those who fail (that is, you can't punish 70 percent of all managers). More important, no one at any level can depend upon anyone else; the "numbers" are jokes. And when "numbers discipline" goes, so does the rest of discipline. Milestones are not met. Promises in general are not kept. Bad news is hidden or distorted. Blaming takes up most of the time, with little time left for doing.

Budgets, revenue projections, milestones, and objectives should be simplified (see S-1 and S-2). But what there is should be (1) prepared at the bottom and passed up, (2) believed in, (3) publicly committed to, and (4) subject to severe discipline if missed.

To move fast requires trust—period. Trust, though essentially interpersonal or one-on-one, is exhibited on a day-to-day basis by not signing up for what you can't deliver on.

Not a Plea for Timidity

The times do not permit timidity. They demand a new aggressiveness. So the conservatism I suggest does not mean setting unchallenging goals. To the contrary, goal setting should involve all sorts of peer pressure, and be done in the context of understanding the programs of competitors, which require us to respond energetically in return.

"Stretch" (within limits; see S-2) and fast movement are a must. But then when you commit to support manufacturing by April 27, at a cost of $70,000, with an installed system, you'd best deliver a working system—on April 27, for $70,000. And if you don't, there should be some substantial consequence, regardless of the reason for the miss.

Appeals

To support the integrity of goal setting, there must be a genuine, not phony or "paper only," opportunity for the manager to appeal any objective shoved down his or her throat.

You, as training officer, "get" an objective to support 50 percent growth in the minicomputer segment aimed at financial service institutions. You meet with the sales boss and come to understand the request. You go through several possible ramp-up scenarios, but you just can't do what's demanded in the next 120 days.

There must be, this prescription urges, a genuine, semi-formal (or formal) channel for you to appeal the request, up the line two or three levels if necessary. Ninety percent of the success of execution depends on commitment to the goal. If it is truly not achievable, commitment will not be there, and perhaps the whole plan will collapse like a house of cards.

Such an appeals process is not, as some suggest, tantamount to letting people off the hook. To the contrary, it puts them squarely on the hook. First, no manager will use it often (unless he or she has a very bad—unrealistic—boss); one does not lightly go over the heads of one or two bosses to challenge a target. More important, the system is a symbol of the overall seriousness with which the process of goal setting—and accepting—is taken. It says, in effect: "Don't sign up for what you can't do. If you do sign up for an undoable chore, you are a lousy manager, and you probably won't be with us long."

INFRASTRUCTURE MUST LEAD GROWTH

"We must take advantage of this narrow window of opportunity to launch the [new product or service]." That's an increasingly common statement. And it's true. Yet there is a major caveat. If the machine doesn't quite work yet, if the sales force isn't well trained in its special features, if distributors have been chosen promiscuously, if adequate spares are not appropriately positioned— well, not only will the product launch go poorly, but the firm's reputation will be set back immeasurably, perhaps irreparably if it is a small firm.

Thus, there is a second form of conservatism—ensuring that growth at any cost and opportunity at any cost does not become the company's watchword. Growth (new-product launches, etc.) must be preceded by skills/capabilities development.

All too many firms—Atari is a recent example—take advantage of what they see as a once-in-a-lifetime opportunity; they pour the product out upon the world, then play catch-up with sales training, distribution center development, and distributor selection. It doesn't work.

Indeed, this strategy of conservatism, which demands that basic skills/ capabilities development precedes growth, is more important in these volatile times than ever before. First, there are more temptations (little windows of opportunity) than ever before. You must regularly seize them; but if you get into the habit of doing so without doing your sales and service development home-work, you are doomed to short-term project failure and long-term loss of reputation.

Second, with more products and services—and more good ones—available to the consumer, quality, service, and reliability/responsiveness (C-2 through C-4) are increasingly the only effective differentiating strategies; you can't play catch-up on quality and service. Given competitive alternatives, the customer will not let you get away with more than one lapse. That is, the skills/capabilities, per se, are *the* most valuable strategic weapons—they can't be "assumed" to follow a clever product's launch.

Loving Growth—with Good Sense

Let me reiterate that all of the above is not a plea for slow growth, or a rejection of opportunism. Opportunistic growth is increasingly essential to any organization's health. A firm is never static—it is either growing or stagnating. While growth for growth's sake at the extreme is silly, growth alone provides an expanding opportunity structure for everyone in the firm. Moreover, stagnation, absolute or relative, is enervating, negatively affecting every element of the firm. Excitement (growth) spurs performance; contraction doesn't.

I am simply insisting in this part of the prescription that the growth should be led by, and governed by, infrastructure development:

► Lead with upgrading the skills of the work force. Teach factory people to be flexible; invest in equipment that abets that flexibility *before* you need it.
► Upgrade the skills of the sales force continuously—*before* the need arises; provide the sales force with tools ahead of the market need.
► Engage in distribution system/distributor upgrading *before* the specific market requirement arises.
► Budgets should emphasize ongoing skill/capability development as the essential strategy (also see the section in S-3 dealing with strategy).

The firm should be looked at as an ever-improving packet of necessary capabilities. If this conception becomes second nature, then the company will indeed be ready to take advantage of almost any market opportunity that comes along, with foreknowledge that it can execute to support the idea.

A WORLD TURNED UPSIDE DOWN

This prescription constitutes a new view of organizing and of strategy development in particular: the company as a set of skills being continuously elaborated, to be applied as needed to market opportunities. The traditional view of strategy is to let the product, product family, or market drive all thinking, with skills in a secondary or supporting role. One does "what makes sense" based upon a static market analysis—filling in behind market opportunities with requisite support skills.

Paradoxically the "rightness" of that idea—conquering or reconceiving markets—is precisely what requires us to reject a "market conception" approach today. The company simply must be ahead of itself in capabilities in order to exploit these fast-appearing/fast-disappearing market/product opportunities. Essential skills must be in place before the fact.

3M has epitomized such an approach. It is a finely tuned machine designed to invent new markets. All of its organizational paraphernalia, from incentive schemes to management development techniques to approaches to factory development, constitute one giant exercise in skill/capability development—which is then directed opportunistically at fast market creation. Likewise, the development of responsive, field-centered marketing mechanisms at Frito-Lay and Campbell Soup (see C-4) is a strategy of "skill development in search of market enhancement opportunities."

The pragmatic implications are twofold. First, as observed, budgets and strategies—and individual evaluations—should emphasize capability development. Second, growth targets for products/markets should be conservative—that is, governed by the status of skill development/readiness.

FIRST STEPS

1. Ensure that each formal and informal review (operations reviews, performance evaluations) emphasizes promises kept—for instance, budget targets, milestones. No small breach of promise can go unnoted, regardless of extenuating circumstances (see also S-5). (In today's world "business as usual" has become a meaningless phrase; every circumstance is an extenuating circumstance—*promises must be made in light of expected extenuating circumstances*.) After due process is observed, fire those who don't get this message, especially those who don't come through on acts of cross-functional support, major or minor (if a pattern exists).

2. Devote two-thirds of budget preparation and strategy formulation/review to skill/capability/infrastructure development. Consider a single forthcoming product. Are growth projections driven by the availability of needed skills/capabilities/infrastructure or by "window of opportunity" logic? Reassess the project in light of an "infrastructure-driven" approach.

S-5

SUMMARY

Today's new realities (let alone common sense) require us to:

▶ Demand total integrity—of the Boy Scout/Girl Scout/"squeaky clean" sort—in all dealings, with people and systems, inside the firm and out.

▶ Eliminate Mickey Mouse rules and regulations (see also P-10, L-8) that induce cheating and game playing, which then spread to all the firm's affairs.

Integrity has been the hallmark of the superior organization through the ages. Be that as it may, today's accelerating uncertainty gives the issue new importance. People on the front line must be able to deal quickly across traditional functional barriers; sole-source arrangements must be made with suppliers in the face of uncertain future demands. Successful organizations must shift from an age dominated by contracts and litigiousness to an age of handshakes and trust.

Set absurdly high standards for integrity—and then live them, with no fuzzy margins. A deal made on a milestone (see S-4) which is subsequently missed is grounds for dismissal, especially when it involves support for another function or a vendor/customer. A person who is genuinely—and legitimately—surprised by his or her annual performance appraisal provides grounds for dismissal of the person's boss.

528

S-5

Demand Total Integrity

Without doubt, honesty has always been the best policy. The best firms on this score have long had the best track records overall—Johnson & Johnson, IBM, S. C. Johnson (Johnson Wax), Hewlett-Packard, Merck, Digital Equipment.

Yet once more, this very-nice-to-do for all times is a must-do for tomorrow. Quality and flexibility—and constant innovation—are chief among the new winner's watchwords. These traits require wholesale involvement by employees and a willingness to work together. Barriers between functions must fall, as must adversarial relations between labor and management, suppliers and buyers, sellers and distributors, sellers and customers.

Involvement by all and nonadversarial relations must necessarily rest on a cornerstone of trust, which in turn can only be engendered by total integrity. If a promise (even a minor one) is not kept, if ethics are compromised, and if management behaves inconsistently, then the strategies necessary to survival today (see C-1 through C-4, for instance) simply can't be executed.

This prescription once more reveals a paradox—namely, that the uncertainty of the environment can be swiftly dealt with only if the firm can fall back upon the certainty of relationships among people and among groups—in other words, upon trust and integrity.

INTEGRITY IN DEALINGS WITH THE FRONT LINE

Integrity means living up to commitments, inside and outside the firm. As discussed in C-3, in a world of exploding product and service offerings, keeping your word takes on added significance. It might at first seem that, faced with stiff new competition, you must make outrageous promises to get the deal. While I hardly advocate being the slowest in town, I do urge very conservative—high-integrity—behavior. With more, often newer, firms, there is more uncertainty surrounding the buyer's purchase, regardless of the offsetting joy of having more choices. With more uncertainty the norm, reliability is worth more than ever, especially when it comes to that all-important repeat business.

Routinely "over-delivering" to the customer cannot be achieved without more cooperation (among functions in a firm) and greater commitment within the firm—which again stems from integrity. Engendering wholesale commitment from everyone involves making "deals" (compacts) and living up to them. Chief among the "deals" is a commitment to lifetime employment (if performance remains acceptable) for some substantial share of the work force (see P-7). The vendor equivalent is sole-sourcing, as long as performance meets agreed-upon goals.

Quite simply, if we are going to ask people to be flexible (C-4), be responsible for constant innovation (I-10), take risks, and perform a host of tasks (P-1), we must provide a relatively certain future. It is inconsistent—or a pipe dream—to ask people to "step out and take risks" (speak up, change things, blow the whistle on poor quality or service) and then confront them with a capricious, never-ending, nickel-and-dime pattern of layoffs or force reductions.

Likewise (see P-10, L-8), it is inconsistent to ensnare people via Mickey Mouse and demeaning rules, and hogtie them with voluminous procedures—and then ask them to take responsibility for quality, maintenance, housekeeping, etc. And it is inconsistent to require much higher commitment and involvement without offering a dollar payoff if the performance is positive (P-6).

All such inconsistencies are abrogations of integrity—that is, they don't amount to a sensible and fair compact between the employee and the firm—especially the firm beset by uncertainty (as almost all are).

Integrity and Quality

High quality of product and high quality of service demand absolute integrity. Providing a superior-quality product or service is a moral and aesthetic act (see C-2), as well as an act that "conforms to specifications." Superior quality stems from pride and enthusiasm for the product or service as much as from good measurement instruments. Top quality also means, of course, not skimping or taking shortcuts in order to meet a production schedule, especially during the last week of the financial reporting period.

Superior quality simply cannot be extracted from a low-integrity organization. That is, unfairness in personnel policies, for instance, directly affects the quality of the product over time. To be treated capriciously by the firm is incompatible with caring about the product religiously.

Integrity and Perks

To use the psychologists' terms, integrity is not only absolute (stealing is bad, period), but it involves "perceived equity." That is, fairness is in the eye of the beholder. Paying bonuses to management and withholding worker bonuses in a problematic year is perceived to be unfair, regardless of the extenuating circumstances (the executive bonuses may have come from cashing in years-old stock options, or be due to extremely good performance in one small part of the business).

In general, the wisest firms avoid excessive executive perks and even the appearance of minor impropriety (an executive "off-site" at a lavish resort following a not-great year). Mars, Inc., is among those paying its managers very well, but avoiding almost all perks, including lavish offices. (It is the officers' special dental plan, covering orthodontics for kids, that causes more anguish on the line than their six-figure salaries. Somehow, the former is more tangible than the latter.)

"SMALL" INJUSTICES—BIG IMPLICATIONS

Integrity may be about little things as much as or more than big ones. It's about executives taking friends, rather than customers, to sit in the company's box seats at the ballpark. It's about pushing salespeople at the end of a quarter to place orders, knowing that many will be canceled within the week—but that the cancellations will count in the next period for accounting purposes.

These "minor" lapses set a tone of disrespect for people, products, systems, customers, distributors, and relationships that can readily become pervasive. That is, there is no such thing as a minor lapse in integrity.

"Squeaky Clean"

IBM has been known to fire an employee for accepting a gratuity from a supplier (a pen set), and then discipline the employee's boss severely as well. As a vendor to Stew Leonard's (he and others have attended our seminars), I am on a mailing list that includes a letter before Christmas asking me not to send any gratuities to anyone in the store. I believe that such rigid behavior around "little" integrity issues is a must.

Go a step further. An employee receives an annual performance evaluation, and is genuinely surprised by his or her low rating. Delve into it, and if it turns out that the supervisor misled the employee, or failed to communicate displeasure along the way, that supervisor should be severely (and officially) warned, and let go if there is a pattern of such behavior.

"Overdoing it" on "little" breaches of integrity pays big dividends as long as you are perfectly consistent (perceived to be even-handed). It pays with people in the firm—it induces integrity in general (living up to all commitments). And it pays with outsiders—suppliers, customers, communities, and even governments.

For example, Milliken's and IBM's squeaky-clean reputations make both firms very desirable to suppliers. Both are downright tough—but also unquestionably fair. You will not lose business for a capricious reason, though you might well lose it for a "minor" breach of promise (by the standards of others), such as a "slightly" missed schedule.

INTEGRITY IS CONSISTENCY

In *Leaders,* when Warren Bennis and Burt Nanus say they observed the highest integrity among their many heroes, they are referring especially to consistency. Visions were clear—and lived with almost frightening consistency, in small as well as in large ways.

Once again, this is a timely issue as well as an issue for the ages. All people must take risks and welcome change, if the firm is to survive. They will only do so when the larger picture (the firm's vision—L-2) is unmistakable.

If it is unmistakable (that is, consistent), then they can take small chances with impunity, knowing that these "tries," successful or not, are consistent with moving the execution of the vision forward. Conversely, if there is no vision, or if the edges of the vision are blurred, you don't know what is "risk in pursuit of the vision" as opposed to "risk for risk's sake." Few of us, mavericks or not, are willing to chance the latter. And a few risk-takers are decisively not the point anyway. We need everyone to be taking risks all the time within the context of the vision.

Hypocrisy: Enemy #1 of Integrity

The boss who preaches quality, but puts wholly unrealistic schedule demands on the plant or operations center, is seen as a hypocrite. Trust, integrity, fairness in dealing with others (all under the gun to do unrealistic things and sign up for unrealistic promises), and quality/service all go kaput.

SYSTEMS SUPPORTS FOR INTEGRITY

Many of the prescriptions in this book, especially those dealing with people and leadership, are enhancers of integrity. Chief among these is removal of bureaucracy and demeaning rules. Silly and demeaning rules invite game playing; it's as simple as that. Likewise, reduction of "layers" on the organization chart (P-8) helps integrity too. In the absence of a lot of paper-pushing middle managers, there's likely to be less delayed action, which is always viewed on the line as being the result of political power plays made for personal reasons—that is, the antithesis of integrity in support of people and quality.

Widespread information sharing (S-3), wholesale people involvement (P-1), and extensive training (P-5) all foster integrity by making front-line people powerful themselves—full-scale, fully informed, participating partners.

Visible management (L-4) is chief among the leadership prescriptions that foster integrity. Integrity, that is, also means "knowing the score." When leaders are perceived to be out of touch (not out and about regularly, for instance), they cannot, in the view of the line, behave with integrity—that is, with consistency or realism. Since they don't know what's going on (in the line's view), their "orders" and policies and nifty new programs often look downright foolish.

Prescriptions S-1 and S-2 touted simplicity—in measures, goals, plans. Simplicity and integrity go hand in hand. If objectives are limited in number and thoughtfully negotiated, the odds of their being meaningful skyrocket. Complex and lengthy skeins of objectives are less well understood, are less likely to be carefully negotiated, and are therefore taken less seriously; in other words, the system lacks integrity.

REPRISE

The systems prescriptions are not a matter of some generic "good practice." They are all in service to the violently changed competitive conditions that now surround us. Moreover, they directly support the other four sets of prescriptions. Without these last five systems prescriptions, much of the power of the first forty will be lost. Though each prescription lays down a major challenge, it is vital to remember that each of the forty-five supports the others; you must somehow address all forty-five at once, even though specific programs will emphasize one or another. That is, the forty-five taken together, and nothing less, constitute the elements of tomorrow's surviving organization.

FIRST STEPS

1. Do not make any commitment, starting right now, internal or external, that you can't live up to (with room to spare)—large or, especially, small.
2. Review delivery promises to ten key customers. Review objectives for the next 90 days that you have agreed to or that you have negotiated with people who report to you, focusing on simplicity—and achievability. Review the achievability of commitments to other functions. Make such reviews a commonplace part of staff meetings, operations reviews, and managerial evaluations, informal as well as formal.
3. Seek out at least one symbolic opportunity each week (preferably small) to emphasize the simplicity/achievability of commitments—to a supplier, to a customer, to another function, to an employee.

Acknowledgments

A nonfiction book is as good as the stories people share. I am first and foremost indebted to the experimenting, risk-taking men and women who are trying (sometimes successfully, sometimes not) to restore American competitiveness and who have let me glimpse their efforts. Likewise I am indebted to the talented reporters for such publications as the *Wall Street Journal, The New York Times, Business Week, Inc., Fortune,* and *Forbes,* and many local papers and journals. I am an inveterate—and unrepentant—user of secondary sources, either directly or as leads for my own investigations; I find the quality of reporting generally to be high—i.e., the facts are straight.

This book grew out of our Skunk Camps. I gratefully acknowledge the role of our participant-customers who kept carping, "Get prescriptive." Well, I've tried—and this book is a work in progress toward that end. I'm also indebted to my close Skunk Camp colleagues, especially Bob Le Duc and Reuben Harris; they are both superb teachers, and our continual reshaping of the seminars together provided another major assist to this effort. Finally, the seminar participants, as mentioned in Part I, more often than not represent America's vital mid-sized ($75 million to $750 million) companies; it was my experience with executives from such firms that triggered my study of these firms' overall contribution to the economy. There is no doubt that these are the bellwether organizations.

I also heartily acknowledge a series of intellectual debts. In this book, I have explored numerous avenues that were new to me, from the history of automation to the history of employment guarantees. Perhaps because of my earlier academic training, I am only comfortable with my empirical efforts when I can find some leading-edge thinkers who are mining the same veins. Among others, then, I doff my cap to James Abegglen, Walter Adams, Warren Bennis, David Birch, Tom Bonoma, James Brock, Dick Cavanagh, Bob Christopher, Dick Foster, Brad Gale, George Gendron, George Gilder, John Groocock, Robert Hall, Jim Harrington, Bob Hayes, Masaaki Imai, Robert Kaplan, Jim Kouzes, Regis McKenna, David Noble, Michael Piore, Brian Quinn, Robert Reich, Charles Sabel, Richard Schonberger, Pat Townsend, Martin Weitzman—and Karl Weick, whose highly original conception of organizational structure remains the single most important influence on my thinking over the years. ("This fits with the unique way Karl sees organizations" is my ultimate test of any idea.)

Another group of people is far too large for me to mention individually—those who have supported me through the years such as Stew Leonard, who exhorts, at exactly the right moment (after I've suffered my tenth consecutive delayed flight), "Keep it up. Keep yelling. Keep talking. Keep writing." Stew will have to stand in for the hundreds I know well, and the thousands who write each year with kind letters of encouragement.

Last but not least are friends closer to home. At the top of the list is my friend (and spouse) Kate Abbe. She believes that there is nothing in life that counts except writing. Her continual and ungentle reminders of that, and support in a million ways, are invaluable. Also invaluable is the contribution of my friend and editor at Alfred A. Knopf, Corona Machemer. Her mastery of detail is impressive, and her damnable questions in the margin have simply reshaped this book several times. Her grasp of the content is at least as good as mine, and her innocent six-word queries have sent many a chapter back to the drawing board (or into the wastebasket); there is no higher tribute.

Kathy Dalle-Molle has checked almost every fact in this manuscript, and has devoted passion and awesome energy to tracing down the most obscure references (and people) imaginable; many of her queries have resulted in valuable elaborations as well. Susan Bright Winn typed and retyped (usually by "yesterday") the formidable manuscript from which this book emerged at least six times—wow!

Jayne Pearl, whose principal activity is the editing of our newsletter, has also been a constant source of creative needling. Jayne and I struggle weekly with my syndicated column, where many of the themes in this book have been born or honed.

Many at Knopf have bent over backwards to bring this book to life in very short order, among them designer Peter Andersen, production manager Andy Hughes, Corona Machemer's assistant, Ann Kraybill, and production editor Melvin Rosenthal. The indexer, Maro Riofrancos, and the compositors at Com-Com also did superior jobs under pressure.

My partners, Debbie Kaplan, Bob Le Duc (mentioned before), and Ian Thomson, continue to encourage and cajole. Debbie, I think, works for Knopf—at least she's asked, "How's the manuscript coming?" many more times than they did.

Finally, one last thanks to the two people to whom this book is dedicated, Roger Milliken and Don Schaefer. When I come across an especially bold idea, one that I think is necessary to our economic survival, I always ask myself, "But could anybody in the real world ever pull this off?" And then I think of Roger and Don—oh yes, it can all be done!

T.P.

The Journal of the Healthcare Forum: Excerpt from "The Power of Owning a High-Quality Market Position Can Be Overwhelming" by J. Daniel Beckham. *The Journal of the Healthcare Forum,* March/April 1987. Copyright © 1987 by *The Journal of the Healthcare Forum.* Excerpt from "Innovator Award Winners" by Julie Herrod. *The Journal of the Healthcare Forum,* March/April 1987. Copyright © 1987 by *The Journal of the Healthcare Forum.*

Little, Brown & Company: Brief excerpt from *The Intuitive Manager* by Roy Rowan.

Pantheon Books, a Division of Random House, Inc.: Excerpts from *The Bigness Complex: Industry, Labor and Government in the American Economy* by Walter Adams and James W. Brock. Copyright © 1986 by Walter Adams and James W. Brock. Reprinted by permission.

Random House, Inc.: Excerpts from *Nobel Dreams* by Gary Taubes. Copyright © 1986 by Gary Taubes. Excerpts from *Kaizen* by Masaaki Imai. Copyright © 1986 by The Kaizen Institute, Ltd. Reprinted by permission.

Scripps-Howard News Service: Excerpt from "Factory Workers' New Design Saved 2-Seater for Ford" by William Allan, copyright © 1986. Reprinted by permission of Scripps-Howard News Service.

Times Books, a Division of Random House, Inc.: Excerpt from *Tales of a New America* by Robert B. Reich. Copyright © 1987 by Robert B. Reich. Reprinted by permission of Times Books.

Viking Penguin Inc.: Excerpt from *Augustine's Laws* by Norman Augustine. Copyright © 1983, 1986 by Norman R. Augustine. Reprinted by permission of Viking Penguin Inc.

Work in America Institute: Material on pages 346 to 350 is based on, and quotes extensively from, *Employment Security in a Free Economy* by Jerome M. Rosow and Robert Zager, © 1984 by Work in America Institute, Inc. Reprinted by permission of Work in America Institute.

Notes

Facing Up to the Need for Revolution

page   3   "Can America make it?": "Rebuilding the US Model," *Financial Times,* May 9, 1987, p. 26.

       This is the General Electric idea: Edwin A. Finn Jr., "General Eclectic," *Forbes,* March 23, 1987, p. 75.

    5   A formidable $41 billion positive trade balance: James Brian Quinn and Christopher Gagnon, "Will Service Follow Manufacturing into Decline," *Harvard Business Review,* November/December 1986, p. 95.

    6   "It will take hard and": Ibid., p. 103.

    7   On the one hand: James R. Norman, "General Electric Is Stalking Big Game Again," *Business Week,* March 16, 1987, p. 113.

       "Certainly most studies suggest that": Michael Porter, "The State of Strategic Thinking," *The Economist,* May 23, 1987, pp. 18, 22.

    8   "Current 'merger mania' notwithstanding": Raymond E. Miles and Charles C. Snow, "Network Organizations: New Concepts for New Forms," *California Management Review,* Spring 1986, p. 62.

       "Restructuring. The magic word": John Heins, "But the Grass Looked Greener over There," *Forbes,* April 27, 1987, p. 54.

   12   "Henry Ford made great contributions": "Business Guru Finds a Following," San Jose *Mercury News,* April 17, 1987, p. 13D.

   14   "they preferred Japanese suppliers": Sylvia Nasar, "Competitiveness: Getting It Back," *Fortune,* April 27, 1987, p. 223.

       GE chairman Jack Welch: Finn, p. 75.

   15   Lee does a thorough: O-Young Lee, *Smaller Is Better: Japan's Mastery of the Miniature* (New York: Kodansha International, 1984), p. 19.

       The folding fan: Ibid., p. 35.

       "Nothing comes harder": Ibid., p. 87.

       Through it was a: Ibid., pp. 154–6.

       Lee concludes: "That reduction": Ibid., p. 156.

       In summary, says Lee: Ibid., p. 169.

   16   "Bigness has not delivered": Walter Adams and James W. Brock, *The Bigness Complex: Industry, Labor and Government in the American Economy* (New York: Pantheon Books, 1986), p. xi.

       "Scientific evidence has not": Ibid., p. 46.

       "a big, sprawling, inert giant": Ibid., p. 35.

   17   "in practically all our activities": Ibid., pp. 39–40.

       In a classic 1956 study: Ibid., pp. 45–6.

page 17 "Cost-cutting opportunities": Ibid., pp. 44–5.

"the Milwaukee-based firm": Jack Thornton, "New Marketing Muscle," *Industry Week,* May 4, 1987, p. 38.

18 "Some 90 percent of those": "California Doing Its Own Thing," *U.S. News & World Report,* December 22, 1986, p. 25.

18–19 "Ostensibly, giant firms might": Adams and Brock, p. 50.

19 "reality and the available": Ibid., p. 52.

"Nor do giant firms": Ibid., p. 54.

Yet another study: Ibid., p. 55.

"A study . . . found the": Ibid., p. 52.

19–20 "The large corporation at risk . . .": Eli Ginzberg and George Vojta, *Beyond Human Scale: The Large Corporation at Risk* (New York: Basic Books Inc., 1985), pp. 218–19.

21–2 ". . . high wage economies can": Robert B. Reich, *Tales of a New America* (New York: Times Books, 1987), pp. 118, 119, 120, 121, 147, 148.

23 "Uniformity has given way": Martin Davis, "Two Plus Two Doesn't Equal Five," *Fortune,* December 9, 1985, p. 175.

24 In September 1986: "Chipping Away," *Financial World,* September 30, 1986, p. 4.

"The way in which market": "IBM Humbled," *The Economist,* January 31, 1987, p. 17.

". . . parallel/multiprocessor computers" market: Dwight B. Davis, "Parallel Computers Diverge," *High Technology,* February 1987, p. 20.

25 The greater good news story: Michael S. Malone, "America's New-Wave Chip Firms," *Wall Street Journal,* May 27, 1987, p. 28.

Take Kitchen Privileges . . .: Caroline E. Mayer, "Cooking Up a Hot Idea," Washington *Post,* January 26, 1987, p. 1 (Business).

26–7 "Stand in the spotless . . .": John Merwin, "McOil Change," *Forbes,* August 11, 1986, p. 91.

C-1

51 ". . . the Japanese pulled . . .": Otis Port, "Making Brawn Work with Brains," *Business Week,* April 20, 1987, p. 57.

"The fastest growing companies": "The Riches in Market Niches," *Fortune,* April 27, 1987, article subhead.

"The car market has become": Bill Saporito, "The Smokestacks Won't Tumble," *Fortune,* February 2, 1987, p. 30.

"There has been an explosion": Rob Hof, "New Gourmet-Food Firms Hope to Dish Up Profits," *Peninsula Times Tribune,* May 11, 1987, p. B-1.

53–4 "Marketing should focus on": Regis McKenna, *The Regis Touch* (Reading, MA: Addison-Wesley Publishing, 1986), pp. 21–3.

56 Economist William Hall: Theodore Levitt, *The Marketing Imagination* (New York: The Free Press, 1983, 1986), pp. 136–7.

58 "One of the characteristics": Robert Christopher, *Second to None* (New York: Crown Publishers, 1986), p. 150.

62–3 "Franklin [Electric Company]": Pat Choate, *The High-Flex Society* (New York: Alfred A. Knopf, 1986), pp. 214–15.

C-2

65 "The best of ours": Jeremy Main, "Detroit's Cars Really Are Getting Better," *Fortune,* February 2, 1987, p. 95.

Percentage of West Germans: "Harper's Index," *Harper's,* March 1987, p. 15.

pages 65–6 "Tennant Company was known": Roger L. Hale, Douglas R. Hoelscher, Ronald E. Kowal, *Quest for Quality* (Minneapolis, MN: Tennant Company, 1987), pp. 11–12.

66 "It has always been remarkable": J. Daniel Beckham, "The Power of Owning a High-Quality Market Position Can Be Overwhelming," *Healthcare Forum,* March/April 1987, pp. 13–14.

67 PIMS researchers now call: "Formulating a Quality Improvement Strategy," *PIMS-LETTER,* no. 31, p. 5.

PIMS assesses both technical: "Product Quality," *PIMSLETTER,* no. 4, p. 4.

In 1985, Dr. John Groocock: John Groocock, *The Chain of Quality* (New York: John Wiley & Sons, 1986), p. 83.

The top third of TRW's: Ibid., p. 85.

68 "The PIMS results for": Ibid., p. 6.

"It would appear that": *Consumer Perceptions Concerning the Quality of American Products and Services* (A study by the Gallup Organization for the American Society for Quality Control, 1985), pp. 12–13.

69 The Rogers Survey, done only: Main, p. 93.

Another important Power survey: *The Power Report,* December 1986, p. 6.

Finally, *Consumer Reports* conducts: James K. Glassman, "The Wreck of General Motors," *New Republic,* December 29, 1986, p. 21.

70–1 "Let me tell you": Laurence Shames, *The Big Time* (New York: Harper & Row, 1986), p. 102.

71 "You can't become emotionally": Steven Prokesch, "Remaking the American CEO," *The New York Times,* January 25, 1987, p. 8 (Section 3).

"I don't think you": James Kouzes and Barry Posner, from the working papers for *The Leadership Challenge: How to Get Extraordinary Things Done in Organizations* (San Francisco: Jossey-Bass, 1987).

"Now step back": H. James Harrington, *The Improvement Process* (New York: McGraw-Hill Book Co., 1987), p. 58.

72 "pour money into computers": Joel Dreyfuss, "Toyota Takes Off the Gloves," *Fortune,* December 22, 1987, p. 78.

In 1960, Toyota's suggestion system: Michael A. Cusumano, *The Japanese Automobile Industry* (Cambridge: Harvard University Press: 1985), pp. 358–9.

73–4 Recall Roger Hale's comment: Hale, Hoelscher, Kowal, p. 31.

74 "Measurement is the heart": H. James Harrington, *Excellence: The IBM Way* (IBM Technical Report, 1986), p. 19.

75 "Data recording comes first": Richard Schonberger, *World Class Manufacturing: The Lessons of Simplicity Applied* (New York: The Free Press, 1986), pp. 18–19.

For instance, with one: Harrington, *Excellence: The IBM Way,* pp. 45–6.

"Western industry must put substantially": Schonberger, p. 215.

76–7 "The billing process consists of": Harrington, *The Improvement Process,* pp. 13–14.

77 "Many teams received credit": Pat Townsend, *Commit to Quality* (New York: John Wiley & Sons, 1986), p. 103.

78 "Champions can . . . come from": Hale, Hoelscher, Kowal, p. 68.

78–9 ". . . I got the phone number": Ibid., pp. 35–6.

79 "As greater quality is built": Norman Augustine, *Augustine's Laws* (New York: Viking Penguin Inc., 1983, 1986), p. 104.

81–2 From Harrington, *Excellence: The IBM Way,* pp. 73, 75, 85.

83 "We have to grant quality": Edward Tenner, "The Meaning of Quality," *Quality: America's Guide to Excellence,* p. 37.

83–4 When Ford designed its pathbreaking: Mary Walton, *The Deming Management Method* (New York: Dodd, Mead & Company, 1986), p. 143.

84 "Seamstresses [who] hold requiem services": Joseph Campbell, *The Masks of Gods: Oriental Mythology* (New York: Penguin, 1970), p. 478.

/ **NOTES**

page 84 "Although Japanese lumbermen": Joel Kotkin, "The New Northwest Passage," Joel Kotkin, *Inc.,* February 1987, p. 94.

C-3

90 Employees even declare that Jim Nordstrom: "Nordstrom Chain Sets Itself Apart with an Old-Fashioned Service Policy," Los Angeles *Times,* September 30, 1984, p. 1 (Business).

91 The PIMS data base once more: *PIMSLETTER,* no. 33, p. 8.

92 The Total Product Concept: Theodore Levitt, "Marketing Success Through Differentiation—of Anything," *Harvard Business Review,* January/February 1980.

95 "[I]t is common . . .": McKenna, pp. 41, 43–4.

C-4

108 "U.S. retailers such as": "How High-Tech Tailors Are Saving a Stitch in Time," *Business Week,* April 14, 1987, p. 92G.

109 "bottom up than top down": Jennifer Lawrence, "Frito Play," *Advertising Age,* March 30, 1987, p. 1.
"Basically there's no such": Ibid., p. 1.
"We are tailoring": Ibid., p. 1.

111 "(1) Reduced order lead times": Louis Stern and Patrick Kaufmann, "Electronic Data Interchange in Selected Consumer Goods Industries: An Interorganizational Perspective," *Marketing in an Electronic Age* (Boston: Harvard Business School Press, 1985), edited by Robert Buzzell, p. 56.
"has pioneered a retailing": James L. Heskett, *Managing in the Service Economy* (Boston: Harvard Business School Press, 1986), p. 67.

112 "transmits [by computer] its production": Davis, p. 20.

114 "All Japanese motorcycle companies": Robert Hall, *Attaining Manufacturing Excellence* (Homewood, IL: Dow Jones-Irwin, 1987), p. 107.

117 "A corrugated box company": Hall, p. 249.

118 "The development of [the] system": Robert Hall, *Zero Inventories* (Homewood, IL: Dow Jones-Irwin, 1983), p. 9.

C-5

123 "American management in the past": Gary Blonston, "The Translator," *Science '85,* July/August 1985, p. 80.

123–4 Natural gas owned by: Walter Wriston: *Risk and Other Four Letter Words* (New York: Harper & Row, 1986), p. 152.

124–5 Despite the hiatus: Nicholas D. Kristof, "Japan Winning Race in China," *The New York Times,* April 29, 1987, p. 41 (Business).

125–8 Material, except on Buckman Labs and IBM, derived from Christopher, pp. 8, 19, 143, 6, 7, 46, 55, 70, 9, 43, 45, 57, 37, 83, 4, 60; and from Lennie Copeland and Lewis Griggs, *Going International: How to Make Friends and Deal Effectively in the Global Marketplace* (New York: Random House, 1985).

128–9 "Several factors explain": Raymond Vernon, "Gone Are the Cash Cows of Yesteryear," *Harvard Business Review,* November/December 1980, pp. 153–4.

130 Coca-Cola took the lime taste: Christopher, pp. 122–3.

131–2 "The Americans still talk": Steven Schlossstein, *Trade War* (New York: Congdon & Weed Inc., 1984), pp. 63–4.

C-6

page 137 "The point about Dayton-Hudson's": Subrata N. Chakravarty, "Federated Chooses Not to Choose," *Forbes,* April 8, 1985, p. 87.

Sears lived by the slogan: Julien R. Phillips and Allan A. Kennedy, "Shaping and Managing Shared Values," in *The Leader-Manager,* ed. by John N. Williamson (New York: John Wiley and Sons, 1984), p. 198.

138 "The three generic strategies": Michael Porter, *Competitive Strategy* (New York: The Free Press, 1980), pp. 35, 41–3.

138–9 A 1985 study: Alex Miller and Bill Camp, "Exploring Determinants of Success in Corporate Ventures," *Journal of Business Venturing,* Winter 1985, pp. 87–105.

140 it turns out that: Groocock, p. 85.

The "straddle" strategy: Levitt, p. 137.

141 "Leadership is heading into": Warren Bennis and Burt Nanus, *Leaders* (New York: Harper & Row, 1985), p. 44.

C-7

146 "The U.S. does more": Michael A. Verespej, "The R&D Challenge," *Industry Week,* May 4, 1987, p. 33.

"Take ceramics, for example": Ibid., p. 33.

148 "When patients understand the": David Perlman, "Medicine That Emphasizes Role of Patient," San Francisco *Chronicle,* September 12, 1985.

150 "on the road *half the time*": McKenna, p. 108.

150–1 "Despite the increased ease": Perry Pascarella, "In Search of Universal Designs," *Industry Week,* July 22, 1985, p. 37.

152 "I've never been surprised": Roy Rowan, *The Intuitive Manager* (Boston: Little, Brown and Company, 1986), p. 97.

160 "Americans have made money": Draft version of *Tales of a New America.*

160–1 "The technical community": David Noble, *Forces of Production* (New York: Alfred A. Knopf, 1984), p. 191.

161–2 "[Harvard's Ramchandran Jaikumar] studies 35": Barnaby Feder: "American technology backfires as much as conquers," *Peninsula Times Tribune,* November 2, 1986, p. D-9.

162 "There's . . . the issue of": Roland Schmitt, "Wanted: Hands-on Engineers," *High Technology,* April 1987, p. 10.

163 "the most efficient engine": Schonberger, pp. 57–8.

"A recent study of production": Dreyfuss, p. 78.

"(1) New American plants often": Hall, pp. 18–19.

164 *World Class Manufacturing* ends with an Appendix: Schonberger, pp. 232, 230, 229.

165–6 "A [major] strength of Japanese": Masaaki Imai, *Kaizen* (New York: Random House, 1986), pp. 36–7.

167–9 "Our largest challenge": Alan M. Kantrow, "Wide-Open Management at Chaparral Steel," *Harvard Business Review,* May/June 1986, pp. 99–101.

C-9

174–5 "Despite the rigidity": Tom Bonoma, *The Marketing Edge: Making Strategies Work* (New York: The Free Press, 1985), pp. 93–4.

175–6 "Consider Dan Siewert": Bonoma, pp. 106–10.

page 177   "The 'visible' half of execution": Amar Bhide, "Hustle as Strategy," *Harvard Business Review,* September/October 1986, p. 65.

179   ". . . Management attempts to": Bonoma, p. 53.

179–80   "Two [real] donut chains": Ibid., pp. 7–8.

I-1

195   "U.S. firms have a": Verespej, p. 33.
"You can't get the": Ibid.
"Where is all this": Adams and Brock, p. 64.
"[Breakthrough] projects the entrepreneurs": George Gilder, *The Spirit of Enterprise* (New York: Simon and Schuster, 1984), p. 246.

197–9   Information from James Lardner, *Fast Forward* (New York: W. W. Norton & Co., 1987), pp. 92, 38, 311, 188, 324.

199   "For God's sake": Christopher Cerf and Victor Navasky, *The Experts Speak* (New York: Pantheon Books, 1984), p. 207.

200   "Because you are a": Paul Hawken, *The Next Economy* (New York: Holt, Rinehart and Winston, 1983), pp. 172–3.

201   Du Pont's loss of leadership: Richard Foster, *Innovation: The Attacker's Advantage* (New York: Summit Books, 1986), pp. 121–35.

202   "At Saclay, outside Paris": Gary Taubes, *Nobel Dreams* (New York: Random House, 1986), p. 48.
"Until Rubbia came along": Taubes, p. 28.

203   "[These firms] are neither": "Factory of the Future: A Survey," *The Economist,* May 30, 1987, p. 14.

204   "Kaisha respond and rarely": James Abegglen and George Stalk Jr., *Kaisha: The Japanese Corporation* (New York: Basic Books, 1985), pp. 9–10.

205   "We shouldn't be afraid": "How to Stop a Russian 'Surge,' " *U.S. News & World Report,* June 15, 1987, p. 43.

I-2

212   "[D]esigners designed a car": Walton, pp. 139–40.

212–13   "With Taurus . . . we brought": Ibid., pp. 140–1.

213   "We went to all": Ibid., p. 143.
"The common way of doing": Ibid., p. 141.

213–14   "One lighting firm": Ibid., p. 142.

214   "In another departure": Ibid., p. 143.
"The prototypes were also": Ibid., p. 143.

I-3

221   "[D]on't get too prepared": From working papers for Kouzes and Posner.

225–6   Young and Rubicam: Eileen Prescott, "An Agency's Turn to Madcap Ads," *The New York Times,* June 7, 1987, p. 8 (Business).

I-4

229   "When we want to": "Productivity and Japanese Management Style" (Meyer Michael Cahn, interviewer), "Maurie" Kaoru Kobayashi, *Japan: The Most Misunderstood Country* (Tokyo: The Japan Times Ltd., 1984), pp. 42–72.

pages 229–30   The Presidio Theaters in Austin: Curtis Hartman, "A Night at the Movies," *Inc.*, October 1986, pp. 101–6.
231   Despite a high batting average: Faye Rice, "The Media Star of Wall Street," *Fortune,* October 13, 1987, p. 100.

I-5

239–40   "Word-of-mouth communication": McKenna, pp. 58–9, 61.
240–1   "Most individuals do not": Everett M. Rogers, *Diffusion of Innovations* (New York: The Free Press, 1962, 1971, 1983), p. 18.

I-6

245   "[T]he entrepreneurs sustain": Gilder, p. 19.
      "The prevailing theory of": Ibid., p. 15.
245–6   "their [leaders'] unfettered and somewhat": Ibid., p. 16.
246   "Curt and Tom were considered": William J. Broad, *Star Warriors* (New York: Simon & Schuster, 1985), p. 32.
246–7   "Any account of Honda's": Richard Pascale, "Perspective on Strategy: The Real Story Behind Honda's Success," *Strategy and Organization* (Boston: Pitman Publishing Ltd., 1984), ed. by Glenn Carroll and David Vogel, p. 42.
247–8   "On December 10, 1984": Taubes, pp. xiii, 6, 8.
249–50   "A few months ago": William Allan, "Factory Workers' New Design Saved 2-Seater for Ford," San Jose *Mercury News,* June 29, 1986, p. 19D.

I-8

259   [Limited founder Les Wexner] actually likes: Steven B. Weiner, "The Unlimited?," *Forbes,* April 6, 1987, p. 77.

I-10

275   "a drug": Porter, p. 18.

P-1

282   A meticulous 1985 study: "Seeking and Destroying the Wealth Dissipators," A. T. Kearney (Chicago).
287   And yet, a poll of: Adam Clymer, "A Times Poll of M.B.A.'s," *The New York Times Magazine,* December 7, 1986, p. 28.
289–90   "It's really amazing": Kantrow, p. 99.
290–1   The *average* workers there: Robert Zager and Michael Rosow, *The Innovative Organization* (New York: Pergamon Press, 1982), pp. 127–30, 139–43.
291   "Traditionally, the welding department's": Hale, Hoelscher, Kowal, p. 76.
292   "In a departure from": Mary A. C. Fallon, "McDonnell looks to rank and file to help set management strategy," San Jose *Mercury News,* November 3, 1986, p. 15D.
293   "The QWL . . . process began": Zager and Rosow, p. 320.

P-2

pages 297–9   From Tom Peters' foreword to *Transforming the Workplace* (Princeton, NJ: Princeton Research Press, 1985), by John Nora, O. Raymond Rogers, and Robert Stramy.
300   "a decision [was reached in 1981] by": Zager and Rosow, pp. 57–8.
300–1   One recent assessment: Ibid., p. 9.

P-4

316   "asked all kinds of": Thomas Melohn, "Screening for the Best Employees," *Inc.*, January 1987, p. 105.
316–17   "has only three Ph.D.s": Imai, p. 34.
318   "I strongly believe in": Melohn, p. 105.
319   "To get your recruiting": Ibid., p. 106.

P-5

323   "We've documented the savings": Michael Brody, "Helping Workers to Work Smarter," *Fortune*, June 8, 1987, p. 87.
324   TRW policy analyst: Choate, p. 217.
      Training magazine's 1986 survey reports that: Jack Gordon, "Where the Training Goes," *Training*, October 1986, p. 49.
325   In four short years: From working papers for Kouzes and Posner.

P-6

333   A Yankelovich poll: Christopher, p. 106.
      "The chief problem of big": Oscar Schisgall, *Eyes on Tomorrow: The Evolution of Procter & Gamble* (Chicago: J. G. Ferguson Publ. Co., 1981), pp. 45–6; and Martin Weitzman, *The Share Economy* (Cambridge, MA: Harvard University Press, 1984), p. 80.
336   At Steelcase, tools for: Robert Levering, Milton Moskowitz, and Michael Katz, *The 100 Best Companies to Work for in America* (Reading, MA: Addison-Wesley Publishing Co., 1984, 1985), pp. 416–22.
      At Publix, a Florida grocer: Ibid., pp. 348–52.
336–7   Andersen Corporation of Bayport: Ingrid Sundstrom, "Profit Sharing Puts Glow in Andersen Corp. Windows," Minneapolis *Star and Tribune*, January 25, 1987, pp. 1A, 7A, 10A.
338   "If a store's employees could keep": Christopher Eklund, "How A&P Fattens Profits by Sharing Them," *Business Week*, December 22, 1986, p. 44.
338–9   Information derived from conversations with Lowe's spokesperson and Corey Rosen, and from *Employee Ownership in America*, Corey Rosen, Katherine J. Klein, Karen M. Young (Lexington, MA: Lexington Books, 1986), and *The 100 Best Companies to Work for in America*.

P-7

345   "If we have too many people": Bill Saporito, "Cutting Costs Without Cutting People," *Fortune*, May 25, 1987, p. 27.
      When a company: Levering, Moskowitz, and Katz, p. 97.
      "marks for the first time": *News from the UAW*, for release May 13, 1987, p. 1.

page 345 Case-IH won: *News from the UAW,* for release May 13, 1987, pp. 1–5.
UAW's historic 1984 agreement: *UAW-GM Report,* September 1984, p. 1.

346 union accepted American Airlines': Jocelyn Gutchess, *Employment Security in Action: Strategies That Work* (New York: Pergamon Press, 1985), p. 14.
the idea of employment security: Jerome M. Rosow and Robert Zager, *Employment Security in a Free Economy* (New York: Pergamon Press, 1984), pp. 17–18.
introduced a minimum: Levering, Moskowitz, and Katz, p. 346.

347 1. Accept management proposed changes: Rosow and Zager, pp. 33–4.
1. Maintenance of productivity: Ibid., p. 35.

348 Different classes of employees: Ibid., pp. 21–2.

350 staffs for 80 to 85 percent: Ibid., p. 64.
which targets for: Ibid., p. 46.
(1) switches assignments: Levering, Moskowitz, and Katz, p. 167.
Shifting people to sales: Rosow and Zager, p. 92.
In 1981–1982: Ibid., p. 92.
Kimberly Clark used: Ibid., p. 92.
During the same slump: Gutchess, pp. 20–1.
Digital Equipment has: Saporito, p. 30.
Its Employee Development Center: Rosow and Zager, p. 70.

351 In the 1981–83 recession: Gutchess, pp. 64–5.

P-8

355 "We have the poorest": "Seven Wary Views from the Top," *Fortune,* February 2, 1987, p. 60.
James O'Toole, professor of: James O'Toole, *Work and the Quality of Life: Resource Papers for Work in America* (Boston, MA: MIT Press, 1974).

359 "Many writers on organization": Ginzberg and Vojta, pp. 29–30.

359–60 "The overall aim": Ginzberg and Vojta, pp. 221, 160–1.

360 A meticulous 1985 study: "Seeking and Destroying the Wealth Dissipators," A. T. Kearney (Chicago).

360–1 "better support with [fewer] people": Schonberger, pp. 39, 43.

361 "William Dowdell, a 45-year-old": Mark L. Goldstein, "What Future for Middle Managers," *Industry Week,* December 8, 1986, pp. 52–3.

P-9

367 "Management excellence cannot": Hall, p. 154.
"Perhaps the biggest change": Schonberger, p. 147.

368 "As a country, the UK": Malcolm Trevor, *The Japanese Management Development System* (Wolfeboro, NH: Frances Pinter Ltd., 1986), pp. 5–6.

371–2 "Consider the following": Jan Carlzon, *Moments of Truth* (Cambridge, MA: Ballinger Publishing Co., 1987), pp. 61–3.

372 "the need for manufacturing engineers": Hall, p. 157.
"Having salaried people": Schonberger, p. 40.

P-10

377 "I find it mind-boggling": "Overheard," *Newsweek,* May 18, 1987, p. 21.
The New York Times recently reported: Prokesch, p. 8 (Section 3).

378 "[Ross] Perot claims he operated": Rowan, p. 9.
"He drives a compact Oldsmobile": Brett Duval Fromson, "A Hero in the Rust Belt," *Fortune,* January 5, 1987, p. 103.

page 379 "How *much* of a head slap": "Getting the Winning Edge Sums Up the Essence of Sports," Kansas City *Star,* January 4, 1987, p. 2 (Sports).

381–2 Upon being questioned: "Now Hear This," *Fortune,* May 25, 1987, p. 14.

383–4 "The miners filed into the pit": " 'This Is About It, Lads,' " *Newsweek,* March 18, 1985, p. 41.

385 "Frank Smith is a good": Hale, Hoelscher, and Kowal, p. 65.

"The emphasis on quality and pride": Levering, Moskowitz, and Katz, p. 420.

L-2

399 "The very essence of": Ezra Bowen, "His Trumpet Was Never Uncertain," *Time,* May 18, 1987, p. 68.

399–400 "Leaders articulate and define": Bennis and Nanus, pp. 33, 21.

400 "We had the chance": From working papers for Kouzes and Posner.

402 "When asked what he": Bennis and Nanus, pp. 29–30.

403 "The controls are not": Working papers for Kouzes and Posner.

"Trust is the lubrication": Bennis and Nanus, pp. 43–4.

403–4 "The leader's job is to": Working papers for Kouzes and Posner.

406 "The leader may have been": Bennis and Nanus, p. 82.

411 "Example is leadership": Mark Green and Gail MacColl, *There He Goes Again: Ronald Reagan's Reign of Error* (New York: Pantheon Books, 1983), p. 8.

"My moment of truth": Working papers for Kouzes and Posner.

418 Stanford researcher Joanne Martin: Ibid.

L-4

431 "Valley Medical Center developed": Julie Herrod, "Innovator Award Winners," *Healthcare Forum,* March/April 1987, p. 59.

L-6

443 "Everybody talks about ["Celtics Pride"]": Alan Webber, "Red Auerbach on Management," *Harvard Business Review,* March/April 1987, p. 85.

"I love 'em all": John Madden: *One Knee Equals Two Feet* (New York: Villard Books, 1986), p. 15.

"The 'visible' half of execution": Bhide, p. 65.

446 "Isn't this beautiful work?": *20 Teachers,* Ken Macrorie (New York: Oxford University Press, 1984), p. 7.

L-7

452 "Dalgliesh had accepted": P. D. James, *A Taste for Death* (New York: Alfred A. Knopf, 1986).

L-8

462 "At Sequent Computer, company president": Working papers for Kouzes and Posner.

S-1

page 483 "Data recording comes first": Schonberger, pp. 221–2.
485 ". . . the manager good at monitoring": Bonoma, p. 150.
486–8 Information from H. Thomas Johnson and Robert S. Kaplan, *Relevance Lost: The Rise and Fall of Management Accounting* (Boston: Harvard Business School Press, 1987).
488 For instance, Schonberger reports on Uniroyal's: Schonberger, pp. 133–4.
"He was responsible for": Groocock, p. 50.
489–90 "The number of believers in zero": Schonberger, p. 13.
490 "[Chairman Jim Robinson] started preaching": Monci Jo Williams, "Synergy Works at American Express," *Fortune,* February 16, 1987, p. 80.

S-2

499 He began "by planning": Cdr. Greg Gullickson, USN, Lieut. Cdr. Richard D. Chenette, USN, "Ch. 12: As the Captain So Is the Ship," *Excellence in the Surface Navy* (Naval Postgraduate School, 1984), p. 51.

S-3

505 "An individual without information": Carlzon, p. 35.
"Promoting information exchange": Schonberger, p. 174.

A Passion for Excellence

THE LEADERSHIP DIFFERENCE

with Nancy Austin

For
KATE ABBE
and
BILL CAWLEY
and the
SKUNKS

In the following pages I offer nothing more than simple facts, plain arguments and common sense; and have no other preliminaries to settle with the reader, other than that he will divest himself of prejudice and prepossession, and suffer his reason and his feelings to determine for themselves; that he will put on, or rather that he will not put off, the true character of a man, and generously enlarge his views beyond the present day.

Thomas Paine,
Common Sense

Foreword

Perhaps five million people have bought copies of *In Search of Excellence,* including its fifteen translations, since its publication in mid-October 1982. If history is any guide, two or three million probably opened the book. Four or five hundred thousand read as much as four or five chapters. A hundred thousand or so read it cover to cover. Twenty-five thousand took notes. Five thousand took detailed notes. (Not all of this is speculation. After his many speaking presentations, Tom is regularly asked to sign books. The number with bent pages and heavy underlining is dispiritingly low.)

In the Introduction we will argue that a revolution is on, that managers in every field are rethinking the tried and, as it turns out, not so true management principles that have often served their institutions poorly. At the heart of revolutions, historically, there have been no more than a handful of people. Perhaps among them today are those five thousand who have underlined key points in *In Search of Excellence.*

But now it's time to enter another phase. The zeal to do something is clear. Video and audio cassettes on the new wave overwhelm the mind and the ad pages of airline magazines. A thousand seminars, all describing radically different approaches to managing, are in the air for the first time in memory. We ourselves have given hundreds of speeches and conducted almost five hundred seminars since 1982. Perhaps a hundred thousand to two hundred thousand people have gone through them. But the question remains: Who's *doing* much of anything differently? And that's not even the most important question. The most important is: How many have sustained the new "it"? *In Search of Excellence* disgorged no magic: it simply said, Stay close to your customers; wander around. The absence of magic—"Practice common sense"—turned out to be its biggest selling point. And its biggest source of frustration: no surefire formulas for productive wandering around, no ten-step guides, how to begin, how to learn, and above all, how to teach yourself to sustain success for decades. And how do you practice excellence if your first name isn't Chairman and his or her last name isn't Kroc or Watson?

A Passion for Excellence is a first step along the path to answering those

559

questions. It is not a how-to book. It is not a book on theory. It is rather an avowed Whitman's Sampler of the passion for excellence observed and cele-brated. The topics we've chosen emerged from experience at five hundred seminars. Each chapter tells paradoxical tales of obsession in pursuing both detail and a dream. Each has scores of examples, as well as suggestions for practical actions that you can start immediately. (As a respected colleague says with certainty, "If you don't get started in the next seventy-two hours, you ain't going to get started at all.") Each stands essentially alone, which means you don't have to read them in order. Our hope is that ten years from now you will be going back and checking your underlinings to see if you're still really doing the things you committed yourself to do.

Many of you are on the verge. You have the instincts, but you have been told for years that those instincts are all wet: "Get the heck back into the office and work on the ten-year plan." "Don't waste your time wandering around with customers. It's not statistically valid." "Learn to draw those charts better. You don't make much of a presentation." "Sure, listen to your people, but then you damn well better tell them how to do it right, to make sure they get it right." "Failure? Not around here; we don't tolerate it." You know that's nonsense. We hope that our accounts of people, in some cases toiling away in big organizations, will give you heart as well as practical, straightforward guidance to innovative new practices.

Who are we and where have we been? Nancy Austin learned about excel-lence at Hewlett-Packard, where she ran the company's management-devel-opment seminars for a uniquely tough-minded set of managers all around the world. She is also the co-author of *The Assertive Woman,* the first book writ-ten to help women take practical steps toward positive, assertive behavior.

Tom Peters was with McKinsey during the research that led to *In Search of Excellence.* He left halfway through the writing of that book, in 1981, to found his own companies. First came the Palo Alto Consulting Center, focused, with colleague Bob Le Duc, on serving a small number of bellwether companies— Apple Computer, People Express, Mervyn's (a Dayton-Hudson subsidiary). It soon became apparent that there was a great hunger throughout the nation—and the world, for that matter—to hear the message of *In Search of Excellence.* Hundreds of seminars followed. With them came the founding of additional companies aimed at spreading the message far and wide. Nancy Austin's company, Not Just Another Publishing Company, along with its Mas-sachusetts cousin, Excel/Media, is responsible for audio, video and print products. A Center for Management Excellence conducts forty-person, four-day workshops a half dozen or so times a year; intense personal and organi-zational evaluation of the wellsprings of strategic competence is the object.

The whole endeavor is a kind of Skunkworks, Inc. Taken from the L'il Abner comic strip, skunkwork is a term that came to the world of business from the Lockheed California Company.* It denotes a highly innovative, fast-

*Where it is called Skunk Works, a registered service mark.

moving and slightly eccentric activity operating at the edges of the corporate world. As we see it, the movement toward developing a new managing approach for America is in its skunkwork phase. The term captures the very essence of what we and newfound colleagues far and wide—from Kuala Lumpur to Dublin to Sydney to Stockholm to Louisville—are up to.

This book is the product of classic skunkwork activity. In the Introduction we'll present twenty or thirty of the companies that have excited us most in the course of the last twenty-four months. They range from the highly visible People Express and Apple Computer to Perdue Farms, the chicken power-house, and Stew Leonard's, a one-story dairy operation, from Milliken & Company and Worthington Industries in, respectively, the battered textile and steel industries to BancOne, the highly innovative regional bank responding so aggressively to deregulation.

In corner after corner—of General Motors and Ford, in single-store oper-ations, in schools, in Big Eight accounting firms—we've unearthed skunk after skunk. It's not that they are implementing what *we* are suggesting. They have been practicing it with passion for years, often achieving remarkable successes in arenas that others have written off as either inexorably declining, hopelessly constrained, or dull—or all three. And they continued to do it in the early eighties, during the worst economic recession since the Great Depression.

Many of us joined together in September 1984, for a seminal event, the First Annual Skunk Camp. Forty brave souls who have been going their own way met in California and swapped tales about the battles fought, the scars accumulated, and the personal and soul-satisfying experiences that have come watching their people become winners, serving their customers better, innovating constantly—and making piles of money for shareholders in the process (or improving the quality of life in their cities or education in their schools). This book is about those skunks. It is about their once lonely lives, and now their banding together. For this is their revolution, not ours.

December 1984   TOM PETERS
Palo Alto, California   NANCY AUSTIN

Contents

CONTENTS

Part V: Leadership 837

Introduction:
A Revolution Is Brewing

At a break during a seminar in San Francisco one of the vice presidents of a giant oil company came up to Tom and said, "I bought your book a year ago, before it became fashionable. I didn't like it very much. I've come to listen to you. I find I don't like what you have to say very much either. But we haven't got a choice."

We think he gives the book too much credit. *In Search of Excellence,* and now *A Passion for Excellence,* do not constitute "the solution" to the problems of American management. But our friend has a point. We find that it is a rare American manager who is complacent these days. All are searching— school and hospital administrators, city managers, factory bosses and bank executives. Why?

We think it's fair to say that we have lived in a house of cards. It was, in fact, pretty difficult for management to mess up an American corporation during the twenty-five years immediately following World War II. William Morris, in *A Time of Passion,* concurs: "Only maligning incompetent management could have shut Americans out of the boom." Thus, in 1946 the United States was blessed with an intact industrial base and seventeen years' worth of unfulfilled consumer demand, pent up during the Great Depression and World War II. From 1946 until the early sixties we opened the spigots full bore, just to meet that domestic demand. The quality of what we made, frankly, didn't matter all that much. Tom remembers when his father bought his first car after World War II, in 1949. If Chevrolet had delivered it minus an axle, his dad probably wouldn't have taken it back, so excited was he at the prospect of having *any* car.

Then, as American demand lost its bloom in the early sixties, our enterprises discovered Europe, which was still not fully rebuilt. American corporations watched their profit-and-loss statements rapidly come to reflect 30 percent or more of sales overseas, and often well over half of their profits.

In the late sixties American management was touted by many, at home and abroad, as the primary asset that America could export to the world. And then came reality: OPEC, the Japanese, social and political unrest, changing concerns as represented by EPA, OSHA, EEOC and other federal agencies, an emerging work force with needs that were substantially different from those of the past. The vaunted American management mystique quickly turned out to be largely just that—mystique. The battering American business took in the seventies and during the 1981–83 recession (is there anyone who thinks the recovery means we're permanently out of the woods?) has humbled virtually every American manager. Nor have public-sector organizations been immune; their performance too has been problematic at best, and much of the reason is surely that their managers adopted, with sadly little reflection, the management techniques that were so highly praised in the industrial sector.

Out of those failures of our organizations, as evidenced by faulty microchips and tanks that can't handle dust, by declining SAT scores and garbage lying about, has emerged the beginning of a fundamental reexamination of managing per se. The landmark *Harvard Business Review* article by Bob Hayes and the late Bill Abernathy, "Managing Our Way to Economic Decline," is the piece that we think of as the cornerstone of the corporate revolution. It attacked the MBA/numbers-only mentality of American managers and the lack of concern in American corporations for such basics as manufacturing. Several other works would qualify as first alarms, including David Halberstam's examination of Vietnam in *The Best and the Brightest* and Daniel Patrick Moynihan's analysis of Great Society failures, *Maximum Feasible Misunderstanding.* All put the knock on mindless systems analysis and began the examination of a misplaced emphasis on paper rather than on people. More recent business books, aside from *In Search of Excellence,* that come to mind include Bill Ouchi's *Theory Z,* Richard Pascale and Tony Athos's *The Art of Japanese Management,* Terry Deal and Allan Kennedy's *Corporate Cultures,* Rosabeth Moss Kanter's *The Change Masters* and Ken Auletta's *The Art of Corporate Success.* Symposia are now regularly held on corporate/organizational cultures, on entrepreneurial revitalization inside and outside the firm and the like. Robert Reich's *The Next American Frontier* and George Gilder's *Wealth and Poverty* taken together—the two contain virtually the same diagnosis, albeit with very different conclusions—suggest that the left and the right are equally distressed.

So a revolution is brewing. What kind of revolution? In large measure it is in fact a "back to basics" revolution. The management systems, schemes, devices and structures promoted during the last quarter century have added up to distractions from the main ideas: the achievement of sustainable growth and equity. Each such scheme seemed to make sense at the time. Each seemed an appropriate response to growing complexity. But the result was that the basics got lost in a blur of well-meaning gibberish that took us further and further from excellent performance in any sphere. We got so tied up in our techniques, devices and programs that we forgot about people—the people who produce the product or service and the people who consume it. (We hasten to add that by "back to basics" we do not intend to bring to mind images of Henry Ford toting a gun, daring his people to go out on strike. When it comes to relations with one's work force, paying attention to one's people, really listening to them, acting on what one hears, and treating them as full-scale partners, we are decidedly not going "back" to basics—though, indeed, as discussed in *In Search of Excellence,* the IBM's and Procter & Gambles have been following these practices for many decades.)

What are the basics of managerial success? Two of the most important are pride in one's organization and enthusiasm for its works. A quick check of the twenty-five leading textbooks on management finds neither in any index. Nor does one find much about such concepts as "naive customer listening," customer perception of service/quality, employee commitment and ownership, internal corporate entrepreneurship (sometimes called intrapreneurship), championing of innovation, trust, vision or "leadership."

That last, the concept of leadership, is crucial to the revolution now under way—so crucial that we believe the words "managing" and "management" should be discarded. "Management," with its attendant images—cop, referee, devil's advocate, dispassionate analyst, naysayer, pronouncer—connotes controlling and arranging and demeaning and reducing. "Leadership" connotes unleashing energy, building, freeing, and growing. As Warren Bennis, a major figure in the current rethinking process, says, "American organizations have been overmanaged and underled." Yet the revolution *is* on, and everywhere we find islands of hope: we see those who have always done it well and have not been bamboozled by apparently inexorable external forces, and those, mounting in number, who have actually turned their organizations around—a clear result of inspired management (which is another way of saying leadership).

At the Core: Paradox

An introduction is a place to deal with common misperceptions. One, concerning this revolution, stands out above all others: it is that we advocate a change from "tough-mindedness" to "tenderness," from concern with hard data and balance sheets to a concern for the "soft stuff"—values, vision and integrity. We have found that when it comes to achieving long-term success, soft is hard. The pressure to perform in the organizations we will describe—from Perdue Farms to the City of Baltimore—is nothing short of brutal: these are "no excuses" environments, where radical decentralization frees people to make anything happen, where training is provided, where extraordinary results are then routinely expected because the barriers to them have been cleared away. There is a certain militancy in the way values are protected and people are empowered to take possession of their own achievements.

The superb business leaders we use as models in this book epitomize paradox. All are tough as nails and uncompromising about their value systems, but at the same time they care deeply about and respect their people; their very respect leads them to demand (in the best sense of the word) that each person be an innovative contributor. Ren McPherson, former chairman of

Dana, went so far as to evaluate even those who held the most mundane jobs almost solely on the degree to which the person (secretary, clerk) contributed innovatively to the job. The best bosses—in school, hospital, factory—are neither exclusively tough nor exclusively tender. They are both: tough on the values, tender in support of people who would dare to take a risk and try something new in support of those values. They speak constantly of vision, of values, of integrity; they harbor the most soaring, lofty and abstract notions. At the same time they pay obsessive attention to detail. No item is too small to pursue if it serves to make the vision a little bit clearer.

We have been forced to deal daily with the central paradox of leadership. One set of attendees at our seminars beseeches us to provide more concrete data. We think we provide a bushelful of it, but they want much more. More practical examples. More details: "What do I do right now?" Another set, equally vociferous, tells us that such details are unimportant. The whole point, they say, is trust, integrity, care; given those, the details will take care of themselves. The paradox: both are *exactly* right. The difficulty: the vast majority of us—some 75 percent, we judge—understand (and live) one way or the other and thus resolve the paradox by avoiding it.

This we can no longer do. We must confront the paradox, own it, live it, celebrate it if we are to make much headway in achieving excellence. We must cultivate passion and trust, and at virtually the same moment we must delve unmercifully into the details. How do we do it, or at least make a beginning? That's what *A Passion for Excellence* is all about.

The Players

In Search of Excellence used a broad brush to paint a picture of excellent performance on eight dimensions in forty-three very large companies. *A Passion for Excellence* etches a finer, bolder portrait of the sources of long-term distinction. And passion it is. Top-flight performance is not dry and deadly; it is spirited, it is emotion-filled. Nor is our focus limited to the chairman and the giant company; we include here managers at every "level," smaller organizations and divisions of larger companies. Our examples penetrate deeper to capture what we now call the "smell" of a customer-(or innovation-) oriented company. And a series of pragmatic questions and suggestions in almost every chapter lead you to analyze where you are, how you got there, and particularly what you might try to do now to construct the easy-to-specify, tough-to-execute, building blocks of excellence on your own turf.

In the last few years we've found excellence in every nook and cranny, overseas as well as in the United States. Here are a few of the friends we've made along the way:

One of the best is a single-store operation, **Stew Leonard's** of Norwalk, Connecticut. Stew does $85 million worth of business—in milk, cheese, rolls and eggs—out of one store. It's a treat to shop there. It's a celebration of imagination and excellence.

Stew's principal supplier is Frank Perdue, chairman of **Perdue Farms.** Perdue turned another commodity—chicken—into gold. Operating out of Salisbury, Maryland, on the economically depressed Delmarva Peninsula, he has built an $800 million enterprise and created seven thousand new jobs along the way. Quality, imagination—and profit—are the keys to his kingdom.

Service businesses have played a huge role in our adventure over the last couple of years. There were few in *In Search of Excellence.* They almost dominate this list. Stew Leonard's is one of them. **Domino's Pizza** is another. In just eight years Tom Monaghan has built a $300 million empire that has become the number two pizza company, right behind PepsiCo's Pizza Hut. It's a delivery-only business, with heretofore unknown levels of service—and an unbelievably turned-on group of young men and women on the payroll.

Talk about turn-on, talk about a fast-growing service company, and, above all, you're describing **People Express,** ranked by some measures as the fastest-growing business in the history of the United States. People Express may offer low airfares, but through the zest and enthusiasm of its young and vital (and wealthy, via share ownership) staff it also provides a service level that some of the "greats" don't match. Don Burr's People Express will be prominent in this book.

Ryder System, a Florida company engaged in truck leasing, also plays a part. The highly profitable and fast-growing $2.5 billion system has taken advantage of deregulation. Its higher value-added services have banished the word "commodity" from yet another business where price is generally considered the only variable.

Another service entrant comes from across the Atlantic. One of the most remarkable turnarounds we've ever observed was crafted by Jan Carlzon of the **Scandinavian Air System (SAS).** In the middle of the 1981–83 recession that clobbered most airlines, Carlzon's company went from losing $10 million a year to making $70 million a year on over $2 billion in sales. The reason (good news, indeed): a return to old-fashioned service excellence, led by Carlzon's boundless spirit.

Retailing has come to intrigue us. What a fast-moving, tough game! It makes high technology look like child's play. The remarkably successful **Limited Stores** of Columbus, Ohio, will be visited in these pages. Les Wexner is providing his shareholders with a 35 percent return on equity and has become the definer of what can be done in specialty retailing. On the much more traditional end we find **Nordstrom,** a Seattle-based retailer. Their return on sales is at the top of the heap. Their formula? Plain, old-fashioned, exceptional service in its billion-dollar business, a decade after such service had been declared uneconomical by almost all others. Another star in the retailing world is **Mervyn's,** the winner in the all-around superb Dayton-Hudson organization. Mervyn's does in a week the total system remerchandising that its competitors take thirteen weeks to do. And interviews with new Mervyn's store people who have come from other chains almost always result in a variation of the same response: "It's like dying and going to heaven." Attention to service also marks a vast grocery store chain: **Giant Food** of Washington, D.C., which has by far the highest return on shareholders' equity among the publicly listed grocery companies. And talk about people and pride: you find both in **Publix,** a Florida-based retailer that, among other things, introduced across-the-board employee ownership long before it was popular to do so (it still isn't).

The United Kingdom is not thought to be the home of much excellence in management these days. But there are exceptions. Say the name of **Marks & Spencer** around a bunch of retailers in any land and they are silenced. Nobody has a better reputation. It's built upon people, and an under-control bureaucracy: that is, they've figured out how to keep the bureaucracy to a bare minimum. We'll observe a bit of their magic as we go along.

Real estate and banking are on this list as well. In banking, which was intentionally omitted from *In Search of Excellence,* we visit a giant star, **Citibank,** which keeps being rated by *Fortune* every year as the most innovative company in America. We believe it deserves the accolade. We'll examine some of the reasons why in our section on innovation. Banking is in the midst of turmoil because of deregulation. As is typical in all parts of the industrial scene, most of the innovation comes where it's not supposed to. **BancOne,** based in Columbus, Ohio, has been decades ahead of its time.

What is the association between warehouse leasing and love? None—if you don't know Trammell Crow and his colleagues. The **Trammell Crow** real estate organization is exciting, vital, fast-moving, based upon extraordinary service to customers—and, yes, love.

Excellence turns up everywhere. We'll talk about several San Francisco Bay Area companies. Take **Sunset Scavengers.** Employees own the garbage trucks. Yes, Sunset Scavengers is a garbage company—most say the best-run garbage company in America. Boss Len Stephanelli's secret: "I love garbage." And Tom Melohn's **North American Tool and Die** in San Leandro, California; Tom avers passionately that his $7 million company is based on caring. Zest and enthusiasm and really *caring* mark all the companies we've looked at.

Success stories found in certain beaten and battered industries provide magnificent examples of what can be done in the face of adverse economic conditions and other "external factors." Perhaps the most excitement we've had during our wanderings has been the time we spent in Spartanburg, South Carolina. Headquartered there is **Milliken & Company.** The $2 billion textile powerhouse has always been a technology leader. In 1980 they added an amazing quality-improvement program, moving from an authoritarian management structure to quality enhancement through participation in management. Has it ever worked! Tens of millions have been added to the bottom line, and factories have been kept humming as improved quality has led to new and bigger orders. (IBM's recently retired vice president for quality, John Jackson, calls Milliken's quality program the most advanced in the nation.)

Pursuit of excellence in steel led us back to Columbus, Ohio, home of BancOne and The Limited; there we also found **Worthington Industries,** whose return on shareholders' equity over the past five years—27 percent— is at the very top of the heap in steel.

Product "maturity" in main-line consumer businesses is a dominant theme of economists and futurists alike—and, we believe, all too often an excuse for premature pruning. We look at the once stodgy **Campbell Soup** and **PepsiCo.** Both are successfully fighting so-called maturity with programs for entrepreneurial revitalization that can serve as models for the rest of industry.

Nor is our focus always the strategies at the very top. In the beleaguered auto industry, we came across an operation that truly shines: **Phil Staley's Ford assembly plant** in Edison, New Jersey. Plant management in companies such as Westinghouse, Dana and GM are featured throughout.

And then some just plain gems, beyond categorization. **W. L. Gore & Associates** of Newark, Delaware: the quarter-billion-dollar company makes, among other things, the breathing synthetic fabric, Goretex. Bill and Vieve Gore's approach to managing people defies ten-word summations. Try the chapter on "ownership" for an exploration of it. **Herman Miller** is a superb office-furniture supplier based in Zeeland, Michigan. Max DePree's view of people will be prominently featured here; he's the Herman Miller chairman.

Bob Swiggett runs a high-tech company, **Kollmorgen.** High tech was a major focus in *In Search of Excellence* and receives less attention here. Swiggett's management style, however, and the path he followed to discover the values of radical decentralization are exactly appropriate for our message. Among our old friends, we've learned more, much more about the bases of customer service at **IBM** and constant innovation at **Hewlett-Packard** and **3M.** And no tour would be complete without featuring **Apple Computer.** Its products define "state of the art," to be sure; but its free-form organization and unbridled enthusiasm may well be the company's most lasting contribution to the U.S. business scene.

In this book we also venture outside the arena of private business. Our biggest foray took us to the Langley, Virginia, headquarters of the **Tactical Air Command, U.S. Air Force.** General Bill Creech thinks centralization and consolidation are the enemy. He has fought them—rapidly and successfully. We'll also talk about the turnaround in the city of **Baltimore,** whose flamboyant mayor, William Donald Schaefer, is a model of leadership and energy, and we'll take a quick look at the worlds of **education** and **health care.** Our conclusions are tentative and speculative, and not based upon the degree of expertise we wish we had, but we think it's important to test the water—and stick our necks out a little too.

So—this is a new walk. We can't wait to share it with you. Dig in. Sample. Cheer—weep. Pull the sheet over your head and privately examine your deepest biases. And, above all, try something—now, this afternoon!

The 1,000 Percent Factor

Winners—even in mundane, declining, battered or regulated environments—don't do only a percent or two better than the norm. They do hundreds of percent better—at least.

In December 1983 Tom traveled to Burbank, California, to visit with Kelly Johnson of the Lockheed California Company, the man who brought the term "skunk work" to American industry.

Johnson and his determined band are responsible for an astonishing share of what flies in the sky. They developed the first of the military jets right after the end of the World War II, the YP- or F-80 (143 days from concept to first and successful flight); subsequently they turned out the F-104, C-130, U-2, SR-71 and others. That's quite a showing, but the output isn't the real story. What lies behind it is. In one instance Johnson got involved in an ailing satellite program. It was a couple of years behind schedule and way above budget; launch effectiveness ran 12.5 percent. While wandering around after taking charge, Kelly discovered, among other things, 1,271 inspectors working with a single subcontractor. In the course of the next year he trimmed that number to 35. He got the program back on schedule, and simultaneously improved launch effectiveness—to 98 percent. In another instance the Air Force demanded that an arch rival of Lockheed's visit with Johnson and his team. The two were working on projects of about equal magnitude and complexity. The competitor was years behind and hundreds of percent over budget, with 3,750 people involved. Johnson was on schedule and under budget, with 126 people. (A formal Rand Corporation study validated these extraordinary figures.)

Tom was so taken by Kelly Johnson's numbers that he took a little white card, calling-card size, and wrote "3,750/126" on it, and then had it plasticized. He keeps it in his wallet. It's a graphic reminder that no matter what he is up to—designing a product, thinking about marketing it, evaluating an addition to staff—Johnson epitomizes what's possible. And, most important, what's possible is a function of *good management* (*read leadership*) alone.

The stories fill shelf after shelf:
- ▶ Frank Perdue earns a margin on a pound of chicken several hundred percent above the industry average; his share runs close to 60 percent, on average, in major urban centers: Norfolk, Richmond, Washington, Baltimore, Philadelphia, Boston and New York.
- ▶ Stew Leonard's sales per square foot, in his astonishing "Disneyland of dairy stores" are fully *ten* times the industry average.
- ▶ A. Ray Smith's Louisville Redbirds, in 1983, twenty-five years after the all too evident demise of minor league baseball, outdraw a quar-

ter of the major leagues and exceed the all-time minor league attendance record (set in 1946) by over 100 percent.

▶ Mervyn's "remerchandises" a $1.25 billion operation a *dozen* times faster than its competitors.

▶ People Express typically opens a new station—e.g. Los Angeles—in ten days, including multiple government approvals, while the industry giants tend to take twelve to eighteen months to accomplish the same task.

▶ Du Pont achieves a safety record 6,800 percent (68 times) above American manufacturing industry average.

▶ Mayor William Donald Schaefer wins reelection in Baltimore against a talented candidate by taking 94 percent of the vote (and every ward).

▶ The Tactical Air Command's Bill Creech takes a sortie rate (flights flown, a good bottom-line surrogate) that had been declining at a rate of 7.8 percent a year (average) for ten years and cranks it up 11.2 percent a year over the next five years, with no push from the budget or other external forces.

The stories we tell in *A Passion for Excellence* are decidedly *not* stories of organizations with 25 percent growth rates given to them from on high. They are stories of baseball diamonds that are the same shape for all competitors—stories of chicken, dairy products and soft goods, as mundane as they come. No outside factors can explain the extraordinary increments in performance. Superb management—leadership—is the only explanation left.

In the past two decades the most exercised part of the corporate body has been the pointing finger. If in doubt, blame it on OPEC, the Japanese, EPA, OSHA, EEOC, etc. Some didn't. Some looked to the talent they were given and seized the moment. They have outperformed the crowd by a long shot. That's the 1,000 percent factor. It's the challenge for all of us.

1

COMMON SENSE

A Blinding Flash
of the Obvious

"What's new?"
Nothing in particular.
"Then why read it?"
Because doing it isn't as easy as it sounds.
"Like what?"
Wandering around, for instance.
"What's so tough about that?"
Have you tried it?
"I haven't had the time."
That's what's so tough about it.
"What else is so tough?"
Listening to customers.
"You are right on that one; it is hard."
Glad to see you agree.
"Darn right. They just don't understand what we're trying to tell them."
Yeah, that's why listening *is so hard.*

And on it goes. It's now been four years since *In Search of Excellence* was written, and six since the research for it was begun. All involved have learned a lot, and yet we've learned nothing. We've learned nothing in that (1) there is nothing new under the sun, and (2) it was "all" covered in *In Search of Excellence:* customers, innovation, people.

But here's the issue. The highest praise we have received came from a colleague at the end of the third day of a four-day seminar for small-business presidents in late 1983. All were sitting around, working on a carafe of young white wine, and he blurted out, "You know what these three days amount to, so far? A blinding flash of the obvious." Right on! Nothing new under the sun, nothing new in *In Search of Excellence,* and nothing new since. Giving everyone in the organization the space to innovate, at least a little bit. Answering the phones and otherwise behaving with common courtesy toward customers. Making things that work. Listening to customers and asking them for their ideas. Then acting on them. Listening to your people and asking them for their ideas. Then acting on them. Wandering around: with customers, your people, suppliers. Paying attention to pride, trust, enthusiasm—and passion and love.

It's common sense, isn't it? But then another good friend says, "I guess the obvious must not be so obvious, or more would practice it." That's right, too: we've often said, only half facetiously, that IBM's only magic is that IBM's people are the lone players in a quarter-trillion-dollar industry who bother to answer the phones consistently. That Disney seems to be the sole player in its big industry that has figured out how to keep a theme park sparkling clean. It turns out that the obvious is not so obvious—and it's a hell of a lot harder to do than we ever imagined!

The Simple Scheme

Many accused *In Search of Excellence* of oversimplifying. After hundreds of post-*In Search of Excellence* seminars we have reached the opposite conclusion: *In Search of Excellence* didn't simplify enough!

In the private or public sector, in big business or small, we observe that there are only two ways to create and sustain superior performance over the long haul. First, take exceptional care of your customers (for chicken, jet engines, education, health care, or baseball) via superior service and superior quality. Second, constantly innovate. That's it. There are no alternatives in achieving long-term superior performance, or sustaining strategic competitive advantage, as the business strategists call it.

Obviously, the two courses of action do not constitute all that's needed. Sound financial controls are essential. Those without them fail, period. Solid planning is not a luxury but a necessity. Moreover, businesses can be temporarily or permanently set back by external forces, such as an overvalued dollar or the loss of access to natural resources. Nonetheless, these other factors are seldom, if ever, the basis for lasting distinction. That is, financial control is vital, but one does not sell financial control, one sells a quality service or product. The lemonade stand, the lemonade, selling and servicing efforts must precede the accountant who adds up the pile of pennies at the end of the day. One seldom sustains superior performance through mere access to natural resources; one sustains it through innovation in resource exploration techniques and subsequent market development. One is battered by an overvalued dollar, but one sustains performance by adding enough value to the product so that it is profitably salable despite international monetary variability. Likewise, in the school, efficient management of the budget is vital; yet a great school is never characterized by the remark, "It has a good budget." The superb school is superb only by virtue of its success in developing its ultimate customer: the student.

It turns out that neither superior customer service nor constant innovation—the two sustaining edges of excellence—is built upon genius in the executive suite, sleight-of-hand techniques or mystical strategic moves on a game board that allow one to gain a five- or ten-year advantage over one's competitors. Both are built, instead, on a bedrock of listening, trust and respect for the dignity and the creative potential of each person in the organization. Thus, customer courtesy means courtesy from the accounting department, from the purchasing department and the engineers, as well as from the sales people. Quality, too, is an all-hands operation. It means quality in all parts of the organization. The winners stun us not by their cleverness, but by the fact that each and every tiny aspect of the business is just a touch better than the norm.

So that is our model: care of customers, constant innovation, turned-on people. Yet one thing is missing, one element that connects all the others. It was a shadow over the pages of *In Search of Excellence,* but was seldom labeled, as many subsequently pointed out. It is leadership. Leadership means vision, cheerleading, enthusiasm, love, trust, verve, passion, obsession, consis-

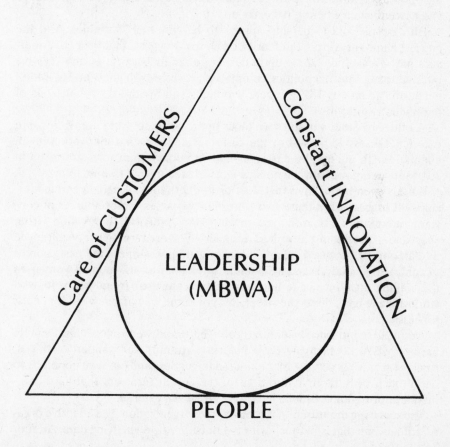

LEADERSHIP (MBWA)

Care of CUSTOMERS

Constant INNOVATION

PEOPLE

tency, the use of symbols, paying attention as illustrated by the content of one's calendar, out-and-out drama (and the management thereof), creating heroes at all levels, coaching, effectively wandering around, and numerous other things. Leadership must be present at *all* levels of the organization. It depends on a million little things done with obsession, consistency and care, but all of those million little things add up to nothing if the trust, vision and basic belief are not there. It seems obvious, doesn't it?

The Adaptive Organization

A regular criticism of *In Search of Excellence* was that it was focused internally (i.e., on management), and did not take into account changes and discontinuities foisted upon the organization by the outside world. It was a bum rap!

We repeat the "error" in *A Passion for Excellence*. That is, in this book you will find no litany of external forces that can affect the enterprise. Our "defense" is that the management practices we describe are aimed at ensuring that the organization is always externally focused, always sensing change and nascent change before it sneaks up.

True, people and leadership appear to be "internal" variables. And the hastiest glance at Akron, Pittsburgh, or Detroit suggests that many of America's past greats have come upon desperate straits because of an excessive internal focus. Internal politics, complacency driven by bigness and a "Members only" mentality led to severe problems and hundreds of thousands of permanently lost jobs.

Yet the two other variables we focus upon, customers and innovation, are external. Obsessive pursuit of the customer and constant innovation mean adaptation. To pursue the customer and to pursue innovation are to be in constant commerce with the outside world, listening and thus adapting.

But it's even better than that. As our in-depth look at people and leadership will suggest, even these two "internal" variables can be sources of constant adaptation. If you are asking for practical innovation from everyone—receptionist as well as designer—you are turning every employee into an outward-focused, adaptive sensor. And guess where the best sources of competitive analysis and assessment often lie: with the men or women on the loading dock or on the line who know what their friend Mary Jo, who works for the bank down the street, just got in the way of a new aid for check processing.

And leadership can be adaptive, too. The brand we propose has a simple base of MBWA (Managing By Wandering Around). To "wander," with customers (at least 25 percent of the time) and vendors and our own people, *is* to be in touch with the first vibrations of the new. It turns out that hard-data-driven information is usually a day late and *always* sterile.

The surviving organization is the adaptive organization. The adaptive organization is one that is in touch with the outside world via living data. All four of our variables—two that you would expect (customers and innovation) and two that are novel (people and leadership)—are focused on sensing change and adapting to it, not via great leaps and genius paper plans, but via constant contact with and reaction to people on the part of every person in the organization. Thus, we will begin by exploring our favorite topic—wandering, listening, staying in touch.

Raise the issue of marketing and the discussion soon becomes technical; no living, breathing customers and their whims intrude upon the heated but wholly sterile debate. Shift to innovation and the same thing is true. Hour after hour of chatter about "technology ramps" and changing demographics ensue; nothing so trivial as the way we continuously dampen the spirit of would-be champions through our questioning routines is raised. Talk of people and productivity and, again, often as not, the language is sterile and depersonalized. Labor intransigence is lamented. Trust and simple listening are never mentioned.

The topic of MBWA is at once about common sense, leadership, customers, innovation and people. Simple wandering—listening, empathizing, staying in touch—is an ideal starting point. Under the deceptively simple heading of MBWA lie the concepts that bring our whole scheme into clear relief.

2

MBWA: The Technology of the Obvious

We were pretty good geologists when we went down there. We found out we weren't nearly as good as we thought we were. . . . From the Brazos River east to the Mississippi . . . We saw bays and estuaries, channels and deltas and bars, lagoons, swamps, growth faults, salt domes. . . . We jumped in the water and felt with our toes the sand of a transgressive overlap.

> *John Masters, president, Canadian Hunter*
> *Exploration, Ltd.*

The greatest problem American business faces is getting the boss back to work watching his customer and his product. Too many bosses are involved with long-range planning meetings. They are too busy playing golf, often to the point that they no longer know what the customer is saying, how he is being treated. They are not on the production floor enough to know how the product is being manufactured or how the buyers are stocking the stores. As a result, we have set ourselves up for a terrific pratfall.

> *Stanley Marcus, former chairman, Neiman-*
> *Marcus (as reported in the* Knoxville News-
> Sentinel, *May 27, 1984)*

Get into the community and find out what their problems are. That's the best politics.

> *The late Senator George Aiken of Vermont, in*
> *1974, on his success at the ballot box*

In our work with groups of all sorts we have commented time and again that we can make a strong case, which boils down to this: the number one managerial productivity problem in America is, quite simply, managers who are out of touch with their people and out of touch with their customers. And the alternative, "being in touch," doesn't come via computer printouts or the endless stream of overhead transparencies viewed in ten thousand darkened meeting rooms stretching across the continent. Being in touch means tangible, visceral ways of being informed. It means a remarkably successful thirty-year veteran geologist/entrepreneur sinking his toes in the sand of a transgressive overlap, instead of totally depending on a computer's interpretation of sophisticated geophysical tools.

In *In Search of Excellence,* Managing By Wandering Around rated a subtitle in "A Bias for Action," the first of eight chapters on the attributes of excellent companies. We know it as the technology of the obvious, the method by which leadership becomes effective in any well-run school, hospital, bank, single-store operation or industrial enterprise.

MBWA: WITH CUSTOMERS

To listen is just that: to listen. Apple's Lisa computer (not a great commercial success, but the machine that spawned the wildly successful Macintosh) was noted for a breakthrough in the "user friendliness" of its operating system software (marked by the "mouse" and a revolutionary reduction in customer learning time). The developer of much of this software was John Couch, a prototypical engineer, with a Ph.D. in computer science from Berkeley, among other degrees. We asked John once about the genesis of his thinking. He was quick to reply: "I bought my dad a computer outlet. I worked in it, for the full two years of the project, at least one and often two days a weekend, doing a full shift on the floor, incognito. I learned about the fears and frustrations of the average first-time user and the more sophisticated one firsthand. I believe it was the single most significant source of what we came up with." Being in touch means just that—being in touch. Somehow. It usually has little to do with statistical surveys—Couch's experience didn't, certainly. But it *is* valid. Currently Apple prides itself on having gotten its entire executive staff (the senior officers) to volunteer for a regular stint of listening in on the toll-free 800 customer call-in number. Whenever an executive participates, she or he gets a commemorative Listening Certificate—with a gold star attached if the executive has the guts to actually answer one or more phone calls.

"Daily Dose of Reality"

Three mornings a week, all executives of Castle find a $5'' \times 7''$ yellow sheet of paper on their desks. The title: "Daily Dose of Reality." Below is the name and phone number of a customer who bought a new piece of equipment from them (they make hospital sterilizers, surgical equipment) about six weeks before. (Better yet—the phone number is for the person who actually uses the equipment.) The routine is stated in full in an internal memo: "We will simply be asking our customers if they are satisfied with our product."

> The objective is threefold: "to let our customers know they are important to us," "uncover problems before they become major irritants," and "give management a daily reminder of where the real world is—with our field reps and our customers."

"Naïve" customer listening. Raw impressions. They are not substitutes for computer printouts—but there are no substitutes for them either. Consider this analysis (in 1983) of the source of many of GM's problems by a Sloan student at Stanford from General Motors:*

They [executives] drive down the highway outside Detroit. All the car company employees and suppliers are virtually required to buy American cars. He looks to his left, looks to his right. "Everybody's still driving American cars" registers at some level. Then he pulls into the company garage. His car is gone over from stem to stern for the next ten hours. When he leaves work he gets in, it starts like a charm: "And the damn things do work." All the tons of market research data that we have don't make up for the lack of *feel*. If even one of the companies or even one car-producing division had moved to California, they would have learned the bitter truth: Californians just don't like American cars anymore. These odd names—Honda, Toyota, Nissan—are all over the highways out here. Even I, and I consider myself pretty darned enlightened, didn't really "feel it" in the most important sense until I moved out to Palo Alto. I started subconsciously counting Japanese cars at intersections. I was incredulous. I'd tell my colleagues about it, back home. They didn't fathom what I was saying, as I hadn't before I came out here and lived it for myself.

If customer listening is the watchword, it should also be opportunistic. The president of Levi Strauss USA had a call, purely social, from a retailer who happened to be in San Francisco (the company's headquarters city). The man sat down and started to pour out his heart about some of the difficulties he had dealing with Levi Strauss (this was during the late 1970's, when the jeans craze led the company to fall behind in satisfying the demand for their product). To the Levi executive's credit, he cut the retailer off early in the discussion, invited him—begged him—to stick around for three or four hours, called in the video cameras and all of the marketing people who were in the headquarters building at the time. Everyone trooped over to the nearest auditorium, and while the audience sat in rapt attention and the video tape

---

*Stanford's and MIT's business schools run year-long programs (e.g., the Stanford Sloan Program) for about forty superfast-trackers, principally from big corporations and federal agencies. The programs were started with seed money from the Alfred P. Sloan Foundation; the student's company nominates and supports the student.

spun, this fellow unloaded and answered questions for a full four hours. A host of copies of the tapes was made, and sent throughout the system.

Now, Apple and Levi Strauss are among the most systematic collectors of market data. Yet none of these examples is very systematic. But, again, each is valid. Here's another, again from a senior executive at Levi Strauss: "We've begun to correct some serious problems, particularly in the service-to-retailers area, over the last couple of years [1983–84]. At the heart of it for me was a commitment I made, following an almost accidental first experience, to spend one Saturday a month on the sales floor of one of our major chain customers, one of my 'executive accounts.' I asked them if they would let me sell blue jeans one weekend. They were delighted. It was quite an eye-opener for me—to sell our own, to watch people decide to buy other people's jeans. We haven't burned the market research data, but I'll tell you it's a different view."

Campbell Soup Chairman Gordon McGovern hasn't burned the computer printouts either, to be sure. But he is going to even greater extremes than Levi Strauss to get in touch. It's a keystone in his effort to innovate based upon listening. *Business Week* (December 24, 1984) reports:

> McGovern recently convened his directors in the back room of a supermarket for a board meeting, after which they roamed the store aisles probing shoppers for comments about Campbell's products. He regularly dispatches company executives to the kitchens of some 300 women across the country, to see how meals are prepared. And he insists that his managers do their own grocery shopping.
>
> McGovern himself can be found every Saturday in his neighborhood supermarket, stocking the family larder. "Gordon's made it his business to be out in the marketplace, getting to know his customers, whoever they may be," says Allen Bildner, president of Kings Super Markets Inc. in West Caldwell, N.J. With the entire food industry scrambling to meet America's changing tastes, McGovern's determination is the key to his dream of transforming Campbell into the nation's most market-sensitive food company—almost an about-face for the once-cautious food processor.

Wandering with "Customers": Urban Government

Mayor William Donald Schaefer of Baltimore has wandered with his constituents for years. Maintaining a feel for his city has long been at the top of his list of priorities. Richard Ben Cramer reported in *Esquire* (October 1984):

"I'm not pleased with this," he'd scolded them [members of the cabinet] many times. "That is NOT . . . GOOD . . . ENOUGH."

PEOPLE, he'd write on his easel. He picked the easel thing up a few years ago, thought it might get the message across. For greater weight, he'd write: PEE-PULL. Or: WHAT IF YOU LIVED

THERE? He wanted the cabinet to have a feel for the citizens they governed.

Sometimes he'd decide the problem was they just couldn't goddam see. He'd be riding around like he does on weekends, with his driver and a cop riding shotgun, and he'd see the potholes, and broken streetlights, caved-in trash cans, dirty parks, housing violations, abandoned cars, crooked traffic signs, dead trees, a missing bus stop, trash at the curb. "What are the bastards doing with the money?" he'd mutter aloud in the Buick. Then he'd get out his pen and his Mayor's Action Memos and tear into the thing:

Get the g-----m trash off East Lombard Street. . . .

Broken pavement at 1700 Carey for TWO MONTHS. . . .

Abandoned car at 2900 Remington. Why?

Then the memos would be on their desks Monday morning, and the trash, the pothole, the abandoned car had better be gone when he drove by again. How'd it get there in the first place?

One time he popped them an Action memo: "There is an abandoned car . . . but I'm not telling you where it is." City crews ran around like hungry gerbils for a week. Must have towed five hundred cars.

That was NOT . . . GOOD . . . ENOUGH: Schaefer called in his cabinet, the best municipal government in America. The mayor held two fingers up, and he poked them at his own glittery eyes.

"Do you know what these are? Do you? These are eyes." The mayor was jabbing at his face now. They thought he might hurt himself.

"I GOT TWO. AND YOU GOT TWO." Then he grabbed a cabinet member and started menacing him with the fingers in the eyes. The cabinet guy's head was burrowing between his shoulders.

"So how come my eyes can see and a smart young fella like you can't see a damn thing, huh? HOW COME?"

But today it's worse. He won't look at them. He is staring down at the table. His head, in his hands, rocks back and forth in sorrow. At his shoulder is the easel with the single word he'd written:

ERR-JEN-C.

Bugging Customers?

Let's pick up on the phrase "They [customers] were delighted [that the Levi's executive wanted to visit]." Often a rebuttal to our persistent suggestions for customer MBWA is that "customers don't want to be bothered," "customers don't want some damn vice president calling once a week to say 'How are you' " (we actually got this comment from the vice president of a phone company in one session). But our experience on such MBWA's is crystal clear: customers are, simply, *always* delighted by the attention.

Joe Baute, the president of Markem (a Keene, New Hampshire, maker of packaging and labeling products), described a new and highly effective twist to the company's annual top-management retreat in 1984: "The focus of the meeting was customers' concerns. We needed data, and decided to do something novel: Each attendee, at some point in the two weeks preceding the meeting, was to spend one full day with a customer, checking out his [the customer's] perception of us. Half our people thought it would be a waste. Several were certain the customers would feel imposed upon. To the contrary, without exception the customers loved it! And this even though we avoided the 'happy customer' problem—visiting only those most likely to tell us we were doing fine—by dividing the pile of candidates into good customers, bad customers and average customers. The debate at the meeting was informed by live impressions, for the first time in memory. Just about all agreed that it was the best meeting we've had. And follow-up has been terrific—and concrete."

An executive of AMP, the remarkably profitable ($1.5 billion in revenues) Harrisburg, Pennsylvania, makers of electrical connectors, tells a similar story. He brought in a dozen tough customers (and three or four AMP people: "We wanted 'them' to far outnumber 'us,' because the purpose was for us to be outnumbered, not for us to tell them why things were this way or that") for an intense weekend discussion. Again, several of his colleagues had argued that the customers wouldn't want to waste time on such an activity; and again, his experience was the converse: "To a man, they were flattered at the attention, and delighted to spend the time. You can't believe how much we learned."

After speaking to a bunch of hospital administrators, Tom had an interview with a new, local Cable TV group, this one specializing in communications with hospitals. As he walked toward the makeshift studio that had been set up in the auditorium, a fellow from the TV company grabbed him and started pumping his hand. It turned out that he was the marketing guy. His story: "I loved your book [*In Search of Excellence*]. The chapter on the customer in particular. As soon as I read it, I went out and started to call our customers, asking the major ones how they liked our programming. They told me! Boy, did I get an earful."

"Naïve Listening"

"Naïve listening" is a term we ran across when talking with the chairman of Allergan, a highly profitable Irvine, California, subsidiary of SmithKline Beckman. About $100 million of the company's $200 million in revenues comes from a product family of ointments and the like aimed at helping patients with eye problems. Chairman Gavin Herbert described the breakthrough that led to the development of a product to help contact-lens users:

"I've repeatedly argued that reading the data and talking to the ophthalmologists is not enough. In the pharmaceutical industry we're overwhelmed by data. All the prescription information comes in by the bushel, rapidly and neatly summarized. We have more than we need. But we miss the basic customer. I've always insisted that our people stay in touch with the users, the patients. In talking with contact-lens wearers, we kept coming across the same problem: 'itchy-scratchy eyes.' Now you know and I know that no ophthalmologist, after twenty years of professional training, is going to write down as his diagnosis 'itchy-scratchy eyes.' It's just not professional language. Yet it *was* the problem. We started working on coming up with something to deal with itchy-scratchy eyes. That was the genesis of this immensely successful product line." (We find it interesting that the company was founded by the current chairman's father, a practicing pharmacist. The family, in fact, lived right over the pharmacy, and the current chairman put in his time behind the counter too. Time and again we discover that the hands-on companies are led by people who got their start in hands-on jobs.)

"Black Box" versus South Bronx

The *Wall Street Journal* (December 12, 1984) reports:
> Westinghouse recently sent 30 hourly workers who produced subway generating equipment to New York to appraise their workmanship on the city's transit system, and underscore the need for reliability. "There's a difference between putting wires into a black box and riding the product through the South Bronx," contends Jack Geikler, general manager of Westinghouse's transportation business unit near Pittsburgh. Westinghouse workers say they see a big change in management's attitudes. "When I joined in 1968, just the notion that you went to see what you made was enough to send shivers up management's spine," recalls Harry Stauffer, a draftsman. Still, attempts to instill more pride-in-product at the workshop level won't necessarily land a contract. Westinghouse just lost a major streetcar contract in its hometown of Pittsburgh to a West German consortium. Nonetheless, asserts Westinghouse's Mr. Geikler, every little bit counts. "We see it as a survival issue. If we don't do these things, we're not going to make it."

Milliken and Company, the textile people, have taken the "naïve" idea and are turning it into a strategic passion. Naïve listening is the source of literally scores of programs. They include getting first-line people from Milliken factories in touch with first-line people in customers' factories. It turns out that, first, "hourly to hourly" is a fine way to sell. (As a friend at Northrop says, "Manufacturers are a helluva lot more credible to other manufacturers than the sales people.") Second, both have clearer notions of the practical problems involved in the use of the product. Milliken is also opening a "customer listening college." (Apple, to get its message through, is spending a huge sum developing a "retailer's college," to teach the Apple way and Apple advantages to the retailing channel.)

Other parts of the Milliken strategy include an internship in manufacturing for all salespeople; a "stand-in-the-customer's-shoes" training program; a program to bring the customer to life (via videotapes of customers using Milliken products, etc.) for the service people—those in the PBX room answering the phones or on the loading dock;* sales training for all senior management (going through a not too shortened form of the normal sales-training program); training all Milliken people to understand customer manufacturing operations (in which so many of Milliken's products are used); inviting customers to come to the Milliken premises and present a history of their company's culture to Milliken people (including hourly people, so that all hands can get a "feel" for major customers); developing joint problem-solving teams with customers that include a heavy representation of hourly people from both Milliken and the customer's operations; having customers visit the specific factory at which their product will be made (and parading them through the factory so that factory people can see live customers);† showing visiting customers a film of the history of the Milliken Company (to give them a feel for what Milliken is all about in a tangible way). Milliken is also introducing extensive and detailed customer surveys through which customers will focus in particular on their perception of the way in which Milliken is responsive to them, and in which everything from phone courtesy through billing is included.

Of course, the heart of the matter is mind-set. Chairman Roger Milliken spends 80 percent of his time on the issue. That's right: eighty! An important customer on a visit finds him, once again, lecturing at the Milliken Customer

---

*This is an extension of the whole MBWA idea. MBWA has become, for us, shorthand for "bringing business—customers, suppliers, etc.—to life," somehow, for *all* hands. A Texas bank is following the Milliken lead. Here are both the logic and the technique: a bank doesn't "lend money"; rather, it lends money so that others can productively employ it—e.g., build factories, restaurants. The bank's innovative program involved bringing the customer to life for the operations people (check processors, management information systems people, et al.) by shooting live footage of new construction financed by the bank, and then showing that footage (often beefed up by a brief interview with the customer) to all those distant from day-to-day contact with customers. The program, an officer reports, has been "a roaring success."

†Customer visits to plants is one of the debated issues. Some staunchly argue that it's "not right"—i.e., "they" will steal "our" secrets. We think they're more likely worried about a potential embarrassment: "They'll see our dirty plants!" None we know who are wholeheartedly committed to customers visiting plants have found any cause for alarm. All view it as an unadulterated plus. A Campbell Soup executive, who had spent his career in sales, was transferred to Pepperidge Farm manufacturing years ago. He said, "We were experiencing some quality problems. My first step was to invite our distributors [customers] into the plants. First, I wanted them to be joint problem solvers with us. Second, I wanted our plant people to understand that there were real customers out there. Some of them literally threw rolls at us. It worked, *and fast.*"

589

Service Center in Spartanburg, South Carolina. "Who's minding the store while you and Tom [Milliken President Malone] are doing this?" the customer asks, somewhat incredulous. Roger doesn't answer directly. Instead he says simply, "But what could be more important for me than to spend time with customers?" Roger Milliken is practicing customer MBWA with a vengeance. As he does, so does the company. (See chapter 16 for more on the importance of symbols.) As one Milliken manager, heavily involved in the new process, puts it: "A customer's problem is almost always solvable. It's up to us to see it as an opportunity. Put simply, the vendor who solves it gets the season's business." (He adds, to the naïve point: "We must constantly guard against the pitfall of being too knowledgeable.")

Really Naïve Listening

In February 1984 Tom spent four days with Milliken's 450 principal officers at their annual top-management retreat. The sole subject was getting closer to the customer—with Tom's connivance, not just listening, but "naïve listening." About a month after the meeting was over, he received a letter from the marketing director (let's get it straight—*marketing* director, not a born-again accountant or lawyer) of the division that manufactures carpets for institutions such as schools and hospitals. In it he described how he is repositioning his product line, focusing on new features, adding some new products. The reason: right after the February meeting and making his commitment to "naïve listening," he had gone out and worked two weeks, on the swing shift, in a customer's hospital. As he said, "Getting close to the customer is a *winner!!* [his emphasis]. I just got back from my second week working in a major hospital as part of the housekeeping staff. What an experience . . . to actually maintain your products (and competitive products) in the environment where they are used. Plus, it gave me an opportunity to do a lot of naïve listening while at this hospital. I worked the second shift (3:00 P.M. until midnight) and actually cleaned carpeting as well as hardsurface floors. I operated all the machinery they used daily, plus handled the same housekeeping problems that our customers face daily. I cleaned every stain from blood to urine, plus a few that I cannot even spell. To be honest, I was stiff and sore and worn out at the end of the two weeks, *but* I plan to do it again at least every six months. What did I learn? [At this point he goes on for about half a page talking about the features that really had come through in the "naïve" setting in which he had placed himself.] Now I can put together my trade advertising as well as my entire merchandising program based directly upon the needs of my customers as I observed them. No more SWAG (Scientific Wild Ass Guess) on what the market needs. I'm learning—from newproduct introduction to maintenance of existing products—exactly what our health care customers require. We can now design products and programs that have a differential advantage for our customers plus get a fair profit for Milliken. . . . I guess if we will just follow the Golden Rule—'Do unto others as you would have them do unto you'—we will become more efficient in our dealings with all people, including our customers!! I know I'm on the road to answering 'Where's the beef?' for the health care market."

What a great story! There's only one nagging problem: How come stories such as this don't describe what *everyone* does naturally? Shouldn't it be like falling off a log, especially for the marketing guy, to go out and spend two weeks at a major customer site, working the swing shift?

A Few (More) Ways to Keep in Touch

Oxford Software is a fine company, profitable, growing fast, with a solid outpouring of new products. At a celebration—a three-day meeting for all hands—of a recent success a secondary objective was to keep people from getting complacent. The chairman began the meeting with a speech. It included just one overhead transparency: a reproduction of a letter from a disgruntled (good, big) customer, telling the chairman that he thought Oxford had slipped of late, was resting on its laurels. Just one letter. Yet it had a truly galvanizing effect. When you eyeball it, see that the guy took the time to write, it's somehow different—very different. The picture is worth not just a thousand words, but more like a million.

Likewise, at People Express there's a highly visible bulletin board in each facility, located where almost everyone must pass by. Good-news customer letters are flaunted on the left side; the right side displays bad-news letters. Of course, the company systematically collects data on customer satisfaction— any sensible organization must. But the visible display of the real, unabridged words of the customer, on his or her letterhead, is compelling far beyond the numbers. It is life in a way that dry statistics can never be.

Test Flying

GE's aircraft engine pioneer, Gerhard Neumann, is a longtime practitioner of customer MBWA. Here is his description from his book *Herman the German* (Morrow, 1984) of the unique approach he took, while a member of General Claire Chennault's World War II Flying Tigers, to improve the reliability of engine repairs:

I asked my squadron mechanics to "volunteer," if this was suggested by me, to test-fly in the single-seat fighter plane whose repair they had just completed. The pilot would sit on the crew chief's lap; neither would be able to sit on a parachute because the cockpit's canopy was not big enough. I had done this myself several times with my tall squadron commander, Major Robert Costello, sitting on my lap, to identify engine problems which showed up only at altitudes of 20,000 feet or higher. The pilots were enthusiastic about my plan. Consequent improvement in quality of workmanship was dramatic. Way past dinnertime, the airfield looked as if it were invaded by glowworms: the twinkling came from flashlights mechanics used to check—once more—the tightness of pipes or connections they had made, in case I might suggest that they "volunteer" to ride in their planes the next day.

Magazine publisher James E. Buerger reports the following in *Travelhost* (September 11, 1983):

Recently I had occasion to visit the national headquarters at Frito-Lay. They produce, among other things, Lays Potato Chips. In their national headquarters they have a large bowl of potato chips, and every one of those chips is perfect. They are literally hand-picked. They are not broken, burned or chipped. They are the finest potato chips that Frito-Lay manufactures. I found this very interesting, to find such perfect potato chips. They brought a point home to me: *that was their business.* [Emphasis ours.] They had brought together the very best that they could do. And because they did, people visiting their national headquarters would have an opportunity to sample the very best of their production. With that in mind, we started doing the same thing. I asked to have the finest magazines that we produce sent to our office each week. And the instructions were that these magazines were our potato chips. I didn't want the burnt ones, or the chipped ones, or the broken ones. I only wanted the ones that were the finest. At first, I was a little shocked. What I was shocked about was that the finest potato chips, the finest magazines, that we were producing were a little burnt and a little chipped. They didn't compare at all to the fine hand-selected potato chips that I had seen at the national headquarters at Frito-Lay.

Amen. Touch. Feel. Taste.

MBWA with Customers:
Some Questions—and Things to Do Now

▶ Do you regularly call your own company and competitors with a simple request (e.g., on product information)? What are differences in response, in detail—days to answer, completeness of answer, courtesy, etc.? Have five people do this with different requests and compare notes. (Less systematically, just make a habit of calling in to your company once every couple of weeks to judge responsiveness. A variation on this theme is to dummy up some stationery and, by letter, make a simple request of your company and competitors.)

► Do you have an 800 toll-free call-in number (even if you are a small company)? If not, why not?

► Must do: Call a minimum of *three* customers per week from a list of fifty or so good, bad and indifferent customers. And get a list of major sales made and lost in the last three weeks. Call one recently gained and one recently lost customer. Ask why it happened. (Have five to ten colleagues—preferably from different functions—repeat this exercise some week, and use the results as the basis for a half-day meeting.)

► Former Marks & Spencer Chairman Marcus Sieff had a simple ritual, reported by Walter Goldsmith and David Clutterbuck in *The Winning Streak* (Weidenfeld and Nicolson, Random House and the Tom Peters Group, 1985). Every Saturday at about 5:00 P.M., for years on end, he would call the heads of four or five stores, chosen randomly, and ask how the day had gone. Likewise, each week, call *three* of your operations that deal directly with customers (sales branches, service offices, retail stores) and ask how the day's business has gone.

► Do you bring customers to life (via video, visits, etc.) for the off-line departments—MIS, accounting, personnel? Do you have members of the off-line functions make occasional (but regular) customer visits, work on the retail floor, etc.?

► Do you conduct occasional intensive customer debriefings (à la Markem, AMP, Milliken) where customers are "called in" (invited in) for multiday "How are *we* doing for *you?*" sessions?

► Do you have set routines and visit patterns which are aimed at the "naïve" part of listening? (E.g., let the customer speak first at debriefings, à la Milliken; visit ultimate users rather than intermediaries, à la Allergan?)

► Do senior managers (and all managers) work in selected customer operations (in a regular job) on a quarterly basis? Do "technical experts" (R&D people, brand managers, designers) regularly visit and work in selected customer operations?

► Are customers regularly invited to visit virtually all facilities? Are people from all customer functions (e.g., manufacturers) invited to visit? Are there regular routines for debriefing (i.e., listening to) customers on these visits?

► Do visitations—yours to customers, customers' to you—go all the way down to the hourly level? And are they regular?

Supplier as "Customer"

It seems that one of the half-dozen traits that we hear exemplify Japanese management (in contrast to management in the United States) is the long-term, almost familial relations between suppliers and producers. But there's no Japanese magic about it: it can happen in the United States—and does in many of the best companies. Again, our friends at Milliken are leading the way, doing virtually all the things we mentioned in connection with customers with their vendors as well, including swapping visits among hourly people from vendor organizations and Milliken organizations, and bringing vendor people into the Milliken operations to learn about things that the Milliken quality-improvement teams are doing.*

Milliken isn't alone. When Tom was in Sweden in 1982, he attended a meeting that included a presentation by Marcus Sieff of Marks & Spencer. Sieff commented on the exceptional family relationships that the company maintains with its suppliers. Tom expected the usual litany about a battalion of quality-control people, a tough legal-contracts section and the like. Instead Lord Sieff said, almost as an aside, "Well, of *course,* I and each of my [top 25 or so] executives make it a hard-and-fast point to visit a minimum of forty suppliers a year." Wow! So it isn't so mysterious after all. (Or is it? That's a lot of time and determination.)

There's a tough side to the M&S equation as well. They simply demand that their suppliers live up to their high standards. Walter Goldsmith and David Clutterbuck again, in *The Winning Streak:*

> M&S maintains a team of inspectors who visit suppliers' premises, ensuring that quality levels are maintained and making suggestions for improvements. It calculates that a one per cent reduction in faulty merchandise more than pays for all the support services it provides suppliers, including substantial help in areas of employee welfare. M&S reasons that good working conditions are a prerequisite for high-quality production. It lays particular stress on canteens, morale and hygiene, and provides free courses for suppliers on a whole range of employee welfare issues. A regular newsletter keeps suppliers up to date on developments that might improve quality directly or through employee motivation.
>
> "All our long-term suppliers are very profitable," claims Sieff, suggesting that that is a result of adopting M&S-style management.

---

*And again, the most common rejoinder we get on this point is "You're giving away your secrets to a potential competitor." Nonsense. The competitor—potential or otherwise—usually knows what you're up to. Besides, this kind of logic assumes that various segments of the channel are mortal enemies—and *that* assumption has gotten a good many of us into a mess. Both the vendors and the Milliken people benefit immensely from this exchange process, and the risks are minimal.

Suppliers who do not fall in line, fall out. A large meat supplier, for example, had very poor working conditions for its employees. "Our business with them was increasing considerably. But they had appalling canteens and lavatories and some of the walls were running with damp. I said I would give them three months to put it right. When I came back there was no improvement. They said, 'You'll never stop doing business with us.' One month later we gave them two weeks' notice."

Only a couple of weeks after we met Marcus Sieff we visited Northrop, where we were doing some consulting, and where our friend Marv Elkin runs the purchasing organization. He's done a remarkable job of changing vendor-producer relationships for the better in the course of the past two or three years. We sat down to chat with him about it a bit, and mentioned Lord Sieff's comment about visits. Now, Marv's an animated fellow, and he leaped up halfway through our description: "That's it! That's it!" Yes, it was. It turned out to be *exactly* what Marv had been doing. He stated that over the past two years, in a program that departed remarkably from the company's previous adversarial relationship with vendors, he had visited over 150 suppliers. Equally important, his visits weren't thinly disguised opportunities to take whacks at the suppliers. They were open-ended, with no set agenda. He asked them to make a presentation on their company's history, their strategy, their work force, their quality programs: "It was just a chance to get acquainted, to learn about them, to show interest (which I desperately had) in them as a whole." It's a program that he's kept up, and gotten others of his own people thoroughly involved in as well. It's been a long first step toward reversing decades of adversarial and negative relationships, where the only senior contact came in the heat of battle and in response to pressing problems. And it came none too soon, because the quality programs that Northrop is having shoved down its throat by the Air Force are now requiring Marv to turn up the heat on his vendors. The groundwork, however, has been clearly—and expensively (in terms of time)—laid by his visits. Now all of them are in a position to work together.

Domino's Pizza Distribution Company (Domino's ingredients and equipment supplier) just says "Thanks." They regularly stage Vendor Appreciation Days. A horde of Domino's people will descend on a Wisconsin cheese maker or a California olive grower and shower the supplier with time and attention. Distribution executive Jeff Smith can't imagine it any other way. "They're part of the family, aren't they," he says, with surprise that anyone could conceive of a different position on the issue. (Interestingly, family relations with vendors are an explicit part of Domino's Distribution statement of its mission. Now, that is rare. But why not?)

That's really about the extent of the supplier-MBWA magic. Wandering around. Keeping in touch. Replacing theoretically adversarial relationships with garden-variety humanness, doing so at all levels of both organizations. And taking time to say thanks in more than a perfunctory fashion.

MBWA with Suppliers:
Some Questions—and Things to Do Now

▶ Do people with functions other than purchasing (e.g., manufacturing, marketing) regularly visit vendors? Do vendors regularly visit *all* your facilities—factories or operations areas, etc.? Does your chief purchasing officer spend 25 to 35 percent or more of his or her time with vendors at *their* locations dealing with other than brushfire problems?

▶ Pick three good (and long) and three rocky vendor relationships. Study them. Have an executive team select one good and one bad per person and visit with each for one to one and a half days. Ask the vendors how *you* are doing as people to sell to. Return and spend a full day analyzing the data. What do they perceive it's like to do business with you? What are the *ten* things that irritate them most about your practices? Can you fix three of the ten in the next sixty days?

▶ To what extent are vendors "part of the family"? Are they (small and large) regularly invited to strategy sessions, company celebrations (formal and informal)? If so, *who* is invited—just the person who sells to you, or members of the vendor's factory, Quality Control department (after all, your success depends on the vendor's QC people)? Is there any air of "can't share this with them because it's too confidential"? Do company newsletters, bulletins (annual reports, even) tell stories about vendors, vendor facilities, company-vendor joint-problem-solving successes?

▶ To what extent are you part of the vendor's "family"? Do your hourly or first-line shop supervisors attend vendor functions? Ever? Regularly? If not, have you ever asked for an invitation for your down-the-line people?

▶ Do you and vendors have numerous, ongoing joint-problem-solving teams that involve hourly people from both sides? If not, why not?

▶ More generally, check around with people in various functions, at various levels. Develop a five-minute questioning routine about vendor relations both in general and in specific terms. What does your little, nonsystematic survey suggest about the role of suppliers in your company? Are they seen as cherished, full-fledged members? Or as necessary nuisances?

MBWA: INNOVATION

PepsiCo was a sleepy company a dozen years ago. Now it's aggressive. But while it spends extravagantly to get Michael Jackson on the tube as an advertiser for Pepsi-Cola in the ceaseless battle against Coke, it places its real bets on development of the likes of La Petite Boulangerie, a bakery chain with six stores in the San Francisco area that is expected to run to three thousand stores, nationwide, just five years from now. Growing new or small businesses is the PepsiCo technique. Its subsidiary Frito-Lay was a fine company with a large share. Yet in the mid-seventies it really began to take off. Changes in the size of the bag, a huge variety of new flavors—in short, innovation—marked the new Frito-Lay.

What's the magic of the PepsiCo transformation? Much of it stems from a form of MBWA, we'd contend. In particular, the unique form practiced by PepsiCo's former chief operating officer, Andy Pearson. He was on the road a lot—probably 40 percent of his time. Much of that time was spent visiting subsidiaries. When he did so, the routine was standard. He ignored the executive suite at first, and headed for the office of the most recently hired members of the brand management staff. "What's up? What've you got going in the test market? How're they reacting to the new umpty-ump flavor?" And so on. Implicit (pretty explicit, come to think of it) was the message that *something* had better be going on. Under his and Chairman Don Kendall's stewardship the company took off like a jackrabbit. (They did the job so well that in 1981 Coca-Cola promoted the dynamic Roberto Goizuetta to chairman just to keep pace.)

To innovate is to pay attention to innovation. At Hewlett-Packard, each engineer leaves the project he or she is working with out on "the bench." Other engineers—including "retired" Bill Hewlett, who according to the old pros was always around and about—take a look at it, play with it, comment on it. More significant, even, is the tone set. Everybody leaves a device out. Everybody gets into the act and plays with everybody else's toys. (And you had darn well better be working on a toy, one that's fun enough and new enough to interest your ceaselessly wandering—and vociferously judgmental—peers.)

MBWA: Problem Solving, a Subset of Innovation

The Rockwell International engineer had a dubious distinction. He had been in charge of a large share of the space shuttle's misbehaving tiles (the ones that popped off during the stress of reentry in the troubled early days of the shuttles). After a discussion about MBWA a couple of years back, he came up to us and said, "I never had a label for it before. But that's it." The story he related was of the obvious—yet not so obvious—variety. It went this way: "Every Monday, it seemed, it would be the same. Another problem had arisen over the weekend. Another foul-up. And then the invariant ritual would begin. Twenty-four hours would pass. I'd arrive the next morning. Like clockwork, a fifty-page report would be lying prominently on my desk, from one of the engineering groups. The thrust of it was always the same: 'It ain't our fault. Two other engineering groups screwed up.' And then another twenty-four hours would pass. The next day's desk fare was also predictable: two more reports, this time numbering a hundred pages each, from the two offended groups [from the previous day] rebutting the accusations and blaming others, including (especially) the first group. We just didn't seem to get anywhere. Finally I had an idea. I started one Friday afternoon. I brought all the top people involved in the program to a cramped, sweaty conference room near my place. These people were from all over. It didn't matter where. After that, every week, on Friday afternoon, we'd sit there and thrash around, from early afternoon until the wee small hours if necessary. We'd go over every problem. We'd figure out what the heck it was each of us was going to do in the next seventy-two to ninety-six hours. We'd review where we'd been in the last ninety-six. It was just as simple as that. You know, it's a fact of human nature: you can bullshit people to a fare-thee-well with a two-hundred-page report, and you can pull the wool over their eyes pretty well with a twenty-five-page one. But it's damn hard, on a Friday afternoon, to do either when you're far away from home and the cigarette smoke has reached the 'can't-quite-breathe' level. It's real hard to sign up for an objective and then come back to that smoke-filled room like clockwork next Friday and report that you couldn't make it to the guy sitting four feet away across the table to whom you made the promise. Truth and honesty win out in such a setting with remarkable regularity. And that was our routine. Every Friday afternoon. And the things that began to occur! In a period of about ten weeks we made more progress than we had in the prior eighteen months."

Now, that's problem solving! No matrix reporting relations. No 16,000-bubble PERT charts. Smoke-filled-room MBWA, instead. We'll see more of it when we talk later about Gerhard Neumann's skunkwork at GE.

MBWA: Innovation
Some Questions and Things to Do Now

▶ Given that concrete experiments are essential to innovation, how—specifically—does your *daily* routine reflect your desire to constantly test and try new things? Are you constantly, like Pearson or the HP people, out on the floor (of the lab, design rooms, MIS coders' space) asking "What's gone on in the last twenty-four (or forty-eight) hours?" (GE's Gerhard Neumann and Lockheed's Kelly Johnson never let more than twenty-four hours pass without thorough "What have you tried that's interesting?" probes of *all* hands.)

▶ Select two projects that are badly delayed, two that are on or ahead of schedule. (Alternatively, select two or three project managers who always seem to bring a job in on time, two or three who don't.) Analyze the information swapping and getting-the-people-together-for-problem-solving routines. Are there any parallels to the Rockwell story? If so, dig a layer deeper: look for fifteen to twenty-five ancillary "trivial" factors that enhance the problem-solving setting (e.g., physical setting, time of day, duration of meetings, record keeping re promises made). How commonplace is the use of the devices you unearthed? If rare, can you induce more widespread use—e.g., by writing up or otherwise communicating these "problem-solving success stories"?

MBWA with Customers (yes, again):
Innovation Source par Excellence

Go back to pages 587–591, where we introduced the concept of naïve listening. The term originated with the chairman of Allergan, in connection with the development of a new product—in other words, with innovation.

Listening/naïve listening. The studies continue to pour in. There are now over eighty that we have unearthed including those reviewed for *In Search of Excellence.* Virtually all of them say the same thing: the lion's share of new ideas comes from the users. (3M adds an important twist: a substantial share of their ideas come in response to the complaints of users. 3M sees the complaint per se as an unparalleled opportunity!) The Milliken people discovered that in virtually every division 50 percent or more of their product ideas came from users. And this was *before* they developed conscious, proactive "naïve listening" programs.

The power of listening: it borders on the bizarre. General Electric has radically increased its share of market in the railroad locomotive business against a tough competitor—the $80 billion General Motors Corporation. In 1980 customers were concerned that GM would achieve a monopolistic position. By 1984 they were again worried about a monopolistic position; only now GE was the worry. At the base of it was a division general manager hellbent upon improving performance. He spurred a marketer to take on a semibootleg project with three engineers quietly borrowed from another operation. They hit the road, doing something that hadn't been done in a decade, talking, naïvely, with principal customers. They held workshops on customer premises. Walls were lined with butcher paper, and lists of desired features were divvied up: these are the features that we at GE will try to provide; this is what you the customer can best do. Out of it came the New Series Design, and then the remarkable new-order growth. The program was so successful that it has now allowed GE to invest over a quarter billion dollars in a new, highly automated factory in depressed Erie, Pennsylvania.

When you hear such stories you ought to be a bit skeptical. We were. But we did the best we could to check the information out, and it appeared to be valid. Then Tom had a unique opportunity to confirm it. He spoke at a luncheon meeting of San Francisco Bay Area business leaders sponsored by the chairman of the Stanford Board of Trustees. One present was Ben Biaggini, then chairman of the Southern Pacific Company. After relating this analysis, Tom turned to Ben, for the SP Railroad had been one of the companies that GE had purportedly "operated upon," and asked, "Is there any truth to this?" To his great dismay, Ben replied, deadpan, "Not a bit." Tom recovered and asked, "OK, what *is* the story?" Ben grinned, and paused for a second, then he proceeded: "To tell you the truth, Tom, it had been a lot longer than ten years since anybody had bothered to ask."

This theme rings especially true for the technology-based industries, where technical arrogance and a "This product will sell itself" mentality dominate many companies—and bring more than a few to their knees. Fred Cox, chairman of successful Emulex, a computer industry player, says, "So many lose because they come to 'own the market.' They start to *tell* the customer what he wants." In computers, Wang has the top growth rate (sales and profits) among the big, higher-end players. Their secret? For the most part it's better listening to the ultimate user. Sandra Kurtzig's ASK Computer, which makes software systems primarily for manufacturers, has gone from $0 to $100 million in no time flat. Almost all agree on the reason. ASK is well named: They ask *and* listen—and then adapt a product to the customer's needs. Digital Switch is a Dallas-based star in telecommunications switch gear. MCI chose it as a major supplier over Northern Telecom when both Digital Switch and MCI were small. The reason, according to one close observer: "NT [Northern Telecom] *told* MCI what they could have. Digital Switch *asked* MCI what they wanted."

3M is so committed to the idea of customer listening for innovation that they've made it their corporate theme/logo.*

A Few (More) Tricks of the Trade

In many companies the best source of ideas is the sales force. Yet so few really listen to their sales force. The common wisdom is that "the sales force rolls over and plays dead in the face of every customer whim." To some extent, of course, that's true: that *is* what the salesman gets paid for, up to a point. But Chairman Bill Keefer of Warner Electric Brake and Clutch, running a highly profitable, $175 million company providing specialty industrial devices (such as clutches for Xerox machines), sees it differently. He knows that his future lies in the development of a large string of new, customer-induced, niche-oriented products (shades of 3M). And he knows that the people most likely to hear what's needed are his salespeople. So he has a boring routine. Each salesperson makes a monthly call report. Not so novel. As part of each call report, there is a requirement to submit the "best three potential product (new or line extension) ideas heard about on a customer premise." Now, this is a bit unusual. But the real novelty? The chairman spends almost

---

*Sometimes our friends explicitly test our credibility when it comes to 3M. The president of a small bank had an idea for an adhesive to keep pothole plugs from popping out in the extreme cold. Having read about 3M's listening proclivity in *In Search of Excellence,* he called them and rapidly got through to a 3M technology executive. A week later, the fellow called our banker friend back to report that they were working on his idea. His comment to us, "By God, they really *do* listen."

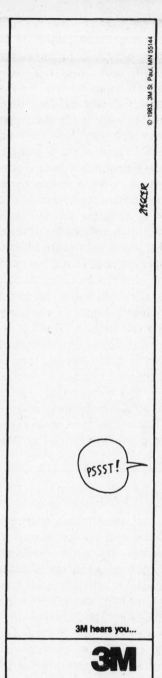
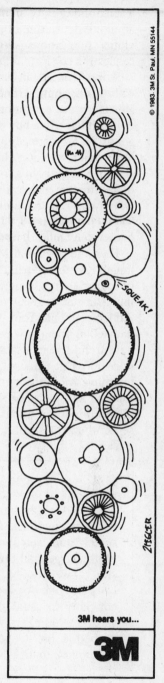

Illustrations courtesy of 3M

a full Sunday each month *reading* those ninety reports. Furthermore, he has an unfailing routine of penning personal notes on thirty or forty of the individual suggestions—notes to people in engineering and manufacturing requesting concrete follow-up within, usually, a five- or ten-day period.

So much of the business of retailing seems to have come to focus on the centralized distribution function, the centralized computer-aided buying function. But there are exceptions. Mervyn's is the shining star in Dayton-Hudson's crown; it has a fine buying organization. Now, buyers these days (like package-goods brand managers) are typical of the hotshot, fast-tracking young men and women who don't have time for the boring task of learning the job on the retail floor. Mervyn's, to some extent, is no exception. Most of its new buyers didn't start on the retail floor. But Mervyn's stays ahead of its competitors by effectively remerchandising its entire billion-dollar-plus operation once a week (see chapter 9, "The Mythology of Innovation"); what Mervyn's does once a week most of its major competitors can barely do in a quarter of a year.

Then the people at Mervyn's take a vital next step. They keep in touch—tangible, visible touch. There's a process called Weekly Store Check. The fleet-of-foot merchandising is accomplished by getting their top hundred or so merchants and executives together once a week to redo things (i.e., create the Ad Supplement). They proceed on the basis of lots of written feedback, lots of data telling them how the stuff they pushed last week is selling this week. They have trend-line analyses from themselves and from their competitors' operations, too. But equally significant, they see it: that same cast of a hundred—executive vice presidents, merchants, buyers—troops together as a group through a single store for a full four hours once a week. They ask questions: "Does this set of things that we put next to that set of things actually make sense when you see it in the store's live format?" "What does it feel like?"

MBWA: The Real-World Loop

MBWA means, among other things, not treating the innovator—designer/buyer/brand manager/product engineer—like a one-dimensional (and weird) being with no interest in the world Out There. Mervyn's gets all the innovators (buyers in this instance) out into the stores—weekly. 3M insists that all their R&D types make regular sales calls. But one doesn't have to go that far. At a seminar with a software company the usual issue arose: The sales types thought the prima donna software designers were flakes, not interested in the real world. We probed a bit deeper, and discovered that given the salespersons' *assumption* that "all software designers are flakes," they did in fact treat the designers like flakes. A designer pleaded: "How do you expect me to be excited about the sales and marketing end? You never give us any information on it—no sales data at all, no customer information except major glitches, in conjunction with which you simply run around calling us a bunch of 'impractical nerd assholes.' " It turns out that this sad tale is an all too common one. The sales types (or the president, who vowed to fix the problem instantly in this case—and did) act out their negative assumptions; thus the "far out" types are not brought into the real-world loop, and they become farther out as a result, with predictable effects on innovation.

Customers and Innovation:
Some Questions—and Things to Do Now

▶ Look at your last ten new products/services. What were the sources of the ideas? Look at key competitors' last ten new products/services. What were the sources of the ideas? (Our experience shows that 50 percent at least will come from customers, *even if you aren't trying hard* to tap this source. Does your evidence match this?) Have the customer-generated ideas led to faster (and more profitable) product development?

▶ Are all customers "hounded" for new ideas in all settings?

▶ Is there a specific and regular mechanism for salespersons to solicit customers' ideas? If so, is there a specific mechanism aimed at making sure that design/marketing/engineering/manufacturing pay attention to these ideas? Do nonsales functions (marketing, manufacturing or operations, accounting) specifically (alone or as part of a team) solicit customer ideas?

▶ Consider giving an award (sales, marketing, engineering) for "best idea garnered from a customer this month." Consider sales (marketing, engineering) contests focused on unearthing new ideas from customers. Consider adding manufacturers/operations people to this crusade (which must start by letting them visit the customers).

▶ Do you treat your designer/buyer types as well-rounded business people? Are they brought into the loop—the store, the factory, the customer's premises—in a way that makes them team members rather than the odd-ball "creative type"? If the answer is yes, then be specific: List 10 ways (or examples within the last 90 days) you've made the designers et al. part of the team.

▶ Are the "idea" people (engineers, brand managers, marketers, buyers) *forced* to visit customers or sales-floor operations regularly? Monthly? How about weekly?

MBWA: PEOPLE

Phil Staley has turned around an old Ford plant in Edison, New Jersey. We'll describe the process in some detail later. Here suffice it to say that every day he wandered the floor. And then he did more: He started barbecuing steaks for his people at one end of the plant. Then he more or less formalized it: he opened—on the floor—a shop of sorts, Staley's Steakhouse. He hangs out there a few hours a day, grilling steak, talking to people, listening.

Jimmy Treybig, Tandem Computer founder, thinks it's important to get people together. So he does. Everybody. Once a *week*. At every Tandem facility, from Santa Clara to Singapore, there is a "beer bust" once a week. No one is required to attend. But anyone can. And most do. Many say that more business is done in those couple of hours than during the rest of the week combined. The leader in the gene-splicing business, Genentech, a South San Francisco company, practices the same routine. Once a week. All hands. Free beer. (Free oysters the week that we were lucky enough to attend.)

We chat with executive after executive (and many nonexecutives). They brag: "Well, we get all our people together once a year. It's a big deal. It's an effort, but it's well worth it." Treybig wouldn't understand that; the Genentech people wouldn't understand it; Phil Staley wouldn't understand it. Hewlett-Packard insists that every division get all hands together, in a common setting, no less than once every two weeks. It's done. The cost—enormous. At least by some measures. It takes a lot of time, and a lot of energy. But how good are you? No better than your people and their commitment and participation in the business, as full partners, and as business people. The fact that you get them all together to share whatever—results, experiences, recent small successes and the like—at least once every couple of weeks seems to us to be a small price indeed to pay for that commitment and sense of teamwork and family. The "return on investment" is probably far and away the best of any program in the organization. Ask Victor Kiam: he started conducting regular all-hands meetings and sharing rituals as part of his turnaround program at Remington (the razor people) a couple of years back. He says it's the best investment he ever made. And if you don't believe him, ask his people.

There are, of course, numerous variations on this theme (we'll look at more of them in Part IV, "People People People"). Each serves to illustrate the imagination that can be applied to this underthought-about area of staying in touch. For instance, People Express has built an internal TV network, WPEX. A daily news show is taped (all "broadcasters" are regular employees—e.g., a pilot just finishing a flight) and transmitted to all the system's locations early the next day. Stock price, customer complaints and praise, and a hundred and one other activities are reported, and, we hear, avidly watched upon receipt. But here's our favorite (partially because it suggests that we *all* have the same problems). George Lucas, of LucasFilm (*Star Wars*, etc.) is just like you and us! His office people fight with his field people, and so on. Lucas has few rules, but one is this: on any LucasFilm softball team, there shall be no more than one person from any one department. Genius! When do you find out that people are human, not narrow-minded "functional bigots," as a colleague calls them? Much more likely over a postgame keg of beer than in a committee meeting.

Boldness!

Most give lip service to getting people together. ASK, HP, Genentech, Dana and People Express put their time (and money) where others put only their mouths, bringing hundreds or thousands together, from far and near, weekly or monthly. S. C. Johnson & Son (Johnson's Wax, etc.), the superb Racine, Wisconsin, company joins the list of the bold. Late in 1984, Chairman Sam Johnson observed that his British subsidiary apparently felt estranged from the Johnson "family feeling" he so cherishes. To rectify the situation, he chartered a 747 and flew all five-hundred employees of the British subsidiary to the United States for a full week! Three days were spent touring U.S. factories and attending a lavish gala in Racine put on by the U.S. work force; two more days were devoted to sightseeing in New York City.

MBWA: People—
Some Questions, and Things to Do Now

▶ How much time do you devote to walking the floor? Be specific: Collect some data for about twenty-five managers—all functions, all levels. How big is the variation? What's the low end: 5 percent? 10 percent? Are you surprised by the pattern?

▶ Wandering is a habit that starts close to home (i.e., the next office). Are the doors open or closed? Or, better yet, do you even have doors? Two examples: An officer in a mid-sized company has a favorite routine. Whenever he takes charge of a new area, he always begins by *personally* removing his door from his office. The message is clear. Another colleague one-ups him: he always moves his desk—again, personally—out into the secretarial bullpen area. More generally, do physical spaces enhance or thwart wandering? (At the highest level of generality, Mars, Inc., for instance, physically attaches *all* administrative facilities to manufacturing plants.)

▶ What is the frequency of "all hands" meetings? Why? Could you do more? We urge you to attend an all-hands session at Dana, Milliken, HP, Tandem or Genentech, for instance, if you can. "Seeing is believing" is probably uniquely applicable to this one.

▶ Can you readily list ten devices, à la LucasFilm, for *forcing* warring tribes into informal contact? If yes, can you list ten more—and put them into practice? This is a constant battle; there are never enough.

MBWA: THE TECHNOLOGY OF LEADERSHIP

MBWA: the technology of the obvious. It is being in touch, with customers, suppliers, your people. It facilitates innovation, and makes possible the teaching of values to every member of an organization. Listening, facilitating, and teaching and reinforcing values. What is this except leadership? Thus *MBWA is the technology of leadership.* We will subsequently argue that leading (a school, a small business, or a Fortune 100 company) is primarily *paying attention,* and that the masters of the use of attention are also not only master users of symbols, of drama, but master storytellers and myth builders. All this can be accomplished only through means that are visible, tangible. The story of the senior manager's ten-minute visit with a neophyte salesman—in the field, in *his* territory—is relayed in minutes around a system spanning six thousand miles. Its effectiveness is many times that of the formal pronouncement, which is viewed by most as written by a committee of staffers.

The Smell of MBWA

Is wandering encouraged or discouraged in your organization? (Look deeply at this. The *implicit* is more important than the explicit.) Do you give lip service to foster wandering, but then get angry and impatient when people take you at your word and are out of their offices—when you want something *now?* Bob Waterman reports a conversation with a long-time Arco executive about inveterate wanderer Chairman Bob Anderson: "If Bob would call you from the field, and if you happened to be *in,* you could detect noticeable disappointment in his voice." Sam Walton of Wal-Mart, too, shows ire when people are in their offices; and a P&G manufacturer reports, "The worst chewing out I got in my career came very early in my managerial days, when a visiting Cincinnati exec wandered by one morning and caught me in my office. He gave me hell and then some." These reports are exceptions. More common is a young brand manager we chatted with. We asked him if he got out to ride with salesmen once a month or so. His reply? "*Once a month?!* You're kidding. If we're not in the office, period, and ready to jump, with data in hand, on a split-second notice, we're in trouble. MBWA around here means bathroom breaks at most." His company's record, we'd add, is nothing to write home about. So, collect *good* data on this. By hook or by crook, get feedback you trust (especially from some entry level types): What is "OK" and "not OK" re wandering—how/how early is the message learned? What, direct and indirect, are the reinforcement devices?

Here are eight ways to fix the "smell," if it discourages wandering:
▶ Publicize the fact that *you* are out wandering 50% of the time, and that your colleagues are, too (if you and they are).

- ▶ Be meticulous in having meetings in other's offices/spaces rather than yours.
- ▶ Evaluate managers in part—and directly—on the basis of *their people's* assessment of how well/how frequently they are in touch.
- ▶ *Fire* a supervisor who doesn't know all his people's first and last names. (McPherson at Dana did this once; this fellow had been in the slot a half dozen years.)
- ▶ Hold meetings and reviews in the field (it gives a further signal that out-of-the-office is the norm).
- ▶ An especially tough one: When you're harried and need some information badly, and only Ms. X has it, and you discover upon calling that she's out on a field visit—*don't* call her in the field and tell her to rush back and get the answer. *Wait!*
- ▶ Start randomly popping into offices and asking the inhabitants why *they* aren't out.
- ▶ If, say, you're a manufacturing boss, make sure you have a second office on the shop floor. If you're an R&D V.P., make sure you have a second (non-headquarters) office in a lab. (S.I. Newhouse, who created the Newhouse publishing empire, *never* had an office or a secretary. He spent 100% of his time in his subsidiaries, roaming in unannounced and seconding an unimposing office to use for the day.)

MBWA pervades every level of the effective organization of every sort—which is to say that leaders exist at every level. We shall return to the subject again directly in the concluding section devoted to leadership. Indirectly it will permeate virtually every intervening page.

3

Integrity and the Technology of the Obvious

"MBWA: The Technology of the Obvious" introduces you to our obsessions with integrity. The issue came clear in mid-1984. Tom read a book he had been asked to comment upon favorably. The words were terrific. They focused on listening, developing empathy for the person on the other side of the table. They emphasized the importance of traveling thousands of miles if necessary to see a person face-to-face, to watch the eyes. Tom, who takes pleasure in giving support for books he likes, demurred in this instance. Why? The book's implicit thrust was that these are *tools* anyone can use to gain immediate advantage over others. We're at a loss to describe the depth of our dismay. We believe in truly listening to the customer, taking the customer's view as *more* important than our own. We believe in truly listening to our people, taking their views as *more* important than our own. But the whole edifice tumbles if one doesn't deal off a base of integrity.

Thus what is not so obvious throughout this book is that virtually every device we suggest is doomed to be useless unless applied with integrity. Worse than useless, most of these devices, used without integrity, will expose you as a hypocrite of the first order.

Install a toll-free number, then don't "overtrain" your people or "overrespond" to customer call-ins. You'll find it won't work. The area code 800 numbers hum only for those who really believe in listening and responding, not those who are merely looking for a PR gimmick.

Paint out the executive parking spots, but treat your people with contempt, and you'll find you stand convicted of a kind of fraud.

Draw your organization charts "upside down" (customers or constituents on top, president or city manager on the bottom) and then provide the same careless service. It won't make an iota of difference. Except that you will become a joke.

In support of innovation, give speeches lauding failures that were good tries, and then demote or sidetrack the first champion whose head pops up; that's it for risk-taking, despite all the fine words.

We are especially at risk in the material we present here. There is little on formal organization structures, on planning or performance appraisal systems. Perhaps with these formal devices you can "get away with" a bit of inconsistency and, yes, lack of integrity, for the formal system is meant to carry the weight.

Not here! Each major element in our model is clearly underpinned by a thousand supporting devices, each insignificant but collectively grand. What gives them the collective coherence, the clarity of vision, is, simply, integrity. Each of a thousand customer-serving devices supports the passionate concern for customers at L. L. Bean. Each of a thousand devices to turn "employees" into owners and heroes at Apple and People Express is in direct support of the passion of Steve Jobs and Don Burr to create a whole new form of equitable organizations for their people.

We will remind you in every chapter that each example lives only as the leader's integrity (leaders at every level) lives within it. As you read on we would ask you to stop and pause, close the door and examine your deepest beliefs about people (and their creative potential and trustworthiness), about wandering, about the importance of the customer's perception, about failure. Especially when a suggestion makes your eyes light up. That's the time to pause. When, for example, you get excited about a listening device, when you want to install it *now,* start *now,* today (which is, after all, what we beg you to do).

Stop, nonetheless. Do you believe in it? Believe what it stands for? Believe that the people who will execute it are trustworthy enough to do so?

If you proceed through these pages simultaneously champing at the bit and reflecting, then we will have accomplished a major objective. And we hope you will have too.

We fight the same battle in our analysis that we are asking you to fight. *We* get excited at the excitement of Milliken president Tom Malone as he describes the details of his Fabulous Bragging Sessions, so integral to Milliken's quality-program success. But then we hesitate. We observe Malone carefully. We observe his enthusiasm, passion, excitement, genuine concern. When he talks of giving out awards personally, we write down the details of everything, including the way he frames them; and then we visualize him giving them out, and we know that he takes pleasure in handing the 157th award of the day to the receptionist or loading dock team. And across our mental screens run the other, all too familiar pictures of the stilted award givers who, from handing out award no. 1 to award no. 200, exude "I wish I were anyplace else but here."

A friend of ours, an outsider, joined us for dinner at our Skunk Camp, mentioned in the Foreword. She spent a half hour with Don Burr of People Express, and with Don Williams, managing partner of Trammell Crow. She knows their towering reputations. Yet her reaction (almost a stunned one, for she has attended far too many "corporate dinners"): "They are such good listeners. They focused on what I am up to, on my small business."

Ah yes, that's it. A million devices, each important—*and* integrity.

2

CUSTOMERS

I'd have to say that [before the events of the last four tough years] our culture in the Ford Motor Company said that there's one central objective in our business, and that's to earn a return on our investment. I think we've now learned there's something else that's central—and that profits will fall to you if you view this as central: Serve the customer. You have to have your costs right, quality right, all those other things that have to be done. But we must always think the customer is the middle of the thrust of what we're trying to do. I think that's what we've learned. I don't think it's much more complicated than that, and I would suggest it to you for your consideration.

> *Edson P. Williams, vice president,*
> *Ford Motor Company general manager,*
> *Ford Truck Operations*

Consumers are statistics. Customers are People.

> *Stanley Marcus, chairman emeritus,*
> *Neiman-Marcus*

The first of the two sustainable strategic advantages we have observed is an obsession with customers. Customers, not markets. Not marketing. Not strategic positioning (whatever that means). Just customers. A "market" has never been observed paying a bill. Customers do that.

Obviously there is a role for marketing, strategy formulation and the like. But ultimately, it all boils down to perceived, and appreciated, and consistently delivered service and quality to customers. Time and again we watch companies sharpen their market focus; we watch them work on quality issues. Progress is made. But it is either fleeting or a fraction of what it might be, because the customer has not become the obsessive focus of all hands—from the mailroom to MIS warren to the sales branch.

We've developed a term, after careful thought: *smell*. Does your company smell of customers? Do you listen to them directly (via MBWA), act on what you hear, listen naïvely (i.e., consider their *perceptions* more important than your superior technical knowledge of service or product)? Do you love your salespersons (i.e., listen to them), despite their efforts to strain your resources—and patience—in response to what you see as customers' whims? Do you look for the dozens (hundreds, really) of tiny bases for differentiation—i.e., a small but measurable difference that is the winning edge for superb cookie makers and aircraft engine makers alike?

IBM, Domino's Pizza, Stew Leonard's, Maytag, Perdue Farms—they seem to live for their customers. They are all good marketers. Or are they? They *appear* to be good marketers, masters of segmentation and strategic positioning, *because* they slavishly put the customer first—in every department in the business.

So the key words in our lexicon are simple ones, such as *courtesy, listening, perception.* We are (sorry to say) a bit self-congratulatory on this issue: that is, we are proud to have a full section in this book called, simply, *Customers.* Not many business or management books do. And all too often business performance reflects this lack of interest by writers, consultants and academics. Tom and Bob Waterman wrote a chapter on the subject of customers in *In Search of Excellence.* We now single it out for fully five chapters. It has become our preoccupation, our obsession. Surely it's obvious that everything necessarily starts with the customer. More specifically, with *common courtesy* toward the customer.

4

Common Courtesy: The Ultimate Barrier to Competitor Entry

Guests

At Disneyland and Disneyworld, every person who comes onto the property (the "set") is called a guest. Moreover, should you ever write the word at Disney, heaven help you if you don't capitalize the G.

Many companies, from Hewlett-Packard and Du Pont to Big Eight accounting firms and banks or truckers newly faced with deregulation, seek to become more "market oriented." Often as not, management kicks off the effort by calling in a large group of marketing professors from Stanford or Harvard or Northwestern to teach market segmentation and the like. The companies love what they hear (the marketing jargon is as complex and scientific-sounding as their own technical jargon), and they go after applications of the new techniques with a vengeance. But not much happens or changes.

Why? We believe that long-term strategic advantage via "marketing orientation" comes principally from some commonsense traits: listening (see the discussion of MBWA with customers in chapter 2); common courtesy (or "uncommon courtesy," as we more correctly call it); slavish devotion to adding value to and differentiating the most mundane of so-called commodities; and superior service and quality. Those traits are, simply, not technique-driven. Moreover, they are not about "marketing." They are about customers. We strongly prefer "customer orientation" to "market orientation"; as we said, markets do not buy products, customers do. The distinction may sound pedantic. We think not. Before a sustained advantage can accrue from finely honed segmentation schemes, one must come to cherish the customer.

Portions of this essay were published under the title "Common Courtesy" in *Hospital Forum* and as "Service Excellence: It's Scarce" in *Florida Trend*.

Advantage comes not from the spectacular, or the technical, but from a persistent seeking of the mundane edge.

We would even go a step further, beyond "customer orientation," to "culture," except that the term, which was discussed in *In Search of Excellence,* has rapidly become the focus of all sorts of gimmickry. And so, in this book, we have scrupulously avoided it. Thus, as mentioned, we chose to use the word "smell." IBM *smells* of the customer in a million tiny ways. So does SAS. And Stew Leonard's. And Perdue Farms, Trammell Crow. Others, despite the application of much marketing technique, do not smell of customers, do not obsessively seek advantages through enhanced closeness to their customers.

T.D.C.: THINLY DISGUISED CONTEMPT

On an all-night flight to Denver our plane stops briefly in Salt Lake City. It is on the ground for only about nine minutes, and then the Salt Lake passengers begin to board. As the new people begin to come down the ramp, the head stewardess turns to her associate and says, "Here come the animals."

A group of hotel company executives complain that they can exert no control over their franchisees, and wonder how McDonald's, operating under the same set of franchise laws, does it. We remind them, none too gently, of a conversation we had heard at a cocktail party the night before. Two officers of the company had stood around talking about the time they would have to "waste," during the next couple of days, meeting with the "franchisee bitch committee." They described it as a committee that "had been put together so the franchisees can blow off steam, can be made to feel that they're part of the company."

A sophisticated design engineer in a technology-based company plays a variation on the theme: "We designed a major fix to be applied in the field to one of our sophisticated machines. Then we engaged in a debate on whether or not we should send a letter out, along with the changes to the manual, explaining why we had done what we'd done. The vote was close to unanimous—'Don't confuse them out there; they're not all that bright.' "

Another engineering-based company, one that gets A pluses for its love of the product, gives their people what they call "product training"—everybody gets it—with great regularity. All are supposed to get a short course in sales. But, one officer explains, "Come hell *and* high water, the product training is done. If a budget crunch comes, though, we always defer sales training. It's implicitly considered 'soft stuff' and therefore expendable." And a receptionist at the same company adds: "Look, when an engineer comes to work here, they begin to train him further midway through the first week. I've been here going on four years, and I have yet to get my first day's training in telephone courtesy."

A few days before Nancy was to leave for a week's vacation in Mexico, she stopped by her favorite photography shop to pick up her newly repaired camera. The salesperson disappeared into the back of the store to look for it, but returned empty-handed, explaining that the camera was not there. Could she be mistaken? Was this really the store that repaired it? (A telephone call the previous day had confirmed that the camera was indeed repaired there and was indeed ready.) A second search ensued. No camera. Nancy finally asked for a loaner to take on vacation (a courtesy normally extended to customers). The salesperson hesitated, then remarked: "How am I to know that you don't already have your camera and are just trying to rip us off? I have to protect the store, you know. And since you don't have the service claim number, how can you expect me to find your camera—if it is here, which I doubt. You should have come in sooner, not just before you have to leave." Everyone's entitled to a bad day, but this was too much. A loaner was eventually granted. Two weeks later the missing camera was found (it had been "misfiled"). P.S. Nancy now has a new favorite photography shop.

"Poor, Dumb Patients"

In *Verdict Pending* (Capistrano Press, 1983), Fredonia French Jacques, a patient representative for twenty-five years, writes about hospital care from the patients' (customers') point of view. Here, a patient speaks for himself:

"I'm brought into this hospital real sick and someone asks me a whole string of dumb questions. I tell them I feel like I'm going to faint and they say, 'I have to ask you a few more questions or else we can't admit you.' I faint and fall to the floor. I come to, and someone's saying, 'You can't lie here!' My wife starts to help me up. The voice says, 'You can't lift him!'

"They take my clothes away. My wife gets told to take home anything that's worth anything: my watch, my ring, my wallet. They say they can't be responsible. I put on this gown split down the back. It doesn't have buttons, and they make you wear it backwards. My backside's always hanging out or I'm clutching at my gown with my only arm. See, the other one has an IV in it and I have to push that pole along every time I get up to go to the bathroom or brush my teeth."

He continued: "They come in and say they're going to take my teeth out. Can't go to surgery with them. Trouble is that they take them out an hour before, so that when I kiss my wife good-bye, there's nothing to buck up against. I'm embarrassed, and they don't give them back until I'm awake, and who knows how many people gawked at me with my mouth hanging open."

In all these vignettes and comments we see one or another of the following: (1) casting aspersions upon the customer; (2) contempt for the franchisee, the field-service person, the receptionist, the people in the stores—that is, all the people truly responsible for the delivery of service to the customer/client; (3) writing off such things as phone courtesy as "obvious," as not requiring thoughtfulness or serious training; (4) "technical hubris"—a belief that technological superiority is the only thing that *really* counts.

We've come to call all these things, and many more, TDC—Thinly Disguised Contempt—for the customer. (And contempt for those who serve the customer, remember, is inevitably handed down to the customers themselves.) It's the biggest barrier to sustainable superior performance—in hospitals, schools, banks, among retailers and manufacturing companies.

The setting now shifts to a classroom at the Stanford Business School in 1983. A team is discussing Disney's obsessive commitment to park cleanliness and customer friendliness. "I've honestly never seen a scrap of trash in either park," a normally skeptical MBA candidate says. She polls the fifty-person class. All agree. Then the team playing the role of the "cynical consultants" rebuts the Disney presentation. They attribute the Disney parks' success to better locations and a couple of good real estate deals. The debate heats up. Many join in. A Sloan Program student, a fast-tracker from General Motors, heads the "cynical consultants" team. He turns serious now; this is no classroom exercise anymore. "*Anybody* can provide a clean park," he maintains. Therefore the explanation for Disney's success must be the real estate, the access to capital, pure and simple. And what about McDonald's? Might cleanliness and uniformly high standards of service have anything to do with their success? Again, "No." Why? "Anyone can do that." Tom, who has been observing this exercise in his professional capacity, is incredulous. He stammers, "Anyone *can,* but only McDonald's *does.*"

As IBM's Buck Rodgers, who retired as IBM's corporate vice president for marketing in 1984, correctly (unfortunately) observes, "It's a shame, but whenever you get good service, it's an exception, and you're excited about it. It ought to be the other way around." We agree. Common decency, common courtesy toward the customer ("Guest") is indeed the exception. Economists may not buy it as the ultimate barrier to competitor entry or as a crucial form of sustainable strategic advantage, but such disparate actors (and extremely successful competitors) as IBM and McDonald's certainly do.

Good Show, Southwest!?

There were four of us in the two rows of seats. The Southwest flight was one hour 35 minutes late leaving Phoenix for San Diego on a Friday afternoon in October 1984. The 2:15 flight was posted on the screen for a 3:20 departure. It was now 3:15. The arriving plane was not at the gate. Tom asked, "When do you *really* think we'll leave?" The check-in counter clerk announced, "Oh, those posted numbers don't mean much. Think of it as within an hour of what they show." "What?" Tom stammered. "I didn't mean it," the clerk said. "Just a joke." Some joke when you're heading home to family on a Friday afternoon! Upon recounting this unpleasant experience once on board, Tom was one-upped. "That's *nothing*," a woman next to him boomed. "I was standing at the check-in counter in Albuquerque [the prior stop]. We had just been told of the first hour's delay. One or two people behind me grumbled, sort of loudly. Right in front of me [she gestured strongly], the [Southwest] counter clerk turned to her colleague and said in a loud and clear voice, 'The passengers are behaving like idiots today.' " As we all chuckled mirthlessly at that, the ultimate one-upper chimed in. She, too, had been part of the Albuquerque delay. "Someone [a passenger] next to me exclaimed, not very loudly, 'This sure as heck makes my life difficult.' The Southwest employee nearest him shot back, 'What do you think it does to *mine?*' as though we passengers were to be blamed for fouling up *his* day." The woman concluded, "I'll be glad when America West [a new airline with a good service reputation] moves in. It'll give these jokers something to think about."

Only four people were part of this conversation. Three had horror stories. Schedule slippage, the lateness was not the point, all agreed. The flippant attitude and disregard for the passengers was. We've all suffered through delays. But being insulted when we express concern is too steep a price to pay.

THE LITTLE THINGS—MAKING A DIFFERENCE AT THE MARGIN

Without a doubt, Tom is a "rational man"—with two degrees in engineering, two degrees in business and a career principally as a business consultant/analyst. This rational man, Tom, flies Delta when he can. The reason? When you arrive at an airport for a connection, late in the day, say, and dragging, there's a living breathing body from Delta who smiles and says as he points, "Hope you had a nice flight. San Francisco is Gate 26, two down on the left." Tom believes *him*—and automatically disregards the CRT display. That's it—completely irrational. Tom, the rational man, is even a bit ashamed of such "reasons." But we've come to think they are critical.

In *Ten Greatest Salespersons,* Shelby Carter, past head of Xerox's sales force, describes the "Windex Man" in his life:

I'll give you a fine example of how a very small, seemingly insignificant thing influenced me as a customer. When our family had just moved into our new home—the whole gang, our six children and two dogs—it was the first day in the house and everything was in an uproar. The kids all poured into the family room, and the television set didn't work. I got out the Yellow Pages and called for a repairman, and he came right out. Well, after he repaired the set, he asked me to come over and look at it. I stepped over the kids, our German Shepherd, the books, and instead of handing me a bill, as I expected, he took out a bottle of Windex spray and cleaned the glass. That impressed me, because he showed me how proud he was of his work and the product he served. From that day on, whenever we needed our TV fixed, I've said to my wife, "Honey, call the Windex guy."

Here's another Windex story. We stop by a local (Menlo Park, California) liquor store, Beltramo's, on Friday evening to buy a case of wine for our office party. At the counter we hand the clerk an American Express card. Amex must be busy in Phoenix or something, because it takes the clerk three or four minutes on the phone to get credit approval. Finally he does get it and hands the card back, and then he picks up a five-cent mint from an old-fashioned candy jar on the counter and drops it in the bag with an accompanying "Sorry for that delay. It was inexcusable. Hope it doesn't happen again. You know we value your business. Come back and see us again soon. And, oh, have a nice party." He's just bought our loyalty for *life!* We will shop with more determination than before at the "nickel-candy-man store." It wasn't the clerk's fault the American Express lines were busy. It was American Express's failing (too few phone lines at a peak hour). But the clerk took it on as *his* problem, not theirs. He didn't say, "Those SOB's at American Express always do this to me at rush hour." Instead he said, "I am sorry for the delay." Oh, we won't drive twenty miles out of our way to buy a single bottle of wine at Beltramo's, but, *at the margin,* we will go out of our way a *little* and pay a *little* more for that courtesy. Excellence is a game of inches, or millimeters. No one act is, per se, clinching. But a thousand things, a thousand thousand things, each done a tiny bit better, do add up to memorable responsiveness and distinction—and loyalty (repeat business) and slightly higher margins.

"People's People Do an Awful Lot of Smiling"

An Eastern Airlines in-house newsletter (provided to us by a People Express employee) describes Eastern's discovery of the People Express secret; it turns out they are more than just a discount airline: "People Express has replaced Eastern as New York's No. 1 airline."

The words, spoken by [Eastern] Miami Agent Pete Rogers to a crowd of fellow agents meeting for recurrent training, had the impact of a sledgehammer. How did Rogers, who isn't an instructor, find his way to the front of the class? And why a slide show about the company's biggest competitor?

The Communications Committee of Eastern's Miami Terminal Employee Involvement group had discussed People Express but nobody knew very much about the low-cost carrier.

"The committee elected 2 people to go to Newark and ride back on People Express," Rogers explained.

Rogers and Deedee Welsh were the chosen couple.

To really test People Express, Rogers and Welsh would create a ruse—posing as newly married on their honeymoon trip to Miami. [Eastern gets an A+ for practicing customer MBWA.]

The pair flew Sept. 14, [1984] on Eastern's Flight 6 to Newark, and put on a great act.

"Honeymooners are either subdued and quiet or confused," Welsh explained. "We chose to be confused. We went to Terminal C at Newark International. That's where People Express operates its international and transcontinental flights. We were directed to the North Terminal, where years ago Eastern began its passenger service."

Everywhere "Mr. and Mrs. Rogers" went they were treated with broad smiles and genuine friendliness. As Rogers told the agents, "People Express people do not look like professionals—but they show an interest in people and are always friendly. Everyone with whom we had contact helped us from the start of our trip to the end. They were polite.

"Deedee and I never expected to run across that sort of thing."

The newlyweds pressed home their case during the remainder of the slide show—showing pictures of People Express' facilities, their customer service managers, their in-flight managers. . . .

Aloft, the "managers" collect the fares and bag-check fees. They sell Cokes for 50¢, beer for $1 and drinks or wine for $2. A snack pack goes for $2. "And they don't care if you buy it or not. They just tell you that if you want something, put your tray table down. Nothing fancy. But the people are always smiling, making the atmosphere friendly," Welsh said.

Rogers explained how he told one of the People Express "managers" he had hoped for some honeymoon champagne once the flight departed. Sorry, the ground employee replied. People Express doesn't have champagne. "But the agent told me he'd take care of us," Rogers said. "When we arrived over Miami, the captain came on the P.A. and announced that the Rogers were starting their married life aboard People Express and thanked us and wished us luck. And the drinks and snack packs we had were complimentary.

"I thoroughly enjoyed the experience. People Express' people made it a fun trip I recommend to everyone in this room."

> Welsh noted that new magazines refer to the Newark-based carrier's passengers as "back-packers." "Look at this picture," she said. "What do you see. You don't see back-packers. Don't those people look an awful lot like Eastern passengers?"
>
> The room was silent.
>
> "Most of those Miami-bound travelers were—*were*—Eastern *passengers.* Now they are People Express *customers.*"

A Citibanker tells of a fifteen-minute effort to get a crisp new $100 bill for an unknown customer who walked in off the street and wanted it to present as an award that afternoon. Our Citibank friend made two phone calls, got the bill, and put it in a little box with a "Thanks for thinking of us" note on his card. The chance visitor soon came back and opened an account; in nine months his major law firm had deposited $250,000 in Citibank's coffers. You can't expect such things to happen often. That's not the point. But *at the margin,* you increase the odds just a little bit with each such act.

Here's another. A friend's VW developed a mysterious clank, and he took the car for repair to a local Shell station, which has a superb word-of-mouth reputation. Well deserved, it turns out. The repairman called a couple of hours after the car was dropped off: "Did you know this part is still under warranty? I called the local VW dealer and he's ready for you right now." Wow! From now on he gets all our friend's repair business—and ours, too. We even stop there for gas, and pay at least a dime a gallon premium. (In a subsequent transaction he talked our colleague out of buying a new battery. No wonder he generally has a two-week queue for service—for which he charges a handsome price.)

THE SOURCE OF COMMON COURTESY: SUPPORT PEOPLE AS HEROES

If common courtesy is the key, then the receptionist, service dispatcher and switchboard attendant are the heroes, not the denizens of executive row. That will be our "obvious" (again) conclusion in Section IV (People, People, People). But the point is so vital to this chapter's argument that we will preview it here—using an unlikely setting as an example.

General Bill Creech led a remarkable turnaround of the U.S. Air Force's Tactical Air Command. TAC has a clear peacetime "product," the sortie, in which the weapon system (plane) and its pilot and support group are tested as a unit in simulated combat conditions, and a peacetime "bottom line," the sortie rate. When General Creech arrived at TAC in 1978, the sortie rate had been falling for ten years at a compound annual rate of 7.8 percent. From 1978 through 1983, it rose at a compound annual rate of 11.2 percent. It used to take about four *hours* on average to get a part to a temporarily inoperable plane. In 1984 the average was eight *minutes*. Since the budget for spare parts actually *decreased* along the way, and other "external" factors became more adverse, the turnaround was a product of management, nothing else. At the heart of it was a simple proposition: planes fly less often than they should because of some failure not of the pilots but of other people. Planes don't fly because, for example, the pickup truck transporting a critical part broke a U-joint in a long-unrepaired pothole while coming across the base. That is, supply and maintenance people and their on-the-job accoutrements (and support people and equipment in general) are at once the problem *and* the opportunity.

Or, as the president of a high-tech company put it to us once: "I'll teach you all you need to know about marketing in one easy lesson—in one easy sentence, in fact: the most important 'marketer' in our company is the man or woman on the loading dock who decides *not* to drop the damned box into the back of the truck."

Amen! And how did General Creech act on this indisputable fact? He motivated, celebrated and virtually canonized the typically unsung support people. He said, "The airplane is the customer for us." And he made heroes out of those whose mundane chores in fact most influenced his "customers' " productivity. (See chapter 14, on "ownership," for more on the turnaround at TAC.)

Like TAC under General Creech, the best customer-serving companies we observe—from Stew Leonard's to Marriott to IBM—overinvest in the welfare and morale of their support people. It turns out that a fire-eating spares department is the key to a truly exceptional Cadillac or Peterbilt (the truck people) dealership. A neglected and demoralized one is the sure sign of a mediocre outfit.

Attacking the problem (opportunity) requires some imagination. Designing measures, competitions, awards and devices for participation for salespeople (or designers, buyers, engineers) is fairly straightforward. It is more difficult to manage genuine (not phony) involvement and awards for customer-support people in the distribution center, MIS and the like. The critical "trick," we observe, is getting them involved directly with customers. Milliken, AMP and several others work to get direct and indirect support people on joint customer/company problem-solving task forces. Successful Davgar Restaurants (over a dozen Burger King franchises in South Florida, every one outperforming the local McDonald's) includes support people in all sales meetings and celebrations. Another route is even more direct: in chapter 14, on ownership, we talk of a bank that got everyone involved in soliciting new accounts at a time of crisis; interestingly, a motivated MIS team, rather than a team of lending officers, won the top prize for new business brought in. General Creech developed clever (and practical) measures of effectiveness for *all* support groups, induced intense and regular subsupport-unit versus subsupport-unit competition and gave numerous and lavish awards for top performances, including regular awards banquets for support people, which surpassed anything done for pilots.

That triggers a final thought. Though we could go on at length on this issue (and shall, indirectly, in the section called "People, People, People"), let us leave you with a question. Most have some familiarity with IBM's lavish off-shore Golden Circle galas for the top 3 percent of its sales force and with Mary Kay's spectaculars for her top saleswomen. Have you ever heard of an offshore bash of similar magnitude for the spare-parts departments, the distribution-center teams or the field-service gangs? If not, why not? There ain't a law that says it can't be done.

Common Courtesy:
One Thing to Do

▶ Commit yourself to performing *one* ten-minute act of exceptional customer courtesy per day, and to inducing your colleagues to do the same. In a 100-person outfit, taking into account normal vacations, holidays, etc., that would mean 24,000 new courteous acts per year. Such is the stuff of revolutions!

Good luck. (And *thank you* for reading.)

5

No Such Thing as a Commodity

In our seminars, as common a question as any has been this one: "For the last decade or so we've heard about the joys of the experience curve [making more—selling more—at a lower price to gain share in order to achieve a barrier to competitor entry via lowest industry cost]. Recently it's come under heavy attack. You maintain that revenue enhancement is more important than cost containment. What's up?"

The senior regional sales manager from John Deere was wearing an odd tie tack. It was in the shape of a cross. The vertical letters spelled out DEERE, the horizontal SOQ NOP. When asked what the letters stood for, his reply was, "Sell on quality, not on price." He added, "It's my toughest job, in down markets, to make my own people realize that the objective is to sell the benefits, not just resort to price [as the only selling leverage]. I tell them a story. I was going after a sale [for Deere] some years ago. It came down to two final contenders. The fellow making the buy called me in to give me one last chance. His message in a nutshell: 'You're just too high on the price side. No hard feelings, and we hope we can do business with you again in the future.' I was about to walk out the door, unhappy to say the least. Then I had an inspiration. I turned around and said, 'Those are nice-looking boots you've got on.' He was a bit surprised, but said, 'Thanks,' and he went on to talk for a minute or so about those fine boots, what was unique about the leather, why they were practical as well as fine. I said to him, at the end of his description, 'How come you buy those boots and not just a pair off the shelf in an Army-Navy surplus store?' It must have taken twenty seconds for the grin to spread all the way across his face. 'The sale is yours,' he said, and he got up and came around his desk and gave me a hearty handshake."

The answer to the question posed at the beginning of this essay has been the subject of books, not a few anecdotes and pages of brief analysis. But let us begin by talking a bit about the sort of evidence that's been accumulated in the past few years. It speaks loud and clear to our point: People who find bases for differentiation and who produce for the higher ends of markets (not just Mercedes makers, but specialty steel makers, washing machine producers, chocolate chip cookie vendors and chicken sellers as well) tend to be winners over the long haul—i.e., the customer *will* pay a tidy premium for things that solve his or her problem and that work and are well serviced.

THE SYSTEMATIC EVIDENCE

(1) The focus for the *In Search of Excellence* research was on seventy-five companies in the United States and Europe. Five (e.g., Amoco) were in the resource-extraction business. For those companies, finding the substance for fewer dollars per barrel or cents per cubic foot may be an appropriate "first principle." Of the remaining seventy, fully sixty-five became and remained winners by focusing on what we now call "revenue line enhancement"—on *quality, service, courtesy, customer listening* and *nichemanship* (solving problems for tailored market segments).* Moreover, of the remaining five—those that fell into the "low cost at all costs" category—four had severe problems during the 1981–83 recession (including onetime darlings of the market—when demand was high—such as National Semiconductor, Data General and Texas Instruments; all three have recently restructured radically to focus on perceived quality, customer satisfaction, listening and, in general, a greater "market orientation"). In fact, the only one in the "low cost" arena that thrived was Emerson Electric. (And, arguably, the Emerson categorization is faulty. It could just as easily be called a company that often follows the "last player in the niche" strategy. In most arenas, they are a specialist producer.)

(2) The *In Search of Excellence* findings, circa 1980, were strongly reinforced in 1983 in a study that concentrated on a different part of the industrial base. An extensive study conducted by McKinsey and Co. for the ABC (American Business Conference)† focused on the management and strategic practices of the forty-five top performers (on a financial basis) in this sector (which includes about fifteen thousand companies); surprisingly, the list was not entirely dominated by technology-driven companies: Dunkin' Donuts, A. T. Cross (the pen people) and Lenox (the china makers) were there along with Millipore, Loctite, Thomas & Betts, Wyle Laboratories. The study showed that management practice in most of these companies was to eschew a low cost-low end position, and instead to provide higher value added products (often costing more to produce), for which they found ready markets. Astonishingly, in fully forty-three of the forty-five cases the following was

---

*We don't want to suggest that cost containment is unimportant to the sixty-five. It's *vital.* But the distinction we like (one not in the microeconomic texts, we'd quickly add) was made by a senior IBM manufacturing executive: "There is a vast difference between 'low cost' and 'competitive cost.' Your cost structure must be competitive. On the other hand, I've never known a company with a low-cost *attitude* that was a winner over the long haul."

†The ABC is a recently formed lobby representing America's "midsize growth companies," companies with sales between $25 million and $1 billion that have doubled or more in size in the most recent five years. (They also have the distinction of having created a huge share of the country's new jobs.)

observed: "Winners compete by delivering a product that supplies superior value to customers, rather than one that costs less. Most strategists have believed that business winners are those that capture commanding market share through lower costs and prices. The winner midsize companies compete on the value of their products and services and usually enjoy premium prices."

(3) These findings—from the research for *In Search of Excellence* and the ABC study—are wholly consistent with analyses made by the PIMS team, which has at its command the most extensive strategic information data base in the world.* PIMS has correlated literally hundreds of variables with long-term financial performance. The single variable far and away the most closely associated with good financial performance over the long haul is "relative perceived product quality." Technically the relative perceived product-quality "score" is deduced by a complex procedure that ranks the importance *to the customer and in the customer's terms* of various quality and service-delivery traits (*other than price*) among principal competitors in a market.

A sample of PIMS output: Those in the lower third on relative perceived product quality had an average ROI of 5 percent; those in the upper third averaged 30 percent. Winners "emphasize customer expectations," "research customer needs," "use customer-based quality performance measures," "formulate QC [Quality Control] objectives for all functions." Losers "downgrade the customer view," "make high quality synonymous with tight tolerances," "tie quality objectives to manufacturing flow," "formalize QC objectives for manufacturing only." The PIMS findings hold as tightly for both North America and Europe, for declining as for growing markets, in slow as in rapid inflation, for consumer as for industrial markets. In short, PIMS finds: "Customers pay more for better products."

Contrary to the conventional wisdom of the past fifteen years, PIMS data suggest that relative perceived product quality is much more positively related to financial performance than market share or relative market share (the latter had traditionally been the preferred variable of the Boston Consulting Group's widely used portfolio-analysis approach to strategy formulation). In fact, evidence from several quarters increasingly suggests that high market share is not an automatic winner. A 1984 *Harvard Business Review* article by Carolyn Y. Woo entitled "Market Share Leadership—Not Always So Good" reported on 112 market share leaders during the period 1972 to 1975. Seventy-one performed well financially (pre-tax return of 40 percent); their focus is on "high value added," "sales support," and "relative quality." Forty-one market share leaders, however, had an average pre-tax ROS (return on sales) of less than 10 percent, and do not focus on the aforementioned traits.

---

*The PIMS (Profit Impact of Market Strategy) data base is managed by the Strategic Planning Institute in Cambridge, Massachusetts.

(4) Another source of systematic reinforcement for the revenue-enhancement/high-value-added notion was the January 1984 *Forbes* "36th Annual Report on American Industry." Here is a small sample of the findings, focusing especially on flat or modest-growth industries, where one might least expect the HVA (high value added) phenomenon to appear.*

▶ *Chemicals.* Specialty chemical producers, as a group, did *40* percent better than diversified chemical producers. The former had a five-year (1978–83) return to equity of 15.8 percent, versus 11.6 percent for the diversified producers. (Perhaps even more to the point, and in support of the high-value-added, "Specialty people win" idea in general: specialty chemical producers did even better over the five-year period than *computer* makers as a group—15.8 percent versus 15.6 percent.) Among the "diversified producers" there's an interesting parallel. Following the 1973 OPEC energy price increases, Dow Chemical became the darling of the chemical industry analysts. It is primarily in "upstream businesses" (bulk building-block commodity chemicals), and almost immediately passed on the price increases to its customers. Du Pont, by contrast, took a walloping; Du Pont is more heavily concentrated in "downstream" (specialty/higher-value-added) businesses and, of course, had been a long-term winner in specialty chemicals, buttressed by its unparalleled research efforts. Now, ten years later, after the OPEC blip has been pushed thoroughly through everybody's system, Du Pont is once again, relatively speaking, the darling, and Dow, belatedly, is mounting a head-long catch-up effort to move a much larger share of its business downstream.

▶ In *steel,* the story is repeated. There are no separate "specialty"/"diverse" categories, but the overall winners by a landslide are Worthington and Nucor—with mini-mills and specialty steels; their equity returns over the last five years are a whopping 27.6 and 23.9 percent (in contrast to a deficit for the industry as a whole). In fact, worldwide, virtually all the winners in the steel industry are in the specialty game. A 1983 trip to Sweden included a visit with Uddeholm's senior officers; they have mounted a substantial turnaround in the last three years, based entirely upon decentralization (increasing independent entrepreneurial units from 5 to 23) and a rapid push toward the specialty/higher-value-added ends of the marketplace.

▶ In the beleaguered *forest products* industry as well no specialty/diverse categories exist. Nonetheless, the two winners, among the big players, by a country mile are specialty people: James River Corporation of Virginia, and Fort Howard Paper Co. in Green Bay, Wisconsin. Far above the herd is $2.4 billion James River, with a 26.7 percent equity return over the past five years (well ahead of IBM). The five-year industry average is just 5 percent. According to *Forbes,* the James River routine consists of "buying

---

*The findings are especially noteworthy, since they were published at the end of the 1981–83 recession and thus cover performance through the toughest of times.

up numerous small mills that had become unsuited to the great economies of scale of the commodity grades, but were ideally suited to the much smaller markets of the specialty grades." (Among smaller forest products companies, none stands above Boise's $125 million Trus Joist. Driven by product technology, they have done well in even the worst of times. One industry securities analyst notes, "They made seven-figure profits at a time when more commodity-oriented competitors were drowning in a sea of red ink.")

► In the *foods* area, it was noted that brand-name foods were taking more and more shelf space (contradicting the conventional wisdom of a couple of years or so ago that all thinking Americans would soon be buying their staples out of big flour bins). This is entirely consistent with our observations in the industry. Campbell Soup, a high-quality but long-dormant company, is undertaking a major restructuring to radically decentralize and attack more specialty markets. Moreover, the long-term Campbell bias is reflected in the first two of the "six pillars" of the new Campbell corporate philosophy: (1) "We want to be in the quality business, first and only—if we can't produce quality, we get out of the category"; (2) "We want to have high-value products—we're not interested in the commodity business." PepsiCo, McCormick (best known for their spices) and others are doing the same: making small-unit entrepreneurial attacks on niche markets, instead of trading thousandths of share points selling "commodities." In the retail channel, analyses that leader Safeway has done suggest that long-term consumer loyalty is based upon the higher-value-added parts/higher-perceived-quality parts of the store—the produce and meat departments; the huge chain, whose CEO was voted one of the top CEOs of 1983, is now moving to a greater reliance upon branded products. In 1983 Giant Food was, as usual, tops among the forty-five publicly traded grocery companies, with a 23 percent equity return. An analyst comments: "[Chairman] Izzy Cohen sees Giant above all as a service company, which is why he isn't worried about the new warehouse supermarkets as competitors. 'You can't build business on price alone. Price will bring "shoppers" but not "customers," ' he says." (Even in fast food, the trend is toward the higher end. The main chains—Wendy's, et al.—are edging in that direction, and the emerging stars include, for instance, Fuddruckers, which features "gourmet hamburgers.")

► In *retailing* the "specialty" category, with a 17.7 percent equity return over the last five years, commands an edge of 40 percent plus over the "general" category, at 12.5. The big winner is The Limited, with a 33.2 percent equity return over five years. Even the tough shoes category has a real star: entrepreneurial U.S. Shoe, which calls itself "the sports car and convertible end of the shoe business." Among the general retailers, too, "higher value added through service" seems to pay—even in the 1980's. In 1983 the performance of Seattle-based soft-goods retailer Nordstrom led the way by a hefty margin. Nordstrom, with a strategy based clearly on superior service in an age of generally low service, earned a 5.1 percent after-tax return on sales in an $800 million operation. By contrast, the after-tax for the May Company, Federated and Dayton-Hudson was 3.9 percent; Nordstrom tops that by fully 30 percent. *The Wall Street Journal* reports, "Prices tend to be high at Nordstrom, markdowns infrequent. . . . but Nordstrom's has a sales formula: Coddle the customers, big and small."

▶ Among *airlines,* USAir and Piedmont share the winner's circle with a 20.9 percent equity return from 1978 through 1983 (in an industry in which the median was in the red during that troubled period). The USAir litany: Smaller is better. According to the simple and clear logic of President Edwin Colodny, "For the price of one big plane, we can have three small planes, and three small planes means three market segments." (Likewise in *trucking,* Miami-based Ryder System, now a $2.5 billion company, has responded to deregulation with a raft of high-value-added services. They will manage a customer's truck fleet, provide creative combinations of equipment, drivers [full or part time] and support on multiple dimensions. The result has been exceptional growth, profitability and a 1984 accolade as "Florida's best-run company.")

▶ And there are a raft of *miscellaneous specialty* companies that are absolute Cadillacs in their industry, and superb performers in general. A few, with their five-year equity returns in parentheses: Deluxe Check (20.9 percent), Snap-On Tools (21.8 percent), Maytag (23.7 percent), Kellogg (27.7 percent). On average the returns on equity of these four companies are 60 percent above their industry's average. Many others, of course, belong in this category, including several privately held firms, such as S. C. Johnson (makers of Johnson Wax, etc.).

Given the beating U.S. industry has taken in everything from cars to microchips—largely, make no mistake, as a result of the relatively poor quality of the American product and unwillingness to listen to the customer (industrial or consumer goods)—it would seem that the point we have been making wouldn't need to be belabored. The revolution now under way in American management involves a renewed focus, in virtually every industry in this country, on quality and quality products aimed at more or less specialized market niches. Gordon McGovern, the Campbell Soup chairman, makes it abundantly clear: "Above all, we've got to teach our people to focus on quality first, cost second."

FROM CHICKEN TO LAUNDROMATS

Our favorite support for our emphasis on value added comes from oddball corners of markets.

There's no better example than Perdue Farms. Frank Perdue has built a three-quarter-billion-dollar chicken business in Salisbury, Maryland. Margins are 700 to 800 percent above the industry average, and his market share doesn't dip below 50 percent in his major markets, which are exceptionally competitive urban areas, such as New York. He says it's simple: "If you believe in unlimited quality, and act in all your business dealings with total integrity, the rest (share, growth, profits) will take care of itself." Perdue, then, quite simply believes that there's no such thing as a limit to quality—even in chickens.

Stew Leonard is Perdue's biggest single-store buyer. Stew runs a dairy store in Norwalk, Connecticut. Selling just a handful of items as compared with typical grocery stores, Stew grosses $85 million in one location. Average grocery store sales run a bit over $300 per square foot. Stew Leonard cashes in at about $3,000 a square foot. The trick? He's made it a delight to shop for chicken, cheese, eggs and muffins. He has a petting zoo for kids; the egg department features a mechanical chicken, "the world's fastest egg layer." On one wall there are over five thousand pictures of Stew's customers prominently displaying Stew Leonard's shopping bags. He happens now to have a picture taken underwater of a customer with a bag on a deep-sea dive, another of a Leonard regular atop the Great Wall of China and so on. Don't tell Stew or his customers that food shopping is a bore!

"Talk about Loyalty"

Sept. 20, 1984

Mr. Stew Leonard
Stew Leonard's Dairy Store
Westport Avenue
Norwalk, CT 06851

Dear Mr. Leonard:

I am a funeral director . . . and am writing to tell you of an event which happened recently.

An elderly woman passed away and requested that some of her most cherished, personal belongings be buried inside a Stew Leonard's shopping bag within her casket. Her relatives stated that your store was her favorite shopping place.

Being a patron of Stew Leonard's myself I have noticed the correspondence from your customers, and felt I should share this story with you.

Sincerely yours,

Out in the West—Park City, Utah—Debbi Fields has a chocolate chip cookie company, which is taking the country—in fact, the world—by storm. Her secret? Over 50 percent chocolate content by weight in her cookies. The profitability? About as high as the chocolate content.

Headquartered in the San Francisco Bay Area is rapidly growing Dreyer's Grand Ice Cream, an $80 million producer, which, characteristically, buys its Oreo cookies at retail (the only option) to put in its Oreo-cookie-based ice cream. Its equity returns stay steady—in the forties.

The J. M. Smucker Co., in Orrville, Ohio, has stayed focused on quality james and jellies. They have top share, over 30 percent, and profits to match, while competing against deep-pocket giants, such as Dart and Kraft.

Houston-based Sysco is a company in an even more mundane business—wholesaling food to restaurants. Their motto, too, sounds as if it came from the IBM book: "Don't sell food, sell peace of mind." Frito-Lay finds the dollars (paid back with a return on top) to have 10,000 salespersons servicing accounts in their presumed low margin business. Sysco, with equivalent audacity, has 2,000 and calls them "marketing associates"; they assure a service level of 98 percent same-day delivery—previously unheard of in the business. They have, literally, *created* a "new" industry segment: They discovered that a large number of customers, *at the margin,* are indeed service-sensitive. They are a fast-growing, highly profitable ($2 billion) giant with equity returns pushing 20 percent in a generally lackluster industry.

The fastest-growing sizable bus company in the nation, Jefferson Lines, Inc., got that way by putting Pac Man on the buses and dreaming up bus-plane/round-the-world tour packages. Says the boss, Donald Prins: "If we could make buses into condominiums and have people live in them, I would do that tomorrow."

Harry D. Oppenheimer, as reported in the *Wall Street Journal* (May 2, 1984), is the man to call if you want tents. He's a high-value-added specialty producer who provided a gold lamé tent for King Saud of Saudi Arabia in the sixties, and under whose tent Pope John Paul II preached in Chicago and Washington. Says a competitor: "They don't do quick and dirty tents. If we're all renting tents for fifty cents a square foot, Harry will get a dollar. He's got a niche."

So, as shown by stars in businesses of every description—from Perdue Farms to Mrs. Field's Cookies, from Dreyer's Ice Cream to USAir, from James River of Virginia to Maytag, from The Limited Stores to U.S. Shoe to Deluxe Checks—there is a sizable market for superior quality, especially quality targeted to a niche. Give the customer something worthwhile and she or he will pay. Mike Kami, an early pioneer of strategic planning at both IBM and Xerox, boils it all down to this: "What is it that makes you distinct and unique?"

As we pointed out above, some of the winners in *In Search of Excellence* were low-cost-at-all-costs producers and had used that strategy effectively. Lowest cost is, after all, a niche of sorts. The worst of all possible worlds is being neither fish nor fowl. A grocery-industry commentator noted at the end of 1983 that "The operators in the middle are extremely vulnerable, stores that have nothing major to distinguish themselves." That was, in fact, at the heart of Sears' problem in the mid-seventies. They gave away their quality-for-a-decent-price image, creating an incredible wedge for K-Mart and Wal-Mart to move in, but only ineffectively maneuvered into the higher end, at least at first. After two or three years of mucking about Sears was not credible at either end of the market, and their unexceptional results for several years reflected the loss of franchise—and uniqueness.

The Floors Sparkle—in the Service Bays

SAS's Group President Jan Carlzon led the remarkable turnaround at SAS with this premise: "We don't seek to be one thousand percent better at any one thing. We seek to be one percent better at one thousand things." It's also the formula that has jacked Carl Sewell and Sewell Village Cadillac of Dallas to the top of the heap in customer ratings (of sales performance, service performance, and as a place you'd recommend to friends) among GM's Cadillac dealers. (In gross dollars, Sewell is number three nationally in sales, number one in service revenue.)

It begins with the look. It is thoroughly professional. The lighting on the showroom floor is sedate. A giant fresh-flower display, changed daily, is in the center of the floor. Office lighting is all from tasteful table lamps, and the waiting room is decorated with antiques. (Carl Sewell uses the same interior designer who did Trammell Crow's lavish Loew's Anatole Hotel in Dallas. Moreover, he is consulted on an ongoing basis by Stanley Marcus, the former chairman of Neiman-Marcus.) A room to the side of the showroom adds a special touch. Called the preview room, it's also decorated with antiques, and it's where you start your Sewell Village Cadillac experience: you begin by viewing a video tape that tells you a bit about Cadillac and a lot about the Sewell Village people and their service philosophy. In other words, you are welcomed to your would-be family.

The prospective buyer is virtually forced to visit the service bays. Had that buyer been dropped in from Mars, he or she would be likely to think the place was a Silicon Valley "clean room." It is no exaggeration to say that you could eat off the floors of the Sewell Village shop. Carl's service manager explains that it's not just for the benefit of customers: "If we want our service people to act like the well-trained professionals they are, we must provide professional working conditions."

Detail after detail mounts up. Sewell Village keeps on hand an incredible 150 "loaners" (cars to be loaned to customers who are having theirs repaired) at an annual cost of well over $500,000. Tom's introduction to the place offers another taste of the thousand "little" things that count. Tom arrived there on a chilly morning in November, 1984. All 225 employees had been invited to turn out. At 6:30 A.M., a popular bluegrass band began to play vigorously. At the ceiling of a temporarily cleared-out service area were thousands of balloons restrained by nets. The band stopped at 7:00 A.M., and Tom gave a speech to all hands, including the receptionist, sweeper, president. At the conclusion of the speech the balloons were released from the ceiling, as at a political convention, and it was off to work for everyone. Not exactly a ritual we've observed with any regularity at car dealerships in general! (And lest you think this was a special for Tom's benefit, the 7:00 A.M. "lecture" is a fairly regular occurrence at Sewell. The visitor before Tom had been Stanley Marcus.)

How do winners differentiate? That's how!

Ted Levitt, the dean of marketing thinkers and longtime professor at the Harvard Business School, opens one important chapter in his 1983 book, *The Marketing Imagination,* with the following: "There need be no such thing as a commodity." And, indeed, that's exactly what we observe. A while back we did a hasty, nonsystematic analysis to test this argument near its limit. The word "commodity" had seeped into the personal- and home-computer business by 1983, and what a disaster it was. Even small personal computers don't seem like commodities to us, and customer response to the relatively high-priced personal computers of reliable and service-oriented companies, such as IBM and Apple, suggests that they certainly needn't be. We wanted to make that point to the president of one sizable personal computer company that was about to head down market. He and Tom both had engineering degrees and were not pros in the world of mass marketing.

To test (make, we hoped) our point, we stopped in early 1983 at a local cooperatively owned grocery store in Palo Alto, California, and priced what any fool (any engineer, at least) would believe was clearly a commodity—one-ply toilet paper. The *generic* type, in a four-roll pack, was going for 79¢ at the time. Then we traveled just two blocks to the nearest 7-11. There we priced Procter & Gamble's Charmin entrant into the one-ply sweepstakes; the tag was fully $1.99. Within two blocks, an "upscale" service-delivery vehicle (7-11) and P&G's long-term devotion to product quality (and squeezability) had added $1.20 (value) to the price of a four-roll package of one-ply toilet paper!* Needless to say, the returns to P&G and Southland (owners of 7-11) exceed those to most co-op stores and generic producers by a tidy sum. Value-added can indeed occur anywhere, as Professor Levitt says. (Another illustration comes from one of the fastest-growing businesses in the Midwest:

---

*Interestingly, each point of differentiation contributed exactly 50 percent of the variation in price: i.e., the Charmin was tagged at $1.39 in the co-op store; thus 60¢ was added by P&G and 60¢ was added by 7-11.

coin-operated laundromats! More often than not, they are the eyesores of the neighborhood. But an enterprising group of high-value-added players has combined a corner laundromat and a *wine bar.* Their logo: "Try our suds while you wash your duds." Game, set, match, to Professor Levitt—and Harry D. Oppenheimer and Frank Perdue.)

We're so strongly in Levitt's corner on this that if we were allowed to be "business czars" for thirty seconds, our first act would be to remove the word "commodity" from the language of commerce. We despise it more than any other word in the business vocabulary.* The problem is that if we label something a "commodity," we often turn it into one. We listen to bankers describing the commercial loan as a commodity, to Big Eight accounting-firm partners calling the audit a commodity. When the label is used, it usually, or often, means that one big step has been taken toward "self-fulfilling prophecy." As a successful forest products wholesaler says, "If you view your product as 'no different from anybody else's' [i.e., as a commodity], then that's what it will somehow turn out to be." Stew Leonard, decidedly, doesn't think he's running "just another dairy store." Levitt, again, is instructive. He admits to an exception to his notion that there's "no such thing as a commodity." "The only exception," he says, "is in the minds of those who express that perception." Amen.

Of course, the closer one gets to the traditional notion of a commodity, the harder one must struggle to create differentiation. Says a DuPont chemical sales manager: "You've got to seek differences—delivery schedule, a snazzier paint job on the gas canisters, anything!" A Pfizer specialty chemical executive sings the same tune: "A lot of people think we're in the bulk chemical business. That's silly. Our objective is to differentiate and head for higher value-added plateaus. We don't want to produce commodities." An ICI (the British-based chemical giant) country boss concurs: "We've got to learn to think about creating differences throughout the distribution process, not about price as the only weapon."

Real Estate, Too!

Trammell Crow has created a vast (and profitable) industrial real estate empire. A lengthy article by Joseph Nocera in the August 1984 issue of *Texas Monthly* chided Crow on the lack of external attractiveness of some of his buildings. At the heart of Crow's success, however, *is* attractiveness where it counts—the result of effective customer listening and differentiation in another of those mundane businesses—warehousing. *Texas Monthly* goes on: "From the start, elements of

---

*"Employee" (as opposed to, say "person") is a close second; see our "People, People, People" section.

Crow's buildings set them apart from his competitors. First, they looked different. Crow intuitively understood that everyone prefers to work in pleasant surroundings, warehousemen included. So he radically reshaped warehouse buildings. Previously, warehouses had been built in long rows, each attached to the next, with loading docks in the front and executives' offices in the rear. Crow built his warehouses independently of each other, so that each stood on its own separate plot of land. Then he moved the unsightly loading docks to the side and put the offices—with windows, no less—in the front. Finally, he spent money on landscaping, which was unheard of at the time. Crow's warehouses were surrounded by trees and flowers and had neatly manicured front lawns. The people who worked in those buildings, unaccustomed to such touches, raved about them. Crow likes to say that one of the keys to his success was that he always followed the dictates of the market 'as we understood it,' and mostly that is true. But with his early warehouses he was doing something more: he was leading people to a market they didn't know existed. ... Crow could work so fast partly because he refused to get caught up in details he considered unimportant. The exact placement of every window didn't matter, because the market he was trying to satisfy didn't much care where the windows were. But when it came to the inside of the building, to details like rugs and bathroom fixtures that he believed his tenants cared about, he could be quite demanding."

We linger over this point because it's proved to be significant to so many we work with. Several have attempted (with varying degrees of success) to expunge the word "commodity" from their language. Milliken, in textiles, has been a leader in doing so.* Thinking about the word, and then thinking about how we get beyond it in *every* market, is step one up the long climb to higher margins. And if it can be done in laundromats. ...

"COST-ONLY" MIND-SET

We've probably gotten our just deserts. In the grocery business, many consumers *have* been moved to buy things out of bins. In the clothing business many *have* been buying off the piles in off-price stores. The chairman of the Hartmarx retail stores (formerly Hart, Schaffner & Marx), a profitable 260-store specialty business, provides an interesting hypothesis: "We've gotten

---

*And has it worked! Their effective quality programs, even in the core of their so-called (previously) commodity grade areas, have time and again led, for instance, to the unprecedented naming of Milliken as a sole source vendor for a product—to such tough customers as GM.

exactly what we deserve. We let service deteriorate in our big department stores, and even in our specialty stores. So, naturally, the consumer went to the off-price store. He says, in effect, 'If I'm going to get rotten service, why not get my rotten service in a warehouse and save thirty percent.' That's the way I look at it too. The industry often gave no distinguishing service, and we reaped the reward—fed-up customers and, now, severe competition."

The evidence favoring differentiation and higher-value-added products and service (in any part of a market) is close to overwhelming. So why *did* we fall for the experience curve? Why did we come to act as if we believed that cost (and, derivatively, price) was the only variable we could manipulate? The reasons are doubtless numerous and will never be clear. We suspect, as we indicated in the Introduction, that, in some subtle respect, the relative historical ease with which the United States gained dominant market position worldwide after World War II is one culprit.* Institutions unintentionally took their eye off the service-and-quality ball;† the focus was simply on making a lot for ever-hungry markets. And this led to any number of outcomes that added up to losing revenue enhancement as a primary strategy. One was a shift in the sixties and seventies to dominance of the executive suite by financially trained executive-administrators, and the exclusion of the people who were closest to the product (and thus to the importance of quality and service)—manufacturers, designers and salespersons.‡ The same type of people also came to dominate business schools, with the result that much of our current business-school logic is implicitly focused on just one variable: cost reduction. Look at Stanford, with its grand number one rank—in a vote by deans—in 1983. Courses in the accounting area outnumber the offerings in manufacturing and sales *combined* by a ratio of about seven to one! Jan Carlzon of SAS provides a personal view: "I said [in a speech], 'When confronted with any big problem, the businessman must either increase revenue or decrease costs. That's all I learned at school.' In response to my saying that, a former economics professor, who was in the audience, put up his hand and rebutted me: 'Mr. Carlzon, as I suspected, you weren't listening! We only taught you *one* thing at the [Swedish] business school—reduction of costs.' "

All of this in turn leads to that hard-to-describe but, we think, most important subject: *mind-set.* It's a central factor, squishy as it may appear to be at first glance. The negative results are all unintended: as one chief executive officer noted, "We act as if cost is the only variable available to us. In our hell-

---

*The Japanese (and Germans) had no such luck. They were late arrivals to the party, and had to win grudgingly given respect via top quality.
†We are haunted by a discussion with a city manager. He came up after a speech in which Tom had been focusing on "living the quality message." He said, "My dad was the *head* of quality control for [a division in a Big Three car company]. He held the job for twelve years, and was only once visited by the division general manager in all that time." Talk about taking the eye off the ball!
‡A wonderful exception is IBM. It is now, and has always been, dominated by former salesmen—not accountants, not "marketeers" (though they call themselves the latter).

bent rush to buy share [via price cutting] to get costs down, we unintentionally give too short shrift to quality and service. So we wake up having, at best, bought great market share, but having, often as not, a marginal or lousy product or service. It's almost always a precarious position that can't be sustained. Somebody's gonna come at you sooner or later. They'll start by clipping away at corners of your market with a little tailoring, and soon they'll have you in full-blown retreat."

Now, this is vital: the experience curve makes exceptional sense *on paper.* Buy share (via one route: cutting price); therefore obtain a low-cost position (by taking advantage of scale economies provided by high share-driven volume); and then fend off the hordes (who won't need much fending off because of the capital required to match the leader's large-scale production facilities). It sounds terrific. *But* mind-set nails us. To gain the share, we discount like crazy in chicken (or watches, calculators and computers—ask an experience-curve-shell-shocked Texas Instruments). And we become "cost freaks," as a friend puts it. We zero in on creating a barrier to competitor entry through more and bigger low-cost production facilities. Controllers are both king and crown prince. Paper-clip counting becomes the most valued (and promotable) skill. Manufacturing and sales types are viewed as crybabies and second-class bumpkins. Service and quality invariably, albeit *unintentionally,* suffer.

"Unintentional" is the key word. No one is for poor quality or service. All wish their people would treat customers with courtesy and would care about making a fine product. But it's jolly tough to get a big business (or a small one, for that matter) to do even *one* thing right. J. Willard Marriott, Sr., still reading complaint cards after fifty-seven years, *still* doesn't think he's got the service right. So the management that focuses obsessively on cost usually ends up, albeit unintentionally (i.e., through omission—a lack of focus), *not* building a "quality fetish" or a "service fetish." That's the harsh reality of big, dumb companies and, as it turns out, of small ones too—inhabited as they all are by that most intractable of all creatures: people in groups.

PIMS comes at the "mind-set" issue in a slightly different fashion, but it nonetheless speaks to the heart of the conundrum with a strong statement on the cause-and-effect chain that constitutes the most effective path to success. It is in direct and explicit contradiction to conventional experience-curve wisdom.

The experience-curve chain of causality says, in effect: (1) Cut the price so as to (2) buy share. Increased share, in turn, allows you to (3) take advantage of economies of scale and thus (4) reduce costs. You eventually (5) obtain a low-cost position which (6) constitutes an effective barrier to competitor entry. PIMS evidence doesn't refute in any sense the desirability of eventually achieving a low-cost position. (Nobody sensible fights a low-cost position.) But the PIMS paradigm is diametrically opposite to the experience curve *from a cause-and-effect standpoint:* It says, *First* achieve a "relative perceived product-quality" edge over your competitors. If you do so, you will gain share. (I.e., there are only *two* ways to gain share: first, the conventional approach of late—rapidly, via murderous price discounting, if you don't screw up the whole market permanently; and, second, more methodically via better relative quality and service.) By gaining share (via relatively higher perceived product quality) you can, indeed, *then* take advantage of economies of scale as appropriate, and achieve low-cost distinction.*

The difference is radical. By the PIMS logic, you *start* from quality and achieve low cost as a result. According to the traditional experience curve approach, you buy your way in with low prices, achieve low cost, and may or may not have acceptable service and quality. If you don't have them, then you're constantly vulnerable to any higher-quality attacker who comes your way; the edge you scrambled so hard for is not likely to be sustainable. We call the distinction "earning your way in" (via quality and service) versus "buying your way in" (via heavy discounting). Only the former, it would appear, is sustainable.

We still think of P&G as prototypical in this regard. Often their dominant position allows for maximum-scale economies (and attendant low cost), yet that position is *always* achieved through "earn in" from higher quality. David Ogilvy, in his marvelous *Ogilvy on Advertising,* argues against competing with P&G. Why? Because of their cost position? Big ad budget? No. The would-be competitor's problem, he says, is that "they [P&G] make better-quality products." Hear, hear!

The cost-only mind-set also seems to lead to an unintentional denigration of innovation. There's something about overly formalized systems, systems run by accountants, that are simply inconsistent with a sea of skunkworks or the highly decentralized environment of Hewlett-Packard, Johnson & Johnson or 3M. We believe, for instance, that the excessive focus on the experience curve (and on the disciplines necessary to exploit it) at Texas Instruments, both in the consumer electronics business and in the "commodity" merchant chip business, led *directly* to the loss of the commanding innovative edge TI once enjoyed. (See chapter 11, "The Context of Innovation," for more on this theme.)

Another, related mind-set problem is that we tend to get conned by the goings-on in the bottom 10 percent of the marketplace, where, indeed, there *is* usually a ready consumer for generic toilet paper, flour out of a bin, or dirt-cheap (albeit often unreliable) home computers. There *is* a "commodity buyer," a person who will buy on the basis of price no matter what, a person who is willing to (or by poverty forced to) settle for close to junk, as long as

---

*All this, we must urgently add, ignores a point that we've made persistently: these economies of scale at the end of the rainbow add up to the most overrated variable in the economist's variable chest. Paper economies are seldom realized in the harsh, cold real world. Smaller, more highly focused and motivated units outperform the larger time and again, in any industry you might choose to review. (Even the popular press is finally picking this up. A major *Business Week* article in October 1984 focused on "Small is beautiful in the factory.")

it's cheaper. It may be 2 percent of the market, or it may be closer to 20. But whenever such a buyer becomes active—in the purchase of toilet paper, groceries, menswear, audits, computers—it seems to drive salespersons, in particular, crazy. They assume that the whole game is lost, the whole market is going to the dogs. Many believe (who among us who've sold for a living doesn't at some level?) that this activity proves that there really *is* only one variable—price. They don't remember the seemingly effortless wins, garnered on the basis of numerous tiny service edges or as a product of a carefully nurtured continuing customer relationship; all that's recalled is a recent dramatic loss because of a bid a nickel too high. There is often overconcern, then, about the need to "shore up the fences" at the bottom. Whatever the reason, it leads many companies at some point to go after the true bottom end. And then we sadly note yet another self-fulfilling prophecy grabbing hold. Our simple observation is that no company—even one that operates through disparate, highly autonomous divisions or groups—can maintain a "quality and service fetish" (of the P&G/Maytag/Marriott sort) in one part of the company and make marginal stuff in another.* The reduced-quality-and-service focus in a given area tends to seep through the company as a whole. A senior brand manager from an old-line European package-goods company once regaled us for an hour with tales of the pernicious side effects of his company's decision to make just a few private-label products, which were not quite up to the business's long-term quality standards. "Somehow," he said, "a lax attitude toward quality began to infect the rest of the company." Ken Melrose, dynamic young chairman of Toro (the lawn-mower people) tells a similar but even more dramatic tale. "When we'd run [in the factory] the other [private-label product], an odd thing would happen. Long after the run, our branded Toro line would be affected. Errors would go way up. We couldn't figure out why to save ourselves." Toro finally decided to get out of the private-label business as a result of the intractable problem. Is there anything to this "mind-set" stuff? Ask Ken Melrose.

Yet another aspect of the experience-curve mind-set is our preoccupation with size and centralization, which is abetted by the dominance of financial officers who focus on paper studies of investments rather than on people. The United States in the past opted for the biggest plants—in automobiles, in steel, in forest products. Yet the evidence is clear. Top quality—and, ironically,

---

*Which is *not* to say that a company can't cover a fairly wide range of a market. For years General Motors went from Chevy to Cadillac; even the low end, though, was a fine car, not at the very bottom of the total automobile market by a long shot. The issue is much more serious and subtle than the little we've said suggests. We've had many vociferous debates about "How far down is too far?" The consensus is, to oversimplify, that there *is* a "too far," that it's probably not quite as far down as you think, and that no amount of organizational and managerial separation will protect your "Maytag/Perdue Farms end" from way down, bottom-end, marginal quality/service pollution.

lower cost, as it often turns out—tend to come from *smaller* units.* So we now see a headlong plunge by automobile companies, as well as the steel makers with their mini-mills and the forest-products vendors, toward the smaller productive unit. It's always been a way of life for Emerson, Dana, 3M, Hewlett-Packard, Milliken.

The truth of the matter is that the analytic models we use are simply not neutral. Analysis always comes down on the side of the big unit and cost control. But as Charles Tandy (founder of Tandy Corp.—Radio Shack, et al.) says, "You can't sell from an empty wagon." Wally Kalina, former chief operating officer at Mervyn's, adds, "Turnover ratios win trophies. Revenue leads to profits." And Bill Andres, recently retired chairman of Dayton-Hudson, notes that if you let the accountants, with their (always) more systematic analyses, win the day, "You'll end up with zero inventory—and, unfortunately, zero revenue." A longtime Macy's follower suggests that their good fortune stems from the same solution: "Overstocking is one of the major reasons for Macy's success."

George Gilder in *Wealth and Poverty* argues that you have no choice but to proceed on "faith" with the new. 3M officers agree. J&J says big productivity gains come, first and foremost, from building small, charged-up decentralized units. Brunswick and Campbell Soup are forgoing a stodgy past to try the 3M/J&J formula, and are loving the early results. The analytic, procentralization, economies-of-scale models are not neutral; their result is an excessive focus on cost that seldom fails to generate a reply of no to innovative proposals.

The experience-curve notion is a terrific one—looked at after the fact, and on paper. Even in reality, there's no doubt that market dominance combined with lowest industry cost is nice if you can achieve it. But quality is the driver; it must come first. You simply make the very best product or provide the best service you can in any category you wish to attack. That, in turn, far more often than not, is what wins customers by the bushel—which in turn allows you to reap whatever benefits there may be in economies of scale.

A Few Questions—and Things to Do Now

▶ Conduct a casual or systematic analysis of your own industry. Who have been the winners over the long haul? Have "low end" people, though darlings for a while from time to time (and usually a different darling each time), become long-term winners? (Consider inviting the Strategic Planning Institute—PIMS—people in for a seminar.)

---

*See the powerful discussion of the focused factory in Steve Wheelright and Bob Hayes's 1984 *Restoring Our Competitive Edge: Competing Through Manufacturing.*

▶ Do you call *any* products or services "commodities"? Take two or three closest to that categorization. Look in every corner—factory quality to delivery to follow-up—for differentiation factors and uniqueness. Study the market leaders in detail. This is obviously a major effort, but well worth it. Involve people for *all* functions; have each conduct detailed customer visits and competitor assessments. (This is vital. *Each* area provides numerous potential sources of differentiation. True—and sustainable—differentiation seldom comes from a single or a few big-bang advantages. It's always—witness Marriott, Disney, IBM—from a thousand things, each done a little better; that's why it's ultimately so hard to beat.) Think about starting with a detailed study of Levitt's *The Marketing Imagination,* Chapters 4, 5 and 6: "Differentiation—of Anything," "Marketing Intangible Products and Product Intangibles" and "Relationship Management."

▶ Do you *accept* commodity-ish/"no different from" language? (Remember our forest-products friends: "If you don't think it's any better, then it won't be.") Do your people, in *any* function, accept it? Do people on the line—back-room operations, factory, distribution center—accept it?

▶ Remember Gordon McGovern of Campbell Soup: "We've got to teach quality first, cost second." A colleague did a survey of a growth company recently. The leaders all knew that their success had come from superior quality. Yet the message had been taken for granted of late (the leaders erroneously assumed that "of course everyone *knows* quality comes first"). The survey revealed that most, down the line, thought that, at the margin, "ship the product to make monthly numbers" was more important than "unwavering adherence to quality standards." How about you? What *really* comes first, where and when it counts—on the loading docks on the very last day of the quarter? How do you *know?* How often do you test your knowledge? (E.g., IBM samples its first-line people quarterly to see if *they* think IBM is living up to its superior-service promise.)

▶ How wide a range of products do you offer? Is there evidence that your lowest-end offerings interfere with higher-end quality standards? (Is there any hard, longtime evidence that more than 5 to 10 percent of any part of the market will go to low-low-end players? If the answer is yes, try again. We are skeptical.)

"Marketing" According to an Iconoclastic Master

Ted Levitt is dean of the marketers, sitting in a senior position on the Harvard Business School faculty. His 1983 book, *The Marketing Imagination,* rings bell after bell:

All energies should be directed toward satisfying the consumer, no matter what. . . . The purpose of business is to get and keep a customer, or, to use Peter Drucker's more demanding construction, to *create* and keep a customer. . . . To do that, you have to do those things that will make people *want* to do business with you. All other truths on this subject are merely derivative.

Cyrus McCormick pioneered the whole idea [of adding service], putting demonstration salesmen to work on wheat farms and providing repairmen in the field. Du Pont pioneered with applications specialists in the textile and garment industry. In all these cases, the "product" that was offered by the "salesman" consisted less of what was manufactured in the factory than of what was provided by way of practical help and advice in the field. "Service" *was* the product and still today in many situations it remains more the product than meets the eye. Customers don't buy things, they buy tools to solve problems.

There is no such thing as a commodity. All goods and services can be differentiated. Though the usual presumption is that this is more true of consumer goods than of industrial goods and services, the opposite is the actual fact. . . . Though it is true that on the commodities exchanges, dealers in metals, grains, pork-bellies and the like trade on totally undifferentiated generic products, what they "sell" is the claimed distinction of their execution—how well they make transactions on behalf of their clients, how responsive they are to inquiries, the clarity and quickness of their confirmations and so on. In short, the "offered" product is differentiated, though the "generic" product is identical. . . . The usual presumption about so-called undifferentiated commodities is that they are exceedingly price-sensitive. A fractionally lower price gets the business. That's seldom true except in the imaginary world of economics textbooks. In the actual world of real markets, nothing is exempt from other considerations. Even when price competition is virulent. The fact that price differences are, prima facie, measurable becomes the usual, and usually false, basis for asserting their powerful primacy.

A product is, to the potential buyer, a complex cluster of value satisfactions. The generic "thing" or "essence" is not itself the product. It is merely, as in poker, the table stake, the minimum necessary at the outset to allow its producer into the game. But it's only a "chance," only a right to enter play. Once entry is actually obtained, the outcome depends on a great many other things.

It is precisely when the buyer has become less dependent on the technical help or brand support of the originating source, that greater attention may be beneficially focused on a systematic program of finding customer-benefiting and therefore customer-keeping augmentations. It is also a time when increasing efforts should be focused on possible price and cost reductions. Thus arises the irony of product maturity: Precisely when price competition gets more severe and therefore price reduction becomes more important is when one is also likely to benefit [the most] by incurring the *additional costs* of special new product augmentation.

Though a customer may "buy" a product whose generic tangibility (like the computer or the steam plant) is as palpable as the primeval rocks, and though he may have agreed after great study and extensive negotiation to a cost that runs into millions of dollars, the process of getting it built on time, installed, and then smoothly operational involves an awful lot more than the generic tangible product itself. What's more crucially at stake are usually a lot of complex, slippery, and difficult intangibles that can make or break the "product's" success. . . . So it makes sense to say that all products are in some crucial respect intangible. . . . Even tangible, testable, feelable, smellable products are, before they are bought, largely promises. . . . The more complex the system, and the more "software" it requires (such as its operating procedures and protocols, its management routines, its service components) and the longer it takes to implement the system, the greater the customer's anxieties and expectations. *Expectations are what people buy, not things.* [Our emphasis.]

The sale merely consummates the courtship, then the marriage begins. How good the marriage is depends on how well the relationship is managed by the seller. . . . The natural tendency of relationships, whether in marriage or in business, is entropy—the erosion or deterioration of sensitivity and attentiveness. . . . A healthy relationship requires a conscious and constant fight against the forces of entropy.

6

"Mere Perception": On the Irreducible Humanness of Customers

We spent four long days with the thirty top managers of a $1.5 billion capital-goods manufacturer. We scrutinized sales problems, marketing problems, manufacturing problems, people problems. When it came time to summarize, six were thought to merit top-level follow-up. However, in five of the six it was noted that persistently the approach was: "We're OK. It's *only* a perception problem." Finally, Tom had had enough. Stepping far beyond the bounds of what's good and proper for a visitor, he virtually shouted, "A perception problem is an engineer's way of saying, 'We've got the right solution, if it weren't for the damned people who invariably get in the way of implementation.' "

A "mere" perception problem. The real problem is that *perception is all there is.* There is no reality as such. There is only perceived reality, the way each of us chooses to perceive a communication, the value of a service, the value of a particular product feature, the quality of a product. The real *is* what we perceive. As the First Commandment of the formal, written Customer Philosophy at a successful forest-products retailer says: "Feelings *are* facts." Or, in the words of Rothchild Venture's Arch McGill (formerly the youngest vice president in IBM's history): "The individual [customer] perceives service in his or her own terms." (We always add to McGill's line: ". . . in his or her own *unique, idiosyncratic, human, emotional, end-of-the-day, irrational, erratic terms.*")

Perception Kills

Ignaz Semmelweis, the father of modern surgical sterilization techniques, committed suicide. Why?

In 1848 Semmelweis, working in a clinic, came up with a simple technique: having a physician wash his hands in a chlorine solution prior to delivery of a baby. It reduced, immediately, the maternal mortality rate in the clinic from

18 percent to 1 percent! Twelve years later, in 1860, in the same clinic, 35 out of 101 mothers died. What happened? Why didn't it take? Semmelweis was perceived as a flake, a disrupter, someone who had extreme political views; he and his unassailable results weren't heeded. Physicians didn't take him seriously, so nobody listened. In June 1865 Semmelweis, in despair, was duped into entering a mental sanatorium, where he killed himself two weeks later. It was another two decades before Lister and Pasteur came along. They apparently wore the equivalent of three-piece suits and otherwise fit the current establishment's mold: they were listened to. Their sterilization techniques were adopted rapidly, and remarkable improvements occurred. The credit and the fame accrued to them. The Semmelweis tragedy is the result of the erroneous "mere perception" of a human being by other human beings. The fact that the field was hard science and that one out of three mothers needlessly died for decades longer than necessary as a result of "mere perception" is simply an indication of its power.

COMPUTER CUSTOMERS ARE HUMAN, TOO

At a seminar for executives of companies that make scientific instruments, the wife of the president of one company (she is fully involved in its operations) related this tale. A friend of hers was about to buy a washing machine; she recommended that her friend buy Brand X. The reason was simple: in her long experience with Brand X machines, she had never had a problem. Her friend, also part of a die-hard engineer/"rational" family, said unequivocally, "No." She was going to buy GE, as she had always done. "Why?" "Well," said the friend, "when they've broken down in the past, GE repair people have arrived immediately." The recommender of Brand X replied, "Yes, but mine has *never* broken down!" Her friend's last word (after all, she was the buyer): "I don't care. It might."

The above could be written off as "housewives" arguing over washing machines. However, a conversation we overheard on the subject of a principal competitor (call it "B") of IBM offers an almost word-for-word parallel. The product was multimillion-dollar systems, and all the people involved were senior technology types. An executive of a third company, Company A, was talking about Company B: "The people at B have really gone overboard on this self-diagnostic stuff. It's efficient, but all human contact is lost. We're not going that route. We're going to show the flag." We reflected on our experience in chatting with IBM customers (versus all other customers). We know both IBM and "Company B" quite well. Company B, according to hardnosed, third-party measures, has better service ratings in several categories than IBM, but it has a less than sparkling service reputation (a reputation, in particular, for arrogance), while IBM's reputation, of course, is great. Why is this so? The answer lies in Company B's highly articulated process for responding to customer problems. People stored away in little cubbyholes, hundreds of miles from the scene, follow a precise manual and escalate their response according to the manual's definition of the customer's need. The only problem is, they never *tell* that customer just how hard they're working for him or ask him if the response meets *his* definition of the need. As we've gotten to know IBM even better in the years since the research for *In Search for Excellence* began, we've become more impressed by their difference in this dimension. They must have a giant stash of little brass bands. When they begin the fix, they tell you. They call you ("The service truck is heading down the driveway right now"). The branch manager takes you to lunch to remind you what they did for you (and how fast they did it). A 3M executive who used to run 3M-Italy describes an IBM "overresponse" to a minor problem. A banker in Minneapolis does the same. A financial-services executive in Columbus, Ohio, tells a similar tale. Yet another service industry executive laments his inability to toss out IBM. "Sometimes they're damned overbearing," he says. "But then my guys say, 'Yeah, but you can count on them.' " In every instance the customer responds to the "humanness" of IBM's response. IBM people, en masse, show up—quickly and with banners unfurled. Telephone calls are immediately made by IBMers to senior people. Often, because of the technical realities, these calls will result in no enhanced practical outcome. But they do show that live bodies at IBM are tracking the difficulty and paying close attention. In fact, many people point out that IBM uses these problem situations as selling opportunities; IBM suggests (seldom without warrant) that the problem may have come about because the wrong machine was being applied to a new or modified application.

Call Him at Home

The tradition of "overresponse" has deep historical roots at IBM. Tom Watson, Jr., speaks of it in *A Business and Its Beliefs:* "In time, good service became almost a reflex in IBM, and Father loved to show what the company could do. In 1942, an official of the War Production Board gave him a perfect excuse to do it. The WPB man called him late on the afternoon of Good Friday to place an order for 150 machines, challenging him to deliver the equipment by the following Monday in Washington, D.C. Father said he would have the machines there on time. On Saturday morning, he and his staff phoned IBM offices all over the country and instructed them to get some 150 machines on the road that Easter weekend. Just to make sure his caller got the point, Father instructed his staff to wire the WPB man at his office or home the minute each truck started on its way to Washington, giving the time of departure and expected time of arrival. He made arrangements with police and Army officials to escort the trucks, which were to be driven around the clock. Customer engineers were brought in and a miniature factory set up in Georgetown to handle the reception and installation

If your failure rate is one in a million, what do you tell that one customer?

Millions of parts go into the machines we build every year. At IBM, we work hard to make sure that everything we make is defect-free, from the smallest circuit to the finished product.

But if an IBM computer or office system ever needs service, we provide our customers with an experienced and widely skilled service organization.

IBM customer service people are on call every day of the year for large companies that have many of our machines and small businesses that may have only one.

Our service people can call on computerized data banks where solutions to thousands of hardware and software problems are stored and instantly available to them.

They also work directly with IBM engineers at our laboratories to help design products that need less service and are easier to maintain.

It's all part of our commitment to deliver fast and reliable service to every customer, every time.

Because when it comes to service, we treat every customer as if he or she is one in a million. **IBM** of the equipment. There were a lot of sleepless people at IBM—and the WPB—that weekend."

Watson goes on, underscoring the importance of the story: "These are not small things. The relationship between the man and the customer, their mutual trust, the importance of reputation, the idea of putting the customer first—always—all these things, if carried out with real conviction by a company, can make a good deal of difference in its destiny."

So everything IBM does is "wrong": they don't use the most efficient techniques, they try to sell you more in response to a problem. Yet it works out beautifully. IBM is paying attention—palpable, human attention. And what is the number one "demographic attribute" of the customer's systems buyer? You got it in one. He or she is a human!

Humanness. Let's look at another variation. There is a classic tale from the annals of marketing. A fine company introduced a cake mix that worked like a charm: Pour the mix into the pan, add water, stick it in the oven and, *voilà*, a beautiful cake! It bombed in the stores. The reason? The cake-making had been taken out of cake-making. So the product was reintroduced. It was purposely made *complicated:* now the user had to add an egg (i.e., participate in the cake-making). The reintroduced product took off like a jackrabbit. Ah ha, you say again: the housewife phenomenon. Yes, *but.* But a major software company, selling IBM compatible software at the highest systems level, also just reintroduced a major product. The problem? The first version of the product had been "too good." The new launch was titled, "A Step *Back* into *the Future.*" Here's the issue: The first version was so good that the ultimate users (in, say, the customer's manufacturing operation) could develop their programs with virtually no assistance from the customer's MIS people. The MIS bunch, who controlled (and bought!) the software, said, in effect, "No way." They didn't like (or buy) the product. The reintroduction essentially took a step back from the state of the art and complicated the product on purpose, so that there would still be a major consultant's role for the friendly people in the customer's MIS department. Now all is well. The product's relaunch is exceeding plan.*

No Plastic Wrappers, Please!

Stew Leonard, Jr., of Stew Leonard's, describes an apropos experience, which surfaced at one of Leonard's many customer-focus group meetings, as shown in Sam Tyler and John Nathan's 1985 PBS film, *In*

---

*And then there are the tough-minded engineers who can't see the need to peddle game software for their personal computers. After all, real men don't eat quiche.

Search of Excellence: "One of the ladies stood up and she said, 'I'll tell you what I don't like.' She said, 'I don't like your fish,' and we said, 'What do you mean, you don't like our fish?' She said, 'Well, it's not fresh. I like to go to a fish market and buy fresh fish.' The fish guy was there, and he stood up and said, 'What do you mean it's not fresh? We get it fresh every morning from Fulton Fish Market, and we get it fresh from the Boston piers every morning.' He said, 'I guarantee you it's fresh!' She said, 'But it's packaged. It's in a [plastic wrapped] supermarket package.' So what we did was to set up a fish bar with ice in it. And we did that right after that meeting. Now there's wrapped fish in one place, but some people like to buy it fresh right off the ice, so it's available across the aisle at the same price off the ice. Our packaged fish sales didn't decrease at all, but we doubled our total fish sales. We were doing about fifteen thousand pounds a week; now we're doing thirty thousand pounds a week."

"Computer Customers": Some Questions—and Things to Do Now

▶ Look at two or three new products or services that recently failed or required an inordinate amount of time to get established/take off. Assess the ways in which they were used by early/trial adopters, the classes of customers who used them first. How (in detail) did actual use vary from that projected by marketers/designers/focus groups/market research? How did you go wrong on attractive features/properties, usability/reliability, etc. (in the customer's eyes)? How could these surprises have been prevented? Did you track early use in enough detail to pick up such issues right away? If so, did you move fast to react?

▶ Take two or three mature or main-line products/services. Do you really know why people repeat purchase (is it the quality of your service à la GE, or something else)? What is the basis/frequency for monitoring your organization's characteristics as *perceived* by those who deal with you?

▶ What role do you perceive service to play in the sale of two or three major products? How do you *know* that your perceptions match the customer's perceptions (i.e., are you doing regular *in-depth* debriefs with major customers at all levels in the user organization—e.g., purchaser, accountant, ultimate user such as first-line person in the factory, intermediate user)?

▶ To what extent does response to problems feature in your thinking? What does response mean? How/how rapidly do you personalize it? Does the customer know how hard you are working for him/her (via what mechanisms, how assiduously practiced)?

UNFAIR!

Ah yes, it is an unfair world in which we ply our trades. Don Burr, chairman of People Express, agrees. He notes, "Coffee stains on the flip-down trays [in the airplane] mean [to the passengers] that we do our engine maintenance wrong." How right he is! In fact, we've often argued that the *only* real distinction of IBM, McDonald's, Disney, Frito-Lay and Marriott is that they are the world's greatest wipers-up of coffee stains; they will not allow you to see a coffee stain and because of it make unfair assertions about the engine maintenance.

Most of our engineer (banker, accountant, manufacturer, designer, whatever) friends unfailingly make some variation on the following response when confronted with Don Burr's statement: "Oh, what a world, in which we must sell our wonderful, marvelously designed, beautifully crafted products and services to *unappreciative people.*" Another—equally plausible— response would be to say, "Wow! What an opportunity!" For the upside of the perception issue is as high as the downside is low. Our colleague Jack Zenger addresses Don Burr's comments about coffee stains: "I've been skiing for over four decades. I've probably been in every resort worth the name in the world. At just one, in the Sierra in California, there's a Kleenex dispenser at the head of the lift line, right before you hop on the chair lift. You can grab a Kleenex and wipe your goggles on your way up the slope." He pauses. "I just can't tell you how many of even my sophisticated friends refer to the place as the 'Kleenex-box resort.' " It's really a superb metaphor. Virtually all business people agree that the be-all and the end-all of business (or ballet or baseball) is repeat business—which only comes as a result of long-term customer satisfaction. *And what's the secret to long-term customer satisfaction? From fast food outfits to department stores; from tentmakers to mainframe computer manufacturers and Boeing's 767, it's the customer's cumulative memory of a long string of "Kleenex-box experiences." Contrariwise, customer satisfaction soon becomes nil after an all too short string of negative "coffee-stain experiences."*

The president of a large technical company, another rational man (with fifteen years of background at IBM), recently ranted and raved in our presence about General Motors. He'd gotten into a Cadillac limousine on a business trip, and forty-five minutes later, emerging from the car, had ripped a finger on a protruding piece of metal near the door. "Damn it," he shrieked, "can't those bastards in Detroit do anything right?" It's not fair: Maybe he would have ripped his hand on a Japanese or German car door, too. But the problem is, he (we) has come to expect tiny problems in large numbers from GM/American cars.

It's not fair. And yet it *is* fair, because *whatever* a customer feels is, by definition, fair. The customer alone pays the freight (or doesn't) for whatever reason or collection of reasons he or she chooses. Period. No debate. No contest.

TOM PETERS

Here's another story we've become particularly fond of—a "Kleenex" story with a vengeance. Major corporate turnarounds are few and far between. A remarkable one is surely that at Scandanavian Air System (SAS), which was accomplished in just three years, and in the midst of the 1981–83 recession-depression. How was it done? SAS's group president, Jan Carlzon, focused attention not on buying new $35 million aircraft but on the "mundane" (read "cost-effective") items that would vault SAS into the number one position as the European businessman's preferred airline. He painted the planes, spruced up the interiors, intensified the customer-service training of personnel, bought more de-icing trucks to put the on-time departure rate at the top of the heap. Carlzon describes his view this way: "SAS has ten million passengers a year. The average passenger comes in contact with five SAS employees. Therefore, SAS is the product of the ten million times the five. SAS *is* fifty million 'moments of truth' per year. Fifty million, unique, never-to-be-repeated opportunities to distinguish ourselves, in a memorable fashion, from each and every one of our competitors. My job is simply to manage the dickens out of the fifty million moments of truth!" He adds, "SAS is the contact of one person in the market [customer] and one person at SAS. *That is SAS.*"

Impersonalness: The Ultimate (Perceived) Discourtesy

We chided a bunch of Pacific Telephone senior managers a while ago. In California (alone, we understand) when you dialed information (411), you'd get a whiny (could be that it only comes across as whiny) canned message: "You *really* can save money on your phone bill if you'll just look it up. . . ." After the message, the information operator invariably answered on the first ring. We said to the telephone folks, "Look, you probably spend billions of dollars to get 'first-ring answering.' But it's all down the drain, because we're so darned annoyed by that dinky little message that we ignore all your technological wizardry and go away mad."

It makes a human being happy to hear the live voice of another human being. That's why we love the Delta Airlines people—the people who point. They may not be any more efficient than a taped message or CRT display, but they're alive. A Pacific Gas & Electric experience provides corroborating evidence. In the midst of storms that knocked out electric service throughout Northern California in 1982, PG&E used to have a taped message that described what was going on in the system—where the repairmen were, estimated time to repair and so on. It was changed regularly, and was in fact quite up-to-date. Complaints, however, were frequent. Then the company changed the routine. A live human being started answering the phone. In reality, the live human being was not as up-to-date and had less specific information than the regularly adjusted taped message. But PG&E got rave notices! People need other people, especially in the midst of uncertainty. It's the difference between calling to get the weather report every day (here the taped message is expected and therefore OK) and trying to get information in an emergency.

American Airlines president Bob Crandall is emphatic on the subject. There had been many complaints about American's response to lost baggage. It turned out that if it wasn't working hours in the locale where a bag was lost, the aggrieved party, upon dialing the lost-baggage number, was confronted with a taped message asking that he or she call back the next morning. So Crandall arranged to have any phone call to the lost-baggage number from any location at any hour answered by a live service rep at a center manned around the clock. The reality was that the live person didn't know any more than the taped message did, and also in effect told the bereft passenger to call back in the morning. But the *real* reality (reality as perceived by the customer) was the sympathetic response that the living person provided—a degree of comfort no tape machine could match.

Long Memories

Oh, the length of the trail we leave behind! Is the memory trail one of Kleenex boxes? Or of coffee stains? Or of but a single coffee stain, *long, long* ago? After a presentation a while back at which Tom had gone through his analysis, a solid candidate for "prototypical rational man" came up to him. He is the senior officer in research and development at the $6 billion pharmaceutical company, Johnson & Johnson, and he had an example of his own to contribute to the discussion. A dozen years before, he had bought an analytic instrument from a fine company. A couple of months after buying it he had a problem with a $2.95 component. The company's response? "First, they mustered their top engineers to try and prove that it was my fault, and that I abused the part and busted it. They were unconscionably tardy in answering my correspondence. They were actually rude over the phone on more than one occasion. Today, fully a dozen years later, I still tell my people, 'Don't you buy equipment from those guys.' Now, I *know* it is not rational, that it is emotional, but it is *life.*" Ah, yes. The little memories—the "mere perceptions"—that pollute forever!*

And of course the flip (positive) side is available for (active) examination. Among a hundred or so presentations during the last eighteen months before trade associations or user groups, in which Tom has been joined by officers of various companies as co-presenters, on only four occasions has a company officer begun his or her speech as follows: "Thank you. I want to thank those of you in the audience who are our customers. We sincerely hope that we will continue to deserve your business in the future." Is it only a coincidence that

---

*A Maryland utility executive laments that many of his industry's problems in Congress were caused by Montana Senator Lee Metcalf, who was still angry because his mother's service was cut off in mid-winter in 1913!

all four executives were from the IBM company, that IBM thought to say those two lovely words, "Thank you"? More: IBM opened a users' meeting Tom attended in Vancouver, B.C., in typical IBM fashion—with a film clip. About 110 companies were represented in the 500-person audience. The film clip consisted of footage shot at the headquarters location of *each* of the customers, with the company's logo prominently displayed. "Mere fluff?" One big technology company vice president says so: "Tom, that's just pat-on-the-back marketing!" Our response: "Yeah. Forty-seven billion pats a year called revenue dollars, seven billion of them after taxes. We'll take it." Memories are made of such stuff.

And How Long Will This Be Remembered?

During our 1984 visit to Ireland an executive passed this on:

HARRODS LIMITED

Knightsbridge   London   SW1X 7XL

Telephone 01-730 1234   Telex 24319   Fax 01-581 0470
Registered Office 87/135 Brompton Road, London SW1X 7XL
Registered in London No 30209

Mr P J Dineen   19.8.80
EIRE

Dear Sir,

We are always seeking to improve upon the despatch of goods by sea and air freight, although standard freight rates leave very little margin for competitive charges. Often freight rates are increased without warning, and this leads to a loss.

On occasion we are able to bulk shipments or obtain a concessionary commodity rate, and, should a saving occur we believe our customers should benefit. I am very glad to be able to enclose a cheque for £217.00 which constitutes the total

saving made on a recent shipment, and I hope that we may have
a further opportunity to serve you very soon.

Yours sincerely

I G Drummond
Manager
Shipping Office

"Unfair!": Some Questions—and Things to Do Now

▶ Look at your own buying habits at home with respect to, say, an airline, a
department store, a plumber. Look at your purchasing habits in your corporate life with respect to a few key suppliers. Sit around as a group and
try to figure out why—over the long haul—you sustain a relationship.
Likewise rerun three or four home/corporate relationships that you have
severed. What are the *perceptual* attributes of your decision to buy/sus-
tain/leave? (Specifically take *one* long "best" relationship, and list a minimum of twenty to thirty attributes of dealing with the supplier that are
attractive. Do the same for *one* recently severed relationship. Now, switch
the game: On the dimensions/traits that surfaced in the above, how do you
rate as a supplier? For a sample of products/services, what are the top ten
"coffee stain" irritants you regularly subject your customers to? The top
twenty "Kleenex boxes" you provide? Are you actively in search of
"Kleenex boxes" to add? "Coffee stains" to clean up? How do you measure yourself/keep up with the above? Especially perceived deterioration?
(P.S.: How well did you do in answering the question? Did you have a firm
enough grasp of the data to do so?)
▶ *Stop!* Commit *ten full days* in the next two months to checking out your
"coffee stain"—"Kleenex box" image. Pick *four major customers* and
spend one full day with each—in a remote location for at least two of the
four. Pick *eight minor customers* and spend one-quarter day with each.
Spend one day with *three recently lost accounts,* another day with *three
accounts recently gained from a competitor.* Spend the remaining two full
days with a group of colleagues from *all* functions, *all* levels (about ten to

fifteen people); invite two longtime customers to attend. What is the "coffee stain"—"Kleenex box" story that emerges? How surprised are you?

▶ Track a routine customer transaction with you, cradle to grave. How many "moments of truth" are involved? Make sure to cover all functions—PBX room, reception, manufacturing, contracts, accounting, delivery, follow-up. Are you actively managing your "moments of truth," especially relative to the "nonmajor" (i.e., nonselling) functions?

▶ Do a "mere fluff" (small signs of courtesy) check. What do you, and your function/company, call customers? Do you have a term? Do you "police" your language? Do you talk about customers regularly in your communications? What is your "Thank you" quotient? Your "logos/pictures" quotient (i.e., to what degree—*very* specifically—do you go out of your way to personalize the trappings of your customer contacts)? Review customer/user meetings. Are they first rate, the very best in the industry show (especially relative to the "mere fluff")? What is the very best user meeting you've ever been to as a customer? What are the twenty-five "little things" you find most attractive? Can you/do you replicate all of them for your company?

Note: All of the above will be hard slogging. Increasing your awareness of the "Kleenex box"-"coffee stain" attributes of a series of transactions is not easy. Keep at it, keep digging. When it looks as if you bought something for "price alone," try again, especially hard. You probably disqualified ten to twenty potential suppliers for "coffee stain" reasons before you reached the list of the last three.

COMPLAINTS *CAN* BE GOLDEN

Joe Girard, the premier car salesman, appeared in *In Search of Excellence*. For ten years in a row he sold over twice as many cars as the number two dealer in the world. He said the key was that he *cared*. Fine. Then Joe stretched it just a bit too far: "I want to sell you a lemon. Then I'll show you just how well I'll perform for you with the service department." We laughed when a seminar participant pointed out that line in a Girard article, a line that we'd missed, frankly. And, then, upon some further reflection, we quit laughing. We thought back to the last ten (senior corporate) slavish IBM devotees we'd chatted with. Surprisingly, not one had very much nice to say about IBM. They pointed out, instead, problems! *But,* they always added that whenever a problem had arisen, fifteen IBM people—eleven of them by parachute—had descended on them within three hours. And they always got the machine up just as the first streak of dawn was about to mark the sky.

IBM doesn't want to sell you a lemon, for sure, but if they do, they make darned sure you know that they are very, very sorry.

And Watson's Assistant Was Already There

We talked to a Hewlett-Packard executive who spent over a dozen years at IBM. He regaled us with story after story. For instance, there was the time when a Union Carbide machine crashed and Mr. Watson, Jr., was going to call on the president of Union Carbide at 8:00 A.M. the following Monday morning for a report on it. Our friend recalls the bus ride at midnight with twenty-two colleagues, heading for the trouble spot, deep in the West Virginia hills. They drove for three hours in blinding rain, snaking through the mountains, in order to arrive at the Union Carbide site in time to get the machine up before Mr. Watson made his in-person call. When they arrived at 4:00 A.M., Mr. Watson's executive assistant was miraculously waiting there to greet them. Where had he come from? How did he get there? Heaven only knows. (Levitation?) But he did. It's the IBM way.

All of the above has led us to broader speculation, to the supposition that there are two kinds of companies. The first, the most typical, views the complaint as a disease to be got over, with memory of the pain rapidly suppressed. The second, exemplified by IBM, views the complaint as a luscious, *golden opportunity*. As the president of IBM's Entry Systems Division (maker of the PC), Don Estridge said: "A live customer on the line. Wow! What an opportunity! What an opportunity to turn him, and make him into a lifelong friend." He added, "It's the ones who *don't* call that worry me."

The logic behind the IBM view of the "joy of complaints" (live customers on the line) is evident in the words of one retail executive: "For every complaint you get, remember, fifty people walk. They don't even bother to tell you they're mad." We've heard the numbers 10, 25, 50 or 150 in this regard. We suspect it varies by industry, though it doesn't really matter. Whether 10 or 2,000 "walk" before picking up the phone, complaints are clearly important. And we are astonished, as are all the business people that we chat with, at just what a *small* world it is. Joe Girard (our car-salesman friend) made the point that each angry person has 250 friends, 100 will hear from him about the rotten experience he had with you. And 50 percent of them, in turn, will tell their 250 friends. A Digital Equipment service executive adds: "There's no such thing as a *small* customer. The least of customers, especially angry customers—and it almost seems inevitable—*always* lives next door to the chairman of the company you've been trying unsuccessfully to sell to for the last fifteen years."

Yet another issue when it comes to complaints is the blithe assessment, "This one is an anomaly." True, at some level each complaint is unique. On the other hand, in our experience in working with companies on this issue and in running our own small business, there is no such thing as a unique complaint. If you get a complaint about a lack of phone courtesy that you can readily explain away as having been caused by a "uniquely busy day," the odds are very high (about $99^{44}/_{100}$ percent) that there are a lot of "uniquely busy days," and that the apparently anomalous complaint is but the tip of an iceberg. Technically (the engineer's/financial person's pristine logic again) each one *is* different; in reality a "pattern of one" invariably turns out to be, sad to say, just that—a pattern.

The availability of information about complaints is vital as well. How easy do you make it for the customer to complain? How rapidly is the whole system made aware of complaints? L. L. Bean, the superb Maine sporting-goods store, updates its product-by-product complaint/problem file *daily* and makes the output available to all hands. People on Nissan's production line in Smyrna, Tennessee, have displays at each workstation, updated regularly, of customer and dealer comments. Caterpillar Tractor and Deere ceaselessly *beg* customers to complain, and then pass on the information about problems with lightning speed. Most, however, make it bureaucratically tough or socially awkward to complain, and they do little with the information once received, on the indefensible basis that it's "too sensitive [i.e., useful to competitors] for widespread dissemination."

There is a last, ought-to-be-obvious point to be made on this subject. If you decide to handle complaints by, say, installing a toll-free 800 "hot line" complaint number, then you'd damn well better follow through, with near perfection! One fellow described an atrocious event to us. Had we not known him fairly well, we wouldn't have believed it. An $800 million high-technology company installed an 800 hot line for customer complaints. But then, our friend says, "They changed the 800 number every three months. That way you'd have to call information and get the 303 area code number. Then you'd have to pay for the subsequent call." In many instances we've come across, people who have installed an 800 number have not realized the substantial degree of training that is necessary for truly effective responses. Milliken & Co. is developing a Milliken Customer College. A principal reason is to train the people who deal with 800 number call-ins and the like on how to respond to customers. The hot line is a magnificent idea, and today's (let alone tomorrow's) telecommunications technology makes it easy to have one—and almost irresponsible not to have one.

We observe time and again that even after a big foul-up you can turn that foul-up into something positive; the disgruntled customer can become a top customer and better friend than ever just by your calling back and saying you're sorry. Astonishingly enough, that's usually all you need to set your-self far apart from (ahead of) the pack.* It's a constant source of amaze-ment to us: Simple common courtesy, such as a personal call after a foul-up, makes you special. It shouldn't (it should be boringly commonplace), but it does.

Have You Gotten Our Letter Yet?

A colleague, Pat Townsend, reports an example of Perdue Farms' response to a customer (remember, this is a three-quarter-*billion*-dollar company): "A friend of mine mentioned last week that he once bought a Perdue chicken that, he discovered after getting home, was all dry and nasty. He took it back to the store and got an immediate refund. Then he decided to write Frank—having seen him on TV—and tell him that he had bought one of his damn quality chickens and it was all dry and nasty. By return mail he got a letter from Frank that not only included profuse apologies and a certificate for a free chicken but also enlisted his help to make sure it never happened again by asking a whole list of specific questions: Where did he buy it? When? Exactly what was wrong? What did he think had happened? What *exactly* did the store say when he returned it? Etc., etc. Two days later an executive of Per-due Chickens *called* to make sure he'd gotten the letter, to make sure that all was well, and to ask some more specific questions. My friend will never buy anything but Perdue Chicken."

---

*While making revisions on this manuscript, Tom was on a flight from Dallas to Detroit. At 11:37 P.M. the plane arrived in Detroit. An overzealous pilot took a corner too sharply. The plane ran off the runway by a couple of feet; it got stuck because of a recent glut of rain. Bad enough. But to make a bad situation worse, the passengers were left on board for thirty-five minutes (until after midnight) while efforts were made to blast the plane's way out, thereby using up all the fuel, and the passengers were cast into darkness. Then the bus shortage hit. The airline rounded up *one* van with an eight-person capacity and proceeded to unload a full plane, one row at a time, for more than two hours. Meanwhile, never *once* in the three hours did the pilot emerge from his cocoon, in person or via the PA system, to say the two simple words, "I'm sorry." (The story pre-sents a golden opportunity to emphasize a point we made before. When we talk of "superior cus-tomer service," we don't mean expensive frills à la Regency Air; we *do* mean the apparently all but lost art of saying "I'm sorry.")

A recent seminar participant recounted an episode in stark contrast to the story above. She had lost some luggage needed for a meeting, instantly. Instant retrieval wasn't physically possi-ble, but she was treated with such courtesy and concern by the airline that she wrote the presi-dent a positive letter about the whole event. Thus there *was* a foul-up and, further, even the thoughtful response failed to result in a fix; nonetheless, the outcome was a big net plus for the company and the customer.

"Golden Complaints":
Some Questions—and Things to Do Now

▶ Pick three customers you lost after a botched transaction (or series of transactions). Spend time with them on the phone, or, if possible, interview them. To what degree did the loss come from the foul-up per se versus the post-foul-up response to the problem?

▶ What is your *exact* method of responding to a complaint? Is it formalized? If so, is there exact adherence to the procedure? How soon and under what circumstances do senior people get involved? How is your personal concern transmitted? How do you handle, if at all, postresponse follow-up ("How'd we do?")?

▶ How easy is it to get in touch with you/your company about a complaint? Do you make it a lead-pipe cinch: big posters with the 800 call-in number very easy to see and with fill-in complaint cards; random sampling of customers 30, 60 and 120 days after a big sale to see "how we're doing," spot calls after a sale to check on same, spot calls/visits to nonmain functions in the customer's operation (how do the first-line *operators* in the factory like the printout format on the new analytic instrument, was the patient's billing handled well?). Do these samples include *seeking out* complaints from big, good customers: "I know you haven't called, but we just modified our billing procedure, and I wanted to check." "We just issued a new manual for the 4261xx; how do your operators like it?"

▶ How is your response to complaints *perceived?* Spend a fair amount of time on this. IBM, for instance, unabashedly does 10 to 100 things to generate the perception of "overkill." Can you say the same? Sample ten complaints. Within how many hours/days did you promise a fix? How many times did you *beat* the deadline? Does the customer know it? (I.e., did you tell him? How many times, and how, in the process of the fix, did you get in touch to say, "We're working on it," or "We just got X done"?)

▶ Sample 20 complaints from small customers. Do your small accounts get the same level of *perceived* service as the large? If so, is it by conscious choice?

▶ If you sell various levels of service packages, do you have a "low end," which, in retrospect, ensures that certain customers—albeit as a result of their own characteristics—will be underserviced (and therefore angry, their "fault" or not)?

▶ Do you have an 800 call-in number? If not, why? If so, (a) is it widely publicized? (b) is it more than adequately manned? (c) are the people involved "overtrained"?

▶ What do you do with complaint information? Are copies of complaint letters, 800 call-in transcripts, etc., circulated to all levels? Is the nature of complaints instantly tallied and summarized (the L. L. Bean approach)?

Do you do multifunction, multilevel post hoc analysis of complaints. If so, how regularly?

▶ How many new products/services or extensions thereof can you attribute directly to follow-up on a single complaint? Or as a response to a pattern of complaints? If the number is small, why? Are there mechanisms for turning the complaint/complaint pattern directly into a new or modified product/service?

▶ Specifically, take the last *five* complaints you've been involved with. Have you rationalized *any* of them as attributable to "special circumstances" (e.g., "a 36-day month"), or have you treated the solo complaint as a likely "pattern"?

▶ Are you a *fanatic* about this subject? Is anybody in the industry/segment better? If so, is it an advantage for them?

DO YOU MEASURE SATISFACTION?

A final issue related to customer perception came to a head in the midst of a four-day seminar with forty company presidents (members of the Young Presidents Organization). We had spent fully a day and a half on the subject of customer perceptions of service and quality. At the end, we evaluated the importance of these ideas, even formalized it with a ballot. Forty out of forty agreed that long-term, total customer satisfaction (and repeat business) was clearly priority number one, the be-all and end-all for any organization in fields ranging from wholesale forest products to fast food franchises, from the manufacture of computer hardware and software to thread making. Then we returned to a discussion we'd had of the IBM measurement process. A large share of IBM's marketing force (all varieties: service, reception, sales, marketing staff) and many nonmarketing people are *directly* evaluated (compensation, bonus, promotion, annual performance review) on the basis of hardnosed, quantitative, external/third party and in-house developed measures of customer satisfaction. (*Not* market share or other surrogate indicators, but "straight satisfaction.") We stuck the two ideas together—hard-nosed measurement and the unparalleled importance of the issue. We then asked the obvious question: "How many of you measure *any* of your people directly on a third-party or impartial, quantitative in-house measure of long-term total customer satisfaction?" The answer? Zero. Thus, forty out of forty say the issue is far and away the most important; yet none of the forty does anything about it.* We suspect it has a lot to do with the idea of "mere perception."

*The day after we wrote the initial draft of this section we tried again, this time only with an audience of 132 (94 of them presidents of small or medium-sized companies). The results? Ditto—all 132 rated long-term customer satisfaction tops in importance; none measured it for purposes of compensation and evaluation.

Fred Cox, chairman of the highly successful Emulex Corporation in Southern California, a computer components maker, spoke to the same issue in early 1984 in addressing technology executives: "We all know and agree that customer satisfaction is the prime reason for being in our businesses. But look at the measures I ran across. I just discovered one called 'return on net capital employed.' Now, what the hell does that mean? I've never seen *any* strategy, *any* plan, *any* annual report that includes a *direct* measure of customer satisfaction. Why?" Why, indeed? We don't happen to be quite the enemy that Fred is of return on net capital employed, but we surely agree otherwise with his comment.

Did Anything Bug You?

Domino's Pizza Distribution Company, the dough makers and equipment suppliers for Domino's Pizza's over 1,200 franchises, *do* measure service systematically—and *weekly,* to boot—in their Ideal Service Survey. They make an extensive phone survey of their customers to ask them how the service and product quality were. The survey not only covers quantitative/technical issues—e.g., response time—but also qualitative ones: "Did *anything* we do bug you?" Monthly evaluation and compensation for all hands (up through the president!) are predicated on the results, which are instantly summarized and made available to everyone; in fact, they are publicly and prominently posted in *all* facilities. President Don Vlcek explains the logic behind the survey: "We believe customer satisfaction is an advance indicator of swings in market share. Why wait for the P&L's?"

Domino's System

Many can see the usefulness of measuring customer satisfaction. However, most in our experience have difficulty taking the next step and tying it to compensation and evaluation. Domino's Pizza Distribution president, Don Vlcek, provided us with a description of the process he uses; read it in the context of an extensive weekly survey system, in which quantitative satisfaction scores are developed on numerous parameters from the lumpiness of the dough to pepperoni freshness to whether the driver closed the franchisee's freezer door at the conclusion of the delivery. Here's Don:

Tying the survey results into the TIPO (Team/Individual Performance Objectives) system: The purpose of the TIPO system is to try to make the monthly bonus be in direct relation to people's and team's performance for that given period. Other purposes are to help the team and people know their priorities and their expected level of performance, which ranges from "crisis level" to "exceptional level." The process is: First, Key [satisfaction] Indicators are developed for each unit and each specific job and are stated in quantifiable terms. Then points are distributed amongst the key indicators in a manner showing how much priority each key indicator has at the present time. The expected level of performance is then determined. If that level is attained, the Team Member receives 80% of the points in that category. Also figured are the level of crisis performance, which would allow the Team Member to receive [a maximum of] 20% of the points available in that category, and the level of exceptional performance, which would result in 100% of all points in that category.

A score of 100 on the national [survey] would set aside 4% of profits for a given period, which goes into a pool to be disbursed amongst Team Members. In that way, a month of high profits in which we have fallen off in customer service might result in having lower bonuses even though the company is making more money; or the reverse. This determination of the pool is done strictly on the performance of the entire team (all divisions of the company).

Individual performance is determined the same way. Every individual has a set of key indicators developed with his or her Team Leader. Their score determines the percent of available bonus they actually receive.

Some jobs are hard to quantify, but not impossible. It must be done to ensure everyone knows his or her priorities, expected level of performance, and how it will be determined. For example, the accounting department exists to perform services for others. We've developed a "rating" system where the users of these services grade them on a scale of 10 *and* comment. No grades can be given without comment. I've noticed this is a great method to motivate peers to get together to coordinate rather than asking their leader for help. Delegation by osmosis!

The expected performance for the Ideal Service Survey is reviewed every six months and set slightly above the average for the last six months. This tends to motivate people to be slightly better every six months. We set the crisis performance at the lowest score received during the last six months, and the exceptional performance at the highest score during the last six months.

Measuring satisfaction is nifty. As you can tell, we are fans of it. But we don't mean to scare you off by our enthusiasm for such highly articulated arrangements. After a talk at a late 1984 seminar, the president of one small company said, "Look, I attended a seminar of yours a year back. After that I forced myself to adopt the simple habit of calling, religiously, three or four customers a week to ask, 'How are *we* doing for *you?*' The result has been nearly revolutionary. They tell me, in no uncertain terms, exactly how we're doing. And then I do something about it." We agree with all but one aspect of his "simple habit." It sounds deceptively simple and therefore commonplace, but he's oh so rare!

"Measurement":
Some Questions—and Things to Do Now

▶ Do you regularly and extensively measure customer satisfaction? by internal surveys? by third-party surveys (e.g., mystery shoppers, regular externally administered surveys)? by third-party or in-house hard measures (e.g., comparative response times—yours vs. those of competitors)? by in-depth customer debriefings (e.g., a two-day, three-person team *not* directly associated with the account doing top-to-bottom, multifunction interviews, partly structured, partly open-ended)?

▶ Do you widely *publicize* satisfaction measures (e.g., in company magazines, on bulletin boards, in annual reports)? Do you set objectives based upon them? Do you *directly* base any part of compensation/evaluation/promotion on them? Do you celebrate satisfaction-measure successes?

▶ Does *every* department or function have "customer satisfaction" measures? (E.g., do the accountants survey their users/"customers" on various aspects of satisfaction?) Note: Developing the notion of "customer" is hard work for internal groups, but it can be done and is worth the struggle.

▶ Do you have any "simple" rituals, like our colleague's weekly calls to ask "How are *we* doing for *you?*"

▶ *Backtrack a moment:* Are you sure you know what customer satisfaction is for *you?* Look ahead to the story of Todd Fraser on p. 96. He wasted two years by first designing *their* (his customers') satisfaction in *his* terms; then he belatedly asked, and got it right!

Note: The process of developing measures that are appropriate and stable is not easy. Try various measures in various locations; experiment for sixty days. Update, revise and hone. It will probably take a year before you are comfortable enough with the nature/validity of a measure to start using it to affect evaluations/compensation.

BUT YOU CAN'T GIVE AWAY THE STORE

Perception is all there is. That's no surprise. All business, from potato chips to washing machines to jet engines, is about people selling to people, whether it's a 17¢ transaction or a $10 billion one.* There is only the cumulative memory, the pattern, the perceived consistency, the perceived level of concern and care and attention and responsiveness.

Seems obvious, doesn't it? But, oh, the rejoinders we get! One important part of total customer satisfaction, we argue, is adapting the service or product to a specific customer's needs. And the wolves howl. They say, "Yes, that's exactly what *all* salesmen want. Redo the product to meet *each* customer's need. We'd have a jillion products—and a totally confusing product line and a wildly noncompetitive cost base." That's not the point at all! Take a $2 million project. Paint the box brown to meet the customer's needs. You win. The situation is so bad (or, conversely, the opportunity so good!) that a *tiny* step in the direction of responsiveness sets you *way* ahead of the pack.

Once we got a question concerning our negative comments about overdoing self-diagnostics in the analytic-instruments world. A company president said, "You mean we shouldn't use self-diagnostics? We shouldn't allow our customers to plug into a modem and diagnose their own problem?" Before we could respond, the president of another (highly successful) company leaped in: "No, that's *not* what they mean at all. The point is the need for human, eyeball-to-eyeball contact—somehow. Maybe not at that time. But you've gotta be in touch. You've gotta press the flesh. You've gotta show the flag. Somehow. Self-diagnostics are fine. But being out of touch is bad news." We couldn't thank him enough. Our sentiments exactly.

"Give Away": Some Questions—and Things to Do Now

▶ Do discussions of service endlessly bog down in cost-of-service issues? Take three or four recent major sales or extensions of contracts. To what extent did you modify product/service traits to meet the customer's perceived needs? Did it take a lot to give the impression of flexibility? Take three or four lost sales: Did you fail to be perceived as flexible in any instance? Could you have gone one-quarter step and have been perceived as forthcoming?

▶ Take one or two particularly pleasing or displeasing experiences with suppliers from whom you buy (or your experience as a consumer, e.g., dealings with a phone company, washing machine purchase and installation). What sorts of flexibility/tailoring-of-package have impressed you? What sorts of inflexibility have irritated you? In the "good news" cases, has the tailoring been expensive to the vendor? Have you paid a premium for the flexibility?

---

*The latter figure is not chosen lightly. GE just won at least that much business in aircraft engines away from Pratt & Whitney. P&W, most say, had the technology edge. GE won on service warranties and spares policy, and because of P&W's hard-headedness (i.e., rudeness and arrogance, it's said, in prior dealings with the Air Force).

▶ In pursuit of automation (e.g., of distribution, service), has the human touch been degraded? If so, what countermeasures are you taking, if any, to keep the human/personal link in transactions? regularly or on a planned but irregular basis? Are any competitors doing it better? What devices are they using?

LEARN TO LOVE YOUR SALESPERSON
EVEN IF IT HURTS

The perception issue. It goes so deep. Feelings *are* facts. Arch McGill is clear on another point: "Marketing is an *art*," the art of selling the benefits of your product and, by contrast, making it clear that your benefits are more relevant than the competitor's. The heart of marketing is not computer-based segmentation. Much as we seem to have ignored it in the last twenty-five years, the heart of marketing is selling. Selling is a fine thing! We love salespersons! We continue to believe that a good candidate for the single most significant strength of the all-powerful IBM Company is the fact that it has *always* been run by former *salesmen.** Salespeople are *people* talking to other *people*. They are people who, in our experience, always live with the certain knowledge—call it terror—that they are going to lose *every* customer between now and tomorrow morning; thus, they take a very different view from ordinary folk of "mere perception" problems.

An interesting discussion with a Citicorp vice chairman and McGill led us to think about the issue of people selling to people. We said we wondered why salesmen have always been so denigrated. (In Tom's old consulting firm, McKinsey, about the worst thing that could ever be said about a consultant was, "He's a bit of a salesman"—it was said about Tom once.) The Citicorp vice chairman agreed that "selling" was looked down upon in his world (at least prior to deregulation). But selling, of course, is where the perception issue really comes to the fore.

The Branch Manager as King

IBM, much as we love and respect it, is a pretty darn bureaucratic company, truth be known. And on many dimensions it's quite centralized, at least within the context of a typical several-billion-dollar division. Yet its customer responsiveness—with nearly four hundred thousand on the payroll—is legendary. How do they do it? At the heart is the autonomy of the (sales) branch manager. It is, simply, his or her responsibility to make things happen for the customer, and break

---

*IBM is alone in this regard among major participants in its industry.

whatever china (i.e., rules) it is necessary to break in the process. There will be no recriminations for a branch manager who moves heaven and earth, and steps on countless toes in the process, to get the customers satisfied.

But heaven help that branch manager who says, "I could've done it, *but*..." And heaven help the field service manager or other support person who says of the branch manager, "I would've helped him or her, *but*..." Neither is long for IBM's world.

IBM is a bureaucracy, to be sure, but there is a pecking order. And the branch manager, responsible for customer satisfaction, is indisputably at the top of it.

Selling—and advertising. Many are as contemptuous of most advertising as they are of salesmen. Many consider it to be "mere fluff"! Most of our technical (and banking, etc.) friends hate it. (Actually they resent the *need* for it. "It should be obvious to any fool that the benefits of this management service [of ours] are overwhelming," is the sentiment just a millimeter below the surface.) They look at it not with thinly disguised contempt but with wholesale contempt. And yet, *is* there a product whose benefit is known before it's been broadly and effectively communicated (i.e., effectively advertised)? Clearly not.

Let's look at it another way. Whether one is a staunch, left-of-center Democrat or far-right-of-center Republican, it would be hard not to agree that President Reagan has done a masterly job of selling his programs and philosophy to America. A *New York Times Magazine* cover story (October 14, 1984) went a long way toward explaining it. It said that Reagan spent "merely" 20 percent of his time formulating programs, and 80 percent "communicating" and—horror of horrors—"selling" them. Communicating, implementing, selling—the bases for changing and establishing perceptions (positive or negative)—*are* the heart of all dealings with customers (constituents, patients, students). Mr. Reagan simply happens to be the first person in the Oval Office in a while who understands that. Superior leadership, make no bones about it, is pure selling, selling in the best sense of the word—i.e., establishing the *perception,* the feeling, the picture, that your view is right, that you listen, hear and understand, that you are worth listening to and following (or buying from).

Furthermore, the *only* great product, by definition, is one that sells (just as it's mandatory to win the election if one is to be considered a candidate for "great president" or "great alderman"). Seldom if ever—and despite, again, the protestations of our technocrat (banker, accountant, etc.) friends—does a product "sell itself" on the basis of its "clear technical merits." The history of innovation is particularly supportive of this point. Many a company has gone down the drain because it has consistently been too far ahead of its time. Varian Associates, the early pioneer in electronics, had, prior to 1983, a dozen bad years. In a speech to security analysts, a Varian executive blamed the largest share of the company's troubles on the fact that Varian engineers have traditionally been about a decade *ahead* of their customers. Mr. Birdseye invented the flash-freezing process in 1912; it didn't garner a profit until 1952. It took fully *forty* years to change the eating habits and food-buying and distribution habits of the nation to prepare us for the benefits of (and need for) flash-frozen products. A product sells only when it fits all elements of the customer's "real time" (i.e., today's) need and context.

"Love Your Salesperson":
Some Questions—and Things to Do Now

▶ Do you honor your salespeople (beyond compensation and the annual-awards gala)? Talk to a friend at Tupperware, or Mary Kay Cosmetics, or The Limited or IBM. Review, *in detail,* the nature and frequency of salesperson celebration. How do you stack up?

▶ What's the *language* surrounding salespeople? Are they seen as second-class citizens? Is "mere salesmanship" the implicit message? Are former salespeople represented to a substantial degree in the ranks of top management? Do all would-be kings or queens do a two-year stint (or more) in sales on the way up? Do top managers still sell (e.g., take a regular turn on the retail floor, do store calls, have assigned accounts)?

▶ What is the role of advertising? Is it seen as a necessary evil or is it exploited to the hilt? Is "overspending" to support the winner brands/services/products the norm? Do you outspend, per sales dollar, the industry/your three top competitors? If not, why not?

▶ Do you *ceaselessly* work on the simple message of product benefits? (David Ogilvy explains, and our experience strongly supports his, that most ads simply fail to communicate—or sometimes even mention—the top one or two [at most] major benefits.) Does every form of communication reflect this? Do any competitors do it more clearly? If so, how? Are benefits in tune with—i.e., not *too* far ahead of—the customer's perceived needs?

EMOTION AND FEEL: BEING HUMAN

It's all about being human. The irritation of a tiny incident of rudeness colors dealings a dozen years later. A simple and genuine "I'm sorry" can make up for a massive (and expensive) technical error.

And it's also about managing by wandering around—MBWA, as we've said before. Yet we shouldn't need to do MBWA, should we? With computer printouts generated in seconds by $250 machines, staying in touch *should* be a simple matter of reading, via electronic spreadsheet, the outcomes of attitude surveys and summaries of market research data. (With two touches of the finger to the HP-150's screen you can instantly turn spreadsheet output into a seven-color pie chart!) And yet we go wrong time and again because we do rely on the numbers and printouts and transparencies alone, and lose our "feel." The only way to enhance feel is to be there. Feel may not constitute statistically significant data by University of Chicago Ph.D. board standards, but what can match the human being in operating in the visual, tactile spheres?

Procter & Gamble exemplifies sophistication in analysis of market data. Yet the biggest payoff from the toll-free "complaint" number the company has placed on all its packages probably did not come from the brand managers' analyses of the phoned-in comments themselves. It probably came when senior vice presidents agreed that they themselves would listen in on the line at least three hours a week. "I can't tell you exactly what I do differently as a result of answering the phone," says one, "but I can tell you that no decision is made quite the same way." Similarly, the deputy director of health in Pennsylvania sent all those who reported directly to her out of the office to work four hours a week in a local service bureau. This is pointedly not a "show the flag" visit by a senior officer; rather, the director insists that each of her people sit on the other side of the glass window and process would-be service recipients, answering complaints and dealing with the same forms that her firstline people have to deal with. "We can sit here talking about too much bureaucracy, too many complex forms, until the cows come home," she notes. "But until you've really been there, regularly, really seen how ridiculous it is to collect this kind of data or that, seen how you're wholly unable to answer the simplest questions because of the bureaucratic procedures that must be followed in order to answer them, until you've done that, until you've felt the frustration, you haven't really begun to get a feel for the situation."

"Mere perception." "Mere communication." "Mere listening." Or should we say, "merely human"? In Chapter 2 we discussed Milliken & Company's development of a revolutionary approach in dealing with its customers: a vast number of commonsense efforts aimed at "getting close to the customer" are being tested and refined. None of their programs is very exotic. Yet a senior—twenty years plus—Du Pont marketing executive, who was a guest at the annual top-management retreat in February 1984 when Milliken people presented those programs, got up spontaneously and said, "In all my years in so-called marketing jobs, I've never seen the likes of this." And all of it is just good common sense. Each device simply *humanizes* the relationship between the seller and the customer.

What Is a Customer?

A Customer is the most important person ever in this office . . . in person or by mail.

A Customer is not dependent on us . . . we are dependent on him.

A Customer is not an interruption of our work . . . he is the purpose of it. We are not doing a favor by serving him . . . he is doing us a favor by giving us the opportunity to do so.

A Customer is not someone to argue or match wits with. Nobody ever won an argument with a Customer.

A Customer is a person who brings us his wants. It is our job to handle them profitably to him and to ourselves.

(A poster that is prominently displayed all around L. L. Bean,
in Freeport, Maine)

In a perfect world, where robots would make the product and sell the product via computer network to other robots in the purchasing organization, none of this would be important. But we're a long way from that. In fact, we'll never reach it. Because any organization, the $45 billion IBM company or Stew Leonard's incredibly successful single store, is purely human, too. The perceptions of human beings are all there is. Let's come to grips with this—it's the essence of managing and marketing. And leading.

Glad He Asked!

Todd Fraser [not his real name] is in a mundane business: plumbing supplies. He has about forty locations in the Southwest. In the last couple of years he's added 50 percent to his revenues, in a no-growth market, and is able to charge premium prices—1 percent to 2 percent above his competitors, a remarkable edge in a very low margin game. How has he done it?

Several years ago Todd was determined to become the "best service company" in his business. To figure out what that meant, he asked his forty branch managers—a sensible enough idea, or so it seemed at the time. They told him: Offer more brand-name products, spruce up the looks of the branches, hire a higher-caliber (and more experienced) salesman, answer the phones more efficiently—*and lower the prices*. It sounded good. Todd did it all. And then waited. And waited. Nothing happened.

A couple of years later his frustration reached the boiling point. Then he got an idea that he now says is "so obvious it's impossible for me to think that I hadn't done it before," and proceeded to carry it out with all his energy. He simply visited his customers and asked them what they wanted, what was bugging them. He patiently devoted a full year to carefully visiting the "bad" as well as the "good" customers of every single branch.

Turns out the branch managers had been out of touch. Some had, literally, he found, not visited a single customer on the customer's own premises in up to five years! Here's what Todd heard: Price was *not* it. Even answering the phones was not it. The problem for the plumbers was the cost of the labor they wasted waiting for an order from Todd (or one of his competitors) to arrive. So Todd promised one-hour service, where the local industry standard was (then) one-half day. He promised a 90 percent "fulfillment factor" (i.e., he guaranteed that 90 percent of the parts ordered would be available instantly), where the standard was 75 percent, and that the remaining 10 percent would be delivered within a day—also far better than his competitors' average. (This last is key: a plumber might be held up several days, while paying his laborers, because of the absence of one little 75-degree bend in an otherwise complete 175-item order.) He promised a maximum wait of fifteen minutes for service fulfillment if the plumber came to the branch. Giant fifteen-minute timers were installed in every branch; if more than fifteen minutes elapsed, the order was filled free of charge. In sum: time is money for the plumber, who turns out not to be all that part-price-sensitive, after all.

The results are history. Todd Fraser did his customers the rare courtesy of "naïvely" asking them what they wanted. And they told him. And then he did something about it. His business was truly revolutionized as a result. Says Todd of the process: " 'Best service' doesn't mean a darned thing. It's best service *in the customer's terms* that counts. And I don't know for the life of me why it took so long to figure that out."

7

Quality Is Not a Technique

There is a central quality which is the root criterion of life and spirit in a man, a town, a building, or a wilderness. This quality is objective and precise, but it cannot be named.

Christopher Alexander,
The Timeless Way of Building

I was brought up by a father who was difficult to satisfy because he always felt something could be made or done better. He was never content with success. . . . It does take eyeball. I'm afraid as great as computers are, they cannot tell you about the quality of your product. The profitability, yes, but not the quality. The human eye, the human experience, is the one thing that can make quality better—or poorer.

Stanley Marcus, former chairman,
Neiman-Marcus

We sometimes think that the average American manager, post *Theory Z* and Phil Crosby's *Quality Is Free,* has a slot directly behind his or her right ear, and in it is a 3½-inch floppy diskette. Say the word "quality," and the manager, seemingly by rote, spits out: "Quality circles, statistical quality control, CAD/CAM/CAE, robotics . . ." And, yes, quality circles can be grand. Statistical quality control is invaluable. Automation is essential. Yet none of the three or a vast array of earlier devices—e.g., job enrichment—is what quality is all about.

This is a short chapter—perhaps surprisingly so. But in fact this entire book is about quality. Because quality, above all, is about *care, people, passion, consistency, eyeball contact* and *gut reaction.* Quality is not a technique, no matter how good.

Any device to maintain quality can be of value. But all devices are valuable only if managers—at *all* levels—are living the quality message, paying attention to quality, spending time on it as evidenced by their calendars. And if managers, at all levels, understand that no matter where the technology leads, quality comes from people (starting in the mail room) who care and are committed. Finally, quality comes from the belief that *anything* can be made better, that beauty is universally achievable—in the collection of garbage, in the services provided by Federal Express or UPS, in the raising of chickens and the making of potato chips, pizzas or French fries, in the design of a retail store or a piece of software or the bypass air intake mechanism of a jet engine. Quality involves living the message of the possibility of perfection and infinite improvement, living it day in and day out, decade by decade.

Ray Kroc once visited a Winnipeg franchise. It's reported that he found a single fly. The franchisee lost his McDonald's franchise two weeks later.

Frank Perdue invested a quarter of a million dollars in "the world's biggest blow dryer, powered by a 727 engine." The reason? Frank thinks the most obnoxious thing in the world is the eight hairs that stick up on a typical chicken wing when it is barbecued. With his new blow dryer, he is able to fluff up the hairs and burn most of them off before the chicken is delivered to the stores. But he is not finished. The new technique on average reduces the eight hairs to two. Frank doesn't think it is enough.

Williams-Sonoma is a very successful gourmet-cookware distributor. Its major business comes via catalog. Bringing in the world's best photographers to take the pictures, Williams-Sonoma puts exceptional efforts into development of the catalog. In 1983 the cover for the Christmas edition was to feature a piece of quiche in a new piece of cookware that Williams-Sonoma had imported. The shot cost tens of thousands of dollars and took a full day. Late in the evening, founder Chuck Williams came upon the scene, then being dismantled. He picked up a fork that was lying about and sampled the quiche that had been featured. The taste wasn't quite right. Without so much as a twinge, he threw out the photography. It wouldn't have occurred to him to have a Williams-Sonoma catalog cover featuring a piece of quiche that didn't *taste* right.

Story after story—from IBM, Hewlett-Packard, the Marriott Corporation, Disney, Mayor Schaefer of Baltimore, Milliken & Co., Stew Leonard's, Trammell Crow, Domino's Pizza, L. L. Bean, Delta Airlines, et al.—has the same theme as that from McDonald's, Perdue Farms and Williams-Sonoma: senior and middle managers alike who live the quality message with passion, persistence and, above all, consistency. Attention to quality can become the organization's mind-set only if *all* of its managers—indeed, all of its people—live it.

Living it means just that. You can't pay attention to it 80 percent of the time or even 95 percent of the time and let it lapse now and then. The only thing that will do is obsession. Tom Watson of IBM understood the connectedness of it all. One of the three principles in IBM's philosophy is excellence in execution in *all* we do. On paper, perhaps, inconsistencies can thrive. But not in sizable human organizations. You can't allow typos in internal memos and then turn around and demand perfection in client reports. There is no such thing as being perfectly conscientious part time.

"Unless I'm misinterpreting the signs, gentlemen, we are approaching the end of the golden age of shoddy merchandise."

Drawing by Weber; © 1983
The New Yorker Magazine, Inc.

The stories, apocryphal or not, that circulate in an organization reveal its devotion (or lack of it) to quality, and serve to inspire its people to live (or not to live) the quality message. Are the stories in your organization about spending $250,000 to cut the chicken-wing hair count? About making sure there isn't a single fly on a food preparation table? Or are they stories like this: "The old man's in favor of quality twelve weeks a quarter. The thirteenth week, though, it's 'Ship the product,' and send it to Australia if we can; the returns take longer"? Or, "Of course the old man's for quality. But he's for everything else, too. I mean, he's never said he's against quality. It's just that he doesn't make a distinction between quality, filling in the forms or [production] line speed"?

Strong Words on Quality Circles

Tom did an unconscionable thing. In early 1984 he was the lunchtime speaker in Logan, Utah, before an audience of seven hundred. Bill Mohr, a respected colleague from Hewlett-Packard, who, with his wife Harriet, had just published a superb book, *Quality Circles: Changing Images of People at Work* (Addison-Wesley, 1983), was presenting a seminar later that afternoon at the gathering. In front of the seven hundred, with microphone in hand, Tom said, "I notice Bill Mohr of Hewlett-Packard is giving a seminar on his book on quality circles. I think what he is doing borders on the *immoral.*" Strong word! He added, "Of course the darned quality circles work at Hewlett-Packard. Ever since Dave Packard and Bill Hewlett opened their fabled garage in 1937, they and their successors and colleagues have, above all, had a bone-deep belief in the ability of *everybody* in the organization to contribute creatively to the betterment of the quality of the products. Given that bedrock, getting HP's quality circles to work is like falling off a log." And then the conclusion: "I come from the so-called humanized/humanistic Silicon Valley. I'm here to tell you that in six out of seven companies that I visit in that valley, Mecca of twenty-first-century management, the average worker wouldn't attend his or her next quality circle meeting if it was the last day on earth. They see it for exactly what it is: another way for management to jerk labor's chain."

Bill and Harriet Mohr's book *is* superb. We heartily recommend it to all. At the same time, we are in dead earnest in our objection. The heart of quality is not technique. It is a commitment by management to its people and product—stretching over a period of decades and lived with persistence and passion—that is unknown in most organizations today.

Quality is about passion and pride. Sometime back Tom spent two days in a series of seminars with managers of a major retail chain. In the course of the meeting the subject of affordable levels of service came up continually. At one point Tom was well launched on a bit of a diatribe about the rotten level of service in retailing in general when an executive vice president, in front of forty of his peers and subordinates, got up and interrupted him: "Tom, sit down and calm down. Or get off our case. It's a changing and complex and highly competitive world. We are no worse than anybody else." We had our graphics people draw up a little logo that illustrated what this fellow was talking about (see page 676). It's a long way from there to L. L. Bean (see page 677)!

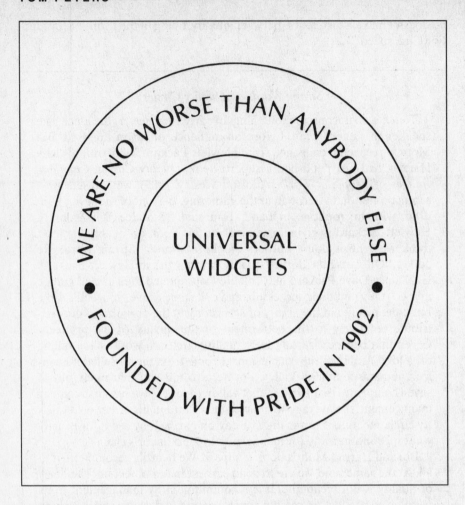

WE ARE NO WORSE THAN ANYBODY ELSE
FOUNDED WITH PRIDE IN 1902
UNIVERSAL WIDGETS

Quality is about people. We will not delve here into the messages discussed in the section called "People, People, People." It is enough to say at this juncture that quality is a function of commitment—from all hands—on the loading dock, at the receptionist's desk, in the design spaces. Without that commitment—and only human beings can give it—you will not get top quality.

W. Edwards Deming taught quality, as it's known today, to the Japanese. He is also thought of as the father of statistical quality control. The principal reason he believes it's important is that the techniques of statistical quality control lead to hugely increased self-inspection (control) by the people on the line. Deming believes, after all is said and done, that quality is primarily a function of human commitment. In a 1983 lecture to college-level business students at Utah State University, he said:

L.L.Bean®
Outdoor Sporting Specialties

THE GOLDEN RULE OF L.L.BEAN

"Sell good merchandise at a reasonable profit, treat your customers like human beings and they'll always come back for more." Leon Leonwood Bean started a company 72 years ago based on this simply stated business philosophy. We call it L.L.'s Golden Rule and today we still practice it.

Everything we sell is backed by an unconditional guarantee that never wears out. We do not want you to have anything from L. L. Bean that is not completely satisfactory. Return anything you buy from us at any time if it proves otherwise.

All of our products are regularly tested by us in the field, as well as in the lab. Each product continues to be made with the best materials, construction and design that we think are appropriate to the needs of our customers. They represent a solid value and deliver a fair return for the money.

The L. L. Bean Customer Service Department operates on L.L.'s belief that "A customer is the most important person ever in this office, in person or by mail." Telephone representatives are available 24 hours a day, 365 days a year for customer assistance and order taking. Your order is shipped promptly, accurately and **L. L. Bean pays all regular postage and handling charges.**

Send us the coupon below or call 207-865-3111 Ext. 39.

© 1984 L. L. Bean, Inc.

☐ **Send for a FREE Christmas 1984 Catalog**

Name_____

Address_____

City_____

State_____Zip_____

L. L. Bean, Inc., 169 Casco St., Freeport, ME 04033

Some of you are students of finance. You learn how to figure and how to run a company on figures. If you run a company on figures alone you will go under. How long will it take the company to go under, get drowned? I don't know, but it is sure to fail. Why? Because the most important figures are not there. Did you learn that in the school of finance? You will, 10 or 15 years from now, learn that the most important figures are those that are unknown or unknowable.

What about the multiplying effects of a happy customer, in either manufacturing or in service? Is he in your figures? What about the multiplying effect of an unhappy customer? Is that in your figures? Did you learn that in your school of finance? What about the multiplying effect of getting better material to use in production? What about the multiplying effect that you get all along the production line? Do you know that figure? You don't! If you run your company without it, you won't have a company. What about the multiplying effect of doing a better job along the line?

People all over the world think that it is the factory worker that causes problems. He is not your problem. Ever since there has been anything such as industry, the factory worker has known that quality is what will protect his job. He knows that poor quality in the hands of the customer will lose the market and cost him his job. He knows it and lives with that fear every day. Yet he cannot do a good job. He is not allowed to do it because the management wants figures, more product, and never mind the quality. They measure only in figures. The factory worker is forced to make defective products, forced to turn out defective items. He is forced to work with defective material, so no matter what they do, it will still be wrong. The worker can't do anything about it. He is totally helpless. If he tries to do something about it, he might as well talk to the wall. Nobody listens.

I can take you to spots, an entire factory with 2,000 people, where conditions have been cleaned up by the management. All the factory workers there are proud of their work. They are turning out almost no defective material. These are happy people. Happy doing a good job.

A dean of a school of business wrote to me to complain that I was a little rough in a speech that I gave to 2,400 purchasing managers in New Orleans. It was a meeting of the International Benevolent Protective Order of Purchasing Managers. They could hear what I was saying. The acoustics were good in the auditorium. There was just one difference between me and the dean. I get around to see what materials come in; he does not. Teamwork is needed between the purchasing department and production and sales. They won't get it, though, because the mandate handed down from management to the purchasing department is to get the lowest price. Top management has to learn something about the entire company. They can no longer play solos or be prima donnas. There has to be teamwork, but the annual system of rating destroys teamwork.

How could someone in purchasing get a good rating for paying a higher price? Even if it saves 10 times as much in production, you do not get a good rating by paying a higher price.

The foreman better not stop the line. He'll hurt production if he does, and he may not be here tomorrow. Fear governs almost everybody. Only perhaps one in 200 are not governed by fear. A millwright, feeling a bearing, informed the foreman that it was getting warm. He suggested that they stop and take care of it before the bearing froze up and scored the shaft. If that happened, they would be down for sure. The foreman knew that the proper thing for the company to do was to stop and work on the bearing. His answer was, "We can't stop now, we must get these castings out today." He didn't make it. The bearing froze and scored the shaft. The line was down four days, but the foreman did his job.

So quality is an all-hands-on proposition. Period.

Let us conclude where we began—with a return to Stanley Marcus's comment on the role of the schooled human eyeball in producing superior quality. In a word, we observe that a disproportionate share of the most effective leaders/managers we've met who have induced a pervasive sense of quality throughout their organizations develop that sense by growing up around the product. They have great gut feel, are tinkerers, tweekers. IBM lives customer service—quality of customer service—with a passion. As one graduate of their eighteen-month sales boot camp put it, "The word 'customer' was heard so frequently that you soon began to dream about them." 3M, too, lives customers and quality. Virtually everyone in 3M's senior ranks grew up with extensive tours in the factory and selling the product. Gerhard Neumann, GE's aircraft engine entrepreneur, was a miracle worker when it comes to quality, service, and speedy design and implementation. His background includes a two-year "dirty nails" stint as a master mechanic's apprentice in Germany. Neumann attributes a great deal of his subsequent success to superior feel developed during that apprenticeship. Ed Carlson turned around United Airlines after moving from the presidency of Westin Hotels to the airline (UAL owns Westin). We attribute a lot of Carlson's success, which focused on cleaning up the bureaucracy and returning to the basics of service and delivery, to the way he got his start: as a bellhop. Dave Thomas has performed miracles in creating the Wendy's organization and making it grow. His formal schooling is limited, and he began his career as a busboy. He says he learned as a busboy that there is no limit to the quality that can be produced in the "meanest" job. Marcus Sieff, chairman of Marks & Spencer, calls himself "a simple third-generation shopkeeper." In sum, it's hard to imagine an organization with a truly exceptional record of quality where a large share of the senior team did not grow up around the product.

(As usual, we must go briefly on the defensive and state that we do not consider such reliance on "the eyeball" to be "soft." One more time: We think the concepts of "soft" and "hard" have gotten badly fouled up. Most seem to believe the "eyeball" is "soft," and that computer output is "hard." Both can be soft, both can be hard. But if our life depended on it, and we had to cast a vote on the "hardness" of Dave Thomas's [Wendy's] "eye" for quality versus ten pounds of MBA-and-electronic-spreadsheet-produced analysis, Thomas would get the nod, no doubt about it.)

So what do you do if you haven't sold or designed or made or serviced the product or delivered the service? Our advice is at once very pragmatic and very abstract. The pragmatic: Get back in touch. MBWA, period. And lots of it. Start now, whether you're chairman or accounting supervisor or assistant sanitation department head in a town of 19,000. The abstract part? Learn, if you can, to trust your gut, to respect passion and enthusiasm and pride. What do you *feel* for your product(s) or service(s)? (And this is as valid a question for an MIS department supervisor as for a Fortune 100 CEO.) There's no winning, no hope of constant improvement, for you or your people, unless there is involvement. You must love (or learn to love) what you do, or else excellence remains an elusive target. Loving what you do or produce is not the exclusive domain of Silicon Valley computer designers, Bloomingdale's buyers or Carnegie Hall harpsichord soloists. During a stay at the Hotel Del Coronado near San Diego, the front entrance was being repaired. We interrupted (rudely to others involved, we're afraid) a busy schedule to spend twenty-five minutes watching a bricklayer at work—because he was an artist, with an artist's passion, and because the quality of his product reflected that.

So measure it, by all means. Reward it. Celebrate it. That love will be readily transmitted. So, sadly, will its absence—even more readily. There is no other route.

8

The "Smell" of
the Customer

"Smell": not "market orientation," but *living* for one's customers. How do you know you're moving in that direction? Or when you've arrived? We have sorted out twenty-two aspects of a true customers-first orientation.* Almost all are missing from most management and even marketing texts. The list is not meant to be exhaustive. It is simply intended to spur you to ask "Why not?" time and again. Indeed, why not? None is exotic. Each is merely sensible.

1. Company bulletins, annual reports and all other forms of printed matter feature stories about working with customers. In particular, joint company/customer problem-solving activities mark all printed material. Customer contact by "noncustomer" functions—R&D, manufacturing, personnel, accounting, MIS—is stressed. Stories about customers, by actual count, occur far more often than any other type. Special bulletins dealing exclusively with customer service exist, from all parts of the company, and are issued regularly (i.e., at least *weekly*). Individual facilities (e.g., each store, each distribution center) are encouraged to develop regular customer bulletins.

2. In a host of ways, unique respect for *sales*people is demonstrated. A disproportionate share of salespeople are promoted to general management. Celebrations for salespeople are special and taken very seriously (e.g., they are *lavish* and attended by almost all of general management). When the salesperson talks, the engineer, manufacturer or MIS person jumps—i.e., failure to "overrespond" to a simple request from sales is a mortal sin. (This is rare, surprisingly. Yet it is arguably the key to the success of the top companies—from Frito-Lay to P&G, from Domino's Pizza to IBM.) Salespeople fill, even dominate, the top executive ranks (a minimum of 50 percent of, say, the top 50 managers have spent a substantial share of their career in sales). Early in their career, young men and women on the move clamor for an

---

*No one company we know, not even IBM or Marriott, lives all twenty-two with equal intensity. Thus the package of traits form an idealized portrait, though each has been derived from empirical observation.

opportunity to be in sales. The company's "hall of fame"—ten past heroes about whom stories are most frequently related—consists principally of salespersons (or perhaps marketers).

3. Customer support people are showered with attention. "Excessive" training is aimed at receptionists, people who answer the 800 toll-free call-in number, the "minor actors" in the service delivery effort (e.g., dispatchers, people on the loading dock). Major celebrations for these people are common, with awards focusing directly on tiny acts of meritorious service to customers. (This is in marked contrast to the normal "technical" focus on manufacturing or engineering/buying/lending in other institutions. In such institutions, the supporting cast tends to be given short shrift.)

4. The importance of the customer pervades every function of the organization. The customer is "alive," through displays of letters (good and bad), film clips and visits, and what-have-you in MIS, accounting, personnel and legal, as well as in the main-line and direct customer support functions. Moreover, the indirect support function members (e.g., in MIS, personnel, accounting) are *required* (not just encouraged) to go out on sales and service calls, serve on joint company/customer problem-solving teams and otherwise engage in *regular,* results-oriented customer activities.

5. There is a special (and friendly/respectful) language associated with customers (à la "Guest" at Disney, "customer" rather than "passenger" or "pax" at People Express). In particular, contemptuous language is simply not permitted.

6. Reviews and reports of all kinds have a disproportionate share of their content aimed at customers and revenue-enhancement activities. Almost every report (manufacturing, MIS, etc.) *begins* with an analysis of the direct impact of any proposed action on the customer. The absence of such a clear tie is an almost sure knockout factor.

7. Visits with customers are exchanged regularly, at *all* levels in the company and customer organization. Customers are invited in to visit all facilities, especially plants or back-room operations. Manufacturers, MIS people, et al. are out visiting customers with some degree of regularity. Customers are invited to many company meetings (both celebrations and policy meetings) and are vigorously encouraged to present their views. Almost no facility is off limits to customers. Factories are open at all times for their visits, which are actively encouraged *and* subsidized (for all levels—i.e., shop floor as well as executive—and functions of the customer operation).

8. Hallway discussions, celebration of heroes—minor and major—overwhelmingly (again, by actual count) focus on support for the customer. Moreover, the customer support stories are invariably *personalized.* They are about particular people and circumstances. That is, the customer is treated as a unique person, *not* as a statistical abstraction.

9. Devices abound for customer listening. Surveys (of customers and our people's views of our customer support skills) are conducted regularly—i.e., at least monthly. Specific training in "naïve" customer *listening* is provided to

R&D people, engineers, manufacturers, accountants (as well as sales and service people). Numerous formal and informal customer feedback devices exist, are used, and are paid attention to. "Iron laws" about time-to-respond (e.g., eight to forty-eight hours) to customer requests and information from customers' feedback surveys are religiously enforced; the response "system" is intrusively overseen by top management.

10. Devices exist to ensure that connections are made (and then acted upon) between sales and engineering and manufacturing. That is, suggestions collected by salespersons from customers are viewed not as "merely the natural tendency of salespersons to snap to attention in response to every customer's whim," but as the tangible rewards of *listening*.

11. Customer satisfaction is measured frequently—monthly at least, and perhaps as often as weekly. Sampling is extensive. Surveys are quantitative as well as qualitative (i.e., response time *and* feelings count equally); the measures are taken very, very seriously. They are reviewed unfailingly by top management: the development of such measures is taken as seriously as the development of budgetary measures or product-reliability measures. Evaluation of people in all functions at all levels is significantly affected by the satisfaction measures. Special, intense "customer satisfaction reviews" are regularly layered on top of the regular evaluation procedures.

12. "Overkill" complaint response mechanisms are firmly locked in place. Unfailingly, they include an "excessive" (as viewed by the rest of the industry's standards) focus on immediacy and personalization of the response. Foulups with big or small customers are not tolerated; even minor glitches are brought swiftly to the attention of top management. Top management, in turn, gets directly involved both with the customer and with correcting what went on. There's a well-documented feeling throughout the company that *anything* untoward that happens to a customer is "somehow" known in the executive suite within minutes (or sooner).

13. Promises to customers are kept, period, regardless of cost in overtime. Achievable delivery dates are set to begin with, and then met. Missing a promised date, no matter how small the customer or order, is the subject of intense top-management scrutiny and severe sanctions. (Every one of our better performers agrees that setting unrealistic delivery times is madness, even if it costs the company a particular job—or even several—to a competitor who promises the moon. Over the long haul, customers respect, above almost all other vendor traits, the ability to keep promises.)

14. The calendars of executives at all levels and in all functions reflect their insistent focus on customers. Visits to customers and time spent with them never run less than 30 percent for senior line management, and not less than 10 percent for indirect function management—accountants, manufacturers, MIS people.

15. Quality and reliability of product and service is an obsession throughout the organization, reflecting virtually the same intensity as that directed to the customer per se. Stories of tiny quality improvements and celebrations of

those who brought them about are abundant. The product or the service-in-use is prominently and "excessively" displayed. Almost all in the company use the product themselves, if possible. Samples are always around for all to see (and use, if possible). An array of T-shirts and caps featuring the product or service, especially a new or enhanced product when it's launched, is in evidence—in *every* corner of the organization.

16. Every element of the organization actively looks for ways that it can specifically contribute to differentiating the product or service. Even ideas that add only minuscule improvement in performance (especially as it's *perceived* by the customer) are the subject of endless reviews, bragging sessions, awards and ceremonies in accounting and personnel, as well as in sales, service, marketing and manufacturing.

17. Manufacturers (or operations people in service companies) are deeply involved in customer activities, especially selling (*directly*) and joint problem-solving teams.

18. The customer's *perception* is what's viewed as most important, rather than a so-called hard-nosed view of reality. We remember well a letter from an executive in a company focusing entirely on manufacturing. Tom had described the IBM approach to disputes with customers, and a respondent was dumbfounded. "You *really* mean that when you're *right* and the customer is way off base you will nonetheless respond to the customer's view—even when it costs you a substantial amount of money?" The very idea that there *is* such a thing as "right," "factual" and "real" is the number one problem we encounter in the technically or financially driven company.

19. There is an explicit philosophy statement, part of or an adjunct to the corporate philosophy statement, that deals with "the way we perceive and treat customers." It is widely distributed and constantly (and explicitly) reinforced in almost every setting, from the Fourth of July picnic to the annual performance review.

20. Executives (and managers at all levels) from *all* functions regularly spend time *performing* all primary customer-support tasks—e.g., working on the loading dock, at the dispatch center, in the spares department, at the distribution center. About a week a quarter is a minimum. At least one visit is in depth—e.g., at least two full days performing the task, for a full shift.

21. Executives in all functions keep track of and manage the bureaucratic (e.g., paperwork) load that gets in the way of customer-contact time for all customer-related functions—e.g., reception, sales, field service, dispatch. "Time in front of (or in direct support of) the customer" is guarded and tracked jealously/measured religiously.

22. The number one "it" is a *passion* for *tiny* customer-related improvements in every department. Accounting people are hell-bent on improving ease of billing. MIS people are determined to improve customer-related information. There is an obsession in every department, in every nook and cranny, to do things just a tiny bit better.

So these are the characteristics we find in companies that truly "smell of the customer." Above all, when we observe these traits in action, we notice that they are lived with intensity, as a matter of reflex. Many, if not most, companies devote some time and attention to developing many of them; the truly distinctive customer service companies are obsessive in pursuit of the least of them. The discourtesy of a single receptionist in Podunk, even in a 150,000-person operation, is cause for top-to-bottom alarm, discussion and decisive action. (Usually such ameliorative action is *not* the disciplining of the receptionist but the disciplining of management—two, three or even four levels above her or him—plus the design of corrective programs aimed at cutting off at the pass an incipient system-wide problem.)

Does your company/organization smell of the customers?

Redefinition of the Mundane

Remember Todd Fraser, who learned that price is less important than 100 percent order-fulfillment in the plumbing supply business? He redefined his highly competitive, low-margin industry in a two-state area. One thousand tiny things vault Stew Leonard (dairy products), Tom Monaghan (pizzas), Carl Sewell (Cadillacs) and Jan Carlzon (airline seats) to the very top of highly competitive, previously-deemed-commodity heaps. Each has won big where it couldn't be done—in theory—by redefining what can be done for the customer.

None is a lavish spender. You can't be if your game is plumbing supplies or dairy products. Each has applied imagination (better yet, the imagination of all his people) to serving the customer better—more personally (via service and product tailoring), with better quality—and each has created virtually a new industry (or a new definition of an old industry). The great mayors (à la Schaefer of Baltimore) and educators (à la Sybil Mobley at Florida A&M—see page 987) have done the same. Each has proven that the customer *can* be served in today's highly automated world where impersonalness has been the all too frequent norm.

We have tried, along the way, to share a little of our emotion. A visit to Stew Leonard's, Perdue Farms or Sewell Village Cadillac redefines forever what *is* possible in a striking and dramatic fashion. We'd conclude by urging every reader to begin his or her own forays to observe superior quality and customer service. Thinly Disguised Contempt is found everywhere. But so, although more rarely, are florists, restaurants, barbershops, machine tool companies that can show us what can be done, and done profitably. We urge you: Become an expert, don't delay. (And then reread this section!)

SOME (MORE) GOOD READING ON CUSTOMERS

There is, of course, lots written on marketing. As one would expect from our discussion, there is little written on our point of focus—customers. Nonetheless, two recent jargon-free books stand out at the top of our "must read" list in support of the points in this section. The first is David Ogilvy's *Ogilvy on Advertising* (Crown, 1984). Ogilvy writes delightfully on the whole issue of bringing products to the marketplace and selling them; on the subject of product differentiation and maintaining client relationships, there is no better work than Ted Levitt's book, from which we extracted heavily, *The Marketing Imagination* (Free Press, 1983).

Robert Shook's *Ten Greatest Sales Persons* (Harper & Row, 1978) at first looks like another garden-variety "how to" book. It's not. Shook writes well and provides biographies and long interviews with Joe Girard, the world's greatest car salesman; Buck Rodgers, former head of marketing at IBM; Shelby Carter, former head of Xerox sales (and a former IBMer as well); Edna Larson, the world's top Avon salesperson; and so on. The message—"Serve the customer" and "The sale doesn't begin until after the sale"—comes through loud and clear, and we often use the book in our seminars.

Mere perception: nowhere else is it dealt with so beautifully as in Fredonia Jacques's *Verdict Pending: A Patient Representative's Intervention* (Capistrano Press, 1983). The odyssey of a hospital patient representative, it has implications far beyond the health care setting. It is about professional human beings dealing with "customers" (patients, in this case); the stories of unimagined "minor" slights that leave irreparable memories are staggering.

We recommend no texts on quality as such; our subject, after all, is not quality per se but its relationship to leadership. Quality itself will always be in the eye of the beholder. Thus the most constructive book on the topic for both of us continues to be Robert Pirsig's *Zen and the Art of Motorcycle Maintenance* (Morrow, 1974). A much more practical look comes from Stanley Marcus (chairman emeritus of Neiman Marcus) in his *Quest for the Best* (Viking, 1979).

3

INNOVATION

The project reminded me of the Flying Tigers in China ... under-manned, overworked, and successful.

> *Gerhard Neumann, on the development of the successful GE Variable Stator Experimental Engine*

The best leaders are apt to be found among those executives who have a strong component of unorthodoxy in their character. Instead of resisting innovation, they symbolize it.

> *David Ogilvy, Ogilvy on Advertising*

The reasonable man adapts himself to the world: the unreasonable one persists in trying to adapt the world to himself. Therefore all progress depends on the unreasonable man.

> *George Bernard Shaw*

Innovating regularly, at all levels, in all functions, is the second basis for sustainable strategic advantage. Our story here is analogous to that of the preceding section, on customers; namely, that traditional management thinking misses the point. For the most part, management writing, and typical discussions even among practicing managers, focus on structures, monetary incentives and planning techniques (e.g., technology forecasting). Our observations—from Stew Leonard's to Trammell Crow to 3M—suggest the emphasis is badly misplaced.

The most significant issues are, again, those concerning "smell" ("smell" of innovation, this time). Is inaction tolerated or not? That is, what's the most commonly asked question in your bank/school/public works department/retail operation? Is it "Why don't you form a task force to look into this?" or is it "So what have you gotten done in the last twenty-four hours?" Are skunks (champions) and skunkworks encouraged or suppressed (in a host of almost always subtle ways)?

The real world of innovating is serendipitous and passion-filled, whether the object is a new banking service or a pharmaceutical miracle derived from basic chemistry. "Managing" it involves MBWA—paying attention to innovation, talking it up, wandering the design spaces, and celebrating the emergence (and even some of the failures) of champions—in a ten-person accounting department or a sluggish $10 billion science-driven company.

So—we beg you to sit back and kick up your feet on the table before delving into this section. The customer section may well have elicited an "Ah, ha, common sense." This will be a tougher take. "Restrain the oddballs [i.e., would-be champions]" has been conventional wisdom for so long that it may be tough to come to grips with the central message here: Champions/skunks, and skunkworks are a must, not a luxury, if constant innovation is truly sought.

9

The Mythology of Innovation, or a Skunkworks Tale

Post-It Note Pads have become a staple in the American office—and a $200 million winner for 3M. The notion originated with Art Fry, a 3M employee who sang in a choir; the bits of paper he used to mark the hymns kept falling out of the books, and he yearned for an adhesive-backed paper that would stick as long as necessary but would leave no trace when removed. From the labs of 3M, the home of Scotch tape, a prototype soon became available. "Great success story," you say? Not quite yet. Major office-supply distributors thought it was silly. Market surveys were negative. But 3M executives and secretaries got hooked, once they actually *used* the little notes. The eventual breakthrough: a mailing of samples to the secretaries of the CEO's of the Fortune 500 under the letterhead of the secretary of the chairman of 3M, Lew Lehr. The time lapse between the germ of the idea and its commercial fruition? Almost a *dozen* years.

The above anecdote would amount to little more than just a charming story were it not similar to stories from Citicorp and Bell Labs, from companies making jet engines or computers, from surgicenters and accounting firms. The course of innovation—from the generation of the idea through prototype development and contact with the initial user to breakthrough and then to final market—is highly uncertain. Moreover, it is *always* messy, unpredictable, and very much affected by the determined ("irrational"?) champions, and that is the important point. It's important, because we must learn to design organizations—those that are public as well as private, banks as well as software developers—that take into account, explicitly, the irreducible sloppiness of the process and take advantage of it, rather than systems and organizations that attempt to fight it.

Unfortunately, most innovation management practice appears to be predicated on the implicit assumption that we can beat the sloppiness out of the

Portions of this chapter were published under this title in the *Stanford Magazine*.

process if only we can make the plans tidier and the teams better organized. Experiments and skunkworks, the zeal of champions, the power gained from exploiting the innovative user (customer) as partner are thought of as fit only for those who aren't smart enough to think far enough ahead and plan wisely enough. As a friend at General Electric says, "When you go through this inordinately messy, sloppy, fouled-up, mucked-up seven-year process of bringing a new product to market, you say to yourself at the end, 'Any idiot could have done it better than that! Let's get organized for the next round.' And in that single phrase, 'Let's get organized for the next round,' lie the seeds of subsequent disaster."

We propose the following (see the chart on the facing page): It *is* a messy world. We hope to demonstrate that. *If* it is a messy world, the *only* way to proceed is by *constant experimentation:* "Don't just stand there, *do* something." *If* constant experimentation is the *only* antidote to a messy world, then we need experimenters—or champions (skunks). And if we need champions, we must realize that the most effective environment for champions is almost always an abundance of *skunkworks,* those small off-line bands of mavericks that are the hallmark of innovative organizations. Finally, and this is the $64,000 issue: *if* the messy-world-experiment-champion-skunkwork paradigm makes sense, then we need to *create a climate* that induces all the above to occur—a climate that nurtures and makes heroes of experimenters and champions.

▶ Datapoint executives insist that a farmer in Arkansas, running an outfit called Chicken Pride, constructed the software that was crucial in the early development of their intelligent terminal business. He reprogrammed some primitive software cassettes and called in seeking additional advice: "What do I do next?" Datapoint engineers were dumbfounded by what he had done already.

▶ More Datapoint, from founder Victor Poor: "There have been surprises, particularly in the way customers apply our products. They use them in ways we never expected when we designed them. The 2200 programmer terminal device, for instance, would emulate any number of terminals. The customers paid no attention to that and started using it in stand-alone computing operations. . . . Very few companies will admit that this is the way products get developed—really. They always tell you their product was planned."

▶ The "technical specs" for a major new Hewlett-Packard test instrument consisted of a picture of an old instrument cut out of an HP catalog, with a hand-drawn sketch stapled to it. The division general manager's response to his engineer's primitive approach: "Do it."

▶ With United Technologies, General Electric, Westinghouse and IBM in the fray, the first "intelligent mobile robot" nonetheless comes from a company that is hardly a household name, Denning Systems, Inc., of Washington, D.C.—the classic "three persons in a garage" operation.

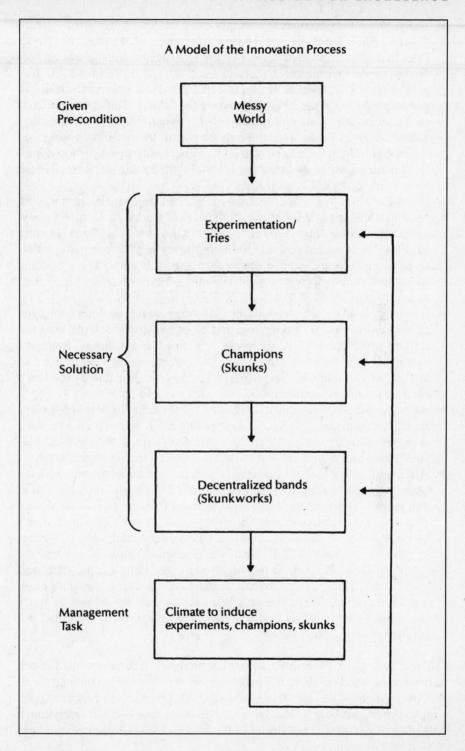

A Model of the Innovation Process

Given
Pre-condition — Messy World

Necessary
Solution — Experimentation/Tries → Champions (Skunks) → Decentralized bands (Skunkworks)

Management
Task — Climate to induce experiments, champions, skunks

▶ The *Nobel Duel* describes the twenty-one-year-long bitterly fought race between Andrew Schally and Roger Guillemin that led to the 1977 Nobel Prize in medicine (divided between them) for the discovery of a brain hormone release mechanism. Others in the field had retired from the fray years before (the mechanism had been fully described, theoretically, in papers published in the 1940's), declaring the Schally-Guillemin race to be an "intellectually barren exercise." Thus, Schally and Guillemin, says author Nicholas Wade, were the only ones with the tenacity to "grind up the millions of pig brains and sheep brains necessary to get the job done." Both prize holders admit that their work involved neither an intellectual nor a methodological breakthrough.

▶ From Ed Finkelstein, architect of Macy's entrepreneurial turnaround: "Some people get worried about duplication of stocks, duplication of buyers. We don't worry about either." And from the *New York Times* (January 17, 1984), in an article on Finkelstein and Macy's: "[The company] insists on having no research staff, no strategic planners. It simply keeps building up its 'well rounded, entrepreneurially minded executives,' as Mr. Finkelstein puts it."

▶ Commodore's Jack Tramiel built the first Vic personal computer prototype in *ninety days*. Adam Osborn, angered by others' fluffy designs, built the Osborn prototype in just *four weeks*. A senior GE gas turbine executive notes that the breakthrough on a major current product came from an intense *sixty-day* small-team effort—after the team was told by the unit's product planning committee that their idea was a loser.

▶ After several embarrassing public failures of the complex, state-of-the-art, liquid-fuel Vanguard, NASA (in a desperate effort to catch up with Russia's Sputnik), turned to Wernher von Braun's much simpler "off-the-shelf" solid fuel military rockets. Success followed almost immediately.

▶ After twenty-five years of studying American industrial innovation, Brian Quinn of Dartmouth's Tuck School said of IBM: "It was difficult to find any successful major innovation that derived from formal product planning rather than the championship process." After years of using Quinn's line with hundreds of audiences, we've heard a demurring voice only once. It came from a senior AT&T executive: "Nonsense. I *know* it's not true for the [Bell] Labs." He pointed to a highly respected Labs vice president and said, "You tell him." The Labs man scratched his chin for ten seconds or so, and then replied, "Well, I've only been at the Labs for a bit over thirty years, but I can't *think* of anything that ever came directly from the new product planning process."

Breakthrough. Optimization. Systems analysis. Technology plan. Such terms are part and parcel of the usual approach to innovation management. Yet from GE, IBM and HP, from Citibank and Mervyn's, from Macy's, Apple, and Raychem, we hear instead about persistence (passion and obsession!), lots of tries, perverse and unusual users, five- to twenty-five-person skunkworks sequestered in dingy warehouses for ninety days, plans gone awry, inventions from the wrong industry at the wrong time for the wrong reason, specs for complex systems on the backs of envelopes. Innovation, it seems, in areas ranging from pure science to the industrial organization, from health care to accounting, just doesn't occur the way it's supposed to. Time and again we roll out the Manhattan Project to illustrate that the concerted effort, well planned, is the only one that wins the day. But it is the Manhattan Project that turns out to be the anomaly.* The computer or financial service prototype—or locomotive(!)—in the garage turns out to be closer to the norm. What's up?

Here we will explore ten popular myths (five "major myths," five "sub-myths") about innovation management. Our case will not be balanced or unbiased. (We've yet to meet an unbiased analyst.) Our objective is to give credence to the sloppy side of innovation, lest the powerful images of the Manhattan Project or the "well-organized" MITI (Ministry of International Trade and Industry)† lead us to fall prey to the myths of rational innovation planning. (Such myths have already damaged many companies, including such stalwarts as GM, U.S. Steel, GE, Xerox, Bell Labs/Western Electric, Sylvania, Westinghouse, RCA, Singer, Texas Instruments.)

We hope we will persuade you to allow for the inherent sloppiness of innovation—indeed, *to take advantage of it.* And if we don't, we do hope you'll at least occasionally scratch your chin and think, They may have a point. The myths we'll examine are these:

1. Myth: Substantial strategic/technological planning greatly increases the odds of a "no surprises" outcome.

Counterpoint: Though you must be thoughtful in order to be in roughly the right arena, **innovation in business (and nonbusiness) is highly unpredictable,** and the context and configuration must be predicated on uncertainty and ambiguity.

2. Myth: Complete technical specs and a thoroughly researched market plan are invariant first steps to success.

Counterpoint: You must move as rapidly as possible to real tests of real products (albeit incomplete) with real customers. That is, you must **experiment** and learn your way toward perfection/completion.

---

*And even that's not clear. Upon publication of some of the material that appears in this chapter, we received several lengthy notes from participants arguing that the Manhattan Project was a classic form of what we were describing: multiple competing groups, crazy champions, skunkworks within larger systems, etc.

†This image, too, is under attack, as in David R. Henderson's "The Myth of MITI," *Fortune,* August 8, 1983. More practically, our friend Ken Ohmae, managing director of McKinsey's Japanese offices, states, "The Japanese [company] winners look more like survivors of a demolition derby than meticulous strategic planners."

3. Myth: Time for reflection and thought built into the development process are essential to creative results.

Counterpoint: "Winners"—e.g., successful **champions/skunks**—are, above all, pragmatic non-blue-sky dreamers who live by one dictum: "Try it, now."

4. Myth: Big teams are necessary to blitz a project rapidly, especially a complex one.

Counterpoint: Small teams—e.g., **skunkworks**—can be many times more efficient than large ones, and can often accomplish the lion's share of even the most complex tasks in a fraction of the time that a large team takes.

4a. Related myth: Strong centralized functions (and, consequently, functional organizations) are imperative if the would-be innovators (from R&D, engineering, merchandising) are to get a fair hearing.

Counterpoint: Commercially viable innovation, though not as orderly, is more likely to occur in radically decentralized organizations. **Smashing engineering, manufacturing and marketing functions together** in outcome-oriented, small-scale groups overcomes the most important source of delays in innovation.

4b. Related Myth: Big projects are inherently different from small projects—or, an airplane is not a calculator.

Counterpoint: Some projects are indeed much bigger than others. Yet the most successful big-project management comes from a **small within big** mindset, in which purposeful "suboptimization" is encouraged.

4c. Related Myth: Product line/product family (and interproduct line) compatibility is the key to economic success.

Counterpoint: Compatibility is vital, but **gaining the last 2 percent in compatibility often costs you the market.**

4d. Related Myth: To win big you must strive to optimize.

Counterpoint: Optimization always wins on paper, and **loses in the real world.**

5. Myth: Customers only tell you about yesterday's needs.

Counterpoint: While "average" customers may reflect yesterday, **lead users**—i.e., forward-looking customers—are usually years ahead of the rest, and are the best source of leading-edge innovation.

5a. Related Myth: Technology push is the cornerstone of business (and presumably American economic) success.

Counterpoint: The "marketing push"—"phony-demand generation," as some see it—versus "technology push" argument has been overplayed. **Lis-**

tening to the market is the winning approach, but it need not mean forgoing sophistication in design.

Myth No. 1: Solid Plans Mean "No Surprises"
Counterpoint: Learn to Live with Uncertainty and Ambiguity

These days attacks on strategic planning are in vogue. It's been too rigid, too bureaucratic, "everyone" says. Let's at least decentralize it, "everyone" agrees. General Electric and Westinghouse, early pioneers, are doing just that. A few have suggested maybe we should even get rid of it. But wait— even as we do it, do we really mean it? The new "in" terms are "innovation" and "production." Now "manufacturing strategy" and "innovation strategy" are proffered as *substitutes* for (additions to?) strategic planning. But wait, again—we're *in favor of* strategic planning, strongly so, but we're not so sure about "innovation strategy." Before industry heads off down this new trail in search of a cookbook panacea, let's at least look at the record of new product and service forecasting. It's hardly spotless.

Anecdotal evidence awaits us by the bucketful. "*We do not consider that the aeroplane will be of any use for war purposes,*" said the British Secretary of War in 1910. The United States lost most of its aircraft early in World War II because we perceived the threat from ground-based saboteurs to be greater than that from heretofore unused sea-launched aircraft (even though we knew full well that the Japanese had carriers), and bunched our planes on the ground accordingly. The French invested billions of dollars (in 1930's money) on the Maginot Line, which was flanked in a matter of hours by the flexible German tank strategy, as the young Charles de Gaulle had predicted.

Go back and look at the first projections for sales of the mainframe computer, developed in the late 1940's. The market was estimated to be a dozen (!): a handful each to the Census Bureau, Bell Labs, Lawrence Livermore Labs. Similar early studies of xerography suggested that a maximum of one thousand machines might be placed. Ironically, these thousand machines were to take on the high-end offset printing market; over twenty years later, Xerox and its competitors still have not decisively beaten that market. (We will accept, tongue in cheek, one variety of success in forecasting: Two wrongs can occasionally make a right. When Xerox introduced the big 9200 machine, it predicted first-year lease placement of about 70,000 units. Scores of market researchers took years to develop the estimate. The actual first-year placements were about 7,000, an error by anyone's standard! However, there's a saving grace: the damnable, idiosyncratic *users* made twice as many copies on the 7,000 as had been estimated to come from the full 70,000.)

What do such anecdotes prove? A little, but not much. You can doubtless match them with your own collection to prove the positive value of forecasting. Ours versus yours. Good laughs. But there's more, lots more.

A Systematic Study

As is often the case, where there's smoke, there's fire. A half-dozen or so thoughtful studies of the process of invention all add up to the same story: the lion's share of invention comes from the "wrong person" in the "wrong place" in the "wrong industry" at the "wrong time," in conjunction with the "wrong user." Perhaps the most systematic analysis is *The Sources of Invention* by John Jewkes and colleagues. At the heart of it are extensive case studies of fifty-eight major inventions, a sample systematically chosen from twentieth-century Europe and America. The fifty-eight range from ballpoint pens and self-winding wristwatches to penicillin, the continuous casting of steel and the digital computer. Jewkes's evidence suggests that at least *forty-six of the fifty-eight* occurred in "the wrong place": they were invented by an individual not in any company, by a very small company, by an individual in an "outgroup" in a large company, or by a large company in the "wrong industry."

Typical among the forty-six is Kodachrome, invented by two musicians. A watchmaker fooling around with brass casting came up with the process for the continuous casting of steel. Dye-making chemists developed synthetic detergents—after soap-making chemists turned the project down as uninteresting. The manufacturers of reciprocating aircraft engines thought the jet engine was useless; the individuals who developed it were finally able to peddle it not, as they "should have," to *engine* makers but to air*frame* makers. The diesel engine was developed solely to haul cars within railyards; all the experts agreed it would *never* be capable of pulling trains long distances.

One of our favorite stories, rather typical of invention in the wrong place, involves the venerable Alfred P. Sloan of General Motors. GM, early in their history, had developed two important new chemical components: freon, the refrigeration agent, and tetraethyl lead, the substance that reduces engine knock. During the 1920s the same researchers wanted to investigate synthetic rubber. Because the inventions had come from the General Motors labs and not one of the expected chemical companies, Du Pont's president wrote to GM, skeptical about their new interest. John Jewkes, et al., who tell this tale in *The Sources of Invention,* quotes the correspondence:

[GM and Du Pont at the time had substantial joint ownership]: "I wonder if it is a wise expenditure of money on the part of GM to go into synthetic rubber investigation. A great deal of work has been done on this
subject by very competent people and well-organized research groups. I
understand that the GM chemical department is neither well-organized
for this purpose nor is the personnel such as would likely prove successful. The same line of thought has so far kept Du Pont from a general
investigation of the subject, and we think that Du Pont is better
equipped for this purpose than General Motors." Mr. Sloan replied as
follows: "You say that General Motors Chemical Department is neither
well organized nor is its personnel such as is likely to prove successful.

This statement may be right or it may be wrong. Frankly, I do not know which it is, but I think that if I had told you six or seven years ago that General Motors Research was working on some chemical scheme whereby we could inject some quantities of some unknown material into gasoline to enable us to increase the compression and produce a fuel of antiknock qualities, you would have said exactly the same thing and would have thought that we were very foolish in mixing up with something that was purely of a chemical or fuel character and had nothing to do with the primary manufacture of motor cars. Then after we had discovered the material you would very likely have questioned the ability of our research department to develop methods of making the material itself in a practical way, yet that was accomplished too. . . ."

In Jewkes's thorough canvassing of the evidence he does come across one study of one industry in which the majority of the innovations is attributed to the right groups at the right time—plastics. But after describing the study in some detail, Jewkes proceeds, in a carefully documented analysis, to challenge it. His conclusion? There is *no* industry group where very much innovation occurred as or when it was supposed to.

An Exception?

We sometimes are told that the principle of invention in the wrong place at the wrong time, by somebody else, does not and cannot hold for pharmaceuticals, where you have a fifteen- to twenty-year development and approval cycle. And we agree that certain stages of the drug development and testing process must be highly systematic. *Invention,* however, particularly in the case of so-called miracle drugs, appears to be just as "messy"—a numbers game, champion-driven and skunkwork-driven—as in the rest of the world. Among the top sellers on the market today is SmithKline's Tagamet, an ulcer drug. The invention of Tagamet embodies the very essence of messiness. The Tagamet team was apparently told to stop working on its area of science three or four times (or five or six, depending on whose version of the story you hear, and we've heard at least a half dozen). One reason, says an informant: the developer was a "disrespected, simple scientist from Glasgow." (He adds, with a touch of awe in his voice, "The same simple fellow subsequently went on to develop the Beta Blocker.") Moreover, the sales potential of the drug, according to a couple of sources, was woefully underestimated at $25 million to $50 million.* It rapidly became a billion-dollar-plus drug (suggesting, as do so many of our examples, that its current description as a "home

---

*Similarly, Upjohn's head of research, Jake Stuki, reports that the ibuprofen family of drugs (Motrin et al.) was at first thought to have little potential: "Market surveys told Upjohn to forgo development before they were ever named, let alone developed."

run" was created *long after the fact* rather than as the result of a preplanned swing for the fences).

Convoluted Paths

Jim Utterback, at MIT, who has studied innovation for over a decade, talks about the special role of *early users*. He concludes that "the initial use and vision for a new product or service is virtually never the one that is of the greatest importance commercially," and he recounts the path to success of invention after invention to support his point. Typical is the case of incandescent lighting. It was first installed in the late 1870's aboard ship, which in retrospect is natural enough. It's dangerous there, in an unstable environment (tossing sea), to have open gas lamps or other forms of flame. Thus the incandescent lamp found a first home, to use Utterback's terms, in a "highly specialized end-use niche." (Likewise, transistors were first used for missile guidance systems; consumer use lagged by twenty years.) And then, in a move that every market research department would have readily predicted, incandescent lighting spread to night baseball! From there it moved to neighborhood lighting, and only fifteen years later did it begin to seep into the home.

Lowell Steele, a GE R&D executive, describes a slightly different twist— the unexpected complications involved in creating the *infrastructure* required to turn a "compelling idea" into a mundane, commercial reality. Here, for instance, is his account of the history of frozen foods (we referred to it briefly earlier): "Clarence Birdseye had his flash of insight in *1912,* but his development of a satisfactory, quick-freezing process was only the first of an excruciatingly drawn out series of steps. Dietetic information had to be developed on the properties of different foods, and new methods were needed for gathering produce. These changes, in turn, required the location of processing plants closer to sources of supply; new techniques and equipment for transferring, storing, and displaying frozen foods; and willingness on the part of both retailers and homeowners to buy adequate storage systems. Even so, the real catalyzing event was the government's decision after World War II to decontrol the price of frozen foods before that of canned goods. In all, it took some *forty years* [our emphasis] before all the pieces were in place for a major new technology to flower!"

In *Patterns of Technological Innovation,* Devendra Sahal has developed a useful term: "technological guideposts." By this he means that some fairly mundane products have become bellwethers for a whole generation of sustained development. He finds that these "super products" that trigger so much subsequent development are seldom from the top tier of exotic technology. Rather they are the *culmination* of many exotic technological advances in a product that is right and *practical for its time*. For example: "A great many advances were centered around a single type of aircraft, the DC-3. Yet it is interesting to note that from a strictly technical view, the

DC-3 was not the most advanced aircraft of its time. It was *singularly lacking in novelty.*" Sahal adds: "The technological guidepost lies in the culmination of prior advances. It is seldom a matter of radical breakthrough." (We think of the Apple II as a more recent product of exactly that sort. It was the right product at the right time. It was a sound product which incorporated advanced but not exotic state-of-the-art technology. Moreover, because of its initial popularity, it attracted any number of effective software writers. Indeed, several have commented that the core of the machine's success was the electronic spreadsheet, first developed by Visicorp. Visicalc—as much as the hardware—really turned the hobbyist's home computer into an effective tool for large numbers of people.)

The path to widespread adoption of an invention, then, is almost always unpredictable—and often lengthy.* Few Hewlett-Packard instrument users did with the instruments what Hewlett-Packard engineers had planned. Scotch tape became a household word only after an enterprising salesman— on his own, at home, during his off hours—invented the desk-top dispenser for a previously narrow-use industrial product. Our strategies for innovation must, then, be based upon *acceptance* of this convoluted process rather than the false hope that "better planning" can magically straighten the maze.

It's Worse than You Think

The evidence is actually frightening. Picking up Utterback's trail again, we find that there is apparently a tendency inherent in organizations to do *exactly* the wrong thing. Following a rigorous study, Utterback concludes: "In 32 of 34 companies, the [challenged market] leader *reduced* investment in the *new* technology in order to pour even more money into buffering up the *old.*" Not only, then, does the leader not embrace the new, but he actually—in absolute and relative dollar terms—reduces his investment in the new in order to hang tight to the old. Utterback's analysis of the turn-of-the-century lighting industry, again, provides a marvelous example. Following the intro- duction of incandescent lighting by small firms, the then leaders spent fifteen years polishing the old technology apple in gas lighting. And they made big bucks at it, because the old technology had not been under challenge and thus yielded big improvements when subjected to renewed scrutiny. In the meantime, however, they *reduced* their investment in the new incandescent lighting. We have seen the phenomenon much more recently. Keuffel and Esser, the premier slide-rule makers (who among engineers didn't carry their K&E with pride?), were not participants at all in the hand-held calculator business. "No names" of the time, such as TI and HP, took the play away from

---

*There is an interesting paradox here. Because of the fact that the path to adoption is uncertain (and often lengthy), one must respond by short-time-frame experiments. That is, the uncertainty is reduced only by constant, rapid tries and adaptations.

K&E. The Swiss watchmakers' response to digital microchip technology is an instant replay.

Technological Hubris

The problems are manifold. Technological and engineering hubris—the engineer-buyer knows best, he or she can predict the use of the product best. Marketing hubris—could all those data on the Edsel be wrong? The issues are organizational, political, habitual, cultural. And they're individual as well.

The potential lost from not listening to would-be champions because they wear the wrong-color suit is a phenomenon of the ages. It goes back hundreds of years, at least. A recent study by William Broad and Nicholas Wade focuses on several giants of science who weren't listened to at the time (and for many subsequent decades—or centuries) because they were not of the then establishment's "right stuff." Ohm (of electricity fame) was disregarded because he was a mere "Jesuit math teacher." Mendel (the pioneer geneticist) was ignored because he did his work at "a little experimental plot in a rural abbey." We mentioned Semmelweis in chapter 6. Even the most inventive have blind spots, in their own back yard, too. Edison did. He fought against the use of alternating current. Marconi, father of radio, fought against wireless telephony. And recently, the wildly creative Nolan Bushnell, then at Atari, could see no value in Steve Jobs's ideas for a new computer, and failed to support it with even a few bucks. Steve, of course, packed up his ideas and (along with Steve Wozniak, similarly unloved at HP) founded Apple.

The causes run deep. Human beings seem to have a need to explain, to write tidy stories. Professor Jewkes puts it this way: "Successful inventors contribute to the romantic aura. . . . It is much more agreeable for them to think of their achievement as the outcome of a flawless chain of brilliant decisions and deliberate planning than as the result of desperate groping and frequent backtracking. . . . Subsequent writers, possessing more complete records of the lucky strokes than of the more numerous failures, and searching for a tidy story rather than a muddled one, carry on the building up of legends."

Are we opposed to central planning? Are we opposed to a central R&D activity? Many have asked that. The answer is no, and yes. One *does* need to make bets on general directions for innovation—the difference, say, between north and northwest. That's great. What's not sensible (it's actually counterproductive) is trying to specify far in advance whether a given course should be 343 degrees or 346 degrees. We also support central research as a good place from which divisions can *steal* ideas. More often than not that's what people at HP, 3M et al. see it as. Finally—another HP view—central research is a marvelous place from which product divisions can *steal* people. And, of course, every now and then, a new product really will come according to plan or from central R&D.

In no sense do we believe we have "proved" that new product or service forecasting is impossible or not useful. If we were in a position to order it done, we'd do so. We just wouldn't bank on it. We'd cover our bets with a bit of eclecticism. Procter & Gamble has done that with its intensive and substantially overlapping brand-versus-brand competition. Mervyn's, Macy's and Bloomingdale's do it with buyer-versus-buyer competition. Smart hospitals are beginning to do it by encouraging internal entrepreneurs to create off-premises walk-in clinics that compete directly with the hospital's service. 3M, Mars, HP, Raychem, Johnson & Johnson, Campbell Soup and others allow several divisions to do about the same thing. Duplication and competition, starting very early in the development cycle, are a hallmark, as well, at IBM.

Never Too Small

These ideas—duplication, purposeful seeding of competing skunk-works, eclecticism, and the like—are often seen by the smaller company, $5 to 100 million, as not workable for them, as only available to an IBM. However, our most successful friends in Silicon Valley, and in banking and in retailing, reject such talk outright. Duplicative development can start in the $5 million company. Experimentation can start in the $200,000 enterprise. In fact, it had better! "Where's the second product or service coming from?" is almost always a burning issue. So you got lucky, hit a home run (or at least a ground-rule double) with the first product or service. It's not enough. Too many founders assume that because they did it right once, they'll likely do it right again, that they are among the chosen few who can hit consecutive home runs. We don't see that happen very often. The true geniuses—the institution builders—start to split their company up, break it into pieces, foster eclecticism, skunkworks and the like at the $5 million mark at the latest (and the $200,000 mark if they are really wise).

"Live with Ambiguity":
Some Questions—and Things to Do Now

▶ We believe it's vital to senior managers—in all businesses, in enterprises of all sizes—to become "expert" on this topic beyond this brief anecdotal analysis. We suggest that you occasionally read biographies of scientists and inventors, or tap the repertoire of Dartmouth's James Brian Quinn or the innovation group at MIT's Sloan School.
▶ More specifically, gather a group of ten to fifteen for a one- to two-day meeting. Include line executives, designers/buyers/engineers and mar-

keters. First review the industry—historically and over the last ten years. Look at both minor and major innovations. Evaluate the sources. (If you can't muster enough evidence, you might even try this on a multicompany basis.) Then on the second day repeat the exercise for your own company. Inviting retired pros in can add immeasurably to the process, we find. Do the results square with what we've presented here?

▶ Repeat the process above for various functions—MIS, manufacturing, accounting. Same story?

Instant results from the above may be limited. It is simply our observation that one needs to examine the process and history of innovation thoroughly to gain personal and group commitment to these notions. Otherwise, the response to most "horror stories" about innovation will be "That's an anomaly" or "You don't understand." Our bet is that the "horror stories," upon semisystematic investigation, will add up to a clear and normal pattern.

Myth No. 2: We Must Begin with a Sound Set of Specs, Mustn't We? Counterpoint: Experiment and Move Fast

---

Innovation in Banking!

Forbes (January 28, 1985) reports:
[Richard Braddock, Citicorp's new top U.S. consumer banker] seems to be coming up with a new product every day or so: a personal computer banking service, insurance centers in branches, a credit card and checking account package. "It's not going to get any less confusing," Braddock says wryly of his myriad new business targets.

A shotgun approach! "Sure," says Braddock, "let the consumer pick the winners. The more things we can try in the marketplace, the better," he says, "as long as we can afford them."

Home-Run Mentality vs Wee Willie Keeler Approach

We call it the "two path" theory. Path One constitutes the "home run mentality." A bright idea is rapidly turned into a $2 million, six-month study—a paper study. The paper evaluation of the study by various interested parties takes another three months. Some sort of a design go-ahead is then given, and technical spec writing, at a cost of another $3 million, takes another six months. The specs are evaluated by several groups during the following four-month period (we're now $7 or 8 million and a year and a half or so into the project). At this stage, a prototype is finally built. It costs $5 to 10 million and takes four to six months. And guess what? In all of history, it seems, from French-fry seasoning at McDonald's to IBM's System/360 computer, the first *and* second prototypes *don't work.* Never! But on Path One, you've invested so much time (and so much money) that competitors are catching up, or have leaped ahead.

So now you enter the "Ignore the misfit data and make the damn thing work" stage. Careers by this time are on the line. And a lot of bucks. And a lot of psychological investment in *the* "one best design." So ignore some of those data that suggest it doesn't work. And as for the rest? Well, competitors have introduced three or four new products or services in the two years you've been at it. Each has several new features. As time went by you got further and further behind. So you have to complicate the product or service, make sure it has every imaginable feature, get it *exactly* right. Remember, this is going to be *the* home run to end all home runs. So you enter the "Make it work" phase. It probably goes on for six months and costs $10 to 15 million more. The whole process has now taken three years and cost $30 million. You'll never scrap it now. You say, "The market's shaking out. It's now or never." The future *always* looks more complicated (and dire) than simplistic recon- structed models of the past. So you think, We must get *all* the features on *this* version or the competitors will steal the market—for good. Falling into this trap is the surest way to bring about exactly the gloom-and-doom result you are trying to avoid. And as you delay and delay in order to craft your home run, six bunt singles and two walks, several by unknown new competitors, put you out of the game for good or cripple you. In the end you finally get to the marketplace with a camel invented by a committee and including every fea- ture known to humankind. It works poorly because of the very fact that so many bells and whistles have been tied to it. But by now it's so late that you *have* to introduce it—whether it works well or not.

In contrast to the home run mentality is Path Two, or the "Wee Willie Keeler" approach. Wee Willie Keeler was a baseball player who played from the 1890's to the 1910's, a consummate opportunist, who said, "Hit 'em where they ain't." He made it into the Hall of Fame stroking only thirty-four home runs in a career that lasted over twenty years.

The Wee Willie Keeler approach is practiced by 3M, Hewlett-Packard, Raychem, Mervyn's, Wang, PepsiCo, Citicorp et al. to a T. How does it work? Start by spending $25,000,* even up to a quarter of a million. Develop a pro- totype, or a big hunk of it, in sixty to ninety *days.* Whether your product or service is a digital switch, a new aircraft or a computer—or a new health ser- vice or a financial instrument or a store format—our evidence suggests that *something* can always be whacked together in that time.

---

*Or $1,500 to $5,000 for a small business.

Then evaluate the prototype; that takes another sixty days. (Also, even at this early point, support—explicitly or tacitly—a second team or skunkwork doing roughly the same thing.) You're already playing with something *tangible,* or a piece of something that's tangible, or, say, a large hunk of primitive software code. Now you take the next little step. Maybe it costs a little more, for a more fully developed prototype, or the beginning of a second prototype. Let's say it costs $100,000 to $500,000. But again you build it fast, in the next ninety days. And this time you can probably get it, or part of it, onto the premises of a user (customer)—not an average user (that *is* a bit away), but a "lead user" who's willing to experiment with you, or at least an in-house lead user (a forward-thinking department). And on the process goes: slightly larger investments, time frames that never run more than sixty to ninety days. It's the "learning organization" or the "experimenting organization."

At each step you learn a little more, but you have harsh reality tests—with hard product/service *and* live users/customers—very early. If it doesn't work, you weed it out quickly, before you have career lock-in and irreversible psychological addiction to the "one best design." Most generally, our experience suggests that the Wee Willie Keeler approach to product or service development, with a sizable dose of duplicate development thrown in, can cut the time it takes to complete the development cycle by 50 percent or more. *And* more products and services ensue. They're not always home runs (or even doubles). Usually, in fact, they're singles or sacrifice flies. And, true, *all* the potential features don't get loaded on the first product. Instead, you introduce another, and another, and another. But you do get there.

Chicken Test!

Here are a couple of Path One "Swing for the fences" examples. First, the Chicken Test. Aircraft engines have to contend with the possible ingestion of flocks of birds. So one of the important things you do to test an aircraft engine is go out at some point to your local chicken farm, buy several gross of chickens, put them into the barrel of a huge (several feet in diameter) "chicken gun," and fire them at the engine. It's the ultimate pragmatic test. Now consider this: Rolls-Royce spends several years and about a quarter billion dollars on a new graphite-based engine, then it fails the Chicken Test. Reworking costs them a big share of a volatile market.

And more of the same: Xerox was determined to get it "exactly right." A twenty-nine-story tower full of MBA's at Rochester armed with powerful multi-hundred-variable models to score would-be product attributes generated and revised marketing study after marketing study in the mid-seventies. Debates raged endlessly. Machine families were going to be perfectly rationalized: Machine A simply was *not* going to cannibalize Machine B. Now, maybe this was a fine strategy for a de facto monopoly with patent protection. But as the analyses continued to be churned out, and as product development continued to lag—and to be continually complicated—competitors took upwards of 50 percent of Xerox's market away. (It took fully ten years—and substantial decentralization—to stem the decline.)

The Wee Willie Keeler approach, or the experimenting approach, is precisely aimed at getting your inevitable "Chicken Test(s)" out of the way early: in the first year, maybe even after the first ninety days, maybe sooner. Every new product fails a Chicken Test or two (or twenty-two) along the way. The burning issue is "When?" At the end of two or three years, by which point there's a whole array of competing products on the market? Or at the end of ninety days, or a hundred and eighty, when damage is still containable, when the design can still be changed?

Eight Per Week/In Just Five Days/A Week versus Thirteen Weeks

Hewlett-Packard, it is said, introduces substantially new products at the rate of eight per week. They are the consummate singles hitters, and sometimes they turn out doubles and triples, even home runs. (Ironically, numerous singles often set in motion a series of developments that become de facto home runs; few home-run swings result in getting on base at all—see Myth No. 1, on the sloppy course of invention.) But HP thinks it has problems: it views its already remarkably short product-development cycles as too long. So the watchword at HP in 1983 became "QTP" (Quick Turnaround Projects). The major instrument whose genesis we mentioned above—the one that emerged from a catalog illustration and a hand-drawn sketch—took, from conception to development and debugged prototype, just seventeen *weeks*. (Remember that Kelly Johnson's development of the first jet aircraft, the YP-80, took 136 days from concept to flying prototype.)

Raychem is another company that does Wee Willie Keeler's kind of work. Raychem is a highly profitable ($700 million) maker of sophisticated products based on materials science. On the occasion of the company's twenty-fifth anniversary, in 1982, Chairman Paul Cook estimated that *200,000* products had gone through the Raychem product line! The company's idea of a winner is a 100% market share, with a 90 percent operating margin, in a $5 million market. It listens to customers, and builds what the customer wants. It comes as no surprise that its motto is "Raychem in Response." Typical was this example we stumbled across. A Raychem field engineer got word of an undersea leak at an offshore oil platform in the North Sea. Within 120 hours (just five days) Raychem had shipped in researchers from Menlo Park, California (headquarters), and Swindon, England (European R&D headquarters), put up a field site on location, developed an honest-to-gosh state-of-the-art new product, prototyped it, debugged it and installed it. (It's now a $10 million or so business; as usual, its ultimate market bore little relation to its first use.) The contrast between Raychem and most of the rest of the "real world" was aptly captured by a participant in a recent seminar: "In our company, at the end of those five days, you'd have been darned lucky to have gotten your travel orders cut to get out of California."

New Ventures Strategy

Allen Michels rapidly built Santa Clara-based Convergent Technologies into a $400 million company. His secret? He started spinning off mostly independent ventures (usually three-person teams) at a very early stage. At the heart of this new ventures strategy, he declares, is the "Try it" orientation. His primary advice: "Think small." "Make decisions and don't contemplate." "Review the day every day and move ahead." Above all, he adds, "Engineers need decisiveness. They mustn't allow themselves to be hung up in pursuit of perfection." In fact, he says, the overarching management challenge is to "nurture rapid decisive activity in a disorderly environment."

Far from the world of HP, Raychem and Convergent Technologies is Mervyn's, the winner by quite a margin in the fine Dayton-Hudson family of retailers. Their winning formula? They accomplish in one week what it takes their prime competitors thirteen weeks or more to do. Every Wednesday morning at 7:00 A.M., fifty-two weeks a year, a hundred Mervyn's people—the president, the executive vice presidents and almost all the merchants (buyers) in the company—march into a giant auditorium. Before them, up on a huge wallboard, are about thirty or so big blank spaces. For the next six hours they will fight, scrap, pull, tug, tear hair. They will assess and interpret the last week's successes and failures. They will turn the blank spaces into the contents of a thirty-page booklet listing items they want to have featured next week in the hundred or so Mervyn's stores in the billion-dollar-plus system. They are developing the *Ad Supplement.* Less than a week later it will be mailed out to approximately fifteen million people! In sum, Mervyn's remerchandises their sizable operation once per week; others are lucky to manage it in 10 to 15 weeks. The magic? None. It's simply what Mervyn's does for a living. It's their (boring? obsessive? passionate?) equivalent of "Raychem in Response."

Turn It to Tin

Howard Head, inventor of Head skis and the Prince tennis racquet, says, "We try to get a prototype made as soon as possible. I want to see an idea. I want to hold it and touch it." That's what it's all about. Such products—early prototypes, even the final products of a Wang or a Rolm—often aren't as "pretty" as the Western Electric or Xerox product. In Tracy Kidder's *The Soul of a New Machine,* about Data General's remarkably quick construction of a super minicomputer needed to compete with DEC, the outcome was described by various DG players as "a wart on a wart on a wart" or "a bag on the side of the Eclipse [the predecessor machine that was being revolutionized]." No, it wasn't pretty. But it was quick, and it got started without muss and fuss.

At HP some R&D managers jokingly argue that a new rule should be instituted: "Anyone developing technical specs more than three pages long will be summarily fired, without right of appeal." (In contrast, a Texas Instruments executive considers some of their recent failures: "[The] number one mortal sin is excessive quantification of the imponderable.")

The late Fred Hooven, holder of over thirty major patents, one-time student of Orville Wright and former senior R&D manager at Ford, used to go on at length about the necessity of getting something built quickly. He talked about the reluctance to experiment and some of the silly reasons he'd heard for failing to do so: "My favorite was when they told me, 'We can't put the engineers and the model shop together because it'll get the drawings dirty.' " He'd argue that getting on with it, doing the next live test or mocking up the next piece would often "take half an hour, whereas sending it 'upstairs' for formal drawings and specifications will take at least four months." That's what we're really talking about: the difference between half an hour and four months! The difference *is* that great.

The phenomenon holds for far more than product development. In process development the experimental way is critical too. An article by Joseph Limprecht and Robert Hayes, "Germany's World-Class Manufacturers," in the November-December 1982 issue of *Harvard Business Review,* argues, for instance, that the American fixation on the home run is a major factory/process issue: "As the auto, steel, and machine tool industries grimly attest, Americans have not been as zealous [as the Germans] in making incremental improvements in mature technologies.... American companies put too much faith in the possibility of breakthroughs." As we review the Milliken, or Perdue Farms environment, for example, we find the contrary. Process breakthroughs are hoped for, but the major management effort is aimed at making, non-stop, the small improvements in performance that inch productivity along.

Analysis I versus Analysis II

The case adds up, on another dimension, to what we call Analysis I versus Analysis II. Analysis I is abstract. It depends on market reports, lengthy technical specs. Analysis II is all about immersion: *Touch. Feel. Do. Try. Fix.* As John Masters, head of Canada's most successful oil and gas wildcatter firm says, "This is so simple it sounds stupid, but it is amazing to me how few oil people understand that you only find oil and gas when you drill wells. You may think that you're finding it when you're drawing maps and studying logs, but you have to drill." We are adamant about labeling this pragmatic immersion process "analysis," because in many quarters today only the abstract stuff is viewed as "analysis." But the scientific method rests foursquare on empiricism, which is to say, the experimenting mentality, not the home-run—on paper—mentality. Get *hard* data. Get it quickly. That's the key. Get market data, of course, but market data from *trying it* with a user as soon as possible. Get technical data, of course, but from *building* a prototype and *handling* it as the real world does, not keeping it bottled up forever in the pristine, sterile, temperature-controlled, dust-free lab or test kitchen.

"Experiment":
Some Questions and Things to Do Now

▶ Take two recent new product or service (or business) introductions that succeeded. Take two that failed or were inordinately delayed. Analyze them in some detail. Are there any differences consistent with the experimenting ideas presented here? Was "test it now" as opposed to later more the mark of the successes? (Assuming that the failure cases were marked by a lack of experimentation, what were the reasons? E.g., lack of coordination between warring functions? delays to get specifications "exactly right" before prototyping? List 10 typical blocks, and what you can do to remove them.)

▶ Repeat the analysis above for the industry as a whole, reviewing the practices of two industry leaders, two laggards, then three or four of the most recent innovations. Did they come from people who move fast? Or from massive, well-planned, multiyear efforts?

▶ Are you willing to gamble on putting a product into a partial test market (e.g., two stores) quickly? Or to seek out a potential "lead user" before the design is finalized? Is such behavior the norm or the exception? (Again, review systematically a handful of successes and failures to aid this analysis.) As a live test, see if you can *halve* the planned time to put two new (under development) services or products into the hands of lead users/test markets. (Remember that there are all sorts of levels of test-market effort. Long before full scale test-market launch you can conduct numerous quick-and-dirty five-person samples to test reaction to bits or pieces of prototypes.)

▶ Most generally, is this—honestly—a "Try it, test it" environment? In new product design? Manufacturing? Operations? MIS? Do most people (the young especially) think that "to get ahead you've got to be constantly trying stuff" or "keeping your nose clean is what *really* counts around here"? Are you sure you can answer this accurately (i.e., from *their* perspective)?

▶ Can you, looking ahead, pinpoint four or five places where you can *test* the experimenting notion? Push a new product team (or factory process improvement team) to try something faster, to cut the bureaucracy and get on with a practical experiment? (If you come up empty on this, get five to

ten of your people together for three or four hours. Our experience is—
unfailingly—that you'll come out of it with twenty to thirty practical ideas
in the next 15 to 30 days.)

Myth No. 3: Creativity (Innovation) Follows from Reflection
Counterpoint: Champions/Skunks a Necessity

Home-run swings take muscle-bound athletes. If innovation took powerful
"thinkers," we would expect to find that those thinkers would regularly climb
to a mountaintop retreat to look out over the pines and accomplish the necessary breakthroughs (and then return, presumably on schedule). If, on the
other hand, the Wee Willie Keeler paradigm is the norm in innovative organizations, as we claim it is, one would expect to find bleary-eyed folks staring
at CRT's or test tubes or mucking about with a nutty fashion designer in forgotten corners of basements and lofts. Instead of tweeds and meerschaum
pipes, one would expect torn dungarees and a determined cast to the eye.

Champions Everywhere—Passion a Must

It turns out that the bleary eyes have quite a role to play. If an endless
series of practical experiments is the "norm" of the truly innovative enterprise (remember *The Nobel Duel:* Grind more pig brains), people called
champions are a necessity.

We've become collectors of stories like these. Formal in-house studies of
research project successes at IBM *always* unearth the presence of a champion. National Science Foundation studies suggest that the champion's role is
crucial in pushing an idea to fruition. MIT's Ed Schon argues most generally,
"The new idea either finds a champion or it dies. No ordinary involvement
with a new idea provides the energy required to cope with the indifference
and resistance that change provokes." John Masters of Canadian Hunter,
looking back on successful projects (and reminding himself of the need to
support lonely champions), adds, "A really new idea at first has only *one*
believer." Brian Quinn, previously cited, concludes that "fanaticism is crucial." And Peter Drucker, looking back on fifty years' experience in all walks
of life in *Adventures of a Bystander,* remarks, "Whenever *anything* is being
accomplished, it is being done, I have learned, by a monomaniac with a mission." Thomas Edison's premier biographer concluded, "What set Edison
apart was that, with all his boundless exaggeration, he conveyed the feeling
that he would succeed. No matter what the obstacles, he would pound away
until he had demolished them." A successful consumer-goods manager
argues that one of his prime criteria for promotion within the brand manager
ranks is that the successful candidate be "a thug"—i.e., determined to beat

down any barriers in his path. A study of Nobel Prize winners suggests that they often give away a few IQ points relative to the rest of the researcher colleagues on top of the heap. Time and again, they are said by their peers to have instead such traits as "peasant toughness," "a streak of brutality" and "killer instincts," and to be "good finishers."

There are crucial implications here. In the halcyon days of Organizational Development in the 1960's and 1970's, cooperation and conflict-smoothing were considered the most desirable traits for any human being working in a sizable enterprise. Our champions, however, are usually not the souls of sweetness and light. As Jewkes put it: "The most inventive spirits have confessed a constitutional aversion to cooperation." In fact, the people who are tenacious, committed champions are often royal pains in the neck (except to their immediate team members, who would often go over the hill for them).

Egotistical. Competitive. Passionate. Persistent beyond belief. These are the most universal traits of those who withstand all the inevitable rebuffs (occasionally personal) and get their "it" to market. (Or get their change in an accounting procedure accepted by the factory managers.) They must be fostered and nurtured—even when it hurts a little (or a lot)—if regular innovation is to flourish.

Failure Goes Hand in Glove

A crucial corollary is that the organization that would nourish champions *must* also tolerate, even celebrate, failures. General George Doriot, the godfather of development along Route 128 in Massachusetts, said in an address to Digital Equipment (one of the first companies he wisely invested in), "If failure can be explained, and it's not based on lack of morality, then to me failure is acceptable." The best of the companies we've looked at explicitly support failures in the sense that they admit that failure along the way is normal. Their philosophies say so, and tolerance for it is fostered through war stories. Setbacks—not sloppy foul-ups, but thoughtful missteps along the way—are considered to be normal. The winners are seen as people who persist. People who fail, sometimes in rather big ways, may get demotions or lateral transfers—but the ranks of corporate vice presidents are densely peppered with those who have *returned* from "Siberia" to bring a critical product to the market or contribute in some other important way. Even egregious failure is thus seen as a natural way-stop on the path to eventual success.

"Champions":
Some Questions—and Things to Do Now

▶ Take *twenty* projects that succeeded—small (mainly) and large, process (all functions) and product (or service); likewise, take *twenty* failures. Are the successes marked more by naturally emerging champions than are the failures? This analysis should best be discussed in a group of five to fifteen, each of whom has done a similar homework assignment (again from all functions).

▶ If champions do mark the successes, how were they nurtured? Was a godfather running interference? Or was grabbing their own territory without aid more commonplace? (We find that *all* environments, innovative or not, spawn at least a few champions. The most innovative are marked by more champions, nurtured consciously by a *network* of past champions-godfathers. The *fewer* champions among the less innovative are lone rangers who broke out without godfathers.)

▶ Take four terrific middle-aged champions. Where did their championing start? Usually the answer is "Very early in their careers"; if so, is championing being encouraged today in the lower levels of the organization? (Incipient or full-blown atrophy is best observed as the absence of champions among the young.)

▶ Be more specific. Evaluate *your* career—alone or with four or five colleagues in a half-day off-site session. Are you all or some of you former champions? If yes, how did it come about (the role of your godfather, etc.)? If no, why/how was your championing thwarted?

▶ Look, specifically, and in a separate exercise, for champions at *lower levels* in *non*-line functions: Are they popping up in MIS? Accounting? Personnel? If not, why not?

▶ How is the word (and idea) of *failure* treated by you and your colleagues? Positively (given that it was a vigorous, well thought-out effort)? Or negatively? Take a project or two you're *most* proud of. Are numerous small failures a part of it? If so, do you tolerate (encourage, in the best sense) such failures by others? One service company marketing vice president says, "We need to fail more quickly around here [i.e., get the inevitable failures out of the way faster]." (Also see a more extensive discussion of failure in chapter 11.)

Myth No. 4: Big, Formal Groups Are Essential
Counterpoint: Skunkworks as the Norm

Giant projects require giant well-integrated groups, it's said. Is the BOF (basic oxygen furnace), by which Japan and MITI, supposedly with malice aforethought (read central planning), battered the U.S. steel industry, a big project? Is GE's entry into plastics and aircraft engines big? The IBM System/360? The Polaris submarine? Of course each is, and yet we'll observe that each was spearheaded by a "skunk" (bootlegger, scrounger) working at the far edges of the traditional corporate structure.

Kollmorgen, Raychem, Convergent Technologies, Macy's and J&J are really nothing more than collections of skunkworks: tiny to modest teams in relatively small divisions performing numerous off-line activities.

Even massive IBM: its Personal Computer (PC) came from one of no fewer than a half-dozen parallel development teams. (Don Estridge's winning team initially consisted of twelve somewhat discredited people working in a rundown facility in Boca Raton, Florida.) And the company's current move toward Independent Business Units (IBU's)—close to twenty have been created in the last two years—is yet another of their continuing efforts to certify non-bureaucratic bunches. To similar purpose were the senior Mr. Watson's constant lauding of Wild Ducks and, more formally, establishment of fifty IBM Fellows, each with a five-year carte blanche to stir things up. Another senior IBMer talks, with relish, about $500,000 that "slipped away." He knew about it, he says, and then again he didn't. The end result was a major new memory device created by a small skunkwork in about 150 days. (Larger groups had been wrestling with the project—unsuccessfully—for years.)

The evidence rolls in: when a practical innovation occurs, a skunkwork, usually with a nucleus of six to twenty-five, is at the heart of it.

Bootlegging marked each step (from the initial technical triumph to the organizational form of the exploitation group) on the way to GE's spectacular successes in aircraft engines and engineering plastics. Their first locomotive and their first off-highway vehicle both got their start from bootleg projects. In fact, every major internally grown business success at GE, from high-tech turbines to the GE Credit Corporation (GECC) and GE Information Services Company (GEISCO), came through a passionate champion, working within a skunkwork operation, always at or slightly beyond the periphery of GE's formal policies and central systems. Then, in the seventies, "planning" was centralized—with deadening effect. When young (just forty-five at the time of his promotion) Jack Welch became chairman in April 1981, and an early act was to dismantle two-thirds of the central (corporate) strategic planning staff. The reason wasn't antipathy to strategic planning (they still do it well in the trenches). Welch had concluded that a return to technological preeminence demanded inducing more entrepreneurial skunks and putting them to work.

Find an industry, look at its principal accomplishments, and you'll invariably find a trail of skunks. Relatively small L. M. Ericcson spurts to the top in the international digital telecommunication switch competition. The origin of the LME product? Twenty disaffected engineers, angry at their bosses, who banded together (within the corporation, but barely) and built the AXE switch—cowing in the process such giant stalwarts as the plodding Siemens. The about-to-be-industry-standard UNIX operating system was created at AT&T/Bell Labs as a hobbyist project using spare computer capacity to build a language to meet the needs of a small group (of two!). (The absence of corporate oversight, says one knowledgeable observer, led to development of a language that "lacked the many compromises and complexities that inevitably afflict large team efforts.")

Name your industry! Mercantile Bank, a highly innovative regional bank headquartered in Dallas, has exploited telecommunications and computer technology much more rapidly than 99 percent of the banking community. It has a vital, high-fee service-producing 600-bank network now. Where did it come from? A big, well-planned, centrally funded MIS-department-driven project? No! One fellow had the idea, and George Clark, the bank's president, had the good sense to let him run with it. The fellow worked on it principally *at home;* it took him about three months and cost but $200,000. His system was simple, practical and to the point. John Fisher, another champion with an effective executive champion protecting him, vaulted BancOne of Columbus, Ohio, to the fore in fee service businesses. With a small supporting cast, he has time and again worked miracles developing, for example, the support system for Merrill-Lynch's revolutionary cash management scheme.

And yet . . . "Sure, Bill Hewlett did it with the hand-held calculator. You can readily imagine someone putting that in his or her pocket, or carrying it home in a brown paper bag. But what about the big stuff?" Well, the GE locomotive is a classic case in point. GE had been building subassemblies. A group wanted to build the whole thing. They were flat out told—not once, but four times—to knock it off. Apparently that was exactly the spur they needed. *They "bootlegged" a locomotive* in an underutilized facility in Erie, Pennsylvania. Locomotives decidedly don't fit in vest pockets.

Let's get even more ridiculous. Consider the development of the basic oxygen furnace (BOF). It turns out not to have been a meticulously planned ten-year 100,000-milestone effort inspired by MITI. BOF technology emerged from Nippon Kokan, then the third largest steel company in Japan (now second, approaching first). And within that steel company, it came from the second and far less respected (disdained, if the truth be known) group of technologists (Thomas rather than Open Hearth engineers). Moreover, within that least respected group, a young fanatic was at the core of it. Pretty much against his superiors' wishes, he went off to Austria to learn about their early experiments with BOF. He came back, commandeered some outdated equipment (an old ladle), carried on BOF experiments "off line." The story is, of course, more complex, especially when we get to the final exploitation of the technology in Japan (a half-dozen to a dozen years ahead of the Americans). But essentially it is, clearly, a skunkwork tale: a small group competing against a stronger and more respected technological group in-house, against bigger companies in Japan as a whole—and led, as is so regularly the case, by a fanatic champion.*

Furthermore, we find the same skunkworkish activities at the heart of *process* improvement as well as product development. Far from being the result

---

*We picked up along the way a case even harder to believe: a breakthrough in aluminum production (at Kaiser Aluminum). A whole pilot plant was built off line, without senior management's explicit awareness.

of the meticulously planned activities of industrial or systems engineers, they usually occur incrementally, as the result of the efforts of four or five disgruntled machine operators or central MIS users who commandeer a couple of industrial engineers or programmers on Saturdays and at nights and redesign a part of a line, or a machine, or a flow process.

The Time It Takes

What are these bunches of six to twenty-five people—these skunkworks—all about? First, most seem to do things in an exceptionally short period of time. Allen Michels of Convergent Technologies talks of regularly telescoping four years' work into one. GE's Gerhard Neumann (aircraft engines) and Lockheed's Kelly Johnson (airframes) regularly reduced development time 50 to 90 percent below the norm—on giant projects. Tom West, Data General's computer project leader, suspects that the crucial breakthroughs in microcoding occurred during the course of a week, and probably a very long weekend. At Hewlett-Packard, the hand-drawn sketch we mentioned earlier was translated into hard product in only seventeen weeks, a year or so less than "normal." Bell Labs executives, recalling the development of the digital switch, refer time and again to "breakthroughs" that took place in the home basements of individuals over a single weekend. Many Xerox executives talk lovingly of the East Rochester skunkworks (a ten- to fifteen-person group sequestered since 1978 in a "leaky third-floor loft" in a deteriorating eighty-year-old building): product after product pours out, often after only a few weeks' effort (one 28-day project has now generated $3 billion in revenue), while hundreds at the main lab are stymied, often for years.*

In sum: when big groups are at their wit's end, they turn to the skunkworks, and near-magical results start to occur in only three or four weeks, or less. Why? Surely one reason is that in such groups there's no passing the buck. The pressure is on. The deadlines can't be evaded, even if they're not entirely real: some of West's colleagues at Data General did chide him for going out of his way to "create dramatic events." West is in good company. Thomas Edison, it is said, had a habit of announcing a product to the press and only afterwards bothering to go about inventing it, while putting himself under the pressure of an absurd self-inflicted deadline.

The Matter of Quality

But what happens with a "quick and dirty" skunkwork product? Isn't the quality lower? Does it ever fit with the rest of the product line? Indeed it

*Others speak less lovingly, for exactly the same reason.

does! In fact, the stuff from skunkworks is usually of *higher* quality, even though it was invented in a tiny fraction of the so-called normal time. What's the reason? Under the pressure of ridiculous deadlines, and suffering limited staffing, the skunkwork seldom reinvents the wheel. A while ago Tom was involved in some "reverse engineering" of a high-technology product. The client's manufacturing costs were about $1,400 a unit, while the Japanese competitors' cost was about $800. It had already been determined that most of the difference was not "better" Japanese technology or cheaper Japanese labor. Tom and his colleagues decided to look at some little part of the machine, such as a small electric motor doing a mundane task. The unit cost ran to an egregious $60. What had happened? The engineers had gone and reinvented the electric motor (in 1980) to get it exactly right for their need. The Japanese, to accomplish the same task, had gone outside to a vendor who supplied a garden variety $2.95 motor; to that they had added twenty-five cents' worth of resistors to change the motor's operating characteristics. The "garden variety" $2.95 motor was developed in about 1940; its reliability is unsurpassed.

Big groups tend to reinvent the wheel, start from scratch with every activity. Small groups *must* improvise—and the improvisation is usually an adaptation of a standard item that's been manufactured flawlessly for years. The IBM PC group went outside to get a disc drive—the first IBM group to do so. And Lockheed's Kelly Johnson insists that one of the fourteen "golden rules" of skunking is the ability to go wherever is necessary—including going to direct competitors—to purchase components.

Small Is Beautiful

Still, we must ask: What is the source of the skunkwork's power? What drives the skunks to success when larger groups founder? We think that it is, above all, a sense of *ownership* and *commitment*. West describes the phenomenon to author Tracy Kidder in *The Soul of a New Machine:* "There's thirty guys out there who think it's their machine. I don't want that tampered with." We'll go into it in some detail in chapter 14, "Ownership"; the point to be emphasized here is the importance of smallness. The small group is, simply, crucial to innovation. Recent studies by the National Science foundation put the optimal size of a research group at about seven. Convergent Technologies says the maximum size of a development team should be two or three; Raychem says five; HP says about six; 3M, no more than eight or ten; Digital, fifteen to twenty. West's team had about thirty. Jewkes observes that the optimal number appears to be under fifty, even for complex projects like aircraft, though Kelly Johnson did go up to one hundred twenty-five, and Gerhard Neumann went even a bit higher. But regardless of what the number is exactly, it is surprisingly small.

The Role of Competition

Also crucial to innovation because of the sense of ownership and commitment it engenders is competition. In the Data General case, competition was encouraged at all levels. It was West's team *versus* the industry (Build the best damned 32-bit minicomputer), *versus* Digital (the hated rival that had gotten there first), *versus* corporate (who had cut off the funding for West's project, forcing it into bootleg status) and, above all, *versus* North Carolina (the large, central, well-funded development group). And finally there was mini-group *versus* mini-group competition within the team (the hardware people *versus* the software people), and occasionally, even one individual *versus* another (Who would get the debugging done first?). The objective in West's words: "to get a machine out the door with your name on it."

Formal recognition of the value of internal competition may have originated at GM in the 1920's, with Alfred P. Sloan's purposeful creation of division overlap. P&G instituted brand-versus-brand competition way back in 1931. As a fairly small company then, they felt that their innovative juices would dry up unless brands were allowed to engage in "no-holds-barred competition." Yes, such competition did (and does) lead to duplication. Yes, it did (and does) mean cannibalization of other P&G products. Yes it did (and does) entail costs. But the positive outcome, making sure that the next product comes from P&G rather than by a competitor, was thought then—and is still thought—to outweigh by far the more readily calculable "downside" costs. 3M states adamantly that they always want the "second product in the category to come from a competing 3M division, rather than from a competitor." Mars' sixty divisions follow the same rule, with virtually no limits: for example, a U.S. division having problems in its own markets shifts its efforts to Australia, where it competes with a Mars subsidiary with a huge share there. Perkin-Elmer, a top performer in the instrument business, talks about "two-site" management: at least two wholly independent centers must be working on anything important. HP divisions, too, compete with one another. The result? An HP computer group introduces products that "should have" come from the hand-held calculator group, and vice versa.

Internal competition *is* darned difficult to manage. There are a great number of subtleties and traps that come with it. A term that we've developed to encompass the opportunity (and focus on the problem) is "(ED)IC"—(*Externally Directed*) *Internal Competition*. Internal competition at Data General—West's "fight" with North Carolina—was aimed at developing hard product to fill a gap in Data General's product line; it did not involve the marketers' view of a product versus the designers' view versus the view of finance staff, in "wars" waged via paper studies with the prime, albeit unspoken, objective of "getting the other staff." True, West wanted to "get" North Carolina, but the only way he could do so (or they could "get" him) was by inventing something that worked or didn't in the real world. On paper, internal competition is not only not necessary but downright wasteful. But in the real world and over the long haul it is the engine of sustained success.

A Pain in the Neck

How *do* you manage "collections of skunkworks"—duplication, internal competition, fanatics? *In Search of Excellence* referred to "leaky systems," a term that comes from Tait Elder, president of the internal venture group at Allied Corporation and formerly of 3M. Tom West of Data General comments that "there are a lot of people pretending this [computer] project doesn't exist." Talk with HP, IBM, 3M, Citicorp, American Express managers about managing bootlegging and their eyes suddenly glaze over. Their response is an important clue. Managing under these conditions involves staying constantly on top of things—but at the same time, one "sort of" (a term we've come to cherish) pretends it's not there. That's also essential, to foster the all-important sense of ownership without which a skunkwork ceases to exist (again, see chapter 14).

Nothing we can say will reduce the agony of managing champions and skunkworks. We cannot tell you how many you need as a function of the size of your company or its position in your industry's life cycle. We cannot tell when you've cut them off too late, when too early. We are most pleased when a seminar participant tells us he's "trying one" or "at least my instinct is not to chop one off if I see it springing up." We are only sure that skunkworks are vital to innovation, whether you are running a 12-person accounts receivable department, a 25-person sanitation department in a small town or chairing a Fortune 500 company. And we do have some ideas about how you can create an environment where skunkworks naturally emerge. Turn to chapter 11, "The Context of Innovation," for those ideas, but be forewarned: they involve very little managing in the traditional sense.

The turned-on band seems to be at the heart, then, of innovation of all sorts—big *and* small, new product (or service) *and* process improvement. Even when big teams are necessary, as for the final assembly and the launch of, say, the IBM System/360 or, surely, a missile system, look for help to a skunkwork when a crisis arises (see Myth 4B Counterpoint: Small within Big). And in sales too: GE managers, HP managers, 3M managers, Citicorp managers all talk about taking new territory with skunkwork sales development operations, calling on "unapproved" segments of markets.

Ten Quick Questions (and Ten Quick Answers) about Skunkworks

1. Can you "appoint" or "designate" a skunkwork?

Yes. Experience from Convergent Technologies, Mercantile Bank, Raychem, Apple Computer, Monarch Marking (Pitney-Bowes) and

---

IBM, among others, suggests you can. On the other hand, the desired end is to achieve an innovative climate from which they "emerge naturally, somehow, at roughly the right time," as a GE manager puts it.

2. *How many people in an ideal skunkwork?*

The evidence suggests a number ranging from 2 to 125, with 5 to 25 surfacing most regularly. (P.S.: Even at the level of 2 to 3, extensive multifunctional experience—manufacturing and marketing as well as design—is a *must,* according to the pros.)

3. *Can you have a part-time leader or part-time members?*

3M would say no. So would we. Ownership and commitment are "it." "Part-time ownership" is a non sequitur (you're either "on the bus" or "off the bus," as Ken Kesey used to say).

4. *Who's the best leader?*

Clear agreement on this: a "tinkerer" with an urge to act, *not* a "blue sky" type. Effective skunkworks have a dramatic outward and pragmatic (customer, action) thrust.

5. *Are there no rules?*

Yes, there are rules and controls. Kelly Johnson insisted, though, that they be extraordinarily simple and to the point, as did GE's Gerhard Neumann. Michels says milestones are great and vital, as long as they don't exceed four or five in number ("and I'm not talking about PERT charts," he adds with emphasis).

6. *Should we expect the quality to suffer?*

No, it will likely be better. But compatibility may suffer a bit. A 5 percent "cost" in lost compatibility (or confusion from partial duplicating) is usually a more-than-fair price for a possible 200–300 percent speedup.

7. *What do we do if they (skunkworks) fail?*

Most will. The Raychem/3M/HP trick is that there's always a next place/project to go to. If there is no pad/fall-back, you won't get many volunteers. (Which is not to say that you should look with favor upon someone who lopes from failure to failure.)

8. *Do you have to offer a big monetary incentive?*

No. HP and 3M, best of the (big) bunch, don't. As Tom West explained in *The Soul of a New Machine,* people do it so they'll get to play "pinball" again: "You win with this machine, you get to build the next" (i.e., participate in an even tougher future assignment).

9. *Do you allow the internal competition between skunkworks to be "unbridled," as P&G calls it?*

No. P&G lies! The powerful P&G quality standard is *always* adhered to. HP is the same. The P&G/HP constraints on competition are two-fold: (1) external focus—Do "it" with live customers, not on paper; (2) the "it" must be of unsurpassed quality, not a cheap low-end product/service aimed at knocking off one of our own high-end market leaders.

10. *What else?*

Kelly Johnson says the skunkworks *must* have purchasing authority, be allowed to buy components on the market, if necessary, rather than from one's own divisions, which may produce a component at a higher price, or one that is more complicated, or too late.

11. (Bonus) *When should I expect results?*

Expect tangible outcomes (not finished products) in sixty to ninety days. If you don't get them, forget it.

"Skunkworks": Some Questions—and Things to Do Now

▶ Personal exercise: Go back at least as far as college. Assess the *five* things *you* are most proud of—being on an athletic team that turned around and surprised everyone, a literary endeavor, a sale to a new major customer. How many of the five were a product of a "skunkworklike" organizational arrangement? (Most find the answer is either "All" or "A majority.") Assess the conditions that lead to the turned-on team/skunkworks creation; the kind of things that fostered high performance. Does the analysis have applicability to your current organizational setting (i.e., do most of the preconditions for effective skunking exist or not)?

▶ Look at the last *ten* innovations (small or large, process or new product/service). How many originated in or were abetted by skunkworks? (If the "winners" have been marked by skunkworks, how—*in detail*—were they started/sustained?) Look at five recently stalled or failed projects: Is there an absence or presence of skunkworks? Look at two *failed skunkworks*. What went wrong? (*No* full-time, volunteer champion? No early customer contact? No freedom to purchase outside? Too much money and thus not enough pressure? Premature corporate intrusion once it started to look like a winner?)

▶ Become a historian! Collect ten great skunkwork tales, from the founder (if applicable) to today. Tell them. Video-tape the stories, if the protagonists are still around. In this and other ways, begin to get "skunking-as-normal-procedure" into the air.

▶ Sit down with a stalled project team in the next ten days. Listen to them—for a full day perhaps. Look for opportunities to get a one- to three-person band to go off and do a quick subproject (semi-skunkwork) to break the logjam. (Such partial and guided starts underpin shifts to more entrepreneurial climates.)

Related Myth 4A: Only Strong Functions Spawn Concern for Innovation
Counterpoint: Smash Functions Together

"Engineers/designers lose out to operations and finance people in divisional organizations." "The division is only interested in short-term profit." "Only a strong functional monolith will keep the engineering/designer/buyer/brand manager (and innovation) at the forefront." So runs the conventional argument. It's a fine argument on paper, but it doesn't hold much water in practice. The functional monolith is, almost by definition, bureaucratic, not commitment/small team/skunkwork/action-oriented.

Division Equals Being Adaptive

For constantly innovating companies—Hewlett-Packard, 3M, Johnson & Johnson, PepsiCo, Raychem, Emerson Electric, Mars, Rolm, Kollmorgen, Citicorp—the division is the solution (and the strategy). J&J constantly creates new divisions. Its corporate watchword is "growing big by staying small." Says J&J chairman Jim Burke: "Decentralization causes creativity, which in turn leads to productivity. That form of productivity [creativity-driven] is giant leaps ahead of all other forms." Likewise PepsiCo prides itself on being "the [world's] biggest small-company environment." IBM people use exactly the same language.

The structure, for these companies, drives and shapes not only their strategy but even the specifics of their product offerings. In fact, for them, the structure *is* the strategy. A Rolm executive speaks to the point eloquently: "The insides of our CBX's [Computer Branch Exchanges] look like us [as a company]—just a bunch of microprocessors on a board talking to each other. [Those of a particular competitor] look like them—inflexible and hierarchical architecture."

Today we are seeing a new wave of radical decentralization aimed directly at increasing innovative vitality. The first such wave—we call it Round no. 1—lasted from about 1950 to 1970, and was generally superseded by the matrix form of organization, designed to control the giants that American corporations had become as single divisions grew larger than the original company was when it divisionalized. This one—"Round no. 2"—is coming largely from mature industries, with major moves at places like Campbell Soup and Brunswick leading the way. Interestingly, these two have turned their backs (explicitly) on portfolio theory. Rather than pigeonholing people and products, they are giving all hands in any division the freedom to create new markets, in any product area, on the J&J/3M/HP model.

Round no. 1 decentralization was *not* always accompanied by "leaning up" the corporate staffs. In fact, it was often accompanied by the growth of central staff and the addition of a "group executive" layer of management. Round no. 2 is invariably accompanied by paring down central staffs. Brunswick's Jack Reichert, for instance, has cut corporate staff, so far, from 560 to 230. He has completely removed the group executive layer; he has also given each division "six-figure spending authority" (up from a tiny amount). The result, in part: "Decisions that once took weeks or months now take hours or days." Round no. 2 is marked as well by a move toward much smaller divisions, and eschews many paper economies of scale (usually unrealized) on both the marketing and the manufacturing/operations sides.

Linking Functions

A vital advantage of the small team/small division approach to organization is the ability to manage, with less muss and fuss, the "pass-off" interfaces (e.g., design to manufacturing or operations) that, we'd judge, account for 75 percent of the delays in the development of new products and new services—in every business from high technology to banking. At HP, the principle of the "triad" development team ensures that the manufacturer and marketer (as well as the design engineer) are full-scale (i.e., full-time) partners in the development process starting *very* early in the design phase. (A former student of Tom's from IBM went so far as to call the Triad "HP's most distinctive positive [relative to IBM] trait.") 3M follows the same principle, putting a full-time manufacturer on the team long before a full-time body can be warranted theoretically (on paper). The enhanced manufacturability and increased effectiveness of the pass-off to manufacturing is huge.

John Masters of Canadian Hunter brought about much of his success with a similar routine—getting the geologists and petroleum engineers to communicate: "We expand the horizons of our engineers and geologists by constant association, by osmosis. We have lunch meetings, management meetings, social occasions. We provide the environment for them to rub together, then let nature take its course. Suddenly an engineer starts to think like a geologist and vice versa."

Interestingly, Ford is taking the same tack. The company now systematically solicits input from all functions, including hourly workers on the line, very early in the design process. First-line people comment on the manufacturability of various parts and are full-scale members even of advance design teams. Said a senior Ford executive in 1983: "We've used the process on our last two new product launches. It's only taken two. Results have been exceptional. I don't think there's a person in the company who would go back to the old way." He also quantified the results: hourly workers provided over seven-hundred *implemented* design changes in one Ford truck (the successful Bronco)!

Milliken Customer Action Teams (CATs) follow a like principle. Salespersons and marketers were regularly bedeviled, in the manufacturing-driven company, by a "we can't stop the line to run new product samples" mentality. Now, the institutionalized reaction is to create a CAT at the drop of a hat. It consists of four or five Milliken people (from sales, marketing, design, manufacturing, accounting) and a handful of customer people. With typical determination, Milliken mounted 1100 (!) teams in the first 15 months of the process, exploiting many untapped market opportunities, and cutting sample delivery time from months (on average) to eight or ten *days.*

It's important that we bring to the surface the prime objection we get to this point: "Won't the 'creative' skill (e.g., geology) suffer if we put these experts on a [short-term results-oriented] business team?" We have, if truth be known, little patience with this one. Of course, the answer is in part yes. Only a pure functional organization will maintain purity of skill. But the "real world" answer is just as clearly "no." Human nature weighs on the side of the discipline: your people want to write papers and be heroes at discipline-based conventions (just as, it's said, most ad copywriters are writing primarily to show off to their peers, not their clients' customers). You don't have to worry about that. The management objective, however, is to deliver real new products or services in a hurry—and most speedup occurs when you allow the real world (e.g., manufacturing) to intrude very early, even if the designers' dreams of grandeur are roughed up a bit.

"Smash Functions Together":
Some Questions—and Things to Do Now

▶ Assess the performance of your decentralized elements—intentional (e.g., small divisions) and unintentional (e.g., skunkworks that have arisen, crash-project team efforts). Specifically, review in depth a half-dozen occasions when decentralized units have pulled the bacon out of the fire. Contrast these occasions—very specifically—with the performance of your more centralized elements. Is there a pattern of performance in favor of the decentralized unit?

▶ Review your divisional (factory, store) structure. Have you *unintentionally* abrogated authority, in a thousand subtle ways, since instituting a "clean" structure perhaps three or four, or ten, years ago? Don't take *your* word for it! Ask the leaders in the field. Make them *demonstrate*—via the accumulation of manuals, etc.—that it is *not* any worse than "x" years ago. (In other words, reverse the normal "goodness" assumption. *You* should assume that you *have* been fouling them up. Make *them* prove to you that you have *not!* Ten gets you one that you lose.)

▶ Take three or four development projects. How many have been delayed because of manufacturing scale-up, hopelessly unrealistic financial-needs assumptions, etc.? At what point do manufacturers (or operations experts), financial planners, etc., get added to teams? Can you speed up their introduction to the teams? Take one team and try it. (Caution: We mean—à la 3M, HP, Ford—*full time* support from the other functions; moreover, support where the "helper's" evaluation is based upon how well the team does, not how zealously he or she guards his or her function's integrity. The point is that the ancillary cast members must be committed to the project, not called in as part-time, dispassionate "experts.")

Related Myth 4B: Big is Different
Counterpoint: Small Within Big

"Hold on a minute," you say. "Maybe I buy in—at Bloomingdale's or Macy's, or for HP's hand-held calculators or a Raychem connector. And you did unearth that story of the GE locomotive. And even Nippon Kokan's BOF success. But what about the 'real stuff'? The truly big projects? The space program? The invention of the transistor at Bell Labs? The MX missile? The Boeing 767? Surely it's different for the giant ones."

Look Again at "Breakthroughs"

First of all, we doubt that big breakthroughs have much to do with development at all. "Big" and "breakthrough," as we discussed earlier (Myth no. 1) are often after-the-fact constructs (even with miracle drugs). Even when we write about relatively "small" big inventions, like Howard Head's metal sandwich ski, with Head as the hero, we are aware that there must have been twenty-five people (more like two hundred fifty, we suspect) who contributed the advances in materials science during the prior two decades that made it possible for Head to conceive of the solution as he did and when he did. The world of computers is similarly indebted to hundreds of important developments from the hardest sciences, from polymer chemistry and surface physics to optics. Evolutionary accidents ("breakthroughs") do occur (which wouldn't negate our point, anyway), but most advances are incremental, and most "breakthroughs" are the so-labeled post hoc results of cumulative innovation. In fact, according to a recent analysis of the space shuttle (and even the moon shot!), no truly monumental technological advances were required to pull it off. Development was, instead, one hell of a task of implementation, of putting known technologies in a new wrapper! (See another parallel in *The Nobel Duel.*)

Big, Yes!/Small Within Big

Even if we assume that there are big projects, that not all "breakthroughs" represent the results of cumulative innovation, we want to suggest that these, too, can be treated to a substantial degree as collections of skunkworks. In particular, the principle we call "small within big" turns out to be "optimal."

The Bell Labs' digital switch and IBM's System/360 were *not*, at first glance, built in skunkworks. That is, each was the organization's main project at the time. Nevertheless, a close look reveals that they were, in fact, thoroughly skunked. That is, most of the "breakthroughs" in the development of each came from champions operating off line, alone or with small teams. At IBM, time and again a 25-person group would go off-site for ten days, usually to a motel ($29.95 per room), and break a logjam that had been holding up the multihundred-person main group for months. Similarly, according to our informants at Bell Labs, the development of the digital switch is replete with tales of breakthroughs that occurred in basements. An executive in Honeywell's successful controls business puts it nicely: "I believe in project planning. It's just that I think of the major project map as a sort of Christmas tree on which I hang skunkworks like ornaments."

Or, consider Boeing's development of the air-launched cruise missile (ALCM). The system was complex. It should have been developed "all at once," undoubtedly with the aid of a 100,000-bubble PERT chart.* It wasn't. The missile was broken down into seven major pieces. Teams of modest size were assembled around the seven substantially autonomous tasks. To outsiders the tasks decidedly did *not* look autonomous. There was a lot of connectedness on paper. However, and this is precisely the point, Boeing *made* the tasks semiautonomous by fiat. Each had a champion. Each was in competition with all the others on several speed and quality parameters. The result? Each of the tasks was accomplished in a remarkably short period of time, relative to the norm. Not all came up roses. When the seven pieces were whacked together, they didn't fit exactly right. So the teams had to spend

---

*If you discern in our attacks on 100,000-bubble charts the zeal of a convert, you're reading correctly. Tom once drafted the world's most complex PERT chart, he thinks. And his ancient master's degree in engineering featured a then-state-of-the-art treatise on combining probabilistic time distributions in multitask PERT (Program Evaluation and Review Technique) design. To repeat a by now familiar refrain: It isn't that *milestones* are bad. It's just that we're in complete accord with the point of view of Allen Michels of Convergent Technologies that we stated in part before: "A group should have maybe four or five milestones. But I'm *not* talking about PERT charts. I'm talking about four or five unassailable things that you sign up to get *done* by a certain time. More complex than that and it doesn't mean anything."

some more time, up to a few months even, getting the interfaces right, despite the effort that had already gone into interface specification. (Boeing hadn't ignored this issue. There had been twice-a-week meetings of a "tiebreaker" group that had sorted out a good many of the interface issues along the way.)

Now many bridle at such "sloppy" retrofitting. And it is true that once the interfaces have been "Rube Goldberged" together, the final design usually isn't as technically "beautiful" as theory-on-paper suggests is possible. But multiple passes usually take much less time, and result ultimately in the development of simpler (more reliable), more practical (if less "beautiful") systems than the single "Get it exactly right the first time" blitz. (The Boeing ALCM was delivered over a year ahead of schedule and well under budget.) That is, using the "multiple pass" route on a "big" project, you wind up with a handful of quickly done, relatively simply designed hunks. Let's say it takes six months to reach that point. Then you take two months to fix the interfaces. Then the five or ten teams go back to work again and polish their individual apples, at the cost of another three months. Then another two months are needed to get the interfaces fixed one final time. You've made two complete "passes" through the system in, say, thirteen months. You probably have a reliable if not "optimal" (beautiful-on-paper) system. The "single pass" (everything depends on everything else), "Get it exactly right the first time" approach is likely to involve a two-year effort to start with—first full pass—and then the damn thing won't work anyway and will likely be too complex, at which point the "all at once" retrofit—which is equally complex—sucks up another couple of years.

"Small Wins"

Our friend Karl Weick wrote a lovely academic paper titled "Small Wins" (*The American Psychologist*, January 1984). It speaks directly to the "small within big" issue:

A series of small wins is also more structurally sound than a large win because small wins are stable building blocks. This characteristic is implicit in [Nobel laureate Herb] Simon's analysis of "nearly decomposable systems" and is illustrated by a fable:

Your task is to count out a thousand sheets of paper, while you are subject to periodic interruptions. Each interruption causes you to lose track of the count and forces you to start over. If you count the thousand as a single sequence, then an interruption could cause you, at worst, to lose count of as many as 999. If the sheets are put into stacks of 100, however, and each stack remains undisturbed by interruptions, then the worst possible count loss from interruption is 108. That number represents the recounting of the nine stacks of 100 each plus the 99 single sheets. Further, if sheets are first put into stacks of ten, which are then joined into stacks of

> 100, the worst possible loss from interruption would be 27. That number represents nine stacks of 100 plus nine stacks of ten plus nine single sheets. Not only is far less recounting time lost by putting the paper into "subsystems" of tens and hundreds, but the chances of completing the count are vastly higher.
>
> Small wins are like short stacks. They preserve gains, they cannot unravel, each one requires less coordination to execute, interruptions such as might occur when there is a change in political administration have limited effects, and subparts can be assembled into different configurations.

Yes, big *is* different. The hand-held calculator and the MX missile are *not* the same. The Boeing 767 and a change in the store format at Mervyn's are *not* the same. On the other hand, championing, the small group, the value of the overtight deadline, internal competition and commitment are keys to all.

"Small Within Big":
Some Questions—and Things to Do Now

▶ Analyze your two or three biggest projects. All stall from time to time. When you've broken out of a slump, what's been the cause? A skunkwork that emerged? Were your two best big programs marked by some form of "small within big," à la the Boeing case?

▶ Look at your two worst big project fiascoes. Were they beset by overcomplexity and "all at once" thinking?

▶ If your analyses in both questions above are congenial with our conclusions, can you do something about it—e.g., break down one big stalled project to get past a hurdle? Now?

▶ What's the nature of the discussion around this issue? Do many (particularly, technical people) pooh-pooh the analysis as "defeatism" (i.e., "What we really need are *better* PERT charts—and better managers!")? If so, can you muster more convincing evidence or begin an experiment right away, aimed at defusing the skeptics or testing the "small within big" view?

Related Myth 4C: Compatibility Drives All
Counterpoint: Last 2 Percent May Cost You the Market

A good plan violently executed right now is far better than a perfect plan executed next week.

General George Patton

Product release is held up another three months. And then another two. And then another forty-five days. "We've got to make sure that the software is *totally* compatible with *all* the rest of the product family," the logic goes. We buy it—up to a point. Product compatibility *is* important, particularly in products related to higher technology systems. But sometimes the last 2 (or 3) percent takes twelve (or eighteen) months. In the meantime ten competitors have approximated the solution, and gotten theirs into the marketplace faster and first. (At Data General, Tom West wrote these lines on the Magic Marker board in his office: "Not everything worth doing is worth doing well.")

IBM announced the System/360, and then they decommitted many of its most important compatibility features in a sequence of a half-dozen separate announcements. Incompatibility still bedevils IBM today, but the System/360 is legend. The Intel 8080 chip, a landmark, was put into the marketplace with many fewer features than had been planned (and promised). Hewlett-Packard engineers, marketers and salesmen lament the incompatibility (and partial overlap) among some products. But another computer maker, which held up production of a product for over six months, saw a major competitor come out with a product that was 75 percent as good (in the area of the principal new feature) and steal the march on an important niche. Several major manufacturers have been delaying products for months while trying to enhance networking and manufacturing interface compatibilities. Meanwhile, a company that is not exactly a household name, On-Line Software International, has introduced a decentralized software product to allow most personal computers to talk to corporate data bases.

In 1982 the Apple III was introduced before compatibility with IBM had been fully worked out—a major error, some said. Only a short while later software packages were developed independently by Base Two, Core Technology, Ergonomic Software, Mesa Graphics, Microlink NESTAR Systems, Protocol Computers, Viking, Soft-Tronics, Softwestern Data, Teksim—to name just a few—to make the Apple III substantially compatible with various IBM systems. Our colleague Bob Waterman went to a major computer systems bazaar at Brooks Hall in San Francisco in late 1982. In his words, "There were fifteen hundred people displaying. Seven hundred fifty of them were turning Apples into IBMs, and the other seven hundred fifty were turning IBMs into Apples."

We're not against compatibility, certainly. But particularly in the extremely fast-paced markets associated with computers, data handling and telecommunications, there are literally thousands of entrepreneurs who will (and do) fill in the spaces, do for you the last 2 percent (and very rapidly at that). Those who wait, trying to get the last percent of compatibility, may well go by the boards.

The same phenomenon, we might add, holds in many other markets, too. That's the reason Proctor & Gamble, 3M, Mars and Johnson & Johnson are so insistent about spurring competition among their divisions and brand managers. Bloomingdale's does the same thing among buyers and for floor space in its stores, and Macy's has done extremely well emulating the practice. In most markets, new things are being developed all the time and the lion's share of this activity is virtually invisible. You frequently don't see it until it's too late. The only way to fight it is to get something out there—*now*—even if it's not exactly tidy in terms of a perfect game plan.

A warning note is in order on this point: premature new-product release can be (and frequently is) disastrous. So when we talk about early release in connection with the last inch of compatibility and newly surfacing competitor products, we're limiting "early" to that—the last inch of compatibility; we're not talking about overall quality or the stocking of supporting spares. All too often a product hits the marketplace with the bugs not ironed out or spares not available, with the result that its technical or fashion advantage is blunted by rotten quality and reliability or insufficient support. Things that get out there ought to work, and ought to have some new features that give you good position in the marketplace. But getting that last possible feature, that last degree of complexity (read overcomplexity), that last degree of compatibility, may cost you more of the market than you would have gained by moving out smartly.

It's never an easy call. In our experience, however, the clear tendency—in all industries—seems to be to err far too much on the side of the optimizers, the perfectionists, the last quarter-percenters, who tend to win around the boardroom table; their case unfailingly looks great on paper, and they always use the argument, "And besides, it will only take another thirty days"; unfortunately, those last 30-day activities always seem to take 120 days—if you're lucky.

"Last 2 Percent May Cost You the Market": Some Questions—and Things to Do Now

► Look at five projects where competitors have gotten the jump on you in the last six to eighteen months. Have you in any instance had the response waiting but on hold while you tried to make it 2 percent (or 1 percent) better? Could you have released it earlier, while maintaining quality standards? Look at three good-news examples, when you have beaten a competitor to the punch. What did you do to speed up release while maintaining quality? Could you do this more often? What are the ingredients? Run an experiment on one or two projects, over the next ninety days, to see if you can noticeably speed up release time.

Myth No. 4D: Optimize!
Counterpoint: Optimization Loses in the Real World

Oh, if it weren't for people! Ten-thousand-person groups would be the most efficient. Oh, if it weren't for people! One-hundred-thousand-bubble

PERT charts and "all at once" execution would be most efficient. Oh, if it weren't for people! Huge amounts of money put into technical forecasting would anticipate competition, customer and technological surprises. Oh, if it weren't for people. De novo invention of every bit of machine innards would be the best way to assure quality. Oh yes, if it weren't for people.

What's optimal? We find that the so-called suboptimal is most often truly optimal (caveat: in the real world). Two "passes" through the system, the second to patch up sloppy boundaries among the skunkworked pieces (e.g., the seven pieces of the Boeing missile), are, it turns out, a heck of a lot faster *and* cheaper than the "optimization" route, and the results are of higher quality, too. Getting 95 percent compatibility and letting the Darwinist market-place do the rest turns out to be optimal, not suboptimal, since getting the last 5 percent may well cost you 50 percent of the market. TI's Mike Lockerd says the key is "intense dedication to what you do, and if it's convenient, be synergistic." (Or, as we rephrase him: Champions/Skunkworks - 1; Matrix/fractionalized responsibility - 0.)

The real problem is the word itself, and our training, especially of engineers and financial/administrative types. When we use the word "suboptimal" to describe a skunkwork, we are implicitly suggesting that the optimal is *possible* in the real world. But what's optimal in the real world is the product of a skunkwork—one that's simple, friendly, timely, fills a practical need and works. Optimal to us is the group that goes outside to buy, off the shelf, highly reliable parts; the group that gets a task that usually takes fifteen months done in fifteen weeks. Optimal is, in sum, the *practically obtainable optimal combination* of technical *and* people resources applied over a finite—i.e., *competitively plausible*—time period. In other words, "suboptimization" *is* "optimal," what we observe when an organization is really humming.

Let's take an example far from U-2's and super minicomputers. A former Unilever brand manager pointed out a surprising fact about Procter & Gamble, the master consumer-goods advertiser. He said, "You know, P&G basically uses just one measure of ad effectiveness: whether or not the ad will be remembered after twenty-four hours—'the twenty-four-hour recall'. The marketing journals serve up a new measure [of ad effectiveness] every month. At Unilever we used each one as it came along. We'd debate endlessly, and the reality was that each new one was pretty good. But when the measures are shifting all the time, most of the debate and discussion ends up being about the measures rather than the ad, and then you're not getting anywhere. The P&G measure may not be the world's best, but they've used it for years. They have developed a feel for what a good ad (or a bad one) is based on that invariant measure." P&G, per our friend's analysis, is following a "suboptimal" procedure—arriving at the true (maximum plausible) optimum. Technically, twenty-four-hour recall may only explain as much as 70 percent of what goes on. But twenty-five measures that explain 90 percent are humanly unmanageable and virtually meaningless. Everyone loses "feel" with so much complexity. There's no time to worry about ad copy because you're so worried about shifting post hoc measures of ad effectiveness. The suboptimal is optimal for P&G; the optimal is suboptimal for Unilever.*

"Optimal Loses in the Real World":
Some Questions—and Things to Do Now

▶ We simply propose that you think back to the last three of four extensive paper studies you've reviewed of savings from centralization, integration, matrixes. Of precision gained from ten more measures of something or other. Of certainty accruing from another four-month delay to collect "all the data." We suspect you'll find that the large majority of such delays or "complexifications" failed to pay off. That in the meanwhile successes that did accrue came from passion-driven, "too small," "underfunded" bands from odd corners of your world. Reflect on all that when next you sit down to review a gee-whiz proposal for a state-of-the-art mega-plant/mega-system/mega-project.

Myth No. 5: Customers Tell You about Yesterday
Counterpoint: Lead Users Are Years Ahead

As we observed in our discussion of MBWA and innovations, we've been able to unearth about eighty studies of sources of new-product ideas. They cover perhaps thirty industries, from bulk commodity chemicals to computers to shoes. In only one instance does the product development department seem to provide the lion's share of the ideas: in a study of bulk commodity chemicals. Analysis after analysis shows, in fact, that the great majority of ideas for new products come from the users. Our own research confirms it, not just in high technology but in the banking, health care and hamburger business as well.

An executive close to the aircraft industry provided a classic example, in this case in the fast-moving area of CAD/CAM (Computer-Aided Design/Computer-Aided Manufacturing). He works with McDonnell-Douglas. Their CAD system was the leader by a mile in the late seventies. But McDonnell-Douglas decided that it was *so* good that they'd keep it proprietary, and thus hold on to their advantage. Our colleague also works with the Lockheed CAD system. Lockheed came late to the marketplace and, positioned well

*Nobel Prize-winner Herb Simon invented the word "satisficing" to describe the real-world process of decision-makers reaching a satisfactory solution to a complex issue. Many have glommed onto it, and would say that's what we're talking about here. We disagree and take exception to "satisficing" because it hints that we *could* do better, and that it's "just good sense" to settle for the "satisfactory." Our point is that the joint technical/human/market "suboptimal" combination *is* truly optimal *within the context* of a real-world competitive environment.

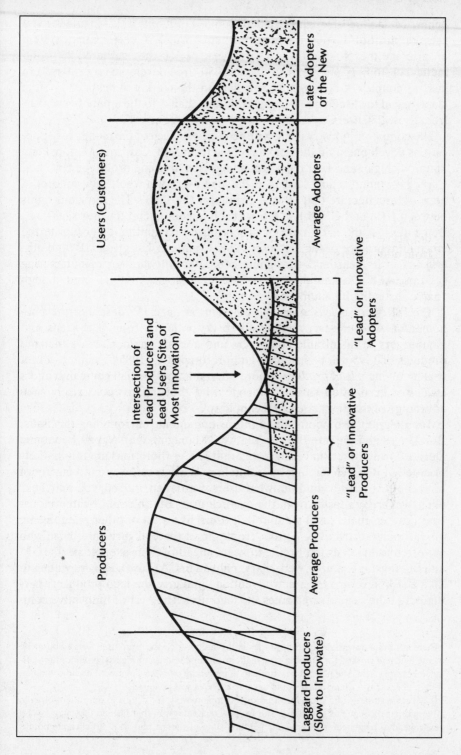

731

behind McDonnell-Douglas, decided to take a different tack—in effect, to let users do most of the development for them. Instead of keeping their system proprietary, they sold it. Over a three-year period they garnered 250 commercial customers. (We refer to them as 250 "free development centers.") In just a couple of years, the very-late-to-the-market Lockheed system leapfrogged the McDonnell-Douglas system, thanks to the input of new ideas from those 250 users.

The computer industry is rife with such cases. Much of the money for applications development in the field has come from MIT, Carnegie-Mellon, Penn State, Michigan and Bell Labs, and all have been prime prototype test sites. Carnegie-Mellon is now serving as the lead user for a whole new concept of network architecture that IBM is testing for the 1990's. The ferocious fights between IBM and GE (when GE was still in computers) for user sites—i.e., Bell Labs—in the early days of decentralized computing demonstrate the crucial importance of the lead user. ASK Computer has given HP (and others) fits in its heartland—designing computer software for manufacturing systems. ASK's essential edge is low technological hubris—and a high "naïve" listening IQ among lead users.*

The key word is *lead user*. The diagram on page 157 describes the phenomenon. After-the-fact analysis for every industry, from blue jeans and hamburgers to mainframe computers and aircraft engines, shows that the products of 1995 will be invented and prototyped ca. 1985 as some sort of a trial involving a *lead producer* (more often than not a small company) and a *lead user* (also often small), someone who thought he could really take advantage of the new, untested technology.†

The diagram also points up an interesting debate surrounding this issue. Bob Hayes and the late Bill Abernathy ("Managing Our Way to Economic Decline") and others have suggested that U.S. corporations are too market-oriented, not driven enough by technology. We agree, *if* we're talking about after-the-fact polls to find out what users want; then, indeed, you only hear about *yesterday's* tastes from the *average* user. But in sophisticated industries (and *all* really are!) we find that users, like a lot of other phenomena, are normally distributed. At the "front" tip of the bell curve are those who are often as much as ten to fifteen years ahead of their average peers (GM and Boeing, for example, were that far ahead in CAD use). They're willing to take a risk in return for a new invention. Similarly, the lead producer (particularly if he's small) welcomes the lead user. The best of innovative com-

---

*There are some downright amusing stories in this arena. A classic "lead user" was a housewife whose husband worked for Corning. One night he brought home a new glass container for a certain laboratory acid. She needed an extra pan to put in the oven, so she used the acid container. It didn't break, as ordinary glass would have. Thus Pyrex was invented.
† The success strategy of a small forest product company we work with is to offer themselves to all (legitimate) comers as a lead-user site for new technology. In that fashion they stay several years ahead of bigger competitors—*and* get their state-of-the-art-plus stuff dirt cheap to boot!

panies—Wang, 3M et al.—are constantly out there probing at that intersection of lead users and lead producers. They pay attention to their own lead users, and how they can better serve them; moreover, they pay attention to what small lead producers are providing to other lead users.* (*In Search of Excellence* rails against most forms of acquisitions. Yet we find that 3M, PepsiCo, P&G, Mars and others regularly acquire *tiny* "lead producers" as a window on new products and technology.) MIT's Eric von Hipple, who has been studying this process intensely for years, sums it up: "Market research, now chartered to seek data and analyze it, would [best] be reoriented to search out data on *user prototypes.*"

"Lead Users Are Years Ahead":
Some Questions—and Things to Do Now

▶ Have every unit analyze the source of new product/service ideas during the last two to three years. (The more detail, the better.) How many come from users? How systematic are your listening devices (debriefing reports, annual debriefing interviews, etc.)? Name five *new* listening devices/programs you have installed in the last eighteen months. Get a group of ten to fifteen people together for a day. Go over the data and form a "next-30-days-action plan" for better "naïve" listening and follow-up. (Incidentally, this can profitably, readily and effectively be done by internal functions—e.g., MIS—with the lead users being certain departments within the company.)

▶ Repeat the above for the industry as a whole. Go back *ten* years, if you can. (If you can't do the exercise, even that's good news: You've learned something about your ignorance in this area!)

▶ Do you seek out "lead users" (especially small, innovative companies) as test sites for *all*(!)/some/a few of your new programs? If not, why not? (By "seek out" we mean on a regular, knee-jerk basis, *very* early in the development cycle.)

Related Myth No. 5A: Technology Push Is the Secret
Counterpoint: Listening Is the Winning Approach

"More scientists in bigger labs" seems to be the watchword, with "better planning, better tools." Massive funding for huge R&D projects to help the United States retain its competitive edge. We expect such an approach won't

---

*The lead-user phenomenon pops up everywhere. The *Wall Street Journal* reports that Campbell Soup keeps in touch with several "impresarios of the restaurant world" in an effort to keep ahead of changing tastes.

work very well, not only because it precludes skunking but because the product that looks best on paper is not always or even often what the customer wants.

We've quoted Arch McGill: "The individual perceives service in his own terms." The customer wants to "feel good" about the product, no matter what it is. A bank chairman in Ohio apologetically admitted that he had bought an IBM system instead of "a much lower priced, technologically superior" Amdahl system. He said, "I simply feel better with IBM." The good feeling can come from the right sort of design, one that incorporates scores of details to enhance user friendliness, to make maintenance easier. It might even come simply from the shape of the package. (For instance, superior package design has long been a closely managed attribute at Raychem, approved in detail by Chairman Paul Cook.)

The point is that all this "stuff" ("stuff" or "fluff"—too many of our technologist/financially trained friends call it the latter) ought to be an up-front part of the *innovation process*. (We are, in fact, making another plea for the skunkwork. A skunkwork often has a much more "holistic" view of the product it's creating. It tends to view it more pragmatically, and out of necessity, in the customer's terms.)

"Listening Is the Winning Approach":
Some Questions—and Things to Do Now

▶ Does your design process have a large dose of "mundane user friendliness" infused into it from the very *start*? (To test the usefulness of this idea, can you point to *five* recent past examples where a competitor has "unfairly" trumped you by paying attention to little, friendly attributes rather than bigger technologically advanced features? Or where you, inadvertently or intentionally, have trumped a competitor this way?)

▶ Does *every* function in the company (i.e., purchasing, accounts receivable, MIS, as well as the more obvious functions) view itself as part of the innovating, new-product development process, with a role to enhance the "friendliness" of every tiny attribute of the product or service as it is presented to the customer? Do you celebrate (and reward) "customer friendliness innovations" from the service, accounting and purchasing departments as enthusiastically as you do those from marketing or design? If not, why not? Can you mount, right now, a contest for innovation success in *every* department, in general or relative to a specific new product?

10

Three Skunks

The life of skunks is seldom chronicled. Most fail. Many are fired. (As IBM's Don Estridge puts it, "You can always tell the pioneers. They're the ones lying face down in the path ahead of you with an arrow in their back.") We've come across three especially good ones, in print and in real life: Tom West of Data General, Kelly Johnson of Lockheed and Gerhard Neumann of GE. To help you understand these three, we want to provide (1) some excerpts from Tracy Kidder's *The Soul of a New Machine,* which talks about Tom West's successful thirty-person band at Data General, (2) a letter Tom received from a fellow who worked with Lockheed's Kelly Johnson for years (which was consistent with our interviews with Kelly and other of his former colleagues), and (3) a brief look at the management practices of GE's Gerhard Neumann, gleaned mainly from his fine 1984 autobiography, *Herman the German.*

Tom West

No one tells the story of a skunkwork better than Tracy Kidder in *The Soul of a New Machine,* an account of the creation of Data General's MV/8000 computer (the Eagle Machine) by the Eclipse Group, at the time a maverick team of engineers, championed by Tom West. The Eagle was to be an enhancement of the existing machine, the Eclipse. The following excerpts trace West's work with the new machine, and his relationships with the young creators (the Hardy Boys and the Microkids), his managers, Ed Rasala (the hardware designer) and Carl Alsing (the software designer), with whose description of West we begin.

West's never unprepared in any kind of meeting. He doesn't talk fast or raise his voice. He conveys—it's not enthusiasm exactly, it's the intensity of someone who's weathering a storm and showing us the way out. He's saying, "Look, we've got to move this way." Then once he gets the VP's to say it sounds good, Tom goes to some of the software people and some of his own people. "The bosses are signed up for this," he tells them. "Can I get you signed up to do your part?" He goes around and hits people one at a time, gets 'em enthused. They say, "Ahhh, it sounds like you're just gonna put a bag on the side of the Eclipse," and Tom'll give 'em his little grin and say, "It's gonna be fast as greased lightning." He tells them, "We're gonna do it by April." That's less than a year away, but never mind. Tom's message is: "Are you guys gonna do it, or sit on your ass and complain? It's a challenge he throws at them. . . .

There was, it appeared, a mysterious rite of initiation through which, in one way or another, almost every member of the team passed. The term that the old hands used for this rite—West invented the term, not the practice—was "signing up." By signing up for the project you agreed to do whatever was necessary for success. You agreed to forsake, if necessary, family, hobbies, and friends—if you had any of these left (and you might not, if you had signed up too many times before). From a manager's point of view, the practical virtues of the ritual were manifold. Labor was no longer coerced. Labor volunteered. When you signed up you in effect declared, "I want to do this job and I'll give it my heart and soul." It cut another way. The vice president of engineering, Carl Carman, who knew the term, said much later on: "Sometimes I worry that I pushed too hard. I tried not to push any harder than I would on myself. That's why, by the way, you have to go through the sign-up. To be sure you're not conning anybody." . . .

Ed Rasala allowed that West made life in the corner of the basement more dramatic—"Definitely more dramatic"—than it usually had to be. . . .

West kept final authority over the circuit designs. But he loosened control over most of the management of their creation. How did the Hardy Boys invent the general plan for the hardware? "Essentially," said Ed Rasala, "some of the guys and I sat down and decided what elements we needed." Over in the Microteam, though never explicitly told to do so, Chuck Holland took on the job of organizing the microcoding job. Holland and Ken Holberger mediated the deals between the Hardy Boys and the Microkids, but in general the veterans let them work things out for themselves. The entire Eclipse crew, especially its managers, seemed to be operating on instinct. Only the simplest visible arrangements existed among them. They kept no charts and graphs or organizational tables that meant anything. But those webs of voluntary, mutual responsibility, the product of many signings up, held them together. Of course, to a recruit it might look chaotic. Of course, someone who believed that a computer ought to be designed with long thought and a great deal of preliminary testing, and who favored rigid control, might have felt ill at the spectacle. Criticism of that sort flattered West. "Show me what I'm doing wrong," he'd say with a little smile.

In fact, the team designed the computer in something like six months and may have set a record for speed. The task was quite complex. . . .

That fall West had put a new term in his vocabulary. It was *trust*. "Trust is risk, and risk avoidance is the name of the game in business," West said once, in praise of trust. He would bind his team with mutual trust, he had decided. When a person signed up to do a job for him, he would in turn trust that person to accomplish it; he wouldn't break it down into little pieces and make the tasks small, easy and dull. . . .

Above all, Rasala wanted around him engineers who took an interest in the entire computer, not just in the parts that they had designed. He said that was what was needed to get Eagle out the door on time. He wanted the Hardy Boys to bind into a real team, and he spoke with evident frustration of engineers who were reluctant to work on boards that someone else had designed, who felt comfortable only when working on their own. . . .

Holberger runs into a problem—he needs to reprogram a PAL. To do that he needs the services of a functioning computer. He hurries to his cubicle and turns on his terminal, which is hooked up to the Eclipse called Woodstock. But a message appears on his screen saying that the program will not run, he'll have to wait—too many other engineers are using Woodstock now. But Holberger can't wait. So through his terminal he broadcasts an EMERGENCY WARNING MESSAGE. Throughout the basement, on every screen of every terminal using Woodstock at the moment, this message now appears. It says, in effect, "Shut down your terminal at once because the system is crashing." From his terminal Holberger can watch the various responses to this false alarm. Some engineers just go on working, he notes with amusement. "The cynical and jaded," he thinks. But enough other users shut down their terminals for Holberger to run the PAL program.

Holberger grinned. "I have the feeling that's the kind of behavior West approves of." . . .

When they had time on their hands to look up from the machine, some saw that they were building Eagle all by themselves, without any significant help from their leader. It was *their* project, theirs alone. West was just an office out of which came "disconnected input and outputs," said one Hardy Boy. He shrugged. It didn't matter. "West may be acting as a real good buffer between us and the rest of the company. Or maybe he's not doing anything."

Alsing listened, and sometimes he smiled. "When this is all over, there are gonna be thirty inventors of the Eagle machine," he predicted. "Tom's letting them believe that they invented it. It's cheaper than money." . . .

They didn't have to name the bigger game. Everyone who had been on the team for a while knew what it was called. It didn't involve stock options. Rasala and Alsing and many of the team had long since decided that they would never see more than token rewards of a material sort. The bigger game was "pinball." West had coined the term; all the old hands used it. "You win one game, you get to play another. You win with this machine, you get to build the next." Pinball was what counted. It was the tacit promise that lay behind signing up, at least for some. . . .

Maybe in the late 1970's designing and debugging a computer was inherently more interesting than any other jobs in industry. But to at least some engineers, at the outset, Eagle appeared to be a fairly uninteresting computer to build. Yet more than two dozen people worked on it overtime, without any real hope of material rewards, for a year and a half; and afterward most of them felt glad. That happened largely because West and the other managers gave them enough freedom to invent, while at the same time guiding them toward success.

West never passed up an opportunity to add flavor to the project. He helped to transform a dispute among engineers into a virtual War of the Roses. He created, as Rasala put it, a seemingly endless series of "brush fires," and got his staff charged up about putting them out. He was always finding romance and excitement in the seemingly ordinary. He welcomed a journalist to observe his team; and how it did delight him when one of the so-called kids remarked to me, "What we're doing must be important if there's a writer covering it."

Engineering is not of necessity a drab, drab world, but you do often sense that engineering teams aspire to a bland uniformity. West was unusual. Alsing, who might have traveled anywhere, but whose life had been largely restricted to the world of engineering, responded most strongly to him. "West," said Alsing, "took a bag on the side of the Eclipse and made it the most exciting project in the company, the most exciting thing in our lives for a year and a half. West never bored us."

Kelly Johnson

H. S. "Blackie" Shanlian worked for decades with the original Kelly Johnson Skunk Work at Lockheed. He wrote Tom about the experience:

Sunnyvale, CA 94089
July 25, 1984

Dr. Thomas J. Peters
505 Hamilton Ave., Suite 201
Palo Alto, CA 94301

Dear Dr. Peters:

It was with great interest that I read your book *In Search of Excellence.* Since I've been in supervision and management at Lockheed for some forty years I saw myself in the many good and some not-so-good situations that you described. . . . The experimental division "Skunk Works" was the brainchild of Clarence L. "Kelly" Johnson. He organized the division in 1943 to design, build and prove the first tactical jet fighter in the United States, XP80. This plane was designed, built and flown 143 days after the project was started. The reason that this project and numerous others following succeeded so well was that Kelly practiced the principles you have analyzed in your book. . . .

First of all, the application of the term "skunk works" to Lockheed's experimental division was on the part of several engineers who were griping about the lack of normally accepted organization in the small group. In the course of time the gripers disappeared but the name stuck. I was one of the charter members of Kelly's team and worked with him for twenty years and so the following comments are from personal observation.

Kelly organized his original team by choosing the best man to be found in each skill, discipline or craft. Each person was told why he had been chosen: He was the best one to be had! Whether it was absolutely true or not, each one believed it and did his darndest to live up to it.

Kelly was the great motivator. He offered to take all 75 employees to see the first flight of the XP80 if the plane was ready to fly in less time than the six months he had quoted the Air Force. When his enthusiastic crew beat his estimate, Kelly kept his word and took everyone to Muroc to see the wondrous first flight of an airplane without a propeller. Milo Burcham, the test pilot, was so impressed by the responses of this first take-off and landing that he then took off and gave the most thrilling exhibition of aerobatic flying that we had ever seen.

Kelly encouraged each person to give all that he could contribute to the program in spite of his job description. At one time I was a shop supervisor in charge of some 25 fabricators and assemblers. Besides supervising my crew I did all the planning, procuring, record keeping, liaison engineering and coordinating with the design engineers. In addition I was the timekeeper, safety man, security man and employment representative and I loved every minute of it.

Kelly practiced positive reinforcement. He gave credit to whom credit was due. We strived to do more than was expected of us so that we could get Kelly's nod of approval. So we became molded into a team that had a common goal.

Kelly advocated the simple solution whether it was in respect to design or keeping of records or in solving problems. Paper work was kept to a minimum. Even Air Force requested forms and reports were minimized. He issued no volumes of procedures or policies. He reiterated his basic philosophy, "Do the best possible job in the simplest way, at the cheapest cost in the quickest time." The application of this philosophy resulted in meeting or beating difficult schedules and in returning monies to the customer because we had been able to do the contracted job cheaper.

Kelly believed in having a minimum staff. There were only two levels of supervision between the vice president and the lowliest hourly paid employee. There was no need for an organization chart. Each one knew to whom he reported, what his job was and when it had to be done, and he did it.

Kelly communicated directly with all of his team, not with just one or two managers. He told all of us his goals, his joys, his fears and his pride in us. After one of his meetings there was nothing that any one person would not do. He not only talked to us but he listened and often accepted our suggestions when they were worthwhile. We respected him and he respected us. It was a pleasure and an honor to be a member of Kelly Johnson's team.

Sincerely,

H. S. "Blackie" Shanlian

Gerhard Neumann

Gerhard Neumann was a guiding force in establishing GE's dominance in jet aircraft engines (against sound, entrenched competition from United Technologies' Pratt & Whitney). His recent (1984) autobiography confirmed stories about him we'd heard for years. It also reinforced our perceptions about the role of skunkworks and passionate champions.

Our perceptions	*Neumann*
Small groups are an advantage.	"The project [to create the Variable Stator Experimental Engine] reminded me of the Flying Tigers in China. . . . undermanned, overworked, and successful!"
Big time savings.	"Normally the job takes 24 months. . . . I was given one year."
Importance of integrated teams.	"All of us were one team: workers, managers, foremen, and engineers."
Isolate team for esprit.	"I insisted this area be painted snow white, in stark contrast to the customary unattractive dark factory gray. Anyone working in the white area could not help but get a feeling of care and importance."

Drama, pizzazz.	"Each morning I stood on top of my desk and got the attention of my [120] associates by ringing a Swiss cowbell. . . . One Friday we ran into a problem whose solution called for a miracle. 'Isn't there anyone who can pull a rabbit out of a hat?' I asked. Under the table in my hat resting on my knees was a live rabbit. I slid the hat into the middle of the round conference table and pulled the astonished bunny by his ears out of the hat. We *did* find a solution that afternoon."
No frills for the boss.	"I moved out of my private office to sit with the troops. . . . I refused to have a rug in my office or a private john next to it—both seemingly essential for all executives in American big industry."
Daily review.	"I updated the assembled team on what we had accomplished during the past 24 hours, what problems had arisen, how many days we had before the next milestone. . . . We held design reviews several times a week. . . . I established [in a bigger group] an IOI (Items of Importance) system: A daily, typed, single-page memo covering the main events of the last 24 hours was mandatory, from every-one reporting to us. (To delegate the writing of an IOI was verboten.)"
MBWA.	". . . my nightly walks through the plant . . . informal discussions during first, second, and third shifts became routine."
Allow team to purchase components, etc., outside.	"I began to encourage competition by outside manufacturers with our own shops."
Importance of "feel."	"My career was helped by my having been fortunate to remain in

my professional field of mechanics and aircraft. I thus had an opportunity to develop a superior *feel* for technical 'go' or 'no go' designs in the real world, regardless of theory or computers."

Obsession.

"Every bit of available time was invested in reading the daily IOIs, studying reports, walking the shops. I will not answer here the question, 'Would you again?' "

11

The Context of Innovation

> My father's real gift and value to U.S. Shoe is not in 'properly segment-
> ing the market'; rather, he has created a beautiful corporate culture
> which rewards risk taking, which supports rather than punishes those
> who have a bad year or two, which allows ideas to percolate upward.
>
> *Michael Barach, responding to a Fortune article
> about U.S. Shoe*

There are some fabled (and somewhat crazy) champions around: Steve
Jobs and Steve Wozniak at Apple, Howard Head, Barney Oliver at HP, Ken
Stahl at Xerox, Tom West, Gerhard Neumann, Kelly Johnson. But while of
great importance, these people are *not* the heart of the matter for the continuously innovative firm, except as real-life symbols of what can be done. The
heart of the matter is turning the crowd in the top 10 percent (if not the top
30 percent) into champions, continually reeling off practical innovations,
small and large, in accounting as well as in product development. Such is the
magic of Schlumberger (its field engineers), The Limited (its store managers), Citicorp (its country managers), Macy's and Bloomingdale's and
Mervyn's (their buyers), 3M and Raychem and HP (their product developers), PepsiCo (their brand managers), Trammell Crow (its entrepreneurial
associates). The tenacious inventor of the Post-It Note Pad at 3M, the developer of Doritos at Frito-Lay, Marriott's entrepreneurial property manager
who created a big win at their Rancho Los Palmas resort in Palm Springs,
California, are our models: "ordinary" people turned into vigorous, enthusiastic experimenters. The environment that transforms them into champions is
the context of innovation, the subject of this chapter.

The Visit

The meeting with the division general manager has been scheduled two
weeks before. He runs a $40 million division, and has a lot on his platter, start-
ing with endless corporate committee assignments. So it takes about that long
for a mid-level engineer to get in to see him. The hour arrives, 10:45 A.M. precisely. You march up to his office. His perfectly coiffed, slightly graying exec-

utive secretary silently motions you to take a seat. Aggressive young staffers shuttle in and out of his sanctuary over the next twenty minutes. Each seems to be carrying a thicker set of briefing papers than the last. Finally it is your turn. You are ushered into the cavernous 30-by-30-foot office. His desk is in the back corner, spotless, even dust-free. It's a beautiful old mahogany desk, rumored to have been used by the company's founder over sixty years ago (sometimes you think the wood must have come from the *Mayflower*). He sits there, perfectly poised, vest buttoned and in a dark blue suit coat despite the August heat. He's tapping his Cross pen lightly on the desktop and talking to his secretary via the intercom, checking on his next meeting, to be held in exactly twenty-five minutes.

Somehow it seems most unlikely that you'd traipse into this Presence and have a little chat about an "interesting screwup" at the lab bench or a vendor's shop or in a preliminary test market. Here you had better have something darn concise to say. And it had best be the good news he wants to hear.

Unfortunately, we find that this scenario comes all too close to the mark most of the time, in big and even small organizations. It stands in stark contrast to the gist of a discussion we had in late 1983 with a group of eight or ten senior people at a major pharmaceutical house on the subject of "nurturing champions." One fellow's name kept cropping up again and again as a prime candidate for Hall of Fame nurturer. He had been the "executive champion" for an extraordinary share of successful new products and new-product champions over a period of decades. He wasn't a genius. Not a brilliant planner. In fact, he had none of the conventional attributes of a "star" performer. But a score of other attributes eventually surfaced, such as the following.

▶ "It didn't matter what had gone on. It didn't matter how bad the news of the day was. Whenever you walked into his office, the first thing he invariably asked was, 'Are you having fun? Are you up to something that's giving you some kicks?' "

▶ "It was interesting. He had a cramped office, with samples of every product he'd ever been associated with scattered about. Also prominently displayed were some of the more egregious failures that he had worked on, and some that a few of the champions he had sponsored had worked on. There was even a plaque, BONEHEAD OF THE YEAR, prominently displayed. And then there was the centerpiece—his pride and joy. His chair. It was—now, get this—an old-fashioned barber's chair! When you'd come in, he'd wander over to it and, with a bit of fanfare, hop in. He'd look you in the eye: 'Now tell me something interesting that's going on.' "

There was no question about whether or not this champion of champions was a tough character. He was: "You wouldn't want to go see him unless you had *something* to chat about. He was no fan of sloppiness or shoddy work. But you felt this guy had been there before. You felt that he understood, that he knew, really *knew*, the inherently messy process associated with innovating." You could see right away, they added, that he loved interesting experiments, and was almost as happy with those that failed as with those that succeeded—as long as you had *learned* something from the failures. In fact, one fellow notes, "I think he really liked the failures *better* if he and you learned something interesting. He always wanted to know exactly what you learned, whether it had taken you a step further down the pike toward dealing with the problem that you had set for yourself. In a way, he considered success to be boring. He wanted you to hurry through your successes, and push up against another stumbling block, defined, really, as a failure. The new barriers were the gist, to be puzzled over, thought about. Then you'd discuss the things that might make sense to move on to next. In a hurry."*

THE ENTREPRENEURIAL ENVIRONMENT

In the years since *In Search of Excellence* was written, we have gotten to know the 3M Company better. 3M was featured in a chapter on autonomy and entrepreneurship in that 1982 book. Tom was frankly proud of that section, feeling that it went far beyond the usual discussion of innovation. It was not about "technology strategy planning," and barely touched upon organizational structure. Instead it talked about the unique composition of a 3M product team and, for instance, the way its members were rewarded and promoted as a group. It was a fine discussion as far as it went. But what we have observed since is much more subtle—and arguably much more important. Let us try to give you a bit of a sense of the context of innovation at 3M.

Sometime ago, Tom visited with a large group of 3M salespeople in the western part of the United States. In preparing for such visits, we routinely ask the organizations involved to send along in advance some information about what they are up to. Usually the most recent annual report is forwarded. Sometimes there will be a statement of philosophy, a recent speech by the president to the security analysts, and occasionally a truncated strategy document. The 3M packet arrived. It must have weighed close to two pounds. What was it? A catalog of every product that the company sold in this area (the health care sector), complete with specifications, and featuring extensive literature on the new ones. New products are "in the air" at 3M. If you want to know about 3M, you've got to get to know their products! They're "into" their products.†

---

*A 3M manager in Sydney, Australia, reacted strongly to this story. He said this fellow sounded like a carbon copy of the man responsible for an "unfair share" of a whole sector's products at 3M. In fact, he thought that was whom we were talking about before we identified the company as a pharmaceutical house.

†3M's was the first product catalog we'd ever received. In July 1984 we received our second. It was from the Raychem Corporation, a 3M clone in terms of innovativeness. Actually, Raychem topped 3M; they came to our office and, unsolicited, gave our staff a product demonstration—of a sophisticated thermal sensor!

Then it was off to the meeting, the monthly "rally" at which the 3M sales force gathers to talk about their products. Part of a program adopted in the last few years, it's aimed at getting the various sales forces (3M has about fifty specialized sales forces) to learn about one another's products. In this instance, it featured a half-dozen or so sales forces in the health care products area. If it had been a big 3M user conference, the sort that the computer industry has, we'd have understood the extensiveness of the displays. But this was just a routine monthly meeting. And yet what a show! Table after table of displays, with all the new products. The feeling went far beyond that, but the inadequacy of our skill at description limits our ability to transmit it to you (and what a contrast to most settings it represents). The "smell" of innovation lies in such tiny things! Everyone was actively testing the products, fiddling ceaselessly with this, that and the other. Everyone was genuinely interested. Getting any of them into the conference room was painful—they preferred playing with products.

Things were going well for them, a good year. Yet they're not in some astounding 40 percent-a-year-growth arena. In fact, the introduction of standardized reimbursement schemes in the health care sector is a bit threatening to high-price players in the field such as 3M. So if they had no reason to be unhappy, they had no reason to be ecstatic either. And yet they seemed genuinely to be having fun. One of the newer groups in the area had garnered enough sales to be automatically elevated to the status of division, in accordance with 3M rules. There was loud cheering when that was announced. Tom was surprised. In most companies such things as achieving divisional status according to a rule don't happen, period. If they were to happen, only the very senior people or executives on the division's payroll would take much note. It would hardly be an occasion for all-hands interest, as was the case here. Another oddity: Products are regularly transferred from one sales force to another with little fanfare (and without the bloody, destructive, demoralizing product-transfer battles we routinely observe). Presentation after presentation, made by senior and junior salespeople alike, focused on that: "We just inherited the blankety-blank product from the blankety-blank division. This is what we are going to try to do with it." Yet another oddity: Tom began his speech with a fairly flippant remark: "It's always a pleasure to talk to the 3M Company. Things are in such disarray. It's the most screwed-up company in America. And I think that's great." Call most groups of people "screwed up" and smiles would turn to frowns; there would be stony silence. Here a cheer went up. 3M people know they're screwed up (in their wonderful fashion), and take great pleasure in the fact.

All small things. For another 3M meeting, this one the 1984 retreat for the company's top 150 managers (the theme was "Commitment to Innovation"—what else?), we were thumbing idly through the agenda, some two or three pages listing various presentations. We were struck by the fact that unfailingly first names were used. Chairman Lew Lehr's presentation was labeled "Lew's Speech." That was the formal designation! Small thing? No, not in our opinion. (Just for the heck of it, we went back and rummaged through our files on other corporate meetings and randomly pulled—from files on banks and insurance companies and pharmaceutical houses—fifteen similar agendas. Five referred to each speaker as Mr. or Ms. such and such. Nine used initials: B. L. Smith, C. N. Jones. The fifteenth used last names alone. None of the fifteen had a first name in it.)

We have also had a chance in these last few years to share the podium with 3Mers at various events. In all settings they own up to (i.e., preach) the messy world of innovation. One speech, made by an executive vice president, Ken Schoen, began this way: "You've got to begin with the unassailable premise: Innovation is a very untidy process." He went on to talk about the value of "gut feel for the customer's needs," which he said "is worth a ton of market research." Further along in his speech, there was another telling off-hand remark: "This week, when we created a new division . . ." The tone was "If it's Monday, there must be a new division." In most companies, creation of a new division takes years and is marked principally by political hassle. On another occasion, Ken joked about having once had to hire a lawyer for his division—in the midst of a head-count freeze, no less—for the express purpose of fighting a corporate lawyer over a product issue. Can you imagine that in most settings? Heresy is not too strong a word. Yet at 3M, that's the way a division manager is *supposed* to act. Nothing, *especially* corporate, is supposed to get in the division's way. It's up to the general manager to make sure it doesn't.

In just this brief discussion, several variables have surfaced: the role of informality, the physical feel of the innovative place, all-hands involvement in new products, having fun, creation of new divisions and shifts of product responsibility as the norm, the role of the general manager as a corporate beater. The language, the feel of a 3M setting, suggest more than a bit about the context of innovation.

Let us now switch abruptly to another extreme case, one that supports our overall point, but which, frankly, scares the daylights out of us. It scares us because it suggests just how big (and deep) the chasm is between the innovators and the noninnovators. Innovating is *the* priority at Hewlett-Packard (as it is at 3M). We were talking to a group of executives who manufacture analytic instruments about the unique HP approach they call the Triad Development Process (see pp. 721–722). At issue was the way the more innovative companies have come to grips with the tough issues of manufacturing scale-up. An HP division general manager who was present came up during a break and said that we'd been right on the mark. He then proceeded to tell a story that suggested we'd missed that mark by a country mile at *least*. We had talked about the need for design engineers to have access to manufacturing from time to time. He said, "Damn it, they did it to me *twice* last week!" "What?" we asked. "Two times my plant manager *shut down the line,* in the middle of an important product run. In both cases, the engineering guys needed some part of a new-product prototype they were working on tested with some important factory equipment." Our reaction: "Holy smokes!"

747

Why? Because, in 99 out of 100 companies (at least), if a new-product engineering guy asked a plant manager to disrupt an important run, he'd be thrown out on his ear. (In nine out of ten companies, the new-product people don't talk regularly to the manufacturing guys, period. Don't live in—or even near—the same home.) Here it was *natural.* Moreover—and most important—it was the *expected* response by the manufacturer. The general manager put on a ritual show of anger at what had gone on, but he knew it was futile as he said it. In the most important sense, he was delighted. Innovating, experimenting, testing things in manufacturing areas—at any time, at almost any cost—simply comes first at HP. It would never occur to manufacturing *not* to accede to the engineer's request. That *is* HP. You don't short a salesperson at Frito-Lay or P&G. You don't get in an engineer's way at HP. And that's that.

"The Entrepreneurial Environment":
Some Questions—and Things to Do Now

▶ We will be more specific in the pages ahead. But at this time we suggest you reflect on the "visit" and the "entrepreneurial environment." Pick, in your mind, two or three innovative departments in your company, or an innovative company you've worked with. Then pick two or three noninnovative spots. Think about the involvement of management in products and innovation in the two sets of examples. Can you "feel" the difference? Try a walk through an innovative group, a noninnovative group (either can be an accounting department as easily as a design department). Does one "look" different from the other? Try to list 10 to 15 "trivial" points of difference in language, physical trappings, etc.

▶ Reflect on the HP "Stop the line" example. To what degree do all functions in your organization "live for innovation"? Could the HP event have happened in your company? Ever? Routinely? Are you sure you can answer (try to collect some hard data around the issue)?

▶ As a first action step, sit with a half-dozen colleagues, preferably from multiple functions, and discuss your findings from these reflections. Be tough on one another: that is, are you really sure that's the way people respond?

LANGUAGE, AND THE TALES YOU TELL

The parallels between HP and 3M are striking, especially in their language; Peters and Waterman (Tom judges) flat out missed it in *In Search of Excellence.* Sit down with a bunch of senior HP people. A couple of executive vice presidents could be present or not. It doesn't matter. Invariably, and usually rather quickly, the talk turns to new products. The undertone is irreverence: a division takes pride in getting a product (often a partial duplicate of a product made by some other division) to the marketplace *before* corporate has figured out whether or not they even want it. Senior management is often the butt of jokes. Publicly—in the very best sense. The message is clear: "Don't wait for the fogies; do it."

Listen to young HPers; the talk is similar: "You learn the first week that you're *nothing* around here until you've been on a successful product development team." Constantly the chatter reinforces the idea that "getting on with it, by hook or by crook, is the way to do things around here." In most companies such bull-in-the-china-shop behavior doesn't occur frequently (especially when youngsters are involved). If and when it does, it's a well-guarded secret, not the subject of constant and public banter among respected elders "designed" to cause emulation by the young.

The openness is vital. We talk to companies with poor records of innovation. We persuade them to discuss in detail a new product that has been brought in. It turns out that the story in the stodgy company is *exactly* the same as in the innovative company: a mess. Experiments. Lucky breaks. A determined (to the edge of irrationality) champion. Bootlegging (products or pieces of products being built off-line). Projects costing $100,000 being done as a series of a hundred innocuous authorizations of a thousand dollars each. So innovation occurs in the same way in the great innovative companies and the not so great. But at the great ones—Raychem, HP, 3M, Citicorp, Macy's, PepsiCo—the language suggests that this sloppy, semi-illicit way of doing things is the *norm,* to be tried by all, to be cherished.

At Bank X (the norm) the bootleg project is a well-guarded secret. At Citicorp, if you're *not* out bootlegging, you're a second-class citizen. And if you're not bragging about it, it's surprising. At Package Goods Company Y (the norm), a test market failure is a closely kept secret. At PepsiCo, the response is: "So what. What the hell are you going to do to fix it? *Now.*" The difference is that the open chatter directly induces the huge number of rapid tries that are *essential* for bringing in a constant stream of winners.

"Language of Innovation":
Some Questions—and Things to Do Now

▶ Interview ten junior people in development, manufacturing, sales and service; talk about ongoing or recent projects. Also sit in on two or three meetings of such people (yes, your presence will change things). Is the talk openly marked by discussions of failures, acknowledgment of the failures of the planning process? Is it marked by juniors' *irreverence* (even with you there, assuming you're a "boss"—second-line supervisor, vice president, etc.) toward *everything,* especially delays? Are illicit/semi-illicit responses (bootlegging, skunkworks) talked about *openly* as *normal* solutions to conundrums? Repeat the process with *very* junior/entry-level people (some with 90 days' experience or less). Does the language of bootlegging, scrounging, surface (it would at HP/Raychem/PepsiCo/Citicorp within a week of hiring!)?

▶ If you are dissatisfied with the results of the above, the *only* way to fix it, we believe, is to purposefully and systematically introduce irreverence into your casual and formal chats, especially with the *very* new. More formal vehicles, such as workshops on innovation that analyze past successes and failures and home in on the role of (and expectation of) scrounging, will help.

Honor Thy Cheaters—in Public

We were talking about the goings-on in innovative companies with a colleague in a not-so-innovative company. He said, "The trouble is, when they get to the top [here], they forget what got them there. Namely, 'cheating.' They become the paragons of virtue, beholden to the controller." In fact, he was talking about a specific boss. And we chatted with the boss subsequently. We reviewed together his five or six most successful projects, those that had led to various promotions. It turned out that every one had involved "cheating," lots of it. By cheating, we don't mean stealing or behaving in an immoral fashion. We do mean bringing people and resources and, often, customers together more rapidly than the bureaucratic rules would allow. Well, it turns out that this boss is an inveterate cheater! The trouble is that he doesn't admit to it or tell anybody about it. And by not telling anybody about it, he fails to inspire emulation of the process that brought him success. He doesn't signal that "this ['cheating,' scrounging] is *the* way." Rather, his words and standard bosslike behavior induce people to follow the petty rules and be good bureaucrats. (We regularly use this experience as a jumping-off point for an exercise. We've gone through it, taking up to half a day, with groups of fifty or sixty: bankers, MIS people, retailers, software-company types. The result, under probing, has been exactly the same everywhere, whether the place is innovative or not. Behind every promotion is a win or two. Behind every win is "cheating," in the best sense of the word.)

In stark contrast to the above, at Raychem the language in an interview with a general manager is peppered with remarks like "Everything takes a champion." . . . "Business plans exist, but they are bullshit." . . . "There's nothing you can't get done overnight." . . . "There's not a damn thing wrong with failure. It's erasable!" Openly and explicitly, people at Raychem *honor* cheating. Demand it, really. A middle-management interview yields similar paydirt: "It's a magic place." . . . "Write your own ticket." . . . "It's a moving target." . . . "Structured people can't survive here." . . . "Anybody can present an idea to [Chairman Paul] Cook." . . . "There is always something going on." . . . And best of all (wouldn't you love to have your people saying this about your group?): "People believe they can make *anything* happen."

An executive in Honeywell's controls group put it well: "I don't tell or order anybody to cheat. Of course I don't do that. What I do is make it a regular point to drop by and chat with the development teams, the marketing guys, the engineers, especially the young ones, some of the manufacturing people involved in new products. I talk about what I used to do when I was their age. I talk openly about some of the shenanigans that I pulled, squirreling away resources, not telling someone I was finished with one project so that I could get time to work on a bootleg job, and so on. I don't demand that they do the same thing. I just tell them what *I* did, and then I get up quietly and leave." Another colleague, a consultant with a major firm, puts it almost the same way:" "I don't sanction it [cheating]. It's just that when people tell certain kinds of stories [about bootleg activity, skunkworks, and the like], I smile a lot. Sort of knowingly."

It's exactly such stories that are at the heart of the innovating—i.e., "Get on with it," "Try it"—process. The best of the innovative companies seem to have vast oceans of tales about how innovation was *really* done. Instead of stressing the buttoned-down attributes, they stress the sloppy attributes, and thus the need to get on with it.

There can, of course, be a more public side to it. Domino's Pizza Distribution Company will honor an innovation/cheater by naming an award after him or her—e.g., the "Dennis Collins Award." The one so honored personally gives out the award when next granted, and the pictures of award winners go permanently into a Hall of Innovation.

Another variety of stories leads us to see yet another dimension of the language equation. We call them "big-end-from-small-beginnings stories," a line that we first heard, in fact, from 3M's international president. In chapter 2 (pp. 596–597) we spoke of the transformation of PepsiCo into an innovative entrepreneurial company. Four or five times recently we've listened to PepsiCo senior managers make speeches (inside and outside the company). They all talk, regardless of the topic of speech, about the need to find small entrepreneurial activities to grow. They invariably recount the history of the Frito-Lay and Pizza Hut start-ups, emphasizing that each grew out of a $500 loan from a mother to a son! Obviously, the notion being touted is that future winners will as likely come from the $5,000 or $50,000 ideas as from the well-planned $10 million development projects.

The lesson from all this is compellingly simple. If you *want innovation, you have got to talk—incessantly—about innovation.* If you want skunkworks, you've got to talk about skunkworks. If you want people to "cheat," you have to talk about the rewards (and honor) of "cheating." If you want people to devote energy to seeking out small, risky ventures instead of merely attaching themselves to today's big-team effort (in the spotlight now), you must tell stories that suggest that the heroes of today were risk-seeking entrepreneurs inside the company who started small and poor, not big and safe.

It boils down to associating yourself regularly with certain kinds of activities as opposed to certain others. In his column in the Spring 1984 issue of

Chief Executive, Robert W. Lear, former chairman of F&M Schaefer (and now a professor at Columbia), reinforces the point:

> In many companies, at many times, the CEO must be the devil's advocate and play a calculated, negative role. There are periods when he must avoid catastrophe, minimize risk, and play the waiting game. A danger is that it can become his management style to be negative. The CEO can come to envision himself as the answerer of tough questions, the insister on compliance with procedures, the setter of high hurdle rates. He can too readily punish those who have tried and failed, too easily reward those who took no risks at all. . . . Product championing by the CEO can be done with a sense of humor. [Admiral] Chester Nimitz, when he was chief executive officer of Perkin Elmer, told me about attending a product development presentation. At the end of the show, he said to the management group, "I hope you have seen me sidling over to stand beside this new product suggestion. I like the idea so much that I want to be identified with it when it becomes successful." How much better that is than "viewing with alarm" and theorizing pitfalls.

So add "sidling over" to your vocabulary. A senior IBM finance person says, "I know where all the bootleg project money is hidden—sorta." Add "sorta" to your vocabulary, too! In *The Soul of a New Machine,* author Tracy Kidder speculated on whether or not Data General CEO Ed de Castro knew about Tom West's skunkwork. The answer? Of course he did—sorta! Said West: "There's a lot of people pretending that this project doesn't exist." Add "pretending" to your vocabulary! This isn't very precise language, but it's key. How often do you use cheat, sorta, sidling over, pretending—or fail?

Sloppy But Not Shoddy

We must stress one caveat here: the fact that sloppiness is one of the essential attributes of innovation decidedly does not imply sanction for sloppy or shoddy thinking or action. To say that 3M honors the sloppy process is to say they respect the irreducible need to try, try, test, test, in order to confront, as rapidly as possible, the numerous roadblocks that always bar the path to a successful commercial product. Paradoxically, this sloppy procedure requires you to know—*exactly*—what you hope to learn from each new iteration or partial iteration. *The more the chaos of the natural world is honored, the greater the discipline required to confront the mess and move forward with alacrity.* Thus, on net, the more innovative the company, the more tough-minded we find management to be: PepsiCo, Mervyn's, Macy's, HP, 3M, Bloomingdale's, Convergent Technologies, W. L. Gore, Kollmorgen and Raychem surely qualify as places for the faint of heart to avoid like the plague. On the flip side the companies that live by a belief that the 100,000-bubble PERT charts will conquer uncertainty and ambiguity are the patsy institutions. There "checking off the boxes," rather than actually doing something, is often acceptable behavior.

"Honor Thy Cheaters": Some Questions—and Things to Do Now

▶ Did you "cheat" to get to where you've gotten? Do you admit it? In public? Do you get specific? With pride? To junior subordinates? Regularly? How about your peers (same seven questions—try it with five peers from five different functions)? If you think you "pass" on this, test your assumptions with very junior people. Do *they* think of you as a "scrounge" or as a "good bureaucrat"? Ask them bluntly! Sit with a half-dozen colleagues: Bring up the last *five* times, specifically (date/place), you "bragged about your bootlegging skills"—past or present. Do you have to go back more than *thirty* days? (If so, you've probably got a problem.)

▶ Are there written stories about the company's bootleg-strewn past? Are there stories of young, nonsenior champions around? Are *all* functions (MIS, accounting, manufacturing, as well as engineering, design, merchandising) covered by your historical sketches of champions? Do your stories *stress* "big ends from small beginnings"? (Are you sure, and if so, are they effective? Casually survey ten people: Would they rather have an ancillary role on a big, visible project team—where they *perceive* they are being more closely watched—or a more central role on a small team?)

▶ Discuss, for a full half day, the words "sorta," "pretend," "sidle over," etc. The language surrounding successful bootlegging is delicate. Do you consciously manage it?

▶ Take several of the phrases from Raychem (e.g., "Everything takes a champion," "Structured people can't survive here," "People believe they can make anything happen"). Construct an "agree"/"disagree" questionnaire using these phrases. Try it, with guaranteed anonymity, on a half-dozen people in three functions (e.g., design, MIS, manufacturing) and at three levels (entry, first-level supervision, department head). What's the result? How does it match with what you think it ought to be?

FOCUS ON FAILURE

We think of the people who are supporters of the "Good tries that fail are OK—even normal" school. The best personalize. They personalize by focusing, openly and in public, on *their* past failures. Pete Thigpen is dealing with the troubles that have arisen at Levi Strauss. To grow into the future they need to try a host of new things. To try is tough. To test is to fail, repeatedly. They need, in Pete's words, to "increase the failure rate" (i.e., get the inevitable—necessary—missteps out of the way as rapidly as possible). A major tool he uses to induce this is relating in every imaginable setting—when he teaches at Stanford, at in-house meetings with marketing staff—and in grim and gory detail stories of his own foul-ups (and he's got a doozer or two). The implicit (darn near explicit) message is "You can foul up, learn from it, and eventually get to the top." Your boy can chop down a cherry tree and grow up to be President, too!

Bill Smithburg, the new chairman of Quaker Oats, is trying to shake up and revitalize that company, a fine but somewhat stodgy institution. He gives a similar high visibility role to failure. He talks regularly about his own failures, and he talks about the failures of all of his colleagues in the senior executive ranks. He adds, "It's just like learning to ski. If you're not falling down, you're not learning."

Even bankers! Ron Terry, chief executive of innovative First Tennessee, says, "Admitting I make mistakes is my greatest strength." He's in good company. Thomas Alva Edison, the peerless inventor, once said, "I failed my way to success." So did Mary Kay Ash, founder of Mary Kay Cosmetics.

Some have included the notion of failing explicitly in their company philosophy. Our favorite is from a small, very successful computer peripherals company, brought to our attention by our colleague Jim Kouzes. One of just a half-dozen points in their formal written philosophy is this: "We tell our people to make at least ten mistakes a day. If you are not making ten mistakes a day, you are not trying hard enough." Depending upon whether you are in retailing or in jet engines, that number may vary from two to forty. But we think that directionally it's right on.

Two points need emphasis here. First, just as sloppy does not mean shoddy, to be a supporter of failure is in no way to be a supporter of slipshod performance. We're talking about *good tries* that fail, well-planned good tries from which one *explicitly* learns something quickly. Second, we'd add that there are absolutely *no* limits to this notion. We've gotten snide asides from time to time: "I certainly don't want my *pilot* to fail ten times a day!" Well, we would just as soon not have our pilot foul up either. Since we're probably as frequent fliers as anyone who will read this book, it is more important to us than to most. But—and it's no small point—we want that person in the front seat of our plane to have screwed up in every way known to man, and to have come back from it. We want his or her career to have been marked by a close call from time to time, so that he or she would have learned indelible lessons from each and every one of them. We feel exactly the same way about the surgeon who does open heart surgery or takes out a gallstone. We want that knife to have slipped a number of times, so that he would have had to come back from every one of the boo-boos to save the patient. And if he couldn't come back a couple of times, we want him to have learned a lesson. (The notion of thinking about failure in terms of surgeons was introduced to us by a European executive of a pharmaceutical company. Tom had gotten side-tracked in a questionable beauty-of-failure argument, and the man came up afterwards: "Listen, the attack on you was nonsense," he said. "Do you want to know what's the most experimental business around? It's surgery. When has surgery made its most rapid advances? In time of war. The extremity of the cases provides an unending stream of 'hopelessness,' where every technique in the world has been tried—and most of the new ones invented. Most of the rest of the learning occurs analogously on patients whose prognosis is worse than grim. 'Try something' is the dictum. Find me a new surgical technique that wasn't learned the hard way, via trial and many an error, and you're a better person than I.")

We have devoted considerable time to the failure issue because we think it is merited. Constant tries are the simple watchwords of innovating. Most fail. And yet, implicitly or explicitly, failure (even tiny) is a dirty word in most settings. We don't talk about it, and we cover it up. Both responses (silence/cover-up) directly impede speed of action and the learning process.

Is It Tough to Tolerate Failure?
The Art of Purposeful Impatience

Some of the most renowned "tough bosses"—Walter Wriston, former Citicorp chairman, Jack Welch at GE, Andy Pearson, former PepsiCo president, and Ed Finkelstein at Macy's—are the most vociferous advocates of "failure-as-normal," even "failure-is-to-be-rewarded". So how come they're so tough? They reserve unlimited contempt for those who have tolerated inaction. To fail, learn and try again *quickly* is seen as normal. To sit and wait for "all the data" to come in is unconscionable. To utter, "I would have gotten it done, *but*... [purchasing wouldn't cooperate, accounting couldn't get the numbers]" is contemptible. Each believes that you get paid to make things happen, regardless of the charts and boxes or the rules and policies that they themselves may have written.

A story is told of Welch. He had asked some purchasing people to work on some tasks. Weeks later he met with them to review progress. To his dismay, they had none to report, only weighty analyses and half-completed efforts at coordination with various departments. Welch was furious. He called the meeting to an abrupt halt, then ordered it reconvened only four hours later. The agenda? To report on progress. He got it, too. More was done in those four hours than had been done in the several weeks preceding them.

To some, all this purposeful impatience may seem a small matter. Our experience suggests that not only is it not small, it is perhaps the biggest distinction between the winners and the losers. Among the losers: (1) a "good presentation" counts as much as a report of concrete action, (2) good logic and lots of data substitute for action, (3) the explanation that it couldn't get done "because" of budget or an inability to get certain people or departments together is considered adequate as long as there is "evidence" demonstrating that "we" tried and "they" were recalcitrant, (4) you "need more staff work," or "need more expensive data," or "should form a committee" (the typical disposition of nine out of ten agenda items at the department, division, corporate or board level). It all adds up to trappings and audit trails being more important than doing.

To what extent do you and your colleagues, team, group, company meet the profile above? Do you accept "I couldn't because . . . ," etc. Or do you demand action, *now?* If you're seeking to move in the latter direction, we'd only remind that to do so will be impossible unless the tolerance for the good try that fails goes hand in glove with *your* program of purposeful impatience. Impatience matched with an abiding fear of the tiniest failure is a design for madness (or high turnover). We've seen it all too many times. It's not pretty.

"Failure":
Some Questions—and Things to Do Now

▶ What do *you* think about failure? First, reflect on the above analysis by yourself, and then with a small group of peers. If you think it's natural (in the best sense, as described here), do you talk about it, and if so, do you personalize your talk (i.e., describe in gory detail some of your own debacles)? Suppose you come out, in your own mind, OK on this score. Is the message getting through? Far down the line? (I.e., for starters, can your direct reports recall, unaided, five specific stories about your foul-ups that you have owned up to?)

▶ Are *tiny* mistakes hidden (and thus allowed, inevitably, to fester into bigger ones) or are they rapidly owned up to? (This is a *very* tough issue to get at. You desperately need "hard facts" to deal with it. You might begin with a handful of case studies of recent major foul-ups. Should the information about the problem, when it was small, somehow have surfaced? If it didn't, why didn't it? Try a success case or two: a minor problem turned around *before* it festered: was there a different sort of openness in the department/group when the minor problem was brought to the surface in a timely way and fixed? You also might try an anonymous survey on the subject—this topic is a big deal and well worth the energy; if you do, make sure you collect specific data about specific cases as well as scores on various questions.)

▶ As a fix, you can mount your own campaign of "failure story-telling." Try to induce your colleagues to do so, too. Moreover, consider a public awards program (with weekly awards) for the "failure brought to the surface most rapidly." Do it for all departments. Post a weekly list of your own "five best" failures each week (indicating what *concrete* things you learned from *each*). Post weekly "this is what we learned from mistakes" bulletins for each new product or project group. Consider a "failure Olympics"—the fastest learning from a neat little experiment that failed. (Again, try to get all departments involved.)

▶ The above is directed at "rapid good tries—failures—from which we learn." There are also "dumb" failures, which need to be brought to the surface rapidly to avoid the snowball phenomenon. Start a quiet campaign of *writing thank-you notes to two or three people a week* who have had the courage to bring uncomfortable information to the surface early. (Try to solicit the participation of colleagues in the campaign, too.)

THE LOOK OF INNOVATIVENESS

The *physical* attributes are hard to overemphasize. We've talked of a barber's chair in contrast to an elegant, spacious office. We've talked of the 3M fetish for using and displaying the product, and Hewlett-Packard's "next-bench syndrome," in which everyone has whatever project he or she is working on out on top of the bench, for everyone else to look at, play with and comment on. Most companies have the obligatory picture of their product in the entrance hall (some don't even have that); fewer have the product—or the pictures of the product—lying about all over the place: in the mail room, on the loading docks and in the MIS department, as well as the design spaces.

These simple practices may seem bizarre (or irrelevant, or "trivial"). "You mean HP engineers really leave their products out for others to play with?" the president of one small company said to us once, incredulously. "My engineers are afraid somebody will steal their ideas. I simply can't conceive of what you're saying. How do they *do* it?" Unfortunately, our lame answer was that "they do it because that's what they've always done." Of course, it's much more than that. The "gold stars" at Hewlett-Packard go to people who cooperate and assist others, not to those who showboat to their own advantage. In fact, one of this fellow's major problems, it turned out, was too much of a push for "grand slam home runs." He gives out irregular $25 to $50,000 awards, and not enough regular $100 prizes. (We'll return to incentive schemes in a moment.)

Another physical attribute of innovative organizations: the engineer, marketer and manufacturer are together in a single location at Hewlett-Packard, from the inception of the project onward. The same holds at 3M. Monarch Marking, a $100 million subsidiary of Pitney Bowes, decides to develop a skunkwork. Boss Bob Vanourek rents an old restaurant, across the road from the company's main facility, and converts it unabashedly into a skunkwork. It is an untidy cubbyhole, which is part of the company (close by) but also slightly separate (not too close). Allen Michels of Convergent Technologies likewise believes that the skunkwork, by definition, must be physically isolated, and sends forth his little teams accordingly, setting them up in separate, Spartan sites.

We talk about this particular trait with many, and the consensus seems to be that the activity should be close enough to get succor from the parent organization and separate enough to induce a feeling of team spirit, a bit of "us against them," and isolation from the bureaucracy. This was a part of the trick with Tom West's group at Data General. His team of Young Turks was squirreled away in a dingy basement far from the direct view from corporate—a setting in marked contrast to the Taj Mahal at the Research Triangle in North Carolina and where the formal development group worked (in competition with West's bunch). And, it's interesting to note, the West team's extraordinary esprit started to unravel when a long-requested (and, previously, long-denied) appropriation came through: individuals were given offices with walls, and the basement hangout was spruced up. The "us against them" spirit was dented a bit by the formalizing changes.

Isolation is important. But so is proximity—in a very special sense. The textile industry is not well known for its R&D. The prime exception is Milliken and Company. Roger Milliken has a passion for constant experimentation in his production facilities. One clear signal of his concern is that Roger's office is in the middle of the splendid Milliken Research Park. Moreover, a prototype shop where manufacturing techniques are tested regularly is right outside Roger's window; and he's proud to declare that when he built the prototype facility he was considered a bit crazy by both his own people and others in the industry. Often as not, you can find Roger wandering through that facility, checking on the latest tests. You can then see Roger's closeness to innovation. While, on the one hand, substantial isolation is good for the skunkwork, on the other, proximity (or not) of the main lab to the boss is a highly visible symbol of the importance (or lack of it) attached to innovation in general. Talking to the president of a small division of a pharmaceutical company reinforced the point. Several years ago he had spent two long days in the central research facilities of a big company with which his own firm was working on a joint venture. The research facilities had been recently moved from the corporate center to a sterile hilltop location twenty-five miles from headquarters. At the end of the two days he paid a call on the company's chief executive officer. "After only two days I knew more about their research than he [the CEO] did," he said. "If you're separated, you just don't quite get around to it." It's no coincidence that this fellow has extreme views on the significance of physical location as a symbol of what's important. You'd better believe his R&D facility is well within a pebble's throw of his office.

758

"Look of Innovativeness":
Some Questions—and Things to Do Now

▶ Do you prominently display the product? In all function areas? Are all hands familiar with the products or services? Especially new products or services? Do you *regularly* have demonstrations and films about new products and services for *all* levels and *all* functions?

▶ Within engineering/design/buyer areas, are new products out and around for all to get involved with, to comment on? Do you have lots of internal meetings where people bring their peers up to date on their projects. (I.e., is sharing or squirreling away the norm?)

▶ Do you pay careful attention to the physical settings of small development teams, focusing in particular on semi-isolation and the Spartanism that helps bring teams together? On the converse side, are design/engineering spaces given prominence in a way that symbolizes directly your (boss, division manager, etc.) strong interest in the design function?

Networking

Silicon Valley is essentially a grand collection of skunkworks, a few of which have become very successful. And their highly visible successes have fueled the flames: The best have in turn expelled many of their best and brightest (as a result of stodginess that invariably accompanies success—even in electronics), a handful of whom are now working on their third or fourth successes (or failures). The Silicon Valley message is a message about the role of critical mass among experiments, champions and skunkworks. With critical mass, networks arise and a near-perpetual-motion machine is possible (e.g., HP, J&J, 3M). Without critical mass—that is, without a certain volume of experiments, champions and skunkworks—the possibility of continuing innovation collapses.

In 1984 Ev Rogers of Stanford and Judith Larsen of Cognos Associates published *Silicon Valley Fever: Growth of High-Technology Culture*. It provides a good model for the individual company as well as a description of the Valley; "networks" are the subject of a full chapter, and the role of "spas"—slightly upscale hamburger joints—is critical. The availability of venture capital is the subject of another chapter; again the critical mass phenomenon plays a vital role, providing a large number of places within the company to "shop." (It's akin to 3M's prodding would-be product champions to try to sell their idea to *any* division that will listen.) Competition between different companies in the Valley plays a major role as well, of course.

Rogers and Larsen contrast critical mass conditions in the Valley on a vast number of individually "trivial" dimensions—e.g., the number of restaurants—with the absence of same in other places:

The close networks that characterize Silicon Valley give the region an advantage over other areas. Nolan Bushnell [then of Atari] illustrated this point: "There's a tremendous amount of networking here in Silicon Valley, unmatched anywhere else. I recently visited a group of engineers in London who were working on a new product in competition with a group here in Silicon Valley. Both started at the same time, but the Silicon Valley team got the jump by six months. Our group included an engineer who had a friend working at Intel. He smuggled out a couple of prototypes of a new chip that was just what they needed. The chip was soon to be on the market, but it wasn't yet in the catalogue. Intel was very happy because there were some immediate buyers. Just that six months shows that we have tremendous advantage here. That's why Silicon Valley is always ahead." Indeed, a Federal Trade Commission report said that the unique strength of the U.S. semi-conductor industry derives from its firms' rapid copying of others' innovative chips.

And:

The equivalent of the Fairchild-Atari old-boy network in the micro-computer industry is the Home Brew Computer Club. This unique organization had its first meeting in March 1975 in the garage of microcomputer enthusiast Gordon French in Menlo Park. Twenty-two [!] microcomputer companies have since been launched by club members, and twenty of them are still in operation. Many are, or were, leading companies in the microcomputer industry: Apple, Cromemco, and North Star, just to name a few. Some of the Computer Kids in Home Brew pioneered in computer software, others like Paul Terrell and Boyd Wilson launched computer retail stores, while other members like Jim Warren founded computer trade shows. When Home Brew was founded it had a regular membership of 500 or so computerphiles, mostly young and male. The purpose of Home Brew (so named because the original members who had computers had assembled them from kits) was to facilitate information-exchange among microcomputer lovers. There were no dues, initiation rites, or bylaws. The typical meeting began with a "mapping period"—individuals with something to announce, trade, sell, or give away would stand up and identify themselves. Then a "random access period" allowed like-minded individuals, such as devotees of the Intel 8080 microprocessor, to break up into small groups for a free-flowing discussion. People exchanged computer programs and circuit designs, information that would in a few years be company secrets. In the mid-1970s Steve Wozniak handed out Xerox copies of his circuit designs for his Apple computer. In return he got peer reinforcement and suggestions for improvement. No one at Home Brew thought that microcomputers would become a competitive industry.

DECENTRALIZATION AND "DISRESPECT"

When it comes to innovation, small, as we have seen, is more beautiful than even we had ever imagined. Virtually *all* successful innovation—in innovative or noninnovative companies, in the factory as well as in the world of new products and services—comes from or is markedly abetted by a skunkwork. So the issue is not the *validity* of the skunkwork as a center of innovation: skunkworks are it. The issue is, simply, *quantity:* have you got *enough* of them to win within a world of twenty-to-one (or worse) odds against new product or service success?

An ancillary point is this, which we've already discussed in part: the language in the air at 3M is "big ends from small beginnings." PepsiCo talks incessantly about giant businesses that came from $500 investments. Innovative companies publicly (and ceaselessly) preach that a little team can make a giant contribution. President Ken Olsen, in a speech to his Digital colleagues summarizing ten years of development success and failure, commented (and it's become a drumbeat theme for DEC since) that not a single substantial, commercially successful project had come from an "adequately funded team." They'd always come, he said, from the scrounging, scrapping, underfunded teams. We want to emphasize that such public discussion (repeated endlessly) encourages people to believe that it's just as important to be a part of a tiny team as to be assigned to the giant, highly visible, "bet the company" team. In fact, perhaps it's more important. (Subsequent promotion of those who took small-team chances will help confirm the rumor.)

The context of innovation is about respect for the reality of the innovation process: the need for lots of tries, lots of failures, lots of scrounging, but *always* action. It's also, therefore, about disrespect. One thoughtful commentator put it this way: "We need the confidence necessary to show disrespect for our own institutions." He had been talking about HP's late-sixties decision to decentralize radically before the move was required by market forces; he viewed that as the prime reason HP had flourished, while his company, once a shoulder-to-shoulder HP peer, had stagnated. J&J's Chairman Jim Burke expressed the same sentiment: "I view my role as saying no to those who would re-centralize things. As soon as any trouble arises, the tendency is, 'Let's bring it back in [to the center] so that we can oversee the fix.' That's the kiss of death." Gordon McGovern's recent radical decentralization of Campbell Soup has the same logic: "We first broke the business into [fifty-two] manageable parts, multiplied the number of people running to an opportunity and with the wherewithal to get things done. We then established with these people a concept which is flexible and rich and open-ended, so they can go out and grab parts of it that we at the top *wouldn't even imagine*."

J&J, IBM (in their new Independent Business Units), Kollmorgen and Gould, among others, give divisions and groups their own boards of directors. The objective is to keep the corporate staff from fouling up the autonomous operations. It's the ultimate wisdom: to know that you are *not* smart enough *not* to intrude *in*appropriately, and hence to create a protective shield *explicitly* aimed at insulating your operators from *you*. IBM puts it this way: The number one task of the IBU is *not* to follow the corporate planning process. Ore-Ida, working with our colleague Bob Waterman, has instituted an internal entrepreneur program, which is rapidly paying big dividends. The *publicly* avowed purpose: "to short-circuit the system." We'll go into more detail on this in chapter 17; here we focus on the extent to which debureaucratization, and an atmosphere in which circumventing the bureaucracy is the norm, are crucial to innovativeness.

Fighting City Hall is not easy, and requires constant vigilance. As Burke says, the tendency is always to slip into the centralizing, consolidating, "Fix it with a PERT diagram" mentality. David Ogilvy merits putting in the last word: "Make sure you have a Vice President in Charge of Revolution, to engender ferment among your more conventional colleagues." How's *your* "purposeful disrespect" IQ?

"Decentralization and Disrespect": Some Questions—and Things to Do Now

▶ We talked before of disrespect by honoring terms like cheating. This section covers, in part, a more formal set of traits. Do you "show disrespect" (1) by the establishment of two- to three (or ten- to twenty)-person skunkworks in *direct* competition with other of your (typically more formal) activities, (2) by fostering decentralization and explicitly *fighting* efforts to centralize after failures, (3) by creating boards of directors or other formal-sounding boards to explicitly "short-circuit" the central planning system and protect fragile small-team innovative efforts from premature or overly extensive central prods? Do you consider such devices—think about this and talk about it with colleagues—as essential or as signs that you "really aren't organized well enough?" (Look at the most innovative parts of your company or the most innovative companies in your business. See if you observe a greater prevalence of these or like devices.) Do you consider such devices as the "luxury" of a giant company, or can you imagine them or a semblance of them in your $25 million division, your three-store operation? (We observe that this process should best begin at the $2 to 3 million mark. At the very latest!)

▶ Do you and your colleagues view your role (especially toward innovation) as a facilitator's role, as opposed to the role of a planner/arranger? Have you visited the spaces of your new project teams a half-dozen times in the last two months? Have you, upon the occasion of or immediately following the visit, done *three* or more specific mundane things to clear Mickey Mouse hurdles out of the team's way? (All functions *should* be in on this. It is wholly legitimate/useful for the accountant, MIS, and personnel person to see her or his role in *exactly* the same way the operator does.) As part of this analysis, go visit a team or two and ask them if you are facilitating, if other departments are facilitating or barrier-building or—worst of all—treating the team with benign neglect (i.e., subjecting it to "merely" the same rules as everyone else). Finally, plan such a facilitation visit in the next *ten* days; set as a specific objective the removal of a minimum of *five* tiny irritants.

"NURTURING" CHAMPIONS AND CREATING HEROES

A successful Bell Labs executive describes his job: "First and foremost, I walk around, I try to remove the petty irritants that impede action. Some team needs $4,000 for a personal computer; I don't want them to go through a six-month capital-appropriation drill. I give 'em the money. Somebody needs the support of a manufacturing engineer for two weeks. I find one."

The companies *best* organized *formally* for innovation (e.g., HP, 3M, J&J, Raychem, Kollmorgen) understand best the need for the interference runners. A 3M executive notes: "The real shortfall is nurturers of champions." And that's from 3M, where every formal procedure and structure is already aligned to maximize innovation.

But it's not enough to sanction cheating, to run interference for champions. Once your rule-breaking, system-short-circuiting team has brought home the bacon, it's vital to *label* them heroes. And it's important to get it straight in the minds of the rest of the organization: to celebrate them as heroes because they got a win *and* because they got it by breaking the rules. Moreover, wild-eyed dreamers need not apply. The innovator/cheater—i.e., the champion/team/skunkwork that brings home the bacon—is, above all, utterly pragmatic. As David Ogilvy says (re advertising): "If it doesn't sell [the product] it isn't 'creative.' " We find that effective product/service developers are pragmatists and exploiters of others' ideas. They are mechanics and tinkerers, with a raging thirst to see the idea work.

Most vital is to nurture champions and create heroes in all phases of innovation. In a discussion with a pharmaceutical company's research managers, we distinguished between two distinct phases of product development: "discovery" and "all the rest." Discovery is the high visibility part. It is a pragmatic business, but does have pure science as its basis. It's the stuff of Nobel Prizes and articles in *Science*. "All the rest" is the "last 90 percent" of the process—clinical tests, approvals and the like. Some companies treat this "last 90 percent" as mechanical and bureaucratic, the work of clerks and automatons. Yet it turns out that a "passionate champion" of this latter sequence of events can cut more time from the total process than can the genius of the discovery phase. For instance, he or she can drum up support for the drug among the members of the medical establishment, push and cajole the clinical testers. All in all, such champions can often reduce the normal clearance time by as much as 75 percent, if they energetically pursue their tasks. A few companies in the industry (which is traditionally marked by a belief in the pure-scientist-as-hero) are wise enough to treat the tail end of the process as equal in importance to the "head." They go out of their way to create a special hero class for those who drive through the "last 90 percent" with alacrity. Moreover, the "last 90 percent" heroes are put on pedestals as high as—or higher than—those of the pure scientist who had the "Eureka" breakthrough in the discovery phase. Similarly, the marked respect at 3M and HP for the whole development team (accountants as well as scientists or engineers) is intended to create a host of heroes among the oft ignored support functions that, in fact, are the real key to timely commercial success.

Incentives—for All Hands

3M is a galaxy of heroes. However, heroes who bring in successful $10 million products are touted nearly as loudly as those with successful $200 million winners. Hewlett-Packard is awash with mini-hero success stories. Surprisingly, much of the momentum for constant innovation can be badly stifled when the rewards for innovation get too *big*. The $100,000 award creates a superstar syndrome. The subtle message is "Only a few people can do it." 3M, HP, Milliken, Wal-Mart, Raychem, Domino's, Dana, The Limited, et al. believe that a large share of the population can and should be innovating—regularly. Winners, big and small, are touted to the skies, but principally via nonmonetary compensation. It seems an iron law: When the rewards structure gets too lumpy (marked by sporadic, big hits), people start hiding things to enhance the probability of their getting the credit and the big one. Sharing, cooperation and emergence of a bunch of tiny, cooperative teams are unintentionally stifled, remarkably quickly.

The innovative companies tend to be innovative from stem to stern. Hewlett-Packard is innovative in the new product area. It encourages skunking to an extreme degree. But you find just about as much skunking going on as well in MIS, personnel and in the factory. An HPer described an occasion when engineering had developed an unwieldy design for a major board. When it got to the factory, one of the manufacturing people realized the incipient problems. His idea? We'll go off, on a brief after-hours bootleg proj-

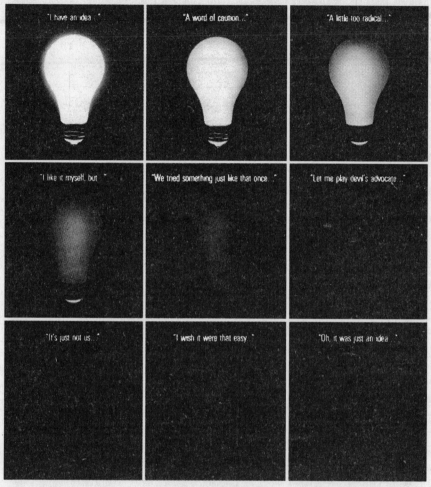

It was just an idea.

An idea is a fragile thing. Turning it off is much easier than keeping it lit.

A company called TRW lives on ideas. So we look for people who have them and for people who won't snuff them out. In recent years TRW has been issued hundreds of patents in such diverse fields as fiber optics, space, lasers and transportation electronics.

Those ideas shone because somebody had them and somebody helped them. And nobody turned them off.

Tomorrow is taking shape at a company called TRW.

A Company Called TRW

© TRW Inc., 1984

ect, and build it differently. His boss's response? Essentially a wink. The complex design failed in the real world of the factory. But the generic tendency to bootleg at HP (in all functions) meant that a better design was instantly available from the wings.

Champions, Heroes, Incentives for All Hands: Some Questions—and Things to Do Now

▶ Are you and your colleagues "hero creators"? Do you, even when it makes you grit your teeth a bit, hail the pain-in-the-neck champion? Do you focus on modest heroism (i.e., lots of mini-heroism)? Do you reserve your top plaudits for the pragmatist-champion, the person(s) *not* involved in the dramatic part of the project, but whose obsessions with the nuts-and-bolts phases may have cut the cycle time most significantly? How (and how regularly), very specifically, do you "post" such acts of heroism? Is everyone, at all levels and in all functions, aware of *exactly* what you think heroism is? Are you sure? Ask. (Developing a program to bring "implementation heroes" or "pragmatist heroes" to the surface and reward them won't be all that easy. It isn't done often, and they are usually less visible—or less findable—than the buyer/research scientist. You will have to mount a treasure hunt of sorts. All can participate—this hunt can be as visible/valuable as the ultimate award. I.e., the headline might read: "An all-out search is being mounted to find the *real* heroes of the 2632AN-3 project.")
▶ Is your definition of innovation limited in any way? Of creativity? Do you consider a minor procedural invention by the receptionist to be true creativity? Think about it—long and hard. Our observation is that the best are "size blind"/"function blind." They reward as frequently, as publicly and as vociferously the tiny innovation as they do the giant one.
▶ Is your award-for-innovation structure (assuming you have one) skewed in the direction of monetary rather than nonmonetary rewards? A few big lumps of money rather than many small lumps? Money for individuals rather than money for teams? If the lion's share of your effort is not going into the second part of these three questions, you are probably blunting your effort. (Remember, attention is the key. Quality senior-officer time spent at an obviously caring, somewhat lavish blowout costing $75 a head for three-hundred "support group innovators" is worth more than $250 surreptitiously added to the paycheck—with FICA, federal, state and city withholding.)

Barber's chairs. Sidling over. Cheating. Disrespect. Praising failure. Creating heroes of rule breakers. The managerial and leadership task implied by all this is not an easy one. As one manager said, "It's a thin line between discipline and chaos. But that's what we get paid for."

12

The "Smell" of Innovation

Just how do you know when your company "smells" of innovation? Here are twenty-three ways:

1. Inaction is *not* tolerated, period! I.e., managers at all levels look harshly askance at phrases like these: "We need more staffing," "We need more data," "Form a committee to look into it," "We coulda gone further, *but* purchasing [etc.] didn't get thus and such for us on time." The most common question is "What have you gotten done in the last 24 to 48 hours?"

2. "Try," "Test," "Quick and dirty," "Get me two [as opposed to 22 or 220] data points and then let's move ahead" are much more common than "Let's get a group together to analyze this," "Let's not be too hasty," "What do X and Y and Z [and L and M and N . . .] think about it?" (Listen *very* carefully to—perhaps quantify—the routine queries and modes of agenda item disposal at formal and informal get-togethers.)

3. This is common: "Why don't you and Joe [in marketing] and Bill [in manufacturing] and Ann [in sales] get together and bring in those two guys from ZZ division *this afternoon* and figure something out? And, yeah, call Dan [customer], maybe, too. He'd have something to contribute. Let me know what you *did*." This is not: "Let's charter a committee and get A and B and C and D to contribute. We'll have E chair it, so that his boss's boss doesn't get his nose bent out of joint. And plan on a formal review with the principals in about eight weeks."

4. Failure is not only tolerated but lauded. We hear this: "Wow, that was a really interesting problem that manufacturing had scaling up the XYZ subassembly. We [engineering] really got caught with our pants down. But it looks like we learned A and B and C. Can we get back to them with a reworked design by tomorrow?" And this: "Boy, the focus group really pounced on that new packaging. Maybe we ought to get another group in. Though I'm inclined to say we flat out blew it. Let's get the gang together this evening and see if we can modify it to respond to those comments, or whether we ought to scrap it and try something else." We don't hear this: "Those SOB's in manufacturing didn't give it a fair shot. I'm not going back to my boss and tell him just yet. I know it's a sound design. We'll get some analysis together and we'll confront them at Thursday's senior staff meeting. We can't

767

let them go on pulling this BS. I told the boss it was a good design, ready to go. And as far as I'm concerned, it still is. Make sure young Dave in your shop doesn't blow the whistle on this."

5. Failures are well-known parts of the background of the star performers, those promoted several times. They talk openly and regularly about "my biggest embarrassment," "my top ten foul-ups of '85" (while making it clear that they kept on trying until they got it right). They are *not* known by phrases like these: "a good presenter," "keeps his head in until all his ducks are lined up with all the players," "never really blew one in the course of the long march to the head of the division," "I don't think he's *ever* made a mistake."

6. The lion's share of the Hall of Fame consists of new product/service champions who are known to have fought through thick and thin (including many rancorous battles with corporate) to bring an idea to market. They are also known to be a tiny bit flaky, yet persistent as all get-out.

7. Despite an avowed tolerance for a bit of eccentricity, *practical* team playing is revered. That is, the Hall of Fame champions are seen as people who despised corporate politics, policies and staffs, yet were marvels at practical coordination and had a masterly ability to recruit top-flight teams and to cadge time and space and other resources from all parts of the organization (usually unofficially) to work on their exciting project.

8. Invention *with* customers (inside user for, say, an MIS or accounting project; regular commercial customer for product/service development) is considered normal. People outside the sales/marketing area are encouraged to engage directly in creative customer contact. Customers are regular members of problem-solving teams (i.e., the organization is accustomed to having them around—in focus groups, for early trials with partially completed products; in pre-design or pre-scale-up brainstorm sessions).

9. "Innovation for innovation's sake" is to some degree rewarded at *all* levels and in all functions. Regular celebrations are held for receptionists, loading-dock teams, accounting sections who create something new or who break time-honored rules or traditions to enhance their performance creatively, and such enhancements are a major component of the *routine* evaluations of *all* people.

10. The physical layout (everywhere) encourages chance and informal communication, especially cross-functional communication. Teams are readily formed, then immediately given temporary (semi-isolated) team space. Numerous social and informal events are aimed specifically at enhancing cross-functional and cross-divisional communication.

11. It is considered normal (almost required) for all hands, especially designers/buyers/brand managers/lending officers/engineers, to devote 10 to 20 percent of their time to bootleg projects. Moreover, it is a plus for others to help out those bootleggers. (It is rewarded, not considered a distraction.) The boss has a formal or semiformal system for keeping track of whether or not his people are bootleggers. He *consciously* and *regularly* rewards

thoughtful and clever bootlegging, even if it results in a dry hole and a little broken bureaucratic china.

12. Most of the stories told to new hires or related by senior management focus on innovating, somewhat crazy champions, bootlegging and other forms of corporate-beating, scrounging resources, getting semi-illicit help from other functions, providing semi-illicit help to other functions. The stories paint the *average* manager as a bit of a rascal.

13. It is considered more valuable (at an early stage in one's career) to get on a little team working on a modest (but wholly "owned") project than it is to "look good" on a trivial tidbit associated with the company's or division's or department's big (but more routine) project. *Senior* heroes are not those who oversee masses of resources (i.e., empire builders). Rather, they are those who leave cushy jobs to take on small but vital future-oriented problems or projects.

14. Quick-hit, small-team (five to ten or even fewer), spur-of-the-moment activity is seen as the normal problem-solving mode, as opposed to "Throw resources at it."

15. Senior (and middle) managers repeatedly show *open* disrespect for their own procedures and structures, regularly encouraging others to subvert the rules.

16. When news of an incipient skunkwork surfaces, the knee-jerk tendency is to wink or smile ("There goes Amy again"), rather than to cut it off at the knees "before it starts working at cross purposes with the ABC team [i.e., the officially designated team]."

17. Well over half of top management (the top twenty-five) has one or more "painful innovative successes" in their background. That is, top management and innovation go together.

18. It is normal for product or service developers to intrude on the orderly functions e.g., operations/manufacturing—i.e., it is routine for a new product developer to disturb a manufacturing operation to get his or her new prototype worked on. The "tiebreaker" in making decisions is always facilitating product development.

19. Insistent championing is so revered that some champions are promoted even though they aren't supermanagers. Again, the "tiebreaker": having "done it" (brought a product or service to market) counts for more than a good administrative record. Conversely, "He doesn't make waves" is the kiss of death.

20. There is a conscious effort to give a solid charter to a small team and then to keep their funding low and deadline pressure high. That is, management cultivates a sense of lean, practical no-nonsense urgency.

21. Milestone/PERT charts are limited to a tiny handful (a dozen, say) of practical, signal accomplishments on which one makes a blood oath to deliver (e.g., "Ship first prototype by September 18"). Vast lists of five hundred to one thousand milestones are unknown.

22. Some product/service and development team overlap is tolerated. Duplication, cannibalization and noncompatibility are not automatically *the* enemies.

23. The company "smells" of its products. Bragging, display and demonstration (in every nook and cranny) is endemic.

As in our discussion of "smell" of the customer, we do not suggest that all top-flight innovators exhibit all these traits with equal vigor. But this list, garnered entirely from empirical observation, will serve, we hope, as a benchmark for a frank assessment of the innovativeness of any organization.

SOME (MORE) GOOD READING ON INNOVATION

Two books do a superb job of capturing, in a global way, the notion of the messy world of innovation. The first, cited extensively in our chapter on "The Mythology of Innovation," is *The Sources of Invention* (2nd ed., W. W. Norton, 1970), by John Jewkes, David Sawers and Richard Stillerman; it includes fifty-eight delightful case studies on major and minor twentieth-century innovations in the United States and Europe. *Readings in the Management of Innovation* (Pitman, 1982), edited by Michael Tushman and William Moore, includes classic articles from leading thinkers in the field, such as Brian Quinn, Jim Utterback and Eric von Hippel, again consistent with the framework provided in "The Mythology of Innovation."

Three very readable books are superior studies of individual examples of the messy, human, emotional world of innovating: Nicholas Wade's *The Nobel Duel* (Anchor/Doubleday, 1981), the story of the race between Roger Guillemin and Andrew Schally for the Nobel prize in medicine, James D. Watson's *The Double Helix* (Atheneum, 1968), his personal account of his and Francis Crick's discovery of the structure of DNA, and *A Feeling for the Organism* (Freeman, 1983), by Evelyn Fox Keller and W. H. Freeman, on the exciting and largely unappreciated fifty-year career of eventual Nobel Prize-winning biologist Barbara McClintock.

The life of skunks has generally gone unrecorded. However, Tracy Kidder's *The Soul of a New Machine* (Atlantic Monthly/Little Brown, 1981) is the alpha-to-omega story of a successful Data General skunkwork that has a bearing on virtually every skunkwork we have observed in industries of all sorts. Gerhard Neumann's *Herman the German* (Morrow, 1984) is the autobiography of the mechanic turned World War II Flying Tiger turned multibillion-dollar aircraft engine business developer for General Electric.

Finally, a couple of more "formal" books on what we call the "context of innovation": Rosabeth Moss Kanter's *The Change Masters* (Simon & Schuster, 1983) nicely describes the setting in which innovation is either fostered or inhibited. Somewhat more specialized is Gifford Pinchot's *Intrapreneuring* (Harper & Row, 1985); it looks at the specifics of developing internal entrepreneurship in the corporation.

4

PEOPLE, PEOPLE, PEOPLE

Now you hear this. Take good care of those people in that speech of yours. In this room are the finest 1,200 people in this country. They deserve the best you can give.

Dave Thomas, Wendy's founder, on the occasion of a speech by Tom Peters to Wendy's franchisees

"Productivity through People" was Tom's favorite chapter in *In Search of Excellence.* Little did he realize that it barely scratched the surface. The power of ownership of the job has become overwhelmingly clear in the last three years, as has the giant gap between those who believe that the average person will be his or her best if given the chance and those who think the opposite.

The "smell" of the customer and the "smell" of innovation have nothing to do with some grand design. They have to do with a thousand tiny things done a little bit better—serving the customer (guest) courteously, honorably, and with distinction; inducing the champion/skunk within almost all of us to come to the fore.

To achieve distinction on either of these dimensions, then, requires not sleight of hand by geniuses but the commitment to excellence (quality, service, make it better/innovation) by everyone. In short, people are the unmistakable base.

How sad! By 1980, as the strategists' view had come to hold sway over the minds of business (and public sector) chieftains and their advisers, "people stuff" had come to be looked at as "soft." But though business schools may deny it, and corporate leader after corporate leader may neglect it, "they," the people in the remote distribution center in Dubuque or Fairbanks, the people cleaning the streets, schooling the young or frying the burgers are what it's all about, what it has always been about, and what it always will be about. Make no mistake about it. "Techniques" don't produce quality products, educate children, or pick up the garbage on time: people do, people who care, people who are treated as creatively contributing adults.

This section consists of three chapters. We begin by looking at the beliefs that managers hold about people. The gulf between those who believe in the humanity of the clerk and those who don't is enormous. From philosophy we turn to "ownership": does the average person view himself or herself as in command, as listened to, as a vital part of the business (city staff, school) or not? We conclude with an essay about celebration (chapter 15, "Applause Applause"). To be human is to be sad, to be glad; to participate fully is to care. Celebration of that caring (manifest—or not—in a host of ways, by every person, every day) is not a footnote; it's at the heart of the success we've observed in organizations from Apple to People Express, from Milliken to The Limited.

We'd ask one favor: before you start to read what follows, find a private room or a lonely tree beside a lake. We ask some very personal questions about what you believe (or don't) about people. A bit of sober self-assessment is pretty much a must if this section is to be of value.

13

Bone-Deep Beliefs

Bert Snider, who runs Bourns, a profitable mid-sized instrument maker, is appalled: "Why, some of [my] new secretaries don't even know what a precision potentiometer is." Why should they? you ask. What is Bert getting at? Nothing less than the dignity of every member of the Bourns "family," the expectation that everyone understand and be an informed part of the business—including the newest of newly hired secretaries. And for Tom Beebe, former chairman of Delta Airlines, for John McConnell of Worthington Industries, for Ren McPherson, former chairman of the Dana Corporation, for Bill and Vieve Gore of W. L. Gore & Associates, for Max DePree of Herman Miller and Tom Monaghan of Domino's Pizza, for Bob Swiggett of Kollmorgen, Stew Leonard of Stew Leonard's and Dave Thomas of Wendy's, the story is the same.

How starkly Bert Snider's attitude stands in contrast to our all too common experience. Tom listens as the president of a $600 million company opens a meeting of several hundred of his people. His vice presidents, naturally enough, are sitting in a neat little row—the first row, of course—in the auditorium. He looms high above them on the podium. He begins his speech: "We've had a good year." Looking down at his vice presidents, he adds, "and I want especially to thank each of you for what you've achieved in your divisions, and I also want to thank the rest of you"—with a sweep of his arm—"who have contributed as well, many not in this room." Tom's stomach turns.

After a speech to business school alumni at Cornell, we are approached by the owner of an old, mid-sized Northeastern business. "You're naïve," he says. "Look, these communities are made up of second- and third-generation union families. They just don't care, don't give a damn, about work, especially about quality." No wonder, we think. No wonder he has problems.

The enemy lurks in our minute-to-minute behavior—and in our language. A chief operating officer of a retailing operation pulled Tom aside to explain why in the midst of reorganizing the company to sharpen the focus on merchandising, he was, contrary to tradition, filling most buyer jobs from outside the company: "Look, to tell the truth, you don't have to be all that bright to run a store." Self-fulfilling prophecy! If the senior folks, even in their most secret confabs, state (and believe) that you "don't have to be that bright," the word will somehow ooze out and spread throughout the organization. (And

"Since we ain't that bright, why put out?" will follow in its stead as surely as the night follows the day.) We talked in an earlier chapter of "thinly disguised contempt" for the customer. What is this but "thinly disguised contempt" for the people of the organization?

We've also discussed something we call the "1,000 percent factor," how a group of a hundred turned-on people can do the same work, faster and of higher quality, that several thousand are unable to accomplish. This chapter, too, is about the 1,000 percent factor.

"BELIEVE IT OR NOT"

John McConnell, chairman of Worthington Industries, runs a steel company with no corporate procedure books. Instead, there's a one-paragraph statement of philosophy, a Golden Rule: Take care of your customers and take care of your people, and the market will take care of you. Hard to believe, isn't it? But it turns out he's not alone. Bob Swiggett of Kollmorgen: "It's all about trust and the Golden Rule." Tom Monaghan, of Domino's Pizza (and new owner of the 1984 world champion Detroit Tigers), says, "Pay attention to the Golden Rule, and the world is yours." Mo Siegel of Celestial Seasonings and, yes, old Tom Watson, Sr., of IBM also hold to the Golden Rule. Steel. Electro-optics. Pizza. Computers. And all of them say it's "just" the Golden Rule.

Tom first met Tom Beebe, the recently retired Delta Air Lines chairman, on a flight from Atlanta to Dallas in early 1983. It was not long after twenty-five thousand Delta employees had banded together, in the midst of the 1981–83 recession, to give the company $30 million to buy a new airplane. Tom asked Beebe about it, a little unbelievingly to tell the truth: "What *is* all this about your people buying you a plane?" Beebe began to describe what had happened, in particular the rolling out of the plane onto the tarmac in Atlanta, with a bright red ribbon wrapped around it. There was wonder in his voice. His eyes misted over. Tom Beebe was sixty-eight then, had been forty years in the industry—and he was not jaded one iota. Only moments later he introduced Tom to Delta's recently retired chief pilot. Upon retirement, the fellow had taken full-page ads in the morning and evening Atlanta papers to thank Delta management for a great career!

Here's Max DePree of Herman Miller describing his lovely "theory fast-ball," derived, in essence, from the fact that Sandy Koufax (the great Dodger baseball pitcher) wouldn't have been worth a hoot without a catcher who could handle that hot fastball. Max says, "Although Herman Miller has become *famous* because of its star pitchers—its designers—we have only been *successful* because of the outstanding catchers who produced and sold their designs." And more Max (this one *is* hard to believe, in a world where it sometimes seems that the only goal is short-term profit improvement): "My goal for Herman Miller is that when people both inside and outside the company look at all of us, they'll say, 'Those folks are a gift to the spirit.' " A gift to the spirit, indeed! And how does Max put this philosophy into practice in his (highly profitable) operations? Obviously, in a hundred ways, but at the head of the list is a bill of rights, what he calls "A Person's Rights." They include: "the right to be needed, the right to understand, the right to be involved, the right to a covenantal relationship [with the company],* the right to affect one's own destiny, the right to be accountable, and the right to appeal." At the heart of it is Max's all too rare understanding of the role of management: "The common wisdom is that American managers have to learn to motivate people. Nonsense. Employees bring their own motivation. What people need from work is to be liberated, to be involved, to be accountable, and to reach for their potential." Leadership as the liberation of talent, rather than restraint by rule, is a common theme in all our winning enterprises.

Bill and Vieve Gore of W. L. Gore & Associates don't talk about "employees" or "workers." They have only "Associates." And the Associates in the organization are bound together by the Gores' four principles: "fairness, which controls destructive dissension; freedom, which allows associates to experience failure; commitment, the power behind the desire to succeed; and 'waterline' or discretion, which reduces the chances for behavior that could damage the company's reputation and profitability." (See p. 925 for more.) And what do the Gores think about the result? Says Bill: "I think my Associates are changing the world." And he really does. With a warm September sun shimmering on the Hudson, Tom listens to Bill talk for a couple of hours about his people. Bill thinks that the people he's gathered in Newark, Delaware, and at his many other locations are the most special people in the world (move over, Dave Thomas). He fervently believes that their way of working together is creating a new wave in the United States.

"I think my Associates are changing the world." That's the depth of commitment that's missing when you hear "and I want to thank the 'other' people, too," or "third-generation union families don't care." There are no "other people" for Bill and Vieve Gore. They assume that all people are capable of caring and contributing *if* management cares and believes in them. Every one of their Associates is right up front—changing the world. Every one of their Associates would be expected, as at Bourns, to know exactly what a precision potentiometer is well before the conclusion of his or her first day on board. Of course everyone must know: unless you understand the business, how can you be a full partner in pushing it (and yourself) forward?

Bill and Vieve Gore couldn't even imagine the kinds of statements people make to us time and time again: "But be honest, Tom/Nancy. You *know* there are 30 percent who would rather *not* know what's going on." In contrast,

---

*DePree makes a distinction between a contractual and covenantal relationship. The former, he argues, is legalistic and formal. The latter is based upon "shared commitments to ideals, values and goals."

Swiggett of Kollmorgen (quoted in *Inc.,* April 1984): "The leader's role is to create a vision, not to kick somebody in the ass. The role of the leader is a servant's role. It's supporting his people, running interference for them. It's coming out with an atmosphere of understanding and trust—and love. You want people to feel they have complete control over their destiny at *every* level. Tyranny is not tolerated here. People who want to manage in the traditional sense are cast off by their peers like dandruff. . . . We preach trust and the golden rule."

Jimmy Treybig left Hewlett-Packard to found Tandem Computer. It makes a fine machine. But its superior reputation is based, above all, upon the extraordinary level of service that has allowed it to compete with IBM effectively from the start—in IBM's traditional markets. At the core of it is Treybig's philosophy: "(1) all people are good; (2) people, workers, management and company are all the same thing; (3) every single person in the company must understand the essence of the business; (4) every employee must benefit from the company's success; (5) you must create an environment where all the above can happen." Simple, to the point, and, unfortunately, rare.

Bim Black revitalized Teleflex, a \$150 million applications engineering company (sophisticated valves, control systems, coatings), by installing a vigorous, decentralized entrepreneurial style in a formerly hidebound organization. A strong people philosophy was at the heart of it:

—People are people . . . not personnel.

—People don't dislike work . . . help them to understand mutual objectives and they'll drive themselves to unbelievable excellence.

—The best way to really train people is with an experienced mentor . . . and on the job.

—People have ego and development needs . . . and they'll commit themselves only to the extent that they can see ways of satisfying these needs.

—People cannot be truly motivated by anyone else . . . that door is locked from the inside; they should work in an atmosphere that fosters self-motivation . . . self-assessment . . . and self-confidence.

—People should work in a climate that is challenging, invigorating, and fun . . . and the rewards should be related as directly as possible to performance.

—When people are in an atmosphere of trust, they'll put themselves at risk; only through risk is there growth . . . reward . . . self-confidence . . . leadership.

Renn Zaphiropoulos heads up about a billion dollars' worth of Xerox's office systems business. Until recently he ran Versatec, a tremendously successful Xerox subsidiary, which he founded. He has lived the Versatec philosophy, and in 1983 he codified it into a written document. It begins: "There is basically one killer [of] successful and productive symbiosis, and it is contempt. Contempt tarnishes someone's self-image. It is also a deadly blow to a person's ego. Criticism should not include contempt. The most commonly practiced crime in industry today is a fundamental insensitivity toward personal dignity. False fronts are one way of displaying contempt. Private parking places are contemptuous towards those who do not have them." Amen! We believe that private parking spaces are a near-mortal sin—along with the executive dining room, and, heaven help us (and they're still around), the executive washroom. As a thirty-five-year veteran of the automotive industry, who runs a substantial piece of North American manufacturing for one of the big three, said to us: "I've never seen people working in a factory angry because they were making nineteen thousand dollars while the plant manager was making seventy thousand dollars. What makes them furious, what demotivates and demoralizes, is that slushy, January twenty-sixth morning, when they arrive for their shift at five-forty-five A.M. They park their car one hundred yards away, amidst the muck and dirt and slush. And then they wander in, finally entering cold and wet through the door that's right next to the plant manager's empty parking spot. That's what certifies them as non-full-scale-adult human beings." Right on! It's the accumulation of little slights that kills—kills the spirit (and with it the possibility of excellent performance).

"Now, come on," you're probably saying. "Are these people for real?" We've asked the same question, over and over again. But the evidence keeps coming in. Even as we are drafting this essay a story appears in *USA Today* (May 16, 1984). Monolithic Memories is a $200 million company in the violently competitive semiconductor business. It just about went bust two or three years ago. In fact, it was so hopeless that the board didn't even bother to bring in a turnaround artist. They just took their vice president for finance and figured, what the heck, he couldn't make it any worse, and since he was a finance guy, he might even help smooth the way as the company went out of business. Now Monolithic Memories is about the fastest growing company in that tough industry. The man responsible: Monolithic's president, Irwin Federman, an accountant raised in Brooklyn. To what does he attribute the turnaround? "Revitalization of the human spirit saved this company."

And across the sea at Marks & Spencer the story is exactly the same. How does the then chairman, Marcus Sieff, begin his speech at a 1982 conference of chief executives in Tylösand, Sweden? "They asked me to give a talk today on 'industrial relations.' I can't do it. I only know about 'human relations.' I've never met an 'industrial.' " The chairman's first stop whenever he visits any Marks & Spencer store is the washroom! Says he: "If the washroom isn't good enough for the people in charge [of the corporation], then it's not good enough for the people in the store."

Respect for all people. Respect is caring and trust. Respect is presence: Can you respect people at a plant if you don't visit the plant (and them) regularly? Of course not. But many, it would seem by their actions, don't understand that. In the winter of 1983 Tom visited Sweden again, and talked with a fellow who runs a mid-sized company that distributes electrical and plumbing parts. He had taken over as general manager when the company was on its way down the tubes and had turned it around in just eighteen months. His focus: Teach people to believe in themselves again; teach them self-respect. To put it into practice, he did something that was unexpected. He started spending time, at the rate of 150 days a year, in the field. The company was a major employer in the smallish town it occupied, and the press got on his case for his odd behavior: "This is a bleeding company. Why aren't you out there 'managing'?" (The assumption being, we suppose, that "managing" means sitting in the office sharpening pencils and doing strategic planning.) His response: "If *I* don't go to the field, if *I* don't treat the field as important, and being out there is the only way I can show that it's important, then why should I expect people in the field to think that they're important?" Why, indeed? The people in the plants of Milliken and Company, peppered throughout the South, think that they're the cat's meow in their communities and in the industry. And where do you find sixty-nine-year-old Chairman Roger Milliken at least a third of the time? Out in the plants, talking to his people, down on his knees fiddling with the machinery. If *you* don't demonstrate that you think it's important, why should the people who are *there* think it's important? They shouldn't. They don't. It's leading by inspiration, by simple example, by showing respect instead of contempt via the executive parking spot. Says Joe Schultz, a successful Lockheed manager: "I have only one rule: You can do anything I do." That may just about say it all.

"Bone-Deep Beliefs":
Some Questions—and Things to Do Now

▶ Spend some contemplative time on this. Alone, with a colleague, in a small group, think about team/group/organizational highs and lows in the past. What has marked the highs and lows in terms of people beliefs? Those of the leader? Of peers for each other? Picture (yes, visually) two or three exceptional bosses: what characterized them (especially, again, their people beliefs)? Repeat for one or two bad bosses.

▶ Spend some time on this, too: Become a "real time" expert. Visit a top performing store, youth league soccer team, Girl/Boy Scout troop. Talk to/observe the coach/manager. What do you feel/see/hear about their people beliefs? (This is *expensive* in terms of time. But what of it? If you are serious about your chosen profession as a manager/leader, how better could you spend your time? A manager, at any level and in any organization, is a "career leader." Yet few spend *any* time systematically observing/studying leaders. We should.)

▶ What is your contempt/respect IQ? Ask your secretary, colleagues, a trusted subordinate (it won't be easy to do). Are there any little (usually unintended) ways that you've fallen into the trap of expecting undignified subservience? (Remember, the little ways are *most* important.)

▶ The $64 question: Do you *really* believe the person on the loading dock is just as important/more important than the buyer/product designer/copy writer? If you do, do you show it? How (name twenty ways in five minutes)? If you don't believe it (welcome to a large club), will you do us the favor of thinking about it? Alone. With colleagues. (We don't spend much/enough time examining our people philosophy, even though all of us—who would dare not?—give lip service to the "people first" conventional wisdom.)

▶ Does everybody who works for you know what your equivalent of a precision potentiometer is? Are you sure? When did you last ask? Can *everyone* cite last quarter's sales and profit figures? The change from last year/last quarter? Describe the last three new products/services launched? Describe the *strategy* in twenty-five words or less? If not, why not? More important: when's the last time you asked?

▶ Do you have a written people philosophy, a bill of rights? If not, have you ever tried to draft one? If so, is it boilerplate, or could most people recite it? (If you can't answer the last question, ask.)

▶ Do you show respect by spending 25–50 percent of your time wandering the shops, back rooms, loading docks? At all hours? If not, why not?

The Bottom Line: A Better Bottom Line— and a Gulf That's Vast

At the outset, we think it's terribly important to set one common misunderstanding aside. This book is about serving customers (or students or patients or citizens) well, providing superior-quality products and services, constantly innovating to come up with new products and services and programs at an unprecedented rate. In other words, we're talking about hard-nosed, bottom-line-oriented management. (Or a better urban environment, a more effective school.) This section on people, too, is about hard-nosed performance improvement.

Among the forty-three companies analyzed in *In Search of Excellence,* we know the Hewlett-Packard Company better than any other. And we can state directly and unequivocally that Hewlett-Packard is the toughest darned setting we've experienced! There's no question about it, it's even downright mean. As our colleague Bob Le Duc said, "HP is the toughest environment I've ever worked in, and I started as field engineer with SOCAL [Standard Oil of California]. They [HP] give you the tools and then they expect results." And that, we think, is *exactly* the point.

The HP's of the world give you the tools and train the daylights out of you; they get rid of the Mickey Mouse regulations that sap your time and stand in the way of top performance; they provide simple and clear and unchanging measures of performance; the expectations are fair and real. And then what have they done? They've done the very worst thing you can do to a living human being: they've created a "No excuses" environment. If you don't get "it" done, that's *your* problem. In other words, through humane and people-oriented management (leadership) they've created a pragmatic, no-nonsense, performance-oriented organization.

There *are* leaders who believe in people. They believe all people *will* contribute if given the chance—and if the Mickey Mouse is kept out of the way, and if the objective/vision is clear and unchanging. Someone asked us whether we thought such leaders would win their jobs by election—if, in fact, that was the way it was done. And, by contrast, whether the leaders of the companies that are not so well run would not be elected. We didn't have an answer, obviously, though we suspect that in both cases it would be yes. But what's clear is this: You can *order* the average person who reports to you to come to work five days a week and work his or her eight-and-a-half-hour day. But you *cannot* order *anyone* to perform in an *excellent* fashion—"excellent" meaning courteous, creative. Excellence, by its very definition and at all levels, is a purely *voluntary* commitment. It ensues only if the job is sincerely "owned." Soft (trust, care for people) is hard (dollars, a well-run city).

There is nothing really new here; trust, care, respect are hardly new ideas. But what borders on the new, to us, is the gulf, in language and intensity of deed, between the Sniders, Beebes, Gores and the others— the lip-service givers, the generators of subtle contempt (by omission much more than commission).

It's not merely that we found some "people people." It's that we found some incredible human beings. We watched Ren McPherson closely in the course of a four-day conference (the first ever Skunk Camp, in September 1984). He wears his passion on his sleeve. And his anger. Sometimes it comes out via a sharp tongue: "Goddammit, there you go again, Tom. Not 'Do this or that for *your* people'! They aren't 'your people.' No! No! No! No! You don't own 'em. Don't you see? It's this subtle stuff." At times even a sharp tongue failed him—he would bury his face in his hands for long moments in frustration. It was then that we felt the vastness of that gulf.

INTEGRITY, ONE MORE TIME

To live the people message, to live leader-as-servant, requires total integrity. Not too long ago, Tom spent time with a Northwestern company that has a week-long gala (called Appreciation Week) in the middle of the summer—to celebrate the fact that they're alive, well, making nifty products that their customers like. Big tents are erected on the lawn among all the facilities, and all people are given extra time off at lunch each day to socialize, enjoy a beer and barbecue. All the offices are open—even the lawyers' and accountants'—and each small unit creates a display describing what its department is up to and how it contributes to the whole. One part of the shindig features an old-fashioned carnival dunking machine, where you throw a ball at a target. At carnivals, when you hit the target, a pretty girl is dropped into the water. Here, instead of the pretty girl, the executives of the company take their turns sitting in the dunking machine. It was the idea of the bright, aggressive and caring manager of this $75 million outfit. Tom

"Help! I'm trapped in an executive vice-president!"

• •

Drawing by Handelsman; © 1975
The New Yorker Magazine, Inc.

thought it was terrific. But the manager revealed that it had caused a great deal of consternation among the senior ranks. Several had complained that "they'd lose their dignity if they were dunked." Dignity? If a three-piece suit with a buttoned vest is the only proof of importance and is all that allows you to "maintain control," then heaven help us. And if it is beneath executives' dignity to be dunked, who would they suggest be dunked in their stead? A "lower level" pretty girl with no dignity to lose? You see the problem.

The boss of Nissan's remarkably successful manufacturing plant in Smyrna, Tennessee makes a habit—without fail, even when dignitaries from afar are present—of wearing the company-issued coveralls to work. We, frankly, have a bias in this direction. Either you're part of the team or you're not part of the team. We don't think the people who work in the plant would expect you to wear coveralls when you make a sales call on a customer, but if you're not comfortable trooping the line—or sitting in your office—in the same kind of clothes your people wear, then you really aren't part of the program. And while there are indeed managers who would look ridiculous in a pair of coveralls, and it's probably best that they not wear them, we wouldn't bet two cents on their ability to run a truly distinctive manufacturing operation.

You don't lose your dignity if you're dunked, or if you wear coveralls. And if you believe in people, you likewise don't lose your dignity if you admit mistakes. The managers of a sizable aircraft producer had made a dumb mistake about parking lots, wiping out a convenient one in order to install some new equipment (that really didn't need to go there). They had, with good reason, gotten most everybody riled up, and the top team had spent hours trying to figure out how to wiggle out of the mess they'd gotten into. Then the manufacturing boss came up with an idea, simple and to the point, and acted on it without telling the rest of the group: he reversed the stupid decision, then heralded the mistake and the remedy on the front page of the company newspaper. To admit screwing up to a fare-thee-well and then having the sense to fix it, and fix it promptly, demonstrates not only self-confidence but the depth of your confidence in others. Conversely, you are being contemptuous of your people if you believe that they can't handle the thought of the top team making a mistake. After all, they are the ones who must live most intimately with your day-to-day, year-to-year mistakes.

Be confident in your beliefs. Live them with integrity. Remember that the "small stuff" is all there is. It's a pretty tough message. If your convictions about people aren't all that clear and strong, then it's tough to be confident and consistent. Maybe that's the secret, for good or ill, after all.

14

Ownership!

Tom and Bob Waterman discussed the Dana Corporation in *In Search of Excellence.* In the last three years we have gotten to know Dana's former chairman, Ren McPherson, much better. This story grows on us as we learn more of it. On page 789 is an advertisement of Ren's that ran for several months in *Fortune, Forbes* and *Business Week:* "Talk Back to the Boss." Dana, an axle manufacturer based in Toledo, Ohio, was once described by its own chairman as having "the rottenest product line ever granted by God to a Fortune 500 company"; for the 1970's it ranked number two in return on total capital among the entire Fortune 500, and though battered along with the rest of the automotive and trucking industry in 1979–81, it has made a remarkable comeback. McPherson's guiding principle was simple: "Turn the company back over to the people who do the work."

The key was the radical decentralization of the personnel, legal, purchasing and financial departments. The reasoning was simple. For instance, per McPherson: "Centralized purchasing *always* looks good on paper, and virtually never works as planned in reality. Yes, we've got some areas where, in theory, we need to purchase centrally in order to get a volume-based price break: certain steel shapes, transportation, energy, and so on. But look, I want my ninety store managers [his term for factory managers] to sign up for their quarterly objectives. And I don't want them to come in ninety days later and say, 'Ren, I would have made it, *but* the guy in purchasing didn't get my steel on time and I had to short my top two customers. Maybe next quarter . . .' I won't accept that. See, I've got the ultimate weapon. I've got ninety very bright factory managers. If seven of them know they need to get together to buy a certain steel shape and get a price break, well, they'll get together. They don't need a corporate daddy to tell them when or how to do it."*

---

*Besides, field people readily know how to "beat" corporate types, and abrogate the benefits of paper centralization. An AT&T manager recalled a time when some purchasing function was centralized. The fellows in the field switching stations started to get shorted (causing service to deteriorate) as a function of the new central group's system-wide inventory minimization program. No dummies they: Subsequently, each time they ordered they'd ask for one or two more than they needed. Pretty soon they had reestablished illicit field inventories. Moreover, since the field was no longer graded on inventory level, they obtained a larger local supply than under the precentralization regime. Inventory climbed, and eventually the experiment was abandoned.

A Dana executive vice president in a speech made in the late summer of 1982, in the depths of the 1981–83 recession, puts it this way: "We have no corporate procedures at Dana. We threw the books away in the late sixties. We eliminated reports and sign-offs. We installed trust."* Trust! Trust and treating people as adults: During the recession Dana had to lay off ten thousand people. Once a week management sent an extensive newsletter to every employee's home, including those who had been laid off. It talked about where the layoffs had been, what the prospects were, and, even more boldly, where the next layoffs *might* occur. What was the result of this up-front approach? There was one indicator that McPherson takes particular pride in. Before the layoffs 80 percent of the employees owned stock in the company, the result of a voluntary stock-purchase program. At the height of the layoffs, the percentage of employees owning shares edged *above* 80 percent, and included all ten thousand people who had been laid off.

While we were working on this chapter, Tom gave a talk that stressed measuring customer satisfaction directly, and then evaluating people on it (see chapter 6), noting that all seem to agree that the procedure would be valuable but few do much about it. Subsequently he got into a discussion with a manager, who said, "But how do we measure customer satisfaction in a meaningful way for the machine operator in the factory?" Not knowing the industry, Tom shot back, "Why don't you *ask* the machine operators what the right measure is? After all, they're closest to it." The manager paused for a moment, and then said, "That's a great idea. You know, we don't naturally do that sort of thing around here—ask people, that is." About three weeks later we got a lovely two-page letter from him. He had asked, he said, "and the ideas were terrific. A couple of people [on the line] even visited a few customers, on their own, to talk about it with them." Efforts were now under way, he added, to collect data in accordance with several of the suggestions. "You hit a sore spot. We've got to get out and do this more," he concluded.

We were both delighted and frustrated: delighted that he did it, *but* why is *asking* such a novel approach for so many? Why in the world would you expect people in a plant to get excited about their "comparative differential negative variance in scrap rate" (vis-à-vis a competitor) when you never share any information about scrap rates with them in the first place? Why in the world would you expect them to be interested in comparative plant profitability if you never tell them how they're doing? Why, indeed? We wonder that our people don't seem interested in the well-being of the business—and yet we have never told them what the hell the well-being of the business is.

What we're talking about here is a phenomenon that we've come to call "all people as 'business people.' " Making everybody part of the strategic information stream of the business; making everybody an owner. Ed Carlson, former chairman of United Airlines, used to talk about countering the NETMA

*Don Estridge, as president of IBM's Entry System Division, used virtually the same language: "We don't need 'checks and balances.' We need trust."

TALK BACK TO THE BOSS.

It's one of Dana's principles of productivity.

Bosses don't have all the answers. The worker who does the job always knows more about it than his boss. But all that he knows can't be used unless he's free to talk about it. Especially to his boss.

At Dana, bosses listen. It's part of what we call humanistic management, giving people the freedom to work well, to grow and to share the rewards.

You can see the results in our productivity. It's more than doubled in the last 7 years.

Productivity alone doesn't produce profits. But we're balancing our output of parts for the vehicular, service and industrial equipment markets we manufacture for. So, as well as increasing productivity, we've improved our earnings year after year.

And that's not bad for a bunch of people who talk back to their bosses.

Dana Corporation, Toledo

PRODUCTIVE PEOPLE

DANA

(Nobody Ever Tells Me Anything) factor. McPherson believes that all should know where the next layoffs are coming from. Treybig of Tandem makes sure that the entire staff, including the newly hired secretaries, has a copy of the complete strategic plan. New secretaries at Bourns are expected to know what a precision potentiometer is (*and* care about it), not because of any technical need associated with their job, but because they're considered full-scale members of the Bourns team. People who are part of the team, who "own" the company and "own" their job, regularly perform a thousand percent better—often many thousand percent better—than the rest. Treat all people as business people and they do become business people—fully involved in the bottom-line orientation of the business and committed to its success.

The illustration below is a calling card: "Sarah Clifton, Supreme Commander." We'll get to Sarah in just a moment. She holds the key to ownership. But allow us to backtrack, and in fact repeat a brief analysis from *In Search of Excellence.* It was buried in an obscure corner. It now occupies a front-row center seat in our thinking: it's at the heart of the issue of ownership.

In Search of Excellence recounted an experiment in which an industrial psychologist brought a bunch of adult subjects to a lab, supposedly to take part in an investigation of garden-variety industrial hygiene, focusing on the effects of noise on productivity. All of them were given some difficult puzzles to solve and some rather dull proofreading to do; while they attempted these two chores, a raucous audio tape consisting of one person speaking Spanish, two people speaking Armenian, a mimeograph machine running, a chattering typewriter and street noise ran in the background. Half the subjects were given a button they could push to suppress the noise. The other half were not. The results? As you might expect, those with buttons to push solved five times more puzzles and made one-quarter as many proofreading errors as those who had no button. The news was that never once (and the experiment was repeated several times) did *anyone* ever push his or her button. The mere fact that people *perceived* that they had a *modicum* of control over their des-

W. L. GORE & ASSOCIATES, INC.

SARAH CLIFTON

SUPREME COMMANDER

1505 NORTH FOURTH STREET
FLAGSTAFF, ARIZONA 86001
PHONE: 602-774-0611
TWX 910-972-0969

tiny—the *option* of pushing the button—led to an enormous improvement in performance. The power that can be unleashed as a result of "mere" ownership (or even the *perception* of it) is awesome!

Let's quickly get away from the industrial psych lab and proceed to the real world: Edison, New Jersey, site of a Ford Motor Company assembly plant. A while back they began an experiment that parallels the one from the lab (and also resembles some Japanese factory techniques). Every person on the line in the huge facility was given a button that he or she could push to shut down the line—quite a gutsy move on the part of the plant manager. The results we're sharing occurred during the first ten months of the experiment (the results since then have been consistent with those at the start). To begin with—no surprise here—Edison, New Jersey, is *not* like an industrial psych lab! People *did* push their buttons at Edison. To be precise, they shut the facility down twenty to thirty times per *day!* The ameliorating news is that the average shutdown lasted only about ten seconds, time enough to make a quality adjustment, a tweek, a twist, a turn, to tighten up a nut or bolt. Now, twenty to thirty shutdowns of about 10 seconds each add up to about 200 to 300 lost seconds a day, essentially unnoticeable. Indeed, productivity in the plant did not change. Three other indicators, however, are worthy of note. The number of defects per car produced dropped during the first months of the experiment from 17.1 per car to 0.8 per car. The number of cars requiring rework after they had come off the end of the line fell by 97 percent. And the backlog of union grievances at any point in the facility plummeted from an average of well over 200 to an average of less than 12.

Moreover, the change in language and attitude was as extreme as the numbers. One old pro on the line commented, "It's like someone opened the window and we can breathe." Or, describing the foremen under the new team-based approach: "They're no longer policemen, but advisers." And along with the opened-up atmosphere came exactly the things you pray for: the side benefits of ownership that are probably at least as significant, if not more so, than the quantifiable indicators. Story after story emerges of the following sort. There had traditionally been difficulties with seat-cover installation. A line employee worked up a method using Saran Wrap in appropriate places to increase slipperiness and thus make it easier to set seat covers. He did the *entire* experiment on his own, at home. He then brought the results to work and shared them with his colleagues. Are we talking about the American automotive industry? Yes, we are. (Similar experiments in Ford's truck plants in Louisville, Kentucky, have been just as successful.)

Now back to Sarah Clifton and her calling card. Sarah worked for W. L. Gore & Associates. She began as a secretary-bookkeeper in one of Gore's twenty-eight factories. Bill Gore doesn't stand on formality. There are no titles whatsoever in the company. Sarah was to go to a meeting in Phoenix to talk about W. L. Gore. She ran into Bill, on one of his many visits, a couple of weeks before the event. "I'm going to this meeting, Billy," she said, "and they're going to want to know who I am. What do I do?"

"Well, Sarah, that's up to you," Gore replied. "What do you want to be?"

"Beats me."

"Well, how about 'Supreme Commander'?" Sarah agreed. Sarah is an "owner" of W. L. Gore & Associates in the deepest sense of that word.

Some go to extremes to ensure not only a sense of ownership but stock ownership as well. Like Dana's McPherson, Publix Super Market's George Jenkins passionately believes that all employees should own shares in the corporation so that they are "working for themselves." So determined was he that he "even gave a raise to the ones who didn't have the money to buy in." Now, that's putting your money where your mouth is!

Ownership. How can we capture the drama, the power of people who have just a *bit* of space and control? Perhaps the best way to bring it to life is through a series of vignettes, small and large. They are but a handful of the stories we've collected about performance of the Ford/Edison sort—not improvement by a percent or two here or there, but a remarkable response to apparently minor opportunities.

SAS. We previously described the turnaround that Group President Jan Carlzon brought about at Scandinavian Air Systems. Here's a tiny piece of the story, per Carlzon: "The objective was to become the number one on-time airline in Europe. I couldn't figure out how to do it. I nosed around trying to determine what group [of people] should be most responsible for it. Finally I unearthed a group that seemed to be as close to the heart of the matter as I could find. I called the fellow who ran the shop and said, 'What will it take to make us the number one on-time airline in Europe? See if you can answer that for me. Come and see me in a couple of weeks and tell me if we can do it.' A couple of weeks later he set up an appointment to see me. He came in, and I said, 'Well, can we do it?' He responded, 'Yes, we can. It will take about six months, and it's going to cost you a million and a half dollars.' I immediately cut him off. It would have been a bargain at five times the price! 'Fine,' I said. 'Get on with it.' He was taken aback: 'Wait, I've got my people with me and a presentation for you. We want to show you just how we're going to do it.' 'I don't care,' I said. 'Go ahead and do it.' To make a long story short, about four and a half months later he called me in with the advance information on the past month's on-time performance. Sure enough, he had jacked us into first place. But that wasn't the only point of his call. He had more: 'And you get half a million of that million and a half dollars back. It only cost us a million.' Now here's my point. If I'd gone down to him, put my arm around him, and said, 'Look, I want you to make us the number one on-time airline in Europe. I'm going to give you two million dollars. I want you to do such and such.' Well, you *know* what would have happened! He would have come back to me six months later and said, 'Well, we've done what you asked, and we've made some headway. We're not quite there yet. It's just going to take another ninety days or so. And it's going to cost another million dollars. And so on.' That's what would have happened.

That's the game. But not this time. He asked for some money, and I gave him what he asked for. And he delivered."*

Quad/Graphics. In an article titled, "Management By Walking Away," *Inc.* (October 1983) reports on successful Quad/Graphics: " 'We don't believe that responsibility should be that defined,' [CEO] Quadracci explains. 'We think it should be *assumed* and *shared.* Nothing should ever be "somebody else's responsibility." Anybody who sees that something needs to be done ought to assume responsibility for doing it. Our people shouldn't need me or anybody else to tell them what to do.' The fact is, Quadracci often *refuses* to tell his employees what to do. For example, when Quad/Graphics' shipping department needed greater back-haul revenue to finance expansion of the trucking fleet, Quadracci handed each of his drivers the keys to one of the company's Peterbilts [trucks]. From now on, he told them, they were owner-operators—partners in a new division called DuPlainville [Quad/Graphics headquarters] Transport, Inc.—and it was their duty to make the rigs profitable on return trips. When the truckers asked what they should take on the back-hauls, Quadracci shrugged, 'How should I know? I don't know anything about driving an 18-wheeler. I'm not going to carry your loads.' With that, he turned and walked away." Amen!

Trust House Forte. Goldsmith and Clutterbuck's *The Winning Streak* reports:

> That there can be autonomy in a centralized organization is borne out by THF's experience in Paris, when it acquired the three grand hotels, the George V, La Tremoille and the Plaza-Athenée.
>
> The unions of the three hotels had campaigned vociferously against a foreign takeover, parading in their chef, bellboy and waiter uniforms outside the hotels to attract public attention. Having won control, Forte discovered that management in the Plaza-Athenée had effectively abdicated, leaving the day-to-day running of the business to the union. In one of those flashes of insight that distinguish the entrepreneurial genius from the normal businessman, Forte offered the post of managing director to the shop steward, who happened to be chief concierge.
>
> The choice was not as irrational as it might have appeared. In analyzing the problems of the hotel, it quickly became clear to the THF representative in Paris that the head concierge had a clearer idea than anyone else of what needed to be done.

---

*A colleague who consults in Japan relates a similar tale: "It was the biggest difference I noticed. In the U.S., if ten people submit proposals and you only have funding for five, what you usually do is fund all ten at fifty percent of what was asked. So when a problem arises, the fellow can lay it on the higher-ups: 'They only gave us half of what we wanted.' In Japan, they'd say no to five groups and yes to five groups. Then the five yes groups have got a problem: They got what they asked for. Now they've got to deliver."

The new managing director introduced a regime of remarkable employee participation, quite unlike anything found elsewhere in THF. An employee consultative committee took over the handling of lateness, absenteeism and other disciplinary matters. An incentive scheme was worked out under which the employees shared with THF all profits above 5 per cent of turnover. In return, the labour force was reduced by 20 per cent. Profits rose dramatically to three and a half times the level on acquisition. The remaining employees saw their annual income double over a five-year period.

Tupperware. Ownership involves the enhancement of pride, pride in ourselves and our close associates. Each of Tupperware's several hundred distributorships has a weekly program called Rally. At Rally, each Tupperware salesperson, during a ceremony called Count Up, marches up front to applause when the amount of their sales for the week is read off (e.g., when "three hundred dollars to five hundred dollars" is read out, you march up if you had sales of $319 for the week). "Count Up" continues until only the week's top five salespersons are left. For them the procedure is different. They come to the front of the room, where there's a giant blackboard. Each walks up to the blackboard and signs her name. End of story. Is that it, you ask? No. But it's *exactly* what we mean by ownership. To sign your name on a big blackboard in front of your peers is the essence of ownership.

Sunset Publications. Ownership means being involved, in *any* way, in the business. Sunset Publications develops cookbooks. Each recipe for a Sunset cookbook is tried in the company's test kitchens in Menlo Park, California—by a half-dozen employees selected from a sign-up list. That's no big deal, you say—but you're wrong! There are, literally, hundreds of people in line to be recipe testers. And the list includes the most senior as well as junior people, people who simply want to be a part of the "live" process. It's a kick to read a cookbook and realize that a recipe, being sent out to a host of customers, is *only* there because *you* tested it and said it was okay. It's a little thing. Or is it?

Alpine Electronics (high-end car stereos) general manager Reese Haggott was taken by the Sarah Clifton story. He didn't go the "Supreme Commander" route, but he did issue each person in this sizable company calling cards (and personalized note pads). The cards had the person's name and the appropriate department—e.g., Joe Doaks, Quality Control, Alpine Electronics. Reese was delighted with the results, and adds, "But it makes so much sense, you know. Remember when you got your first calling cards [we do]? It was a really big deal. 'Hey, I'm real,' you know." Yes!

IBM. Tiny things, even from the granddaddy of it all. An IBMer, a twenty-five-year veteran, hands us his business card. It is the first business card we have seen from an IBMer who has been there for more than twenty-five years. On the calling card is a beautiful blue shield with a gilt edge and gilt embossed printing. It's a printed reproduction of his twenty-five-year pin. It reads "IBM. Twenty-five Years of Loyal Service." Big deal? No. Just another "little way" in which IBM says, "Thanks for the twenty-five years of service." And they want you to be able to share it with everyone you come in contact with. Genius!

Markem of Keene, New Hampshire, has a calendar. Peppered throughout are quotes. Bartlett's? No. Hemingway? No. Michael Jackson? Not even. How about Markem employees: "A full year of quality thoughts from Markem employees to inspire our finest performance [from the cover]." Sample: five to ten days a month are marked by quotes—e.g., January 15, 1985: "Quality is a celebration of commitment."—Barbara Yoerger. Or this from George Scott, April 23, 1985: "The priceless ingredient in every product is the honor and integrity of the person who makes it." Or this, on August 2, 1985, from Jim Lawrence: "Quality is always working one step beyond your best." Ownership!

People Express. Not only has this exceptional airline shattered every record in the book for growth by "respecting people and giving them a good deal," it has established a unique way for its more than three thousand full- and part-time people to work together: Every employee is a "manager"— those who would be termed "flight attendants" on other airlines are "customer service managers" at People Express; in other airlines' cockpits you'll find pilots, but at People Express you'll find "flight managers." And everywhere you look, you find not employees but owners. Everyone in a permanent position is a shareholder. Don Burr, president, CEO and founder of People Express, comments in a Harvard University Case Study: "I guess the single predominant reason that I cared about starting a new company was to try and develop a better way for people to work together. . . . that's where the name People Express came from, as well as the whole people focus and trust. . . . It drives everything we do. I'm not a Goody Two-shoes person, I don't view myself as a social scientist, as a minister, as a do-gooder. I perceive myself as a hard-nosed businessman, whose ambitions and aspirations have to do with providing goods and services to other people for a return."

The airline started out with no hierarchy, and still operates with no vice presidents, no supervisors and no secretaries. Everybody answers the phones and takes care of his or her own correspondence. Everybody works more than one job: People Express calls it "cross-utilization." Flight managers may fly one day and work in the Newark, New Jersey, headquarters the next; customer service managers also take reservations; the six managing officers (the airline's founding group) also work in-flight, as customer service managers, or on the ground, checking baggage or helping customers board.

Don Burr's two favorite words are "awesome" and "empowerment." What the people at People Express have accomplished is "awesome;" what people need is to be "empowered," not managed.

Training Manual

A retailer, who had run a store for six or seven years, personally conducted all the training; she correctly thought it was a vital function. As the store grew to seventy-five employees (with retail's typical high turnover, though hers was far below average), the task became almost impossible. She began to write a training manual, and was thinking about appointing someone to assist her as training manager. But that sounded bureaucratic to her, so she shifted gears and decided to ask her best people in each area if they would like to do some of the training. Would they ever! She was astonished by the outpouring of enthusiasm. Old hands signed up for even the most inconvenient shifts to train a newcomer. It became a major distinction to be chosen/allowed to train. And that enthusiasm—and talent—had been all there, lying untapped, during the prior two years, when the task had been getting beyond her control. Moreover, she readily admitted, "The quality of the training has gone way up, mainly as a function of the enthusiasm the new 'trainers' bring to it."

Baltimore Orioles. Tom was born in Baltimore and is a loyal Oriole fan. The Orioles are well over a hundred wins ahead of the number two team in major league baseball over the last twenty-five years. Yet, until a couple of years ago, they always ranked twenty-sixth out of twenty-six major league teams on the salary scale—i.e., they were at the very bottom, and hence a "no-name" team. The unique factor in the Baltimore system is that all twenty-five players on the roster actually play, and twenty-five no-names playing as a team are, it turns out, a winning team.

Los Angeles Raiders. Tough-guy owner Al Davis, according to an article in the *New York Times* (September 2, 1984), is *loved* by his players yet almost universally hated by the other owners (and not just because he has by far the best won/loss record in the NFL over the last twenty-five years). The *Times* explains why:

He gives his players the impression he cares about them. Chandler, the retired wide receiver, tells the story, about a discussion with Davis for a new contract after Davis had acquired him in a trade from the Buffalo Bills. Chandler had distinguished himself for ten years with the Bills. When they traded him to the Raiders, he felt betrayed. Yet he figured that this would be as good a time as any to cash in.

"I decided that I would go in and ask Al for a lot of money," Chandler said. "The first thing he told me was, 'You're a great receiver. If you had been here your whole career, you'd be going into the Hall of Fame. I've wanted you since you were a senior in college, but we always had Fred Biletnikoff. Now, about the money. There's no way I can pay you more than I'm paying Cliff Branch. Cliff's been with me nine or ten years; he's done a lot for the organization. Loyalty is important to me, more important than anything else.'

"So he paid me the same as Cliff, which was less than I had asked for. But, you know, I came out of that meeting feeling great. Before when I had negotiated for a new contract, the team always made me feel like a C+ player. But they expected you to play like an A player. That wasn't the case with Al. I remember thinking, 'This guy thinks I'm a great player.' When I left his office I couldn't wait to show him he was right.". . .

"It means they're not always in your face," said Dave Casper, the tight end whom Davis traded to the Houston Oilers in 1980 and who resigned this summer [1984] after he was released by the Minnesota Vikings. "If you treat players like dogs, they turn into dogs. That doesn't happen here."

"It means they don't try to turn a team of 45 players into Raiders," said Chandler. "The team is 45 individuals who become the Raiders."

And it means tolerating the unusual nature of many players who have come and gone over the years. . . .

"They don't nitpick you to death here or hammer you all the time," said Lyle Alzado, the defensive lineman who played for Cleveland and Denver before he became a Raider in 1982. "I've been places where a guy would be fined $200 for being one minute late to a meeting and the team would embarrass you by announcing it at a meeting. Here, they treat you like an adult until you prove that you're not."

Butter Sculptures

A tough industrial enterprise in Ireland has a couple of dozen facilities, each with about seventy-five to two hundred employees. One of the managers proposed that once every several months each facility should have an "open house," featuring a garden-variety cafeteria meal for each of their people and members of their families. It was to be held in the canteen at the factory. The results? Amazing on every score. The manager reports that "the people in the canteen [the work force there] are not exactly looked upon as the most creative in the world. They're held in some contempt, frankly. But you wouldn't have believed how they responded to this. I remember, in place after place, seeing an outpouring the likes of which I wouldn't have dreamt. It was more like coming to dinner at a fine hotel in Dublin. Massive, beautiful, extremely elaborate butter sculptures were created. It was a delight to behold." And he is further amazed by the reactions of the families: "It was astonishing. In some cases it was the *first* time in over a *dozen* years of employment that families had ever been to the facility, had ever seen where their husband or wife or son or daughter worked." He adds that the goodwill (and productivity) that has been garnered is substantial. Such small things, such big payoffs!

Mervyn's, the shining star in Dayton-Hudson's tiara, yields a marvelous example of "autonomy by accident." Or at least we call it "by accident." One of the issues in retailing today is that the merchant/buyer element tends to dominate the stores. In other words, company after company has taken the sense of ownership away from the stores. It hurt Sears, especially, in the late seventies; once-proud store managers became second-class citizens (bureaucrats going through the motions to respond to Chicago) and they did all sorts of things, intentional and unintentional, to express their ire. Well, Mervyn's too, is forced to deal with the real world, a world of fast-changing fashion tastes that requires a fairly centralized buying organization. The buyers put together "programs," and the store people execute them. Now a term commonly used to denote a program is a "rounder." "Rounder" is short for a "round rack," the rack that displays an array of skirts, sport coats or what-have-you in a store. The Mervyn's buyer organization, under energetic leadership, has really gotten on with the programs. In fact, buyers have outdone themselves. They've outpaced the stores: "We have 105 programs and only 70 rounders per store." The result? Despite Mervyn's best-laid plans, the store managers still have a lot of flexibility! That is, they have the wherewithal to execute only 70 programs, but 105 have been ordained from on high. So what do they do? They do what *they* think is best with what they have (70 rounders). Their power to make decisions thus remains high. And what does that mean, in turn? A sense of ownership. Store managers who still think they run their stores (and do) are the blessed norm.

Productivity in Research

A department administrator in a research hospital came up to Tom after a seminar he gave for the Association of Western Hospitals. Her story was an involved one, but it boiled down to just a couple of sentences. About a year before, with each of her groups she had taken a new tack on managing. "My approach was to tell people in the department, 'Do whatever you want to as long as it's legal and within the budget.' " She said that she'd provided virtually no guidelines beyond that. The results? "I was astounded. Research productivity in the department, in terms of papers produced and accepted for publication, for instance, increased by a factor of *six!* And all within less than a year. I still can't believe it. Do you think the ownership phenomenon is really that potent?" Yes.

Seattle First (Seafirst), the bank, got in a lot of trouble, principally with some inappropriate energy loans. The response of the new top team, following a Bank of America bailout, was to go back to their knitting, to seek to become, again, a premier regional bank. A basic problem, in addition to a shaky loan portfolio, was a wholesale sense of demoralization throughout the work force. The new chairman, Dick Cooley, came up with an inventive program to counter it, and make some money besides. He divided the entire staff of the bank into nine hundred teams—teams from everywhere: receptionists, people in MIS, those in the various operations departments, as well as loan officers. High visibility contests were run with one target: Bring in new accounts. The effect was spectacular—$500 million in new accounts in ninety days! More significant in terms of the long-term reinvigoration of the institution, the contest winners seldom came from the "right" places—i.e., from the lending departments. In fact, the topmost team came from the MIS department; they thought it was terrific to have a chance to go out and sell business—to their friends, to their neighbors. Ownership!

In *Baltimore,* Mayor Schaefer has launched a host of programs aimed at enhancing citizen ownership. For instance, last year he "sold" potholes to citizens for Valentine's Day. For $35 ($5 for students and senior citizens) you "bought" a pothole. The city patched it and painted a heart on the finished product; then they sent a card with a picture of your repaired and Valentined pothole to the loved one of your choice. The program was a smashing success. The mayor also insisted that communities, even destitute ones, buy into urban improvements. Richard Ben Cramer in *Esquire* (October 1984) reports an exchange between a vocal community group and the mayor:

"What are you going to do?" they demanded.
Schaefer: "Wait a minute. What are *you* going to do?"
"What do you mean? *We're* not supposed to do it."
Schaefer's chins tucked, and his eyes started shining. "You want a playground?"
"We are *entitled* to playgrounds."
"You gonna maintain it?"
"*We* can't maintain it."
"Then . . . we're not gonna build it."
Pretty soon he started demanding that the neighborhood group buy the swings, or the jungle gym. "It'll cost you $1,000," he'd say. "I don't care if you gotta sell cookies. Just get it." If there was no neighborhood group, they had to make one. Then hold the bake sales. Then buy the swings. Pretty soon, in a couple of neighborhoods, then a half dozen, then

a few more, people stopped to show him their playgrounds. They showed him how they'd changed the city's plans to make it more like they wanted it. And they showed where they wanted the city to put a recreation center for the older kids. Could the city kick in part of the money?

Even the [Irish] *Post Office*... A very aggressive retailer has taken on a collateral duty as chairman of the Post Office in Ireland. For St. Patrick's Day in 1984 the Post Office did something very special: each local branch sent St. Patrick's day cards to their subscribers—a card that was signed by all the people at the branch. The chairman, a real pepper-pot, couldn't be more enthusiastic: "Typical were the clerks I run into in central headquarters. Before, I'd ask them what they do, and I'd get, 'I'm a clerk.' *Now* I ask and they reply, proudly, 'I work for the Post Office.' They're no longer ashamed. It's pride. Pride is everything, you know." We didn't know when we started. But we're beginning to learn.

Ownership: MBWA with Customers

The *Wall Street Journal* (December 12, 1984) reports from Sparrows Point, Maryland:

When Robert Felts's supervisor at Bethlehem Steel Corp. here asked him to visit a customer, the veteran line operator jumped at the chance. But there was one problem: The client was in East Texas, and Mr. Felts had to fly for the first time in his life.

"I didn't like that. And they put me on four planes to get me there," he recalls with a shudder.

Mr. Felts's adjustment is only a small part of a general upheaval in traditional management-labor roles in the country's basic industries. Increasingly, management is turning to hourly workers for help with problems formerly handled only by field engineers and select executives. Employees like Mr. Felts are calling on customers and, in some instances, even visiting foreign competitors to determine firsthand how their own products stack up....

[G]eneral manager *John G. Roberts* is largely credited with starting the employee visitation program. "Management still has to make the tough economic decisions. But these are easier to make when employees understand the issue and also trust management," he says.

The Sparrows Point main office is also educating its work force about the steel market by distributing a weekly business news roundup throughout the plant. A recent issue reported that foreign steel was getting a 31% share of the domestic steel market in July and August.

The program seems to be working. For line operators here, the priority for years was to churn out so many tons of steel each hour with quality a secondary concern. But that changed for Tony DeLuca, a mill worker, during a recent trip to a client. "A foreman there said, 'You guys at Sparrows Point are garbage rollers,' and that really hit my pride," he says. Other steelworkers recall how they were jolted after seeing defects in Bethlehem sheet steel show up in their customers' products.

"You're especially aware when you go to warehouses of customers and see all that foreign steel wrapped up in pretty packages," says steelworker Greg Blackenship. "We know what we're doing now. Before we were just rolling steel."

Customers say they generally appreciate the visits, which let them air grievances with workers who are actually responsible for the product. The visits also show the supplier's commitment, they add. Dale Aulthouse, a purchaser for High Steel Structures Inc. in Lancaster, Pa., a big Bethlehem client, says he was ready to switch to a competitor because Sparrows Point management apparently wasn't heeding his complaints about flaws in Bethlehem's steel plate.

A visit by Sparrows Point plate workers, he says, was a "last-ditch effort." When the steelworkers saw the problem their defects were causing, they were "practically in tears," Mr. Aulthouse says. The defect was resolved overnight.

H. H. Robertson, a highly profitable UK specialty steel producer: According-ing to the *Financial Times,* November 14, 1983, "Efficient production is not the whole story. Robertson's managing director, Cliff Dyer, felt a year ago that the company was missing orders it should have won and decided to use a radical organizational tool to change things. He developed the 'ginger group' program. Each group is ad hoc and formed for a specific project, or likely order. It comprises the key people concerned, irrespective of rank in the company. Thus, design, sales, production, cost accounting and purchasing might all be asked to join, often with junior people brought in. The system has broken down interdepartmental barriers, producing a fluid, creative approach that Dyer describes as 'analog' [organization]—as opposed to the 'digital' organizational structure with segregated functions with formal communications between departments which bogs down many managements." Let people have the tools—and watch out. The results have been smashing.

Monarch Marking, principally a maker of labels for retailers, has a bunch of exciting programs. One involves their smallest division, which sells labels for industrial use—e.g., tag wires in an aircraft's electronics area. Until the new boss took over, the division had been in a state of rapid decline in an apparently decrepit market, falling from $9 million in sales to $4 million in a three-year period. As of late 1983, the new man's been in charge for about two years; sales—in the face of the recession of 1981–83—had vaulted to $23 million. What's going on? A hopped-up organization with everybody involved. For instance, once a week there's a series of "partnership meetings" for all hands. Everyone participates. Everyone is treated as a full-scale business person and partner. *Everyone* goes out and visits customers—regularly. The leap from $4 million to $23 million in sales has not come via one or two superproducts; it's come from an outpouring of tiny products. Most were developed by the most unlikely people, and in the most unlikely places once intensive customer contact (listening and inquiring) by all hands was begun. All participate and all have come to feel responsible for serving even better the customers they have. Tiny things: for instance, a flashy letterhead (pride, again!). The manager even made a trip to Las Vegas for the sole purpose of picking up some old silver dollars (he could have obtained them via courier, but he made the trip personally as a symbolic gesture). Now, when something good happens (some small success), he gives out one of those precious silver dollars.

Paint and Potties

A tough old nut, sporting a close-cropped crew cut in the 1980's, ran the Buffalo, New York, foundry for General Motors. He turned it around—and in just eighteen months. The secret? He began with a bucket of paint and an innocent query, "Is there any reason why a foundry can't be white?" There wasn't. And it mattered to his people. An officer at Memorex, and another from Hewlett-Packard, both with exceptional records, apply the same "magic." Colleagues say of each: "Whenever he arrives someplace, he always begins the same way— paints it up. Makes it a place you'd be proud of."

And the potty part? We mentioned before that Marcus Sieff of Marks & Spencer speaks often of having the washrooms up to snuff. Ed Carlson, the UAL turnaround genius in the early seventies, also preached the importance of clean washrooms—if they're not clean enough for you (the honcho), then they aren't clean enough for your people. A. Ray Smith turned the minor league Louisville Redbirds into a sparkling winner at the gate. His formula? Clean washrooms—"a place you'd be proud to take the family." And after a Dayton, Ohio, speech to Hewlett-Packard customers sometime back in which Tom had been talking about "bone-deep belief in people," the seventy-year-old-plus (he'd estimate) manager of several foundries outside of Cleveland came up to him, pulled him aside and said, "I liked what you said. But you were much too abstract. It's clean washrooms. Start by cleaning up the washrooms. If the goddamned place stinks to high heaven and looks like hell, if you wouldn't piss in it yourself, where's the pride, where's the care going to come from? How do you preach pride in product with any credibility at all when the smell from the head seeps onto the shop floor? Too goddam few people understand that. You tell 'em that."

What is the common denominator of this series of stories—stories that range from the Irish Post Office to an Irish canteen, from embossed lettering on an IBM calling card to "partnership meetings" in a forgotten division, from the sale of potholes to the citizens of Baltimore, to signing your name on a blackboard or testing a recipe? Ownership. Being a full-scale business person/partner, inexorably involved in a hands-on way in the output of the organization, particularly output directed toward customers for those not used to customer contact. Pride. Enthusiasm. Redefinition of a mundane job (e.g., working in the canteen) in a way that turns the performer of a "routine" task into a valued expert. Recognition and respect, in a host of small ways, especially for seldom acknowledged people and functions. Being part of a charged-up group with a pragmatic goal, sufficient resources and a fair time frame in which to achieve it, but no handed-down-from-on-high approach to getting there. The chance to set yourself apart as a winner.

These stories are also about integrity and guts. Integrity in that the leaders we've mentioned here believe in the capacity of people. Integrity in that they give recognition and opportunity, but not in a gimmicky or frivolous way. Chairman Bill Lane and his colleagues at Sunset have encouraged recipe testing not as a "gimmick" to involve people, but because they sincerely believe that their people can perform a genuine service. Guts in that these leaders are giving up control in not specifying the steps to the goal and in resisting the impulse to step in, to retract the grant of ownership opportunity before a fair effort has been made—one that will invariably include missteps along the way.

And what are the stories *not* about? They are *not* about expensive programs. Our friend Jim Kouzes conducted a seminar for engineering managers a while back. After a discussion of issues such as the granting of autonomy and ownership, one of his engineer-manager students summed it up: "All this [stuff is] free. And it works."* These are not tales of exotic programs, involving plans that take months. They are tales that result from the application of plain common sense in pursuit of giving people ownership of their jobs. You could start on any one tomorrow, or this afternoon.

---

*Actually his student said "All this shit's free." And our friend Jim put it on a T-shirt, of which we were early, proud recipients.

Quality for Your People's Sake

Want superior quality? Courtesy? Pride transmitted to the customer via enthusiasm and care?

Davgar Restaurants (a successful Burger King franchisee with fifteen outlets) uses Heinz ketchup, rather than a second-rate substitute. They use butter instead of margarine. Is there a clear market advantage? Why, heavens no. They don't even tell their customers they're doing it. Nutty? No to that, too. They say, "Our people know they are serving the best. In a hundred ways they transmit their pride to our customers."

Delta Airlines cleans up all their *ground* equipment with a passion, according to a former manager—yet no customer ever sees it. Why do they do it? "It makes you [their support people] feel part of a quality effort."

Being the best by a country mile makes your own people feel like all-stars. And all-stars usually rise to the occasion, perform like all-stars. "Treat me C–," says one employee, "and you'll get a C– effort. Treat me as an A+ and you'll get an A+, or at least my very best effort."

"Ownership" Some Questions—and Things to Do Now

▶ Review the stories we've just told. Talk with colleagues at all levels, in all departments, and collect similar cases within your own group/division/ company. Briefly write up fifteen to twenty-five of them. Look for the common variables: manager attitudes, team leader, problem to be solved. What can you learn? Do you allow autonomy or create small, self-sufficient problem solving teams, à la SAS, H. H. Robertson, Quad/Graphics? Do you enhance ownership via tiny marks of pride as do Sunset, Tupperware, IBM, the small retailer? Do you look to hiving off little divisions (instead of cutting them off) à la Monarch? Do you ensure that operators—à la Mervyn's—still have "space" left in their jobs? Analyzing these cases is serious business. A full day or two, at a minimum, could be usefully spent on this subject, with a group of ten to fifteen colleagues. The end product might be a detailed, thirty- to sixty-day plan to experiment with some efforts like these. The plan should also include a plan within a plan to get *all* managers (1) to search for examples like these, and (2) to develop their own plans for rapid experimentation.

▶ What is the status of information availability at the lowest levels in the organization? Is detailed comparative information on each unit's performance available to all? Are ten to twenty important output indicators, updated at least weekly, available to *everyone*—indicators that go from the individual to the team to the corporate level? When you develop new indicators, do you ask—at the *lowest* level—for guidance and ideas? For starters, does everybody at least receive and understand the annual report?

▶ *Stop:* another big request for a commitment is coming! Take a first or second-level supervisory job in three areas that are critical to you. Spend two days with each of the three supervisors, "shadowing" them and extensively debriefing them. (Better yet, take on a supervisor's shift for one full week—preferably an off-hours shift.) Write up a ten- to fifteen-page description of what the job is like, focusing on constraints and Mickey Mouse versus output orientation. (Or get two or three colleagues to join you in this effort. After your "shadowing" or performing the job, go off-site for one and a half to two days and do the same analysis on butcher paper.) In any event, pass the analysis back to the supervisors and have them grade you on it. Then get together with them and a half dozen of their colleagues and spend one day assessing your analysis and developing a game plan for "first step" thirty-day changes to enhance ownership of the jobs you looked at and similar jobs.

▶ Find 50 (!) little marks of respect—of the Sarah Clifton/IBM calling card and Tupperware blackboard variety—in use in your organization. Can you? Can you find 25 *new* ones introduced in the last *six* months? If not, . . .

▶ Find 50 (!) little marks of *dis*respect. (E.g., language, facilities, restricting information, demeaning rules, blatantly exhibited perks for senior people, "little" differences in benefits.) If you come up short, keep trying. They're there! Next: Eradicate some (five within the first ninety-six hours after the exercise). Repeat the exercise once every three or six months.

These exercises constitute hard work, and lots of work, especially if viewed as "in addition to" work. We contend, however, that this is the "it," not the "in addition to." Ownership is pivotal in achieving superior quality, service and innovation, and there can be nothing more important. If you *disagree,* try to explain why (to yourself, and to your people).

The Basics of Ownership

Our good friend Julien Phillips brought the following to our attention from the *Wall Street Journal* (February 8, 1984):

Medical-supply companies plan to introduce a patient-controlled analgesic device in the U.S. hospital market this year. A few hospitals, including the University of Kentucky Medical Center in Lexington, are testing the infusion pumps. What is different about the pump is that it gives patients some control over their own pain medication. Currently, hospital staff members can be pretty stingy with painkillers. Fear of an overdose or addiction means "physicians tend to under-prescribe, then nurses tend to under-administer," says Terrence Murphy, a professor of anesthesiology at the University of Washington pain clinic in Seattle. "No great harm is done. The patient is just a lot less comfortable than he might be."

Not only do patients control pain better with the pump, they use *less* painkiller to do it. In one test, patients recovering from abdominal surgery were randomly assigned either shot therapy or pain pumps. The patients on the pumps used 31.5% less painkiller than the patients getting shots. Mr. Lonnie Weddington, a patient in Kentucky, says that even though pain medicine was available from his pump every six or eight minutes, he used the pump rarely.

Researchers say that's not surprising. Certain psychological dimensions of pain are eliminated simply because the pump is there, they say; when a patient knows he has a way to control pain, he actually hurts less. Because they hurt less, patients on the pump are "more willing to cough, get up and do all the other things that are needed post-operatively," says Eulene Boyle, a nurse at the University of Kentucky Medical Center's intensive-care unit. In theory, Dr. Bennett says, patient-controlled analgesia reduces recovery time after surgery, but studies have yet to prove that. The patient-controlled analgesic device saves nurses a great deal of time. A nurse at a Chicago hospital says that normally she has to open a double-locked cabinet, sign a medicine sheet and account for every bit of painkiller each time she gives a shot.

People who oppose the pump aren't convinced it's safe to give a patient control over narcotics. One head nurse at a Chicago hospital says flatly, "I wouldn't have it on my floor." She fears patients might become dependent on the pump. "Fear of dependence or addiction is incredibly overblown," says Arthur Lipman, professor of clinical pharmacy at the University of Utah. "People in pain aren't junkies looking for a fix." He says that at the University of Utah medical facility, where the pump is being tested, patients "go off the machine at least as soon as they go off the shots." The second big concern is accidental overdose. But Dr. Bennett of Kentucky says the pump's design makes both overdoses and addiction nearly impossible. After the pump delivers a small dose of the narcotic, the patient is "locked out" of the pump for as long as the doctor has decided beforehand. If the patient presses the button during a lock-out period, no painkiller is delivered.

The simple story here *is* our story. Ownership, the promise of it. Ownership, the nonabuse of it (patients use 31.5 percent *less* painkiller). And, sadly, predictable resistance to it. To allow ownership is risky—to the nurse or any manager. Pain relief for patients is a major "perk" for the nurse (nurse as savior). Likewise, *telling people how to do their job* is a "perk" for managers at all levels, and thus ownership is a threat to what is traditionally the essence of the manager's job.

THE ISSUE OF SCALE (AGAIN)

In our discussion of customers and innovation, we observed small groups producing higher quality, more personalized service and faster innovation than larger entities. It turns out that scale—small scale, via team organizations and decentralized units—is a vital component of top performance. The bottom line: ownership is inevitably lost in big groups.

What does "ownership" look like when the *whole* organization is involved? There's no better place to go for an answer than to W. L. Gore & Associates. It's the home of Sarah Clifton, Supreme Commander. It's the home of Bill and Vieve Gore: "We can't run the business. We learned over twenty-five years ago to let the business run itself. Commitment, not authority, produces results." Bill Gore calls the "structure" of the company a "lattice organization." Everybody depends on everybody else. He adds, "Certain attributes of the lattice can be defined: no fixed or assigned authority, sponsors rather than bosses, natural leadership defined by followership, person-to-person communication, objectives set by those who 'must make them happen,' tasks and functions organized through commitments. We don't manage people here, People manage themselves." And boost themselves, too: "People promote themselves here. They promote themselves every time they take on a new responsibility, every time they get a big sale, every time they come up with a new invention. We have a host of heroes around here." (In fact, he refers to the whole process as "creating heroes.")

"We organize ourselves around voluntary commitments." Do they ever! When you come on board W. L. Gore & Associates, you aren't given an assignment at the outset. You *find* an assignment. You try a bunch of jobs, in any area you think might fit. You actively seek a "sponsor," because no one stays on permanently unless he or she finds a sponsor. Bill calls it the "mentoring system." The sponsor is responsible for your development and, with other sponsors, for your ongoing evaluation, compensation, etc. How many years until you become a sponsor? If you're a natural leader and people gravitate to you, you could become a sponsor in thirty, sixty or ninety *days*. It's happened. The winners end up being sponsors for many and being sponsored by many. Significantly, your worth is assessed principally by your peers—a hard group to deceive.

A while back Tom was talking about Gore with a sophisticated audience. After the speech an executive from another company came up and pounded him on the shoulder: "It's true. But you understate. [We've heard it so many times—we talk about the remarkable turnaround at Ford in Edison, New Jersey, and somebody visits there and sends us a detailed letter saying that we understated.] My daughter was hired off the street by the Gores. She came up with a neat idea, and within just thirty days of hiring she had been given more than three thousand dollars to play with. It might not work out and she knows that. But she also knows that if she does a decent job she need not fear failure. I'd also add that she's had no business experience, but that she's already become a mentor to some in her group. This has *all* happened in four months. They mean what they say."

The issue that we want to focus on with the Gore story is the issue of teams and scale. In a word, ownership and commitment, pride and enthusiasm, and an "all people as business people" attitude are virtually impossible in a giant, overly specialized organizational unit. Bill Gore is a hard-nosed scientist; he was a senior research executive at Du Pont when he left to found his company with Vieve over twenty-five years ago. He believed in the efficiencies of scale, and he initially let his factories grow like wildfire to achieve those efficiencies. He's backed off now, and backed off radically. These days Bill Gore illustrates what he means by optimal size with complex charts and graphs. But originally he learned his lesson through tough observation of what was going on. He says: "As the number [of people in one of his facilities] approaches two hundred, the group invariably turns into a *crowd* in which individuals grow increasingly anonymous and significantly less cooperative." Now the Gores almost religiously limit the size of their facilities to 100 to 150 people.

We regularly observe that such "small" plants, which do not pass any tests for "efficiencies of scale," outperform the bigger ones time and again. Milliken & Company maintains that the "right" number is about 200. 3M says 200 to 300 is the limit, and HP and Digital Equipment say no more than 300 to 400. Emerson Electric and Dana limit the size of their plants to about 500. GM now says that if it ever builds anything new, the limit will be around 300, while for Volvo the magic number is 500 or less. None of these is a number derived from theoretical science; rather, each is based upon years of experience with the failure of giant operations to live up to their promised (on paper) performance levels.

The essence of ownership is giving people some space. And the corollary that almost automatically goes with it is that it is smaller organizational units that make it possible to do so.

Rush Week

That's right, "rush week"—fraternity/sorority jargon. The unparalleled growth of People Express had resulted in over 4,000 people on the payroll by late 1984. Senior management became concerned that the earlier zest might begin to wane. Their solution was to "reorganize" into teams of 200 to 300 people. The teams were to be roughly constituted around aircraft types (e.g., 737's, 747's). Each team would do its own scheduling within some general parameters.

The remaining issue was how to divvy up team membership. People's managing officers hit upon the rush-week theme. Each team captain would set up a recruiting booth in the crew space at Newark Airport's North Terminal (the location of company headquarters) and sign up volunteers. It was as simple as that. And it worked. Team captains (i.e., People executives) manned the booths and resorted to all sorts of inducements in the course of the week, especially as one team's membership surged ahead of another's. New recruits had their pictures taken with their new team captain. One team sent off to a Houston restaurant (many of People's senior people are Houston refugees) for special Nachos. By Wednesday the pace was feverish, and even the initially reticent pilots were joining in the frenzied competition.

The net result was a gigantic running start for the new form of organization—and confirmation of the bedrock principle of ownership and involvement at People Express, even in the face of increasing numbers.

Teams

Japanese corporations have very large manufacturing facilities in many instances. But their distinctive trait is the team. The focus is on groups of ten to twenty people (they're called "sections" in Japan) that are given exceptional autonomy; the American experience with reliance on teams, though not so widespread, is just as decisive. The Gores believe in teams. And so do two other very special people to whom we'll now turn—Bob Swiggett of the Kollmorgen Company, and Bill Creech, recently retired commanding general of the U.S. Air Force's Tactical Air Command (TAC). All three cases exemplify the vital importance of the sense of ownership that goes with small turned-on teams. More significantly to our mind, all three leaders are hardnosed rationalists who have come to their conclusions almost unwillingly. Gore, as we've seen, was a senior scientist at Du Pont. Swiggett is an MIT-trained engineer, and Creech is an Air Force warrior-bureaucrat. Yet they have caused *revolutions* in organizations ranging in size from $250-million-a-year W. L. Gore & Associates through $400-million-a-year Kollmorgen to TAC, with tens of billions of dollars in assets. Each had a bias that said centralization, consolidation and efficiencies of scale are vital. Each changed that view. Their odysseys, then, are as important as the outcomes themselves.

The Kollmorgen story is an exciting one. A manufacturer of printed circuits, DC motors and controls, and electro-optic devices, Kollmorgen had some fine early successes, and with the successes came complications in manufacturing (apparently inevitable), and also the opportunity to take advantage of efficiencies of scale. Led by the Swiggett brothers, Bob and Jim, the company proceeded down the path of more centralization, more automation. By the late sixties, they were ready to install what was called the IBM System

70: state-of-the-art computer-driven factory control. In Bob Swiggett's words, "We were going to put this business on line, real time. We were going to know where every part was. We were going to have scheduling. Loading algorithms. We were smart. We weren't willing to trust our gut." And install the system they did. The result? Bob Swiggett explains: "Statistically we got what we wanted. But the foremen became preoccupied with their printouts instead of our customers." Quality deteriorated, schedules weren't met, and the company plunged downward. Disaster loomed.

Salvation, it turned out, lay in the company's files from the recent past—data from a bunch of unheralded efforts that had involved a fruitful team approach to rapid product development and manufacturing. After the early success, Kollmorgen had found it had become the new big guys in the printed circuit business; suddenly small guys started doing to Kollmorgen what Kollmorgen had done to the big guys of a generation before: moving faster, listening better and being more adaptive to customer needs. As a partial solution, Kollmorgen had created what was called the Proto [prototype] Department, which regularly accomplished in *one* week the product modifications and advances in manufacturing that it took the main-line part of the organization fully *ten* weeks to complete. (Remember the 1,000 percent factor?) "The Proto guys," says Bob Swiggett, "had one game, to satisfy the customer. The others were playing departmental games, like who has the best score for efficiency. The customer was just a job number."

The Proto "method" had been used on numerous occasions, whenever crisis demanded it, but though the results had always been positive, the team efforts had been perceived as "one off" activities, anomalies (it's a common engineer's bias). Now, however, as overall disaster approached, Bob Swiggett recalled the past and considered turning to the teams in a wholesale fashion. The idea was to organize the *entire* company into small production/product/customer-oriented teams. Team Manufacturing was to replace the System 70. System 70 would be scrapped.

Team Manufacturing was installed in 1968. In a six-month period—"a chaos of empire shattering," says Swiggett—the organization was transformed into a structure consisting of six teams of seventy-five persons each. The results were dramatic. Within the same six months, Kollmorgen's output per employee more than *doubled,* and on-time delivery to customers rose from less *than 60 percent to well over 90 percent.**

Now, nearly fifteen years later, the teams are embedded in numerous small divisions (in effect, a second layer of teams) that are highly autonomous

---

*In the April 1984 issue of *Inc.* Lucien Rhodes describes a trip Bob Swiggett made to the Harvard Business School shortly before Kollmorgen made the shift to Team Manufacturing: "He packed his bags and went to Harvard to consult 'the world's leading guy on control.' Said Swiggett, 'I talked for quite a while. He was very patient. Then he said, "Here you are in the modern age with computers, control theory, and you just spent two hours on how you want to abdicate your responsibility. Forget this team manufacturing stuff." ' " Fortunately, Swiggett went his own way.

profit centers. The objective? That each division be "strong enough to go public." New divisions are created regularly—as needed, with little fanfare—in an approach reminiscent of 3M's. Each has its own board of directors to both guide it and insulate it from distracting corporate intrusions.

The focus on the contribution of each person in the organization extends with astonishing uniformity throughout Kollmorgen's world. Tom had the opportunity to meet with the head of its Irish operations. Now Ireland is hardly the home, in general, of vigorous, new-wave management. And yet the Kollmorgen organization of Ireland is a joy to behold, looking more like Apple in Cupertino, California, than like its neighbors. Tom's first opportunity to speak with the head of the operation came at a very proper dinner (among the guests was the Prime Minister of Ireland). "There are two exceptional people I'd especially like you to meet when you visit us," said the "boss" of Kollmorgen/Ireland. The design engineers or the like, Tom supposed. No. The first was "the fella who cleans up the washrooms. He'd stand in a group like this as a man of extraordinary integrity." The other was a person who had been with the company for a long time and who now ran the supply room.

So strong is the emphasis on the team and the development of the whole person in this man's operation that young men and women in the town where Kollmorgen/Ireland is headquartered are spurning college to go, instead, to what they've dubbed Kollmorgen College—the training program that has been installed in the organization. Our colleague gets his greatest pleasure from turning young men and women fresh off the streets into responsible contributors. The payoff? The real new-product heroes (each division of Kollmorgen, even overseas, is wholly responsible for the generation of its own set of new products) are a couple of unschooled eighteen-year-old tinkerers: "They'll grab hold of those ideas [from the formal, "scientific" product developers], and quicker than a wink turn them into practical prototypes. It's my eighteen-year-olds that are doing the real work." As our colleague was saying this, Tom was reminded of a couple of similar stories from Japan. The head of Mitsubishi Electric states that the most innovative research in his company (very sophisticated) has come from some recent high school graduates, "with many fewer preconceptions than the rest—and a willingness to listen before they act." And at Kyocera Corporation, which makes 70 percent of the ceramic packages for semiconductors, the chairman talks ceaselessly about "maximizing the output from the 50 percent person," the average person in the company's employ. His secret weapon: *teams!* An article in the April 16, 1984, issue of *Business Week* reported that "the corporation is divided into groups of 10 to 20 employees, in a system that president and founder Kazuo Inamori calls 'amoeba management.' Each group keeps separate accounts and is expected to make a profit, measuring production and value against cost." Kyocera has been voted the best-managed company in Japan.

Teams and ownership work miracles for Gore. They work for Kollmorgen. For Kyocera. But do they work in a truly giant organization? Well, when Tom returned from the visit to Ireland during which he met the head of Kollmorgen/Ireland, awaiting him was a delightful four-page letter from an unexpected source: General Bill Creech, the four-star general who commanded the United States Air Force's Tactical Air Command (TAC) until October 1984. Amazingly, Creech's story sounds a lot like Bill Gore's and Bob Swiggett's and Kazuo Inamori's.

We've seen in chapter 4 (pp. 622–623) something of the turnaround at TAC—an organization of 113,000 people. Central to that not so minor miracle was Creech's realization that the Air Force (like most of the rest of America's organizations—schools, hospitals, private corporations) had been ill-served by the "centralization/consolidation disease of the 1960's," which he calls "dehumanizing." Centralization, he says, "creates functional 'stovepipes,' long on management theory and short on overall mission responsibility. Centralization wants one thing of a type, not many. There's little or no stress on competition. Centralization prizes 'one-of-a-kind,' not 'competitive' sub-elements. . . . The theory was that if you had all the inputs [the so-called functional stovepipes], the output would 'take care of itself.' " While Creech talks ceaselessly about the importance of leadership, he also believes that leadership can't do it all: "Even the best leaders get submerged and stymied in organizations that are highly centralized, highly consolidated." His solution was to shift from the highly centralized and specialized (input-driven) structure he inherited to an output-focused organization he called POMO (Production-Oriented Maintenance Organization). And with it in place, the remarkable reversal occurred. Keep in mind that he had no "outside" help. He had (1) no more people, (2) no positive change in weapon systems mix (i.e., no easier-to-maintain planes), (3) fewer parts available, and (4) a work force with *less* experience than had been available, on average, during the previous ten years. You can't just explain the change away by any set of external factors.

What is the POMO magic? It's quite simple—some might say it's obvious. First and foremost, management's focus was shifted from the higher level (input-based) unit—the wing—to the lower level (output-oriented) unit—the squadron. Each "production unit" (squadron)—shades of Kollmorgen's team manufacturing or Kyocera's teams—now does its own scheduling. It has its own decentralized computers, much to the dismay of the central MIS people (just as in industry). Squadron-versus-squadron comparison numbers are readily available, and intense squadron-versus-squadron competition has been introduced. Though the Air Force always deploys or fights as a squadron, the centralization logic of the sixties and seventies had led to squadrons literally being abolished. Colorful aircraft tail markings were not allowed. Squadron patches were forbidden. Even the fabled 94th, the Eddie Rickenbacker squadron, disappeared—history, unit pride and all. Now the colorful pennants, tail markings and arm patches (along with mugs, ties, tie tacks, T-shirts and a host of other paraphernalia) are back, and sprouting up everywhere.

Many other things happened in the wake of the change in organizational philosophy. Maintenance was reorganized; the decentralized squadron became self-sufficient. Parts were made available on the flight line. (In an Air Force dominated by "efficiencies of scale" there had been one depot, no matter how many miles it was away from the flight line. Unfortunately, this led to frequent non-sorties because there were no parts available.) Creech's motto was "Organize as you will fight." He wanted his "squadron supervisors to train as wartime leaders." Previously his NCO's "had evaluated themselves by the thickness of their carpets." MBWA was introduced: "I insisted that specialists of all skills get back to the flight line." Other terms were "cross-utilization," "on-scene supervision" and "immediate [parts] availability."

But the reincarnation of the squadrons wasn't even the half of it. Creech went yet a level lower: the long-neglected support people in maintenance and supply became his obsession. First he created coherent aircraft maintenance units (AMU's) at the squadron level. The units were given decent facilities, in contrast to the second-rate quarters previously accorded them. Tiny details counted: Artwork (done by the men) was hung in the facilities (previously it had been implicitly assumed that only pilots cared about such things); one AMU now has a self-executed wall mural on the history of aviation. The maintenance and supply people were given recognition. The NCO in charge of an aircraft is now a "dedicated crew chief"; highly visible bulletin boards inside and outside an AMU facility include pictures of that AMU's dedicated crew chiefs—always next to their planes. The team leaders/dedicated crew chiefs are now directly in charge of their people's evaluation. (Previously evaluations were done way up the line by an officer unfamiliar with the outfit.)

The output of the AMU's is highly visible. Walls are dotted with sizable charts showing trend lines with key readiness and quality-improvement indicators. The most vital are posted on big boards outside the unit, visible to all who drive by (i.e., all one's competitive peers). Competitions among supply and maintenance units have been introduced. In fact, each wing has a sizable trophy room wholly devoted to trophies and plaques won only in supply and maintenance competitions. Regular award banquets for supply and maintenance people are now commonplace.

Thus the "least" of activities are now heralded and the subject of competition. General Creech even instituted a semiannual base-by-base "drive-by" (a takeoff on the spectacular aircraft "fly-by"), a triumphant parade of pickup trucks, jeeps, parts trailers and other support vehicles. Top-management attendance (i.e., base commander et al.) is 100 percent.

Does this ownership stuff count for much? Well, you have the overwhelming statistics from TAC, Kollmorgen et al., to support the point. But perhaps the last word, and the best, comes from one of Bill Creech's noncommissioned officers. The general asked him what the difference was between the old, specialist organization and the new organization, in which the plane and the sortie are the "customer," where the supervisor ("designated crew chief," remember) "owns" the plane. The NCO's to-the-point reply: "General, when's the last time you washed a rental car?" We think that may say it all. None of us washes our rental cars. There's no ownership. And there's no ownership if you're a specialist, no matter how well trained, if you're responsible only for two square feet of the right wing of a hundred planes. Only whole planes fly. Only "owners," especially in competition and with flags flying, will go all out to make a whole plane fly. Creech had, pure and simple, made that NCO a proud owner—with (and this is vital, too) the wherewithal to get the job done.

One last point, as we move beyond TAC and Kollmorgen and our focus on teams: the speed of the transformations. Many ask, "How long does a turn-around take?" A $50 million outfit (then), Kollmorgen, had a revolution in results in six months. The Creech revolution—in a $35-billion operation—was well under way in a year, and remarkable results were evident after just two years. To build a sustaining new "culture" may (will) take decades, but to get a running start—with dramatic changes in output—takes only months.

Creech's Laws

General Creech, as he prepared to turn over his command in the fall of 1984, published a set of fifteen "organizational principles." Here they are:

1. *Have a set of overarching principles and philosophies. Have an overall theme and purpose.*

2. *Use goals throughout*—goals at *all* levels, from crews to senior command. There should be darned few of them—in general, paperwork should be kept to a minimum—and they should be clearly achievable—i.e., most people should end up as winners.

3. *Measure productivity at several levels.* But "don't strangle in paperwork." Also: "Micro-information should not be used to micro-manage [that is, it should be used primarily to spur peer-versus-peer competition]." All information should be "oriented to the product"—i.e., the aircraft sortie.

4. *Create leaders at many levels.* With this goes a plea to "get leaders [e.g., dedicated crew chiefs] where the action is. Staff supports the line. Not vice versa."

5. *Match authority and responsibility and instill a sense of responsibility.* "Ninety-nine percent will accept responsibility if authority goes with it," and authority should always be product (i.e., aircraft)-oriented, not function-oriented. "I'm not wild about accepting responsibility without authority," says the general. "Why should my people be?"

6. *Set up internal competition and comparison where feasible.* "Reward success" is the key corollary. The resultant pressure is high: "Nobody wants to report that his unit is last, month after month."

7. *Create a climate of pride.* "Instill individual dignity. Provide challenge and opportunity to each. Intangibles matter."

8. *Create a climate of professionalism.* "Esprit is the critical measure."

9. *Educate, educate, educate.* By means, first and foremost, of *regular* feedback.

10. *Communicate, communicate, communicate.* Do *not* depend on the formal hierarchy; skip down several levels—regularly.

11. *Create organizational discipline and loyalty.* This is vital, but will inevitably "stifle initiative." Hence, specific devices must be in place to lead people to disregard the system and reward initiative.

12. *Provide everyone with a stake in the outcome.* Make each job meaningful. Reward good performance (lavishly) in all areas.

13. *Make it better.* Create a sense of individual and organizational worth. Create an "optimistic organization." Provide a climate for continuous change. Above all: "The leader is not just a scorekeeper and steward. He is responsible for creating something new and better."

14. *Make it happen:* "Vigorous leadership at all levels is the key." The leader is at once responsible for creating "the dynamic spark" and simultaneously "working the details" that make it happen.

15. *Make it last.*

We talked of Edison, New Jersey, where the Ford Motor Company gave a shut-down-the-line button to each of its people. We talked about Sarah Clifton, Supreme Commander. But the magic of Ford at Edison is not just— or even primarily—the button. It's Phil Staley trooping the line, it's his pride and enthusiasm and zest. And in addition to decentralization, unit flags, intense competition and crew ownership of the aircraft/sortie/customer, the story of Bill Creech's turnaround at TAC is likewise the story of intangibles that go beyond team structure per se. Read Creech's Laws again. Note the emphasis on pride and enthusiasm. "You need pride," Creech says. "There are no poor outfits—just poor leaders." As additional evidence, he provides a homely example, from another service—the Navy's helicopter carrier *Iwo Jima.* In a remarkably brief period it went from "worst to first" in its squadron, he reports. The "magic" used by the commanding officer? "You know how he did it? He had the crew paint the whole damned ship from one end to the other. He started preaching pride."

More than a Label

In their discussion of unsuccessful companies in the chapter called "Success versus failure" in *The Winning Streak,* Walter Goldsmith and

David Clutterbuck vividly illustrate the importance of the trade names that give people (at every level) their working identity:

When Jaguar was renamed 'large car assembly plant number one', its founder, Sir William Lyons, marched into the boardroom and removed his portrait from the wall. He had no intention of presiding, even on canvas, over the undermining of the principles of grace, pace and space on which he had built the company and its reputation.

John Egan, the sixth chief executive in eight years, describes what happened: "In 1975 an attempt was made to subjugate Jaguar, along with other marques such as Rover, Land-Rover, Triumph, Austin Morris, MG and so on, under the ill-fated Leyland Cars umbrella.

"At one stage Jaguar flags at the entrance to the factory were torn down. Only Leyland flags were allowed to be flown on the premises and telephonists were threatened with disciplinary action if they answered callers with 'Good morning. Jaguar Cars.' Instead they were supposed to say, 'Good morning. Leyland Cars,' and if any further address was needed, 'Large assembly plant number one.' Worse still, the then two constituent factories of Jaguar were put into two quite separate organizational units within Leyland— the Power and Transmission Division and the Body and Assembly Division—hardly an appropriate fate for one of the most famous marque names in the world motoring industry."

Sir Michael Edwardes' . . . genius was to recognize immediately that no progress was possible unless famous marque names were re-created as a focus for group and individual loyalty.

It's so important not to get off track in this chapter, especially in this section on teams. Because teams can work only if the leader believes in his or her people. And that belief, perhaps surprisingly, tends to be best reflected in a focus on the mundane sources of pride—a newly painted ship, or the butter sculptures that appear when people are allowed to celebrate, with their families, in their facility. Some will move to decentralization/teams, but then fail to give the team leaders the tools to do the job; not believing in them, they don't trust them with parts on the flight line or responsibility for scheduling. And this is probably worse than making no change—it smacks of hypocrisy, among other things.

So it's paint and potties.* It's stimulation through competition. It's fun and enthusiasm. General Creech is thoughtful about it. He says he's been accused

---

*And more: Staley's turnaround in Edison features a strong dose of additional fans and water-coolers—and the removal of time clocks. A dramatic Western Electric plant turnaround features extra pay phones in the coffee-break areas, awnings over the doors to keep out the rain, and lights in the parking lot.

of merely creating a five-year "Hawthorne effect."* He adds, "If you wish to call it a 'Hawthorne effect,' then so be it." We agree with him. So be it. But we'd go further—much further. We think the best leaders are, perhaps above all, perpetual creators of Hawthorne effects. Sam Walton, the Wal-Mart boss, makes the opening of every one of his stores—over seven hundred now—exciting *and* different from the one before. The $64 question—and the gut-wrenching issue—all of us must face as leaders is: Are we, as Mr. Sam (Walton) is, capable of creating yet another Hawthorne effect after the seven hundredth opening? Of making our teams into excited, turned-on, prideful, enthusiastic, competitive owners of the job, responsible for the output, wholly aware of *all* the statistics and information that affect the enterprise? Of making the organization an exciting place to be?

"Teams":
Some Questions—and Things to Do Now

▶ Seriously consider a radical restructuring (whether you are in charge of twenty-seven or seventy-five or seventy-five thousand) into a team-based organization. Begin by going back into your own history—personal and professional. Look at the things that worked—athletic teams, Girl/Boy Scout troops, army squads, college groups, alumni fund-raising—and the work environment. Do you find any pattern? If so, take the next step and begin to codify the supporting devices: à la TAC, did the unit have the full wherewithal to get on with the job? Was unit competition a part of it? Were flags, pennants and other symbols of pride part of it?

▶ If this is a serious endeavor (as we think it ought to be), have ten to twenty people at various levels perform the same analysis. Then go off-site for a day or two (or a long weekend) and assess the data—personal and professional.

▶ Look at some first steps (read the account of Sam Neaman and McCrory's in chapter 17): Can you start the team process *somewhere?* It need not be a likely or highly visible place. E.g., can you, as did the retailer described on page 796, construct a team of pros to train others in a critical skill? Can you form a SWAT team of MIS people to actually *help* a small facility somewhere? Following the H. H. Robertson example (see page 801), can you form a few multifunction service teams in a group to help problem/opportunity customers? Can you give a team the charge to "somehow" make better use of a facility or asset à la Quad/Graphics and the back-haul

---

*The Hawthorne studies in Western Electric's bank wiring rooms in the thirties revealed that simple attention paid (e.g., by management) led to dramatic productivity increases. For instance, in an examination of the effects of industrial hygiene, lighting levels were increased. Not surprisingly, productivity increased. When the experiment was completed, the lights were turned down. To the researchers' surprise, the productivity went up again, not down. Many more experiments were done to corroborate this finding. All added up to the same thing: Pay attention, stimulate the system, and effectiveness increases.

(see page 793)? Two cautions: First, don't take on too much too soon. The would-be leaders (if this is foreign stuff) will take lots of coaching (your time), and you don't want this to be viewed as a flash in the pan. We're suggesting, à la Swiggett, that you think of it as a way of life. Second, make sure the team has a thirty- to sixty-day output objective; above all, we are *not* talking about landing a new prime customer, adding a new service, installing a new (up and running, debugged) support system.

▶ Finally, the usual caution: This is a big deal! We are suggesting action, but also sober and serious reflection, about the way you organize for results. If this reflection comes *easy*, either you've already done it or you haven't dug deep enough. You've got to go through some form of the marathon runner's wall of pain on this, we suspect.

MORE ON TRUST: WE HAS MET THE ENEMY AND IT IS US

The story up to this point has been positive, the story of the enhancement of individuals, of flag-bearing teams and small units. The negative side is that we are our own worst enemy; that is, we get in our own way. Actually, it's worse: It's a double-negative story. Not only do we get in our own way, but we don't mean to. In other words, there is little stupidity, little irrationality, little malicious intent among us. It's rules, in fact, that trip us up and strip our Sarah Cliftons or NCOs of the sense of ownership—rules that invariably were instituted for sound, rational reasons.

Thoughts of Sarah Clifton forced themselves into our consciousness soon after we were called upon to assist an Eastern aircraft manufacturer with a $750 million operation. The problem was quality. After some study, our decision was to focus all our energy on but a single topic—the life and times of the first-line manufacturing supervisor in a several-thousand-person manufacturing organization. We determined to take that one job and tear it apart, second by second, minute by minute, hour by hour, to answer the question: What's it *really* like to be a first-level manager in this place? The procedure involved an intensive, seventeen-hour-a-day, four-day-long off-site retreat with the top twenty people and two of us. This is typical of what we found: The first-line supervisor was responsible for some twenty-five to thirty-five people, and had $1 million at least, and often up to $4 million worth of capital equipment, under her or his control. And yet, characteristically, this supremely responsible individual didn't have the authority to buy an $8.95 can of paint to clean up his or her people's work space. An "owner"? Hardly. He or she was responsible for the quality of the product, for the company's number one asset, its people (twenty-five or more of them), and several million dollars' worth of capital, but was not *trusted* with $8.95 unless the facility manager signed off on it. As one small businessperson said, "We make people responsible for all that's important, then we treat them like children, and then we're utterly dismayed when they turn around and behave and respond like children."

In this case, we decided to do something about the situation. At the end of a lengthy day's deliberations we agreed to give that first-line supervisor $25 in unquestioned spending authority. You may laugh at the lack of largesse (as many have in many groups), but that's not the punch line. After the fateful decision was made, one vice president raised his hand and said, "I want to go on record, before we do this, as saying that you know and I know what they're going to do with those twenty-five bucks—they're going to go out and buy handguns." (And you wonder why the quality wasn't so great!) So we facetiously suggested another solution. "Leave it at $8.95, if you wish," we said. "We'll make but one suggestion. Write the rule if you must—for reasons of control, etc.—but add a little parenthetical expression in *red*, at the end: 'We're doing this because we don't trust you.' If you can stomach that language, then leave the proposed rule in."

It is claimed that such demeaning rules are necessary to ensure "fiduciary responsibility." But although a forty-three-year-old, high-school-educated, first-line manufacturing supervisor may not know the nuances of fiduciary responsibility all that well, she or he surely is an expert on the meaning— exactly—of the word "trust." And trust—make no mistake about it—is what it's all about.

We could bore the reader with the full contents of a four-inch-thick file folder labeled "The $8.95 syndrome." Instead, we'll mention just one other example. A plant manager for a Big Three auto maker in Europe employs three thousand people in a major urban center (it makes him the biggest employer in the city). He was solicited a while back to supply musical instruments for a school band. The cost would have been a few hundred dollars. But he had to write Detroit for approval, which took weeks. He couldn't say yes on the spot. Talk about revealing someone's powerlessness to his peers and people and the community! Talk about demeaning! Talk about demotivating!

Such abominations can—and do—happen in the very best of companies. We spoke earlier about Renn Zaphiropoulos and his concern for individual dignity. In 1984 Tom went through a presentation with him that included the $8.95 paint-bucket analysis, and they and several of Renn's people were sitting around his office afterwards. They decided—and it attests to Renn's integrity (and guts) that he agreed—that they'd run an on-the-spot check. Three or four of his people from the secretarial pool, the copier room and so on were called in and asked to come up with the most demeaning regulation they could name. What an eye-opener! The procedure for leaving a $1 IOU in petty cash to buy stamps and the form required to purchase more than five pads of paper were nothing short of gruesome. Renn was stunned. And that's the point. The very best of us are shocked at how quickly the web of individually trivial but cumulatively demeaning Mickey Mouse can spread.

Sometimes assaults on ownership do seem to border on the malicious, though even then, malicious is not exactly the right word. It's more likely frustration or thoughtless insensitivity. After a daylong seminar, we talked to a fellow who runs a middle-sized (about six hundred employees) timber-products wholesaling and retailing operation. He had just taken a tough strike. In the midst of the strike there had been some incidents of apparent arson—a couple of small fires, one of which almost destroyed a $15,000 facility. Now, what such actions prove, in our view (and in the view of most with whom we've shared this story), is that most of life's phenomena follow bell-shaped curves. That is, given a cast of six hundred, you will probably find one or two real turkeys. We have not a shred of sympathy for the arsonists. Neither, naturally, did the manager of the operation in question. But his response was, nonetheless, wholly inappropriate—the worst imaginable, we believe. Because when the strike was over, he did the one thing that might indeed turn 20 percent of the workforce into potential arsonists. He instituted draconian inspection procedures—essentially going through the pockets of his people as they entered the facilities to work, to see if they had lighters or matches. And in so doing, he severely and unnecessarily alienated the 598 out of 600 who were *not* arsonists. He treated the 598 like children or worse—like criminals. In such ways do we all too regularly shoot ourselves in the foot (or heart).

There comes a special time when we weep at the $8.95 paint-bucket (and band-instrument and pocket-inspection) stories. During the course of a several-days-long program with some presidents of small companies, we spent a pleasant afternoon over a bottle or so of wine talking about their experiences with allowing their people a little bit more control. There's one story that we remember particularly clearly. This executive, we'd judge in his late fifties, was coming late to this subject of treating people with respect. The experiment he launched consisted of taking a couple of his facilities—an old plant and a foundry—and giving them $2,000 a month apiece to spend any way they wished. There were only two strictures: the plant manager could not sit on the committee that decided on the nature of the expenditure, and the composition of the expenditure committee had to mirror the proportion of managerial to nonmanagerial people in the facility's population. He recalled the first month of the experiment. He'd granted the $2,000. The likely nature of the expenditure had been the subject of much flippant chatter among the senior people, several of whom thought our friend was a bit batty ("They'll buy handguns"). What *did* the people in those old facilities choose to do? Well, one group took the $2,000 and built a memorial garden outside the plant. It honored past members of the work force who, over the course of several decades, had died in industrial accidents and in foreign wars.

Yes, these are the same beings of a lower order who are not responsible enough to spend $8.95 wisely. Yet, given $2,000, what do they do with it? Buy handguns? No, a memorial garden for former colleagues. And that *is* the nature of the average human being in the work force, if given an opportunity to shine.

Two "Knockout" Factors—
and What to Do about Them

Again and again in our seminars, two hurdles to achieving a people/ownership orientation, in the sense talked about here, arise. "Sure, *I* believe this stuff," says the division general manager (or big-company CEO), "but the unions get in the way." And: "Sure, *I* believe this stuff, but I can't bring first-line supervisors along. They are so threatened by enhanced 'ownership.'"

Let's take unions. First, we agree. Unions *do* get in the way. The question is why? We aren't sure we buy very often (ever?) the "*My* hands are clean, *theirs* are dirty" argument. We are in agreement with pollster Daniel Yankelovitch, Walt Kelly (in *Pogo*) and Gary Bello of Clark Equipment, who said, respectively: "The work ethic [in America] is alive and well, urgently wishes to express itself, and is hobbled at every turn by management"; "We has met the enemy and it is us"; "Management gets *exactly* the work force it deserves, not one iota more and not one iota less."

In a nutshell, we think *you* are the problem. There is no doubt that unions, nationally and on a company-by-company basis, vary greatly. For instance, Ford's great progress on employee involvement in the early eighties was spurred on in part by a lucky happenstance: the advent of a new Ford industrial relations VP and a new head of UAW at Ford with no Ford history. Neither carried bad prior baggage to the table. Principally, however, we agree with Ren McPherson, the former Dana head. *The* issue, he states adamantly, is management getting *its* house in order. One of his former colleagues added, "Look, let's take [union] work rules. They're awful. Right? Well, I'll tell you the union-contrived work rules pale by comparison with the crap we used to send out from the executive offices and try to enforce through the foreman." Amen. Look ahead to chapter 17, on debureaucratizing. We observe the possibility of a 95 percent-plus reduction in bureaucracy—even in the Army. Management, unlike foreign policy, is ripe for unilateral disarmament; let's clean up our act first.

An advance in management-union relations began, belatedly, to happen on another dimension in the 1981–83 recession. For the first time in memory, cuts in middle management occasionally matched (or, in rare instances, exceeded) layoffs on the line from a percentage standpoint. Yet this promising start was, we believe, generally inadequate. It is a rare company that couldn't enhance its management by cutting yet another 25 to 75 percent of its horribly bloated middle management. Again: "Let's get our own house in order" is the message.

Finally, it's important to *persist* if progress is to be made. We believe that the attitude of *people*—i.e., the work force—toward quality and productivity are *the* issue in steel and autos. Yet a recent analysis we made of public speeches by auto executives finds *people* missing. Automation, unions, unfair competition and that old devil Washington still win the word-count prize by a country mile. But if you listen to, say, Ren McPherson or Phil Staley of Ford or Bob Strammy of GM or Bill and Vieve Gore, you find the insistent theme is people. Tom has known Ren McPherson well for five years, and still has no idea what his views are on automation, because McPherson doesn't talk about it. We think, then, that most who view unions as the problem don't view people as the solution, to begin with. They don't really, deep down, believe that "stuff" is worthy of no. 1 priority status. And sure enough, they reap less than superb union relations as one reward.

And what of that other objection—recalcitrant first-line supervisors? To begin with, we agree. First-line supervisors *are* threatened by enhanced ownership on the line. Their traditional control vehicles are thrown out; they must transform themselves from order givers to cheerleaders and facilitators. The problem is major, and the solution to it is that the response must be major as well. In the hell-bent and sometimes faddish plunge into increased participation and ownership, we often skip over the role of the supervisor. Shop-floor or back-room operations teams are trained in group problem solving, but the supervisor is ignored. Such a situation will inevitably come back to haunt you.

Our ultimate solution is radical, but must be stated. We see little need, over the long haul, for the traditional first-line supervisor. Team leaders (temporary or permanent) selected by the work group are proving a brilliant alternative. But we won't belabor that here, for the issue in this brief section is what to do if you *do* have traditional supervisors. Our answer is threefold: training, careful use of new promotion opportunities and separation.

First, training. The supervisor is being asked to change, and change radically. You must provide *excessive* help. Expensive and extensive retraining is a must. It was at the heart of McPherson's reason for setting up Dana U., his pride and joy. And, of course, the key to superb training is not leaving it to the trainers. If the issue is big (and it usually is) and if it is the block to performance improvement (and it usually is), then senior management *must* be involved in the program's design *and* delivery. It's simply far too important—especially the element that deals with supervisorial training—for the frequently second-rate training department. (While a good bit of the substance of this book is related to this issue, you might turn at this point to the chapter on "Coaching" for some more detailed suggestions.)

Second, use promotion wisely. When a new first-line supervisor job opening comes up, don't get overwhelmed by an attack of (largely appropriate) sympathy for an old hand who played the game well by the old rules. Promotion is *the* swiftest and clearest signal of altered priorities to vast numbers of people. First promotion *must* go to those who are learning fastest to play the game by the new rules. Anything less spells delay or disaster. (See also chapter 16, "Attention, Symbols, Drama, Vision—and Love.")

Finally, separation. *If* your training is sound and intense, *if* you set out clear new expectations and if *you* live up to them, then (and only then) the time will come when you can separate those who can't or won't play by the new rules. And you must. Our only caveat here is fairness. Did you really give the old hand a good shot? And this fairness issue always falls on the senior managers' shoulders. Did you preach the new way but inadvertently fail to practice it in a thousand tiny acts, thus giving hopelessly mixed signals to the shop floor? Unfortunately, that is most often the case.

Finally, another word of warning: following our guidelines—all of which we have learned from others, the real people pros—not only will *not* make life easy but will not even make the problems go away rapidly! Often as not, even the most enlightened new boss—e.g., division general manager—is fighting decades of tradition. Expect a five-to-ten-year struggle at a minimum. Progress, we observe, from colleagues at Ford, TAC, Milliken et al. can come almost overnight. Victory, however, is elusive.

A pithy summation on the issue of demeaning regulations—and it speaks clearly to the matter of nonmaliciousness—comes from a senior manufacturing person at IBM. "Our systems are the scar tissues of past mistakes," he says. Ah, yes. And each layer of that scar tissue—the initial system that was developed—made perfectly rational sense when created. Yes, each layer is rational, or microrational. Every line on every form makes sense—taken alone. It's the thousands of lines taken together that, unintentionally, add up to a macro-illogic (the same macro-illogic based on micro-logic that General Creech so successfully fought at TAC).

How does sense deteriorate into nonsense? Suppose you have a dozen facilities (stores, distribution centers, plants, bank branches, or what have you). There's a fire in one of them. You put together a SWAT team of your best people to analyze why it occurred. They do a super job (you can depend on it—after all, they're your best and brightest). They come up with a 35-page report, concluding with 42 recommendations about what to do to avoid the problem in the future. The recommendations are without exception solid and sound. As a responsible leader, you want to make sure that *everybody* can take advantage of this wisdom. So you pass it along, in the form of hard-and-fast rules, to *all* of your twelve facilities. Great (so far). And then a major computer failure occurs in another location six weeks later. Another bright and aggressive SWAT team is instantly mounted. Another 30-page (more likely 300-page) report and another 26 (or 86) recommendations. Again, all sound. Again, everyone should have the opportunity to take advantage of this wisdom. Again, 26 "recommendations" (or at least 20) are added to the rule book. At the end of five, or ten, or, heaven help us, seventy years, the Sarah Cliftons of the world are trying to work according to 950-page rule books. That's when we get in trouble. Ownership is reduced to about zero.

The systems come to take on a life of their own. The systems end up having little to do with what we are trying to accomplish. Tiny distortions are added by each person who holds the job (in accounting, purchasing, MIS). These are the ten things George wanted to measure when he was the accounts receivable person, or Ellen when she was the reports person for this part of the bank. A senior manufacturer from the Northrop Corporation stated it nicely: "Our systems get detached from the way people build a plane. Systems, after all, are supposed to mirror and abet the way things are done, are supposed to make things easier. Yet the systems, so often, don't look like the creature that we are attempting to build."

And one other point. As the head of several top Hickory Farm franchisees said to us, "Let's call them what they are. They aren't rule books. They're *excuse* books. Nobody reads the damned things unless there's a screwup. And then they only read them to figure out who to blame the foul-up on." Amen! Tom was an officer in the Navy for five years. They say the Navy is run by U.S. Navy Regulations. Tom, to this day, has yet to read the first word of Navy Regulations. And he never will—that is, unless the Navy tries to come back and accost him for some horrible misdeed of twenty years ago. Then he'll read them. You bet. And his objective? You've got it—to figure out whom he can blame the sin on!

Dee Hock, the former chairman of the highly innovative Visa organization, puts it this way: "Substituting rules for judgment starts a self-defeating cycle, since judgment can only be developed by using it. You end up with an army of people who live by rote rather than reason, and where reason cannot be depended upon." Above all, we desperately *want* people to exercise judgment. We want maximum "creativity"—from the person handling the mail, in the PBX room, on the loading dock. And we do mean creativity. We want that person on the loading dock to be alert for a box that has a toe mark where it inadvertently got kicked. And we want him or her to have the "ownership" (both the care and the power) to do the right thing when that box comes along—i.e., cast it aside. We want the PBX operator to feel a sense of ownership and to behave creatively *whenever* a call comes in—to break his or her back, just a little bit, to respond courteously to a difficult/impolitic/irritable query, to take an extra forty-five seconds to try to direct the caller to the right person. *That* is creativity! As one manager commented, "Creative design teams are a dime a dozen. A well-functioning, well-oiled and creatively courteous PBX room or loading dock crew is as rare as a smog-free day in Los Angeles." A nice epilogue is provided by former HEW Secretary John Gardner: "Don't let form triumph over spirit."

"The Enemy Is Us":
Some Questions—and Things to Do Now

▶ Analogous to our aircraft manufacturers and $1 IOU vignettes, conduct two levels of analysis. First, in depth. Select one to four critical "hourly" or first-line supervisory jobs. Collect as much information as possible on "how it feels to live there" (e.g., interviews, anonymous questionnaires, collection of all the procedural material that governs the job, performing the job for two shifts). Have four or five colleagues do the same thing. Spend *two full days,* preferably off-site, going through your analysis in detail. What does it tell you in general? Specifically? Then, make long- and short-term action plans—both remedial and proactive. Begin, during the two days, by taking twenty *concrete* actions (e.g., decidedly *not* "Form a committee to cut paperwork by 20 percent") that reduce demeaning irritants. Set up a plan to continue this process, with you directly in charge (no delegation). Proactively, set in place a process to review future procedures with an eye toward minimizing the demeaning ones (again, you as boss must be *directly* in charge). Take the results of the off-site and review it with the affected people. (The odds are that they will be delighted that you tried, but appalled by how little you still know. But it *is* a start.) Plan to involve them directly in future rounds.

▶ The second level of analysis is less in depth, but just as important. For this one, call a group of twenty-five together (all the same level—e.g., hourly, then first-line supervisors; other variations are mixed levels, new hires with ninety or fewer days' experience, etc.). Have each one offer up "the most demeaning and annoying rule/regulation/form/procedure with which I must live." (This takes guts.) Then change something, on the spot, relative to at least 50 percent of the ideas; promise rapid action (within ten working days) on the rest. Repeat the exercise regularly; perhaps form regular councils to offer up ideas.

(At a third level, more casually, develop a planned habit of spending one hour every three weeks with one randomly chosen person—an MIS new hire, a new dispatcher; repeat, more informally, the "most demeaning rule" exercise—and act on it.)

The suggestions above are not in any sense a "best approach" to attacking the issue. They all do, however, contain two elements that are musts for any such effort: (1) you must dig into the detail, and (2) you and you alone must then *act* on what you find. (Interestingly, regardless of your level—second-level supervisor or vice president, you will find, we guarantee, much more than you think. Our experience is wholly consistent on this point: Once you allow yourself to really get into the process, you will discover vast avenues for improvement within your purview.)

15

ApplauseApplause

To talk about people, we've focused on philosophies, on ownership, on teams and on the pernicious effects of petty rules. Now we turn to a subject that is most conspicuously absent from management textbooks: Fun, Zest, Enthusiasm. (All three words deserve to be capitalized.) All of us learn how to enjoy things before the age of six. And then we observe joy later on—among the members of the county's top Girl Scout cookie-selling troop and the city's top youth league soccer team, at the top Limited store, the top Wang sales branch and in the bakery crew at Stew Leonard's "Disneyland of Dairy Stores." But all too often our instinct for zest is driven out of us by our formal education, especially professional education. Life, and surely life in organizations, is not supposed to be fun.

We've often commented that we have a secret hypothesis (it's one that we don't wish to test, since there's a good chance that we're wrong). The hypothesis is that over the entrance to the Harvard Business School (or the business/professional school of your choice), there's a giant stone lintel. Deeply inscribed in the granite are the following lines: "All ye who enter here shall never smile again. American business/education/etc. is damned serious stuff!" And yet time and again, whether the evidence is the unit flags on the flight line at TAC or the smiles on the faces of the people at Nordstrom, we've observed that winners *are* people who have fun—and produce results *as a result* of their zest.

The Limited is as fast-growing (and profitable) a big company as exists anywhere. It prides itself on a remarkably lean corporate staff. Yet on the staff of The Limited Stores is a full-time manager of nonmonetary compensation and incentives. One of her products? A lovely magazine called *ApplauseApplause*. It comes out once a month, and it praises, by name and with pictures, the actions of hundreds of Limited associates. That's what we call celebration. The holder of the job, Lynn Buckmaster-Irwin, says, "I consider a new contest a week to be a minimum." There's always something going on at The Limited. Fun, zest, enthusiasm—and unparalleled results.

We've seen some extravaganzas in the way of celebrations. We've attended a Tupperware celebration, and a celebration of the IBM Golden Circle, which

---

The chapter title was blatantly lifted from The Limited biweekly magazine of the same title.

honors the top 3 percent of its sales force. We've seen film footage of Mary Kay's galas. Talk about shows! The Limited Stores has a doozer, too, in a class with the best. It has an annual celebration for its top 100 store managers (out of about 600). They are invited to the annual President's Club meeting; it always takes place in August, in Vail, Colorado. It's a gala. The highlight is the presentation of awards. The 100 managers to be honored are brought to the top of a mountain on a chair (ski) lift. There, at the mountaintop, the awards ceremony takes place, with video cameras recording every second of it. A memorable occasion, to put it mildly. And the film? It's used to spur on the whole system.

Think big! We talked about the Scandinavian Air System (SAS) and its remarkable (1981–83) turnaround. What a prize Group President Jan Carlzon gave his people. At Christmas in 1982, all sixteen thousand SAS employees received a gold watch. Moreover, there was a lavish, three-country blow-out (SAS is owned by Sweden, Norway and Denmark). There were several thousand people at each party. A ride home in a private limousine was provided to each person at the end of the night. That's a celebration!

Think big, even if you're small(er). Oxford Software is a $10 million company based in New Jersey. It had a lot of growth, a lot of profit, and passed a big hurdle—the $10 million mark—in 1983. In January 1984, Chairman Judd Shanker decided to celebrate. He took *all* 125 employees (that's right, including the clerks from the mail room and the receptionists) to Acapulco for four fun-filled (and work-filled) days. Memorable!

The Spirit of the Thing

The spirit of the thing lives in the details.
Mies van der Rohe

Raychem's record of innovation is virtually unmatched in American industry (as are its margins). Nonetheless, the senior team began to fret about some incipient calcification about three years ago. They decided to do something about it.

Each year, Raychem's top officers head for Pajaro Dunes, in Watsonville, California, an exclusive housing development at the north end of Monterey Bay, for a three-day retreat and strategic review. The year 1981 was no different. Same quarters as always. Same players (there had been almost no turnover among the top team in the twenty-five years of the company's existence).

For the opening afternoon meeting, Chairman Paul Cook began with a strategic overview. It stressed changes in the environment, the tough constraints on all sides. It wasn't doom and gloom, but it was hardly upbeat, either. Then Cook stopped, virtually in mid-sentence, and almost shouted (about his own presentation), "What a bunch of BS."

He said it was time for a reassessment. Time to take a radical second look at the company. Time to scrape off the barnacles and begin anew.

The dozen or so participants were stunned, and even more so when the next sound was that of helicopters hovering over the house and then landing on the beach (no small feat, since clearance from about five agencies was required). The whole bunch was herded out of the house with virtually no explanation. They were asked to take with them the Sony Walkman that each had been given as a memento upon arrival.

At sunset the helicopters took off and headed across Monterey Bay and down the Pacific toward Big Sur. Each passenger was asked to turn on his Walkman and plug into the aircraft's sound system. The strains of Bach blended with the Pacific sunset, and with Paul Cook's voice. He explained that the next few days would be different. That the constraints were off. It was all to symbolize a new beginning, a new look. He set out a handful of concise, memorable (and challenging) goals for growth and innovation.

The helicopters landed, and a startling three days of intense exchanges and exotic fanfare began. The meetings had traditionally consisted of rather dry presentations by the managers to Cook and President Bob Halperin. This time, a dozen presentations had been written by Cook and Halperin themselves. They led each discussion. No sacred cows were left untouched.

The days were also broken up in a number of ways. One day, on a walk down to lunch, the team hiked past the Pfeiffer Big Sur parking lot. There stood two elephants! Each had a giant pennant affixed to it trumpeting one of the (concise and memorable) goals that Cook and Halperin were using as themes for the meeting (and, indeed, for the next ten years). Another evening was Sheik of Araby night. Raychem's top bunch (almost all engineers) dressed up in splendid Arabian costumes; one highlight of the evening was a camel race! Live camels, of course (four of them), and (of course) each bedecked in a blanket with one of the new goals inscribed on it. (And, again, their presence requiring fancy footwork through many a regulatory maze.)

There was a host of little touches as well. A daily "newspaper" was put together between the hours of midnight and 4:00 A.M., then delivered; it highlighted memorable business and nonbusiness events of the previous twenty-four hours. On the last day an impressive videotape of the three days was shown (all events had been filmed).

The result? A group that had grown a bit too complacent, a bit too familiar with each other, passed an emotional watershed. Three years later the event was still referred to in the course of everyday decision making, and many of the little events were regularly recalled to invoke the "spirit of the camels and elephants meeting."

We spend a good bit of time giving presentations at company meetings of all sorts. We are above all impressed by the attention and intensity with which IBM, SAS, The Limited, Mary Kay et al. approach theirs. Clearly they consider them "strategic"—we think that's the right way to put it. Another way: Muck up a Golden Circle—even as a vice president at IBM—and you've had it. In a million tiny ways, IBM—and The Limited et al.—show that the event is not a distraction from normal routine. This is an "it," a serious (as well as fun-filled) main event of the year.

A Very Golden Circle

IBM celebrates, lavishly, the success of the top 80 percent of its sales force. All attend gala Hundred Percent Club multiday meetings. But the show for the top 3 percent, the Golden Circle, is something else. It tends to be at an exotic site—Bermuda or Majorca, for example.

Every detail is taken seriously. (As a "service provider"—i.e., speaker—Tom has never been through such a mill: you either agree to a host of demanding requests, from the 35-mm slide format and rehearsal schedule to arriving exactly on time days ahead of time, or you can forget it.) The daily "shows," says an Emmy Award-winning producer who attended a 1984 Golden Circle, are "Broadway caliber." Speakers tend to be those who have recently performed exotic deeds. The meeting Tom attended featured a fellow (who was on the cover of the then current *National Geographic*) who had discovered an old sunken ship in the Arctic Sea. The other featured speaker had recently led the first expedition to go around the earth the "wrong way"—via the two poles.

Small acts of celebration were impressive. About ten of the Golden Circle participants had made twenty Hundred Percent Clubs in the course of their career. Interspersed in the goings-on were film clips of them and their families, about five minutes long each, showing their home, hobbies—e.g., skydiving—and so on; the films were "production quality," no expense spared.

It's difficult to describe all the special touches, from the handsome name tags to the short films, put together in twelve hours, featuring the prior afternoon's recreational activity. The show was simply first-class and all the attendees (even the speakers!) felt as if they had been part of a memorable event.

And there's one more thing: top IBM management was present throughout, and presided over a massive and spectacular black-tie awards banquet. How can we impress upon you the difference in approach between IBM or The Limited and so many of the corporate "celebrations" we attend? Alas, most give the celebration lip service, and then delegate it way down the line, showing up for a one-day-out-of-four cameo appearance.

(Incidentally, the lavishness of Golden Circles is not a luxury of IBM's current positive cash flow. Mr. Watson, Sr., was known in 1915 as a "collector of salesmen," and the lavishness preceded by decades IBM's ability to pay.)

There's no limit to celebration—large or small. We've come across all sorts:

▶ The facing page exhibits samples from the new *Quality News* from the Paul Revere Companies (insurance). Shown are some recent headlines and the scoring systems and awards program. Also note the lovely—and bizarre—team names. No, it's not against the Ten Commandments to have fun! (Even in insurance.)

▶ Paul Revere again! Our friend Pat Townsend reports: "We have begun the PEET program. It stands for 'Program for Ensuring that Everybody's Thanked.' The system is this: Each Monday morning, each of the seven members of the executive committee, including the president, gets his PEET sheet. It lists three quality team leaders along with some highlights of what their team has been up to of late. It also notes who visited this particular team leader last, and when. The executive committee has made the commitment to find at least five minutes for each of their assignments some time during the week."

▶ In response to *In Search of Excellence,* a service group at Digital Equipment discussed enhancing the morale of the company's operation through hoopla. Said a senior and somewhat "traditional" manager several months later: "It was the best thing we've done in years. For one thing, the entire senior staff dressed up as reindeer to sing Christmas carols to the troops. Boy, did they get a kick out of it. It was the talk of the halls for weeks. I was amazed."

▶ The head of a 15-person accounting department in a little electronics firm came up to Tom after a speech: "Wow! Hoopla is it. I've gotten into the habit of finding, *at least once per week,* an event of *some* sort to celebrate. It can be somebody's birthday, but preferably—and we've gotten good at finding these—some positive accomplishment at work. The celebration doesn't need to be dinner at an expensive restaurant, it can be a box of doughnuts. But we celebrate. And it does work! The morale of the place has turned around in just three months." (Hawthorne effect? You bet. The issue? Keep it up. How long? No more than forty or fifty years.)

▶ A manager of several small facilities in the South decided to cut back the workweek from five days to four for several months. The objective was to spend the fifth day figuring out how to make the facilities better places to work. Some of the things that came out of the discussions amazed us (and him). In one of his oldest facilities, there was an energetic boss who led the

The Paul Revere Companies
Our policy is quality

Here's how the Quality Recognition Program works...

Bronze Award

When a team meets the qualification criteria for the Bronze Award, each team member receives a Bronze cloisonne lapel pin which recognizes each team member's contributions to "Paul Revere Quality."

Silver Award

When a Quality Team reaches the Silver Award, each team member Silver-plated lap off his or her Revere Q each S rec

Gold Award

When a Q reaches th each te Gold R

Names of new Bronze Team Members —

FAFFANOOSE: Virginia Quitadamo, Barbara Lyseth, Madeline Crocker, Martha Baker, Alfreda Owens, Elizabeth Young, Diane Buthen, Gloria Steele, Evelyn Mercon, Rita Desroches, Dorothy Gonyea, Carmella Monfreda, Dorothy Olen, Janet Mercon, Marrion Lamarche. **PAT'S POURRI:** Pat Townsend, Selma White, Ray Perkins, Sally Hanscom, Mary Gablaski, Rick Perez, Marybeth Lucey, Evie Frederickson, Karen Todd, Cheryl Alderman, Kathy Gaucher. **YTILAUQ:** Mark Reger, Jane Domings, Timothy McNamara, Sandy Schiltz, Donna Euwart, Gerry Rochon, Robert Murphy, Ray Martinez, Beverly Labrie, David Moorefield, Diane ... Andonian, Nellie ... , Paula Bechard, ... , Doreen Evans, ... n Riccutti, Julie ... th Melyonowski, ... g, Lynda Hadley,

Cooperation Breeds Quality

In order to improve the morale of the clerical staff and the sales force in the Supervisor Donna Tod grams. One provides clerical staff who displ who make an effort at A recognition plaque

Seven-Up Gold

Straight to Gold! Orv Miller and his Quality Team, the *Seven-Ups*, received their Bronze, Silver, and Gold pins all at once from Aubrey K. Reid.

How'd they do it? Orv credits the fact that the Quality Has Value process "allows non-management people to get involved." A decision was made to remove some phrasing from the Voluntary Accident Program for AVCO Corporation — phrasing that had been the cause of some expensive lawsuits in the past.

More Teams Bronzed

Twenty-three additional Quality Teams had attain Bronze status by March 28, and have been reco by the company with individual member.

One of these, the "Gophers" dec ty, by adopting the strategy of think the time, and never doing anything tions. Team leader Bette Ostenf members of the *Gophers* "now feel this company; that they count and th feel more a part of the Paul Rever to weekly meetings, the team also h ment" Quality meetings, because something will make a difference, it to talk about.

Regina Prentiss and Bette Spe sions," and their team goal is to ob in the department. Everything they discuss and improve upon leads to this goal. Everyone is excited because "they themselves are doing the changing and implementing, so they feel more important and better about themselves."

OCTOBER GOLD TEAMS: Audrey Arrington and *Systems-Addicts*, Tom Junell and *Mr. T's Team*, Janet Burns and *The A Team*, Gary MacConnell and *ISD Mgmt*, Ken McNulty and *Ken's Kost Kontrollers*, Marrion Lamarche and the *All Stars*, Jayne Bryce and *Lucky 13*, Bette Ostenfeld and the *Gophers*, Shirley Salah and *Shirl's Girls*, Marge White and *The Mighty Eight*, Loxie Woodcock and *Supply-We Deliver*, Barbara Harper and *B's Guys and Dolls*, Irene Liberty and *Liberty Belles*, Sally Freeburn and the *Support Team*, Isabella McKinlay and *George's Candi-Kanes*, Pat Diceeare and *Renewal Crediting*, Kay Roberts and *Special K's* way by building a "potato shack." She took a small unused shed in the back of the plant, and turned it into an eating facility and recreation area. People got heavily involved. It made all the difference in the world to morale—and productivity.

▶ In a textile factory the factory manager came up with an ingenious solution to a problem. He wanted to buy new, fairly expensive chairs for each of his on-line people (for their workstations). He decided to delay the buy, and in a remarkable fashion: anybody who exceeded the target output per hour and then some (about a 25 percent premium) for a month would "win" a chair. The chair was awarded in a unique way: the plant boss brought the chair to his own office, then the line person came and sat down in the chair, and the boss rolled him or her back out to the workstation.

▶ Executive recruiters would like as not be near the top of anyone's list of "stodgy" types—they seem to get paid in part for being stodgy. Virtually the best of the bunch is Russell Reynolds Associates, where a special routine is practiced. One year Russ Reynolds went to Paris and bought old French taxicab horns (they're quite beautiful) and had one placed in each of his offices. Now, whenever a job is placed, the horn is blown. Ceremonially. Even executive recruiters can celebrate!

We've come to label these celebrations, both small and large, the "technology of enthusiasm," and we chose the word "technology" for a particular reason. When it comes to production or backroom operations, we're capable of analyzing problems thoughtfully. When it comes to marketing, we can quick as a wink generate analyses by the ton. But when we talk about rewarding enthusiasm, celebrating, and the like, the eyes usually glaze over. What we're suggesting is that you can be just as thoughtful, just as meticulous and systematic in developing programs that substantially boost the enthusiasm in your organization, as you are when you test-market your new widget.

The Rolm Corporation (recently acquired by IBM) has been a remarkably profitable and fast-growing company, successfully challenging the giant AT&T in the PBX market. A Rolm officer put it this way: "The leader is not a devil's advocate. He is cheerleader." Cheerleader, indeed. Cheerleading is not merely legitimate; it's at the core of most successful organizations. It always has been. We've noticed it, in sports teams and the like, since we were kids. Now let's apply it, as the best have, to business and other organizations.

We've talked of Tom Monaghan, the Domino's Pizza (and Detroit Tigers) boss. Tom, we're proud to say, is a fan of *In Search of Excellence*. In fact, when Tom (Peters) first met him, he pulled out the little black notebook that is his business bible and said that he had the eight main points from the book written down in it. Then he apologized! "I hope you won't think I've committed a sacrilege," he said, "but I've changed it a little bit." How? He had added his own ninth point: "Have fun."

EIGHT COMMON QUESTIONS ABOUT
CELEBRATIONS—AND SOME ANSWERS

1. *Can you have too many prizes, or banquets, and thereby cheapen the whole process?*

Yes and no. One award is too many if it isn't given with conviction and for generally perceived merit. But if these two attributes (conviction and merit) are in place, the sky is the limit. Paul Revere's quality program includes team awards (e.g., bronze, silver, gold) for various levels of accepted suggestions. Soon teams began to go beyond gold. So now it's double bronze, double silver, etc. An Apple manufacturing manager has a trinket bag in her desk. When something good is done, the doer gets a trinket. A Milliken manufacturing manager is a former football player. A common football award, for a lineman, is a gold star permanently affixed to the helmet (e.g., for an unassisted tackle). He uses the same device at Milliken to great effect. He's comfortable with it, and believes in it. It shows. It works.

Do you have any talented sailor friends? Go into their home and you'll find, unfailingly in our experience, a big trophy case in the living room, or close to it. They may be bankers or brokers, but they can never get too many loving cups. And they never tire of showing them off.

2. *But isn't it hard to design meaningful awards for people other than, say, salespeople (based on sales dollars) or engineers (based on patents registered)?*

No. Or, rather, yes. It *is* harder, since we have so underexercised our imagination in this area. But it can be done. Anywhere. Each Milliken department has a scoreboard posted for all to see. In one instance it may note "X days since an order-entry error," in another, "Y days since a below-standard order was produced." One trick here: the people closest to the job know the job best, *and* its impact on others, so have them specify the standards for achieving the award. Our experience is that they will be tougher on themselves than a manager would be, *if* it is clear to them that the objective is not to subsequently use the standards against them (punish them for not achieving a certain standard), and if it is clear that management is sincere in its approach to the program.

3. *How do you get secretaries, loading-dock teams, etc. involved in "big" events where celebrations of company successes are in order?*

Invite them! It may come as a surprise, but there is no iron law that says (1) celebrations can't be held for support functions or (2) support people can't be feted at sales banquets. Milliken marketing meetings include the whole team—every support function. Bill Creech at TAC, remember, held regular banquets and awards nights for his supply and maintenance teams.

4. *But engineers (accountants, bankers) don't go for this stuff, do they?*

Try them! The parties at MIT are as festive as at any other school, and the singing is just as loud. In professional societies, the desire for recognition is as great as at Mary Kay. We are all suckers for brass bands and pats on the back.

5. *But I don't feel right rushing around with balloons in my hand. What do I do?*

First, we suspect that over time you can come to feel right. We've seen it happen among the macho, "Not me" pilots at People Express and the engineers at Raychem and the manufacturers at Milliken. But if you don't feel right, don't do it. Do something that feels appropriate. A friend, an executive, is a bibliophile. When something special occurs, he gives out a carefully selected first edition of a fine book. Many recipients aren't bibliophiles, yet it is clear that he has personally invested time and trouble in selecting the gift. Even those who read no more than the *Reader's Digest* are unfailingly touched.

6. *But isn't there a role for punishment, the negative stuff, as well as rewards and celebrations?*

The answer is twofold. First: there is a role for punishment—minor to major—when continuous poor performance merits it. Second, however: the celebration serves a dual purpose, for it is a strong, indirect "punishment" to those who do not win accolades. The best "awarders"—IBM, Tupperware, Mary Kay, Milliken—provide awards to almost all who participate in their programs ("showing up" awards). But just as clearly, they provide special awards to the top 60 percent, 25 percent, 5 percent, 1 percent. Failing regularly to be in the "top 60 percent," especially in situations where one is surrounded by one's peers, is a powerful stimulus to better performance—without being labeled as a loser. As one senior manager puts it, "You quickly get tired of walking out of group celebrations with 'honorable mention.'" (We'd hasten to add, though, that the honorable mention *is* valuable. It's a lot better than "no show.")

7. *How do I convince my boss that we ought to spend possibly hundreds of thousands of dollars on a single bash for, say, our salesforce?*

Beats us! No short-term cost/benefit analysis will provide justification. You simply must believe in people and believe that people like to be around one another and share one another's successes. Sorry. We have never had a shred of luck with our clients on this. We think that if you could smuggle that reluctant dragon into an IBM or Limited celebration, you could make a believer out of him or her. Short of that, we're stymied, too.

8. *What should the average prize be? What's the role of money?*

For one thing, people will work eighteen hours a day for months for a T-shirt if the context is meaningful and the presenter is sincere. For another, big cash awards can be horribly disruptive, leading to "Hide the idea," "Screw the other guy" and "Don't help *them*" behavior. We observe that small gifts or sums of money and equal gifts (monetary or otherwise) to *all* members of a team are the most effective. Put simply, I will be delighted with your $250 award, provided that awards are plentiful and I can picture myself winning one too. I will be resentful of your $1,000 or $3,000 award, especially if such awards are granted infrequently. I'll figure I was just as deserving as those who received them, especially if I think I aided you in any tiny way (the tiniest of assists leads to a wholesale feeling of "He couldn't have done it without me").

INTEGRITY, AGAIN!

Throughout this section of the book we have come back again and again, explicitly and implicitly, to integrity. It is nowhere more important than in this matter of applause and celebration. Tom Monaghan didn't learn about zest at the Harvard Business School. He learned it from life, and his endorsement of joy and celebration comes from within.

Now, there is a chance that our quieter friends could view this section with alarm. In part, that's the point! You can't fake this stuff. People have great built-in BS meters, they've been through the mill before. If you don't believe it, if you're behaving in an even slightly manipulative fashion, they'll see through you in a flash. On the other hand, we do think you can learn to appreciate the power (and beauty) of *genuine* celebration. At least you can let those who *are* comfortable begin now. Watch what happens. You may (we predict you will) be pleasantly surprised. We'd also reiterate that celebration and extroversion are not handmaidens. Jan Carlzon is a consummate showman. Tom Monoghan is actually quite shy. Yet both exude zest and excitement and involvement. And both really *care*. They celebrate because they genuinely appreciate what their people have accomplished. It's plain as day from the gleam in their eye and the genuineness of their greeting.

SOME (MORE) GOOD READING ON PEOPLE

There is a vast number of books on "managerial psychology," but on the issue of ordinary people working in organizations we find few works in any field to be enlightening. There are a couple of remarkable exceptions. Our favorite, with nothing a close second, is Robert Townsend's *Further Up the Organization* (Knopf, 1984). It's succinct. It's plausible (Townsend turned Avis around years ago). And it's right on target (we think).

More encyclopedic is *The One Hundred Best Companies to Work For in America,* by Robert Levering, Milton Moskowitz and Michael Katz (Addison-Wesley, 1984). The book consists of one hundred vignettes of fine companies—from the grocery business to the computer business, with every stop in between; many are also profiled in our book.

Mary Kay Ash's *Mary Kay on People Management* (Warner, 1984) is a personal saga of people management from which anyone can learn. There's a tendency by some to write it off as "a bunch of new-to-the-work-force-women-conned-by-pink-Cadillacs." Wrong! The toughest truck dealers around could learn invaluable lessons from Mary Kay if they were willing to open their ears.

James Fallows's *National Defense* (Random House, 1981) is not a "people management book," but it fills the bill better than any we know on the "people" issues involved in debureaucratizing; we use several chapters in our seminars to show in graphic terms how sensible, reasonable human beings responding to the real world can get themselves into hopeless, irrational tangles.

Finally, we would recommend a subscription to *Inc.* Its profiles on business persons leading $50–$500 million enterprises, virtually one a month, are a constant source of inspiration to us.

5

LEADERSHIP

The leader must have infectious optimism. . . . The final test of a leader is the feeling you have when you leave his presence after a conference. Have you a feeling of uplift and confidence?

Field Marshal Bernard Montgomery

Make it *fun* to work in your agency. When people aren't having any fun, they don't produce good advertising. Encourage exuberance. Get rid of sad dogs who spread doom. What kind of paragons are the men and women who run successful [advertising] agencies? My observation has been that they are enthusiasts.

David Ogilvy, Ogilvy on Advertising

16

Attention, Symbols, Drama, Vision—and Love

"All business is show business." Those words were uttered by Jan Carlzon, of the Scandinavian Air System (SAS). We agree. All business *is* show business. All leadership *is* show business. All management *is* show business. That doesn't mean tap dancing; it means shaping values, symbolizing attention—and it is the opposite of "administration" and, especially, "professional management."

As we said at the beginning of this book, for the last twenty-five years we have carried around with us the model of *manager* as cop, referee, devil's advocate, dispassionate analyst, professional, decision-maker, naysayer, pronouncer. The alternative we now propose is *leader* (not manager) as cheerleader, enthusiast, nurturer of champions, hero finder, wanderer, dramatist, coach, facilitator, builder. It's not a model of what might be, or a prescription for the impossible. We've learned it in real-time, from people who've done it in glamour industries and those who've won in extremely adverse situations—in low-growth or no-growth industries or the public sector. We've learned it from Bill Hewlett of Hewlett-Packard; from Steve Jobs of Apple; from Buck Rodgers and Don Estridge of IBM, from Jim Treybig of Tandem. Others we've learned so much from are Bill and Vieve Gore of W. L. Gore & Associates; Roger Milliken of Milliken & Co.; Ren McPherson of the Dana Corporation; Jan Carlzon of SAS; Frank Perdue of Perdue Farms; Sam Walton of the Wal-Mart Corporation; Willard Marriott (Sr. and Jr.) of the Marriott Corporation; Sam Johnson of the S. C. Johnson Company; Jim Rinehart, former General Motors hero at Packard Electric and now chief executive officer of Clark Equipment; Bob Stramy, a GMer who launched the new Livonia, Michigan, Cadillac engine plant; Phil Staley, plant manager of Ford's Edison, New Jersey, assembly operation. And Mayor William Donald Schaefer of Baltimore and General Bill Creech of the Air Force. From all these people we've learned nothing about magic. We've learned, instead, of passion, care, intensity, consistency, attention, drama, of the implicit and explicit use of symbols—in short, of leadership.

ATTENTION

We think our colleague Bob Waterman said it first: "Attention is all there is." Ren McPherson, who made the key to the turnaround he guided at Dana "turning the company back over to the people who do the work"—that is, the first-line people—adds: "When you assume the title of manager, you give up doing honest work for a living. You don't make it, you don't sell it, you don't service it. You don't stand on the loading docks in the cold, or sit in the PBX rooms answering the phones hour after hour." Putting the two statements together, we say that as long as the manager doesn't do "honest work" (and we agree), the only thing he's got left is using his calendar, his day-timer, to pay attention to what's important.

Ah! How do we make this tough? How do we make it complicated enough to seem plausible? Attention *is* all there is. We're coming out of a twenty-five-year period during which managers were said (by all the consultants and teachers) to be powerless, confounded by multiple stakeholders, multiple constituencies, swirling and uncontrollable "external forces" and trapped in the middle—whether the manager was chairman (trapped between the EPA, an angry board and the Japanese) or first-line supervisor (trapped between the union's grievance committee and middle management). We think this is nonsense. The manager is shockingly powerful. Remember when you were a nineteen-year-old on your first job? You darn well knew what your manager (who was probably all of twenty-two) ate, and when his eating habits changed. You were a manager watcher par excellence. We all were. Managers are powerful. People pay attention to the obsessions (or—and here's the rub—lack of them) of managers.

Attention is all there is. Milliken & Company has long been way ahead of the pack, even the Japanese, in the manufacturing technology of textiles. The source of their prowess? Here's an example. Once every three or four years there's a show of textile machinery from all over the world. In 1984 it was in Milan, Italy. The average sizable company sent four or five people for three or four days. Roger Milliken sent a hundred and fifty of his people for the full ten days! He accompanied them. At the end of each long day of wandering the floors, they had a three- or four-hour meeting that usually lasted way past midnight to swap ideas. Roger Milliken wouldn't misspend a single penny knowingly. He's hardly extravagant. Yet he *is* extravagant when it comes to his strategic obsession—keeping Milliken's plants at or ahead of the state of the art.

Sam Walton has accumulated a personal fortune well in excess of $2 billion (said *Forbes* in 1984) while boosting the Wal-Mart Corporation from $40 million to over $6 billion in a decade (with equity returns staying near 40 percent). He thinks retailing is all about stores (an almost novel idea in the systems-and-merchandising-dominated 1980s). Years ago, Mr. Walton began making a point of visiting every one of his stores at least once a year; that was when he had only eighteen. The number by early 1985 was close to seven hun-

dred fifty; and he was still visiting each one at least once a year! And hitchik-
ing with Wal-Mart Trucks across the country, greeting each store manager
and spouse by name at annual meetings, wandering down to share doughnuts
at 2:00 A.M. with his people in the distribution centers. Do the store people
know he's interested? You bet!

Bill Hewlett constantly wandered the engineering spaces at Hewlett-
Packard, as did Barney Oliver, his head of R&D for forty years. Today,
though neither is any longer on active duty, a twenty-four-year-old student at
the Stanford Business School (a cooperative engineering student from
Hewlett-Packard) can still say, "Believe me, each and every one of us [the
eighty thousand people on the payroll] thinks that Bill or Barney is likely to
stop by our desk any minute and ask about the prototype we're working on."
Absurd! But repeated time and again, in other places. The McDonald's franchisees expected Ray Kroc within the hour even when they knew he was in
the hospital.

Terry Deal and Allan Kennedy, in *Corporate Cultures*, recount this story
about the present chairman of the General Electric Corporation:

> When Jack Welch was an up-and-coming group executive, he had a
> special telephone installed in his office with a private number which was
> made available to all the purchasing agents in his group. If an agent ever
> got a price concession from a vendor, he could phone Welch and the call
> would come in on his telephone. Whether he was making a million-dollar
> deal or chatting with his secretary, Welch would interrupt what he was
> doing, take the call, and say, "That's wonderful news; you just knocked a
> nickel per ton off the price of steel." Then, straightaway, he'd sit down
> and scribble out a congratulatory note to the agent—a profoundly messy
> and ambiguous motivational procedure. But Welch not only made him-
> self a hero by the symbolic act, he also transformed each and every pur-
> chasing agent into a hero, too. [Later, Deal and Kennedy go on to
> analyze what went on.] Welch could have attacked the problem of high
> costs in a number of ways. He could have appointed a task force to study
> the problem and come up with solutions. Or he could have hired consul-
> tants to do the same. Or he could have reassigned his best managers to
> head up the purchasing function. What he chose to do was install a tele-
> phone in his office. Suppose no one called? Suppose people called but
> the impact on purchasing costs was negligible? It took courage to pursue
> such an unconventional, culture-reinforcing approach to the problem—
> the courage to trust others in the culture to do the right thing!

Extraordinarily successful Seattle Seahawk coach Chuck Knox would
doubtless identify with the Welch story. A large part of the (positive) reversal
of Seahawk performance between 1982 and 1984 was moving from the bottom of the heap to the top in "turnover ratio." (That is, they used to lose many
more fumbles than they took from opponents, and have many more passes

intercepted than they intercepted.) In a late 1984 TV interview, Knox gave what was, in his view, a prime reason for the shift: "I began starting every practice with a five-minute drill on some aspect of turnovers. I just wanted them [the team] to focus, each and every day, in some way or other, on the importance of the turnover deal." Just five minutes. But constant—and up front—repetition. I.e., attention.

Tom spent an exciting day with Kelly Johnson, founder of the original Skunk Works at Lockheed. Beyond the imposing outcomes that Johnson achieved lies an even more impressive story, one that includes chapters like this. In our rather extensive experience with big development projects we've found that the major development issue is invariably manufacturing scale-up. That's a semitechnical way of saying that the engineers (designers) seldom if ever talk to the manufacturers (builders), and vice versa. So Tom asked, in the course of a wide-ranging discussion, "Mr. Johnson, how did *you* beat the manufacturing scale-up issue? How did you solve the problem of getting the manufacturers to talk to the engineers?" His response? "What problem?"

"Well, sir," Tom began, "in every *other* company we know it's a major problem."

"It's not a big thing," he said. "At about six-thirty A.M. most every morning I'd get the manufacturing supervisors together and let them moan about what the engineers had done to them during the last twenty-four hours. Then at seven A.M. I'd get all the engineering gang together and let them jaw about what the manufacturers had done to them. At seven-thirty, for about a half an hour, no more, we'd get 'em all together, decide what the problems were, and what we'd do about them now." He concluded: "If you do that sort of thing, five or six days a week, fifty or so weeks a year, for forty years, all those problems you talk about go away." Indeed!

Or, consider this. A major tire company follows standard industry procedures: cosmetically defective tires (not ones that would cause safety problems) are put on sale at a radical discount. There's even a name for them—"blemmies" (from blemish, of course). The company is running a 6 percent "blemmie" rate. A new person becomes honcho. He finds this unacceptable: "Let's discontinue the discount sales," he says. But nothing much happens; after all, it's a time-honored tradition, dating back decades. The people don't really believe him. Then he heads out to a plant and spends two full days there, in shirt sleeves, slicing up blemmies with a carving knife. Mysteriously, in a multithousand-person operation, the blemmie rate plummets from the historically immutable 6 percent level to 1 percent in a matter of weeks, and it never goes back up.

Who Gets Promoted: An (Unsung) Attention Getter

Calling promotion an "unsung" tool may surprise some. It surprises us, to tell the truth. But it expresses an honest observation. Perhaps the best and clearest signal of what's important, what is being paid attention to, especially in times of change, is who gets promoted, when and for what. Yet as Tom's former colleague at McKinsey, the renowned Arch Patton, once stated, "Promotion is *the* most underutilized managerial tool."

If an organization is not tiny (having, say, thirty or more people on the payroll), promotions occur regularly—at least three or four a year, in even the very small outfit. The issue? Will you use promotion *consistently,* to tell a consistent story about values and priorities (or shifting priorities if apropos)?

So often in times of change we (all too understandably) waste a promotion to reward a loyal soldier who performed honorably under the old scheme or value set. Now, we are all in favor of rewarding loyal soldiers. But do it with a raise or a medal signifying a fine and loyal past, not with a relatively scarce promotion that singularly signals your colleague's fit with the (new) value set and course for the future.

There are two additional points worthy of note in this connection. First, we urge senior bosses to get heavily involved in making and certifying promotions, even three or four or more levels down. It was said that GM's legendary Alfred Sloan would often miss policy meetings but never a personnel meeting. And with a 250,000-person outfit at the time, he would regularly spend three or four hours on the appointment of a chief engineer in a small facility. He viewed such time (attention) as his most significant contribution to the enterprise—i.e., it was his primary means of signaling certain concerns. (How different from most of today's organizations, where promotions even two levels down are rubber-stamped by a boss who simply notes that "the process"—often ungainly and mechanical—has been followed.)

Second, promotion is a wonderful tool for the *non*chairman, a marvelous way (the best we know) to sow the seeds of revolution from other than the very top. The best way to instill your agenda is via numerous unsung promotions to the first and second levels. You can quietly, in only a few years, create a substantial new look. General Bill Creech, for instance, is open about having nurtured a large group of fellow "enemies of consolidation and centralization" and having seeded them in as many vital command slots as possible throughout the Air Force.

Promotion *is* attention. We suggest you not allow even one of these inevitably offered up (yet still scarce) opportunities to go to waste.

It's "just" a matter of paying attention. *You* might not know what your priorities really are; *you* might not even remember what breakfast cereal you eat. But your people know. The problem is that your people *do* pay attention to you! We were once called in to work with a company that was having a terrible problem: the chairman was determined to enhance entrepreneurship, but the message was not getting through. As consultants we spent a lot of the chairman's money reanalyzing his strategy, checking his structure and job descriptions, and dissecting each one of his business subsystems (capital budgeting and the like). They all looked great, aimed at the right target. Out of sheer desperation, we looked at the only other thing we could think of left to look at—his calendar, the way he spent his time. We looked at the meetings he attended, and did a detailed content analysis of the agenda over a period of several months. We looked at the visits he made and the people he talked to and the order in which he talked to them while at a site. He was even kind enough (or brave enough) to allow us to run a phone log on him for several months. The net? He was "Mr. Entrepreneurship"—in the speeches he made on the Fourth of July—but he spent barely 3 percent of his total time on his presumed objective. His attention wasn't there. And his people knew it.

Another project, with a major construction company, revealed a similar problem—one that was amenable to an obvious solution. The company, which was run by engineers (who liked to talk about engineering problems), had gotten badly overextended in new overseas areas. Yet a detailed, minute-by-minute (for months) analysis of the agendas of top management's weekly meetings suggested that about 80 percent of their time was spent *not* talking about overseas implementation issues, but about the nuts and bolts of the engineering problems, with which they felt more familiar (and which they apparently had more skill dealing with). Over a twelve-month period meeting agendas were shifted until 70 percent of management's attention was focused on implementation. And things changed radically.

How does change come about? First, and not so obvious, it's a matter of the *quantity* of attention paid to the matter at hand rather than the quality, odd as that statement may sound. When the senior folks (at the store level, the department level, the division level or the corporate level) start to focus on a newish "it" (entrepreneurship, overseas implementation), then the rest of the organization starts to pay attention to "it." And what gets attended to gets done. Thus, if you want to focus on quality, focus on quality, *period.* If you haven't focused on quality a lot before, you won't know exactly what to talk about at first. Conversations will drag, will be abstract. It doesn't matter a whit. Everybody will eventually get the drift—that you're focused on quality (and *not* some other, former priority—an equally important message). It doesn't have to be a *good* conversation about quality, just a conversation about quality. In some fashion, pay significant attention to the blemmies, and *somehow* the blemmie rate goes down. Not because of a specific program you invented, but because of the energy that comes to be focused on "it."

There it is again: "the mere Hawthorne effect." Productivity goes up "merely" because attention is being paid to people and not because some mechanical (real) improvement (like brighter lights) has been installed. And they're right! Hawthorne it is. But "mere"? No!

Attention as Symbolic Behavior

Attention *is* symbolic behavior. One difficulty we find in dealing with this subject stems from baggage that comes along with the word "symbolic" for the hard-nosed, rational manager. Somehow, given the macho jargon of Western management theorizing, describing an executive's behavior as "symbolic" suggests something other than the "tough-minded stuff of decisive strategic decision-making." But symbolic it is. As a result of our "symbolic" attention—symbolic of our concern and our priority—others become engaged. (And let us pointedly remember, symbols—paying attention—are all the manager, who doesn't drive a forklift, has.) So it is with Marriott's reading of the complaint cards, Milliken's concern with the factory, Perdue's obsession with the hairs on a chicken wing and quality in general. The annual day-timers of these leaders (observed in retrospect) are simply (not "merely") the *only* valid measures of the concerns they have, concerns that will eventually lead to down-the-line promotion or demotion, favor or disfavor.

Mars, Inc., executives make a fetish of physically attaching every administrative facility to a factory, furnishing the facilities in Spartan fashion, prominently displaying next to the desk the white coats to be worn without fail in going into the factory. Truth be known, those few dozen white coats don't really have a whole lot to do with either the spotlessness of the factory or the Mars quality record. And yet they have everything to do with it. They make it crystal clear what the primary concerns of top management are.

Experts agree that the only thing that distinguishes mankind from the rest of the planet's creatures is our use of language and reasoning power—i.e., the manipulation of symbols. Leadership (management) *is* symbolic behavior, whether you're talking about Martin Luther King's trek to Selma, Alabama, or Jack Welch's special phone for purchasing agents. And that's all it is—not because symbols constitute a "good" variable to manage, but because they're the *only* variable we have at our command, whether we recognize it as such or not.

Now, this is at once a very good news story and a very bad news story. Good news, because it doesn't involve capital spending—every second is an honest-to-gosh "symbolic opportunity." Bad news because of *exactly* the same fact: *Every* minute *is* a symbolic opportunity. It's an opportunity that you consciously or, more likely, unconsciously choose to grasp *or* squander. What's the old man (or supervisor) interested in? Who's he talking to? What are the changes since yesterday? Why's he talking to Dick about that, rather than Jim? What do the marginal notes on the memos look like? Who's he chewing out now? Why? How come Harriet got a pat on the back for her presentation and Dave didn't get one for his? How come he chose white paint instead of blue? It was quality last week, now he's off on costs—and it's only three days later. We knew it wouldn't last. Remember—again—that the manager can't really *do* anything much of value. He can only suggest (symbolize) what's important by the way he behaves. And the myriad *subconscious* actions, those that end up as marginal notes penned on memos, are *more*—much more—important cumulatively than so-called strategic decisions. So you're in favor of quality. So you make a couple of "strategic" decisions to reinforce that, spending a bit of capital on robots. So what? The quality message will get across only if it ends up as marginal notes penned on memos day after day, year after year.

Attention: Turnarounds

Substantial turnarounds are few and far between. Not surprisingly, each involves a strong leader, a leader who is obsessive about paying attention to his theme. SAS's Jan Carlzon finds no opportunity too small to hammer on the service theme. You can't get him to talk about airplanes. He talks about passengers. He focuses on the language: SAS is no longer an "asset-oriented business" but a "service-oriented business," no longer an "airplane-oriented business" but a "customer-oriented business," no longer a "technically oriented and financially oriented business" but a "market-oriented business." The stories he tells are stories about mundane service improvements. That's it: minute by minute, day after day.

Ren McPherson, architect of the remarkable Dana turnaround we've described, is the same way. People—that's his theme. He gives but one speech on management, regardless of setting. It focuses on the enhancement of productivity in manufacturing through people on the line, period. There is no way you could miss it.

Andy Pearson, as chief operating officer at PepsiCo, was, along with Chairman Don Kendall, the guiding light behind the extraordinary PepsiCo turnaround. SAS turned toward service, Dana turned toward increasing manufacturing productivity through turned-on people, PepsiCo turned toward enhancing entrepreneurship. And Pearson was another broken record. No matter what the PepsiCo audience, he was always jawing about action, about test markets: "What are you up to?" "What's been going on in your test market in the last ninety-six hours?" At a dinner (a social occasion nominally), the subject, sure as can be, became not baseball or philosophy or $150 million capital expenditures but what was going on in the test markets for Pizza Hut, La Petite Boulangerie, Frito-Lay.

Most senior corporate officers are broad-minded, with eclectic interests and lots of different things to talk about. Not Frank Perdue, who talks solely about chicken and its quality. Not Debbi Fields, who talks about her cookies. Not Ray Kroc, who talked about Quality, Service, Cleanliness, and Value. Herman Lay (Frito-Lay founder) was a broken record on the subject of the perfect potato; Bill and Vieve Gore are the same about their "Associates," and so is Roger Milliken on textile technology. The turnaround artists—Carlzon, McPherson, Pearson et al.— are the same: one-track minds, obsessive.

It all adds up to this: *Every* system, *every* seating arrangement, *every* visit is symbolic behavior. Questioning routines: What's the first question the boss invariably asks? Market-oriented people ask about marketing. Financially oriented people ask about finance. (DuPont people ask about safety!) Want to change your strategic emphasis? Determined shifts in time-honored questioning habits can be a big part of it. Seating arrangements. Who gets invited to what kinds of meeting? In "staff-oriented" organizations, a disproportionate share of staff gets invited to meetings. Want to take the emphasis off staff? Quit inviting staff people to meetings! Visits: Who gets visited, in what order? What functions first? Junior or senior people first? How much time is spent with what level people in which functions? The word gets around—at approximately the speed of light (some argue faster).

Got a problem? Symbolize your concern by paying obsessive attention to it. In a straightforward, no shortcuts fashion. Put time on it, and on all appropriate players, year in and year out, decade in and decade out. The remarkable cleanliness of Disney's parks is merely a matter of a lot of people trying to do cleanliness better. The secret is, they don't sell gum in the parks! Disney *is* a thousand people dreaming up a thousand thousand "no gum" ideas.

Attention:
Some Questions and Things to Do Now

Analysis

1. Review your calendar, if you keep one in detail, for the last year, the last 90 days in more detail, the last 30 days in great detail. What does it tell you about your (1) substantive priorities, (2) MBWA proclivities—visits, in the office or out?

2. Repeat no. 1 for your chron file: What do your replies to your correspondence tell the world? (Don't be defensive. Do it privately.) They may tell the world that you're busy with 46 conflicting priorities. *All* are legitimate. But maybe you can do better in the future. Cut it to 43? or 10? How about two?

3. Repeat no. 1 for your visits (MBWA). Whom do you visit at a site? In what order? Is there a regular pattern? What does that tell you about your priorities?

4. Repeat no. 1 for your phone log.

5. If no. 1 through no. 4 fail for lack of data, plan to accumulate this data for the next 30 to 90 days, starting today.

6. Get a colleague to note carefully remarks/queries at a series of meetings over the next 7 to 14 days. What do you ask/talk about? About service? About factories? About financials? (Don't assume, when analyzing the data, that the "financial focus" was "just because it was budget time." We are *all* broken records. We create, subconsciously in the main, opportunities to ask about our pet topics. Believe it!)

Next Steps

Treat no. 1 through no. 6 as studies in *variable* behavior. You *can* redo your calendar, your visitation pattern, your phone focus, your meeting routines. It will be damned hard work! (Stopping smoking or shedding twenty pounds permanently is child's play by comparison.) It necessarily—or best—begins by having the analysis of the past in front of you. Redo the calendar, to the tune of *only* 10 percent (2 days) next month. Rework *one* visit routine. Make a note of *one* variation in meeting routine. Enlist, if you can, a trusted colleague to work through this with you. To do so is not a sign of weakness. This is not kid stuff. This is the "it" of strategic skill development.

And that leads us to our next subject: symbol *management,* and the leader (manager) as dramatist. Each one of these symbol-using activities (which is what they are) is a minidrama. It has nothing to do with Theory X or Theory Y, extroverted personalities or introverted personalities. It has to do with the economical (symbolic, dramatic) use of time—the economical use of each and every phone call, the order of each and every item on the agenda of every minor meeting.

ATTENTION PLUS: SYMBOLS AND DRAMA

Symbols and drama. We've mentioned Renn Zaphiropoulos's feelings about private parking spaces. In December 1983, one month before he assumed a more senior position within the Xerox group—president of the Information Products Division in Dallas, Texas—Renn made his first appearance before the three hundred assembled members of his new management team. His number one priority in this opening speech? To make the point that there would be no unnecessary distinctions among individuals in the division—none of those petty privileges that not only serve no productive purpose but are in fact damaging to the sense of self-worth of those who do not have them and to their personal dignity. In this spirit, Renn directed that in each of the three facilities of the division all reserved parking spaces be painted out. By the time he actually took over in January, 1984, each and every one of the "executive" parking spaces was gone. Symbolism? You bet. "Strategy" in action? You'd better believe it.

Symbols. Drama. Our colleague Jim Kouzes recounts the following. Corning Glass had focused its energies on decorative glass for most of its history. Now it was faced with a declining market. Arthur A. Houghton, Jr., was the newly appointed chief executive officer. He wanted to move Corning toward higher technology. His approach? He went down to the warehouse containing some of the most ornately beautiful glass Corning had ever produced (it was lying fallow in inventory). He had a lead pipe with him. He proceeded to smash several hundred thousand dollars' worth of glass into smithereens. He wanted to make it clear that he was up to something new. He did!

General Bill Creech, architect of the turnaround at TAC, has a superb sense of symbols and the dramatic. On an inspection visit soon after he took over he came across a supply office in disrepair, the epitome of the second-class status to which supply people had been relegated (and the issue toward which he was directing so much energy). The supply sergeant, a fifteen-year veteran, occupied a government-gray chair with a torn back (mended with electrical tape) and only three casters—the fourth leg was propped up on a block of wood. Creech ordered his aide to have the chair boxed and sent to TAC's Langley, Virginia, headquarters. Soon thereafter the general held a major ceremony. The three-star general—Creech has four stars—who headed logistics was "awarded" the chair, and told that it was now *his* chair, until the supply operation was cleaned up.

An executive came up to us after a meeting with a McDonald's competitor. He had worked at McDonald's for quite a while some years back, and remembered a time when founder Ray Kroc had gotten irritated because his crew chiefs (shift managers) weren't, in his opinion, spending enough time out at the counter with the customers: "He sent an order around. It was a while back, you know, when the tables and chairs were wooden. The order was to be executed immediately (and it was): '*Saw* the back off each manager's chair.' Ray figured that might keep them a little less comfortable while desk sitting." Apocryphal or not, it's a tale that reveals the importance of keeping in touch at McDonald's. And it's still told—pointedly—today.

A Nordstrom brother was out on one of his regular store inspection tours. He visited a shoe department. Wandering into the back room, he noted that there were lots of gaps along the shelves (indicating stockouts, and Nordstrom's, above all, prides itself on customer-satisfying "overstock," by others' standards). He asked the clerk why the gaps were there. "Don't worry," the young man replied, "I've got them on order." He produced the order forms as proof. Nordstrom picked up the order forms, rolled each one up carefully, walked over to the back-room shelves, and placed the appropriate forms in the empty spaces. "Why don't you wrap these forms around the customers' feet if they ask for the out-of-stock items?" he said, and walked out. That night after work the young man raced to the nearest warehouse to pick up replenishment stock. The (symbolic) story lives today!

Entrepreneurship can also be spurred by symbols. GE was singled out as the paragon of strategic thinking for fifteen years (the entire history of the high-visibility strategy movement, in fact). We noted earlier that when Jack Welch became chairman in 1981, one of the first things he did was dismantle much of the strategic planning staff. Welch hadn't given up on strategic think-ing. Rather, he sent it back to where it belongs—to the strategic business units and divisions. In addition to breaking up the central staff, he accom-plished a major (symbolic) change in the location of strategy review, which used to be full-dress affairs held in corporate headquarters in Fairfield, Con-necticut. The staffs were invariably the heroes of the hour (overwhelmingly outnumbering the line), and sharpshooting among staffs was rampant. Welch simply moved the strategic reviews to the field. Immediately the "heroes" were making their case on *their* turf. Small point? No, a big one.

Drama. Real-life drama. Set your mind in that direction.

Domino's Pizza lives by and owes its phenomenal success to its 30-minute (maximum) "We deliver anywhere" pledge. Domino's Pizza Distribution, therefore and logically enough, must *never* allow a franchise to run out of dough. "Shutting a store down" is the number one sin. It nearly happened a while back, and Distribution President Don Vlcek got a call telling him about the probable disaster. His ready response (in a low-margin business): "Char-ter a plane. Get it there!" Charter they did, get it there they did.* In another instance, Vlcek's lieutenant, irrepressible young Jeff Smith, did have a store shut down for lack of dough. He went out and bought a thousand black arm bands and his whole team wore them in mourning for quite a time afterwards. The message, at Domino's, is clear—and memorable.

And again (with planes, no less). Stew Leonard's, as we noted, is Frank Per-due's biggest single-store customer. Stew wanted to change his chicken-packaging technology a while back, and Frank's people were the only ones expert in the new techniques. So Frank, without a second thought, sent two Lear jets up to Connecticut to fetch fifteen of Stew's chicken packers down to Salisbury, Maryland, for schooling at Perdue Farms' headquarters.

What is such behavior? "Real"—to a point. "Symbolic"? Dramatic? All of those. The stories of Vlcek and the charter, Smith and the armbands, and Per-due and the Lears will be remembered ten years from now, likely thirty years from now, and every time they're told the message will be reinforced: Domino's Distribution *means* franchise service; Perdue Farms *means* quality and customer service. It's at the very heart of the culture/value/strategic strength transmission process.

---

*From time to time we get rebuttals to this: "But you can't afford to deliver the average load of dough by plane!" Of course not. And, indeed, Vlcek had to make up the charter fee by cutting back somewhere else to meet his profit targets. The point is that the story transmits graphic evi-dence about exactly what comes first, what the "tie-breaker" is, about just how far you *must* go to live the *chief* strategic value of the institution. (And if you have to go that far, then you're sad-dled with the issue of how to find the money; but at the time of decision, the story teaches "Think customer first, budget second.")

We believe that in a slightly less dramatic form, "charter opportunities" quite literally occur five hundred to five thousand times a week. Remember, every opportunity to meet with thirty people (or one person) is an opportunity to let them know exactly what's on your mind. Every casual conversation is interpreted endlessly. Every tiny change on your calendar is an indicator of the importance (or lack of it) you assign to a given activity. And such power is available way down the line, not only to Fortune 500 CEO's or the entrepreneur-owners of $20 million companies. When you are nineteen, the "boss," that twenty-two-year-old, is God.

If you choke on that idea, more power to you—as a decent human being. We're glad you don't regularly think of yourself as a deity. But still, listen (and recall your own experience). Whether you are twenty-two and a first-line supervisor or the CEO, your every action is watched, and watched closely and charted by "your" people. Inconsistencies are noted. Small deviations are the subject of intense Kremlinology. Patterns are assessed and updated daily, if not more frequently. Stories are remembered for years. It might not make you comfortable, but you know darned well it's true.

Drama also has a number of other connotations. SAS's Jan Carlzon, remember, stated that "all business is show business." Stew Leonard has turned shopping into an event. Carl Sewell has done the same with car buying. A. Ray Smith, in the midst of decline all around him, has made the Louisville Redbirds into a minor league team outdrawing many of the majors; the edge, as we noted, is clean rest rooms and a show every night. Little Scandinavian Design has founded "Scandinavian Design University" to teach "stage direction." Tupperware, The Limited, Mary Kay Cosmetics, and IBM unabashedly stage dramatic events to motivate their people. Even "conservative" Milliken & Co. stages regular Fabulous Bragging Sessions (see pages 878–881).

We are emotional creatures. We feel pride, we feel slights. Our life *is* a drama to each of us. The winners are institutions and leaders that own up to that reality and live with us as humans—not as automatons.

Language

Attention and symbols and drama are about signaling, of course—about the creation of a "language of attention." Language is fundamental. Sometimes it is specific words. Disney, McDonald's, Gore, Wal-Mart, Dana and People Express eschew "worker" or "employee" in favor of "cast member," "crew member," "associate" and "person." At People everyone is a "manager." Disney calls every customer "guest."

The conscious use of certain words is a vital form of paying attention. And we all get the opportunity to choose our vocabulary. We all call our people or our customers *something*. But do we all use the opportunity to use labels to shape new and positive and strategically important ways of seeing things?

(It's especially crucial here to keep in mind the matter of integrity. To shift from "employee" to "associate" means nothing unless you treat each person as a respected peer rather than a hired hand. On the other hand, if you do believe your clerks are associates/peers/self-managers, then using the word is yet another—and significant—mark of respect.)

Stories

In talking of Domino's Pizza and Perdue Farms, we have introduced the role of stories. There's a lot of psychological literature that we could bring to bear on our discussion of this; *In Search of Excellence* covered some of it. It turns out that human beings reason largely by means of stories, not by mounds of data. Stories are memorable, stories about real people doing real things. Remember Ray Kroc's visit to a McDonald's franchise in Winnipeg? He finds a single fly. Even one fly doesn't fit with QSC&V (Quality, Service, Cleanliness and Value). Two weeks later the Winnipeg franchisee loses his franchise. You'd better believe that after this story made the rounds a whole lot of McDonald's people found nearly mystical ways to eliminate flies— every fly—from their shops. Is the story apocryphal? It doesn't really matter. Mr. Kroc *did* do things *like* that.

Just as Forrest Mars has done things *like* throwing candy bars at his officers after finding a single miswrapped one on a candy counter. A former Mars manager recounts the tale—to him as fresh as if it had happened yesterday— of Mr. Mars visiting a chocolate factory in mid-summer. He went up to the third floor, where the biggest chocolate machines were placed. It was hotter than the hinges of hell. He asked the factory manager, "How come you don't have air conditioning up here?" The factory manager replied that it wasn't in his budget, and he darn well had to make budget. While Mr. Mars allowed as how that was a fact (the fellow had to make budget), he nonetheless went over to a nearby phone and dialed the maintenance people downstairs and asked them to come up immediately. He said, "While we [he and the factory manager] stand here, would you please go downstairs and get all [the factory manager's] furniture and other things from his office and bring them up here? Sit them down next to the big chocolate machine up here, if you don't mind." Said our Mars colleague: "The guy figured out that it was probably a pretty good idea to air-condition the factory, sooner rather than later. Mr. Mars told him that once that had been completed, he could move back to his office anytime he wanted." The stories are memorable. They teach. And they're a darn sight more efficient than policy manuals!

A Procter & Gamble manufacturing manager remembers a call in the middle of the night. It came from a district sales manager, soon after this fellow (now a fifteen-year vet) had become a manager: "George, you've got a problem with a bar of soap down here." Down here, George explains (in 1983), was three hundred miles away. "George, think you could get down here by six-thirty this morning?" Our informant adds, "It sounded like something more than an invitation." And, finally, he concludes, "After you've finished your first three-hundred-mile ride through the back hills of Tennessee at seventy miles an hour to look at one damned thirty-four-cent bar of soap, you understand that the Procter & Gamble Company is *very, very,* serious about product quality. You don't subsequently need a detailed two-hundred-page manual to prove it to you." We suspect this story is true or close to it. The point is, our friend believes it. He repeats it. It lives. (And if P&G were not living the quality message, day in and day out, such stories would either not exist or not be regularly transmitted.)*

The Impact of Stories
A Study

A colleague, Alan Wilkins, studied the impact of stories told in two companies with very different track records in the same industry. The first company was a strong performer and sustained its growth; the second had suffered severe setbacks for the past five years. Could the stories told in each have affected performance? Wilkins says yes. In the high-performing company, managers placed clear emphasis on their management philosophy (the "high story" company); 98 percent of the stories told were favorable to the company's interests. In the "low story" company, only about 50 percent of the stories were favorable. The basic business philosophy in the high story company was overwhelmingly clearer to all employees—managers, technicians, secretaries—than in the low story company. Wilkins discovered that the managers in the low story company confused their people on priorities, while their counterparts in the high story company "had close to a passion for [consistently] communicating a philosophy."

Wilkins concluded that some kinds of stories were powerful ways to motivate, teach and spread enthusiasm, loyalty and commitment; others served an equally powerful purpose: to perpetuate cynicism, distrust and disbelief. Themes that hindered performance included "sinking ship" stories (this company is inept, failing, unable to cope in a changing environment, what's the use?); "trickster" stories (this world is sinister and the only way to survive is to live by your wits; you're on your own, buster); "unjust company" stories (the system is unfair, managers

---

*Even as this chapter was being written, a P&G manager at a seminar told us that he became a believer when he saw an hourly P&G employee at a Jif peanut butter plant bring a shopping bag full of jars of Jif to work. The fellow had noticed while shopping that the labels on the Jif in the store had been mounted off kilter and he had been *unable* to leave them there, so he had bought them all, assuming P&G would pay him back. Indeed they did. "You'd have had to see it to believe it," our friend said. How many others do you suppose he's told that story to?

can't be trusted); and "rule" stories (recounted as a way to establish or justify rigid rules rather than to share a perspective). Unlike the helpful variety, these stories tend to encourage sabotage (how to hurt the company), destructive competition among groups or individuals (deliberately encouraging noncooperation, asking only "What's in it for me?"), and high turnover ("I give up; I'd be better off someplace else").

So if you come across close at hand such stories as those described above listen carefully; don't dismiss them as ridiculous and untrue. The stories may *not* be factual, but that's wholly beside the point. What is valuable about them is that they reveal underlying beliefs or doubts people feel but are unwilling to confess to you directly. So take the time to lean in and listen close. Care about the stories you hear and treat them as the crucial company heartbeats they are. In fact, the drift of stories over time is arguably the single best measure of corporate vitality.

Following the first layoffs in decades, the tone of stories of *all sorts* throughout one company turned sour. Suddenly *every* policy was interpreted through a new lens; management was seen as uttering doubletalk. Such a problem is not a "morale problem." It's a strategic problem of the first order. Quality decline soon matches "morale" decline. Stories are so powerful that a decade's work can be undone in six weeks. And, sadly, it may take years (and/or a change in management) to undo the damage.

The storytelling, per se, is vital. In the innovation section we noted the way a Honeywell officer explains how he encourages skunkworks: "I never *tell* my people to cheat. I just go down and chat with them. I merely describe to them what I did when I was a young man their age."

Once you realize the importance of stories, you can begin to think of yourself, in part, as a story-trail creator. Domino's Pizza Distribution, again: Don Vlcek recalls the speed and impact with which a certain story traveled through his system. He was visiting a distribution center. He noticed some unacceptably lumpy dough. As he tells it, "The quality wasn't right. We couldn't let it go out. I stopped, I rolled up my sleeves and I worked with the local team to fix the procedure. In twenty-four hours, the news had traveled twenty-five hundred miles! I got a call from one of my centers on the other side of the continent: 'Don, we heard about what you did. That's great. That's the kind of commitment to quality we need. We're behind you out here. We'll redouble our efforts.' You had to have been there to believe it." No, Don, we do believe it. Your tale has too many parallels to be coincidence.

Stories as *pictures.* How do we say this, get this right? We follow, remember, by example. King's march to Selma, Gandhi's march to the Ganges, Mao's "long march": none had much strategic—"hard"—significance. And yet each played a significant part in changing the face of a nation—the United States, India, China. USC's Warren Bennis describes Jim Rouse, city builder and rebuilder, at work, talking about teaching: "I wanted them to understand my vision. They'd come to me with plans. I'd correct the plans. They'd come back. It would be worse. This went on three or four times. Finally, when they came to see me again, I had plane tickets. Go visit [X] and [Y], look at it. It's what I mean! It worked." Bennis adds a corroborative note about Robert Redford (in the role of director) as he began shooting *Ordinary People*. He called his crew, gave them an audiotape of Pachelbel's "Canon," and said, "Ride around until you see a place that *feels* and *looks* like this *sounds*. That's where we'll begin." And a successful banker says, "A relationship with a customer is more than return on assets. I can feel a relationship when it's right. My job is to transmit that picture to my people: 'This [X, Y, Z] is what a good relationship looks like.' "

Stories and Changing Focus

Stories—or their absence—are most important at times of change. HP, DuPont, Raychem are attempting to shift focus somewhat from research/technical excellence to market/customer service excellence. Traits enhancing the former are currently enshrined in stories of all sorts. Traits desirable for achieving the latter are not—almost by definition. That is, HP has few or no Hall of Fame members who drive through sleet, snow and mud to deliver a seventeen-cent part. (IBM has a host of them, on the other hand.) HP's Hall of Famers, instead, beat down the barriers of physical science to develop a splendid new product in record time. Developing—partly spontaneously and partly through guidance—a revised or enhanced Hall of Fame (especially one that includes the factory floor and the MIS center) is arguably *the* most vital step in any major change. Quite simply, the new or modified thrust is not credible until there is a tapestry of legends to support it.

"Soft is hard" is what it's all about. We act as if the hard (tough) stuff were the formal rule book. That is *exactly* wrong. The hard stuff is the Mars story about air conditioning. The values of any organization live most humanly through stories, pictures. If we are serious about ideals, values, motivation, commitment, we will pay attention to the role of stories, myths, pictures of our vision. Bill Moore of Recognition Equipment calls it "seeing the glory." (Business people, do us a favor right now. Picture what it would be like to be served well on a flight. Translate that picture into your own company. You're on your way!)

Symbols, Drama, Language Stories:
Some Questions—and Things to Do Now

Analysis

1. Do you use symbols naturally? Dissect the last two or four visits you've made, the last two or four meetings in your office, the last two or three committee meetings you have attended. Have you consciously and in detail managed the settings: who gets invited, seating arrangements, order of agenda items, content of agenda items, location of meeting? If not, why not? Each is an opportunity to symbolize (or not) strategic concerns.

2. Do you have a conscious and well-thought-out process for managing your involvement in the rewarding process? Do you select factories to visit, sales branches to visit, workstations to visit so as to signal your approval for specifics on their performances? If you do (nice going!), do you go the next step and personally involve yourself in the selection and format for the awards/rewarding process?

3. Check the number of hourly people with whom you've come in *close* (more than ten-second "How are you") contact. What's the number/occasion? Does it adequately reflect your concern with issues of quality, service, cost reduction? Do you consciously balance the number of hourlys versus the number of supervisors?

4. Have you a spontaneous or planned vehicle for learning about real-life "mini-dramas" of customer service or innovation excellence (not the $7 million contract but the $7,000 one)? Do you collect and use those stories of real-life, down-the-line winners in your discussions with senior executives? With lower-level people?

5. Have you ever done a "language audit" (casually is good enough)? How are employees described? (Customers? Customer problems? Persistent champions?) Does *your* (and your colleagues') language show passionate pride in the institution, its products, its people, its customers? If not, why not?

6. Are you aware of the "top three" stories making the rounds of your organization today? How do they depict you and your colleagues? What do they disclose about your perceived interests?

7. Take *one* recent visit. Dissect it, minute by minute, starting in the planning phase. If you were a man from Mars (or an hourly in the Podunk plant), how would *you* interpret the whole affair? What values and concerns would it reveal/reinforce—e.g., as a function of whom you visited, in what order, and *exactly* what you talked about with whom?

Next Steps

Again, each of the items above is about "cheap" (except in terms of time) variables. You can manage *any* of them. The objective is to get your minute yet closely observed actions in line with your (doubtless) noble objectives. Select any of the seven and begin to work on modest 5 percent changes in the pattern *this* week.

Attention, Symbols, etc.: When It All Fits
Du Pont and Safety

Du Pont's safety record is seventeen times better than the chemical industry average, and sixty-eight times better than manufacturing as a whole. The fixation on safety at Du Pont goes back to the early days of the company, over one-hundred-eighty years ago, when it began as an explosives maker. This fetish spills over to produce and sustain excellence in manufacturing—and quality. That, along with Du Pont's almost equally strong devotion to research and development, is the foundation of the company's almost singular record of success.

Du Pont's fetish provides a marvelous opportunity to see all the levers—stories, language, attention—pointed in one direction. Safety is pervasive at Du Pont, defying all formal categorization. In fact, when we were talking about this notion with a senior DuPonter, he said, "It's important that you not spend too much time looking at the formal attributes, the procedures, the structures. The pervasiveness goes so far beyond that." Well, what are the symbols? Where do you see them? In the annual report, which unfailingly includes, early in the document, a major section on safety, with extensive statistics (this we've never seen before in any other annual report). Virtually every meeting, regardless of the subject matter, begins with a report on safety. Any accident, no matter how minor, must be reported instantly; the report is automatically on the chairman's desk within twenty-four hours after the accident occurs. In addition, the chairman receives an accident report from the entire $35 billion system every day.

But even all this fails by a long shot to convey the depth of commitment. At the time of our discussion in the summer of 1984 there had been a recent and relatively minor accident somewhere in the system. Our informants tell us that Chairman Ed Jefferson (remember, he's running a $35 billion business) came back to it on three separate occasions in the course of two consecutive executive meetings, irritated that it should have happened and determined to find out why.

Du Ponters are as obsessive about *off*-the-job accidents as they are about on-the-job accidents. Naturally, this obsession results in the post-

---

ing of the customary "Drive safely" signs, but—much more significantly—it also affects the annual evaluations of every unit manager, no matter how senior. In 1984 a directive went out through the system refocusing on off-the-job safety. The cause wasn't anything so grand as a rash of fatal traffic accidents; it was a rash of minor athletic accidents—e.g., a few twisted knees in summer softball games—that led to time off the job.

It goes further. Much further. Senior managers readily acknowledge that, indirectly but surely and swiftly, incentive compensation and evaluation are *radically* affected by any accident that might occur—so much so that one twenty-five-year hand comments: "If I had to choose between losing a major account and taking a minor on-the-job lost-time accident, it would be easy. I'd prefer the loss of the account."

Du Pont initiates a high visibility program to improve manufacturing quality, quality in the marketing organization, quality in various departments. It is meant to be pervasive. One thing is left out: safety. Why? Safety is far too important to be part of a "mere" program. Safety is beyond such seasonal vagaries.

In the halls of the Hotel Du Pont, across the road from the company's headquarters, Tom heard two Du Pont people chatting. They were talking about a meeting on safety they had just attended. Now, we've spent many days in many halls in many hotels across from many corporate offices, and that was the first time either of us had ever heard the word "safety."

A walk past the marketing communications department (marketing!) yields more confirmation. What's exhibited outside? Evidence of product or customer successes? No. There's a glass display case containing all sorts of safety gear that can be bought—for the employee's home. Flares, signs, to put up behind your car if you have an accident, first-aid kits and the like. You simply can't travel more than twenty feet in any direction at Du Pont without running into the safety message.

The result has been enviable: the safety record itself and a massive spillover into the entire area of product quality and manufacturing technique. The real point of this brief discussion, however, is what holds it all in place. The focus on customers at IBM is a function of many formal procedures; at Du Pont the same is true of safety. But more significant by far is the explicit and regular *attention* paid to the "it" of the company in ways that one just doesn't see in other organizations. "It" pervades the language and stories of people at all levels: the for-certain notion that one would rather lose an account than confront even a minor accident. Is this stuff—symbols, attention, language, stories—powerful? Take a trip to Wilmington and listen to the Du Pont story. You'll never ask the question again.

PREACHING THE VISION

Attention, symbols, drama. The nuts and bolts of leadership. More is called for than technique. You have to know where you're going, to be able to state it clearly and concisely—and you have to care about it passionately. That all adds up to vision, the concise statement/picture of where the company and its people are heading, and why they should be proud of it. The elements of a successful vision, we believe, lurk in our sections on Customers, Innovation and People, tailored of course to your organization's specific circumstances. The issue here, in our discussion of leadership, is not, then, the substance of the vision, but the importance of having one, per se, and the importance of communicating it consistently and with fervor. Bill Moore took on the presidency of Recognition Equipment when it was near death's door. In just a couple of years he turned it around. In an interview published in the "Speak-out Series" (1983) of the *Electronic Engineering Times* he speaks eloquently on leadership:

▶ The leader's got to have a vision of where he plans to take the company.
▶ [He] has to be able to *dramatize* that vision for his organization.
▶ If there is one role the CEO should play, it is that of "chief salesman."
▶ Too often a chief executive hesitates to get up and perform the role of cheerleader or stem-winder.
▶ Simple and direct communication should be the watchword. When you get caught up in the planning fetish, you make the business much too complicated for the average person to understand.
▶ As most of us know, it's rare that one can ask the question "What are you trying to do in this company?" and get the same answer from the guy on the production end as you get from the guy in marketing. But if you keep it simple and direct, you have a chance to achieve that consistent understanding.
▶ I think we'd all be better off if we spent more time articulating our corporate plans and less time on perfecting them.

Vision, then, comes first. General Walter Ulmer, unconventional and highly effective U.S. Army combat commander: "The essence of a general's job is to assist in developing a clear sense of purpose . . . to keep the junk from getting in the way of important things." Bourns CEO, Bert Snider: "The CEO's prime task is teaching his people what the company is all about and then getting them to teach their people. . . . It seems that a lot of CEO's don't appear to have a clear vision of what their company is about. All the ruckus about strategic planning can be reduced to a very simple idea: knowing exactly what you want to do with your company. Then you convey that." Successful Casa Bonita (restaurants) founder Bill Waugh: "My main job as president is to share the values and business philosophy. . . . The value system has to be taught through more than just manuals and reciting the values. It has to be taught through example."

Even if you're small, vision—and the teaching of it—comes first. Hamburger U. Dana U. Disney U. When we think of the top corporate training schools, we think of the unabashed culture shaping of IBM, Disney, McDonald's, Dana, Marriott et al. Yet Apple opened Apple University at an early date. They wanted to teach the Apple values—and Apple's special brand of enthusiasm—on their own turf, in their own way. We mentioned that Scandinavian Design, a modest (in size) but immodestly successful retailer of furniture, launched Scandinavian Design University early in its history. Its objective is to unabashedly teach the company's culture and generate enthusiasm: "Stage direction, lighting, theatrics, excitement. It's the way we do things."

Most will agree that Ronald Reagan has done an astonishing job on this dimension. A *New York Times* (October 14, 1984) report suggests that the magic is exactly vision, belief and dramatization: "He [an effective president] must embody a dream and values. . . . He [Reagan] is a true believer. He repeats [his simple dream] again and again because he believes every word of it. . . . [He has a] gift for narrative and storytelling. . . ." (The *Times* said all this with some implicit criticism, but read Bill Moore, et al. again: vision and communication of that vision through attention, symbols, drama, are the key, *not* perfection of plan.)

The Reagan phenomenon raises a point often overlooked: the empowering vision will inevitably be one that stresses the positive (e.g., "America's back"). Invariably, the effective visions—from People Express's Precepts to Apple's Values to Johnson & Johnson's Credo (see p. 907)—stress contribution to customers and community, growth of every employee in the company, constant seeking of the new (innovation), striving for top quality. The most effective visions tap the inherent pride that resides in virtually the entire population.

On the other side of the coin, the successful visions are also realistic, within grasp. The most effective leaders from all walks of life—the classroom, the battlefield, the corporation—have set down challenging *but achievable* visions. In the worst of times, one can always strive for doable minor improvements. Bernard Montgomery and George Patton inherited dispirited armies in North Africa. Both began their campaign by focusing on internal discipline—housekeeping, uniform maintenance, physical fitness. The avowed objective was to teach their soldiers that they were winners, could accomplish things. Nothing is more demoralizing and ultimately useless than an unachievable vision.

Concocting a Vision

Visions cannot be "concocted"! Many ask us, "How do I go about writing up my values?" The implicit question is, "What formula did General Johnson use to develop the J&J Credo?" There is none, of course. It must come from the market and the soul simultaneously. It must be felt passionately before it's published. People Express has had remarkable success, in the face of extraordinary growth, in transmitting their "Precepts." However, it is clear that the now written precepts are a passionate (and market-wise) expression of the implicit values that were within Don Burr when he founded the company. The precepts are sharper; but the unarticulated vision was there much earlier.

A vision must always, we observe, start with a single individual. We are wary, to say the least, of "committee visions." That does not mean (and again the People Express experience is confirming) that a major team effort of rewriting and buy-in should not ensue. It usually should. But the raw material of the effective vision is invariably the result of one man's or woman's soul-searching. Time for soul-searching can indeed be put aside—and should be. But above all, this process is not amenable to straightforward analysis and group process techniques.

Finally, visions are not just for presidents! From a Ford plant in Edison, New Jersey, to a Crown Zellerbach paper plant in St. Francisville, Louisiana, and Domino's Pizza Distribution Company we find clear and effective visions at lower levels of organizations—down to single clinics and class-rooms and five-person accounting departments. *If* the vision is at odds with the central view of things, executing it will be tougher, no doubt of it. However, we continually find pockets of excellence in the worst of companies— and pockets of superlative performance in the best; most are marked by a leader (at any level) with a vision that is clear and compelling.

You Can't Have It All

"Attention is all there is." I.e., if you want to create a constantly inno-vative environment, you must pay close to full-time attention to inno-vation.

Now, here's the rub: full-time attention to innovation means, by defi-nition, less than full-time attention to customers (the other of our two bases for lasting distinctive performance). The implication is clear: you can't have it all!

This issue first arose when many interpreted the *In Search of Excel-lence* message as meaning that the forty-three exemplary companies scored "perfect 10's" on all 8 "basics" presented in the book. This, of course, is not so. IBM is awesome on customer service, and a bit bureau-cratic at the innovation game; HP is the reverse. P&G scores top marks on the quality angle of customer closeness, but has also slowed a step on innovation; in roughly the same industry, PepsiCo has the reverse imbalance.

To survive in business (or in running a school, a city) you must score at least C+ at all aspects of business: financial controls, customer ser-vice, innovativeness, etc. We do, however, find that A+ behavior on all the key dimensions is a virtual impossibility. Moreover, to even seek A+

---

behavior on all major dimensions causes confusion as to just what the real number one priority is. Seeking to "get better" on all dimensions is fine (e.g., IBM's third of three precepts—excellence in execution), but seeking unmatched multidimensional greatness is not fine.

In fact, we bridle at corporate philosophy statements that say "Be the best at *everything*"—lowest cost producer, most innovative producer, highest value added producer, all-segment coverage, etc. Philosophies, we observe, are worse than useless if they constitute an undoable charter; they become pipe dreams or worse, a form of hypocrisy. (Again, let us be clear. A "program of the year" for 1985–86 to "focus on innovation" is fine, even if you're an IBM. It means "Let's improve." But the program must not conflict, at the deepest level, with the three basic IBM precepts, which clearly call slavish customer service the king, the ultimate tie-breaker. We saw a classic example of a company that understands itself in this regard. As noted, when Du Pont launched a major "quality" program, *safety* was not included. Why? Safety, the Du Pont sine qua non, is *too important* to be part of a "mere" program.

The issue best comes to life, as always, via mundane example. Raychem and HP (see pp. 173–174) gladly shut down a manufacturing line to fiddle with a prototype. Terrific, we say. It's near the heart of their skill as remarkably rapid innovators. But guess what? Such behavior translates into less reverence (than at a P&G or IBM) for meeting shipment schedules. Likewise, the IBM slavish devotion to making things smooth for customers gets in the way of HP-like innovation.

This issue is a devilish one. You can take bits of our advice in each chapter, apply them now and, we are certain, things will get better. But relative to the hoped-for towering distinction and dimension of clear uniqueness, think twice before taking on all the challenges/opportunities we present.

Finally, note that this discussion has not involved people. People are the "exception" (but not really, as we will see in a moment) to the rule. Either of the strategic distinctions (customers, innovation) rests upon a bedrock of belief in the dignity and worth and creative potential of each and every person in the organization. Thus IBM's "customers first" philosophy rests upon their precept number one—respect for the individual. Likewise, HP's "innovation first" philosophy rests foursquare upon the "HP Way" of treating people.

. . . AND LOVE

In an article in the August 1984 issue of *Texas Monthly,* reporter Joe Nocera wrote: "Several years ago Trammell Crow was invited to speak at the Harvard Business School. After his speech, the floor was opened for questions. 'What is the secret of your success?' asked one of the students. 'Love,' said Trammell Crow."

You have to have a vision, and you have to care—passionately. During a February 1984 seminar a young man, an undergraduate at Utah State University, asked Tom what he thought the most important criterion for career success might be. He clearly wanted a systematic answer. Tom turned and went to the board and wrote, in foot-and-a-half-high letters, one word: "Passion." That is, you gotta love what you do, you gotta care. Mr. Marriott, Sr., could not have read those complaint cards for fifty-six consecutive years if he had not loved the hotel business. Ray Kroc was serious: "You've gotta be able to see the beauty in a hamburger bun"; all his stories are hamburger stories— love stories about hamburgers, really. Debbi Fields, founder of the wildly successful Mrs. Fields Cookies, says, "I am not a businesswoman, I'm a cookie person."

Love translates into joy. Donald Trump (of Trump Tower in New York City and New Jersey Generals fame) has Broadway's Flo Ziegfeld and builder Bill Zeckendorf as role models because they created "glamour and pageantry" and "brought joy to what they do." Observe a meeting of a thousand Tupperware distributors, men and women. They are unabashed enthusiasts. They have fun doing what they're doing. They enjoy each other's company and success. Bill Moore says of the turnaround at Recognition Equipment: "I can't overemphasize the role of enthusiasm in making this process work."

Love in the Cooking

In an interview in the October 1983 issue of *Northwest Orient* magazine, André Soltner, of Lutèce in New York, one of the world's premier restaurants, puts it this way: "I am more than thirty years a chef. I know what I am doing and each day I do my absolute best. I cook for you from my heart, with love. It must be the same with service. The waiter must serve with love. Otherwise, the food is nothing. Do you see? Many times, I will leave my kitchen and go to the tables to take the orders myself. It starts right then and there. That feeling the customer must have is relaxation. If not, then his evening is ruined. Mine, too, by the way. How can he love, if he's not relaxed? People ask me all the time what secrets I have. I tell them there is nothing mysterious about Lutèce. I put love in my cooking and love in the serving. That is all."

Even garbage! Len Steffanelli runs San Francisco's Sunset Scavengers, the widely acclaimed model of an excellent garbage company in a giant industry. Steffanelli loves his garbage as much as Steve Jobs loves his [Apple] computers. Visit Steffanelli's office. Look at the mementos (e.g., a collection of ceramic pigs and garbage cans). Listen to him. He cares. (The flip side, of course, was aptly expressed to us by a service company executive. "If *you* [the executive] don't even love your product," he said, "why would you expect your people to?" Why, indeed?)

Successful North American Tool & Die's chairman, Tom Melohn, talks with Nancy. She asks him what he looks for in a prospective employee. Melohn scribbles something on a table napkin, hides it momentarily, and asks Elli Parrnelli, the office manager who makes the hiring decisions along with Melohn, what she looks for. She answers without hesitation: "Someone who's a caring person." Nancy adds that as Melohn looks at Parrnelli and nods his agreement, his eyes are filled with tears.*

Vince Lombardi, the Green Bay Packers legendary coach, didn't shy away from caring either. He spoke to an American Management Association group shortly before his death: "Mental toughness is humility, simplicity, Spartanism. And one other, love. I don't necessarily have to like my associates, but as a man I must love them. Love is loyalty. Love is teamwork. Love respects the dignity of the individual. Heartpower is the strength of your corporation."

Empathy

We have found no more eloquent source on what it means to care than this from a speech given a number of years ago to the Armed Forces Staff College by a former commander of the U.S. Army's blood-and-guts 101st Airborne, the late Lieutenant General Melvin Zais:

> I will stop providing you with pearls of wisdom and I will elaborate on one. The one piece of advice which I believe will contribute more to making you a better leader and commander, will provide you with greater happiness and self-esteem and at the same time advance your career more than any other advice which I can provide you. And it doesn't call for a special personality, and it doesn't call for any certain chemistry. Any one of you can do it. And that advice is that *you must care....*
>
> How do you know if you care? Well, for one thing, if you care, you *listen* to your junior officers and your soldiers. Now, when I say listen, I don't mean that stilted baloney that so many officers engage in and stand up to an enlisted man and say, 'How old are you, son? Where are you from? How long you been here? Thank you very much. Next man.' That's baloney. That's form. That's pose. I can remember when I asked my son, when he was a cadet at West Point, how he liked his regimental commander, and he paused awhile and with that clean-cut incisiveness that most midshipmen and cadets evaluate people, he said to me, "He

---

*Ah, sadness and cynicism! Nancy used this vignette in an article for a New York-based magazine. It was cut from the final copy with the editor's cryptic note: "Too emotional."

plays the role." Wow! That was damning! "He plays the role." And I noticed this officer in later life, and he postured a great deal, and he always stood with his knees bent back, and he always turned one toe out, and he always wore special little things around his collar. And, you know, he always turned sideways, and I knew what he meant when he said, "He plays the role." Well, I'm not talking about that kind of stuff. I'm talking about listening, ... listening ... 'cause the little soldier won't come out and tell you that everything's all wrong. He'll be a little hesitant. If you ask him if he's getting along all right and he just shrugs, he's getting along lousy. If he's not enthusiastic in his response, there's something wrong. You better dig a little deeper.

To care, you must listen. You care if you listen to him [your soldier]. *Really* listen to him! You care if you *really* wonder what he's doing on his off-duty activities. When you're about to tee-off on Saturday afternoon, when you're at the club at happy hour, if you're wondering, if there's a little creeping nagging in the back of your head, "I wonder, I wonder what the soldiers are doing." Do you do that? What are the airmen doing? What are the sailors doing? Where do they go?

You care if you go in the mess hall, and I don't mean go in with white gloves and rub dishes and pots and pans and find dust. You care if you go in the mess hall and you notice that the scrambled eggs are in a puddle of water and twenty pounds of toast has been done in advance and it's all lying there hard and cold, and the bacon is lying there dripping in the grease and the cooks got all their work done way ahead of time, and the cold pots of coffee are sitting on the tables getting even colder. If that *really* bothers you, if it *really* gripes you, if you want to *tear up* those cooks, you care.

It's little things. When I was in Vietnam, a quartermaster captain was bragging to me about the ice cream that they made at Camp Evans and were taking out to the soldiers at the fire bases. And I said, "That's great." And he said, "Sir, would you like to see where we make it?" And I said, "Yeah, I'd like to, very much." And I went there and they had these machines and it was pouring out into these gallon containers. And he was very proud. He said, "We get it out there every day." And I said, "That's great." I said, "What do you carry it out there in?" He said, "Oh, these containers." I said, "Yeah, but how do the soldiers *eat it*? You know, they're all in little dugouts. They're not all lined up in the mess hall. They don't have mess kits out there and things like that." He said, "I don't know, sir." I said, "*I* know how they eat it. They pass that damn thing around and they stick their fingers in it and each one grabs some. Get some Dixie cups and send them." He said, "*Dixie cups?*" I said, "Yeah, Dixie cups." ...

And I can't make you do this. But you really, you really need to *like* soldiers. You need to be amused at their humor, you need to be tolerant of their bawdiness, and you have to understand that they're as lousy as you let them be, and as good as you make them be. You just have to really like them and feel good about being with them.

Finally, the general quotes from a newsletter he had written while commanding the 101st Airborne:

> You cannot expect a soldier to be a proud soldier if you humiliate him. You cannot expect him to be brave if you abuse and cow him. You cannot expect him to be strong if you break him. You cannot ask for respect and obedience and willingness to assault hot landing zones, hump back-breaking ridges, destroy dug-in emplacements if your soldier has not been treated with respect and dignity which fosters unit esprit and personal pride. The line between firmness and harshness, between strong leadership and bullying, between discipline and chicken, is a fine line. It is difficult to define, but those of us who are professionals, who have also accepted a career as a leader of men, *must* find that line. It is because judgement and concern for people and human relations are involved in leadership that only men can lead, and not computers. I enjoin you to be ever alert to the pitfalls of too much authority. Beware that you do not fall into the category of the little man, with a little job, with a big head. In essence, be considerate, treat your subordinates right, and they will literally die for you.

Personality: Roadblock to Success?

Is there a certain kind of person who alone can exhibit the leadership traits we have described and praised? The wonderful answer is no. Or, nearly so. That is, the leaders we've learned from are neither unfailingly extroverted nor unfailingly introverted. They *are* visionaries, but then, as Jan Carlzon (SAS) says, the visions are often quite garden-variety: "We had a vision: to be the 'businessman's preferred airline for Europe.' But everyone else has had that vision. The difference was, we executed."

Ah, there's the key. These leaders seem to pay *equal* attention to soaring ideals ("a gift to the spirit"—Max DePree; "the perfect potato"—Herman Lay) *and* the details of execution (Rodgers of IBM: "Above all, we want a reputation for doing the little things well").

Tom once wrote a short column for the *Wall Street Journal* entitled "Ideas, Plans and Actions." It suggested that the best leaders were comfortable moving back and forth between (or working simultaneously with) the highest abstractions (visions, ideas) and the most mundane details (minute-to-minute actions). Even their language illustrated the point. Ren McPherson, Marcus Sieff and Jan Carlzon talk of vision, but invariably illustrate their visions with stories of a specific first-rank person at the retail counter, on the line or in the Podunk factory.

Many (Walton of Wal-Mart, Carlzon of SAS, Watson of IBM, Mary Kay Ash of Mary Kay Cosmetics) did/do see "all business as show business." Yet a Stanford student chided Tom severely for using that phrase. "It cheapens the whole process," he said. "Look," Tom replied, "it's not *my* fault. I'm using Watson's and Carlzon's *exact words.*" That leads, indirectly, to our last point. All of life *is* show business. Our life, to each of us, is a spell-binding drama, and we play, day in and day out, the lead role. Time and again, we are put upon, are not fully appreciated or loved, are misunderstood. Thus, we would argue that the specialness of Perdue, Gore, Staley, DePree, McPherson, Melohn and Walton is that each allows (encourages) humanness, the very essence of it, to pervade his organization. Each creates "places to go," "places to be." Commitment, passion, zest, energy, care, love, and enthusiasm can be readily expressed. And unashamedly so. And that *is* their distinction.

If you're not quite there, getting there takes some nerve. It *does* mean letting go of paper control, the comfort of ten staff reports before acting, before siting a rest room. But we urge that every manager give it a shot. Start with a two-week stint on the graveyard shift at a customer facility. Start with a graveyard shift in your own operations department. Goethe said that in order to understand the world it's necessary to select an *Eckchen,* a small corner of it, for contemplation. We sorely need, in managing our enterprises, to get beyond our almost total dependence on committees, staff, reports, and rules. We need desperately to select an *Eckchen,* to begin to get back in touch. We need to begin (again?) to depend, instead, on people—the power of commitment, ownership, verve, zest, enthusiasm, celebration, and love.

Take a look at your calendar—now. Are you *living* your proclaimed priorities—when it comes to people, to quality, to innovation, to service? Have you painted out a parking spot today? Have you held a celebration? Have you eliminated at least one unnecessary rule or form? Have you responded to a customer's complaint or query? Have you shared doughnuts on the loading dock at 2:00 A.M.? If no to all the above, you're out of touch. You're not living values connected to sustainable strategic excellence, no two ways about it. And there's *nothing* to stop you, darn it. No Capital Appropriations Committee is in your way. Only *you* stand in your way, you and the vestiges of the management theories that we and others have foisted on you in the past, "proving" to you that you should—instead of buying doughnuts at 2:00 A.M. for the distribution center team (as Sam Walton does)—hunker down, call in the staff and review yet another 600 clever overhead transparencies. We're sorry. We were wrong. Terribly wrong. But *you* should have known better! Now is the hour.

17

Transformations and Enhancements: Small Wins, Debureaucratizing and Pockets of Excellence

Attention. Symbols. Drama. Language. Stories. Vision and love. These are the stuff of effective leadership, much more so than formal processes or structures. But another thread needs to be pulled into this tapestry. In discussing strategic distinction, we argued that it is, above all, built upon a base of one thousand things done just a bit better. Subsequently we suggested that such a strategy leaves no choice: the thousand little things will come only from "ownership" at all levels of the organization, from the executive suite to the newest hire on the loading dock.

Missing in all this is any practical suggestion on how to move methodically toward a systemwide overhaul. We gave advice on shifting calendar content, on listening to customers, on supporting good tries that end in failure. But just how do you get the whole thing started? Our answer is the *small win* (and a system for generating a *string of small wins*) and debureaucratizing (that is, consciously policing, nipping in the bud, or rolling back the excessive regulations—and regulators—who get in the way of ownership). Thus these two tools constitute opposite approaches in a sense: building winners and ownership and adding momentum, on the one hand (small wins); and keeping people from becoming losers or disenfranchised on the other (debureaucratizing). We find both are essential elements of either enhancement of already good performance or transformation of an unsatisfactory situation.

SMALL WINS: THE EFFICIENT PATH TO SUCCESS

In some respects this represents a new tack. In most respects it doesn't. Our focus when it comes to initiating change and leading it is unfailingly on the mundane, the trivial, taking advantage of the typical nine-minute act that Professors Henry Minzberg and John Kotter find so characteristic of the general manager in *The Nature of Managerial Work* and *The General Managers,* respectively. That we tout "Small is beautiful" should come as no surprise.

Let's be concrete. We want to offer an example, one that we now use as the primary vehicle for teaching implementation in our executive seminars (the ones known as Skunk Camps). It's the story of Sam Neaman and McCrory's told in Isadore Barmash's *For the Good of the Company.** Neaman was brought into the ailing McCrory's chain in the sixties by Chairman Meshulam Riklis. His background included experience as a garment manufacturer in Europe and owner of a steel plant in Mexico. Here he describes his start:

> I had no [formal] authority, but here was my opportunity. It was a store that had lost money. I wanted to know what it took to make a good store, so I said to John [the store manager], "Look, we are going to form in this store a group of people, a team, and you'll be the quarterback. You and they will visit all the competition in town and write up what you find. You'll check out merchandise and write it up. Every evening you'll hold classes with a blackboard and will have a consultation with everyone. I want to know the sum total of our know-how by taking a sampling of a group of people dedicated to finding out what they can do thinking together. For weeks they studied the store. They had a tough time agreeing with each other, but they did. The spirit was sky-high; excitement was beyond description. Why? For the first time they were given a chance to express themselves as individuals and as a group, each one giving the best that he knew. Not a nickel was spent. Every change was made from what we had in the store. Floors were changed, aisles widened, walls painted. It was a new store, a pleasure to the eye.
>
> What put that store across? They knew they had to visit all the competition and then visit our store with a cold eye. They applied what they learned. Up till then, they had to look at the eyeball of the boss and guess what it was he wanted. All I did was ask them to use their senses and their heads, and I got a damn good store.
>
> Over the next two years, it reduced its losses and then started making money. After all the hustle and bustle, the whole company became aware of it. The chairman and his entourage came running to see what was happening. Now everybody jumped on the bandwagon. Now everybody wanted a district—every vice president, the executive vice president, even the chairman. . . .
>
> Show the people a way. That's what I did. I even had a place to send everyone. Indianapolis. "Go to Indianapolis. Go there, look at the store,

---

*The McCrory's example was used in *In Search of Excellence* to illustrate the general point about experimentation, but was never analyzed. We have vaulted it into a preeminent position; here we subject it to intense analysis.

and learn. It was put together by people like you, using spit and polish and only their own normal talents." A little while later, in the home office, I changed the pattern. To a variety-chain vice president, who was in charge of buying, I said, "All right, Joe, you don't have to go to the Midwest. Do me an Indianapolis right here in New York. You have seen it can be done. But I don't want you to copy it. We will keep Indianapolis as a sort of school." I told him to give me his version of a good variety store in Flushing. Well, several weeks later he invited me to the store and I found one of the most beautiful retail stores I have ever seen. I immediately invited a few others to see it. You would never have believed that this horrible store could be the attraction of the neighborhood and the jewel of the company. Sales began rising right away, and the store became our best in New York. But what it also did was to challenge the other home office executives to go out and do an Indianapolis. As the parent company began to brag more and more, I extended the variations, I used the idea of the Indianapolis stores as a visual aid, getting the people to bring it into shape, then bringing others to see what they did. This became a substitute for writing memos or giving instructions on the phone. Instead, I said, "Come look and see. This is the new company—nothing else is—this is it!" I instructed every district [10 to 15 stores] that it must have its own model store. Every district manager would have to reflect all his knowledge in one store and from that "Indianapolis" improve all the stores in his district. The idea caught on like wildfire. They did it evenings, Sundays, holidays. The Sundays became big shindigs with beer and food provided by the store's restaurant manager. They had the year of their life getting the chain in shape, all 47 districts.

Before analyzing this, we want to answer the question, "Why listen?" McCrory's long-term record is arguably not worth emulating. But true though that might be, the fact remains that the results represented by this brief vignette are exceptional. Sam Neaman was a miracle worker. His efforts with some six-hundred stores led to a remarkable increase in profitability in a short period of time. It was a personal clash with the headstrong Riklis that led to a breakup between the two, and dashed hopes for the project Neaman had so auspiciously begun.

We will break our analysis into two parts. First we want to talk about Indianapolis as a simple experiment. Then we will talk about the experimenting process per se. Indianapolis is, in the scheme of things, a "small win," or to put it better, a small win made up of many even smaller wins. What are its attributes?

The Small Win: Doability

Above all—and this theme runs through our whole discussion of leadership, subtly and sometimes explicitly—the small win is about *doability*. It's about tasks (and subtasks) that can be done by "real people." Mr. Neaman turns the average performer into a star. Or, better stated, he *allows* the average performer to *find* that there *is* a star within him. He began with a single store. Moreover, it wasn't a high visibility store. It wasn't being looked at under a microscope by top management as *the* "experiment." Neaman trundled off, without portfolio, and dug around for several weeks, observing the ins and outs of the McCrory system. And then he happened upon Indianapolis. He had learned enough to be ready to take a next step. But he didn't begin with a call to the architects, a plea for capital expenditures for a new store. He didn't begin with an arrogant, brash "Throw the existing turkeys to the wolves" attitude. He began with the idea that the people in this store were all worth saving; they had simply been misled. (Tom Watson, Sr., took that same view with the disheartened and disoriented C-T-R [Computing-Tabulating-Recording] Company, which he inherited in 1912. He didn't fire people. He said they had the stuff within them to become winners. It's been the approach of IBM ever since.) It was *their* show. He told people to go out and *look* at the local competition. Not do competitive analysis in the "on paper" (abstract, sterile) sense, but have real people (e.g., the woman who sells purses at McCrory's in Indianapolis) go out to the store next door and take a look at the counter where the same goods are being sold. (As one senior manager said to us, "I'll bet, and it would pretty much hold for us, it was the first time that anybody like that had really taken that kind of a look at a competitor.")

Then Sam introduced one heck of a routine. *All* hands gathered together *every* evening—five evenings in a row each week—to look at what they had learned that day, to talk about it, to debate what it meant. Real-time feedback, based on real-time collection of tactile data. Not systematic market research, but *real* people collecting *real* impressions about *real* things about which (it turned out—as it always does) they knew a lot. Neaman knew who the experts were: the people in those underled McCrory stores who hadn't been allowed out or hadn't had the motivation to go out, who had not been asked their opinion in years, if ever. His focus was on the tangible. Not *analysis* of purse departments, but *visits* to purse departments. How do *they* display the merchandise? The vehicle and process, the nightly meeting, was vital. It wasn't easy. Doubtless the discussions were forced or stilted at first. People had gone through twenty-five years of learning *not* to talk, *not* to speak up. How did he get them to speak up? He did it by putting them to work in areas where they were legitimately expert. He didn't tell them to expound a retail philosophy. He told them to talk, in nuts-and-bolts terms, about something they understood—their twenty-five square feet of turf. (The words of Dana's Ren McPherson echo in our ears: "When I'm in your twenty-five square feet, I'd better listen.")

So the focus was on doability, tangibility, *speed* (24-hour feedback, low budget, real people talking about actual experience). No staff or "experts" were allowed to meddle. *Self-analysis* was essential.

Neaman's wonderful term is "guided autonomy." The "guided" part was based on his clear vision. Not a clear vision in terms of shelf-display algorithms. But a vision such that he would *know* when he had a "beautiful store." It was perhaps mystical, maybe Zen-like, but certainly real to him. And he rapidly made the *possibility* of it real to others. And the autonomy? (It sounds a lot like "ownership.") The group of locals—"People like you, using spit and polish and only their normal talents" were his words—was to figure out how to get from here to there. He gave them spirit: beer busts on the weekend, yes, but mainly a purpose. It was *their* game, *their* store to fix, *their* store to build. The company was in trouble. There was no capital available. They weren't going to get $2 million to build a spanking-new store. Lamenting the fact that Penney's had a better nationwide distribution system wasn't going to do them a bit of good. They had to figure out a way to turn the store around—on their own. He was rigid in only one thing. He clearly dictated the outline of the process, the daily feedback sessions based upon analysis of real-time data. So the three pillars were *vision,* ("guided") *autonomy* and a rigid real-time *process.*

A "learning system" is vital. Learning is an inadequate word; a constellation of terms like real-time, momentum-building is better. And make sure the learning "system" or process encompasses (and generates) many small wins. Get people to make daily assessments; then act on those assessments. (Incidentally, the small-win, quick-feedback process actually *generates* practicality. Go out once a year with a call for suggestions, or focus on the few big $5,000 awards, and you reap what you sow: big, largely impractical suggestions. Develop a system that "demands" a suggestion a week and process it in a few days and, lo and behold, you induce practical and implementable suggestions—e.g., a new way to hold a welding iron.)

Consider another pair of words: *opportunity* and *constraint.* Managers, according to the consultants and the academics, are "constrained." Neaman, said, in effect, "The heck with constraints." He got his people to look at that Indianapolis site and the Indianapolis process as an *opportunity:* "Figure out what *we* (you) can make of this."

Finally, an "experiment" does not have to be a present or future event. Interestingly, it can have happened in the past. Here's how it works. At Hewlett-Packard, most managerial skills—R&D, manufacturing, etc.—are taught by a vehicle called "best practices." The best practitioners are sought out and a composite of their work patterns (not rules) is used as a model. An IBM officer, assigned the task of being the quality "czar" of a division, took the same tack. Frustrated by his inability to define quality based upon textbook analysis, he sought out the "best receptionist" and so on; these real-time models became his operational definitions of top quality. Such devices need not be the province of superstars alone. In our experience, the *worst* of organizations have top performers, worthy of emulation. Thus a marvelous way to "save steps" and get on with a new program is to ferret out bits of good news from the past: e.g., one receptionist who does the job well. Though these obviously must soon be matched by new good news, they should at least help you to hit the ground trotting.

Ownership and the Small-Win Process—Natural Diffusion

Let's move to the small-win process per se. Here's where the true genius of Neaman shows itself. What was Neaman's trick? We think, above all, it was *patience,* the fact that he wouldn't let people *copy* Indianapolis. Neaman said others could come and *look* at Indianapolis, *visit* Indianapolis, *touch* Indianapolis, *feel* Indianapolis, but they could *not* copy Indianapolis. Indianapolis became a model, a symbol, a story, a small win. It was, moreover, a tangible example, and therefore what was most important—given the way humans process information—was that it was *real.* A staff-generated book on "how to do an Indianapolis" would *not* have been real.

This point is vital because it touches on the single most important reason why most new programs fail. Many—ranging from quality circles to rejuvenated factories—do develop an Indianapolis, one shining star that's touted because of some powerful and extraordinary champion. But then there's a horrible tendency to say, "Boy, oh boy. We've got a winner. Let's take advantage of it—*now!* Let's write down *exactly* what happened at Indianapolis. Let's write it up as a case study. Let's turn it into a book, a procedures book." What you're saying, of course, is: "Let's shove it down the throat of each of the leaders of the five-hundred ninety-nine other stores." By doing so, you kill the fatted calf because the magic, it turns out, isn't the *specific* techniques of Indianapolis; it's the sense of *ownership* and *commitment* so patiently developed—allowed to develop—within the Indianapolis operation/context.

At the Dana Corporation, Ren McPherson's vision of "turning the company back over to the people who do the work" was his own form of guided autonomy. McPherson hammered away on productivity, ranted and raved about it, lived it—his calendar vividly illustrated what *his* priority was. But he didn't *tell* his people what to do. In fact, he made his central staff's mission the exact opposite of what the staff's mission usually is. At Dana, staff ceased to be enforcers. They became leaders of a natural diffusion process. That is, they became people who went out on the road to find good-news stories and to tell other people about them. They were *not* to suggest explicitly that what worked in Toledo ought to work in Dayton, but simply to tell the people in Dayton what happened in Toledo—and let them learn from it if they could, if it made sense in *their unique* setting. Now the staff *did* become "experts." They became experts in diffusion. They became experts in exposing people to other people's experiments. And, in two annual Hell Weeks, success stories were swapped with memorable intensity.

Eschewing "participation through mandate" is, of course, basic to what Neaman did. After a successful "Indianapolis" became visible, he then unearthed an aggressive headquarters person who volunteered to "do" a Flushing. And then a few more came aboard. He let the process take its course. He nudged, to be sure. But he nudged by providing people access, the opportunity to become excited. He did not mandate. The process took a long

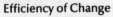

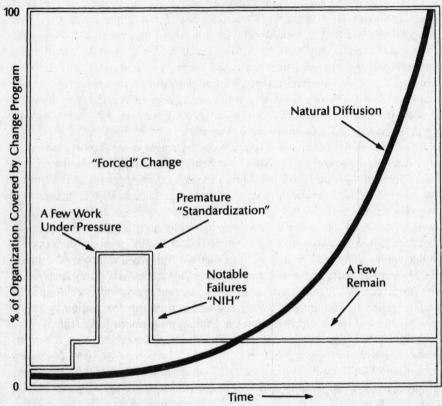

time. The people who were impatient after seeing the startling Indianapolis success were doubtless dissatisfied. They wanted to sweep the Indianapolis experience through the system; the result would undoubtedly have been an out-and-out disaster. There would have been some initial change for the better, to be sure, but things would soon have leveled off. The upshot: just one more program shoved down the throats of the operators by a smart-aleck corporate staffer, one more great hope shattered by year's end.

We've drawn up a conceptual chart to illustrate the McCrory phenomenon. The overall point is that the natural diffusion process, albeit slow at the start, is a process that is ultimately more efficient—*and faster*—than the one following the principle of "Change by mandate." You nudge a program into existence—i.e., cause/create an Indianapolis. Then, having decided to go the "Force it" route, you send in the staff. You draw up a manual—mandate it. People do, indeed, listen. There *are* additional successes. But because the program has been mandated, two things happen. Commitment is vitiated (NIH—Not Invented Here—at work), and there are some failures (because Indianapolis *was* unique—each location is). Soon the vultures descend (in all change programs, the vultures are close at hand): "See? See? I told you Indianapolis was a fluke. Great market. Dumb guy in charge before. Neaman's the only reason it happened. He forced it." The skeptics (always far outnumbering champions in the early days) have a field day. And the program peters out. A little of the good is left, but the system in general returns to rest close to where it was before.

Now let's look at the alternative to the mandate: natural diffusion. The start is usually painfully slow, an exponential curve, as pictured. Finding the second and third "champion" (inducing him or her to come out of the woodwork) is often agonizing. But then the diffusion process begins to take hold, and the champions (even including skeptics, who are unfailingly good "straw-in-the-wind watchers"; more on that later) queue up. Failure is by and large avoided because near champions—who are committed and ready—are the early proponents; they make it happen. Then as news of their results spread, there are more and more successful experiments to learn from in a non-threatening situation. The odd conclusion, of course, is that the natural diffusion path turns out to be *more* efficient, speedier. Those who said "we haven't got the time to wait for volunteers to surface" are ultimately proved wrong.

We want to stress that natural diffusion does not stand in the way of planned forums (à la Milliken's Fabulous Bragging Sessions, discussed on p. 878) or a traveling staff with videotapes spreading good news (à la Dana). In fact, these devices constitute exactly what *can* be a consciously managed "technology of diffusion" aimed at maximizing the speed of spreading the word and maximizing peer pressure. But what is maximized by management is, precisely, diffusion—not a forced march.

After Flushing (success no. 2) was completed, Neaman did indeed go another step in turning up the flame under the "guiding" process. But the increased heat was wholly consistent with his guided autonomy model. Remember, he had forty-seven districts of ten to fifteen stores each. He insisted (now that he had demonstrated, via Flushing, that Indianapolis was not a fluke) that each district have its own "Indianapolis." Each of the forty-seven was to have one model store among the ten to fifteen. He assumed at this point that a district boss could find at least *one* would-be champion among his branch managers. And from those (one in ten to fifteen), the natural diffusion process would flow again, stepped up in pace a bit. And so it happened.

Let's shift focus to these vital champions for a moment. The single most important piece of advice we think we can offer to would-be major-change managers is the following: For heaven's sake, go after the easy stuff first! What's the thrill of beating your head against a brick wall? Sam Neaman found *someone* he could work with at Indianapolis. Then he found someone else who was ready to roll, who did Flushing. Then he sought one in fifteen (one per district): These were the champions, the handful of people who, even in the worst of circumstances, in the most bureaucratic and stifling environments, *do* want to get on with "it" urgently. In our experience such champions *always* exist. So begin with the people on the ten-yard line. Give them a big push to help go the last ten yards and score a touchdown. It's absolutely vital. What a previously defeatist system needs most is momentum and a handful of believable successes and new role models. What it needs is to understand that there *can* be winners. What it needs is to see that there are incipient champions who *can* be successful in this (previously) stodgy environment. Mr. Indianapolis became a champion. Mr. Flushing became a champion. Then the one in ten to fifteen became champions.

The chart on the facing page illustrates this. We find that in any system there are some "lunatic" champions out on the fringe. They'll unfailingly do their own thing, often successfully. But, perhaps surprisingly, they really aren't the heart of the systemwide change process, as we've described it. Why? Because they'll always be considered lunatics by their peers, decidedly not "just like you and me." The fact that they behave strangely—albeit effectively—is of little comfort to the rest of the gang. But what we want desperately is the next group, the group that we view as between the five- and the fifteen-yard line. They're about ready to charge. They're energetic. They're would-be champions/skunks. They haven't yet been wholly beaten down. Push *them* to be the champions of the Indianapolises, or Flushings, or of the first store in each district. They, by dint of their location on the distribution, are *not* lunatic fringe. They are not *quite* "just like you and me." But they decidedly *are plausible, credible* role models. And then, once there are a few credible wins and winners in the system, and once we've been smart enough to celebrate them (yet not force the example they set down others' throats), *then* the next group will catch on. They are, say, the next 20 percent of the distribution—they are seducible, still far from being hardened skeptics. *Now* you do have the ball rolling! The key is *always* to go after the next bunch of the nearly converted. Proving that the true skeptics are indeed truly skeptical achieves nothing, except that you've dented your pick and probably permanently diminished your credibility (and failed to appreciate the vital importance of building a fragile momentum).

(An odd thing does frequently occur. The most hardened skeptics are *not* the last to come on board. Straw-in-the-wind watchers that they are, the hardened skeptics—the laggard tail of the normal distribution curve—will often jump on the bandwagon as momentum builds and progress appears to be more than fleeting. It's the center of the distribution, the neither angry nor particularly seducible bunch, that is more likely to climb on last.)

And the job of senior managers in all this? Go back to the previous chapter. They're in charge of the *symbols*. In charge of finding and nurturing that original Indianapolis into being, and making darned sure *it* doesn't fail. You need that first small win, and you need it desperately. To this end, spending a *full* year of your life on a "trivial" Indianapolis, just one store out of six-hundred, is likely the highest and best use of your time. (Similarly, spending a

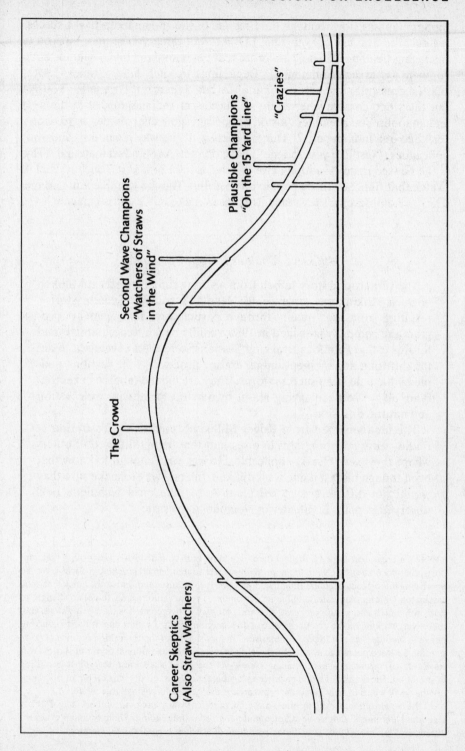

month planning how to make the first *day* of the Indianapolis trial a success is likely the best use of your time.) Others will think you're nuts; but you're managing (leading) the delicate process of beginning to build a winning environment. (One sage commented: "Beginnings are such delicate times.") After that (successful) start you become historian. Symbolist. Dramatist. You get out the video camera when there's a success at Indianapolis, or at the next Indianapolis. You are noter, poster, publicist, visible cheerleader, hero anointer. "See our Indianapolis?" This is a *picture* of the way it can be—and your colleagues ("just like you and me") have done it. As Sam Neaman said, "This *is* the new company—nothing else is—this is it." Look at it. Touch it. Feel it. Watch that film. See those people on that film. They're just like you and me. They're no different. They made it. You can make it. We can all make it.*

Milliken's Fabulous Bragging Sessions

The turnaround story (albeit from a strong running start) at Milliken bears a striking resemblance to Neaman's routine. Success stories, resulting from the "quality through participative management" program the company launched in 1980, rapidly began to accumulate, and forums called Fabulous Bragging Sessions were then developed to aid the diffusion and momentum-generating process. At the sessions, people by the bale swap success stories. They are indeed fabulous, exemplifying all we've been saying about ownership, small wins, celebration and natural diffusion.

The idea emerged from Roger Milliken's continuing frustration at finding nifty new programs in one plant that hadn't diffused to others where they were clearly applicable. He was wise enough to know that even though his last name was Milliken, the one way to make sure they would not diffuse was to *tell* plant A to take on a technique he'd observed in plant B. (Shades of Neaman, to be sure.)

---

*There's a great deal of psychological theory, relating both to individuals and groups, that supports the observations we've made here. With respect to individuals, psychology focuses on the overriding importance of commitment, if motivation is to be sustained, and of the quick feedback associated with human-scale, tangible achievements. The literature on resistance to change (in both individuals and groups) suggests that the best way to overcome it is taking tiny steps, and, moreover, working on the positive ("we can do something right"), rather than trying to confront negative feelings directly. "Social comparison" theory speaks to the critical importance of competition between peers, and systematic research focuses on the exceptional power of stories ("little knots of meaning")—e.g., Indianapolises—as the most significant way of transmitting information. The dominant strain in current learning theory heralds the importance of role models; the small win is exactly about the rapid creation of plausible, positive role models.

At the organizational level, the most powerful theories now speak to the importance of "organizational learning." What we've talked about here, under the heading of Sam Neaman's "guided autonomy," is a model for the textbook paradigm of efficient organizational learning.

So the Fabulous Bragging Sessions (more formally, Corporate Sharing Rallies) were born—out of the notion that it was essential to get people together somehow to share war stories. Here are some of the elements, some of the things Milliken's people have learned along the way:

1. Frequency. *Corporate* Fabulous Bragging Sessions are held every ninety days. Held less frequently and the momentum is lost. More frequently and they eat up too much time, even by Milliken's tolerant (on this dimension) standards. Each session lasts almost two full days.

2. Structure. In the course of the two days a hundred or more teams will present ideas or success stories. Teams will come from any of Milliken's scores of facilities, and may travel several hundred miles to make a five-minute presentation. Attendance at the sessions is wholly voluntary (the practical limit has been the size of the facility). Several hundred people usually show up, and many more are waiting in the wings.

3. Few "rules." Milliken President Tom Malone did have to install three. First, no negatives. Plain and simple, no criticism of any team's presentation is allowed (this reminds us of the Gores, who quite literally outlaw the term "devil's advocate" at W. L. Gore & Associates). The second rule is that there is no such thing as a "big" idea or "small" one. Ideas are evaluated on their quality, and a fine idea that brings in a small savings in a clerical department is considered as much a winner as an idea that generates a giant improvement in a factory. Third and finally, "I coulda done it [done it better], *but* . . . [e.g., but MIS wouldn't help out]" is not allowed. You are responsible for making your "it" happen, period.

4. Themes. Each quarter's bragging session has a major "theme." One time it's sales enhancement. Another time it's quality enhancement, or what Milliken calls its "center-cut program" (a program through which they attempt to surpass their customers' quality standards by 70 percent or more). The next quarter it's cost reduction. All in all, the sessions rotate through about a half-dozen themes, around which all the presentations at any session are focused.

5. Tangible objectives. Each improvement is to be reported with a quantitative outcome indicator, but the quantitative indicators are not "audited" by any outsider to the group. Honesty is up to the presenting team. As Malone says, the last thing people are likely to do around their peers is inflate an outcome. "They'd BS me at the drop of a hat," he notes, "but not each other."

6. Voting. Milliken wants to make sure that teams/people don't "win" just on the basis of clever presentation. So several criteria have been developed for voting on projects. One of them does focus on the quality of the presentation, but the rest stress various aspects of the idea per se. (Malone asserts that peers are exceptionally tough on one another. After the early sessions he found himself voting almost all presentations "excellent." Peers, however, did not.)

7. Everyone a winner. While several ascending grades of awards are given to those who have the outstanding presentations, everyone and every team goes home with a framed certificate simply for participating. Moreover, there's a subtle ritual that Malone engages in which speaks a thousand words. He usually finds an outside speaker to come in for a couple of hours very near the end of the session. During that time Malone and his colleagues are hard at work, signing and framing every award certificate. The grand finale is an awards ceremony, during which, on the spot, each participant is handed (by Malone or chairman Roger Milliken) his or her framed and signed certificate.

The corporate Fabulous Bragging Sessions at Milliken are only one element, albeit the most dramatic, of Milliken's extraordinary quality enhancement program. In addition, sharing/bragging sessions are held within each facility prior to each quarterly corporate extravaganza; Malone visits scores of these as well. Teams with top ideas may end up presenting several times: once or twice within their facility, at the corporate sharing session, and to the corporation's senior management group. Each corporate president's council meeting, in fact, is kicked off by several stellar teams making presentations.

The effort is by "all hands." In each facility the secretaries and loading-dock bunch will likely form teams, as will the people running the giant weaving machines. Malone reports that it was tough at first to figure out how to get the sales and marketing people involved (a common lament of those who are working quality circle programs and their kin), how to move them beyond the traditional role of the salespersons-as-Lone Rangers. Nonetheless, he decided to plunge ahead, and the results have been gratifying. The salesperson is made "chairman" of a CAT (Customer Action Team) that includes participants from various supporting disciplines. Very tough targets—for instance, to double sales with a particular customer within ninety *days*—are set. "Doesn't this mean that the team goes after 'small' customers?" "You bet," Malone says. "But getting the involvement and getting the point across that such objectives can be set and met is what it's all about, after all, isn't it?"

Another intriguing element in Milliken's program is the extent to which it has come to include a "bottom-up push." As you might guess, some old-school supervisors didn't exactly leap aboard. To Milliken's delight, these supervisors' people ganged up on them: "We want to present. Why can't we? Everyone else is. We want to go to the Spartanburg Session." Time and again the reluctant dragons were dragged in from below.

It's vital to note here that the ongoing personal attention (quantity and quality) paid to the quality program by Roger Milliken, Tom Malone and the senior Milliken team is the crucial ingredient that's absent in most similar programs. Most quality drives are kicked off with great gusto and then lose momentum. There are several reasons. Flagging attention is one. Another is the fact that most focus only on the so-called substance (some dramatic outcome), not the *process* necessary for sustaining all-hands commitment to the goal. Milliken's program, at the end of four years, is *still* picking up steam. Much of the reason is the continued energy directed at the process generating and sustaining momentum—the Fabulous Bragging Sessions and all that surrounds them.

The Management Role in Small Win-Induced Transformations— a Summary:

▶ Ferret out would-be champions and would-be sites for first and subsequent experiments.
▶ Sanction experiments "caught in midstream" or just getting under way.
▶ Sanction the notion of experimenting.
▶ Label the experiment a success (if warranted), or a part of the experiment a success; "toast" the results in notable ways and become chief publicist of partial and wholesale experimental success(es).
▶ Buffer new experiments and would-be champion-experimenters from intrusive staff, not only those obvious stiflers who have an apparent need to say no, but also those who *like* what they see and want to prematurely pry (for good and well-intended reasons).
▶ Arrange peer pressure (competition, visits, publicity) that is rapidly transmitted to people in similar settings.
▶ Work hard to keep the NIH phenomenon from arising; for example, as Neaman did, by allowing no exact replicas or premature (forced) implementation of ideas.
▶ Be sure that first or early champions cannot be denigrated as "crazy" (as nonplausible role models) and that first successes are not distinguished by extraordinary environmental circumstances (somebody builds a ninety-story office building right next to an old store).

The Small-Wins Process:
Some Questions—and Things to Do Now

Analysis

1. Review a priority program dealing with enhancing a strategic skill, especially one that's stalled. Are you taking on the world, or have you identified a potential champion and a potential "Indianapolis"? If the latter, is your Indianapolis site marked by "Sam-like" traits: (1) not of such darned high visibility that all eyes are upon it, (2) *your* obsessive attention, (3) doable/visible

positive outcome within the next 90 (30? 15?) days? Try again. Are you *really* committed to making the Indianapolis a success? Are there *any* (be honest, now) higher priorities on your agenda? Do you know the "real people" in your Indianapolis well enough to be able to answer this question and predict the outcome?

2. The process: Do you have one? How are you recognizing Indianapolises? How do you seek them out? Support them? Hide them from probing bureaucrats? Do you celebrate with real fanfare? How often? Is your staff still focused on "cop tasks," or are they aimed at "managing the diffusion process"? Do you have an explicit, well-planned, thoughtfully construed process for conducting Fabulous Bragging Sessions/Hell Weeks? How often do you get your "experimenters" together? (If the answer is less often than once every three weeks, think about it.)

3. What is your visitation record re those experiments? Last 120 days? Last 15 days? Last week?

4. What, *explicitly,* have you done to publicize/reward/give prizes to your new heroes? Are heroes credible?

5. How "public" are you with your support of the experiments? Are you on videotape? Do you *unfailingly* (i.e., at every *in*appropriate opportunity) speak, in story form, of early successes?

6. When's the last time you talked to a "champion"? If "over forty-eight hours ago" is the answer, why so long?

7. How do you keep your finger on the pulse re how many of your colleagues/subordinates are starting *their* Indianapolises? Is it prevalent? If not, why not?

8. Do you (and colleagues) regularly talk about the Indianapolises in your organization?

Next Steps

Pick one important program, seek out an Indianapolis demonstration activity to get it off stall. Look for a would-be champion "on the ten-yard line," not a skeptic (even if the champion is ranked "too low," according to the formal structure). Within the next 5 to 10 days, say, plan for inducing an Indianapolis with *some* results in the next 30 to 45 days. Talk with your colleagues about urging one Indianapolis into being in each of their top priority/opportunity areas.

Marv's Meetings: Small Wins, Big Outcome

Cross-functional noncommunication is at the heart of most management problems. It is the genesis of the matrix structure—so beautiful on paper (it solves all those nasty communications problems) but invariably horrendous, at least in practice. Well, let's just take a look at one more place with obvious cross-functional problems and look at their (definitely nonmatrix) solution. We work from time to time with the Northrop Corporation's $1.5 billion Aircraft Division, where the materiel/purchasing function is run by Marv Elkin, whom we introduced earlier. The materiel/purchasing function is important in any organization, but in the world of advanced avionics and the like it's especially important—probably 70 percent of the cost of the aircraft comes from outside purchases. Well, different functions don't talk to one another—*anywhere*. In hospitals the nurses don't talk to the doctors. In banks the lenders don't talk to the operations people. As we said before, in industrial companies the engineers don't talk to the manufacturers. Salesmen everywhere are seen to be self-serving blowhards. And, of course, *nobody* talks to the purchasing guy!

Elkin, however, has found a way to beat the rap. What is it? Oh, oh, is it b-o-r-i-n-g. He has a bunch of programs going. They are called FIN-MAT, TECH-MAT, Q-MAT. So what does that jargon mean? The first, FIN-MAT, is a team that involves supervisors from the finance area (FIN) and the materiel (purchasing) area (MAT). In the second, TECH stands for technology; in the third, Q stands for the quality organization. FIN-MAT simply means that the finance people *meet* with—i.e., talk to—the materiel people. What could be simpler? *Or rarer?* It works this way. Sometime in 1983 Elkin got the idea that the best way to overcome the seemingly God-given barriers would be to have people meet and learn to appreciate each other. So he got together with the head of finance and suggested that they take about thirty people—the top fifteen managers in each area—and go off-site for two or three days "just to discuss things." They did. It was a revelation for all involved: each found out the other function was made up of human beings with reasonable objectives. An agenda of doable cooperative tasks began rapidly to emerge. At least as important, people got to know others, so they could call on them as colleagues, not adversaries, when a problem came up. They decided to continue the dialogue. They went off-site once a month. ("It's hard to do a 'Gotcha' on a guy you've been drinking beers with once a month," Elkin says.) At last count, they had been doing so for fourteen consecutive months.

Well, it's working! Now they'd never think of abandoning it. They no longer go off-site; that was, Elkin admits, "a con": "It's the only way I know to get 'em away from the phones." He adds, "Now that they've gotten used to the program, we can do it on premises. Moreover, the program was at first dictated. That is, I insisted that my people go, and [the finance person] did the same. Now, as the program is well under way, we've made it voluntary." What's the result? Has attendance dropped off from thirty to four die-hards? To the contrary: Elkin was so pleased with the process and the results that he decided to do the same thing with technology people, and then with the quality group. Hence TECH-MAT and Q-MAT. Each has followed the same course.

Now, what's the big deal? None, we suppose. But let's look at it again. There are a bunch of factors at play here. The first one obviously is leadership. Elkin was bound and determined to make it work. He paid attention. Second, as discussed in the Neaman case, he looked for an "easy opening": namely, the finance man, who was a solid individual who believed the same things Elkin did. Elkin didn't go after the most recalcitrant fellow; he went instead after the colleague who was the most sympathetic. Third he (they) didn't really have any objective other than "making things better." The meetings weren't for the purpose of browbeating or "getting your [the other guy's] act together." Fourth, the effort was marked by *intensity* and *persistence.* Once a month. Month in and month out. When will they be "finished"? Never, we presume (hope). And they do, too.

Degrees of Winning

The small-win theme pervades this book—especially the extensive discussions of "ownership" (in the section on People). This is because we know of no other sure fire way to generate momentum and create a winning tradition, especially when a turnaround is required, than through small wins that turn all hands into winners—*and at their own pace.* Winning is a key word. Almost all of us believe we're winners. Tom and Bob Waterman reported a study in *In Search of Excellence* that suggested that almost 100 percent of us think ourselves in the top 1 percent of the population on cooperativeness, in the top 25 percent on leadership; and even when an objective skill is the subject—i.e., athletic talent—about 75 percent of us put ourselves in the first quartile. Yes, almost all of us think we're (very) hot stuff. Yet most of our organizations go out of their way to disconfirm that daily.

We're not talking about a Pollyanna's world view here. Mars, Inc., is hardly a "soft" company, yet every person gets a weekly 10 percent bonus—including the president (in a $6 billion company)—if she or he comes to work on time each day! And, yes, it *is* quite an accomplishment to get up five mornings in a row and show up on time with the car's battery run down and the latest bout of the flu about to set in.

Most of the companies we think highly of proceed according to what we call a "degrees of winning" principle rather than a "degrees of losing" one. Moderately good performance is touted. It's true at Tupperware, Disney, McDonald's, Mary Kay Cosmetics, The Limited Stores, Mars Inc., Milliken, Stew Leonard's, People Express and Hewlett-Packard. Even IBM. IBM works like the devil to make sure that fully 80 percent of its sales force is successful. Now, of course, it does offer special recognition for the top 3 percent—the members of the Golden Circle. But more important, to our minds, is the fact that fully 80 percent are celebrated as members of the Hundred Percent Club.

Creating Winners: Are "They" Ready?

We hear the following time and again: "Many companies are now highly centralized and autocratic. You recommend, almost without caveat, radical decentralization and greatly enhanced doses of autonomy. But isn't it true that some people aren't ready for it immediately? Or ever?"

That is, are people ready to do an Indianapolis? There are two sides to the answer. The first is to acknowledge that the problem does exist. Speaking of the encouragement of numerous, sometimes duplicative product-development teams at Hewlett-Packard, a division general manager says, "We can only allow the apparent chaos because of the bone-deep belief we all share in superior product quality and the way in which people should be treated." Indeed, we do, flatly, find that there is little worse than creating autonomous teams willy-nilly, before beliefs to guide the teams is clear.

There is, then, a necessary order: values first, autonomous teams second. For instance, Campbell Soup, as we noted, is undertaking radical (for them) decentralization right now. But before launching the transformation, Chairman Gordon McGovern took all his senior colleagues through a lengthy and agonizing reappraisal of the company's value system, in which respect for quality stands out at the very top. Johnson & Johnson may have the most radically autonomous units of any company we've investigated. At the same time, it has as rigorous, regular and tightly articulated a value-review process as any we've observed—an annual, intense review of its credo called the Credo Challenge. Also, J&J's Statement of Strategic Direction is clearly autonomy-guided-religiously (almost literally)-by-the-Credo. (See chapter 18, on coaching.)

The same line of reasoning holds for individuals as for teams. The creative party giving of the autonomous Tupperware salesperson becomes "magic" only because she is "overtrained" in the Tupperware Way before ever being allowed to conduct her first house party. That is, Tupperware ensures beyond a reasonable doubt that the first independent try will indeed result in a small win. Likewise, the "harshness" of, say, IBM's full liability policy (salespersons are docked out of *salary* for prior commissions earned on IBM equipment that is removed from a customer's premises while that customer is one of their accounts) only works as well as it does (and does not create nightmarish conditions) *because of* the superb training that salespersons receive. That is, they are "ready"—fully prepared—to deal with their tough environments. We, in fact, have become great fans of the IBM, Tupperware or Disney sort of "boot camp." Substantial autonomy without prior training "overkill" is a sure prescription for disaster.

The important flip side of the "Don't give them premature autonomy" issue is widely misunderstood. First, most people *are* responsible—*now;* are ready for *far* more autonomy than we commonly suspect. (Neaman's story is fine evidence.) It's also essential to note that it is not a fair or symmetrical world. The analyst's bias, albeit unintentional, is almost always on the side of "They're not ready *yet.*" And the analyst is dead right! The new general manager, the superbly prepared Tupperware house party giver and the Disney ticket taker alike *will* make a host of mistakes early in the game. The only way to be fully "ready to be there" is to have been there—a classic catch-22.* So one must be terribly careful not to allow "They're not ready yet" to hold sway forever.

The early days following the granting of enhanced autonomy, then, no matter how well planned, will always be marked by minor—and often major—glitches. However, the experience we've had with scores of people who have granted increases of autonomy is that in almost every instance—and here's another rub—*if* it's done with goodwill (a genuine belief that it will work), the results are positive. Most managers, *if* they've given it an honest go, are literally shocked at the amount of responsibility that units and teams with a new sense of ownership take on and the speed with which they take it on. In fact, much of the "problem" arises because teams do so well, making it readily apparent to the supervisor that he is less needed than he thought!

DEBUREAUCRATIZATING

We spend 30 percent of our days in off-site senior management meetings. At each, it seems, some fair share of the time is spent railing against unnecessary bureaucracy. And it should be. We have said that there are only two paths to lasting strategic dominance: constant innovation and superior customer service. Further, each is wholly dependent not upon mystical techniques but upon ownership—i.e., the creative contribution of each person in the organization. And what most gets in the way of ownership—on the loading dock, in the mail room? Unnecessary bureaucracy. So, logically, inescapably, cleaning up the bureaucratic gunk *must be* the number one strategic priority.

At each meeting we attend, top management promises to do something "serious" about it; maybe even something quantitative: "Cut the paper by 25 percent." And then they appoint a low-level committee to carry out this so-called prime directive. By doing so, they ensure that next year at this time *nothing* will have happened.

If you're gonna do it, you gotta do it! (Profound, eh?) No ifs, ands and buts. The *Newsweek* cover story of August 1984 illustrated this point in even the heartland of bureaucracy. General Walter Ulmer, who has no stomach for

---

*This reminds us of the old saw: Good judgment is the product of experience; experience is the product of bad judgment.

bureaucracy, reduced "several feet of local regulations [theretofore perceived as unalterably imposed by higher-ups] to less than two inches." In the processed-steel industry, Worthington Industries' John McConnell, Sr., never had corporate policy manuals to begin with. As a young man working for other companies, he decided that policy books and rules restrict rather than guide. If he ever had his own company, McConnell determined to treat people the way he would have liked to have been treated as an employee. The Worthington Industries philosophy fits on one small card, and reads simply: "We treat our customers, employees, investors and suppliers as we would like to be treated." Period.

Remember Ren McPherson, who in 1969 produced a one-page operational philosophy statement to replace Dana Corporation's hefty collection of corporate policy manuals? Add Marcus Sieff of Marks & Spencer, who began his tenure as managing director by taking a one-year "sabbatical," as he calls it. He spent the entire period, with virtually no exception, reducing the company's paperwork. He eliminated 80 percent of it, or, he judges, 27 million pages a year. Sieff brought that year to a memorable close by piling the 5 tons of useless paper into a massive heap, striking a match, and hosting a company-wide bonfire.

General Principles for Operation
Simplification at Marks & Spencer:

1. Sensible approximation—the price of perfection is prohibitive.
2. Reporting by exception (only when absolutely necessary).
3. Manuals—no attempt is made to legislate for every contingency and every eventuality. (Before simplification there were thirteen instruction manuals, and now there are two small booklets: *Guide to Staff Management* and *Store Regulations*).
4. Decategorization—people have been removed from water-tight compartments and placed in general categories.
5. People can be trusted, so checks can be eliminated. This, in turn, saves time, staff and money, and leads to increased self-confidence and a sense of responsibility among staff. Control can be effectively exercised by selective and occasional spot checks, which are usually more satisfactory and productive and certainly less costly than a whole series of permanent control systems and continuous routine checks.

A friend at Hewlett-Packard concurs. Since a major body of sound psychological research has reached the conclusion that we can hold only a half-dozen things in mind at once, our friend insists that his assistants never use more than half a dozen measurement parameters when they measure something. He says, "Look, I want *everyone* to be a businessperson. That means everybody—the most junior clerk—has got to understand how the business works, totally. So we only measure half a dozen things. People become familiar with them, can see how they interrelate, how they vary as a function of what we're up to. If some smart-aleck young analyst comes along and wants to complicate it, I say, Fine. Five measures are the maximum. Do you want to prove to me that you have two better measures? Don't bother. You just go ahead and add your two, but then get rid of two existing ones. We simply won't let the total go above five."*

CONTROL IS NOT A FORM

We had just been through another discussion of Willard Marriott Sr.'s habit of reading complaint cards. An executive in a mid-sized health care firm piped up: "Control is not administration. It's not control via forms. It's *exactly* those fifty-six years of card-reading." Control? Formal? Informal? A former Marriott regional vice president, once a property manager, adds: "It may be 'informal control' to you, but it's got teeth. Mr. Marriott's habit meant that you had one hundred forty property managers working twenty-eight-hour days, fifteen-month years, to make sure that the old man had a very, very, very light reading load!" Du Pont, as we noted, demands that all accident reports be on the chairman's desk in Wilmington, Delaware, within twenty-four hours of the occurrence. Control is the knowledge that someone who is interested and cares is paying close attention.† Real and effective control comes from a *small* number of *simple* rules (or measures) that are *directly* consistent with the organization's vision. Mr. Marriott Sr.'s complaint-card reading is perfectly consistent with his and Bill Jr.'s vision of Marriott's hotels as those that best serve the customer.

Even when one does feel the pressing need to venture in the direction of "rulism," it need not mean the 175-page manual. In fact, there need not be anything "ordered" at all. Hewlett-Packard—(and IBM to a lesser extent)— runs almost every aspect of the company according to so-called best practices. There isn't a rule book. Instead, HP captures the best ways of doing things—for the receptionist, the design engineer, the manufacturing foreman. They actively collect these best practices and put them together in what we like to call "storybooks," chockablock with hard-edged examples of how real

---

*Goldsmith and Clutterbuck made a similar point in *The Winning Streak:* "One immediate observation of most of our successful companies, which contrasts with many unsuccessful companies, is that they try hard to keep central controls to a minimum. . . . That doesn't mean that the controls are lax. Quite the opposite, in fact. As a general rule, it seems that the fewer controls exercised by the centre, the more strictly line managers are expected to adhere to them."

†The ultimate: in Singapore, strongman Prime Minister Lee Kuan Yew reads the quarterly grade transcripts of each young man and woman the state has sent to the university on a special fast-tracking program to prepare for public service. "Do your homework" takes on special meaning, via this "informal" review!

people ("your peers") best perform common tasks in accordance with the "HP Way."

Milliken and Company has taken the same route. In their effort to improve customer listening skills, most units have launched several experimental programs. They want to share results widely, yet abhor excessive rules; moreover, they don't want to shove one person's/groups's experience down another's throat (see the preceding chapter). So they've taken to constructing a master binder. Stories (good-news outcomes—usually small—of successful experiments) are collected and regularly added to the binder. What a lovely alternative to a 300-page rule book in bureaucratese on "how to listen to customers," put out by a "genius" (or a committee of geniuses) on a corporate marketing staff!

A small retailer, running a $4 million store, invented a similar routine. Her objective was to describe to new employees how the store did business and what it stood for. She tried to write a rule book, but that wasn't the way she really wanted to run the store, and besides, the thing immediately began to get lengthy—fifty pages before she had batted an eye. So she chose an alternative approach. She got all of her people together, some seventy-five, on about five occasions. She had them submit their best stories, orally or in written form, about when they were most proud of the way they had presented themselves to their customers and fellow employees. Those stories, edited down, formed a thirty-page booklet of "examples of how we do things." They are the heart of the company's training program, and constitute both its philosophy and its book of rules. Moreover, the document is a *living* one: people are proud to add to it, to get their examples into it, and so they constantly offer up new material. (Lo and behold, the store has a problem with the length of "the book" because people keep adding stories—or "rules"!)

It Takes Guts

We have never seen a form or manual that couldn't be reduced by 50 to 75 percent. But it does take *guts* to give up on the paper. Paper is a form of security, and something *is* lost when it's given up, something that must be replaced by mushy old trust (abetted by prior training and development). And it takes guts of another sort, as well: A friend runs a forty-person establishment. Someone was fired (for, it seems to us, just causes), and for a while it appeared that the separated employee might file a suit, which, though frivolous, would have been expensive and time-consuming to defend. One day her lawyer sat our friend down and took her through the routine she *must* follow, he said, in order to avoid such eventualities in the future. It turned out that if she followed through exactly, she would have to accumulate an FBI-like dossier on each of her people. She refused flatly, because to do so would be in complete contradiction to the people-oriented philosophy behind her

> fine and spirited (and profitable) business. "I'd rather be sued and lose than become an undercover agent spying on our people" was her conclusion. And it took guts.

Control Is Not a Form:
Some Questions—and Things to Do Now

▶ Anti-Mickey Mouse Brigade I: This afternoon or tomorrow stop in on a first-line person (this will take about one-half hour). Ask him or her what the dumbest form/dumbest rule/dumbest report/biggest minor irritant is in the daily routine. What are you going to *do* about it? (Can you get rid of it/revise it on the spot? You likely can.) Repeat the exercise once per week for ten weeks. Repeat once per month—forever. Have your assistants (and/or your secretary) do the same thing (and perhaps empower them to act on what they find). Variations: Purposefully mix visits to more senior first-line people and to the most junior (week 1, 2 or 3 impressions are invaluable). Try it outside your area of responsibility—you and a colleague supervisor (or VP) can probe each other's area usefully.

Report on it: Post a big scoreboard on "Mickey Mouse removed." How about an anti-Mickey Mouse Hall of Fame for those who remove the "dumbest rule/form/etc."—best (i.e., worst) of the month, year. Blue ribbon, red ribbon, gold awards for ten forms demolished, silver for five. And a meeting with the president for twenty-five! (Why not?)

▶ Anti-Mickey Mouse Brigade II: Repeat the above with a team focus: e.g., get teams together to decide on the "three dumbest and most amazing rules." Etc. (Our experience shows this *does* work. First-line people have an acute and fair sense of what's needed and what's not, and will rarely propose removal of useful rules/forms, unless we've been keeping them in the dark and not telling them what we're up to in the first place.)

Caveat: This process *will* work. Beware. It snowballs. If you're not serious, you will be overwhelmed. Backing off is high hypocrisy.

▶ Report in the Annual Report—quantitatively—on progress made in debureaucratizing!

▶ Consider replacing a large share of your procedure books with "best practices" books. Or highlighting a strategic program (à la Milliken) with a "significant recent wins" book.

▶ Pencil in 10 percent of your calendar time to work directly on anti-Mickey Mouse activities. Do *two* things *today*. Do *two* things tomorrow. Do a minimum of *five* this week.

WHAT GETS IN THE WAY: STAFF SIZE, LAYERS

One of the regular rejoinders we get to all this is, "I'm really a good guy. We do all this Mickey Mouse only because the EEO or OSHA requires it." But the fact is that while the EEO, OSHA and others *do* obligate us to do some reporting, our overzealous, overstaffed middle managements tend typically to take a fairly simple request for a report and turn it into a 97-line requirement for information from all the company's operating units. And another fact is that you can invariably (and this is said after four years' experience in Washington) drive a Mack truck through any regulation. Yes, *something* is required, but seldom what staffers, justifying their existence as "OSHA experts," tell us is required.

The most important deterrent to debureaucratizing is often simply the layers of staff that get in the way. Moreover—worst of all—it's the layers of *intelligent* staff. One division general manager of a smaller concern notes: "The problem is, the [central] staff guys are *smart*. If they were dumb, and if they asked dumb questions, we could ignore them. But they're smart, and they ask smart questions, smart questions that can tie us up for days, if not weeks and months. And if it were just one request, that would be fine, but it's multiple staffs, with multiple centers of intelligence, asking multiple series of smart questions that really keep us from getting the job done." Every line on every form and every form itself has a "champion" just as tenacious as any "product champion," who believes that life itself revolves around that particular packet of data.

There is, then, a lot that can be said for simply cutting staff. We find so many companies that do so much better with so many fewer people. Our journey through the terrible recession of 1981–83 was peppered with stories of company presidents who had cut their staffs, often by up to 80 percent. The only noticable difference in output, they'd tell us time and again, was *better* staff work. Said one, "I went to every management development course that came along. It seemed that each one would encourage me to add a specialist to help me with some task at which I was deficient. My dad, a wise soul who had founded the company, shook his head every time I'd add another one. Brother, was he right. We find that we're living a lot better—more effectively as well as more efficiently—without seventy-five percent of them."

The other piece of improvement is fewer layers. It makes decision-making simpler and faster. But a word of warning: Right after a reduction in layers too much will be bucked upstairs for decisions. You'll be appalled. But if you have the guts to refuse to decide—i.e., the guts to buck the decisions right back down—the system will soon learn that you are serious. The prime benefit of flat organizations is what we call their "self-defense" properties. That is, *none* of us is smart enough to keep our hands out of our subordinates' business. But if the span is wide (at least twice as wide as you think wise is a good rule of thumb), then you simply don't have enough hours to interfere, though most of us try desperately to do so at first. Flat structure, in a word, automatically breeds ownership, whether you like it or not. "But what if 'they' aren't ready?" We dealt with that one in the preceding chapter. They usually are—and in any case in the flat organizations your role shifts dramatically from monitor/decider to coach/teacher/developer (see chapter 18). The issue, it turns out, is this: Are *you* ready? Because your new number one objective—like it or not—*must* be getting "them" ready once you've decided to make your move.

"Upside Down" or *"Right Side Up"*?

How do you draw your organization chart (if you feel you must have one)? "Right side up?" or "upside down?" "Huh?" you ask. Look at this one:

CUSTOMERS

First-line people who design, make, sell and service products for customers.

First-line people in direct support of first-line people who support customers.

Other

An "upside down" organization chart, to be sure. "No," screams Ren McPherson (we can still hear the echo in our ears). "The other [standard] one's 'upside down.' This one's 'right side up.' " McPherson introduced us to the reversed chart. He used it at Dana. We've since come across them at Wal-Mart, Nordstrom and SAS, all fine performers.

> The "reverse" chart is a simple depiction of business success. The customer comes first. Our first-line people in line functions who support him come next. Below them come first-line people in support functions (MIS, accounting, personnel). Finally management (called "other" here).
>
> We don't necessarily suggest you adopt some version of this chart. To do so willy-nilly could be gimmickry of the worst sort. The four companies we mentioned live for their customers and first-line people; given that, the chart is a fine confirmation and reinforcement.

The few illustrations we provide aren't meant to serve as specific advice for anyone. But they *do* suggest that there are *radically* different approaches to organizing—i.e., more than one way to skin a cat. In *In Search of Excellence* it is noted that Ren McPherson had been able to reduce the corporate staff at Dana from 600 to 150 while the company was simultaneously growing from $1 billion to $3 billion. In 1984, several years after his departure, the staff is down to the low eighties, and the layers of management, which he reduced from eleven to five, remains at five. Similarly, *The Winning Streak* reports that British Steel's then Chairman Ian MacGregor began his realignment efforts there by cutting central staff from over 1,000 to 170, and moving them from a "Taj Mahal" in London to a very modest situation.

But let's take an even more extreme example: Mars, Inc., is a complex business: sixty divisions, almost two-thirds of its sales overseas. Divisions are allowed to compete openly with one another. Moreover, each one of those sixty divisions faces tough outside competitors. In other words, it's a prototypical multi-industry, multisegment, multiproduct, multinational enterprise. It's a clear case, in a characteristically low-margin business, of a situation commonly believed to require strong centralized control—"checkers checking checkers," as a frustrated chemical-company colleague puts it. Yet somehow Mars runs a highly profitable $6 billion enterprise with a corporate staff of just twenty officers and twenty secretaries (in a nondescript building without a sign on it, at the end of a road that you can barely find *with* a map, in McLean, Virginia).

Or, yes, an even *more* extreme example: Nucor Steel, based in Charlotte, North Carolina. Chairman Ken Iverson manages to run a $552 million company (as of 1984—with a five-year return on shareholder's equity of over 23 percent) with a corporate staff, including secretaries, of less than a *dozen!* And make no bones about it, Iverson sees his lean form as perhaps his most vital strategic weapon. He was asked a while back what he could do if he were called upon to run one of the giant steel companies. His immediate response: "The biggest hurdle would not be the union. It would be the management with its deeply ingrained method of operation—all those layers. You'd have to tear it all apart and start over again."

Part of the issue *is* sheer numbers. Mars, Nucor, Dana et al. have fewer people on their staffs. But numbers may be a less significant part of it. At least as important is *where* these staff people are. At Dana, for instance, very few of the victims of the reduction from six-hundred to eighty-five were laid off. Instead, they were given the opportunity to go to where the action was—to the plants. Mars doesn't necessarily have fewer accountants per dollar of revenue. The accountants are where they can best support the company as businesspersons—in the plants, in the small divisions. A funny (nice) thing happens. Remember one of our themes: "All people as business people." Accountants (lawyers, etc.) *can* learn to act as members of a profit-making team, not just as referees or cops. A senior controller in retailing was able to get about 75 percent of his people out of corporate headquarters. "Time and again," he said, "I would send them out to the field for close to permanent duty, as part of a 30- or 40-person profit-making team. Once they became full-scale members of the team, and I made it clear that the primary dimension of their evaluation would come from what that profit-center boss thought of them, then suddenly they became business people—not just 'accountants.' "

All this is easier said than done, of course. In headquarters-focused companies, the sole objective is to reduce the number of feet between you and the chairman. Most big companies, sadly, fall into this category. Decentralizing only works effectively—and attracts the best people to the field—when the reward system (e.g., subsequent promotions) starts to say "to be in the boondocks is to win." At HP, Citicorp, GE (today, under Jack Welch), the unmistakable be-all and end-all is creating "wins" as far from headquarters as possible. And implicit in this fact is a reward structure based on "good deeds performed," wherever, rather than "a good presence" close to headquarters.

Staff as Support

January 1, 1984, was independence day for seven regional companies—the remnants of the Bell System. One, say most experts as of the end of 1984, has fared better than the rest (though most have done well): U.S. West, the Denver-based regional.

Above all, it's said, U.S. West is more aggressive, more entrepreneurial. We know at least one reason for it. Each of the seven regions (which made up the twenty-two former operating companies of the Bell System) got a "bonus" upon formation: 3,000 central-staff people from the old AT&T central apparatus. Most organized them as AT&T had, as centralized operations. U.S. West did not. It stuck by CEO Jack McAllister's "rule of 100." The staff of U.S. West would not exceed 100, period. Such an iron law was mandatory, he felt, to induce the decentralized entrepreneurship he cherished.

So what do you do with the other 2,900? The answer was simple (to McAllister). Form a wholly owned support subsidiary consisting of the

2,900. Moreover, keep the U.S. West central staff out of the act. Have the subsidiary chaired (on a rotating basis) by the head of one of the three decentralized operating companies that the 2,900 are designed to support (the other two operating company heads constitute the rest of the "board"). Thus McAllister took a giant step toward (1) enhancing incipient but fragile entrepreneurship (by keeping the central staff *very* lean—100 for a $10 billion business) and (2) putting support people in clear support of those whom they are supposed to support (the three line operating companies). So simple. So rare.

"Staffs"/"Layers": Some Questions—and Things to Do Now

▶ We don't want to suggest a "study" on optimal staff size. You will do what is appropriate when you think it necessary. We would suggest a "pre-first step." Become a student of spans of control and staff size. Seek out some organization in your industry (and outside it) known for especially lean staffs and flat organizations. Visit them, see how they survive. Try to begin to observe other ways of life. This is a big deal. It's worth your investment.

▶ Consider relocation of staff, even on a temporary basis. Check back in your experience to times when "staffies" have been assigned as full-time members of business-unit teams, with evaluation coming from the business-unit leader. Did it affect their behavior? Did they become more "business-oriented"? If so, as we suspect you'll find, consider an experiment with several accountants, etc., going out to a field unit (under the field leader's control) for three to nine months. Revisit the results and consider more sweeping changes.

PULLING IT TOGETHER: POCKETS OF EXCELLENCE

And if I'm not chairman or division general manager? Or even if . . . ? This is a book for chief executives and a book for first-line supervisors. It is a book for Fortune 100 executives. And for those who run garages and corner stores. The two strategic distinctions—superior customer service/product and constant innovation—are the key for CEO and supervisor. What makes his or her outfit unique on these dimensions is a valid question for Chairman Jack Welch of GE, Stew Leonard of Stew Leonard's and the head of an accounts-receivable section in a $20 million division of a $100 million company. The lessons of leadership are available to anyone and amenable to instant action.

So—if you're not chairman, we suggest subversive acts. Don't answer the mail from headquarters. It works! The logic is this: if we are even half right when it comes to the power unleashed via ownership (see chapter 14), then giving people in your unit some room will likely—and quickly—result in substantial improvement in performance. It's your best defense. People with the best store, sales branch, department, crew are seldom fired for lousy paperwork. Ren McPherson said of his own odd practices on the way up: "I came close to being fired six times [the first time for sharing results—e.g. profitability numbers—with all the people in his plant, at the time an unheard-of act of ownership enhancement]. But when they came right down to it, they had a tough time firing the fellow with the top performing outfit." A former IBMer, then a market forecaster, tells another story that's apropos: "One Sunday I was doing some repair projects around the house when it occurred to me that most of the people providing me with data were subsequently not promoted, or left. The best seldom answered my queries. I talked to my boss about it the next day, and he replied, 'Of course. To get to the top of the heap, they [the best] spend more time with customers and have little patience with bureaucracy. Once they are on top of the heap we're hardly going to ding them, except perfunctorily, for tardy paperwork. Only the marginal ones, scared for their jobs, are slavish devotees of requests from headquarters. They're petrified of accumulating the tiniest black mark.'"

Oil or Paper?

A colleague in Kuala Lumpur reports on a bureaucratic insurrection. Years ago the head of Royal Dutch/Shell Malaysia had had enough. He gathered up a vast stock of requests sent out to him by Shell headquarters. He knew the board was meeting in The Hague. He hopped a flight and went there unannounced—highly irregular behavior in general, and even more irregular given the staid nature of that board. He arrived at the meeting, and, for all practical purposes, barged in. He opened the suitcase on the spotless, orderly table and dumped out thirty pounds of forms, asking as he did so, "Do you want me to fill these out or hunt for oil?" We have no report of the immediate reply. However, we do know that the Malaysian boss did go on to head the Royal Dutch/Shell Group, and to lead it through a necessary and profitable overhaul.

Insurrections don't always lead to eventual promotion to the top. But they surely can lead to a dramatic performance improvement in a part of the organization. Our evidence is clear. Even if the company is not an exciting one, we observe *pockets of excellence*. Excellence is what you, the supervisor (or vice president), create on *your* turf. We see great factories in rotten manufacturing companies, super buyer areas and great stores in moribund retailing establishments, a fine and aggressive specialist/lending operation in an unduly conservative bank. It can be done and it is done. The principal tools are the small win—semi-surreptitious creation of Indianapolises à la Sam Neaman, or Westborough, Massachusetts, basement bunches à la Tom West's Data General skunkwork in *The Soul of a New Machine;* and debureaucratizing—creating a void in an otherwise oppressive and constricted system.

In this we are *not* Pollyannas. The fact that your store (or department within a store) is great does not mean the qualities that make it so will spread to the rest of the company. Major overall corporate transformations tend to be top-down, not bottom-up. But that is no excuse for not getting on with it among your people.

Small Win as Demonstration

"It's so tough to convince top management of the rightness of the 'new way' [Whatever it is]." Top management got there through pragmatism. Logic will seldom be decisive to them, even yours. Demonstration may be. A small win is a demonstration. Don't fight City Hall! Do it. Demonstrate it. (Via your own Indianapolis.) We don't believe in fighting, especially old pros. We do believe in the process of demonstrating that alternatives *are* possible.

There is one guaranteed "win" from all this: you'll feel better about yourself! Serving customers, innovating, celebrating, inducing ownership and local heroism through a string of small wins and by cutting out the Mickey Mouse is likely to be a damn sight more satisfying than being a "good steward" of one part of an aging and stultified bureaucracy. We think it's important to picture yourself looking in the mirror at age fifty (or thirty-five, or sixty). What will you see? "A good steward"? One who "did his forms well and made good presentations"? Or something a little more exciting?

We dwell on this last point because of a sense of sadness. We recently ran into an executive vice president of a $10 billion company. This fellow ran a $3.5 billion portion of it. And yet his direct response to our remarks was, "But *I* can't do anything. The chairman is flatly opposed to most of the things you speak about." Had it been the first time it had happened, we could have written it off. But it was more like the forty-first.* How sad! *Not* "how sad that the

---

*Two of the saddest came from the public sector. Both concerned MBWA. A city manager of a town of 500,000 said, "The supervisors would think I'd lost my marbles [if I spent 50 percent of my time doing MBWA]." We referred him to the actions of Mayor Schaefer of Baltimore. A county school superintendent uttered virtually the same words, suggesting painful consequences from the reaction of his board if he were to start wandering the schools.

chairman opposes." But "how sad that this fellow [in his mid-fifties] *perceives* that he can't do anything about it." Perhaps pitiful is a better if harsher term. (And then there is the chairman who can't do "it" because of the government, the securities analysts or the board.)

It *can* be done. Mayor Schaefer has done it with a city. Bill Creech did it in the Air Force. Phil Staley did it with an old Ford plant. And the accountant we described on p. 894 did it with an accounts-receivable section in a stodgy company.

18

Coaching

Virtually every day, a couple of the engineers in my section get calls from competitors inviting them out to lunch to talk about their futures. A key aspect to my job, obviously, is to keep this group motivated, enthusiastic. . . . The best managers are the ones whose people want to get up in the morning and work for them. The secret is making it clear to your people that you care, that you're really interested in them as individuals. They need to know that you appreciate their efforts and that their accomplishments are recognized.

Hewlett-Packard Research & Development
section manager

Perhaps if there has been one failing within our organization over the years, it is that we haven't tried to dispel the notion that our success comes out of a computer. It doesn't. It comes out of the sweat glands of our coaches and players.

Tom Landry, head coach, Dallas Cowboys

Has the leader a right to mold and shape? Of what use is aging, experience, and wisdom if not to be the leaven for those who are younger? Of what use is pain if not to teach others to avoid it? The leader not only has the right; if he is a leader, he has the obligation.

Harry Levinson, The Exceptional Executive

There is no magic: only people who find and nurture champions, dramatize company goals and direction, build skills and teams, spread irresistible enthusiasm. They are cheerleaders, coaches, storytellers and wanderers. They encourage, excite, teach, listen, facilitate. Their actions are consistent. Only brute consistency breeds believability: they say people are special and they treat them that way—always. You know they take their priorities seriously because they live them clearly and visibly: they walk the talk.

The trick is demonstrating to people, every day, where you want to take your organization. It begins with a shared understanding of purpose, made real and tangible through consistent "mundane" actions. It's being amazingly consistent that counts, ignoring the charge (which will be leveled) that you are a broken record. Some of the brightest and best-trained managers we know miss the boat entirely on this score. Once they've said it, they've said it, is their feeling. But the only thing that convinces people that you really care, that you take personally your commitment to them, is unflagging consistency. And it is a commitment: for instance, virtually all the best-performing organizations believe in promotion from within their own ranks. At the 275-store Publix SuperMarkets chain everyone on the retail side of the business (including the company's officers) started his or her career bagging groceries.

Fine performance comes from people at all levels who pay close attention to their environment, communicate unshakable core values, and patiently develop the skills that will enable them to make sustained contributions to their organizations. *In a word, it recasts the detached, analytical manager as the dedicated, enthusiastic coach.*

Coaching is face-to-face leadership that pulls together people with diverse backgrounds, talents, experiences and interests, encourages them to step up

"*I understand you've learned some new tricks since you were here last.*"

Drawing by C. Barsotti; © 1981
The New Yorker Magazine, Inc.

to responsibility and continued achievement, and treats them as full-scale partners and contributors. Coaching is not about memorizing techniques or devising the perfect game plan. It is about really paying attention to people— really believing them, really caring about them, really involving them. New Orleans Saints coach Bum Phillips observes: "The main thing is getting people to *play*. When you think it's your system that's winning, you're in for a damn big surprise. It's those players' efforts."

To coach is largely to facilitate, which literally means "to make easy"—not less demanding, less interesting or less intense, but less discouraging, less bound up with excessive controls and complications. A coach/facilitator works tirelessly to free the team from needless restrictions on performance, even when they are self-imposed.

In these next few pages we will talk about some of the most vital aspects of coaching: visibility, listening, limit-setting, value-shaping, skill-stretching. To develop one's skill in these areas is not easy; it does not often come naturally and must be worked at. But, oh, the rewards that can follow! Think back on your career, starting as far back as elementary school. Almost all of us can name a handful (but only a handful) of superior coaches—teachers, sports or nonsports activity leaders, bosses—who have contributed disproportionately to our development, almost as if they had laid a magic hand on you. They drew from within you a best that you couldn't have conceived of.

Tom remembers two such people. The first was Ned Harkness, who led almost anti-athletics Rensselaer Polytechnic Institute to NCAA titles in hockey and lacrosse. He became Tom's lacrosse coach at Cornell after the tragic death of the former head coach. Tom had played the sport, as all good Baltimoreans do, since age six. Yet his skill grew more under Harkness in a week or two than it had in the prior decade. Harkness knew his stuff—was technically commanding. But much more important, he instinctively (it seemed) knew his players' limits. He pulled you to those limits (which in Tom's case were well short of stardom) and beyond, but never pushed you to discouragement. And, above all, you knew he cared, cared individually about what was going on in your head as you faced tiny (and not so tiny) defeats and exhaustion, as well as occasional victory.

Tom's other all-star coach was Dick Anderson, captain of a Navy Seabee (construction) batallion to which Tom was assigned as an ensign in 1966. Again, the result was the same: almost instant growth and flowering. Dick was a demanding taskmaster (all the best coaches are), but he was demanding because he cared (you could feel it and smell it) and because he was hell-bent on cajoling the best from you, a best you didn't even know you had. Also, as in the Harkness case, he had a fine sense of limits. He pushed and nudged, and occasionally ranted and raved. But just as zealously he guarded you against a big fall and religiously avoided pushing you too far.

Moreover, when his somewhat irreverent charge (Tom) would run afoul of those above him, Anderson, an avowed breeder of skunklike instincts, would be there, quick as a wink, to protect him vigorously from the bureaucrats above (and then he'd chew Tom out unmercifully in private for having played his hand so awkwardly).

The Manager as Teacher

The Center for Creative Leadership in Greensboro, North Carolina, has long been associated with emerging perspectives on the subject of leadership. As part of the Center's Research Sponsor Program, successful managers were asked to talk about their best teachers. In most cases, they turned out to be a former boss. The following were the most frequently mentioned characteristics of these managers-as-teachers.

► They counseled. *They gave younger managers constructive advice and feedback. They used younger managers as sounding boards.*

► They excelled. *Whether in finance, production or marketing, these managers were the best in some aspect of their business.*

► They gave exposure. *They made sure that the work and accomplishments of young managers were seen. They opened doors for them.*

► They provided latitude. *They gave young managers the freedom to try, the courage to fail. They involved them in important tasks.*

► They were tough taskmasters. *They challenged; they demanded excellence.*

Nancy encountered her first bona fide coach shortly after her college graduation, in an unlikely setting. Robert Liberman, a research psychiatrist who ran a unique and innovative treatment center in California, was Nancy's first boss when she was a member of his research team. Bob was, above all, a superb teacher. A soft-spoken man, he never ranted or raved, but made his presence felt quietly and always supportively. He particularly urged people to reach for "firsts"—acting on a new idea, writing a difficult article, organizing and leading new staff-training programs, working with a new patient—and devoted enough time, usually daily, to make sure that the "first" wouldn't be the last. If a staff member doubted his or her ability to work successfully with a new patient, Liberman would take the time to sit down with him or her and rehearse the first meeting in detail, asking questions, encouraging, nudging, listening, even role-playing the part of the patient. When that first meeting finally came, he would show up just before, to offer a word or two of encouragement, and again after, to ask how things had gone, and to spend time debriefing the meeting if the staff member wanted him to. He had the gift of being around when you needed his help the most—and not around when you needed to go it on your own. He was a master momentum-maker.

It's because of the profound effect of these coaches on our lives, and the profound effect our research suggests great coaches can have on organizations as well as individuals, that we will push you to examine this topic with us. It may seem that coaches can have but a tiny number of charges or pro-tégés, but, surprisingly, they have the ability to affect *many* people. A few years back, Tom was with a group of about twenty-five McKinsey partners from all over the world. They were being led through an exercise to identify top coaches in their McKinsey careers. The number who identified the same two or three people, in this 1,000-consultant, 175-partner operation, was startling. Just a few had affected so many, often in the deepest ways.

Coaching by Wandering Around

At Herman Miller, the superb office furniture company, there's a term called "roving leadership." Chairman Max DePree describes roving leaders as "those indispensable people in our lives who are there when we need them." DePree goes on: "Roving leadership is the expression of the ability of hierarchical leaders to permit others to share ownership of problems—in effect, to take possession of a situation. It demands that we be enablers of each other." Coaching is the process of enabling others to act, of building on their strengths. It's counting on other people to use their own special skill and competence, and then giving them enough room and enough time to do it.

Coaching at its heart involves caring enough about people to take the time to build a personal relationship with them. Easy to say, tough to do. Relation-ships depend on contact. No contact, no relationship. The best coaches know this: they lavish time and attention (occasionally to their personal detri-ment)—time and attention that others never quite get around to spending on a consistent basis—on people. They also make sure people see enough of one another to impart a vital sense of continuity, momentum and urgency, and to focus attention on the long term. They find reasons *every day* to get the whole team together—hundreds at times, à la Kelly Johnson or Gerhard Neu-mann—and to underscore the point that "we're all in this together for the long run, so we damn well better do what we can to help each other out." Armchair coaches and Monday-morning quarterbacks, on the other hand, wait until the opponent has scored and only 37 seconds remain on the clock before they step in or get people together. But by then it's too late. Coaching is a real-time endeavor. Michigan assistant football coach Alex Agase puts it this way: "If you really want to advise me, do it on Saturday afternoon between one and four o'clock. And you've got twenty-five seconds to do it, between plays. Not on Monday. I know the right thing to do on Monday."

You have to be there when games are played, and the only way to do that is to do it. Plan to spend the lion's share of your time out of your office, not behind your desk. Show up in your team's floor space. Better yet, move your desk there. That's what all Milliken bosses, up to and including division pres-idents, are encouraged, none too gently, to do. Listen. Spread rampant enthu-siasm and pride. Encourage tries. Get the whole group together often—say, every day.

Participating directly—seeing with your own eyes and hearing with your own ears—is simply the only thing that yields the unfiltered, richly detailed impressions that tell you how things are really going, that give you the minute-to-minute opportunities to take another couple of steps toward building trust, toward making room for people to innovate and to contribute, and toward making your strategic priorities clear. It's the awesome power of personal attention, and it is communicated in one way only: physical presence.

Coaching is tough-minded. It's nurturing and bringing out the best; it's demanding that the team play as a team. And should it finally become clear that there are prima donnas who won't forgo the "I" in favor of "we," you have to handle that one, too—by letting them go. The chairman of a giant, multidivisional aerospace company that manufactures integrated systems made it clear that divisions must cooperate if long-term customer relations were to be maintained. The boss of his most profitable division retorted that the top spot on the short-term dollar scorecard protected him against all the " 'Love they neighbor' bullshit," as he ungently put it. The chairman had had enough. The fellow was sacked, and given less than twenty-four hours to be off the premises.

Coaching, Contribution and Career Mazes

Coaching goes far beyond the short-term need to help someone learn the mechanics of preparing a budget and setting a proposal up. It is the principal means through which people learn what makes their organization tick, what it stands for, and how they can contribute to it over time. *Perhaps surprisingly, the more elbowroom a company grants to its people, the more important on-the-job coaching becomes.* Hewlett-Packard, W. L. Gore & Associates and People Express have crafted distinctive environments that do without the traditional "career path" structures found elsewhere. In these organizations we find instead "career mazes"—loosely defined hierarchies and wide-open fields of opportunity for people to develop skills, contribute directly and receive recognition. Such companies demand that people focus not so much on the climb to the top, and encourage them instead to keep their eyes on making a sustained personal contribution to producing, selling or servicing products, and to building the spirit and commitment of all hands—and this holds for people at all stages of their careers and in every job category. A middle manager in Hewlett-Packard's oldest manufacturing division describes the difference in focus: "I'd been managing a fifty-person department for about a year, and I was thinking about my next step. I'd just turned thirty; a lot of my friends from school were running bigger operations in their companies. I think I'm as capable as they are, and I guess it started to bother me. So the next time I saw my boss I told him about my concerns, asked him what I could do to move up. He thought about it for a minute, and his answer surprised me. He smiled and said, "What's your hurry? The best way to move up here is to do the best you can with the job you've got. I know it takes time to get used to the way we do things here, but trust us a little bit. Pay attention to how you can contribute now; have fun! That's the way people move up.' And the funny thing is, he was right. I realized he always took the time to lend a hand, help me out. In fact, everyone seemed to be aware of what I was working on, how I was contributing. HP just takes a real interest in people. They assume you're here for the long run, and they personally give you the help and feedback you need. They don't leave it to somebody else."

COACHING AS VALUE-SHAPING

Every coach, at every level, is above all a value-shaper. The value-shaper not only brings company philosophy to life by paying extraordinary attention to communicating and symbolizing it, he or she also helps newcomers understand how shared company values affect individual performance.

Shaping Values

Effective shared values are a well from which come leadership and the ways customers and colleagues appraise your company and its products and services.

Johnson & Johnson articulates its business principles in a document called "Our Credo," reproduced on page 907. It clearly sets out the company's responsibility to customers, employees, communities and stockholders. First given to employees in 1947, these guiding principles have been renewed over the years, in part through Credo Challenge meetings. Chairman Jim Burke comments:

A generation later, in 1975, some of us became concerned as to whether, in fact, we were *practicing* what we preached.

We had become a large and complex corporation, with well over 100 companies around the world, each with its own separate mission. In corporate headquarters we were concerned that the Credo perhaps had greater meaning to us than to those who were ultimately responsible for managing our various businesses around the world.

So we tried an experiment. We invited twenty-four of our managers from the United States and overseas here for a meeting to challenge the Credo. I opened the meeting with the observation that the document was hanging in most of our offices around the world. If we were not committed to it, it was an act of pretension and ought to be ripped off the walls. I challenged the group to recommend whether we should get rid of it, rewrite it, or commit to it as is. The meeting was a turn-on, a genuine happening, as these managers struggled with the issues that the Credo defined. What we discovered was that we had a set of guiding principles far more powerful than we had imagined.

This was the beginning of a series of Credo Challenge meetings to include all of our key management from around the world. Dave Clare, our president, and I chaired these sessions over the next three years. The basic philosophy is unchanged. Many words stayed the same; others were changed substantively, some just modernized. Some of the responsibilities were expanded to take cognizance of a much more complicated world.

[Then, on September 29, 1982], . . . we learned with a terrifying suddenness that inexplicably someone had chosen one of our products—Tylenol—as a murder weapon. Thus began what was to become for us an unremitting nightmare, and one that required literally dozens of people to make hundreds of decisions in painfully short periods of time. Even when we had time for careful consideration, most of our decisions were complicated, involving considerable risk, and we had no historical precedent to rely on.

As you know, we have received much praise for our handling of the "Tylenol Affair." Certainly we are proud of the heroic job done by our people at McNeil Consumer Products and all of those from their sister companies who worked so tirelessly to help them during those difficult weeks. However, all of us at McNeil Consumer Products and Johnson & Johnson truly believe that the guidance of the Credo played *the* most important role in our decision-making. Ask yourselves, with a statement like that, if we had any alternative but to do what we did during the Tylenol tragedy. Ask yourselves how the Tylenol consumer, the Johnson & Johnson employee, the public, the stockholder would have felt. What would *your* attitude today be toward Johnson & Johnson if we hadn't behaved the way we did?

And, of course, the important thing that the Tylenol affair reaffirmed is the intrinsic fairness of the American public. A remarkable poll by the Roper organization taken three months after the tragedy showed 93 percent of the public felt Johnson & Johnson handled its responsibility either very well or fairly well. *But* the public also gave very high marks to the Food and Drug Administration, the law enforcement agencies, the drug industry in general, *and* the media! The public knew that all of these institutions were working—together—and in their interest! And what did *our* customers do? They gave us back our business. A year ago tonight we had but a fraction left of one of the most valuable consumer franchises ever built. Our latest Nielsen, taken in July–August [1983] shows Tylenol has regained over 90 percent of the business we enjoyed prior to the tragedies.

Burke's words are exhilarating—to us. To many they will seem like flowery nonsense. "Surely," many (most?) say, "there's more to J&J than that." There

Our Credo

We believe our first responsibility is to the doctors, nurses and patients,
to mothers and all others who use our products and services.
In meeting their needs everything we do must be of high quality.
We must constantly strive to reduce our costs
In order to maintain reasonable prices.
Customers' orders must be serviced promptly and accurately.
Our suppliers and distributors must have an opportunity
to make a fair profit.

We are responsible to our employees,
the men and women who work with us throughout the world.
Everyone must be considered as an individual.
We must respect their dignity and recognize their merit.
They must have a sense of security in their jobs.
Compensation must be fair and adequate,
and working conditions clean, orderly and safe.
Employees must feel free to make suggestions and complaints.
There must be equal opportunity for employment, development
and advancement for those qualified.
We must provide competent management,
and their actions must be just and ethical.

We are responsible to the communities in which we live and work
and to the world community as well.
We must be good citizens — support good works and charities
and bear our fair share of taxes.
We must encourage civic improvements and better health and education.
We must maintain in good order
the property we are privileged to use,
protecting the environment and natural resources.

Our final responsibility is to our stockholders.
Business must make a sound profit.
We must experiment with new ideas.
Research must be carried on, innovative programs developed
and mistakes paid for.
New equipment must be purchased, new facilities provided
and new products launched.
Reserves must be created to provide for adverse times.
When we operate according to these principles,
the stockholders should realize a fair return.

Johnson & Johnson

is—and there isn't. Yes, J&J has a structure (albeit a very loose one) and tough reporting standards. Yet J&J *is* that Credo. We have gone out of our way to corroborate the Tylenol story, talking to media investigators who were on the scene, lawyers, lower-level J&J employees. All had been impressed by the strength of the institution (though it was devastated by the tragedy per se). "Seeing" a value live—at J&J, IBM, People Express, Apple, HP, Gore—is remarkable, yet will always remain impossible for the skeptic and cynic.

Look in the Mirror First

How can you reduce the risk that your actions contradict your stated values? The first step (again and again) is to appraise honestly and critically the way you spend your time. This theme pervades every chapter in this book. We revisit it here because coaching is made up of actions, not words. You will unfailingly see your behavior reflected in that of your team: they *see* what's really important to you. Look for the *tiniest* inconsistencies (the tiniest are the *most* important, it turns out): Do you sit in your office talking about quality, yet spend the bulk of your time on factory visits reviewing inventory levels? Take an unflinching look at what your calendar says about what really matters to you. Like it or not, that's the sincerest—and only—measure. And the reason (again, it's absolutely vital to the whole issue of leadership) is this: any closely held value, no matter how well concealed (even from yourself), inevitably prompts action that is consistent with it, because *all* your people are boss watchers, boss students, boss anthropologists of the first order. If you say innovation is important but you don't tolerate the minor missteps that inevitably go hand in glove with innovation, your true priority will be as evident as if it were emblazoned on banners and streamers. If you preach trust but impose demeaning limits on purchasing authority—e.g., the ability to buy office supplies or the $8.95 bucket of paint—your people get the message in a flash.

Take the time to judge how well your hard work furthers your company's core values and expresses your beliefs. (And we do mean *hard* work. Almost all managers *do* work hard. Few are slothful in our experience. Yet most squander their effort through inconsistency.) Look for the ways you trip yourself up—how you get in your own way without meaning to. It will help you anticipate where problems and setbacks will likely occur in the coaching process.

Doing the Right Thing: Trust and Integrity

Shaping values for others means attaching more importance to integrity than skill: even if people don't know exactly how to do something, if they do know precisely where their bosses (and their company) are coming from, they can rely on *themselves* (and you can rely on them) to affirm that direction in day-to-day activity. Trust (proffered by one's own boss) and integrity of vision is learned only by example, not from procedure manuals, training courses or Labor Day speeches. It's learned when the off-hours chatter, belly up to the bar, reflects the same respect for the individual as the carefully crafted speech. Effective value-shapers protect their company's integrity at all costs, at all times. They are unmerciful when it is betrayed. Yet the hardest part is mustering the courage to give others a chance to "do the right thing" in the first place. *If* you've communicated shared values, acted consistently, *and* provided training and coaching, you won't need to intervene so often to "fix" things. Your people will keep their promises *if* you keep yours.

Where we find integrity and trust, we also find aggressive cooperation. The best coaches spend as much time developing the team's ability to believe in what each member can contribute as they do working with individual players. It sets the tone for the way people should aim to work together, and trust evolves in the process. When everyone is headed in the same direction, there's every reason for team members to trust one another, every reason to anticipate innovative action and creativity.

The Coach as Storyteller

Nothing reveals more of what a company really cares about than its stories and legends—i.e., its folk wisdom. We've seen (in chapter 16) that leaders use stories to persuade, symbolize and guide day-to-day actions; there's simply nothing better than a story to tell people what they really want to know about "how things work around here," or to illustrate the right thing to do in a given situation. They can lend believability and impact to a company's philosophy (in fact, they are almost the only routes to believability)—they will highlight, with lightning speed, any gaps between what a company says it values and what it actually holds dear. That is, you are simply as good or as bad, as consistent or as inconsistent, as your stories. You can like that or not. You can ignore it or manage and guide it. But it *is* a fact.

Stories engage. They help put current decisions and events into an overall framework that is readily understood, and they embellish a company philosophy in a unique way. The common memory created by swapping tales imparts a sense of tradition and continuity, and sparks interest as nothing else can. Listening to a company's stories is the surest route to determining its real priorities and who symbolizes them. At L. L. Bean and Nordstrom, the stories are about customer service. At Publix Super Markets and People Express they're about pride of ownership, and at Perdue Farms, Maytag and J. M. Smucker, about quality. Stories are a rich, colorful tapestry that illustrates what's most important to the organization; effective value-shapers use stories to convey the successes and the mistakes so that others can learn from them, and to build enthusiasm and involvement.

COACHING OPPORTUNITIES

One-Idea Club

Stew Leonard (of Stew Leonard's dairy store) solicits his people's ideas regularly. One unique way is via regular visits to competitors. There aren't many stores that compete with Stew across the board, but sometimes he will come across an interesting department like one of his (e.g., bakery goods), or an interesting store in another business (e.g., a florist). When he does, even if it's three hundred or four hundred miles away, he's likely to grab fifteen of his people (including hourly people, even very recent hires) and hop into the 15-person van that he uses for just such occasions.

Off they go to Stew's challenge to join the One-Idea Club. The issue? Who will be the first to come up with *one* new idea for Stew's gleaned from the competitor's outfit? Next, can *everyone* come up with at least one new idea? (It *must* be implementable immediately upon returning home.) That's almost all there is to it—but not quite. Even though Stew Leonard's is at the top of the heap, none of his travelers is allowed to talk about anything that Stew's does better than the competitor they're visiting. The point is for each person to find at least one thing that the competitor does better than Stew's. "It's so darned easy to fall into the trap," Stew says, "and grouse that 'Those guys don't know what they're doing with this, or that.' We have a rule. We just don't allow that. You should be able to find at least one thing that the competitor does better. Often as not it'll be a tiny thing. But that's the way *you* get better." The new ideas gleaned are communicated throughout the store in the company newsletter, *Stew's News.*

The parallel to Sam Neaman's routine is close. Keys include: self-analysis, hourly-person-as-expert, eyeball analysis, looking for the small and the immediately doable, a vehicle for swapping notes (the van ride in this instance), rules about the process (e.g., the "no derogation" rule), and an overall approach that is, again, guided autonomy. And it works!

What's Stew up to? He's teaching, leading, coaching. He's turning everyone into a fully empowered expert in retailing and competitive analysis, into an owner, into a winner, and into an enthusiast ("We can make it better" and "Wow!" are Stew's two favorite expressions).

Coaching isn't limited to what you personally teach. What can you lead your people to learn from customers, suppliers and colleagues in other parts of the company? How can you take advantage of day-to-day opportunities as part of your coaching game plan? The list below is a starting point:

—Have people regularly attend meetings they wouldn't ordinarily (e.g., concerning unfamiliar specialties—accountants to marketing and vice versa) to gain firsthand exposure to other colleagues' work.

—Start your own One-Idea Club inside or outside the company.

—Have your team observe you in real time as you handle customer complaints, make formal presentations, wander around.

—Rotate people through other jobs and functions, with temporary—but real (i.e., having palpable output)—assignments; e.g., set an objective of having every team member able to perform everyone else's job.

—Encourage enrollment in continuing education programs and participation in your best internal training programs and classes; make sure implicit penalties for "being away from the job" are not levied.

—Have your people co-lead company courses and seminars.

—Spring for memberships in professional associations.

—Encourage people to make presentations on their projects inside and outside the company, especially to other functions and divisions.

—Get people to serve on temporary multifunction task forces (volunteer them to others, on a *non*-quid-pro-quo basis).

—Invite colleagues at all levels in other departments to spend time with your people to explain what they need from your group (and encourage them to invite your people to visit them).

—Follow Roger Milliken's example (see p. 840) and send one hundred fifty of your people, not just two or three, for the full ten days of a trade show.

—Invite someone from another department or company (e.g., a customer or vendor) to work in your department for a while.

Every opportunity to involve people in the business in its broadest sense is a coaching opportunity, and none is too small to overlook. If learning a new skill is important to your team's success, focus on it. Use every device you can think of to facilitate learning.

Caution: Most will not volunteer for out-of-sight assignments because they assume (stories, again) that out of sight is out of mind. Through your evaluation of your people and by seeding a few (positive) stories of your own, you must demonstrate by action that to engage in these nonroutine activities is a short- and long-term plus.

Look in the Mirror Again

We *told* you this was important! A colleague says, "The best coaching opportunity is getting people involved with how *you* do your own job, showing them how what *you* do gets you a little further toward a goal. I had a boss once who used to set aside a little time every day for 'coaching.' He'd talk about the importance of quality, all the right things. But then he ran into trouble. As soon as he finished 'coaching,' he'd go back to 'doing his real job.' So if it was time to ship products, and if there was pressure to get the products out the door, he'd press to do it, even if the product was scratched or damaged. To him, 'coaching' and 'doing his job' were two different things. It didn't take us long to figure out what really mattered to him. He'd talk a great game, but the one he played was totally different. He couldn't understand why our product-quality record wasn't terrific, since he talked quality a lot. He didn't realize that we paid more attention to how he handled quality issues in his own job than to what he said in his 'coaching' sessions."

A familiar story, this. To your team, you *are* your enacted priorities, no more and no less. The mundane, minute-to-minute choices you make as you do your own job are the most powerful teachers. Your people won't miss a beat. So look in the mirror again. You are coaching all the time, like it or not; on and off the field you set the example that others will follow. Do you walk the talk?

Leadership and Expertise

Leadership and expertise, or the perils of professional management. The boss of Domino's Pizza, Tom Monaghan, can flip a pizza with the best of them. Don Vlcek, president of Domino's Pizza Distribution Company (the dough providers), is a Grade A dough maker. David Ogilvy, throughout his career, would return to copywriting, and he's a fine writer. At the age of seventy-eight, McKinsey's legendary leader, Marvin Bower, is still a new-business generator—and per hour spent, there's none better (he recently brought GM into the fold). In a word, walking the talk is massively enhanced if you are "of the business," as a good friend puts it. Living the basic values—e.g., people, customers— does come first. But, frankly, it only becomes coherent and full of life for your people if you understand what the context is. "The astute professional manager can manage anything" has been the common litany. "Nuts," we say. "To know is to be credible" is more correct. But to know is *not* enough: supercoaches know the business—are expert—*and* live the more abstract values passionately. Neither is sufficient alone.

FIVE COACHING ROLES

How do you know what approach to take in coaching? What to emphasize? What to leave alone for the time being? Where do you start?

An HP marketing manager observes that "to coach well, you have to be flexible. What works with one person doesn't with someone else. It depends on knowing the person and understanding the situation." In short, sometimes coaching is not coaching but counseling, or sponsoring, or confronting, or educating.*

It's a paradox. Writer John McPhee observed of Deerfield's legendary headmaster Frank Boyden that his values were simple, yet it took a complex person to live simplicity in an ambiguous world. That is, the great coaches, as we've said, live simple values. But the art is to bring these simple values to life for each different person with whom one comes in contact and whom one attempts to influence.

Educating, Sponsoring, Coaching, Counseling and Confronting

We want to be very concrete. In our work with exceptionally talented leaders and coaches, we've discovered that they make dozens of intuitive judgments daily about how to work with their people. Sometimes they focus on removing barriers to performance. Other times they immerse themselves in a situation and exert a great deal of influence on the way it turns out. There are times when they help people work through personal or performance problems, and there are times when the only requirement is to provide straightforward information. In some situations the coach is the dominant figure, while in others the team practically forgets he or she is there.

It turns out that successful coaches instinctively vary their approaches to meet the needs of this person at this time, or that group at that time. They perform five distinctly different roles: they educate, sponsor, coach, counsel and confront. Each approach is executed with the intensity we have come to expect, always toward the same goal: to facilitate learning and elicit creative contributions from all hands to the organization's overarching purpose. Let's take a closer look at the five roles. We summarize the hallmarks of each before digging into the roles individually.

*We want to acknowledge Robert Dyer's pioneering work in this area, for contributing so much to our thinking on this subject, and for being one of the first to conceive of coaching as a collection of roles.
We appreciate the special inventive contribution of HP's excellent management trainer, Pat Lingen, to the material in the following chart.

EDUCATE
TIMING
When goals, roles, or business conditions change
To orient a newcomer • When you are new to a group
When new skills are needed

TONE

Positive, supportive
Emphasis on learning and applying specific new knowledge

CONSEQUENCES

New skills acquired • Confidence increases
Perspective on the company or organization is broadened

KEY SKILLS

Ability to articulate performance expectations clearly
An eye for recognizing real-life "learning laboratories"
Ability and willingness to reinforce learning

SPONSOR

TIMING

When an individual can make a special contribution
To let an outstanding skill speak for itself

TONE

Positive, enthusiastic
Emphasis on long-term development and contribution to the company
Future focus • Polishing, fine-tuning

CONSEQUENCES

Showcase for outstanding skill, contribution
Greater experience • Promotion

KEY SKILLS

Debureaucratizing • Dismantling barriers to performance
Ability to develop collegial relationship
Willingness to let go of control
Willingness to provide access to information and people

COACH

TIMING

For special encouragement before or after a "first"
(e.g., first-customer visit, first board meeting)
To make simple, brief corrections

TONE

Encouraging, enthusiastic • Preparatory, explanatory

CONSEQUENCES

Enhanced confidence, skills, better performance

KEY SKILLS

Ability to express genuine appreciation • Ability to listen

COUNSEL

TIMING

When problems damage performance • After educating and coaching
To respond to setbacks and disappointments and speed recovery

TONE

Emphasis on problem solving • Positive, supportive, encouraging
Structured • Two-way discussion

CONSEQUENCES

Turnaround • Enhanced sense of ownership and accountability
Renewed commitment

KEY SKILLS

Willingness to listen • Ability to give clear, useful feedback

---

CONFRONT

TIMING

Persistent performance problems are not resolved
An individual seems unable to meet expectations despite educating
and counseling
An individual is failing in his or her current role

TONE

Positive, supportive • Firm
Clear focus on need to make a decision and time at which decision
will be made
Calm

CONSEQUENCES

Reassignment • A chance to succeed in another position
Current job is restructured, responsibilities curtailed • Dismissal

KEY SKILLS

Listening • Ability to give direct, useful feedback
Ability to discuss sensitive issues without overemotionalizing them

EDUCATING

When Ren McPherson wanted to enhance productivity at Dana, one of the most important things he did was to insist that entire divisions—each, say, a 1,500-person operation—get together at least quarterly to share corporate operating results, to keep up with developments throughout the corporation. As we pointed out in our chapter on ownership, McPherson acted upon the assumption that all, including the new hire of eight days ago—have the potential to be a full business partner if he treated them that way. If we can get people involved on a weekly, monthly or quarterly basis, we can encourage them to see themselves as a real part of the organization—in both its successes and stumbles.

Dana Corporation's Forty Thoughts to Put into Practice

Dana, under the leadership in the 1970's of Ren McPherson and today of chairman Gerry Mitchell, added an important chapter to the book on American management. As noted, one of McPherson's first acts as chairman was to reduce the company's existing policy manuals to a one-page operational philosophy. In the mid-1970's that single page was culled to become "The Dana Corporation's 40 Thoughts"—not by the chairman but by a group of Dana employees acting entirely on their own initiative. They wanted to make it even easier for everyone at Dana to read and remember what made the company tick. The "40 Thoughts" are still vital to Dana's remarkable productivity:

Remember our purpose—to earn money for our shareholders and increase the value of their investment • Recognize people as our most important asset • Help people grow • Promote from within • Remember—people respond to recognition • Share the rewards • Provide stability of income and employment • Decentralize • Provide autonomy • Encourage entrepreneurship • Use corporate committees, task forces • Push responsibility down • Involve everyone • Make every employee a manager • Control only what's important • Promote identity with Dana • Make all Dana people shareholders • Simplify • Use little paper • Keep no files • Communicate fully • Let Dana people know first • Let people set goals and judge their performance • Let the people decide where possible • Discourage conformity • Be professional • Break organizational barriers • Develop pride • Insist on high ethical standards • Focus on markets • Utilize assets fully • Contain investment—buy, don't make • Balance plants, products, markets • Keep facilities under 500 people • Stabilize production • Develop proprietary products • Anticipate market needs • Control cash • Deliver reliably • Do what's best for all of Dana

---

Now reflect on this for a moment. We observe (and commend to you) that educating is *not* principally about jamming techniques down the neophyte's throat, whether the neophyte is a new hire, new manager or new vice president. The prime education is "You belong," "You can contribute." Once that message is genuinely transmitted, and absorbed, *then* the "technique-learning process" can be shortened by 60 to 90 percent, for there is suddenly the will to learn.

So leaders-as-educators treat every person—full time, part-time and temporary—as a full-fledged team member (for reasons of profitability and performance as well as humanity). They facilitate the sense of belonging (ownership) by providing a full complement of training, free access to information about how things are going throughout the company, and by making performance expectations clear, consistent, simple and concrete. Even industries that face cyclical and seasonal manufacturing problems can use the educating role to affirm the full-partner status of their people, regardless of their tenure.

Educating well ("overeducating" by most of the world's standards) at the beginning—bringing newcomers into the organization and making them a part of it in a short time—is the bedrock for sustained creative contributions. Educating is not about giving instructions. It's acting on a deep-down belief in the potential of every person to contribute, over time, by providing the tools, the elbowroom and frequent, concrete, believable feedback about progress. It means giving people a chance to experiment a little bit from the start and to learn the difference between mistakes and disasters, between satisfactory and exceptional.

When Should You Educate

—When you want to introduce a newcomer—at any level—to your organization, philosophy and way of doing business.
—When people need specific information that will enable them to contribute as fully involved partners day to day.
—When performance expectations are unclear.
—When people need information about changing goals, strategies, roles or responsibilities.
—When people successfully apply their current skills and want to concentrate on expanding their ability.
—When you want people to learn a specific skill.
—When company business values are misinterpreted, ambiguous or unobtrusive.

Educating the Newcomer

At North American Tool and Die, based in San Leandro, California, on-the-job education begins with the *interview* process! Candidates are asked to spend two or three days working (with pay) to see where they would best fit in. During that time the candidate learns about the precision machine parts business, meets most of the company's eighty people, gets hands-on exposure to several jobs, and is immersed in the North American way of doing things. President Tom Melohn meets with every recruit, often for an hour or more, to answer questions and to talk about what he believes in: profitable growth, sharing the wealth and having fun. Hiring decisions are reached by consensus, and the candidate is given equal voice. "If the person will fit in with our way of doing things, he or she knows it after those two days," Melohn observes. "Then they can't wait to go out and start on something. We want to get people involved from the very beginning; we want them to know that's important to us."

So the best education processes begin long before the hiring decision is made: each interview or plant tour is an opportunity to make your priorities clear and understandable, to reinforce expectations, and to get the newcomer involved in the whole of the business. We met Donna Ecton, vice president of administration at Campbell Soup Company, when we researched the best companies for women for *Savvy* magazine's June 1984 cover story. Campbell scored high on our list, and so did Donna's approach to her new position (she had come to Campbell from Citibank): she had spent her first quarter working in the company's processing plants, "packing pickles, working the graveyard shift, eviscerating chickens, and listening to people." In less than a year, she had worked at every one of the company's ninety operating units. The (senior) newcomer's investing time in getting to the roots of the business is oh so rare.

Training and Beyond

Educating the newcomer often begins with a formal orientation program. The best firms focus on the company's history, evolution, current product lines, business philosophy, how each individual contributes to the organization's success. The newcomers are unfailingly taught by top management. Intel President Andy Grove says his new-hire orientation teaching is his most significant contribution to the $1.2 billion company. The entire top team at People Express devotes four to eight hours a week to in-house classroom orientation. They believe it is the best way to ensure that People traditions do not become attenuated in the face of incredible growth. But the real orientation begins when the newcomer starts his or her new role and depends on peers and managers to do the lion's share of the educating on the job. Harry Levinson, in *The Exceptional Executive,* enhances the theme:

> Although always imperative, the need for closeness is most crucial at the beginning of a relationship with the organization. It is at this point that people become "attached," and the attaching process must take place at

a time when they are most confused about the new job and the strange organization. They are more heavily dependent then than at any other time in their organizational careers. Unless someone takes them in hand, they literally cannot begin their work, let alone become part of the organization.

An adequate orientation reduces anxiety. Much of the turnover among newly employed people is due to their concern that they might fail, their feeling of desertion about being left to 'muddle through,' and their impression that no one really cares about them.

One more point, one more time: all the training in your power to provide won't matter a whit unless you believe the individual *wants* to contribute, and unless you give him or her a chance to contribute—creatively—from the start. The first step is to make this belief crystal clear. Make it tangible and believable through concrete example and by encouraging early participation.

Experience is still the best teacher. At HP, newcomers are often invited to sit on temporary task forces convened to address a particular issue, resolve a problem or streamline a system. It's a way to draw people in immediately and to convince them that the company is dead serious about wanting their participation and full contribution in the most complex business decisions. The beauty of harnessing brief, practical task forces as educational opportunities is that they build in real accountability without excessive risk. The odds overwhelmingly favor the newcomer's successful contribution—the group is kept small but diverse, the group is focused on a particular task, and is held responsible for contributing to a fully implemented solution. It's a small slice of organization life that showers full-scale responsibility on newcomers.

As a newcomer to HP, Nancy was a member of a small, multifunctional task force formed for the purpose of reviewing, redesigning and implementing a new performance evaluation system throughout the company. The six-person group was made up of two senior people from operating divisions, a representative from the sales regions, a corporate senior vice president and two senior personnel managers. Meetings were held regularly over a three-month period, each lasting half a day; minutes were published and distributed the same day.

The real work of the task force, however, was done between meetings, when the members worked with managers from all over the company to incorporate their "best practices"—particularly innovative approaches or effective solutions developed in a division or region and worthy of company-wide attention—into the task force recommendations (see chapter 17). Here the real learning occurred: Nancy spent a considerable amount of time with line managers in HP divisions and regions, was exposed to a broad cross section of the company's business, and learned firsthand how the HP Way is put into action at the operating level, where it counts. These meetings were first-class testing grounds for a newcomer's impressions and ideas. Almost every conversation would yield some new information: "Oh, we wouldn't do it that way here." "Why not?" "Well, because the HP Way is different. Here, we do it this way, because equity is so important. . . ." A better education couldn't be designed. Accountability was also an important feature of the experience, and felt most acutely when task force progress and result were reported to line and senior managers. This was a no-nonsense occasion, when the expectation that the task force produce real results was evident.

Pritchard Services Group, now a successful $325 million diversified health services company in the UK, was originally best known as a cleaning company. Despite its size, Pritchard regularly takes on cleaning contracts that other companies would consider too small to bother with. The reason? As reported in *The Winning Streak,* these contracts provide a superb training ground for inexperienced managers, who can make mistakes and learn from them without excessive risk, and who can develop the practical entrepreneurial skills and mind-set that breathe life into this large corporation.

Educating the New Manager

Somehow it's easier to imagine educating individual contributors than to think in terms of following the same approach in educating newly promoted managers to perform well in their roles. Take a minute or two and review the "Educating the Newcomer" section, replacing "newcomer" with "new manager" as you go. Our point is simple: new managers, though now responsible for others' welfare and destiny, need the same clear expectations about performance and accountability, *and* the chance to make mistakes through hands-on experience. New managers need to know and work from corporate objectives, know how to work with their new teams and more experienced managers, know how to build peer relationships and how to resolve conflicts. Educators can exert tremendous positive influence on new managers' development *if* they will recognize the obvious early confusion and at the same time the unparalleled opportunity to mold behavior. It's easy to rationalize leaving new managers alone to fend for themselves under the rubric of "hands-on experience," but we believe strongly that this is a mistake and a tragic waste precisely because what's being inadvertently taught is that managing (leading) effectively is not the special skill we know it to be. When we say in effect "Well, you know your job, so go manage," the implicit message is that there's nothing more to it, that any dummy (who's made it this far) can do it, that if you're uncomfortable it's because you're weird. Let's be blunt: how many new managers are given the same level of training in "shaping corporate values" as they were given when they were learning engineering or fashion buying? The latter was the subject of four years (or more) of collegiate training and big doses of corporate refurbishment. The former nets two weeks of training at the most, and yet the skills to be assumed and the responsibility (i.e., for corporate value maintenance and transmittal) are awesome.

(Incidentally, this is an area where IBM has shone brightly: new manager training, which (1) begins with a refocusing on values, and (2) is *never* delayed due to "job exigencies" is expensive, intensive and superb.)

When Everyone's a Newcomer: Culture Shock

In baseball: The major league umpires threaten to walk out again only minutes before the fifth and final game in the battle between the Chicago Cubs and the San Diego Padres for the National League pennant. The team members are introduced, the national anthem is sung; there are no umpires. At last the men in blue appear, reporting to work without a contract. Later in the game, the attorney for the Umpires Union, Richie Phillips, comments to a television reporter, explaining the umpires' presence: "I trust Peter Ueberroth [the new commissioner of baseball and arbitrator for the binding arbitration the umpires agreed to in their negotiations just before the 1984 World Series]." Phillips speaks of trust not once but three times in a thirty-second interview. And Ueberroth, for his part, is equally confident. "We'll settle before the Series," he says calmly, optimistically—and it is a promise, not a threat.

In electronics: During the 1981–83 recession, Kollmorgen Corporation, like so many others, was forced to lay off hundreds of people. But the company believes in commitment—they wanted these people back and they wanted them to know it. So Kollmorgen did an unusual thing: Each week every Kollmorgen division manager held "news conferences"—open forums to which everyone, including those who had been laid off, was invited. The news conferences drew standing-room-only crowds, and each week division managers were asked to explain exactly what the company was doing to get their people their jobs back. The managers shared every bit of information they had, including what progress had been made *and* where the next layoffs might occur. Trust and truth in real time—giving the people all the information even when it is the hardest thing imaginable to do—is the heart and soul of educating.

When conditions change, new standards must be set, new skills learned, new roles taken, old records broken. Educators are essential at these times, to point the way, to articulate progress, and to share what was previously considered unsharable. It's as much a new beginning—a new mind-set—as any newcomer faces. In fact, though our topic here is education, the deeper theme, again, is trust. Peter Ueberroth gained it quickly by prior reputation and by acting in an unheard-of, new fashion—genuinely listening to both sides—and he can lose it just as quickly. Kollmorgen earned it through years of consistency and through openly sharing all news—regularly. Both used trust and mutual respect as the basis for timely action in a crisis. Trust is always important, but never more so than in times of rapid change.

Accountability and Support

The education process works when it is characterized by accountability and unwavering support. People need to know exactly what their roles are and what results they are expected to produce. They need to see that mistakes are allowed and expected as a part of learning. The effective educator prefers a bit of daring and persistence to unimaginative perfection, and supports learning by paying vigilant attention to each successful (and unsuccessful) try. Progress is recognized and reinforced every tiny step of the way.

The need for support and active guidance in the learning process is well understood by anyone who remembers what the first few weeks of a new job (supervisor of the cleaning crew or vice president) are like: strange, confusing, uncertain and, all too often, lonely. Harry Levinson underscores the point: "Despite its importance, the most glaring deficiency in contemporary organizational functioning is the almost universal inadequacy of support. This is evident in the repetitive response to a simple question. If one asks people in almost any organization, 'How do you know how well you are doing?' 90 percent of them are likely to respond, 'If I do something wrong, I'll hear about it.' Too often this topic is discussed as if praise were the answer; it is not. What people are saying in such a response is that they do not feel sufficient support from their superiors. Praise without support is an empty gesture." Support is reflected in real, active help in accomplishing work, in providing training, in full disclosure of information about the company's financial health and key measures of output, and in the conviction that trust and confidence is reciprocated between leader and newcomer. Exerting pressure to perform without giving such support is hopelessly destructive, and all too common.

The educator role requires the ability to:

- ► Articulate *consistent* performance expectations and objectives.
- ► Find a "learning laboratory"—task forces; real but low-risk projects—where practical experience can be acquired without heavy penalties or losses.
- ► Give balanced, believable, timely feedback about the specifics of day-to-day performance so people know where they stand and how they're doing.
- ► Provide access to all information that people need to be full partners in the enterprise—and then some.
- ► Explain (most effectively by storytelling) the difference between an acceptable performance and an exceptional one.
- ► Spend enough time to be a useful facilitator and source of support.
- ► Give meticulous attention to planning the education process.
- ► Confident educators do one thing more. They have lived their values with integrity and transmitted those values; the newcomer, new manager or person faced with crises has thus been exposed to bedrock. Given that, the exceptional educator inculcates flexibility. In the terms of our innovation

section, he or she encourages skunking and "cheating." He or she is intolerant of "I could have done it, but . . ." That is, the educator has taught the values so well that he or she expects (demands, really) that the newcomer or new manager bend silly rules to get the job done. This is the ultimate subtlety in the education process.

Educating:
Questions—and Things to Do Now

▶ How well do you educate newcomers? Go ask the last three people you hired about their respective orientations. Were they treated as colleagues and team members? (Collect specifics from them.) Or ignored (i.e., treated as students going through a required mill)? Was your organization's philosophy communicated clearly? (How can you tell?) Did they receive support and clear guidance? Did they develop a sense of accomplishments early? (If so, how?) Did you (as chief orienter) point out how to approach various people in the organization, what the barriers to action are and how to deal with them, what idiosyncrasies exist in the company and how to respond to them? Did you spend enough time, personally, with the newcomers to listen to their first reactions and to reinforce your guidance accordingly? What changes would *they* make in the way they were introduced to the organization? Incorporate their suggestions into the orientation program, but—much, much better—build them into the way you work with all newcomers.

▶ Here comes a big request: Share information vital to your business or organization—Annual Reports, Quarterly Reports, monthly operating results, measures of weekly or daily quality performance, comparative performance (among divisions or units)—with everyone on your team, to the lowest level. Do all hands know, on a *weekly* basis, how their group is performing according to the ten or fifteen most important measures of output? How it stacks up with other groups? Do they know what the measures mean and how they were arrived at and why?

▶ Devote one week to judging your organization's health by tuning in to its stories. This is best done when you are out of your office, wandering around, listening. (If you are new to MBWA, be aware that it will take some time before people share stories; such self-disclosure depends on long-standing trust.) Lead company seminars; it's one of the best ways to hear, firsthand, what the group has to say about their company's beliefs and philosophy. Try to understand why the beliefs persist (e.g., "Nobody listens to salespersons around here," or "Manufacturing can do no wrong"). What kinds of examples (stories) are used to support their beliefs about how your organization runs? Do the beliefs and stories reflect your own impressions? If not, why not?

▶ Facilitate getting information *across* organizational or departmental bounds quickly by scheduling same-level management staff meetings to occur within twenty-four hours of each other, every week. Instead of staff meetings that pop up on an apparently random basis throughout your organization (i.e., at times convenient for each individual group but inconvenient for the organization as a whole), scheduling same-level meetings in tandem means that everyone knows when information is being shared and has access to it much faster. For example, the general manager of a Hewlett-Packard division holds his meeting with his seven functional managers on a Monday morning; they, in turn, meet with their own teams Monday afternoon, and their staffs, meet with their groups by Tuesday afternoon. As a result, the 2,000-person division is fully and consistently informed on a routine basis within forty-eight hours of the general manager's meeting.

▶ Volunteer to teach in your organization's new-hire orientation program. Participate at least once a month, for three or more hours.

▶ Give new *staff* members hands-on orientation experiences by having them spend at least a week working alongside line operators and providers of direct customer service within their first month on board. Request that they write a short (no more than two pages) summary of what they learned from the experience.

▶ Spend some contemplative time on this question: Does your orientation of newcomers serve to "tame" them or prepare them for long-term contribution? The former emphasizes controlling, limiting and restricting; the latter assumes the newcomer is a highly useful resource for innovative ideas and new approaches. What does your orientation say about your beliefs?

What's So Special about You?

Information sharing, as we've said time and again, is an extraordinarily sensitive topic. It shouldn't be! "But there will be leaks" was a rejoinder we heard recently, relative to a discussion about sharing detailed operating information with supervisors. Our nasty response took these two tacks. First, "Oh yeah? And where do most leaks come from? Vice presidents. Ever hear of a leak from a maintenance supervisor?" Second, "And why should a forty-six-year-old, nineteen-year vet on the line have any more inclination to leak than you, a thirty-eight-year-old, six-year vet department head?"

Obviously, there are some few areas of information—e.g., acquisition-related, pre-patent application—where secrecy is called for. Other than that, it is a "simple" matter of trust: You've either taken care in recruiting and developing people, and thus trust them, or you haven't. This strong view, which we hold deeply, doesn't even include the most practical rejoinder to pro-secrecy arguments; namely, there are few important facts that competitors can't get a pretty good fix on by legitimate and legal means. With rare exceptions, the result of most stringent secrecy programs we've observed is mainly to restrict desirable intra-company information flow.

SPONSORING

Sponsoring makes it possible for people to take charge of their environments after they've received a full complement of training and encouragement. Sponsors grant practical autonomy by removing obstacles to performance; sponsoring assumes that the key skills are already in place and have only to be applied.

The key to sponsoring is not to grant too much autonomy too soon and thereby invite failure rather than pride in steady achievement. Although we find that it is much more common to underestimate what people can handle than to overestimate, this point is nonetheless too important to overlook. It's just as bad to give so much room that people feel abandoned as not to give enough. They'll observe that you are out of touch with reality, that you don't understand what they can actually accomplish without your support and personal leadership. They'll conclude that you don't care if they get beaten up unnecessarily. And, of course, they'll be dead right. Sponsoring is not the all too common lack of attention masquerading as "giving people room to grow." Sponsoring is personally *guided* autonomy—and you're the chief guide. Although somewhere near the heart of sponsoring is letting go of the impulse to overcontrol the situation, it never means letting go of the individual.

The Sponsor's Commitment

Everyone at W. L. Gore & Associates has a sponsor, and often more than one, depending on the scope of the Associate's interests and responsibilities. Sponsorship is the pivotal concept in the Gore "lattice" organization (see page 779).

The sponsor's role is defined within the context of Gore's four guiding principles. Successful participation as an Associate (and sponsor) depends on observing and perpetuating them:

1. Fairness. Each of us will *try* to be fair in all dealings—with one another, with our suppliers, with our customers, within our communities, and with all the people with whom we have transactions or agreements. Fairness is seldom clearly defined, but if a sincere effort is made by all, it generates a tolerance that preserves good feelings among us.

2. Freedom. Each of us will allow, help, and encourage his or her Associates to grow in knowledge, skill, the scope of responsibility and the range of

activities. Authority is gained by recognized knowledge or skill. It is a power only of leadership, not of command.

3. Commitment. Each of us will make his or her own commitments—and keep them. No Associates can impose a commitment on another. All commitments are self-commitments.

We organize our enterprises—projects, functions and work of all kinds—through commitments. Therefore, a commitment is a serious matter, amounting to a contract that must be fulfilled.

4. Waterline. Each of us will consult with appropriate Associates who will share the responsibility of taking any action that has the potential of inflicting serious harm on the reputation, success or survival of the enterprise.

The analogy is that our enterprise is like a ship that we are all in together. Boring holes above the waterline is not serious, but below the waterline, holes could sink our ship.

Sponsors at W. L. Gore & Associates voluntarily take a specific, personal interest in the activities, well-being, progress, accomplishments, personal problems and ambitions of the people they sponsor. Sponsors help newcomers get started and vigilantly follow their progress. Sponsors also take the lead in compensation decisions, an especially important role because everything at Gore is done in teams, and the results may not be clear until months or years later. Sponsors, acting together in small committees, evaluate the relative contribution of comparable groups of Associates, and act as positive advocates for the value of each person's individual contribution to the enterprise.

Sponsors and Mentors

Sponsoring and mentoring. The difference may appear to be merely semantic, given conventional usage, but we believe it's useful to differentiate. We called this trait mentoring at first, but then discarded the word for two reasons. First, mentoring has been gobbled up by the psychologists; it's become an "in" word. Who knows what they mean? Second, and more significant, "mentoring" has come to suggest cult-of-personality problems: e.g., the Bill Agee-Mary Cunningham fiasco. If the mentor dies, the mentored one(s) die also: e.g., "Reed's people" versus "Theobald's people" at Citicorp in 1984. (Reed became chairman, at the end of a two-person race, and his "people" quickly came to receive a lion's share of the top slots.) Sponsoring is broader. We steal it unabashedly from Bill and Vieve Gore. The sponsor at Gore is not only responsible for an Associate's development "down" (e.g., practical skill-building), but also responsible for "selling" an Associate laterally and up—i.e., sponsorship occurs wholly within the context of the *organization's* philosophy and needs. Mentoring, often as not, deteriorates into a "Follow *my* flag" relationship.

When Should You Sponsor?

—You assess an individual's ability as consistently high or exceptional.
—You want to prepare someone for promotion or increased responsibility.
—Your main focus is to fine-tune already good technical, administrative and leadership skills and performance.
—Exposure to other areas of the company is necessary to broaden experience.
—You want to alert your colleagues to a promising performer.
—You want to enable people to contribute without stifling them.

The Sponsor Relationship

Sponsoring reflects your direct responsibility for guiding and developing in new contexts the particularly strong skills your people possess. Building on strength is key. Warren Bennis's new study of leadership isolates five factors that mark superb leaders. At the top of the list: they build on strengths rather than focus on weaknesses.

Sponsorship should start early, and almost all superb senior leaders have been superb sponsors throughout their careers. They have understood that the best leaders follow that easy-to-state, hard-to-follow (because ego will be ego) folk wisdom: Promote people who are better than you, then watch them shine as they make *you* look good. (David Ogilvy cemented this notion symbolically. Upon promoting someone to the position of office manager at Ogilvy & Mather, Ogilvy would send the new manager a wooden Russian matryoshka doll from Gorky—the kind that opens to reveal a smaller doll inside, which in turn opens to reveal another. Inside the smallest, the new manager will find this message: "If each of us hires people who are smaller than we are, we shall become a company of *dwarfs*. But if each of us hires people who are bigger than we are, we shall become a company of *giants*.")

The result of the work of the clever and committed sponsor is that when he or she reaches a senior position, all elements of the organization are seeded with his or her talented charges; change of focus thus becomes much more rapidly and effectively achievable.

What Sponsorship Is Not

Sponsoring can be many things, but the following are the antithesis of sound sponsorship.

—Encouraging an individual to become too dependent on you.
—Using the sponsoring role to control rather than to guide and to support performance.
—Shielding people from mistakes or bad news (i.e., dishonesty).

—Telling an individual what he or she wants to hear.
—Becoming involved in the personal decisions an individual must make.
—Applying the sponsor role only to people just like you, avoiding those with different backgrounds or professional goals.
—Confusing sponsoring with parenting.
—Pitting your people against one another in the name of "healthy competition" or survival of the fittest.

Again, we'd stress the difference between the mentor (as popularly conceived) and the sponsor. Sponsoring is the best way of rapidly pushing talented performers to achieve. It is the very core of effective management/leadership development. If you are wise, you will push your most talented charges out into green fields and expect to reap a reward only indirectly, over time. Mentoring, we observe in the real world, often deteriorates into hoarding and, eventually, backbiting politics as "Jones's candidate" contends with "Smith's candidate."

Positive Sponsorship

Positive sponsorship deals with helping people become sensitive to but not enslaved by—a fine balance—your company's norms and prevailing philosophy. The skills addressed in sponsoring are much more subtle, for the most part, than those you address in other coaching roles, because sponsoring assumes that you are moving beyond raw skills and abilities that are already substantially developed and applied. It may, then, focus on the gentle arts: knowing when to shut up, when to stop digging into a problem, when to give in and when to stand and fight, and knowing the limits of skunklike behavior. Many managers refer to these as "street smarts," the kind of understanding that develops over time and cannot be learned in classrooms. The role of sponsorship is to acknowledge unabashedly the subtle norms and to push your best and brightest to come to understand them, take them into account, and use them to achieve.

A fair share of sponsoring—again—involves making philosophy and core values explicit. The best sponsors sit down with an individual to discuss a particular decision and show why it was chosen over other alternatives, or why a course of action turned out to be a mistake. (At Gore & Associates, this consultation involves several sponsors for critical "waterline" issues.) Others spend time talking about how they approach their own jobs with an eye to highlighting the reasoning that underlies decisions.

We have devoted such substantial space to this role because effective leadership is, after all, no more than developing other leaders who both cherish the organization's philosophy (if it is a sound one) and yet test it and adapt within it at every opportunity. An organization is as good as the consistency *and* vitality of its leadership cadre. Almost without exception the most effective leaders at the top are those who started early looking for others to sponsor. When they were department heads in a single retail store, they were determined to look for a would-be superstar to follow in their footsteps. In fact, they were confident of promotion from the start, and were wise enough to realize that their path to glory lay in creating a swath of newly anointed heroes in their wake.

Sponsoring takes time—lots of it. The wise realize that it is the only surefire path to success. (And even if success does not surely follow, at least—no small thing—one can look back on a slate of people developed and enhanced. In the deepest sense—when the light goes on over the mirror—who could ask for more?)

Profile of a Good Sponsor

Like the other four development tasks, sponsoring requires constant attention. Short spurts of attention won't help, but the following will:

—Treating people as colleagues.
—Being on the lookout for opportunities to help people learn and experience other jobs and new responsibilities.
—Making company norms and philosophy explicit and understandable; helping people understand them (their power *and* their limits) within the context of their current activities.
—Regularly discussing an individual's career plans and goals with him or her in the context of recent accomplishments and pratfalls.
—Not being threatened by an individual's exceptional skill or ability.
—Desperately and passionately wanting your people to succeed.

To live this profile takes guts, above all. The gutsiest move imaginable (whether you are a first-line supervisor or chairman) is to give an only somewhat junior person the encouragement and opportunity to push his or her substantial skills to the limit. It *is* scary. It *is* threatening. It is also the *only* path to development of a truly talent-rich organization.

Sponsoring:
Some Questions—and Things to Do Now

▶ There is only one exercise for sponsoring. Do your managers take the kind of broad, sincere interest in people that the sponsors at W. L. Gore & Associates do? How about you? Could you describe the especially strong skills that each of your people possesses? When does each of your people sparkle the most? With whom do they work the best? What experiences does each of your people find the most rewarding? (Sponsoring is tailored to each individual's strengths—not providing the same collection of experiences for everyone alike.) Take the time to answer these questions for each of your people. Put together a real development plan for each person and sit down to discuss what each wants to achieve, what his or her ambitions are. A paper program is not enough!

COACHING

Is There a Leader in Your Company?

In an open memorandum to the "outside directors and trustees of all the organizations not in the Fortune 1000", Robert Townsend, author of *Further Up the Organization,* posed one question: "Ask yourself if you have a leader as a CEO." Do you have a leader in your company?

LEADER	*NON-LEADER*
Carries water for people.	Presides over the mess.
A coach appealing to the best in each person; open door; problem-solver and advice-giver; cheerleader.	Invisible—gives orders to staff—expects them to be carried out.
Thinks of ways to make people more productive, more focused on company goals; how to reward them.	Thinks of personal rewards, status, and how he or she looks to outsiders.
Comfortable with people in their workplaces.	Uncomfortable with people.
No reserved parking place, private washroom, dining room or elevator.	Has them.
MBWA (manages by wandering around).	No MBWA.
Arrives early—stays late.	In late—usually leaves on time.
Common touch.	Strained with blue collars.
Good listener.	Good talker.
Simplistic on company values.	Good at demonstrating his command of all the complexities.

Available.	Hard to reach from below.
Fair.	Fair to the top; exploits the rest.
Decisive.	Uses committees, consultants.
Humble.	Arrogant.
Tough—confronts nasty problems.	Elusive—the artful dodger.
Persistent.	Only when his own goodies are at stake.
Simplifies (makes it look easy).	Complicates (makes it look difficult).
Tolerant of open disagreement.	Intolerant of open disagreement.
Knows people's names.	Doesn't know people's names.
Has strong convictions.	Vacillates when a decision is needed.
Does dog-work when necessary.	Above dog-work.
Trusts people.	Trusts only words and numbers on paper.
Delegates whole important jobs.	Keeps all final decisions.
Spends as little time as possible with outside directors, outside activities.	Spends a lot of time massaging outside directors.
Wants anonymity for himself, publicity for his company.	The reverse.
Often takes the blame.	Looks for a scapegoat.
Gives credit to others.	Takes credit; complains about lack of good people.
Gives honest, frequent feedback.	Info flows one way—into his or her office.
Knows when and how to fire people.	Ducks unpleasant tasks.
Weeds the garden.	Likes to get bigger and more complex.
Goes where the trouble is to help.	Interrupts people in crisis and calls them to meeting in his or her office.

Sees growth as by-product of search for excellence.	Sees growth as primary goal.
Has respect for all people.	Thinks blue collars and pink collars are lazy, incompetent ingrates.
Knows the business, and the kind of people who make it tick.	They've never met him or her.
Honest under pressure.	Improvises, equivocates.
Looks for controls to abolish.	Loves new controls.
Prefers eyeball to eyeball instead of memos.	Prefers memos, long reports.
Straightforward.	Tricky, manipulative.
Consistent and credible to the troops.	Unpredictable; says what he thinks they want to hear.
Admits own mistakes; comforts others when they admit them.	Never makes mistakes; blames others; starts witch hunts to identify culprits.
No policy manuals.	Policy manuals.
Openness.	Secrecy.
Little paperwork in planning.	Vast paperwork in planning.
Promotes from within.	Always searching outside the company.
Keeps his promises.	Doesn't.
Plain office.	Lavish office.
Thinks there are at least two other people in the company who would be good CEO's.	Number one priority is to make bloody sure no one remotely resembling a CEO gets on the payroll.
Focused to the point of monomania on the company's values and objectives.	Unfocused except on self.
Company is No. 1.	Self is No. 1.
Sees mistakes as learning opportunities.	Sees mistakes as punishable offenses.

You *now* know more about leaders and leadership than all the combined graduate business schools in America.

You also know whether you have a leader or an administrator in your CEO's office.

There are subtle differences between coaching and sponsoring. Coaching teaches people how to contribute and participate as active, full partners; sponsoring begins when outstanding skill has begun to speak for itself.

Effective coaching means creating winners, keeping the faith in the thick of turmoil, building momentum, finding tiny glimmers of light (to reinforce) in the midst of darkness, building on the strength that ninety-nine out of a hundred have.

We've learned about coaching from participants in our seminars. Here's what they've said about the characteristics of good coaches:

Challenges me to do my best.
Sets a good example.
Never divulges a confidence.
Explains the reasons for instructions and procedures.
Helps me polish my thoughts before I present them to others.
Is objective about things.
Lets me make my own decisions.
Cares about me and how I'm doing.
Does not seek the limelight.
Won't let me give up.
Gives personal guidance and direction, especially when I'm learning something new.
Is empathetic and understanding.
Is firm but fair.
Keeps a results orientation.
Makes me work out most of my own problems or tough situations, but supports me.
Lets me know where I stand.
Listens exceptionally well.
Doesn't put words in my mouth.
Is easy to talk to.
Keeps the promises he or she makes.
Keeps me focused on the goals ahead.
Works as hard or harder than anyone else.
Is humble.
Is proud of those managers he or she has developed.
Gives credit where credit is due.
Practices MBWA.
Never says "I told you so."
Corrects my performance in private.
Never flaunts authority.
Is always straightforward.
Gives at least a second chance.
Maintains an Open Door Policy.
Uses language that is easy to understand.

Lets bygones be bygones.
Inspires loyalty.
Really wants to hear my ideas, and acts on them.
Lets me set my own deadlines.
Celebrates successes.
Is open and honest.
Doesn't hide bad news.
Gives me enough time to prepare for discussion.
Is enthusiastic.
Follows through.
Is patient.
Wants me to "stretch" my skills.
Gives me his or her full attention during discussions, won't be distracted.
Has a sense of humor.
Handles disagreements privately.
Reassures me.
Makes me feel confident.
Tells me the "whole story."
Says "we" instead of "I."
Makes hard work worth it.
Can communicate annoyance without running wild.
Is courageous.
Insists on training.
Is a stabilizing influence in a crisis.
Gets everyone involved.
Wants me to be successful.
Is optimistic.
Operates well under pressure, or in a rapidly changing environment.
Has a reputation for competence with his or her peers.
Has a good understanding of the job.
Is tough and tender.
Believes we can do it.
Sets attainable milestones.
Communicates philosophy and values.
Is perceptive—doesn't require that everything be spelled out.
Has a strong sense of urgency.
Preserves the individuality of his or her team members.
Thinks and operates at a level above that expected.
Wants to make the organization the best in the industry.
Is willing to act on intuition; believes feelings are facts.
Empowers us.
Is there when we need him or her.
Enjoys his or her job.
Likes to spend time with us.

This list has one stunning characteristic: there is absolutely nothing new on it. Leaders want to do all these things. Most get distracted by the technical aspects of their job. They don't get around to it. New managers find that time spent doing those things "doesn't feel like work." No leader practices all these traits all the time. What they best do (usually intuitively, because most leadership training is so shoddy) is realize that these are the "it." Effective leadership *is* full-time people development. Moreover, it doesn't take an extroverted personality, or special flair or a flashy style, to coach well—it only takes consistent attention and vigilant action. In coaching, the name of the game is execution.

When Should You Coach?

—When you assess an individual's administrative, technical or leadership ability and performance as moderate.
—When you want to encourage people to discover what they can do by "pushing" themselves.
—When you want to develop teamwork.
—To express confidence and support.
—When recognition and credit are due for innovativeness.
—When reassurance is all that's needed for successful performance.
—When you want to develop each individual's skill and foster individual performance.
—To celebrate the accomplishments of a team or an individual.

Demanding PepsiCo Is Attempting to Make Work Nicer for Managers

The Wall Street Journal, October 23, 1984, reports:

Can PepsiCo Inc. become a nicer place to work without losing the edge that has helped make it a highly profitable, $8 billion food and soft-drink company?

Its management thinks so. Although PepsiCo prizes the fast pace and demanding standards that make it so competitive, it worries about battle fatigue in the ranks. Says Andrall E. Pearson, the company's president: "We probably attract people who give ulcers, rather than those who get them."

Accordingly, PepsiCo has decided that a bit more back-patting and hand-holding are in order—but not so much, mind you, that standards slip. The time is ripe to focus on such "soft stuff," Mr. Pearson explains, because the company has recently rebounded from a financial slump. Wall Street is touting its stock and earnings are headed for record levels.

But the principal motivation came last spring, when two surveys of PepsiCo's top 470 executives turned up some troubling job alienation. Many managers complained that they didn't feel cared about as people, that they didn't know enough about what was happening in the company as a whole, and that they weren't told how they were doing in their jobs.

As a consequence, Mr. Pearson told executives at a big May meeting in the Bahamas that they need to give more feedback and demonstrate a "real interest" in subordinates.

Although the company doesn't claim to have made enormous strides in six months, it has started tinkering with a corporate environment that is often criticized for encouraging individualism at the expense of the collective effort. . . .

PepsiCo will try to convince its solid achievers that it cares about them as well as its fast-track stars. It will try to better inform such employees of specific career paths to promotion, and limit job changes to those that are necessary.

In addition, the company wants to emphasize the value of coaching and training, management traits that aren't rewarded now. In the future, promotions and pay will be based partly on how well an executive furthers the development of subordinates.

According to J. Roger King, the new head of personnel, PepsiCo hopes to accomplish all this without sending managers to "sensitivity" training courses. "There are a lot of workshops where you dip people in and bring them up clean," Mr. King says. "I call it the bathtub theory of training. Two hours later they're dirty. It doesn't work because you can't take it to the workplace."

Instead, he favors on-the-job changes that, while slight, may change attitudes and behavior. In the past, for instance, January bonus checks have been distributed with a handshake but few words. This year, the employee's supervisor will review performance and try to explain precisely what determined the size of the bonus.

At annual merit-increase reviews, the company will be more specific in showing what kinds of behavior are rewarded. The forms for such reviews have been rewritten: Instead of dwelling on generalities, they now ask how a manager is doing daily, how effectively he is planning for the long term, what he is doing to develop subordinates, and how his own personal development is progressing.

After the Turn-On, What?

Each summer, thirty thousand Mary Kay consultants convene in Dallas, Texas, for a "seminar"—an extravaganza by any standards. There are countless awards. Applause floods the Convention Center. Mary Kay Ash steps to the stage and addresses the sea of people before her. She urges, cheers, directs, pushes, advises and convinces virtually all of the thirty thousand consultants that they can go out and do anything.

This is coaching, to be sure, although many managers dismiss such grand-scale events as "mere" theatrics or show business. We've said that all business *is* show business—yes, a matter of symbolizing and shaping values and beliefs. After the turn-on of the big event, what? How does coaching work day to day, minute to minute?

Support (versus Praise)

Coaching does include praise—expressing approval or admiration, applauding, commending and lauding small (and large) victories. No coach can build a successful team without dipping into these reserves. But warm words of reassurance are not enough. Coaching is the act of helping the team withstand the tough times and the inevitable setbacks along the way, maintaining momentum, and building small successes into a solid track record. Support is shown by the personal commitment of the coach, proven through his or her stubborn, imaginative interest (not just friendliness or congeniality) in helping each individual progress. Support is sometimes proven through direct intervention— when a talented individual strays off track and wants (needs) forth-right, active, palpable help or more information. At other times, the most supportive act is to stay out of the way, allowing people to discover for themselves how best to handle a situation: quiet but assertive trust that they will overcome difficulty is the essence of support. Praise *without* support is mere platitude.

Coaching is ongoing leadership, frequently unobtrusive. We like the imagery of former Stanford basketball coach Dick DiBiaso. He calls it "floor coaching": the coach as part of the team, observing, making notes, critiquing play, offering suggestions for improvement, challenging, working *for* the team, alongside. It's a subtle process. A former IBMer stresses the point: "Coaching isn't always noisy and obvious. The best coach I ever had used to come around and ask, 'How's such and such going?' or 'What do you think the customer wants?' Those questions were perfectly aimed. I'd leave those little meetings believing I'd come up with the answers. Only later did I realize that he directed my attention with those questions of his, used them as rudders to steer me in a certain direction. He never once came out and told me what to do; he led me there and made me feel like I'd figured it out on my own. He was never impatient, or too busy to listen. But I think what I appreciated about him most was that he never asked me to do something I didn't have the ability to do, even if I didn't realize it. He knew me well enough to judge my reach; that was his credibility. If he had put me in situations where I failed, I would have doubted *his* ability as a coach more than mine as a player. I knew he wanted me to succeed and that we could count on each other. After talking with him, I felt empowered."*

As vital a point here as any is "He never asked me to do something I didn't have the ability to do." Coaches stretch you to your limit, a limit often beyond what you thought possible. *Great* coaches stretch you *exactly* to that previously unknown limit, but no further. Because their chief concern is turning you into a successful person, to have you experience *some* stretch and *lots* of success, to build momentum and enthusiasm for further accomplishment.

General Douglas MacArthur said he learned one thing, above all, from his almost equally celebrated father, a Civil War hero: "Never give an order that can't be obeyed." I.e., the ultimate loss is to push your people beyond their capacities. Business's classic "stretch target" more often than not leaves us appalled. It's stretch for stretch's sake, creating "can't win" situations (read "creating losers"). IBM's sales goal negotiation process, on the other hand, is great. It's tough, but the manager is marked down badly if his or her people aren't successful (i.e., if they are allowed to commit to too much). He or she is paid, says IBM, to get it roughly right—stretch, to be sure, but not excess.

Mary Kay Ash, in her book *Mary Kay on People Management,* reprises the "stretching" theme with her account of a telephone call from a "consultant", (her term for Mary Kay field people) in Michigan, who was not doing well in her business.

> We talked for a while, and I finally told her, "Here's what we're going to do. We're going to have a special contest just for you. I want you to book ten beauty shows for next week, and after you've held them, I want you to call me back and tell me how you did."
>
> "Ten shows?"
>
> "That's right," I answered. "I want you to call each hostess in your datebook, and say that you just talked to Mary Kay. Tell her that I've established a contest for you, and then let her know how much you want to win it. Finally, ask her to be a hostess for next week." Based on what she told me, I knew her problem: she was giving only one or two beauty shows a month. I also knew that former hostesses would be the most receptive to her request, giving her a better chance to book more beauty shows. With enough exposure, I felt she would do well. She just needed to gain confidence.

*This IBM account is hardly random. IBM is the rare institution that views leadership (and coaching) as teachable, and goes about doing so with a vengeance. Moreover, while "developing subordinates" is a new wrinkle in PepsiCo's formal evaluation process, it is the paramount success criterion for IBM managers at all levels.

At the end of the following week she called me back to report $748 in sales. Although it was not among the highest sales recorded that week, it was by far a record for her. Even though she hadn't booked all ten shows, she was elated and seemed to have snapped out of her depression.

Educating supplies the knowledge and training needed to perform. Coaching guides that performance in real time, shapes it, refines it, carries it forward, makes it matter. No more detached, cynical naysayers, but people who operate from feelings, who inspire others, who count on their teams to perform, who see that performance is rewarded and appreciated. Coaches know they will never have perfect information and they act anyway. They take one step, try something, move forward to listen and encourage.

> I would like to suggest that in a day when so much energy seems to be spent on maintenance and manuals, on bureaucracy and meaningless quantification, to be a leader is to enjoy the special privileges of complexity, of ambiguity, of diversity—but especially the opportunity to make a meaningful difference in the lives of those who permit us to lead.
>
> *Max DePree, Herman Miller, Inc.*

Coaching:
Some Questions and Things To Do Now

▶ Reflect on this: alone, or with a colleague, or in a small group, think about team, group or organizational highs and lows in the past. What has marked the highs and lows in terms of people beliefs? Those of the leader? Of peers for each other? Picture (yes, visually) two or three exceptional coaches/bosses: What characterized them (especially again, their people beliefs)? Repeat the exercise for one or two bad bosses.

▶ Do you show substantial *support* for your team (as opposed to using praise or pressure alone)? How do you think your team members would evaluate your willingness to understand their problems and to do something about them (recall Mary Kay Ash's tangible support for the sidetracked consultant)? Evaluate how much real support you provide for your team. Think of at least three occasions when you applied pressure to perform, but without support; three times when you provided praise without support; and three times when you provided support and praise or pressure. How did the consequences of each approach differ? Why? Which approach was the most successful? Least successful?

► Visit a store, department, company or other organization that you particularly admire, and observe the manager/leader/coach very carefully. What does he or she do that enables the other people to perform? Plan to spend at least two or three hours observing. Do the same at the next sporting event you attend: Watch the coaches. Football, basketball, swimming or soccer are all good choices with plenty of opportunities to watch coaches in action. (Better yet, take a week "off" and attend a pro football summer camp—practices are usually open. Watch a Don Shula of the Miami Dolphins work with his staff and players.) How do they interact with their teams? When do they work with an individual? How does the style vary from one person to another? How does the coach behave during time-outs and during play? Make this a systematic study. Write down your impressions along with two or three ways you can apply them in your interactions with your team. (I.e., so you want to be a great leader? *Study* great leaders. Devote time to it. After all, whether as supervisor of the night maintenance crew or chairman of the board, your career *is* leadership. Have you studied it as you studied accounting? Physics? If not, why not?)

► Do you, de facto, know what your team expects from you as a coach? Ask each person individually how he or she wants to work with you as a leader/coach. Do your impressions of your team members' abilities coincide with theirs? If not, is this a surprise? Or do patterns develop—e.g., do you tend to overfocus on administrative responsibilities and underfocus on helping your team members expand their skills or trying them out in new areas?

► Do you define coaching as showing up when there are problems? Do your people feel that they hear from you only when something has gone wrong? Ask two or three of your team members this question (it will be hard to do).

► Do you have an Open Door Policy? (I.e., do people *use* the open door?)

► Do you show up to provide real-time encouragement before an important event for one of your team members? And after to find out how it went?

► Find twenty-five little behaviors of yours that show you care about your team, that convey genuine respect and care beyond lip service. Be specific.

► Find twenty-five little behaviors that show indifference to your team (welcome to a very large club). You may not intend to communicate noncaring or noninvolvement, but your team members are the best judges. If you aren't sure, ask one or two of your team to help you (this can be very tough but extremely helpful).

► Follow Donna Ecton's example (VP, Campbell Soup, then at Citicorp) and infuse your team with enthusiasm by renaming a company district or territory, e.g., from District 12B South (who can take pride in a name like that?) to the Superstars or other name that you and your team devise. Create symbols to go along with the name, and use it the way professional athletic teams use their colors, names and mascots to generate ownership and care.

To Scream or Not to Scream

Indiana basketball coach Bobby Knight rants and raves—in practices and at games. And wins. San Francisco Forty-niner Coach Bill Walsh is so cool and collected that he is regularly called "cerebral," "the professor." He wins. Both are respected by their players. Both have an extraordinary degree of compassion for their players, albeit exhibited in almost diametrically opposing ways.

This is not the place to review the thousands of papers and monographs written about leadership and personality. It is, however, the place to underscore again that *we* observe that no one personality type is associated with coaching and leadership success. We *do* believe that compassion, empathy and a belief in the ability of the average team member is a must. But this belief can come in wrappers of all descriptions.

COUNSELING

Problems arise. They fester. They must be fixed. "Tough-minded" managers take pride in "stepping up to the plate on tough personnel issues." Yet most, we find, stink as counselors. For counseling is about frankness *and* (equally) about compassion. It is the acid test of whether you really live up to the spirit of the "belief in people" you doubtless espouse. Poor counseling—too early or too late, too harsh or too soft, too perfunctory or dragged on forever—puts your beliefs on display as nothing else does.

It is April 24, 1984, and Herman Miller's Max DePree addresses the Annual Scanlon Plan Associates Conference in Raleigh, North Carolina. His themes are leadership, followership and, particularly, "ownership." DePree characterizes ownership, above all, as full-scale *accountability,* reaching for one's potential and "taking full possession of a situation," including sharing the ownership of problems. Counseling is the delicate but vital leadership role that leads people to seek and accept accountability.

All people have the *right* to know where they stand, "to be accountable," in Max DePree's words. This means your caring enough to let someone know in a timely fashion when performance is off track. It takes self-confidence and skill to lead people to recognize problems, as well as successes, in a constructive way. But as a veteran manager said to Nancy recently, "It's downright cruel to allow people to flounder when you can see what's happening and you don't do anything to turn it around. There's no excuse for that kind of insensitivity. None."

The Art of Listening

Mary Kay Ash describes how she handled a personal problem of one of her executives:

Sometimes listening by itself may not be enough—some people must be prodded if you are to find out what they're thinking. But a word of caution: Be subtle, or you'll come across as being intrusive. Sometimes a thin line separates invasion of privacy from concern and interest. With this in mind, when I sense a problem, I'll ask a question or two, then be quiet and listen for a response. Sometime ago, for instance, the work habits of one of my executives, whom I will call "Bill," began to falter. He had always submitted his reports promptly, but for several consecutive weeks he had been arriving at the office late, at the committee meetings he had contributed very little—all of which was quite uncharacteristic of him. One day while he was in my office explaining why a report was late, I decided it was time to have a heart-to-heart talk with him. I stood up from my desk and walked around to pour him a cup of coffee.

"How do you like your coffee?" I asked.

"Black would be fine."

I put his cup on the table in front of the sofa and sat down. He automatically sat down beside me. "Bill," I said, "you're one of our key people, you've been with us for twelve years, and I feel we have become good friends in that time."

"I feel that way, too, Mary Kay," he said in a soft voice.

"I'm concerned about you, Bill. You've always been so conscientious about your work that we've come to depend upon your contributions. But lately you just haven't been yourself. . . ."

He didn't respond, so I stopped talking and took a sip of coffee. He seemed tense, and I offered to pour some more coffee for him. "No, that's all right," he answered.

"Is something wrong at home?" I asked.

His face grew red, and after a few moments he nodded his head. "Is there anything I could do to help?"

He proceeded to tell me how upset he was because his wife's doctor had discovered a tumor on her upper back—and he wanted to tell me because he knew it was affecting his work. I'm certain it was necessary for him to release his bottled-up feelings; we must have talked for over an hour. He seemed to feel much better at the end of the conversation, and later his work improved immensely. While I didn't solve his personal problem, it was good for the two of us to talk about it.

Just how far a manager should go in discussing an employee's personal problems is something only the individuals involved can

> determine. I don't think a manager can work with a person day in and day out and not develop some sort of personal relationship.

The counseling role at its best leads people to understand and overcome problems that get in the way of top-notch performance. It's a question of always taking the time—*now*. Some problems turn out to be no more than small glitches and can be solved in fifteen minutes; many others will be the predictable result of incomplete information or simple misunderstanding. Others will require months of intermittent effort to unleash the potential of someone whose superior skills are shackled by an unwillingness to be a partner or team player. Counseling is *overkill* in all these situations.

When Should You Counsel?

—When an individual has a solid track record but isn't performing as well as usual.
—When performance isn't improved by educating or coaching.
—When an individual asks for your help to solve a personal problem.
—When an individual is "stuck," unsure about how to proceed.
—When people are having trouble coping because your organization is growing very fast or is experiencing major change.
—When an individual used to success experiences failure or disappointment and seems unable to bounce back, especially after his or her role has been broadened by promotion.

Counseling and Major Change

In a volatile environment marked by economic turbulence or fundamental change, even the very best will stumble before finding their sea legs. The same is true in industries that undergo major technological revolutions every few years as a matter of course. Counseling provides needed support and stability at these times by helping people discover how they can continue to contribute to their organization as it rolls with the punches; it also prepares people emotionally for the uncertainty to come. Even positive change needs to be facilitated by the willingness to counsel: Reducing bureaucracy to give each individual more freedom and a real stake takes some getting used to. Staff layers are reduced and real accountability replaces the "way we've always done it around here." It may sound like an unadulterated good. But it feels like a whole new ball game, and people have the right to expect sustained support and clearly articulated goals.* Counseling at its best can help people move through a period of change with their self-respect intact, which in turn can speed up the entire pace of change dramatically.

The *Right* to Counsel

Before you take on the counseling role, ask yourself if the situation really calls for it. The first step is to give the individual a reasonable chance to turn things around under his or her own power, with your wholehearted support, without your interference. Counseling is *not* meddling—"involvement without the right or an invitation." Too soon is as disastrous as too late. You have the right to counsel when and only when you're invited, or performance problems threaten to undermine an individual's ability to contribute over time in spite of conscientious education and coaching. The right to counsel is *earned* by your demonstrated and repeated willingness to educate and coach first. If you pass that tough first test and the problems persist, it's time to extend a purposeful hand: "I want you to be effective, and I know that you want to be effective. Let's see how we can work together to achieve that."

A Counseling Sequence

What follows is a counseling approach that we've learned from the collective experiences of Hewlett-Packard, Gore & Associates, People Express and Dana managers. Their problem-solving model is characterized by the kind of care, sensitivity and respect for people that we see reflected in everything they do. Its unique attribute is the combination of hardheaded practicality (putting the organization first, as you must do for the sake of others) and compassion.

Preparation

Getting ready to counsel has mainly to do with defining the key issue as you see it: improving working relationships, bringing slipped project schedules back into line, improving customer-service track records. Develop a focus on objective behavior and measurable results that the individual *can do something about.* Hazy interpretations are always misunderstood, and are rarely, if ever, very helpful. Worse, they betray a sincere desire to help by making you appear out of touch with real achievements as well as real setbacks.

---

*GM confronted this during the early days of the 1984 merger with Ross Perot's EDS. The non-bureaucracy of EDS came as such a shock that hundreds of GM's senior MIS department people sought out unions as a buffer from straightforward transfer to EDS.

Schedule the Meeting

Some times are better than others for a counseling discussion. Counseling is a promise you must keep: Don't squeeze it between staff meetings. Don't cancel your first two tries. Pick a time when you both can give it your full attention, but do it during working hours. Conducting a counseling meeting after hours over a drink doesn't work. Superior counseling is not a warmed-over negative innuendo or two eased in between beers.

Top-notch counselors have very strong feelings about how much advance notice to give someone they will counsel. In a nutshell: not much. The reason? "People usually know when things aren't going well, even if they haven't asked for help," comments one manager. "You don't tell them on a Friday that you want to meet on Monday or Tuesday. Do you know what kind of a weekend they're going to have trying to second-guess what's on your mind? I'd want to be treated with more courtesy than that." The recommended alternative: ask the individual early in the day if he or she can meet with you that afternoon.

State the Problem

The counseling process begins with a face-to-face discussion that you open with a brief, straightforward statement of why you wanted to meet. At this point you don't have to agree on the problem—just that you have something to talk about. This is not the time for drama. Open the discussion, and then listen.

Listen

The most important part of counseling is listening. Nothing matters so much as your full attention. See what you can learn. Face up to a hard question: How have *you* contributed to the problem situation? A manager who's been there comments, "It's tough to admit that you're part of the problem. It's easy to convince yourself that you've been coaching just right. But you've probably gone too fast or too slow, maybe held on too tight. If you listen, you'll find out." What's at the root of the problem?

When the Problem Is Personal

Counseling requires special sensitivity and genuine respect when the problem is personal in nature: family troubles, illness, alcohol or drug abuse, money problems. It can be tough to know how to help in situations like these, whether your interest will be seen as interference (it usually is) or your reserve mistaken for callousness (it usually is). Reassure the individual that you want to do what you can to help; be sure that people know what outside resources are available (e.g., counseling support, financial counselors or advisers). An empathetic ear and an open door may be the most genuine signs that you care.

Put Together an Action Plan on the Spot

Once you know where you're headed, build the means to get there. What needs to happen, and when? What will your role be? Do you both agree? Before the meeting ends, set up another one to check on how things are going, to see how you can help and support progress.

What Counseling Is Not

Counseling has boundaries that must be respected. Counseling is not:

—An opportunity for you to practice psychiatric therapy.
—A one-shot activity.
—An off-the-cuff discussion.
—Punitive.
—Solely concerned with personal problems.
—The Personnel Department's business.
—An opportunity to review an individual's whole life.
—A one-way mini-lecture by the counselor.
—A brief, hurried activity.
—Intended to solve all an individual's problems.

Profile of a Good Counselor

How well do you perform the counseling role? The following characterize a good counselor:

—Is easy to talk to.
—Listens well.
—Helps people solve problems but does not overcontrol.
—Shows empathy when discussing problems.
—Is receptive to feelings.
—Can keep a confidence.
—Is perceptive in recognizing when help is needed.
—Wants people to do well.
—Builds self-esteem and confidence.
—Is interested in what the other has to say, not just what he or she wants to hear.
—Takes the other seriously.
—Is willing to spend time.
—Is receptive to the idea of others.
—Gives the other his or her full attention.
—Encourages another try.

In the "People, People, People" section we stressed ownership almost exclusively. In the customer and innovation sections, we stressed top-to-bottom attention to the customer's perception and inculcating the right to fail (a prime precursor to regular innovation). All three of these bases for distinctive performance emanate, more fundamentally, from genuine trust, care, respect and integrity on the part of leaders at all levels. Not mollycoddling, but sincere respect for the potential of the person.

The chief indicator of wholesale respect by you (the boss) for me (a person) is your willingness to give unabashedly of yourself as a counselor. It is via the act of counseling—a tremendous commitment on the part of *every* manager—that one best sees the willingness to take care and give respect beyond lip service.

No one disagrees: "All problems are people problems." Yet few put their calendars where their mouth is. Counseling meetings are delayed time and time again in the less effective companies. Failure to devote genuine concern and energy to counseling isn't a major black mark when senior managers evaluate junior managers. "Oh, boy, we waited too long, again [to address a problem]" is the common hallway lament in the mediocre performers. At IBM, if you wait too long, your days, to be blunt, are numbered. IBM says in a hundred ways, "Put the time in, *now.*"

Like most of our "common sense" traits, this one, too, takes time. Even, heaven help us, time away from MBWA with customers and the shop floor. Nonetheless it may be the most distinctive mark of the star performer. Counseling, done with genuine care, *is* respect. Without it, the trust that breeds true ownership—throughout the entire organization—is simply not possible.

Counseling:
Some Questions—and Things to Do Now

▶ Think back and reflect on the first major setback you experienced in your career. How did your boss handle it? What was (or wasn't) done to make you feel stronger and wiser, rather than weaker and less confident? How specifically can you learn from your own experience and apply it tangibly with your team members? What would you do differently as a counselor from the ways you were counseled earlier in your career? What would you do the same ways? Why?

▶ If yours is a company in an industry that undergoes dramatic changes in short periods of time, have you adequately protected your people from its volatility by being aware (very closely aware) of the skills, achievements, talents and weak spots each person possesses (essential if you are to help an individual develop a long-term career)? If you can't describe, in detail, each person's skills and vulnerabilities, sit down within the week and talk at length with each of your team members. A large part of successful counseling is keeping up with potential problems before they arise, and protecting people from unexpected shocks or setbacks. Listen to what your people tell you. Review their performance records. What skills can be highlighted and stretched? What areas need to be strengthened? How can you help people stay in front of technological or industry changes rather than play "catch up" later? (P.S.: You *can* find the time. Our friend Marty Davidson, of the highly successful Southern Pipe and Supply, has an annual 45-minute meeting, on the road, with *each* of his *five hundred* employees, in forty locations.)

▶ Reflect again on your own career. What obstacles were the most difficult for you to overcome? Why? How can your experience be applied as you work with your team?

▶ When you counsel an individual, do you show respect for him or her by listening more than talking and advising? (If you said yes, try again. Are you sure? Most of us think we're good listeners, but aren't.) Do you treat the problem as important? Do you try to help the individual organize his or her feelings and impressions?

▶ Do you overprotect people so they cannot accept full ownership of situations (including problems)? Have you tried to hide or soften bad news? Do you encourage overdependence on you as a result? What do you imagine would happen if you gave clear, direct feedback about the problematic consequences of a situation?

CONFRONTING

Don't live with a problem—face it honestly and correct it. Excuses interest no one except our competition. Never tolerate commitments in words instead of in spirit.

Hewlett-Packard group manager

This comment captures what we mean when we say that HP is a tough, no-excuses environment. Serious problems are taken seriously and addressed cleanly. The company assumes that performance problems can be solved, but only within the context of the HP Way, the company's operating philosophy.

There may come a time when a company has done all it can do to help people turn around a persistent problem. Alternatives have to be faced squarely and honestly. The last-ditch confronting role is for that purpose. It facilitates choice and makes the alternatives crystal clear.

When Should You Confront?

—When performance consistently falls below expectations or deteriorates.
—When counseling does not resolve problems.

—When an individual seems unhappy and unable to perform in his or her role.
—When an individual's behavior is disrupting a team's performance or contributes to others' decisions to transfer or leave the company.
—When an individual is unable to meet performance expectations even though they are clear and understood.
—When reassignment or termination are the only remaining options.
—When the consequences of continued inappropriate behavior or low performance must be explained.

Confronting low performance is probably the toughest responsibility to carry out, but the alternative, observed all too frequently, is worse. Unaddressed, chronic, serious difficulty not only demoralizes the organization but undermines an individual's confidence and may make it nearly impossible for the person to bounce back. That's the crime of refusing to act, and act quickly. (Quite simply, nothing reduces the manager's credibility faster than the unwillingness to address an obvious problem. Our people rightly ask, "What in the hell is he or she [boss] waiting for?")

Confrontation Defined

Confronting does *not* mean a tough battle, clash or personal attack, an *unplanned* hostile discussion, browbeating or threatening.* It never means treating people badly. Done by the best, it is in no way an opportunity for a frustrated leader to unload on someone else. Confronting is a form of counseling in which the alternatives and consequences are clear and close at hand. Provided the individual understands performance expectations (i.e., you performed your educator's role well), and provided you have done everything you can (effectively coached and counseled) to foster improvement, confronting can be a constructive, caring response to an individual's chronic low performance—a face-to-face meeting where you bring an individual's attention to the consequences of unacceptable performance, which include reassignment or termination. Confronting recognizes that a change is imperative.

When Loyalty Isn't Enough

Inc. magazine reports in the January 1982 issue:

Warren joined Diemakers Inc. shortly after it was started in 1960. There was only one person working with him when the company

---

*There is an unexpected benefit of this. We note that "alumni" (who failed to be promoted or were released) of the companies who counsel and confront most effectively end up being among the companies' biggest fans, once the initial pain has passed.

gave him the title of die-casting supervisor. But, in the next ten years, Diemakers grew from 40 to 150 employees, and Warren's staff swelled to 6.

Warren was a proud man who worked hard for the firm, and he was only a few years away from retirement. But as his responsibilities grew, Warren had trouble keeping up. Employees began taking their problems to the department's strongest manager, the second-in-command.

"We had a situation that outgrew the individual, and we should have dealt with it directly," says George Spalding, president of the Monroe City, Mo., diecasting company. Instead, Diemakers' management never confronted the supervisor about his limitations. Warren's feelings of frustration and failure mounted until he finally retired. . . .

Why do so many entrepreneurs and managers fail to confront these problems? The most common excuse is that other problems of running the company are more important.

"When you're trying to stay on top of a growing company, you tend to ignore this kind of problem, especially if the employee is at a low level in the organization," says Diemakers' Spalding. "But you can't overlook it because disgruntled people at any level can cause havoc in a company."

The other reason, of course, is the unwillingness to face the pain even if, in the long run, it might make things easier for all concerned.

"Don't kid yourself," said one chief executive. "Confronting a loyal employee about his limited capability makes for a very bad day. But if you can't address these situations, you're in the wrong job yourself. Most chief executives who don't take action think they're being good guys. The truth is you're a lousy guy for doing that."

Once more, this is a vital step beyond lip service in showing true respect for all your direct reports (whether division general managers or down-the-line team members). To allow a problem to fester beyond the limits of good sense exposes you as noncaring. You are not thought sympathetic because you let a problem drag on. (Properly handled confrontation is, of course, an art. Pull the string too quickly and all fear your capriciousness: "There, but for the grace of God, go I." Pull it too slowly and you demonstrate the lack of being in touch with your people.)

A Confronting Process

Consider the person who has contributed consistently over time—the last decade or more—and who is clearly giving the task his or her full attention, but who recently has been outrun by state-of-the-art technology and is unable to keep up. Or think about the manager who loves the technical side of his or her work but doesn't like the people side, and whose team consistently suffers as a result. Consider as well the person who believes more strenuously in quantification and methodology than in paying attention to customers, innovative practices or people—a "forlorn existence," according to Max DePree. Each of these situations might be best handled with confronting, depending on the answers to a few hard questions:

—Has this person been given every reasonable chance to succeed?
—Have company resources been used well to improve performance?
—Does this person understand what contribution is expected?
—Have you given honest and timely feedback?
—Is it possible to restructure the job to take advantage of this person's strengths?
—Can this individual contribute to the company in other ways?

Your answers will help you determine whether confronting—to effect a clear, focused change—is necessary. One manager observes that "the hardest decision you have to make is when you've done enough counseling and you have to ask: Have you really worked hard enough? Was your heart in it? What can my team and my company live with? The clear-cut decision doesn't exist."

No Surprises

Except for the rare circumstance that demands on-the-spot action, the occasion for confronting low performance should never be the first time an individual realizes that there's a problem. The individual has the right to know where he or she stands, and to have the means to judge how serious a problem might become if it is not turned around. By the time you decide that the time and solutions are limited, you both should be very familiar with the issues.

The Discussion

Once you are committed to a course of action, express yourself directly. Words like "sometimes," "maybe," "sort of" or "a little" confuse and perplex. Your language must convey respect *and* clarity. The intention to do what is best for the individual, his or her colleagues and the company should govern what you say. Focus feedback on the value that hearing your comments will have to the recipient, not on the release they may give you.

Be brief: Give only as much feedback as the individual can hear and use. This is not the time to review tiny details of performance or to over-focus on "just the facts." Look the individual in the eye and try to put yourself in his or her place: how would you want to be treated?

Focus on positive alternatives: This is the part of the discussion you have to be precise about before you start. If the individual has a good track record up to now, a reasonable alternative might be to find another role in the company that he or she could perform successfully. When that isn't possible, decide beforehand what arrangements you can make, and stick to them.

At minimum, your feedback in confronting unacceptable performance begins a limited period of reevaluation that may lead to major changes in job focus, so it is never a discussion that is held without very careful thought.

Paradox—Again

We have urged that you make the time for counseling and confronting, that you not put off the unpleasant meeting. To do so is injurious to all three parties: you, the confronted person, his or her colleagues. Be decisive. But, as we've also said with equal vociferousness, be methodical. And patient: Give every chance. Proceed step by step.

In effect, our advice is paradoxical: Be methodical and patient, but be decisive to be fair to all. We don't apologize for the paradox. Living with it, explaining it, and understanding it is what you get paid for. The "answer" to the paradox is your own (and your organization's) deeply held definition of trust, care, respect, fairness, due process, decisiveness and integrity all rolled into one. No wonder it's so delicate, so vital.

The dilemma is clear: Most of us probably don't think of a counseling meeting delayed *a* day as a "strategic issue," i.e., as a vital test of integrity (and care, trust, respect, etc.). It is. Our people are people watchers. It is exactly in these delays that the core of our philosophy, which will subsequently impact every strategic outcome, is most on display.

Confronting:
Some Questions—and Things to Do Now

► Carefully assess, for all your team members, their capabilities as well as their limitations. Can you anticipate situations where an individual is being outrun or trapped in a job he or she cannot do well—before serious failure occurs? Are you allowing someone to flounder unnecessarily? Pay special attention to those on your team who have recently taken on greater responsibility. How are they doing? Do you see any indication that this new, broad area of responsibility may be beyond the individual's reach? (An outstanding sales representative, for example, may be promoted to sales manager and subsequently fail because he or she liked the specialist role but not the supervisor/leader role.) Are you enough in touch to know who may be faltering in their jobs?

▶ How can you prepare people for the disappointments that may come their way? (E.g., when a new job isn't as rewarding as it seemed, when someone else gets the promotion, when an individual experiences his or her first failure.) What "shock absorbers" can you tap to help people cope with important changes in their careers before and after they happen? Resist the impulse to accentuate the positive or praise the individual's successes if he or she is, in fact, coping with failure: Allow yourself to hear what the person has to say about the circumstance. Are you comfortable giving people the opportunity to discuss their feelings with you—without fear or excessive embarrassment—about the impending change? If not, why not? Can you accept the individual's feelings and restrictions?

▶ How can you help an individual facing failure or major job changes to take control of his or her situation as much as possible? How can you engage the individual in joint problem solving?

▶ Do you find that you have to confront low performance frequently (i.e., is it your most often used approach)? After periods of no contact especially, do you attempt to resolve problems by confronting alone? If you do, consider the cost of your "hit-and-run" behavior, as one colleague so aptly described it. Are people in your department more dependent on you than you would prefer? Do they feel they must check with you before making any decision? (If you don't know, ask them.) If confronting is your most frequent form of contact, one price you pay is that you won't have a capable group who can act independently. Instead, they look to you for direction, even on tiny matters, because they want to avoid your wrath. Does your group experiment a little bit? Try something new? If not, look to your interactions with them. Are you educating? Coaching? Counseling?

We have devoted such substantial space to the five coaching roles because we know it to be a very special and powerful form of guidance, one for which there are no substitutes. The best coaches set in motion a continuing learning process—one that, we find, helps people develop a tolerance for their own struggles and accelerates the unfolding of skill and contributions that would not have been possible without the "magic" attention of a dedicated coach. Coaching is *not* a simple rubric. Done well, it is the best a leader can give.

19

Doing MBWA

We began with the technology of the obvious—MBWA; we explored MBWA with customers, suppliers, MBWA and innovation, MBWA and listening (to customers, as an unparalleled source of innovation), MBWA and leadership. That was introduction. Now we come full circle—to the process of *doing* MBWA. Leading (more so than managing) is a hands-on art. Coaching is the essence of leading—developing those with whom we work. Coaching *is* MBWA (or vice versa, we're not sure which, or whether it matters). This apparently obvious (we said it ourselves) trait/skill/process deserves a closer look.

First, it seems fair, honest, appropriate—and obvious to the many wounded among readers—to begin by saying that MBWA ain't as easy as it may sound! Doing it well is an art. However, it is an art that can probably be learned—and it is clearly unrelated to having an "outgoing" personality. In fact, arguably the best wanderers are the introverts who start with the ability to listen, because listening, and not tap dancing or pronouncing, is at the heart of effective MBWA.

There is a certain inappropriateness, frankly, to our use of the term "MBWA." In a way it makes the physical act of the wandering, per se, seem the most significant point. That is vital—but MBWA as we see it is much more. It is, as we have said, really a code word for all the aspects of leadership we have stressed. That's why it turns out to be so tough.

To begin with, as the effective leader wanders/coaches/develops/engenders small wins, a lot is going on—at least three major activities, usually all at once. They are (1) listening, (2) teaching and (3) facilitating. Listening is the "being in touch" part, getting it firsthand and undistorted—from suppliers, customers and your own people. Varieties of listening was the subject of chapter 2, "MBWA: The Technology of the Obvious." The very act of listening suggests a form of caring. MBWA is also a "teaching" (and "coaching") act. Values simply *must* be transmitted face-to-face. The questioning routines, order of visits and a host of other variables add up willy-nilly to the teaching of values. Finally, the wanderer can also be of direct help! The role of the leader as servant, facilitator, protector from bureaucracy (and bureaucrats) is the third prime MBWA objective. That is, often as not, you'll find a project or team stalled for want of 250 square feet of space in which to build a prototype, or an extra $15,000 travel budget to invite ten would-be customers for a weekend-long evaluation of a projected service. You can relieve the bottleneck on the spot, but only if you're there. As we said, the three roles are usually being performed simultaneously, even in a twenty-minute drop-in visit to a team, accounting group, or what have you.

SPACE: REDUCED OR ENHANCED

Let's talk about MBWA as leadership, talk about the art, and talk about the difficulty. For starters, MBWA is all tied up with *delegation,* which we still find to be, by a country mile, the toughest issue in management. Let's consider two people, one of whom (the good guy) we'll mention by name. Both are connected with high tech companies. Both are wanderers. So far so good. But one wanders, and the result is the enhancement of the performance of those with whom he comes in contact. The other is a bull in a china shop; he seems to do about as much harm as he does good.

The "good guy" is a fellow by the name of Barney Oliver, former head of Research and Development at Hewlett-Packard. First, Barney is a brilliant scientist. Second, he's tough as nails, and intellectually demanding. And yet he was the personification of effective MBWA in HP Labs, the heart of its "next bench syndrome," which in turn is the heart of open and participative (albeit tough-minded) communication.

Barney would wander, we are told, with extraordinary regularity. And he'd stop and chat. And, indeed, you had darn well better have something worthwhile to chat about! He'd look at what you were working on and ask the toughest questions imaginable. He didn't shy away from anything. (MBWA *doesn't* mean, then, that most subjects are *verboten.*) He spoke his mind. But the consensus, among twenty-seven-year-olds and fifty-seven-year-olds alike, was that when Barney had finished with you, (1) you'd learned a heck of a lot, of both lasting and short-term significance, and (2) *the project you were working on was still yours*—Barney had not taken away the space, had not in any sense told you what to do or what the next steps should be.

Mr. Bad Guy also wanders in technical spaces. He also knows what he is talking about, and isn't afraid to speak his mind. But when he departs, invariably the consensus is that little is left in his wake. You get the tough-minded dialogue, but the conclusion is his *telling* you, directly or indirectly, almost exactly what you ought to do next (and had better do—given his authority). One blitzed survivor commented, "In six minutes he essentially took away a project that I'd been working on for four months. When he left, it was suddenly his project, not mine."

The important point in the above is the combination of tough-mindedness and space left enhanced (or diminished). Both wanderers are tough. MBWA is *not* about *not* speaking your mind. Good wanderers don't ramble around saying only things like "Howya doin'," "How're the kids?" "Looks like you're doing OK." It's fine to ask about the kids and the spouse if you know there are kids and a spouse (and you should, in fact, find out before you go down and do your wandering). But "gee-whiz socializing," per se, is decidedly not the prime objective of MBWA. It's to find out what's going on, to find out what's bugging people, and, indeed, to guide and direct by a questioning routine that conveys your value set—the sorts of things that "are important around here."

But there's a fine line between instilling your value set (via tough-minded, focused questions) and "managing" a project, and it's a line not easy to establish or maintain, because whether you are a first-line supervisor or CEO, your innocent question is so readily turned into a command—a stone tablet delivered from the mountaintop. Superior wanderers set parameters and draw mental pictures of what a good outcome would look like ("dramatizing the vision," as Bill Moore of Recognition Equipment puts it) instead of "suggesting" that "these three courses of action ought to be followed." Superior wanderers leave the "victim" enlarged, not diminished. They give him or her more freedom to try more things—within the parameters of the vision.*

Domino's Pizza Distribution Company president Don Vlcek demonstrated that fine line in the following story. He was on one of his regular field trips, and a supervisor was complaining that in the process of delivering dough to one particular shop, delivery people had repeatedly broken an exposed basement window. Vlcek whipped a $20 bill out of his pocket and said, "Buy some plywood and cover it—permanently." Afterwards, he talked to the supervisor about the episode: "We don't have any rules that prevented *you* from doing that. I expect you, within reasonable limits, to do what needs to be done." Let's look at what Vlcek did. He "taught" the young supervisor (by "a picture"—i.e., whipping out the $20 bill on the spot) what he ought to be up to— direct problem solving on his own. Yet he left the young man bigger, not smaller: "*You* do what's necessary and right, and let no Mickey Mouse get in your way." This was hardly a carte blanche to go out and buy Mercedes delivery trucks, but it was *guidance:* space-enhancing advice.†

---

*Tough-minded Tom West, hero of Tracy Kidder's *The Soul of a New Machine,* was a master. He set three or four crystal-clear guiding parameters for his team of youngsters developing a computer at Data General. Then he stayed out of the way, devoting the lion's share of his time to protecting them from corporate interventions. His ultimate genius was in *not* intruding, in the face of awesome outside pressures, during the critical debugging phase (all the more impressive given that debugging was his area of expertise). He left the space for his lads and the subsequent exhibition of the power of ownership to produce results was awe-inspiring.

†This story brings to mind a typical rejoinder we hear: "Show him he can spend $20 on window glass, and tomorrow he'll spend $100 on his girlfriend, if there's no explicit rule book." We believe it's the worst sort of straw man and reveals our interlocutors' complete lack of trust in their people.

"Space":
Some Questions—and Things to Do Now

▶ This will not be easy! If you're up to it, select four or five down-the-line people with whom you've had more or less regular contact. Sit down individually with them and talk about your style, as a space eater or enhancer. (You might have an outside consultant do this for you. It is one of the rare cases when a clinically trained outsider may be helpful.) As a second best, gather a group of two or three trusted peers and spend a half-day talking about how all of you come out on this dimension. (You might try doing the data collection by talking to a trusted colleague's people and getting some feedback on him or her—though it won't be easy.) Alternatively, start your data collection for the future (i.e., now). Have a trusted colleague go with you on your wanders and give you feedback (or have your secretary do so by, say, sitting in on meetings; any setting is fair game).

▶ Repeat the process for you and your colleagues as a management team. The tone set by the team is at least as important as that set by an individual.

▶ Suppose you and your team come up as space eaters par excellence, then what? There are some gimmicky aids (gimmicky, but not silly), such as (a) talking last, not first; (b) consciously using "What do you think?" and avoiding "Why don't you try X, Y, Z?"; (c) pushing your "pupils" to give you a detailed narrative, so that they expose their reasoning to *themselves*, with you continually interjecting "And then what did you try?" rather than "Why didn't you do thus and such at that point?"; (d) not forcing them to blame others, via questions such as "Did purchasing get you the parts on time?"; (e) leading them to generate the next steps with indirect (at most) guidance, with queries such as "And what should that fact lead us toward in the way of tests?"; and (f) asking them to stop by and tell you what was tried, or to give you a call, if it would be helpful, when the next step is taken, thus instilling urgency but not forcing a next step or specific milestone. It boils down to thinking ahead some, and trying to replay (ahead of time) what a typical question from you sounds like. (Is it truly a question, merely aimed at stimulating thought? Or is it a piece of rigid "advice"?) Just "thinking about it" is a very useful first step. Few of us do so, regularly or systematically (and even if we do, we readily forget to what degree our innocent *question*—not direction—sounds like a direct order to those ten years or two rungs more junior).

FREQUENCY

The simplest point to make about MBWA—and the toughest to get most of us to act on—is one that has to do with frequency: If you are not a regular wanderer, the onset of wandering will be, in a word, *terrifying*. Terrifying for you *and* terrifying for those with whom you come in contact (this is true whether you are a first-line supervisor, a small business person or chairman of a Fortune 500 company). Nonwanderers' infrequent forays usually amount to "state visits," prepared for by the "subjects" months in advance, with the result that what one beholds bears no relationship whatsoever to reality. MBWA is decidedly *not* about "state visits." It is a method for keeping in touch, getting real impressions, reinforcing strategic themes. The fact is that the most vital function of MBWA, *listening,* is not accomplished effectively in the "state visit" or "Select the good customer to visit" mode.

Both sides contribute to the problem. Suppose the sales vice president or regional sales manager is going to descend upon a local branch. He tells the top people there five weeks ahead of time. They set up some calls for him, because he thinks he ought to go out on calls. They pick patsy customers, who love the company. He learns nothing. Then he leaves. Two weeks later, routinely, the branch bitches to headquarters about not getting more support. Yet the sales manager's "MBWA experience" has told him that everything is rosy, so what's this about needing an extra $150 worth of tools for each person's kit? All the customers *he* saw were happy as clams.

The best (only?) way to beat the state visit rap is by wandering often, regularly, every day of the year. Barney Oliver was at first a terrifying figure to

On his tenth anniversary with St. Joseph's Hospital in Stockton, California, our friend Executive Vice President Ed Schroeder was presented with this wonderful "MBWA award"—bronzed size-13 shoes!

young and innocent engineers, but the fact that Barney was wandering around a good part of every day meant that eventually they got used to having him around. (It was never *easy* to have him around, but you did get used to it.) Given the size of HP Labs, and the company's geographic spread, he could hardly be an every-day visitor to every work space. But the real power of the regular wanderer was demonstrated by an amazing comment from a twenty-four-year-old HP engineer: "I know that Dave and Bill and Barney [Packard, Hewlett, Oliver] have been out of active management for quite a while now. But let me tell you, each of the [many thousands of] engineers on HP's payroll still believes today [this was 1983] that any one of the three is liable to stop by in the next five minutes." That's what frequency is all about: expectation, not mere statistical probabilities.

And, yes, it *will* be awkward at first. One president of a small company said, "Well, look, if I make the effort to go down on the shop floor, they [the people down there] have got to make the reciprocal effort and give me honest feedback." Why? Why in the hell should your people be committed to giving you "honest feedback" if your last three visits were to lay people off? So you read *In Search of Excellence* and suddenly you think wandering is a great idea—so what? You can't expect your people to give you a birthday cake the first time out. (Or even the twenty-first.) You *earn* honest feedback. And the main way you earn it is by the frequency of your wandering (*and* by what you do after you return home—more on that in a bit).

By frequency we mean exactly that. In order to visit each of the over seven hundred Wal-Mart stores at least once a year, Sam Walton takes a minimum of three full days a week; much of the rest of his time is spent visiting distribution centers, riding with Wal-mart drivers, and visiting suppliers. Robert O. Anderson, Arco's chairman, averaged about five hundred miles a day during his fifteen years as CEO of that company. *Quite frankly, we believe that any supervisor—accounting, first line in the factory, engineering, merchandising, information systems or Fortune 500 CEO—probably ought to be out of the office 75 percent of the time, and in the field (if he or she has multiple, dispersed geographical sites) at least 50 percent of the time.*

And note: Doing away with the state visit doesn't mean that you should be afraid to *advertise* the fact that you are out wandering. The best way to have people think that you might come by is to let them know you are out and about—*listening*—most of the time.

"Frequency":
Some Questions—and Things to Do Now

▶ How often are you out of your office? Be specific. Look at your calendar for the last sixty to ninety days. Break it down into meetings, visits and other. Take the meeting component and break it down into formal and informal, making note of the location of each meeting. Go over each in-office/in-headquarters event and ask yourself if it could have taken place as readily on the other person's turf: e.g., why not have the R&D review in the labs, rather than in your office?

Could visits have been used more productively? Look at each. Could one or two (or five or six) brief "walk-throughs" of another field facility or another department have been added?

▶ Now look ahead sixty days. First, look at booked, must-do events: Can some be held at "their place" rather than "your place"? Look at your currently unprogrammed time; can you put "Don't book" in 25 percent of it, and save the time for spontaneous "wandering"?

▶ Think about putting a checklist or two in a reachable desk drawer (or even in your wallet). On it (them) note, for instance, your top twenty-five customers, your top twenty-five vendors, twenty-five upcoming milestones for project teams, twenty-five facilities or departments. Systematically plan to "do" two from each list each week (two customer calls, two departmental "drop-ins"). You might even use a desk-top personal computer for this. Have your secretary, if you have one, bug you about the lists (she or he should have duplicates), or even give you weekly gold stars if you get all of your "MBWA 'to dos' " completed.

▶ Repeat all the above as a team: analysis, meeting location shifts and checklists. Make your *team* MBWA Scorecard a regular (first?) agenda item when you get together for staff meetings. Force group feedback at least weekly.

TRAPPINGS OF MBWA

Trappings are vital. Anderson's (Arco) routine is highly instructive. Above all, he didn't travel with a retinue. There weren't seven hovering note-takers from staff in attendance, shaking their heads and clucking as they thought he would at forms not filled out appropriately.

The order or sequence of wandering is vital. Mr. Anderson's habit was to arrive at a district field office and immediately head for an ongoing, routine meeting of junior geologists and geophysicists discussing a minor property. He didn't begin with an hour-and-a-half, behind-closed-doors visit and strategic review with the district supervisor. He hopped in, virtually unannounced, and looked in on whatever was happening at the time. Andy Pearson followed about the same routine at PepsiCo. When he arrived, he'd drop in on a junior assistant brand manager, ask him, "What's up? What's going on?" or stop in on a meeting far down the line that was pretty routine. The bosses came later. A fellow who runs a mid-sized construction company has a similar ritual. One of his vice presidents remarks: "Whenever he arrives at a construction site, it's automatic. He makes a beeline for the crane operators or the welders. The site boss is last on his list." Senior people *will* get their time. They always do. *Starting* at the "lower" levels shows those people the importance you attach to them—that they are not, in fact, "lower" at all, but are vital to the organization.

Bank Wanderer

A manager of several branches of the retail part of Chase Manhattan decided to manage less by form and more by wandering. She didn't tell people when she was going to arrive, not in the state-visit sense, but she did give them a little warning. She'd stop at a phone booth before hitting a site and say, "See you in half an hour." When she arrived she'd go up to somebody in the operations area, look at what he or she was doing, and spend a little time chatting about it. The tail end of the visit would be the branch manager.

There are some other, smaller points to be made in connection with the trappings of MBWA. One president of a small business asked us, "What do you *wear* when you do MBWA?" Our answer? "Whatever feels comfortable." What we mean is that if you're a three-piece-suit wearer, and the vest is always buttoned and the cuffs of your shirts are monogrammed, wandering around in overalls is apt to make you look a bit of a fool. On the other hand, if you *can* pull it off—i.e., comfortably—we're all for overalls if you're in a plant. We heard a story about a well-run GM plant where the manager was a wanderer supreme. His relationships with his people were terrific. His costume for wandering was almost always the same (what it was, in fact, when he was sitting at his desk—unless the brass from Detroit were about to show up). It was a satin baseball warm-up jacket with the insignia of the UAW local on it; he wore that and a baseball hat pushed back on his head as he ceaselessly trooped around.

It is a little easier to be informal—and to listen—if you can wear informal clothes and not look strange in the process. But there are a lot of jerks who wander around in baseball jackets, so that doesn't mean everything, to put it mildly. And if you are one of the true buttoned-down types, and you are always seen in pictures in the company newspaper wearing a three-piece suit (even on the softball diamond), then don't suddenly head out to the field with a T-shirt on; if you do, people will probably think, "Ah, he's practicing wandering. Been to one of Peters' seminars." And that decidedly is not the point.

"Trappings":
Some Questions—and Things to Do Now

▶ Think about the trappings when various people visit you. Analyze two or three recent visits in detail. Do the trappings make a difference? How?

What are the smart-aleck remarks you make after visits of higher-ups? Could the visitors have avoided the faux pas that led to your snide assessments? How? Now, turn your attention to yourself (and yourself and your colleagues as a group). To what extent do you manage/think through the "trappings" issue—e.g., order of visits, formality of note taking, clothes? Do you consider this a useful exercise, or low priority, or silly? If you don't take it seriously, ask yourself why. The greatest world leaders have unfailingly been fanatics about trappings.

MAINTAINING THE CHAIN OF COMMAND

Except for the matter of leaving space (or, better yet, enhancing it) the toughest issue in MBWA has to do with abrogation (or not) of the chain of command. A score of points could be made. Quite simply, the best of the MBWAers do not abrogate the chain of command. But wait: Of course they *do*, in a way. Let's not kid ourselves. Wandering down, skipping two or five or six, or, heaven help us, ten layers *is* violating the chain of command. Regardless of your purpose. You're there to hear it firsthand, and you're there to do some teaching firsthand. No bones about it. But there *are* degrees.

Consider former Chairman Ed Carlson of United Airlines. Soon after taking over the ailing airline, he hit the field, asking very direct questions—in detail, for his objective was to clean up the bureaucratic mess he had inherited. He took endless notes, usually on scraps of paper, and stuffed them into his pocket. He never told people down the line what to do or change, he never fixed what he disliked (unless it was a matter of safety) on the spot. But what he did do—and this is vital—was *promise* that he would get back to people in a very short time (five working days at most). And he promised he would get back with *action*, not the announcement of the appointment of a six-month task force or study group. When he returned to home base, he played it straight: he let the chain of command know what he had found and that he wanted action taken, immediately. Then he initiated correspondence with the down-the-line people he had chatted with on his wanderings, letting them know that something was up, and had his staff check religiously to make sure that action was taken, and taken within the promised time.

Of course an abrogation of the chain of command was involved here. Carlson's unabashed objective was to skip steps, get on directly and rapidly with debureaucratizing, using himself in a highly visible fashion to make his point. (He called it "visible management".) But the implementation was done in a relatively traditional if uncommonly rapid fashion. In sum, to make MBWA credible one must promise fast action and then make damn sure that it occurs within the proposed time frame; but to do so does not mean (or should not mean) impetuously issuing the order to the first-line person on the spot.

Again, frequency is a key issue. The screams about violating the chain of command will be particularly loud at first. Your presence (even if you're a second-line supervisor) is initially awkward. People overlisten to you and overinterpret the subtle inflections in your voice. Many a million-dollar program has been started, or stopped, because of a frown by a division general manager at the wrong second (and because, it turns out, he had a fly land on his nose). And that *will* happen. But it will happen less—this is a simple law of nature—the more you are around. People will figure out what sort of person you are when they've had a chance to be exposed to you. Your managers will come to accept the fact that you're not going to destroy the chain of command only when you repeatedly demonstrate that you won't.

An Adventure in Excellence

An experienced wanderer recalls the first time he ventured out from the safety of his office to begin what was for him an utterly unfamiliar experience: "I was out of touch. I wanted to see with my own eyes what was going on in my division, but I never had the time. People came to me, but they never seemed to be very comfortable. Finally I decided to go to them. I came out of my office, turned the corner, headed for the coffee urn. It was break time, and everybody crowded around it, talking about the new product we'd just introduced. A supervisor in manufacturing thought the production time could be cut by 20 percent if two changes were made; one of the design engineers agreed. Another engineer joined the discussion—now a debate—and as I reached them, the whole group was involved in how the production cycle could be improved. Then they noticed me. The conversation thudded to a stop. Just like that. I could see the surprise on their faces: 'What's *he* doing here?' I didn't know what to do with my hands, so I shoved them in my pockets. It was awkward as hell. Our place is informal, but I had a meeting that afternoon, so I was wearing a tie—everyone else wore open collars or T-shirts. For a minute I seriously considered going back to my desk. But I didn't see how I could back up. Someone handed me a cup of coffee. I yanked my hands out of my pockets to reach for the cup—and loose change, car keys, a little tin of aspirin and a button fell to the floor. They all stared, didn't know what to do. I reached down for the keys and collided halfway with a supervisor, who was reaching for them at the same time. He grinned as he handed them to me. I had to smile. Two or three of the others collected the change. My boss's secretary retrieved the aspirin tin and remarked, 'Here, you'll probably need these in a few minutes.' I took a deep breath, gulped my coffee, loosened my tie, tried to look casual. I decided this wandering-around stuff was for the birds, it couldn't work. I was there to listen, and they didn't tell me anything. I'd be better off preparing for my meeting, getting all my charts ready. But I came back the next day, just to give it one more shot. How could it be worse than yesterday? People didn't open up and tell me about what they were concerned about that time, either, but I kept at it. I was determined, I'll tell you. I went around to see people at their desks. I was learning a lot. I was having fun! I realized that these people knew a hell of a lot more about what our company stands for, where we're heading, how our products could be improved, than I gave them credit for. They knew much more than how to do a given job. I didn't even know what half of them actually did. Now it's a regular thing with me—wandering around. A couple of my peers used to criticize me for not being at my desk enough. 'Why aren't you managing?' they'd ask! Well, now *they're* out more, too. Its amazing what we've learned from just simple listening."

A vital subpoint, in connection with this issue, is the necessity of assuring and accomplishing the absolute protection of those who talk with you. The objective is to find out what is going on, to listen especially to the clerks, the MIS gang, the assistant branch manager, the junior buyers and the people on the loading dock. There is a tendency among "real people" (those on the loading dock and in the PBX room) to be frank, interestingly enough. And it is vitally important, especially in a tradition-bound organization, to make sure that the provider of frank feedback isn't shot or exiled to Siberia after your visit. A lot of first-line supervisors don't take too kindly to an hourly person mouthing off to a vice president (or even a third-level supervisor) about the rotten state of the housekeeping ("The toilets stink"). A lot of second-line supervisors don't take kindly to first-line supervisors doing the same thing. So the all-pro wanderers are crystal clear on this point. If they find even the slightest hint that something negative has happened as a result of someone speaking out (and they actively listen to the grapevine to check), the person responsible is fired or demoted or sent to Siberia. The MBWA process rests, foursquare, on absolute integrity. If the integrity is not there, it all becomes a very bad joke. And, once again, the frequency of visits is involved. At first it will be tough enough for people to open up. But once they hear that you wander regularly (50 percent of the time), that you do get back to people quickly, and that you do watch out for the people who have spoken up, then gradually, the process will begin to work.*

Bourns' Bert Snider summarizes nicely: "There's always a chance that a foreman, for example, will think the CEO is screwing things up by getting involved. But I think there's a danger only if the foreman is singing a different song from the CEO. If they're all singing the same song, the CEO is only

---

*This is an extraordinarily thorny issue. We talked with one Fortune 500 president. He wears his integrity on his sleeve, in a company where it's sadly uncommon. People—junior clerks in the Austin, Texas, operation—*do* open up with him regularly. He is continually astonished at the havoc he creates when he inadvertently lets a clerk's name slip in subsequent conversations with his peers.

reinforcing that song in people's minds. If it's a song they've never heard before, then, yes, they'll be confused."

"Chain":
Some Questions—and Things to Do Now

▶ Do you have an *exact* routine for getting back to everyone who talks to you? Does it include a harsh (for you) deadline for action—e.g., forty-eight to seventy-two hours? Do you meet your deadline? How do you handle the standard chain of command in asking for follow-up? Do you ensure that they conform to your promised deadline? How do you (if you do) ensure that subtle negative action is not taken against those who speak out (e.g., that snide remarks about "George airing our dirty linen with the boss" don't follow in the wake of a frank exchange about quality with a foreman)? Most important: do you play slavish attention to and "manage" these issues?

LISTENING, TEACHING, FACILITATING: SOME (MORE) SUGGESTIONS

Listening is best done on somebody else's turf. That is why we urge wandering. There are, however, many ways to do it, even on the other person's turf. One is to gather people together in formal question-and-answer sessions. That's not bad. Ren McPherson, the former Dana head, used to do a lot of this, sometimes gathering fifteen hundred people together in the same room and taking questions with all present. It's useful, because the group as a whole takes the measure of the "boss" in this kind of a setting. Is he or she trying to pull the wool over our eyes? Is he or she being straight with us? What is he or she hiding? Why? Small, impromptu get-togethers with cross sections of five or ten people are also helpful. Again, the trick is in the word "impromptu"—the people attending should be picked at the last minute, on the spot. A carefully crafted and preselected group merely sets you up to hear what some supervisor thinks you want to hear. Also vital are wandering the line and going out on calls with sales and service people.

Some other listening rituals: Our colleague Jack Zenger reports that the president of the Syntex Corporation makes a habit of eating breakfast at the same table in the company cafeteria about twice a week. It's well known that he will be there, and that anybody is welcome to come up and sit with him. Note also, however, that nobody came and sat with him at first. Then, probably out of sympathy, a few brave souls ventured to do so. And it's only now—after twenty years—that it has become comfortable. That's MBWA for you!

Bill Moore's turnaround at Recognition Equipment also involved breakfast—a ritual that became known as Biscuits with Billy. Four or five mornings a week he was there in the company cafeteria, to chat with all comers. What did they chat about? Anything, everything, and nothing. His mere presence implied that he wanted to listen and keep in touch. He shared heretofore sensitive data about small gains and small losses, making it clear that everybody was part of the team effort. His self-confidence and frankness conveyed a badly needed "Someone's in charge here" sense to the whole organization. Above all, Moore is neither a time waster nor a "How ya doin' " type. Times were tough and he was taking tough-minded action. So the breakfast vehicle became a vital, frank, and practical daily "state of the corporation . . . and you and me [Moore]" interchange.

Listening is the number one objective of MBWA. Teaching is almost as important, however, and it emphatically does *not* mean telling people what to do (that delicate point again). It does mean telling people in a direct, no-nonsense fashion what it is you think is important about the world—their world and yours. It can as readily be accomplished by the regular pattern of your questioning routine as by a formal speech, but it is a big part of the MBWA process.

Wandering activity is, in this regard (and above all), a golden opportunity. The pattern of your questioning—and variations therein—*will* be noticed and interpreted, have no doubt about it. Everything about what you are up to—your dress, the order in which you talk to people, the things you focus on in your questions, the things you *fail* to focus on—will be, even if you *are* a regular wanderer, the subject of endless speculation. You have just two choices in the matter: to go about it in an erratic fashion or to go about it systematically. We would highly recommend the latter because it would mean that you will in fact be teaching what you want to teach and not something else.

By systematic we don't mean planning every second of your visit. We do mean making sure that your two or three simple messages are the focus of everything you do: the questioning pattern, the visiting pattern while on the site, etc. Tom followed Frank Perdue around for a day in Salisbury, Maryland, in the summer of 1983. In the course of that day he gave half-a-dozen impromptu talks, always on the same subject—product quality. It is what he's been jawing about for forty years, but he still takes every opportunity, no matter who's the target, to reinforce his point of view.*

On the other hand, we have followed many managers around who squander their opportunities. One colleague was involved in a life-and-death quality program: Get it better or lose a $100 million contract renewal. Several solid successes had been chalked up, and more were coming in every day. Yet in the course of a four-department visit, he missed opportunity after opportunity. In one of the four instances he said nothing about quality. In two others it was an afterthought. Only in one was quality an up-front topic. In no instance did he attempt to build momentum by giving accounts of the suc-

*And if you knew Frank, you'd know it surely wasn't for Tom's benefit!

cesses in other parts of the organization. Instead he became involved in putting out a series of routine brushfires on a variety of issues. It is not that he wasted time, but that he failed to use the time to hammer home his over-arching priority.

In the first chapter in this section we looked at the leader (plant manager or MIS boss) as dramatist. Coaching, teaching and transmitting values, more than any other responsibility of leadership, demand dramatic skills. However, it is vital that the show you put on not be fraudulent in any way, that you do not merely act a part. Your people will judge your integrity. And they will get it right! The smallest inconsistencies or hypocritical acts will be noted. The story is not a wholly negative one, of course. If you do act with total integrity, the MBWA process is the best and, in a sense, the only way in which to truly demonstrate it. That is, your people will judge your integrity by the cast of your eye (Napoleon said, "If you wish to lead people, speak to their eyes"), the firmness of your grip, and a multitude of other little things. You cannot fake it. Nor can you *convey* it except in person. A videotape helps, but it is no substitute for all the millions (literally) of bits of data that we process when we observe a person face-to-face.

There is an important point about communication behind all this. We have had many people, particularly in connection with such MBWAing as a day-long ride-around with a single salesman, say, "Look, it's such low leverage. I have got seven hundred fifty (or seventy-five hundred) people in my com-pany. To spend one day with *one* salesman is too darned expensive." We think such a view is wrongheaded. The worldwide rumor mill will be grinding away *seconds* after that day comes to an end (if not before). Every item of your conversation will be known four thousand miles away about half an hour after it occurs—at the most. As one wise soul said about such visits: "The sound of the old man's voice travels at the speed of light around here." It trav-els at the speed of light *everywhere.* So the teaching that takes place on that day will not be lost—that is, unless it is lost through your squandering the opportunity.

MBWA's big three are listening, teaching and facilitating; we've talked of the first two and, peripherally, the third. Facilitating is Ed Carlson promising action within about five days after a visit. But even that's somewhat indirect. So what's direct facilitation? A successful senior manager at Bell Labs has it right: "My job? Run the Xerox machine for a team at three A.M. the morning their project is due for review. I spend half my time just asking dumb ques-tions: 'What's bugging you?' 'What's getting in the way?' It turns out it's sel-dom big stuff. It's usually petty annoyances. A small group needed a personal computer, and was being dragged through an almost full-blown capital budget review to get one. I got them one in forty-eight hours. And so on. Running interference and kicking down small hurdles. And, you know, you can only do it if you're out there. Nobody will come to you with this stuff. They think it's 'too trivial' to bother you with! They think they ought to be able to do it them-selves. So they'll tie themselves up in knots for a week on some little nit."

The only addendum we have to that is to point out that it's the small stuff that is almost always—because of its cumulative effect—at the heart of major problems. As an IBM systems manager said, "How does a project come to be delayed by a year? One day at a time."

MBWA is not easy, and it shouldn't be easy. Estimating conservatively, we'd bet a thousand variables are at play! We have described only a handful. MBWA exposes you. Your ability to listen is exposed. Your honesty and integrity (or lack of it) are exposed. Your consistency is exposed to the scrutiny of the toughest watchers of all—hourly people. You can bullshit a vice president with ease. But it's almost impossible to BS somebody on the loading dock. They have been there and back. Your vision (or lack of it) is exposed. Your statements have coherence (or not) relative to the basics of that vision. Jan Carlzon's hammering home his vision of SAS's transformation from a "broker of assets" to a "service company" was and is the theme of a thousand thousand impromptu chats.

Putting major effort and energy into learning MBWA and practicing it is worth the candle, but it won't be easy. In fact, it will be hard. If you haven't done much of it, we can guarantee that the first few days, weeks, months, and perhaps years, will be just plain awful. Few will trust you: "What's he up to?" "How long will it take for this 'wander phase' to pass?"

And ah, yes, how *do* you find the time? You are already busy. You already have forty-seven more legitimate priorities than you can deal with. Maybe you can play a game with yourself. A friend wanted to free 20 percent of his time for wandering. Together we did an analysis of his calendar for the week after next. He had some twenty-nine scheduled meetings; moreover, the phone log revealed that another fourteen people had requested meetings that he'd not been able to squeeze into his docket. The solution was simple: "Dave, cut your meetings to seventeen." His obvious (and reasonable) rejoinder: "Why seventeen?" The rebuttal: "Well, look, you could have had forty-three [the twenty-nine he was going to have plus the fourteen he hadn't been able to schedule], but you only had twenty-nine. Neither the forty-three nor the twenty-nine makes any sense at all as a number. So the seventeen can't make any less sense than the twenty-nine! Right? And it has a nice ring to it, seventeen, doesn't it? It sounds precise, sounds like you've given it a lot of thought."

Who among us can say that our calendar—in any way, shape or form— really makes sense? Perhaps it does reflect, directionally, our strategic priorities. But the set of a week's meetings can hardly be called "optimal." It's mostly random and reactive. And the only way to change it, unfortunately, is to change it. Not through immutable logic, there's none available. But just by doing it. And, perhaps, like our friend Dave, you can at least take some comfort in the fact that the new schedule makes no less sense than the previous one. That we can guarantee you. So what are you waiting for? . . . "Uh, Mr. Arnold, sorry to interrupt your reading, but your ten-forty-five is here."

20

Excellence in School Leadership

... in his valley in western Massachusetts, Frank Boyden, who is 86, continues his work with no apparent letup, sharing his authority by the thimbleful with his faculty, traveling with his athletic teams, interviewing boys and parents who are interested in the school, conducting Sunday-night vesper services, writing as many as 70 letters a day, planning the details of new buildings, meeting with boys who are going home for the weekend and reminding them of their responsibilities to "the older traveling public," careering around his campus in an electric golf cart, and working from 7 a.m. to midnight every day. If he sees a bit of paper on the ground, he jumps out of his cart and picks it up. . . .

In 1966, in *The Headmaster,* author John McPhee wrote those words about Frank Boyden, of Deerfield Academy. Boyden had begun his tenure there in 1902. He had fourteen students, and had induced most of them to come by leaping into a borrowed horse and buggy and heading out to the farms surrounding Deerfield to do hands-on recruitment. Boyden, said McPhee, had "no plan, no theory." He was an "educator by intuition." In one of the seventy letters a day that he wrote in 1953 Boyden stated, while turning down a request to give a speech, "I have no definite topic. I would not quite know how to approach any other than an educational subject, and in my work have just gone ahead from day to day without any particular theory or any particular policy except a real personal interest in the boys, in their work, in their activities. I'm afraid you would be very definitely disappointed in any effort which I might make." In conversations with McPhee, Boyden made the same point: "My philosophy—I can't express it really: I believe in boys. I believe in keeping them busy, and in the highest standards of scholarship. I believe in [creating] a very normal life."

Boyden *did* have a distinct philosophy: for the kids. And everyone had to buy in. The Deerfield faculty had inordinate demands placed upon it. "I'm not running this school for the faculty," said Boyden. "I'm running it for the boys." To achieve his dream, Boyden was omnipresent. In 1902 ". . . he set up a card table beside a radiator just inside the front door of the school building. This was his office, not because there was no room for a headmaster's office anywhere else but because he wanted nothing to go on in the school without his being in the middle of it. Years later, when the present main school building was built, the headmaster had the architect design a wide place in the first-floor central hallway—the spot with the heaviest traffic in the school—and that was where his desk was put and where it still is. . . . If the mood of the student body at large is poor, he will sense it, and when one boy is disturbed, he will see it in the boy's face, and he will think of some minor matter they need to talk over, so that he can find out what the difficulty is and try to do something about it. He has maintained his familial approach to education despite the spread of bureaucracy into institutions and industries and despite the increased size of his own school [from 14 boys to over 500]."

While tough on his teachers and demanding exceptional commitment, he gave them almost total freedom to teach as they pleased in the classroom. His philosophy, notes McPhee, was the essence of simplicity. Yet the sensitivity and intensity required to execute it was remarkable. McPhee adds that he was "in the highest sense, a simple man, and he has spent his life building a school according to elemental ideals, but only a complicated man could bring off what he has done, and, on the practical plane, he is full of paradox and politics. Senior members of the faculty, in various conversations, have described him as 'a great humanitarian,' 'ruthless,' 'loyal,' 'feudal,' 'benevolent,' 'grateful,' 'humble,' 'impatient,' 'restless,' 'thoughtful,' 'thoughtless,' 'selfish,' 'selfless,' 'stubborn,' 'discerning,' 'intuitive,' and so on."

Who was this Frank Boyden? He was an original. Or was he? In 1983 Sara Lawrence Lightfoot wrote a book called *The Good High School,* the culmination of years of research, in which she analyzes six schools. Two were tough urban schools, George Washington Carver High School in Atlanta and John F. Kennedy High School in New York City. Two were suburban: Highland Park High School, near Chicago, Illinois, and Brookline High School, in Boston. Two were "elite": St. Paul's School and Milton Academy. In this essay we shall focus on three of the six principals—Dr. Norris Hogans of Carver, Robert Mastruzzi of JFK, and Bob McCarthy of Brookline—the three who face the toughest environments, radically different from Boyden's peaceful valley in western Massachusetts.

We shall attempt to take the framework and findings of *A Passion for Excellence* and apply them to the school setting. To this effort we bring only our commonplace experiences as high school students and a handful of seminars we've held with school administrators; we are admittedly taking a leap beyond our area of expertise, for three reasons. First, school leadership and management are obviously important, and the subject of excellence in education is appropriately high on the national agenda. Second, we were struck as if by lightning by the traits shared by Boyden, Hogans, Mastruzzi, McCarthy, and, say, Ray Kroc, Willard Marriott, Frank Perdue, Tom Watson. As we read McPhee's tale of Frank Boyden, age eighty-six, heading out to his football field in his golf cart late at night, in the rain, to replace the divots that had been dug up during the afternoon's junior varsity game, and as we read about his discussing in great detail with a junior varsity high school coach the unsatisfactory nature of recent postgame receptions, we were struck by the parallel to Willard Marriott's years of reading every complaint card received from a Marriott Hotel guest, to Forrest Mars checking out the displays of M&M's in local candy stores, and to Ray Kroc's ceaseless effort to move quality, service, cleanliness and value one step further at McDonald's.

The third reason stems from the fact that we have regularly been accused of merely rediscovering "common sense"—and the fact that the charge is true, because "common sense" has not been practiced much lately in most of today's businesses. We suspect the same is true in schools, and Sara Lightfoot confirms our suspicions: In most schools, she writes, "Teachers are typically cast in low positions in the school's hierarchy and not treated with respectful regard. In the worst schools, teachers are demeaned and infantilized by administrators who view them as custodians, guardians, or uninspired technicians. In less grotesque settings teachers are left alone with little adult interaction and minimal attention is given to their needs for support, reward, and criticism." Oh, how the bells of familiarity ring. Lightfoot adds that only if teachers are treated as adults, will they, in turn, treat students as adults through "mature and giving relationships." So obvious! And yet it recalls that "obvious" (and sadly unusual) comment from the president of a small company in the private sector: "If you want your people to treat your customers with courtesy, doesn't it follow that you must first treat your people with courtesy?" True. Obvious. And rare. In factory or school, it seems.

VISION/SYMBOLS/PRINCIPAL AS SALESPERSON

McPhee says that Frank Boyden devoted his life to "developing the character of the school." Lightfoot observes in Norris Hogans a "clarity of vision and purpose." In general, in the six schools she surveyed, Lightfoot notes a "clear authority and vivid ideological stance." At Brookline, Principal Bob McCarthy had his faculty devote an inordinate amount of time to development of a written philosophy; honing the four hundred words required months and months of debate, as the meaning of each semicolon was examined in detail.

School Philosophy of Brookline High School

1. *Education Presumes a Climate of Care*
The schoolhouse must be a kind of home which offers its inhabitants a sense of belonging, of individuality strengthened by expectation, of security born of respect. As in the home, the student should feel known

---

but revered; the teacher, exposed but esteemed. Reason for excellence need not preclude acceptance of human foibles; neither should devotion and understanding be devoid of rigor. Care is by nature compensatory, seeking to provide that which would otherwise be lacking.

2. *Thoughtfulness Is the Social as Well as the Intellectual Aim of Education*

The habit of reflection is the ideal trait of the educated mind, taking for its concern what others may be satisfied to take for granted. Education should foster this habit, should teach us patience in the understanding and construction of ideas. But it should also teach us to consider feelings, to anticipate the probable effect of our actions and words on others, and to temper these when they augur injury. Education is thus forethought rather than afterthought, abiding thought rather than sporadic thought.

3. *No Style of Learning or Teaching Is Privileged*

Learning and teaching are two sides of the same coin. Both rely on a sense of timing, a state of readiness, a heightened sensibility which enables one to see or say or think something not seen or said or thought before. Readiness is achieved in different ways, depending on what there is to be learned. Sometimes it requires painful and protracted effort—thinking, reading, watching, writing, talking, doing. Other times it is attained effortlessly, almost inadvertently. Either way, timing is critical. Knowing how to learn or how to teach is essentially knowing when to press and when to wait. Styles of learning and teaching are characterized by their mix of pressure and patience. Thorough education will expose teachers and students to a range of styles so that they come to know their own.

4. *Learning Is a Mixture of Pleasure and of Pain*

The love of learning is an acquired taste, an addiction for the tart rather than the sweet. To learn is to change, and to change can be both exhilarating and wrenching. As creatures of habit, we must approach learning with trepidation, not expecting those who learn to experience a smooth trajectory of triumphs, nor those who teach to effect unrelieved excitement about their subject. While it is true that what is most easily learned is usually hardest taught, it is also true that love of learning cannot be taught; it can only be exemplified. As is so often averred, teaching requires patience. Let it also be said that what teaching requires, learning must learn.

5. *Education Examines Not the Individual but the Species*

The value of learning lies not so much in its immediate utility as in its generality. Schools are instituted and maintained to serve their communities as havens of learning, not as microcosms of the marketplace. Here students are apprenticed to life in its ideal form, life that is devoted to inquiry, touched by beauty, informed by justice, guided by reason, girded by simplicity, graced by elegance. At the very least, graduates should exhibit competency in the exercise of certain skills—computation, composition—but the aim is to make them literate about the full array of human achievement, so that they will know what it means to do any thing well.

As the best companies are imbued with philosophies, so apparently are the best schools. But the parallel doesn't stop there. Effective and lasting corporate philosophies are in truth about "the obvious" and "common sense." Success lies in the fact that they are lived with intensity. Likewise, the best school philosophies are simple and to the point, as the Brookline statement suggests. Remember that Boyden, who had the clearest philosophy of all, said that he had none except "I believe in boys." Lightfoot discovered that the philosophies in the six schools she observed were, above all, marked by "a universal concern for civility, order, and structure." Bob McCarthy's at Brookline focused on "[developing] a sense of community." High schools (even the good ones) are often marked by a lack of physical and emotional security— on the part of teachers at least as much as students; all six of Lightfoot's school leaders focused first on achieving a sense of security. None took disciplinary infractions lightly, and the toughness was respected by all concerned. McCarthy at Brookline came into a rapidly deteriorating situation. Violence had been on the rise, and was being largely ignored by administrators and faculty, who, Lightfoot reports, would turn the other way and pretend not to see what was going on around them. McCarthy, despite being the model of a delegating and participative manager, nonetheless began his reign by visibly "showing anger." He challenged the "pretense of complacency": "I would not accept breaking up fights as part of my job. I would show those kids how angry I was." Students and faculty alike breathed a long-pent-up sigh of relief when he did.

The philosophy or vision is quickly turned into symbols by the best school leaders. Norris Hogans (who happens to be black) faced an even tougher task than McCarthy at his largely black Atlanta school in a deteriorated neighborhood. Personal presence is the key, Lightfoot notes: "He dominates the school. Hogans is a man of great energy. He walks about the campus in perpetual motion looking severe and determined, always carrying his walkie-talkie. Hogans does not want to be out of touch with any corner of his sphere. There is a sense of immediacy about him, an unwillingness to wait or be held back." It began on day one. Lightfoot observes that "Hogans's first response to the aimlessness and laziness [that he found at Carver] was to show them who was in charge. He started the first faculty meeting with fighting words:

'You're either part of the team or you are not.' Tough standards of behavior and decorum were stressed for the faculty." He also began with an immediate attack via the symbolic—on the shabby physical environment. Lightfoot comments, "The physical environment matched the deteriorating human spirit. Roaches were running around like cats. . . . There was dirt and filth everywhere. . . . The band instruments were all broken up. . . . Athletic trophies were falling out of the broken glass cabinets! Hogans said incredulously, 'I can't believe no one stood up and screamed about it!' " He took immediate action to get on with a highly visible cleanup.

All of Lightfoot's good principals are showmen, visionaries, masterly users of symbols and supersalesmen. Consider Hogans, in perpetual motion, with his walkie-talkie in hand, or crisscrossing the country with an impressive slide show promoting the new programs in his school. Some of his faculty, notes Lightfoot, have suggested that he spends too much time promoting. We suggest that the amount of time he spends is entirely consistent with what we've learned about leadership. The slide show and the "selling" of the school everywhere, not merely in Atlanta, have their greatest impact not on the outside world, but on the school itself, as generators par excellence of pride and self-confidence. Hogans's routine recalls Ren McPherson's "Talk back to the boss," and "Give them [the bosses] hell" ads in national media, ads directed mainly to his own people as part of his program of "turning the company back over to the people." Hogans's salesmanship also takes him into the Atlanta community, where he has invested huge blocks of time and forged exceptional relationships. At the heart of the "new Carver" is his Free Enterprise Day. Lightfoot states that "It is a public event that symbolizes Carver's new image. Vocational education no longer has to be linked with tough and menial work for people of low status, but can be seen as training for jobs of choice, skill, and honor. On the cover of the program for Free Enterprise Day there is a workman's hand 'laying the foundation to success.' " In a remarkable feat, Hogans talked the Boy Scouts of America into letting all of his boys and girls become Explorer Scouts. The explorations take place in the world of work, as each student heads into the community for a work-study program, proudly wearing the bright white Explorer jackets that Hogan was able to cadge from his various and obsessively nurtured sponsors.

Mastruzzi at Kennedy is at least as dedicated to showmanship, salesmanship and the use of symbols. He often refers to his school as the "big top," and many of his faculty members refer to him as the "master of ceremonies." Lightfoot delighted in a school plastered from one end to the other with signs of all sorts focusing on educational excellence. As she carried out her interviewing, Mastruzzi and his senior colleagues had just completed an intense eighteen-month effort to sponsor and host the New York State Special Olympics; as in the case of Hogans's traveling show, the real aim of this visibility-enhancing effort was to induce pride *within* the halls of Kennedy.

Like Marriott, Mastruzzi is obsessed. His particular fetish is attendance, and it is regularly and visibly demonstrated. As in the private sector, he could be criticized for not having a subtle and sophisticated system for measuring the quality of his service. But as is the case with Marriott, the energy focused on a single factor makes it a credible indicator of the success of the school's endeavors. Computerized attendance records are to schools what computerized accounting systems are to private sector organizations. Yet Mastruzzi has a hand-done attendance count given to him once a day, within a couple of hours of the opening of school. Lightfoot declares that "his 'fetish' with attendance figures reflects the dual concern for image and essence. High attendance rates are critically important, says Mastruzzi, 'because unless kids come to school, they won't learn.' However, he is equally concerned about the *appearance* of high attendance scores. He believes they are a quick indicator of a school's goodness, a visible and measurable sign. In September 1982, the attendance figures reached 84.5%, and the morning that I [Lightfoot] arrived in early October the principal has just offered his effusive congratulations to the students over the public address system. 'I got on the PA and told them how great they are. They should be rewarded for their sense of responsibility and commitment.' " Free McDonald's hamburgers are given to kids in various classrooms and at various times for particularly good attendance records.

The symbols—vision made visible—are important for the tough schools like Kennedy, Carver, and Brookline. They are just as important for the academies, such as Milton, which Lightfoot also studied. Headmaster Jerry Pieh "admits that his behavior is grounded as much in stylistic, temperamental qualities as in a philosophical stance. 'Style first, then philosophy. I want to set a tone that is permeating the environment. It is not so much a campaign or a clear philosophical view. I want my actions to speak.' " McPhee found the same in Boyden: "Boyden's strategy is best exemplified by his showmanship and his pantoscopic attention to detail. It has been said that a thousand details add up to one impression, and at Deerfield it was the headmaster who added them up. He thought in pictures. Once a picture seemed right, he wanted to keep it that way. Anything that marked it or changed the focus irritated him." McPhee goes on to offer numerous examples of the headmaster's fetish for the tiny and symbolic details that reinforce the image: "A lengthy and expensively produced concert program once arrived from the printer with one name misspelled. 'Miller' had been set as 'Millar.' The headmaster had the program reprinted. He staged basketball games as if he were the manager of La Scala. . . . Once, in the 1920's when Lewis Perry, of Exeter, made a visit to Deerfield [at the time Deerfield was a poor second cousin to Exeter] the headmaster assigned each of a number of boys a pose to strike while Perry walked by; one was to be reading busily at his desk, another browsing through a newspaper in a master's living room, a third straightening his belongings. Some boys had two assignments, in the way that spear carriers disappear from stage one moment and return a bit later as messengers or pages."

Boyden simply lived his message: " 'If you keep floors and walls nice, it's like having your shoes shined and a clean shirt on.' He has been seen mopping floors. He has the gym floor kept like polished brass and classroom floors polished every day. There were no dirty window panes. 'Bob,' he once said to a coach, 'I was in your locker room after practice today and there was some tape on the floor.'

"He is essentially conservative with money, but he will spend any sum to get what he wants. Cut flowers appear regularly in vases all over the campus and there is a single rosebud on each table in the school store. . . . The details have long since added up to a place that is incomparably impressive to the eye. Even the grass is a little greener there, growing in fourteen inches of top-soil, and for many years the headmaster went around with a jackknife digging plantain out of his lawns."

Boyden had one or two fetishes like Mastruzzi's attendance fetish. For his first sixty years as headmaster, until his hearing became too impaired, he personally gave out every grade to every student: "There were no report cards. Each boy had a private talk with the headmaster six times a year and was told where he stood. In these talks the headmaster drew the boys out, getting their reaction to their courses and thus learning where the strength of his faculty was as well. 'Personality counts in teaching at the secondary level,' Boyden said. 'Personality rubs off. The boys are conscious of meeting a colorful and active mind.' " Boyden also believed in keeping in touch via school meetings for all students. And again he did it to a fare-thee-well. How frequent were the meetings? Once per day! From Boyden's world at Deerfield and Pieh's at Milton to Mastruzzi's at JFK and Hogans' at Carver, the message is the same: a crystal-clear and simple vision, the headmaster as chief salesman inside and out, and the constant, blatant, consistent, obsessive use of symbols. It is the foundation on which all else rests.

Paint

In our analysis we have talked about the "paint and potties" phenomenon. A substantial number of the best business leaders, from factory boss to chief executive, have had a continuing concern about the physical details. People like Ray Kroc, Forrest Mars and a foundry manager from Cleveland contend that getting the (not so little) physical details right sets much of the tone. In the use of symbols by school leaders, we observe the same. Norris Hogans at Carver began with an attack on the roaches. The sparkling white Explorer jackets were not another "detail," but a major part of his program to demonstrate new attitudes as well. Frank Boyden was seen at night, in the rain, replacing the divots on the football field, and insisted upon a fresh rose on each table in the school store. McCarthy, at Brookline, had a thing about instantly cleaning up any graffiti. If graffiti are around, discipline is likely to be lax, and learning minimal.

McCarthy's philosophy, once discipline was in hand, was focused on the enhancement of a sense of community. At the heart of it was a participatory

Town Meeting structure, involving students and faculty in making decisions on school policy. He also gave greatly increased autonomy to his housemasters, who run 500-person "schools within a school," and symbolized all these major changes with physical "details." Sara Lawrence Lightfoot reports:

> Another indication of educational engagement is audible rather than visual. I am surprised not to hear the harsh sounds of bells that indicate the beginning and end of class periods. The day's rhythms appear to be internalized by both faculty and students, who do not rely on the external alarms. Despite the absence of bells, all the classes I visited started easily on time and without much fanfare. The only time when bells are used is to mark the home room period, a largely procedural event. It seems to me that a school that was not serious about education could not proceed without bells. They would be a needed enforcer of student and teacher behavior. Instead, Brookline students show surprise when I inquire about the lack of bells. Says one to me in mock alarm, "This isn't a prison, you know! We're not Pavlov's dogs!"

Again the specifics of the analogue to industry are eerie. Ren McPherson used virtually the same words to describe the removal of all time clocks at the Dana Corporation as he masterminded its exceptional turnaround. Attention to the physical trappings (visible and audible) is a major part of tone setting and philosophy reinforcement in factory and schools alike.

Pictures

Related to vision and symbols, and to the use of physical trappings, is thinking in pictures. We regularly find that our best private-sector leaders have a literal picture of their vision. Bill Moore, Recognition Equipment, as we noted, talks about "dramatizing the vision," "seeing the glory." Norris Hogans at Carver believes that "before they can learn, they must be strictly disciplined and mannerly." Thus, when he took over the school—fraught with disciplinary problems and moving toward chaos—he focused on achieving in reality his image of a disciplined school: "Radios and basketballs are confiscated by the vice principals, boys can't wear caps or walk around with afrocombs stuck in the back of their hair, and girls are not allowed to wear rollers in their hair." What Hogans is attempting to achieve, says Lightfoot, is "visible conformity and a dignified presence." Mastruzzi's continued reference to "the big top" gets to the same point. And Boyden of Deerfield thought "in pictures." Once a picture seemed right, he wanted to keep it that way.

There is much talk these days about visualization—it has become almost a separate subfield of psychology—in which the "subject" pictures an outcome (an eventual win) and/or, for example (in athletics), every single step of a race. While none of the leaders we have worked with or read about have used the process scientifically, most seem intuitively to do so. Within their head is a picture of what a positive outcome would look like, and of what the individual components of it are. They attempt to set the picture and, as leaders, to paint it for others. They are, then, as Mastruzzi says, "masters of ceremonies." The private-sector analogue? SAS's Jan Carlzon's "All business is show business."

MBWA

No matter how often we talk about Managing by Wandering Around, it always seems odd to be doing so. It seems so natural that one should be in touch. But it appears that it's not. After a presentation to hospital administrators, a seminar devoted solely to MBWA, a leader of a small rural hospital came up to us: "But, you know, they don't teach us that in school." We didn't know then, but we're learning.

When we talk with school leaders, the sad nonobviousness of MBWA quickly surfaces. The differences between the superb and the not-so-good teacher, they unfailingly tell us, center on intensity of involvement and empathy. Perhaps the biggest indicator of that is the amount of wandering the teacher does (and, of course, all that wandering stands for). The involved teacher is constantly pacing the classroom. The noninvolved teacher is most often seen hiding behind the desk. The same thing holds true of vice principals, principals and administrators. Some (most, we fear) just don't seem to be able to find the time to get out. Others (the exceptional ones), with the same clamoring constituencies on their backs, do. Lightfoot was struck that Norris Hogans of Carver "walks about the campus in perpetual motion." The image of Boyden that seems to have struck McPhee was "the small man in the golf cart." Lightfoot describes Mastruzzi at Kennedy as a very physical person, comfortable with himself: " 'He doesn't draw back from you,' says a dark-skinned black boy who claims that his junior high school teachers were often repelled by and afraid of students of darker hue. 'They'd never touch you. Sometimes I felt like I was diseased . . . but I've seen Mastruzzi reach out to all kinds of kids.' The principal's powerful example makes it difficult for others to express their fears or distaste towards certain groups. 'Mastruzzi is not just asking for tolerance among groups,' claims an ardent admirer, 'he's asking for respect and friendship.' "

In our chapter called "MBWA: The Technology of the Obvious," we focused on MBWA with customers, suppliers, one's people. In excellent schools it is the same. Hogans of Carver and Mastruzzi of Kennedy spend huge amounts of time in the community. Boyden of Deerfield wrote *seventy* letters a day, mainly to alumni, and spent inordinate amounts of time—on the road, in his eighties—with admissions directors and officers of the colleges to which Deerfield sent its boys, and with members of the local community. (As is so often the case, the astonishing consistency of the superb leaders shows up in the tiniest details. McPhee reports, "A Massachusetts state policeman once said, 'The headmaster is the only person of importance around here who calls us all by our first names.' ")

Two more Boyden stories illustrate the pervasiveness of his wandering around and his involvement. The first describes the fabled, daily Deerfield Evening Meetings:

He listens to the noise level in a group of boys and watches the degree of restlessness; he can read these things as if they were a printed page. This is one reason he believes in meetings that involve the entire school. "You must have your boys together as a unit at least once a day, just as you have your family together once a day," he says. Evening Meeting is a Deerfield custom. The boys sit on a vast carpet in the anteroom of the school auditorium and listen to announcements, perhaps an anecdotal story from the headmaster, and reports of athletic contests and other activities. "Junior B Football beat the Holyoke High School junior varsity 6-0 this afternoon," says the coach of Junior B Football. "Charlie Hiller scored the touchdown with two minutes left in the game." In the applause that follows this one low-echelon athlete gains something, and so does the school. On Sunday evenings, there is a vesper service, or Sunday Night Sing, as it is called, in which the boys sing one hymn after another, with a pause for a short talk by a visiting clergyman or educator. The luster, or lack of it, in their voices is the headmaster's gauge of the climate of the student body for the week to come, and he accordingly chides them or exhorts them or amuses them or blasts them at Evening Meetings on succeeding days, often shaping his remarks around one of several precepts—"keep it on a high level," "be mobile," "finish up strong"—which he uses so repeatedly and effectively that the words continue to ricochet through the minds of Deerfield graduates long after they leave the school.

Here is an average afternoon in the headmaster's life:

The headmaster wakes up from his midday nap and decides to take a quick look around the school before lunch. He believes correctly that the more people see of him—students and faculty alike—the more smoothly his school will run. "You won't see any confusion anywhere, I'm sure," he says. (Recently, he was scheduled to go on a complicated journey from Deerfield to Worcester to Chicago and back to Deerfield. He went to Worcester but decided to backtrack to Deerfield. It was 5 p.m. when he reached the campus, and at that time the greatest concentration of students happened to be in the gymnasium. He walked into the gym, stayed two minutes, walked out of the building, and went on to Chicago.) Getting into his golf cart, he shoots at full throttle along

Albany Road, which goes through the center of the campus and forms a right angle with the long town street. He loops, twists, drives with his hands off the wheel, dives downhill, shaves trees, goes up the left side of the street into oncoming traffic, and waves and honks to people without regard to obstacles rapidly approaching. He has never actually known how to drive a car, but he used to swirl around Deerfield in an old Pontiac he had, going everywhere at top speed in second gear, because that was the only gear he knew how to find.

Wandering around, staying in touch, keeping out of the office. It's the mark of the superb factory manager, hospital administrator, division manager, city manager and also, apparently, school leader.

FOR THE KIDS

When Peters and Waterman "discovered" the "close to the customer" principle in business, they couldn't have been more embarrassed. How obvious. How trite. We are no longer embarrassed. We now talk about answering the phone, listening "naively" to customers, and the like with the fervor of crusaders. Why? Because we've found that everyone gives lip service to "close to the customer," but few live it with the intensity required to give it any meaning.

In the school world, it seems to us, "for the kids" is an exact analogue. Of course they are the educational target, just as customers must be the object of every manufacturing service operation. But for whose benefit? For the parents'? For the community's? For the nation's? For the school board's? And how many administrators say, "But I know best; I've had the training"? It's the same sweet line that we hear from so many engineers: "But *we* know best the value of this feature. The product will sell itself."

Much of the success of school leaders like Mastruzzi and Boyden is in the fact that they really *do* live "for the kids." Likewise, the magic of any superb teacher, it turns out, is empathy for each child and where each child is in his or her unique development. In our chapter called "Mere Perception" we argue that each and every customer (whether for a jet engine at several million dollars or a hamburger at sixty-nine cents) is different and must be treated differently, must be responded to in his or her own terms. The great companies do so. In the same vein the great teachers and schools do so, and despite the numbers—over five thousand students at Kennedy—they manage to personalize their school's delivery of education.

Bob Mastruzzi at Kennedy views his objective as turning every kid into a winner, a young man or woman who feels that he or she *can* win. It reminds us of Bill and Vieve Gore at Gore & Associates and Ren McPherson at Dana, all of whom say their objective was to have each of their people be an innovative contributor (and who base evaluations, remember, even of the receptionist, on innovative contributions to the job). Says Lightfoot of Mastruzzi, "His passion seems to be reserved for the kids as he reminds me of the Special Olympics motto, 'you're all winners.' 'I believe that is true for all the kids here at Kennedy,' he says forcefully. 'Each year I tell the faculty to increase their expectations of students. You ask for more and you get more.' ... Hogans is the same. His pet Free Enterprise Day is aimed at getting kids into the community with the understanding that they can be winners.

Moreover, Hogans also emphasizes that being a winner doesn't mean being a doctor or a lawyer; it means doing passionately and enthusiastically whatever work you do. Likewise Mastruzzi:

Winning has more to do with being a good, caring, and generous person than with visible and lofty achievement. It is an inclusive, rather than exclusive, educational vision—one that does not focus superior or prideful attention on a narrow band of top achievers, or create a school image based on their great successes. Rather, it is a vision that asks for "extra human effort" on the part of *all* students and asserts that they are all equally capable of becoming good citizens. Says Mastruzzi proudly, "There is an unbelievable emphasis on doing something for somebody else." As an example, Mastruzzi points to a now traditional holiday ritual. At Christmastime, Kennedy's students collect hundreds of gifts for needy children. The students wrap each gift and deliver the presents themselves. Last year the presents were given to a home for mentally retarded children, and this year they will probably arrive at an institution for the severely handicapped. The personal attention of gift wrapping and the presenting of gifts is central to the act of giving. It is not a distant, paternalistic gesture. It is an immediate act of charity. Each year the principal offers the same message of charity to the graduating seniors. He rehearses the words to me with great feeling, "I tell them, you need to leave your school with a sense of appreciation for other human beings. That is the primary lesson we teach at this school. I don't care if you are going to Columbia University pre-med, or if you have been tops in our Honors program. If you don't give a bit of yourself to someone else, you are a failure!"

Kids as Adults

Bob McCarthy at Brookline says it most simply: "I see kids as emerging adults. The more dignity and respect you give them, the more it will come back to you." The single most significant message of *A Passion for Excellence* is this: Treat your people as adults, and they will respond as adults, conscientiously and creatively. Treat them as mindless automatons, treat them with contempt, and they will respond with contempt for you and your product, will respond as automatons. It's as simple as that and as complex as that. It's the obvious again. But it's the obvious that is ignored in schools as well as in the world of goods production and services delivery.

Throughout Lightfoot's analysis there is a contrast between the atmosphere of Brookline, Kennedy and Carver before and after the arrival of McCarthy, Mastruzzi and Hogans, respectively. Before, all three schools were fearful places, with staffs and students distant from one another, stand-offish. Now, though all three current principal-administrators are tough as nails and moved quickly to instill discipline and ensure stability, all three staffs feel comfortable, confident, a part of a community, a community in which students are full-time, adult, contributing members—and so do their students. Reports a JFK commentator about Mastruzzi: "He is very physical, very demonstrative, and it affects all of us. Even the kids hold hands in friendship and support. . . . It's amazing."

The comment is made of Boyden at Deerfield that he did not, as does the traditional headmaster, "see the schoolboy as his enemy." In the same vein, Lightfoot describes Kennedy's approach to absenteeism: "Instead of searching for reasons why students do *not* come to school, they believe that the faculty must find ways of getting them there." In other words, instead of student as thief, ne'er-do-well, demotivated urchin, the notion is student as winner, student as full of potential, student as good. Hence, it's the faculty's prime task to make the rewards of coming to school sufficient to induce the student to attend. As we've pointed out before, "Management [the faculty] gets exactly the work force [student body and attendance] it deserves, not one iota more and not one iota less."

Earlier, we made it clear that the Hewlett-Packards of this world are among the toughest environments of all. Remove the excuses (e.g., the bells as McCarthy did at Brookline), get rid of the Mickey Mouse, and suddenly "it" becomes the employee's (student's) responsibility. There's no way to get off the hook. Empathy means care and concern, but it does not mean softness. Treat students as adults, *expect them to respond as adults,* and they will. Lightfoot makes this clear: "By empathy I do not mean something sentimental and soft. As a matter of fact, the empathetic regard of students is often communicated through tough teacher criticism, admonitions, and even punishment." McCarthy comes through as perhaps the most empathetic of Lightfoot's six principals; nonetheless, "[His] first administrative move was to express outrage at the frequent eruptions of violence. He insisted that parents come to witness student punishments. And he developed a disciplinary committee that would respond immediately to acts of transgression." McPhee tells us, "A new boy at Deerfield cannot have been there very long before the idea is impressed upon him that he is a part of something that won't work unless he does his share," and Boyden was clear on the point: "We just treat the boys as if we expect something of them. . . ."

AUTONOMY/EXPERIMENTATION/SUPPORT
FOR FAILURE

These excellent principals are tough disciplinarians. And yet they are the grantors of autonomy in the classroom. They facilitate the process of treating students as adults by first treating the faculty as adults.* Mastruzzi is apparently charismatic. But Lightfoot, an able and experienced commentator, thinks his secret is not charisma at all. His faculty's commitment "does not seem to be an expression of idol worship, but a reflection of their connection to a communal process. When people [at Kennedy] refer to 'feelings of connection,' they often talk about the autonomy and independence that Mastruzzi permits and encourages. 'He allows a scope, the space to develop our own thing,' says one assistant principal. Another points to the way that Mastruzzi protects his faculty from 'the arbitrary regulations of the central authority. . . . He serves as a buffer between outside and inside. If it weren't for him we'd feel more constrained. We have a great deal of freedom here.' Some observers believe Mastruzzi is able to encourage autonomy among his faculty because of his own deeply rooted self-confidence. 'He is the most secure principal I have ever known. He likes to see strength, not weakness, in the people who work for him,' says a relatively new faculty member who believes there is a 'fair exchange' between the freedom the faculty enjoy and the commitment that Mastruzzi expects."

Supporting good tries that fail is also important to Mastruzzi. Lightfoot goes on: "One enthusiast claims that Mastruzzi not only encourages faculty creativity and autonomy, but he also allows people the room to make mistakes. He is 'forgiving' and believes that people often learn from repairing the damage they have created. The coordinator of student affairs, Pamela Gino, recounts a disastrous story of the first rock concert she organized for students at Kennedy. She had expected a couple hundred students and 800 showed up, many high on alcohol and marijuana. 'A lot of those kids think you can't listen to rock unless you're high. Booze and rock go together.' Not expecting a great number of students, nor their inebriation, Gino had not planned for adequate security; and it became a chaotic, treacherous evening. 'After it all, I felt a tremendous letdown, a real sense of failure,' remembers Gino. 'But I also had learned a lot about how to plan for that kind of event. I knew I could do it better given a second chance.' Mastruzzi greeted her request for a second chance with healthy skepticism and a battery of critical questions, but he allowed her to try again. The second rock concert was a 'great success . . . he's a generous man. He sees failure as an opportunity for change,' beams Gino."

---

*Talking of philosophies with a California elementary school principal led to this sad comment, "You talk of IBM's first principle [respect for the individual]. Well, I've been in education over twenty years, and I've never seen one school philosophy or district philosophy that even *mentions* the teachers or employees, let alone puts them first."

In the private sector a critical attribute of the champion- and autonomy-inducing companies is senior administrators who work to "beat the system," even if it is their own system. Mastruzzi at Kennedy is a master: "He spends a fair amount of energy figuring out ways to circumvent policies and directives that, he believes, distort the educational experiences of teachers and students. Even though he finds the external intrusions 'pernicious' he recognizes why they are necessary in a large, diverse city school system. He believes they were established to monitor the poor schools, the ineffective administrators, and the lazy teachers. But in trying to protect against inferior schooling, these 'central authorities' have limited the freedom of the better schools and distorted the essential human encounters that shape education." The source of Mastruzzi's success as a buffer and a shield is his self-confidence, the sheer guts to get on with it.

Brookline is the Hewlett-Packard or 3M among this collection of schools. McCarthy, as we have noted, has granted autonomy at all levels. He is uncompromising about disciplinary issues, yet he immediately established a Fairness Committee to deal with the problems. Both students and faculty sit on the committee, and their recommendations for action, notes Lightfoot, "are binding. There are no empty gestures. This is real power and decision-making." In our description of the Raychem Corporation we noted the language that marks the innovative company. In particular, we sat through interviews in which first- and second-line supervisors said things like "people believe they can make anything happen." Similarly, one Brookline housemaster, contrasting McCarthy with his predecessor, says, "with [the predecessor], the housemasters were like lieutenants. The metaphors were very male, very military. . . . But McCarthy has opened the door for housemasters. Lincoln House students are *my* students. I can make all the decisions about them." Lightfoot adds, "and to watch him [the housemaster of Lincoln House] in action, one sees a person with a wide range of responsibilities and tasks. The job does not seem glamorous. His office is functional, cluttered with papers and books, empty of aesthetic expression, and open for people seeking attention and help."

FAMILY

Bob McCarthy of Brookline says, "I have always found that the more power you give people, the more responsibility they take." His objective is to "create a school structure that will increase the sense of community." Lightfoot notes that "community" is a word that pops up again and again when McCarthy speaks. It similarly dominates the language of Norris Hogans at Carver, Bob Mastruzzi at Kennedy.

In our investigations of organizations in the private sector, time and again we see the unabashed use of the word "family" among those who exhibit a passion for excellence. We sense family feeling at Delta Airlines, at Hewlett-

Packard, at Gore: There is no shame in talking about the workplace as a community, as a family. Likewise, Boyden talks about Deerfield as a family, Mastruzzi about creating the conditions of nurturance at Kennedy that are typically found in the family.

In an effective family unit all members are full-scale participants. Boyden had an obsession about ensuring that each student played on athletic teams. A heightened sense of competitiveness? Perhaps, but much more than that. McPhee notes, "When a boy at Deerfield chooses a sport, he automatically makes a team that has a full schedule of games with other schools." That is, everyone is required to participate—but as a full-scale member. Playing time and "making the team" are guaranteed.

Discipline

In *In Search of Excellence,* "loose-tight" was the awkward term Tom and Bob invented to describe the leadership of their excellent companies. That is, leaders in those companies had simple, crisp and clear visions, but the intensity and clarity of the shared values behind those visions allowed lots of room for autonomy, creative expression, and love, care and empathy. And so it is, it seems, with leaders in schools.

Norris Hogans, thrust into an impossible environment in Atlanta, began with a focus on discipline. He said that it was necessary to establish discipline before learning could ensue. At the same time, he says to his students, "If I didn't love you as I do, I wouldn't do this . . . I wouldn't come down so hard on you. And I won't stand for any negative attitudes. There is no time for that." The example of Boyden, once again, sums it up: McPhee reports:

> Most schools have detailed lists of printed rules, and boys who violate them either are given penalties or are thrown out. A reasonable percentage of expulsions is a norm of prep-school life. Deerfield has no printed rules and no set penalties, and the headmaster has fired only five boys in 64 years. "For one foolish mistake, a boy should not have a stamp put on him that will be with him for the rest of his life," he says. "I could show you a list of rules from one school that is 30 pages long. There is no flexibility in a system like that. I'm willing to try a little longer than some of the other people do, provided there is nothing immoral. You can't have a family of three children without having some problems, so you have problems if you have 500. If you make a lot of rules, they never hit the fellow you made them for. Two hours after making the rule, you may want to change it. We have rules here, unwritten ones, but we make exceptions to them more than we enforce them. I always remember what Robert E. Lee said when he was President of Washington College, which is now Washington and Lee. He said, 'A boy is more important than any rule.' Ninety percent of any group of boys will never get out of line. You

must have about 90% as a central core. Then the question is: How many of the others can you absorb?

SENSE-OF-THE WHOLE/RHYTHM, OR PASSION, INTENSITY, ENTHUSIASM

A two-star general who runs a highly effective Wing organization in the Air Force's Tactical Air Command talks of a superbly performing unit as having "rhythm." Boyden of Deerfield says, "The thing I have tried to build is a unity of feeling." Lightfoot talks of the optimism and spirit in the language of the teachers, students and administrators alike at JFK High School. She talks likewise of the sense of "immediacy" when one is around Norris Hogans at Carver. David Ogilvy quotes Howard Johnson, former president of MIT, on great leaders; he says they have a "visceral form of spiritual energy."

We think that most who have written about leadership have missed the boat. We don't know what the essence of goodness is in fast food restaurants or great high schools. But we think the essence of leadership is the same in both: not shortness or tallness, not sweetness or harshness. Such variables are seldom predictors of success or failure. But something else. Vision, energy, empathy, persistence, passion, attention to detail, a picture of the goal . . . These are not the factors that we have discussed in management for the past several decades. Yet we believe that they are as amenable to "hard" analysis as are the themes of MBO and performance appraisal. We just have to start collecting the right "data."

One must be around that which works, which sings, which has rhythm, which has passion, which has enthusiasm, before one can understand just how broad the gulf is between not the winners and the losers (that's defeatist talk) but things that are humming and things that aren't.

A Personal Note from Tom

After I entered a private junior high school in 1955, my mother took on a new job—teaching the fifth grade in a nearby suburban elementary school. It had students from ethnic and socioeconomic backgrounds other than she had been used to. She taught there—contrary to her initial plans—for almost twenty years, and occasionally I acted as her bumbling assistant. The memories are vivid.

First, she was totally involved. She was on her feet all the time (doing MBWA). There was no reason for her to have a desk, though the school system provided one. She was never behind it. She paced about the room, nudging, cajoling, pushing, pressing. Above all, she had a passion for her students. The letters that she still receives, twenty years later now, from both good and bad, successful and unsuccessful, attest to that.

Her room was a hotbed of creativity. Everyone was allowed to express himself or herself with a unique project. At the same time, the seeming chaos was embedded in a context of extraordinary discipline: total respect was to be shown by each student for every other student—or else! No rudeness was tolerated. Not only did the discipline and creativity not conflict with each other, but they went hand in glove. The discipline of care and concern for one another was the necessary foundation upon which the less venturesome were willing to step out and try a little bit of something new.

A passion for the material was evident as well. (Joseph Epstein's *Masters: Portrait of Great Teachers* underscores this point. Above all, each master teacher is marked by great passion for his or her subject. The technical excellence—i.e., mastery—is there, too, of course, but it is the passion which is decisive, which alters the lives of so many students.) My mother was appalled by the new math (the very best of us are often appalled by the new twists), but her love of learning knew no bounds. Certainly I learned more of Maryland's history, one of her special passions—the school was located halfway between Baltimore and Annapolis—and more of an appreciation of where I was within the universe, from working for her as an elementary school assistant than I did in my private high school.

Nothing is more important to our society, by definition, than the education of our youth. Nothing in pursuit of educational excellence is more important than studying the models of things that work. Frank Boyden's Deerfield and Sara Lightfoot Lawrence's six good high schools—and Tom's mother's fifth-grade classroom—are models from which we suspect all of us can learn.

The Marine Corps of Business Schools:
Pride, Poise and Results

It's 1:00 A.M. as Tom teeters bleary-eyed down the steps of the Cessna 310 in Tallahassee, Florida, after completing a long, long day and a choppy, three-hour flight from Mansfield, Ohio. The poised young man (all of nineteen) dressed in a well-kept, conservative business suit, greets him crisply. "I'm Dan Callis, a junior accounting major from Clinton, Maryland. Welcome to Florida A&M's School of Business and Industry." We've just gotten our first taste of Sybil Mobley's extraordinary accomplishments as dean of a once unknown black business school, now the home of four hundred exceptionally talented students (over half were Merit Scholarship finalists) and first stop on the recruiting trail for almost all of America's giant corporations.

Dean Mobley decided that the usual business school offerings on debits and credits and the intersection of supply-and-demand curves were not enough. Business is about social commerce among people; for the holder of a BS degree who is just starting out, black or white, poise and confidence are more decisive predictors of a successful future than lightning-fast speed with a calculator or PC keyboard.

Thus Sybil's school looks more like a business than a school—beginning with her own office and its reception area. Its accoutrements include thick carpets and the sort of furnishings more common to the offices of Fortune 100 chairmen than schoolrooms. Even the names of student lounges (e.g., the Bull and Bear) are all introduction to business and business terminology, while the main hallway on each floor of the new building is named after one of the world's business thoroughfares (e.g., Wall Street, Threadneedle Street). Each floor/hallway will soon feature a mural—not "just a mural" but a work of art. The one that depicts Des Voeux Road, Central, in Hong Kong, already in place, is exciting—and lavish, a gift from Chase Manhattan Bank. It's all designed, along with a curriculum that teaches the nuts and bolts and tenor of business, to turn out students who feel like confident, would-be winners as they approach the business environment.

Once-a-year internships are another big part of the program. Each student spends a substantial hunk of his or her time each year in a no-nonsense, real-world internship—every one individually-crafted by Mobley and her aggressive senior staff. Even more impressive is the day-to-day organization of the students. Each one is assigned to a team, which is organized as a company and involved in recruiting and promoting students as well as accomplishing certain tasks. *Everything* is done by the teams, from the generation of publications to the running of the dorms. (Sybil was adamant about putting the dorms on a profit-making basis. When her student company/teams took over, they quickly saw that the only way to do so was by laying off the custodial staff, with students taking on the chores on a rotating basis. Lay them off they did, and, typically, Dean Mobley got heavily involved in the fracas that ensued. She won, as is her habit.)

One focal point of the teams' effort is the weekly (or more frequent) visits to the school by corporate heavyweights (and others, such as Tom)—each one a grueling and exciting eighteen-hour series of seminars, interviews and speeches orchestrated by the students. Who comes? The managing partner of Touche-Ross preceded Tom by less than seven days. In the last few months the list has included Chairman Jim Burke of Johnson & Johnson, Chairman Jack Welch of GE and Governor Bob Graham of Florida.

One of the student "companies" is wholly responsible, on a rotating basis, for each visit, from airport greeting to departure. Dinner with a dozen students starts things off. As is true throughout the experience, these students are *prepared.* It is not even slight exaggeration to say that they are more ready than the *best* of interviewers Tom has confronted since the publication of *In Search of Excellence.*

The next day begins with a tour. The dean gives lots of running commentary, to be sure, but a student host is a prominent part of every activity. Next, at 10:00 A.M. sharp, you are shepherded into the campus TV facility for your appearance on a student panel show. Called *Today's Leaders Face Tomorrow's,* it is modeled after *Face the Nation,* and is carried locally on a cable network. The questions are not pap, not student-plays-sycophant-with-hot-shot-corporate-chieftain. They are tough. In Tom's case, every article critical of *In Search of Excellence* had been studied with a fine-tooth comb. *Every* question was hardball! (When a corporate exec is involved, critical reportage and the company's balance sheets are scrutinized in an effort to unearth pointed questions.) If one survives the ordeal, it's on to lunch and the postlunch Forum, where the guest speaks his or her piece for an hour to all students in assembly (remember this happens sixty or seventy times a year). Next, it's on to "wrap-up." Here, twenty-five students, chosen randomly from among the members of the hosting "company," grill you for another hour. Again, the preparation has been awesome; the questions are tough. Again, the setting is vital: the SBI (School of Business and Industry) boardroom, which is no pale imitation of the Fortune 100 model, but the hushed, plush real thing. The twenty-five students who take their seats and proceed to grill a business luminary in this setting are not going to be intimidated by the business world "out there."

It is Sybil Mobley who has made all this happen. Her passion for her task and for her students is palpable. No detail escapes her attention. She exudes energy, on the run, crisscrossing the country in pursuit of support, recruiting, cajoling money from alums. And yet she always has time for a personal tête-à-tête with a student. In her we saw Frank Boyden personified. Her mission is noble. Her results must be seen to be believed.

21

What Price Excellence?

To fight a bull when you are not scared is nothing. And to not fight a bull when you are scared is nothing. But to fight a bull when you are scared—that is something.

Anonymous bullfighter

I seldom think about politics more than eighteen hours a day.

Lyndon Johnson

One is happy as a result of one's own efforts, once one knows the necessary ingredients of happiness: Simple tastes, a certain degree of courage, self-denial to a point, love of work, and above all, a clear conscience.

George Sand

A passion for excellence means thinking big and starting small: excellence happens when high purpose and intense pragmatism meet. This is almost, but not quite, the whole truth. We believe a passion for excellence also carries a price, and we state it simply: the adventure of excellence is not for the faint of heart.

Adventure? You bet. It's not just a job. It's a personal commitment. Whether we're looking at a billion-dollar corporation or a three-person accounting department, we see that excellence is achieved by people who muster up the nerve (and the passion) to step out—in spite of doubt, or fear, or job description—to maintain face-to-face contact with other people, namely, customers and colleagues. They won't retreat behind office doors, committees, memos or layers of staff, knowing this is the fair bargain they make for extraordinary results. They may step out for love, because of a burning desire to be the best, to make a difference, or perhaps, as a colleague recently explained, "Because the thought of being average scares the hell out of me." (Manny, you needn't worry.)

Doing better than average takes tenacious preparation. You need an invigorating purpose you can call your own, one you care enough about to justify investing your steadfast interest—one that, we hope, makes you happy, because you'll live with it day in and day out. It has to be worth your full attention. It has to be worth the time and effort it takes to master the basics and be diligent on the details, the little things that prove yours is an environment where things happen, where the only thing you like as well as listening is acting without delay, where people are committed to finding a few more ways to get things done the way they want them to be done. The good news? You can start now. The bad news? You'll never finish. As Admiral Hyman Rickover put it, "Good ideas and innovations must be driven into existence by courageous patience." Exactly.

Courage and self-respect are the lion's share of passion: It's hanging in long after others have gotten bored or given up; it's refusing to leave well enough alone; it means that anything less than the best you can imagine really bothers you, maybe keeps you awake at night. It usually means sticking your neck out: daring to give your best shot to something you care about and asking others to do the same *is* self-exposing. It asks you to pick sides, to wear your passion on your sleeve, to take a position and remain true to it even under the scrutiny of an audience, when the wish to please, to be accepted, welcomed, can compromise the clearest inner vision. Passion opens you to criticism, disappointment, disillusionment and failure, any one of which is enough to scare off all but the bravest souls. But the passionate, courageous, self-respecting people we know, when challenges or risks loom before them, regard them as something to be faced. As writer Amy Gross reasoned in her essay on courage, "One person sees a mountain as a mountain. Another takes it personally, as a thing to be climbed, or else. Awful as the climbing might be, the or-else is worse."

Bottom-Linemanship

On the op-ed page of the Sunday, May 20, 1984, issue of the *New York Times,* Norman Lear wrote:

America is suffering from an unhealthy emphasis on success as measured by The Numbers. The tendency to boil the world down into analytic abstractions distorts and oversimplifies the richness of life. It insists upon evaluating the world through ratings and lists, matrices and polls, the bottom line, winners and losers.

Success is not a destination. It is a journey. Robert Louis Stevenson once said, "To travel hopefully is a better thing than to arrive." There is only one arrival in life—and that is at the end of life. All the achievements, the moments of success, are merely milestones along the way.

Television is perhaps the most dramatic example of the failure to continue traveling hopefully. The name of the game for the networks is: "How do I win Tuesday night at 8 o'clock?" When the only criterion for airing the show is how it may rate against the competition in the short term, it isn't good for network business in the long term. And so, despite the threat of audience erosion from the new technologies, we see the networks scrambling—not to innovate, but to imitate, because innovation requires risk-taking, and risk-taking is antithetical to winning in the short term. With painful predictability, the networks putter with the same tired formats, adding more sex here and more violence there—more mindlessness—in an effort to grab the viewers' attention quickly.

If the heads of the three networks were standing in a circle with razors to each other's throats, they could not be committing suicide more deliberately. Just as, it seems clear now, the Big Three were doing all those years ago in Detroit, when they refused to innovate, to build small, fuel-efficient cars; refused to sacrifice a current quarterly profit statement to invest in the future, and meet the threat of the imports from abroad. Or the steel companies, when they wouldn't modernize. Or the labor unions in both industries, when they fought only for added wages and benefits—instead of fighting to protect their members' jobs in the long term.

There are no villains in all of this. It is a matter of climate. The average network programming executive is trapped. Imagine yourself in his job: You wake up and read that your network didn't have one show in the Top 10. Your palms sweat. On your way into the office, you pick up The Wall Street Journal, which now prints an analysis of projected earnings based on ratings. Your network's projected earnings are down. You walk into the office and a warm Xerox copy of last night's overnight ratings is on your desk. You didn't win a single time slot. Now your first appointment of the day is with tomorrow's Rod Serling or Paddy Chayefsky, who has a fresh, innovative idea. You are in no condition to hear a new idea. What you must have, and quickly, is a new version of something that is working on one of the other networks. You are a victim—trapped.

TV must, of course, pay attention to business and prosper economically. But when it overlooks the human essence, that spirit that defies the marketplace and its economic calculus of motives, it does so at its own peril.

. . . We have been raising generations of children to think that there is nothing between winning and losing. The notion that life has everything to do with succeeding at the level of doing one's best is lost to these kids. If we really believe that we are on this planet for the long term, we will encourage our youth to understand that not everyone catches the brass ring on the carousel of life. The rest of us better enjoy the ride for its own sake, or life has no meaning at all.

Passion doesn't have to be flashy. Garden-variety, everyday passion is the stuff of excellence, the sort of stuff you need when you face the prospect of managing by wandering around, for instance. Being visible takes guts. There you are, a regular person, stepping out from behind your desk, where it's safe. You have to believe that the stepping out is worth the trouble. It does take courage—the ability to face up to difficulty in spite of doubt, the ability to say good isn't good enough, the ability to learn from the losses, to celebrate the successful tries, to resist the impulse to use managing by wandering around as an opportunity to *tell* people how their jobs *ought* to be done, and—maybe most important—to realize that even if you fail the first time, there's reason to try again, that the sting is brief.

It takes some getting used to. From the moment you know it's excellence or bust, you're in for the distance. You'll need a generous supply of both altruism and action to dip into: a passion for excellence goes bad when it relies too much on either. Altruism without the personal drive to make it into something tangible gets stuck, doesn't go anywhere. Action for its own sake can be transmuted into ruthlessness, particularly when a little cynicism is added. Excellence is optimistic. It's believing that something can be done, that it's worth fighting for, worth trusting others to play a part. And there is a benefit: Even recent medical findings suggest that optimism is *good* for you. Duke University Medical Center scientist Redford Williams, while exploring Type A personalities—hard-driving, impatient, relentless folks, thought to be more prone to heart attacks—found that one element stood out as more dangerous than any other: "We suggest that 'cynicism,' better than any other word, captures the toxic element in the Type A personality. We're finding that some components of Type A behavior are far worse than others."

From cookies to computers, real estate to basketball, not a cynic among the winners. We can promise you that they're good at faith, the kind that gets them over inevitable disappointments and setbacks, the kind that propels them when they feel—as they sometimes do—that their small efforts don't count for much, their organization is too brittle, their chief executive officer (or boss) is unsympathetic, their industry decaying. At these times, there is only the passionate belief that something distinctive can be forged nonetheless—if not throughout the organization, then in their tiny part of it: a pocket of excellence. This, they know, can be done. It has been done, in tough places—auto factories, steel mills, retail stores, banks—where handfuls of self-respecting innovators thrive among the bureaucrats.

Consider network television again—that business with the bottom-line, short-term (overnight) focus. Todd Gitlin writes in *Prime Time* (published in 1984) about the hugely successful and distinctive *Hill Street Blues:*

> In network television, even the exceptions reveal the rules. Everything emerges at the end of a chain of *ifs. If* a producer gets on the inside track; *If* he or she has strong ideas and fights for them intelligently . . . *If* the

producer is willing to give ground here and there . . . *If* the network has the right niche for the show . . . then the system that cranks out mind candy occasionally proves hospitable to something else, while at the same time betraying its limits. As Universal Studios executive Jennings Lang once said about the work of the writer Howard Rodman, 'Every department store needs a boutique.' In the early eighties, *Hill Street Blues* was network television's most conspicuous boutique. This intelligent, literate ensemble police series with its rough texture and intertangled plots, its complex mix of crime melodrama and absurdist comedy, was commissioned by the same network executive who brought America *Real People, The Brady Brides,* and *Sheriff Lobo.* As the networks scrambled to cash in on the presumed trend toward national discipline, Fred Silverman at NBC wanted a down-and-dirty cop show. But because he assigned the notion to two particular writer-producers at the right moment in their careers; because they were working for the right company; because they caught some of the richness of American life at that moment; because they made the right choices of director, line producer, and cast; and because they took some chances and fought for them, what Silverman got was *Hill Street Blues,* at its best a mature and even brilliant show that violated many conventions, pleased critics, caught the undertow of cultural change, and ran away with the Emmys. Then, in defiance of virtually all predictions, after puny first-season ratings *Hill Street* in its second and third seasons also became NBC's top series hit. . . . *Hill Street*'s achievement was first of all a matter of style. Thirteen principal characters and several other regulars careened through this show, making it, by conventional wisdom, overpopulated. To thicken the plot further, most of the episodes were written in four-show blocks, with at least four major stories running concurrently, each starting at a different moment and often not resolving at all.

Such a pocket of excellence is hospitable to innovative, creative and sometimes risky new ventures. When *Hill Street* was renewed for its second half-season, co-executive producer Greg Hoblit quipped that it was "the lowest-rated show renewed in the history of television." The dogged persistence of the show's creative team—their single-minded focus on delivering a "messy-looking," real-sounding, inventively written television product and their acceptance of its cost—began to pay off.

There will be disagreements with the boss along the way, as there were between the *Hill Street* producers and the network censors, the programming executives, just about everyone. But this was a passionate group. They believed they could do it, believed it could work in their industry. Small pockets can yield sizable rewards.

All the same, sticking with it day in and day out is plain difficult, and not only because of the organizational waves a passionate endeavor can make. Even a pocket of excellence can fill your life like a wall-to-wall revolution.

We have found that the majority of passionate activists who hammer away at the old boundaries have given up family vacations, Little League games, birthday dinners, evenings, weekends and lunch hours, gardening, reading, movies and most other pastimes. We have a number of friends whose marriages or partnerships crumbled under the weight of their devotion to a dream. There are more newly single parents than we expected among our colleagues.

Such profound trade-offs don't have to be a part of the bargain. Lost sleep, some late nights and probably a few weekends do go with the territory. Divorce does not. There is no requirement that the cost of excellence is suffering. But there is also no guarantee that the process will be graced by a personal and professional "balance," where things work out nicely on both fronts with little wear and tear on either, thank you. We are frequently asked if it is possible to "have it all"—a full and satisfying personal life and a full and satisfying, hard-working, professional one. Our answer is: No. The price of excellence is time, energy, attention and focus, at the very same time that energy, attention and focus could have gone toward enjoying your daughter's soccer game. Excellence is a high-cost item. As David Ogilvy observed in *Confessions of an Advertising Man:* "If you prefer to spend all your spare time growing roses or playing with your children, I like you better, but do not complain that you are not being promoted fast enough."

Some have built their organizations with the active participation of their families. Stew Leonard's, Marriott, Mrs. Field's Cookies—all are new "family" businesses. When the cost of excellence is shared by husbands, wives, children or grandparents, rewards are, too. The cruel division between the love of work and love of family blurs, softens and bends. In other organizations, family and friends are welcome at all events, including annual organization performance reviews.

When you have a true passion for excellence, and when you act on it, you will stand straighter. You will look people in the eye. You will see things happen. You will see heroes created, watch ideas unfold and take shape. You'll walk with a springier step. You'll have something to fight for, to care about, to share, scary as it is, with other people. There will be times when you swing from dedicated to obsessed. We don't pretend that it's easy. It takes real courage to step out and stake your claim. But we think the renewed sense of purpose, of making a difference, of recovered self-respect, is well worth the price of admission.

SOME (MORE) GOOD READING ON LEADERSHIP

Quick, go out and get *Leaders,* by Warren Bennis and Bert Nanus (Harper & Row, 1985). Warren is a good personal friend, and has struck gold with this book. His descriptions of forty leaders—from symphony orchestra conductor to movie director to Fortune 500 chairman—focus on the themes that we develop throughout the leadership section here. The six case studies in Michael Maccoby's *The Leader* (Simon & Schuster, 1981) also support our conclusions on the importance of "people-oriented" leadership at all levels.

Corporate Cultures, by Terry Deal and Allan Kennedy (Addison-Wesley, 1982) remains the first, most thorough and best description of corporate "culture" we've ever read. It is also exceptionally readable, filled with pragmatic anecdotes of leaders at all levels.

John Kotter's *The General Managers* (Free Press/Macmillan, 1982) is a data-rich analysis of several hundred highly effective general managers. Kotter finds that their success stems from a series of factors seldom discussed in traditional management texts; the ways these leaders deal with information and people are especially consistent with our observations.

For the true student of leadership (and we believe that *every manager* at *every level* should be a true student of leadership), there's no better source than James MacGregor Burns's *Leadership* (Harper & Row, 1978). In particular, consistent with Warren Bennis's work and ours, Burns speaks of the "transforming leader," one who goes beyond dealing with the day-to-day problems of managing a sizable concern (such as a country) and focuses on the development of a new level of awareness among, often, tens of millions of people.

Finally, we would strongly suggest that the would-be effective leader become a reader of biographies. Ken Auletta's *The Art of Corporate Success* (Putnam's, 1983) is the unusual story of Jean Riboud of Schlumberger, one of the world's most profitable corporations; the portrait is that of a remarkably complex person (in other words, a real-world leader, not one from the world of texts on leadership). Another example is William Manchester's *American Caesar* (Little, Brown, 1978), which provides an extraordinary perspective on General MacArthur; the best part, to our minds, is the account of MacArthur's masterly management of post-World War II Japan (the subtlety of effective leadership has never been made more apparent to us).

Acknowledgments

Nonfiction authors who are even half honest with themselves know that the acknowledgments section should be almost as long as the book. If that's true in general, it holds many times over for us. This book *is* those we've met.

We have listened to a thousand stories, each of which has come from someone who has been thoughtful enough to share an experience with us, to explain it in depth. Virtually all we included were marked not only by hard facts, but also by a genuine enthusiasm and caring on the part of the teller.

In September 1984 our partner Bob Le Duc's first Skunk Camp was held. What a gathering! Bill and Vieve Gore of W. L. Gore & Associates, Stew Leonard and Stew Jr. from Stew Leonard's, Frank and Jimmy Perdue from Perdue Farms, Don Burr of People Express, Tom Melohn from North American Tool & Die, Don Williams from Trammell Crow, Jerry Gallagher from Mervyn's and Dayton Hudson, Tom Malone of Milliken & Co., Ren McPherson from the Dana Corporation, John McConnell, Jr., from Worthington Industries, Ken Schoen from 3M, skunk Ken Stahl from Xerox, Don Vlcek of Domino's Pizza, Manny Garcia from Burger King, Donna Ecton from Campbell Soup, and many others attended. Several special friends couldn't be with us because of crises at the last minute (among them, Karen Strand from the Dana Corporation, Bob Stramy from General Motors, and Phil Staley from Ford). Seldom, if ever, have we learned so much or felt so much.

But that experience is but the tiniest part of all we have benefited from: Getting to know Bill Creech, the four-star general who turned around a huge part of the Air Force. Meeting Dean Sybil Mobley of Florida A&M's School of Business and Industry, who has performed true miracles in transforming an underfunded Southern black business school (she now has everyone from Jim Burke of Johnson & Johnson to Roger Smith of General Motors beating down the door for an opportunity to talk to her students). It's visiting Sweden and finding master showman (by his own admission) Jan Carlzon, who reversed SAS's fortunes; feeling the intensity of his concern for people (on another trip to Sweden) from Marcus Sieff, former chairman of Marks & Spencer.

How lucky we've been! To spend time with today's great entrepreneurs: Les Wexner of The Limited, Merv Morris of Mervyn's, Dave Thomas of

ACKNOWLEDGMENTS

Wendy's, Trammell Crow of Trammell Crow, Tom Monaghan of Domino's Pizza, Roger Milliken of Milliken & Co.

But maybe even these people aren't the most important who've shaped our thinking. Most important are those whose names are absent from these pages. Tens of thousands have attended our seminars. They're often enmeshed in stodgy, bureaucratic organizations. Yet they've had the guts to try again, after years of depression and suppression of their ideas. They're out wandering, and proud of it. Out nurturing skunks. Out celebrating their people's successes.

Inspiration has come from unexpected quarters. We are not fans of the executives who populate the upper floors of most of the Fortune 500 companies. We have become special fans of those, most often in the mid-sized or smaller companies, who are making the American economy grow. Consider the bakers, for example. We met them at a meeting of the American Bakery Association (that's bakers, not bankers, which most people thought we meant when we reported on it). How inspiring! The bakers are down-to-earth business people. They understand about customer service and people—and innovation, too. The bakers, and Peterbilt truck dealers, all 225 employees of the Carl Sewell's Sewell Village Cadillac. Those are the ones who've given us ideas, hope and the courage to speak out about what's important.

How to pinpoint our indebtedness to some? Well, we could mention Don Burr and Bill Gore, who really believe they are creating important new forms of organization, and we believe they are, too. We are convinced by their ideas, to be sure, but above all, by their passion, and by the array of extraordinary people who work with them from whom we've also learned so much. And our minds return time and again to the image of Ren McPherson at our Skunk Camp. Despite the cast of stars scattered around him, whose hearts (and records) are unfailingly on the side of the angels, we would watch Ren bestir himself every forty-five minutes: "Bullshit." Someone (sometimes one of us) had just used the word "employee," rather than "person." And Ren simply wouldn't let it pass. He shouldn't, we shouldn't, and America shouldn't.

On the facing page is the "official portrait" from that first Skunk Camp. The players and their organizations are identified below the picture. Our heartfelt thanks to each and every one of them.

We're often hard on the academics. They have been much kinder to us than we to them. We've been highly critical, often in public. They've been supportive. Tom's close personal friend and colleague at Stanford, Associate Dean Gene Webb at the Business School, has remained a staunch supporter (though tried sorely on many an occasion). There's no way that Tom can thank Gene enough for his steadfastness. Warren Bennis of USC, Jim Kouzes of Santa Clara, Brian Quinn of Dartmouth, Wick Skinner of Harvard, Rosabeth Moss Kanter of Yale, and Andy Van de Ven of Minnesota stand out as special colleagues from academia. They and many others are trying new things in the beleaguered business schools. There's a special category of "miscellaneous friends" ("miscellaneous" only because they defy categorization).

998

1. Dick Jackson
   First Georgia Bank
2. Jake Kerr
   Lignum, Ltd.
3. Barry Roach
   Raychem
4. Donna Ecton
   Campbell Soup
5. Paul Sakamoto
   *Mountain View-Los
   Altos, CA School
   District*
6. Sam Tyler
   The Tom Peters Group
7. Ren McPherson
   The Dana Corporation
8. Bob Le Duc
   The Tom Peters Group
9. Manny Garcia
   Davgar Restaurants
10. John McCoy
    Bancone
11. Melissa Manson
    The Tom Peters Group
12. Mara Nieman
    The Tom Peters Group
13. Don Williams
    Trammell Crow
14. Peter Vaill
    George Washington Univ.
15. Pete Mesa
    *Milpitas Unified
    School District*
16. Kathy Johnson
    *Association of
    Western
    Hospitals*

17. Jim Perdue
    Perdue Farms
18. Nancy Badore
    Ford Motor Co.
19. Don Burr
    People Express
20. Frank Perdue
    Perdue Farms
21. Bill Benak
    Levin Metals Corp.
22. Don Vlcek
    *Domino's Pizza
    Distribution*
23. Joe Stegmayer
    *Worthington
    Industries*
24. Ian Thomson
    *The Tom Peters
    Group*
25. Dale Miller
    Zenger-Miller, Inc.
26. Tom Malone
    Milliken & Co.
27. Stew Leonard, Sr.
    Stew Leonard's

28. Tait Elder
    *Allied
    Technologies*
29. Ed Prell
    Bell Labs
30. John McConnell, Jr.
    *Worthington
    Industries*
31. Ken Schoen
    3M
32. Tony Schulte
    Random House
33. Jerry Gallagher
    Mervyn's
34. Tom Melohn
    *North American
    Tool & Die*
35. Tom Peters
    *The Tom Peters
    Group*
36. Jerry Porras
    Stanford Univ.

37. Stew Leonard, Jr.
    Stew Leonard's
38. Nancy Austin
    *The Tom Peters
    Group*
39. Barbara Demere
    *The Tom Peters
    Group*
40. Bill Gore
    *W. L. Gore &
    Associates*
41. Vieve Gore
    *W. L. Gore &
    Associates*
42. Debbie Henken
    *The Tom Peters
    Group*
43. Ken Stahl
    Xerox
44. Debbie Kaplan
    *The Tom Peters
    Group*
45. Christy Miller
    *The Tom Peters
    Group*
46. Dee Young
    *The Tom Peters
    Group*
47. Henry Haskell
    *Kal Kan
    Foods, Inc.*

ACKNOWLEDGMENTS

One of these is Bob Schwartz of Tarrytown, who is deeply concerned with new forms of managing. His support has meant more than he'll ever know.

And then there are those who have given us courage at exactly the right moment. Tom was down and out after a brush with many too many of the (inappropriately) complacent, publicly advertised "greats" of the Fortune 500. He spent the next day with Chairman Jim Burke of Johnson & Johnson, President Wayne Calloway of PepsiCo, and Don Estridge, who is now vice president for manufacturing at IBM. Never has anyone's spirit lifted so fast.

Our partners and cohorts in crime not only have "provided support through the long hours," but have tested, pushed forth and insisted that we *live* the ideas that we talk about. Among them: Stewart Clifford, Linda Devillier, Debbie Henken, Melissa Howard, Debbie Kaplan, Bob Le Duc, Christy Miller, Gail Miller, John Nathan, Mara Nieman, Jeff Newcomb, Malka Rosen, Kathy Swan, Ian Thomson, Sam Tyler, Marilyn Van Wichen, and Dee Young.

And now a word for those who worked directly on the book. Corona Machemer is our editor at Random House. We must do one of two things: either say "thanks" and stop there, or write fifteen pages of tribute. To do less than the latter would severely denigrate her contribution. Corona's technical contribution has been exceptional—what one would expect from a fine editor, and more. Her impeccable sense of organization has been equally thoughtful—again, at some level, what one would expect from a superb editor. What has made the relationship radically different, however, has been her passionate involvement with the ideas we present. This book is about enthusiasm and passion and ownership and pride and care and trust and listening and courtesy and another dozen terms of the same sort. Corona's dedication to what these words represent is doubtless more strenuous than even our own. She has forced us to dig deep to test the strength and consistency of our beliefs. Time and again she's caught us napping, tested us, and led us to revise what we were doing. The integrity of her work, we believe, shines out from every page. Thanks, Corona. We didn't know such contributions were possible.

Bob Bernstein and Tony Schulte at Random House have made the relationship with our publisher a wholly rewarding one. In the best of worlds one's publisher becomes one's family. That's exactly what's happened at Random House, and we're thankful indeed.

Our technical support at Random House and at home has been more than helpful, and always there when we needed it: thanks to Susan Winn and Linda Dee for getting the whole manuscript together; to Sono Rosenberg for her heroic and masterly copy-editing; to Jo Metsch for her brilliant design work; to Sallye Leventhal, for doing just about anything that had to be done; and to Dee Young, for researching and correcting and her sense of humor.

The book is dedicated to Kate Abbe and Bill Cawley and the skunks. You've read of the skunks. As for Bill and Kate, they've been supportive, yes, but that's the least of it. We both read a lot, and we are inured to the "and thanks to Mary Jo who put up with us when we were cranky" stuff. Kate's and Bill's belief in the possibility of a world in which human beings treat each other decently is what the book is about, what they're about, and what we have tried to live up to. Both Kate and Bill are living demonstrations that you can care about people, care about what you do, and be exceptionally successful at it.

We conclude with a tribute to someone that neither of us knew, the late Lieutenant General Melvin Zais, U.S. Army. One of our many unsung supporters sent Tom a letter three years ago. Attached was an audiotape of an Army general giving a speech to the Armed Forces Staff College on leadership. Unfortunately, in the swirl of things, the letter got detached from the tape, and has been lost. The tape remains, and on a hot summer day in 1983, Tom got around to listening to it. He listened and wept. We now use it at all of our Skunk Camps. You've read some of the words in the book. General Zais's advice is clear: "You must care." To listen to it, a sometimes halting speech by a general who jumped with the 101st Airborne, to listen to him talk of love and care and trust and humility on the part of those who lead still brings on an emotional reaction each time we hear it. Tom Melohn of North American Tool & Die, talking about his people, broke down in front of television cameras during the filming of our January 1985 PBS special. The intensity and passion of Zais and Melohn is inspiring. General Zais, we thank you so much. Finally, our most heartfelt acknowledgment goes out to all of you whom we have not had the opportunity to meet, but who are giving us the most steadfast support by living this message. We trust that we will have the chance to get acquainted with you in the years ahead.

Acknowledgments

Grateful acknowledgment is made to the following for permission to reprint previously published material:

Thomas Larry Adcock: Excerpt from "They Also Wait Who Stand and Serve," by Thomas Larry Adcock, which previously appeared in *Northwest Orient* magazine, October 1983. Used with permission of the author.

American Psychological Association: Excerpt reprinted from "Small Wins: Redefining the Scale of Social Problems," in *The American Psychologist,* Vol. 39, January 1984, pp. 40–49. Copyright © 1984 by the American Psychological Association. Reprinted by permission of the publisher.

Basic Books, Inc.: Excerpt from *Silicon Valley Fever: Growth of High-Technology Culture,* by Everett M. Rogers and Judith Larsen. Copyright © 1984 by Basic Books, Inc. United Kingdom rights administered by George Allen & Unwin (Publishers) Ltd, London. Excerpt from *The Good School: Portraits of Character and Culture,* by Sara Lawrence Lightfoot. Copyright © 1983 by Basic Books, Inc. Reprinted by permission of the publisher.

Business Week: Excerpt from "Campbell Soup's Recipe for Growth: Offering Something for Every Palate." Reprinted from the December 24, 1984, issue of *Business Week,* by special permission, © 1984 by McGraw-Hill, Inc.

Capistrano Press, Ltd.: Excerpt from Fredonia F. Jacques: "Verdict Pending: A Patient Representative's Intervention" reprinted with permission for World English Language Rights. Garden Grove, Calif.; Capistrano Press Ltd., 1983, pp. 57–58.

Center for Creative Leadership: Excerpt from "Participative Management," by E. J. Cattabiani and R. P. White; *Issues and Observations,* August 1983; © 1983 Center for Creative Leadership, Greensboro, N.C.

Chief Executive Magazine: Excerpt from "The CEO as Champion," reprinted with permission from *Chief Executive* (Spring 1984, No. 27). Copyright © Chief Executive Magazine, Inc., 645 5th Avenue, New York, NY 10022. All rights reserved. Single copy, $7.00.

Crown Publishers: Excerpts reprinted from Ogilvy on Advertising, by David Ogilvy. Text copyright © 1983 by David Ogilvy and compilation copyright © 1983 by Multimedia Publications, Inc. Used by permission of Crown Publishers, Inc.

Dana Corporation: "Dana's 40 Thoughts" reprinted courtesy of the Dana Corporation, Toledo, Ohio.

Dow Jones & Company, Inc.: Excerpts from the February 8, 1984; October 23, 1984; and December 12, 1984 issues of *The Wall Street Journal.* Reprinted by permission of The Wall Street Journal, Copyright © Dow Jones & Company, Inc., 1984. All rights reserved.

Farrar, Straus & Giroux, Inc.: Excerpts reprinted by permission of Farrar, Straus and Giroux, Inc., from *The Headmaster* by John McPhee. Copyright © 1966 by John McPhee. This material originally appeared in *The New Yorker.*

Grosset & Dunlap, Inc.: Excerpt reprinted by permission of Grosset & Dunlap, Inc., from *For the Good of The Company,* copyright © 1976 by Isadore Barmash.

Harvard Business Review: The following excerpts, by Theodore Levitt (except where noted): Excerpt from Chapter 2, "The Globalization of Markets," as adapted in *The Marketing Imagination,* by Theodore Levitt. Copyright © 1983 by The Free Press. "The Globalization of Markets" by Theodore Levitt (May/June 1983). Copyright © 1983 by the President and Fellows of Harvard College; all rights reserved. Excerpt from Chapter 3, "The Industrialization of Service," as adapted in *The Marketing Imagination.* Copyright © 1983 by The Free Press. "The Industrialization of Service" (September/October 1976). Copyright © 1976 by the President and Fellows of

ACKNOWLEDGMENTS

Harvard College; all rights reserved. Excerpt from Chapter 4, "Differentiation—Of Anything," as adapted in *The Marketing Imagination*. Copyright © 1983 by The Free Press. "Marketing Success Through Differentiation—Of Anything" (January/February 1980). Copyright © 1980 by the President and Fellows of Harvard College; all rights reserved. Excerpt from Chapter 5, "Marketing Intangible Products and Product Intangibles," as adapted in *The Marketing Imagination*. Copyright © 1983 by The Free Press. "Marketing Intangible Products and Product Intangibles" (May/June 1981). Copyright © 1981 by the President and Fellows of Harvard College; all rights reserved. Excerpt from Chapter 6, "Relationship Management," as adapted in *The Marketing Imagination*. Copyright © 1983 by The Free Press. "After the Sale is Over" (September/October 1983). Copyright © 1983 by the President and Fellows of Harvard College; all rights reserved. All excerpts reprinted by permission of the *Harvard Business Review*.

IBM Corporation: Advertisement reprinted courtesy of the IBM Corporation.

Inc. Magazine: Excerpt from "The Employee Who's No Longer Useful." Reprinted with permission, Inc. magazine, January 1982. Copyright © 1982, by Inc. Publishing Corporation, 38 Commercial Wharf, Boston, MA 02110.

Johnson & Johnson: Jim Burke's Ad Council speech, and Johnson & Johnson Credo. Reprinted courtesy of Johnson & Johnson.

Little, Brown & Company: Excerpts from *The Soul of a New Machine*, by Tracy Kidder. Copyright © 1981 by John Tracy Kidder. By permission of Little, Brown & Company in association with the Atlantic Monthly Press.

L. L. Bean, Inc.: "The Golden Rule of L. L. Bean," reprinted courtesy of L. L. Bean, Inc.

McGraw-Hill Book Co.: Excerpt from *A Business and Its Beliefs: The Ideas That Helped Build IBM*, by Thomas Watson, Jr. Copyright © 1963 by the Trustees of Columbia University. Used with permission of McGraw-Hill Book Company.

Herman Miller, Inc.: Excerpt from speeches by Max DePree, courtesy Herman Miller, Inc.

The New York Times Company: Excerpt from "Molded in Al Davis' Images," by Michael Janofsky, *New York Times*, September 2, 1984. "Bottom Linemanship," by Norman Lear, *New York Times*, May 20, 1984. Copyright © 1984 by The New York Times Company. Reprinted by permission.

Nordstrom: Advertisement reprinted courtesy of Nordstrom, Seattle, Washington.

Random House, Inc.: Excerpts from *Inside Prime Time*, by Todd Gitlin. Copyright © 1983, 1985 by Todd Gitlin. Reprinted by permission of Pantheon Books, a division of Random House, Inc. United Kingdom rights administered by International Creative Management. Material adapted from *The Winning Streak*, by Walter Goldsmith and David Clutterbuck. Reprinted by permission of Random House, Inc., and Weidenfeld (Publishers) Ltd. *The Winning Streak* will be published jointly in the United States and Canada by Random House, Inc., and Not Just Another Publishing Company, Inc.

H. S. Shanlian: Letter reprinted courtesy of Mr. H. S. "Blackie" Shanlian.

The Sterling Lord Agency, Inc.: Excerpt from "Can The Best Mayor Win?" by Richard Cramer. Reprinted by permission of the Sterling Lord Agency, Inc. Copyright © 1984 by Richard Cramer. The excerpt first appeared in the October 1984 issue of *Esquire* magazine.

Texas Monthly: Excerpt from "The Eccentric Genius of Trammell Crow," by Joseph Nocera. Reprinted with permission from the August issue of *Texas Monthly*. Copyright © 1984 by Texas Monthly.

Robert Townsend: quotes from Robert Townsend's Alfred A. Knopf open memorandum on "Leadership."

Travelhost: Excerpt from "The Choicest Potato Chip," by James E. Buerger, Publisher of Travelhost Magazine.

Utah State University School of Business: Excerpt from W. Edwards Deming's speech, "Transformation of Management Needed: Must Remove Deadly Obstacles," reprinted courtesy of Utah State University School of Business, George S. Eccles Distinguished Lecture Series, 1982–83.

Warner Books: Excerpt from *Mary Kay on People Management*, Copyright © 1984 by Warner Books, Inc. Reprinted by permission of the publisher.

A Guide to Key Concepts

Index for Thriving on Chaos

INDEX

Index for *A Passion for Excellence*

Brookline High School (Boston, Mass.), 970, 971–73, 975, 976–77, 981–82
Brunswick, 641, 721
Buckmaster-Irwin, Lynn, 826
Buerger, James E., 592
Burger King, 623, 804
Burke, Jim, 720, 761, 762, 905–06, 988
Burns, James MacGregor, 996
Burr, Don, 569, 609, 651, 795, 861
Bushnell, Nolan, 700, 760
Business and Its Beliefs, A (Watson), 647, 649
Business Week, 585, 639n, 787, 811

Callis, Dan, 987
Campbell Soup, 571, 585, 589n, 629, 630, 641, 642, 701, 721, 733n, 761–62, 885, 918
Canadian Hunter Exploration, Ltd., 582, 709, 721
Carlson, Ed, 676, 788, 802, 962, 967
Carlzon, Jan, 569, 633, 637, 652, 685, 792–93, 827, 835, 839, 846, 851, 986
Carman, Carl, 736
Carter, Shelby, 619–20, 686
Casa Bonita, 859
Casper, Dave, 797
Celestial Seasonings, 778
Center for Creative Leadership, 902
Change Masters, The (Kanter), 566, 770
Chase Manhattan, 961
Chayefsky, Paddy, 992
Chennault, Claire, 591
Chicken Pride, 690
Chief Executive, 752
Citibank, 570, 622, 692
Citicorp, 666, 689, 702, 703, 926
Clare, Dave, 906
Clark, George, 713
Clark Equipment, 821, 839
Clifton, Sarah, 790, 791–92, 794, 807
Clutterbuck, David, 593, 594, 793, 816, 888
Coca-Cola, 596, 597
Cognos Associates, 759
Cohen, Izzy, 629
Colodny, Edwin, 630
Commodore, 692
Confessions of an Advertising Man (Ogilvy), 995
Convergent Technologies, 706, 712, 714, 715, 724n, 758
Cook, Paul, 705, 734, 750, 827–28
Cooley, Dick, 799
Corning Glass, 732n, 849

Corporate Cultures (Deal and Kennedy), 566, 841, 996
Costello, Robert, 592
Cox, Fred, 600, 662
Cramer, Richard Ben, 585, 799
Crandall, Bob, 653
Creech, Bill, 571, 573, 622–23, 809, 812–15, 816, 843, 849, 898
Crick, Francis, 770
Crosby, Phil, 672
A. T. Cross, 626
Crow, Trammell, 570, 635–36, 862–63
Trammell Crow, 570, 609, 616, 633, 673, 688
Crown Zellerbach, 861
C-T-R (Computing-Tabulating-Recording) Company, 871
Cunningham, Mary, 926

Dallas Cowboys, 899
Dana Corporation, 568, 787–88, 789, 840, 873, 893, 916
Dart, 632
Data General (DG), 626, 707, 716–17, 735–38, 752, 758, 770, 956n
Datapoint, 690
Davgar Restaurants, 623, 804
Davidson, Marty, 948
Davis, Al, 796–97
Dayton-Hudson, 560, 569, 602, 641, 706, 798
Deal, Terry, 566, 841, 996
de Castro, Ed, 752
Deerfield Academy, 913, 969, 975, 976, 977, 978–79, 982, 985, 986
Delta Airlines, 619, 652, 673, 777, 778
DeLuca, Tony, 801
Deluxe Check, 630, 632
Deming, W. Edwards, 676, 678–79
Denning Systems, Inc., 690
DePree, Max, 571, 778–79, 866, 903, 939, 941, 951
Detroit Tigers, 832
DiBiaso, Dick, 937
Diemakers Inc., 949–50
Digital Equipment, 657, 710, 761, 830
Digital Switch, 600
Dineen, P.J., 654
Disneyland/Disneyworld, 578, 615, 618, 642, 651, 673, 682, 847, 851
Domino's Pizza, 569, 613, 662, 673, 681, 777, 778, 832, 912
Domino's Pizza Distribution Company, 595, 662–63, 751, 850, 854, 861, 912

ABOUT THE AUTHOR

Tom Peters is the co-author of *In Search of Excellence* (with Robert H. Waterman, Jr.) and the author of *Thriving on Chaos, Liberation Management, The Tom Peters Seminar* and *The Pursuit of WOW!*. Though he is founder and chief of the Tom Peters Group in Palo Alto, California, he and his family spend much of their time on a farm in Vermont, thanks to the information technology revolution.